HOW TO AVOID LAWYERS

A Step-by-Step Guide to Being Your Own Lawyer in Almost Every Situation

HOW TO AVOID LAWYERS

A Step-by-Step Guide to Being Your Own Lawyer in Almost Every Situation

by
Don Biggs

LEGAL CONSULTANTS: *Stephen L. Bluestone, J.D.*
& Jerry M. Dale, J.D.

Garland Publishing, Inc.
New York & London
1985

Copyright © 1985 by Garland Publishing, Inc.

15 14 13 12 11 10 9 8 7 6 5 4 3

LIBRARY OF CONGRESS CATALOGING IN PUBLICATION DATA

Biggs, Don.
How to avoid lawyers.

Includes index.
1. Forms (Law)—United States. I. Title.
KF170.B47 1984   347.73'55   84-18636
ISBN 0-8240-7285-5   347.30755
ISBN 0-8240-7284-7 (pbk.)

Cover design by Jonathan Billing
Forms design by Jonathan Billing and Geoffrey Braine

Published by Garland Publishing, Inc.
136 Madison Avenue, New York, New York 10016

Paperback distribution to bookstores by Kampmann and Co., Inc., New York

Printed in the United States of America

Contents

Foreword   xi

Acknowledgments   xiii

Using This Book   xv

I
LIVING WITH THE LAW

1 What This Book Can Do for You   3

2 The Basis of American Law   4

3 Organizing the Law   8

4 The Court System   9

5 Finding and Working with a Lawyer   12

6 Staying Out of Court   15

7 If You Must Go to Court   21

II
LANDLORD-TENANT

8 The Most Hated Document in America   27

9 Lease Agreements   30

Lease Agreement—Unfurnished Apartment   F1

Lease Agreement—Furnished Apartment   F5

Lease Agreement—Unfurnished House   F9

Lease Agreement—Furnished House   F13

Seasonal Lease Agreement— Furnished Country/Seashore House   F17

Extension of Lease   F21

Parking Space Lease   F23

Storage Space Lease   F25

10 Short-term Leases— Monthly Tenancy Agreements and Subleases   32

Lease Agreement—Monthly Tenancy of Unfurnished Apartment   F29

Lease Agreement—Monthly Tenancy of Furnished Premises   F31

Lease Agreement—Sublease of Unfurnished Apartment or House (for use by landlord)   F33

Lease Agreement—Sublease of Unfurnished Apartment or House (for use by tenant)   F35

Lease Agreement—Sublease of Furnished Apartment or House   F37

Permission to Sublet   F39

Permission to Underlet   F41

11 List of Furnishings/Rental Application   34

List of Furnishings   F43

Rental Application   F45

12 Forms for Departing Tenants   35

Notice of Intent to Vacate   F47

Departing Tenant Cleanup Letter   F49

Transfer Clause   F51

III
ACCIDENTS AND INJURIES

13 Looking Out for Number One   39

14 Auto Accident Reports   42

Auto Accident Report   F53

Minor Accident Report   F77

15 Boating/Marine Accident Report   47

Boating/Marine Accident Report   F83

Float Plan   F95

16 Miscellaneous Accident Reports   49

Building Accident Report   F97

Street/Sidewalk Accident Report   F103

Defective Product Accident Report   F107

Animal Accident Report   F111

Public Transportation Accident Report   F115

Attorney's Accident Work Sheet   F119

17 Authorizations to Inspect Medical Records   51

Authorization to Inspect Hospital Medical Records   F137

Authorization to Inspect
Physician's Medical Records   F139

**18 Request for a Copy of
Police Blotter and/or
Accident Report**   52
Request for a Copy of Police
Blotter and/or Accident Report   F141

19 Using a Power of Attorney   53
Retainer and Power of Attorney   F143
Power of Attorney   F145

**20 Release of All Rights and
Claims**   54
Release of All Rights and Claims   F147

IV
HOMEOWNER-CONTRACTOR

**21 Improving on Home
Improvement**   61

**22 Agreements Between
Homeowner and
Contractor**   65
Agreement Between Owner and
Contractor   F149
Alternate Articles   F153
Agreement Between Owner and
Contractor—Short Form   F155
Alternate Articles   F157

**23 Two Forms: Authority to
Represent the Owner;
Revocation of Authority to
Represent the Owner**   69
Authority to Represent the Owner
(for use with Form 22.1/F149)   F159
Authority to Represent the Owner
(for use with Form 22.3/F155)   F161
Revocation of Authority to
Represent the Owner   F163

**24 Agreement Between
Contractor and
Subcontractor**   70
Agreement Between Contractor
and Subcontractor   F165

**25 Two Forms You Can Easily
Use Yourself**   71
Job Estimate Work Sheet   F167
Bid and Proposal   F177

**26 Contractor Forms
Pertaining to Payment and
Completion**   72
General Waiver of Liens   F179

Waiver of Lien   F185
Receipt for Conditional Payment   F187
Contractor's Affidavit of
Completion   F189

**27 Why Not Be Your Own
Contractor?**   74

V
ARBITRATION

**28 Avoiding the Arbitration
Trap**   81

**29 Handling Your Own
Arbitration**   86
Agreement for Submission of an
Existing Dispute to Arbitration—
One Arbitrator   F191
Demand for Arbitration—
One Arbitrator   F193
Guidelines for Arbitration—
One Arbitrator   F195
Agreement for Submission of an
Existing Dispute to Arbitration—
Three Arbitrators   F199
Demand for Arbitration—Three
Arbitrators   F201
Guidelines for Arbitration—Three
Arbitrators   F203
Model arbitration agreements for
insertion in a contract:
—Agreement Using One
Arbitrator   F207
—Agreement Using Three
Arbitrators   F209
Petition for the Appointment of
Arbitrator   F211

VI
GETTING YOUR
CONSUMER RIGHTS

30 Introduction   93

**31 How to Avoid Buying
Trouble**   94

**32 Buying Smart—Learning
Your Warranty Rights**   96

**33 When You Go Shopping—
Protecting Your Consumer
Rights**   98
Comparison Shopping Checklist   F213
Warranty Comparison Checklist   F215

34 The Art and Technique of Making Complaints   101

35 Meeting (and Using) the Uniform Commercial Code   112

36 Revocation of Acceptance: Getting Rid of a Lemon   117

     Notice of Revocation of Acceptance   F217

37 Friends You Didn't Know You Had   125

     Federal Trade Commission consumer notice and form   F219

     Consumer Complaint Report   F223

     Consumer Questionnaire   F225

38 Other Federal Agencies and Consumer Groups   130

     Consumer Product Complaint Form   F227

     Telephone Log   F229

VII

CONSUMER-SIZE JUSTICE

39 Taking Your Case to Small Claims Court   137

40 Making and Filing Your Complaint   139

     Summons and Complaint   F231

41 Rules of the Court   144

42 Evidence and Witnesses   147

     Application for Subpoena   F235

     Subpoena Duces Tecum   F237

43 Out-of-Court Settlement   153

     Agreement   F239

44 Trying Your Case   157

     Declaration and Notice of Motion to Vacate Judgment   F241

45 Collecting Your Award   162

     Petition for Writ of Execution   F243

     Writ of Execution   F245

     Petition for Order to Answer Written Interrogatories   F247

     Summons to Answer Interrogatories   F249

     Plaintiff's Interrogatories in Aid of Judgment   F251

     Garnishee Summons   F295

46 Small Claims Courts— State by State   169

VIII

YOUR PERSONAL LOVING ARRANGEMENT

47 Writing Your Own Contract   175

48 Agreement in Contemplation of Marriage   178

     Agreement in Contemplation of Marriage   F297

     Exhibit A   F325

     Exhibit B   F327

49 Agreement to Live Together   216

     Agreement to Live Together   F329

50 Agreement Between Husband and Wife   219

     Agreement Between Husband and Wife   F357

IX

PREPARING YOUR OWN WILL

51 Nobody Lives Forever   223

     List of Important People and Papers   F359

52 Minimizing Your Federal Estate Taxes   231

     Declaration of Gift   F363

53 Evaluating Your Estate   240

     Informal Estate Evaluation   F365

54 The Anatomy of a Will   244

     Document to Be Kept with the Last Will and Testament   F371

55 Nine Wills   252

     Will of husband leaving entire estate to wife, if surviving, otherwise to adult children; appointment of wife as primary executrix   F379

     Will of wife leaving entire estate to husband, if surviving, otherwise to adult children; appointment of husband as primary executor   F383

     Will of husband leaving entire estate to wife, if surviving, otherwise in trust for minor children; wife appointed primary executrix   F387

     Will of wife leaving entire estate to husband, if surviving, otherwise in trust for minor children; husband appointed primary executor   F391

viii / CONTENTS

Will of husband having no children leaving entire estate to wife, if surviving, otherwise certain bequests and devises; appointment of wife as primary executrix F395

Will of wife having no children leaving entire estate to husband, if surviving, otherwise certain bequests and devises; appointment of husband as primary executor F399

Will of unmarried man having no children leaving entire estate to female cohabitant, if surviving, otherwise certain bequests and devises; appointment of cohabitant as primary executrix F403

Will of unmarried woman having no children leaving entire estate to male cohabitant, if surviving, otherwise certain bequests and devises, appointment of cohabitant as primary executor F407

Will of unmarried man or woman having no children, making certain bequests and devises, appointment of executor or executrix F411

56 Two Wills Using Tax-Free Interspousal Transfer and Life Income Trust Provisions of the Economic Recovery Tax Act of 1981   254
Will of husband F415
Will of wife F421

57 Custom Fitting Your Will   256
Last Will and Testament Provisions F427

X

CREATING YOUR OWN TRUST

58 A Measure of Trust   263
Declaration of Gift F433

59 The Anatomy of a Simple Trust   272

60 Twelve Trusts (and Two Revocations)   275
Revocable Trust: One trustor, appointment of one trustee F435

Revocable Trust: Two trustors, appointment of one trustee F439

Revocable Trust: One trustor, trustor as initial trustee, provision for appointment of successor trustee F443

Revocable Trust: Two trustors, trustors as initial trustees, provision for appointment of successor trustee F447

Revocable Trust: One trustor, appointment of one trustee, provision for successor trustee, payment of trust income to primary beneficiary commencing upon death of trustor, payment of trust income and/or principal to secondary beneficiary upon death of primary beneficiary F451

Revocable *Inter Vivos* Bypass Trust: One trustor, appointment of one trustee F455

Irrevocable Trust: One trustor, appointment of one trustee F459

Irrevocable Trust: Two trustors, appointment of one trustee, trust income to surviving trustor for life, then to secondary beneficiary or beneficiaries F463

Ten-Year Reversionary Trust (Clifford Trust): One trustor, appointment of one trustee F467

Two-Year Reversionary Charitable Trust: One trustor, appointment of one trustee F471

Irrevocable Charitable Remainder Trust: One trustor, appointment of one trustee F475

Irrevocable Charitable Remainder Trust: Spouses as trustors, appointment of one trustee F479

Revocation of Trust (for trusts having one trustor) F483

Revocation of Trust (for trusts having two trustors) F485

61 Creating a Custom-made Trust   285
Optional Trust Provisions— First-Step Clauses F487

Optional Trust Provisions— Second-Step Clauses F489

Optional Trust Provisions— "Stand-Alone" Clauses F491

Optional Trust Provision—For Use with Two-Year Charitable Trust F493

Optional Trust Provision—For Use with Ten-Year Clifford Trust F495

XI

SELLING YOUR OWN HOUSE

62 You Can Do It Better   291

63 Helping Your House Sell Itself   293
Exterior Checklist F497

Interior Checklist F509
Appliance/Equipment Checklist F525

64 What's So Special About Your House? 295
Fact Sheet F533

65 Pricing Your House 306
Selling Price Comparison Survey F543

66 Advertising Your Home 315

67 Showing Your House 319
Telephone Log F545
OPEN HOUSE Flyer F547

68 Helping Your Buyer Finance Your Home 324
Estimated Purchase Data F549
Loan Comparison Data F551

69 Avoiding the Due-on-Sale Clause 334
Lease Agreement with Option to Purchase F553

70 Negotiating the Sale 343
Agreement to Purchase Real Estate F561
Counteroffer F563
Earnest Money Receipt F565

71 Closing 349

XII

USING THE FREEDOM OF INFORMATION AND PRIVACY ACTS

72 Your Right to Know 355

73 Federally Held Information Only 357

74 The Freedom of Information Act 359

75 The Privacy Act 368

76 Systems of Records 373

77 Filing a Privacy Act Request 376
FBI Privacy Act/FOIA Request F567
CIA Privacy Act/FOIA Request F569
Privacy Act/FOIA Request F571
Sample Format for Privacy Act Records Release Appeal F573
Sample Format for Privacy Act Records Amendment Request F575

Sample Format for Privacy Act Records Amendment Appeal F577
Model Format for Privacy Act Lawsuit to Effect Amendment of Records F579

78 Filing an FOIA Request 383
Freedom of Information Act Request F581
Sample Format for FOIA Records Release Appeal F583
Model Format for FOIA Lawsuit to Effect Release of Records F585

79 Additional Sources of Information 392

XIII

PERSONAL, FAMILY, AND FINANCIAL FORMS

80 Direct Mail Forms 429
Form letter requesting the Direct Mail Marketing Association (DMMA) for less mail F587
Form letter requesting the removal of name from mailing list F589
Notices Not to Add Name to Mailing List F591
Form letter requesting the DMMA for more mail F593

81 Medical Forms 430
Uniform Donor Cards F595
Special Medical Power of Attorney F597
(List of) Emergency Names and Numbers F599

82 Rental Agreements 432
Auto/Truck Rental Agreement F601
Boat Rental Agreement F603
"Open" Rental Agreement F605

83 Real Estate Forms 433
Rent Receipt F607
Notice of Rent Due F609
Notice of Overdue Rent F611
Notice to Quit Premises F613
Furnishings Inspection and Inventory F615
Property Management Agreement F619

84 Employment Application 434
Employment Application F621

85 Bills of Sale 435
Bill of Sale of Boat (Individual Buyer and Seller) F625

Bill of Sale of Boat (Joint Buyers and Sellers) F627

Bill of Sale of Personal Property (Individual Buyer and Seller) F629

Bill of Sale of Personal Property (Joint Buyers and Sellers) F631

86 Selling Your Own Car 436

Fix-up Materials Shopping List F633

Offer to Purchase Motor Vehicle F635

Receipt for Nonrefundable Deposit F637

Bill of Sale of Motor Vehicle (Individual Buyer and Seller) F639

Bill of Sale of Motor Vehicle (Joint Buyers and Sellers) F641

Odometer Mileage Statement F643

87 Financial Forms 448

Credit Application F645

Personal Financial Statement F649

Joint Financial Statement F653

Promissory Note F657

Installment Note F659

Series Promissory Note F661

Security Agreement F663

Chattel Mortgage F665

Request for Reason for Adverse Credit Action F669

Request for Disclosure of Credit Information F671

88 Attorney Forms 450

Power of Attorney F673

Miscellaneous Power of Attorney Clauses F675

Affidavit of Attorney F677

Auto Dealer's Powers of Attorney F679

Revocation of Power of Attorney F681

Retainer F683

Contingent Fee Retainer F685

Retainer of Attorney by Executor F687

Affidavit F689

89 Living Will 452

Living Will F691

Living Will (with pregnancy clause) F693

Living Will (for use after diagnosis of a terminal condition) F695

XIV **GLOSSARY** 453

XV **INDEX** 477

XVI **LEGAL FOOTNOTES** 489

XVII **FORMS** 495

Foreword

Remember the famous Fram oil filter commercial: "You can pay me now . . . or pay me later"? Paying "now" meant buying a new oil filter (about $4). Paying "later" meant a complete engine overhaul (about $400). The ad was a clever version of the old proverb "an ounce of prevention is worth a pound of cure." Preventive maintenance is the key to trouble-free motoring. Preventive medicine has become one key to good health. And preventive law is one key to "legal health."

Preventive law is what *How to Avoid Lawyers* is all about. Make no mistake. This massive manual of forms and advice is not a how-to for jailhouse lawyers or aspiring Perry Masons. It hardly mentions criminal law, and, except for small claims court, does not instruct a reader on representing himself. To this extent the title of this highly useful (and usable) book may seem misleading to some, but it may also be instructive, for the truth is that most lawyers spend more time preventing problems than they do fighting lawsuits. Preventive law has long been the staple product of lawyers working for wealthy clients and business organizations. The poor, on the other hand, only use lawyers in a crisis. The middle class are, well, in the middle. Deterred by fear, ignorance and lawyers' high hourly rates, most people do not take full advantage of lawyers to prevent legal problems. Most adults do not even have a will, a basic preventive law document.

Don Biggs wants to change that. In 500 pages of clear text and 700 pages of forms, he enables the reader to write a will or trust, sell a house, use the Freedom of Information Act, complain about products, use small claims court, deal with contractors, and much more. This is the most complete legal manual for nonlawyers that I've seen, as well as the most usable. The section on wills is 37 pages long, not counting 25 pages on trusts, plus 73 pages of will forms and model provisions. The section on real estate sales is even longer. The forms are designed to be photocopied and can be removed from the book, if that is necessary to get a clean copy. The forms are conveniently keyed to the text.

Two lawyers have reviewed and approved everything in the book. This (nonpracticing) lawyer noticed nothing amiss. The book strikes reasonable balances between caution and boldness, economy and completeness. An overly cautious author would constantly tell the reader to check with a lawyer, and warn about variations in state law. He might be so vague that the book would not be very helpful in specific situations, or so complete that a multivolume work would result that is suitable only for libraries. An overly bold author would generalize too easily from limited information.

The book is the best of its kind and a bargain to boot. I suspect that among its buyers will be many lawyers.

WILLIAM A. BOLGER
Executive Director, National Resource Center for Consumers of Legal Services

Acknowledgments

I can never fully express my appreciation to the numerous people who spent many hours with me and who gave of their wisdom and good offices in making this book possible.

I shall always be grateful to this book's primary legal consultants, Stephen Bluestone and Jerry M. Dale, both of them busy attorneys in private practice who gave unselfishly of their time and experience, often spending evening hours and weekends reviewing this book's manuscript and legal forms to assure accuracy and completeness.

To these, too, and many others who could not be named, my special thanks:

Ruth Adams, Allan Adler, David Bell, Milner Benedict, Jonathan Billing, Joseph Binns, Linda Briggs, Marian Ciaccio, Shirley Cobert, Jeff Conrad, Hon. William Corbo, Hon. Alan Cranston, Dan Cutero, Sebastian Dangerfield, Helen Deckert, Hon. David Durenberger, Patricia E. Dunston, Jean G. Feldman.

Mark F. Ferber, Keely Fitzpatrick, Ken Foster, Lawrence A. Glendell, Hon. Barry M. Goldwater, Jr., William V. Gullickson, Irwin Hall, Diana Jones, Eldon Jones, Kric Kampnann, Gene Karpinski, Hon. Glen C. Kenton, Roger S. Kepier.

Prof. David F. Linowes, Karen E. McCaffrey. Grady McGregor, Marjorie Mahle, Ralph Nader, Hon. Stuart Nemser, Ramon J. Palacios, Michael Percheck, Hon. William Proxmire, Isadore Ringel, Kathryn Rosich.

Hon. Ira Salzberg, Hazel D. Stebbins, Joseph Teisan, Armand W. Thayer, Hon. Robert S. Trimble, D. Edwin Venery, Donald H. Venable, Gordon Weel, Lila Weingarten, Virginia Welsh, Andria Wiley, George L. Wilhelm, Dave Wright, Caril Young, Mary Youngblood.

My thanks also to legal researchers Robert Brinkerhoff, Susan Freeman, David D. Jordan, Irving Nissen, and Julia L. Strayhorn.

Finally, my deep appreciation to Geoffrey H. Braine, editor of this book, for his thoroughness, many, many invaluable suggestions, and for being such a pleasure to work with.

Using This Book

This book is organized into two main parts:

- Text, comprising the first 494 pages, which encompasses thirteen descriptive text sections, the Glossary (Section XIV), Index (Section XV), and Legal Footnotes (case annotations and legal citations for attorneys—Section XVI).
- Pages containing legal forms, contracts, and agreements, which make up the second portion of the book (Section XVII) and are numbered F1 (for forms page one) through F696.

ESSENTIAL THAT YOU READ TEXT

The text comprising this book's various sections is based upon the extensive legal research and the consultation of attorneys, judges, court clerks, government officials, consumer organizations, and nonprofit "watchdog" groups that constantly monitor and report on the administration's conduct of your government.

In addition, the text (as well as the forms) has been thoroughly reviewed by both of this book's primary legal consultants. Don't throw away the benefit of that effort, wisdom, and knowledge by ignoring this book's text when making use of any of its forms.

SAMPLE FORMS AND LETTERS INCLUDED WITH TEXT

In addition to the explanatory text, many sections of this book also contain sample letters and completed sample forms to be used in completing various "fill-in-the-blanks" forms, contracts, and agreements provided in the second portion of this book. These sample letters and forms have been kept close to related text for convenience and understanding, rather than placed with the uncompleted forms in the back of the book.

FORMS ORDERED AND NUMBERED BY CHAPTER

Forms contained in the second half of this book are ordered in the same sequence as they are described in the text. For quick and easy reference, these forms are numbered both by the chapter within which they are described and by their order within that particular chapter. Form 9.2, for example, is the second form described in Chapter 9; Form 16.5 is the fifth form referred to in Chapter 16. This form number may be found (along with the form page number) at the top outside corner of each form page.

FORM FORMAT DESIGNED FOR TYPEWRITER USE

In most cases we have designed this book's forms so that either a 10-pitch typewriter (10 letters to the inch) or a 12-pitch typewriter (12 letters to the inch) may be used. In a few cases, however, space limitations have required that we utilize a format more suited to a 12-pitch than to a 10-pitch typewriter. Thus, it would be a good idea before attempting to complete any form using a 10-pitch machine to make sure that information will fit in the space provided.

ORIGINAL FORMS NOT TO BE USED

In using this book, make *photocopies* of the original agreements, contracts, and forms that you want to use, making sufficient extra copies so that you will have duplicates for practice "work copy" forms. When you have completed filling out your "work copy" form, transcribe the data onto a "final" photocopy, which you will then use as your "official" form. Make at least one photocopy of your completed "final" form for your files.

All forms are printed on perforated pages for easy removal. After you have made photocopies of any form, either return it to its original spot (between the book's pages) or tuck it into the pocket that has been provided inside the back cover of this book.

I

LIVING WITH
THE LAW

1 What This Book Can Do for You

How to Avoid Lawyers is a book of legal action. It does more than merely hand you an instruction manual with a bit of information with which to defend yourself within the legal jungle. It gives you the weapons you need to take the initiative in dealing with landlords and merchants, insurance companies and home-improvement contractors, attorneys and creditors, and courts and the federal government.

These pages do more than remind you that you should have a will; they give you the information *and* the forms *and* the specific paragraphs you need so that you can have the protection of a custom-made will, now, tonight, before you go to bed.

One section of this volume provides complete contract forms you can use in dealing with home-improvement contractors, plus nearly all the forms, contracts, and agreements that you need to act as your own contractor, a move that can save you more than half the entire cost of a new home.

Another section of this book shows you how to establish a wide range of simple tax saving, privacy-protecting trusts that allow you to transfer assets to anyone you choose immediately after your death—and even before your death—outside of your will and outside of probate. You don't even need to have a will to make use of such trusts.

Section VIII has suggestions about agreements covering living together and marriage, gives you the agreement forms, and supplies specific paragraphs that you can use in defining your own loving arrangement.

Section XI shows you how to sell your own house more quickly than most real estate agents could do the job, and how to keep the customary six-percent sales commission for yourself and use that money to lower the price of your house and the down payment required to buy it.

You'll find guidelines and detailed agreements for do-it-yourself arbitration that can save you time and legal fees—and resolve previously unsolvable problems without going to court.

You'll learn how to shop for warranty protection as well as product features and price, how to complain without pain, how to make a store take back a "lemon" without resorting to lawyers or threats—and how to *win* in small claims court and COLLECT on your award.

Section XII of this book provides guidelines and forms that will enable you to file formal requests for federal data under provisions of the Freedom of Information Act, and shows you how to use the Privacy Act to learn the contents of any files on you maintained by the federal government—and how to correct errors about you (a not uncommon occurrence) that may exist in federal files.

While this book won't turn you into an attorney, with proper use it can allow you to become your own legal "paramedic," learning to take legal action the way an intelligent person learns how to perform CPR (cardiopulmonary resuscitation). It is also a book of legal "preventive medicine," its readily available information and legal forms are immediately useful and can often prevent major complications when you are faced with a potential legal problem.

While no book can ever substitute for a good attorney, many legal procedures and forms are simple enough, and relate to situations that are simple enough, so that very often no attorney is needed if you have sufficient information and use the proper legal form.

Many of the forms in this volume can be used without an attorney. Others, related to more complex issues, are useful in acquainting you with what is involved so that you can make more intelligent use of a lawyer when you consult one.

As explained thoroughly in the preliminary section, Using This Book, all of the ready-to-use forms —found in Section XVII—are ordered and coded by chapter number, with their use described and, on occasion, illustrated within each corresponding chapter—the description of their use often including a series of suggestions based upon the advice of this book's legal consultants. Though many of this book's forms are quite simple, and some are even very short, none should be used without first reading, and making sure you understand, the related text.

2 The Basis of American Law

Learning your way around in the law—staying out of trouble and successfully parrying occasional little legal sorties by antagonists—requires a certain acquaintance with the law's background, traditions, and sometimes peculiar way of looking at things.

You don't need the kind of legal training that might turn you into a courtroom jungle fighter—just a general knowledge, like the knowledge of auto mechanics that allows you to get your stalled car started or the knowledge of electricity that enables you to repair an appliance.

The practical basis for modern American law can be traced to the laws of Moses and Christ, to the early civilizations of the Greeks and Romans, and, more directly, to the first English codes that had their beginnings around A.D. 600. Interestingly, the early English codes imposed fines for the commission of crimes, fines that were paid by the criminal to the victim—something we are just getting around to again today, although with the state being the recipient of the criminal fine and then, in some jurisdictions, paying compensation to victims of robbery, assault, etc.

To early English law we owe our tradition of juries, professional judges, the principle of legal precedent, judicial review, and the grand jury system for the indictment of suspects in criminal offenses. The American colonies, having been settled by British subjects, looked to English "common" law as the foundation of their own laws once free of the prerogatives of the crown, a crown that often denied them many of the rights they had known at home.

English common law still governs much of how we live and do business with each other today, although "common-law" marriage (marriage without a ceremony presided over by a religious or civil official) is probably the most frequent and familiar reference to common law today.

The personal rights and obligations of a valid common-law marriage (originating in a "common-law" state) are recognized today by every other state, but there is no such thing as "common-law" divorce. Once a couple is married in common law, a court must sever even those bonds of matrimony if either party decides to remarry legally.

The Declaration of Independence, along with its twenty-eight accusations against the king of Great Britain, made the first few thumbprints on the continually changing block of modeling clay comprising American law when it declared it self-evident that "all Men are created equal" and "are endowed by their Creator with certain unalienable rights, that among these are Life, Liberty and the Pursuit of Happiness."

It was not until eleven years later, in 1787, that the Constitution was signed and America got around to living under what we now think of as the law of the land.

The Constitution made heady reading:

- It established the Senate and the House of Representatives and set the qualifications for membership in each.
- It established rules for impeachment.
- It established rules for national elections.
- It established rules for procedure in the House and the Senate.
- It enumerated the powers and limitations of Congress.
- It defined and listed the qualifications for the offices of President and Vice-President.
- It provided for the Supreme Court and other federal courts and listed the jurisdictions of each.
- It also established the relationship of states to the federal government and established certain rights of citizens.
- And finally, it set down the means of ratification by the states.

The Constitution was far from a shoo-in. Delegates to the Constitutional Convention questioned whether the lower house should be elected by the people instead of by state legislatures and whether the Presidency should be a three-man troika. Virginia's Edmund Randolph shouted that a one-man Presidency "would be the foetus of monarchy!" Even Ben Franklin had his doubts about the wisdom of a one-man office of the Presidency, saying that some future President, presiding alone, might prove corrupt. The term of office was initially set at 6, then 11, 15, 7, and, finally, 4 years.

Thirty-nine of the convention's fifty-five delegates were on hand to sign the Constitution on September 17, 1787. Two refused to sign, and one, delegate Patrick Henry, refused even to attend the Constitutional Convention because he "smelled a rat."

Many delegates from states ratifying the Constitution felt that individual rights weren't adequately covered by the document. It was only with the promise that individual rights amendments would be added later that enough votes were obtained to secure ratification.

The first ten constitutional amendments are, of course, the Bill of Rights. They touch our lives so significantly on a daily basis that we have included them here.

Article I

Congress shall make no law respecting an establishment of religion, or prohibiting the free exercise thereof; or abridging the freedom of speech or of the press; or the right of the people to peaceably assemble and to petition the Government for redress of grievances.

Article II

A well-regulated militia being necessary to the security of a free State, the right of the people to keep and bear arms shall not be infringed.

Article III

No soldier shall, in time of peace, be quartered in any house without the consent of the owner, nor in time of war but in a manner to be prescribed by law.

Article IV

The right of the people to be secure in their persons, houses, papers, and effects, against unreasonable searches and seizures, shall not be violated, and no warrants shall issue but upon probable cause, supported by oath or affirmation, and particularly describing the place to be searched, and the persons and things to be seized.

Article V

No person shall be held to answer for a capital or other infamous crime unless on a presentment or indictment of a Grand Jury, except in cases arising in the land or naval forces, or in the Militia, when in actual service, in time of war or public danger; nor shall any person be subject for the same offense to be twice put in jeopardy of life or limb; nor shall be compelled in any criminal case to be a witness against himself, nor be deprived of life, liberty, or property, without due process of law; nor shall private property be taken for public use without just compensation.

Article VI

In all criminal prosecutions, the accused shall enjoy the right to a speedy and public trial, by an impartial jury of the State and district wherein the crime shall have been committed, which district shall have been previously ascertained by law, and to be informed of the nature and cause of the accusation; to be confronted with the witnesses against him; to have compulsory process for obtaining witnesses in his favor, and to have assistance of counsel for his defense.

Article VII

In suits at common law, where the value of the controversy shall exceed twenty dollars, the right to trial by jury shall be preserved, and no fact tried by a jury shall be otherwise re-examined in any court of the United States than according to the rules of the common law.

Article VIII

Excessive bail shall not be required, nor excessive fines imposed, nor cruel and unusual punishments inflicted.

Article IX

The enumeration in the Constitution of certain rights shall not be construed to deny or disparage others retained by the people.

Article X

The powers not delegated to the United States by the Constitution, nor prohibited by it to the States, are reserved to the States respectively, or to the people.

You have only to consider a few recent years' major news stories to become aware of the reach of the Bill of Rights into today's affairs. Cases involving search and seizure, federal handgun legislation, the use of uninformed adults and children in medical and psychological research, protection against disclosure of personal data contained in computers, and abortion are only a handful of cases recently or presently before the Supreme Court for interpretation of one amendment or another of the Bill of Rights.

With ratification of the Bill of Rights, four years after ratification of the Constitution, the shape of American law was refined again and seemed, for the moment at least, to satisfy the needs of the people for personal rights guarantees.

For a time, at least, it was as though the framers of the Constitution were able to step back for a moment to gain better perspective of what they had formed and were able to say, "Not bad, not bad at all!"

Within five years the Eleventh Amendment, exempting the state from lawsuits, was ratified. In 1804 the Twelfth Amendment, dealing with election of the President and Vice-President, was also ratified.

Then, in 1865, the Thirteenth Amendment, which was to set in motion forces that ground the nation under the heel of civil war, became part of the Constitution. The Thirteenth, proposed by Congress in January and ratified by the states before the end of December, provided the following:

> Neither slavery nor involuntary servitude, except as a punishment for crime whereof the party shall have been duly convicted, shall exist within the United States, or any place subject to their jurisdiction.

Three years later the states ratified the Fourteenth Amendment, granting citizenship to blacks:

> All persons born or naturalized in the United States, and subject to the jurisdiction thereof, are citizens of the United States and of the State wherein they reside. No State shall make or enforce any law which shall abridge the privileges or immunities of citizens of the United States; nor shall any State deprive any person of life, liberty, or property without due process of law; nor deny to any person within its jurisdiction the equal protection of the law.

(It was under provisions of the Fourteenth Amendment that the Supreme Court decided in 1978 [*Regents of the University of California* v. *Allan Bakke*] that Bakke, a white man, had been illegally denied admission to the university's medical school because of his race.)

Within a few years of ratifying the Fourteenth Amendment, further amendments approved by the states granted the right to vote regardless of race (the Fifteenth), authorized the federal income tax (the Sixteenth), provided for the direct election of senators (the Seventeenth), and instituted national prohibition (the Eighteenth Amendment, repealed thirteen years later, in 1933). Then, in 1920, the Nineteenth Amendment gave women the right to vote.

The Equal Rights Amendment, which would have been the Twenty-seventh Amendment had it been ratified, would have provided equal rights for women:

> Equality of rights under the law shall not be denied or abridged by the United States or any state on account of sex.
>   The Congress shall have the power to enforce, by appropriate legislation, the provisions of this article.
>   This amendment shall take effect two years after the date of ratification.

In all, more than 2,700 amendments to the Constitution have been proposed by Congress, but only 26, including the 10 amendments of the Bill of Rights, have obtained the necessary approval by three-fourths of the states for ratification.

As much as they seem to offer, the promises of the Constitution are often not fulfilled, and it has remained for the Supreme Court to interpret the meaning of the Constitution as it daily applies to individual freedoms, equal rights, taxation, and almost every other aspect of ordinary life.

In addition to the Constitution, there are other far more prolific, if less profound, sources of American law. The members of the House of Representatives and Senate spend much of their time in Washington each year grinding out new federal laws faster than anyone can read, understand, or implement them. The recent Ninety-seventh Congress passed, and the President signed into law, 1,358 pieces of new federal legislation.

Any new federal law can abruptly increase your taxes, affect your chances for job promotion, determine where your children go to school, specify how you receive medical care, and in other ways significantly change the way you live your life.

In addition to Congress, yet still within the federal system, are agencies of the government like the U.S. Treasury, Department of Health and Human Services, Department of Defense, Federal Aviation Administration, Department of Agriculture, and so on, whose regulations have the force of law.

The Tenth Amendment to the Constitution, you recall, declares, "The powers not delegated to the United States by the Constitution, nor prohibited by it to the States, are reserved to the States respectively, or to the people."

The states, of course, have never shown any hesitancy about enacting laws of their own, generally following the same principles adhered to by the federal lawmaking machinery.

States are prohibited by the Constitution from entering into treaties, from coining money or issuing currency, from seceding from the federal union, and, except for one (Texas), from dividing like an amoeba to form additional states.

The joint congressional resolution providing for the admission of the Republic of Texas into the federal union in 1845 states:

> New states of convenient size, not exceeding four in number, in addition to said state of Texas, and having sufficient population, may hereafter, by consent of said state, be formed out of the territory thereof, which shall be entitled to admission under provisions of the federal Constitution.

So what? Well, for one thing, that would mean four new governors and eight additional senators representing Texans' interests in Washington. Imagine the helplessness of any President visited by a delegation of ten twangy-voiced senators who share the same language and purpose—ten thinly disguised clones of Lyndon Johnson. Why, the federal government would be powerless against anything like that!

Of course, that joint resolution did not promise anything about more congressional representatives, that being based on population. But given Texans' way with numbers, it shouldn't be any time at all until the new states have the largest congressional delegation in Washington.

Although the states might still pass laws that are unconstitutional, such as the former Virginia law prohibiting marriage between men and women of different races, it is an almost sure bet they'll be struck down by the Supreme Court, as was Virginia's miscegenation law in 1957.

Finally, counties, cities, towns, and villages all enact laws of their own, some of them more for publicity, or even in jest, one suspects, than with any thought of serious enforcement.

In New York, for example, it is illegal for children to collect old cigar butts. A city ordinance in Tulsa makes it a violation of law to open a soft-drink bottle unless an engineer is present, and Los Angeles forbids hunting moths under a streetlight.

"UNWRITTEN" LAW

There is another source of law, often called "unwritten" law. For years the most commonly mentioned unwritten law was the supposed unwritten law that if a man came home and found another man in bed with his wife, he could do away with either—or both —and get away with it. But even that unwritten law was based more on the belief that no jury would convict the husband than on confidence that the state would look the other way and pretend the killing never happened.

Today's so-called unwritten law most often comes into existence as the result of decisions by judges, *precedents* upon which future cases are decided.

The rule of precedent is so strong that attorneys often spend days, sometimes even weeks or months in important cases, in law libraries looking for previous judicial decisions bearing on their clients' cases— looking for favorable precedents that the judge hearing their case will be bound to follow.

If a lawyer can find a series of precedents favoring his client's very similar case, he can almost count on a favorable decision by the judge. If the judge's decision does happen to depart from a strong body of precedent, the lawyer can be fairly sure the judge's decision will be overturned by an appeals court.

Unwritten law, the "real" unwritten law of history, was the body of law formulated by prophets, priests, and tribal wise men and handed down verbally from one generation to the next. Most of that unwritten law has since been written down and was the basis for much of what became written law in the United States and other countries.

Today in the United States the term "unwritten law" is pretty much a misnomer; although so-called unwritten law is not based upon enacted statutes, it is transcribed in court records—based upon the written decisions of judges.

RELIGIOUS LAW

There is one final source of law that deserves looking at, although you will not find it in any list of statutes passed by a lawmaking body nor among the compilation of judicial precedents referred to by attorneys in law libraries.

That law is religious law. While no American can expect to be fined or sent to jail for a violation of religious law, it often comes into play in major, everyday issues and can influence laws passed by Congress and the states. The effect of the Catholic Church's "law" against abortion is but one example.

For many Americans, Hebrew law, Muslim law, and the laws of other religions are a part of everyday life and are adhered to with as much dedication as any United States law is respected by the most law-abiding citizen.

③ Organizing the Law

Law—the whole body of federal, state, county, and municipal legislation and so-called unwritten law—generally falls into two categories: criminal law and civil law.

CRIMINAL LAW

In *criminal law*, although the victim may be an individual, the offense is against the law of the state, and it is the state that initiates legal action—*The People v. Smith.*

You probably don't need to worry too much about being arrested and having to face trial for a violation of criminal law—you can hardly hold up a bank without realizing it, nor can you inadvertently steal your neighbor's silverware for sale to a trafficker in stolen goods without knowing that you're committing a criminal offense.

But you do have some cause for concern. Suppose you're selling vacuum cleaners and become a bit carried away in claiming to a prospective customer what your vacuum cleaner will do. You might think it's sales enthusiasm, but unless your vacuum cleaner will do everything you said it will do, the prosecuting attorney might call it fraud—and that's a criminal offense.

Or if you obtain a bank loan and it can be shown that you knowingly failed to disclose certain debts or misrepresented your income (especially if you later default on the loan), you might be prosecuted for fraud as a violation of criminal law.

Also, if you injure someone or are responsible for the injury of others due to your direct negligence, your negligence could be found to be so gross that you might be prosecuted for criminal negligence. A contractor whose shoddy workmanship resulted in the collapse of a building that injured its occupants could be prosecuted for criminal negligence.

CIVIL LAW

Civil law comprises those laws that govern affairs between private parties. Court proceedings within the framework of civil law often involve damages, or injuries by one person to another, or disputes between parties over contracts.

In civil law the complaining party initiates the legal action—*Jones v. Brown, Thomas v. the ABC Corporation,* or, in the case of divorce, *Williams v. Williams.*

The U.S. government, states, counties, and municipalities can also bring civil suit. You may read about a case involving *The Federal Communications Commission v. the XYZ Broadcasting Company* or even, as increasingly happens, one government agency against another, *The Environmental Protection Agency v. the U.S. Army Corps of Engineers.*

The first listed party, by the way, is the one bringing the case to court and is called the *plaintiff.* The second listed name is the party being complained against, the *defendant,* who is defending himself against the complaint.

Sometimes an offense comes within the bounds of both criminal and civil law. If I steal your car and damage it, the theft can be prosecuted by the state as a violation of criminal law, but you can also bring suit against me under civil law for damaging your car.

Within the framework of civil law most defendants come to grief in court over disputes involving negligence or contracts. Consequently both of those categories of civil law will be dealt with more fully in Chapter 6, Staying Out of Court.

4 The Court System

Perhaps one way of looking at the court system is to compare its jurisdictions (legal authority to act) to those of law enforcement agencies. We know that a police officer from San Francisco cannot exercise his authority in Atlanta; we also know that a Pennsylvania state trooper can make an arrest anywhere in his state, just as a sheriff has jurisdiction throughout his county.

Generally, police officers, county sheriffs, and state police can exercise their authority over a fairly wide spectrum of law enforcement, from issuing traffic tickets to conducting criminal investigations and answering calls in connection with domestic disputes.

Agents of the Federal Bureau of Investigation can also act throughout a wide spectrum of law enforcement, although their authority, their *jurisdiction*, is limited to federal matters. They can, of course, make an arrest anywhere in the United States.

Then there are other federal officers, such as U.S. Treasury agents, who have jurisdiction anywhere in the United States, but whose authority is limited to actions specifically falling within the responsibility of their department, in this case the Treasury Department.

The analogy isn't perfect, but it does give some idea of how the system of courts in the United States is organized. At each level there are general courts (often called general sessions courts) and specialized courts. In each instance their jurisdictions are limited to specific geographical areas.

LOCAL COURTS

If someone sues you for property damage or personal injury and the amount claimed is less than $3,000, the case will probably be heard in your municipal general sessions court. The same court would hear cases involving credit disputes, nuisance suits, and disagreements over contracts that do not involve amounts above the court's statutory limit. Claims above a set limit must be brought in a state court.

Municipal traffic courts, police courts, juvenile courts, and family relations courts all have jurisdictions limited to specific areas of the law. If you receive a traffic ticket and want to contest the citation, your case will probably be heard in a traffic court.

STATE COURTS

You're likely to find yourself in a state court if you are involved in a trial related to violation of state criminal or civil laws—and especially if you're a party to a lawsuit in which the amount of damages claimed is in excess of the maximum limit imposed on municipal and county courts.

There are also several types of specialized state courts. Two of these are *Courts of Claims*, where civil suits against the state are brought, and *State Courts of Appeals*, sometimes called *Appellate Courts*, where the "losers" of lower court decisions can appeal for review of their case and possible reversal of the lower court's decision.

Each state also has its own *State Supreme Court*, which hears cases turning on some aspect of the state's constitution and, in those states not having appellate courts, hears appeals of lower court decisions.

In an appeal a complete transcript of the original trial, plus opposing lawyers' briefs containing citations of relevant precedents and laws, are presented to the judges. Attorneys for both sides may also make oral arguments.

In an appeal there is no jury, no witnesses are heard, and no new evidence is presented. The judges of the appeals court, usually a chief justice and two associate justices, review the transcript and attorneys' briefs and hear any oral arguments opposing lawyers may care to make. They then consider relevant laws and the original trial judge's handling of the case and finally decide whether the appeal is sustained or denied.

It's important to note that an appeals court's consideration of a case is not a new trial. If the appeal is sustained, the appeals court can reverse the original court's decision, granting a new trial. It may also reduce the amount of damages awarded or do whatever else the judges decide is required in order for justice to be done.

In every state there are also courts, usually called *Probate Courts*, but sometimes also called *Surrogate* or *Orphans Courts*, whose special authority gives them jurisdiction over the administration of wills and estates.

If you leave a will when you die, the executor you have named will present your will to a probate court, along with an inventory of your estate's assets and liabilities. The court will determine if your will is valid, will place a legal notice in newspapers, and will hear all claims against the estate.

If you don't leave a will, the probate court will still have jurisdiction over your estate and, in effect, will write a will for you, based on state laws. It will also appoint an administrator whose legal responsibility is much the same as that of an executor who would have carried out the responsibility of probating your will if you had written one.

In many states the legal costs of probating a modest estate range from $500 to $750, but in others the legal cost of probate can be considerable, perhaps

20 percent of an estate valued between $15,000 and $30,000. Those costs, mostly for lawyers' fees, are in addition to the substantial taxes that are levied against large estates (see Section IX).

FEDERAL COURTS

The basic and broadest segment of the federal court system is organized into ten districts, plus the District of Columbia—ninety-four courts in all, at least one in each state.

U.S. District Courts are the courts of original jurisdiction within the federal court system. They are empowered to try:

- All civil cases involving claims over $10,000 where the suit involves citizens of different states, and civil cases between citizens of different states where foreign citizens or foreign countries are also involved.
- Criminal cases in which federal laws are alleged to have been broken.
- Cases involving admiralty (marine and maritime) law.
- Certain cases involving income tax, copyright, patent, and trademark law.

Although each year U.S. District Courts receive more than 100,000 new civil cases and more than 50,000 criminal cases, only about 15 percent come to trial.

Many civil cases are settled by negotiation before trial, and a great number of criminal cases are settled by plea bargaining wherein the accused agrees to plead guilty to a lesser charge to avoid going to trial and risking conviction for the more serious crime of which he was originally accused.

Above the ninety-four U.S. District Courts sit the eleven *U.S. Courts of Appeals*, one for each of the ten districts plus the District of Columbia, which hear appeals from the decisions of U.S. District Courts. The Supreme Court, of which more later, can also hear appeals directly from district courts in cases that involve the constitutionality of a federal or state law. Bankruptcy cases are dealt with in special *Federal Bankruptcy Courts*.

As in the case of local and state courts, the federal court system includes a number of courts whose jurisdiction is limited to specific areas. The *U.S. Court of Claims* hears cases involving claims against the federal government. The *U.S. Customs Court* hears cases involving alleged violations of customs law. There is also a *U.S. Court of Customs and Patent Appeals*, which hears appeals from customs courts and, in the instance of patent litigation, hears appeals from district courts.

Appeals from the semijudicial decisions of regulatory agencies like the Interstate Commerce Commission can also be heard by the federal appeals courts and even by the Supreme Court if they involve constitutional questions.

U.S. SUPREME COURT

The Supreme Court, whose prime duty is the day-to-day interpretation of the Constitution, has often been described as a kind of Constitutional Convention sitting in continuous session. "We must never forget," said Chief Justice John Marshall in 1834, "that it is a *constitution* we are expounding . . . intended to be adapted to the various crises of human affairs."

Although the chances of a case involving any specific individual *ever* reaching the Supreme Court are slight, it is the Supreme Court, perhaps, that influences our lives more profoundly and more frequently than any other because its decisions, turning on a point of constitutional law as they do, affect the daily lives not only of every U.S. citizen but also of every resident of the United States.

During 1943, in the midst of World War II, the Supreme Court determined that "compelling the flag salute and pledge . . . invades the sphere of intellect and spirit which is the purpose of the First Amendment," thus outlawing the requirement of many schools that students daily pledge allegiance to the flag.

Until one day in 1962, students in many public schools began each day with a prayer. On the following day, because of a Supreme Court decision based upon First Amendment separation of church and state, such prayers were outlawed.

In January of 1973, the Court ruled that during the first three months of pregnancy states must leave the decision on abortion to a woman and her physician, thus overturning restrictive laws of several states.

Appearing before the Supreme Court on July 8, 1974, attorney James St. Clair argued that a President was not required to hand over certain tape recordings sought by special prosecutor Leon Jaworski in his investigation of former White House advisers charged in connection with the Watergate break-in.

On July 24 the Court unanimously found that the President must obey a judge's order (to furnish the tapes) to provide evidence required for a fair trial for the accused. Executive privilege, said the Court, must yield to due process of law.

On August 9, largely on the basis of evidence revealed by the tapes, Richard Nixon resigned as President of the United States.

In a more recent decision (*Exxon v. Governor of Maryland*), the Court affirmed the right of that state (and by implication, others) to prohibit oil producers from operating retail service stations within the state —a law passed by the Maryland legislature on evidence that oil producers were favoring company-owned stations.

In a more controversial case (*Zurcher, Chief of Police of Palo Alto, California v. Stanford Daily*), in May 1978, the Court found that law enforcement agencies may legally obtain search warrants to search the home or other property of individuals and organizations *not* accused of any crime if police believe the party is in possession of evidence required for an investigation.

In his dissent Justice Stevens expressed concern that "countless law-abiding citizens—doctors, lawyers, merchants, customers, bystanders—may have documents in their possession that relate to an ongoing criminal investigation. The consequences of subjecting this large category of persons to unannounced police searches is extremely serious."

Many attorneys and civil rights organizations interpreted the decision to mean that police, armed with search warrants issued by any friendly judge or magistrate, could now invade the homes and offices of innocent parties and rummage through their personal letters, files, photos, financial records, and other documents as though they were common criminals. It was a far-reaching decision that no one except police and prosecuting attorneys seemed to like.

As we mentioned in Chapter 2, the Court, in 1978, determined that Allan Bakke, a white man, had been illegally denied admission to the University of California at Los Angeles Medical School because of his race.

Although the Supreme Court also found that race may be considered as one factor in a university's admissions policy, the decision forced the immediate abolishment of quota-related admissions programs at more than 150 colleges and universities across the United States. However, the final result is sure to be even more widespread, forcing changes in hiring and on-the-job training programs—changes that are expected to affect the employment and career advancement of millions.

Thus, the form of the law of the land, initially shaped by the framers of the Declaration of Independence and the Constitution, is still being shaped and refined.

In recent years the Supreme Court has handed down an average of 170 decisions per year. To qualify for review, a case must have four affirmative votes. The Court accepts very few of the nearly 4,000 petitions filed each year and hears oral arguments in only about 150 of these. The remainder are decided without hearing oral arguments. The nine justices of the Court are appointed by the President, confirmed by the Senate, and, once sworn into office, serve for life or until retirement.

Least numerous, but often the most complicated and time consuming, are original jurisdiction actions coming directly before the Court as a result of litigation between the United States and a state or between two or more states.

When California was sued by Arizona in 1952 over Colorado River water rights, two court-appointed special masters (officers of the court) heard more than 100 witnesses, took depositions from 240 others, and produced a final report containing more than 26,000 pages. Briefs and other documents filed by the states required another 4,000 pages.

Oral arguments were heard in 1961 and 1962, and the Court's decision, for Arizona, was handed down in 1963, six years after the case was originally filed.

All of the Court's hearings are held in public, and its decisions are always handed down in public. Sitting from the first Monday in October until their work is completed, usually by July 1, the Court alternately hears oral arguments for two weeks and then retires for two weeks for deliberations and opinion writing.

The Supreme Court building is open to visitors all year long. Tours are conducted several times each day during the week, and no matter how many government officials and VIPs a notable case brings to the courtroom, seats are always available for the public.

⑤ Finding and Working with a Lawyer

Finding and working with a lawyer is easier and cheaper today than ever before, thanks to a June 1977 Supreme Court decision (*Bates* v. *State Bar of Arizona*) that state bar association prohibitions against lawyer advertising violate First Amendment rights of free speech. In New York the Court's decision has been credited with reducing lawyers' fees for an uncontested divorce from an average of $750 to between $150 and $200.

Although a full page of small ads for lawyers appeared in the *Los Angeles Times* (mostly due to aggressive selling efforts by the newspaper), there has been little evidence of widespread unethical lawyer advertising warned against by the American Bar Association (ABA). Apart from one Chicago attorney who briefly advertised himself as the "world's most creative lawyer," most attorney ads have been limited to describing a lawyer's type of practice plus an occasional listing of minimum fee schedules for routine cases.

Although lawyer ads resulting from the Supreme Court's decision have lowered costs and made it easier to find various types of legal specialists, you're still faced with deciding when you should consult an attorney.

WHEN TO CONSULT A LAWYER

It's a good idea to consider consulting an attorney whenever—

- You seriously injure someone or damage property.
- You are injured or your property is damaged.
- You need to reestablish your credit rating after severe financial reverses.
- You are charged with a criminal offense.
- You are sued or want to sue someone.
- You plan to buy or sell real estate.
- You plan to establish a business.
- You write a will or establish a trust.
- You are involved in a contested divorce or custody proceeding.

Since many people sell their own houses, write their own wills, and form their own corporations, it may seem like legal overkill to consult a lawyer about some of the matters we've listed above.

But consider the alternatives: a possibly invalid contract, a costly award for damages, or some other unforseen and expensive legal complication, perhaps years after you thought everything was settled and done with.

FEES

Consider, too, the fees charged by many lawyers during 1984 for routine legal services. The fees listed in the table below do not include court costs, and it should be noted that these fees are lower in some rural areas.

TYPICAL LAWYER FEES (1984)

Settlement of a residential sale—to seller	$100/$200
Settlement of residential purchase—to buyer who is more concerned with assurance of clear title	$200/$300
Uncontested divorce	$150/$300
Simple bankruptcy	$150/$250
Name change	$100/$150
Formation of corporation	$150/$250
Partnership	$100/$150
Simple apartment lease	$100/$150
Draw simple will	$150/$200
Simple adoption	$150/$250

And if you need further inducement, many lawyers who advertise today offer the first half hour or hour consultation without charge.

Obviously not all legal matters lend themselves to a fixed fee. There are several traditional bases on which attorneys determine fees for handling a case:

- **By the Hour:** Ranging from $50 to $100 per hour in many metropolitan areas on fairly routine matters for which no advance time requirement can be determined.
- **Contingent Fee:** Based upon successful representation of the client in a personal injury or property damage claim. The contingent fee is often 33⅓ percent of the amount awarded if the case does not go to trial, 40 percent of the amount awarded if the attorney takes the case to trial. You pay no fee (but still must pay court costs) if the attorney fails to obtain an award in your favor.
- **Predetermined Percentage of the Amount Involved:** Collection of debt, 25 percent of the first $1,000

collected, 15 percent of the next $4,000 collected, etc. These fees are usually plus court costs.
- **For Reduction of Real Estate or Personal Property Assessment:** Usually 50 percent of the first year's tax reduction.
- **For Sale of a Business:** Commonly 3 percent of the selling price.

Of course, you and your lawyer can negotiate any fee for handling a case that seems fair to the two of you. It has been a long tradition in rural areas, and it is becoming increasingly popular in cities, for lawyer and client to barter for legal services—for example, the client agreeing to paint the lawyer's house, repair his or her car, or provide the labor to fix up an attorney's summer cottage in exchange for legal work.

In the future it may be as easy to join a prepaid legal plan as it is today to sign up for prepaid medical care. In 1978 the United Automobile Workers (UAW) announced a prepaid legal plan for present and retired Chrysler workers—and the union can be expected in the future to push for similar benefits in negotiating new contracts with other auto makers. Soon after other unions follow the UAW's example, private plans should become widely available.

FINDING A LAWYER

For years the most common way of finding a lawyer has been to ask a friend. Today, however, with society's greater mobility, our friends are either moving away from us or we're moving away from them. Thus we turn elsewhere. The source many of us think of first, a local bar association's lawyer referral service, is often the worst way to find a lawyer.

Lawyer referral services almost always provide the names of listed attorneys that happen to be next up on the rotation list. The lawyers' names that you are given may be attorneys whose offices are inconvenient to get to or who are not particularly interested in your type of case.

If you don't know a lawyer or have a trusted friend or relative who can recommend one, you can contact your insurance agent, employer, accountant, banker, physician, or landlord.

When attorneys look for attorneys, they turn to the national lawyers listing published in the *Martindale-Hubbell Law Directory*, which is an eight-volume directory done by states. Not all lawyers choose to be listed in the directory, however.

The most useful portion of Martindale-Hubbell (as called by lawyers) is the section made up of law firm advertisements listing the firm's name and address, phone number, type of practice, members' biographies, names of certain clients, and even bank references.

Each advertisement's biographical sketch lists education, professional organizations and honors, publications, public offices held, and even social fraternities and country clubs; in one instance we came across membership on a regional squash team.

Yes, lawyers have been advertising for years, but only to each other; *that* has always been considered ethical.

Your own public library probably has the multivolume Martindale-Hubbell. Another place to look would be in the law library of the county courthouse.

There are two additional sources of lawyers that you should check: lawyer ads and law clinics. In researching this book we found attorney ads in most major city newspapers. The ads were small and in many respects less self-congratulatory than ads in Martindale-Hubbell. Most included the type of practice that the lawyer had and occasionally listed representative minimum fees.

Law clinics are a recent and increasingly available source of legal advice. Established to provide quick, low-cost legal service to the vast numbers of people who have fairly routine matters to be handled, law clinics are staffed by lawyers and paralegals (lawyers' assistants). Often they see clients on a drop-in basis. Many law clinics do not charge a fee, or collect only a token charge, for an initial consultation.

It was the law clinic of Bates and O'Steen, in fact, that was responsible for the suit that led to the Supreme Court ruling that it was a violation of First Amendment rights of free speech to prohibit advertising by attorneys.

Bates and O'Steen ran afoul of the state bar of Arizona when they opened a law clinic in Phoenix during 1976 and placed an ad in that city's *Arizona Republic*. The Arizona Bar Association took the two lawyers to court, charging they violated a State Supreme Court ruling that stated:

> A lawyer shall not publicize himself, or his partner, or associate, or any other lawyer affiliated with him or his firm, as a lawyer through newspaper or magazine advertisements, radio or television announcements, display advertisements in city or telephone directories, nor shall he authorize or permit others to do so in his behalf.

Bates and O'Steen appealed an Arizona State Supreme Court censure to the United States Supreme Court and won the reversal of the Arizona high court's decision, thus opening the way for lawyer advertising and for the proliferation of low-cost law clinics, which must advertise to make themselves known to large numbers of prospective clients.

By mid-1978, law clinics, many of them with storefront offices in low-income areas, were flourishing in many cities.

One unforeseen side effect of the Supreme Court's decision has been to place competent legal service within the reach of low-income families, who are now taking unscrupulous landlords, loan sharks, and dishonest merchants to court in growing numbers.

One Florida lawyer, Stuart Stein of Fort Lauderdale, doesn't sit in his law clinic office waiting for clients to come to him; he takes his office where the clients are. Stein has fitted out his white van as a mobile office and sets up shop on weekends at drive-in swap meets and flea markets. His van bears the sign, *Law Office, Stuart L. Stein, Swap Shop Annex.*

Stein gives initial consultations without fee to clients sitting with him on folding chairs at a card table in the shade of an awning stretched out from the side of his van. "If a client wants to talk in private," says Stein, "we just go into the van and close the door."

WORKING WITH A LAWYER

Before making an appointment with a lawyer, write down everything you feel is important about your case: damages, injuries, circumstances, names, dates, times, places, etc. Section III's law forms will be a big help since they are related to many of the most common types of legal cases.

If you've been served papers of any kind, make several copies so that you can give the originals to your lawyer and still have a set for your files. Also make copies of any bills, receipts, complaint letters, medical records, and correspondence and give one set to your attorney.

Don't withold any information from your lawyer. Lawyer–client relationships are confidential, and no court can force an attorney to reveal anything a client has disclosed. Better to reveal some stupid thing you've done, possibly even something you're ashamed of and would never do again, than to risk losing your lawyer's confidence or risk losing your case in court because an opposing attorney caught your lawyer off-balance with surprise evidence that could not be prepared for because you did not tell him or her the whole truth.

Don't expect your lawyer to work for free, he or she has to earn a living just as you do. Don't be surprised if your attorney asks for a "retainer" before beginning work on your case. A retainer is simply a part payment of the attorney's estimated fee to cover the cost of initiating your case.

If you cannot pay anything at all at the moment, admit it; your attorney may be willing to defer payment or may handle your case without fee. If you truly have no funds, your community's legal aid society may refer you to an attorney who will provide legal service at no charge. Many excellent lawyers perform this kind of no-fee service for the public good, especially where the outcome of a case may establish a precedent that will have wide benefits for others.

By following this volume's legal consultants' advice, and by making use of many of its forms, you should be able to handle many routine matters on your own and more easily avoid some of the legal pitfalls that too often bring people into court. Better still, you'll know how to find and work with a good lawyer when you need one.

⑥ Staying Out of Court

The United States is the most lawyered nation in the world: 462,000 attorneys, one for every 465 men, women, and children in the nation.

Our 462,000 attorneys may be too few. One adult in two has some problem with the law each year, and a 1978 federal survey revealed that 70 percent of those needing legal services were either underrepresented or not represented at all.

All too often having a good attorney and winning your day in court can be so costly and time-consuming that being the legal victor is still a "no-win" situation. Better to stay out of court in the first place.

When most of us think of "staying out of court," we're considering ways of avoiding being hauled before a judge or jury; yet the other half of avoiding litigation consists of conducting our affairs so that we're not forced to haul *someone else* into court to obtain redress for real or imagined injustice.

While not all of the legal snares presented in this chapter can be avoided by the use of one of this book's law forms (a knowledge of the law being your best defense), many of the forms, such as bills of sale, contracts with workmen, auto accident diagrams, and simple auto/truck rental agreements, can help prevent legal problems or can considerably ease them if they do occur.

Since the time when those accused of crimes were put to trial by fire or somehow expected to remain cool, rational, and immune to the tortures of the rack if innocent, the law has acquired a patina of mystery little different from the rituals of witch doctors.

Indeed, "*Coram nobis, coram nobis; ignoranta legis non excusati, flagrante delicto, ab initio, absque hoc; ad damnum, ad damnum . . .*" and you're cursed *ad vitam.*

Or, "*Chimera, chimera; coram ipso rege, inter alia, brutum fulmen, ante litem motam, amicus curiae, volenti non fit injuria, de minimum non curat lex, nemine dissentiente, nemine dissentiente . . .*" and all your wishes are fulfilled.

Yet the law is basically founded on logic and equity. Most of us get into trouble with the law because we haven't done something we should have done or because we did something we shouldn't have done.

To make things especially confusing, we live under a three-tiered system of federal law, state law, and local law, all of it constantly changing and all of it subject to varying interpretations.

There is no way any book could consider every contingency that might bring the reader into court. Even if it were possible, the law would be changed between the time a book was written and the time it was printed—and changed again before it reached readers' hands.

Better then, instead of putting a microscope to the law, to consider the law's sometimes confusing logic in an attempt to develop an intuitive feel for the law that will warn us when we're beginning to tread on thin ice.

TORTS

Tort is a term you're likely to hear tossed around almost any lawyer's office if you sit in the waiting room for more than five minutes. A tort is simply a legal wrong *not* arising from a contract. Any breach of an individual's right to privacy, his or her right to reasonable peace and quiet, or his or her right to be left alone is a tort.

Assault, trespass, unlawful conversion, and defamation of character are *intentional* torts. Negligence is an *unintentional* tort. Anyone who commits a tort is legally responsible for all damage that directly results from his or her action.

Negligence

Undoubtedly the most common causes impelling Americans into court are in the area of unintentional torts termed negligence. Negligence is a failure to exercise the degree of care (which the court determines) an ordinary and prudent person would exercise under the same circumstances.

The highway is the most popular arena for Americans to practice court-determined negligence; fully one-third of all courtroom litigation each year is made up of auto accident lawsuits.

Beyond driving with care to steer clear of the courtroom, consider the following:

> You are driving at the 35 m.p.h. speed limit down an avenue in your hometown when a badly worn tire on your car blows out, causing you to veer into another auto, damaging the other car and injuring its driver.

Are you liable? Yes, because it could be shown that your tire was obviously worn and unsafe to drive on. Since a prudent person would not drive on such a tire, you could be found negligent.

> You are driving at the 35 m.p.h. speed limit down the same street and your recently checked brakes fail, causing you to hit another car, damaging it and injuring its driver.

Are you liable? No, because the brake failed due to a hidden defect and you could show that you exercised the degree of care (by having your brakes checked) that a prudent person would normally exercise.

You are driving down a street at night and because of a moment's inattention you hit the rear of an auto that is double-parked with its lights out.

Are you liable? Yes, in some states, because as a driver you are supposed to have control of your car at all times.

You are driving down a street at night and because of a moment's inattention you hit the rear of an auto that is double-parked with its lights out.

Are you liable? No, in some states, because the other driver's illegal double-parking and/or failure to have his lights on could be determined to be *contributory negligence*—thus making him ineligible to collect.

You are driving down a street at night and because of a moment's inattention you hit the rear of an auto that is double-parked with its lights out.

Are you liable? Maybe, in some states, which hold that judgments for damages may be awarded against the driver who is "most liable" for the accident. Yet in other states damages may be awarded in *proportion* to the degree of negligence—a "comparative-negligence" state.

In an Alabama case the driver of a car experienced engine trouble at night on a two-lane road that was not lighted. He left his car to seek help when the battery ran down, abandoning the auto in the roadway without setting out flares. The stalled car was struck from the rear by another auto.

The driver of the stalled auto was held liable for damage to the other car and for the injury of its driver. In handing down his decision the judge stated that if the driver of the stalled car had set out road flares, even though they may have burned out before the second car came along, the driver of the stalled car would have exercised **ordinary** care—and not been held liable.

You lend a friend your car. While driving it, he is injured or damages the property of another because of a hidden defect you were unaware of.

Are you liable? In some states, no, because you loaned your car to your friend for *his* convenience without receiving anything of value *and* without knowing of any defect that would make the car unsafe. In other states, yes, the owner is liable except in instances of theft or unauthorized use.

You *rent* a friend your car. While driving it, he is injured or damages the property of another because of a hidden defect you were unaware of.

Are you liable? In most states, yes, because you allowed him to use your car for a *consideration*, thus requiring you to exercise *great* care—in most states meaning that you are liable for almost any defect.

After you have had a few too many drinks at a neighborhood bar, you offer to drive a friend home. He knows you have had too much to drink, but he accepts the ride anyway. On the way to his house, and because of your drinking, you have an accident that injures him.

Are you liable for your friend's injury? No, because he knew that you were intoxicated before he got into your car and your car was the (proximate) cause of the accident.

Encountering a friend who is obviously intoxicated in a neighborhood bar, you offer to drive him home. On the way to his house you stop for some cigarettes, leaving him in the car with the key in the ignition. While you are in the store, he slides into the driver's seat, drives away, and has an accident that destroys your car.

Is your friend liable? In most states, no, because by leaving him in the car with the key in the ignition, you were guilty of *contributory negligence* and thus are unable to collect.

You and a friend are returning home from a night baseball game, and you drive into a large pothole that you were unable to avoid. Driving into the pothole caused you to lose control of your car and hit a tree, damaging your car and injuring your friend.

Is the city liable? Yes, if a city or state can be shown to have allowed a large pothole to remain unrepaired under either of the following conditions:

1. For an unreasonable time after it was reported.
2. After it should have been noticed and repaired in the normal course of inspection and maintenance.

You still might have a case if you had driven into the pothole in the daytime, although the city could argue that you had an opportunity to see and avoid the hole. The important thing to remember is that ultimate liability for your friend's injury and the damage to your car might well rest with the city, not with you.

Of course the highway isn't the only place where you can encounter a potential legal problem. Consider the following cases:

A customer in your store trips on a piece of torn carpet and falls, sustaining an injury.

Are you liable? Yes, if it can be shown that you were aware of the torn carpet or (as in the case of the pothole above) that the tear existed so long that you *should* have known about it.

A friend visiting your home falls down your

basement steps when a weak step gives way as he puts his weight on it; he is injured.

Are you liable? Not if the (hidden) weakened condition of the step was unknown to you. The burden of proof is upon your friend to show that you knew of the defect. The condition of the weakened step, not being readily visible, will almost surely be found by the court not to involve negligence on your part.

A passerby trips and falls on a broken portion of the sidewalk in front of your home and is injured.

Are you liable? Yes, a homeowner is responsible for maintaining the sidewalk in front of his house in a safe condition. This responsibility also includes removal of ice and snow within a reasonable time after they have accumulated. The law in some states is less clear if you rent, but many courts would absolve the renter of responsibility for an unsafe sidewalk if he had given notice to the owner.

You install a swimming pool in your backyard and place a three-foot fence around it. You keep the gate locked, but one weekend while you are away neighborhood children trespass on your property, climb the pool fence, and one of them drowns while swimming.

Are you liable? In some states, yes, because courts have found that swimming pools are an especially "attractive nuisance" and that children can easily climb a three-foot fence. In a similar case involving a five-foot fence the homeowner was found not liable.

In defense against claims resulting from alleged negligence, most courts will give weight to the following principles:

1. *Contributory Negligence*: The plaintiff may not recover because, along with the defendant, he failed to exercise ordinary care and thus contributed to the defendant's negligence.
2. *Comparative Negligence*: Many states have adopted the principle that a court's decision in awarding damages should reflect the comparative negligence of the parties. If the plaintiff is 25 percent negligent, he may be awarded 75 percent of the damages he sustained. In a state adhering strictly to the principle of contributory negligence, he would be awarded nothing, even if he were judged to be only 1 percent negligent.
3. *Assumption of Risk*: A plaintiff may not recover because the law presumes that he was aware of the peril and accepted the risk. A wrestling fan at a ringside seat who is injured when a contestant is thrown into his lap is presumed by the court to have accepted that risk. A baseball fan who is injured by a hit ball is presumed to have accepted that risk also.
4. *Imputed Negligence*: The plaintiff may not recover because the damage or injury resulting from negli-

gence may be imputed to him. In the classic textbook case, when a guest in a speeding auto neither warns the driver to slow down nor threatens to get out of the car (at the first safe opportunity one hopes) unless the driver slows down, the passenger relinquishes his right, in many states, to recover damages if he is injured in an accident in which the driver is judged negligent.

Conversion

Conversion is the unauthorized use or control of property to the exclusion of the owner's rights.

You borrow a friend's car to go to the beach. While legally parked at the beach, a hit-and-run driver seriously damages your friend's car.

Are you liable? No, because your use of the car was within the bounds of the purpose for which the car was loaned—the use was *authorized*.

You borrow a friend's car to go to the beach, but leave the beach early because of rainy weather and decide to go by your office to catch up on some work. While the car is legally parked at your office, a hit-and-run driver damages the car.

Are you liable? Yes, because your use of the car to go to your office was not the *purpose* for which the car was loaned—the use was **unauthorized**. Thus, you are liable whether or not the damage was due to your negligence.

If the use or possession of property by someone other than the owner is *authorized*, the user is normally required to exercise *ordinary* care. However, if the use is **unauthorized**, the user is held responsible for the exercise of *extraordinary* care (also termed by some courts as *great care*), which for all practical purposes means that in most courts an individual found to have made unauthorized use of property will be held liable for any damage, whether the user is negligent or not.

Bailment

Bailment is a written or unwritten agreement that *authorizes* a person (or persons) to possess the property of another (the owner) for a *specific* purpose or use. The following cases illustrate the degree of responsibility of the *bailee* (one to whom property is bailed) under varying circumstances.

A friend who is going out of town asks to leave his camera with you for safekeeping. You put the camera on a shelf in your bedroom closet. Your house is broken into while you are at work, and the camera is stolen.

Are you liable? No. Since you were in possession of the camera solely for the benefit of its owner, you are required to exercise only ordinary care and would be liable only if you could be shown to be guilty of gross negligence.

> You ask a friend who is going out of town to lend you his camera so that you can take some photographs. You put the camera on a shelf in your bedroom closet. Your house is broken into, and the camera is stolen.

Are you liable? In some states, yes. Since the camera was in your possession solely for *your benefit*, you are required to exercise great care, not just ordinary care, while in possession of the camera. If you had locked the camera in a desk drawer, the court might have accepted that as *great care* and absolved you from liability.

If your friend had left his camera with you for safekeeping and you made use of it without his permission, that would have been *conversion* and you would be liable for anything that happened to it.

> You leave your car in a parking lot and receive a claim check stating that the management's maximum liability for damage to your car shall not exceed $25. While driving your car in the lot, an attendant loses control of the car and seriously damages it.

Does the $25 limit on your claim check restrict the amount of damages you may collect from the owner of the lot? No. The parking lot owner is liable for any damage that results from his (employees') failure to exercise ordinary care.

> You leave your car in a parking lot and are asked to leave the key so that the car may be moved by the attendant. Later, when you return to the lot, you discover that your car has been stolen.

Is the parking lot owner liable? Probably. Many courts have held that his failure to return your auto established a *prima facie* case of negligence on the part of the owner. However, a few courts have determined that the lot owner was merely renting parking space and that the owner was not liable for the car's theft.

> A parking lot owner is generally not responsible for any damage, such as that caused by fire or flood, that is beyond his control and that is not the result of his negligence. If you leave your car at a garage for repair, or leave clothing with a tailor for cleaning or repair, neither will be held liable for loss or damage unless negligence can be proved. Although the bailee is responsible for his negligent acts, he is not the insurer of your property.

Nuisance

A nuisance is an intentional or unintentional activity that upsets the peaceful enjoyment of life. A noisy, all-night discotheque or a pollution-generating industrial plant may be liable for damages as a *public nuisance* because it affects the life of the community.

A nuisance that discomforts or damages the life of an individual or a household is a *private nuisance* and is also actionable in court.

> Your neighbor's dog, barking in the late hours night after night, disturbs your sleep. You have spoken to your neighbor asking that he make some attempt to quiet the dog, but he has refused.

Is your neighbor liable for damages by maintaining a nuisance? Yes. Your right to peaceful sleep has been disturbed. If your neighbor refuses to stop his dog's late night barking, you may obtain a court order requiring him to stop the nuisance, and you may also collect damages (for being unable to report to work on time due to lack of sleep, for example).

If your neighbor ignores the court's injunction, he can be held in contempt of court and can be fined and ordered to pay additional damages. A similar cause for action would exist if your neighbor played a radio excessively loud during late evening hours—generally held to be after 11:00 P.M.

If you've lived with a nuisance for a long time, or if its existence, such as a discotheque next door, was in evidence when you moved in, the court would probably not turn a sympathetic ear to your plea.

Assault

An assault is a threat against the personal safety of a person with *apparent intent and ability* to forcefully inflict bodily injury. For an assault to have taken place, no actual touching need have been done. An actual touching or application of force is called *battery*; hence the oft heard phrase *assault and battery*.

> During a card game with several new acquaintances at a business convention, one of the players angrily accuses you of cheating and, picking up a handy beer bottle, threatens to "break your skull open" unless you return his money.

Is he liable for assault? Yes, because he had apparent intent and ability to carry out his threat of bodily harm.

> You engage in a heated disagreement with a garage owner over what you feel are excessive charges. He angrily orders you to "get the hell off my property" and, picking up a tire iron, advances toward you. In order to evade his expected blow, you step backward, trip over a piece of equipment, and are injured.

Is the garage owner liable for your injury? Yes, because your injury was directly related to the assault, flowing from your reasonable belief that the garage owner intended and was able to inflict bodily harm.

NOTE: If the apparent means *and* intent to carry out a threatened attack cannot be proved, your fear would probably be determined to be unreasonable and you could not collect.

The above examples of negligence, conversion, bailment, nuisance, and assault, all of them torts of one form or another, cannot begin to anticipate every legal eventuality that might bring you, either as a plaintiff or defendant, into court. But they do cover some of the areas of courtroom conflict that commonly result in litigation.

CONTRACTS

There is yet another area of law that each year brings many of us into court, the area of law known as *contracts*. Disagreements over contracts include suits over leases; sales of homes, businesses, and real estate; guarantees and warranties; and contracts to perform a wide range of services.

Contracts can be written—as in the case of a lease, a contract for the sale of real estate, or a contract for home improvement work to be done by a contractor. Just as valid is an unwritten or implied contract—such as the implied contract when you get into a taxi that the car is safe to ride in and that the driver is sober and duly licensed, or the implied contract between you and your surgeon that when you're finally unconscious on the operating table, he, and not some intern or medical student, will actually perform the surgery.

For a contract to be valid in the eyes of the law, all of the following conditions must be met:

1. It must be entered into *voluntarily*; a "shotgun" contract, like a shotgun marriage, may hold up while you're in range of the shotgun, but it will never hold up in a court of law.
2. The parties must have the *legal capacity* to enter into a contract. An individual who has been declared insane cannot enter into a valid contract; neither can some, but not all, minors. Generally, however, a contract entered into by a minor can be enforced against a corporation or an adult who is a party to that contract, but cannot be enforced against another minor who is a party to the contract.

   Although marriage is a contract, the legal age for marriage varies from state to state and is often different from the minimum age at which persons may enter into other legally valid contracts.
3. There must be an *offer* and an *acceptance* of the offer. Each party must contribute something toward the creation of the contract; if I agree to paint your house for $2,000, that's a valid contract. If I merely promise to paint your house out of the goodness of my heart—even though I may put it in writing—there's no contract and my promise is not binding under law.
4. The subject and purpose of the contract must be *lawful*. Smith and Jones cannot sign a valid contract for Smith to transport Jones's truckload of stolen goods from one place to another.

Although it is a very good idea for any contract to be written down, if for no other reason than to make sure that both parties understand what they're agreeing to, the common types of contracts that *must* be written are contracts involving real estate and contracts that will not be fulfilled within one year of the agreement. Generally, however, verbal contracts are valid—the major problem you're likely to have in enforcing a verbal agreement being proof that it existed at all.

Contracts should provide for payment of court costs and legal fees by the "loser" if court action is required for enforcement of the agreement, unless, of course, such awards are unlawful in the state in which the contract was drawn.

Bills of Sale

You incur a risk of liability for damages if you fail to adequately describe an item listed in a bill of sale.

If you sell a car and fail to note any major, hidden defect that would adversely affect its safety, utility, or value, a court could find you liable for damages and require you to pay a specific sum to the buyer or, worse, hold you liable for damages and/or injuries resulting from an accident in which the car's hidden defect was a significant factor.

To collect, the buyer would have to prove that you knew of the car's faulty condition and willfully concealed it; sizable judgments have been awarded in such cases.

If you are selling a car, describe it adequately in the bill of sale. Include make, model, year, color, engine, and total miles, plus any major accessories, such as air conditioner, radio, stereo, CB, etc.

By listing accessories you protect yourself from their loss if you have to take the car back for any reason, such as nonpayment or payment with a check that bounces. If the bill of sale lists a radio, the car better have one when you repossess it or else the buyer legally owes you one.

A car, or most any other item for that matter, sold "where is, as is" can be sold without there being any representation as to condition or fitness for use.

Auto Rental

If you rent a neighbor's pickup truck some weekend to haul building materials for a do-it-yourself home improvement project, make sure you have a rental agreement that states how much you'll be paying and what you will be using the truck for. That way, so long as you use the truck as described in the agreement, you'll be liable only for the exercise of ordinary care in utilizing the truck. (And check your own auto insurance to make sure you're covered driving the truck; some policies limit *other vehicle* coverage to other passenger cars, not trucks.)

Notes and Interest

If you lend money to someone and take a promissory note, make sure that any interest is no more than the legal rate in your state. The courts of *some* states have determined that a promissory note that specifies a rate of interest higher than the state's legal rate is illegal and thus unenforceable.

You obviously don't expect a friend or relative to renege on a note, but in the event of your friend's or relative's death a court could rule that the "illegal" note gives you no claim against the debtor's estate.

"Legalese"

There's a very real effort being made, mostly by banks and insurance companies who are competing for your business, to simplify two of the most widely used types of contracts—loan agreements and insurance policies.

There is even an attempt underway, resisted by real estate interests, to introduce a simplified and easy-to-understand lease agreement.

During the summer of 1977, New York State passed a law that requires that all consumer agreements be "written in nontechnical language and in a clear and coherent manner using words with common and everyday meaning." This law is under attack by attorneys in that state. They claim that the law, passed by a state legislature whose membership is 41 percent lawyers, is "ambiguous and conflicts with existing law."

Writing in *One L*, a book describing his first year at Harvard Law School, former creative-writing teacher Scott Turow observed:

> In reading cases I soon discovered that most judges and lawyers did not like to sound like ordinary people. Few said "I." Many did not write in simple declarative sentences. They wanted their opinions to seem the work of the law, rather than that of any individual. To make their writing less personal and more impressive, they resorted to all kinds of devices, "whences" and "heretofores," roundabout phrasing, sentences of interminable length.

Turow's observation is confirmed by Washington, D.C., attorney Ronald Goldfarb, who conducts seminars for lawyers and judges to help improve their writing. Goldfarb says, "I have to brainwash Harvard Law School graduates to write simple, straight sentences that don't go on for pages."

One law professor wrestling with pervasive legalese, David Mellinkoff of the University of California at Los Angeles, terms most lawyers' writing, "wordy, unclear, pompous and dull. It's not the most precise way; it's the most *imprecise* way because it isn't common usage."

Commenting on the fact that much legal language in use today is "boiler plate" run up on preprinted legal forms or hidden away in law libraries, Mellinkoff asserts that "forms are the only way lawyers stay in business." But there is a crumb of reason in lawyers' love of arcane and complicated legalese. If a lawyer uses an old form, the chances are that it has already been interpreted by several courts, providing a legal precedent to tell him or her what the words actually mean.

That's the reason some of the forms in this book are included just as they are—their validity and meaning have already been determined by judicial opinion. To revise a form's wording extensively, ponderous though it may seem, would invite legal difficulties over the possible meaning of newly inserted words or phrases.

As we stated earlier, this chapter's purpose is to acquaint you with the logic of the law so that you can more easily avoid some of the circumstances that each year result in thousands of dollars in awards for damages and injury.

Whenever you believe that you may be involved in any situation that may lead to court, follow the previous chapter's advice on finding and working with a lawyer.

7 If You Must Go to Court

In a very real sense every civil court is a court of last resort in that neither of the parties would be there if there was any other way to resolve their disagreement.

Quite often, after a plaintiff has filed suit and the defendant learns that the plaintiff "really means business" and is serious about taking him to court, a compromise is reached to save both parties time and legal costs. So if a lawsuit comes to trial, it's almost always because there is no other way for the problem to be resolved.

Whenever you feel there is no other remedy for a civil wrong, you should consult a lawyer about taking your case to court. You should be as sure as possible that you have a valid case and that your claim warrants the time and expense of filing suit.

Before you see a lawyer, write down your complaint as clearly as you can. This will help you put your facts in order and will help you remember what you need to know. It's important for you to be able to establish the exact date on which the wrong took place because each state has established a *statute of limitations* for various types of complaints that sets a time period after which a claim may be unenforceable.

Assemble all receipts, bills, warranties and guarantees, contracts, letters, photos, and so on that pertain to your complaint. Make copies so that you can give a complete set to your attorney.

Also list the names, addresses, and phone numbers of everyone who might serve as a witness or who may have knowledge of the case. Finally, make sure you have the name and address of the party you intend to sue.

If you and your attorney agree that a suit should be filed, what follows is what you can expect to happen.

THE COMPLAINT

Based upon the evidence you have presented, your lawyer will draw up a complaint (or petition) describing the circumstances of the case and naming the defendant. The complaint will probably ask that a specific sum be paid for damages.

Actually, before filing a complaint an attorney will sometimes contact the defendant in an attempt to reconcile your differences before taking the case to trial.

If efforts at reconciliation fail, or if your lawyer feels that it would be useless anyway, he or she will file the complaint with the clerk of the appropriate court, that being a municipal or state court, or possibly a federal district court, where the defendant lives or where the wrong took place.

SUMMONS AND SERVICE

When the complaint has been filed with the clerk of the court, he issues a summons that directs the defendant to respond within a specific time, usually within thirty days. The summons will usually state that if the defendant does not respond within the required time, the plaintiff may obtain a default judgment against him in the amount of the claimed damages.

The defendant must receive legal notice of the suit. This requirement is generally determined to have been met when he receives a copy of the summons—usually served (delivered) by a local constable, sheriff, federal marshal, process server, or, in some jurisdictions, the plaintiff's attorney. In some states summons may be served by certified mail (see page 139).

Many defendants feel that they must sign for or be touched with the summons in order for service to have been accomplished. However, a summons may sometimes be considered to have been legally served if it is delivered to the defendant's home or place of business, or even published in a newspaper.

DEFENDANT'S ANSWER

As soon as a summons is served, the defendant should contact an attorney and assist him in preparing his response, called an *answer*, to the complaint.

If you are ever served with a summons, you should get your facts in order and marshal all possible evidence that could be used in presenting your side of the case before you see an attorney.

If you honestly feel the disagreement has arisen due to a misunderstanding, or if you are willing to compromise with the plaintiff, your attorney might suggest that you authorize him to contact the plaintiff, offering to "meet him halfway."

If you and your attorney feel there is no other recourse than to defend against the complaint, he or she will draw up and file an answer that will probably deny most of the complaint's allegations. Just as the complaint must be filed with the clerk of the court, so must the answer. Your lawyer will also send a copy of the answer to the plaintiff's attorney.

Normally, a date for the trial will be set soon after the defendant's answer has been filed. As a practical matter though, because court *dockets* (lists of cases to be tried) are so crowded, it may be months or years before the case comes to trial.

JUDGE OR JURY

The plaintiff when filing a complaint, and/or the defendant when filing an answer, may request that the case be heard either by a judge sitting without a jury or by a jury. Often in suing a corporation the plaintiff will feel that he or she stands a better chance of winning the case if the trial is heard by a jury, which the plaintiff assumes to be proconsumer. Either side, however, may elect to have the case heard by a jury.

Usually in civil litigation, unanimous agreement by a jury is necessary to decide a case.

DISCOVERY

Between the time when the date for the trial is set and the date on which it begins, sworn *depositions* (statements relative to the case) will usually be taken by the attorneys for both sides, generally in the attorneys' offices.

Deposition taking is part of the pretrial process of discovery designed to help eliminate courtroom surprises, improve the chances of a fair trial, and provide a last-ditch opportunity for the plaintiff and defendant to reach a compromise.

Both attorneys have the right to question witnesses from each side, and all testimony is taken down in writing. Copies of witnesses' depositions will be in front of each attorney during the trial, and any witness's departure from them will almost immediately be pounced on by the attorney who believes he may gain an advantage by exposing an "error" on the part of a witness.

Since depositions are given under oath, any falsehood makes the witness liable to criminal prosecution for perjury. The deposition itself may be entered into evidence, usually in instances where the witness cannot be present.

THE TRIAL

After discovery depositions have been taken and pretrial motions, such as Summary Judgment motions, have narrowed the issues as much as possible, the next step in the contest between plaintiff and defendent is the trial.

In preparation for trial the attorney for each side may prepare a trial memorandum stating his view of the case, citing what he believes are relevant laws, the decisions of other judges and juries in similiar cases (precedents), plus arguments he believes will influence the court's decision in his client's favor.

If an attorney's citing of precedent in a very similar case is strong enough, the judge is almost bound to follow precedent rather than risk the chance that a decision against the client with precedent on his side will be overturned by an appeals court.

In a 1978 Albany, N.Y. case, the state court of appeals handed down a decision affirming a lower court decision that police may enter a private home to make an arrest without a warrant even though there is no danger that the suspect will escape. The state decision was in direct opposition to a 1978 decision by the U.S. Court of Appeals (Second Circuit in New York) that held that such warrantless entry was against the law.

Both cases will probably find their way to the U.S. Supreme Court with respect to Fourth Amendment protection against unreasonable search and seizures. In the meantime all such warrantless arrests must be upheld in state courts and thrown out in local federal courts.

To get back to our routine civil trial—if a jury is to hear the case, it must be selected just before the trial. Each attorney has the right to reject certain prospective jurors without giving cause, called *peremptory* challenges. Either attorney may also call for a juror to be excused by showing cause, such as admitted bias, prejudice, related past experience, etc.

Once the jury has been selected and sworn, the attorney for the plaintiff makes his opening statement, setting forth his client's complaint and asking for the redress his client seeks.

The attorney for the defendant then makes his opening statement, arguing why he believes the plaintiff's complaint should be set aside and a decision rendered in favor of the defendant.

Once the attorneys for the plaintiff and defendant have made their opening statements, the attorney for the plaintiff may call his side's witnesses. They are sworn, directed to the witness chair, and questioned by the plaintiff's attorney to elicit answers that he hopes will build the credibility of his client's case. This "friendly" questioning is called *direct examination*.

The following "unfriendly" questioning of each witness by the opposing attorney is called *cross-examination*.

After the plaintiff's witnesses are questioned under direct examination, then cross-examination, and then redirect, each witness is questioned under direct examination by the defendant's attorney and then under cross-examination by the plaintiff's attorney.

After the evidence and witnesses for each side have been presented to the court, the attorney for the plaintiff makes his final argument, citing the strong points of his client's case, attempting to tear down the arguments presented by the defense, and then again asking for whatever damages are being sought. After the plaintiff's attorney's final argument, the attorney for the defendant makes a rebuttal argument.

Finally, the plaintiff's attorney gives his closing statement, making any last-minute arguments that he feels will influence the judge or jury.

In a jury trial the judge will then instruct the jury with respect to relevant law, after which they retire to the jury room to reach their verdict.

Traditionally, juries have been composed of "twelve men tried and true" (actually twelve persons), but recently some jurisdictions have been functional with fewer numbers, six or eight, in certain civil cases. Twelve, however, is still the normal number, and unanimous agreement is usually required for a verdict.

Not long ago if a judge heard a case without a jury, he would retire to his chambers to consider relevant law, attorneys' briefs, and the trial proceedings and then hand down his decision. With today's crowded court calendars, a judge hearing a case without a jury will often call for the next case to be heard and then hand down his decisons on all cases heard that day at some later time.

APPEAL

If the "losing" attorney feels that an error of law has been made by the judge that affected the outcome of his case, he may appeal the judge's decision to an appellate court.

There is no jury in an appeals court. Three appeals court judges, a chief justice, and two associate justices hear opposing attorneys' oral arguments and take their written briefs under advisement. No witnesses are heard and the judges' decision is based upon the transcript of the trial.

As we pointed out in the chapter on courts, an appeals hearing is not a new trial. In sustaining an appeal the appellate court can reverse the original court's decision, granting a new trial, or it may reduce the award for damages or do whatever else it feels is required for justice to be done.

COST OF GOING TO COURT

The expense of taking a case to court will include your lawyer's fees, court costs, the cost of taking your side's depositions, and possibly witnesses' travel expenses and fees for expert witnesses.

In a major suit, specialists may be called by your lawyer to give expert testimony regarding unsafe product design, shoddy building construction, and the like. Your attorney might also want to present testimony by medical or handwriting experts or the testimony of private detectives whose observations over a few weeks or months might prove that the injured party was not injured nearly as seriously as claimed in the suit.

In an appeal one of the major expenses beyond attorney's additional fees will be for the preparation of a verbatim transcript of the trial, which was taken down but not typed by the court reporter. These costs are so high, running into hundreds and sometimes thousands of dollars, that this expense alone often inhibits appeals which might otherwise be made.

There is one consolation: you can almost exclude your chances of ever having to pay these costs as a *defendant* by taking out adequate auto, home, business, and personal liability insurance. But if you sue someone else, then the expenses of going to court are yours to pay, and only you can balance the cost against the possible benefits to be gained.

WITNESSES

If you ever take a case to court you may have friends or neighbors who saw or heard what happened and who may volunteer to testify on your behalf. Even though they may be eager to come into court for your side, it's important that the court clerk issue a *subpoena*, which "commands" them to appear at the trial and give testimony.

A witness can recieve two kinds of subpoenas: a subpoena merely requiring him or her to testify or a subpoena *duces tecum*, which directs the witness to bring certain documents (appraisals of value, letters, receipts, photographs, etc.) to court.

If your friendly witness is not under subpoena and is unable to appear, the trial will go on without him or her. However, if your witness has received a subpoena and is unable to appear, your attorney can usually receive a postponement of the trial until such time as your witness can be there.

A witness under subpoena also receives certain travel and per diem allowances from the court and, in accordance with many employer personnel policies, does not suffer pay losses or time away from work penalties.

LANDLORD-TENANT

⑧ The Most Hated Document in America

"You resent it *every* time you have to sign a lease because you know that, more often than not, the landlord has language in there that lets him walk all over your rights," so says Leon B. Jennings, president of the National Rental Tenants Association (NRTA).

Could be. How do you like this provision from a commonly used New York lease?

> This lease agreement is conditioned upon the landlord's being able to secure possession of said premises from existing tenant, if any, by the commencement date hereof, and if the landlord is unable to deliver possession of said premises to the tenant at said commencement date for any reason, such right of possession by the tenant shall be postponed until such time when said premises shall be put in suitable physical condition for occupancy, or until such time when the landlord is able to legally deliver possession, without any liability on the part of the landlord to the tenant for any postponement.

In other words, if the apartment isn't made available to you for six months, you have no cause of legal action and can kiss the required security deposit, plus first and last month's rent, goodbye.

Perhaps you'd be more comfortable with this provision from an Illinois lease:

> The landlord, his agents or employees shall and may at any reasonable hour of the day or night, and without requirement for advance notice to the tenant, enter in and upon said premises for the purpose of inspection and repair and for any other proper purpose.

A lease, before we go any farther, is one of those documents known within the legal profession as an *adhesion contract*—a contract printed as a standard form, submitted by one party to the other on a take-it-or-leave-it basis, often presented in situations where the buyer's position is significantly weaker than the seller's. Where leases are concerned, some landlords like to operate on the assumption that it's always a seller's market.

Leases, like many other legal documents, contain a lot of archaic language: words like *covenant*, which we usually associate with pacts made with the devil, and an abundance of *premises* and *demise* and *agents and assigns*—terms that many of us believe no ordinary, honest person would *ever* use.

But we're stuck with that language for a while because those words, and worse, are written into the law. You cannot just casually go around substituting some other word for *covenant* in a lease, for example, as long as the **law** related to leases turns on the word

covenant in certain key areas like landlord and tenant obligations.

If you occasionally rent out your cabin in the woods or at the seashore, you may not think of yourself as a *landlord*, but whether you use a written rental agreement or not, that's what you are under the law, even if you feel more like an *owner* than a landlord.

There are, of course, good landlords, but, even so, given the fact that most leases are drawn up by landlord's lawyers and real estate boards, it's a good idea to scrutinize any lease you intend to sign. If you really need the apartment or house you're considering, you may not be able to do much about some of the lease provisions, but at least you'll know what you're getting into.

One of the first provisions of most leases follows:

> The landlord covenants that the tenant, on paying aforesaid rent and performing the covenents and conditions of this lease, shall and may peaceably and quietly have, hold and enjoy the demised premises for the term aforesaid.

—meaning that as long as you pay the rent and live according to all the conditions set down by the landlord, you can stay.

Another common provision is:

> The tenant covenants and agrees that the demised premises shall be used exclusively for a private residence.

If you plan to use your apartment for work, as a psychologist occasionally seeing clients there, for example, get the landlord's written permission before you sign the lease. If your work doesn't disturb other tenants and won't bring hordes of people into the building or create problems in the parking lot, he'll probably be willing to approve.

And now the gloves come off:

> This lease is granted upon the express condition that in the event the landlord, his agents or assigns shall deem objectionable or improper any conduct on the part of aforesaid tenant or occupant of said apartment, said landlord, his agents or assigns may give the tenant five (5) days notice of landlord's intention to terminate this lease and tender return of the rent paid on account of the unexpired term, and upon expiration of said notice this lease shall terminate as effectually as if such date of expiration were the date fixed herein for its termination, and thereupon said landlord, his agents or assigns shall have full license and authority to reenter and have full possession of said premises, either with

or without legal process; and in consideration of the above letting, the tenant consents that said landlord, his agents or assigns shall not be liable to prosecution for damages for so resuming possession of said premises.

In a further recitation of the landlord's rights, many lease provisions declare:

It is expressly agreed that if the operation of the elevators, the furnishings of heat or of any service shall cease by reason of accident, strike, repairs, cleaning out boilers, alterations or improvements to be made or done to any part of the apparatus or appurtenances belonging thereto, or any cause beyond control of the landlord, the obligations of the tenant under the terms of this lease shall not be affected thereby, nor shall any claim accrue to the tenant by reason thereof.

Better hope for a warm winter, a cool summer, and a second-floor apartment, because you're obligated to go right on paying penthouse rent for a cold-water walk-up until it's convenient for the landlord to put things right.

In many standard leases there are some twenty additional paragraphs of covenants by the tenant and disclaimers by the landlord, some of which follow:

The tenant shall not drive nails into the walls or woodwork of said premises or allow the same to be done.

This is often used as an excuse for failure to return a tenant's security deposit.

The tenant agrees that the storerooms are provided and maintained gratuitously by the landlord, and their use is not appurtenant to the premises hereby demised. The tenant hereby expressly agrees that if the same be made use of by himself, his family or servants, such use shall be at his or their own proper risk, and that the landlord shall in no event be or become liable thereby for any loss or damage to persons or property by reason of such use, whether such property be contained in the storerooms, in the demised premises or in any portion of said building.

This is like a sneak rider on a piece of legislation. The paragraph starts talking about storerooms and concludes by absolving the landlord of responsibility for damage to the tenant's property *in the demised premises or in any portion of said building.*

That four months prior to the expiration of the term hereby granted, prospective new tenants shall be admitted at reasonable hours of the day to view the premises until rented; and the landlord or landlord's agents or assigns shall also be permitted at any time during the term to visit and examine them and show them to prospective tenants at any reasonable hour of the day and whenever necessary for any repairs or alterations to same or to any part of the building.

This paragraph says nothing about advance notice to the tenant, but it does state that the landlord or his army of "agents or assigns" may enter the premises *whenever necessary for any repairs or alterations.* Tenants who have fought rent increases, formed tenant organizations, or otherwise irritated landlords have found their apartments being visited at all hours of the day and night under provisions of this clause.

The landlord shall not be liable for failure to give possession of the premises upon aforesaid commencement date by reason of the fact that said premises are not ready for occupancy, or due to a prior tenant wrongfully holding over, or for any other reason. In such event the rent shall not commence until possession is given, but the term herein shall not be extended.

So the landlord has got your security deposit and your first month's rent (paid at the time of signing the lease), doesn't have the apartment available, and you can't get your money back to move someplace else.

It is agreed and covenanted by the tenant that in consideration of letting the premises heretofore described that upon default made in any of the covenants, agreements and conditions, or of the rules and regulations herein, that then this lease, at the option of the landlord after five (5) days' notice of such option shall be served in writing upon the tenant, shall and will expire immediately at the expiration of said notice, and the landlord shall be entitled to immediate possession of said premises. . . ."

Drive a nail into a wall or let the landlord deem any of your conduct improper or objectionable, and out you go.

Remember the good old days when a security deposit was to assure that the tenant left the premises in good condition "excepting normal wear and tear" when moving out? Gone, gone forever, if some landlords have anything to say about it:

The tenant has deposited with the landlord the sum of $_____ as security for the faithful performance of and compliance with all of the terms, covenants and conditions of this lease. If the tenant fails to comply with each of said terms, covenants and conditions . . . the security shall belong to the landlord as part payment for the disbursements, attorney's fees, costs and expenses that the landlord may undergo for the purpose of regaining possession of the premises and preparing same for renting.

Back to square one: if the landlord deems any of your conduct "objectionable or improper," it can cost you not only your apartment, but your security deposit as well!

And just in case you thought you had any protection left at all:

The landlord shall not be responsible for the loss of or damage to property, or injury to persons, occurring in or about the demised premises, by reason of any existing or future condition, defect, matter or thing in said demised premises or the property of which the premises are a part. The tenant agrees to indemnify and save the landlord harmless from all claims and liability for losses of or damage to property, or injuries to persons occurring in or about the demised premises.

In case you hadn't guessed it by now, these citations comprise what is known in the trade as a *landlord's lease.* But all isn't lost! A landlord can no more absolve himself of liability for negligence than can the owner of a parking lot or any other business.

You'd be better off not having anything to do with a landlord who presented you with the kind of lease we excerpted above, but if you're really desperate for a place to live, find out what you're getting into and familiarize yourself with this section's advice and forms.

There are a few other lease provisions you might run across from time to time, such as:

No animals, birds or pets of any kind shall be permitted, kept or harbored in the demised premises without the written consent of the landlord.

This provision is outlawed in some cities. Often as not, permission to keep a pet is fairly easy to obtain. The requirement that permission be in writing infers the landlord's right to cancel permission if he later decides that he doesn't like your pet—or you.

Three others commonly encountered are:

All persons shall be properly attired when appearing in the lobby, corridors, elevators and other public areas of the building and grounds. In the event that the landlord shall at any time deem the attire of the tenant, his guests or invitees to be improper, the landlord shall have the right to terminate this lease by giving the tenant five days' written notice to vacate the premises leased hereunder.

The landlord may modify, discontinue or change the character of the telephone service furnished to the tenant in any manner without affecting the obligations or covenants of the tenant herein contained, and without rendering the landlord liable for damage by reason thereof.

The landlord shall have a lien upon all personal property of the tenant moved in and located upon the demised premises, or in the aforesaid building, and should tenant attempt to remove such property while there shall remain any amount due and owing, the landlord is hereby empowered to seize and detain the same until said landlord shall be fully paid for such rent as shall then be, or thereafter become, due under the terms of this lease.

In addition to prohibitions against children and pets, you might also be handed a lease that restricts what you can do with and on a balcony (no hibachi cooking, for example), that prohibits you from placing radio or TV antennas out your windows, that forbids flower pots on window sills, and that restricts your installing shades, blinds, or draperies that are different from those supplied by the landlord (that's so everything looks oh so nice and uniform from the outside).

A few final considerations before we consider a really decent lease:

Prior to signing a lease and moving in, make a list of all defects and damage and get the landlord's agreement, *in writing*, to make repairs either before you occupy the apartment or by a specific date.

You might also take photographs of every room, especially any cracked walls, nail holes, broken fixtures, stained or burned carpets, etc. Take photos again immediately after your furniture has been removed. The front page of that day's newspaper temporarily taped to various walls will prove the photos were taken the day you moved out and not one day before.

Although a lease may state that an apartment is being turned over to you in a *clean* condition, that doesn't legally mean that it must be free of rats, roaches, silverfish, and other crawly things.

Staying beyond the expiration date of your lease can make you a *holdover tenant*. In some states the terms of the lease remain in effect on a month-to-month basis; in other states the lease is automatically extended for a period equal to its original term.

Try to inspect an apartment you're thinking of moving into at a time that is likely to be the most noisy or during a time when quiet is most important to you. Try to meet a few tenants of the building, especially the people who occupy adjoining apartments. You can always note a few names from building mailboxes and phone later to introduce yourself.

Find out if there's a tenant organization in the building or, if not, in the area. Check out the reputation of landlords who own buildings you're considering.

Keep all receipts for carpet shampoo machines, floor polishers, etc. They will be useful if you have to go into small claims court to get your security deposit refunded.

Some leases contain a *transfer clause*, releasing you from the lease in the event you are transferred by your employer. If you think there's a possibility you may be transferred, ask your landlord to add the transfer clause provided on page F51 (Form 12.3).

If you anticipate trouble obtaining refund of your security deposit, in the presence of a witness ask the landlord or his agent to inspect the apartment with you before you move out. If the landlord is repeatedly "too busy," note his statement in your formal letter requesting refund. In addition to giving your landlord this letter, also send him a copy by registered mail, return receipt requested.

You will notice that each of our ready-to-use leases (pages F1–F42) provides for two witnesses each for the landlord and tenant(s). This is because in some states (Florida, for example) two witnesses to each signature are required. If your state doesn't require witness signatures on leases, it's a simple matter to "white them out" before making photocopies for use. If you're not sure of your state's requirements and don't have time to check, go ahead and obtain witnesses' signatures; the lease will not be invalid merely because it has witnesses' names on it.

This section of *How to Avoid Lawyers* describes several types of leases, subleases, rental applications, lease renewals, parking space leases, storage space leases, etc., all of which can be found at the start of the Forms section at the back of the book. Check the Contents for quick access to the lease forms you need.

⑨ Lease Agreements

UNFURNISHED AND FURNISHED APARTMENTS

There may not be an Easter Bunny, but there are fair, decent, easy-to-read leases for both unfurnished and furnished apartments that landlords and tenants can live with.

About half as long as the usual *landlord's* lease, they contain a couple of "covenants," but not a single "demise," and not once mention the landlord's legions of "agents and assigns." After what we've just seen in Chapter 8, they're a joy to behold!

If you're a landlord, we commend them to you. When the word gets around that you're using a "white-hat" lease, we expect you'll have the pick of the best tenants in town.

If you're a tenant of an unfurnished apartment, make a photocopy of the **Lease of Unfurnished Apartment** (Form 9.1, starting on page F1) and give it to your landlord some sunny morning, or give it to a prospective landlord when you tell him you'll look around at a few other apartments and will get back to him—maybe.

The **Lease of Furnished Apartment** (Form 9.2, starting on page F5) is similar to that of the unfurnished apartment, except for provisions listing furnishings, requiring their good and proper care by the tenant and specifying the means of compensating the landlord for damage to furnishings caused by negligent acts of the tenant.

An inventory of furniture and other household items received by the tenant should be a part of the lease and signed by the landlord and tenant. The **List of Furnishings** (Form 11.1 on page F43) will serve for this purpose.

UNFURNISHED AND FURNISHED HOUSES

The ready-to-use leases for the rental of an **unfurnished house** (Form 9.3, page F9) and a **furnished house** (Form 9.4, page F13) have been prepared for homeowners who may be away for military service or some other reason and who want to earn income by renting their house while living elsewhere.

Tax advantages are significant, and although there will be some wear and tear, your house will probably fare better occupied than it would standing vacant. Occupancy will discourage vandalism, and there will be someone present to order repairs if the roof begins to leak or other work needs to be done.

It's important to have a good agent—and this need not necessarily be a real estate or commercial property management agent—representing your in-

terests. Your lawyer would be a good possibility if he or she has the background and inclination. So would an attorney who happens to live nearby who can keep an eye on the property. Check with your neighbors, insurance agent, lawyer, and banker.

See your insurance agent to discuss adjustments in your homeowner's coverage. Check to make sure there are no safety hazards, and install fire extinguishers, smoke alarms, dead-bolt door locks, and secure window latches if you don't already have them. Instruct renters in the safe use of any tools and equipment, such as power lawn mowers, that you leave for their convenience. As landlord, you can be held liable for injury or loss to tenants resulting from inadequate security, dangerous conditions, etc.

The lease for a furnished house differs little from that for an unfurnished one—only with respect to its being for a furnished rather than unfurnished house. The primary differences can be seen in paragraphs 2, 11, and 12, plus its stipulation for the addition, as a part of the lease, of the **List of Furnishings** (Form 11.1 on page F43).

Beyond taking the precautions previously noted, for a furnished house you might also want to do the following:

As a landlord, photograph each side of the house's exterior, outbuildings, and the grounds. Also take several photos of each room and any items that are valuable or particularly important to you. It's a good idea to do this, anyway, so you'll have a record if you ever have to make insurance claims.

As a tenant, photograph any furniture or portions of the house that appear to be damaged or worn and for which you would not like to be held responsible. If you notice damage or wear after you move in, take a picture to give to the landlord or agent whenever you see him or her.

SEASONAL LEASE FOR A FURNISHED COUNTRY/SEASHORE HOUSE

The lease for a furnished house in the country or at the seashore contains all of the routine provisions for the lease of any furnished house, but takes into account the shorter term common with this type of lease.

In our ready-to-use **Seasonal Lease** (Form 9.5, page F17), the amount of security deposit is left open, the tenant agrees to pay for utilities on a monthly basis, and the tenant is responsible for compliance with housing and land-use codes that may apply to the area where the house is located.

EXTENSION OF LEASE

Since there are likely to be few changes required for the renewal of a lease, the form for its extension (Form 9.6, page F21) is relatively simple.

The form's third paragraph contains a provision for any increase or decrease in the rent or to confirm that there is no change in the amount of rent due. Space is provided for any revision of other terms.

PARKING SPACE LEASE AND STORAGE SPACE LEASE

The ready-to-use **Parking Space Lease** (Form 9.7, page F23) can be used for the rental of apartment or office parking space or for the rental of parking space to or from a neighbor.

Use the **Storage Space Lease** (Form 9.8, page F25) if you have a garage or other space that you'd like to rent out to earn extra income. Use it too if you need to rent extra space for your own needs.

This agreement is a bit longer than required for some purposes, but it serves for a wide range of uses: inside or outside boat or vehicle storage, rental of a garage, or even rental of a room in someone's house or apartment, basement, or barn.

If you'll be a storage space *tenant*, a quick call to your insurance agent might extend your coverage at little or no additional cost.

If you plan to be *lessor*, also check with your insurance agent to see whether you might need additional coverage for liability, theft, or fire.

10 Short-term Leases—Monthly Tenancy Agreements and Subleases

MONTHLY TENANCY AGREEMENTS

Unfurnished Apartments

The monthly tenancy agreement is used, obviously, for month-to-month rental. Form 10.1 (page F29), Monthly Tenancy Agreement for Unfurnished Apartment, is an example of a short-form lease that, in fact, covers most of the contingencies provided for in the much longer leases we're used to signing. With the tenant and landlord both giving up a number of paragraphs, the balance of "terror" remains about the same as in a longer agreement.

Furnished Premises

The short-form lease that serves for rental of furnished premises (Form 10.2, page F31) could be used for the short-term rental of a house, cabin, or cottage, since it does not anywhere specify "apartment." As landlord or tenant you still may want to make use of the List of Furnishings (Form 11.1).

SUBLEASES OF UNFURNISHED APARTMENT OR HOUSE

For Use by Landlord

Form 10.3 (page F33), Sublease of Unfurnished Apartment or House, would be used by the landlord or landlord's agent:

1. In compliance with an agreement granting to the landlord sole authority to arrange any sublease.
2. At the request of the tenant.

Since most of the routine provisions of a lease are contained in the original document, a sublease can be quite brief. If you sublease, be sure you read and understand the original lease; once you sign the sublease, you will be bound by all the provisions of the original contract. Any changes or exceptions to terms of the original lease can be noted in the space provided.

For Use by Tenant

Form 10.4 (page F35) is the form to use if you have leased an apartment or house and the landlord has given you permission to make your own sublease arrangements. Remember, you are still responsible to the landlord for all provisions of your contract with him.

Provisions of the sublease make the subtenant responsible to the tenant for compliance with all terms, conditions, covenants, and agreements of the original lease, but the tenant remains responsible to the landlord.

The tenant's sublease contains provision for a security deposit by the subtenant and for the monthly payment of all utilities by the subtenant, since gas and electricity may remain in the tenant's name. If they are to be in the subtenant's name, this stipulation won't present a problem anyway.

If you want to move out of an apartment or house before your lease has expired, see if the landlord will release you if you can locate a replacement tenant. That's better for you than the continuing responsibility of a sublease.

SUBLEASE OF FURNISHED APARTMENT OR HOUSE—FOR USE BY TENANT

If you're going to be away from home for a few months and want to sublease your apartment or house, Form 10.5 (page F37)—Sublease of Furnished Apartment or House—can be used.

Although security deposits are generally an amount equal to one month's rent, you may want to require a sum greater than the monthly rate you'll be charging, since you're putting your easily damaged possessions at risk.

Be sure to let your insurance agent know that you'll be renting your house or apartment furnished so that he or she can advise you about taking out additional insurance. Figure the cost of any extra insurance into the rental rate.

You'll probably need an agent to receive rent and utility payments, keep an eye on your home, and generally look after your interests. Your lawyer might be a good person if he or she has the background and is interested. You might also contact your bank or insurance agent. Be sure that both the subtenant and your agent know how to contact the landlord for maintenance and repairs.

Take photographs of each room, each major appliance or piece of furniture, and if subleasing a house, its exterior and grounds. Store valuable paintings, antiques, and the like.

PERMISSION TO SUBLET

Form 10.6 (page F39)—**Permission to Sublet**—is a quick and simple form to use if you want to sublet your leased apartment or house and need your landlord's written permission.

It protects the landlord fairly well, especially if he knows where to reach you. Note that the permission retains your legal obligations to the landlord under terms of the original lease.

PERMISSION TO UNDERLET

Form 10.7 (page F41)—**Permission to Underlet**—is used to authorize a tenant to rent a *portion* of a leased apartment or house to an additional person when written permission of the landlord is required for such action.

Another way of handling the whole thing is simply for the landlord to allow the new person to sign as an additional tenant on the original lease.

11 List of Furnishings/ Rental Application

LIST OF FURNISHINGS

Form 11.1 (page F43), a ready-to-use list of furnishings and receipt, may be used by owners leasing to tenants or by tenants leasing to subtenants.

A good way to compile a list of furnishings is to start in one corner of each room and circle the room listing each item as you go. General descriptions such as:

- Sofa, three cushion, green
- Carpet, biege wool, 9 × 12
- Dresser, rosewood, five-drawer
- Mixmaster, model No. 337

will probably be sufficient IF you take photographs of each wall, each significant piece of furniture, and any carpets, plus any damage to any of the above evident prior to your move-in. You should have the photos and list anyway for making insurance claims. In your list be sure to note any damaged or worn items.

This would also be a good time to make a list of serial numbers of valuable items, such as cameras, lenses, stereo equipment, TV, sewing machine, typewriter, binoculars, watches, appliances, etc. If you don't have sales receipts for these, just about the only way you'll get them back from police if they are stolen is to have a record of serial numbers or to have marked them as suggested by *Operation Identification*.

In many areas of the country, Operation Identification is sponsored by police and sheriff's depart-ments. They lend community residents, at no cost, small electric engraving tools with which to engrave their initials, social security number, or other identifying mark on valuable "stealables" such as television sets, typewriters, cameras, etc., so that they may be positively identified by their owners if stolen and later recovered by the police.

RENTAL APPLICATION

The ready-to-use **Rental Application**, Form 11.2 (on page F45), conforms to fair credit reporting statutes.

As a prospective tenant interested in moving into a building, you might want to ask the landlord, or his agent, for a copy of the lease, letting him know that you would like to compare it with others before making up your mind. No *reasonable* landlord would balk at giving you a copy of his lease to study. If one does, it's a strong sign that he's probably not the kind of person you'd want to do business with.

As a landlord using this form, you stand to gain points when prospective tenants compare the fairness of this application with those used by others.

Extra space has been provided above this form's title to allow landlords to insert the top of their business letterhead so that, when reproduced, the form will contain the building name, address, phone, etc.

12 Forms for Departing Tenants

NOTICE OF INTENT TO VACATE

Mail copies of the **Notice of Intent to Vacate** (Form 12.1, page F47) to your landlord in accordance with the requirements of the applicable provisions of your lease. At least one copy should be sent by certified mail, which, for your own protection, should be "return receipt requested." A second copy should be mailed first class.

Be sure to note under "forwarding address" the address to which your security deposit refund should be mailed.

Keep two copies of the completed notice so that you will have one copy to give to a lawyer in the event you are forced to initiate legal action to obtain your refund.

DEPARTING TENANT CLEANUP LETTER

OK landlords! We've made it easy for you and left plenty of space at the top of this ready-to-use letter (Form 12.2, page F49) so your printer can insert the printed portion of your letterhead. If you want to, you might just retype this letter on your letterhead, leaving out the "Dear Tenant" so that you can type in individual names.

TRANSFER CLAUSE

Add the transfer clause (Form 12.3, page F51) to your lease in the space provided at its end if you expect that during its term there's a possibility that you'll be transferred by your employer.

Actually, few people pay attention to it anymore. The courts have decided time and time and time again against landlords who tried to hold tenants with job transfers to the term of a lease. Then, too, it's pretty easy to get a job-transfer letter to give a landlord even if you're moving just because you don't like the place.

III

ACCIDENTS AND INJURIES

13 Looking Out for Number One

Very soon after you're involved in any kind of accident resulting in property damage or injury, an attorney or adjuster from the other party's insurance company will probably be around to see you, all smiling and polite and offering to pay you some piddling sum "to compensate you for any inconvenience"—for which you will be expected to sign a document releasing the insurer and its client from all future claims.

DON'T MAKE *ANY* STATEMENT ABOUT THE ACCIDENT.

DON'T SIGN ANYTHING.

The adjuster will probably try to gain entry to your home by saying something like, "May I come in and discuss our offer with you?" or anything else that he or she thinks will gain entry to your living room. The insurance company knows that you will feel obligated to be polite (as you would be to a guest) and to listen to whatever the adjuster has to say, to discuss the accident, and to enter into conversation as you would with a friend.

STOP THE ADJUSTER AT THE DOOR. It's easier to get rid of the adjuster if you don't let him in.

The adjuster may tell you that your refusal to make a statement indicates that "you have something to hide" or that your refusal to discuss the incident "will make it impossible for us to settle your claim."

TELL THE ADJUSTER THAT YOU WILL NOT DISCUSS YOUR CLAIM AT THIS TIME.

The adjuster may even appear to go along with your statement, saying, "I can understand that," but then attempt to continue the conversation, at first asking apparently harmless questions like "What day was that?" and then gradually leading you into increasingly hazardous areas.

THE ADJUSTER PROBABLY HAS A CASSETTE RECORDER IN HIS OR HER POCKET, PURSE, OR BRIEFCASE. DO NOT DISCUSS YOUR CLAIM.

Since he's offering to compensate you for any "inconvenience," it might be amusing to look at the release he'll expect you to sign in exchange for your $50 check. It will probably contain harmless little phrases such as:

I know that this paper is much more than a receipt. It is a release. I am giving up every right I have.

or

In exchange for $_____, which I have received, I do hereby release and forever discharge _____

and his, her or their heirs, executors, administrators and assigns from each and every right and claim which I may now have, or hereafter have, on account of any injuries or illnesses suffered by me which may later be shown to be the result of _____.

or

I acknowledge that payment of the sum I have received is not an admission that anyone is liable to me for anything.

It's all "just a matter of form," as the insurance adjuster will tell you.

When initially contacted by the insurance adjuster, tell him that you are not prepared to discuss your claim and that you will be in touch with him or her later.

If you have been involved in an accident in which you or anyone in your vehicle was injured or in which your property suffered major damage, you should probably contact a lawyer. Most lawyers don't charge for an initial consultation, or make only a minimal charge, so you have little, if anything, to lose.

If you do hire a lawyer to prosecute your claim, he will probably represent you on a "contingent fee" basis, meaning that if he obtains a monetary judgment in your favor, he will receive a percentage of any sum you are awarded, but that if he is unable to obtain a monetary judgment in your favor, you need pay him nothing except, perhaps, nominal costs.

If you have sustained an injury, or even if you are not yet aware of an injury but have been rear-ended in an accident likely to produce a whiplash injury, see a doctor as soon as possible.

Don't try to treat any accident-related aches and pains yourself because taking aspirin or soaking in a hot tub may temporarily mask symptoms of a serious injury. See a doctor! If you *don't* see a doctor and later attempt to make a claim for injuries, pain, or time lost from work, your claim won't carry much weight in court.

If you hire a lawyer, follow his advice precisely. If you do not have a family physician in whom you have full confidence, ask your lawyer to recommend a physician to you.

DO NOT allow yourself to be examined by a physician working for or recommended by an insurance adjuster. The adjuster may tell you that the company cannot settle your claim until you have been examined by its physician. Not true.

DO NOT settle your claim until you have been discharged by the physician who is treating your injury.

DO NOT sign any form that will allow the inspection of medical records by the other driver's insurance company.

FOLLOW YOUR LAWYER'S ADVICE TO THE LETTER. DO NOT DO ANYTHING UNLESS YOUR LAWYER TELLS YOU TO.

DO NOT SIGN ANYTHING—DO NOT SAY ANYTHING.

WARNING: *No longer can you count on your own insurance company to be your friend in need. If you are sued in connection with an accident in which you're alleged to be at fault, your insurance company will defend you because it has to pay if a judgment is awarded to the other party.*

But you can be sure your insurance company's FIRST consideration is to SAVE MONEY and that it will be looking for ways NOT to pay, even if it means leaving you holding the bag. Your insurer will most probably be looking for ways to cancel your coverage, to increase greatly the amount of your deductible, and to increase your insurance rate if it is unable to cancel your coverage altogether.

If you are involved in an accident that could result in a major claim against you for injury or property damage, consult your attorney even BEFORE you present a claim to your insurance company. Treat an interview with any representative of your insurance company as you would an interrogation by the police, have your attorney present.

PROTECTING YOURSELF —A MATTER OF FORM

If filling out some of the accident report forms we have provided seems like a bother, you're right: it can be. But so is having a $600,000 judgment against you when your liability coverage stops at $300,000. And as you know from reading the newspapers, juries are making huge awards these days.

One should obtain as much information as possible *at the scene* of the accident and fill in as much of the report as you can *later*. It could make the difference in whether you keep your house or not—and even in the event of a relatively minor accident, it could determine whether you'll face an insurance rate increase.

If you are injured, or if your property is damaged, a good investigation, based upon a completed accident report with witnesses' names, etc., can facilitate a quick, out-of-court settlement as well as save you money. Remember that in most states an attorney will charge you one-third of the amount awarded if your claim is settled out of court but will charge you at least 40 percent if a suit must be filed.

A well-documented claim, especially if the defendant's insurance policy limits are much lower than a potential jury award, can mean the difference between long, costly, and drawn-out pretrial and trial procedures and a quick settlement.

Then, too, if you're on the receiving end of an injury, the facts you note on one of our ready-to-use forms could make the difference between your being compensated or not for medical expenses, loss of work, permanent disability, and pain and suffering. Having all of the facts is especially important if your accident is **work-related**, since your employer, or at least your employer's insurance company, may suddenly become your adversary in court.

ANOTHER WARNING: *Many insurance adjusters will try and adjust you right out of your claim by trying to get you to make what is known as an "admission against interest"—in essence, a statement admitting liability that can be used against you in trial whether in a suit **by** you to recover damages or in a suit **against** you by another party. Adjusters operate on the tendency of people to admit wrongdoing immediately after an incident—a tendency often caused by feelings of guilt or sorrow resulting from possibly causing an injury. Restrain this tendency.*

Information you fill in on one of this section's accident report forms can be the basis upon which a "negligence attorney"—who is paid only if he or she wins your case—may decide to represent you.

The three chapters that follow in this section explain the proper use of the following ready-to-use accident report forms (found in the Forms Section on pages F53–F118):

- **Auto Accident Report/Minor Accident Report**—for accidents that take place on the road.
- **Boating/Marine Accident Report**—for accidents that take place afloat.
- **Building Accident Report**—for such things as falling down steps when you trip on a torn carpet or worn rubber stair tread—or having the ceiling drop on your head when water from a leaking air conditioner or radiator upstairs loosens plaster.
- **Street/Sidewalk Accident Report**—to deal with the consequences of injuries from the hazards of uneven or icy sidewalks, missing manhole covers, or falling flowerpots.
- **Defective Product Report**—for setting down the circumstances of electrical shocks and of appliances that fly apart when you turn them on and that have arms and levers that injuriously *zig* when they're supposed to *zag*.
- **Animal Accident Report**—works equally well whether your well-behaved pet or the monster next door is the "injurer" or the "injuree." You can also use it if you're bitten by a spider or kissed by a frog.
- **Public Transportation Accident Report**—to use when filing a claim for injuries sustained aboard trains, planes, buses, subways, etc.

Each form has its own instructions, but there are some general comments that apply to all.

You do not have to be planning to sue for negligence in order to make use of an accident report form: for instance, you will need to set down all the data in order to make a claim under provisions of your own medical insurance.

Whenever you plan to use a form, make two photocopies—one as a "work" copy that you will fill in with pencil for easy corrections; the second copy to fill in with a typewriter, using the work copy as a guide. Always retain the **unsigned** original as a master for making additional reproductions for lawyers, insurance companies, etc. Sign each reproduction with your legal signature, but **not** the original from which you make copies.

The accident reports can help you most if you have them with you when you need them. Make a photocopy of the auto accident report and keep it in the glove compartment of your car. Take the boating accident report with you when you go boating. Make copies of any other reports you think you might need and keep them handy.

NOTE TO ATTORNEYS: *Extra space has been provided at the top of a number of the accident report forms so that you can neatly affix the printed portion of your letterhead before taking the form to your printer for photocopy reproduction of accident report forms bearing your firm's name. Just white out the Garland Publishing logo (GP) and the form number at the top of the form to allow for adequate space for the insertion of your letterhead.*

14 Auto Accident Reports

Earlier we noted that lawsuits involving auto accidents make up almost one-third of all courtroom litigation. In all, nearly 4 million of us will be involved in auto accidents during a typical year.

Although even a minor accident can be a major inconvenience (and not inconsiderable expense if you carry the usual $100-deductible collision coverage), it's nothing compared to the grief you can encounter if you're involved in a major accident, especially if there is bodily injury.

Your first line of defense is to "drive defensively," but driving defensively is a defense that can be easily breached. Often as not, if you have a collision, the other driver will be at fault.

Remember that litigation related to any accident you may be involved in isn't merely a case of you or your insurance company deciding whether to go to court; there is a distinct possibility of your being **taken** to court, even if you're convinced you weren't at fault.

Beyond having adequate insurance, your second, third, fourth, and fifth lines of defense will be to collect pertinent facts:

Take the right immediate actions and get the facts down on paper as quickly as you can before memory fades so that your observations cannot later be challenged as merely hazy recollections by an opposing attorney if you're taken to court.

Nowhere that we know of, except in this book, will you find an accident report that's designed to protect YOU, that's designed to serve as a tool for your defense, and that takes into account the fact that you may be hassled and shook up when you have to fill it out.

Yes, the ready-to-use **Auto Accident Report** (Form 14.1, pages F53–F75) is a long one, almost overwhelming when you first look at it. And, yes, it includes space for much more information than you'll probably need or be able to obtain at the scene immediately. *But*, except for witnesses' names, most of the form can be completed using check marks —and it's arranged in order of priority: first things first.

To prepare for the worst, we have assumed that there are injuries. The form's first two pages provide for the names, addresses, and phone numbers of up to twelve witnesses—because witnesses will often move on or become just about impossible to sort out from onlookers. Once lost, the opportunity to obtain the names of favorable witnesses can almost never be regained. And just one favorable witness can save your neck!

This volume's auto accident report form can protect you from possible lawsuit better than almost anything else. Was the driver of the other vehicle wearing glasses when he got out of his car? Some judges have found a driver to be guilty of contributory negligence if he or she was supposed to be wearing corrective lenses while driving and wasn't wearing them at the time of an accident.

Were seat belts in the other vehicle readily available for use, or, as in the case of more than half of all cars, were they pushed down between the rear of the seat and the seat back, thus not readily available? Some courts have determined the owners of cars whose seatbelts were not readily available to be guilty of contributory negligence in accidents resulting in the injury of passengers riding in the car.

Passengers riding in autos with readily available seat belts but who did not make use of them and were subsequently injured have also been found guilty of contributory negligence.

In all of these cases, your liability for injuries to occupants of another car might be greatly reduced, or in a few states even eliminated, if you could show that seat belts were not being used. This volume's auto accident report form provides space to note such information—and now you know one more thing to look for.

NEVER underestimate the seriousness of an accident. Very often the symptoms of serious injuries —whiplash and brain concussion, to name just two— do not show up right away.

Whenever you're involved in an auto accident, there are three cardinal rules to follow:

1. Immediately write down the time. If necessary, later on your lawyer can use the exact time of the accident to help determine whether it was raining, whether the street was wet, how heavy the traffic may have been, whether the sun may have been in your eyes, whether a traffic signal was working, etc.
2. Write down the license number of the other vehicle.
3. Check yourself, your passengers, the occupants of the other vehicle, and any involved pedestrians to determine if anyone was injured. If so, call for medical assistance.

After you've taken care of these musts, you can begin to fill in the essential elements of the form **Auto Accident Report** (pages F53–F75). Don't worry too much about immediately calling the police. In nearly every urban auto accident the police promptly receive any number of calls reporting the collision. For some reason people love to report accidents.

If you need to make a copy of the accident report or any other form in this book for use by anyone other than yourself, begin by making two photocopies of the blank form. Use one copy as a "work" copy, which you'll fill in with pencil so you can make clarifications as you go along. Then fill in the "final" copy with a typewriter if at all possible, using the completed work copy as a guide. DO NOT SIGN THE "FINAL" COPY.

Next, make photocopy reproductions of the unsigned final copy, then sign the **reproductions** of the final copy and give the signed reproductions to your insurance company, lawyer, or whoever needs a signed accident report. By retaining the **unsigned** final copy you will be able to make as many additional sets of completed forms as you need without eventually being forced to make a copy of a copy of a copy, etc.

Examine the form now, from beginning to end, then go through the form again as you read the following comments pertaining to each section. Next make a photocopy or similar facsimile of every page so you'll have a copy of the form *in your car* if you have an accident.

SECTION-BY-SECTION REVIEW OF THE AUTO ACCIDENT REPORT FORM

To save flipping back and forth as we refer to various pages of the **Auto Accident Report**, make a photocopy of it first (in addition to the one you'll need for your car's glove compartment).

EMERGENCY MEDICAL SERVICE

In many urban areas people who depend on public services for medical care have learned that the fire department responds much more quickly to life-and-death calls than the police. If you call the police, they may or may not come; if you call the fire department—they'll come. Firemen are also generally better trained, more experienced, and better equipped to give emergency medical care than are police.

Be SURE, when the operator has connected you with the fire department, to tell them you're reporting an **accident** involving a possibly major injury and NOT, repeat, NOT a fire.

NOTE: *Always wait for police in the event of bodily injury or death resulting from an accident in which you're involved. Even if injuries do not occur, check with police to find out if an accident report must be filed.*

Now is the time to investigate and obtain the proper numbers to call for fast medical assistance in the area where you live. Insert these numbers in the space provided on the top of the first page of the accident form. And do it **now.** (If I were out of town and had an auto accident resulting in injuries that I believed were imminently life-threatening, I'd pull the nearest fire alarm and get back to doing what I could for the injured.)

ACCIDENT DATA— Time of Accident

The minute you have an auto accident write down the time. Later you can transfer it to the space provided on the first page of the accident form. The exact time can help establish weather, amount of light, road conditions, traffic density, and many other factors that might help your case.

WITNESSES

Space is provided for the names, addresses, and phone numbers of twelve witnesses. One recommended approach to witnesses is to ask, "May I have your name so you could tell my insurance company what happened?" Also, in requesting addresses, ask, "Where do you live?" rather than the more formal (and somehow more threatening) "What is your address?" Also ask, "Is there a number where I could call you?" rather than, "What is your telephone number?" In requesting a witness's occupation (not essential to obtain at the scene), ask, "What do you do?" rather than, "What is your occupation?"

If you encounter resistance from a witness, move on before others notice and emulate his refusal. Also, the more time you spend with a witness, the more likely others are to drift away. If you can't get a name, get an auto license number if possible; your insurance company can follow up on it later. Also, if you have an uninjured passenger or two in your car, make use of them—put them to work too.

If you have a business card, give one to every witness you talk to, especially those who refuse to provide their names. Fairly often someone who declined to give a name and address will phone later and volunteer to give a statement on your behalf. Don't worry about revealing your employer and occupation; you can be sure the opposing attorney will find out anyway as a part of his investigation.

INJURIES—Other Vehicle, Pedestrian/Other

These two sections are self-explanatory once you take a minute to study them. There may be more than one item to mark under a particular heading. For example, if the right front passenger (RFP) had to be carried from the scene *and* was also partially ejected from the vehicle, you'd need to make two notations. Use an **X**, a check mark, a circle, or whatever is most convenient to fill in the blanks in these sections.

SAFETY EQUIPMENT (APPARENTLY) USED

There probably will not be more than one item to mark under any one heading in these sections. For example, if the driver of the other car (DVR) was not wearing a seat belt (or utilizing any other passive or active restraint system) mark the line for no restraint used under DVR.

This can be extremely important: Check the other vehicle as soon as possible to determine whether seat belts (lap belts) were readily available. The Traffic Safety Administration estimates that only 20 percent of all people use seat belts, so the chances are eight out of ten that anyone in the other car who was injured wasn't wearing a seat belt—"contributory negligence" according to many judges, and a factor that might greatly reduce, or even possibly eliminate, a judgment against you for injuries.

If you discover seat belts pushed down between the seat and seat back, or lying on the seat buckled to prevent a buzzer from going off, point this out to the investigating officer and ask him, in the presence of witnesses, to confirm your findings. If the police officer is reluctant to investigate, point out that in court you will state that you requested him to check the other vehicle and that he refused—and that your attorney will question him under oath.

You certainly should complete the section that applies to the use of safety equipment in your vehicle at the time of the accident. However, you may find it more convenient to fill in this data at your convenience rather than at the scene of the accident, when you will have many other details to be concerned with.

Remember that if you are riding in someone's car not wearing a seat belt that was readily available and your head goes through the windshield in an accident, you (or your survivors) could lose all right to claim damages because of your contributory negligence in not wearing the belt. It's been so decided more than once.

NOTE: *Consider buying an inexpensive Instamatic-type camera and keeping it in the trunk of your car for use in the event of an accident. A photo of missing seat belts, of buckled belts on a seat, or of minor damage that is later claimed (or made to be) major could make the difference in whether a judgment goes for or against you.*

OTHER VEHICLE—Vehicle/Driver

Insertion of information in these two sections of the accident form is self-evident.

OTHER VEHICLE—
Vehicle Condition

This section could be important. An expired inspection sticker might denote contributory negligence in the case of a brake failure, for example. Checkmark the appropriate condition(s).

OTHER VEHICLE—
Driver Apparent Condition

If the other driver wasn't wearing corrective lenses and his driver's license required him to do so while driving, he might be found guilty of contributory negligence.

INJURIES—Additional Vehicles

These two sections (one for each of two additional vehicles—#1 and #2) are identical to the **INJURIES—Other Vehicle** section described earlier.

ADDITIONAL VEHICLES

The completion of these eight sections (four sections each for two additional vehicles—#1 and #2) is straightforward.

INJURIES—Your Vehicle

Same as in **INJURIES—Other Vehicle**, although you may want to complete it later, especially if occupants of your vehicle are family members.

INJURED PERSONS

Fill in names, addresses, etc. You may have to get this information later from police or from the hospital to which the injured have been taken. If you miss this information altogether, don't worry; someone will surely be in touch with you—to talk about your paying for damages.

If, for example, an injured person was the center front passenger (CFP) in the other vehicle, write in CFP alongside Other Vehicle under the appropriate person's name and address.

ACCIDENT DIAGRAM

Fill in the dotted lines in the accident diagram to indicate appropriate roadways. In the sample accident illustrated in the completed accident diagram below, your vehicle, #1, was struck on the left side by vehicle #2 as you proceeded through the intersection. Your vehicle was also struck from the rear by vehicle #3 when you stopped upon being struck by vehicle #2. The 1 indicates the position of a pedestrian also struck by vehicle #2 just prior to that vehicle's striking your vehicle. The arrow and **N** indicate the direction north.

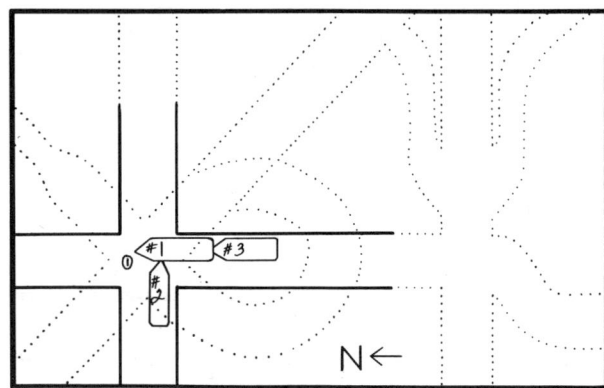

TRAFFIC CONTROL

Mark the lines appropriate to the traffic control conditions at the scene of the accident.

TRAFFIC SIGN/SIGNAL

Check the appropriate lines to indicate the existence, position, condition, and visibility of any traffic signs and signals at the site of the accident; you may need to mark a number of these.

ROADWAY

Checkmark the appropriate blanks in these three sections to describe the prevailing road **conditions, grade and curvature,** and **defects** (if any) at the scene of the accident; in some cases you may need to mark more than one in a section.

VEHICLE MOTION/DIRECTION

Mark the appropriate lines in these three sections to describe vehicular motion at the time of the accident. It's possible that you may need to fill in two lines within a section: making U-turn from parked position, passing while changing lanes, etc.

TYPE OF COLLISION—
Collision with Vehicle/Fixed Object

Check the appropriate blanks in these two sections.

SKIDDING

Mark the appropriate lines to indicate your estimation of the moment of skidding (if any) relative to the application of the brakes for **your vehicle,** the **other vehicle,** and two other **additional vehicles** (if applicable).

VEHICLE DAMAGE

Circle the appropriate number(s) on the automobile diagrams to indicate any damaged areas on **your vehicle,** the **other vehicle,** and two other **additional vehicles** (if applicable).

WEATHER CONDITIONS

Indicate the weather conditions at the time of the accident; you may need to mark more than one line here.

LIGHT CONDITIONS

Mark the lighting conditions present at the time of the accident.

VISION OBSCURED

Checkmark your best estimate of the manner in which the vision of any of the other drivers was obscured (if at all); you may need to mark more than one blank in each of the three sections provided. Additionally, indicate how your vision was obscured (if at all) during the accident.

DRIVERS' ACTIONS

Four headings provide for your actions, the actions of the other driver, plus two additional drivers (A#1 and A#2). You will probably need to mark more than one line for each driver involved.

PEDESTRIANS' ACTIONS

Check the appropriate lines to indicate the actions of up to four pedestrians (P#1, P#2, P#3, and P#4).

YOUR VEHICLE

This section of the form contains information that need not be filled out at the scene of the accident. If your vehicle was defective in some way, mark the appropriate blank under **Vehicle Condition** so you'll remember to discuss that item with your attorney. Under **Driver Condition,** also indicate the appropriate lines so that you can discuss those items with your attorney. Be sure to mention any way in which you believe you might have been at fault so that your attorney won't be surprised and caught off guard in the courtroom.

MANNER OF ACCIDENT

Here is your chance to include information that you feel may not have been adequately noted elsewhere in this report. For example, you might want to note that the accident was work-related, why you feel the accident took place, what you tried to do to avoid the accident, or what the other driver did that you feel caused the accident. If there was a related road defect that appeared to you to have existed for some time, this is the place to elaborate on that observation.

WARNING: *Don't make statements at the scene of an accident to **anyone** except police. An apparently curious bystander might be a passenger from the other driver's car or a runner for an ambulance-chasing attorney who could end up representing the other side. You might find your most offhand statement being used against you by the opposing lawyer's "witness" (runner) if you have to go to court.*

*However, it is also true that statements you make for the police accident report **can** be used against you in court. For instance, a police officer may refer to the report to refresh his or her memory when giving testimony at the trial. Your opponent's attorney and insurance company will have had access to the report prior to trial and can be counted on to ask the police officer questions that will damage your case. It will be up to your attorney to object to such questions before the officer has a chance to answer.*

*Remember that you are **not** required by law to "witness against yourself" in answering police questions at the scene. Be sure that any statements you make to investigating police are made only in the course and scope of the investigation and that you do not needlessly incriminate yourself.*

PERSON FILLING OUT REPORT

The information to be inserted here is especially important since the person filling out the report may not have been involved in—or even present at—the accident.

The auto accident report, as well as those reports that follow, can serve as the "other half" of the **Attorney's Accident Work Sheet** (see page F119). It might well be completed by a law office associate, paralegal, or even a member of your family if you're in the hospital.

As with any legal form in this book that might be needed by someone other than yourself, make two photocopies of the blank form. Use one copy as a "work" copy, then fill in the "final" copy using the work copy as a guide. Then make a photocopy of the **unsigned** final copy. Sign the **reproduction** of the final copy and give it to your attorney or insurance adjuster **ONLY**. Save the unsigned final copy to make additional reproductions later, if needed.

NO FAULT INSURANCE: *In some jurisdictions, despite the intense lobbying of trial lawyer organizations, the right to sue the person at fault in an automobile injury case has been altered in line with a concept referred to as no fault insurance. The basic premise of this concept is to have automobile insurance against injuries instead of against liabilities for adjudicated fault (i.e., fault determined judicially). In other words, one is covered in an automobile accident (subject to the statute of limitations) regardless of one's liability in that accident. The ordinary procedure requires the injured party to make a claim upon his own insurer, restricting, but not necessarily eliminating, his or her right to make a claim against the other party. As no fault insurance has been applied in many variants from jurisdiction to jurisdiction, local laws should be carefully examined.*

MINOR AUTO ACCIDENT REPORT FORM

Fortunately not all auto accidents are major ones, but you can easily become involved in a minor accident that can result in an insurance claim. In many states auto accidents causing more than $200 or $300 damage must be reported to the police.

Our ready-to-use short-form auto accident report—**Minor Accident Report** (Form 14.2, page F77) —can be used in setting forth the details of your insurance claim and in gathering the data needed to fill in whatever report form is used by the local police. (*Note:* this form should only be used when there are no injuries resulting from the accident.)

Notice that the form requires the name of your insurance company. Most states now require that vehicle owners carry liability insurance, and they verify coverage with any insurance company listed in an accident report.

If you have a minor auto accident, check with police to learn if you are required to fill in a report. Your failure to submit a report could come to light when the other driver files an insurance claim.

If you've read the above-described instructions for the long-form auto accident report, you will have no trouble completing this short form.

15 Boating/Marine Accident Report

More than 2,000 people die in boating accidents in the United States each year, not counting a few hundred more who simply vanish with their boats, drowned or maybe living a new life somewhere with a different name and all the same old problems.

About 400 men and women drown each year when they fall overboard—experienced boaters mostly, hardly the kind who would trip over the shadow of rigging on the deck. They must have thought falling overboard couldn't happen to them because hardly a one was wearing a life jacket. Life jackets are for kids and landlubbers, so they aren't the ones who drown.

Another 800 or so die annually when their boats capsize or break up. They probably thought capsizing happens to someone else too, because, like the men and women who fall overboard, almost none was wearing a life jacket.

Others die in "safe places," the kinds of waters where you'd let your kids go boating without too much concern: state parks, along slow-moving rivers, in tiny inlets, and in the clean, blue waters of mountain lakes in Maine, Missouri, and Montana, among others.

Injuries run to seven or eight times the number of deaths, many of them the burns and concussions that take place before anyone knows what happened. One-third of all who fall overboard are so seriously injured that they're all but helpless when it comes to assisting their rescuers in getting them back on board.

Lawsuits by guests and passengers against owners and by boat owners against boat yards and manufacturers run into the millions each year.

But boating is safer than we've made it seem: a kitchen can easily be more dangerous than a catamaran, a bathtub more lethal than a motorboat, and a backyard swing more deadly than any sloop or ketch.

This book's **Boating/Marine Accident Report** probably can't save your life (for a form that *could* save your life, see this volume's search and rescue **Float Plan** on page F95), but it can help to reduce, and perhaps prevent, the kind of devastating financial loss that often follows a lawsuit resulting from an accident or injury afloat.

Our ready-to-use Form 15.1 (page F83) can help you assemble information that will aid the Coast Guard, sheriff, or police in locating a missing boat. It can also serve to pull together data that will be essential for making an insurance claim for property damage or medical costs, for helping your lawyer defend you against a lawsuit, or for helping build a strong case if you're the plaintiff.

There is space for more data than will usually be relevant to any one accident; just fill in as many of the appropriate blanks as possible. Read through the form once; then go over it again step by step while you read the following instructions.

You might want to make several photocopies of the form to carry aboard your boat.

NOTE TO INSURANCE AGENTS: *You might want to have the Boating/Marine Accident Report reproduced with your letterhead at the top to give to clients who have boats insured through you. Just white out the Garland Publishing logo, along with the form number at the top of the page, and carefully affix your letterhead prior to photocopying. The cost is negligible and use of the form might help reduce your assured's liability in the event of accident or injury. In any case, the thought would be appreciated, a feeling of being in good hands.*

STEP-BY-STEP INSTRUCTIONS FOR THE BOATING/MARINE ACCIDENT REPORT FORM

As done with the previously described Auto Accident Report in an effort to save this book from unnecessary wear and tear, we strongly suggest that you make a photocopy of the **Boating/Marine Accident Report** form (starting on page F83) that you can refer to as you read through the following instructions.

ACCIDENT DATA—
Date/Time of Accident

Fill in both the date and time of accident if known at the time the report is filled out. If either of these is unknown when the report is made, leave them blank to be filled in later.

TYPE OF ACCIDENT

Check the appropriate space to indicate the type of accident. If it's a collision, fill in the type of object—other boat, pier, buoy, bridge, rocks, etc. The line between **overdue** and **missing** is a gray one, depending upon such things as weather, length of voyage, etc. A boat on a 500-mile voyage would hardly be classified as missing if it was only three or four days overdue. However, a fisherman out on a river might be classified missing if he wasn't heard from for 48 hours.

VESSEL/BOAT—
Vessel Description
Fill in as much information as possible, based upon your own knowledge. For additional data, check with the marina where the boat was kept, the boatyard where it was maintained, the place where it was purchased, the state boat registry, etc. Two sections —one section for each of two boats (#1 and #2)—are provided for this information and the information described below.

Owner/Captain
Fill out as much of this section as possible, given your level of knowledge. Check the marina and boatyard for additional information.

Voyage/Activity
The data to be inserted in this section is especially important to searchers in the event a boat is overdue or missing. Check friends, marina, and boating supply store for chart purchases (these may be of particular help); talk to owners of boats at slips near where the boat was berthed.

Crew/Passengers
List names and addresses if known. If more than seven were aboard, make additional photocopies of this section.

Navigation/Communications Equipment
Mark the appropriate items to indicate the type of equipment believed to be aboard.

Safety/Survival Gear
As above, checkmark the safety/survival equipment that, to the best of your knowledge, was aboard the vessel at the time of the accident.

Stores/Rations
First indicate by check mark whether the stores/ rations to be described and quantified are those present at time of departure or those on hand at the time of the accident. Then, insert the requested information, if available.

MANNER OF ACCIDENT
Describe what happened, if known. If the boat is missing or overdue, leave it blank and fill it in later. NOTE: If necessary (and if it will help clarify things)

continue description of the accident into the space provided for the diagram.

DIAGRAM OF ACCIDENT
Use this space to draw a diagram of the accident if it was a collision with another boat or a fixed object. Indicate north by using an arrow with an **N** at its point. If possible, indicate the direction of both the wind and the current. Mark boats #1 and #2, and indicate the length of each.

INJURED PERSONS
Obtain the names and addresses of any persons injured in the accident. Fill in the type of injury and, if applicable, the name of the hospital each of the injured was taken to. If there are more than a total of five injured persons involved in the accident, you will have to make additional photocopies of this section.

WITNESSES
Obtain the names of crew/passengers who observed any accident taking place aboard—or of persons aboard other boats or ashore who saw the collision, explosion, capsizing, etc. Use binoculars to note numbers and/or names of nearby boats if possible. Actually, obtaining the names of witnesses ashore or aboard other boats is often impossible. However, if more than four witnesses' names are obtained, make additional photocopies of this section.

WEATHER
Indicate whether the weather being described is weather at the point of departure or in the area of the actual or suspected accident. Whether data is based upon forecast or actual reported weather in the area should be noted here as well. Adequate space for a narrative description of the weather follows.

PERSON FILLING OUT REPORT
This is an important section in that the person filling out this report may not have been involved in—nor a witness to—the accident.

Date of Report
List the date on which the report is filled out, not the date that the report is submitted to the Coast Guard, sheriff, insurance company, etc.

16 Miscellaneous Accident Reports

BUILDING ACCIDENT REPORT

If you rent an apartment, the form **Building Accident Report** (Form 16.1, page F97) is good to have handy in the event of injury in your building. It will help you catalog items that you or your attorney can use to establish landlord liability—such things as torn carpets, faulty stair treads, poor lighting, wet floors around electric washing machines and dryers, etc.

NOTE: *Always take photos of hazardous conditions that cause an accident so you'll have evidence to present in court, because the landlord's first action will be to repair the condition as quickly as possible after the incident.*

It is also a good idea to take photos of a hazardous condition to give to the landlord BEFORE an accident, since once the landlord knows you have proof of negligence, he or she will fix the condition in a hurry.

Our form is a fairly good checklist for landlords and building owners too. Make several copies and take a walk through your building to note (and, we hope, correct) any situation that might leave you exposed to damages for negligence in the event of a personal injury in your building.

In the **Building Common Area** section of this form you may need to check more than one item, basement and laundry room, for example.

Copies of this form should be in the hands of all tenants, property managers, and building superintendents.

STREET/SIDEWALK ACCIDENT REPORT

If you expect to file an insurance claim or sue for negligence due to injury on a sidewalk or street, take a look at our ready-to-use **Street/Sidewalk Accident Report** form (Form 16.2, page F103).

Your insurance company will have its own form for you to complete when making a claim for medical payments, disability, or loss of income. By filling in as many blanks as possible on our form, you will have almost all of the information about the accident and injury that your insurance company will ask for. More importantly, perhaps, the completed report form can provide essential information to your attorney, should you have good cause to file suit for negligence.

Be sure to note (and photograph if possible) street and sidewalk defects—your insurance company and/or attorney may want to enter a claim or file suit against a building owner who failed to maintain the sidewalk, or even against the city for negligence in failing to maintain the street. After all, if you trip and fall and are injured because of a sidewalk slab raised by the growing roots of a tree, the building owner can hardly claim he didn't have the time to notice the uneven condition of the walk.

DEFECTIVE PRODUCT ACCIDENT REPORT

The accident report for a defective product (Form 16.3, page F107) is an important one to complete before filing a claim for injury due to such a product. It's also a good form to fill in before making a complaint about a defective product, even if there has yet to be an injury.

Not all products will have serial or model numbers or warranties, nor will weather be a factor in the use of many products. Just fill in what's appropriate in the **Defective Product Accident Report**. To record extensive injury data, use the Hospital Care or Out-Patient Care pages from the **Attorney's Accident Work Sheet** (Form 16.6, starting on page F119).

For more about dealing with sellers and manufacturers of defective products, see Section VI and Section VII.

The *Consumer Product Safety Commission* (1111 18th Street, N.W., Washington, DC 20036) would like to recieve a report of any injury caused by a product. The commission would appreciate your mailing a copy of your completed accident report.

ANIMAL ACCIDENT REPORT

Whether someone is injured by an animal or whether an animal is injured in an accident, the form **Animal Accident Report** (Form 16.4, page F111) works equally well. Just fill in the appropriate blanks; as there probably aren't many licensed spiders—nor wasps with shot records on file with the local vet—this form should cover most, if not all, accidents involving animals. If more than three injured persons are involved (and let's hope not!), the Injured Persons section may be photocopied.

PUBLIC TRANSPORTATION ACCIDENT REPORT

As with the previously described forms, the **Public Transportation Accident Report** (Form 16.5, page F115) is easy to complete and includes almost everything you'll need when filing a claim for any injury associated with public transportation.

You may not be able to fill in all the blanks. Just obtain as much information as possible as soon as you can, then contact your insurance company or an attorney when you've got everything together. If you're involved in an accident as a public transportation passenger, it would be a good idea to get the names and addresses of as many other injured passengers as possible. Your attorney or insurance company may want to contact them later as witnesses, or you and several other injured passengers may want to hire the same attorney to handle your case.

If space for more than three witnesses is needed, simply photocopy an extra copy of that particular form page and note "injured" by the name of any injured passenger.

By becoming familiar with this and other accident reports now, you will have a good idea of what to look for and write down if and when you are involved in an accident.

ATTORNEY'S ACCIDENT WORK SHEET

The **Attorney's Accident Work Sheet** (Form 16.6, page F119) is relatively routine, straightforward, and easy to complete. It provides space for more data than will be required for many cases, yet is broad enough so that it can be used for a fairly wide range of negligence litigation. Combined with the appropriate accident report, it provides the basis for a complete case file.

NOTE TO NONLAWYERS: *Be sure to fill out the appropriate accident report **and** complete as much as possible of the **Attorney's Accident Work Sheet** before you see your lawyer. No use sitting in his office while he's charging you $75 to $100 an hour to ask questions you could have answered ahead of time.*

---

17 Authorizations to Inspect Medical Records

AUTHORIZATION TO INSPECT HOSPITAL MEDICAL RECORDS

The form Authorization to Inspect Hospital Medical Records (Form 17.1, page F137) authorizes a *hospital* to permit the inspection of its medical records on the person named in the document.

The name and address of the hospital should be typed in the space provided after CUSTODIAN OF RECORDS. The name and address of the person or organization being given authority to inspect records (usually an attorney, but sometimes an insurance company) should be typed in the second set of lines. And usually the name of the person signing the document will be typed in above *Name of Person*, but not always. For example, a parent would sign for release of medical records of an injured child.

Unlike *every* other medical release form in current use, this volume's form restricts release of medical records to those **specific** records related to the specified injury and date of treatment or confinement. Hospitals and doctors' offices are all too careless in handing over their **complete file** on an individual, thus exposing him or her to unwarranted and unlawful invasion or privacy. The limitation that is a part of this volume's form puts medical care agencies on notice to disclose ONLY the specified records.

The body of the form provides for the signature of the individual giving the authorization, and also provides for the signature of a witness. If there is no requirement in the jurisdiction where the hospital is located that the document be notarized, have a witness sign in the space provided, but do not photocopy *the notary portion* (the back side) of the form so that a records clerk won't tell you, "I'm sorry, but you'll have to have this notarized first." (Such is the power of the printed form.)

If the document must be notarized, if you're going to mail it to a hospital, or if you merely feel that the added psychological weight of the notary seal will be needed to overcome the reluctance of a part-time or not-too-well-informed clerk, leave the notary portion attached and have the release notarized.

If you do plan to have the release notarized, place a strip of white paper over the "Witness line" before making a photocopy—so you-know-who won't tell you, "I'm sorry, but you'll have to have this witnessed first."

ATTORNEYS: *You may want to have this form printed with, and without, the notary portion for use in various jurisdictions. When mailing the form, use of the notary portion will probably help eliminate delay in compliance with your request.*

AUTHORIZATION TO INSPECT PHYSICIAN'S MEDICAL RECORDS

As distinct from the previously described form, this form (Form 17.2, page F139) authorizes a *physician* to permit the inspection of his or her medical records on the person named in the document.

The name and address of the physician should be typed in the space provided near the top of the form. As before, the name and address of the person or organization granted the authority to inspect records should be typed in the second set of lines, while the name of the person signing the document will usually be typed in above *Name of Person*, but not always.

To repeat, unlike *every* other medical release form in current use, Authorization to Inspect Physician's Medical Records restricts release of medical records to those **specific** records related to the specified injury and dates of examination and treatment. Doctors' offices and hospitals are all too careless in handing over their **complete file** on an individual, thus exposing him or her to unwarranted and unlawful invasion of privacy. The limitation that is a part of this form puts physicians on notice to disclose ONLY the specified records.

Note that the previously detailed suggestions concerning the notarization and witnessing of Authorization to Inspect Hospital Medical Records also apply equally for Form 17.2.

18 Request for a Copy of Police Blotter and/or Accident Report

Form 18.1 (page F141), **Request for a Copy of Police Blotter and/or Accident Report,** requests that police provide a copy of the "police blotter," their brief record of the incident and any arrest made, plus a copy of the accident report submitted by the investigating officer.

It is important to remember that you are **not** required by law to "give testimony against yourself" in answering questions put to you by police at the scene of an accident. Statements you make for the police accident report **can** be used against you in court—the opposing attorney and insurance company will have had access to the report and can be counted on to call police officers to the witness stand to ask questions based upon police report information that they hope will be damaging to your case.

Answer police questions truthfully and as briefly as possible. Volunteer nothing. Keep in mind that your answers, plus other data on the police report, can help avoid a lawsuit and can aid speedy out-of-court settlement of your claim by the other driver's insurance company if your responses clearly indicate that the other driver was at fault. And, of course, use of information from the police report "cuts" both ways. Your attorney can subpoena the police officer to testify—and the report can give a pretty good idea of what the officer is going to say.

Some police departments, because certain information contained in police accident reports may be covered by the federal or state privacy acts, restrict **full** copies of reports to those involved in an accident and will want the notarized signature of anyone requesting a copy of the report by mail.

But if you, as one of the drivers involved in the accident, walk into the station, show identification, and sign our request form there, you should have no trouble obtaining copies of the blotter and report for a nominal fee. If you're going to take the request form to the police station yourself, cut off the notary portion before submitting it.

19 Using a Power of Attorney

RETAINER AND POWER OF ATTORNEY

The document by which a client usually formalizes the hiring of an attorney to prosecute his or her claim for injury in an accident is called a **Retainer and Power of Attorney**, which sets forth the key details of the case, name of the plaintiff(s), name of the attorney(s), a brief description of the claim, and the name of the defendant(s).

The retainer portion of the document also specifies the various percentages of any sum awarded the client that will be due the attorney at various stages of the claim's prosecution. Often an attorney will receive 10 percent of an out-of-court settlement but may receive as much as 50 percent of any award granted as the result of an appeal.

The power of attorney portion authorizes your lawyer to act in your stead in dealing with the other party and in representing you in court. It also authorizes your attorney to "accept" (subject to your approval) an out-of-court settlement offer from the other party. This accepted settlement offer will be binding even if you change your mind prior to signing a release of claim (see pages 54–57).

The **Retainer and Power of Attorney** may, or may not, need to be notarized, depending upon the jurisdiction. Your lawyer may have his or her own form or may choose to use our ready-to-use form (Form 19.1, page F143), which is easier to understand and to complete than any we have seen.

POWER OF ATTORNEY

The form **Power of Attorney** (Form 19.2, page F145) is similar to the previous form but does not contain a retainer. Thus, it may be used by attorneys and clients who have negotiated a separate fee arrangement. As with the **Retainer and Power of Attorney**, it may, or may not, need to be notarized.

20 Release of All Rights and Claims

When the courtroom contest is over and the judge's decision and award have been handed down, or when your lawyer has emerged from the battlefield of negotiated settlement, someone is going to shove a document titled **Release of All Rights and Claims** under your nose and say, "Sign!"

Your lawyer may be the one who hands it to you, after the two of you have agreed that the amount offered is all you're going to get, or it may be given to you by someone from the opposing side's insurance company or law firm.

Having stood the test of time and repeated assault, every word of the "enemy's" release form is considered by its lawyers to be *sacred*. There will be no changes or revisions or notes in the margin as often happens with other contracts and agreements.

Any release of rights and claims reads like a ripoff, but if the settlement or award is fair and you're willing to accept it, then the other side has a right to all the protection it can get against resurrected claims —sort of like making sure you get the negatives when you pay off the blackmailer.

It would probably be a good idea to at least glance at this book's **Release of All Rights and Claims** (Form 20.1, page F147) so that if you're ever a claimant and are handed something similar, you'll be aware that what you're being asked to sign is purely routine despite appearances.

Be sure that any settlement you accept is one with which you're satisfied because, once you sign, you have, just as the form says, given up every right and claim you have.

We said it before: DON'T SIGN **ANYTHING**, EXCEPT ON THE ADVISE OF **YOUR** LAWYER.

ATTORNEYS: *This volume's Release of All Rights and Claims is relatively standard, its language having been revised in line with recent "plain-language" guidelines.*

FILLING OUT YOUR RELEASE OF ALL RIGHTS AND CLAIMS FORM

The **Release of All Rights and Claims** is simple, almost deceptively simple, to fill out. In the Sample of Form 20.1/F147, starting on page 56, we have inserted a letter in each blank space to aid you in the filling out of the ready-to-use form at the back of the book. These letters refer to the following instructions and comments:

A: Attorney's office or insurance carrier (hereafter designated A or IC) types in **name** of claimant.

B: A or IC types in **age** of claimant.

C: A or IC types in the **legal** address of claimant.

D: A or IC types in, **in words**, the amount of the settlement.

E: A or IC types in, **in figures**, the amount of the settlement.

F: A or IC types in the **name** of the person or organization making payment to the claimant.

G: A or IC types in the **address** of the person or organization making payment to the claimant.

H: CLAIMANT, **in his or her own handwriting**, writes in the word "release."

I: A or IC types in the **name** of the person or organization being released.

J: A or IC types in the **address** of the person or organization being released.

K: If possible, CLAIMANT briefly describes the accident or injury, date of same, and his or her resulting injuries, disabilities, and/or illnesses. CLAIMANT may wish to write the description on a separate piece of paper first, then rewrite it in the space provided.

   If CLAIMANT is unable to write the description in his or her own words, he or she can dictate same to A or IC who can assist and then later type in CLAIMANT'S description. This is obviously a less satisfactory procedure.

L: CLAIMANT writes in, **in his or her own handwriting**, the word "release."

M: CLAIMANT, **in his or her own handwriting**, writes in "Yes."

N: CLAIMANT, **in his or her own handwriting**, writes in "A release of everything."

O: CLAIMANT, **in his or her own handwriting**, writes in "Yes."

P: CLAIMANT, **in his or her own handwriting**, writes in "Yes."

Q: CLAIMANT signs the release with his complete, legal name over the words, THIS IS A RELEASE.

R: CLAIMANT, **in his or her own handwriting**, fills in the date of his or her signature.

S: A or IC types in the **name** of claimant.

T: A or IC types in, **in words**, the amount of the settlement.

U: A or IC types in, **in figures**, the amount of the settlement.

V: A or IC types in the **date** on which the witnesses saw the claimant sign the release.

W: Witnesses sign in the appropriate spaces.

X: A or IC types in the **addresses** of the witnesses.

The NOTARY will fill in, sign, seal, and date the notary portion of the release.

NOTE: *Sufficient copies of the release should be prepared to provide at least one "original," signed by the claimant, for each of the following: plaintiff, defendant, attorney for plaintiff, attorney for defendant, defendant's insurance carrier, and (if appropriate) the court.*

Sample of Form 20.1/F147

Release of All Rights and Claims

I, _____A_____, age ____B____, residing at _____C_____

_____C_____,

in exchange for _____D_____ ($ ___E___), which I have received from

_____F_____ _____G_____,

do hereby forever _____H_____ and discharge _____I_____

_____J_____,

and their heirs, executors, administrators, successors and assigns, from every right and claim which I may now have, or may hereafter have, on account of any injuries, disabilities and/or illnesses suffered by me as follows:

_____K_____

_____K_____

_____K_____

I hereby acknowledge that by signing this _____L_____ I am forever settling in full for any injuries, disabilities and/or illnesses which I have previously had, which I now have and which I may have in the future, either on account of the specific occurrence mentioned above, or because of any other occurrence in the past, or because of both, even though I do not know that I already have had, have now or may in the future have such injuries, disabilities and/or illnesses, and even though they are not mentioned specifically in this release; and I do this regardless of what any person or persons may have told me about my injuries, disabilities and/or illnesses, or about anything else.

I KNOW THAT DOCTORS, LAWYERS AND OTHERS MAKE MISTAKES AND I REALIZE THAT WHAT OTHER PEOPLE MAY HAVE TOLD ME COULD BE WRONG. I REALIZE I AM TAKING THE RISK THAT THEY MIGHT BE WRONG ABOUT MY CASE, AND IF THEY ARE WRONG, IT IS MY LOSS AND I CANNOT BACK OUT OF THIS _____L_____ AND SETTLEMENT.

I am signing this _____L_____ in exchange for the money which I am being paid, and I have not been promised anything else.

I realize that payment of the above-mentioned money is not an admission by anyone that anyone is liable to me for anything.

CLAIMANT: Please answer the following questions in your own handwriting:

1. Have you read this paper from beginning to end? _____M_____

2. What is this paper you are signing? _____N_____

3. Do you realize that signing this paper forever settles and ends every right and/or claim which you may now have for any damages as well as for past or future medical treatment, care, cure, maintenance and/or wages?

_____O_____

4. Are you satisfied with this settlement? _____P_____

THEREFORE, I am signing my name upon the words, THIS IS A RELEASE, which is printed below to show that I understand and mean everything which is said in this paper.

Signature: _____Q_____ THIS IS A RELEASE

Dated this ___R___ day of ___R___, 19 _R_.

Sample of Form 20.1 (Continued)

CERTIFICATE OF WITNESSES

WE, THE UNDERSIGNED, do hereby certify that the **Release of All Rights and Claims** set forth on the reverse side of this paper was executed in our presence by _____ S _____ and that said claimant acknowledged that he or she fully understood the contents and that it was a release of everything and that he or she executed the same as his or her free act and deed in exchange for _____ T _____ ($ __ U __), as therein set forth, and for that only.

WITNESS our hands and seals this _____ V _____ day of _____ V _____ , 19 __ V __ .

_____ W _____
Signature

_____ X _____
Address

_____ W _____
Signature

_____ X _____
Address

_____ W _____
Signature

_____ X _____
Address

* *

CERTIFICATE OF NOTARY

STATE OF   )

) ss:

COUNTY OF   )

On this _____ day of _____ , 19 _____ , before me personally came and appeared said claimant, _____ , known, and known to me, to be the individual described in and who executed the foregoing document, and who duly acknowledged to me that he or she executed same for the purpose therein contained.

IN WITNESS WHEREOF, I hereunto set my hand and official seal.

_____
Notary Public

My commission expires: _____

IV

HOMEOWNER-
CONTRACTOR

21 Improving on Home Improvement

This section, Section IV, includes every form normally associated with home-improvement contracts or, for that matter, with home construction. Reviewing the forms before signing an agreement with any home-improvement contractor will show you what to look for and avoid—which provisions you may want to include and which provisions you may want to revise or exclude altogether.

If you're ever going to build a home, this section's forms and advice will provide the guidelines you need in deciding whether to act as your own contractor, subcontracting out most of the actual building and thereby saving almost half the cost of your house in the process.

The forms of Section IV include two forms of agreement between owner and contractor, an agreement between contractor and subcontractor, forms for a contractor's bid and proposal, job estimate work sheets, several forms for waiver of lien, a receipt for conditional payment, and a contractor's affidavit of completion—plus paragraph-by-paragraph explanations of many of these forms.

As a homeowner, you're likely to find yourself talking with a contractor about home improvement work on your house when:

- You believe you'd like to have some work done and have called in a contractor.
- You've responded to an ad offering special seasonal rates, such as a reduced end-of-summer swimming pool constuction price.
- You've been contacted by phone, letter, or personal visit by a home-improvement salesperson soliciting work for his or her company, supposedly at a bargain price.

A fourth way, not too common, but perhaps one of the best, might present itself when you least expect it:

Soon after moving into a typical three-bedroom tract house in a still developing suburb several years ago, we set to work converting the house's two-car garage into a living and office space. A contractor replaced the garage's overhead doors with sliding glass ones and added electrical outlets. We then built walls for a separate office, installed paneling, and finally put down carpet. Just as we were fitting the final corner of carpet, we happened to glance outside and spotted a big truck and crew down the street blowing insulation into a recently completed, but still vacant, house.

Figuring the worker was already *there* and that we might be able to make a deal on the spot, we went down to where he was. We made a cash agreement, and two hours later our new living area was insulated better than the rest of the house. We also had *extra* insulation added over the ceiling of our entire home. The cost was about one-fourth of the amount we would otherwise have had to pay.

Which brings us to another point. One money-saving way to locate someone to do home-improvement work is to get in the car and check out carpenters, electricians, plumbers, roofers, etc., working on nearby construction. The people you'll find are usually well qualified to do small jobs or to work along with you. By making the contract yourself, you eliminate the middle person. On bigger jobs, talk to the subcontractor whose specialty you need.

It seems almost redundant to warn you about "fly-by-night" con persons who'll take your money and run, but people keep getting ripped off. Therefore take note of this WARNING: Very carefully check out anyone who comes around, or who phones, offering to do home-improvement work. Do the following:

- Ask the contractor, **and** the Better Business Bureau, how long he's been in business and under how many corporate names.
- Be sure to get his or her street address. A post office box number isn't enough if you have to find the owner or take legal action.
- Find out if the contractor is licensed by the city or county. Do so by calling the licensing bureau at the city hall or county courthouse.
- Investigate if complaints about the contractor have been made to the local consumer affairs office or Better Business Bureau.
- Determine the company's credit rating by asking your bank, or a business-owner friend, to obtain a credit report.
- Be sure you know the name of the owner or principal officer.
- Finally, obtain the names of half a dozen people for whom the contractor has done work. Two are not enough; anyone can get two relatives, friends, or even employees to pose as satisfied customers.

DECIDING WHAT YOU WANT

Before calling in anyone to give you bids on your planned addition or improvement, make sure you have a pretty good idea of what you want:

- What size room?
- How many windows and doors and where?
- What about electrical needs?
- How will you heat it and cool it?
- What kind of flooring?
- What kind of wall covering?
- What about storage space?
- What type of roof?
- What kind of roofing material?
- What kind of exterior?
- What size swimming pool and where?
- What type of construction?
- What kind of protective fence?
- What type of driveway resurfacing material?
- How much and what type of landscaping?

One thing that helps is to visit a few lumber yards and large hardware and building supply houses to look over doors, windows, wall paneling, bathroom fixtures, roofing materials, floor covering, etc., so that you'll have a fair idea of what you want. Many suppliers will be glad to estimate the retail cost of materials for you. (Your contractor will, of course, be buying at a lower price.)

Ask for any pamphlets, brochures, or specification sheets on the materials you're interested in. Also ask for stock numbers, catalog numbers, and samples of tile, flooring, paneling, roofing, etc.

At home, write a list of all the materials you would like the contractor to use. Next, draw up a sketch of what you want done. Make several photocopies of the sketch and materials list so you can give one to each contractor you'll be talking with. Keep one set for yourself, and keep a set to give to your bank if you're planning to finance the work.

Decide how much you can spend, and if you don't have the cash, find out how much you can finance and pay for on a monthly basis. (See page 63 for information on financing.) Decide when you want the work to start and when you want the job to be completed.

When you finally know what you want and how you're going to pay for it, you're ready to look for someone to do the work.

FINDING A CONTRACTOR

When taking the initiative in locating someone to do home-improvement work, you might contact:

- A friend or someone at work who has recently had a similar job done.
- An officer at the bank that holds the mortgage on your house.
- The contractor who originally built your house. If it isn't practical for him to do the work, he can give you the names of subcontractors or individuals you might be able to use.
- Workmen and subcontractors at nearby construction sites.

Talk to at least three contractors and obtain three bids. If you're planning to finance the work at your bank or a credit union (usually much cheaper than having the contractor finance it), you will probably need three bids anyway.

NOTE: *Make sure that any contractor you sign an agreement with supplies a performance bond issued by an insurance company to assure his "performance" of the contract. Otherwise the contractor could take the money and run, and you'd wind up with nothing more than a debt due your bank.*

OBTAINING BIDS

Based on your sketch and list of materials, the contractor can work up a bid, which should include:

1. A description of the work to be done
2. An estimate of the cost of:
   - Building permits, licenses, etc.
   - Insurance, surety bond, etc.
   - Labor
   - Materials
3. Proposed starting date
4. Proposed completion date

Based upon the bid, plus such other factors as the proposed starting and completion dates and the contractor's reputation, you can begin negotiations with whomever you've tentatively selected to do the work.

NEGOTIATING A CONTRACT

Many contractors will offer you their own contract form, a printed form that is slanted in the contractor's favor. The contractor isn't necessarily trying to put anything over on you; it's just that contractors usually buy forms sold by office or legal supply houses, and since contractors are the buyers, the forms are heavily weighted in their favor. (Just as leases sold in the same way are weighted in favor of landlords since landlords, not tenants, buy the forms.)

Just because a form is printed doesn't mean that it's "standard." Read the contract, and if in doubt about *anything*, ask the contractor to clarify it for you. If you object to an item, ask the contractor if he'd be willing to modify or strike out that provision. Both parties must initial any changes that are made on the contract itself.

As a point of good negotiating technique, make sure that whenever you object to a provision, you have an alternate ready to offer. If you would like to have a provision added, write it out and ask that it be included in the agreement.

If the contract involves anything over $5,000, or maybe less if you're not sure you understand the agreement, have a lawyer check it over before you sign.

The contract should include the name and address of the owner, the name and address of the contractor, and the address and a brief description of the property. It should also include the following:

1. A precise description of the work to be done—not just "repair roof," "resurface driveway," or "add room, 12′ × 14′." The description should include the type of construction and list the major materials to be used: the type and, if practical, the brand and quality level of roofing, exterior siding, paint, windows and doors, hardware, fixtures, flooring, etc.
2. A provision that all materials shall be new and of good quality and that all work shall be by skilled workers and be of good quality.
3. A statement that the contractor will obtain and display all appropriate notices and permits. (You will have to pay for the cost of any survey.)
4. A statement guaranteeing that the contractor will carry liability and workmen's compensation insurance. This will protect you against suits for injury to workmen and against injury or damage caused by the contractor or his workers. Ask for a copy of the policy or get a letter from the insurance company confirming the coverage.
5. A "performance clause" stating that the contractor will complete the job by the date promised and that, in the event he fails to complete the work on time, the contractor shall pay a penalty of, say, $35 a day until the work is completed.
6. A statement that the contractor has obtained a *surety bond.** This will help protect you against suppliers' and workers' liens and will make sure you get what you paid for.
7. A statement that all changes from the original agreement by either the contractor or homeowner must be in writing.
8. A guarantee that during the first year following completion of the work the contractor shall correct in a timely manner any materials or workmanship not meeting the provisions of the contract.
9. A provision stating that should you cancel the contract before work begins, you must pay the contractor a specified percentage, usually 10 or 20 percent, of the job's estimated cost. This is to compensate the contractor for time already spent and for possible loss of work that was declined in the expectation of doing your job.

*A surety bond is a type of "insurance policy" in which the bonding company makes itself responsible for the fulfillment of the contractor's obligations—his obligations to you and to his suppliers, employees, etc., with respect to the job. If, for example, the contractor fails to complete the job according to specifications, the bonding company will make sure that it's done by someone else or that you receive satisfactory financial compensation. Then they'll go after the contractor.

Many home-improvement contractors wish they'd never heard of the term "surety bond" and will tell you that obtaining a surety bond will force them to substantially increase the amount of their estimate. Not necessarily so; contractors with good performance records are highly "bondable" at very low cost. Contractors with poor performance records, on the other hand, are almost unbondable—thus making a contractor's willingness to be bonded a fairly good indication of the company's performance history.

Bonding companies, by the way, are listed in the yellow pages of your phone book under "Bonds–Surety." Although the contractor pays the bonding company, you might find a surety bond an interesting document to look at just the same.

There are a number of additional provisions that should be a part of an agreement for any major home-improvement work. These are exhibited in detail in the contract **Agreement Between Owner and Contractor** (Form 22.1, page F149) and are explained in Chapter 22. A short-form contract for less extensive work is also provided (Form 22.3, page F155).

FINANCING

It's probably a good idea to pay cash if you have the money—unless the **interest rate** is *less* than you expect the **inflation rate** to be during the loan payment period. If the inflation rate is greater than the interest rate, anything you borrow is "free" money, regardless of how high the interest rate is.

If you're not going to pay cash, talk to the bank that holds the mortgage on your house. If you have enough equity, your mortgage can be rewritten to include the home improvement. Just make sure the bank doesn't figure any new mortgage at a higher interest rate on the **entire amount** owing on your house. That could be very expensive.

You might also consider a second mortgage to pay for major home improvements. You'll pay a higher interest rate than on a first mortgage, but since the dollar amount is less, the actual cost might be lower. Remember though, payments on a second mortgage are *in addition* to your regular monthly first-mortgage payments.

You might also consider a loan from any credit union you're qualified to join or from the commercial bank you do business with.

The contractor might offer to finance the work. But be careful: the interest rate he'll have to charge will probably be quite a bit higher than you would pay at any bank or credit union.

Watch out for any interest rate that seems unusually low. Make sure that you're not being quoted an "add-on" interest rate. An "add-on" rate of 5 percent of the price for the job will really cost you about 10 percent simple interest.

With *simple interest*, you pay interest only on the amount still owed. With *add-on interest*, you pay as much interest the last month as you did the first month, even though you have repaid almost all of the money.

IDEA: *There is yet another financing method you might try if you and your bank get along well together. In considering a home-improvement loan your bank will be very interested in two things:*

1. *Your ability and intention to repay the loan.*
2. *The increase in the value of your house as a result of the home-improvement work.*

The bank really doesn't care who does the work as long as there is an appropriate increase in the value of the property. Therefore, if you obtain three estimates and then find there is no way you can make up the difference between the $8,000 the bank will lend and *the $10,000 that the job will cost, your bank might well lend you the $8,000 and let you do the work yourself.*

The bank will probably want to take a look at the house before and after, but you should have no trouble getting the bank to agree and might find that the total cost is less (labor being what it is) than the $8,000 the bank was willing to loan you.

LIENS

It is possible that you could pay your contractor in full and then end up having to pay for the job a second time. This can occur because of a provision of law in most states, usually called a "mechanic's lien," that gives unpaid suppliers, subcontractors, and workers the right to enforce payment by filing claims against the property.

There are ways you can help protect yourself against a mechanic's lien:

1. Deal with a reputable contractor.
2. Require a *surety bond.*
3. Obtain from the contractor the following:
   A. When the work is half completed, a signed, notarized list of the names and addresses of all suppliers, subcontractors, and workers.
   B. When the work is completed, but before the final payment, a *waiver of lien* (see Chapter 26) signed by all of the suppliers, subcontractors, and workers listed by the contractor.
4. Obtain from the contractor a sworn, notarized *affidavit of completion* (see Chapter 26) stating that there are no unpaid bills or that all unpaid bills will be paid in full by the contractor.

If you've followed the suggested precautions, there is not much chance of a lien being filed against your property. However, if one is filed, it will usually be a simple matter for your lawyer to obtain a release of lien. A lien is only a formal *claim* by the lienor; the lienor will still have to file a lawsuit, go to court, prove the claim, and obtain a judgment in order to enforce the lien.

A lien is most often the result of a dispute between the contractor and a supplier or subcontractor. It is the responsibility of the contractor to have it released without delay.

DISPUTE WITH THE CONTRACTOR

Insufficient progress, inferior materials and workmanship, and departures from drawings and specifications are the most common causes of disputes between owners and contractors. Many of these can be quickly resolved if you have a concise, comprehensive contract setting forth the terms. In this way both owner and contractor know where they stand and what the decision most likely would be if the case went to court.

If you do have a problem with the contractor that cannot be resolved by talking it over, write him a fairly informal letter outlining the problem and asking him to rectify it.

If the contractor doesn't correct the problem within a reasonable time, which might vary depending on the nature of the problem and how fast the contractor's workers are "building the problems into the job," you should write a more formal complaint demanding correction by a specific date.

This second letter should be sent via registered mail, return receipt requested. In the lower left-hand corner it should bear the notation that a copy has been sent to your lawyer, whose name and address should also be listed.

Remember that in almost any dispute your signed agreement with the contractor will be the final word. You can sign the most one-sided contract in the world, and, except for violations of law of the most gross inequity, a court of law is likely to enforce the agreement. A reputable contractor and a concise, equitable contract are your best protection.

The following pages will guide you through most of the legal forms you're likely to come into contact with in connection with home-improvement work. Some forms are supplied for possible use; others are provided for the information they provide.

22 Agreements Between Homeowner and Contractor

The long-form agreement between homeowner and contractor, **Agreement Between Owner and Contractor** (Form 22.1, page F149), can serve for home construction or a major home-improvement project involving considerable expense and several subcontractors. The **short-form** owner–contractor agreement (Form 22.3, page F155), discussed later in this chapter, is probably all you'll need for not-so-major jobs involving just one contractor. Either form can serve as a basis for comparison when you're reviewing an agreement offered by any contractor or architect.

THE LONG-FORM AGREEMENT

If you're doing business with a builder or home-improvement contractor who doesn't have an agreement form of his own, you and your contractor will probably agree that this volume's form will meet your needs.

You'll notice that we offer two choices for the contract's final articles (Articles 20, 21, and 22): one choice containing a provision for arbitration (see **Alternate Articles**, Form 22.2), the other without an arbitration clause (as in our long-form agreement, Form 22.1). See Section V, Arbitration, before deciding on which set of articles to use.

Prior to reading our article-by-article instructions concerning the form **Agreement Between Owner and Contractor**, you should make a photocopy of the forms themselves (Forms 22.1 and 22.2). You will then be able to refer to them, while reading our comments, without undue flipping back and forth between sections of this book.

The following descriptions and instructions may appear to repeat certain remarks made earlier. The earlier remarks were general comments, whereas the following information pertains to each of the particular articles of our long-form agreement.

Opening Proviso

The agreement's opening paragraph is self-explanatory, just make sure the address shown for the contractor is a **street** address and not a post office box number. Phone numbers usually aren't noted in this portion of a contract, but we've provided for them as a matter of convenience.

Article 1: Description of the Work

In this article the contractor provides a fairly detailed description of the work to be done, referring to specific materials, dimensions, plans, and specifications.

Drawings, plans, and specifications become a part of the agreement when initialed by the owner and contractor. For a relatively simple job, you might make the drawings, depending upon your skill. For extensive work, the contractor or an architect can draw up plans based upon discussions with you.

In stating your requirements, specify both **design** and **performance** specifications and be very descriptive, such as, "solid walnut sufficient to hold a 2′6″ expresso coffee maker."

Article 2: Payment

Include the total cost of the work, following that with a payment schedule. A typical home-improvement contract to be fulfilled by a small contractor might call for the following schedule:

- One-third upon commencement of work.
- One-third when the job is half completed.
- One-third upon satisfactory completion **and** presentation of appropriate waiver(s) of lien.

On home construction, if you're dealing with a well-established and reputable builder, you might work out an agreement to pay:

- One-fourth when the excavation is complete, the foundation is complete, and utility lines are in place.
- One-fourth when the walls are up and the job is under roof.
- One-fourth after the electrical, plumbing, and mechanical work (such as heating and air conditioning) is complete and the interior walls are closed in.
- One-fourth upon satisfactory completion of finish carpentry, painting, final grading, landscaping, etc., **and** upon presentation of waiver(s) of lien.

Article 3: Liens

Final payment, as explained above and on page 72, should be keyed to obtaining waiver(s) of lien from the contractor. Forms for *waiver of lien* (Forms 26.1 and 26.2) are provided starting on page F179 and are discussed in Chapter 26.

Article 4: Timely Completion of the Work

Specify dates by which certain portions of the work shall be completed. It's easy enough to tie these dates in with the payment schedule specified in Article 2.

The penalty to be paid by the contractor for any delay he is responsible for should be keyed to the overall cost of the job, plus any expenses and inconvenience you would incur as a result of the delay.

Actually, this provision isn't all that enforceable. The contractor has plenty of "outs" and can always get a supplier to say that delivery of materials was held up for one reason or another. Still, the performance clause should be a part of every construction agreement. It will not be found very often in contracts presented by many home-improvement contractors.

Article 5: Surveys and Easements

You pay the cost of any surveys, but surveys will not be relevant to most home-improvement contracts unless the work gets close to the property line. A fence, of course, is at the property line. Usually a survey that you already have will be sufficient.

Although common law generally grants you an easement across the property of another in order to obtain access to your property, it would be a good idea to see your lawyer to obtain a written easement to include permission for any construction, such as a roadway, putting up a gate, or bridging across a culvert on the property of another. You'll need this before a contractor begins any work.

Article 6: Licenses, Permits and Building Codes

The contractor can generally obtain required permits easily—he does it all the time. Usually there won't be any problem as long as what you're trying to do meets zoning regulations. In some residential areas, home builders are required to meet esthetic requirements—for example, allowing only colonial or contemporary style homes. Other requirements state that a minimum number of square feet be included or that a specific amount be spent on the construction of any house. This is to guard against the lowering of property values.

Article 7: Materials and Equipment

Although this provision calls for new materials, there may be instances where you'd rather specify used bricks and might want to panel an interior wall with weathered wood from a barn. However, expect to pay more for used barn siding and bricks than for the same material new.

Article 8: Samples

Working from samples is a good idea, but don't hold your contractor too slavishly to specific samples because he may be able to save you money on very similar items that he can obtain at a greatly reduced price.

Article 9: Labor and Supervision

Requiring skilled workers will help protect you against faulty workmanship. If you do give instructions to a foreman, as also provided for in this article, try to put all but the most minor instructions in writing. The temptation will be there, but when you're visiting the work site, avoid giving any directions to workers. It puts them in an awkward position and is in violation of this article.

Article 10: Alterations and Changes

This provision protects both owner and contractor. After the contractor starts work, you're almost sure to think of things you'll want to change; it happens all the time. Either write down and sketch out any changes you'd like made, or tell the contractor what you want and let him make up any drawings and specification changes that you can "OK" and initial. This qualifies as "written approval."

This article also protects you against the surprise of additional expenses when the contractor presents the final bill. Any changes that are not in writing, you do not have to pay for—unless they were required to meet building codes or other regulations. Ask the contractor to let you know early on if he'll have to incur additional expenses to comply with laws or codes.

Article 11: Correction of Deficiencies

Beyond requiring the contractor to correct deficiencies and departures from specifications, this article provides what is, in effect, a warranty for one year following completion of the work. Such a provision is not always found in home-improvement contractors' agreements.

Article 12: Protection of the Work

The determination of "reasonable" protection of the work is greatly affected by the area. Some locations almost require a 24-hour guard; in others merely locking up tools and equipment is sufficient. In regard to damage or injury caused by the contractor, he would be responsible for his own negligence anyway, but it's nice to have it spelled out. And it can save trouble if something does happen.

Article 13: Cleaning Up

Most contractors do clean up satisfactorily. The trick here is to keep your eyes constantly open for things you want him not to haul away. On a job of any size there are all kinds of items that you'll want to keep: odd lengths of 2″ × 4″ and 4″ × 4″ lumber, less-than-full-size pieces of 4′ × 8′ plywood and paneling, leftover cement blocks and bricks, etc. You'll especially want the contractor to leave any extra roofing, asphalt or vinyl floor tile, and paint so that you'll have a perfect match if anything is damaged later on.

TREASURE TROVE: *When it comes to cleaning up when the job is done, some contractors act as though they took lessons from whoever it was that dreamed up the idea of sweeping dirt under the rug, only in the case of contractors the rug is likely to be your front lawn.*

Not long after we moved into a new house a few years ago, we discovered, after a trip home from the nursery with a load of shrubs and trees, that the 4-

inch-thick sod that made our yard look so smooth and green covered what seemed like a truckload of broken cement blocks, pipe, odd lengths of wood, cement reinforcing rod, and yards of barbed wire, all of which we had to dig up, pull out, cut, and break into bits before we could dig a hole big enough to plant anything.

The bulldozer had graded it nice and level, but nobody bothered to pick up all the junk that had accumulated over the more than three months it had taken to construct the house.

To avoid having to transplant a cement block, scrap lumber, and a garden laced with barbed wire before you can plant your rose bushes and evergreens, let the contractor know you're on to the quick and easy trick of sweeping the debris under the sod and ask him not to let it happen—something he'll assure you his people would never do. With luck, maybe they won't.

Article 14: Contractor's Liability Insurance

Most contractors of any size carry insurance as a matter of course. However, if you're working with a small contractor who may not be well financed, you should obtain confirmation of coverage from his insurance company.

Article 15: Owner's Liability Insurance

As this article states, contingent liability coverage is at your option. We suggest you discuss it with your insurance agent. The agent might also be the best person to obtain verification of coverage from your contractor's insurance company: insurance agents know what to look for to make sure you're protected.

Article 16: Fire Insurance with Extended Coverage

You'll want to obtain, or increase, fire insurance anyway, so you might as well take care of it as early as you can—while construction is going on.

Article 17: Owner's Right to Terminate the Agreement

We hope that you never have to terminate an agreement. If you must, you're in for a hassle. It would probably be a good idea to talk to an attorney before going very far under the provisions of this article.

Article 18: Contractor's Right to Terminate the Agreement

The contractor would probably rather sell his pet pickup truck than leave a job, and he'll do almost anything he can to work out a problem. But he cannot work without money. If you and your contractor have a dispute to settle but would like to maintain progress with the job, consider making payment using

our Receipt for Conditional Payment (Form 26.3, page F187) as discussed in Chapter 26.

Article 19: Assignment of Rights

This article is designed to protect you against waking up some morning to find that your job is being done by XYZ Contractors when you signed an agreement with ABC Construction Company. Under the provisions of this article the contractor you sign with is prohibited from assigning the agreement, and with it your job, to anyone else. He is also prohibited from pledging your payments to a bank or any other lender, creditor, person, company, etc.

You are also prohibited from assigning the agreement, so the contractor doesn't find that, instead of satisfying you, he has to start all over again with someone who may have leased or purchased your property—and who has very different ideas about what he or she wants.

OPTIONAL PROVISIONS: *The following paragraphs present a series of optional articles that allow the parties to decide whether to resolve disputes through arbitration or by taking the disagreement to court.*

In its original form, the contract does NOT provide for arbitration, and its last two articles, Access and Inspection and Attorney Fees (Articles 20 and 21), make no reference to arbitration.

Optional articles for arbitration of owner–contractor disputes are provided on page F153 under the heading Alternate Articles. These articles are titled Access and Inspection, Arbitration, and Attorney Fees and are numbered 20, 21, and 22. To provide for arbitration of disputes related to the contract, substitute these three alternate articles for the two original, final articles of the contract.

Article 20: Access and Inspection

Here's your chance, if you suspect you're not getting what you're paying for, to have an architect or another contractor examine the work and render an opinion. This proviso also allows you to name a representative to keep an eye on the job and take necessary action if you have to be away.

The first optional Article 20 (in Form 22.1) does not contain a provision for arbitration in the event of a disagreement between the contractor and anyone ordering the removal of materials or the taking down "of any portions of the work failing to meet drawings, specifications, laws, regulations or building codes."

The dispute here will probably be over whether the work actually does, or does not, meet specifications, building codes, etc. Although the article doesn't say so, the best way to settle an argument about codes is to get a building inspector to examine the work.

The best way to resolve whether the work meets specifications is for a contractor or architect, as noted earlier, to examine the work and render a *written* opinion—a form of voluntary conciliation (if it works!).

The second optional article on Access and Inspection (see Form 22.2 on page F153) **does** provide for arbitration, but in using it—and its related alternate articles—you will be giving up your right to go to court, a tactical advantage that might be one of the contractor's strongest motivations to settle a dispute—settling in order to avoid the disclosure that a public trial would bring.

Note, however, that in the event a dispute is settled through arbitration, Alternate Article 22, Attorney Fees, provides for the defendant's payment of the plaintiff's attorney fees in the event that a court order must be, and is, obtained to enforce the arbitrator's decision.

Article 21: Attorney Fees/Arbitration

Article 21 in Form 22.1, clarifying payment of attorney's fees, will appear unless you elect to use the optional Article 21, Arbitration (see Form 22.2).

Use of the attorney's fees article provides a homeowner of only modest financial resources with a convincing means of using the threat of legal action to enforce compliance with the agreement (thus, perhaps, actually *avoiding* a need to go to court) since the "loser," presumably the contractor if you know that you are right on a particular issue, will end up having to pay court costs plus your attorney's fees.

Although "loser pays court costs and attorney's fees" is a practice followed in many states, there are others in which an order for payment of attorney's fees of the victor is not routinely issued by the court. Thus, the article on attorney's fees establishes that the "winner's" attorney's fees shall be paid by the "loser."

The key words in this article are "and is." If no judgment is obtained against the defendant to enforce the agreement, then your attorney's fees will not be paid by the defendant. So, in spite of this article, don't threaten legal action unless all else fails and you're very sure you can prove to the court that you are right.

The optional Article 21, relating to arbitration, appears only within the **Alternate Articles** (Form 22.2, page F153). Rather than deal with the potential advantages and disadvantages of arbitration here, we

suggest you check Section V, Arbitration, before deciding whether to make it a part of any homeowner-contractor agreement you sign.

NOTE TO READER: *Should you still wish to use the above-described optional articles (Articles 21, 22 & 23 —Alternate Articles, Form 22.2) after carefully reviewing Section V, simply photocopy the complete agreement and the optional articles and adhere the photocopied alternate articles to the photocopied agreement form—replacing the "old" articles with the optional ones. Photocopy. Your new* **Agreement Between Owner and Contractor** *is now ready for use.*

SHORT-FORM AGREEMENT

You and most any contractor you sign up to do a less-than-major job will probably agree that our **short-form** owner–contractor agreement (thirteen articles instead of the long form's twenty-one) is probably all that you will need. This is possible because the short form doesn't have to make provision for several subcontractors or complicated jobs where thousands of things can go wrong, nor do the projects it's used for involve such large sums of money that people feel they need a Mandarin contract to protect themselves against every possible contingency.

In all, however, **Agreement Between Owner and Contractor—Short Form** (Form 22.3, page F155) is quite practical; it's just a sort of *Reader's Digest* condensation of the long-form agreement. Rather than dragging you again through each provision of this form, paragraph by paragraph, we suggest that you just refer to the long form's explanation of any short-form paragraph about which you have questions.

As in the case of the long-form agreement, we've also provided an alternate set of articles for the short form (**Alternate Articles**, Form 22.4, page F157) that contains an arbitration provision. These alternate articles (14 and 15) may be inserted on Form 22.3, replacing the Attorney Fees provision (Article 14). After assembly, you can photocopy your new **Agreement Between Owner and Contractor—Short Form**. Note, however, that you should carefully review Section V, Arbitration, before deciding on whether to use these alternate articles.

23 Two Forms: Authority to Represent the Owner; Revocation of Authority to Represent the Owner

AUTHORITY TO REPRESENT THE OWNER

Use our forms **Authority to Represent the Owner** (Forms 23.1 and 23.2, pages F159 and F161) to appoint someone to represent you under the provisions of the **Agreement Between Owner and Contractor**. This written authority will permit access to and inspection of the work by anyone you name and will allow that person to issue instructions to the contractor.

In the event that you question the quality of the work, give a copy of this authority to any appropriately licensed individual—architect, contractor, engineer, etc.—whom you would like to have evaluate the work.

Note that there are **two** forms of the **Authority to Represent the Owner**. One form (Form 23.1, page F159) refers to Article 20 of the **long-form** agreement between homeowner and contractor; the other form (Form 23.2, page F161) refers to Paragraph 7 (or Article 7) of the **short form** of this agreement. Be sure to use the right authority.

Whenever you use either of these forms, give one signed copy to your representative and another one to your contractor.

REVOCATION OF AUTHORITY TO REPRESENT THE OWNER

You will need our form **Revocation of Authority to Represent the Owner** (Form 23.3, page F163) if you replace one representative with another or if, for some reason, your original representative doesn't work out.

Until you give a copy of this form to the contractor, he is legally off the hook—and you're legally required to pay—for any additional expenses incurred upon the instructions of your representative.

Three copies of this form have been provided.

24 Agreement Between Contractor and Subcontractor

Our **Agreement Between Contractor and Subcontractor** (Form 24.1, page F165) is similar to **Agreement Between Homeowner and Contractor—Short Form** (Form 22.3, page F155), with the exception of the following specific contractor/subcontractor provisions:

- *Paragraph 8* provides for subcontractor's receipt of a fair share of any fire insurance claim payments made to the contractor.
- *Paragraph 12* provides for the subcontractor to assume toward the contractor certain responsibilities that the contractor has assumed toward the owner with respect to materials and labor.

- *Paragraph 13* provides that the contractor shall be bound to the subcontractor in the same manner as the contractor is bound to the owner with respect to plans, drawings, and specifications.
- *Paragraph 14* provides protection for the subcontractor in the event of arbitration of any dispute to which the subcontractor may be a party.

If after reading Chapter 27 you decide to take advantage of the possible savings in building your own home, then you'll be signing agreements as contractor with the various carpenters, electricians, excavators, stone masons, etc., who will be your **subcontractors** on the job.

25 Two Forms You Can Easily Use Yourself

JOB ESTIMATE WORK SHEET

The job estimate work sheet we are providing you with is the type that a contractor would use in costing out a fairly major job. It provides for more than you would ever want to face paying for and lists almost all the subcontractors and materials involved in the construction of a house.

If you're planning to build a house yourself, or to act as your own contractor (more on this in Chapter 27), this work sheet should give you a fairly good idea of the amount of work and the potential cost involved.

The **Job Estimate Work Sheet** (Form 25.1, page F167) is an "in-house" form rather than a bid like the previous one; consequently, it isn't given to customers and it isn't signed.

BID AND PROPOSAL

For small jobs, the **Bid and Proposal** (Form 25.2, page F177) is a very convenient form to use, whether you're a homeowner or a contractor. Couple it with the short-form **Waiver of Lien** (Form 26.2) and you're in business.

This is a perfectly okay form for interior painting, fence installation, minor electrical work, etc., done by an individual contractor helped by an employee or two.

If you're a moonlighting carpenter, roofer, painter, etc., who wants to make a professional first impression, this form can help. To allow enough space for the insertion of your printed name, address, and phone number at the top of this form, just white out the GP logo and form number prior to photocopying.

26 Contractor Forms Pertaining to Payment and Completion

GENERAL WAIVER OF LIENS

The enclosed **General Waiver of Liens** (Form 26.1, page F179) is an example of the type of signed, sworn waiver of liens that you should obtain from your contractor before making final payment under the provisions of any owner–contractor agreement. Be sure the lien waiver requirement is a part of any payment schedule included in any agreement. For example:

- One-third upon commencement
- One-third when the work is half completed
- One-third upon satisfactory completion *and presentation of appropriate waiver(s) of lien*

See page 65 for a more specific schedule appropriate for the construction of a house.

If you fail to obtain a signed, sworn waiver from your contractor, you are subject (under the mechanic's lien statutes of most states) to the filing of a lien by any supplier, worker, or subcontractor involved with the job, even though you have a receipt from the prime contractor stating that his bill is "Paid in Full." Avoid the problems and expense of contending with a mechanic's lien by having your contractor provide a signed, sworn **General Waiver of Liens** similar to the one we have provided.

The first blank of the **General Waiver of Liens** should contain a fairly complete description of the job, the best thing here being simply a duplication of the job description from the **Agreement Between Owner and Contractor**. The address should be copied from the same document.

The signatures of all subcontractors and suppliers, along with the dates of signing and signatures of witnesses, should be placed in the appropraite spaces. Any listed items not appropriate to the job should be lined through and initialed by the contractor, as follows:

NAME	DATE	WITNESS
~~Ornamental Ironwork~~ *DHS*		

If this form's list seems unnecessarily long (it's designed to accommodate construction of a house), consider using the shorter **Waiver of Lien** (Form 26.2, page F185) described below.

Under **Certificate to Obtain Payment**, the contractor should fill in the date, plus your name in the blank immediately following "I hereby certify unto." The signature portion should include the name of the contracting company, the contractor's signature, and the title of the person signing, in this manner:

D. G. Shook Contracting Co., Inc.

By *D. G. Shook*

Title   President

The certificate of notary should be completed before you accept the waiver.

WAIVER OF LIEN

Form 26.2—**Waiver of Lien**—is the short version of the **General Waiver of Liens** and may be all you'll need for jobs done by a single contractor, such as a roofer, electrician, painter, or landscape gardner.

This form contains all the I's, Our's, and We's to accommodate its use by small contractors, who are more likely than large ones to be individuals or partnerships. This is a good lien waiver to use if you've hired an individual to do a job for you.

RECEIPT FOR CONDITIONAL PAYMENT

When you want to pay the contractor to keep the job moving while the two of you work to resolve a problem (which the two of you feel you *can* resolve), use the enclosed **Receipt for Conditional Payment** (Form 26.3, page F187).

There is always a chance that you will not be able to settle your differences, but the use of this form at least helps protect you against the contractor later claiming, perhaps in court or before an arbitrator, that by making payment you implied acceptance of the work as it stood.

The receipt's second paragraph fixes a specific date for correction of any work and puts the contractor's commitment in writing.

CONTRACTOR'S AFFIDAVIT OF COMPLETION

You should receive an affidavit similar to the enclosed Contractor's Affidavit of Completion (Form 26.4, page F189) when your contractor presents his final bill for payment. In this form he makes the following commitments:

1. He has completed the work according to the plans and specifications set forth in the agreement between owner and contractor.
2. He agrees to promptly pay in full all workers and suppliers and to obtain releases of lien from each. (This paragraph takes into account the fact that the contractor may need to receive final payment from you in order to have funds with which to make final payment to suppliers and workers.)
3. He agrees to hold the owner harmless from any loss or damage in the event of the contractor's failure to pay all creditors and obtain lien releases.
4. He has neither pledged nor assigned the agreement nor any funds due or to become due under the agreement.
5. He has supervised the work and has the right to sign the Affidavit of Completion.

NOTE: *On new construction in some jurisdictions you may need to take a copy of the Contractor's Affidavit of Completion to the city hall or county courthouse and request that a building inspector visit the site and issue a Certificate of Occupancy. This certificate will usually be placed close to the electrical junction box and may be needed to obtain, or maintain, fire insurance.*

27 Why Not Be Your Own Contractor?

With the average newly constructed house costing close to $92,000 during mid-1984,* and with home mortgage interest rates in most areas of the United States close to 14 percent during the same period, it's worthwhile to consider every possible way of reducing the expense of building the house you would like to own.

If you're willing to take on the part-time job of acting as your own contractor (signing up and scheduling the subcontractors who will do the actual building), you can achieve long-term savings of more than half the cost of building the house and may even eliminate the need to make any down payment at all. But count on this phase of the job taking you six to eight months.

By following through on this chapter's proposals and making use of this section's homeowner–contractor forms and agreements, you won't necessarily be breaking untrodden ground; you'll simply be joining the ranks of other homeowners who today build more than 20 percent of all United States single-family dwellings by acting as their own contractor.

By acting as your own contractor, you can expect to save close to $50,000 in the long run, including mortgage interest savings, on a $75,000 house. These savings result (1) from eliminating contractor office expense and profit, (2) from builder discounts you'll be able to obtain on construction materials, carpeting, heating and air-conditioning equipment, and appliances, and (3) from reduced mortgage interest because of a smaller mortgage loan than would otherwise be possible.

OK, so you're willing to think about playing contractor for half a year. What does a contractor do? In one sense, he doesn't do anything; on the other hand, it's the contractor who makes everything happen.

This isn't the place to tell you how to function as a contractor; there are other books and even short-term schools for that, which we'll tell you about later. Generally, though, a home-building contractor is a middleman. Unless he is a large developer, he usually doesn't own any construction equipment nor have a large payroll.

One thing, perhaps the most important thing, that a contractor does is to line up and coordinate the efforts of the "baker's dozen" or so of subcontractors who actually prepare the lot and construct the house.

The subcontractors usually employed by the home contractor do the following:

- Clearing and excavating
- Foundation and/or slab construction
- Framing
- Roofing
- Masonry—brick and stone work
- Plumbing
- Electrical work
- Mechanical work—heating, air-conditioning, and duct work
- Insulation
- Siding
- Dry wall installation
- Tile work
- Painting
- Flooring
- Landscaping

Actually, the same subcontractor might fulfill several functions. A masonry contractor might install the footings, foundation, and slab and later might come back to lay brick, put up stone walls, or construct a fireplace and chimney. Depending on local union rules, the same electrical contractor who does the wiring might return to install electrical heating and air conditioning—but may put out the sheet-metal duct work to a sub-subcontractor who does only that.

Your biggest job as your own contactor will be to contract with and schedule the subcontractors who wil be putting up your house. You will need:

1. To locate subcontractors (through the phone book, your mortgage lender, trade associations, local unions, construction materials suppliers, etc.).
2. To obtain bids based upon blueprints and specifications.
3. To select each "sub" based upon the amount of his bid, reputation, and availability for your job.
4. To negotiate and sign agreements with each.
5. To coordinate the arrival and departure from the site of the "subs" involved. This is extremely important. Dry wall cannot go up to close in walls until the electrical wiring and plumbing are installed and inspected; finish carpentry, flooring, and painting cannot be done until the dry wall is up.
6. To frequently check the work to make sure it's being done according to specifications and to

---

*Each Monday *The Wall Street Journal*, in a box headed "*Buying & Selling*," publishes the national average conventional mortgage interest rate on new homes and the average price of new homes for the previous seven days.

assure that the materials you selected are being used.

The most time-consuming part of acting as your own contractor will be devoted to the tasks just described. But perhaps the most personally demanding part of the job will be acting as peacemaker and smoother-over of ruffled feathers and bruised egos when subcontractors clash over whose fault something may be or over who has priority access to some part of the house to get a portion of the work done.

Being your own contractor is not the easiest job in the world. It takes an almost day-to-day knowledge of what's going on, and it requires someone who can get along with, and not be walked all over by, some pretty adept walkers-over.

The biggest cost of building/buying a house is *not* the expense of construction: it's the *interest* you pay the mortgage holder. But we'll look at the cost of interest last, since it's a factor related to your mortgage amount and the total expense of construction.

SAVINGS ON MATERIALS

On the average, construction materials cost makes up about 35 percent of the total outlay of building a house. Staying with our $75,000 example, construction could be expected to cost about $26,250. The customary 10 percent builder's discount on materials would result in a $2,650 saving.

You should have no trouble obtaining the builder's discount when acting as your own contractor—sellers don't want to lose that $25,000 worth of business. If you did, though, it would be a simple matter to go down to city hall or the county courthouse and take out a business permit as a builder, or to incorporate as a builder.

Builder's discounts on appliances, heating and air-conditioning equipment, and carpeting range from 30 to 40 percent, but we have not factored in this potential saving, just to keep our estimate conservative.

SAVINGS ON CONTRACTOR PROFIT

The savings that you'll make on contractor profit are a substantial part of your total reduction in building costs. On a national basis, contractor profits on single-family, new home construction average about 8 percent. Thus, on our $75,000 sample house that saving would total about $6,000.

We have not estimated any saving at all due to the elimination of contractor administrative and office expenses since these are costs that, to some extent at least, you will be saddled with also.

SAVINGS ON LABOR

Depending on how well qualified you are to perform certain jobs and how much time you have available, savings on labor can be your biggest variable.

Let us assume one day's labor per week during a typical 7-month construction period (28 days × 8 hours = 224 hours). With this schedule you'll be performing about 20 percent of the total labor required to build your house. Local building codes may require that electrical work and plumbing be done by a licensed professional; however, many codes merely require that such work be "supervised" by a licensed professional. In any event, there is still plenty of relatively unskilled "rough" work you can do.

Aside from saving money on whatever labor you perform, one of the biggest advantages of being on the job as a worker is that you know what is going on. People will not be so inclined to "goof off" or do less than adequate work when you are often right there. Workers will get to know you as a person (just as you'll get to know them). There is less tendency to cheat a "person" than there is to cheat someone who is merely an "owner." And perhaps most important, you'll have the satisfaction of having contributed part of the labor toward the building of your own house.

CLICK! *Try to keep a camera handy while construction is in progress. Photograph the site before excavation begins, and photograph key steps in the construction progress, zeroing in on crucial areas that are important to the building's structural soundness. Then if something sags, cracks, or collapses later, you have a chance of being able to prove whether the work was, or wasn't, done properly. Photograph wiring and plumbing before the walls are closed in so that you'll know where lines have been routed.*

That you're taking pictures every step of the way will not be lost on the subcontractors, and they might not be so inclined to cut corners if they know you have photos of what is usually out of sight and never seen by the owner.

Taking into account the National Association of Homebuilders estimate of construction labor costs as being about 15 percent of total construction expense, the saving you would achieve by performing 20 percent of the necessary labor on a $75,000 house would be 20 percent of an $11,250 labor cost—or about $2,250.

SAVINGS BEFORE INTEREST

Thus far, by acting as your own contractor on the building of a $75,000 house, your savings would add up roughly as follows:

Savings on materials:	$2,650.00
Savings on contractor profit:	6,000.00
Savings on labor:	2,250.00
Total pre-interest savings:	$10,900.00

SAVINGS ON INTEREST

On a $75,000 contractor-built house financed with a $60,000 first trust (mortgage) at 14 percent annual interest over the 30-year period common during 1984, you would pay a total of $195,934 interest:

Total paid over 30-year mortgage:	$255,934
Amount financed:	60,000
Total interest:	$195,934

On the same **owner**-built house, costing only $65,000 (but still *valued* at $75,000), with a $50,000, 14 percent, 30-year mortgage, you'd pay $163,278 interest:

Total paid over 30-year mortgage:	$213,278
Amount financed:	50,000
Total interest:	$163,278

Thus, the 30-year savings in interest made possible by the $10,900 reduced construction cost achieved by acting as your own contractor would be $32,656:

Interest on 30-year, $60,000 mortgage:	$195,934
Interest on 30-year, $50,000 mortgage:	$163,278
Savings on interest:	$32,656

Total long-term savings, on both interest and construction expense, would be more than half the cost of building the house:

Savings on construction:	$10,900
Savings on interest:	32,656
Total owner–contractor savings:	$43,556

SWEAT EQUITY

Bankers use the term "sweat equity" to refer to the estimated dollar value of an owner-contractor's contributions in labor, materials, or other savings toward the total worth of a newly constructed house.

In the $75,000 house example, the owner–builder's sweat equity is approximately $10,000, an amount equal to the total saving achieved through owner labor, reduced material costs, and the elimination of contractor profit.

Since these savings are obtained without reducing the **value** of the house, mortgage lenders are willing to give an owner–builder full credit for sweat equity toward meeting requirements for the down payment. The owner–contractor has two options:

1. Combine sweat equity with an amount of cash equal to the normal 20 percent down payment, reducing the amount of the mortgage to obtain a substantial saving in interest (as was demonstrated above).
2. Reduce the amount of cash needed to meet down-payment requirements by combining sweat equity with sufficient cash to fulfill normal down-payment requisites. Some mortgage lenders will allow an owner-contractor to combine sweat equity with private mortgage insurance (see Section XI, page

326) so no cash at all need be paid to the lender to meet down-payment requirements.

Even though full credit is given by lenders for an owner-contractor's sweat equity, the owner must still meet the usual good credit requirements and have an income that provides a satisfactory ratio of monthly income to monthly mortgage payments.

WORKING WITH AN ARCHITECT

Soon after you have arranged your financing but well before you purchase a building site or start lining up subcontractors, you should talk to several architects. Select the one who designs the type of house you want to build and with whom you seem to have the best rapport.

Since you'll otherwise be going it alone by acting as your own contractor, you need someone who not only can design your house, but who can also hold your hand throughout the entire construction period, guiding your choice of building site, materials, and design, and even helping you select, schedule, and monitor some of your subcontractors.

The architect need not necessarily draw up costly, individual plans for your house. You might find that you would be happy using plans for a house he has previously designed or "off-the-shelf" plans he has readily available. Ask the architect about plans for prefab houses that meet local building codes or can be made inexpensively to meet local codes. These homes have the advantage of going up more quickly and thus requiring less of your time as a contractor.

A NOTE ABOUT INTERIOR DECORATORS: *Some interior decorators are more aware of home-owners' needs than some architects. They will be more likely than architects to suggest, for example, that kitchen sinks and counters and bathroom basins be raised three inches or so above the usual height to "save backs" or to suggest that the electrical outlets and switches be placed in practical and individualized locations, etc. As one of this book's legal consultants put it, "Architects deal with appearance; a good decorator deals with practicality."*

HELPFUL SOURCES OF INFORMATION ON BEING AN OWNER-CONTRACTOR

Several books and pamphlets have been published to help people build their own house. Your local library will probably have some in its stacks. We recommend the following:

- *Enjoy and Build It Yourself!* by George Hicks. $12.95 from Acropolis Books, 2400 Seventeenth Street, N.W., Washington, D.C. 20009

- *Designs for Low Cost Homes* by the U.S. Forest Service. $1.75 paperback from Consumer Information Center, Dept. 155-J, Pueblo, Colorado 81009
- *Guide to Manufactured Homes* by the Home Manufacturers Council. $6.25 from Home Manufacturers Council, Fifteenth and M Streets, N.W., Washington, D.C. 20005.
- *From the Ground Up: The Shelter Institute Guide to Building Your Own House* by John Cole and Charles Wing. $9.95 paperback from Little, Brown & Co., 34 Beacon Street, Boston, Massachusetts 02106.

There are also several schools where prospective owner–contractors can learn the skills and techniques needed to perform and supervise nearly every task associated with building a house. For more information, write or phone the nearest school:

Chino Housing Improvement Program
539 Flume Street
Chino, CA   95926
916-342-0012

Colorado OBC
P.O. Box 12061
Boulder, CO   80302
303-449-6126

Denver OBC
5835 West Sixth Avenue
Unit 4D
Lakewood, CO   80214
303-232-8571

Durango OBC
P.O. Box 3447
Durango, CO   81301
303-247-2417

Hanford Adult School
120 East Grangeville Boulevard
Hanford, CA   93231
209-582-4401

Michigan OBC
1505 East Eleven Mile Road
Royal Oak, MI   48067
303-545-7033

Minnesota OBC
2615 South Sixth Street
Minneapolis, MN   55454
612-339-5104

Northwest OBC
1139 34th Avenue
Seattle, WA   98122
206-324-9559

Shelter Institute
P.O. Box 811
Bath, ME   04530
207-442-7938

For information about possible new schools in your area, and for a free copy of *Owner-Builder* magazine, phone or write:

Owner-Builder Center
1516 Fifth Street
Berkeley, CA   94710
1-800-547-5995

ARBITRATION

28 Avoiding the Arbitration Trap

When you mention arbitration, most people will not be familiar with what you're talking about. They'll have heard the word often enough, usually in connection with a labor dispute that someone is trying to "arbitrate" so that workers won't go out on strike, but they'll probably still not know really what you're talking about.

In fact, most of us probably still believe that arbitration is a word representing something that *never* touches us directly—like "treaty"; after all, ordinary people don't sign treaties. Yet ordinary people **do** go into arbitration, and by going into arbitration instead of into court, most of us could save time, money, and aggravation—by handling our own do-it-yourself arbitration arrangements.

Remember that unlike mediation and conciliation, which are attempts to bring parties together in a voluntary agreement, arbitration requires that the disputing parties make a prior agreement to accept the decision of the arbitrator (or arbitrators), who, after hearing both sides of the case, will render a decision that is **binding**.

If you think the idea of binding arbitration is scary, just compare it to the alternative—the expense, the time, and the inconvenience of going to court, plus the weight and far-reaching effect of a legal judgment—and the idea of going into arbitration doesn't seem so bad after all.

For arbitration to work, there has to be a certain amount of good will: a readiness to be fair and a desire neither to be vindictive nor to take the other party for all the traffic will bear, but merely to seek an equitable solution to a problem whose resolution has somehow slipped beyond the reach of the people involved.

Given good will, arbitration can often be your quickest and cheapest way to a fair resolution whenever you get into a serious dispute—and in the process can often save a business or personal relationship that could be destroyed by going to court.

That's the good news. The bad news about arbitration is that the colossus of arbitration, the American Arbitration Association (AAA), administers a far-reaching industry-oriented arbitration program that can perhaps best be described as a set of loaded dice frequently handed to consumers on a take-it-or-leave-it basis by growing numbers of corporations.

Unless you're very careful about signing any contract containing an AAA arbitration clause, you could be stepping between steel jaws as quick and final as any bear trap. The bait of the AAA arbitration bear trap is a deceptively simple paragraph (italics ours):

Any controversy or claim arising out of or relating to this contract, or any breach thereof, shall be settled by arbitration in accordance with the rules of the American Arbitration Association, and judgment upon award rendered by the Arbitrator(s) may be entered in any court having jurisdiction thereof.

What this paragraph means, pure and simple, is that once you've become a party to an agreement containing this clause, you're legally subject to and *bound* by the decision of the **AAA** arbitrator.

One thing the AAA's arbitration clause *doesn't* tell you is that the arbitrator who decides your case will almost certainly be an individual who is a member of the industry you're having a problem with. A disagreement with your home builder is likely to be heard by a contractor; your problem with a manufacturer is likely to be settled by an executive from another, similar manufacturer; and your dispute with an insurance company is likely to be decided by an insurance company executive—all of them members of the AAA's panel of arbitrators.

Given the utmost honesty, the arbitrator who decides your case will still be laboring under the corporate mental set and attitudes of the industry he represents. It's sort of like having your suit for police brutality judged by a policeman or having your claim for medical malpractice settled by a physician.

According to the AAA, its arbitration clause is a part of millions of contracts, and increasing numbers of insurance companies, home-improvement contractors, manufacturers, and other corporations are quietly adding AAA arbitration clauses to agreements you'll be expected to become a party to if you want to buy their products and services.

It should be fairly obvious that corporations insert AAA arbitration clauses in their contracts because AAA arbitration clearly benefits the corporations. Hence, arbitration is a subject you need to know something about.

If you've become a party to an agreement containing an AAA arbitration clause (such as in a Sears Allstate auto insurance policy, for example) and a problem arises that goes into arbitration, each party is given a list of a dozen names or so from which to select an AAA arbitrator, rating his or her choices one, two, three, etc. If either party feels that a particular person is unacceptable, he or she draws a line through that name. The AAA then attempts to assign an arbitrator who is acceptable to both parties.

The list of arbitrators offered by the AAA briefly outlines the background and current employment of each. However, the data you're given on each potential arbitrator contains no information at all about his or her previous decisions or the amounts of any awards—nor will the AAA make any of that information available to you.

On the other hand, it's not very difficult for an executive of the company with whom you're having a problem to make a few phone calls (possibly to friends within a potential arbitrator's own company or to those who've been subject to his or her previous decisions) to learn which possible arbitrator is likely to decide in his company's favor.

Today's corporate arbitration "defendant" might be the company that supplies tomorrow's arbitrator; the executive who hears your case might find himself on the other side of the fence one day—a fact that we doubt many industry arbitrators are completely able to forget.

As an individual, your access to the corporate network is probably limited. Therefore, by agreeing to the AAA's form of arbitration, you relinquish access to precisely the kind of useful information normally available to your lawyer in attempting to place your case before a possibly friendly judge. And, of course, you're completely giving up your right to a public trial and to have your case heard before a jury.

Here's what the AAA's *Business Man's Guide to Arbitration* has to say about its arbitrators (italics ours):

> To serve the *business community* with arbitrators representing all fields of specialization, the American Arbitration Association now maintains a National Panel of Arbitrators numbering some 37,000 men and women in 1,600 communities of the United States. Usually *nominated by leading figures in their industries, trades and professions*, arbitrators are added to the panel after careful checking of qualifications and reputations.

The elimination of a possibly embarrassing public trial is another strong inducement for corporations to include an arbitration clause in contracts with consumers. According to AAA president Robert Coulson, "The general privacy of arbitration proceedings is an asset in preventing a company's credit standing and reputation from being endangered . . . arbitration is generally without appeal and secret, meaning that nobody's troubles are exposed in public."

One of the AAA's own publications, *Arbitration for Buyers and Sellers*, points out that "the preference for arbitration might be particularly strong where one or both parties might be harmed by public knowledge of failure or inability to perform contractual obligations."

Another AAA publication, *The Lawyer and Arbitration*, reminds business lawyers that, apart from convenience, the next reason (for inserting an arbitration clause in contracts) is the privacy of arbitration: "The good name of a company and the reputation of its product are often its most valuable assets, representing heavy outlays for advertising. These may be lost, if as a result of public trial, the firm's credit

standing or business ethics are cast in doubt. Differences are resolved through arbitration with less danger that the parties may be hurt by publicity."

It doesn't take a genius to figure out that by surrendering the right to have your dispute settled before a judge and jury in public trial you are giving away a strong inducement, perhaps the **strongest** inducement, for a corporation to offer you a settlement **out** of court: avoidance of public disclosure that could lose customers—and that might encourage others to file additional lawsuits against it.

The Roman emperor Vegetius reputedly said, "Let him who desires peace prepare for war"—particularly good advice when you're dealing with a corporate Goliath.

The AAA presents its form of arbitration as a time-saving, money-saving way of settling disputes that might otherwise result in a protracted trial, risky disclosure, and costly legal fees.

It is true that your dispute might be heard and decided upon by an AAA arbitrator more quickly than by a judge and jury, and possibly for lower legal fees, but to what end is it if you suffer a significant monetary loss compared to what you may have obtained in open trial?

Another disadvantage that you face by signing a contract with an AAA arbitration clause is the fact that the arbitrators are quite reluctant to award punitive damages. We've been told of one case in which a bad roofing job resulted in a leak that caused (while the homeowner begged and pleaded with the builder to correct the fault) serious water damage to a fine rug and damaged hi-fi equipment when plaster fell on it due to the leak. The family was also forced to stay home from work in order to empty buckets of water and mop up, all because the contractor refused to correct his faulty workmanship.

The arbitrator did make an award—an order for the contractor to fix the leak. But there was no compensation for harm done to the carpet and hi-fi, and nothing in the way of punitive damages to compensate the homeowner for distress, anxiety, loss of sleep, etc.

Although AAA arbitration may be concluded in less time than a public trial, there's no assurance that lessened arbitration time (perhaps at the risk of a greatly reduced financial settlement) would eliminate or even reduce legal costs.

There is little to suggest that you would be less than foolhardy to enter into AAA arbitration without an attorney. If anything, you'll probably have greater need for legal counsel during AAA arbitration than you would in a courtroom where the judge, legal precedent, rules of evidence, the swearing of witnesses, and a public trial give you a measure of protection.

Although the AAA's commercial arbitration rules are too long to quote here in their entirety, there are a few you should know about (italics ours):

Section 12. APPOINTMENT FROM PANEL—If the parties have not appointed an Arbitrator and have not provided for any other method of appointment, the Arbitrator shall be appointed in the following manner: Immediately after the filing of the Demand or Submission, the AAA shall submit simultaneously to each party to the dispute an identical list of names of persons chosen from the Panel. Each party to the dispute shall have *seven days from the mailing date* in which to cross off any names to which he objects, number the remaining names indicating the order of his preference, and return the list to the AAA. If a party does not return the list within the time specified, all persons named therein shall be deemed acceptable. From among the persons who have been approved on both lists, and in accordance with the designated order of mutual preference, the AAA shall invite the acceptance of an Arbitrator to serve. If the parties fail to agree upon any of the persons named, or if acceptable Arbitrators are unable to act, or if for any other reason the appointment cannot be made from submitted lists, the AAA shall have the power to make the appointment from other members of the Panel without the submission of any additional lists.

Section 16. NUMBER OF ARBITRATORS—If the arbitration agreement does not specify the number of Arbitrators, the dispute *shall be heard and determined by one Arbitrator*, unless the AAA, in *its* discretion, directs that a greater number of Arbitrators be appointed.

Section 24. ATTENDANCE AT HEARINGS—The Arbitrator *shall maintain the privacy of the hearings* unless the law provides to the contrary. Any person having a direct interest in the arbitration is entitled to attend hearings. The Arbitrator shall otherwise have the power to require the exclusion of any witness, other than a party or other essential person, during the testimony of any other witness. *It shall be discretionary with the Arbitrator to determine the propriety of the attendance of any other person.*

Section 26. OATHS—Before proceeding with the first hearing or with the examination of the file, each Arbitrator *may* take an oath of office, and if required by law, shall do so. The Arbitrator *may, in his discretion,* require witnesses to testify under oath administered by any duly qualified person or, if required by law or demanded by either party, shall do so.

Section 37. WAIVER OF RULES—Any party who proceeds with the arbitration after knowledge that any provision or requirement of these Rules has not been complied with *and who fails to state his objection thereto in writing, shall be deemed to have waived his right to object.*

Section 42. SCOPE OF AWARD*—The Arbitrator may grant any remedy or relief which he deems just and equitable and within the scope of the agreement of the parties, including, but not limited to, *specific performance of a contract*. The Arbitrator, in his award, shall assess arbitration fees and expenses in favor of any party and, in the event any administrative fees or expenses are due the AAA, in favor of the AAA.

Section 47. ADMINISTRATIVE FEES†—As a nonprofit organization, the AAA shall prescribe an administrative fee schedule and a refund schedule to compensate it for the cost of providing administrative services. The schedule in effect at the time of filing or the time of refund shall be applicable.

Section 51. DEPOSITS—The AAA may require the parties to deposit in advance such sums of money as it deems necessary to defray the expense of the arbitration, including the Arbitrator's fee, if any, and shall render an accounting to the parties and return any unexpended balance.

The courts have not yet fully determined whether your acceptance of an AAA arbitration clause in a contract can be forced upon you as a condition of doing business with a particular company. However, a number of courts *have* set aside the arbitration clause in a number of contracts, finding them to be "adhesion contracts"—contracts presented as a standard form on a take-it-or-leave-it basis—and have further questioned whether those contracts were, in fact, voluntary and uncoerced agreements.

Beyond questioning the equality of bargaining power in such agreements, the courts have also questioned them on the basis of [depriving the consumer of] due process [of law], a serious Constitutional question.

The question of take-it-or-leave-it arbitration clauses may soon be resolved, but in the meantime if you're ever handed a contract to sign containing an AAA arbitration clause, you might refuse to sign the agreement until (1) the other party has supplied you with a copy of the AAA's arbitration rules that the other party **guarantees in writing** are the arbitration rules that apply to **that particular** contract and (2) you have had an opportunity to consult an attorney.

Since the other party has included the AAA's arbitration clause in its contract because it clearly believes such a clause to be to its advantage, you or your attorney might wish to propose:

- That instead of using one AAA arbitrator, *a panel of three arbitrators* (not necessarily from the AAA) be utilized: one arbitrator named by each party to the dispute, with a third arbitrator to be selected jointly by the other two. A decision by *any two of the three* arbitrators would be binding.
- That the hearings be open to any person or persons acceptable to *either* party.

---

*"But the fact that the relief was such that it could not or would not be granted by a court of law or equity *is not ground for vacating or refusing to confirm the [Arbitrator's] award.*" (Uniform Arbitration Act, Sec. 2, Par 5.)

†The administrative fee of the AAA is based upon the amount of each claim and counterclaim as disclosed when the claim and counterclaim are filed, and is due and payable at the time of filing.

Amount of Claim	Fee
Up to $10,000	3% (minimum $100)
$10,000 to $25,000	$300, plus 2% of excess over $10,000
$25,000 to $100,000	$600, plus 1% of excess over $25,000
$100,000 to $200,000	$1,350, plus ½% of excess over $100,000
$200,000 to $5,000,000	$1,850, plus ¼% of excess over $200,000

Where the claim or counterclaim exceeds $5 million, an appropriate fee will be determined by the AAA.

- That it be agreed that all witnesses be sworn and subject to the same penalties for perjury as would witnesses testifying before a court of law.
- That no award be made by the arbitrators that could not be made by the court of jurisdiction.
- That the cost of a transcript shall be borne equally by both parties to the dispute.

The corporation will probably complain that you are being difficult (which you are) and unreasonable (which you are not), but you are simply standing up for your rights. If the company objects to what you propose, it can always strike the entire arbitration clause from the contract.

And, of course, you can take your business elsewhere. Top consumer-rated State Farm Mutual, for example, follows the arbitrator selection method described here and sees no need to force the AAA's arbitration rules upon its customers.

Perhaps one of the most important advantages of handling your own arbitration is that you avoid the AAA's stacked deck of corporate-thinking arbitrators. With the freedom to select their own arbitrators, both parties can draw upon a wide range of friends, priests, clergymen, neighbors, fellow farmers or miners or mechanics—or lawyers—or experts from any profession or field of endeavor. That, perhaps, is one of the strengths of handling one's own arbitration: the reliance of each of us upon our own good sense, and our trust, if we're not always in agreement, in the honesty and good will of those around us.

We still question the worth and risk of arbitration in disputes between parties of greatly unequal strength and resources, between an individual and a General Motors, for example, or between a small business and a large corporation. But in other disputes, such as between an individual and a small, local business or between two individuals, arbitration is worth considering.

Since arbitration is sort of an "extrajudicial" judicial proceeding that can carry all the weight of a court decision, arbitration is, in itself, increasingly subject to law.

The following is a typical state statute that defines the powers and limits of arbitration (italics ours):

Submission of controversy; agreement to arbitrate.

Persons desiring to end any controversy, whether there be a suit pending therefore or not, may submit the same to arbitration, and agree that such submission may be entered of record in any court. Upon proof of such agreement out of court, or by consent of the parties given in court in person or by counsel, it shall be entered in the proceedings of such court; and thereupon a rule shall be made, that the parties shall submit to the award which shall be made in pursuance of such agreement.

Notwithstanding any other provisions of law, the parties may enter into a written agreement to arbitrate which will be as binding as any other agreement. If, after entry into such agreement, either party refuses to cooperate in the appointment of an arbitrator or arbitrators, then after ten days' notice *on the motion of either party*, the court which has jurisdiction of the claim shall act for the party so refusing or failing to agree to the appointment, then the arbitration shall proceed and be as binding as if both parties had cooperated throughout the proceedings. Neither party shall have the right to revoke an agreement to arbitrate except on a ground which would be good for revoking or annulling other agreements.

Submission irrevocable; power of court over it.

No such submission, entered or agreed to be entered of record in any court, shall be revocable by any party to such submission, without the leave of such court; and such court may, from time to time, enlarge the term within which an award is required to be made.

How award entered as judgment of court.

Upon the return of any such award, made under such an agreement, whether any previous record of the submission, or a rule thereupon, has been made or not, it shall be entered up as the judgment of the court, unless good cause be shown against it at the first term after the parties have been summoned to show cause against it.

For what award may be set aside.

No such award shall be set aside, except for errors apparent on its face, unless it appears to have been procured by corruption or other undue means, or that there was partiality or misbehavior by the arbitrators or umpires, or any of them. But this section shall not be construed to take away *the power of courts of equity* over awards.

Now, there are three interesting precedents you should know about:

1. The courts have determined (as you would expect) that an arbitration award procured by fraud may be set aside.
2. An arbitration award may be set aside if the arbitrator(s) admit improper evidence *even though the arbitrator(s) state that the award was determined before such evidence was received.*
3. An award may be set aside where it is shown that the arbitrator(s) refused to hear competent witnesses offered by either party.

These precedents should be kept in mind in view of the AAA's suggestion, in its publication *Nine Ways to Cut Arbitration Costs*, that a record of arbitration hearings *not* be made (italics ours):

> Don't order a transcript unless you really need it. Court reporting is expensive. Transcripts delay the award. The arbitrator can't start writing his opinion until he gets the record. Furthermore, arbitrators feel obliged to read every word. That means study time at the per diem rate. In some cases, transcripts are worth what they cost. But most of the time they serve only to double the total expenses of arbitration.

We must point out that one of the best means at your disposal of proving fraud at the hearings, of proving that improper evidence was admitted, or of proving refusal by the arbitrator(s) to hear competent witnesses is through **recourse to the record.** Remember what we said about appeals courts in Chapter 7, "No witnesses are heard and the judges' decision is based upon the **transcript of the trial.**" Without a transcript (of which more later), quite a few of your means to appeal the arbitrator's decision go right out the window.

The courts have also determined that *when* an arbitrator or arbitrators set down legal principles upon which an award is decided, the award may be set aside if the court determines that the arbitrator(s) appear to have acted "under a mistake." However, following the AAA's advice might eliminate this basis for asking the court to review the award of the arbitrator(s) (italics ours):

> Sometimes parties don't really need long opinions. Parties can ask the AAA to request the arbitrator to simplify or eliminate his opinion. In a few cases, it may be appropriate for the arbitrator to handwrite his award and a brief opinion at the close of the hearing, delivering it to the parties at once. *If you don't need an opinion as a guideline for the future, consider the possibility of eliminating it. The arbitrator's bill will be substantially smaller. The dispute may be resolved sooner.*

The arbitrator's written opinion, stating his or her basis in law for making the award, may be your only lifesaver if you feel you have been wronged by the proceedings.

NOTE: *One very simple way of cutting the cost of making a record of the hearings (and we would think obvious to the AAA) is for both parties to agree that a cassette recording of the hearings be made, but not transcribed, unless either party disputes the validity of the award on the basis of a claim that would be supported by the transcript. Recordings may be held in custody of the arbitrator(s) at the end of each day's hearings or may be held by the clerk of the court of jurisdiction until the award is made and accepted by both parties.*

If it becomes necessary to transcribe the recordings, this may be done by a court reporter designated by the arbitrator(s) or by the court. The recordings may also be used by the arbitrator(s) for review of testimony if desired.

Handled in this way, recordings of the hearings should be no more than a few dollars—merely the cost of the cassettes themselves.

---

29 Handling Your Own Arbitration

There needn't be anything particularly complicated about arbitration, especially when compared to other methods of settling difficult disputes. Parents have arbitrated arguments between brothers and sisters for years. Priests, tribal chiefs, and kings have all been arbitrators. In history, a leader's ability as an arbitrator has often been a measure of his greatness.

Today we cannot expect to have a disagreement settled by arbitration without any expense at all, but if both parties can agree to arbitrate, the procedure can serve quite well at a far lower cost, and much more quickly, than if the dispute is taken to court.

If your dispute is a complicated one requiring special knowledge to understand what is involved and if both parties are members of the same profession or trade (such as contractor and subcontractor), a trade or professional association that both belong to is often a good source for a knowledgeable arbitrator. If the dispute is more general, or between individuals or between an individual and a business, consider selecting a lawyer or lawyers to arbitrate your disagreement.

No matter whom you and the other party agree on, the two of you and the arbitrator should discuss what the fee will be. If you select an attorney, he or she will probably charge you an hourly rate, since it's impossible to tell beforehand how much time the hearings, the arbitrator's deliberations, and the writing of the decision will take.

Arbitration, by the way, is one of the few instances in which an attorney can serve conflicting parties. In even the friendliest of uncontested divorces the attorney representing one spouse will almost always refuse, on grounds of ethics, to represent the other.

This section's forms provide for arbitration by one arbitrator and also for arbitration by a three-member panel. Additionally, there are guidelines for hearings conducted by one or by three arbitrators, as well as **Demand for Arbitration** forms for hearings held under either system.

In all, this section includes nine forms—almost everything you'll need for making your own arbitration arrangements:

Hearings Before One Arbitrator

1. Agreement for Submission of an Existing Dispute to Arbitration—One Arbitrator (Form 29.1 on page F191).
2. Demand for Arbitration—One Arbitrator (Form 29.2 on page F193).
3. Guidelines for Arbitration—One Arbitrator (Form 29.3 on page F195).

Hearings Before Three Arbitrators

4. Agreement for Submission of an Existing Dispute to Arbitration—Three Arbitrators (Form 29.4 on page F199).
5. Demand for Arbitration—Three Arbitrators (Form 29.5 on page F201).
6. Guidelines for Arbitration—Three Arbitrators (Form 29.6 on page F203).

Miscellaneous

7. Model arbitration agreements for insertion in a contract: Agreement Using One Arbitrator (Form 29.7 on page F207) and Agreement Using Three Arbitrators (Form 29.8 on page F209).
8. Petition for the Appointment of Arbitrator (Form 29.9 on page F211).

Although the forms for do-it-yourself arbitration are of two types, those for hearings heard by a single arbitrator and those for hearings heard by three arbitrators, they're similar enough so that one explanation can serve for both types of forms. Where there is a difference, we'll point it out.

COMPLETING THIS SECTION'S FORMS

As with other forms in this volume, the original printed form should be removed from the book and photocopied. Make two photocopies of each form you plan to use: one copy as a work form and the second copy to serve as your typed "original."

Many photocopy services have equipment that will easily produce "both sides" copy. If the service, or your office or home machine, is incapable of producing two-sided copies, simply make sufficient one-sided copies of the form, turn over your "master" to copy the form's second side, and then place the one-sided copies in the machine's paper tray to be run through a second time. Voilà, you now have "two-sided" copies of your form.

At the bottom of the appropriate page of each arbitration form you will find the front panel (that's the portion in **Olde English** type) set horizontally. In completing each form's front panel, just fill in the appropriate names after "Agreed to Between" and "and," or beneath "BETWEEN" and "and," or following "TO," etc.

Finally, fold the form in thirds as you would an 8½″ by 11″ business letter. The front panel should then be easily visible.

AGREEMENT FOR SUBMISSION OF AN EXISTING DISPUTE TO ARBITRATION

The first portion of Forms 29.1 and 29.4 requires a brief description of the dispute. Keep this description to the bare bones of the dispute so the parties will have as little as possible to disagree about here. This isn't the place to try to make your case—the time for that will come later.

> **Example:** Elizabeth Smith claims that her auto, repaired by Sunshine Auto Body shop, has decreased in value due to poor workmanship and materials used by Sunshine Auto Body. Sunshine Auto Body claims that Ms. Smith's auto was repaired using good workmanship and materials and that its value has not been depreciated because of the work performed by Sunshine Auto Body.

Selection of Arbitrator(s)

In selecting one arbitrator to hear a case, you'll have to be resourceful in finding someone both parties can agree on. There's a lot to be said for selecting a lawyer. A good lawyer will have the ability to help both parties reduce the dispute to its basic elements, perhaps enabling them to reach agreement on some points along the way. A good lawyer will also be able to ask questions that will elicit relevant information and will know what constitutes evidence and what does not, etc., etc.

In single-arbitrator situations, however, finding an attorney satisfactory to both parties is not always easy. You probably would not accept the other party's regular lawyer as arbitrator, and the other party probably wouldn't accept yours. You might think you could call your local bar association for recommendations, but that can prove very unsatisfactory. We made test calls in several cities and they all turned out disappointingly the same:

> "Hello, I wonder if you could give me the names of a few attorneys who might serve as arbitrator."
>
> "Huh?"
>
> "I said, I wonder if you could give me the names of some attorneys who could serve as an arbitrator; you know, to arbitrate a dispute?"
>
> "Gee, we don't have anything like that. Arbitrator? Do you want a criminal lawyer or a divorce lawyer or something?"
>
> "Maybe you could just give me the names of some attorneys."
>
> "Well, you'd have to tell me what kind of a case it is first. Is it a criminal case or a divorce case or a negligence case maybe—you know, was there an accident?"
>
> "Not really. I just need the names of a few lawyers I could call."
>
> "Well, you'd have to tell me what kind of case it would be first."
>
> "Thank you."
>
> "Oh, you're very welcome."

If you really can't agree on someone to conduct one-arbitrator hearings, probably the simplest and quickest thing to do is use Form 29.9 on page F211 to petition the court to appoint an arbitrator to hear the case (see page 89 for instructions on completing this form). The cost of obtaining a court-appointed arbitrator will be minimal, and the problem will be solved to the satisfaction of any reasonable person.

The method of selection for **three** arbitrators is simplicity itself. You name your arbitrator and the other party names theirs. The two arbitrators get together and name a third arbitrator, satisfactory to themselves, who acts as *umpire*—one who will have somewhat more authority than either of the disputant-named arbitrators. When three arbitrators conduct hearings their award must always be by at least a majority (see **Guidelines for Arbitration**).

Costs

The costs of three-arbitrator hearings obviously will be greater than for one-arbitrator hearings and normally will be reserved for arbitration of a major dispute, perhaps with a corporation, in which you would want to name as "your" arbitrator an attorney with extensive experience in the area of the dispute.

While no paragraph can provide for *all* contingencies, the **Costs** provision in our form is relatively inclusive and should not give rise to any difficulties.

Procedure

Again, no paragraph can cover all contingencies, but there is little room for rational disagreement here. The location of the hearings in the county and state of the appropriate court of jurisdiction may be an inconvenience to one or both parties. If it's an inconvenience to *both* parties, they might agree that hearings be held elsewhere, or possibly alternating between a location convenient to one party and then convenient to the other. (*Warning:* This would involve additional time and travel costs for the arbitrator(s), thus increasing the expense of arbitration.)

Award

There is little room for reasonable objection as concerns the **Award** provision.

Signature and Date

Both parties must sign the agreement. If either party is signing on behalf of a business, the signing individual should note his or her title (president, owner, partner, etc.) after his or her name and type in the name and address of the business underneath both. The agreement must be dated.

DEMAND FOR ARBITRATION

The **Demand for Arbitration** (Forms 29.2 and 29.5 on pages F193 and F201) is filled in and "filed" by the complaining party, who sends it via United States registered mail, return receipt requested, to the defending party. This is more than ritual, since defending parties have been known to move that a court set aside a **Demand**, in fact set aside a whole arbitration agreement, on grounds that it was not filed, or was not filed within a reasonable time.

The **Demand** also provides the arbitrator(s) with a starting place to begin hearings, and if an arbitrator must be appointed by the court, the document includes information that the judge will need if he or she is to appoint a knowledgeable arbitrator.

In filling out the **Demand for Arbitration**, first write or type in the name and street address (not post office box) of the person or business upon which you are making the **Demand**. Next, fill in the date of the **Arbitration Agreement**, or agreement containing the arbitration clause upon which you are basing your **Demand**, in the space provided in the form's first paragraph.

Statement of Complaint

Here the complaining party sets down his or her complaint:

> The Rite-Way Roofing Company contracted to reroof my house at 219 Pinocchio Lane, Tulsa, Oklahoma, with "Diamondback" shingles and contracted to complete the work on or before August 15, 1980. I paid the company a one-half deposit of $950.00 and they have not been back to finish the job after completing only about one-fourth of the work.

This statement notes the basic points of the complaint: who was supposed to do the work, what was supposed to be done, what materials were to be used, where the work was supposed to be done, how much was paid, when the work was supposed to be done, and what it is the complaining party believes the defending party failed to do.

Nature of Claim or Relief Sought

Here the complaining party states what he or she wants the defending party to do:

> I want my $950.00 promptly returned or I want the work completed within fourteen (14) days.

Naming of Arbitrator

In the case of **one-arbitrator** hearings, the parties will follow the procedure outlined on page F195. In the case of **three-arbitrator** hearings, the complaining party fills in the name and address of the person who he or she is naming as "his" or "her" arbitrator.

Date

Fill in the date upon which the document is signed and mailed.

Signature

The complaining party signs the **Demand**. If the complaining party is signing on behalf of a business, the individual's title (president, owner, partner, etc.) should be filled in beneath that person's name, and the name and address of the complaining business should be added in the space provided.

Front Panel

At the bottom of the page of each arbitration form you will find the front panel (that's the portion with **Olde English** type) set horizontally. In making use of the **Demand for Arbitration**, for example, just fill in the defendant's name and address beneath the word "TO."

Be sure to address the **Demand** to a particular individual as well as to the name of the company (at its business address):

```
Inger Bergesen, President
Econo-Flex, Inc.
4338 Upsala Blvd.
Thief River Falls, MN 56701
```

or

```
Lee C. Jones, Owner
Sup-R-Mart Bargain World
77438 State Line Highway
Karnak, IL 60532
```

Certificate of Service

The **Certificate of Service** may be needed by the arbitrator(s), or possibly by a judge, in the event of a motion by the other party to set aside the arbitration agreement or to set aside an award by the arbitrator(s).

You don't especially need to sign the **Certificate of Service** at the bottom of the **Demand** that you mail to the defending party. (But why not? No harm done.) You should, however, sign the **Certificate of Service** on copies of the **Demand** that you mail to "your" arbitrator and/or to your attorney. While not conclusive, later proof of this mailing can lend credence to your assertion before the court that the **Demand** was indeed mailed—and mailed within a reasonable time.

GUIDELINES FOR ARBITRATION

There are two sets of **Guidelines for Arbitration**, one for hearings conducted by **one arbitrator** (Form 29.3, page F195) and one set for hearings by **three arbitrators** (Form 29.6, page F203).

As with the other one-arbitrator and three-arbitrator forms, the **Guidelines** are quite similar. They should be signed by both parties to any arbitration agreement at the time of signing that agreement so that the **Guidelines** become a part of the agreement, thus avoiding a future dispute over procedures to be followed in conducting the hearings.

The final provision of the **Guidelines**, INTERPRETATION AND APPLICATION, is a loophole big enough to throw this book through, since it permits the arbitrator(s) to translate the provisions quite freely. This is a necessity if they are not to be 10,000 words long to allow for *every* contingency—a length which wouldn't meet every contingency anyway.

NOTE: *Before presenting your case, or testifying as a complaining or defending party in any arbitration or court proceeding, you might want to look at Chapter 44, **Trying Your Case**, in the section of this book titled **Consumer-Size Justice**. It contains much useful information about witnesses, evidence, and general courtroom and hearing conduct.*

ARBITRATION AGREEMENT FOR INSERTION IN A CONTRACT

Our two arbitration agreements (Forms 29.7 and 29.8) are self-explanatory and similar. These easy-to-use forms are ready for insertion into any already existing contract to which you are a party, as well as for future contracts that you will prepare or be presented with.

The first, **Agreement Using One Arbitrator** (page F207), should serve quite well for simple contracts not involving large sums of money. For complex contracts or those that do involve large amounts of money—hence more open to varying interpretation that can give rise to dispute—we suggest you consider using **Agreement Using Three Arbitrators** on page F209.

PETITION FOR THE APPOINTMENT OF ARBITRATOR

Form 29.9, **Petition for the Appointment of Arbitrator**, is the form to be used when parties in dispute are unable to agree on an arbitrator to conduct one-arbitrator hearings. Unlike similar documents (a petition for appointment of a judge pro tempore, for example), this petition does not specify a **complainant** or **defendant**.

Prior to completing the petition, study the completed sample **Petition for Writ of Execution** (pages 165–166) and **Petition for Order to Answer Written Interrogatories** (pages 167–168) in Section VII, Consumer-Size Justice.

To fill in the form, first type or print on the line at the top the **name of the court of jurisdiction**. This is likely to be something such as:

THE CIRCUIT COURT OF JEFFERSON COUNTY

or

SUPERIOR COURT OF THE CITY OF SPRINGFIELD
Civil Division

or

MUNICIPAL GENERAL SESSIONS COURT

An easy (and free) way of determining the court of jurisdiction is to go to the city hall or county courthouse, show the **Arbitration Agreement** and **Demand for Arbitration** to the clerk of the court, and ask him or her to write down for you the name of the appropriate court. Fill in the name of that court since the **Petition** is being addressed to the judge of that court. (At this time, the clerk of the court can also tell you how many copies of the **Petition** you are to submit, as well as the amount of the filing fee associated with this type of petition.)

Next, under the phrase "IN THE MATTER FOR ARBITRATION BETWEEN," fill in the name, street address, and phone number of each disputant. Normal legal practice would be to fill in the name of the complainant first, followed by the name of the defendant. Since we have avoided labeling a "complainant" or "defendant," either name could be listed first.

In the space provided in the **Petition's** first paragraph, fill in the date of the appropriate **Agreement for Arbitration**, or the date of the contract containing the provision for arbitration that is referred to in the **Petition**.

Next, each party should sign the **Petition** on one of the lines provided following "We ask for this:" and then should print or type his or her name beneath his or her signature.

Before signing the Petition ask the clerk if both parties' signatures should be notarized. Some judges, especially when the parties are not represented by counsel, like to have the notarization. Other judges have no preference.

Now, type or print the name of the judge, followed by the name of the court, beneath the word "TO" on the front panel at the bottom of the page. For example:

Hon. William G. Crim
Circuit Court of
Jefferson County
Chatam, Arkansas

Also fill in the date on which the **Petition** is signed and submitted to the court.

Finally, photocopy the final copy of your **Petition** the required number of times plus one. Attach a copy of the **Agreement for Arbitration** (or contract containing the appropriate arbitration clause) plus a copy of the **Demand for Arbitration** to each copy of the **Petition**. The judge will need a copy of the **Demand** to get some idea of the nature of the dispute for guidance in appointing a knowledgeable arbitrator.

When you give the **Petition** to the clerk, you will be "filing" it with the court, so there will be a **filing fee**, generally about $35—the sum usually charged by the court for filing a divorce or any other civil suit.

At that time the clerk will give your **Petition** a number, writing it usually after the words "In Chancery," which will be placed in the white space to the right of the parties' names on the **Petition** (see the Glossary—Section XIV—for an explanation of "In Chancery"). Use that number when inquiring about your **Petition**.

Probably a few days or weeks after you file the Petition the judge's clerk will give you the names of several possible arbitrators. Then, after both parties have met with a number of them and there is agreement on a particular arbitrator, as well as agreement on his or her (probably hourly) fee, the parties should advise the clerk of the name of the person selected. Then the judge will issue an order appointing that person to arbitrate the dispute.

VI

GETTING YOUR CONSUMER RIGHTS

30 Introduction

It would be a fairly straightforward proposition for this section to provide you with composites of the forms you need to take a case through small claims court. But we feel we're serving you much better if we can keep you from having to go there at all. So, departing from a strictly "forms" format, we've added several extra chapters that we hope will help you:

1. Buy smart, using the **Comparison Shopping Checklist** (Chapter 33).
2. Learn how to use your warranty rights and how to make "best buys" using the **Warranty Comparison Checklist** (Chapter 33).
3. Present an organized, articulate, and well-organized complaint (Chapter 34).
4. Revoke your acceptance of a defective product and obtain a full refund using your **rights of "implied" warranty** granted by law (Chapter 36).

Using this section's information will save you a lot of grief. It will help you save time—and it will help you save money. However, this section will not be the most exciting material you've ever read. Included excerpts from the **Uniform Commercial Code** can be downright boring—but they do put powerful weapons in your hands and prepare you to deal effectively with large retailers and manufacturers.

If you suspect that we're tending to overtrain you for survival in the marketplace, consider this:

- More than fifty-three cents of *every* auto repair dollar is wasted, often through mechanic incompetence and outright fraud.
- More than 75 million purchases each year are believed by buyers to provide "significantly less" than paid for.
- More than 15 million households responding in a national 1973 survey reported the belief that they had been cheated or deceived in connection with the purchase of a product or service during the previous year.
- Although nearly all states have consumer protection legislation on the books, there is very little litigation under these statutes because consumers don't know how to use them.
- Many product warranties do not inform you of your full legal rights and would have you believe that the manufacturer's only obligations are those stated in the warranty.
- A national study of warranties commissioned in 1973 by three major trade associations revealed that only 17 of 106 warranties examined met all of the industries' *own* guidelines.
- Many corporate consumer complaint mechanisms have been deliberately designed to "cool out" complainants and cause them to "drop out" of the complaint process.
- A recent study of industry-financed "consumer action panels," presented by manufacturers as having been established to assist consumers, revealed that such panels exist primarily to serve industry, *not* consumers.
- When consumers take problems to third parties, such as action lines, city, county, and state consumer agencies, and Better Business Bureaus, they usually come away unsatisfied.

Usually, when a business creates problems for consumers, either through deception, failure to provide complete information, or outright fraud, they know exactly what they're doing. That means you have to be sufficiently assertive in pressing for your rights to make such policies unprofitable. Like the coach who felt that "winning is the *only* thing," many business managers operate on the basis that profit is the *only* thing, so you have to "hit them in the profit," where it hurts.

31 How to Avoid Buying Trouble

Avoiding consumer hassles and preventing yourself from being taken advantage of depends as much upon smart buying, articulate complaining, and knowing your rights, as being judged *not guilty* in a criminal trial depends upon your being innocent. Neither your innocence nor smart buying are guarantees of justice, but they can help a lot.

Having the facts on your side and having them lined up in an impressive array can often be enough to convince the other party of the futility of ignoring your claim. Like having an arsenal of nuclear weapons, your well-organized facts are an *effective* deterrent against being ripped off.

Meet Sam, the television man, who could just as well be Pete, the appliance peddler:

"Listen," says Sam confidentially, leading you down to one end of the counter and shifting his cigar to the other side of his mouth, "with them small claims cases you got to be smart.

"You get a summons and right away you mail the people one of these form letters, see, like this one here. It says, 'We have received information that your television set is not working correctly. Please bring it in so that we may service it properly.'

"So right away the letter implies that the small claims suit is the first time that we, top management, have heard of the problem. And now we got something to show the judge. If it's a big set, they probably won't bring it in—you just don't go across town that *easy* with a big TV. Besides, it might get damaged in transit, if you know what I mean.

"If they *do* bring the set in, we put it on the shelf for a while. In the meantime that old warranty is running out, right?

"Eventually we send them a postcard saying it's ready. That uses up maybe five days if you mail it toward the end of the week, and it takes them a few more days to get by and pick it up.

"So say we get dragged into court. We tell the judge, 'Your honor, we sent them this letter, and they failed to contact us.' Or we tell the judge, 'They brought the set in and we serviced it.' That shows 'good faith,' so the most that happens is the judge tells them to let us service it again.

"Listen, if people would just follow my advice they'd never have one of them small claims suits go against them, but you got to set the customer up *before* the case goes to court. That way they ain't got a chance—right?"

Let's shift the scene to Washington, D.C., the paneled boardroom of a well-financed trade association representing major manufacturers of a widely sold category of consumer products. The executive committee is in session prior to the association's annual convention, to be held this year in Hawaii. The group's full-time executive director is next on the agenda:

"Gentlemen, as you are aware from our newsletter and from the questioning some of you recently received when testifying before House and Senate committees, a number of consumer groups have mounted a well-organized campaign for increased government control of our industry.

"Basing their case for this unwarranted intrusion upon what they allege to be widespread consumer dissatisfaction with our products, they are proposing legislation which would impose costly warranty revisions as well as require the institution of expensive repair and service programs.

"We believe we have developed a response to this situation that will defuse the issue and thereby reduce this danger of increased bureaucratic control. It is a program, by the way, which our lobbyists on the Hill tell us will provide them with ammunition to give our friends in Congress to use in combating this interference with free enterprise.

"The program to which I refer is MADCAP, the *Manufacturers and Dealers Consumer Assistance Program.* John Enright of our public information office deserves full credit for that name, by the way. I think you'll agree that it has a nice ring to it.

"MADCAP is similar in its essential elements to comparable programs presently being inaugurated by other trade groups. It provides evidence of 'conscientious industry self-regulation,' while at the same time serves effectively as a consumer 'cool-down' mechanism that offers hope of complaint resolution while involving the complaining party in time-consuming correspondence, forms completion, answering questions, and so on.

"At every step, initiative on the part of the complaining party is required, and, in most cases, we believe that individual's energy and resolve will soon become exhausted and he or she will drop out of the process, thus eliminating the need for profit-reducing expense on the part of our members.

"Examples of the program's forms, letters, questionaires, and so on, as well as dealer and distributor instructions and samples of MADCAP ads and dealer window stickers, are in the large, three-ring binders before you.

"We are looking forward to a favorable vote by the association's general membership at the convention in Hawaii."

How do you build an arsenal of evidence to defend against these kinds of local shopkeepers and national corporations?

Begin protecting yourself before making a major purchase by practicing "defensive buying." Set up a file in which you can start collecting store ads, brochures, and manufacturer's magazine advertisements. Beyond telling you what a product is supposed to do, ads and brochures are **legal documents** (the *courts* have ruled this)—they are as binding upon the seller or manufacturer as any signed contract would be.

One of the most important—and overlooked—legal documents related to any important purchase is the warranty. There's no law that says that **any** product has to be sold with a written warranty, but where a warranty is offered, it's every bit as relevant to your buying decision as quality, features, price, and appearance.

Several manufacturers may offer almost equally priced similar products, but one may provide a full warranty while another offers only a limited one. One manufacturer's warranty might include a five-year protection clause, while another manufacturer's warranty is only good for two years. One warranty may provide a money-back or lifetime guarantee, while the other does not. There is, for example, a vast difference in warranties offered with widely sold, similarly priced hi-fi stereo equipment.

If a product requires service or if you have an unresolved complaint, your warranty can be your single most effective weapon in obtaining repairs—or in winning your case in small claims court.

But it wasn't always so. Until passage of the Magnuson-Ross Warranty Act in 1975, warranties were often vague, deceptive, and frequently not honored by too many sellers and manufacturers. Evidence introduced at Federal Trade Commission (FTC) hearings prior to the promulgation of the 1975 warranty act revealed that an auto manufacturer's new-car warranty explicitly did not extend to "service items," that it failed to enumerate those items the auto maker considered to be "service items," and that it was deceptively using the term in an extremely broad and uncommon sense to exclude the myriad items that were included in many other manufacturer's warranties using the same terminology.

Although the Uniform Commercial Code, adopted by all states except Louisiana since 1968, provides that certain warranties are implied (the so-called "implied warranty," of which more later), industry representatives at the FTC hearings objected to proposed warranty text that would have informed you of that fact:

> This warranty gives you specific legal rights. You also have implied warranty rights. In the event of a problem with warranty service or performance you may be able to go to small claims court, a State court or a Federal District Court.

A number of other industry representatives, undoubtedly concerned about the health of overworked judges, warned that the inclusion of such information in warranties would "encourage litigation in already congested courts." Other corporations and trade associations argued that the provision of such information to consumers would be "in conflict with the intention of the warranty act to encourage informal settlements."

In opposing the proposed text, the National Association of Home Appliance Manufacturers admonished:

> Encouraged by a written warranty to seek redress in court, unable in many instances to find the proper court, and finding in most instances that the assistance of a lawyer is necessary, a dissatisfied purchaser would be rewarded only with disillusionment and frustration. Unfortunately, the frustration and disillusionment and resulting animosity would be directed against the warrantor . . .

We fail to see how a dissatisfied customer would be any *less* frustrated and disillusioned by being kept ignorant of information about possible recourse to law, but corporate concern about the possibility of being hauled into court *does* say something about its fear of unfavorable judicial precedent, time-consuming court appearances, costly awards, and adverse publicity. (All of which serves to give you some indication of how potent a weapon a small claims or other lawsuit really is.)

We could, by the way, find no mention in the hearings record of any industry participant suggesting that perhaps customer frustration and disillusionment might be reduced simply by taking care of customer complaints and by turning out better merchandise.

The warranty text finally adopted, with any reference to the existence of implied warranties removed, reads:

> This warranty gives you specific legal rights, and you may have other rights which vary from state to state.

Actually, your implied warranty rights are much the same in every state except Louisiana, which has not adopted the Uniform Commercial Code. But in pressing for the above text, corporate interests have managed to make the issue of obtaining your implied warranty rights seem so complex you'll be convinced you'd need a (costly) lawyer. In reality, all you may need is a little effort—plus the information in this book.

32 Buying Smart—Learning Your Warranty Rights

A September 1974 report issued by the staff of the House Interstate and Foreign Commerce Committee, Subcommittee on Commerce and Finance, stated, on the basis of an extensive investigation, that no significant warranty improvements had been made by industry since 1969:

> Any actions taken on the part of manufacturers and trade associations to clean up warranties during the past five years appear to have had minimal results. These certificates, often marked WARRANTY and printed on good quality paper with a fancy filigree border, in many cases serve primarily to limit obligations otherwise owed to the buyer as a matter of law. This is done by disclaimers and exemptions and by ambiguous phrases and terms. All too often warranties shroud and effectively cover up the obligations of the seller.

In commenting on the committee staff's findings, its chairman, Representative John Moss, stated that "it is all but fraud when a guarantee declares in large print that the manufacturer is giving protection to the buyer and in the fine print attempts to take away common-law buyer protection."

Prior to the warranty act, warranties were often not available for inspection before you bought the product—"The warranty comes in the [sealed] box." The 1975 warranty act requires that the seller make available the **text**, not necessarily the actual certificate, of any product selling for more than $15 that has a warranty.

There's no requirement that a warranty be offered with any product, no matter how highly priced, just the requirement that if one is offered for a product selling for more than $15, you would be able to inspect its text before making your purchase.

There are several kinds of warranties. Since the protection they offer varies widely, their provisions can be a major factor in the ultimate cost of whatever you buy. Two common types of written warranties are **full** warranties and **limited** warranties.

FULL WARRANTY

The provisions of a full warranty include the following:

1. A defective product will be repaired or replaced free, including removal and reinstallation if necessary.
2. The product will be fixed within a reasonable* time after you complain.
3. You do not have to do anything unreasonable (such as ship your washing machine back to the factory) in order to obtain warranty service.
4. The warranty is good for **anyone** who owns the product during the warranty period.
5. If the product can't be fixed—or hasn't been after a reasonable* number of tries—you get your choice of a new one or your money back.

When reading any full warranty, note whether it applies to the entire product or just to certain parts, such as the motor or compressor in an air conditioner or the picture tube in a TV set.

LIMITED WARRANTY

A limited warranty, on the other hand, is "limited":

1. A limited warranty covers only parts; you pay for labor.
2. It covers only the **original** owner.
3. It may require you to return a heavy product to the store or an authorized warranty repair center for servicing.
4. It may allow only a **pro rata** refund or credit—you get a smaller refund the longer you have the product.
5. You may be required to pay a service charge for handling.

These are the *minimum* requirements for a limited warranty. There's nothing to keep a manufacturer from including some of the features of a full warranty in its limited warranty, nor is there any restriction upon additional goodies, such as free maintenance checkups or free periodic adjustments, which a warrantor can offer—another reason for reading your warranty carefully. (Extra benefits can, of course, be offered with a *full* warranty.)

IMPLIED WARRANTY

In addition to any full or limited warranty (or combination of these warranties), your purchase will almost always be covered by an additional **implied** warranty under terms of the Uniform Commercial

---

*At this writing the FTC has yet to determine what a "reasonable" time or "reasonable" number of tries is, but most consumer organizations we've contacted report that so far most companies offering full warranties are being, well—reasonable.

Code (UCC). The Uniform Commercial Code, adopted between 1958 and 1968 by all states except Louisiana, came about through the need for a uniform code to regulate all aspects of commercial transactions. Previously, differences in various states' commercial codes made settlement of disputes between buyers and sellers in different states almost impossible to resolve in court.

Implied warranty provisions of the Uniform Commercial Code give you the following kinds of protection:

- **Warranty of Merchantability:** The *seller* warrants that the product you buy is fit for the *ordinary* uses for which the product is intended. A toaster must toast, a clock must keep time, etc. If it doesn't, you have a legal right to a full refund.
- **Warranty of Fitness for a Particular Purpose:** If the *seller* advises you that a product you buy is suitable for a *particular* purpose, this advice creates a warranty that the product will serve for that purpose. A seller who advises you that a vehicle will tow a 5,000-pound trailer, or that a well pump will raise water 500 feet, warrants that the product is suitable for that purpose.

  A good point to remember here is to put your requirements in writing or take someone along to the store with you to act as a witness when you ask the advice of the salesperson about a product's suitability for the particular purpose for which you plan to use it.
- **Protection Against Consequential Damages:** The *manufacturer* must not only repair or replace the product under terms of any written or implied warranties but must also bear the cost of reimbursing you for damage caused by the product. If you buy a hot-water heater that leaks and damages your house or household goods, the *manufacturer* is liable for that expense.

  Note: The manufacturer can avoid this contingent liability by expressly excluding consequential damages within the text of any written warranty or sales agreement. However, you may want to look elsewhere when you discover this exclusion in the warranty of any product you're considering.

EXERCISING YOUR WARRANTY RIGHTS

The warranty is one of the most important considerations of any major purchase you make, so when the salesperson wants to demonstrate Dynamic-Electric's new Tangle-Matic washing machine, tell him or her you'd like to read the warranty too.

Under the often liberally interpreted warranty of merchantability, you might successfully sue if a product fails or breaks down after its full or limited warranty has expired. Your implied warranty rights don't end when your written warranty expires.

For example, if you buy a new car with a 12-month/12,000-mile limited warranty, you may be able to obtain repair or replacement of its automatic transmission beyond the warranty period simply because no reasonable person would buy a new car with the expectation that its transmission would break down after 13,000, or even 20,000, miles of normal use. Your implied warranty rights could also be brought to bear if an appliance with a 90-day warranty breaks down after four months of normal use.

To exercise your rights successfully in court under the warranty of merchantability or warranty of fitness for a particular purpose, you must be able to show that you gave the seller a reasonable number of opportunities to repair or exchange the product. Too often a lawsuit is your only means of obtaining redress under your implied warranty rights, so make sure you obtain *evidence* of your attempts to obtain repair or replacement.

When you're ready to begin shopping for a major purchase, bring our **Comparison Shopping Checklist** and our **Warranty Comparison Checklist** (Forms 33.1 and 33.2) with you to the store and you may never have to see the inside of a small claims court. And if you do have to go to court, you'll be in a strong position to win. Chapter 33 describes in detail how to fill out these two handy, ready-to-use checklists.

A chapter dealing more fully with implied warranties (Chapter 35) and a chapter expounding on how to get your implied warranty rights *without going to court* (Chapter 36) begin on pages 112 and 117, respectively.

33 When You Go Shopping— Protecting Your Consumer Rights

Now that you're ready to go shopping, you'll find that filling out our **Comparison Shopping Checklist** (Form 33.1, page F213) and **Warranty Comparison Checklist** (Form 33.2, page F215) will help you decide what to buy. If necessary, after your purchase you can use the forms' data in presenting a well-documented complaint or in filing a suit in small claims court.

COMPARISON SHOPPING CHECKLIST

Make enough copies of the **Comparison Shopping Checklist** so that you'll have one for each store you plan to visit. You might need more than one form for a particular store if you expect to examine several similar products, say, various models of washing machines, while you're there.

You don't need to note the serial number of every item you're considering, just the serial number of the one you finally receive. You should note the model number, though, to make sure that what you bought is what you get.

The checklist provides space for noting most aspects common to any major purchase. Use space at the end of the form to note specific features of any refrigerator, washing machine, auto battery, air conditioner, chain saw, sewing machine, set of tires, clothes dryer, etc., that you're planning to buy.

Once at the store, complete the form in the presence of the salesperson. This will serve to put him or her on notice not to make extravagant claims and that you are keeping a record of all price quotations and delivery and installation promises.

WARRANTY COMPARISON CHECKLIST

Although there are minimum standards for warranties offered with products selling for more than $15, there is no limitation on the maximum protection you can be offered. Some manufacturers offer longer, better warranties than others, making the warranty you receive as valid a consideration as price, quality, and features.

The **Warranty Comparison Checklist** contains space for noting more than you might think you ever wanted to know about warranties, but when the time comes to buy, the warranty comparisons you'll be able to make will help you base your decision on all the important facts, not just some of them.

Again, make a good number of photocopies of this checklist before going out on your shopping expedition. You may only need to fill out a few of the blanks at the store itself—the blanks pertaining to the manufacturer; product name and model number; seller (store) name and address; salesperson name, department, and phone number; and the availability of the warranty text in the store—but **only** if you're able to bring a copy of the warranty home with you to fill out the balance of the checklist. Otherwise, you'll just have to fill it out in front of the salesperson, who, by now, *really* knows you *really* mean business.

Warranty Comparison Guidelines: Filling Out Your Checklist

To get the most out of your **Warranty Comparison Checklist**, familiarize yourself with these step-by-step guidelines as you look through the form itself (the numbers below corresponding to those within the checklist):

1. No explanation is needed.
2. Sometime you might find yourself considering something that includes both a product and a service, such as installation of new kitchen cabinets. In that case you'll have two warranties to consider.
3. The product designation may be both a model number and a name, such as Custom DeLuxe or Super-Matic II. Note both name and model number. Some services, such as auto painting, are offered in various quality levels, for example, Standard or Premier, and since those terms don't always mean the same thing, the warranty can be a good basis upon which to compare services. (The shop's Standard paint job may specify two coats of paint and offer a two-year warranty, while its Premier paint job may specify one coat of primer and three coats of paint and offer a five-year warranty.)
4. Note the name and address of each particular store, since different stores within the same chain may offer various models of similar items—and at different prices.
5. No explanation is needed.
6. FTC regulations require that the text, not necessarily the actual warranty certificate, of each

offered warranty for any product selling for more than $15 be available for your inspection in the store. You may want to think twice about buying from anyone who does not have warranties available for you to read.

7. FTC regulations require that the text of warranties for mail-order products selling for more than $15 be included in the catalog or be offered, via return mail, by the seller.

8. Note if the name of the warrantor is different from the manufacturer. If you're not satisfied with what you have read, ask the salesperson to clarify it.

9. See the definitions of full and limited warranty on pages 96–97. Some products are offered with both full and limited warranties on different components, and for different lengths of time. For example, the following could be the warranty for a sewing machine you just purchased:

> Full five year warranty on sewing machine head. Full two year warranty on electrical equipment of sewing machine and mechanical adjustments. After one year and until five years from date of purchase, limited warranty on all electrical and mechanical parts and adjustments. Manufacturer will furnish replacement under limited warranty for any defective parts. You will be charged for labor.

10. No explanation is needed; see 9.

11. No explanation is needed; see 9.

12. Some parts and components may carry a "lifetime" guarantee. A "money-back" guarantee might also be offered.

13. Make sure that costly-to-replace components, such as TV picture tubes, motors, and compressors, are covered.

14. Usually, parts and components excluded from warranty coverage will not affect the utility of a product, but they can affect your enjoyment of it. Note this excerpt from a stereo component manufacturer's warranty:

> This product is warranted free of defects in construction and workmanship except for cabinets, grilles and other finish items.

(There are, by the way, tremendous differences in warranties offered by the manufacturers of similarly priced stereo equipment. Read those warranties very carefully.)

15. Some limitations can be reasonable:

> . . . when product is . . . installed . . . operated . . . maintained . . . in accordance with instruction manual.

> . . . when used for private household purposes.

16. Make sure that warranty coverage for any product that you might resell during the warranty period, such as a refrigerator or air conditioner, can be exercised by subsequent owners. When you buy a warranted product as a gift, list the recipient's name on the receipt so he or she can obtain warranty service without any problem.

17. Warranty commencement date is important if you're buying something that can't be installed or used for some time. Gifts that are purchased early need to have their receipts dated to begin the warranty commencement date on the day of giving. Many stores are happy to do this.

18. Are you required to have the product serviced as specified by the manufacturer, installed by the seller, or inspected regularly? Must the product be used, or not used, in a particular manner?

19. The return of owner registration cards can be legally required as a precondition to your exercising warranty rights, but this requirement must be clearly disclosed within the warranty.

There are valid reasons for requiring warranty registration cards, such as the need to establish the identity of the original owner, for product recall, etc. But, regardless of what the card might have you believe, you *do not* have to answer those questions about income, educational level, and whether you'd rather go to a party or read a book.

Complaints about warranty registration card requirements are becoming so widespread that consumer organizations have come to believe that they are being used as a device to deter warranty claims. First, there's the chance that you won't send in the required card, so that eliminates you as a source of warranty service. Second, increasing numbers of consumers report sending in the cards and then failing to receive the necessary **warranty validation card**, which must be shown to obtain warranty service. In reporting on the problem (in its September 1978 issue), the editors of *Motorhome Life* stated that "given the frequency of this occurrence one wonders if some manufacturers don't deliberately use this ploy to discourage warranty claims."

If you do decide to buy a product from a manufacturer who requires a warranty registration card, make several copies before sending in the original card by registered mail, return receipt requested. And don't wait too long before sending a follow-up letter and copy of the original card—registered mail, return receipt requested.

20. Does the warranty or owner's manual include a list of authorized warranty repair agencies? If not, how about a toll-free number you can call?

21. Can an authorized service station approve an exchange or refund? If not, who can?

22. No explanation is needed.

23. Here is one widely sold stereo hi-fi equipment manufacturer's consequential damage exclusion:

> Incidental and consequential damages caused by malfunction, defect or otherwise, and with respect to breach of any express or implied warranty, are not the responsibility of the manufacturer, and, to the extent permitted by law, are hereby excluded, both for property damage and, to the extent not unconscionable, for personal injury. The above includes, but is not limited to records, tapes and other high fidelity equipment

and components. Some states do not allow the exclusion or limitation of incidental or consequential damages, so the above limitation or exclusion may not apply to you.

But there are some good guys around too. Here is one popular manufacturer's consequential damage provision from its home freezer warranty:

If promptly reported to your nearest retail sales store or warranty service center, we will reimburse you up to a total of $100.00 for the value of food, as verified by us, lost while stored in the freezer when used for private household use as a result of defects that occur during the first year following the date of purchase.

24. Referral of a warranty dispute to an industry-related "consumer action panel" CAN be legally required as a precondition to your taking legal action. However, this fact must be clearly disclosed in the warranty, *and* the panel must meet FTC standards and must normally render its nonbinding decision within forty days.

34 The Art and Technique of Making Complaints

We've never seen it listed in any compilation of phobias, but *querelophobia*, the name we've just made up for "fear of complaining," is probably one of the most common phobias in America. Most of us want to be liked; most of us want to be thought of as reasonable; and very few of us enjoy starting an argument.

Most of us refrain from complaining if we can. We will walk around hating ourselves for not doing anything in a situation where we know we have every right to complain. Scores of medical and psychological research papers have been written about the harm that *not* taking action in that kind of situation does to us. But we don't have to tell you about that—you've been there!

Complaining isn't so bad once you get your feet wet. We'll help you get organized, show you the ropes, and introduce you to a few guerrilla tactics. We won't go so far as to say complaining is *fun*, but it's a lot better than just sitting there and "taking it."

There are all kinds of resources available to complainers: consumer organizations, media "action lines," Better Business Bureaus, federal agencies, arbitration groups, industry and trade association "consumer action panels," corporate customer service offices, and company complaint departments. All of these have contributed much toward making things better for consumers. They are responsible for a lot of good legislation, and many have obtained redress for consumers when nothing else could except, perhaps, a complicated lawsuit.

Since the effectiveness of consumer organizations varies widely and new ones are always cropping up, and established ones change their addresses, it's difficult, if not impossible, to recommend specific organizations. However, on pages 131–133 (see Chapter 38) we have provided a list of each state's primary, state-sponsored consumer agency—agencies that can serve as contact points for reaching nearby consumer organizations.

Whether you make use of a consumer group depends a lot on how competent you feel you are in handling your own complaint and how willing you are to engage in the extra phone calls, correspondence, and written explanations you'll need to go through if a consumer group is going to work effectively for you. It depends, too, on whether you're willing to put up with a bad air conditioner, a washer that doesn't wash, or an auto transmission that won't shift, for the time it takes for a third party to evaluate your problem, make an investigation, and get back to you.

Almost any time you enlist a consumer group to work on your behalf, you can count on two weeks to a month additional time spent in resolving your complaint. Consumer groups are overworked and understaffed. They do the best they can.

Statistically, third-party action on your behalf has only one chance in three of resolving your complaint in a way that's satisfactory to you. Third-party resolutions, especially those proposed by Better Business Bureau arbitrators and industry consumer action panels, are almost always a compromise—a compromise you'd probably never accept if offered directly by the store or manufacturer.

For solving your problem, nothing can approach the potential of your own personal action in obtaining (as the pain-reliever commercials say) fast, effective relief. If you handle your complaint yourself and if you're well organized, articulate, and appear to be determined, your chances of a relatively prompt, completely satisfactory resolution are better than two out of three.

Your town might just have the best consumer group in the nation (there are a few terrific ones we'll tell you about later), so check around and ask friends, but don't discount what you can do. Don't deprive yourself of the opportunity for self-reliance—nor of the joy of winning! Remember, nobody cares as much about solving your problem as you do!

We do advise, though, that you keep consumer groups informed. City, county, state, and federal agencies need to know about your problem so that they can investigate unethical businesses and propose legislation to reduce consumer difficulties.

All you need do, at the time you make your **second** complaint effort about a particular problem, is to send consumer groups copies of your complaint letters, store or manufacturer responses, and any other relevant documents. In a brief note tell them you are writing because you feel they would want to know about your problem and that, while you would appreciate any help they may be able to offer, you realize they may not be in a position to assist you directly and you are proceeding on your own pending any offer of assistance from them.

ORGANIZING YOUR COMPLAINT

Getting your complaint organized is fairly simple. We recommend five basic steps:

1. **Determine what you want.**

Do you want your money back, an exchange, a repair, a billing correction, or possibly reimbursement for wages lost because you stayed home from work to wait for a delivery truck that didn't come?

2. **Find out WHO has authority to give you what you want.**

If you're dealing with a large department store, the complaint department would be an obvious place to start, but first find the salesperson you bought from. Often he or she will be happy, off the record, simply to "make a switch," exchanging the item you have for another one and taking yours out of stock as "damaged" or whatever.

If you feel a complaint department is giving you the runaround, don't hesitate to contact the store's manager.

If you're having trouble with a manager who refuses to give you the owner's name, you can often get it by visiting the business licensing bureau in your city hall or county courthouse.

If your difficulty is with the local manager for a large national corporation, you can obtain the president's name and corporate headquarters address from *Standard & Poor's Register of Corporations* in your public library. Once you have an executive's name, you can check the alphabetical listing of *Standard & Poor's Register of Corporations, Directors and Executives.* The *Register* often includes fairly extensive biographies of many executives that contain information on colleges attended, clubs and organization memberships, and corporate boards on which he or she serves or has served. His or her home address is often included as well. There just may be information about an executive in the *Register* that you could use to obtain some leverage. At least it will help give you the measure of the person you're dealing with.

3. **Write down the specifics of your purchase.**

- Model number and name, such as Tornado-Matic or whatever
- Serial number
- Date purchased
- Price
- How paid—cash, charge, check, etc.
- When delivered
- Apparent condition when delivered
- Salesperson's name
- Store where purchase was made

Read your warranty before you complain so that you can refer to specific provisions.

4. **State the reason for your complaint.**

Briefly describe what is wrong with the product or service.

5. **State the date by which you expect action to be taken.**

This date will depend upon when you made any initial verbal complaint: yesterday or two weeks ago.

It will also depend upon what you view as a practical amount of time to rectify the problem. If a required repair is a major one, or if you suspect that factory authorization may be required or that parts must be shipped from an out-of-town warehouse, then you might specify a fairly distant date, say, two weeks or so.

COMMUNICATING YOUR COMPLAINT

The preceding complaint procedure applies whether you're visiting the store, making a phone call, or writing a letter. If your first contact doesn't produce a satisfactory response, subsequent communications will still include these basic points, although you may escalate your demands due to continuing inconvenience or expense.

Whatever the case, before you initially complain, decide what method to use: phone call, personal visit, or letter.

Telephone

A phone call is quick and easy. It doesn't take a lot of time, and you can phone from home or work. If the seller really wants to please, a brief call may be all that's needed. Also, you can often talk on the phone to a top executive who would never see you if you turned up at the office—and you can talk long-distance.

The person you talk to might ask to call you back after he or she has had a day or two to look into the problem. If that happens: (1) get the person's name, department, and phone number; and (2) ask the person to give you a specific day on which he or she will contact you. If you are not called on the promised day, wait one day and then phone, reminding him or her of their promise to contact you the previous day. Restate what you want and make it clear that you expect the situation to be taken care of within whatever you consider to be a reasonable time. If you don't receive an answer by **that** date, send a registered letter to the store's owner, or corporation's president, stating *what* you want and *when* you want it.

Here's how your (the complainant's) end of a typical phone call might go, after you've found out who can handle your complaint:

"Mr. Smith, this is Pat Wilson and I'm calling to ask that you replace the electric heater that I recently bought in your store or that you refund the money I paid for it.

"The heater is a Sol-Ray model GS-2152, which I bought for $38.95 on November 26. I paid cash and have my receipt.

"Although the heater has a thermostat, it will only operate for a few minutes, even with the thermostat turned all the way up. Even then, the cord becomes almost too hot to touch.

"It will be in your store in a few days, and if you will tell me who can handle an exchange or refund, I will bring the heater with me."

This phone conversation indicates that you assume the store will naturally want to satisfy your request. Your reference to the cord that becomes almost too hot to touch warns the manager of possible liability for consequential damages in the event of fire, and your statement that you will be in the store in a few days implies that you are probably a regular customer—someone the store wouldn't want to offend.

Personal Visit

You can see whom you're dealing with when you make a personal visit. You become more than just a remote voice. It's more difficult to deal with you in a routine, impersonal manner. If the person you're talking to says he can't help you, you can ask to see someone who can. You can persuade, cajole, use humor, talk in a loud voice, create a scene, etc.

You can optimize the benefit of a personal visit by dressing and conducting yourself as though you just might be someone with connections and influence—someone to reckon with. I'm not talking about being pompous and overbearing or wearing job interview clothes to the country hardware store. Just don't show up at a corporation's regional office in jeans and a dirty T-shirt.

When making a personal visit, you can also "take it with you." If your problem is with a small appliance or clothing, you'll have it with you to exchange. If a toaster doesn't toast, take a few pieces of bread along to demonstrate, etc. Take along copies (keep the originals) of relevant documents. If you resolve your complaint, you can walk out with your new toaster or with a refund.

A special advantage of making a personal visit is that you can take someone with you to act as a witness in the event of difficulty. The presence of your witness will not be lost on the store's representative either.

The disadvantages of a visit are that it takes time, requires dressing the part, and may involve some expense. As with making a phone call, a visit doesn't get quite as much "on the record" as you might like.

Letter

One of the good things about sending a letter is that it forces you to organize your thinking and then gives you time to polish and rewrite what you want to say until you're satisfied with the way it reads. When writing a letter, you can obtain help that won't be available when talking on the phone or presenting your case in person.

A letter is "on the record," and copies can later be sent to corporate headquarters, consumer groups, or your attorney and can be presented as "evidence" to the judge in a small claims suit.

Just as your appearance will be judged when you present your case in person, the appearance of your letter, perhaps more than the justification of your

complaint, can influence a decision in your favor. If you write a letter:

1. Use a typewriter. Beg, borrow, or steal one if you have to, but DON'T send a handwritten complaint letter.
2. Use a printed letterhead of some kind. If you work and can get away with using an office letterhead for writing your complaint, do it. If you can't use a letterhead from your place of business, have a personal letterhead printed. Your letterhead should be:

a. On good quality "rag"-content white paper.
b. On standard 8½" × 11" business size to fit No. 10 envelopes, which you'll also need.
c. Printed in staid-looking, black type with your first name, middle initial or name, and last name centered above the address, such as these:

David R. Lewis
406 Avenida Presidio
San Clemente, California 92672

or

Ellen P. Westerman
Apartment 4-G
235 East 84th Street
New York, New York 10028

Ask the printer to show you some letterheads he's done for lawyers and accountants. They'll be of the type that you'll want to use. (Use of your phone number is optional and can be placed anywhere the lawyers and accountants place theirs.)

4. Use only a black typewriter ribbon, and use black ink for the signature.
5. If at all possible, write your letter so that it fits on one page.

Printed letterheads do not cost nearly as much as you might think, and they'll probably double the effectiveness of any written complaint.

Whatever method you use to communicate your complaint, be brief, be calm, be businesslike, be determined—and stick to the facts.

TECHNIQUES AND TACTICS

The following paragraphs contain specific tactics you can employ in your initial complaint letters and phone calls (sample letters may be found at the very end of this chapter). Beyond that, providing examples of your possible responses to stores' and manufacturers' possible responses would be more complicated than charting Henry the VIII's family tree.

Before we look at various tactics, both yours and theirs, there is one thing you should never forget: From the moment you begin comparison shopping and start to collect advertisements, brochures, receipts, and warranties, from the moment you write your first complaint letter and receive your first reply, think of it all as EVIDENCE. *Your case will stand or fall—you can get what you want or be taken ad-*

vantage of—based upon the EVIDENCE *that you have a strong case.*

There *are* people you'll buy from who will be happy to make an exchange or refund or see to it that repairs are promptly made, that your account is corrected, and that deliveries are made on time. But there are others who will give you the "sunshine treatment," like car dealers who will take your car in for warranty repairs, let it sit on the back lot a day or two, and then phone to say it's fixed and ready to go. They are the brothers and sisters of Sam the television man who feel they know how to beat the "rap" in small claims court. They're great builders of "evidence" too.

Practitioners of the sunshine treatment trap themselves in the end, though, because if you're *persistent*, you'll soon have a file of four or five unproductive repair attempts on the record—evidence for a strong case in small claims court.

Then there are the experts at giving you the runaround. Your best defense is to learn, before you make your initial complaint, who can give you what you want. If you suspect you'll be shunted from person to person, department to department, phone the company's office ahead of time and tell them you are "Mr. Witherspoon's secretary" or "Mr. Cartright's assistant" and that "we have to write a letter to your president (or manager), but we seem to have misplaced his (or her) name."

If you expect or are having trouble, send a complaint letter to the top executive, with copies to "lower downs." It's a bit more difficult to put you off then, because management knows that *you* know that *they* know of the problem and that they can't claim ignorance later on.

If you begin to get the feeling you're being given a runaround, make every future communication by letter and specify that replies be by mail. Unethical merchants love to deal with you on the phone because, if the case gets to small claims court, it will be your word against theirs.

And there are those who, especially on the telephone or face to face, are virtuosos at playing, "We've certainly never had *that* complaint before!" Their declaration is delivered in a sort of indignant, "surely-you-must-be-joking-but-in-very-bad-taste" kind of voice accompanied by suitable haughty and injured facial expressions.

"We've certainly never had that complaint before!" is perhaps the meanest form of psychological warfare because it attempts to make you feel inadequate and vaguely guilty for even bringing the matter up.

Most of the time you won't have to resort to "tactics" in presenting and following up your complaint. The majority of business people want to handle your problem as fairly and promptly as possible.

But if you're not being dealt with fairly, do not waste weeks of valuable time nor subject yourself to inconvenience by playing by the guilty party's rules. If your problem is with the phone company, for example, and they're giving you a hard time, play by **your**

rules: let them deal with you by **letter** and refuse to discuss the matter over the phone—"I'm not free to discuss that with you right now; just put whatever you need to say in a letter."

Whenever you get the runaround, get your complaint **on the record** (so that it's evidence) and escalate the pressure of your complaint rapidly.

If your initial phone call, visit, or letter (see sample letter on page 107) fails to produce a response indicating willingness to resolve your problem, make your second contact a rather formal letter to the company's owner or president or local manager and send it by registered mail, return receipt requested (see our second sample letter on page 109). If you have an attorney, or a friend who happens to be an attorney, note in the lower left-hand corner of the letter that a copy has been mailed to that law firm:

cc: **Williams, Matthews and Myer**

We don't advise following his example, but one person we know who works in Manhattan's financial district has for years been marking his complaint letters with "cc: Chambers, Park, Fulton and Wall" —the names of four consecutive stops on one of New York's major subway lines.

Despite what we said earlier about not counting on third-party organizations to help resolve your complaint, you can write them as a matter of **tactics.** Rather than merely writing a litany of cc's at the bottom of letters to the offending company:

cc: **Better Business Bureau**
cc: **Chamber of Commerce**
cc: **Hometown Consumer Protection Agency**
cc: **XYZ Trade Association**

—something that might just be considered an idle threat (everybody threatens to "call the Better Business Bureau")—you can *really* write those groups (see our third sample letter on page 110). Just be sure to *send copies* to the company you're having trouble with, with the implied threat of more to follow. That's something the "bad" guys will want *stopped.* And the only way for them to stop it is to take care of your complaint.

If you've paid for the product or service by check (charge purchases whenever you can), the back of your canceled check will reveal the name of the company's bank. In a subsequent conversation with the manager or president of the company you're having a problem with, you might mention that you're "surprised that the East Bank of The Mississippi would have you as an account." No business person likes to offend someone who might be in a position to endanger his or her reputation at the bank.

One complainer we know turned her knowledge of the problem company's bank to good use. She had encountered more than $600 in extra expenses due to a bad engine overhaul on the family car. She looked at the canceled check to learn the name and branch of the company's bank and promptly went there to apply for a loan. When they asked what she needed the money for, she said, "Well, you see, I had this engine overhaul over at ABC Auto Service. It was no good and they won't fix it, so I've had to spend a lot of extra money. . . ."

Guess who received a phone call that same afternoon from ABC Auto Service offering to install a new engine the next day—and for free?

THE ART OF COMPLAINING

Thus far we've been talking mostly about the techniques, the formulas, of complaining. But, just as there is an art beyond the formula of selling, an art beyond the procedures of medical diagnosis by which a physician determines what's really wrong with the patient, and an art by which a perceptive attorney senses the mind of the judge, the mood of the jury, and the mental state of the witness, so there is an art of complaining that can obtain results against all odds.

The art goes with the technique. Part of it is being sensitive to the state of the person you're dealing with. Are they harassed, upset by something that happened before they started talking to you? Is there something you can say or do to show that you understand *their* situation?

Part of the art of complaining is being easy to communicate with, being the kind of person the individual who is handling your complaint will not want to avoid talking to again because you've been hostile or made them feel embarrassed or defensive in some way. Your purpose is not to teach them a lesson or show them how wrong they are; all you want, really, is for your complaint to be taken care of. That's all!

The person you're dealing with (if you've picked the right person) is in a position to help you. That person carries a lot more weight within the company than you do.

Anyone who is in a position to help you (by using personal authority to make a refund, by making an "off-the-record" exchange from stock, by fixing your appliance first, by waiving a service charge, etc.) is also in a position to hurt you—by holding to the letter of your warranty, by "losing" your paperwork, by keeping your car or TV or air conditioner a few days or weeks longer than really necessary—just to "get even" for what he or she feels is your rudeness or unreasonable attitude. Maybe that's not the way things *should* be, but it's the way things are.

It may seem out of place when you're in the middle of your third attempt to obtain the warranty service you paid for when you bought the product, but—be nice!

BEYOND COMPLAINING

We're in favor of carrying complaining only so far. Your first complaint gives the seller an opportunity to remedy the situation if he wants to. Your second complaint, which should probably be a registered letter, return receipt requested, to the company president or owner, gives top management a chance to correct a mistaken clerk or manager. After that, if you begin to feel that your complaint will never produce satisfactory results, you're free to declare war.

As you now know, you can sue in small claims court on the basis of a written warranty, plus your implied warranty rights granted by law. Advertisements, brochures, and even salespersons' claims, especially if you have a witness, can also serve as the basis for a lawsuit.

Not long ago, Hibbing, Minnesota, bookkeeper Steve Lastovich saw a TV commercial for a Ford four-wheel drive pickup bouncing up dry creek beds and plowing through rough, off-road backcountry. Lastovich was so impressed he went right out and bought one. After his first weekend of "four-wheeling," Lastovich's truck barely made it into his Ford dealer with several hundred dollars worth of damage.

When the dealer and Ford told him "no deal" on warranty repairs, Lastovich went to small claims court, lost there, and appealed.

After viewing a videotape of the commercial in his courtroom, the judge ruled that claims made in the commercial should be considered part of Ford's warranty for the truck. The jury promptly awarded Lastovich $500 in damages plus $175 in court costs.

Consumer groups report that buyer problems with warranty service constitute a "horrendous" percentage of complaints they receive. "If you've got a problem with a new car, most of the time it's your tough luck. The bastards won't give an inch" is how one consumer group director describes the situation.

Part of the problem is that United States auto makers do not fully reimburse dealers for their cost of making repairs, often haggle about time spent on repairs, and "disallow" warranty repairs the dealer has made in good faith. Dealers also complain that the manufacturers are "slow pay" when it comes to reimbursing them for warranty work.

Some dealers try to fight the manufacturer-controlled system by adding a bit of extra time to whatever amount was required to accomplish the work—just to break even. Unfortunately, this adds up to inconvenience and expense for the buyers of American-made cars.

Throughout this section we've tried to help you *avoid* having to go to small claims court—through smart buying, through knowledge of your warranty rights, and through learning the art and technique of successful complaining. However, it just might seem that now, finally, if your complaint is still unresolved, the time has come to take the company to court.

But if your problem is with a *product*, not a service such as construction work or auto repairs, there may yet remain one last step in avoiding litigation—that final step is your *Revocation of Acceptance* as provided for by law under provisions of the **Uniform Commercial Code.**

Revocation of acceptance doesn't apply to all product purchases—not to used items, for example—but it does apply to enough of your purchases so that in almost every instance where you have a substantial problem with a product you've bought from a merchant or manufacturer, you can revoke your acceptance and demand a full refund.

Sample Letter—Initial Complaint

DAVID R. LEWIS
406 AVENIDA PRESIDIO
SAN CLEMENTE, CALIFORNIA   92672

November 1, 1984

Mr. Dan Rogers, President

XYZ Motors, Inc.

24775 Imperial Way

Stadium, California   90313

Dear Mr. Rogers:

I am writing to ask that you make prompt arrangements for repair of the automatic transmission on my 1984 Grand Slam Coupe, purchased new from you on September 23.

Upon taking delivery of the car it was immediately apparent that the transmission would not shift into high gear. I returned the car to your shop the following day, September 24, and described the problem to your service manager, Mr. Philip Driver. Your shop kept the car three days, and Mr. Driver phoned me on September 27 to say that it was repaired and ready to go.

After two days the transmission again ceased to shift into high gear. The car has been back in your shop with this same problem a total of four times--on September 24 and on October 3, 9, and 28--and it still fails to operate properly.

The above defect is a great inconvenience and so far has resulted in more than $175 of auto rental costs directly related to the time the car has been in your shop and unavailable for my work.

Enclosed you will find copies of the four work orders related to the transmission defect, plus auto rental receipts for the cost of a replacement car.

Initial Complaint (*Continued*)

Mr. Dan Rogers
November 1, 1984
Page 2

 I feel that you have an obligation to make prompt and proper repair of the transmission, and since my next visit will be the fifth to your shop in an effort to obtain service, I feel that you should provide me with a replacement auto until such time as you have accomplished repairs.

 Please contact me no later than Friday, November 10.

Sincerely,

David R. Lewis

David R. Lewis

Sample Letter—Follow-up Correspondence

DAVID R. LEWIS
406 AVENIDA PRESIDIO
SAN CLEMENTE, CALIFORNIA   92672

November 15, 1984

Mr. Harlow Sputtering, President

Goliath Motors Corporation

Goliath Building

Detroit, Michigan   48555

Dear Mr. Sputtering:

I am writing in an effort to solve a problem I am experiencing with one of your dealers, XYZ Motors, Inc., of Stadium, California.

Since taking delivery of a new, 1984 Grand Slam Coupe from XYZ Motors on September 23, I have been forced to return the car for service on four occasions due to a detective transmission that will not shift into high gear. XYZ Motors appears to be either unable or unwilling to fix the problem.

I have enclosed copies of the four XYZ Motors work orders plus a copy of my letter to Mr. Dan Rogers, which has gone unanswered. Please have a responsible official of Goliath Motors contact me no later than November 30 with respect to arranging repairs on my car.

Sincerely,

David R Lewis

David R. Lewis

cc: Williams, Matthews and Myer

Goliath Motors zone office, Los Angeles, California

Mr. Dan Rogers, XYZ Motors, Inc., Stadium, California

Sample Letter—Third-party Organization

ELIZABETH T. LEWIS
406 AVENIDA PRESIDIO
SAN CLEMENTE, CALIFORNIA 92672

June 6, 1984

Ms. Bernice T. Bradley
Executive Vice President
National Association of
   Outerwear Manufacturers
1735 K Street, N.W.
Washington, D.C.   20006

Dear Ms. Bradley:

I am writing in an effort to resolve a problem with one of your members, Sunnyvale Rainwear Crafters, of Salton City, California.

On April 2, 1984, I purchased a "parchment tan," size 12 "Hi-n-Dri" raincoat from the Sunnyvale Rainwear store at 214 Rodeo Drive, Beverly Hills, California.

Each time I have worn the coat in the rain, water has readily passed through the material, allowing my clothing to become very wet--just as though the fabric had never been treated to repel water.

I returned the coat to the store manager, Ms. Lisa Domel, on April 14, explaining the problem. She told me that "this is very unusual" and that she would have to return the coat to the head office in order to "have it tested" since it was entirely possible that I had "damaged the fabric in some way."

I have since visited the store on April 24, May 7, and May 21 and each time have been informed by Ms. Domel that she has received no word from the head office.

Third-party Organization (*Continued*)

Ms. Bernice T. Bradley
June 6, 1984
Page 2

I am sure that the N.A.O.M. desires good relations between consumers and
its members and hope that your association may assist me in resolving this
problem. A photocopy of my sales receipt is enclosed.

Please telephone me at 717-223-7756 if you have any questions.

Sincerely,

Elizabeth T. Lewis

Elizabeth T. Lewis

cc: Ms. Lisa Domel
     Sunnyvale Rainwear, Inc.
     214 Rodeo Drive
     Beverly Hills, California 90213

35 Meeting (and Using) the Uniform Commercial Code

The **Uniform Commercial Code (UCC)**, adopted between 1958 and 1968 by all states except Louisiana, came about through the need for a uniform code to regulate all aspects of commercial transactions. Previously, differences in various states' business and commercial codes made settlement of disputes between buyers and sellers in different states difficult, and sometimes almost impossible, to resolve in court.

The code came into being as a result of the cooperative effort of the National Conference of Commissioners on Uniform State Laws and the American Law Institute, and was offered to the states for consideration in 1956.

Massachusetts was the first state to put the UCC into effect, in 1958. The last was Mississippi, having enacted legislation calling for it to take effect on April 1, 1968. Arizona, Idaho, and South Carolina also put the code into effect that year on January 1. (See pages 119–120 for a table listing each state's effective date for the Uniform Commercial Code, as well as the appropriate statutory provisions.)

Under a few key provisions of the UCC, which we're going to quote in all their stirring detail on the pages that follow, you can return a defective product to the seller and obtain a full refund.

The UCC also makes it possible for you to obtain reimbursement for removal and storage of the item until its return is accepted, and to be reimbursed by the seller for consequential damages caused by a defective product—an important provision, since consequential damages (brought about by a defective heater that set your house on fire, for example) could be far greater than the mere cost of replacing or repairing the defective product.

When cases involving violations of the code have gone to trial, consumers who've won favorable judgments have also been awarded court costs and attorney's fees.

So there's an ample war chest of motivations you can use under provisions of the Uniform Commercial Code that can induce a seller to give you your money back for a bad product as soon as he learns:

1. That you know exactly what your rights are.
2. That you have a valid case.
3. That you intend to be persistent.

You can forcefully make all of these points in one relatively simple step using Form 36.1 (page F217)—once you have a working knowledge of the six UCC sections on the following pages. They're written with the lawyer's natural desire to provide for *every* contingency, which sometimes leads to writing that is about as interesting as reading a set of operating instructions, which, in a way, is what they are—operating instructions for the law.

Much of the seeming ambiguity and a lot of what might be confusing has been fairly well clarified by court decisions, which we'll present following the relevant sections of the UCC (emphasis ours):

UNIFORM COMMERCIAL CODE

Sec. 2.314. Implied Warranty: Merchantability; Usage of Trade

(a) Unless excluded or modified (Section 2.316), a warranty that the goods shall be merchantable* is implied in a contract for their sale *if the seller is a merchant with respect to goods of that kind.* Under this section the serving for value of food or drink to be consumed either on the premises or elsewhere is a sale.

(b) Goods to be merchantable must be at least such as

  (1) pass without objection in the trade under the contract description; and

  (2) in the case of fungible† goods, are of fair average quality within the description; and

  (3) *are fit for the ordinary purposes for which such goods are used;* and

  (4) run, within the variations permitted by the agreement, of even kind, quality and quantity within each unit and among all units involved; and

  (5) are adequately contained, packaged, and labeled as the agreement may require; and

  (6) *conform to the promises or affirmations of fact made on the container or label if any.*

(c) Unless excluded or modified (Section 2.316) other implied warranties may arise from [the] course of dealing or usage of trade.

Note: An individual making an *isolated* sale of goods would not be defined as a "merchant" within the scope of this section, therefore no warranty of merchantability results.‡

*Merchantable—having at least an ordinary or average quality, being reasonably fit for the general purpose for which an item is manufactured and sold.

†Fungible—those goods which are assumed to be uniform; any one unit equivalent to any other. Grain and gravel of a given kind, for example, would be considered fungible goods.

‡Notes on pages 112 through 114 are adapted from West Publishing Company's *Uniform Commercial Code Annotated.*

Sec. 2.315. Implied Warranty: Fitness for Particular Purpose

Where the seller *at the time of contracting* has reason to know *any particular purpose for which the goods are required AND that the buyer is relying on the seller's skill and judgment to select or furnish suitable goods*, there is unless excluded or modified under the next section an implied warranty that the goods *shall be fit for such purpose.*

Note: When a buyer specifies a particular brand, he or she is not relying upon the seller's skill and judgment, thus no warranty under this section would apply.

Sec. 2.316. Exclusion or Modification of Warranties

(a) Words or conduct relevant to the creation of an express warranty and words or conduct tending to negate or limit [a] warranty shall be construed wherever reasonable as consistent with each other; but subject to the provisions of this chapter on parol or extrinsic evidence (Section 2.202) *negation or limitation is inoperative to the extent that such construction is unreasonable.*

(b) Subject to Subsection (c), to exclude or modify the implied warranty of merchantability or any part of it the language must mention *merchantability* and in the case of a writing must be *conspicuous*, and to exclude or modify *any* implied warranty of fitness the exclusion *must be by a writing and conspicuous.* Language to exclude all implied warranties of fitness is sufficient if it states, for example, that "There are no warranties which extend beyond the description on the face hereof."

(c) Notwithstanding Subsection (b)
    (1) unless the circumstances indicate otherwise, all implied warranties are excluded by expressions like "as is", "with all faults" or other language which in common understanding calls the buyer's attention to the exclusion of warranties and makes plain that there is no implied warranty; and
    (2) when the buyer before entering into the contract *has examined the goods or the sample or model as fully as he desired or has refused to examine the goods there is no implied warranty with regard to defects which an examination ought in the circumstances to have revealed to him; and*
    (3) an implied warranty can also be excluded or modified by [the] course of dealing or course of performance or usage of trade.

(d) Remedies for breach of warranty can be limited in accordance with the provisions of this chapter on liquidation or limitation of damages and on contractual modification of remedy (Sections 2.718 and 2.719).

(e) The implied warranties of merchantability and fitness shall not be applicable to the furnishing of human blood, blood plasma, or other human tissue or organs from a blood bank or reservoir of such other tissues or organs. Such blood, blood plasma or tissue or organs shall not for the purpose of this Title be considered commodities subject to sale or barter, but shall be considered medical services.

Note: A professional buyer examining a product in his field will be expected to have, during the course of his examination of the product, noted all the defects that a professional ought to have discovered, while a nonprofessional or consumer would be held only for having noted such defects as a layman would reasonably be expected to observe.

Sec. 2.608. Revocation of Acceptance in Whole or in Part

(a) The buyer may revoke his acceptance of a lot or commercial unit whose non-conformity *substantially impairs* its value to him if he has accepted it
    (1) on the reasonable assumption that its non-conformity would be cured and it has not been seasonably cured; or
    (2) without discovery of such non-conformity if his acceptance was reasonably induced either by the difficulty of discovery before acceptance or by the seller's assurances.

(b) Revocation of acceptance *must occur within a reasonable time* after the buyer discovers or *should* have discovered the ground for it and before any substantial change in condition of the goods which is not caused by their own defects. It is not effective until the buyer notifies the seller of it.

(c) A buyer who so revokes has the same rights and duties with regard to the goods as if he had rejected them.

Note: Since revocation of acceptance will normally only be resorted to after attempts at repair or adjustment have failed, the reasonable time period noted in Subsection (b) has been determined in many cases to extend:

- Beyond the time within which notice must be given.
- Beyond the time for discovery of nonconformity after acceptance.
- Beyond any contractual time for rejection after tender.

Sec. 2.715. Buyer's Incidental and Consequential Damages

(a) Incidental damages resulting from the *seller's* breach include expenses reasonably incurred in inspection, receipt, transportation and care and custody of goods *rightfully rejected,* any commercially reasonable charges, expenses and commissions in connection with effecting cover and any other reasonable expense incident to the delay or other breach.

(b) Consequential damages resulting from the seller's breach include
    (1) any loss resulting from general or particular requirements and needs of which the seller *at the time of contracting had reason to know* and which could not reasonably be prevented by cover or otherwise; and
    (2) injury to person or property proximately resulting from any breach of warranty [of merchantability or warranty of fitness for a particular purpose].

Note: *Particular* needs of the buyer must generally be made known to the seller, but *general* needs must only rarely be made known to charge the seller with knowledge of the buyer's needs. The buyer's need for merchantable goods is assumed to be known by the seller.

Sec. 2.719. Contractual Modification or Limitation of Remedy

(a) Subject to the provisions of Subsections (b) and (c) of this section and of the preceding section on liquidation and limitation of damages,

(1) the agreement may provide for remedies in addition to or in substitution for those provided in this chapter and may limit or alter the measure of damages recoverable under this chapter, as by limiting the buyer's remedies to [the] return of the goods and repayment of the price or to [the] repair and replacement of nonconforming goods or parts; and

(2) resort to a remedy as provided is optional unless the remedy is expressly agreed to be exclusive, in which case it is the *sole* remedy.

(b) Where circumstances cause an exclusive or limited remedy *to fail of its essential purpose*, remedy may be had as [is] provided by this Title.

(c) Consequential* damages may be limited or excluded *unless* the limitation or exclusion is *unconscionable.†* Limitation of consequential damages for injury to the person in the case of *consumer goods is prima facie unconscionable* but limitation of damages where the loss is commercial is not.

Let us now consider the major rights and obligations that the previous sections of the code set forth as law.

Section 2.314 states, in subparagraph (b), (3), that a product you buy has to be fit for the purpose for which such products are ordinarily used. A television set has to perform in the ways that a television set is reasonably expected to perform. BUT, under subparagraph (a), for there to be a warranty of merchantability you must have purchased the product from a **merchant** who normally sells goods of that kind. There is no warranty of merchantability if you buy the TV set from an individual through a classified ad or a 3" × 5" card on a bulletin board.

The product also has to do at least what the label or text on the container says it will do. If a cleaner container states the product will allow you to "rinse away grime" after you've let something soak in it for ten minutes, then you have to be able to rinse away the grime after your grimy pot or whatever has soaked in the cleaner for ten, not thirty, minutes—even though a cleaner that required a thirty-minute soak might otherwise be determined to be "merchantable" under this section.

*Consequential—resulting from or an outgrowth of a defect in the non-conforming goods.

†Unconscionable—unscrupulous, unreasonable, beyond the conscience of a reasonable, scrupulous person.

Though the seller often has recourse to the manufacturer (in the case of a defect originating in the factory, for example), *your* recourse is almost always initially to the seller, who is almost never in a position to pass the buck to the manufacturer, telling you to "write to the factory" or some such.

Section 2.315 says that if at the time of purchase you tell the salesperson about your particular need and the salesperson suggests a particular product, which you buy, then the *implied warranty of fitness for a particular purpose* applies and you can get your money back if the product fails to meet that particular purpose, even though the product might otherwise be merchantable.

Shoes, for example, are ordinarily used for walking, but if you go into a store and tell the salesperson that you want jogging shoes for running *and* you follow the recommendation of the salesperson, then the shoes must serve for running. However, if you go into the store and say, "I want a pair of Brand X running shoes," and buy them, no warranty of suitability applies since you did not rely upon the seller's skill and judgment in making the purchase.

So if you buy a specialized product, even though you know what you want, see if you can, perhaps by asking the right questions, get the salesperson to recommend the brand you want to buy anyway. If the product costs a lot of money, like an underwater camera, it wouldn't hurt to have a friend along.

Incidentally, the principle of warranty of suitability for a particular purpose can be used to find really well-made, durable products if you're willing to pay the price. They still "make them like they used to"; it's just that they've been priced out of the ordinary market.

If, for example, you live on a farm miles from nowhere and can't get repair service, or if you live someplace like New York City where appliance service is hard to come by, expensive, and often not very good anyway, consider buying a *commercial* washing machine instead of one manufactured for household use. A machine made for use in a laundromat will be much more durable than a household model due to the more stringent warranty of suitability for *that* particular purpose.

The same benefits could be gained by purchasing a commercial food freezer or blender or other appliance. There is a commercial grade available, though not widely advertised, for almost *every* product you can think of. Trade journals of the business or profession that use them are a good source of names.

Section 2.316 states that any negation or limitation upon a written warranty is inoperative to the extent that it is unreasonable and that any written limitation with respect to the warranty of merchantability must contain the term "merchantability" and must be conspicuous. Also, any exclusion or modification of any implied warranty of fitness must be in writing and conspicuous. For a writing to be "conspicuous" within the definition of this title of the UCC, it must be larger than, or a different color from, the type used for the remainder of the warranty.

Section 2.608 states that you can revoke your acceptance of any product that is defective to the extent that its purpose is *substantially* impaired. You can't revoke your acceptance of a TV set just because the light in the channel selector won't work.

Under this section you can also revoke acceptance of a product, obviously defective upon delivery or installation, that you kept, relying upon the seller's assurances that the defect would be repaired. Of course, you can revoke your acceptance if a product has a substantial defect that you could not reasonably discover in the store or when it was delivered. BUT, under subparagraph (b), you must revoke your acceptance within a reasonable time.

As a practical matter you should ordinarily give the seller three or four opportunities to repair or replace the product before you start taking steps to revoke acceptance. Make sure that you get each repair or exchange attempt "on the record," either by making or confirming it in writing. Also be sure to report promptly to the seller, while sending written confirmation, all unsuccessful repair attempts so that you will have good evidence for revocation of acceptance or a lawsuit in small claims court.

Section 2.715 allows you to collect for consequential damages caused by a defective product and, among other things, to collect for the cost of removal and storage of goods rightfully rejected.

Under subparagraph (b), (2), consequential damages could range from tearing your clothing on the sharp, unfinished edge of a desk to the destruction of your house caused by a gas heater shown to be substantially defective in a manner *that could reasonably be expected to have caused the explosion.* Consequential damages also include injury resulting from a substantially defective product.

Section 2.719 provides that an agreement (or warranty) may limit your claim for damages to repair or replacement of the product. BUT, under subparagraph (b), where the remedy of repair or replacement *fails of its essential purpose,* that is, if after a reasonable number of tries they're still unable to fix it and will not exchange it for a new one, you can get your money back no matter what the warranty says and no matter what the seller tells you.

WARNING: Subparagraph (c) points out that the agreement (warranty) CAN exclude manufacturer's and seller's liability for consequential damages. Courts have determined that, with respect to a written warranty, any exclusion or limitation of consequential damages must be part of the warranty and must be conspicuous.

Here's a typical clause limiting liability for consequential damages:

Our obligations with respect to this product are limited to replacement or repair of defective parts and equipment, or at our option, to refund the purchase price without further liability. We are not responsible for consequential damages.

Regardless of what the warranty or sales agreement says or what the seller or manufacturer tells you, liability for consequential damages for *personal injury* cannot be waived by prior agreement, as any attempt to do so would be unconscionable according to subparagraph (c).

Guidelines and instructions pertaining to the proper completion and use of the legal form **Notice of Revocation of Acceptance** (Form 36.1) may be found in the following chapter. But before we go on to that form and describe how to use it, let's briefly scan some court decisions—court decisions that can help give you a feel for the legal lay of the land as far as revocation of acceptance and consequential damages are concerned and that will provide you with some clues as to how a judge might decide your case.

These decisions, handed down by different judges in different states, aren't necessarily consistent since judges do not always see the law in exactly the same way. Furthermore, lawyers write for lawyers, and legal writings and court decisions tend to compress the language to save space. In an attempt to clarify things just a bit, we have sometimes added our own words in brackets, added articles, made use of *italics,* and changed punctuation to make some sentences easier to follow. [Decisions were selected from West Publishing Company's *Uniform Commercial Code Annotated.*]

The purpose of this section establishing [the] implied warranty is that [an] enterprise which causes losses should shift them from individual [buyer] victims and distribute them widely on those [sellers and manufacturers] who benefit from activities of enterprise. (1964)

Generally, no implied warranty exists as to characteristics or defects of property which are *obvious and discoverable by ordinary examination* . . . (1962)

Goods purchased by sample must substantially conform to the sample and must be merchantable. (1958)

Warranty of merchantability of goods sold is applicable only when goods are bought by *description* from a seller who deals in such goods. There is *no sale by description* when the goods are present and there is an opportunity [for the buyer] to inspect. (1963)

A dealer who sells articles which ordinarily are used in only one way impliedly warrants fitness for use in that particular way, and such implied warranty is one of merchantability. (1960)

Implied warranty of merchantability means that a product is reasonably fit for the purpose intended; it does not imply absolute perfection and there is no duty on the part of the manufacturer to furnish tools which will not wear out. (1968)

The manufacturer of products is strictly liable in tort to the ultimate consumer for injuries or damages resulting from defective products, even where only damage to [the] article sold or to other property of the consumer is involved. (1965)

The manufacturer is responsible for economics or commercial losses where the product is not suitable for [the] use for which it was advertised. (1967)

To recover from the *manufacturer* on [the] theory of implied warranty, it is necessary to establish that there was a defect in the object sold *as it left the manufacturer.* (1967)

The implied warranty will not be waived under a clause in a contract indicating that all agreements are set forth in the written contract and [that] no warranty is attached thereto except as expressly set forth.   (1959)

Whether plaintiff's [the buyer's] action against the manufacturer was for negligence or breach of sales warranty, plaintiff [the buyer] was required to establish, by proof greater than mere surmise or conjecture, that his injury resulted from an unreasonably dangerous condition of the product involved for which the manufacturer was responsible.   (1964)

The buyer may not recover from the seller for consequences that reasonably could have been avoided by the buyer.   (1961)

Damages for breach of warranty are not recoverable for harm that [the buyer] plaintiff should have foreseen and could have avoided by reasonable effort without undue risk, expense or humiliation.   (1959)

An express warranty ordinarily excludes an implied warranty, since the seller has a right to define his liability and provide for the measure of damages or the manner of fulfilling the warranty.*   (1921)

The knowledgeable use of a defective article deprives [a buyer who is the suing] party from consequential damages upon breach of warranty.   (1963)

It was no defense [by the defendant seller] in [an] action against [the seller] cart vendor for injuries sustained by customer [the plaintiff] when his tooth broke off as he bit into a hard-crusted sandwich sold to him by the vendor for lunch, that the tooth was weak, since the vendor took the customer as it found him.† (1963)

When it is shown that a defective product came in a sealed container, it is inferable that the product reached the injured consumer without substantial change in condition in which it was sold.   (1967)

Where a householder purchased a household stepladder, the purpose was impliedly made known to the seller by the very nature of the article and by circumstances surrounding the transaction.   (1963)

Where the sale of steel was "as is" and without warrant, law of implied warranties that goods shall correspond to description was inapplicable.   (1962)

A retailer who sells a hair preparation in a sealed can does so under implied warranty that the product is suited and fit for the purpose for which it was manufactured and sold.   (1963)

Where alleged disclaimer of implied warranties in a purchase order was in smaller type than the rest of the purchase order and thus was not conspicuous, implied warranties were not withdrawn as a matter of law.   (1966)

Where it would have cost several hundred dollars to remove a defective building stone from the purchasers' house and would have left them without their money or any covering for the house, the buyers could both rescind [their acceptance] and recover damages. (1959)

Where [a] provision of [a] sale contract that [a] warranty therein was in lieu of any and all other warranties, express or implied, was merely in the same color and size of other type in the contract, [the] provision was not "conspicuous" . . . and was ineffective as a disclaimer.   (1964)

For a breach of the seller's implied warranty of merchantability, the buyer may recover the loss of profits resulting from the breach, if [the loss of profits is] not speculative.   (1964)

Punitive damages are not recoverable for a breach of warranty.   (1958)

---

*That's the way it *used* to be. The principle of implied warranty wasn't born yesterday; it was only through continuing consumer action and, finally, the UCC that implied warranty became the force that it is today.

†We warned you that some of this was gobbledygook. What the decision means is that if you bite into food and something in it breaks your tooth, you have a pretty good chance of collecting from the seller if you go to court—at least if your case is heard by the judge who rendered this decision.

36 Revocation of Acceptance: Getting Rid of a Lemon

You now know the important provisions of the Uniform Commercial Code well enough to put them to work for you. Our form **Notice of Revocation of Acceptance** (Form 36.1, page F217) provides the framework for revoking your acceptance of a defective product in a way that presents your complaint and your demands such that the seller is well aware that you know your rights, have a valid complaint, and are determined to press for a prompt resolution of your problem.

The form for **Revocation of Acceptance**, by the way, very closely follows the design, format, and tenor of legal documents prepared by lawyers, used within the court system, and often served by sheriffs, marshals, and officers of the court. This chapter will provide you with guidelines for completing the form, as well as two sample completed forms for your perusal. First, however, carefully read the following instructions pertaining to the *how's* and *when's* of signing, copying, and serving your **Notice of Revocation of Acceptance**.

BEFORE AND AFTER COMPLETING THE FORM

Make a photocopy of the blank form on page F217. Most copy centers now have equipment that can duplicate the form on both sides just as it appears here. If you cannot locate a copy center that can duplicate the form on both sides, find a copy machine that uses paper from trays. Run one side of the form, place the one-sided copy on the top of the paper tray facedown, turn over your original from this book, and run the machine again—you'll have a two-sided copy from a one-sided copier.

When you've completed the form, make six copies **before** signing it. Then:

1. Sign your *original* and "serve" it on the seller or seller's representative, such as the store manager.
2. As soon as you've served your original, sign one of the copies and send it via *registered mail, return receipt requested*, to the owner of the business. Send this second copy even though you may have served the original on the owner as well.
3. Sign a third copy and mail it to your attorney, if you have one.
4. Sign the other copies for later use, possibly in small claims court.

If the seller hasn't responded as demanded by the dates specified, you may want to consider taking your case to small claims court (see Section VII).

GUIDELINES FOR COMPLETING YOUR REVOCATION OF ACCEPTANCE

The following paragraphs for revoking acceptance for failure to meet the implied *warranty of merchantability* and/or the implied warranty of *suitability for a particular purpose* should be used to complete your form. In accordance with our directions, type the Revocation's four key sections—PLEASE TAKE NOTICE, STATEMENT OF COMPLAINT, DEMAND, and PLEASE TAKE FURTHER NOTICE. Required information pertaining to your particular product and situation should be inserted within the paragraphs as indicated by the bracketed instructions.

We are assuming that by the time things reach the point where you must revoke acceptance, what you're really interested in is a full refund so you can take your business elsewhere—although under the UCC you could ask for an exchange in lieu of getting your money back.

PLEASE TAKE NOTICE

If a product fails to meet the implied warranty of **merchantability**, type the following paragraphs at the start of your Revocation:

PLEASE TAKE NOTICE:

Pursuant to Sec. 2.608 of the Uniform Commercial Code, [INSERT APPROPRIATE STATE CITATION, SEE PAGE 119], I hereby revoke my acceptance of [DESCRIBE PRODUCT], purchased for [WRITE OUT AMOUNT AND USE FIGURES AS ON A CHECK] from [NAME AND ADDRESS OF SELLER] on [DATE OF PURCHASE].

The aforementioned [NAME OF PRODUCT] is substantially impaired within the definition of Sec. 2-314 of the Code, and attempt to remedy defects under provisions of the warranty has failed "of its essential purpose," Sec. 2.719 (b).

On the other hand, type the following text for revocation of acceptance of a product that fails to meet the implied warranty of **fitness for a particular purpose**:

PLEASE TAKE NOTICE:

Pursuant to Sec. 2.315 of the Uniform Commercial Code, [INSERT APPROPRIATE STATE CITATION, SEE PAGE 119], I hereby revoke my acceptance of [DESCRIBE PRODUCT] purchased for [WRITE AMOUNT AND USE FIGURES AS ON A CHECK] from [NAME AND ADDRESS OF SELLER] on [DATE OF PURCHASE].

The aforementioned [NAME OF PRODUCT] is substantially unfit for the particular purpose of [DESCRIBE
PURPOSE], for which it was purchased in reliance
upon the skill and judgment of [NAME OF SALESPERSON],
a salesperson at [NAME OF SELLER'S BUSINESS].

STATEMENT OF COMPLAINT

The following guidelines will aid you in writing a
STATEMENT OF COMPLAINT for a product that
fails to meet the implied warranty of **merchantability**.

1. Describe the substantial defect and how it impairs
   the product. Also relate your attempts to have the
   product repaired. Give dates of repair attempts
   and note all unsuccessful attempts, broken promises, and "no shows" by repair people.
2. Include the names and dates of contact with all
   company personnel with whom you discussed the
   problem.
3. Also note any incidental or consequential damages
   and include dollar estimates of the costs.

Use these guidelines for a STATEMENT OF
COMPLAINT for a product that fails to meet the
implied warranty of **suitability for a particular purpose**:

1. Describe the manner in which the product is unfit
   for the particular purpose for which it was bought.
2. Describe as accurately as possible the recommendation of the salesperson advising the purchase of the product.
3. Relate any attempts to exchange the product for a
   more suitable one or to obtain a refund.

DEMAND

In this third section of your Revocation, use the paragraphs below if your product is small (such as a
toaster) and can easily be returned to the store:

DEMAND:

No later than [SET REASONABLE DATE], I must receive a full refund of the purchase price of the
aforementioned [NAME PRODUCT], which I hereby offer
to return to you.

You may telephone me at [TELEPHONE NUMBER] between the hours of [GIVE APPROPRIATE HOURS] to make
arrangements to accept return of the product and
issue a full refund.

For a large product, such as a washing machine,
that must be disconnected and picked up by the
seller, type these paragraphs:

DEMAND:

No later than [SET REASONABLE DATE], you must
pick up the aforementioned [NAME PRODUCT] from my
[HOME, OFFICE, OR OTHER LOCATION] at [ADDRESS].

You may telephone me at [TELEPHONE NUMBER] between the hours of [GIVE APPROPRIATE HOURS] to make
arrangements to pick up the [NAME PRODUCT].

I must receive a full refund of the purchase
price no later than five working days after your
acceptance of my revocation as evidenced by your removal of the [NAME PRODUCT] from the aforementioned
premises.

PLEASE TAKE FURTHER NOTICE

Retype the following paragraphs for a product that
fails to meet the implied warranty of **merchantability**:

PLEASE TAKE FURTHER NOTICE:

If the above demand has not been satisfied by
the date specified, I shall commence proceedings
against you under Sec. 2.314, Sec. 2.608, and Sec.
2.719 of the Uniform Commercial Code.

Pursuant to Sec. 2.715, I may be awarded costs
of removal, transportation, and storage of a rightfully rejected product, plus other reasonable expenses incident to your delay or any other breach
of the above-cited provisions of the Code.

I shall also be entitled to an award of attorney's fees in any judgment proceedings against you.

Note: You may choose not to employ the second
paragraph above, relevant to Sec. 2.715, if the product is a small item such as a blender or other lightweight appliance.

For a product that fails to meet the implied warranty of **fitness for a particular purpose**, use these
paragraphs:

PLEASE TAKE FURTHER NOTICE:

If the above demand has not been satisfied by the
date specified, I shall commence proceedings against
you under Sec. 2.315, Sec. 2.608, and Sec. 2.719 of
the Uniform Commercial Code.

Pursuant to Sec. 2.715, I may be awarded costs
of removal, transportation, and storage of a rightfully rejected product, plus other reasonable expenses incident to your delay or any breach of the
above-cited provisions of the Code.

I shall also be entitled to an award of attorney's
fees in any judgment proceedings against you.

Note: You may choose not to employ the second
paragraph above, relevant to Sec. 2.715, if the product is a small item such as a blender or other lightweight appliance.

Front Panel

Now go to the front panel of the form (printed at the
base of the back side of the form) and complete the
portion to be filled in under *IN THE MATTER OF*.
This portion of the form is really a condensed version
of the PLEASE TAKE NOTICE paragraph inside.

For an appliance failing to meet the implied
warranty of **merchantability**, *IN THE MATTER OF*
should read:

IN THE MATTER OF

Revocation of acceptance
of substantially defective
[PRODUCT NAME] pursuant to
Sec. 2.314 and Sec. 2.608
of the Uniform Commercial
Code, [INSERT STATE CITATION].

Whereas, the revocation of acceptance for a product
failing to meet the implied warranty of **fitness for a
particular purpose** should read:

IN THE MATTER OF

```
Revocation of acceptance
of substantially defective
[PRODUCT NAME] pursuant to
Sec. 2.315 and Sec. 2.608
of the Uniform Commercial
Code, [INSERT STATE CITATION].
```

Under *TO*, fill in the name of the owner or manager of the store, plus the name and address as shown on the store's business license. This information can be obtained from the city or county licensing bureau.

TO

```
Arthur C. Smedley, President
Art's Appliance City, Inc.
2341 North Enterprise St.
Bloomingdale, PA 19168
```

In the case of an individual ownership, list the owner's name as:

```
Arthur C. Smedley, Owner
```

or

```
Arthur C. Smedley d/b/a*
```

A partner's name would be followed by "Partner."

Two completed samples of the **Notice of Revocation of Acceptance**—the first for a washing machine that fails to meet the implied warranty of **merchantability**, and the second for a washing machine that fails to meet the implied warranty of **fitness**

for a particular purpose—can be found on pages 121–124.

Using State UCC Citations

When completing both the first section (PLEASE TAKE NOTICE) and the front panel of your Revocation, insert the appropriate citation for your own state's enactment of the UCC from the table below.

As a resident of Georgia, for example, you would state:

PLEASE TAKE NOTICE:

```
Pursuant to Sec. 2.608 of the Uniform Commercial
Code, Ga. Code Ann. 109A-1-101 to 109A-10-106, I
hereby revoke my acceptance of . . .
```

Or if you were a resident of Oklahoma:

PLEASE TAKE NOTICE:

```
Pursuant to Sec. 2.608 of the Uniform Commercial
Code, 12A Okl.St.Ann. SS 1-101 to 10-104, I hereby
revoke my acceptance of . . .
```

Although all of the states in the following table have adopted the Uniform Commercial Code, some do provide additional protection. Kansas, Maine, Maryland, Massachusetts, Vermont, and West Virginia prohibit manufacturers from imposing *any* limitation upon the duration of an implied warranty. In all, more than half the states have some kind of implied warranty provision that extends beyond the duration of any written warranty buyers may receive.

UNIFORM COMMERCIAL CODE

State	Date	Statutory Citation
Alabama	1967	Code of Ala., Ttl. 7A SS 1-101 to 10-104
Alaska	1963	A.S. SS 45.05.002 - 45.05.794
Arizona	1968	A.R.S. SS 44-2201 to 44-3202
Arkansas	1962	Ark. Stats. SS 85-1-101 to 85-9-507
California	1965	West's Ann. Comm. C. 1101 to 10104
Colorado	1966	C.R.S. '73, SS 4-1-101 to 4-11-102
Connecticut	1961	C.G.S.A. SS 42a-1-101 to 42a-10-104
Delaware	1967	6 DEL C. SS 1-101 to 10-104
District of Columbia	1965	D.C.C.E. SS 28:1-101 to 28:10-104
Florida	1967	F.S.A. SS 671.1-101 to 680.10-105
Georgia	1964	Ga. Code Ann. 109A-1-101 to 109A-10-106
Hawaii	1967	HRS 490:10-101 to 490:10-104
Idaho	1968	I.C.S. 28-1-101 et seq.
Illinois	1962	S.H.A. ch. 26, SS 1-101 to 11-108
Indiana	1964	Burns' Ass. St. SS 19-1-101 to 19-507

(continued)

*d/b/a—"doing business as," a phrase commonly used in many parts of the United States.

UNIFORM COMMERCIAL CODE (*Continued*)

State	Date	Statutory Citation
Iowa	1966	I.C.A. SS 554.1101 to 554.10109
Kansas	1966	K.S.A. SS 84-1-101 to 84-10-104
Kentucky	1960	KRS 355.1-101 to 355.10-102
Maine	1964	11 M.R.S.A. SS 1-101 to 9-507
Maryland	1964	Code 1957 art 95b, SS 1-101 to 10-104
Massachusetts	1958	M.G.L.A. c. 106, SS 1-101 to 9-507
Michigan	1964	M.C.L.A. SS 440.1101 to 440.9994
Minnesota	1966	M.S.A. SS 336.1-101 to 336.10-105
Mississippi	1968	Code 1972, SS 75-1-101 to 75-10-104
Missouri	1965	V.A.M.S. SS 400.1-101 to 400.10-102
Montana	1965	R.C.M. 1947, SS 87A-1-101 to 87A-10-103
Nebraska	1965	Neb.U.C.C. SS 1-101 to 10-104
Nevada	1967	N.R.S. 92.001 to 92.196
New Hampshire	1961	RSA 382-A:1-101 to -29-A:9-507
New Jersey	1963	N.J.S.A. 12A:1-101 to 12A:10-106
New Mexico	1962	1953 Comp. SS 50A-1-101 to 50A-9-507
New York	1964	McKinney's Uniform Commerical Code, SS 1-101 to 10-105
North Carolina	1967	G.S. SS 25-1-101 to 25-10-107
North Dakota	1966	NDCC 41-01-02 to 41-09-53
Ohio	1962	R.C. SS 1301.01-1309.50
Oklahoma	1963	12A Okl. St. Ann. SS 1-101 to 10-104
Oregon	1963	ORS 71.1010 to 79.5070
Pennsylvania	1964	12A P.S. SS 1-101 to 10-104
Rhode Island	1962	Gen. Laws 1956, SS 6A-1-101 to 6A-9-507
South Carolina	1968	Code 1962, Ttl. 10.1 to 10.10
South Dakota	1967	SDCL 1960 Supp. 1-101 to 10-102
Tennessee	1964	T.C.A. SS 47-1-101 to 47-9-507
Texas	1966	V.T.C.A., Bus & C. SS 1.101 to 9-507
Utah	1966	U.C.A. 1953, 70A-1-101 to 70A-10-104
Vermont	1967	9A V.S.A. SS 1-101 to 9-507
Virgin Islands	1965	T. 11A V.I.C. SS 1-101 to 9-507
Virginia	1966	Code 1950, SS 8.1-101 to 8.11-108
Washington	1967	RCWA SS 62A.1-101 to 62A.10-104
West Virginia	1964	Code 46-1-101 to 46-10-204
Wisconsin	1965	W.S.A. 401.101 to 409.507
Wyoming	1962	W.S. 1957, SS 34:1-101 to 34:10-105

First Sample of Form 36.1/F217

Notice of Revocation of Acceptance

PLEASE TAKE NOTICE:

Pursuant to Sec. 2.608 of the Uniform Commercial Code, 12A P.S. SS 1-101 to 10-104, I hereby revoke my acceptance of American Eagle, Inc., Tangle-Matic washing machine, model No. XL-401, purchased for three hundred and eighty-two dollars ($382.00) from Art's Appliance City, Inc., 2341 North Enterprise Street, Bloomingdale, Pa. 19168, on June 15, 1984.

The aforementioned washing machine is substantially impaired within the definition of Sec. 2.314 of the Code, and attempt to remedy defects under provisions of the warranty has failed "of its essential purpose," Sec. 2.719 (b).

STATEMENT OF COMPLAINT:

The washing machine delivered and installed by Art's Appliance City has never operated properly in that (1) it will not fill to the proper water level and (2) water will not drain from the machine when the wash cycle is completed.

Attempt to secure repair was made by telephone call on June 18, upon which date a serviceman came to inspect the machine and left after remarking, "It sure looks like you got a problem here." Two additional attempts to secure repair were made on June 21 and June 24 when personal visits were made to Art's Appliance City. Two promises by Ms. Louella Snip to "have someone get out to take care of it this afternoon" were not kept, and no serviceman appeared. The machine is not merchantable within the definition of Sec. 2.314 of the Code and all attempts to secure repair have failed, see Sec. 2.719 (b).

DEMAND:

No later than July 15, 1984, you must pick up the aforementioned washing machine from my home at 885 Primrose Path, Bloomingdale, Pennsylvania.

You may telephone me at 479-6433 between the hours of 9 A.M. and 5 P.M. to make arrangements to pick up the washing machine.

I must receive a full refund of the purchase price no later than five working days after your acceptance of my revocation as evidenced by your removal of the washing machine from the aforementioned premises.

First Sample of Form 36.1 (*Continued*)

PLEASE TAKE FURTHER NOTICE:

    If the above demand has not been satisfied by the date specified, I shall commence proceedings against you under Sec. 2.314, Sec. 2.608, and Sec. 2.719 of the Uniform Commercial Code.

    Pursuant to Sec. 2.715, I may be awarded costs of removal, transportation, and storage of a rightfully rejected product, plus other reasonable expenses incident to your delay or any other breach of the above-cited provisions of the Code.

    I shall also be entitled to an award of attorney's fees in any judgment proceedings against you.

Signed: *Lee A. Moorehouse*
Lee A. Moorehouse
885 Primrose Path
Bloomingdale, Pennsylvania 19168

Notice of Revocation of Acceptance

IN THE MATTER OF

Revocation of acceptance of washing machine substantially impaired within the definition of Sec. 2.314 of the Uniform Commercial Code, pursuant to Sec. 2.608 of the Uniform Commercial Code, 12A P.S. SS 1-101 to 10-104.

TO

Arthur C. Smedley, President
Art's Appliance City, Inc.
2341 North Enterprise Street
Bloomingdale, PA 19168

Dated _____ July 5, _____ 19 84 _____

Second Sample of Form 36.1/F217

Notice of Revocation of Acceptance

PLEASE TAKE NOTICE:

 Pursuant to Sec. 2.315 of the Uniform Commercial Code, Ill. S.H.A. ch. 26, SS 1-101 to 11-108, I hereby revoke my acceptance of model MX-1 Tangle-Matic washing machine that I purchased on October 30, 1984, for four hundred and fifty-two dollars ($452.00) from Al's Appliance Heaven, 4593 South Broadway, Aberdeen, Ill. 60919.

 The aforementioned washing machine is substantially unfit for the particular purpose of washing clothes, for which it was purchased in reliance upon the skill and judgment of Elton Wiggins, a salesperson in the employ of Al's Appliance Heaven.

STATEMENT OF COMPLAINT:

 When attempting to use the washer after installation by personnel from Al's Appliance Heaven: (1) the washer failed to fill to the proper level and (2) the machine only operated on "spindry" cycle.

 On November 4, the day after installation, I telephoned your office and described the problem to a woman who identified herself as Jane Friedman and who stated that a serviceman "would be right out." No serviceman arrived on that date.

 On November 5, I again telephoned your office and spoke with a man who identified himself as Hank Harmon, sales manager. Mr. Harmon stated that a serviceman "would be right out." When your serviceman arrived four hours later he inspected the machine and told me, "Gee, you sure got yourself a problem here. I got to talk to the boss." There was no further response to my complaint.

 On November 9, I wrote you a letter detailing the problem with the washer and describing my attempts to obtain repair service. You did not reply to my letter.

DEMAND:

 No later than December 15, 1984, you must pick up the aforementioned washer from my home, 421 Willow Road, Aberdeen, Ill. 60919. You may telephone me at 312-4478 between the hours of 9 A.M. and 5 P.M. to make arrangements to pick up the washer. I must also receive a full refund of the purchase price no later than five (5) working days after your acceptance of my revocation as evidenced by your removal of the washer from the aforementioned premises.

Second Sample of Form 36.1 (*Continued*)

PLEASE TAKE FURTHER NOTICE:

    If the above demand has not been satisfied by the date specified, I shall commence proceedings against you under Sec. 2.315, Sec. 2.608, and Sec. 2.719 of the Uniform Commercial Code.

    Pursuant to Sec. 2.715, I may be awarded the costs of removal, transportation, and storage of a rightfully rejected product, plus other reasonable costs incident to your delay or any other breach of the above-cited provisions of the Code.

    I shall also be entitled to an award of attorney's fees in any judgment proceedings against you.

Signed: *Louis S. Wasserman*

Louis S. Wasserman
421 Willow Road
Aberdeen, Illinois 60919

Notice of Revocation of Acceptance

IN THE MATTER OF

Revocation of acceptance of substantially defective washing machine pursuant to Sec. 2.315 and Sec. 2.608 of the Uniform Commercial Code, Ill. S.H.A. ch. 26, SS 1-101 to 11-108.

TO

Albert J. Higgins d/b/a
Al's Appliance Heaven
4593 South Broadway
Aberdeen, Illinois 60919

Dated _____ November 15, _____ 19 84 _____

37 Friends You Didn't Know You Had

Two of the most effective consumer organizations in the United States are not consumer organizations at all; they are small, low-budget government agencies that administer laws affecting commerce—the Interstate Commerce Commission (ICC) and the Federal Trade Commission (FTC).

Neither agency has the staff nor budget to prosecute individual consumer's claims concerning problems with a product or service, or with a particular retailer or manufacturer; yet, on the basis of information from consumers, they have been able to order unethical businesses to cease unfair, deceptive, and fraudulant practices, have secured refunds for consumers, and have levied fines against the guilty.

One major public benefit of their actions has been their effectiveness in countering, to some degree, the continuing multimillion dollar campaign of industry lobbyists, trade organizations, and corporations working to weaken existing consumer laws and prevent the passage of new legislation that might reduce profits in any way.

FEDERAL TRADE COMMISSION

Although it's not a "consumer" organization—it also protects corporations from each other—the **Federal Trade Commission (FTC)** is the government agency industry most loves to hate. After glancing at a few fairly recent case histories, it is easy to see why.

In January 1978, after numerous consumer complaints and a thorough investigation, a complaint order was issued against the Ford Motor Company charging that Ford knowingly sold cars and trucks with a major defect (piston scuffing) without disclosing the defect to prospective buyers.

In issuing the order, the FTC pointed out that Ford also failed to disclose the existence of a program quietly established to compensate highly assertive customers who threatened court or other action possibly harmful to Ford and that Ford "falsely represented, by the offering for sale of its vehicles, that they did not have any latent defect which substantially affects their reliability, durability or performance" and that "notwithstanding its knowledge of the problem, Ford failed to disclose the possibility of substantial damage to its engines through piston scuffing, and the nature and extent of repairs which may be necessary to correct it."

Also in 1978, after consumers and store owners complained of price fixing and illegal tie-in sales, Levi

Strauss & Company, makers of the widely sold denim jeans, agreed to an FTC consent order to end any such practices by the company.

In October 1979, Horizon Corporation, a Tuscon, Arizona, land sales organization with sixty-seven sales offices throughout the United States, was found by an FTC Administrative Law judge to have "perpetrated a series of vicious frauds appropriating nearly four hundred million dollars from thousands of consumers for virtually worthless land." The company was ordered to cease its unfair practices, and the judge stated that the refunds "may well be the sole remaining hope for consumer relief."

Also during October 1979, General Motors was ordered to alter a wholesale compensation plan for sales of frequently sold "crash parts" that, according to findings of the FTC, "illegally discriminated against those [independent repair shops] which compete with GM dealers in repairing crash damaged autos and light trucks."

Earlier that same year General Motors was also ordered by the FTC to cease an engine-switching practice that put Chevrolet engines in some Buick, Oldsmobile, and Pontiac cars without informing buyers. A related class-action lawsuit filed by Chicago attorney Charles A. Boyle resulted in a settlement in which GM offered to pay buyers of the engine-switched cars a $200 rebate and extend owners' warranties in exchange for dropping out of the suit. Boyle appealed the settlement, and the court-approved GM offer was reversed.

And in November 1979, in actions similar to others taken nearly every month of the year, the FTC sent questionaires to manufacturers of "maintenance-free" auto batteries, "all-season" tires, and "high-potency" vitamins asking for substantiation of the products' advertising claims.

Though the FTC is usually unable to help individuals settle a specific dispute, you can help yourself and help the FTC help others by advising them of problems with products and services. Only then will the FTC be aware of the particular problems that exist and just how widely they exist.

Here's a current case that was brought to the FTC's attention by consumers:

Seemingly not having learned much from consumer outrage as a result of its engine-switch deception, General Motors, before the ink was dry on the FTC engine-switching stop order, began installing a lightweight, less expensive, inferior automatic transmission (the THM 200, designed for GM's minicompact Chevette) in heavier cars that were supposed to have the more sturdy THM 350 turbohydramatic transmission.

According to Attorney Boyle, representing car buyers in a second suit against GM, "the inferior transmission was installed in at least 50,000 Buicks, Oldsmobiles and Pontiacs," and GM "intentionally concealed, suppressed and failed to disclose" the substitutions.

Mounting consumer complaints to the FTC, many from car buyers who experienced difficulty with the lightweight transmissions in larger cars—and who faced frequent and costly transmission repairs—caused the FTC to begin its own investigation of the problem. As part of its investigation, the FTC, at this writing, is making a notice and form available to consumers (it's our numbered Form 37.1, on page F219, so you can detach it from this book and use it).

If the FTC finds that the transmission substitution materially affects the reliability, durability, or performance of GM cars, the company could be ordered by an Administrative Law judge to offer refunds or some other compensation to buyers of the GM cars.

Any FTC action would be independent of the class-action suit filed against GM by Boyle, but an FTC finding against the auto maker could affect the outcome of consumers' lawsuits against GM.

FTC-administered Law

Although it has a broader mandate today than when it was established more than sixty years ago, all of the actions outlined above were taken under authority of the original **Federal Trade Commission Act of 1914,** which states:

> The Commission is hereby empowered and directed to prevent . . . unfair methods of competition in or affecting commerce and unfair or deceptive acts or practices in or affecting commerce.

Currently, the FTC administers and enforces a wide range of laws that benefit you as a consumer:

- The **Clayton Act of 1914,** which forbids mergers or acquisitions that might substantially lessen competition or tend to create a monopoly.
- The **Wool Products Labeling Act of 1939,** which protects producers, manufacturers, distributors, and consumers from undisclosed substitutes and mixtures in spun, woven, knitted, felted, or other types of wool products.
- The **Fur Products Labeling Act of 1951,** which protects consumers and others against misbranding, false advertising, and false invoicing of furs and fur products.
- The **Textile Fiber Products Identification Act of 1958,** which protects consumers and others against misbranding and false advertising of the fiber content of textile fiber products.
- The **Fair Packaging and Labeling Act of 1966,** which prevents unfair and deceptive packaging or labeling of certain consumer commodities.
- The **Truth in Lending Act of 1969,** which requires full disclosure of related credit terms before a consumer

credit account is opened or a credit transaction (finance agreement or loan, for example) is completed.

An amendment to the Act limits credit card holders' liability for unauthorized use to $50 on cards issued on or before January 25, 1971, with no liability on cards issued after that date unless the credit card issuer takes several steps, such as notifying the card holder of limited liability, providing a postage-free means of notification of loss, and providing a means of card holder identification—either a signature, photograph, or thumb print.

- **Fair Credit Reporting Act of 1970,** which is designed to ensure that a consumer's credit report will contain only accurate, relevant, and recent information and will be confidential unless requested for appropriate reason by a proper authority.
- **Magnuson-Moss Warranty/Federal Trade Improvement Act of 1975,** which authorizes the FTC to represent itself in court (on behalf of consumers and others), to put into force substantive Trade Regulation Rules in the consumer protection area, to obtain civil penalties and (monetary) consumer redress for violations of the Federal Trade Commission Act, and to pursue any unlawful act "affecting commerce" rather than only those acts defined as "in commerce."
- **Fair Credit Billing Act of 1975,** which provides consumers with an opportunity to dispute errors in billing statements and to require creditors to correct such errors.
- **Equal Credit Opportunity Act of 1975,** which is designed to ensure that consumers are not denied credit for reasons of sex, marital status, age, race, religion, or national origin.

If you experience problems with manufacturers, lending institutions, retail stores, or services in **any** of the above areas, the FTC wants to hear from you. Just remember that generally the FTC's job is mostly "fire prevention" and control of "forest fires" that threaten a broad consumer area. Rarely, if ever, can the FTC rush to put out the fire of a particular, individual consumer complaint. But data from individual consumers is essential if the FTC is to know where the forest fires are and where fire prevention measures need to be taken.

To advise the FTC of a consumer problem, write to:

Federal Trade Commission
Office of the Secretary
Correspondence Branch
Room 701
6th Street and Pennsylvania Avenue, N.W.
Washington, DC 20580

or use Form 37.2, **Consumer Complaint Report,** on pages F223–F224. Enclose copies of any correspondence, receipts, warranties, etc., that will document your complaint. And be sure to enclose your *return address.*

FTC Reports and Booklets

When it comes to information, the FTC likes to give every bit as much as it likes to receive. The FTC will send you a catalog listing a number of free booklets on how to handle and, even better, how to *avoid* problems in nearly all of the areas noted above: truth in lending, fair credit and credit reporting, warranties, fair packaging, product labeling, etc.

Perhaps the best news is that the FTC catalog includes National Technical Information Service (NTIS) order numbers for detailed reports submitted to the FTC by manufacturers in response to the commission's advertising substantiation program and other investigations. The reports are a gold mine of not generally available, hard-core, bottom-line data for anyone considering a major purchase OR experiencing difficulty with product performance, reliability, or durability, or with a particular warranty or manufacturer.

This is the kind of data that tells you whether a particular laundry detergent *really* gets clothes brighter, which television manufacturer's set *really* provides more lifelike color or is more reliable, whether a particular tire maker's new steel-belted radial *really* lasts longer and is more blowout resistant, and, most important of all, whether that deoderant the guy in the TV commercial didn't use yesterday and may not use today will *really* leave him sleeping alone until he takes a shower and switches to another brand.

In short, the FTC advertising substantiation data tells you, as Ed McMahon would be sure to say, *everything* that *anybody* would *ever* want to know about *any* of the products listed.

Here are a few sample listings:

Manufacturer	NTIS Order Number
AIR CONDITIONERS	
Ford Motor Co.	PB 207 387
General Electric Co.	PB 207 388
National Union Electric Corp.	PB 207 389
Crutcher Resources Corp.	PB 207 390
Fedders Corp.	PB 207 391
Sears Roebuck & Co.	PB 207 394
White Consolidated Industries	PB 208 443
Borg-Warner Corp.	PB 208 823
McGraw Edison Co.	PB 208 824
Chrysler Corp.	PB 208 825
Whirlpool Corp.	PB 208 826
Trane Corp.	PB 208 827
City Investing Co.	PB 208 829
Raytheon Corp.	PB 212 283
Westinghouse Electric Corp.	PB 213 784
Carrier Corp.	PB 214 350
AUTOMOBILE TIRES	
Delta Tire Corp.	PB 222 388
Armstrong Rubber Co.	PB 222 455

Atlas Supply Co.	PB 222 602
Montgomery Ward & Co.	PB 222 630
J.C. Penney Co.	PB 222 640
Uniroyal, Inc.	PB 222 642
B.F. Goodrich Co.	PB 222 677
R.H. Macy & Co., Inc.	PB 222 793
Spartan Industries, Inc.	PB 222 809
Dunlop Tire & Rubber Co.	PB 222 811
Mobil Oil Corp.	PB 222 819
General Tire & Rubber Co.	PB 222 847
Michelin Tire Corp.	PB 222 864
Phillips Petroleum Co.	PB 222 809
S.S. Kresge Co.	PB 222 902
Firestone Tire & Rubber Co.	PB 222 903
Sears Roebuck & Co.	PB 222 969
Goodyear Tire & Rubber Co.	PB 224 596
Bridgestone Tire Co. of America	PB 237 592

Additional data is also available on antiperspirants, automobiles, cold remedies, color television, hair shampoo, pet food, soaps and detergents, power lawn mowers, etc., etc., etc.

The FTC may not often be able to put out individual complaint backyard brush fires, but it's still the best consumer organization you've got going for you. If it weren't a government agency, we'd say, "join today," and include its membership form on the very next page. *Use* the FTC and support it through letters to your state's congressmen and senators.

To obtain the FTC's free publications catalog, write to:

Federal Trade Commission
Distribution and Duplication Branch
Room 128
6th Street and Pennsylvania Avenue, N.W.
Washington, DC 20580

Orders and inquiries to the National Technical Information Service should be addressed to:

National Technical Information Service
Department of Commerce
5285 Port Royal Road
Springfield, VA 22161

INTERSTATE COMMERCE COMMISSION

With several exceptions, the **Interstate Commerce Commission (ICC)** is charged with regulating interstate surface transportation within the United States. The key words are **interstate** and **surface**. While the ICC is involved with railroad, water, truck, and bus transportation with respect to licensing and fitness and as an alternative channel for consumer complaints other than the carriers themselves, what it hears most about from the public is complaints about movers.

According to ICC investigators, "weight bumping," falsifying the weight of a household goods shipment to increase charges, takes place in about 10 percent of all moves.

The practice is simple enough to carry out by filling a truck's fuel tanks **after** loading a householder's goods or by having three or four men climb onto the truck for its second weighing. Filling tanks can add as much as 1,000 pounds, and four men can add about 800 pounds, to the cost a consumer will pay—all clear profit for the mover. Weight bumping, according to the ICC, costs consumers about $20 million per year.

The ICC is your best advocate when it comes to dealing with movers. The commission has been articulate and persistent in representing consumers on Capitol Hill, so the laws are there IF you take a few simple measures to protect yourself. The ICC has made that easy to do if you know what to do.

As part of its effort to crack down on weight bumping, the ICC, in January 1981, charged forty-five movers with 9,000 violations of ICC regulations, which, according to then ICC Chairman Dan O'Neal, "include deliberate padding of bills."

The ICC also reports that in 22 percent of all moves actual charges were 10 percent or more above the amount estimated. The commission has proposed that written estimates provided to householders by movers be binding on the carrier as part of an effort to reduce "low balling," deliberately giving a householder an artificially low bid to obtain the business, then charging more for the actual shipment.

The commission is also cracking down on movers who refuse or unreasonably delay paying householders for lost or damaged goods. In January 1980, for example, a federal district court, ruling on a suit filed by the ICC, ordered Trans-American Van Service, Inc., to pay approximately $25,000 in loss damages owed to consumers that were never paid.

To that end the commission publishes several free booklets that tell how to select a mover and explain what movers are required to do in making

estimates, weighing your shipment, handling your household effects, compensating you for loss or damage, and delivering your shipment. To obtain them, write for the following titles:

- *Summary of Information for Shippers of Household Goods*
- *Lost or Damaged Household Goods: Prevention and Recovery—Public Advisory No. 4*

Each year the ICC makes available a seventeen-item evaluation that rates movers on accuracy of estimates, on-time performance, promptness in settling damage claims, etc. To obtain a free copy of this evaluation of the nation's twenty largest movers, ask for *Performance Data, Twenty Largest Movers* for the most recent available year. The commission also publishes an annual *Summary of Shipments Transported and Complaints Received; Household Carriers.*

You can obtain free copies of all these booklets and reports by sending a request to:

Interstate Commerce Commission
Office of Communications and Consumer Affairs
Washington, DC 20423

The ICC would like to hear from you about your "moving experience" with any ICC-licensed mover of household goods. To file a report, complete the official ICC **Consumer Questionnaire** (Form 37.3) on page F225.

The table below shows the ICC's summary of shipments transported and complaints received during 1978. Data for more recent years is not available because, according to informants, "the administration is trying to figure out a way to make the movers look better."

HOUSEHOLD GOODS CARRIERS: SUMMARY OF SHIPMENTS TRANSPORTED AND COMPLAINTS RECEIVED, 1978

Carrier	Shipments Delivered	Shipper Complaints	Loss and Damage	Delay in Service	Charges and/or Estimates	Percent of Shipments Resulting in Complaints
Aero Mayflower World-Wide Moving Service	128,543	3,687	35%	46%	19%	2.8%
Allied Van Lines	218,382	3,018	38	38	24	1.4
American Red Ball	24,640	624	33	50	17	2.5
Andrews Van Lines	6,390	69	39	53	8	1.1
Atlas Van Lines	69,711	813	33	49	18	1.2
Bekins Van Lines	101,504	2,313	28	51	21	2.3
Burnham Van Service	17,414	125	23	58	19	0.7
Fernstrom Storage & Van	2,294	28	49	19	32	1.2
Global Van Lines	39,738	804	34	48	18	2.0

The table columns "Loss and Damage", "Delay in Service", "Charges and/or Estimates" fall under heading "Distribution of Complaints by Reason".

(continued)

HOUSEHOLD GOODS CARRIERS: SUMMARY OF SHIPMENTS TRANSPORTED AND COMPLAINTS RECEIVED, 1978 (Continued)

Carrier	Shipments Delivered	Shipper Complaints	Distribution of Complaints by Reason			Percent of Shipments Resulting in Complaints
			Loss and Damage	Delay in Service	Charges and/or Estimates	
King Van Lines	13,547	291	39	42	19	2.1
Lyon Moving & Storage	30,204	214	32	45	23	0.7
National Van Lines	10,699	291	39	33	28	2.7
Neptune World Wide Moving	5,496	45	52	25	23	0.8
northAmerican Van Lines	122,684	2,838	27	49	24	2.3
Smyth Van Lines	18,522	267	38	43	19	1.4
Trans American Van Service	2,590	270	45	43	12	10.4
United Van Lines	117,059	1,443	40	40	20	1.2
Von Der Ahe Van Lines	4,136	76	39	56	5	1.8
Wheaton Van Lines	26,850	363	33	50	17	1.4
Total:	1,230,963	21,421	36%	43%	21%	1.7%

38 Other Federal Agencies and Consumer Groups

U.S. CONSUMER PRODUCT SAFETY COMMISSION

As its name suggests, the main thrust of the U.S. Consumer Product Safety Commission is to reduce injuries and save lives. It participates in industry efforts to develop voluntary product safety standards and negotiates and monitors corrective action plans for products that may present a substantial hazard to consumers. In addition, it informs consumers about product hazards.

Through decisions of an Administrative Law judge, the commission can levy civil and criminal penalties and may ban a hazardous product for which no feasible safety standard exists that would adequately protect the public. In addition, it administers and enforces four federal statutes:

- The **Federal Hazardous Substances Act**, which is mainly a labeling act requiring labels that warn consumers about the hazards of using and storing products such as household cleaners, solvents, and other flammable, poisonous, or caustic materials.
- The **Flammable Fabrics Act**, which establishes flammability standards for clothing, bedding, and other materials.
- The **Poison Prevention Packaging Act**, which mostly involves child-resistant closures for drugs and other hazardous substances.
- The **Refrigerator Safety Act**, which sets refrigerator closure standards designed to prevent child entrapment in refrigerators and freezers.

The commission doesn't regulate products that are regulated by other agencies. Foods, drugs, cosmetics, and medical devices are regulated by the Food and Drug Administration (FDA), and motor vehicles come under the National Traffic Safety Administration.

The Product Safety Commission needs to hear from you if you know of an article intended for use by children or adults that you believe presents an **unreasonable** hazard. Use the **Consumer Product Complaint Form** (Form 38.1 on page F227) to advise the commission whenever you encounter such a product.

U.S. OFFICE OF CONSUMER AFFAIRS

A part of the Department of Health, Education and Welfare, the **Office of Consumer Affairs (OCA)** in early 1980 established the Federal Complaint Coordinating Center to develop voluntary standards for complaint handling procedures. On the basis of suggestions from consumers and business, the Complaint Coordinating Center will publish recommended procedures for handling consumer complaints.

Though we're fairly certain the OCA isn't planning to establish the "Famous Complainers School," it does want to hear from "people who know how to complain" and who have suggestions to offer that it can use in developing complaint handling guidelines. Remember, **suggestions** about improved complaint handling procedures, NOT complaints of your own about products, services, etc. Write to:

Director
Federal Complaint Coordinating Center
621 Reporters Building
Washington, DC 20201

The Office of Consumer Affairs does have some suggestions of its own about making complaints that get results. For the OCA's free, 80-page *Consumer Resource Handbook*, write:

Consumer Information Center
Dept. 635-H
Pueblo, CO 81009

If you add a request for a free catalog, you'll also receive an excellent, giant catalog of government consumer publications.

The primary responsibility of the Office of Consumer Affairs is to provide advice for the President and government agencies regarding consumer interests. OCA people spend a fair amount of their time on Capitol Hill testifying before House and Senate committees considering legislation that will affect consumers.

The OCA staff is small though, less than 50 at this writing, so you're still pretty much on your own, OCA-wise, when it comes to actually making and following up a complaint.

OTHER CONSUMER ORGANIZATIONS

In the beginning of this section we suggested that you generally not count on help from consumer organizations in attempting to resolve a problem with a product or service, or a manufacturer or retailer.

Within almost any consumer group you contact, people will consult, follow procedures, adhere to policies, and, finally, after several weeks delay, may only be able to refer you to yet another group or agency. And almost any consumer group you contact will have a backlog of previous complaints to be dealt with before it can get to yours.

The record shows that well-organized consumers have a far better success rate when prosecuting their own complaints than that which is achieved when working through third-party groups. We don't know all the reasons for this, but we suspect that, in part, it's simply that nobody cares as much about resolving your complaint as you do.

Of course, there are effective consumer groups that can step in and help resolve your complaint; the problem is finding them.

One such group is San Francisco Consumer Action (SFCA), a volunteer group made up of dues-paying members, many of whom had no specific consumer complaint when they joined but who wanted to work through SFCA to improve conditions for all consumers.

When a consumer asks SFCA for assistance, the group first makes sure the complainant has informed the merchant of the problem. If the merchant fails to respond or responds negatively, SFCA writes a letter suggesting a specific resolution. If *that* fails, the merchant is visited by a delegation (usually six or eight) of the organization's members, who, along with the complainant, attempt to negotiate a settlement. If *that* fails, members picket the store until a resolution is achieved.

According to SFCA's John Pound, about 20 percent of all disputes taken up by the group are settled on the basis of a letter from SFCA to the merchant. Nearly 80 percent of the remaining cases are settled during a store visit by a delegation of members. Only half a dozen times a year is the group forced to picket.

State Consumer Protection Agencies

Since it's nearly impossible for us to know of all of the other "SFCAs" around the country, we have provided the following list of each state's primary, state-sponsored consumer agency. Each of these agencies may serve as a contact point for reaching a nearby consumer organization—an organization that may be able to assist you if your previous, well-organized, individual efforts fail to gain satisfactory results.

ALABAMA
Governor's Office of Consumer Protection
138 Adams Avenue
Montgomery, AL 36104

ALASKA
Office of the Attorney General
Chief, Consumer Protection Section
Pouch "K"
State Capitol
Juneau, AK 99801

ARIZONA
Economic Protection Division
Department of Law
159 State Capitol Building
Phoenix, AZ 85007

ARKANSAS
Chief Counsel
Consumer Services Division
Office of the Attorney General
Justice Building
Little Rock, AR 72201

CALIFORNIA
Director
Department of Consumer Affairs
1020 N Street
Sacramento, CA 95814

COLORADO
Office of Consumer Affairs
Office of the Attorney General
112 East 14th Avenue
Denver, CO 80203

CONNECTICUT
Department of Consumer Protection
State Office Building
Hartford, CT 06115

DELAWARE
Director
Consumer Affairs Division
Department of Community Affairs and Economic Development
200 West 9th Street
Wilmington, DE 19801

DISTRICT OF COLUMBIA
Director
Office of Consumer Affairs
1407 L Street, N.W.
Washington, DC 20005

FLORIDA
Consumer Counsel, FTP Office
Department of Legal Affairs
State Capitol
Tallahassee, FA 32304

GEORGIA
Administrator
Governor's Office of Consumer Affairs
104 State Capitol
Atlanta, GA 30334

HAWAII
Director of Consumer Protection
Office of the Governor
250 South King Street
602 Kamamalu Building
P.O. Box 3767
Honolulu, HI 96811

IDAHO
Deputy Attorney General
Consumer Protection Division
Office of the Attorney General
State Capitol
Boise, IO 83720

ILLINOIS
Chief
Consumer Protection Division
Office of the Attorney General
500 South Second Street
Springfield, IL 62706

INDIANA
Chief
Consumer Protection Division
Office of the Attorney General
215 State House
Indianapolis, IN 46204

IOWA
Assistant Attorney General in
  Charge
Consumer Protection Division
Iowa Department of Justice
1209 East Court
Des Moines, IA 50319

KANSAS
Chief
Consumer Protection Division
Office of the Attorney General
State Capitol
Topeka, KS 66612

KENTUCKY
Chief
Consumer Protection Division
Office of the Attorney General
Room 34
State Capitol
Frankfort, KY 40601

LOUISIANA
Director
Governor's Office of Consumer
  Protection
P.O. Box 44091
Capitol Station
Baton Rouge, LA 70804

MAINE
Assistant Attorney General
Division of Consumer Fraud and
  Protection
Office of the Attorney General
State House
Augusta, ME 04330

MARYLAND
Chief
Consumer Protection Division
Office of the Attorney General
1 South Calvert Street
Baltimore, MD 21202

MASSACHUSETTS
Director
Consumer Complaint Division
Executive Office of Consumer
  Affairs
1 Ashburton Place
Boston, MA 02108

MICHIGAN
Chief
Consumer Protection and
  Antitrust Division
Office of the Attorney General
Law Building
Lansing, MI 48902

MINNESOTA
Director
Office of Consumer Services
Department of Commerce
Metro Square Building
7th and Roberts Streets
St. Paul, MN 55101

MISSISSIPPI
Chief
Consumer Protection Division
Office of the Attorney General
Gartin Justice Building
P.O. Box 220
Jackson, MS 39205

MISSOURI
Chief
Consumer Protection Division
Office of the Attorney General
Supreme Court Building
Jefferson City, MO 65101

MONTANA
Administrator
Department of Business
  Regulation
805 North Main Street
Helena, MT 59601

NEBRASKA
Assistant Attorney General for
  Consumer Protection and
  Antitrust
Department of Justice
State Capitol
Lincoln, NE 68509

NEVADA
Chief
Consumer Affairs Division
Department of Commerce
2501 East Sahara Avenue
Las Vegas, NV 89104

NEW HAMPSHIRE
Chief
Consumer Protection Division
Office of the Attorney General
State House Annex
Concord, NH 03301

NEW JERSEY
Director, CALA
Division of Consumer Affairs
Department of Law and Public
  Safety
1100 Raymond Boulevard
Newark, NJ 07102

NEW MEXICO
Director
Consumer Protection Division
Office of the Attorney General
P.O. Box 2246
Santa Fe, NM 87501

NEW YORK
Chairman
State Consumer Protection
  Board
Twin Towers Office Building
99 Washington Avenue
Albany, NY 12210

NORTH CAROLINA
Division Head
Consumer Protection Division
Office of the Attorney General
Justice Building
P.O. Box 629
Raleigh, NC 27602

NORTH DAKOTA
Assistant Attorney General and
  Counsel

Consumer Fraud Division
Office of the Attorney General
State Capitol
Bismark, ND 58501

OHIO

Chief
Consumer Protection Division
Department of Commerce
180 East Broad Street
Columbus, OH 43215

OKLAHOMA

Administrator
Department of Consumer Affairs
Room 460
Jim Thorpe Building
Oklahoma City, OK 73105

OREGON

Administrator
Consumer Services Division
Department of Commerce
Salem, OR 97310

PENNSYLVANIA

Director
Bureau of Consumer Protection
Office of the Attorney General
State Capitol
Harrisburg, PA 17101

RHODE ISLAND

Director
Rhode Island Consumer Council
365 Broadway
Providence, RI 02902

SOUTH CAROLINA

Coordinator
Office of Citizens Service
Governor's Office
State House
P.O. Box 11450
Columbia, SC 29211

SOUTH DAKOTA

Secretary
Department of Commerce and
    Consumer Affairs
State Capitol
Pierre, SD 57401

TENNESSEE

Assistant Attorney General for
    Consumer Protection
Office of the Attorney General
Supreme Court Building
Nashville, TN 37219

TEXAS

Chief
Antitrust and Consumer
    Protection Division
Office of the Attorney General
P.O. Box 12548
Capitol Station
Austin, TX 78711

UTAH

Assistant Attorney General for
    Consumer Protection
Office of the Attorney General
Room 236
State Capitol
Salt Lake City, UT 84114

VERMONT

Chief
Consumer Affairs Division
Vermont Public Service Board
120 State Street
Montpelier, VT 05602

VIRGINIA

Assistant Attorney General
Division of Consumer Counsel
Office of the Attorney General
Supreme Court Building
825 Broad Street
Richmond, VA 23219

WASHINGTON

Chief
Consumer Protection and
    Antitrust Division
Office of the Attorney General
1266 Dexter Horton Building
710 Second Avenue
Seattle, WA 98104

WEST VIRGINIA

Chief
Consumer Protection Division
Office of the Attorney General
State Capitol
Charleston, WV 25305

WISCONSIN

Chairman
Governor's Council for
    Consumer Affairs
State Capitol
Madison, WI 53702

WYOMING

Chief
Consumer Affairs Division
Office of the Attorney General
Capitol Building
Cheyenne, WY 82002

Nearly all state consumer protection agencies prefer that your complaint be in writing. All suggest that you at least have informed both the seller and manufacturer about your problem before contacting them for assistance.

Many state agencies claim a high success rate, 80 or 90 percent, but that depends on how you spell "success." Some agencies do not get into the act unless there's obvious, prosecutable fraud. Others seem to define success as *any* compromise that you're willing, in desperation, to accept.

Admittedly, much of any agency's success potential depends a lot on the strength of state consumer laws and upon whatever powers are given it— some can prosecute, some can levy fines, and others can only mediate.

Waiting time varies from two to six weeks, but several states, notably New Jersey with more than 100 offices, have branches that can work with you. Several states have separate consumer protection divisions devoted to credit, insurance, land sales, agriculture, and landlord–tenant problems.

The most common complaints are about auto repairs and sales, major appliance repairs and sales, home repairs, credit, and mobile homes.

When you contact a state consumer protection agency, enclose copies of your initial complaint letters, plus any replies, along with your telephone log (Form 38.2, page F229), receipts, canceled checks, warranties, and anything else you feel would be useful. Some agencies have toll-free telephone numbers (not listed here due to frequent changes), which you can obtain by calling information.

AT SOME POINT AFTER YOU HAVE A FAIRLY COMPLETE FILE, ADVISE YOUR STATE'S CONSUMER PROTECTION AGENCY ABOUT YOUR PROBLEM—EVEN IF YOU'VE RESOLVED IT. THAT WAY THEY'LL BE AWARE OF THE MERCHANT'S NAME AND THE PRODUCT OR SERVICE INVOLVED. THIS WILL HELP THEM HELP OTHERS AND PERHAPS OBTAIN IMPROVED LEGISLATION AND STRENGTHEN THEIR ABILITY TO RESIST INDUSTRY LOBBYING.

VII

CONSUMER-SIZE JUSTICE

39 Taking Your Case to Small Claims Court

Small claims court is a pussycat. The clerk of the court will bend over backward to help you complete the required forms, show you how to state your complaint, and even advise you about evidence and witnesses. And the fees are small, often less than you'd pay for a couple of dinners at McDonald's.

Since the amount involved in a suit is comparatively limited (85 percent of all small claims suits are for amounts less than $500; see the table on pages 170–171 for maximum limits set by each state), the judge usually isn't inclined to make a "federal case" out of the trial, and procedures are directed more toward fairness than strict legal procedure.

Many small claims court judges are justices of the peace or judges who rotate between small claims and general sessions court duties. They usually go out of their way to help you feel at ease and state your case. I've seen judges in small claims courts question corporate defendants in the manner of a plaintiff's attorney instead of that of a judge, and on occasion suggest to a plaintiff, "You probably want to object to that, don't you—I thought so—sustained."

In several states neither side may be represented by an attorney (see the table on page 170), so in those jurisdictions, at least, you won't have to worry about going up against Perry Mason. In other states, either side *may* be represented by an attorney, but you still don't have to use one if you don't want to.

In some states a corporation *must* be represented by an attorney. That's not necessarily the cause for concern that at first it might appear to be, since the increased expense of having a lawyer appear in court might just make the corporation all the more inclined to offer a fairly decent out-of-court settlement before the trial.

Finally, small claims courts have a better record of settling disputes in consumers' favor than any other mechanism. The decisions have been in favor of consumers about 75 percent of the time, not so much because judges in those courts have any particular proconsumer bias but because most of the time consumers who have gone to the trouble to go to small claims court are right.

If you add the above figure to the large number of cases where initiation of a small claims suit brought an out-of-court settlement from a company that previously refused to acknowledge a consumer's claim, it becomes apparent just how potent a consumer weapon the small claims lawsuit really is.

For corporations, almost any small claims suit is bad news. To begin with, your suit means that someone from the company has to *be* there—has to set aside time from other tasks, get to the courtroom, sit through a bunch of other cases until your case is called, and testify to questions in front of a room full of the other consumers (potential ex-customers) plus, sometimes in major cities, a courthouse reporter or two who have wandered in for the momentary want of something better to do. No matter how you slice it, it costs a company money when you file a small claims suit.

Even if you lose, there's a certain amount of satisfaction in making them appear in court, *finally* pay attention to you, and put up with the expense and embarrassment of a public hearing.

You can imagine the meetings—"Who allowed this situation to get out of hand?"—and memos and costs involved for a large corporation like Exxon or General Motors or the phone company just to send someone to represent the company at a small claims hearing. If you've been given the corporate runaround, it is almost a joy to contemplate—no, it *is* a joy to contemplate.

Another thing no major company likes to contemplate is the possibility of a potentially expensive legal precedent. Suppose you were the first to take General Motors to small claims court for "sneaking" a Chevrolet engine into your new Oldsmobile or were the first to take Firestone to court because your Firestone 500 tires didn't hold up. Quite often a company will settle out of court rather than risk a judge's decision that, over the long run, could cost far more than the amount of any award to you.

There are, of course, cases where a company will fight. It will fight if you won't settle out of court. It will fight if there's a potentially costly precedent involved AND it's *sure* that it will win (then the precedent would be in *its* favor). And the company will fight if it's convinced it's right—but not always. Sometimes winning still costs more than buying you off with an out-of-court settlement. If your suit is against a local business or an individual, chances are better than fifty-fifty that there will be an attempt to make an out-of-court settlement before trial.

Remember that the **Magnuson-Moss Warranty Act** was passed by Congress "to provide minimum disclosure standards for written product warranties; to define minimum Federal content standards for such warranties; to amend the Federal Trade Commission Act in order to improve its consumer protection activities; and for other purposes." Except possibly with respect to paint used by a contractor, or parts used by a plumber or mechanic, the Warranty Act can't help you much when it comes to problems with services such as auto repair, dry cleaning, painting, carpentry, etc.

And, as with the Warranty Act itself, implied warranty provisions of the **Uniform Commercial Code** apply only to **products**, so in the event of a service, or in a number of other nonproduct areas that can't be resolved through negotiation or arbitration, a small claims suit may be your best way to settle the matter.

If you've followed the procedures for buying and complaining described earlier, you'll have warranties, receipts, bills of sale, copies of correspondence, names of salespersons and repairpersons, and a log of phone calls made in an attempt to obtain repairs or resolve the difficulty—in short, the makings of a strong foundation on which to base a suit.

Just as there are procedures to follow in making a well-organized complaint, so are there certain steps to be taken if you want to increase your chances of winning in small claims court. And winning is not just obtaining an award in your favor; it is *collecting* on your award from the defendant.

The following chapters will guide you on each step of taking a case through small claims court, providing you with the necessary forms. The forms are composites that follow those of your local court and contain space for information you'll be asked to supply. For this section's forms we've created the state of New Bedford and Putnam County.

Small claims court can be an excellent recourse when:

- You're having trouble getting your money back for poorly done auto, appliance, or home repairs.
- Your cleaner or laundry has lost your favorite suit or dress.
- A parking lot attendant has dented your car.
- Your landlord fails to fulfill lease requirements or won't return your security deposit when you move.
- A product causes damage or injury.
- Failure to make a delivery or service call causes you to lose wages because you were away from work.
- You suffer damage or loss as the result of a negligent act or acts of the defendant (a landlord, merchant, the driver of a vehicle, etc.).
- You are owed money (within the maximum limit of the particular small claims court).

In order for a suit to be brought before small claims court:

1. Your dispute must be such that it can be satisfied by an award of money.
2. The amount sought must fall within the maximum limit set by your state.

Before taking a case to small claims court you must determine five things:

- **Who to sue**—generally, the name and address of the company and name of the owner/president as they appear on the business license, not necessarily as they appear on the front of the store or on the company letterhead. In the case of a suit against an individual, his or her complete name and home address will be required. If you cannot get the company's legal name from its business license, which is supposed to be conspicuously displayed on the wall, contact your city or county licensing bureau or county clerk. With corporations, write or phone your state's secretary of state asking for the corporation's legal name.
- **Where to sue**—in order to collect on any award resulting from your suit, the defendant must have assets within the jurisdiction of the court. For example, as a California resident you can sue and collect on a judgment against a company incorporated in Delaware with headquarters in Chicago if the company is licensed as a "foreign" corporation to do business in your state.

  In some states you must sue a defendant in the court of the district where he or she lives. In other states you may sue where the defendant lives or works, or wherever the defendent can be found and served, or, in a case involving injury, where the injury itself occurred.
- **What to sue for**—damages that can be defined in terms of money.
- **How much to sue for**—maximum amounts that may be awarded by small claims courts are established by law in each state.
- **When to sue**—if all else fails and you can show the court you have made a conscientious effort to resolve the dispute prior to bringing your case to court.

40 Making and Filing Your Complaint

The first form you are likely to encounter in filing a small claims suit is the **Summons and Complaint**. This is the form that, when signed by the judge or clerk of the court, summons the defendant to court.

As its name suggests, the **Summons and Complaint** also includes your complaint and a statement of claim stated in dollar terms. It is usually served on the defendant—handed to him or her—by a deputy sheriff, marshal, or constable, although in some jurisdictions a small claims **Summons and Complaint** may be "served" by registered mail, return receipt requested.

Despite the official-looking nature of the form, YOU are expected to fill it out. This can best be done at home or work on a typewriter. Probably the most intimidating thing about the **Summons and Complaint** is its legalistic and unfamiliar form. Here is what you must fill in:

1. Your name and address as plaintiff.
2. The defendant's name and address.
3. Your **Statement of Complaint** (sometimes called the **Statement of Claim**).
4. The dollar amount of your claim.

That's it!

Your **Statement of Complaint** obviously bears some thinking about. If you have already written several letters of complaint—something that you should have done so you'll have evidence of your previous attempts to resolve the problem—you already have a good description of the nature and history of your complaint.

Briefly describe the nature of your complaint and briefly describe its history—the defendant's inability or refusal to correct your complaint. Also state the amount sought. This would include the cost of:

- Repairing or replacing a product.
- Having poorly executed work such as painting roofing or auto repairs redone.
- Having damage, caused by a defective product or faulty work, repaired.
- Reimbursement for expenses directly related to the complaint, for example, taxi fares or auto rental if poor workmanship made your car unusable.
- Reimbursement for the cost of physical injury.

Include everything you can think of that is at all reasonable. First, because the defendant may propose an out-of-court settlement before trial and any such offer is likely to be a compromise, you might as well start as high as you can. Second, you'll want to include every reasonable expense because the judge may award something less than the amount you've asked for.

You may be asked to complete several copies of the **Summons and Complaint**, possibly one copy for the court, one for the defendant, one for the sheriff's or constable's office, and, of course, one copy for yourself. In any event, make and keep an extra copy for your files.

There are a few parts of the form, in addition to the plaintiff's and defendant's names and addresses and the **Statement of Claim**, that you should know about. The most obvious is that portion generally called the "return," on which the deputy sheriff, constable, or marshal notes, on the *court's* copy, the date and manner of serving the summons. The latest date upon which the summons may be served (and still meet requirements of prior notice with respect to the given trial date) is the date shown after "Returnable" on the front panel of the summons or subpoena.

Some states allow what is known as "mail service." The serving of a summons by certified mail may be performed by the sheriff's department, constable's office, marshal, plaintiff's attorney, the clerk's office, an ordinary citizen, or, in a few jurisdictions, the plaintiff. If mail service is permissible in your state, you will be asked to sign a certificate (similar to that on top of the following page) for each summons you mail.

There is also a place on the **Summons and Complaint** for the docket number for your case. This is your suit's number on the court's list of cases, and you should use it whenever referring to your case.

The docket number will be filled in by the clerk after you have given him or her the completed **Summons and Complaint**. The clerk may give you the docket number and trial date at the time of filing, or they may be assigned later and filled in by the clerk, who will then mail a copy to you.

In lieu of sending a copy of the **Summons and Complaint** by return mail, the clerk might just give you back one of the copies you've handed to him or her and then mail you a postcard **Trial Notice** (see bottom of page 140).

A clerk of the court or notary will also probably swear you to the truth of your statements. For this reason do not sign the form until you give it to the clerk.

When you pick up the form, find out the amount of the filing fee and any charges for serving the summons. Bring this amount with you in cash when you come to the courthouse to file your suit.

PUTNAM COUNTY DISTRICT COURT

Certificate

"I hereby certify that a true and correct copy of the **Summons and Complaint** in _____ vs. _____

_____, Docket # SC _____ was mailed to (each of) said defendant(s) on _____, 19 ___."

(Signed) _____

☐ Deputy Sheriff ☐ Plaintiff's Attorney

☐ Plaintiff's Agent ☐ Plaintiff ☐ _____

The following completed sample copy of a typical small claims **Summons and Complaint** is provided as it would be filled in by the plaintiff, clerk of the court, and sheriff, with the clerk's and sheriff's data added by hand, as they frequently are. A blank **Summons and Complaint** (Form 40.1, page F231) should be photocopied and used as a work form before going to the courthouse.

These forms, as is the case with many in the court system, are not particularly well organized, nor are they consistent in style or format with those to follow—the way you'll probably find it to be with the forms used by your local court.

Generally within this section we have used *Mason vs. Arthur C. Smedley, d/b/a Art's Appliance City,* but some material differs to provide a wider range of information than we would be able to furnish by attempting to present the forms as though all related to a specific case.

NOTE: *In some states, especially those having higher small claims limits, a **pretrial hearing** is held to make a preliminary determination of the validity of the claim and to attempt to achieve an out-of-court settlement to avoid the time and expense of an actual trial.*

PUTNAM COUNTY DISTRICT COURT

TRIAL NOTICE   DOCKET # SC _____

vs.

is scheduled for trial on _____ before the Division of Small Claims, Putnam County District Court, 101 Courthouse Square, Sommerton, N.B., at _____.

_____
District Court Clerk

Sample of Form 40.1/F231

Summons and Complaint

STATE OF NEW BEDFORD

COUNTY OF PUTNAM

TO: Arthur C. Smedley d/b/a
Art's Appliance City
35 Clark Street
Sommerton, N.B. 10560

YOU ARE HEREBY SUMMONED to appear and state your defense to the annexed complaint of:

Robert B. Mason
25 Calkinstown Road
Hinkley, N.B. 10531

Plaintiff, in a civil action, Small Claims Division, of Putnam County District Court, to be held at the Putnam County Courthouse, 101 Courthouse Square, Sommerton, N.B.

TAKE NOTICE that unless you appear before the court on _August 1, 1984_ at _10:00 AM_, a judgment by default may be entered against you for the money damages demanded in the statement of claim. If this occurs, your wages or bank account may be attached or withheld, or any personal property owned by you may be taken and sold to pay the judgment.

Hon. _George Bradford_
Presiding Judge, Putnam County District Court at Sommerton

Robert B. Mason
Attorney or Plaintiff

25 Calkinstown Road
Address

Hinkley, N.B.   10531
City/Township   *Zip*

Janet Hodge
Clerk or Deputy Clerk

(Bring this **Summons and Complaint** with you at all times.)

Sample of Form 40.1 (*Continued*)

PUTNAM COUNTY DISTRICT COURT, DIVISION OF SMALL CLAIMS

101 Courthouse Square, Sommerton, N.B. 10560

Robert B. Mason
_____
Plaintiff

25 Calkinstown Road
_____
Address

Hinkley, N.B.   10531
_____
Township   Zip

vs.

Arthur C. Smedley d/b/a
_____
Defendant   Art's Appliance City

35 Clark Street
_____
Address

Sommerton, N.B.   10560
_____
Township   Zip

No. SC 3-80-57954
_____

STATEMENT OF CLAIM

That American Eagle, Inc., Tangle-Matic washing machine sold to the Plaintiff by the Defendant d/b/a Art's Appliance City, for $387.95 on March 3, 1984, will not operate and that, though contacted by the Plaintiff on four occasions in an effort to obtain repair or replacement of the washer, the Defendant has failed to take any remedial action whatsoever. Plaintiff demands return of the full purchase price plus $120.00 for two days' lost wages occasioned by absence from work to admit Defendant's repairman, allegedly dispached by the Defendant, who failed to appear. Plaintiff also demands $25.75 reimbursement for cost of clothes commercially laundered due to the inoperative condition of washer.

Judgment will be claimed in the sum of $ ____533.70____ together with interest and costs of suit.

STATE OF NEW BEDFORD)
) ss:
COUNTY OF PUTNAM   )

_____Robert B. Mason_____, Plaintiff, being duly sworn on oath, says the foregoing is a just and true statement of the amount owed by the Defendant to said Plaintiff.

Robert B Mason
Plaintiff

_____
Attorney for Plaintiff (*if any*)

_____
Address

_____
Township   Zip

Subscribed and sworn to before me this __20th__ of __May__, 19_84_.

Janet Hodgin
Deputy Clerk/Notary Public

My appointment/commission expires: __September 20, 1986__.

Sample of Form 40.1 (*Continued*)

INSTRUCTIONS TO DEFENDANT(S)

You may come with or without a lawyer. The Statement of Claim indicates whether the Plaintiff has a lawyer. If the Plaintiff does have a lawyer and you wish either to dispute the claim or to attempt to arrange a compromise settlement, it would be in your best interest to have your own lawyer.

If you wish to have legal advice and feel that you cannot afford to pay an attorney, you may contact the Putnam County Legal Aid Society, 751-1775, or the New Bedford University Law Students in Court Project, 387-7000, to ask for help. Act promptly.

If it is impossible for you to appear on the date set for trial, notify the Clerk of the Division of Small Claims in person or by phone, 569-4189. The Clerk will assist you in requesting a new date. In arranging this new date you may wish to consider that the court holds sessions on weekdays at 10:00 A.M., Thursday evenings at 6:30 P.M., and Saturday mornings at 9:00 A.M. If you do not appear on the new date, judgment may be entered against you.

If you have witnesses, photographs, receipts, writings or other evidence bearing upon this claim, you should bring them with you at the time of the hearing.

If you wish to have witnesses summoned, contact the Clerk at once for assistance.

If you admit the claim but desire additional time to pay, you must come to the hearing in person and state your circumstances to the court.

A CORPORATION MAY APPEAR ONLY THROUGH AN ATTORNEY.

(Bring this **Summons and Complaint** with you at all times.)

I served the within **Summons and Complaint** on _____ said defendant by giving (him) (her) a copy thereof.

_____
Sheriff's Deputy

The said defendant not being found, I served the **Summons and Complaint** _____ by June 5 1984 leaving a copy thereof at the place of abode with a competent person residing therein, of the age of sixteen years or more.

Robert Dempsey
Sheriff's Deputy

I served the within **Summons and Complaint** on _____, (he) (she) being the _____ of _____ said _____, by giving (him) (her) a copy thereof.

_____
Sheriff's Deputy

_____, being _____ of _____ and the _____ said _____ (he) (she) not being found, I served the **Summons and Complaint** _____ by leaving a copy thereof at the abode or place of business with a competent person of the age of sixteen years or more.

_____
Sheriff's Deputy

No. SC 3-80-57954

Summons and Complaint

Robert B. Mason
25 Calkinstown Road
Hinkley, N.B. 10531

vs.

Arthur C. Smedley d/b/a
Art's Appliance City
35 Clark Street
Sommerton, N.B. 10560

Amount of Claim $ 533.70

Dated May 20, 19 84

Returnable July 20, 19 84

On your initial visit to the courthouse to pick up necessary copies of the Summons and Complaint, ask at the court clerk's counter if there is a *pro se* clerk, a deputy clerk whose main responsibility is to assist small claims plaintiffs and defendants and others with the preparation of their cases.

Smaller counties and towns that don't have a *pro se* clerk usually have someone who takes an interest in *pro se* work who will be extremely helpful. Fill in and take along a completed copy of this book's Summons and Complaint (Form 40.1), and you'll probably have everything the clerk will need to know in order to help you.

Before you've finished working with the clerk, ask if you can have, or buy for a nominal amount, a copy of the **Rules of the Court**. All courts have written procedural rules to follow. In federal civil courts these are called, aptly enough, the **Federal Rules of Civil Procedure**. State and other civil court rules may be called **Rules of Civil Procedure, Rules of Civil Practice and Procedure, Rules of the Court**, etc.

Small claims courts have their own rules in each state, sometimes with additional rules that apply only in a particular court. The **Rules of the Court** for *your* court define the procedures and conduct you **must comply with** in presenting your case. The **Rules of the Court** tell you what you may and may not do, and what you must and must not do.

If the clerk is unable to give you a copy of the rules, find out if you can at least read and possibly photocopy certain portions that appear to bear most directly on your case.

The following composites are based upon several courts' rules gathered for this book. They do not touch upon all, or even most, areas; they are included to give you a feel for what to expect and what to look for in studying your own court's rules.

Rules of the Court relating to small claims are important, too, for what they *do not* say, giving the judge more leeway than he or she might have in general sessions court where rules are more extensive.

Each state's **Rules of Civil Procedure** normally spell out discovery measures, such as the posttrial use of verbal or written interrogatories designed to discover assets of a defendant who appears unwilling or unable to pay a judgment.

Ordinarily, court rules compel such a defendant to answer, under oath, all reasonable questions asked in such an interrogatory. But since most small claims court rules are silent on the subject, this section contains a *Petition for Order to Answer Interrogatories* similar to that used in many courts for obtaining a judge's order that the defendant answer.

The **Rules of the Court** will take on greater meaning later on and you may want to come back and read them again, but this is as good a place as any to present them.

RULES OF THE COURT AND INFORMATION FOR LITIGANTS
State of New Bedford, County of Putnam

JURISDICTION
1. Meaning

Jurisdiction is (1) the power to hear and decide a particular case and render some judgment in the case, and (2) decide the facts from evidence, (3) apply the law to the facts, and (4) render a judgment based upon the conclusion reached from the law and the facts.

Jurisdiction is given to a court by law. It cannot be waived or given by consent of the parties. A court cannot refuse jurisdiction given to it, nor can it assume jurisdiction not given to it by law.

2. Necessity for

A judgment rendered by a court which has no jurisdiction is invalid. It has no force or effect, grants no rights and binds nobody. If, however, a court has jurisdiction, its judgment in the case is **not** void even if it is wrong. Jurisdiction includes the power to decide the case correctly or incorrectly.

AMOUNT IN CONTROVERSY NOT OVER $500*
1. In General

The Small Claims Court has jurisdiction in all civil cases in which the amount in controversy is $500 or less, exclusive of [not including] interest, unless exclusive original jurisdiction to try a particular case is given to the County District Court.

2. Amount in Controversy

The amount in controversy in a case is not the amount a party is entitled to recover. It is the amount of the plaintiff's claim as determined by the pleadings, whether written or oral, original or amended, upon which the parties go to trial and the largest amount for which judgment can be rendered upon the pleadings.

If a plaintiff's pleadings assert a claim for no more than $500, the Small Claims Court has jurisdiction. The latest pleadings in Small Claims Court determine the amount in controversy. Therefore, even though the plaintiff's original pleadings assert a claim for more than $500, if he amends his pleadings before trial to reduce the amount to $500 or less, the court has jurisdiction to try the case.

If you feel you're entitled to $600, but your small claims court maximum is $500, consider reducing your claim to $500 and filing in small claims court.

*This amount may be higher or lower in various states.

Attorney's fees and other costs associated with bringing your suit before a regular court could eat up the $100 difference anyway. It can be made obvious to the judge from the nature of your claim that you're really owed more than $500 and you stand a pretty good chance of being awarded the full amount of your claim.

3. Counterclaim of Defendant
If the defendant files a counterclaim against the plaintiff in a case, the defendant's claim may not be for more than $500. The amount of the counterclaim is determined by the amount the defendant seeks to recover under his pleadings.

Where the plaintiff files a claim against the defendant, and the defendant files a counterclaim against the plaintiff, the amount in controversy is not determined by adding together the two claims. The court's jurisdiction of each claim is controlled by the maximum amount each party seeks to recover.

If the plaintiff's claim is for $500 or less, and the defendant's counterclaim is for more than $500, the court has no jurisdiction to hear and decide the counterclaim, but it has jurisdiction to try the plaintiff's claim.

The above rule is not universal, though it is coming into increasing acceptance. In many jurisdictions a counterclaim in excess of the small claims maximum automatically moves **both** suits, the original suit and the counterclaim, to a court having higher limits, even though the amount of the initial suit was less than the small claims maximum. However, growing numbers of courts are following the above-quoted rule to reduce the filing of counterclaims merely as a defendant's tactical maneuver to delay a case and wear down the plaintiff.

VENUE
1. Meaning
Venue means the county in which a plaintiff has the legal right to file and try his suit, regardless of the defendant's objections. Venue does not mean the same thing as jurisdiction. It is possible, therefore, for a court to have jurisdiction to try a case, but not have venue.

2. Basic Rule of Venue
All suits brought in Small Claims Court must be brought in the county in which the defendant resides, except that when the defendant has contracted to perform an obligation in a particular county, the suit to recover on that obligation may be brought in the county where the defendant contracted to perform it or, in the case of a tort, where the act was committed. The defendant may file a plea to have the case transferred to the county of his or her residence.

The privilege of being tried in one's own county is a valuable right, and before a defendant may be sued elsewhere, the case must come clearly within one of the exceptions to the basic rule.

3. Corporate Agency or Representative
The plaintiff may bring suit in the county where the defendant corporation, association or joint stock company has an "agent" or "representative." An "agent" or "representative" is more than a mere employee or servant of the defendant. He is a person who transacts the defendant's business in the county of suit in more or less regular and permanent manner. He handles the commercial or business transactions having to do with the corporate affairs of the defendant. He is subject to the control of the defendant, but has some discretionary power, and is authorized to act for the defendant in promoting its affairs.

The mere fact that a nationwide soft-drink company has a local bottling plant in the county of suit, or that a nationwide auto manufacturer has a local dealer in the county of suit, does not mean that it has an "agent" or "representative" there. On the other hand, a person or corporation authorized to make contracts in behalf of the defendant is the defendant's "agent" or "representative." It is not essential, however, that the local person have the authority to make contracts on behalf of the defendant.

COSTS AND FEES
7. Recovery of Attorney's Fees
The general rule is that, unless provided for by statute or by contract between the parties, attorney's fees incurred by the plaintiff are not recoverable against the defendant in a suit upon contract or in tort [see glossary]. If the plaintiff's suit is based upon a contract or promissory note which provided that the defendant shall pay a certain attorney's fees in the event of his failure to perform, the plaintiff may recover a reasonable attorney's fee as part of his claim. A statute provides that a plaintiff may recover a reasonable attorney's fee in addition to his claim and costs if his suit is based upon valid claim for services rendered, labor done, material furnished, overcharges on freight or express, lost or damaged freight or express, or stock killed or injured, or suits founded upon a sworn account or accounts, if the defendant failed to pay the claim within thirty (30) days after it was presented to him for payment by the plaintiff.

When the plaintiff is entitled to sue for and recover an attorney's fee, the amount of the fee becomes a part of the amount in controversy, and if the amount of the plaintiff's claim exceeds the fee and $500, the court does not have jurisdiction.

CAUSE OF ACTION
1. In General
When a person suffers a loss or injury by the wrongful act of another, he has a cause of action to recover his damages. It is the aim of the law to protect every person against the wrongful act of every other person, and the law has provided an action for injuries done by disturbing a person in the enjoyment of any right or privilege he has.

CONTINUANCE AND POSTPONEMENT OF TRIAL
1. In General
For good cause shown, supported by affidavit, the judge may continue any suit to the next regular term of his court or postpone the suit to some other day of the term. The affidavit setting forth the reason for the continuance or postponement may be made by either party or his attorney. The granting or denial of a motion for continuance rests within the sound discretion of the judge, but before any judge may exercise his discretion, he must be presented with a sworn

motion setting forth good cause. A case may be continued or postponed also by consent of the parties or by operation of law.

PLEADINGS
1. In General
The purpose of a pleading [the body of the plaintiff's claim] is to inform the court and the party being sued of what the pleader's contentions will be when the case is tried and to give fair and adequate notice to the party being sued of the nature of the cause of action asserted against him so that he may adequately prepare his defense. The pleadings must set forth enough facts to enable the judge to determine that a good cause of action probably exists. The plaintiff's petition should be so certain and specific that, accepting the truth of the facts alleged in it, the court can render judgment on it.
2. Exception
The purpose of an exception is to furnish the defendant a means by which to force the plaintiff to make his pleadings more clear and specific and to furnish a better, more complete and more definite statement on the matters upon which the plaintiff relies for relief sought from the court. A [motion for] exception must point out the particular pleading being excepted and must clearly define the specific defect, omission, obscurity, duplicity, generality or other alleged insufficiency of the plaintiff's pleading.

As plaintiff, the message for you here is to make your claim specific enough to prevent the defendant from entering a successful motion of exception, thus placing you in the position of stepping into some innocent-looking quicksand along the path of explanation and clarification the defense asks the judge to order you to travel.

EVIDENCE
4. Plaintiff's Evidence in Chief
The plaintiff's "evidence in chief" is evidence which supports his case, and his evidence in chief must prove at least a prima facie case. A *prima facie* case is one that will entitle the plaintiff to recover if no evidence to the contrary is offered by the defendant.
Since the plaintiff has the burden of proving his claim or cause of action, he is entitled and should be permitted to present all of the competent evidence he has which is relevant to proving the facts of his case, even though he may have more than one source of evidence which tends to prove the same fact.
5. Defendant's Evidence in Chief
The defendant's "evidence in chief" is evidence which supports his or her defense to the plaintiff's claim. Except for a *summary judgment* [see Glossary], a judgment may not be rendered against the defendant before the defendant has had an opportunity to present a defense and has rested his or her case.

JURY
1. In General
If either party wants a trial by jury [usually six jurors in small claims cases], he must, at least one calendar day before the date on which the case is set to be tried, file a request for trial by jury and pay a jury fee of $5.50. When the request is made and the fee paid, a jury will be summoned as in other cases in Small Claims Court.
2. Verdict
When a case has been tried by jury and a verdict has been returned by the jury, the Judge must announce the verdict in open court and note it in his docket and render judgment on it.

JUDGMENT
1. In General
The judgment must clearly state the decision as to the rights of the parties in the case and which party has to pay costs, and it must direct the issuance of whatever process that may be necessary to enforce the judgment.
2. Costs
The party who wins the case is entitled to recover costs, unless the law expressly provides otherwise.
3. Specific Articles
When the judgment is for recovery of specific articles of personal or real property, their value must be separately assessed, and the judgment must be that the plaintiff recover the specific articles if they can be found, and if they cannot be found, that the plaintiff recover their value as assessed with interest at the rate of 7 percent from the date of the judgment.

APPEAL
1. In General
When the amount in controversy, not counting costs, is more than $50, the dissatisfied party may appeal from a final judgment to the County District Court and the trial in the County court is *de novo* [a new trial].

If you're handed a copy of the **Rules of the Court** that looks like a major city telephone book, don't be intimidated. Many of the rules deal with qualifications and conduct of the judge, hiring of personnel, and other administrative matters that have nothing to do with your case.

Turn to the table of contents and zero in on what you need to know. Ask permission to use the courthouse copying machine (there's usually one in the law library for public use) to reproduce material you'd like to take home.

42 Evidence and Witnesses

EVIDENCE

Before you go to the clerk's office to file your suit, spend some time thinking about evidence. Your receipts, warranties, and complaint letters are documentary evidence. You can also present documentary evidence in the form of photographs.

If a defective product, poor workmanship, or damage must be repaired, bring estimates—three if you can manage it. If you have medical bills, bring those.

The best evidence is physical evidence. I wouldn't try to bring a washing maching half full of water into the courtroom, but if you have a toaster or portable TV that doesn't work, bring it with you, plus an extension cord long enough to reach a wall outlet.

If you have a bad example of auto body work, park your car as close to the courthouse as you can. Judges have been known, particularly if it's a nice day, to step out into the street for a firsthand look at what you've been talking about.

WITNESSES

Witnesses can provide evidence in several ways:

1. A witness can appear and give testimony.
2. A witness can appear to give testimony and can bring documentary or physical evidence to court.
3. In many states a witness may make and sign a sworn statement that you can present as evidence in a **small claims** court. (Ask the clerk of the court if this may be done in your state.)

Potential witnesses might be people who were with you when you made the purchase, who saw the smoking refrigerator, or who witnessed the damage or injury. Potential witnesses might also be experts qualified to evaluate your problem, pass judgment on the quality of repairs, and make valid estimates of repair costs and fair market value.

If a body shop has done a bang-up job on repairing your collision-damaged car, you might bring photos plus several estimates for having the work done properly. But if yours is a farily costly claim, you might also offer to pay a body shop its regular hourly rate to have a qualified person appear as an expert witness to describe the problem and estimate the cost of putting it right. (If you win, the defendant will have to pay the expense of your expert witness's testimony—that's part of "court costs" borne by the loser.)

If you do use an expert witness in a situation like this, make sure you get someone who does the work rather than a shop owner or service manager who the opposition might point out really has not personally exercised the relevant skill for some time and is thus unqualified to testify.

The use of an expert witness is often good tactics. In some jurisdictions, however, an expert witness MUST be used to establish (prove) the necessity of repair or replacement and the reasonableness of certain damages claimed.

Whomever you use, even if it is your neighbor or best friend who is glad to help, ask the clerk of the court to issue a subpoena, which is an order of the court requiring the witness to appear.

There are several reasons for this. First, if for some reason an important witness who has received a subpoena fails to appear, you can probably ask for and obtain a continuance (a postponement of the case), something which would be more difficult to do if your witness was just coming in on his or her own.

Second, many union contracts call for, and many employers will voluntarily pay, a worker who must be absent from the job due to a subpoena requiring an appearance in court. Testifying on your behalf without a subpoena might cost your witness a day's pay or loss of vacation time or sick leave. In other cases a subpoena simply provides your witness with an unarguable reason for having to be away from the office.

Another way of using the witness subpoena is to have the court order some of the *other* side's people to appear at the hearing. If Art's Appliance City sent a repair person who just looked at your washer and said, "You sure got yourself a problem here," and left, subpoena the repair person and ask him or her about that. You could subpoena Art, too, and require him to bring along his repair and service records so the court could determine if he has many repeat service requests, if he has sufficient repair personnel to service the amount of business he does, and whether his people made more than one unsatisfactory visit to your home.

If your car was the victim of poor mechanical work at XYZ Motors, you can subpoena the mechanic who worked on the car (whose name or initials should be on the work order), as well as the service writer, service manager, and even the owner—to ask them questions about "service policy" as it affects your unsatisfactory experience.

You'll want to give calling in the other side's people a bit of thought, making sure that you have a strong case and that you have some questions to ask them when they get there. But you can see the increased motivation for the president of XYZ Motors to settle out of court when he contemplates some of the things that could happen if you get his mechanic on the witness stand. Then, too, it can be fairly inconvenient and costly for a business if three or four people have to go to court. All the more reason to settle with you if they can.

There will usually be a nominal charge for serving each witness subpoena, plus a witness fee, probably about $10 per witness, that the court pays out—using your money.

If you win, you will be reimbursed these as well as other court costs because in handing down his decision the judge almost always grants any award "plus costs," which means the defendant will have to pay the expense of your costs (except your attorney's fees, if any) in addition to the amount of the award.

There are two common types of witness subpoenas:

1. **Subpoena for Witness**, which merely requires that the witness appear at the date and time specified and be prepared to give testimony.
2. **Subpoena Duces Tecum**, which requires that the witness bring to court bookkeeping journals, sales records, work orders, other documents, physical evidence, or whatever else may be specified in the subpoena.

As plaintiff in a small claims suit, you may be asked by the clerk to complete an **Application for Subpoena** and/or the court's forms for **Subpoena for Witness** or **Subpoena Duces Tecum**.

The following completed samples of **Application for Subpoena** and **Subpoena Duces Tecum** should aid you when you fill out photocopies of our ready-to-use Forms 42.1 and 42.2 (pages F235–F238)—forms that may serve as work sheets and should be brought in to court to help you complete *their* forms. Note that an ordinary **Subpoena for Witness** would be the same as the **Subpoena Duces Tecum**, but simply without the *duces tecum*.

Sample of Form 42.1/F235

STATE OF NEW BEDFORD

Application for Subpoena

June 3 _____, 19 84

TO: Hon. JUDGE of the
_____ Putnam _____ County District Court
Division of Small Claims

Robert B. Mason   Arthur C. Smedley d/b/a
25 Calkinstown Road   vs.   Art's Appliance City
Hinkley, N.B.   10531   35 Clark Street
                                         Sommerton, N.B.   10560

No. ___ SC 3-80-57954 ___

I HEREBY REQUEST that you issue a subpoena for each of the following witnesses, represented to reside within the jurisdiction of said court where the suit above described is pending.

Name	County	Address	D.O.S.*
David K. Lowen	Putnam	45 Front Street Sommerton, N.B. 10551	
Louella Snip	Burr	365 Columbus Circle Slapes Corners, N.B. 10566	

Arthur C. Smedley d/b/a Art's Appliance City
35 Clark Street, Sommerton, N.B.   10560

The Defendant to produce at trial all sales, service and other records

pertaining to the sale of American Eagle, Inc., Tangle-Matic washing

machine to Plaintiff on March 3, 1984.

Such subpoena(s) to be made returnable no later than the ___ 1st ___ day of ___ July ___, 19 84 .

(Signed) _Robert B. Mason_

† _____ Plaintiff _____

*Date of subpoena to be filled in by clerk of the court.

†Show Plaintiff, Defendant, or Attorney for Plaintiff or Defendant.

Sample of Form 42.1 (*Continued*)

No. _____ SC 3-80-57954

Application

for

Subpoena

Robert B. Mason
25 Calkinstown Road
Hinkley, N.B.   10531

vs.

Arthur C. Smedley d/b/a
Art's Appliance City
35 Clark Street
Sommerton, N.B.   10560

Putnam County District Court
Court
Division of Small Claims

Putnam
County, New Bedford

Filed ___3rd___ day of ___June___, 19 __84__

Sample of Form 42.2/F237

(Bring this **Subpoena** with you at all times.)

STATE OF NEW BEDFORD

𝔖𝔲𝔟𝔭𝔬𝔢𝔫𝔞 𝔇𝔲𝔠𝔢𝔰 𝔗𝔢𝔠𝔲𝔪

No. _____SC 3-80-57954_____

_____Mason_____ vs. _____Smedley_____

TO ANY SHERIFF, CONSTABLE OR OTHER PERSON WHO IS NOT A PARTY AND WHO IS NOT LESS THAN EIGHTEEN YEARS OF AGE, A CITIZEN OF THE STATE OF NEW BEDFORD, GREETING:

YOU ARE HEREBY COMMANDED TO SUMMON _____

_____Arthur C. Smedley_____

to be and personally appear at __10:00__ o'clock, __A.M.__, on the __15th__ day of __July__, 19 _84_; before the HONORABLE JUDGE of the District Court, Division of Small Claims, __Putnam__ County, New Bedford, held within said county at the courthouse thereof, ____101 Courthouse Square, Sommerton____ _____, New Bedford, then and there to testify and say the truth on behalf of the __XXXXXXXXXXXXXXXXXXX__ in the above-styled and -numbered case, now pending before said Court, and there to remain from day to day, and from term to term, until discharged by said Court.

Said named witness is further commanded to produce at said time and place above, as now set forth, the following books, papers, documents and/or other tangible things, to wit:

Invoice, sales agreement, credit sales contract and all delivery, installation and warranty repair service call records pertaining to the sale of American Eagle Inc., Tangle-Matic washing machine to Plaintiff on March 3, 1984.

HEREIN FAIL NOT, and make due return thereof, showing how you have executed same.

Issued and given under my hand and seal of said Court at office, this __7th__ day of __June__, 19 _84_.

Clerk ____Cyrus T. Hammer____

_____Putnam_____ County, New Bedford

By ____*Peter Ryan*____
              Deputy

··

RETURN

Came to hand the __9th__ day of __June__, 19 _84_, at __10__ o'clock __A__ M., and executed the __13th__ day of __June__, 19 _84_, at __2:30__ o'clock __P__ M., by delivering to the within-named witness at __residence__ in __Putnam__ County, New Bedford, in person, a true copy of this Subpoena.

(Signed) ____*Damon Jennings*____
          * ____*Deputy Sheriff*____

*Show Sheriff, Constable, Marshal or Citizen.

Sample of Form 42.2 (*Continued*)

ACCEPTANCE OF SERVICE

The undersigned witness named in the Subpoena acknowledges receipt of a copy thereof and hereby accepts and waives service of such Subpoena.

(Signed) *Arthur C. Smedley*

June 13, 1984
Date

RETURN ORIGINAL TO CLERK OF THE COURT

(Bring this **Subpoena** with you at all times.)

No. SC 3-80-57954

Subpoena Duces Tecum

Robert B. Mason
25 Calkinstown Road
Hinkley, N.B.   10531

vs.

Arthur C. Smedley d/b/a
Art's Appliance City
35 Clark Street
Sommerton, N.B.   10560

Issued   June 7, 19 84

Cyrus T. Hammer
Clerk

Putnam County District/SCD
Court

Putnam
County, New Bedford

By *Peter Ryan*
Deputy Clerk

43 Out-of-Court Settlement

As we have implied, a small claims lawsuit is the greatest attention-getter in the world. Your complaints may have gone unanswered, your phone calls may have gone unreturned, but now, once the other party has been served with a summons to appear in court, you cease to be invisible.

If you have filed a suit against a company, their first response is likely to come from its attorney or local manager, either apologizing profusely for "this little misunderstanding" or aggressively pointing out that you "don't have a leg to stand on" and that you'll regret it if you persist in "making a fool out of yourself."

Step two, whether it's a "little misunderstanding" or "you don't have a leg to stand on," will possibly be an offer of an out-of-court settlement. They'll probably try a token offer, say $50 if you've sued for $250, or will offer at most about half of the amount you've asked the court to award.

Only you know how little you're willing to settle for, but if you've included every possible reasonable expense you can think of in your **Statement of Claim,** you'll be starting high anyway.

There is one thing to say for an out-of-court settlement: it will save you a lot of time and inconvenience and may not be the comedown it at first appears to be, since the judge may not award the full amount you've asked for anyway. A good rule of thumb might be to give serious thought to accepting any offer that equals 70 percent of your claim—and if you're offered more than that, take it.

The defendant's attorney, if there is one, is in a difficult position at this point. He has to do something to show the client that he is worth the money he is being paid or has been charging by way of accepting a salary or retainer fee. He (or she) is under pressure to come up with some kind of settlement that is less than the amount you're suing for. If you will not settle, he will try that much harder to shoot you down in court, both to prove his worth to his client and to "get even" with you for making him go to trial. About 75 to 90 percent of civil suits are settled out of court anyway, so nobody is really expecting you to take the case all the way to trial.

As plaintiff, you're on the spot too. If you do not accept a reasonable settlement offer, almost the first thing the judge will ask is, "Why wasn't this settled out of court?" Unless you've got a really good reason for not accepting an offer of about 70 percent, you'll be hard pressed to convince his honor you've been "reasonable." He or she might just award you 50 or 60 percent of the amount claimed and say, "Next case."

There are, of course, times when you will not be prepared to settle for anything less than the full amount claimed. There can be instances when you'll be able to convince the judge you deserve every penny you've asked for. If you're out $387.95 for the cost of a washing machine, plus $120 in lost wages for days you missed work to admit a repairman who never showed up and $25 for the expense of clothes that had to be sent to a commercial laundry, you can very easily point out to the judge, "Your honor, I can't *afford* to lose this money." The same could hold true with respect to warranty work on a car or unsatisfactory work done on your home.

Whether settlement for the full amount seems reasonable to the judge depends on the merits of your case, but in more practical terms it also depends upon the defendant's history before the court, the amount of money involved, and your financial resources compared to those of the defendant.

If you do receive a pretrial settlement offer that is acceptable you can say, "OK, when do I get the money?" If you get the money, all of it, before the trial date, you can cancel the trial. If you don't obtain full payment prior to the trial, get the settlement agreement in writing.

The settlement agreement (Form 43.1, page F239) specifies the amount and means of payment and gives you protection that you can go back into court with if the defendant should default. The completed sample settlement agreement on page 156 should be used as a guide to aid you in completing a photocopy of our ready-to-use blank form.

PRETRIAL MANEUVERS

An out-of-court settlement offer is not the *only* thing you might receive before the trial. You could get a copy of a letter similar to this from the defendant or the defendant's attorney to the court:

FETTERMAN, FREEMANTLE AND FLEISCHER
Law Offices
1285 Downey
Sommerton, N.B. 10560

```
Clerk
Putnam County District Court
Division of Small Claims
101 Courthouse Square
Sommerton, N.B. 10560

RE:  BROWN VS. SMEDLEY
     OUR FILE NO. 1215

Gentlemen:
     Kindly be advised that we represent the Defend-
ant in the above matter, which is returnable May 20,
1984.
     In order to permit us to confer with the Defendant
and investigate the circumstances of this case, will
you kindly continue this matter for one month.
```

A copy of this request is being sent to the Plaintiff.

Sincerely,

Walter P. Fetterman

The opposition may not even bother to write you —sending you a copy of their letter requesting a delay of the trial. Their request could be an honest effort to determine the merits of the case—and possibly advise their client to settle—or it might be the opening shot in a campaign of delay and inconvenience designed to wear you down.

In any event, your first step is to show the opposition that you intend to be firm and not allow yourself to be manipulated. As soon as you receive a copy of correspondence similar to that above, you can respond promptly with a letter of your own to the court:

Dear _____:

We are in receipt of correspondence from Walter P. Fetterman, attorney for the Defendant in small claims action Docket No. SC 3-80-57954.

As plaintiff we have no objection to counsel's request for a continuation of one month to provide time to confer with the Defendant.

We trust that the time requested will be sufficient for the purpose stated and that no further delay will be required.

A copy of this letter is being mailed to the attorney for the Defendant.

Very truly yours,

It's probably a good idea to send a "between-the-lines" message to the opposition that it probably won't pay to play games with you. To accomplish this, mail a letter similar to the following to the defendant a week or so after the trial date has been set.

Dear _____:

I regret that we were unable to resolve the problem of my new car's transmission. As you are aware from having been served with a summons and complaint, our dispute will be settled in Putnam County District Court, Division of Small Claims, on July 25, 1984.

If the trial date is inconvenient, I would be happy to agree to a continuance if you will give me three or four days notice to reschedule my work. You can reach me at my office (351-1100) during business hours or at my home (456-1414) any evening until 10:00 P.M.

Otherwise, I expect that this matter will be resolved at trial on July 25.

Sincerely,

Another possibly valid move that the defendant might make is to file an **affirmative defense** with the court, setting forth an item-by-item refutation of each and every claim made by the plaintiff. The techniques of affirmative defense writing are a bit beyond the scope of this book—writing an affirmative defense in a small claims suit is just as exacting as writing an affirmative defense to a multimillion dollar claim. However, the following are a few of the least complicated affirmative defenses that a defendant might use:

- Plaintiff's contributory negligence
- Duress by plaintiff
- Fraud by plaintiff
- Illegal (and thus unenforceable) contract
- Statute of limitations
- Prior award in arbitration
- Assumption of risk (for a hazardous activity) by plaintiff
- Discharge of defendant's debt in bankruptcy
- Absence of consideration (such as payment)
- Lack of venue
- Lack of jurisdiction

There are a few other maneuvers more common to trials before regular courts that a defendant might use as part of a campaign to wear the plaintiff down. One move might be to file a motion with the judge for permission to take sworn depositions or to submit written interrogatories to the plaintiff consisting of a long list of questions (as a tactical move, the longer, the better) asking for all sorts of detailed information about the claim: dates, damages, circumstances, descriptions, witnesses, etc.

A part of the normal civil litigation discovery procedure, the written interrogatory provides the opposition with a lot of information about the strong and weak points of your case: what you know and what you don't know, what evidence you have and don't have, etc.

Another source of delay, a **counterclaim** by the defendant will almost always induce the judge to grant a continuance or two without question. A wily defendant, especially a wily defendant with a wily attorney, will often come up with a seemingly valid counterclaim if for no other reason than to delay the trial and wear you down.

There can be a similar cause for delay, if, for example, a contractor-defendant's lateness in completion of a job results in litigation, and the late job completion was because of overdue delivery of materials by a supplier who failed to meet a contracted-for delivery date. In that kind of a situation the contractor-defendant might file a **cross-claim** (lawsuit) against the supplier in an effort to pass along any liability for late completion due to the supplier's tardy delivery of materials.

You'll probably never be faced with a written interrogatory in a small claims case, whether you're a plaintiff or a defendant. If you are, the stakes are probably high enough to make it worth your while to hire an attorney.

Another step the defense might take, also not often part of a small claims suit but still possible with permission of the judge, is to file a **Notice to Take Deposition** on the plaintiff. Under this procedure the defense can bring the plaintiff (or any of the plaintiff's witnesses, for that matter) before the defendant or defendant's attorney to take down statements, under oath and recorded by a stenographer, in response to questions put by the defendant or defendant's attorney. (But two can play at that game. If faced with such action by the opposition, you can file a motion with the court to take deposition on the defendant.)

The taking of depositions is a customary procedure in normal civil suits, and it's quite possible that a good attorney can convince the judge that the *only* way he or she can prepare a defense that will result in justice is to take your deposition, and those of your witnesses, prior to trial.

You will seldom be faced with written answers, counterclaims, written interrogatories, and depositions in a small claims suit because the damages claimed usually aren't great enough to justify the expense and trouble and because in many states attorneys are not permitted to participate in small claims litigation.

Sample of Form 43.1/F239

Agreement

IN ACCORDANCE with the terms set forth herein,

_____ Robert B. Mason _____, Plaintiff, and _____ Arthur C. Smedley _____

_____, Defendant, in the action of _____ Mason _____ vs. _____ Smedley _____

_____, Docket No. _____ SC 3-80-57954 _____, in _____ Putnam County District _____

Court, Division of Small Claims _____, agree that the above action between them is

hereby settled without trial for the sum of $ _____ 533.70 _____ to be paid by the Defendant to the Plaintiff _____
on or before June 25, 1984 _____.

It is further agreed that prior to the date for trial the Plaintiff shall advise the court of this Agreement and discontinue the above action.

The Plaintiff shall have the right, in the event of default of payment of the above sum, to collect same from the Defendant, in addition to court costs, interest and reasonable attorney's fees.

Robert B. Mason
_____
Plaintiff

Arthur C. Smedley
_____
Defendant

Dated _____ June 20 _____, 19 __84__.

44 Trying Your Case

When the date set for the trial approaches, contact the clerk to make sure the case has not been postponed. On the day of the trial check the court's docket, which is usually posted outside the courtroom door. The docket will list your name vs. the defendant's and might list a tentative time for the trial. You may find that only fifteen or twenty minutes is allowed for hearing your case.

No matter how much we might say here, you can learn much more about trying your case by visiting the judge's court sometime when he or she is hearing cases. Not only will you get firsthand knowledge of the procedure, but you'll develop a feel for how the judge operates—whether he asks a lot of questions, whether he asks to see a lot of documentary evidence, or whether he likes to move through the docket at a fast pace or sometimes seems to like to "settle into" a case, probing for circumstances that might not at first be evident from the plaintiff's or defendant's initial statements.

In one sense at least, a part of trying your case will be anticlimactic because this is where all of your record keeping, letter writing, and remembering to think "evidence" is going to pay off. Other considerations aside for the moment, if you can document your claim, it will be just about impossible for your opponent to square his or her defense with your proof.

These are the steps your hearing is likely to follow:

1. The clerk will call your case and determine if the plaintiff and defendant are both in court.
2. As plaintiff, you will be called forward, sworn, and asked by the judge to state your complaint. At this time you will advise the judge of any documentary or physical evidence you have to present and/or any witnesses you wish to have called. The judge may ask questions while or after you state your case.
3. The judge will allow the defense to cross-examine you and any of your witnesses.
4. The defendant will state his or her case and present any evidence or witnesses. The judge may ask questions.
5. The plaintiff will be given an opportunity to cross-examine the defendant and any defense witnesses.
6. After hearing both sides, the judge may hand down a decision and judgment immediately or might reserve decision and judgment until later, in which case the plaintiff and defendant will receive copies of the judgment in the mail.

Remember, the court's *decision* may be in favor of the defendant or plaintiff. The court's *judgment* may be an award of money to the plaintiff or defendant. If there is no counterclaim, the judgment for the defendant often notes that he may "go hence" or "go forth," meaning that he is not found liable and is "free."

When going into trial remember that the odds are in your favor; 75 percent of all small claims cases are decided for the plaintiff. This occurs so often, in fact, that around the courthouse J.P. is said to stand for "judgment for the plaintiff" as much as for Justice of the Peace when it comes to rendering judgment in what lawyers (bound to playing with words as they are) traditionally refer to as "small clams" court.

Several days before the trial, in fact as soon as you're fairly certain that you're not going to accept an out-of-court settlement, write down a brief outline of what you want to tell the judge:

1. What the problem is.
2. What steps you took to resolve the problem.
3. What the defendant did or did not do.
4. How the problem has affected you: inconvenience, injury, loss of wages or time at work, cost of repairs or replacement, etc.
5. What you want—in dollar terms.

Remember that you should be prepared to "prove" your claim, using physical evidence, documents, and expert or other witnesses whenever possible.

It is okay to refer to notes when stating your case, just keep them short enough to fit on a three-by-five card. And *don't* write anything on the card that you would not want the opposition to see. Sometimes the defense attorney will ask if you mind if he or she looks at your notes—just a ploy to shake you up a bit.

In stating your case be direct, be brief, be unemotional, be logical. Don't go on and on, don't make slurs about the defendant, don't make accusations. *Just state the facts.* And be respectful.

EVIDENCE

If you plan to present bills, receipts, work orders, warranties, correspondence, cancelled checks, etc., have clean, legible **copies** well organized and ready to give to the judge, but do not hand the judge your evidence unless he or she asks for it. If you have a series of bills or other documents listing amounts of money, prepare a tabulation showing dates or numbers, followed by a total.

Do not forget photographs. If bad bodywork on your car will show up in a photo, take one and bring it to court. The same goes for bad construction work, water damage, etc. If you have physical evidence, such as clothes ruined by your cleaner or laundry, bring them.

WITNESSES

Never subpoena or call a witness unless you are **sure** he or she will help your case. Never ask a witness a question unless you are **sure** what the answer will be.

There are two kinds of witnesses. **Friendly** witnesses are "for" your side and appear willingly on your behalf. They can be people who were with you when you made a purchase or attempted to have a problem rectified, who saw the damage or injury occur, etc. There are also "neutral" friendly witnesses, such as experts qualified to evaluate your problem (such as bad workmanship or damage) and make a realistic estimate of the cost of putting it right.

And then there are **unfriendly** witnesses, maybe a mechanic or service manager or executive of the defendant company who would rather not testify at all and certainly not in any way that would help your case.

If you have subpoenaed any witnesses *duces tecum*, ask questions that will provide facts from the record—"What was the date of the last service call?"; "What part does the work order show was replaced?"; etc.

By all means feel free to discuss with friendly or expert witnesses ahead of time any questions you are going to ask—as well as what answers you are after. Lawyers do it all the time. And remember: **never** ask a question unless you know what the answer is going to be.

DRESS

What to wear for the trial is one thing you'll learn by visiting the judge's court ahead of time. I've seen major-city small claims judges wearing enough black robes to sit on the Supreme Court and I've seen judges in equally big cities hear cases wearing regular business clothes. Rural and small-town small claims judges have been known to hold trial wearing blue jeans and a work shirt right off the ranch or farm.

Generally, you're pretty safe appearing in court the way you would ordinarily dress for work. I wouldn't exactly advise you to show up wearing greasy overalls or a white chef's hat (certainly not wearing greasy overalls *and* a white chef's hat), but if you're a construction worker, or a waitress, or a nurse, or a plumber who might have to go directly from court to your job, no judge is likely to hold it against you if you do not appear dressed for a job interview.

Be clean and be neat. Visit the judge's court ahead of time just to make sure your judge doesn't like to have his court look like everybody there has gathered for a funeral. If in doubt, ask the clerk.

JUDGMENT

The form of the court's judgment can be anything from a postcard to a legal-size document that could pass for a treaty between nations. But beyond any "Greetings," "Wherefore," and "Whereas," the judgment will include:

1. Whether the court's decision is in favor of the plaintiff or defendant.
2. If in favor of the plaintiff, the amount of the award, almost always "plus court costs" and almost never to include attorney's fees.

If the court finds for the defendant, the judgment will state:

1. Judgment is entered in favor of the defendant who shall "go forth without delay."
2. The defendant shall be entitled to court costs.

Remember that the judgment is not money. All the judgment is, is a hunting license authorizing you to collect the amount of the award from the defendant if you can—and you might have to go to court to do it.

An example of a typical small claims judgment form may be found on the following page.

DEFAULT BY THE DEFENDANT

If the defendant fails to appear, the judge, upon hearing the plaintiff's case, is very likely to issue a **default judgment** against the defendant. A default judgment may either take effect immediately or may be issued with a stay of a few weeks to give the defendant time to enter a motion to vacate the judgment and request a new trial.

Remember that in many jurisdictions, service of the Summons and Complaint may be legally accomplished by mail. Consequently, it is possible that the defendant may not show up for or even know of the trial. It's entirely possible, too, that some day you may be on the receiving end of a default judgment handed down on the basis of a trial that you were unaware of. If you're ever the "victim" of a small claims court default judgment, YOU will be the one who will have to complete and file any motion to vacate that judgment—and you'll have to do it within a relatively short time after the judgment was entered. You will need to show "good cause" in your motion to set aside the judgment **and** must have what the court determines to be a "meritorious" defense.

The completed sample **Declaration and Notice of Motion to Vacate Judgment** on page 160 will serve as a guide for completing Form 44.1 (page F241). Fill in blanks of our ready-to-use form before contacting the clerk to file an actual motion in your local court.

Sample Small Claims Judgment Form

STATE OF NEW BEDFORD

No. _____

_____)
Plaintiff   )   PUTNAM COUNTY DISTRICT COURT
)
)   DIVISION OF SMALL CLAIMS
                  vs.   )
)
)   101 Courthouse Square
)
_____)   Sommerton, N.B. 10560
Defendant   )

𝔍𝔲𝔡𝔤𝔪𝔢𝔫𝔱

This day in the above-entitled and -numbered case, whereas _____ is Plaintiff and _____ is Defendant, came the Plaintiff in person, and the Defendant, though duly served with process, failed to appear or answer in this behalf, but wholly made default; and the pleadings, evidence and argument having been heard and fully understood, it is the opinion of the Court that Plaintiff is justly entitled to a judgment against Defendant as hereafter set out:

It is therefore, accordingly ordered, adjudged and decreed by the Court that the Plaintiff, _____ _____, do have and recover of the Defendant, _____, the said sum of $ _____ with interest thereon at the rate of 8 percent per annum, together with his costs in this behalf expended, and that he have his execution forthwith.

_____
Judge
PUTNAM COUNTY DISTRICT COURT

No. _____

𝔍𝔲𝔡𝔤𝔪𝔢𝔫𝔱

vs.

Dated _____ 19 ___

Sample of Form 44.1/F241

STATE OF NEW BEDFORD

No. _____ SC 3-80-57954 _____

Robert B. Mason	)	PUTNAM COUNTY DISTRICT COURT
Plaintiff	)	
	)	DIVISION OF SMALL CLAIMS
	)	
vs.	)	101 Courthouse Square
	)	
Arthur C. Smedley	)	Sommerton, N.B. 10560
Defendant		

𝔇eclaration and 𝔑otice of 𝔐otion to 𝔙acate 𝔍udgment

WHEREAS I, the undersigned Defendant in the above-styled action; that on _____ December 15, 1983 _____ judgment was entered against me; I was not present at the trial and did not notify the court before trial that I could not be present because:

_____ I did not receive any summons or notice of the above action whatsoever _____

_____

_____

I believe I can prove to the Court that the facts support my defense, to wit: _____

_____ that the debt claimed by the Plaintiff, Robert B. Mason, has been paid in full _____

_____

_____

_____

WHEREFORE, I request that said judgment against me be vacated and the case be tried on its merits. I declare under penalty of perjury that the aforesaid statements are true and correct.

(Signed) *Arthur C. Smedley* _____
Defendant

Executed this _____ 21st _____ day of _____ January _____, 19 _84_ .

Sample of Form 44.1 (*Continued*)

NOTICE OF MOTION

To: Robert B. Mason

25 Calkinstown Road

Hinkley, N.B. 10531

PLEASE TAKE NOTICE that on the _____21st_____ day of _____January_____, 19 _84_, _____
_____I_____ will move the Court for an order vacating the judgment heretofore entered in this case and for trial forthwith.

Arthur C. Smedley
Signature of Moving Party

Dated this _____4th_____ day of _____January_____, 19 _84_.

* *

COURT ORDER

The above motion is hereby _____Granted_____, and trial is set for the _____13th_____ day of _____February_____, 19 _84_.

Walton Green
Judge
PUTNAM COUNTY DISTRICT COURT

Dated this _____2nd_____ day of _____February_____, 19 _84_.

No. _____ SC 3-80-57954

Declaration and Notice of Motion

Robert B. Mason
25 Calkinstown Road
Hinkley, N.B. 10531

vs.

Arthur C. Smedley d/b/a
Art's Appliance City
35 Clark Street
Sommerton, N.B. 10560

Dated _____ January 21, 19 _84_

45 Collecting Your Award

There's no need, if the judge hands down a decision and award in your favor while you and the defendant are both in the courtroom, for you to approach the defendant and say anything. It has been a bad day for the defendant, so just nod on your way out and let it go at that.

Within a few days, if the judge announced a decision in court, and within a few weeks, if he or she reserved decision, you will receive a postcard or other form of judgment. Either way, give the defendant ten days or so after the decision has been rendered to make a move to pay you.

If you have not received payment within ten days of the court's decision date, send the defendant a letter similar to the following, enclosing a photocopy of your copy of the judgment.

```
Dear _____ :
     As you will note from the enclosed judgment
against you, I have been awarded the sum of
$ _____ by the Putnam County District Court,
payable immediately.
     To avoid additional expense and the possibility
of further legal action, please mail a check or
money order for the above amount to me at the fol-
lowing* address:

                    Your name
                    Street Address
                    City, State    Zip

                         Sincerely,


Encl:  Final Judgment dated _____
       Putnam County District Court
```

If the letter fails to obtain payment within ten days or so, inform the clerk that the defendant has failed to satisfy the judgment and then file a **Petition for Writ of Execution**. Some jurisdictions use a printed form; in others the petition is prepared by the plaintiff or in attorneys' offices. Use the completed form sample on page 165 as a guide for filling in the blank petition—Form 45.1 on page F243. If your state does not use a printed petition, ask the clerk if you can use our form as a model for preparing the petition yourself.

If you fill in the appropriate spaces on our **Writ of Execution** (Form 45.2, page F245), the clerk will have everything needed to prepare your **Writ** for you.

When the clerk gives you your Writ, you will have to take it to the sheriff, marshal, or constable to be carried out (executed) for you. Ask the clerk which office (sheriff, marshal, or constable) to con-

tact, and possibly even which individual to see, about executing your Writ.

Sheriffs, constables, and marshals have other things to do, so do not expect any one of them to go out to the defendant's house or place of business the next day to seize the defendant's property. A marshal or constable will normally, by law in some jurisdictions, receive a percentage of any amount collected as the result of his or her seizure and sale of the defendant's property. The sheriff's department will only receive a nominal fee.

Since the constable's or marshal's gain will be slight for collecting on a small claims judgment, he or she will possibly be "too busy" to get around to your case. It's all the same to the sheriff though; whether it's a multithousand-dollar or five-hundred-dollar case, his fees, like the court clerk's fees, are pretty much the same regardless of the amount involved.

There's no hard-and-fast rule to follow when it comes to persuading the sheriff, marshal, or constable to collect on *your* judgment. As they are all elected officials, if you happen to have some political influence, now's the time to use it. Then, too, you might take time to have coffee or lunch with whoever will be carrying out the Writ and reason with him or her, explaining the case's importance to you. If you live in the county, you are a potential favorable voter, campaign contributor, or political antagonist.

The sheriff might tell you that the defendant appears to be "judgment proof," that is, he or she may not have any assets that can be seized and sold by the court. In most states a person's home, furnishings, clothing, tools of a trade, and car used to travel to and from work cannot be taken to satisfy a judgment. Or it may be that the sheriff always seems to be "too busy" to execute your judgment.

However, there are still a couple of things you can do.

USING THE INTERROGATORY "MONEY HOOK"

One highly effective step you can take, especially if the defendant has been giving you the runaround or is just being plain mean—or if the amount of money involved is worth it—is to file a petition asking the court to order the defendant to submit to verbal or written **interrogatories**—questions put to the defendant, under oath, as a means of discovering what assets he or she may have that are subject to sale by the court.

A summons to answer **verbal** interrogatories calls the defendant into court (more likely into the office of an attorney named by the court) to answer questions

---

*Or, if you use a printed letterhead, "at the above address."

put to him or her by you or by your lawyer if you have one.

Increasingly, because of the work load facing judges, courts are making use of private attorneys to "stand in" for judges in performing certain judicial functions. Many divorce hearings, for example, are held before these attorneys, called, when acting on behalf of the court, "commissioners." The interrogatory may be held in the office of a commissioner, where legally it's the same as if it were held in court before a judge.

Prior to responding to verbal interrogatories, the defendant will be placed under oath. Refusal to answer a question can result in citation for contempt of court. Lying can result in conviction for perjury. Both are punishable by sentence to jail.

Because of the fees that must be paid to the commissioner (for his or her time), to the stenographer, and for preparation of the transcript, verbal interrogatories are fairly expensive, often running to several hundred dollars.

A second approach is to obtain an order requiring the defendant to submit responses to **written interrogatories**, often called **Plaintiff's Interrogatories in Aid of Judgment** or, occasionally, **Plaintiff's Interrogatories in Aid of Execution**. Once you have the judge's order, written interrogatories may be served on the defendant the same as any other court document. There will be no commissioner's fee involved and no cost for a stenographer or for preparation of a transcript. The defendant's responses to the written interrogatories must be signed and sworn to, so their legal weight is the same as answers given before a judge or commissioner. (See the written interrogatories on pages F251–F294. These are suitable for plaintiff's use in most small claims cases.)

All told, using the interrogatory involves three steps:

1. PETITION for **Summons to Answer** [verbal] **Interrogatories**

   or

   PETITION for order to answer written **Plaintiff's Interrogatories in Aid of Judgment**

2. ORDER to answer verbal interrogatories

   or

   ORDER to answer written interrogatories

3. SUMMONS to answer verbal interrogatories

   or

   SERVING of written interrogatories on the defendant

If you use a written interrogatory, the defendant will be given a specified time within which to answer all questions in the interrogatory. As with the verbal interrogatory, failure to respond can result in citation for contempt of court. Proven failure to tell the truth can result in conviction for perjury.

Forms 45.3, 45.4, and 45.5 will allow you to use either method, verbal or written, of submitting the

defendant—now legally termed the **judgment debtor** —to interrogatories in aid of your judgment.

As with other petitions, some states use a printed form for the **Petition for Order to Answer Interrogatories**. In other states the petition is prepared by the plaintiff or the plaintiff's attorney. The completed sample petition on page 167 will serve as a guide for filling in your state's form. Ask the clerk whether you should fill in the blanks under **Order of the Court**. Some judges want it done; others do not. Our blank petition (Form 45.3, page F247), **Petition for Order to Answer Written Interrogatories**, may be used as a work form for use with either verbal or written interrogatories. If your state doesn't use a printed petition, ask the clerk if you can use this book's model in preparing your own.

The **Summons to Answer Interrogatories** (Form 45.4, page F249), for use by the court to summon the defendant to answer verbal interrogatories, is a form that you very probably will not have to fill out, but you'll still need to provide the clerk with all the information required to complete the court's form. Use our blank form for this purpose.

At the beginning of Form 45.5, **Plaintiff's Interrogatories in Aid of Judgment**, may be found two cover sheets. The first (page F251) provides for the use of the questions as a verbal interrogatory. The second (page F252) allows the same questions to be used as a written interrogatory.

As a written interrogatory, use the questions and answers "as is," attached to an appropriate cover sheet (patterned after our second cover sheet). You will only need to insert the proper years in questions 96 and 97.

To complete the cover sheet for written interrogatories (beyond providing the appropriate court name and address) you'll need to ask the clerk to tell you:

1. Your state's relevant rules of civil procedure so you can fill in the proper numbers (he'll probably know them without even looking them up).
2. The required method of service.
3. Who may legally serve the papers.

To use the questions as a verbal interrogatory, first ask the initial question, set in capitals, and then, after you have the defendant's response, develop each question using the follow-up material that asks for specifics.

The 100-question interrogatories, in jurisdictions where such extensive form interrogatories are allowed, is quite complete, far more extensive than is required for the majority of small claims cases. But the judge will probably go along with it—other small claims judges have. After all, you can explain, you **do** have a judgment in your favor that remains unpaid, and you **did** obtain a **Writ of Execution** that **failed** to result in satisfaction of your judgment. Actually, neither the judge nor the clerk will probably ever read your interrogatories anyway. (Soon, the interrogatory's length may not be that much out of line. Increasing numbers of states, encouraged by various consumer organizations, are raising their small claims limits so that, before long, a small claims judgment of $1,000 or even $2,000 might not be at all uncommon.)

You can be sure the defendant will read it though, and not like what he or she sees—one reason for using the form we have furnished. Beyond the form being a time-consuming nuisance to respond to, the defendant probably knows by now that, an interrogatory being part of the public court record, all of his or her personal, family, and financial answers will be available to anyone in town curious enough to stop by the clerk's office to look. The defendant's answers will also be available to others, such as hostile former spouses and the IRS—precisely the people that the defendant may especially NOT want viewing the information.

Soon after reading the interrogatory the defendant may well decide to pay your judgment rather than answer its questions—a decision a lot of defendants have made.

GARNISHMENT

Another collection step you might take is to obtain a court order to garnish a portion of the defendant's wages—require his or her employer to deduct a percentage of salary each payday toward payment of your judgment. This doesn't always work for a number of reasons:

1. If another creditor has an earlier garnishment, you'll have to "stand in line" until the earlier garnishment is satisfied.
2. Several states do not allow garnishment, and in many others the portion of an individual's salary exempt from garnishment is so great that using that method would not be practical.
3. There are those debtors who, expecting to be sued, protect themselves from garnishment by asking a friend to quickly file suit claiming money owed. The debtor's friend obtains a default judgment and follows that up with a garnishment of his friend's wages—which he promptly returns to his friend shortly after each payday. No other creditor will be able to touch the debtor's wages with a garnishment until the first one is "paid in full."

The garnishee, by the way, is not the defendant; it is the person or firm that is ordered to pay the defendant's money to the plaintiff. The garnishee, usually the defendant's employer, must be within the jurisdiction of the court. If the defendant's employer is out of state, the garnishment order cannot be served.

IF the defendant is employed, and IF his or her salary, commissions, etc., have not already been garnished, and IF the employer is located within the jurisdiction of the court, and IF the amount of money due you is worth the trouble, by all means consider talking with the clerk about obtaining a garnishment from the court.

You can say this for a garnishment: receipt of the summons as garnishee may prompt the defendant's employer to have a heart-to-heart talk with him or her about the importance of paying obligations—and just might result in your being paid, maybe even in full, without your actually having to exercise the garnishment.

As with obtaining a writ of execution or order for the defendant to answer interrogatories, your first step in obtaining a garnishment should be to see the clerk of the court to find out what your court's requirement is for issuing the order.

Although we shall not take you step by step through a **Petition for Garnishment** of the defendant's wages (you'll probably only need to ask the clerk or fill out a simple form anyway), we have provided a sample **Garnishee Summons** (Form 45.6, page F295). This form is particularly informative since it's both a summons and an order. Its limitations, as concerns sums of money exempt from garnishment, will give you a pretty good idea whether its use would be practical in your case (note, though, that these "exemptions" are only typical of *many* states' codes—not all). Notice that the document is signed by the clerk of the court rather than the judge. The form has been left blank for use as a work sheet to provide the clerk with information needed to complete the court's **Garnishee Summons.**

Sample of Form 45.1/F243

STATE OF NEW BEDFORD

No. _____SC 3-80-57954_____

In the PUTNAM COUNTY DISTRICT COURT, DIVISION OF SMALL CLAIMS:

_____Robert B. Mason_____)
Plaintiff)
)
)
)
)
vs.)
)
)
_____Arthur C. Smedley_____)
Defendant

Petition for Writ of Execution

TO THE HONORABLE _____Walton Green_____, Judge:

YOUR PETITIONER, _____Robert B. Mason_____, Plaintiff in the above-styled and -numbered case, respectfully shows Your Honor that on the _____15th_____ day of _____August_____, 19 _84_, judgment was awarded by the _____Putnam County District Court, Division of Small Claims_____ in favor of Your Petitioner against said Defendant in the sum of _____five hundred and sixty-three dollars_____ _____ ($ _563.00_), which amount was due and payable in full on the _15th_ day of _____August_____, 19 _84_; that said judgment has not been satisfied; and that Your Petitioner is entitled to recover said sum.

WHEREFORE Your Petitioner asks for a **Writ of Execution** against the estate, real and personal, of the Defendant, and that sufficient real and personal property of said Defendant be seized and sold to satisfy the claim of Your Petitioner and be applied to the satisfaction thereof.

And Your Petitioner will ever pray, etc.

Robert B. Mason
Plaintiff

* *

CERTIFICATE OF NOTARY

STATE OF NEW BEDFORD)
) ss:
COUNTY OF PUTNAM)

BEFORE ME, the undersigned, on this day personally appeared _____Robert B. Mason_____, who, first being duly sworn, made oath that (he) (she) is cognizant of the facts stated in the foregoing petition and that they are true.

GIVEN UNDER MY HAND, this _____15th_____ day of _____September_____, 19 _84_.

Marion Bates
Notary Public

Sample of Form 45.1 (*Continued*)

ORDER OF THE COURT

WHEREAS, on this _____16th_____ day of _____September_____, 19 _84_, came _Robert B. Mason,_ _____Plaintiff_____, petitioning the Court for a **Writ of Execution** for the reasons set out in said petition, the same having been duly considered, the Court is of the opinion that the reasons stated are good and sufficient to order said **Writ**. It is therefore, considered, adjudged and ordered that the petitioned **Writ** be granted forthwith.

_____
Judge
PUTNAM COUNTY DISTRICT COURT
Division of Small Claims
Sommerton, N.B.

No. _____ SC 3-80-57954

Petition for Writ of Execution

Robert B. Mason
25 Calkinstown Road
Hinkley, N.B. 10531

vs.

Arthur C. Smedley d/b/a
Art's Appliance City
35 Clark Street
Sommerton, N.B. 10560

Dated _____ September 15, _____ 19 __84__

Sample of Form 45.3/F247

STATE OF NEW BEDFORD

No. ___SC 3-80-57954___

In the PUTNAM COUNTY DISTRICT COURT, DIVISION OF SMALL CLAIMS:

___Robert B. Mason___) *Plaintiff*)))) vs.)))) ___Arthur C. Smedley___) *Defendant*)	**Petition for Order to Answer Written Interrogatories**

TO THE HONORABLE ___Walton Green___, Judge:

YOUR PETITIONER, ___Robert B. Mason___, Plaintiff in the above-number and -styled case, respectfully shows Your Honor that on the ___15th___ day of ___August___, 19 __84__, judgment was awarded by the ___Putnam County District Court, Division of Small Claims___ in favor of Your Petitioner against said Defendant in the sum of ___five hundred and sixty-three dollars___ _____ ($ __563.00__), which amount was due and payable in full on the __15th__ day of __August__, 19 __84__; that said judgment has not been satisfied; and that Your Petitioner is entitled to recover same.

WHEREFORE Your Petitioner asks that an **Order to Answer Written Interrogatories** be issued by the Court to the Defendant requiring said Defendant to answer questions contained in said Interrogatory in aid of aforesaid judgment against the Defendant.

And Your Petitioner will ever pray, etc.

Robert B. Mason
Plaintiff

* *

CERTIFICATE OF NOTARY

STATE OF NEW BEDFORD)
) ss:
COUNTY OF PUTNAM)

BEFORE ME, the undersigned, on this day personally appeared ___Robert B. Mason___, who, first being duly sworn, made oath that (he) (she) is cognizant of the facts stated in the foregoing petition and that they are true.

GIVEN UNDER MY HAND, this ___15th___ day of ___October___, 19 __84__.

Marion Bates
Notary Public

Sample of Form 45.3 (*Continued*)

ORDER OF THE COURT

WHEREAS, on this ____2nd____ day of ____October____, 19 _84_, came ____Robert B. Mason,____ ____Plaintiff____, to petition the Court for an Order to answer **Plaintiff's Interrogatories in Aid of Judgment**, for the reasons set out in said petition, the same having been duly considered, the Court is of the opinion that the reasons so stated are good and sufficient to issue said Order.

It is, therefore, considered, adjudged and ordered that the petitioned Order be granted forthwith.

_____
Judge

PUTNAM COUNTY DISTRICT COURT
Division of Small Claims
Sommeton, N.B.

No. ___SC 3-80-57954___

Petition for Order to Answer Written Interrogatories

Robert B. Mason
25 Calkinstown Road
Hinkley, N.B. 10531

vs.

Arthur C. Smedley d/b/a
Art's Appliance City
35 Clark Street
Sommerton, N.B. 10560

Dated ___October 1,___ 19 _84_

46 Small Claims Courts— State by State

The table on pages 170–171 lists the following important aspects of small claims courts in each of the fifty states plus the District of Columbia, the Commonwealth of Puerto Rico, and the Virgin Islands: maximum limit, fees, method of serving summons, minimum age for filing suit, and whether an attorney *may* represent or *must* represent represent the plaintiff or defendant. For instance, in certain states (Arizona, Colorado, Illinois, and a few others) an attorney must represent a corporate defendant—a possible plus for consumers since such a requirement adds to a corporation's cost of defending a suit and may thus encourage a favorable offer to settle out of court.

Several states (Iowa, Kansas, Louisiana, and Wyoming) have $100 maximum limits for small claims suits—hardly worth the effort. Business interests in those and other states are applying pressure to legislators in an effort to combat consumer efforts to raise small claims limits to compensate for inflation. The maintenance of small claims limits at low levels would, of course, discourage small claims suits by consumers who feel they have been taken advantage of.

Maximum limits vary widely—from a low of $100 in four states to maximums of well over $1,000 in others. Most states, except those with strong industry efforts to retain low limits to discourage troublesome small claims suits, are attempting to keep up with inflation, so the maximum small claims limit in your state might be higher today than the amount shown.

We have not attempted to include in the table "everything you need to know about small claims courts." The following are additional items you should ask the clerk about when you visit the courthouse.

Venue

Your suit must be filed with a court having *venue* over the defendant. Usually this is within the district that includes his or her residence or place of business. Some states allow you to file where you live; others allow you to file anywhere at all in the state and permit the defendant to be served anywhere in the state. Where you file can sometimes be a matter of tactics—easier for you, harder for him—but just as often the defendant may be able to obtain a change of venue to the district of his or her residence or place of business—harder for you, easier for him.

Some states allow a suit to be heard in the district where the "thing" of the case, the act that is the basis of the suit, took place or was supposed to have taken place.

Jurisdiction

You will also have to file with a court having *jurisdiction* (authority) over your case. Obviously the court has no jurisdiction if the amount you're seeking exceeds the maximum limit established for small claims courts. In some areas small claims court jurisdiction is limited to certain types of cases. Thus, you'll need to make sure that the court you file in has both venue and jurisdiction.

Statute of Limitations

Since the *statute of limitations*—time within which legal action must be brought—is nowhere less than one year, you'll probably be initiating your suit well within the time stipulated by your state. The statute of limitations varies from state to state for different kinds of actions, such as breach of contract, property damage, personal injury, etc.

Waiting Time

The time between the date of filing and the date of the trial is, obviously, the *waiting time*. This time varies from a few weeks to several months, even within the same state. If you're interested in a quick trial and your local district court has a long waiting time, ask the clerk if another court might be able to hear your case at an earlier date.

Transfer

In many states a counterclaim by the defendant or a cross-claim by another party for an amount in excess of the small claims maximum will automatically *transfer* the case to a court having higher limits—usually a regular county district or municipal court. As a matter of tactics, a counterclaim resulting in transfer increases the plaintiff's costs, delays the trial, and gives the defendant's attorney more leeway to attack your case with courtroom karate. This is a defense strategy you should be aware of.

Appeal

The cost of an *appeal*, compared with the relatively modest maximum judgments allowed in most small claims suits, usually makes an appeal impractical. In some states only the defendant can appeal; in some states neither side can appeal; and in still others an appeal results in a new trial (trial *de novo* in legalese) held in a regular session of the county or municipal court.

THE JUDICIAL MECHANISMS FOR SMALL CLAIMS LITIGATION IN THE UNITED STATES

The following table presents key information about each state's judicial mechanism for handling small claims litigation. In some states small claims are handled by different types of courts in rural areas than in urban areas. Maximum amounts can vary, too, between rural and urban courts.

Two of the most commonly listed types of courts are Justice of the Peace (JP) and Small Claims Court. JP courts abound in rural areas, particularly those of

the south and southwest. They're less formal—more comfortable about "just doing what's right" than sticking to the letter of the law. JP judges, frequently nonlawyers, will just as often go by what they know about the defendant's and plaintiff's reputations as by any arguments presented in court.

Small Claims Courts are often special sessions of regular county district and municipal courts. Since those judges preside over regular sessions most of the time, their working methods tend to be more like those of a regular court, sticking to formal procedures, perhaps by habit as much as anything else, when hearing small claims cases.

STATE-BY-STATE JUDICIAL MECHANISMS FOR SMALL CLAIMS LITIGATION

State	Type of Court[a]	Maximum Limit	Fees[b]	Method of Serving Summons[c]	Minimum Age for Filing Suit	Attorney for Individuals[d]	Attorney for Corporations[e]
Alaska	SC	$1,000	2	1, 2	18	2	3
Alabama	JC	300	2	1, 2	21	2	2
Arizona	JP	500	1	1	21	2	3
Arkansas	JP / M	200 / 500	1	1, 2, 5	21[f]	2	2
California	SC	500	1	7	21[f]	1	1
Colorado	SC	500	1	4, 7	18	2	3
Connecticut	SC	750	1		1	2	2
Delaware	JP	1,500	1	2	19	2	2
District of Columbia	SC	2,000	1	3, 6	21	2	2
Florida	CTC	1,500	4	1, 7	18		
Georgia	SC / JP	Varies / Varies	1	3	18	2	2
Hawaii	SC	300	1	1, 6	21	2	2
Idaho	SC	200	1	4, 6	21	1	1
Illinois	SC	1,000	1	6	18	2	3
Indiana	JP	500	1	2	21	2	3
Iowa	JP	100	1	1, 2	19	2	2
Kansas	SC	100	1	1, 2	18	2	2
Kentucky	JP	500	1	1, 2	18	2	2
Louisiana	JP[g] / C[h]	100 / 5,000	1 / 1	2 / 2	21 / 21	2 / 2	2 / 2
Maine	SC	200	1	8	20	2	2
Maryland	SC	10,000	1	1, 2	21	2	2
Massachusetts	SC	400	1	2, 7	21	2	2
Michigan	SC	300[i]	1	4	21	2	2
Minnesota	CC	300[i]	1	9	21	1	1
Mississippi	JP	200	1	1, 2, 4	None	2	2
Missouri	MA	3,500	2	2	21	2	2

(continued)

STATE-BY-STATE JUDICIAL MECHANISMS FOR SMALL CLAIMS LITIGATION

State	Type of Court[a]	Maximum Limit	Fees[b]	Method of Serving Summons[c]	Minimum Age for Filing Suit	Attorney for Individuals[d]	Attorney for Corporations[e]
Montana	JP	300	1	1, 2, 4	19	2	2
Nebraska	JP	200	1	8	19	1	1
	SC	500	1	4	19	1	1
Nevada	SC	300	1	4, 8	21[f]	2	2
New Hampshire	SC	300	1	7	21	2	2
New Jersey	SC	200	2	2, 6	21	2	2
New Mexico	SC	2,000[j]	1	1, 2	18	2	2
New York	SC	500	1	7	21	2	3
North Carolina	MA	300	2	1	18	2	2
North Dakota	SC	200	1	6, 4	18	2	2
Ohio	SC	150	1	4, 6	21	2	2
Oklahoma	SC	400	2	6	21[f]	2	2
Oregon	SC	500	1	1, 2, 4	21	2	2
Pennsylvania	SC[k] JP[l]	500	1	1, 2, 6	None	2	2[m]
Puerto Rico	SC	2,500	1	8[n]	21	2	2
Rhode Island	SC	300	1	8	21	2	2
South Carolina	MA	200[o]	1	1	21	2	2
South Dakota	SC	500	1	8	18	2	2
Tennessee	JP	3,000	3	1	18	2	2
Texas	JP	150[p]	1	1, 2	18	2	2
Utah	SC	200	1	1, 2	21[f]	2	2
Virgin Islands	SC	300	1	3, 4	21	1	1
Vermont	SC	250	1	4, 7	18	2	2
Virginia	CNOR	3,000	1	1, 4	None	2	2
Washington	SC	100[q]	1	4, 7	18	1	1
West Virginia	JP	300	1	2	18	2	2
Wisconsin	SC	500	1	1, 2, 8	21	2	2
Wyoming	JP	100	1	7	21	2	2

[a]*Type of Court*: SC, Small Claims; JP, Justice of the Peace; MA, Magistrate's; MM, Mayor's or Municipal; JC, Justice Court; C, City Court; CTC, County Court; CC, Conciliation Court; CNOR, Court Not of Record.

[b]*Fees*: 1, Under $10, including service and summons; 2, over $10 but under $15, including service and summons; 3, over $15 but under $25, including service and summons; 4, over $20 but under $30, including service and summons.

[c]*Method of Serving Summons*: 1, Personal by sheriff; 2, personal by constable; 3, personal by marshal; 4, personal by qualified party; 5, left at current or most recent residence; 6, certified mail; 7, registered mail; 8, first class mail; 9, personal by plaintiff.

[d]*Attorney for Individuals*: 1, Prohibited; 2, optional.

[e]*Attorney for Corporations*: 1, Prohibited; 2, optional; 3, required.

[f]Age 18 for women. [g]Outside New Orleans. [h]In New Orleans. [i]Up to $500 in some areas. [j]In counties with populations over 100,000. [k]In Philadelphia. [l]Outside Philadelphia. [m]Attorney required in Philadelphia. [n]Or any written communication. [o]Higher in some areas. [p]$200 for wages or labor. [q]Up to $200 in populous counties.

YOUR PERSONAL
LOVING
ARRANGEMENT

47 Writing Your Own Contract

You may not believe in marriage agreements, but once you're married you *have* a marriage contract—written by the state—and the only way you can better its terms is to write one of your own.

In a sense, getting married without writing a marriage agreement is like dying without having a will, and thus having your property distributed according to the laws of intestacy instead of according to your own wishes and the needs of your heirs.

In many jurisdictions, for example, if a married man owns real estate, even though he may have purchased it prior to marriage, he can't sell it without his wife's signature. And according to long-standing domestic relations law, determination of state of residence and choice of domicile is the sole prerogative of the husband, and a wife may be readily divorced for desertion if she refuses to follow her husband.

But just as the wishes of an individual expressed in his or her Last Will and Testament are generally regarded by the courts as prevailing over the laws of intestacy, so are the stipulations of a written marriage agreement generally regarded as prevailing over most provisions of a state's marriage and divorce law.

As with the laws of intestacy, the state imposes most of the terms of its "marriage contract" only when the parties have neglected to write an agreement of their own. Thus, a well-written marriage contract can largely prevail over a state's domestic relations law (also called family law) in matters of separately owned and jointly owned property, separate incomes, shared and separate financial responsibilities, bank accounts, alimony, etc.

The courts of all states require a husband and wife to support each other in time of need, and all require that parents provide for the care and support of their children.

The laws of the few community-property states —Arizona, California, Idaho, Louisiana, Nevada, New Mexico, Texas, and Washington—not only vary widely with respect to the maintenance of separate property and incomes of spouses, but are changing rapidly (generally toward granting greater freedom of choice). Residents of those states should consult an attorney familiar with those states' current community-property statutes.

Even in the most "hard-line" of community-property states, gifts to either party almost always remain the separate property of each, so that annual "gifts" between husband and wife can result in individual ownership of substantial separate property.

PROTECTION FROM WHIM OF THE COURT

Because a marriage contract permits you, in effect, to write the law of marriage and divorce of your state as it applies to you, such a contract provides protection from the whim of the family law equivalent of the "hanging judge" of pioneer days, known for sentencing most defendants, whatever their crime, to "hang by the neck until dead."

A written marriage agreement also defends its parties from the actions of strict constructionist (and sometimes overly moralistic) judges who hold to the letter of the law in handing down judgments based upon marriage and divorce statutes written scores of years ago when wives stayed home and did as they were told and when husbands were seen as properly the sole provider.

MAINTAINING INDIVIDUALITY

Not long ago I attended a magnificent wedding in one of Los Angeles' most prominent churches. As part of the ceremony, the bride and groom each took up a lighted candle and stepped together before the altar and with their small flames lighted a larger candle that had been placed there. Then they blew out their *individual* flames.

A few months later I overheard the following conversation in a shopping mall as one married couple in their mid-twenties ran into the female half of a couple with whom they were apparently close friends.

"Hey, listen; tomorrow night we're going to that movie you've been wanting to see. Why don't you come with us?

"Gee, I'd *love* to, but Jack has to work."

To me, both of these actions symbolize one of the greatest distortions of marriage—that when you marry it should somehow be the end of individuality and that from then on you should exist solely as half of a couple.

Yet there is probably no area of our lives that is more open to our own control and that is more important for us to control than that portion of our existence that we share intimately with another person. Unlike work, unlike school, and unlike the daily touch-and-go relationships we have with friends, acquaintances, and co-workers, which are "public," the relationship that we share with someone we're married to or live with is completely "private."

While there is nothing about a marriage ceremony that *must* affect how a couple relates to each other, the fact is that society begins to treat men and women differently immediately after marriage. And newly married couples tend to think of themselves differently soon after marriage because a lifetime of conditioning takes over in spite of almost everything they do. Before many years go by, some partners begin to feel that "something is missing" and that the empty "calories" of their relationship are leaving some important needs unfulfilled.

But the "empty calorie syndrome" is something we may be seeing less of in the future. Marriage counseling, which was the standard way of addressing such problems not long ago, is quietly being supplemented or replaced with *preventive medicine* based upon a prescription that couples can write for themselves: a marriage contract.

One of the most beneficial and disaster-preventing aspects of working out an agreement before marriage is that it helps the couple face the fact that marriage is not made in heaven and that it is not necessarily "until death us do part." When you start sorting out, for example, the rights and responsibilities of each partner in the event of divorce, it helps you take a realistic look at some of your other expectations of marriage.

In writing your own marriage agreement, begin alone. Start by listing, as free as possible from the influence of "shoulds" and "should nots" of traditional marriage, all of your own nonnegotiable demands: those freedoms, those people in your life, those activities, and those things that you must have. List, too, those things that must not be allowed to intrude into your relationship. List the circumstances necessary to keep you from feeling that you are being taken advantage of by your partner or by the marriage.

When you and your partner have each spent a week or so separately shaping the framework of your own part of a marriage contract, exchange papers and then, using the various provisions provided in the back of the book (Forms 48.1, 48.2, and 48.3) and the sample agreement beginning on page 200, jointly put together the first draft of your own agreement. Even if your contract is never hammered into a "court legal" document, the two of you will have had an opportunity for your relationship to gain authenticity, openness, and honesty, instead of leading you blindly into a never-never land of radiant unreality.

Writing a marriage agreement is not easy. Many of us have been so locked in by parents, schools, our respective church, and Madison Avenue into unconscious beliefs of what marriage "should" be that it's hard for us to imagine a relationship that departs from our preconceived idea of society's norm.

If there is any one thing worth remembering in facing marriage or in writing your own marriage agreement, it is that individual uniqueness is best fulfilled in individual and unique ways. Even more so than in our work, this is true of our intimate relationships with each other.

The best approach to writing your own contract is to make it as brief as possible, including only those things that must be a part of the agreement. For example, there's probably no need, if a couple intends to share housekeeping responsibilities equally, to set forth in detail who will do which tasks unless you really believe that arguments about who does the laundry and who does the vacuuming are likely to lead to serious difficulty. One of our agreement's general provisions for the sharing of housekeeping responsibilities will probably fill any need for such a clause.

On the other hand, provisions of an agreement that deal with separate or jointly owned property, financial support of the parties, the care and education of children, details of alimony or payments in lieu of alimony, or each party's Last Will and Testament must be quite detailed and, so far as possible, written in language that has withstood the test of litigation.

With regard to separately owned and jointly owned property, an agreement must not only serve the immediate needs of the parties, but also must be able to withstand attack by relatives and others who may lay claims to the estate of either party in the event of death.

KINDS OF AGREEMENTS POSSIBLE

Three types of agreements are discussed in the following chapters:

1. **Agreement in Contemplation of Marriage**—for use by couples who plan to marry in the near future.
2. **Agreement to Live Together**—for consideration by couples who may or may not plan to marry but who want to define the rights, responsibilities, and privileges of their relationship.
3. **Agreement Between Husband and Wife**—for couples who are already married and feel a need to define their relationship more clearly, who want to specify the separate and jointly owned property of each, and who may want to place their relationship on a new footing of equality, increased independence, and mutually shared responsibility.

Interestingly, provisions of the various agreements are not very different. Although in most states there is a lot of difference under the law between marriage and living together without marriage, there are few rights and responsibilities of marriage that cannot be incorporated into an *Agreement to Live Together*.

In most states the major difference between a *Marriage Agreement* and an *Agreement to Live Together* is that for an *Agreement to Live Together* to have the maximum possible legal validity, no aspect of the couple's sexual relationship (such as whether it is to be closed or open with respect to each party's right to have additional relationships) should be mentioned. This is because the statutes of many states stipulate that any agreement based upon a "meretricious" relationship (that is, upon unlawful sexual relations or in which the sexual services of either party are deemed by the court to be a part of the agreement) are often declared invalid and of no force or effect. On the other hand, *marriage* contracts stating husbands' and wives' mutual agreement that either may have additional sexual relationships outside the marriage have been upheld in some courts.

At this writing cohabitation is outlawed in four states: Arkansas, Arizona, Florida, and Georgia. Thus, an **Agreement to Live Together** would almost surely be thrown out of court in any of those jurisdictions.

A number of states, wishing to avoid the thorny legal thicket of *Marvin v. Marvin,* are considering legislation that would specifically eliminate legal protection of any kind for either party of a couple who live together without a written agreement setting forth the rights, responsibilities, and privileges of each.

CONTRACTS NOT ALWAYS WHOLLY ENFORCEABLE

As with the law of cohabitation, the sands of marriage and divorce law are rapidly shifting under the tide of social change. However, the law of contracts still remains a rocklike cliff facing the sea with only barely perceptible alteration from year to year.

Thus, any attempt to write an agreement that binds marriage and divorce law to contract law in a single, comprehensive, wholly enforceable marital contract can sometimes be an almost impossible task—almost impossible because provisions that some courts will enforce, others may not, and because judicial interpretations of what may be "against public policy" (and thereby unlikely to withstand the test of litigation) vary from court to court and are changing from day to day.

The demand, then, in drafting a marriage agreement that will serve the personal, financial, and other needs of its parties and yet withstand the possible test of litigation is to tread the sands of marriage and

divorce law as closely as possible in the straight and narrow footsteps of contract law.

The result, in attempting to fit the needs and wishes of the parties to the concepts of the courts, is an agreement that in many respects is much more "legalistic" than might otherwise be necessary—a sort of dotting all the legal i's and crossing all the t's so that the agreement will hold up in court.

ENFORCEMENT BY COURT

While the court may enforce those terms of a marital agreement dealing with separate and jointly owned property that comply with applicable law, protecting it, for example, from attack by creditors or would-be heirs, there are only three actions that the court can take under family law:

1. Award child custody
2. Grant a divorce or separation
3. Award money or property from one party to the other—including alimony and/or maintenance and/or child support

ADVICE BY ATTORNEY

After you and your partner have written a marriage agreement using options provided by this book, perhaps combined with others that you have written, you should obtain legal counsel if you want to make sure that your agreement, or at least certain parts of it, will be upheld by the court.

There will obviously be some cost involved, but you will have saved perhaps 90 percent of the legal expense of preparing such a contract by approaching an attorney with your agreement already drawn, saying, in effect, "We've already given this agreement a lot of thought and have determined that this is what we want. We're asking for your advice primarily to assure that certain provisions comply with the laws of this state." (See **Advice by Counsel,** page 194.)

If significant amounts of property are involved or if certain provisions of an agreement may be considered "contrary to public policy," then each party should obtain separate, independent legal counsel for the agreement to have the optimum chance of withstanding attack before the court. (See **Independent Counsel,** page 194.)

48 Agreement in Contemplation of Marriage

The following pages illustrate each and every provision that we have provided for inclusion in our **Agreement in Contemplation of Marriage**. Some provisions are those that you *must* include if the agreement is to have any legal validity at all. Others are provisions that you *may* want to include, and still others are provisions that you *may not* want to include at all, preferring to let the agreement remain silent on certain subjects.

If discussion of a particular provision tends to make you uncomfortable, your discomfort may be a signal that the particular area could later become a pressure point along a hidden fault line in your relationship and thus *especially* needs to be dealt with on the basis of real feelings—free of the "shoulds" and "should nots" of how you may think you and your partner are *supposed* to feel.

A number of clauses have blanks providing for the inclusion of parties' names, percentage of household expenses to be shared by each, etc. These have been filled in merely by way of illustration, and *no* suggestion should be inferred from any of the amounts or other specifics that we have inserted.

Generally, the options provided for a particular heading (say, **Household Expenses** or **Care and Support of Children**) repeat the titles for that heading for ease in assembling a master copy of your agreement. They are numbered to the right of each heading. Additionally, the agreement is comprised of six articles:

- Article I: Conditions of the Agreement
- Article II: Property and Financial Provisions
- Article III: Children
- Article IV: Possible Dissolution of the Marriage
- Article V: Testamentary Provisions
- Article VI: General Provisions

Where several options of a particular provision happen to be the first item in a given article, we have repeated the article number and title above each option, also for ease in putting together your master copy. In a few instances alternate provisions bear headings that are different from each other and that are not numbered as options. These we will present together and comment on under a combination of the two headings.

Before putting together the final draft of any agreement, both partners should go over their previously written lists of nonnegotiable demands and other needs to make sure that any clauses *not* provided by this book's agreement can be added to the final form of any contract.

Despite its somewhat legalistic language, made necessary by the need to adhere as closely as possible to the family law statutes and legal precedents established in various states, the agreement makes for fairly straightforward reading.

AGREEMENT IN CONTEMPLATION OF MARRIAGE

On the agreement's first page, list the names and addresses of the parties, filling in their first names on the first line of the second paragraph as shown below. The third paragraph's "consideration" (each party receiving something for that which is given) is deemed necessary by many judges in order to make the contract binding under law.

Agreement in Contemplation of Marriage

THIS AGREEMENT in comtemplation of marriage is made this __15th__ day of __March__, 19__84__, by and between

__John Smith_____, of

__126 West Elm_____ __4-A__
Street Address   *Apt. No.*
__Fairview__   __Kansas__   __66425__
City   *State*   *Zip*
hereinafter referred to as _____ __John__ _____, and

__Mary Jones_____, of

__4416 North Washington_____ __3-C__
Street Address   *Apt. No.*
__Fairview__   __Kansas__   __66425__,
City   *State*   *Zip*
hereinafter referred to as _____ __Mary__ _____.

WHEREAS __John_____ and __Mary_____ are contemplating marriage, and each party wishes to settle between themselves questions of separate and jointly owned property; separate and joint financial responsibilities; children, if any, and their care, financial support and education; location of domicile; the sharing of household space, expenses and housekeeping responsibilities; the gainful employment and education of each party; the names of each; the possible incapacitation of each; possible dissolution of the marriage; maintenance and support; alimony; and the death of either party; and

WHEREAS, for and in consideration of the sum of twenty dollars ($20.00), and other good and valuable consideration, the receipt whereof is hereby acknowledged, and in further consideration of the parties entering into this agreement and making the mutual covenants herein contained to be performed by the parties, the parties hereto mutually agree and covenant as follows:

ARTICLE I: CONDITIONS OF THE AGREEMENT

In the initial article of the contract the parties sort of weigh in, stake out the boundaries, and establish the rules of their relationship—how high the net will be, where the foul lines shall be drawn, etc. Many of this article's provisions (practically all, as a matter of fact) are considered by attorneys to be essential if the agreement is to have maximum legal validity.

Neither Party Presently Married

Option 1 may be used for agreements between parties who have never been married and who want to establish that they will be of legal age when married under terms of the agreement. *Option 2* may be used for agreements between parties who may have previously been married and who are now divorced and free to enter into a new, valid marriage.

Neither Party Presently Married (1)

___John___ hereby states that *he* is not presently married and has never been married, is ___twenty-two___ (_22_) years of age and is competent to enter into a valid marriage, and ___Mary___ hereby states that *she* is not presently married and has never been married, is ___twenty-two___ (_22_) years of age and is competent to enter into a valid marriage.

Neither Party Presently Married (2)

___John___ hereby states that *he* is not presently married and that if previously married has received a final decree of divorce and is competent to enter into a valid marriage, and ___Mary___ hereby states that *she* is not presently married and that if previously married has received a final decree of divorce and is competent to enter into a valid marriage.

Purpose

Two options. *Option 1* makes no reference to religious belief; *option 2* does.

Purpose (1)

The purpose of the parties for entering into a state of matrimony under the laws of the State of ___Kansas___ is to receive public recognition of the relationship between them as defined by this agreement and to receive mutually the benefits thus obtained.

Purpose (2)

The purpose of the parties for entering into a state of matrimony within the embrace of their *religious faith* and under the laws of the State of ___Kansas___ is an expression of their *religious belief* and their love and commitment to each other.

Voluntary

There is no option here. The clause must be included to establish the voluntary nature of the agreement.

Voluntary

Each party acknowledges that this agreement is being entered into voluntarily and that it is not the result of duress, coercion or undue influence.

Marriage as a Condition Precedent

No option here either. The clause establishes that the agreement shall become effective only upon the parties' marriage to each other.

Marriage as a Condition Precedent

This agreement shall become effective immediately upon the marriage of the parties to each other, but shall have no force or effect until that time.

Declaration of Principle

Two options. *Option 1* may be used for agreements that in subsequent pages will emphasize the partners' independence. *Option 2* does not stress independence quite so strongly.

Declaration of Principle (1)

The parties value and accept the principle of independence and of the equal distribution of responsibility and authority between them and that each is a fully equal *and independent* partner in their relationship with each other.

Declaration of Principle (2)

The parties value and accept the principle of independence and of equal distribution of responsibility and authority between them and that each is a fully equal partner in their relationship with each other.

Waiver of Rights/Acceptance of Obligations

The first option, **Waiver of Rights,** is usually thought of by attorneys as the "clean-slate" clause since it establishes that the stipulations of the *agreement* are intended by the parties to take precedence over the traditional rights, duties, and privileges of marriage. In it the parties waive nothing that cannot later be written into and made a part of the agreement.

The second option, **Acceptance of Obligations,** is almost the opposite of the above provision. If used, it can limit options that the parties might later wish to make a part of the agreement.

Waiver of Rights (1)

Both parties hereby waive, relinquish and renounce whatever rights, duties, obligations and privileges which either might have which may be derived from or related to a state of matrimony between them, other than those which are included in and made a part of this agreement.

Acceptance of Obligations (2)

Both parties voluntarily and fully accept all legal, moral and religious duties, rights, obligations and privileges derived from or related to a state of matrimony between them.

Openness Between Parties

Option 1 does not refer to religious sharing, which is included in *option 2*. Apart from that the two options are the same.

Openness Between Parties   (1)

Both parties anticipate and expect the sharing of each other's emotional and sexual lives to the extent as may benefit both, without infringing upon the privacy, independence or solitude of the other.

Openness Between Parties   (2)

Both parties anticipate the sharing of their religious faith and experience and each other's emotional and sexual lives to the extent as may benefit both, without infringing upon the privacy, independence or solitude of the other.

Sexual Nonexclusivity/Sexual Exclusivity

Option 1 establishes both parties' freedom to have intimate relationships in addition to the one within the marriage; option 2 excludes this possibility. These provisions, like certain others on the following pages, need not be included in the contract at all, thus allowing the marriage agreement to remain silent on the issue of sexual exclusivity.

Sexual Nonexclusivity   (1)

Each party recognizes the right of the other to be open to, and to maintain, additional emotional and sexual relationships beyond the one existing between them, neither party expecting nor demanding sexual exclusivity.

Sexual Exclusivity   (2)

Each party anticipates and pledges complete sexual fidelity during the marriage, each party promising to forsake all other such relationships out of love, commitment and deep personal belief.

Names of the Parties

Under option 1 there is mutual agreement by the parties that each shall retain his or her own name after the marriage. Option 2 provides for the taking of a new surname by the parties after their marriage, which might be, for example, a composite of their premarital surnames.

Names of the Parties   (1)

The parties agree that neither shall change his or her name as a result of the marriage. We shall continue to be known, respectively, as __John Smith__ and __Mary Jones__ .

Names of the Parties   (2)

The parties agree that, following their marriage, they shall both adopt the surname of __Smith-Jones__ , being known, respectively, as __John Smith-Jones__ and __Mary Smith-Jones__ .

Note: Parties wishing to follow the tradition of the wife accepting her husband's surname upon marriage need no contractual provision for this purpose, since it would normally occur if there were no written agreement between them.

Present Employment of the Parties

We note five options. The inclusion of one of these options is important to establish each party's ability to provide for his or her own financial support as well as establish some important ground rules for the marriage.

Option 1 lists the occupations and incomes of both parties. Option 2 lists the occupation and income of one party, recognizes that the other party is presently not employed and may or may not become employed, and states the purpose for obtaining employment or for not becoming employed. Option 3 lists the occupations and incomes of both parties and notes the intent of one party to terminate employment and the purpose therefore. Option 4 states that neither party is employed and that one or both parties plan to seek employment. Option 5 states that neither party is presently employed—as might be the case with full-time students or a retired couple.

Present Employment of the Parties   (1)

(a) The parties acknowledge their understanding that _____ __John__ is presently gainfully employed as _____ __an accountant__ with an approximate annual income of $ __40,000__ and presently intends to continue such employment, and that;

(b) __Mary__ is presently gainfully employed as __a nurse__ with an approximate annual income of $ __20,000__ and presently intends to continue such employment.

Present Employment of the Parties   (2)

(a) The parties acknowledge their understanding that _____ __John__ is presently gainfully employed as _____ __an accountant__ with an approximate annual income of $ ___ __40,000__ and presently intends to continue such employment indefinitely, and that;

(b) __Mary__ is not employed and _____ __does not__ plan to become employed during the next ____ __four years__ in order to __attend medical school__ .

Present Employment of the Parties   (3)

(a) The parties acknowledge their understanding that _____ __John__ is presently gainfully employed as _____ __an accountant__ with an approximate annual income of $ __40,000__ and presently intends to continue such employment, and that;

(b) __Mary__ is presently gainfully employed as __a nurse__ with an approximate annual income of $ __20,000__ , but that he/she presently intends to terminate such employment __September 1, 1981__ in order to __enter medical school__ .

Present Employment of the Parties   (4)

The parties acknowledge their understanding that neither is presently gainfully employed and that __John__ shall diligently seek gainful employment so that __Mary__ may __remain home to take care of the children__ .

Present Employment of the Parties (5)

The parties acknowledge that neither party is presently gainfully employed and that neither presently plans to become gainfully employed.

Children by Previous Marriage

Each of the three options establishes both parties' knowledge of the existence of previous children of either party and acknowledges any responsibility for child support and for time that a child of either may spend with the parties.

Option 1 states the obligation of one party to pay child support. Option 2 states that one party shall receive child support. Option 3 acknowledges that a child of either exists and will be spending a specified amount of time with the parties. (The matter of parties' responsibility for child support will be dealt with in a forthcoming portion of the agreement, Article III: Children.)

Children by Previous Marriage (1)

The parties acknowledge their understanding that __John__ has previously been married and has a child or children born of or adopted during such marriage for whom he/she is obligated to provide $ __300.00__ per __month__ in financial support and who shall, for approximately __three months__ of each year, live with the parties.

Children by Previous Marriage (2)

The parties acknowledge their understanding that _____ __Mary__ has previously been married and has a child or children born of or adopted during such marriage for whom he/she has a right to receive child support in the amount of $ __300.00__ per __month__ and who shall, for approximately _____ __three months__ of each year, live with the parties.

Children by Previous Marriage (3)

The parties acknowledge their understanding that _____ __John__ has previously been married and has a child or children born of or adopted during such marriage for whom he/she receives no child support and who shall, for approximately __three months__ of each year, live with the parties.

Note: The various paragraphs under the above headings may be combined under **Children by Previous Marriage** to accommodate a wide range of situations.

Previous Children

Similar to the above provisions, this clause clarifies the existence of a previous child who may not have been born of a marriage.

Previous Children

The parties acknowledge their understanding that __Mary__ _____ has a child or children adopted during or born of a previous relationship for whom he/she _____ __receives no__ child support and who shall, for approximately __twelve months__ of each year, live with the parties.

Incapacitation of Either Party

This clause confirms each party's intention to care for and support the other in the event of incapacitation. This is a requirement of most states' marriage law anyway.

Incapacitation of Either Party

The parties agree that in the event of incapacitation of either party during the marriage the other party shall assume complete responsibility for the care and financial support of such party to the extent of his or her income, assets and time.

Use of Living Space

The living-space clause provides for equal authority in determination of domicile and the parties' use of living space. It also recognizes that one party or the other may need to be absent from time to time.

Use of Living Space

(a) The parties agree to live together at a residence of their mutual choice, recognizing, however, that it may be necessary or desirable from time to time for one to live away from the other for a period of up to several months as determined by the educational, employment or other needs of either party. Each party hereby waives whatever right he or she may have to determine solely the domicile of the parties, and the parties further agree that;

(b) The parties shall have equal right to use of all living space in their home and that all decisions regarding its use shall be by mutual consent only, except that the right of each party to the quiet enjoyment and security of shared living space shall take precedence over all other uses.

ARTICLE II: PROPERTY AND FINANCIAL PROVISIONS

If it can be said that there is a bread-and-butter article of the agreement, that pertaining to property and finances is it. Not necessarily because it deals with money and property (every article does that to a perhaps surprising degree), but because it is the here-and-now portion of the contract rather than one that deals with future possibilities.

This article of the agreement contains more headings than any other, twenty in all, including disclosure of the parties' financial circumstances, separation of the parties' property, individual waivers by each party of rights to the property of the other, ownership of jointly and separately held property, joint and separate bank accounts, the sharing of household expenses, existing financial obligations of the parties, credit transactions of the parties, joint tax returns, financial support during the marriage, and almost a dozen other items.

If the future husband and wife cannot agree here, then there will not be any Article III, IV, or V of the agreement dealing with future conditions.

In litigation concerning the property and financial relationship of the parties, the court will look to the contract, but the court will also carefully look *beyond* the contract to determine fairness and equity. In this respect, full and complete disclosure of each party's financial situation to the other is almost essential to the upholding of an agreement by the court.

Disclosure

Two options. *Option 1* is much less specific than option 2 and should only be used for agreements where the property of the parties is minimal. *Option 2* is usually considered adequate for all but the most complex financial situations involving considerable assets. The core of option 2, of course, consists of Exhibits A and B, completed by the parties and attached to and made a part of the agreement. Forms for Exhibits A and B (Forms 48.2 and 48.3) are provided on pages F325 and F327, and sample exhibits are part of the completed sample agreement beginning on page 200.

Option 2 would be essential for parties whose agreements are governed by the laws of community-property states (Arizona, California, Idaho, Louisiana, Nevada, New Mexico, Texas, and Washington). The parties must have the advice of qualified legal counsel regarding their desires to keep individually owned property and individual income separate after marriage. Even then there is no assurance that the courts of those states will uphold property provisions of the agreement.

Disclosure (1)

Each party has made a full and complete disclosure of his or her assets, liabilities and net worth to the other.

Disclosure (2)

Each party has made a full and complete disclosure of his or her assets, liabilities and net worth to the other by means of documents which are attached hereto and made a part of this agreement as exhibits: the disclosure of _____ John _____ being **Exhibit A,** and the disclosure of _____ Mary _____ being **Exhibit B.**

Present Property of the Parties/Separate Property

Titled somewhat differently, these provisions indicate the parties' intent to keep separate all property owned by each party prior to the marriage or acquired by either party after the marriage. In community property states neither of these provisions (nor any others) may serve to entirely meet the parties' wishes in this respect.

Present Property of the Parties

Each of the parties has acquired all of his or her separate property independently of, and without the assistance of, the other and desires to keep separate all of his or her real and/or personal property, whether now owned or hereafter acquired, free from any claim by virtue of a marriage between them.

Separate Property

(a) For all purposes of this agreement, as used herein, the term "separate property" shall mean, with respect to a party hereto, all of such party's right, title and interest, legal or beneficial, in and to any and all property and interests in property, whether real, personal or mixed, wherever situated, and regardless of whether now owned or hereafter acquired, and;

(b) Each party shall, during his or her remaining lifetime, retain the sole ownership of all of his or her separate property, and shall have the exclusive right to dispose of any and all of such property during his or her remaining lifetime, by *inter vivos* or testamentary transfer, or by any and all other dispositions, and/or to encumber, pledge or hypothecate same, without any interference on the part of the other in such manner as shall be determined at the sole discretion of such owner thereof, as if their marriage had not taken place.

Waiver by Future Husband/Waiver by Future Wife

These twin provisions serve to further express the parties' intent that individually owned and individually acquired property be kept separate after the marriage. Rights to inheritance, alimony, support, etc., waived in these paragraphs are provided for in subsequent clauses. These waivers are further examples of "clean-slate" provisions indicating the parties' intent that the stipulations of the agreement should take precedence over the traditional rights usually accorded to husbands and wives by the law.

Waiver by Future Husband

Except as specifically provided herein, _____ John _____ hereby waives, relinquishes and releases all right, title and interest in and to any and all separate property of _____ Mary _____, accruing to, or vesting in him, or in which he may otherwise be entitled as husband of _____ Mary _____, or her widower, heir-at-law, next of kin or distributee, upon or by virtue of a termination of the marriage of the parties by death, divorce, dissolution, annulment, or otherwise, including, but not limited to such rights as curtesy, statutory or other allowances to a spouse of a decedent, distributions by way of intestacy, rights of election to take against the will of _____ Mary _____, or against any other alimony, support and/or other property settlement.

Waiver by Future Wife

Except as specifically provided herein, _____ Mary _____ hereby waives, relinquishes and releases all right, title and interest in and to any and all separate property of _____ John _____, accruing to, or vesting in her, or in which she may otherwise be entitled as wife of _____ John _____, or his widow, heir-at-law, next of kin or distributee, upon or by virtue of a termination of the marriage of the parties by death, divorce, dissolution, annulment, or otherwise, including, but not limited to such rights as dower, statutory or other allowances of a spouse of a decedent, distributions by way of intestacy, rights of election to take against the will of _____ John _____, or against any other alimony, support and/or other property settlement.

Property Held as Tenants by the Entirety

This clause states the parties' intent that they shall have the right, under the agreement, to possess jointly owned property as tenants by the entirety—and that in the event of the death of either during the marriage such property shall pass outright to the survivor. Transfer of ownership of such property should also be provided for in each party's Last Will and Testament. The clause also specifies that in the event of divorce each party shall become a tenant in common with the other.

It is pursuant to this clause of the agreement that the husband and wife could jointly own any property such as a house, condominium, land, automobiles, boats, etc. Pursuant to other provisions of the agreement (but not necessarily under the laws of the few community-property states), either party could, of course, also separately own other real and/or personal property.

Upon the *death* of the husband or wife of a couple owning property as tenants by the entirety, the survivor is usually entitled to the whole property. Upon the *divorce* of a couple owning property as tenants by the entirety, a tenancy in common is usually created.

Property Held as Tenants by the Entirety

(a) Any other provisions of this agreement to the contrary notwithstanding, _____John_____ and _____Mary_____ may, during the marriage, acquire property or interests therein, in both names, with or without rights of survivorship. In such event, the signatures of both parties shall be required to sell, transfer, convey, pledge, encumber or hypothecate such jointly held property; and, upon the death of either party, any and all such property jointly held by both parties with rights of survivorship shall pass outright to the survivor in accordance with applicable law. Entry into such arrangements shall not in any way be deemed a waiver of or abandonment of this agreement or any part hereof.

(b) Upon termination of the marriage of the parties by divorce, dissolution, annulment or any other means while both are living, each party shall become a tenant in common with the other party and thereby entitled to an undivided one-half interest in said property. Should either party have contributed more than one-half toward the purchase, maintenance or improvement of such property, said party shall be entitled to a special equity in such property according to his or her respective contribution.

Partition of Community Property

Parties whose agreements are governed by the laws of community-property states need to include a proviso for partition of community property. Such a clause expresses their intent that income or property of either that is derived from separately owned property or from the labor of either party shall remain separate. Our legal consultants point out that the courts of some community-property states may declare this provision invalid, although it may be upheld in others.

Partition of Community Property

The parties hereby agree that, if at any time after their marriage, either shall have or acquire any property which shall be derived from or related to separately owned property, or which is income from such property, or which is derived from or related to the labor of either party, then, upon request of either party, the parties will promptly execute such documents and instruments as may be required by applicable law to partition such community property into the separate property of the parties.

Right to Make Voluntary Transfers Not Waived

Under the terms of voluntary transfer, the parties retain their right to make voluntary transfers of property between them without such transfer being deemed an abandonment of other provisions of the contract providing for separation of individually owned property.

This is an important paragraph for inclusion in the agreements of parties whose contracts are governed by the laws of community-property states since the laws of most of those states stipulate that *gifts* to either party remain the separate property of the recipient.

Right to Make Voluntary Transfers Not Waived

Any other provisions of this agreement to the contrary notwithstanding, each party shall have the right to voluntarily transfer or convey to the other any property or interest therein which may be lawfully transferred or conveyed, during his or her lifetime, or by will or otherwise upon death; and neither party intends by this agreement to limit nor restrict in any way the right and power of the other to receive any such voluntary transfer or conveyance. All such ostensible voluntary transfers or conveyances shall be deemed to be voluntary gifts from the transferor to the transferee and shall not in any way be deemed a waiver or abandonment of this agreement or any part hereof.

Joint Bank Accounts

Two provisions in regard to joint bank accounts follow. *Option 1* provides for the establishment of joint bank checking and/or savings accounts requiring the signatures of *both* parties for the withdrawal of funds. *Option 2* provides for the establishment of such accounts requiring the signature of *either* party for the withdrawal of funds.

Joint Bank Accounts (1)

Any other provisions of this agreement to the contrary notwithstanding, the parties may, from time to time during the marriage, establish joint bank checking and/or savings accounts as tenants by the entirety requiring the signatures of both parties for the withdrawal of funds from such accounts. Upon the death of either party, any and all sums in any such bank accounts jointly held by both parties shall pass outright to the survivor in accordance with applicable law.

Joint Bank Accounts (2)

Any other provisions of this agreement to the contrary notwithstanding, the parties may, from time to time during the marriage, establish joint bank savings and/or checking accounts requiring the signature of either party for the withdrawal of funds from such accounts. Upon the death of either party, any and all sums in any such bank accounts jointly held by the parties shall pass outright to the survivor in accordance with applicable law.

Separate Bank Accounts

This clause states the parties' intent that under the agreement each shall have the right to maintain individual bank accounts as "separate property." It is an important clause for parties whose agreements are governed by the laws of community-property states, although our legal consultants point out that there is no assurance that the courts of those states will uphold such a provision in every case.

Separate Bank Accounts

The parties agree that each may, from time to time during the marriage, establish various bank savings and/or checking accounts which shall be "separate property" under terms of this agreement and that all funds deposited therein, and all income derived therefrom, shall be "separate property" of the party in whose name such funds are held. The parties further agree to instruct any bank holding funds as provided for in this paragraph, that such funds shall be the separate property of the party in whose name such funds are being held.

Household Bank Accounts

Under *option 1* equal deposits are made by the parties in accord with their agreement elsewhere in the contract to share equally the payment of household expenses. *Option 2* provides for deposits by the parties in a stated ratio—which will probably be the same ratio in which the parties agree elsewhere in the contract to pay for household expenses. With *option 3* the deposits of either party shall be regarded as the property of both. This clause may be used by parties who agree elsewhere in the contract that one of the parties will provide for the payment of all household expenses.

Household Bank Accounts   (1)

(a) The parties agree that they may, from time to time during the marriage, establish various jointly held bank checking accounts for convenience in the payment of household expenses and which require the signature of either party for the withdrawal of funds, and that;

(b) Funds shall be equally deposited therein by both parties in accord with their agreement to equally share payment of household expenses, and that;

(c) Upon the death of either party, any and all such sums in any such jointly held accounts shall pass outright to the surviving party in accordance with applicable law.

Household Bank Accounts   (2)

(a) The parties agree that they may, from time to time during the marriage, establish various jointly held bank checking accounts for convenience in the payment of household expenses and which require the signature of either party for the withdrawal of funds, and that;

(b) Funds deposited therein shall be deposited _____ sixty _____ percent by _____ John _____ and _____ forty _____ percent by _____ Mary _____, and that;

(c) Upon the death of either party, any and all sums in any such bank accounts jointly held by the parties shall pass outright to the surviving party in accordance with applicable law.

Household Bank Accounts   (3)

(a) The parties agree that they may, from time to time during the marriage, establish various jointly held bank checking accounts for convenience in the payment of household expenses and which require the signature of either party for the withdrawal of funds, and that;

(b) Any and all funds deposited therein by either party shall be deemed the equal and undivided property of both, and that;

(c) Upon the death of either party, any and all sums in any such bank accounts jointly held by the parties shall pass outright to the surviving party in accordance with applicable law.

Existing Financial Obligations

It is important to have a clear understanding about outstanding debts when getting married. The following clause states each party's acceptance of responsibility for payment of his or her antenuptial debts. It also sets forth each party's agreement to indemnify the other for legal costs or damage resulting from nonpayment of any antenuptial debt by either. The third subparagraph specifies that a party who pays an antenuptial debt of the other shall have an interest in the property of that party until such time as the party paying the debt of the other has been reimbursed.

Existing Financial Obligations

(a) Each of the parties acknowledges that he or she is presently indebted to various persons and/or business entities as described by each in the hereinabove-mentioned disclosures to each other. With regard to these financial obligations, the parties hereby agree that they shall each individually be responsible for the payment of all antenuptial debts existing at the time of marriage, _____ John _____ paying for all antenuptial debts incurred by *himself* on *his* behalf, and _____ Mary _____ paying for all antenuptial debts incurred by *herself* on *her* behalf.

(b) Each party agrees to indemnify the other for all damage and cost incurred by reason of any suit against said party for debts which the other party has agreed in subparagraph (a) hereof to be responsible.

(c) In consideration of payment of any antenuptial debt of one party by the other, the party whose debt is thus paid agrees that the party satisfying such debt shall be entitled to a special equity in the property of the other, equal in value to the amount of any such debt so paid.

Credit Transactions by the Parties

The key words in the terms of the credit clause are "solely by virtue of his or her assets, liabilities, income and credit history." If credit is granted on the basis of the assets, income, and credit history of both parties, then it's possible that both will be held liable for payment of the debt regardless of what the parties' agreement may say.

This is an additional provision whereby the parties may further indicate to the court their intention and wish that their property remain separate.

Credit Transactions by the Parties

The parties hereby agree that when either party enters into a transaction where credit is extended to such party, and such party becomes a debtor on the basis of credit extended solely by virtue of his or her assets, liabilities, income and credit history, then such party shall be fully and individually liable for the timely payment of any such obligation and shall hold the other party harmless from any such obligation and indemnify him or her in the event that he or she shall ever be required to satisfy same.

Taxes

As with the preceding provision, this clause emphasizes the parties' intent that separate property be considered as such—while retaining their right under the agreement to file joint tax returns without inviting the court to consider such action an abandonment of the separate property provisions of the agreement.

Taxes

Any other provisions of this agreement to the contrary notwithstanding, the parties recognize that the Internal Revenue Code and regulations thereunder, and other codes and regulations of the several states and of foreign nations, do, in certain instances, provide substantial savings in taxes paid by married couples filing joint returns. If such be the case, the parties hereby agree that the filing of any such joint returns, and/or the combining of their separate incomes and deductions, shall not in any way be deemed a waiver of, or abandonment of, this agreement or any part hereof, and that each party shall be fully responsible for the payment of his or her portion of any federal, state or other taxes attributable to his or her income or personal or real property.

Household Expenses

Option 1 provides for the equal sharing of household expenses and may be keyed to option 1 of **Household Bank Accounts**. Under *option 2* either party pays all household expenses. This proviso may be keyed to option 3 of **Household Bank Accounts**. *Option 3* provides for the shared payment of household expenses on an agreed-upon ratio, say 60:40, and may be keyed to option 2 of **Household Bank Accounts**.

These provisions also *define* household expenses for purposes of the agreement.

Household Expenses (1)

(a) The parties agree to equally share responsibility for payment of household expenses, which for all purposes of this agreement, as used herein, shall mean mortgage or rent payments on the residence of the parties, all maintenance and improvement of same, utilities, food, shared entertainment and travel and medical expenses. The parties also agree that the mutually agreed-upon purchase and maintenance of household furniture, draperies, carpets, appliances, etc., shall also be "household expenses" for all purposes of this agreement and shall be shared equally by the parties, and the parties further agree that;

(b) Distribution of any such jointly owned property between the parties in the event the marriage is dissolved *vinculo matrimoni* by divorce, annulment, or any other means during the lifetime of both parties shall be carried out as provided for under **Possible Dissolution of the Marriage** as set forth herein, and that;

(c) The parties may determine, from time to time, to equally share the cost of insurance on their residence and its contents and the costs of medical and hospitalization insurance on both parties.

Household Expenses (2)

(a) _____John_____ agrees to provide for payment of all household expenses during the marriage and to establish and adequately fund a joint bank checking account from which either party may withdraw funds for convenience in the payment of household expenses. For all purposes of this agreement, "household expenses" shall mean mortgage or rent payments on the residence of the parties, all maintenance and improvement of same, utilities, food, shared entertainment and travel and medical expenses. The mutually agreed-upon purchase and maintenance of household furniture, draperies, carpets, appliances, etc., shall also be "household expenses" for all purposes of this agreement, and;

(b) Distribution of any such jointly owned property between the parties in the event the marriage is dissolved *vinculo matrimoni* by divorce, annulment, or any other means during the lifetime of both parties shall be carried out as provided for under **Possible Dissolution of the Marriage** as set forth herein, and;

(c) _____John_____ also agrees to provide for payment of insurance on their residence and its contents and for medical and hospitalization insurance on both parties.

Household Expenses (3)

(a) The parties agree to share responsibility for the payment of household expenses as follows:

(i) _____John_____ shall provide for the payment of __sixty__ percent of all reasonable household expenses, and

(ii) _____Mary_____ shall provide for the payment of __forty__ percent of all reasonable household expenses, and the parties agree to establish and fund a joint bank checking account for convenience in the payment of household expenses. For all purposes of this agreement, "household expenses" shall mean mortgage or rent payments on the residence of the parties, all maintenance and improvement of same, utilities, food, shared entertainment and travel and medical expenses. The parties also agree that the mutually agreed-upon purchase and maintenance of household furniture, draperies, carpets, appliances, etc., shall also be "household expenses" for all purposes of this agreement and shall be shared in the same proportion as provided for under (i) and (ii) hereinabove, and the parties further agree that;

(b) Distribution of any such jointly owned property between the parties in the event the marriage is dissolved *vinculo matrimoni* by divorce, annulment or any other means during the lifetime of both parties shall be carried out as provided for under **Possible Dissolution of the Marriage,** as set forth herein, and that;

(c) The parties may determine, from time to time, to share the cost of insurance on their residence and its contents and the costs of medical and hospitalization insurance on both parties. Any such insurance shall be paid for by the parties in the same proportion as "household expenses," as provided for under subparagraph (a), (i) and (ii), hereinabove.

Revision of Shared Household Expenses

Used with any of the three options pertaining to household expenses, the revision clause provides for a revision in the proportion of household expenses paid by each party when there is a substantial change in the ratio between their incomes.

Revision of Shared Household Expenses

The parties agree to revise the proportion of household expenses shared by each, and of household, medical and hospitalization insurance paid by each, whenever there is a substantial revision in the ratio between the incomes of the parties, so that the proportion of such shared household and insurance expenses remains closely related to the ratio between the individual incomes of the parties.

Financial Support

Under *option 1* each party pays for all expenses related to his or her own personal financial support during the marriage. This may be keyed to option 1 of Household Bank Accounts and option 1 of Household Expenses.

Option 2 is concerned with each party's payment of all expenses related to his or her own personal financial support during the marriage and further provides for either party's acceptance of responsibility to pay a set percentage of the expenses of the personal financial support of another person, such as a relative, during the marriage.

Option 3 is similar to option 2 but sets forth either party's acceptance of responsibility to pay a set percentage of the personal financial support of two, rather than one, additional persons.

Option 4 provides for the parties' sharing, in various proportions, the expense of the personal financial support of another person.

Option 5 provides for either party to pay for the entire cost of his or her own financial support, plus the financial support of the second party to be shared at a set proportion. This option may be combined with option 2 under Household Bank Accounts and option 3 under Household Expenses.

Note: The apportionment of shared expense for the financial support of children of the parties is taken care of under Article III: Children.

Financial Support (1)

The parties agree to each be fully responsible for the payment of all expenses related to his or her own personal financial support and maintenance during the marriage.

Financial Support (2)

(a) The parties agree to each be fully responsible for the payment of all expenses related to his or her personal financial support and maintenance during the marriage, and;

(b) _____John_____ agrees to be responsible for payment of ___fifty___ percent of the expense of the personal financial support of ___Mary's mother___ during said marriage.

Financial Support (3)

(a) The parties agree to each be fully responsible for the payment of all expenses related to his or her own personal financial support and maintenance during the marriage, and;

(b) _____John_____ agrees to be responsible for payment of ___seventy-five___ percent of the expense of the personal financial support of _____Mary's aunt Louise_____ during said marriage, and further;

(c) Agrees to be responsible for the payment of ___twenty-five___ percent of the expense of the personal financial support of ___Mary's sister Blanche___ during said marriage.

Financial Support (4)

(a) The parties agree to each be fully responsible for the payment of all expenses related to his or her own personal financial support and maintenance during the marriage, and further agree that;

(b) Each party shall be responsible for the financial support and maintenance of _____John's father_____ as follows:

(i) ___John___ shall be responsible for payment of ___eighty___ percent of such financial support and maintenance, and

(ii) ___Mary___ shall be responsible for payment of ___twenty___ percent of such financial support and maintenance.

Financial Support (5)

(a) _____John_____ agrees to be fully responsible for the payment of all expenses related to ___his___ own financial support and maintenance and agrees to be responsible for payment of ___sixty___ percent of all expenses for the personal financial support and maintenance of _____Mary_____, and;

(b) _____Mary_____ agrees to be fully responsible for the payment of ___forty___ percent of all expenses related to ___her___ own personal financial support and maintenance.

Revision of Shared Financial Support

Used with any of the immediately preceding paragraphs, this clause provides for revision in the ratio of shared financial support whenever there is a substantial change in the ratio between the parties' individual incomes.

Revision of Shared Financial Support

The parties agree to revise the proportion of financial support hereinabove-apportioned between the parties whenever there is a substantial revision in the ratio of incomes between the parties, so that the proportion of shared financial support remains closely related to the ratio between the individual incomes of the parties.

Gainful Employment and Education

Complete employment and educational autonomy within the bounds of the parties' stated agreement to meet specified expense and financial support commitments are the terms of *option 1*. *Option 2* provides for complete employment and educational autonomy, except for the responsibility of either party to provide for payment of all household expenses and expenses of financial support of both parties. Under *option 3* there is a work-study agreement between the parties. They agree to share responsibility alternately for the support of both.

Gainful Employment and Education (1)

The parties agree that each shall have full autonomy regarding the choice of occupation, employment, career and education during the marriage, while in no way waiving nor renouncing the binding nature of their agreement providing for payment of household expenses and financial support as set forth herein.

Gainful Employment and Education (2)

The parties agree that each shall have full autonomy regarding the choice of occupation, employment, career and education during the marriage, while recognizing the binding agreement of _____ _____John_____ to provide for payment of household expenses, financial support and maintenance as set forth herein.

Gainful Employment and Education (3)

(a) The parties agree that each shall alternately be responsible for the payment of all reasonable household expenses and for the financial support and maintenance of both parties during such times when the other party is enrolled in school, namely: _____John_____ shall be responsible for payment of the household expenses, financial support and maintenance of both parties during such times as _____Mary_____ shall be enrolled substantially full time in school diligently pursuing the educational goal of __chemical engineer__; and _____Mary_____ shall be responsible for payment of the household expenses, financial support and maintenance of both parties during such times as _____John_____ shall be enrolled substantially full time in school diligently pursuing the educational goal of __Ph.D. in business administration__. The enrollment of either party in school and the responsibility of the other for payment of household expenses, financial support and maintenance shall be determined solely by mutual consent.

(b) If after one party has provided for payment of the household expenses, financial support and maintenance of both parties for a period of approximately _____two years_____ so that the other may be enrolled in school pursuant to subparagraph (a) hereof, and then the party having been enrolled in school fails to provide for payment of the household expenses, financial support and maintenance of both parties for a subsequent equal period of time, the party failing to fulfill such obligation shall be indebted to the other party for a sum equal to one-half the amount reasonably expended for the household expenses, financial support and maintenance of both parties during the previous _____two years_____.

Home Care and Maintenance

With *option 1* the couple equally shares home care and maintenance in terms of time, effort, and expense.

Option 2 allows for one party to be responsible for all home care and maintenance in consideration of the other party's acceptance of the responsibility to provide for the payment of all household expenses and for the entire cost of support and maintenance of both parties. This provision could be keyed to option 5 under **Financial Support** if the employed party agrees to provide for 100 percent of the support of the stay-at-home party. This option may also be keyed to option 2 under **Household Expenses** and option 3 under **Household Bank Accounts**.

Option 3 separates each party's commitment for time and effort from his or her commitment for shared expense so that the two may, for example, share time and effort 50:50 and share expense 60:40.

Option 4 provides for payment by one party to the other for acceptance of the responsibility for home care and maintenance, plus the sharing of home care and maintenance on a separate, shared basis.

Home Care and Maintenance (1)

The parties agree to share equally, in terms of time, effort and expense, the responsibility for all housekeeping and the care and maintenance of their living space and any real property jointly owned or used.

Home Care and Maintenance (2)

In consideration of the obligation herein accepted by _____ _____John_____ to provide for payment of household expenses and for the financial support of _____ __Mary and her children__ during the marriage, _____ _____Mary_____ hereby agrees to accept responsibility for the housekeeping, care and maintenance of shared living space, with such assistance as _____John_____ may voluntarily provide.

Home Care and Maintenance (3)

The parties agree to share the responsibility for the housekeeping, care and maintenance of shared living space and any real property jointly owned or used as follows:
(a) _____John_____ accepts responsibility for _____fifty_____ percent of the necessary time and effort and _____sixty_____ percent of the reasonable expense for the care and maintenance of shared living space and any real property jointly owned or used, and;
(b) _____Mary_____ accepts responsibility for _____fifty_____ percent of the necessary time and effort and _____forty_____ percent of the reasonable expense for the care and maintenance of shared living space and any real property jointly owned or used.

Home Care and Maintenance (4)

(a) It is agreed by the parties that _____Mary_____ shall be responsible for the necessary time and effort for the care and maintenance of shared living space and any real property jointly owned or used during the marriage, for which he/she shall be paid the weekly sum of $ __100.00__ by _____John_____ in addition to any other sums provided by _____John_____ for household expenses, maintenance and the personal financial support of _____Mary_____ as herein provided, and;
(b) _____John_____ accepts responsibility for _____sixty_____ percent of the reasonable expense for the care and maintenance of shared living space and any real property jointly owned or used, and that;
(c) _____Mary_____ accepts responsibility for _____forty_____ percent of the reasonable expense for the care and maintenance of shared living space and any real property jointly owned or used.

ARTICLE III: CHILDREN

A fairly brief portion of the agreement deals with half a dozen or so basic areas regarding children, including mutual agreement not to have children, care and support of children of the marriage, care and support of previous children of either party, education of children, religious instruction of children, names of children, and rights of children. These, of course, are not all of the possible provisions that might be included, and you may want to write a few of your own.

As you might expect, the court's primary concern when looking at the provisions of this article in the event of litigation will be the welfare of any children. Courts have been quick to declare provisions of marriage agreements invalid that they feel infringe upon the rights of a child or that tend to disadvantage a child in any way.

Of course, if you agree *not* to have children, and neither party has previous children, you can choose this article's first paragraph and happily go to the next article, Possible Dissolution of the Marriage.

Mutual Agreement Not to Have Children

This clause establishes the parties' mutual agreement not to have children and specifies the waiver of traditional rights of parenthood that the parties mutually agree to relinquish in the event that a child is born of the marriage—unless both parties agree in writing to parent a child.

Subparagraph (d) acknowledges that the court may deem certain provisions of the agreement not to have children "contrary to public policy" and therefore includes the mother's request that the court nevertheless enforce this paragraph to the letter.

Mutual Agreement Not to Have Children

(a) Each party agrees that no children shall be born of the marriage, nor shall any children be adopted by either party during the marriage, unless both parties mutually agree in writing, and;

(b) It is further agreed that if a child is born during the marriage without the written agreement of both parties, then the wife waives all right to child support and the husband waives all right to visitation, and;

(c) _____Mary_____ agrees to inform _____John_____ _____ immediately upon obtaining knowledge that she is pregnant, and further agrees that the withholding of such information from _____John_____ shall be deemed a waiver by her of child-support payments in the event of divorce, annulment or dissolution of the marriage by any other means during the lifetime of both parties, and;

(d) _____Mary_____ realizes that the Courts look upon with disfavor as being contrary to public policy, agreements containing the provisions in subparagraphs (a), (b) and (c), hereof, but she strongly urges that those provisions be enforced to the letter. This provision shall be null and void where for medical reasons the wife must deliver a child.

Care and Support of Children

We have noted seven options in regard to the care and support of children. *Option 1* provides for equal participation in the care and financial support of children.

Under *option 2* one party accepts responsibility for the care of children in consideration of the other party's acceptance of responsibility for the financial support of such children, as well as for the person who accepts responsibility for their care.

Option 3 calls for the equal sharing of the care and financial support of any children of the marriage, plus equal sharing of the care and financial support of any *previous* child of *either* party.

With *option 4* there is equal sharing of the care and financial support of any children of the marriage, plus equal sharing of the care and support of the previous children of each of the parties.

Option 5 provides for equal sharing of the care and financial support of the previous children of *either*

party—although the parties have mutually agreed (above) to have no children of their own.

Option 6 provides for equal sharing of the care and financial support of previous children of *each* party—although the parties have mutually agreed (above) to have no children of their own.

Option 7 is similar to option 5, but it does not state that a previous child of either party was necessarily born of a marriage.

Care and Support of Children   (1)

The parties agree to share fully and equally all responsibilities related to the care and financial support of any and all children whom they may mutually agree to have or to adopt during the marriage.

Care and Support of Children   (2)

In consideration of the agreement by _____John_____ to provide for payment of all household expenses and for the financial support and maintenance of _____Mary_____ and any and all children whom the parties may mutually agree to have or to adopt during the marriage, _____Mary_____ agrees to accept primary responsibility for the care of any such children.

Care and Support of Children   (3)

(a) The parties agree to share fully and equally during the marriage all responsibilities related to the financial support and care of the children of _____John_____, of whom he/she is parent by previous marriage or by adoption, and;

(b) Further agree to share fully and equally all responsibilities related to the financial support and care of any and all children whom they may mutually agree to have or to adopt during the marriage.

Care and Support of Children   (4)

(a) The parties agree to share fully and equally during the marriage all responsibilities related to the financial support and care of the children of _____Mary_____, of whom she is parent by previous marriage or by adoption, and the children of _____John_____, of whom he is parent by previous marriage or by adoption, and;

(b) Further agree to share fully and equally all responsibilities related to the financial support and care of any and all children whom they may mutually agree to have or to adopt during the marriage.

Care and Support of Children   (5)

The parties agree to share fully and equally during the marriage all responsibilities related to the financial support and care of the children of _____John_____, of whom he/she is parent by previous marriage or by adoption.

Care and Support of Children   (6)

The parties agree to share fully and equally during the marriage all responsibilities related to the financial support and care of the children of _____John_____, of whom he is parent by previous marriage or by adoption, and for the financial support and care of the children of _____Mary_____, of whom she is parent by previous marriage or by adoption.

Care and Support of Children   (7)

The parties agree to share fully and equally during the marriage all responsibilities related to the financial support and care of the children of _____Mary_____, of whom he/she is parent.

Education of Children

This provision stipulates public school education through high school for any child or children of the parties and required determination by the parties, no later than a child's junior year in high school, whether additional education should be provided and how it is to be paid for. (You may want to write an education clause of your own, perhaps providing for private primary and/or secondary school and perhaps naming a particular institution.)

Education of Children

It is mutually agreed by the parties that any child or children of them, or of either of them, shall have the benefit of a public school education up to and through the high school level and that the parties shall mutually determine no later than during each child's junior year in high school whether it is desirable that such child have additional education and the manner of paying therefore.

Religious Instruction

Option 1 specifies that children of the parties shall receive religious instruction in a specific religious faith. *Option 2* states that children of the parties shall be free of religious influence by the parents and shall seek their own religious instruction. *Option 3* specifies that any child or children of the parties shall be free of religious influence by the parties, but that a previous child of either may continue to receive religious instruction if deemed by the parent to be in the best interests of the child. *Option 4* is similar to option 3, except that it provides for the instruction of each child in possibly different religious faiths as deemed in the best interests of each child by each parent.

Religious Instruction (1)

It is mutually agreed by the parties that any child or children of them shall receive instruction in the _____Lutheran_____ faith and be encouraged by the parties to continue in that faith.

Religious Instruction (2)

It is mutually agreed by the parties that any child or children of them shall receive no religious instruction from either parent, nor from any religious organization recommended by either parent, it being agreed by the parties that any child or children of theirs may seek his or her own religious instruction without influence or hindrance of either parent and that it shall be up to each child to pursue his or her own religious interest.

Religious Instruction (3)

(a) It is mutually agreed by the parties that any child or children of them shall receive no religious instruction from either parent, nor from any religious organization recommended by either parent, it being agreed by the parties that any child or children of theirs may seek his or her own religious instruction without influence or hindrance of either parent and that it shall be up to each child to pursue his or her own religious interest, it being further agreed between the parties, however, that;

(b) Any child of _____Mary_____, of whom he or she is parent by previous marriage or adoption, may be instructed in the _____Catholic_____ faith, this being deemed in the best interests of the child by _____Mary_____.

Religious Instruction (4)

(a) It is mutually agreed by the parties that any child or children of them shall receive no religious instruction from either parent, nor from any religious organization recommended by either parent, it being agreed by the parties that any child or children of theirs may seek his or her own religious instruction without influence or hindrance of either parent and that it shall be up to each child to pursue his or her own religious interest, it being further agreed between the parties, however, that;

(b) Any child of _____John_____, of whom he is parent by previous marriage or by adoption, may be instructed in the _____Lutheran_____ faith, this being deemed in the best interests of such child by _____John_____, and, that;

(c) Any child of _____Mary_____, of whom she is parent by previous marriage or by adoption, may be instructed in the _____Catholic_____ faith, this being deemed in the best interests of such child by _____Mary_____.

Names of Children

This clause provides for the surname of any child or children of the parties. Parents should key this clause to **Names of the Parties.**

Names of Children

It is agreed by the parties that any child whom the parties mutually agree to have or to adopt during the marriage shall bear the surname of _____Smith_____.

Rights of Children

This is an important clause for establishing the parties' intent not to infringe upon the rights of any children of either of them.

Rights of Children

The parties recognize that they might, during the course of their marriage, mutually determine to have or to adopt a child or children and hereby agree that the provisions of this agreement are not intended to govern nor affect the rights of any such children in or to the separate property of either party hereto, and the parties further agree that all such rights in and to such separate property and/or financial support shall be governed by applicable law.

ARTICLE IV: POSSIBLE DISSOLUTION OF THE MARRIAGE

Not many years ago, the fact that, prior to marriage, a man and woman made provision in an agreement for the possibility of divorce was enough to get the agreement, or at least that portion of it, thrown out of court.

Until very recently, any waiver of alimony or support by a woman was also considered good reason, by many judges, for declaring a marriage agreement "contrary to public policy." The courts' concern may not have been so much for the rights of the wife in such cases, but more likely a desire that she not become an added burden upon the state's welfare rolls.

Today, in most states, written agreements containing provisions for possible dissolution of a marriage, and waivers of rights to alimony and/or support, are usually upheld by the courts as long as judges are convinced that the parties understand the possible consequences of the waivers.

The following three provisions—Waiver of Alimony and Support; Waiver of Alimony, Provision for Child Support; and Waiver of Alimony—are all "clean-slate" provisions, waiving certain rights normally granted under family law so that mutually agreed upon stipulations of the marriage contract may take precedence to avoid, in effect, a "jurisdictional dispute" between marriage law and the marriage agreement. There is nothing waived in any of these provisions that cannot be written into and made a part of the agreement.

A second paragraph, **Advice of Counsel**, immediately follows each waiver and states that the preceding waiver was granted by each party only after receipt of legal advice from independent counsel. Such provisions have greatly increased the courts' acceptance of waivers of rights to alimony and support.

Though titled differently, the three following provisions are actually options regarding alimony and support. If you choose one, you exclude the others.

Waiver of Alimony and Support

In this provision both parties waive any right to receipt of alimony or support in the event of the dissolution of the marriage.

Waiver of Alimony and Support   (1)

(a) In accordance with the parties' full and complete acceptance of the principle of independence and equal responsibility and authority between them, and in further accordance with the parties' waiver and relinquishment of whatever rights, duties, obligations and privileges which either might or could have derived from or related to a state of matrimony between them, other than those which may be included in and made a part of this agreement, each party hereby waives, relinquishes and renounces whatever right he or she may have to alimony, maintenance or support in the event the marriage is dissolved *vinculo matrimoni* by divorce, annulment or any other means during the lifetime of both parties.

(b) The parties recognize that the Courts look upon with disfavor as being contrary to public policy, marriage agreements anticipating dissolution of the marriage or the waiver of alimony and/or support by either party. The above notwithstanding, the parties strongly urge the Court to enforce this agreement to the letter.

Advice of Counsel

In connection with provisions of the above paragraph, **Waiver of Alimony and Support**, and particularly regarding the waiver, relinquishment and renouncing of whatever right either party may have to alimony, maintenance or support in the event the marriage is dissolved by divorce, annulment or any other means during the lifetime of both parties, each party hereby acknowledges receipt of specific advice pertaining thereto by separate, independent counsel of each party's own choice, each paying for his or her own counsel's advice and aid. Each party acknowledges that as a part of such advice his or her counsel has thoroughly discussed current _____

_____ Kansas _____ statutes concerning the dissolution of marriage and of alimony in connection therewith, as well as pertinent judicial decisions.

Waiver of Alimony and Support, Provision for Child Support

In this provision both parties waive any right to receive alimony or support, but they mutually agree that the party having primary custody of any child or children shall receive from the other party a set percentage of the cost of maintenance and support of any child or children.

Waiver of Alimony, Provision for Child Support   (2)

(a) In accordance with the parties' full and complete acceptance of the principle of independence and equal responsibility and authority between them, and in further accordance with the parties' waiver and relinquishment of whatever rights, duties, obligations and privileges which either might or could have derived from or related to a state of matrimony between them, other than those which may be included in and made a part of this agreement, each party hereby waives, relinquishes and renounces whatever right he or she may have to alimony, maintenance and support in the event the marriage is dissolved *vinculo matrimoni* by divorce, annulment or any other means during the lifetime of both parties except that;

(b) The party having primary custody of any child or children whom the parties may mutually have agreed to have or to adopt during the marriage shall receive from the other party a monthly sum equal to _fifty_ percent of the reasonable cost of the maintenance and support of any such child or children until reaching eighteen (18) years of age.

(c) The parties recognize that the Courts look with disfavor as being contrary to public policy, marriage agreements anticipating dissolution of the marriage or the waiver of alimony and/or support by either party. The above notwithstanding, the parties strongly urge the Court to enforce this agreement to the letter.

Advice of Counsel

In connection with provisions of the above paragraph, **Waiver of Alimony, Provision for Child Support**, and particularly regarding the waiver, relinquishment and renouncing of whatever right either party may have to alimony, maintenance or support in the event the marriage is dissolved by divorce, annulment or any other means during the lifetime of both parties, each party hereby acknowledges receipt of specific advice pertaining thereto by separate, independent counsel of each party's own choice, each paying for his or her own counsel's advice and aid. Each party acknowledges that as a part of such advice, his or her counsel has thoroughly discussed current _____ Kansas _____ statutes concerning the dissolution of marriage, and of alimony in connection therewith, as well as pertinent judicial decisions.

WARNING: *Because of the involvement of the rights of children, both parties must actually receive advice of counsel. A mere recital to that effect is insufficient.*

Waiver of Alimony

In this provision both parties waive any right to alimony. The clause is silent on the matter of support and/or maintenance.

Waiver of Alimony (3)

Each party hereby waives, relinquishes and renounces in perpetuity his or her right to receive any type of alimony, whether it be temporary, permanent, continuous, lump sum, rehabilitative, periodic or otherwise, from the other party, regardless of whether or not either party has experienced a substantial change in his or her financial circumstances.

(b) The parties recognize that the Courts look upon with disfavor as being contrary to public policy, marriage agreements anticipating dissolution of the marriage or the waiver of alimony and/or support by either party. The above notwithstanding, the parties strongly urge the Court to enforce this agreement to the letter.

Advice of Counsel

In connection with provisions of the above paragraph, **Waiver of Alimony**, and particularly regarding the waiver, relinquishment and renouncing of whatever right either party may have to alimony, maintenance or support in the event the marriage is dissolved by divorce, annulment or any other means during the lifetime of both parties, each party hereby acknowledges receipt of specific advice pertaining thereto by separate, independent counsel of each party's own choice, each paying for his or her own counsel's advice and aid. Each party acknowledges that as a part of such advice, his or her own counsel has thoroughly discussed _____Kansas_____ statutes concerning the dissolution of marriage, and of alimony in connection therewith, as well as pertinent judicial decisions.

Payments in Lieu of Alimony (and Support)

This clause provides for payments in lieu of alimony to be made by one party to the other in the event of dissolution of the marriage and further states the *amounts* of such payments, the *terms* of payment, and the *conditions* related to receipt of such payments.

Payments in Lieu of Alimony (4)

While the parties contemplate a long and lasting marriage terminated only by the death of one of the parties, they also recognize the possibility that their marriage may be terminated by way of divorce or dissolution during the lifetime of both. In the event of such termination of the marriage *vinculo matrimoni* during the lifetime of both parties by way of divorce, annulment or any other means, regardless of which party hereto shall initiate such action, the parties hereby specifically agree:

(a) _____Mary_____ shall not receive any alimony, support or separate property which might otherwise be available to him or her in accordance with applicable law.

(b) _____Mary_____ shall accept from ___John___ _____, in limitation of alimony and support, and in lieu of and instead of any obligation of _____John_____ for the costs and attorney's fees of _____Mary_____, payments as set forth below for a period equal to the number of months of marriage between the parties, or ten (10) years, whichever is less, and subject to the provisions of paragraph (d) hereof:

(i) For the first ___thirty-six___ months from and after issuance of the final decree of dissolution (termination date) of the marriage, _____Mary_____ shall receive the sum of ___eight hundred dollars___ ($800.00) per month;

(ii) Thereafter, the sum of ___five hundred dollars___ ($500.00) per month.

(iii) The aforesaid sums shall be payable by ___John___ _____, by depositing a check therefore in the mails

of the United States Postal Service, first class, postage prepaid, on or before the first day of each month to such address as _____Mary_____ may from time to time designate in writing to _____John_____. The first such monthly payment shall be made for the first calendar month following the termination date of the marriage.

(iv) It is further agreed that the maximum monthly payments made by _____John_____ hereunder shall at no time exceed ___two___ percent of the net worth of _____John_____.

(c) It is hereby agreed by the parties that all payments made pursuant to provisions of the immediately preceding subparagraph (b) shall, for federal income tax purposes, be deemed and considered by both parties as payments of alimony or as payments in lieu thereof, and;

(d) All such obligations of and payments by _____John_____ _____ shall terminate conclusively and forever upon the first occurrence of the death of or the remarriage of ___Mary___ _____, or his/her continuously residing with an adult of the opposite sex other than a blood relative; and no obligation of any kind as set forth in this paragraph, **Payments in Lieu of Alimony**, shall survive such first occurrence of said events, and;

(e) It is further agreed that such obligations of ___John___ _____ shall be legal and binding obligations of and upon the estate and property in which _____John_____ had a legal or beneficial interest prior to death, and;

(f) _____Mary_____ hereby specifically recognizes and agrees that he/she shall have no right to receive additional payments of alimony or support in any manner at any time and upon the occurrence of any event from and after the aforesaid termination of marriage, and that he/she shall have no right to receive any separate property of _____John_____ at any time, or upon the occurrence of any event, and _____Mary_____ further recognizes and ratifies his/her waiver, relinquishment and release of all such rights, and;

(g) The parties recognize that the Courts look upon with disfavor as being contrary to public policy, marriage agreements anticipating dissolution of the marriage or the waiver of alimony and/or support by either party. The above notwithstanding, the parties strongly urge the Court to enforce this agreement to the letter.

Advice of Counsel

In connection with provisions of the above paragraph, **Payments in Lieu of Alimony**, and particularly regarding the waiver, relinquishment and renouncing of whatever right either party may have to alimony, maintenance or support in the event the marriage is dissolved *vinculo matrimoni* by divorce, annulment or any other means during the lifetime of the parties, each party hereby acknowledges receipt of specific advice pertaining thereto by separate, independent counsel of each party's own choice, each paying for his or her own counsel's advice and aid. Each party acknowledges that as a part of such advice, his or her own counsel has thoroughly discussed _____Kansas_____ statutes concerning dissolution of marriage, and of alimony in connection therewith, as well as pertinent judicial decisions.

Compliance with Applicable Law

The following paragraph should be included in any agreement that contains the above provision, Payments in Lieu of Alimony, to which it refers.

Compliance with Applicable Law

Each party further acknowledges that he or she has sought meticulously to comply with applicable law concerning marital agreements regarding alimony, dower and curtesy rights and property rights, and that, among other things, each:

(a) Has fully and fairly advised the other, and been advised by the other, of their respective financial situations, and;

(b) Has a fair understanding of the financial status of the other and specifically understands that the other party is possessed of certain assets, as set forth in the annexed **Exhibits A** and **B**, which are made a part of this agreement, and;

(c) Considers the proposed payments in limitation of alimony or support as more than he or she would presently regard as fair under the current and probable future circumstances of each party and, in sum;

(d) Considers and believes after full and fair examination of the other's finances and after the advice of independent counsel that each has made a full disclosure to the other, each has a reasonable approximation of the financial situation of the other, and each considers the payments in limitation of and in lieu of all further obligation under provisions of said paragraph, **Payments in Lieu of Alimony**, to be more than fair.

Support *Pendente Lite*

This clause sets forth the terms for payment of a predetermined weekly amount by one party to the other during the time that any divorce or other litigation for dissolution of the marriage is pending.

Support *Pendente Lite*

The parties realize that in the event of dissolution of the marriage *vinculo matrimoni* by divorce, annulment or any other means during the lifetime of both parties, this agreement does not govern nor provide for support payments for the period beginning with the initiation of legal proceedings by either party for termination of the marriage and ending with the issuance of the final decree of termination in accordance with applicable law. To the extent enforceable and valid under _____Kansas_____ law, the parties agree that support *pendente lite* shall not exceed _____ ___two hundred dollars_____ ($__200.00__) per week and that each party shall bear his or her own costs and attorney's fees related thereto.

Child Support in the Event of Dissolution of the Marriage

This provision *may* flow from any of the above waivers used in combination with **Payments in Lieu of Alimony**, but it may also be used even though none of those provisions are a part of the agreement.

Child Support in the Event of Dissolution of the Marriage

(a) The parties shall attempt to arrive at a sum which they mutually agree shall constitute reasonable monthly payments for support of any child or children whom the parties, by mutual consent, may agree to have or to adopt during the marriage, in the event of legal separation of the parties or dissolution of the marriage *vinculo matrimoni* by divorce, annulment or any other means during the lifetime of both parties. In the event that they are unable to agree upon such a sum, the Court shall decide the issue, and;

(b) The parties each agree that neither party shall attempt to include an amount which would have been used for alimony in the sum designated for child-support payments. This provision also applies to temporary child support.

Child Custody

With *option 1* the court determines child custody in the event the parties are unable to agree upon a custody arrangement. *Option 2* provides for a wide range of custody provisions as agreed to by the parties.

Child Custody (1)

The parties shall attempt, in the event of dissolution of the marriage, to arrive at an agreement for the custody of any child or children whom the parties may mutually agree to have or to adopt during the marriage. Such agreement shall take into consideration the best interests of any such child or children and the ability of each parent to provide for the financial support and care of any such children. In the event the parties are unable to agree upon child custody, the Court shall decide the issue.

Child Custody (2)

(a) It is agreed between the parties that _____Mary_____ shall have primary custody of any child or children whom the parties mutually agree to have or to adopt during the marriage, subject to the following conditions:

(b) _____John_____ shall have liberal visitation rights with any such child or children and shall give _____Mary_____ reasonable advance notice of each visit, so that plans may be made by _____Mary_____ so that the children will not be disturbed to their detriment, unless the parties have agreed to a fixed schedule which may be adhered to without notice to _____ ___Mary___ by ___John___, and;

(c) _____John_____ shall have custody of any such child or children for a _____two-month_____ period during the summer and _____all_____ of every other Christmas vacation and up to one week every other Thanksgiving. _____ _____Mary_____ shall have liberal visitation rights during all periods of custody of any such child or children by __John__.

Removal of Children from Jurisdiction of the Court

This provision states the parties' mutual agreement that, in the event of dissolution of the marriage, neither shall attempt to remove a child from jurisdiction of the court without written permission of the other.

Removal of Children from Jurisdiction of the Court

It is mutually agreed by the parties that, in the event of dissolution of the marriage, neither party shall attempt to remove from the jurisdiction of the Court, without the written permission of the other party, any child or children whom the parties mutually agreed to have or to adopt during the marriage.

ARTICLE V: TESTEMENTARY PROVISIONS

By the time you begin working on this portion of the agreement, the most difficult part of negotiating the contract is usually behind you and both parties can concentrate on whatever measures they feel are necessary to assure for each other those things that previous contractual commitments, at minimum, provide and whatever additional property or funds they would want the other party to receive in the event of death.

Obviously, a practical way to do this is in one's **Last Will and Testament**, but it's important that each party's Will avoid conflict with the agreement. If that happens, there can be unnecessary expense and delay in carrying out the stipulations of either, and both might be in jeopardy of successful attack by would-be heirs.

Thus, this article's provisions must conform to earlier, relevant provisions of the agreement; then, each party's Will must conform to relevant provisions of this article's stipulations.

Agreement Between the Parties

Option 1 provides for mutual agreement of the parties specifying the value of property that one party is to receive upon the death of the other. This provision may be *duplicated* in the contract as from husband to wife and as from wife to husband.

Under *option 2* each party waives his or her right to take from the estate of the other and stipulates a perdetermined amount that each party agrees to accept upon the death of the other in consideration of his or her waiver of any right to take against the estate of the deceased party.

Either of these options should also be provided for and referred to in the **Last Will and Testament** of each party.

Agreement Between the Parties (1)

(a) In the event that the marriage shall be terminated by the death of _____ John _____, and if at the time of such death the parties are living together as husband and wife, then, upon such death, _____ Mary _____ shall receive from the estate of _____ John _____, or from trust funds in which _____ John _____ may have a beneficial interest, together with all other funds and/or property which _____ Mary _____ _____ may receive upon, and by virtue of the death of _____ John _____ (from, without limitation, joint bank accounts with or without rights of survivorship, other jointly held assets, life insurance and other property held in trust for the benefit of _____ Mary _____), a sum which shall be equal to the lesser of _____ one hundred thousand dollars _____ ($_____ 100,000.00) or _____ fifty _____ percent of the gross estate of _____ John _____, for Federal Estate Tax purposes, and;

(b) Any additional sum which may be needed to achieve said amount of $_____ 100,000.00 _____ or said _____ fifty _____ percent, as the case may be, shall be distributed to _____ Mary _____ _____ by the executors of the estate of _____ John _____ and/or trustees of said estate, as the case may be, in cash or other forms of property capable of being converted to cash without material reduction in value, and such distribution shall be made as soon as practicable after the death of _____ John _____ _____, but no later than six (6) months after the date of such death, and;

(c) The provisions required under subparagraphs (a) and (b) hereof shall be set forth in the **Last Will and Testament** of _____ John _____, or if an *inter vivos* trust agreement contains substantially all of the dispositive provisions concerning

the assets of _____ John _____ at his or her death, then upon the request of _____ Mary _____, at any time during their marriage, _____ John _____ shall deliver to _____ Mary _____ a copy of the portion of such then current will and/or trust containing such provisions. The said obligation to set forth said provision in the said will and/or trust shall be an additional obligation of _____ John _____, but failure to perform such additional obligation shall have no effect upon the existence or validity of the obligation of _____ _____ John _____ to make provision and payment as set forth in subparagraphs (a) and (b) hereof, and;

(d) In the event that at the time of the death of _____ John _____ _____, the parties shall have not been married, or shall not then be living together as husband and wife, or the said marriage shall have been dissolved prior thereto, the obligations set forth hereinabove shall be null and void and of no force or effect whatever.

Agreement Between the Parties (2)

(a) In the event the marriage shall be terminated by the death of _____ John _____, and if at the time of such death the parties shall be living together as husband and wife, then _____ _____ Mary _____ accepts as full discharge, settlement and satisfaction of any and all other statutory and/or other right, title and interest which *she*, as *widow*, heir-at-law, next of kin or distributee, upon termination of the marriage by death might or could acquire by virtue of the death of _____ John _____, the provisions of any **Last Will and Testament** of _____ John _____ _____, and hereby waives, relinquishes and renounces any right which *she* may have to share in the estate of _____ John _____ by way of intestacy, *dower* or right of election to take against the estate of _____ John _____, and;

(b) In consideration of the agreement of _____ Mary _____ _____ as provided in subparagraph (a) hereof, _____ John _____ hereby agrees to take out and maintain in force during the marriage, life insurance which will pay an amount not less than _____ one hundred thousand dollars _____ ($_____ 100,000.00 _____) to _____ Mary _____ in the event of the death of _____ John _____ by illness or accident, or, alternatively, to make an *inter vivos* gift to, or to establish an irrevocable trust for the benefit of, _____ Mary _____ in said amount, and;

(c) In the event the marriage shall be terminated by the death of _____ Mary _____, and if at the time of such death the parties shall be living together as husband and wife, then _____ _____ John _____ accepts as full discharge, settlement and satisfaction of any and all other statutory and other right, title and interest which *he*, as *widower*, heir-at-law, next of kin or distributee, upon termination of the marriage by death might or could acquire by virtue of the death of _____ Mary _____, the provisions of any **Last Will and Testament** of _____ Mary _____, and hereby waives, relinquishes and renounces any right which *he* may have to share in the estate of _____ Mary _____ by way of intestacy, *curtesy* or right of election to take against the estate of _____ Mary _____, and;

(d) In consideration of the agreement of _____ John _____ _____ as provided in subparagraph (c) hereof, _____ _____ Mary _____ hereby agrees to take out and maintain in force during the marriage, life insurance which will pay an amount not less than _____ fifty thousand dollars _____ ($_____ 50,000.00 _____) to _____ John _____ in the event of the death of _____ Mary _____ by illness or accident, or, alternatively, to make an *inter vivos* gift to, or to establish an irrevocable trust for the benefit of, _____ John _____ in said amount.

Life Insurance

Each party acknowledges his or her commitment to obtain and maintain in force life insurance payable to the other party. This provision may be used in combination with, or independently of, any of the other provisions of this article. The amounts of insurance coverage, as was also indicated in **Agreement Between the Parties (2)**, above, need not be the same.

Subparagraph (b) may be eliminated if the agreement is not to be bilateral.

Life Insurance

(a) _____John_____ hereby agrees to take out and maintain in force during the marriage, life insurance which will pay not less than _____one hundred thousand dollars_____ ($_100,000.00_) to _____Mary_____ in the event of the death of _____John_____ by illness or accident, or, alternatively, to make an *inter vivos* gift to, or to establish an irrevocable trust for the benefit of, _____Mary_____ in said amount, and;

(b) _____Mary_____ hereby agrees to take out and maintain in force during the marriage, life insurance which will pay an amount not less than _____fifty thousand dollars_____ ($_50,000.00_) to _____John_____ in the event of the death of _____Mary_____ by illness or accident, or, alternatively, to make an *inter vivos* gift to, or to establish an irrevocable trust fund for the benefit of, _____John_____ in said amount.

ARTICLE VI: GENERAL PROVISIONS

Article VI contains many of the general provisions that are found not only in this volume's marriage agreement, but in many other types of agreements as well. They have become routine provisions because over the years, as various types of contracts have been tossed out of court due to the *absence* of one or another of them, they have been added, one by one, to the deck of cards dealt to players in the drawing up of contracts.

These "one-size-fits-all" clauses are what lawyers call "boiler plate" (routine), but essential if the boiler is to withstand the heat and pressure of litigation.

Independent Counsel/Advice by Counsel

Though titled differently, the following two provisions are separate options—if you select one, you must exclude the other. Note, too, that **Advice by Counsel**, which follows, is quite different from **Advice of Counsel**, which appears following the waivers of right to alimony or support in **Article IV: Possible Dissolution of the Marriage.**

Option 1, **Independent Counsel**, states that the parties have received the advice of separate, independent counsel concerning the agreement. The employment of separate, independent counsel by the parties may be *essential* for the upholding, in litigation, of certain provisions of a marriage agreement, especially with respect to portions of the agreement that

may be considered "contrary to public policy," in which the assets and educational level of one party may be vastly different from those of the other party, and where, in their financial dealings with each other, the parties are playing for really high stakes.

Option 2, **Advice by Counsel**, states that the parties *jointly* obtained legal counsel and that such counsel has explained to both any statutes relevant to marriage, alimony, divorce, support, etc.

Note: If you use this option, then make sure that **Advice of Counsel** does not appear following any of the waivers of right to alimony and support in Article IV, since those **Advice of Counsel** provisions refer to *separate* and *independent* counsel of each of the parties.

Independent Counsel (1)

(a) The parties hereto jointly and severally acknowledge that each has consulted with separate and independent legal counsel with respect to the legal and other effects of this agreement, the rights and privileges waived and granted hereby, and all other matters pertaining thereto, and;

(b) Both parties further jointly and severally acknowledge their complete understanding of such legal and other effects of this agreement, and;

(c) Each of the parties hereby warrants and represents that the legal counsel of each party executing this agreement was and is the sole and exclusive legal counsel consulted by such party with regard to the matters contained herein, and;

(d) Each acknowledges his or her understanding that he or she is relinquishing and waiving certain rights which might or could have great value in consideration of the provisions of this agreement, and each does so willingly and free of all duress or coercion.

Advice by Counsel (2)

(a) The parties hereto acknowledge that they have jointly obtained the advice and counsel of an attorney with respect to the legal and other effects of this agreement, the rights and privileges waived and granted hereby, and all other matters pertaining hereto, and;

(b) The parties acknowledge that as a part of such counsel's advice, said counsel has thoroughly discussed _____Kansas_____ statutes concerning the dissolution of marriage, alimony, support, dower and curtesy rights and property rights, as well as pertinent judicial decisions, and;

(c) Each party acknowledges his/her understanding that he/she is accepting certain rights, duties and obligations hereby, and is also waiving certain rights which might or could have great value in consideration for the provisions of this agreement, and each does so willingly and free from all duress or coercion.

Headings

Self-explanatory. This provision is considered essential.

Headings

The headings of the several paragraphs hereof are inserted solely for the convenience of reference and shall have no further meaning, force or effect.

Partial Invalidity

Self-explanatory and essential.

Partial Invalidity

If any portion of this agreement is held to be invalid or unenforceable, all other provisions hereof shall nevertheless remain in full force and effect.

Fair and Equitable

This provision needs no explanation or comment—other than its being an essential provision of the agreement.

Fair and Equitable

Each party acknowledges that this agreement is fair and equitable.

Parties Bound

Self-explanatory and essential.

Parties Bound

This agreement shall inure to the benefit of and be legally binding upon the parties hereto, and the heirs, executors, administrators, successors and assigns of each of them, but shall take effect only in the event the parties become legally married to each other.

Enforcement by Court

This provision strengthens the parties' earlier requests that all provisions of the agreement be enforced by the court even though some may be considered "contrary to public policy." It is an essential part of the agreement.

Enforcement by Court

The parties hereto strongly urge the Court to enforce this agreement to the letter, even though some provisions contained herein may be void as against public policy and even though a substantial change may have occurred in the financial circumstances of either or both parties.

Entire Agreement

This paragraph specifically provides for future revision of the agreement, something which you will almost surely want to do as your circumstances change and, of course, as you and your spouse change. Since the agreement is written and signed by both parties, so must any revisions be written and signed by both parties. The need for legal counsel remains. This section is a must in the agreement.

Entire Agreement

This agreement contains the entire understanding and agreement between the parties, and no amendment or future understanding shall be binding upon either party unless reduced to writing and executed by both parties.

Evidence

Self-explanatory and considered essential.

Evidence

Neither party shall object to this agreement being entered into evidence in any action for permanent separation, divorce, dissolution of the marriage, or other similar action in any Court of law.

Execution of Documents

The mutual commitment of the parties to cooperate with each other and the attorney(s) of each in keeping the agreement current and as legally valid as possible is covered in this section, which is a necessary part of the agreement.

Execution of Documents

Each party shall, at any time and from time to time, upon the request of the other party, execute, acknowledge and deliver any and all documents which may be necessary or advisable to carry out the intentions and provisions of this agreement, including, but not limited to, such instruments as may be required by the laws of any jurisdiction now in effect or hereafter enacted which may affect the property or other rights of the parties *inter se*, or between the parties hereto and third parties; and further, specifically including all portions of this agreement, or amendments thereto, in recordable form, which may, at the option of either party, be filed of record with any Court in any county wherein is located any separate property of either party hereto.

Counterparts

Another essential provision of the agreement.

Counterparts

This agreement may be executed in one or more counterparts, each of which shall be considered as an original.

Governing Law

Since laws of the state in which the parties may later reside may conflict with laws of the state in which the agreement was written and executed (sure to be the case when parties move from a non-community-property state to a community-property state), it is especially important to include a proviso "governing law."

The following provisions will probably be honored between non-community-property states, but they will almost surely not be honored if the parties move from a non-community-property state to a community-property state. They are likely to be honored if the parties move from a community-property state to a non-community-property state.

Generally, though, the only area of conflict between non-community-property and community-property states regarding the agreement would probably be limited to litigation that would involve community property/separate property questions.

Option 1 may be used by parties having little real and personal property AND who now reside in a non-community-property state and who have no expectation of ever residing in a community-property state.

Option 2 is much more likely to prevail and is suggested by this book's legal consultants. The provisions are considered essential.

Governing Law (1)

This agreement shall be construed and governed in accordance with the laws of the State of _____Kansas_____ .

Governing Law (2)

(a) This agreement shall be executed and delivered in the State of _____Kansas_____ , and the provisions hereof shall be construed and enforced in accordance with the laws of said State, regardless of any change of domicile by either or both parties, and;

(b) Any and all actions brought in any Court of law relating directly or indirectly to the marriage or any terms of this agreement, shall be brought in the appropriate Court of the State of _____Kansas_____ , and;

(c) Such Court shall have exclusive jurisdiction and venue thereof, and;

(d) Both parties hereby specifically agree to submit to the personal jurisdiction of such Court, regardless of their respective domiciles or residences, at any time any such action is brought.

Resident Agent

The **Resident Agent** clause lists the names and addresses of the parties and the name and address of the resident agent of each. In good faith compliance with **Execution of Documents**, above, each party should keep the other, and the agent of the other, advised of his or her current address. Each party usually names his or her attorney as resident agent, but anyone of legal age residing in the state of jurisdiction may generally serve as resident agent. Your bank trust officer might, for example, be an alternative choice, but you should avoid anyone who is a beneficiary of your will or anyone who is likely to move out of the state of jurisdiction.

This clause dealing with parties' addresses, and the names and addresses of resident agents, may seem like legalistic overkill, but it's entirely possible that you and your spouse may, in the future, amicably decide to live apart or that other circumstances, such as military service, might intervene.

Resident Agent

Each party hereby makes, constitutes and appoints the following as his or her resident agent for service of process and other notices as herein provided, waives his or her right to service by publication, and agrees that any and all such service may be made on:

(i) The party personally,
(ii) Said designated agent, or
(iii) By certified or registered mail.

PARTY	REGISTERED AGENT
John Smith	Fred Brown
126 West Elm, Apt. 4-A	515 East Main
Fairview, Kansas 66425	Fairview, Kansas 66425

Mary Jones	Ann Johnson
4416 N. Washington,	614 East Main
Apt. 3-C	Fairview, Kansas 66425
Fairview, Kansas 66425	

Execution of Agreement

This portion of the agreement is comprised of the date of execution, the signatures of the parties, and the signatures and addresses of witnesses. Strictly speaking, the *signing* of a document is not always synonymous with *executing* a document, since the signatures of witnesses or attestation by a notary public (or both!) may be required for proper *execution*.

Requirements for proper execution of various legal documents may vary between states, as does, for example, the requirement for witnesses to a **Last Will and Testament**: two witnesses in some states, three in others. If ever in doubt and unable to obtain the advice of an attorney, you can opt (as attorneys often do to provide maximum protection for clients) for legalistic overkill—signatures of *several* witnesses *and* attestation by notary public (the *works!*).

Execution of Agreement

IN WITNESS WHEREOF, the parties hereto set their hands and seals this _____15th_____ day of _____March_____ , 19 __84__ .

Witness
2375 S. Hemlock

Fairview, Kansas 66425

John Smith (Seal)

Witness
22 E. Sunflower Lane

Fairview, Kansas 66425

Witness
4156 Lincoln Road

Fairview, Kansas 66425

Mary Jones (Seal)

Witness
994 S. Oak

Fairview, Kansas 66425

Attestation of Notary

The attestation of each party's signature by a notary public serves to authenticate the signatures of the parties, important in the case of death or disappearance of either since certain provisions of the agreement deal with the separate property of each, with waivers of rights to inherit, and with the inheritance of property by the other party and by children.

Attestation of Notary

STATE OF Kansas   )
) ss:
COUNTY OF Franklin)

On this _____15th_____ day of _____March_____,
19 _84_, before me personally came and appeared _____
_____John Smith_____, who, first being duly sworn, stated that *he* has read the foregoing **Agreement in Contemplation of Marriage** and that he signed same for the purpose therein contained.

IN WITNESS WHEREOF, I hereunto set my hand and official seal.

Ellen Porter
Notary Public

My commission expires: _____January 6, 1985_____

STATE OF   Kansas   )
) ss:
COUNTY OF Franklin)

On this _____15th_____ day of _____March_____,
19 _84_, before me personally came and appeared _____
_____Mary Jones_____, who, first being duly sworn, stated that *she* has read the foregoing **Agreement in Contemplation of Marriage** and that she signed same for the purpose therein contained.

IN WITNESS WHEREOF, I hereunto set my hand and official seal.

Ellen Porter
Notary Public

My commission expires: _____January 6, 1985_____

Affidavit of Counsel

The affidavit of counsel can be important in litigation involving provisions of the contract that might be deemed contrary to public policy, such as the parties' agreement not to have children, their waivers of rights to alimony or support, or their waivers of rights to inherit. In some cases the parties' ability to present proof of separate independent legal counsel in preparing the agreement may make the difference between those provisions being upheld by the court or being declared invalid.

Option 1 states that the attorney has provided *separate* and *independent* counsel to *one* of the parties to the agreement. You will need to make *two* photocopies of this, one for each party's attorney. *Option 2* declares that the attorney has *jointly* counseled both parties to the agreement. *Note:* Each affidavit includes an **Attestation of Notary**.

AFFIDAVIT OF COUNSEL   (1)

The undersigned hereby certifies that he/she is and has been legal counsel to _____John Smith_____ in connection with the preparation, review and execution of the foregoing **Agreement in Contemplation of Marriage;** and

The undersigned further certifies that he/she has consulted with and rendered independent legal advice to said client concerning provisions of the aforesaid **Agreement in Contemplation of Marriage**, the financial, legal and other effects thereof, and has thoroughly discussed _____Kansas_____ statutes concerning the dissolution of marriage, and of alimony in connection therewith, as well as judicial decisions related thereto.

IN WITNESS WHEREOF, I hereunto set my hand and seal this _____15th_____ day of _____March_____, 19 _84_.

Fred Brown (Seal)

George Adams
Witness
2375 S. Hemlock

Fairview, Kansas 66425

Jane Welch
Witness
22 E. Sunflower Lane

Fairview, Kansas 66425

Attestation of Notary

STATE OF Kansas   )
) ss:
COUNTY OF Franklin)

On this _____15th_____ day of _____March_____,
19 _84_, before me personally came and appeared _____
_____Fred Brown_____, who, first being duly sworn, stated that he/she executed the foregoing **Affidavit of Counsel** for the purpose therein contained.

IN WITNESS WHEREOF, I hereunto set my hand and official seal.

Ellen Porter
Notary Public

My commission expires: _____January 6, 1985_____

AFFIDAVIT OF COUNSEL   (2)

The undersigned hereby certifies that he/she is and has been legal counsel to _____John Smith_____ and _____Mary Jones_____ in connection with the preparation, review and execution of the foregoing **Agreement in Contemplation of Marriage;** and

The undersigned further certifies that he/she has consulted with and rendered legal advice to said clients concerning provisions of the aforesaid **Agreement in Contemplation of Marriage,** the financial, legal and other effects thereof, and has thoroughly discussed _____ ____Kansas____ statutes concerning the dissolution of marriage, and of alimony in connection therewith, as well as judicial decisions related thereto.

IN WITNESS WHEREOF, I hereunto set my hand and seal this ____15th____ day of ____March____, 19 __84__.

Ann Johnson (Seal)

Bob Adams
Witness
___4156 Lincoln Road___

___Fairview, Kansas 66425___

Susan Green
Witness
___994 South Oak___

___Fairview, Kansas 66425___

Attestation of Notary

STATE OF Kansas)
) ss:
COUNTY OF Franklin)

On this ____15th____ day of ____March____, 19 __84__, before me personally came and appeared _____ ____Joan Harris____, who, first being duly sworn, stated that he/she executed the foregoing **Affidavit of Counsel** for the purpose therein contained.

IN WITNESS WHEREOF, I hereunto set my hand and official seal.

Ellen Porter
Notary Public
January 6, 1985
My commission expires: _____

EXHIBITS A AND B

Use these exhibits in combination with option 2 of **Disclosure** (page 182). List all real and personal property that the parties agree shall remain the separate property of each.

Exhibit A

It is mutually agreed by ____John Smith____ and ____Mary Jones____ that all of the following listed real and personal property was acquired by ____John____ independent of and without the assistance of ____Mary____, and shall hereafter be the separate property of ____John____.

1. 1980 Ford Fairlane 4-door sedan
2. 1978 Ford pickup with tool box
3. Sears 48-inch wood turning lathe
4. Montgomery-Ward 19-foot aluminum boat
5. Johnson 50-horsepower outboard motor
6. Remington 12-gauge and 14-gauge shotguns
7. Fifteen hand-painted duck decoys
8. One moose decoy
9. ITT Little Zapper microwave oven
10. Philco color TV console
11. Chrome and formica dinette set
12. Dark brown Bark-Lounger chair

Acknowledged:

John Smith (Seal)
Mary Jones (Seal)

Exhibit B

It is mutually agreed by ____John Smith____ and ____Mary Jones____ that all of the following listed real and personal property was acquired by ____Mary____ independent of and without the assistance of ____John____, and shall hereafter be the separate property of ____Mary____.

1. Mary's clothing
2. Shell collection
3. Toastmaster oven/broiler
4. Eureka vacuum cleaner
5. Sears washer
6. Sears dryer
7. 1975 Volkswagen Beetle
8. Bell & Howell 8mm movie camera
9. Bell & Howell 8mm movie projector
10. 12-inch Sony color TV
11. Kitchen pots and pans
12. Head skis, poles, etc.

Acknowledged:

John Smith (Seal)
Mary Jones (Seal)

SAMPLE MARRIAGE AGREEMENT

Our sample marriage agreement—comprised of selected provisions of those just described—may be found at the end of this chapter (pages 200–215). It is presented merely as an example of an agreement that _could_ be devised using only those clauses that you have just examined. You will probably not want to limit your agreement to only those provisions, preferring to discard some and to write others of your own.

The sample agreement is not offered as in any way comprising the "best" agreement for anyone.

Some of the clauses included were made a part of the sample because they happen to be the most complex of several options offered or because they relate to other provisions in a particularly exacting manner. The numbers in parentheses next to the subheadings of the agreement indicate the number of the option we have chosen from those previously illustrated. They have been retained in this completed sample agreement for the sake of clarity.

COMPLETING YOUR MARRIAGE AGREEMENT

All of the provisions, *en blanc*, for an **Agreement in Contemplation of Marriage**, as previously described, can be found starting on page F297 (Forms 48.1, 48.2, and 48.3).

To devise your own marriage agreement, begin by making four photocopies of each page of these blank provisions:

- One copy for him.
- One copy for her.
- One copy for use as a working draft on which you'll fill in details by hand as they're negotiated.
- One copy on which you will type final details for use as a master copy of the agreement.

Assembling Your Master Copy

You will notice in examining the pages of blank marriage agreement provisions that there is about an inch of space between each of them. This is so that when you have selected the provisions that you're going to use and have separated them (a razor blade and straightedge work best), you'll have about one-half of an inch of overlap for use when pasting them together. (Use rubber cement for the best seal.)

Plan on making each completed page approxi-mately legal size. Don't worry too much, though, about making pages exactly the proper length because when you make photocopies all pages will come out of the copier at precisely the same dimensions.

After you've assembled your master copy, run each page through the typewriter again to number each page about half an inch from the bottom. You need not be concerned about the line showing where you have joined various provisions to each other. Most recently made photocopy machines are relatively "shadowless," and those kinds of lines show very little, if at all.

Next, go through your typewritten master copy page by page and, using a typist's correction fluid, white out the numbers appearing to the right of the headings of some of the provisions. Allow these numbers to remain until the last minute, though, because they're a handy reference when discussing various clauses over the phone with your partner or attorney.

Make four photocopies of your typewritten master: one for you, one for her or him, one for your attorney, and one for her or his attorney. If both parties use the same attorney, only three copies of the master are necessary.

When the agreement is signed, each party should also initial every page at the bottom—close to the last word on the page (see our completed sample agreement). This is not so much to prevent him or her from sneakily substituting a page later on as it is to prevent tampering by a would-be heir in the event of the death of the husband or wife.

Your agreement should be kept in a safe place: an office safe, a safe deposit box, or perhaps left with your attorney. Since you're out to make the copy center rich with this agreement, make yet another copy of the signed contract to keep handy at home for reference —and for flaunting at each other to settle arguments.

Sample of Form 48.1/F297

Agreement in Contemplation of Marriage

THIS AGREEMENT in contemplation of marriage is made this _____ 21st _____ day of _____ June _____ ,
19 _85_ , by and between

_____ William Richard Wooten _____ , of

158 East 59th Street	4-D	New York	New York	10035
Street Address	Apt. No.	City	State	Zip

hereinafter referred to as _____ William _____ , and

_____ Ashley Freemont Harper _____ , of

241 Central Park West	PH-4	New York	New York	10023
Street Address	Apt. No.	City	State	Zip

hereinafter referred to as _____ Ashley _____ .

WHEREAS _____ William _____ and _____ Ashley _____ are contemplating marriage, and each party wishes to settle between themselves questions of separate and jointly owned property; separate and joint financial responsibilities; children, if any, and their care, financial support and education; location of domicile; the sharing of household space, expenses and housekeeping responsibilities; the gainful employment and education of each party; the names of each; the possible incapacitation of each; possible dissolution of the marriage; maintenance and support; alimony; and the death of either party; and

WHEREAS, for and in consideration of the sum of twenty dollars ($20.00), and other good and valuable consideration, the receipt whereof is hereby acknowledged, and in further consideration of the parties entering into this agreement and making the mutual covenants herein contained to be performed by the parties, the parties hereto mutually agree and covenant as follows:

ARTICLE I: CONDITIONS OF THE AGREEMENT

Neither Party Presently Married   (2)

_____ William _____ hereby states that he is not presently married and that if previously married has received a final decree of divorce and is competent to enter into a valid marriage, and _____ Ashley _____
_____ hereby states that she is not presently married and that if previously married has received a final decree of divorce and is competent to enter into a valid marriage.

Purpose   (1)

The purpose of the parties for entering into a state of matrimony under the laws of the State of _____ New York _____ is to receive public recognition of the relationship between them as defined by this agreement and to receive mutually the benefits thus obtained.

Voluntary

Each party acknowledges that this agreement is being entered into voluntarily and that it is not the result of duress, coercion or undue influence.

Marriage as a Condition Precedent

This agreement shall become effective immediately upon the marriage of the parties to each other, but shall have no force or effect until that time.

Declaration of Principle   (1)

The parties value and accept the principle of independence and of the equal distribution of responsibility and authority between them and that each is a fully equal and independent partner in their relationship with each other.

Waiver of Rights   (1)

Both parties hereby waive, relinquish and renounce whatever rights, duties, obligations and privileges which either might have which may be derived from or related to a state of matrimony between them, other than those which are included in and made a part of this agreement.

1

Sample of Form 48.1 (*Continued*)

Openness Between Parties   (1)

Both parties anticipate and expect the sharing of each other's emotional and sexual lives to the extent as may benefit both, without infringing upon the privacy, independence or solitude of the other.

Names of the Parties   (1)

The parties agree that neither shall change his or her name as a result of the marriage. We shall continue to be known, respectively, as _____William Richard Wooten_____ and _____Ashley Freemont Harper_____.

Present Employment of the Parties   (1)

(a) The parties acknowledge their understanding that _____William_____ is presently gainfully employed as _____architect_____ with an approximate annual income of $_____40,000_____ and presently intends to continue such employment, and that;

(b) _____Ashley_____ is presently gainfully employed as _____decorator_____ with an approximate annual income of $_____25,000_____ and presently intends to continue such employment.

Children by Previous Marriage   (1)

The parties acknowledge their understanding that _____William_____ has previously been married and has a child or children born of or adopted during such marriage for whom he/she is obligated to provide $_____300.00_____ per _____month_____ in financial support and who shall, for approximately _____four_____ _____months_____ of each year, live with the parties.

Incapacitation of Either Party

The parties agree that in the event of incapacitation of either party during the marriage the other party shall assume complete responsibility for the care and financial support of such party to the extent of his or her income, assets and time.

Use of Living Space

(a) The parties agree to live together at a residence of their mutual choice, recognizing, however, that it may be necessary or desirable from time to time for one to live away from the other for a period of up to several months as determined by the educational, employment or other needs of either party. Each party hereby waives whatever right he or she may have to determine solely the domicile of the parties, and the parties further agree that;

(b) The parties shall have equal right to use of all living space in their home and that all decisions regarding its use shall be by mutual consent only, except that the right of each party to the quiet enjoyment and security of shared living space shall take precedence over all other uses.

ARTICLE II: PROPERTY AND FINANCIAL PROVISIONS

Disclosure   (2)

Each party has made a full and complete disclosure of his or her assets, liabilities and net worth to the other by means of documents which are attached hereto and made a part of this agreement as exhibits; the disclosure of _____William_____ being **Exhibit A**, and the disclosure of _____Ashley_____ being **Exhibit B**.

Present Property of the Parties

Each of the parties has acquired all of his or her separate property independently of, and without the assistance of, the other and desires to keep separate all of his or her real and/or personal property, whether now owned or hereafter acquired, free from any claim by virtue of a marriage between them.

Separate Property

(a) For all purposes of this agreement, as used herein, the term "separate property" shall mean, with respect to a party hereto, all of such party's right, title and interest, legal or beneficial, in and to any and all property and interests in property, whether real, personal or mixed, wherever situated, and regardless of whether now owned or hereafter acquired, and;

(b) Each party shall, during his or her remaining lifetime, retain the sole ownership of all of his or her separate property, and shall have the exclusive right to dispose of any and all of such property during his or her remaining lifetime, by *inter vivos* or testamentary transfer, or by any and all other dispositions, and/or to encumber, pledge or hypothecate same, without any interference on the part of the other in such manner as shall be determined at the sole discretion of such owner thereof, as if their marriage had not taken place.

2

Sample of Form 48.1 (*Continued*)

Waiver by Future Husband

Except as specifically provided herein, _____ William _____ hereby waives, relinquishes and releases all right, title and interest in and to any and all separate property of _____ Ashley _____, accruing to, or vesting in him, or in which he may otherwise be entitled as husband of _____ Ashley _____ _____, or her widower, heir-at-law, next of kin or distributee, upon or by virtue of a termination of the marriage of the parties by death, divorce, dissolution, annulment, or otherwise, including, but not limited to such rights as curtesy, statutory or other allowances to a spouse of a decedent, distributions by way of intestacy, rights of election to take against the will of _____ Ashley _____, or against any other alimony, support and/or other property settlement.

Waiver by Future Wife

Except as specifically provided herein, _____ Ashley _____ hereby waives, relinquishes and releases all right, title and interest in and to any and all separate property of _____ William _____, accruing to, or vesting in her, or in which she may otherwise by entitled as wife of _____ William _____, or his widow, heir-at-law, next of kin or distributee, upon or by virtue of a termination of the marriage of the parties by death, divorce, dissolution, annulment, or otherwise, including, but not limited to such rights as dower, statutory or other allowances of a spouse of a decedent, distributions by way of intestacy, rights of election to take against the will of _____ William _____, or against any other alimony, support and/or other property settlement.

Property Held as Tenants by the Entirety

(a) Any other provisions of this agreement to the contrary notwithstanding, _____ William _____ and _____ Ashley _____ may, during the marriage, acquire property or interests therein, in both names, with or without rights of survivorship. In such event, the signatures of both parties shall be required to sell, transfer, convey, pledge, encumber or hypothecate such jointly held property; and, upon the death of either party, any and all such property jointly held by both parties with rights of survivorship shall pass outright to the survivor in accordance with applicable law. Entry into such arrangements shall not in any way be deemed a waiver of or abandonment of this agreement or any part hereof.

(b) Upon termination of the marriage of the parties by divorce, dissolution, annulment or any other means while both are living, each party shall become a tenant in common with the other party and thereby entitled to an undivided one-half interest in said property. Should either party have contributed more than one-half toward the purchase, maintenance or improvement of such property, said party shall be entitled to a special equity in such property according to his or her respective contribution.

Right to Make Voluntary Transfers Not Waived

Any other provisions of this agreement to the contrary notwithstanding, each party shall have the right to voluntarily transfer or convey to the other any property or interest therein which may be lawfully transferred or conveyed, during his or her lifetime, or by will or otherwise upon death; and neither party intends by this agreement to limit nor restrict in any way the right and power of the other to receive any such voluntary transfer or conveyance. All such ostensible voluntary transfers or conveyances shall be deemed to be voluntary gifts from the transferor to the transferee and shall not in any way be deemed a waiver or abandonment of this agreement or any part hereof.

Joint Bank Accounts (2)

Any other provisions of this agreement to the contrary notwithstanding, the parties may, from time to time during the marriage, establish joint bank savings and/or checking accounts requiring the signature of either party for the withdrawal of funds from such accounts. Upon the death of either party, any and all sums in any such bank accounts jointly held by the parties shall pass outright to the survivor in accordance with applicable law.

Separate Bank Accounts

The parties agree that each may, from time to time during the marriage, establish various bank savings and/or checking accounts which shall be "separate property" under terms of this agreement and that all funds deposited therein, and all income derived therefrom, shall be "separate property" of the party in whose name such funds are held. The parties further agree to instruct any bank holding funds as provided for in this paragraph, that such funds shall be the separate property of the party in whose name such funds are being held.

AJH WRW

3

Sample of Form 48.1 (*Continued*)

Household Bank Accounts   (2)

(a) The parties agree that they may, from time to time during the marriage, establish various jointly held bank checking accounts for convenience in the payment of household expenses and which require the signature of either party for the withdrawal of funds, and that;

(b) Funds deposited therein shall be deposited _____ sixty _____ percent by _____ William _____ and _____ forty _____ percent by _____ Ashley _____, and that;

(c) Upon the death of either party, any and all sums in any such bank accounts jointly held by the parties shall pass outright to the surviving party in accordance with applicable law.

Existing Financial Obligations

(a) Each of the parties acknowledges that he or she is presently indebted to various persons and/or business entities as described by each in the hereinabove-mentioned disclosures to each other. With regard to these financial obligations, the parties hereby agree that they shall each individually be responsible for the payment of all antenuptial debts existing at the time of marriage, _____ William _____ paying for all antenuptial debts incurred by himself on his behalf, and _____ Ashley _____ paying for all antenuptial debts incurred by herself on her behalf.

(b) Each party agrees to indemnify the other for all damage and cost incurred by reason of any suit against said party for debts which the other party has agreed in subparagraph (a) hereof to be responsible.

(c) In consideration of payment of any antenuptial debt of one party by the other, the party whose debt is thus paid agrees that the party satisfying such debt shall be entitled to a special equity in the property of the other, equal in value to the amount of any such debt so paid.

Credit Transactions by the Parties

The parties hereby agree that when either party enters into a transaction where credit is extended to such party, and such party becomes a debtor on the basis of credit extended solely by virtue of his or her assets, liabilities, income and credit history, then such party shall be fully and individually liable for the timely payment of any such obligation and shall hold the other party harmless from any such obligation and indemnify him or her in the event that he or she shall ever be required to satisfy same.

Taxes

Any other provisions of this agreement to the contrary notwithstanding, the parties recognize that the Internal Revenue Code and regulations thereunder, and other codes and regulations of the several states and of foreign nations, do, in certain instances, provide substantial savings in taxes paid by married couples filing joint returns. If such be the case, the parties hereby agree that the filing of any such joint returns, and/or the combining of their separate incomes and deductions, shall not in any way be deemed a waiver of, or abandonment of, this agreement or any part hereof, and that each party shall be fully responsible for the payment of his or her portion of any federal, state or other taxes attributable to his or her income or personal or real property.

Household Expenses   (3)

(a) The parties agree to share responsibility for the payment of household expenses as follows:

(i) _____ William _____ shall provide for the payment of _____ sixty _____ percent of all reasonable household expenses, and

(ii) _____ Ashley _____ shall provide for the payment of _____ forty _____ percent of all reasonable household expenses, and

the parties agree to establish and fund a joint bank checking account for convenience in the payment of household expenses. For all purposes of this agreement, "household expenses" shall mean mortgage or rent payments on the residence of the parties, all maintenance and improvement of same, utilities, food, shared entertainment and travel and medical expenses. The parties also agree that the mutually agreed-upon purchase and maintenance of household furniture, draperies, carpets, appliances, etc., shall also be "household expenses" for all purposes of this agreement and shall be shared in the same proportion as provided for under (i) and (ii) hereinabove, and the parties further agree that;

(b) Distribution of any such jointly owned property between the parties in the event the marriage is dissolved *vinculo matrimoni* by divorce, annulment or any other means during the lifetime of both parties shall be carried out as provided for under **Possible Dissolution of the Marriage**, as set forth herein, and that;

(c) The parties may determine, from time to time, to share the cost of insurance on their residence and its contents and the costs of medical and hospitalization insurance on both parties. Any such insurance shall be paid for by the parties in the same proportion as "household expenses," as provided for under subparagraph (a), (i) and (ii), hereinabove.

Revision of Shared Household Expenses

The parties agree to revise the proportion of household expenses shared by each, and of household, medical and hospitalization insurance paid by each, whenever there is a substantial revision in the ratio between the incomes of the parties, so that the proportion of such shared household and insurance expenses remains closely related to the ratio between the individual incomes of the parties.

A7H WRW

Sample of Form 48.1 (*Continued*)

Financial Support (4)

(a) The parties agree to each be fully responsible for the payment of all expenses related to his or her own personal financial support and maintenance during the marriage, and further agree that;

(b) Each party shall be responsible for the financial support and maintenance of _____Ashley's mother_____ as follows:

(i) _____William_____ shall be responsible for payment of _____sixty_____ percent of such financial support and maintenance, and

(ii) _____Ashley_____ shall be responsible for payment of _____forty_____ percent of such financial support and maintenance.

Revision of Shared Financial Support

The parties agree to revise the proportion of financial support hereinabove-apportioned between the parties whenever there is a substantial change in the ratio of incomes between the parties, so that the proportion of shared financial support remains closely related to the ratio between the individual incomes of the parties.

Gainful Employment and Education (2)

The parties agree that each shall have full autonomy regarding the choice of occupation, employment, career and education during the marriage, while recognizing the binding agreement of _____William and Ashley_____ to provide for payment of household expenses, financial support and maintenance as set forth herein.

Home Care and Maintenance (3)

The parties agree to share the responsibility for the housekeeping, care and maintenance of shared living space and any real property jointly owned or used as follows:

(a) _____William_____ accepts responsibility for _____fifty_____ percent of the necessary time and effort and _____sixty_____ percent of the reasonable expense for the care and maintenance of shared living space and any real property jointly owned or used, and;

(b) _____Ashley_____ accepts responsibility for _____fifty_____ percent of the necessary time and effort and _____forty_____ percent of the reasonable expense for the care and maintenance of shared living space and any real property jointly owned or used.

ARTICLE III: CHILDREN

Mutual Agreement Not to Have Children

(a) Each party agrees that no children shall be born of the marriage, nor shall any children be adopted by either party during the marriage, unless both parties mutually agree in writing, and;

(b) It is further agreed that if a child is born during the marriage without the written agreement of both parties, then the wife waives all right to child support and the husband waives all right to visitation, and;

(c) _____Ashley_____ agrees to inform _____William_____ immediately upon obtaining knowledge that she is pregnant, and further agrees that the withholding of such information from _____William_____ shall be deemed a waiver by her of child-support payments in the event of divorce, annulment or dissolution of the marriage by any other means during the lifetime of both parties, and;

(d) _____Ashley_____ realizes that the Courts look upon with disfavor as being contrary to public policy, agreements containing the provisions in subparagraphs (a), (b) and (c), hereof, but she strongly urges that those provisions be enforced to the letter. This provision shall be null and void where for medical reasons the wife must deliver a child.

Care and Support of Children (1)

The parties agree to share fully and equally all responsibilities related to the care and financial support of any and all children whom they may mutually agree to have or to adopt during the marriage.

Education of Children

It is mutually agreed by the parties that any child or children of them, or of either of them, shall have the benefit of a public school education up to and through high school level and that the parties shall mutually determine no later than during each child's junior year in high school whether it is desirable that such child have additional education and the manner of paying therefore.

5

A7H WRW

Sample of Form 48.1 (*Continued*)

Religious Instruction   (3)

(a) It is mutually agreed by the parties that any child or children of them shall receive no religious instruction from either parent, nor from any religious organization recommended by either parent, it being agreed between the parties that any child or children of theirs may seek his or her own religious instruction without influence or hindrance of either parent and that it shall be up to each child to pursue his or her own religious interest, it being further agreed between the parties, however, that;

(b) Any child of _____ William _____, of whom he or she is parent by previous marriage or adoption, may be instructed in the _____ Lutheran _____ faith, this being deemed in the best interests of the child by _____ William _____.

Names of Children

It is agreed by the parties that any child whom the parties mutually agree to have or to adopt during the marriage shall bear the surname of _____ Wooten _____.

Rights of Children

The parties recognize that they might, during the course of their marriage, mutually determine to have or to adopt a child or children and hereby agree that the provisions of this agreement are not intended to govern nor affect the rights of any such children in or to the separate property of either party hereto, and the parties further agree that all such rights in and to such separate property and/or financial support shall be governed by applicable law.

ARTICLE IV: POSSIBLE DISSOLUTION OF THE MARRIAGE

Waiver of Alimony and Support   (1)

(a) In accordance with the parties' full and complete acceptance of the principle of independence and equal responsibility and authority between them, and in further accordance with the parties' waiver and relinquishment of whatever rights, duties, obligations and privileges which either might or could have derived from or related to a state of matrimony between them, other than those which may be included in and made a part of this agreement, each party hereby waives, relinquishes and renounces whatever right he or she may have to alimony, maintenance or support in the event the marriage is dissolved *vinculo matrimoni* by divorce, annulment or any other means during the lifetime of both parties.

(b) The parties recognize that the Courts look upon with disfavor as being contrary to public policy, marriage agreements anticipating dissolution of the marriage or the waiver of alimony and/or support by either party. The above notwithstanding, the parties strongly urge the Court to enforce this agreement to the letter.

Advice of Counsel

In connection with provisions of the above paragraph, **Waiver of Alimony and Support**, and particularly regarding the waiver, relinquishment and renouncing of whatever right either party may have to alimony, maintenance or support in the event the marriage is dissolved by divorce, annulment or any other means during the lifetime of both parties, each party hereby acknowledges receipt of specific advice pertaining thereto by separate, independent counsel of each party's own choice, each paying for his or her own counsel's advice and aid. Each party acknowledges that as a part of such advice his or her counsel has thoroughly discussed current _____ New York _____ statutes concerning the dissolution of marriage and of alimony in connection therewith, as well as pertinent judicial decisions.

Payments in Lieu of Alimony   (4)

While the parties contemplate a long and lasting marriage terminated only by the death of one of the parties, they also recognize the possibility that their marriage may be terminated by way of divorce or dissolution during the lifetime of both. In the event of such termination of the marriage *vinculo matrimoni* during the lifetime of both parties by way of divorce, annulment or any other means, regardless of which party hereto shall initiate such action, the parties hereby specifically agree:

(a) _____ Ashley _____ shall not receive any alimony, support or separate property which might otherwise be available to him or her in accordance with applicable law.

(b) _____ Ashley _____ shall accept from _____ William _____, in limitation of alimony and support, and in lieu of and instead of any obligation of _____ William _____ for the costs and attorney's fees of _____ Ashley _____, payments as set forth below for a period equal to the number of months of marriage between the parties, or ten (10) years, whichever is less, and subject to the provisions of paragraph (d) hereof:

(i) For the first _____ twenty-four _____ months from and after issuance of the final decree of dissolution (termination date) of the marriage, _____ Ashley _____ shall receive the sum of _____ six hundred dollars _____ ($ 600.00) per month;

(ii) Thereafter, the sum of _____ three hundred dollars _____ ($ 300.00) per month.

6

ATH WRW

Sample of Form 48.1 (*Continued*)

(iii) The aforesaid sums shall be payable by _____ William _____, by depositing a check therefore in the mails of the United States Postal Service, first class, postage prepaid, on or before the first day of each month to such address as _____ Ashley _____ may from time to time designate in writing to _____ William _____. The first such monthly payment shall be made for the first calendar month following the termination date of the marriage.

(iv) It is further agreed that the maximum monthly payments made by _____ William _____ hereunder shall at no time exceed _____ one _____ percent of the net worth of _____ William _____.

(c) It is hereby agreed by the parties that all payments made pursuant to provisions of the immediately preceding subparagraph (b) shall, for federal income tax purposes, be deemed and considered by both parties as payments of alimony or as payments in lieu thereof, and;

(d) All such obligations of and payments by _____ William _____ shall terminate conclusively and forever upon the first occurrence of the death of or the remarriage of _____ Ashley _____, or his/her continuously residing with an adult of the opposite sex other than a blood relative; and no obligation of any kind as set forth in this paragraph, **Payments in Lieu of Alimony**, shall survive such first occurrence of said events, and;

(e) It is further agreed that such obligations of _____ William _____ shall be legal and binding obligations of and upon the estate and property in which _____ William _____ had a legal or beneficial interest prior to death, and;

(f) _____ Ashley _____ hereby specifically recognizes and agrees that he/she shall have no right to receive additional payments of alimony or support in any manner at any time and upon the occurrence of any event from and after the aforesaid termination of marriage, and that he/she shall have no right to receive any separate property of _____ William _____ at any time, or upon the occurrence of any event, and _____ _____ Ashley _____ further recognizes and ratifies his/her waiver, relinquishment and release of all such rights, and;

(g) The parties recognize that the Courts look upon with disfavor as being contrary to public policy, marriage agreements anticipating dissolution of the marriage or the waiver of alimony and/or support by either party. The above notwithstanding, the parties strongly urge the Court to enforce this agreement to the letter.

Advice of Counsel

In connection with provisions of the above paragraph, **Payments in Lieu of Alimony**, and particularly regarding the waiver, relinquishment and renouncing of whatever right either party may have to alimony, maintenance or support in the event the marriage is dissolved *vinculo matrimoni* by divorce, annulment or any other means during the lifetime of the parties, each party hereby acknowledges receipt of specific advice pertaining thereto by separate, independent counsel of each party's own choice, each paying for his or her won counsel's advice and aid. Each party acknowledges that as part of such advice, his or her own counsel has thoroughly discussed _____ New York _____ statutes concerning the dissolution of marriage, and of alimony in connection therewith, as well as pertinent judicial decisions.

Compliance with Applicable Law

Each party further acknowledges that he or she has sought meticulously to comply with applicable law concerning marital agreements regarding alimony, dower and curtesy rights and property rights, and that, among other things, each:

(a) Has fully and fairly advised the other, and been advised by the other, of their respective financial situations, and;

(b) Has a fair understanding of the financial status of the other and specifically understands that the other party is possessed of certain assets, as set forth in the annexed **Exhibits A** and **B**, which are made a part of this agreement, and;

(c) Considers the proposed payments in limitation of alimony or support as more than he or she would presently regard as fair under the current and probable future circumstances of each party and, in sum;

(d) Considers and believes after full and fair examination of the other's finances and after the advice of independent counsel that each has made a full disclosure to the other, each has a reasonable approximation of the financial situation of the other, and each considers the payments in limitation of and in lieu of all further obligation under provisions of said paragraph, **Payments in Lieu of Alimony**, to be more than fair.

Support *Pendente Lite*

The parties realize that in the event of dissolution of the marriage *vinculo matrimoni* by divorce, annulment or any other means during the lifetime of both parties, this agreement does not govern nor provide for support payments for the period beginning with the initiation of legal proceedings by either party for termination of the marriage and ending with the issuance of the final decree of termination in accordance with applicable law. To the extent enforceable and valid under _____ New York _____ law, the parties agree that support *pendente lite* shall not exceed _____ one _____ hundred and fifty dollars _____ ($ 150.00) per week and that each party shall bear his or her own costs and attorney's fees related thereto.

AFH WRW

Sample of Form 48.1 (*Continued*)

Child Support in the Event of Dissolution of the Marriage

(a) The parties shall attempt to arrive at a sum which they mutually agree shall constitute reasonable monthly payments for support of any child or children whom the parties, by mutual consent, may agree to have or to adopt during the marriage, in the event of legal separation of the parties or dissolution of the marriage *vinculo matrimoni* by divorce, annulment or any other means during the lifetime of both parties. In the event that they are unable to agree upon such a sum, the Court shall decide the issue, and;

(b) The parties each agree that neither party shall attempt to include an amount which would have been used for alimony in the sum designated for child-support payments. This provision also applies to temporary child support.

Child Custody (1)

The parties shall attempt, in the event of dissolution of the marriage, to arrive at an agreement for the custody of any child or children whom the parties may mutually agree to have or to adopt during the marriage. Such agreement shall take into consideration the best interests of any such child or children and the ability of each parent to provide for the financial support and care of any such children. In the event the parties are unable to agree upon child custody, the Court shall decide the issue.

Removal of Children from Jurisdiction of the Court

It is mutually agreed by the parties that, in the event of dissolution of the marriage, neither party shall attempt to remove from the jurisdiction of the Court, without the written permission of the other party, any child or children whom the parties mutually agreed to have or to adopt during the marriage.

ARTICLE V: TESTEMENTARY PROVISIONS

Agreement Between the Parties (2)

(a) In the event the marriage shall be terminated by the death of _____ William _____, and if at the time of such death the parties shall be living together as husband and wife, then _____ Ashley _____ accepts as full discharge, settlement and satisfaction of any and all other statutory and/or other right, title and interest which she, as widow, heir-at-law, next of kin or distributee, upon termination of the marriage by death might or could acquire by virtue of the death of _____ William _____, the provisions of any **Last Will and Testament** of _____ William _____, and hereby waives, relinquishes and renounces any right which she may have to share in the estate of _____ William _____ by way of intestacy, dower or right of election to take against the estate of _____ William _____, and;

(b) In consideration of the agreement of _____ Ashley _____ as provided in subparagraph (a) hereof, _____ William _____ hereby agrees to take out and maintain in force during the marriage, life insurance which will pay an amount not less than one hundred thousand dollars ($ 100,000.00) to _____ Ashley _____ in the event of the death of _____ William _____ by illness or accident, or, alternatively, to make an *inter vivos* gift to, or to establish an irrevocable trust for the benefit of, _____ Ashley _____ in said amount, and;

(c) In the event the marriage shall be terminated by the death of _____ Ashley _____, and if at the time of such death the parties shall be living together as husband and wife, then _____ William _____ accepts as full discharge, settlement and satisfaction of any and all other statutory and other right, title and interest which he, as widower, heir-at-law, next of kin or distributee, upon termination of the marriage by death might or could acquire by virtue of the death of _____ Ashley _____, the provisions of any **Last Will and Testament** of _____ Ashley _____, and hereby waives, relinquishes and renounces any right which he may have to share in the estate of _____ Ashley _____ by way of intestacy, curtesy or right of election to take against the estate of _____ Ashley _____, and;

(d) In consideration of the agreement of _____ William _____ as provided in subparagraph (c) hereof, _____ Ashley _____ hereby agrees to take out and maintain in force during the marriage, life insurance which will pay an amount not less than twenty-five thousand dollars ($ 25,000.00) to _____ William _____ in the event of the death of _____ Ashley _____ by illness or accident, or, alternatively, to make an *inter vivos* gift to, or to establish an irrevocable trust for the benefit of, _____ William _____ in said amount.

47H WRW

8

Sample of Form 48.1 (*Continued*)

Life Insurance

(a) _____ William _____ hereby agrees to take out and maintain in force during the marriage, life insurance which will pay an amount not less than _one hundred thousand dollars_ ($_100,000.00_) to _____ Ashley _____ in the event of the death of _____ William _____ by illness or accident, or, alternatively, to make an *inter vivos* gift to, or to establish an irrevocable trust for the benefit of, _____ Ashley _____ in said amount, and;

(b) _____ Ashley _____ hereby agrees to take out and maintain in force during the marriage, life insurance which will pay an amount not less than _twenty-five thousand dollars_ ($_25,000.00_) to _____ William _____ in the event of the death of _____ Ashley _____ by illness or accident, or, alternatively, to make an *inter vivos* gift to, or to establish an irrevocable trust fund for the benefit of, _____ William _____ in said amount.

ARTICLE VI: GENERAL PROVISIONS

Independent Counsel (1)

(a) The parties hereto jointly and severally acknowledge that each has consulted with separate and independent legal counsel with respect to the legal and other effects of this agreement, the rights and privileges waived and granted hereby, and all other matters pertaining thereto, and;

(b) Both parties further jointly and severally acknowledge their complete understanding of such legal and other effects of this agreement, and;

(c) Each of the parties hereby warrants and represents that the legal counsel of each party executing this agreement was and is the sole and exclusive legal counsel consulted by such party with regard to the matters contained herein, and;

(d) Each acknowledges his or her understanding that he or she is relinquishing and waiving certain rights which might or could have great value in consideration of the provisions of this agreement, and each does so willingly and free of all duress or coercion.

Headings

The headings of the several paragraphs hereof are inserted solely for the convenience of reference and shall have no further meaning, force or effect.

Partial Invalidity

If any provision of this agreement is held to be invalid or unenforceable, all other provisions hereof shall nevertheless remain in full force and effect.

Fair and Equitable

Each party acknowledges that this agreement is fair and equitable.

Parties Bound

This agreement shall inure to the benefit of and be legally binding upon the parties hereto, and the heirs, executors, administrators, successors and assigns of each of them, but shall take effect only in the event the parties become legally married to each other.

Enforcement by Court

The parties hereto strongly urge the Court to enforce this agreement to the letter, even though some provisions contained herein may be void as against public policy and even though a substantial change may have occurred in the financial circumstances of either or both parties.

Entire Agreement

This agreement contains the entire understanding and agreement between the parties, and no amendment or future understanding shall be binding upon either party unless reduced to writing and executed by both parties.

Evidence

Neither party shall object to this agreement being entered in evidence in any action for permanent separation, divorce, dissolution of the marriage, or other similar action in any Court of law.

AJH   WRW

Sample of Form 48.1 (*Continued*)

Execution of Documents

Each party shall, at any time and from time to time, upon the request of the other party, execute, acknowledge and deliver any and all documents which may be necessary or advisable to carry out the intentions and provisions of this agreement, including, but not limited to, such instruments as may be required by the laws of any jurisdiction now in effect or hereafter enacted which may affect the property or other rights of the parties *inter se*, or between the parties hereto and third parties; and further, specifically including all portions of this agreement, or amendments thereto, in recordable form, which may, at the option of either party, be filed of record with any Court in any county wherein is located any separate property of either party hereto.

Counterparts

This agreement may be executed in one or more counterparts, each of which shall be considered as an original.

Governing Law (2)

(a) This agreement shall be executed and delivered in the State of _____ New York _____, and the provisions hereof shall be construed and enforced in accordance with the laws of said State, regardless of any change of domicile by either or both parties, and;

(b) Any and all actions brought in any Court of law relating directly or indirectly to the marriage or any terms of this agreement, shall be brought in the appropriate Court of the State of _____ New York _____, and;

(c) Such Court shall have exclusive jurisdiction and venue thereof, and;

(d) Both parties hereby specifically agree to submit to the personal jurisdiction of such Court, regardless of their respective domiciles or residences, at any time any such action is brought.

Resident Agent

Each party hereby makes, constitutes and appoints the following as his or her resident agent for service of process and other notices as herein provided, waives his or her right to service by publication, and agrees that any and all such service may be made on:

(i) The party personally,

(ii) Said designated agent, or

(iii) By certified or registered mail.

PARTY	REGISTERED AGENT
William Richard Wooten	Marvin C. Kaplan
Apt. 4-D	Suite 1218
158 East 59th Street	124 East 42nd Street
New York, N.Y. 10035	New York, N.Y. 10017
Ashley Freemont Harper	Randall J. Swain, III
Apt. PH-4	Suite 44
241 Central Park West	19 Rector Street
New York, N.Y. 10023	New York, N.Y. 10006

A7H WRW

10

Sample of Form 48.1 (*Continued*)

Execution of Agreement

IN WITNESS WHEREOF, the parties hereto set their hands and seals this _____21st_____ day of _____June_____, 19 _85_ .

Eva Putnam
_____
Witness
_____
35 Clark Street   Apt. 9-C
_____
Brooklyn, N.Y.   11201

Curtis Parker
_____
Witness
_____
277 North Avenue
_____
New Rochelle, N.Y.   10801

Howard Britton
_____
Witness
_____
212 East 68th Street   Apt. 2-B
_____
New York, N.Y.   10021

Lydia Taylor
_____
Witness
_____
22 Woodside Road
_____
Greenwich, Conn.   06830

Ashley Freemont Harper (Seal)

William Richard Wooten (Seal)

* *

Attestation of Notary

STATE OF   New York   )
) ss:
COUNTY OF   New York   )

On this _____21st_____ day of _____June_____, 19 _85_ , before me personally came and appeared _____William Richard Wooten_____ , who, first being duly sworn, stated that he has read the foregoing **Agreement in Contemplation of Marriage** and that he signed same for the purpose therein contained.

IN WITNESS WHEREOF, I hereunto set my hand and official seal.

Gale Simon
_____
Notary Public

My commission expires: _____September 27, 1986_____

11

Sample of Form 48.1 (*Continued*)

STATE OF   New York   )
)   ss:

COUNTY OF   New York   )

On this _____ 21st _____ day of _____ June _____, 19 __85__, before me personally came and appeared
_____ Ashley Freemont Harper _____, who, first being duly sworn, stated that she has read the foregoing **Agreement in Contemplation of Marriage** and that she signed same for the purpose therein contained.

IN WITNESS WHEREOF, I hereunto set my hand and official seal.

Gale Simon
_____
Notary Public

My commission expires: _____ September 27, 1986 _____

* *

AFFIDAVIT OF COUNSEL   (1)

The undersigned hereby certifies that he/she is and has been legal counsel to _____ William R. Wooten _____
in connection with the preparation, review and execution of the foregoing **Agreement in Contemplation of Marriage;** and

The undersigned further certifies that he/she has consulted with and rendered independent legal advice to said client concerning provisions of the aforesaid **Agreement in Contemplation of Marriage**, the financial, legal and other effects thereof, and has thoroughly discussed _____ New York _____ statutes concerning the dissolution of marriage, and of alimony in connection therewith, as well as judicial decisions related thereto.

IN WITNESS WHEREOF, I hereunto set my hand and seal this _____ 21st _____ day of _____ June _____, 19 __85__.

Marvin C. Kaplan _____ (Seal)

Howard E. Bolton
_____
Witness
     212 East 68th Street   Apt. 2-B

     New York, N.Y.   10021

Curtis Pember
_____
Witness
     277 North Avenue

     New Rochelle, N.Y.   10801

Sample of Form 48.1 (*Continued*)

Attestation of Notary

STATE OF   New York   )
)   ss:

COUNTY OF   New York   )

On this _____ 21st _____ day of _____ June _____, 19 __85__, before me personally came and appeared _____ Marvin C. Kaplan _____, who, first being duly sworn, stated that he/she executed the foregoing **Affidavit of Counsel** for the purpose therein contained.

     IN WITNESS WHEREOF, I hereunto set my hand and official seal.

Gale Simon
_____
                   Notary Public

My commission expires: _____ September 27, 1986 _____

* *

AFFIDAVIT OF COUNSEL   (1)

     The undersigned hereby certifies that he/she is and has been legal counsel to _____ Ashley F. Harper _____ in connection with the preparation, review and execution of the foregoing **Agreement in Contemplation of Marriage**; and

     The undersigned further certifies that he/she has consulted with and rendered independent legal advice to said client concerning provisions of the aforesaid **Agreement in Contemplation of Marriage**, the financial, legal and other effects thereof, and has thoroughly discussed _____ New York _____ statutes concerning the dissolution of marriage, and of alimony in connection therewith, as well as judicial decisions related thereto.

     IN WITNESS WHEREOF, I hereunto set my hand and seal this _____ 21st _____ day of _____ June _____, 19 __85__ .

Howard Bolton   *Randall J. Swain II*
_____   _____ (Seal)
Witness

     212 East 68th Street   Apt. 2-B

     New York, N.Y.   10021

Curtis Parker
_____
Witness

     277 North Avenue

     New Rochelle, N.Y.   10801

13

Sample of Form 48.1 (*Continued*)

Attestation of Notary

STATE OF   New York   )
) ss:

COUNTY OF   New York   )

On this ____21st____ day of _____June_____, 19 __85__, before me personally came and appeared ____Randall J. Swain, III____, who, first being duly sworn, stated that he/she executed the foregoing **Affidavit of Counsel** for the purpose therein contained.

IN WITNESS WHEREOF, I hereunto set my hand and official seal.

_____
Gale Simon
Notary Public

My commission expires: ____September 27, 1986____

Agreement in Contemplation of Marriage

Between

William Richard Wooten
Apt. 4-D
158 East 59th Street
New York, N.Y. 10035

and

Ashley Freemont Harper
Apt. PH-4
241 Central Park West
New York, N.Y. 10023

Dated _____June 21,_____ 19 __85__

14

Sample of Form 48.2/F325

Exhibit A

It is mutually agreed by _____William Richard Wooten_____ and _____Ashley Freemont Harper_____ that all of the following listed real and personal property was acquired by _____William_____ independent of and without the assistance of _____Ashley_____, and shall hereafter be the separate property of _____William_____.

1. William's clothing

2. William's jewelry, including gold Rolex and stainless steel Rolex watches

3. 1979 Volkswagen Rabbit

4. Drafting instruments, tools, and equipment

5. Nikon F-2 camera and six lenses

6. Furniture, including teak desk, four teak bookcases, teak dresser, teak bedside table, teak dining table and eight chairs, black leather sofa and chair, bed with teak headboard

7. Appliances, including Mixmaster model 337, Electrolux vacuum cleaner, Curtis-Mathis portable color TV, Mr. Tea tea maker, Singer sewing machine

8. Two paintings by Paul Klee, Rampant Sphinx and God of the Spanish Plain

Acknowledged:

William Richard Wooten (Seal)

Ashley Freemont Harper (Seal)

15

Sample of Form 48.3/F327

Exhibit B

It is mutually agreed by ___William Richard Wooten___ and ___Ashley Freemont Harper___ that all of the following listed real and personal property was acquired by ___Ashley___ independent of and without the assistance of ___William___, and shall hereafter be the separate property of ___Ashley___.

1. Ashley's clothing

2. Ashley's sable coat

3. Dyna-Gym machine

4. Portable greenhouse

5. Digital bathroom scale

6. Super 3600 Vitamix

7. Antique grain grinder

8. Horse, three-year-old bay

9. Smith-Corona portable typewriter

10. Antique furniture, four rooms, appraised at $38,000.00

11. Jewelry, appraised at $18,500.00

13. Sterling flatware, appraised at $11,000.00

Acknowledged:

William Richard Wooten (Seal)

Ashley Freemont Harper (Seal)

16

㊽ Agreement to Live Together

Since both a marriage agreement and an **Agreement to Live Together** define what two people want from a relationship, there's not a great deal of difference between the two agreements. True, there are many reasons for living together that differ from the reasons for marriage, but between people who agree to have a *contract* for living together and people who agree to have a *contract* for marriage, the differences are few.

What all this means is that, except for certain areas of the agreements that deal with differences in how the law treats the two kinds of arrangements, the contracts are pretty much the same because committed people who live together and committed people who marry want many of the same things.

Except for those few states where cohabitation is illegal (Arkansas, Arizona, Florida, and Georgia), there are few rights, duties, obligations, and privileges of marriage that cannot be included in and made a part of an **Agreement to Live Together**. However, there is nothing short of marriage that will allow a couple to legally file a joint federal income tax return, nor is there any way that either of a live-together couple may claim the federal marital estate tax deduction.

WIDE APPLICATION

As with the previous chapter's marriage contract, this volume's **Agreement to Live Together** offers a selection of options that easily make it suitable for use by a wide range of partners—from high school graduates to college students to more experienced, previously married, relatively affluent professionals.

Even though you will likely be consulting an attorney about the legal aspects of your agreement, you and your partner can gain valuable insight into what you expect from living together and from each other by using this volume's agreement as a basis for your own understanding. And by taking an essentially complete document to your attorney you will save much of the usual cost of drafting such an agreement.

CHILDREN

The legitimacy of a child born to a live-together couple seldom presents legal difficulties if properly prepared for. Birth certificates now issued by many jurisdictions no longer give any indication of a child's legitimacy or lack of it. Our **Agreement to Live Together** contains a provision for acknowledgment of

paternity by the father, as well as several slightly different provisions to provide for the financial support and care of any child born of the relationship.

Obviously, any live-together couple planning to have a child should consult a lawyer as well as a gynecologist/obstetrician before going ahead with their plans. Often, a temporary change of residence so that a baby may be born in a more "friendly" state can prevent later difficulties.

Although a live-together couple cannot file a joint income tax return, the father or mother may claim the usual federal income tax deduction for support of a dependent child. Even the *nonparent* party of a live-together couple may claim a deduction for support of a child of the other partner provided that the dependent child *resides* with the person claiming the deduction and that the person claiming the deduction provides *more than half* of the financial support of such child. The child must also have less than $1,000 dollars annual income and be under eighteen years of age.

COMMON-LAW MARRIAGE

If you and your partner live together in any one of fourteen states, it's possible that you may become married to each other (in a so-called "common-law" marriage) even though you haven't planned to. For this to happen, two conditions must be met.

First, you must reside in one of those states that recognizes a common-law marriage created within its borders: Alabama, Colorado, the District of Columbia, Georgia, Idaho, Iowa, Kansas, Montana, Ohio, Oklahoma, Pennsylvania, Rhode Island, South Carolina, and Texas.

Second, you and your partner must "hold yourselves out to be married" by telling people that you are married, by filing a joint tax return, by stating on the birth records of a child that you are married, by stating in an employment application, credit application, insurance application, or lease that you are married, etc.

If these conditions are met, even inadvertently, you could be married without intending to be.

NEED FOR WRITTEN AGREEMENT

Although the courts of some states have, on occasion, awarded rehabilitative support and/or a portion of the value of assets acquired by a live-together couple to one of the parties in the event of dissolution of the relationship, the laws of many states in this regard are vague or nonexistent.

In the wake of *Marvin v. Marvin*, a number of states are considering legislation that would disallow financial protection for either party of a live-together couple unless they have properly executed a written Agreement to Live Together.

PROVISIONS OF AGREEMENT

It would be needlessly repetitive for this chapter to comment on every provision of the following **Agreement to Live Together**, since a very close approximation of nearly every clause appears in the previously described **Agreement in Contemplation of Marriage**. For this reason, Chapter 48 should be studied before proceeding with the **Agreement to Live Together**. It should be noted, however, that option numbers of corresponding provisions of the two agreements *do not always coincide*—something to keep in mind when studying the illustrative descriptions of provision options for the **Agreement in Contemplation of Marriage** (in Chapter 48) in regard to your choice of individual clauses in your **Agreement to Live Together**. Additionally, there are several provisions that are unique to the **Agreement to Live Together** and that deserve consideration here.

Future Marriage Not a Condition Precedent

The clause states the parties' mutual understanding that neither has made nor expects any commitment of marriage.

Future Marriage Not a Condition Precedent

The parties mutually and severally acknowledge that neither has made nor expects any commitment, promise or offer of marriage now or at any time hereafter, in consideration of, nor in any way related to nor derived from, any of the promises, covenants or effects of this agreement.

Names of the Parties

Option 1 provides for the parties' agreement that each shall continue to be known by his or her separate name, thus establishing their intent NOT to hold themselves out to be husband and wife. *Option 2* provides for the parties' mutual agreement to be known by a chosen name—which may, in some states, result in their being deemed legally married under common law.

Names of the Parties (1)

The parties agree not to hold themselves out to be husband and wife and further agree that each shall continue to use his or her own name, being known, respectively, as ____John Smith____ ____ and ____Mary Jones____.

Names of the Parties (2)

The parties agree that they shall use the surname of ____ ____Smith____ and shall be known during the herein-described relationship as ____John Smith____ ____ and ____Mary Smith____.

Paternity

This clause provides for the father's commitment to acknowledge paternity of any child born of the relationship. (Other paragraphs of the agreement provide for the father's financial support and care of any such child.)

Paternity

In the event of the birth of a child to ____Mary____ ____ during the herein-described relationship or during the nine months immediately following the termination of said relationship, ____John____ agrees to execute, within ten days of the birth of any such child, an affidavit acknowledging paternity of such child, unless advised by ____Mary____ that he is not the father of said child or it has been medically determined that he is not the father of such child.

Means of Dissolution

This provision states the means by which the parties mutually agree the relationship may be dissolved. This provision may not be upheld in litigation if the parties reside in a state that recognizes common-law marriage created within its borders.

Means of Dissolution

(a) The parties mutually agree that the herein-described relationship may be dissolved by either party at any time by the initiating party's moving his or her personal property from the parties' shared living space to a separate living space, and;

(b) The parties further agree that any such action will not be taken capriciously, nor in the heat of argument, but only after diligent, considerate and thoughtful efforts to achieve reconciliation, taking into account the feelings of the parties and the possible effects upon any child or children of the parties.

TAILORING YOUR OWN AGREEMENT

All of the provisions (plus several options of many provisions) of the **Agreement to Live Together** can be found grouped together in Form 49.1 (pages F329–F355). Nearly all of these provisions are similar to those of the previously described marriage agreement, and the preceding chapter describing individual paragraphs of that agreement should be studied before beginning to negotiate an **Agreement to Live Together**.

You will probably want to exclude some of our provisions, preferring to let the agreement remain silent on certain issues, and you will also probably want to write a number of provisions of your own for addition to the contract.

Exhibits A and B (Forms 48.2 and 48.3, pages F325 and F327) from the **Agreement in Contemplation of**

Marriage may be used in conjunction with the second option of **Disclosure** in your **Agreement to Live Together.**

Refer to the sample marriage agreement (starting on page 200) as a guide for completing various portions of the **Agreement to Live Together** and read page 199 of Chapter 48 for suggestions in actually putting together your agreement, as well as for advice pertaining to the page numbering, photocopying, initialing, and storage of your agreement form.

50 Agreement Between Husband and Wife

There are probably more reasons why a husband and wife of some years would want to negotiate a marriage agreement than there are reasons why an about-to-be-married couple, or a couple planning to live together, would want to negotiate such a contract.

About-to-be-married couples and those making plans to live together are usually starting out comparatively fresh, at least with each other. There may be things that they want to *establish* between themselves, but there are usually few areas of the relationship that they want to *change*.

So the task facing a husband and wife in negotiating a marriage agreement is more demanding because any contract worth negotiating is going to require giving up old habits, accepting new values, and relating to each other in significantly different ways. If at least one of the parties did not strongly feel a need for these changes, there would have been no thought of negotiating a new contract.

In a way, feeling a need to change an unwritten (and, in many cases, unspoken) marriage agreement may not be so surprising, because if they have grown emotionally and in other ways, both husband and wife will have changed considerably from the persons they were on the date of their wedding.

Often, for a husband and wife, negotiating a marriage agreement—an agreement for a new marriage, really—is one of the best ways of acknowledging where it feels good and where it hurts. The headings of the various provisions of the preceding **Agreement in Contemplation of Marriage** make a pretty good checklist for marital dietary deficiencies and possible allergies.

But, just as frequently, a new marriage agreement can be the celebration of a better, more spontaneous, more independent, and even closer relationship between a husband and wife. Surely the freely achieved attainment of the equality and other role-emancipating aspects of marriage offered by certain options of this volume's marriage agreement can be something to celebrate.

Most of the necessary provisions for an **Agreement Between Husband and Wife** can be found in the preceding **Agreement in Contemplation of Marriage** (pages F297–F323). Some of the key provisions, though, cannot, for they can only be written by you, based upon where you have been with your lives together—and where you have determined you now want (and need) to go.

The first page of a possible agreement (Form 50.1, page F357) might provide a starting point.

PREPARING YOUR OWN WILL

51 **Nobody Lives Forever**

Most of us like to believe we care for those who are close to us: our spouse or the person we live with, our children, other members of our family, friends we've developed an affection for over the years, and those who have helped us in one way or another.

We like to think that about ourselves, but we don't like to think about dying; we try to push that reality off into some far corner of our minds. To seriously consider making a will, to actually *do* something about it, is uncomfortable, so we put it off. (More than 70 percent of the 2 million adults who died in the United States during 1983 left no wills—if you've been procrastinating, you're not alone.)

But think about this: if you die without leaving a will, you'll have absolutely nothing to say about who receives your personal belongings, real estate, cash, stocks, or any other assets. Unnecessary legal fees, court costs, taxes, and other expenses could eat up much of your estate, leaving very little for those to whom the court finally awards the remainder.

If you're married and die without a will, you'll almost surely create unnecessary hardship and expense for your spouse and children.

If you're living with someone and die without a will, there's an almost 100 percent chance that he or she will receive nothing at all from your estate—even though you may have wanted him or her to have everything.

Even if you're single and own three times the amount of money you'd be able to raise if you sold everything you own, you still need a will. Suppose, for example, you get hit by a bus and the court determines that the bus company was negligent and your estate is awarded $100,000? Suppose you die in a plane crash flying home for Christmas, and the court, in one of those cases you read about, awards your estate $1 million? Without a will that money could go to people you hardly know—cousins, aunts, and uncles—instead of someone you really care more about.

But having a will is especially important for both husband and wife, even if one or the other has little or no property. Suppose, to cite just one example, you are in an auto or airplane accident while accompanied by your spouse. If you are named as beneficiary in the will of, say, your husband, and it can be shown that following the accident you survived him, even by one minute, you will have legally inherited whatever was left to you in his will. If you die shortly thereafter (as a result of the same accident, let's assume) without having written a will of your own, the state will determine how your property will be distributed—and your estate will likely be open to costly and time-consuming litigation by relatives and others who claim a portion of it.

If you die without a will (called dying *intestate*) and you're married, the probate court will award only one-third to one-half of your estate to your spouse and will divide the remainder among your children. Unnecessary taxes could force the inopportune sale of your business interests, real estate (except perhaps your home), and much of your personal property. This can be a particular hardship on your family since a will could have allowed your business to remain in operation to provide long-term income.

In many states even if your spouse is appointed as guardian of your children's property (a common practice), he or she will practically have to get a court order *every* time it's necessary to spend a dime of their portion of the estate—even when it's for their own medical expenses or education.

When you die intestate, everything doesn't "automatically" go to your spouse. Joint ownership of your house or other assets doesn't necessarily mean that they will "automatically" go to your spouse either.

There is *no* need to allow any of the potential problems we've mentioned to arise when they can be easily avoided with a will, plus possibly a simple trust or two.

A will, which we'll describe in detail later on, is simply your declaration of how you want your property distributed after your death. Your will can be revoked and can be changed *as many times as you want.* It is completely confidential during your lifetime (even the witnesses to your signature don't have to know its contents); it doesn't have to be filed with any court or government agency until you die; and, except in Louisiana, it doesn't have to be in any particular format as long as it meets simple legal requirements. There is a traditional way of writing a will though, and there's no particular reason not to follow it.

This section explains and illustrates how several ready-to-use wills for simple estates can be filled in and properly signed before witnesses to eliminate almost immediately many of the problems, needless expenses, and unfairness that can arise if you die without a will.

These wills, found in the Forms section at the back of the book, include:

1. Will of husband leaving entire estate to wife, if surviving, otherwise to adult children; appointment of wife as primary executrix (Form 55.1 on page F379).
2. Will of wife leaving entire estate to husband, if surviving, otherwise to adult children; appointment of husband as primary executor (Form 55.2 on page F383).

3. Will of husband leaving entire estate to wife, if surviving, otherwise in trust for minor children; wife appointed primary executrix (Form 55.3 on page F387).
4. Will of wife leaving entire estate to husband, if surviving, otherwise in trust for minor children; husband appointed primary executor (Form 55.4 on page F391).
5. Will of husband having no children leaving entire estate to wife, if surviving, otherwise certain bequests and devises; appointment of wife as primary executrix (Form 55.5 on page F395).
6. Will of wife having no children leaving entire estate to husband, if surviving, otherwise certain bequests and devises; appointment of husband as primary executor (Form 55.6 on page F399).
7. Will of unmarried man having no children leaving entire estate to female cohabitant, if surviving, otherwise certain bequests and devises; appointment of cohabitant as primary executrix (Form 55.7 on page F403).
8. Will of unmarried woman having no children leaving entire estate to male cohabitant, if surviving, otherwise certain bequests and devises; appointment of cohabitant as primary executor (Form 55.8 on page F407).
9. Will of unmarried man or woman having no children, making certain bequests and devises; appointment of executor or executrix (Form 55.9 page F411).

Appropriately selected, any of the above documents can serve as a good will—maybe not a *great* will, but a good will—and can accomplish for you much of what even the best will can do. It can certainly provide for those you care about infinitely better than no will.

If you still don't have a will, complete and properly execute, as directed in this section, the most nearly appropriate will *as soon as possible*. Then, once you've taken that step, make an appointment with an attorney for help in drawing up a better will.

In addition to the aforementioned wills, this section will illustrate how a fairly wide range of individual will provisions (provided in the back of the book) can be used as separate paragraphs to amend and tailor one of the previously mentioned wills to "create" a will that fits your needs more closely. Simply photocopy several copies of each desired paragraph, using one as a work copy and one as a final copy; affix the completed final copies to one of the ready-to-use will forms—replacing or adding provisions as necessary—with adhesive; then photocopy each completed page to assemble your "printed" will according to simple legal requirements outlined later.

ASSETS THAT REMAIN OUTSIDE YOUR WILL

There are a number of assets that remain outside your will for probate purposes (they do not pass to your heirs through your will and thus are immediately available after your death) but that are still counted as part of your will for estate tax purposes.

1. Proceeds of life insurance; these pass directly to the beneficiary you have named without being mentioned in your will.
2. Assets that you have placed in trust for a named person or institution (more on trusts in Section X).
3. Property jointly owned by a husband and wife, IF wording of the deed meets certain legal requirements.
4. U.S. government savings bonds cannot be transferred by will but may be made payable to another person or to your estate upon presentation of proof of your death.

These assets, which are not subject to the delays of probate, should be thoughtfully planned with the assistance of an attorney and an insurance advisor to ease the financial circumstances of your family since they can provide immediate cash for living expenses, plus money to obtain a clear title to your home in the surviving spouse's or cohabitant's name.

Since creditors are often given several months during which to present claims against the estate (*see* the table on pages 227–228) and because legal requirements may take additional time, from six months to as much as four or five years may elapse before an estate is distributed according to the dictates of a will.

TERMINOLOGY YOU NEED TO KNOW

Before we begin taking a typical will apart, examining it paragraph by paragraph to gain an understanding of the meaning and function and requirements of each portion, we need to take a brief look at some of the terminology, find exactly what a will can and cannot do, review basic federal estate taxes, and answer some often asked questions about wills, estates, and inheritance.

Years ago, "will" and "testament" meant different things. Today, like "kith and kin," "will and testament" are almost always found together, a "last will and testament" being a person's declaration of how he or she desires his or her personal and real property to be distributed after death. A will may contain other instructions, such as those for burial, but it must always distribute *some* property in order to be a will.

As we pointed out earlier, a will may be revoked, may be amended, and may be replaced by another will at any time. Your will is completely secret during your lifetime, and even the witnesses to your signature don't need to know what's in your will.

An amendment to a will is called a *codicil* and to be valid must meet all the same legal requirements as the original will with respect to the maker's sound mind, age, witnesses, etc. A codicil is normally used to make a simple change in a will, such as the name of an executor. For extensive changes a new will should be written.

Nearly every will begins, "I, _____, being of sound and disposing mind. . . ." These exact words are not required, but their exact meaning—that the maker of the will is conscious of his or her acts, is of sound memory, is aware of what this property is and who he's giving it to, and is aware that he is making (presumably) a Last Will and Testament—is always found in the opening paragraph of any standard will.

Some wills also continue to say, "and not acting under the duress, menace or fraud of any person or persons . . ." but this phrase is falling into disuse since anyone under undue influence would not be aware of it or would be acting out of fear anyway.

A person who makes a will is termed a *testator* if male and a *testatrix* if female.

The person named by the testator or testatrix to administer his or her estate may be called an *executor* if male and an *executrix* if female (the more modern term is *personal representative*). There may be more than one executor—an individual and a bank, for example—acting as coexecutors.

An individual's *estate* is his or her interest in real and personal property. You don't have to be dead to have an estate; if you own anything, you have an estate now.

The term *personal property* includes an individual's clothing, vehicles, jewelry, books, equipment, tools, objects of art, home furnishings, cash on hand, money in checking and savings accounts, stocks and bonds, etc.

The term *real property* refers to real estate, such as your home, land, a ranch, farm, etc.

In directing the distribution of property the phrase "give, devise and bequeath" is almost always used. Legal precedent has established that you *bequeath* personal property and that you *devise* real estate. *Give* is thrown in for good measure (and perhaps for good meter).

The "rest, residue and remainder" of an estate are just that, whatever remains after all taxes, expenses, and other costs have been paid and all devises and bequests have been made. If the maker of a will leaves his or her entire estate to one person after all taxes and costs have been paid, then the "rest, residue and remainder" often constitute the main body of the estate. If there are many bequests and devises, the "rest, residue and remainder" might be quite modest.

The disposition by will of one's personal property is termed a *legacy*, and an individual receiving a legacy is called a *legatee*.

Assets of an estate are often left to children of the maker and/or to grandchildren, *per stirpes*. If, for example, a parent were to leave an entire estate to three children, "or to the children of any of my deceased children [i.e., grandchildren] *per stirpes*," then if **one** of the three children predeceased the maker, each of the two **surviving** children would receive one-third of the estate and the two children of the **deceased**

child, being grandchildren of the maker, would each receive one-sixth of the estate.

Now, if the estate were to be distributed to the maker's three children *per capita* and all three were alive at the time of the maker's death, each would receive one-third, just as before. But if one child predeceased the maker, leaving only two, then those two would each receive one-half of the estate.

Community property is that property, real and personal, of either one of a married couple that is considered under the law of some states to be owned equally by both, **solely on the basis of their marriage to each other.** In a community-property state almost all property acquired by either spouse **after** the date of their marriage, whether earned through the efforts of the husband or the wife, is considered *community property* (for a listing of community-property states, see the table on pages 227–228).

General exceptions to the community-property rule are gifts, real and personal property inherited after marriage, and property obtained by the husband or wife through the sale or exchange of noncommunity property.

Upon the death of either spouse, only the decedent's half share of community property may be distributed by will. Either spouse may relinquish community rights through a prenuptial (also called antenuptial) or postnuptial agreement.

Strictly speaking, to *probate* a will is to prove its authenticity and proper execution, but use of the term has been broadened to include all of the procedural judicial steps relating to a will. In some jurisdictions, by the way, a probate court is termed a *surrogate* court.

In probate matters there are two types of guardians, both types usually named by the deceased and appointed by the court. A *guardian of the person* acts in the stead of deceased parents to care for minor children. A *guardian of the property* (or *guardian of the estate*) is responsible for administering and managing property for the benefit of his or her charge, usually a minor child. Both types of guardianship are usually terminated when a minor child comes of age.

A *trustee*, as the name suggests, is a person or institution named by the decedent to administer and manage a trust established in the name of a beneficiary of his or her will. Trustees are often given wide discretionary powers over the management and distribution of the trust, and with very large estates they are sometimes required to administer trusts over several generations. For this reason, institutions such as banks are often named as trustee or cotrustee, with a law firm or family member sharing the responsibility.

A *trust* is a right in real or personal property held by one person, a trustee, for the benefit of another. A *testamentary trust* is created by will; an *inter vivos trust* is created by the *trustor* during life. A trust may be revocable or irrevocable, each type having different tax aspects—to be explained in Section X, Creating Your Own Trust.

Here are a few other terms related to wills and estates:

An *administrator* (or *administratrix*) is a person appointed by the court to administer the estate of someone who dies without a will. The administrator acts in lieu of an executor and divides the property of the deceased, not according to his or her wishes but in compliance with the laws of the decedent's state of legal residence.

A *dower* is that portion of a husband's estate, usually one-third to one-half, that by law belongs to his surviving wife and from which she cannot be disinherited. (Dower does not apply in community-property states.) The recipient of a dower is a *dowager*. (Now you know where that term comes from.)

A *curtesy* is a surviving husband's "dower." Fewer states guarantee a husband's curtesy than guarantee a wife's dower—another thing that would change if the ERA were ever to pass. (Curtesy does not apply in community-property states either.)

An *heir* (or *heiress*) is someone who, by law and/or line of descent, would inherit part of the estate of someone who dies without a will.

With respect to probate matters, *issue* is used most commonly to refer to descendants of the deceased or to descendants of beneficiaries of the deceased.

To *disinherit* is, by willful act, to deprive an heir or heiress of property that he or she would otherwise received from the estate of the decedent.

To *contest* a will is to question its authenticity, legality, or proper execution, or to oppose or question certain of its provisions. Disinherited heirs are frequent contestors of wills.

With respect to wills, an *abatement* is the reduction of or, more often, the complete extinction of a bequest. A bequest of cash might *abate* because there was insufficient money in the estate to fulfill it. The maker of a will may give preference to a particular bequest by directing that it "not abate until all other bequests have been fully abated." In other words, "Pay the preferred bequest first."

COMMON QUESTIONS ABOUT WILLS

Who Can Make a Will?

Anyone making a valid will must be of sound mind and must meet the minimum age requirements of the state of his or her legal residence. In some states (see **Requirements for Wills in the United States** on pages 227–228) an individual may distribute personal property by will at a younger age than is required for the distribution of real property.

A blind, deaf, or physically incapacitated person may make a valid will. An individual who uses alcohol or other drugs to excess may also be found capable of making a valid will. A convict or exconvict, though often deprived of other "civil rights," may make a valid will. The right to make a will is not a right of common law; it is granted to the citizens of each state by statute.

What Is My State of Legal Residence?

Generally, but not always, your state of legal residence is the state where you make your home. If certain advantages, such as the absence of state income tax, inheritance taxes, or personal property taxes, are worth the effort, you may be able (best with the help of a lawyer) to establish legal residence in one state yet live in another.

What Kinds of Wills Are There?

Holographic wills, those written entirely in the hand of the maker and signed by him or her, need not be attested to by witnesses. Although accepted by close to half of the states (see the table starting on the following page), such wills should be drawn only in dire emergencies.

Oral wills (also called *nuncupative* wills) are recognized by a number of states, but usually within very narrow limits. The only oral wills accepted in many jurisdictions are those made by service personnel in anticipation of combat or deathbed wills made by individuals in anticipation of imminent death —and who die as anticipated.

A *joint* will is a will made by more than one person, usually a husband and wife, containing provisions that are agreed to by the makers. When the first maker dies, the will is probated as his or her will. When the survivor dies, the same will is then probated with respect to the estate of that person. (This will was not recommended by any attorney we consulted.)

A so-called *standard* will is the type of will executed by nearly all persons in the United States and is the type presented in this book. It is usually typewritten and is attested to by the required number of witnesses (see pages 227–228 for the number of witnesses required by each state).

Can I Disinherit My Spouse?

Except by written marital agreement, one generally cannot. The laws of most states require that a spouse receive one-half or one-third of the decedent's estate. If a married person's will leaves less than that portion to his or her surviving spouse, the survivor may elect to petition the probate court to receive the minimum required by the state. Interestingly, husbands may disinherit wives in twelve states, but wives may disinherit their husbands in only two (see next page).

Can I Disinherit My Children?

Yes, but generally not by omission in most states. A child whom you wish to disinherit must be mentioned by name, such as, "I make no provision in this will for my son Thomas because of my many previous financial gifts to him" or "I make no provision for my daughter Nimona because she has been generously provided for by her [deceased] husband." Grandchildren, parents, cousins, aunts, uncles, brothers, sisters, and other blood relatives may be disinherited by omission.

REQUIREMENTS FOR WILLS IN THE UNITED STATES

	Age[a]				Witn. Req.	Comm. Prop. State	Months for Creditors' Claims After Death	Oral Will Accepted	Holo- graphic Will Accepted	Husband May Disinherit Wife		Wife May Disinherit Husband	
	Males		Females							Real Prop.	Per- sonal Prop.	Real Prop.	Per- sonal Prop.
Alabama	18	21	18	21	2	No	6	Yes	No	Yes	No	No	No
Alaska	21	21	21	21	2	No	6	Yes	Yes	No	Yes	No	Yes
Arizona	21[b]	21[b]	21[b]	21[b]	2	No	4	Yes	Yes	Yes	Yes	No	No
Arkansas	18	18	18	18	2	No	6	Yes	Yes	No	No	No	No
California	18	18	18	18	2	Yes	4	Yes	Yes	No	No	No	No
Colorado	17	21	17	21	2	No	6	No	Yes	No	No	No	No
Connecticut	18	18	18	18	3	No	12	No	No	No	No	No	No
Delaware	21	21	21	21	2	No	9	Yes	No	No	Yes	No	Yes
District of Columbia	21	21	18	18	2	No	6	Yes	No	Yes	No	No	No
Florida	18	18	18	18	2	No	3	Yes	No	No	No	No	No
Georgia	14	14	14	14	2	No	6	Yes	No	Yes	Yes	No	Yes
Hawaii	20	20	20	20	2	No	4	No	No	No	No	No	No
Idaho	18	18	18	18	2	Yes	4	Yes	Yes	No	No	No	No
Illinois	18	18	18	18	2	No	6	No	No	No	No	No	No
Indiana	21	21	21	21	2	No	6	Yes	No	No	No	No	No
Iowa	21	21	21	21	2	No	6	Yes	No	No	No	No	No
Kansas	21	21	21	21	2	No	6	Yes	No	No	No	No	No
Kentucky	21	21	21	21	2	No	6	Yes	Yes	No	No	No	No
Louisiana	16	16	16	16	3	Yes	NSL[c]	Yes	Yes	No	No	No	No
Maine	21	21	21[d]	21[d]	3	No	12	Yes	No	No	No	No	No
Maryland	21	21	18	18	2	No	6	Yes	No	No	No	No	No
Massachusetts	21	21	21	21	3	No	NSL	Yes	No	No	No	No	No
Michigan	21	21	21	21	2	No	18	Yes	No	Yes	Yes	No	No
Minnesota	21	21	21	21	2	No	4	Yes	No	No	No	No	No
Mississippi	21	21	21	21	2	No	6	Yes	Yes	No	No	No	No
Missouri	21	21	21	21	2	No	6	Yes	No	No	No	No	No
Montana	18	18	18	18	2	No	4	Yes	Yes	No	No	No	No
Nebraska	21	21	21	21	2	No	18	Yes	No	No	No	No	No
Nevada	18	18	18	18	2	Yes	3	Yes	Yes	No	No	No	No
New Hampshire	18[b]	18[b]	18[b]	18[b]	3	No	6	Yes	No	No	No	No	No
New Jersey	21	21	21	21	2	No	6	Accepted	No	No	Yes	No	Yes
New Mexico	21	21	21	21	2	No	4	No	No	No	No	No	No
New York	18	21	18	21	2	No	7	Yes	No	No	No	No	No
North Carolina	21	21	21	21	2	No	6	Yes	Yes	Yes	Yes	No	No
North Dakota	18	18	18	18	2	No	3	Yes	Yes	Yes	Yes	Yes	Yes
Ohio	21	21	21	21	2	No	4	Yes	No	No	No	No	No
Oklahoma	18	18	18	18	2	No	2	Yes	Yes	No	No	No	No
Oregon	21	21	21	21	2	No	4	Yes	No	No	Yes	No	Yes
Pennsylvania	21	21	21	21	2	No	NSL	Yes	Yes	No	No	No	No
Rhode Island	18	21	18	21	2	No	6	No	No	No	Yes	No	Yes
South Carolina	21	21	21	21	3	No	5	Yes	No	Yes	Yes	No	Yes
South Dakota	18	18	18	18	2	No	4	Yes	Yes	Yes	Yes	Yes	Yes
Tennessee	18	18	18	18	2	No	6	No	Yes	No	No	No	No

(continued)

REQUIREMENTS FOR WILLS IN THE UNITED STATES (*Continued*)

	Age[a] Males		Females		Witn. Req.	Comm. Prop. State	Months for Creditors' Claims After Death	Oral Will Accepted	Holo- graphic Will Accepted	Husband May Disinherit Wife Real Prop.	Per- sonal Prop.	Wife May Disinherit Husband Real Prop.	Per- sonal Prop.
Texas	21[b]	21[b]	21[b]	21[b]	2	Yes	6	Yes	Yes	No	No	No	No
Utah	18	18	18	18	2	No	3	Yes	Yes	Yes	Yes	No	Yes
Vermont	21	21	21	21	3	No	NSL	Yes	No	No	No	No	No
Virginia	18	21	18	21	2	No	NSL	Yes	Yes	No	No	No	No
Washington	21[e]	21[e]	21[e]	21[e]	2	Yes	4	Yes	No	No	No	No	No
West Virginia	21	21	21	21	2	No	6	Yes	Yes	No	No	No	No
Wisconsin	21	21	21[f]	21[f]	2	No	NSL	Yes	No	Yes	Yes	No	No
Wyoming	21	21	21	21	2	No	3	No	Yes	No	No	No	No

[a]Legal residence determines minimum age requirements. Note that minimum age requirements are broken down by minimum age at which an individual can distribute personal property (*first age*) as opposed to the distribution of real property (*second age*).

[b]Or married.

[c]No statute of limitations.

[d]Or married woman or widow.

[e]Or married and over 18.

[f]Or married woman over 18.

What Other Limitations Are There?

Generally, the court will not enforce instructions that are contrary to public policy, that seem to be unduly eccentric, or that attempt to defraud or ignore creditors.

As stated earlier, life insurance benefits, U.S. savings bonds, and trusts established for beneficiaries during your life (called *inter vivos* trusts) pass directly to beneficiaries outside your will.

What Can My Will Be Used For in Addition to the Distribution of Property?

Your will can be used to convey instructions for your funeral and burial, to name guardians for the person and property of your minor children, to declare your desire with respect to the religous upbringing of your minor children, to establish trusts, and to instruct an executor and trustee in the administration and management of your estate for the benefit of your spouse, children, or other beneficiaries.

What Happens with My Will When I Die?

Generally speaking, your executor will contact an attorney, who will contact the clerk of the probate or surrogate court (depending on what it's called in your area) and who will make arrangements to present your will for probate (proving).

The court will want:

1. A copy of your death certificate.
2. The original copy of your will—the only copy that can be proved.

3. An inventory of the assets and liabilities of your estate.
4. The presence of at least one witness to the signing of your will who will be put under oath to attest to the authenticity of your signature, OR the introduction into evidence of a notarized "self-proving affidavit" (see pages 249–251) that can eliminate the need for court appearance by any witness to the signing of a will.

After your will has been proved, the judge will usually confirm your naming of an executor, and in the case of minor children if your spouse does not survive you, the judge will examine, and probably approve, the person or persons you have named as guardian or guardians.

The court will also publish legal notice of your death in local newspapers to notify creditors and start the clock running on the time during which creditors may present claims against your estate— see **Requirements for Wills in the United States** on pages 227–228.

There are those who follow death notices closely and who quickly mail "past due" bills to the address of the deceased or who promptly put into the mail overpriced Bibles or other items supposedly ordered by the deceased. In many cases the purchases are highly suspect. Few athiests buy white, genuine leather-bound, gold-embossed Bibles costing hundreds of dollars, but often such items are paid for without question by the bereaved family or by executors unfamiliar with the personal beliefs and interests of the deceased.

In some jurisdictions the court will appoint an appraiser or appraisers to evaluate the worth of your estate. Their fees are paid by the estate, a well-entrenched "rip-off" that your executor may not be able to do much about in some parts of the country. These political-appointee appraisers often act as "bloodhounds" for unethical furniture, auto, and antique dealers who approach bereaved families with ridiculously low offers to "take these things off your hands" while the family has still not recovered from its loss and is easy prey to be taken advantage of.

In more enlightened areas the executor of an estate may select any appraiser he or she chooses from an approved list of usually qualified and honest appraisers. Appraisers are used by the court so that taxes, both state and federal, can be based upon something other than value stated by a member of the family. The selection of an appraiser is one of the areas in which an attorney experienced in estate matters can be of help to your executor.

Usually, the court will permit the wife of a deceased husband to draw an allowance from the estate for day-to-day living expenses until such time as the will has been proved, the decedent's debts have been paid, and the executor is finally authorized to begin distribution of property as directed by the will.

A federal estate tax return must be filed by your executor within nine months of your death if the value of your estate is above a specific amount. State inheritance and succession taxes also must usually be paid within a set time.

What Is the Cost of Probating a Will?

Court costs associated with probate are relatively modest for most estates, often no more than $200 or $300. Attorneys' fees and executors' fees in many states are, by custom, based upon a percentage of the value of an estate, with the percentage charged scaled downward as the value increases. In "percentage" states, the attorney or any nonfamily executor is authorized to charge the state-specified amount, one reason why banks love to act as executors.

There is, of course, no law that stipulates that an attorney–executor **must** charge a percentage of the value of an estate for serving as executor. Increasing numbers of states are doing away with "percentage of appraised value" guidelines, and an increasing number of fair-minded attorneys, even in "percentage" states, are charging on a normal hourly basis, rather than on the basis of an estate's value, for serving as executor.

In describing what military bureaucrats would probably term a "worst case scenario," the May 1, 1982, issue of *Changing Times* magazine noted that "in some parts of the U.S. it can cost more than $10,000 or more to settle a simple, uncontested $100,000 estate, and the job can take months or years. Why? Critics say exorbitant legal fees and archaic court procedures are usually to blame. All too often lawyers collect thousands of dollars for routine paperwork that family members could do themselves if they knew how."

Many people name their husband or wife, son or daughter, or a trusted relative or friend to serve as executor of their estate. It's especially important for people who live together or who frequently travel together to name an additional person to serve as **alternate executor** in the event both should die in the same accident.

If you feel the need to nominate an attorney to serve as executor or coexecutor of your estate, ask the attorney if he or she will charge the estate an agreed hourly rate rather than a percentage of the value of the estate.

If you live in a jurisdiction where the practice of using do-nothing, political-appointee appraisers is followed, you can count on your estate being billed an unreasonably high amount, whatever the size of your estate.

DUTIES OF AN EXECUTOR AND AN ATTORNEY IN ESTATE PROBATE AND ADMINISTRATION

The tables on page 230 list the usual duties of an executor and attorney involved with the probate and administration of an estate. If your estate is a modest one, you may be able to combine the duties of executor and attorney under the responsibilities of a competent and responsible family-member executor.

LIST OF IMPORTANT PEOPLE AND PAPERS

You can smooth the way for administration of your estate by completing this section's List of Important People and Papers (Form 51.1, page F359). This form provides for listing the location of your will and such other important documents as insurance policies, trust agreements, savings account books, military and veterans benefit papers, stock certificates, medical records, etc.

The list also makes provision for the names and addresses of people who should be contacted in the event of your death: the executor of your will, your attorney, your employer, physician, insurance agent, banker, certain friends, your grown children, and possibly your former spouse.

You may want to make several copies of the list, giving one to the executor of your will and one to your attorney, with additional copies going to your spouse, an adult son or daughter, and a good friend.

EXECUTOR RESPONSIBILITIES

Locate will

Obtain death certificate

Assure compliance with funeral instructions, if any, in will

Open safe deposit box

Take control of personal property

Probate will and obtain appointment as executor

Make inventory of assets and liabilities of estate

Arrange for life insurance benefits payable to estate

Arrange for payment of debts of estate

Arrange for collection of debts due estate

Arrange for appraisal of property of estate

Keep an accounting of estate transactions

Determine which, if any, assets should be sold

Liquidate or continue operation of business interests

Arrange for transfer of stocks and bonds from name of decedent to name of executor

Comply with instructions of will regarding assets held in trust

Determine decedent's right to employment, government, and other insurance and benefit plans

Arrange distribution of property in accordance with will

Prepare, sign, file, and pay federal, state, and other estate taxes

Initiate and/or defend legal action affecting estate

Prepare, sign, and file decedent's federal income tax return

Submit final accounting to probate court

ATTORNEY RESPONSIBILITIES

Prepare petition for probate

Obtain order for probate

Obtain order for access to safe deposit box

Publish notice to creditors

Prepare notices to creditors whose claims are rejected

Prepare petition for family allowance

Prepare petitions, at executor's request, for sale of assets

Obtain partial and final decrees of distribution

Prepare documents for transfer of real property

Prepare receipts for signature of beneficiaries receiving real and personal property

Assist, at executor's request, with preparation of tax returns

Prepare other petitions and court documents as required

Prepare petition and obtain order for final discharge of executor

52 Minimizing Your Federal Estate Taxes

Under provisions of the **Economic Recovery Tax Act of 1981 (ERTA)** (effective January 1, 1982), your estate has no federal estate tax liability at all for any portion of your estate transferred to your spouse under your will. The previous law, the **Tax Reform Act of 1976**, imposed a tax on the greater of $250,000 or one-half of the adjusted gross value of an estate transferred to a decedent's spouse under terms of a will.

The 1981 Act considerably simplifies estate planning and saves considerable money, especially for wealthy individuals' estates, but there is some "trickle down" that benefits more modest estates.

Since there is no federal estate tax on what the Internal Revenue Service (IRS) likes to call "interspousal transfers" under a will, there is a reduced need to buy life insurance specifically to help defray the cost of estimated federal estate taxes.

Especially important to the self-employed is that, under provisions of the Act, ownership of a family business can now be transferred to a spouse under terms of a will without federal estate tax liability, often eliminating any need to sell the business in order to meet estate taxes.

The 1981 Act also provides a substantial increase in the value of an estate that is exempt from federal estate tax liability. The gross value of an estate that escapes federal estate tax liability is also raised each year through 1987 (see table below).

EQUIVALENT TAX EXEMPTION TABLE

Year	Federal Estate Tax Credit	Equivalent Tax Exemption
1982	$62,800	$225,000
1983	79,300	275,000
1984	96,300	325,000
1985	121,800	400,000
1986	155,800	500,000
1987 and after	192,800	600,000

So, if you die during 1984 leaving an estate of $325,000, your estate will have no federal estate tax liability at all. It will probably have a liability for the payment of other federal taxes, though, such as your personal income tax.

If you were to die during 1984 leaving an estate valued at **more** than $325,000, it could still escape federal estate taxes based on the amount transferred to your spouse under terms of your will:

Gross value of estate:	$1,325,000
Transferred to spouse under terms of will:	$1,000,000
Remainder (tax free):	$325,000

While the **Economic Recovery Tax Act of 1981** progressively increases the value of an estate that is exempt from federal estate tax by increasing the amount of the *estate tax credit* (as indicated by the **Equivalent Tax Exemption Table**), it also progressively reduces the tax rate on large estates. Beginning in 1985 the maximum estate tax rate on estates of $2.5 million or more will be 50 percent, a substantial saving for the wealthy. For estates valued at less than $2.5 million, the **Unified Rate Schedule** established pursuant to the **Tax Reform Act of 1976** remains in force.

BUT, even though the tax *rate* remains the same under the 1981 Act as it was under the 1976 Act, it applies to *fewer* estates each year through 1987 because the *value* of an estate that is exempt from tax increases annually up until that date.

Under the 1976 Act an estate valued at $175,625 would be taxable at the rate shown on the **Unified Rate Schedule** (see page 232). Estates of persons dying during 1984 would not be taxable under the Schedule unless they were valued at greater than $325,000.

ESTATE TAX REDUCTION THROUGH GIVING

One way to reduce your federal estate tax liability is to give away part of your estate before you die, since what you no longer own can't be counted as part of your estate. The **Economic Recovery Tax Act of 1981**:

1. Allows unlimited "interspousal gifts" (gifts between husband and wife) free of gift tax liability.
2. Raises from $3,000 to $10,000 the amount that any person can give to any number of individuals each year.
3. Raises from $6,000 to $20,000 the amount that a married couple can give to any number of individuals each year. (There is no requirement that either spouse actually provide any part of the gift, so long as *both* spouses concur in the gift.)
4. No longer includes in the value of an estate gifts made within three years of the giver's death. (However, the value of gifts of life insurance made within

UNIFIED RATE SCHEDULE

Column A: Taxable Amount Over	Column B: Taxable Amount Not Over	Column C: Tax on Amount in Column A	Column D: Rate of Tax on Excess Over Amount in Column A
0	$10,000	0	18%
$10,000	20,000	$1,800	20
29,000	40,000	3,800	22
40,000	60,000	8,200	24
60,000	80,000	13,000	26
80,000	100,000	18,200	28
100,000	150,000	23,800	30
150,000	250,000	38,800	32
250,000	500,000	70,800	34
500,000	750,000	155,800	37
750,000	1,000,000	248,300	39
1,000,000	1,250,000	345,800	41
1,250,000	1,500,000	448,300	43
1,500,000	2,000,000	555,800	45
2,000,000	2,500,000	780,800	49
2,500,000	3,000,000	1,025,800	53
3,000,000	3,500,000	1,290,800	57

three years of the giver's death are still counted as part of the decedent's estate. The value of the insurance gift is based upon its loan or cash value—NOT upon the face value of the policy.)

Under provisions of the 1981 Act, you can give as many gifts as you would like, without limitation as to individual or total value, to your husband or wife without incurring a gift tax liability. You can also give as many gifts as you would like to as many different individuals as you may wish during any year without incurring gift tax liability—as long as the value of gifts given to any one individual during any year does not exceed $10,000.

You could, for example, give $10,000 to your married son and also give $10,000 to his wife during any year without incurring a gift tax liability. During the same year you could also give $10,000 in gifts to any number of other individuals without incurring any gift tax liability at all.

If a married couple concur in the giving of any gift or gifts, the annual amount that can be given free of tax liability during any year is doubled. In the case cited above, a married couple concurring in their giving could give $20,000 to their married son and $20,000 to his wife during any one year free of gift tax liability.

While in most cases it may be more blessed to give than to receive, under the **Internal Revenue Service Code** it is extremely blessed to receive, since a recipient has no federal tax liability for the amount of gifts that he or she may receive.

To clear up one point of occasional misunderstanding, the giver—except the giver of a charitable contribution—cannot deduct the amount of a gift from his or her taxable personal income.

DEDUCTION FROM LIFETIME ESTATE AND GIFT TAX CREDIT

If, for some reason (such as sure knowledge of your impending death or dire need on the part of the recipient) you wish to give more than $10,000 to an individual during a given year, you can still escape federal gift tax liability for the excess amount of the gift by deducting the excess from your "lifetime" equivalent tax exemption (see the Equivalent Tax Exemption Table).

Assuming a gift of $15,000 made during 1984 ($5,000 above the maximum tax-free gift allowed by the 1981 Act), you could deduct $5,000 from your $325,000 equivalent estate tax exemption to eliminate a gift tax liability for the $5,000 excess.

This action would reduce your total estate tax exemption equivalent by the $5,000 "used up," thus making your estate liable for estate taxes if you were to die during 1984 *and* the value of your estate exceeded $320,000.

The amount of the $5,000 exemption thus used up would carry over to each successive year as the exemption equivalent increases annually through 1987, so that no matter when you die and no matter what the exemption equivalent may be during the year of your death, the $5,000 deduction will still be made from your total estate tax exemption equivalent.

QUALIFYING GIFTS

For a gift to qualify under the $10,000 annual exclusion per recipient provided for by the **Economic Recovery Tax Act of 1981**, it must meet three criteria:

1. The gift must be available for the immediate use and benefit of the recipient. (A gift of future interest, such as property given in trust, would not qualify.)
2. The value of the gift must be readily verifiable.
3. The identity of both the giver and the recipient must be readily verifiable.

Remember that while every individual may give up to $10,000 per year per recipient without liability for gift tax, a husband and wife may combine tax exclusions to make any number of gifts of up to $20,000 per year, per recipient, without incurring gift tax liability. Thus, a married couple may combine their individual $10,000 tax exclusions in making a $20,000 gift even though the assets may have been earned by or owned by either spouse.

SAVING MONEY BY GIVING IT AWAY

You'll want the advice of a qualified advisor before making decisions about giving, personal investment programs, and estate planning, but there are a number of tax and money-saving provisions of the **Economic Recovery Tax Act of 1981**, the **Uniform Gifts to Minors Act**, and the **Internal Revenue Code** that you should know about.

Gifts to Children

As noted previously, anyone can give up to $10,000 to any individual, or number of individuals, free of gift tax liability during any year; a married couple can give $20,000.

However, one advantage of making gifts to children, especially when they are quite young, is that although the gift itself is not tax deductible, personal income tax need not be paid on interest, dividends, or other income earned by the gift as long as the total annual income of the child does not exceed the minimum amount that must be reported on a personal federal income tax return.

Even if a personal income tax liability is created as the result of interest, dividends, or other income earned by gifts to a child, the tax *rate* is almost always much lower than if the same income were to be taxed to the giver. A gift of $3,000 that earns, say, 10 percent annually and is compounded tax free will have become $7,782 in ten years.

Generally, gifts to children are placed in trust in a simple-to-open custodianship account with a bank or

brokerage house. Prior to opening such an account, you'll need to obtain a social security number for the child so that interest and/or dividends earned by gifts may be reported to the IRS by the bank or brokerage house. And, of course, a personal federal income tax return will have to be filed if the child's income exceeds the minimum tax exempt amount—$1,000 as of 1984.

Gifts to children are deemed as qualifying as "gifts of present interest" under provisions of the **Economic Recovery Tax Act of 1981** if—

- Both the property and its income are expended by, or for the benefit of, the minor before attaining the age of majority.
- Any portion of the property or its income not disposed of by the minor's attaining the age of majority passes to the minor on that birthday.
- In the event the minor dies before attaining the age of majority, the property and its income are payed either to the minor's estate or to whomever the minor may appoint under a general power of appointment.

State-by-State Variations: The legal definition of a "child" varies from state to state. In some states the age of majority is 18; in others it may be as high as 21. Since many states are revising their age of majority upward due to increased auto accident deaths resulting from the sale of liquor to youths under 21 years of age, you should determine your state's current age of majority before establishing a giving plan for the benefit of any child. In some states, by the way, the age of majority for males is different from the age of majority for females.

Warning: All gifts placed in a custodianship account for a child become the property of the child for him or her to do with as he or she pleases—free of any control by the custodian, parents, or anyone else—when the child reaches the age of majority.

Note: More complete information on trusts, plus forms suitable for the establishment of trusts and trust funds for children and others, are provided in Section X, Creating Your Own Trust.

Gifts of Securities

Under current law, gifts of securities to a child, or to anyone else for that matter, may be valued, for purposes of the $10,000 annual gift tax exclusion of the 1981 Act, at their original acquisition cost to the giver rather than at market value on the date of transfer.

If, for example, you purchased securities for $9,000 some time ago that on the date of transfer as a gift to the recipient had a market value of, say, $18,000, the "value" of the securities for gift tax purposes remains at $9,000, your original cost.

However, when the recipient sells the securities, his or her acquisition value is deemed by the IRS to be the *giver's* original acquisition value and a capital gains tax liability to the recipient is created by any increase in the value of the securities over the giver's acquisition cost.

Gifts of Real Estate

Ditto. Gifts of real estate are also valued for gift tax purposes on the basis of their value when acquired by the giver rather than at their market value on the date of transfer to the recipient.

A home-building lot valued at $9,000 when acquired by the giver, but worth $15,000 on the date of transfer as a gift to the recipient, will be valued at $9,000 for purposes of the annual gift tax exclusion. As with gifts of appreciated value, the difference between the giver's acquisition cost and the value when sold by the recipient will be taxed to the recipient's personal income.

Gifts of Life Insurance

Normally, life insurance benefits immediately and directly pass to your beneficiaries outside your will (not probated), but the amount of such payments to beneficiaries by the insurance company is counted as part of your taxable estate. A $100,000 payment to any beneficiary (other than your spouse) adds $100,000 to the taxable value of your estate.

But if the beneficiary **owns** the policy, he or she receives the proceeds of the policy at your death without the proceeds being counted as part of your estate. Making use of this provision of the 1981 Act, you could take advantage of several options.

You could, for example, each year give to each of your children sufficient funds to pay the premiums on separate life insurance policies on yourself, each policy naming a different child as beneficiary. In that manner, an individual having, say, five children could leave them a total of $500,000, $100,000 each, immediately available upon his or her death free of the delays of probate and without adding to the taxable value of the estate. But for the proceeds of the insurance policies to remain outside an estate and not increase its taxable value, the **beneficiaries** must **OWN** the policies.

Taking advantage of another option, you can give ownership of any currently in force life insurance policy to any individual, free of gift tax liability, as long as the loan or cash value of the policy is less than $10,000.

Larger Gifts

If you'd like to make a gift larger than $10,000, say, a $75,000 house to a son or daughter or to parents, you can buy a house (let us say for cash just to keep things simple) and then sell the house to the recipient, taking a note, due in one year, for the value of the house. Then, during each subsequent year over the next several years, forgive up to $10,000 of the amount of the note and write a new note, due in one year, for the remainder.

Similar giving arrangements came under scrutiny beginning in 1977 (the first year following the **Tax Reform Act of 1976**), the IRS claiming that such arrangements were nothing more than a disguised gift, taxable in the year during which it was made.

Federal tax courts have since determined that such gifts may be made and can qualify under the annual exclusion. If you're planning to make such a gift, here's what our legal consultants advise:

1. Obtain an appraisal of the property.
2. The note should be negotiable and secured by the property.
3. The note should be interest-bearing for the going, current rate of interest for such notes.
4. Use a single note that is reduced by $10,000 each year and replaced by a new one, rather than a series of $10,000 notes, one of which is forgiven each year.
5. Properly record the mortgage and deed relating to the transferred property.

Our legal consultants also advise that if you do make such a gift, you also make provision through your will, through a trust, or through the purchase of life insurance, naming the recipient of the gift as beneficiary to assure that the house won't be lost at your death due to the recipient's inability to pay off the note.

Charitable Gifts

Charitable gifts made through your will may be deducted from the taxable value of your estate, just as charitable gifts made during your lifetime may be deducted from your income during the year given.

You recall that with ordinary gifts the acquisition cost to the giver is used as the basis for the value of a gift on the date of transfer to the recipient, even though its value may have appreciated since acquisition by the giver.

With **charitable** gifts, the giver may take a deduction from income for the year during which the gift is given, for the **appreciated** value of the gift, **without** paying a capital gains tax for the increased value of the gift.

If, for example, you acquired securities some time ago at a cost of $8,000 that today, several years later, are worth $24,000, you may take a charitable income tax deduction for the $24,000 appreciated value of the securities without incurring a capital gains tax liability for the securities' greater value.

So, in making the above charitable contribution, you would save money two ways by giving it away. You would obtain a charitable deduction of $24,000 from current income, and you avoid payment of personal capital gains tax on the $16,000 increase in the value of the securities.

The same principle would apply to other **charitable** gifts of real estate, works of art, etc.

WARNING: *The laws of many states prohibit your giving more than one-third or one-half of your estate to charity if you are married or have children. Such provisions of your will may be set aside by the court if contested by your heirs.*

Statutes relating to wills may be changed at any time, so determine the law of your state before planning major charitable testamentary gifts. (Of course, you can often get around such laws by creating an inter vivos trust giving property to a charitable organization while retaining possession and use of the property during your lifetime.)

Unmarried Cohabitants

Unmarried cohabitants are deprived of benefits of the marital estate tax exclusion, just as they are deprived of many other income tax benefits available to married couples. But with the number of couples living together beginning to exceed the number of married couples in certain age brackets, growing numbers of life insurance companies are willing to concede that cohabitants do, indeed, have an "insurable interest" in each other and will write policies on male and female cohabitants with premiums for each policy to be paid by the other. Nontaxable gifts may also be made by one cohabitant to another, and living trusts may also be established.

Gifts for Educational and Medical Expenses

The Economic Recovery Tax Act of 1981 permits an unlimited gift tax exclusion to the giver for any amount paid directly to an educational organization for tuition and to a health care provider for medical care or services. The exclusion is granted without regard to the relationship between the giver and the recipient.

PAYMENT OF GIFT TAX

You will incur a gift tax liability if, during any year, you give more than $10,000 to any one individual. A married couple will incur a gift tax liability if, during any year, they give more than $20,000 to any one individual.

If you want to give more than $10,000 to someone during a single year and do not wish to deduct the excess amount from your lifetime equivalent tax exemption, as previously explained, you can pay the gift tax as provided for by the 1981 Act.

Payment of gift tax is based upon rates shown in the **Unified Rate Schedule** on page 232. On a gift of $15,000 ($5,000 over the exempt amount), the gift tax liability would be $1,800 plus 20 percent of the $5,000 excess ($1,000) for a total gift tax of $2,800. Total tax on a $50,000 gift would be $8,200 plus 24 percent of $10,000, a hefty total of $10,600.

If you do incur a gift tax liability during any year, you'll need to file an IRS Form 709, **United States Gift Tax Return**. The gift tax return must be filed and any gift tax paid "no later than the 15th day of the fourth month following the close of the calendar year" (which reads like April 15 to us). However, for a year in which the donor dies, the gift tax return must be filed

and any gift tax paid no later than the due date for filing the deceased donor's estate tax return.

Just to make sure that everything about computing your possible gift tax liability is perfectly clear, we include the IRS explanation, "Gift taxes are computed by applying the unified rate schedule to cumulative lifetime transfers and subtracting the taxes payable for prior taxable periods." Got that?

For additional information on computing estate and gift taxes, ask the IRS (via a toll-free 800 number in your local phone book) for IRS publication 408, **Federal Estate and Gift Taxes**.

While you've got them on the phone, you might as well ask for a copy of **Instructions for Form 706, United States Estate Tax Return**, along with a copy of Form 706, the actual estate tax return. The instructions include information that can be useful in estate planning. Both the form and its instructions could be placed in any file of documents to be given to your executor.

FINDING A FINANCIAL PLANNER: *About now you may be getting the idea that what we've been writing about barely scratches the surface as far as the potential benefits of financial planning are concerned. You're right.*

But what to do? You could turn to your lawyer, accountant, banker, insurance agent, or a stockbroker—and you should—but probably not as your financial advisor. The mere fact of being an attorney, CPA (certified public accountant), banker, insurance agent, or stockbroker doesn't necessarily make a man or woman a competent financial advisor.

Obviously, stockbrokers and insurance agents see the world of financial planning through different and somewhat myopic eyes. Bankers like to base your financial plan in their trust department, and, of course, attorneys and accountants may not know as much about securities and insurance as your particular financial planning needs might require.

But turn to all of the people we've listed for their recommendations. Any of these professionals worth the framed certificate on his or her wall should know the names of several personal financial planners, one of whom may be right for you.

While you're turning, turn to friends, co-workers, neighbors, your dentist and doctor (notoriously bad investors who need financial planning assistance the way a leaky boat needs a bilge pump), and even to the president or financial chief of the company you work for, who may be able to give you the names of financial planners used by your employer's top executives.

If you still haven't been able to locate a satisfactory financial advisor, you can write to two national organizations, both of which will send you the names of financial planners in your area:

The International Association of Financial Planning
Suite 120-C

*5775 Peachtree Dunwoody Road
Atlanta, Georgia   30342
(404) 252-9600*

*The Institute of Certified Financial Planners
9725 East Hampden Avenue
Denver, Colorado   80231
(303) 751-7600*

Membership in either of these organizations doesn't guarantee that an advisor is highly qualified. The Institute of Certified Financial Planners designation of **Certified Financial Planner (CFP)** *means only that the member has passed a correspondence course in estate planning, insurance, investments, taxes, and retirement and employee benefits.*

One way to evaluate a financial planner's credentials is to ask about professional training and certification in related fields. There's no law in any state that prevents anyone from calling himself or herself a financial planner, but you can find out if a financial planner is a licensed stockbroker, real estate agent, certified public accountant, or an attorney. None of these are assurance of expert financial planning, but they are a measure of the planner's general background and professional attitude.

Though a law degree is no guarantee of financial planning ability, there is one advantage of using a lawyer–financial planner: confidentiality of the attorney–client relationship that is protected from court and IRS probing.

When interviewing a prospective financial planner, you should ask if he or she receives commissions or fees on securities, limited partnerships, insurance, real estate, or other investments that you purchase. Not that receipt of such fees and commissions is unethical, but you should be informed of any such arrangements.

Other questions you'll want to ask are:

- *How many clients does the planner personally service and how large are they? If most of the planner's accounts are larger than yours, or if there are too many accounts to service yours properly, your planning may not receive the attention it needs.*
- *What types of clients does the planner serve? Are they people like you, or are they corporations, investment clubs, and very wealthy individuals?*
- *How long has he/she been acting as a full-time financial planner? What is his or her track record? Ask for the names of two or three client references.*
- *What resources does the planner have for dealing with complex issues such as taxes, trusts, and estate planning? What specialists does the planner consult with and what are* **their** *qualifications?*
- *How does the planner charge for his or her services: by the hour, a percentage of the amount invested, a percentage of your plan's growth/income, an initial fixed fee for a basic plan with an hourly or monthly charge for continuing follow-up?*

You should also be prepared to answer a number of questions that will help the planner best determine how to advise you:

- *What are your financial goals?*
- *How much are you worth and in what types of assets?*
- *What is your income and what are your expenses, liabilities, and responsibilities?*
- *What are your career and long-term life expectations?*

One warning: beware of financial planners, sometimes affiliated with an insurance company, brokerage house, mutual fund, or financial planning franchise operation, who do little more than grind out computer-generated "customized" financial plans to get new customers.

For a continuing inside look at what's going on in the financial planning business, subscribe to:

*Financial Planner Magazine
Suite 120-C
5775 Peachtree Dunwoody Road
Atlanta, Georgia   30342*

If you're in a hurry to find out as much as you can as fast as you can, ask for the magazine's annual index, and then order half a dozen back issues featuring the information you're most interested in.

OTHER RELEVANT TAX PROVISIONS OF ERTA

There are several major provisions of the **Economic Recovery Tax Act of 1981** that may also figure in your estate planning.

The Act stipulates that if the value of your ownership of a closely held business exceeds 35 percent of the adjusted gross value of your estate, your estate will have fourteen years in which to pay estate taxes attributable to *that* interest. Assuming a total gross estate valued at $500,000, with $180,000 (36 percent) of that value comprised of stock in a closely held corporation or in some other nonincorporated business, your estate would have up to fourteen years in which to pay any estate tax attributable to your $180,000 interest in the closely held business.

During the first four years following your death, your estate would be required to pay only *interest* on the tax due and thereafter could pay the tax in as many as ten equal installments of principal and interest. A special interest rate of 4 percent would apply.

Under provisions of the Act, farmland, wooded land, and other land used in a closely held business on the date of your death and for five of the eight years prior to your death may be valued for estate tax purposes at its "special-use value" rather than at its "highest and best value," such as its value as a residential development.

The special-use valuation requirement is met if the land is "employed"—in other words, used—by you or a member of your family during five of the eight years preceding your death. For *this* purpose of the Act, family members are designated as your spouse, parents, brothers, sisters, children, stepchildren, and the spouses and lineal descendants and their spouses of those individuals.

Under the Act, the value of qualifying land may be reduced for estate tax purposes by as much as $750,000 from its highest and best use during 1983 and thereafter.

The Act provides that "terminable interests" designated through your will to your spouse be considered as an interspousal transfer and thus deducted from the taxable value of your estate.

Okay, but what is a "terminable interest"? Under IRS definition, a "terminable interest" consists of assets that an individual may use during his or her lifetime (in other words, from which he or she may derive income) but that he or she may not transfer— give away, sell, or convey through a will, for example.

Thus, under terms of the 1981 Act, you could establish a trust through your will specifying, for example, that its **assets** be held in trust for your children, but that **income** from the trust be paid to your spouse during his or her lifetime. The income from such a trust is now a qualifying "terminable interest," is not taxed to your estate, and is income tax free to your spouse.

Additional information, as well as instructions for the completion of forms for the creation of such a trust, are provided beginning on page 267 of the following section, Creating Your Own Trust.

Provisions of the **Economic Recovery Tax Act of 1981** relating to wills, estates, gifts, and trusts are many and complex, and you should consult with a well-qualified attorney or estate planning specialist before engaging in anything beyond the most basic estate planning.

DECLARATION OF GIFT

It's entirely possible, perhaps even likely, that planned giving could play a major part in the formation of your estate program—gifts to children, gifts of real estate, securities, and insurance all having been touched upon earlier in this section.

If you expect to make substantial gifts as a part of your estate plan, you may want to consider making use of Form 52.1, Declaration of Gift, on page F363. The completely filled-in and notarized declaration can:

- Place on the record a gift of your property that the Internal Revenue Service or probate court might otherwise argue should be counted as part of your estate.
- Eliminate claims by acquisitive heirs that the gift recipient's possession of your stamp or coin collection, or boat or fur coat, was the result of theft or borrowing rather than receipt of the item as a gift from you.
- Eliminate claims that property given to an indi-

vidual shortly before your death was not *legally* transferred to the recipient and thus is part of the "rest and remainder" of your estate for distribution to heirs.

- Help the recipient avoid difficulties with the IRS should he or she be questioned, in connection with a tax audit, for example, about ownership of certain assets that appear to be inconsistent with the recipient's reported income.
- Prove legal ownership, should the time come when the recipient may need to sell or transfer your gift to someone else.

One way of avoiding these kinds of problems— for the recipient, for your estate, and perhaps for yourself—is to make a formal record of the transfer by using the **Declaration of Gift**.

The declaration records the date of gift, the names of the giver and the recipient, the value of the item, and a brief description of the item. The accompanying Certificate of Notary eliminates any question that the declaration may be forged or perhaps may have been completed before or after the actual date on which you made the gift.

Our legal consultants point out that the declaration is an ideal means of recording the gift of cash, jewelry, a stamp collection, silverware, valuable antiques, or works of art, etc. In the case of most gifts, except cash and securities, it's a good idea to obtain a written appraisal of the gift's value from a qualified appraiser—or two or three appraisers if the gift is costly and its value is likely to be disputed.

The obtaining of a written appraisal is especially important when making a charitable contribution of a work of art, antique, or collection of one kind or another, since it's almost as hard for the IRS to accept the value of those kinds of charitable deductions as it is for some people not to step on a crack in the sidewalk.

Note the value of the gift in the appropriate place on the declaration and attach a copy of the appraisal. Give the original declaration to the recipient; place one copy with your important papers; and give one copy to your attorney, the executor of your estate, and/or your tax consultant.

CAUTION: The Declaration of Gift should not be counted on to serve as a legal instrument for the transfer of title or ownership of property, such as real estate, securities, an auto or boat, etc., for which other means of transfer are traditional and legally required.

A sample declaration describing the gift of real estate is provided on the following two pages. Since the Declaration of Gift can also be utilized in relation to the establishment of simple trusts, a declaration and completed sample are also provided in the following section. That section's completed sample (on page 271) describes the gift of personal property and may also be of interest.

Sample of Form 52.1/F363

Declaration of Gift

TO ALL TO WHOM THESE PRESENTS SHALL COME OR MAY CONCERN, KNOW THAT on this __3rd__

day of ___April___, 19 _85_, I, ___Tilden P. Holladay, Sr.___,

of ___Lazy B Ranch, Box 14, Star Route___ ___Gunlock___ ___Utah___ ___84733___,
               Street   *City*   *State*   *Zip*

being of sound and disposing mind and memory, do hereby irrevocably give, bestow and deliver up to ___

___Tilden P. Holladay, III___,

of ___318 Trinity Lane___ ___Ogden___ ___Utah___ ___84401___,
               Street   *City*   *State*   *Zip*

all of my right, title and interest in the following described property valued at ___eight thousand
seven hundred dollars___ ($ _8,700.00_):

The Southwest Quarter (SW/4) of the Northeast Quarter (NE/4) of

Section Thirty-Seven (37), Block G-12, G. C. & S. F. Ry. Co., Box Elder

County, Utah, and containing forty (40) acres, more or less.

IN WITNESS WHEREOF, I hereunto set my hand and seal on the date above mentioned.

Tilden P. Holladay, Sr.

* *

CERTIFICATE OF NOTARY

STATE OF   Utah   )
) ss:
COUNTY OF   Iron   )

On this ___3rd___ day of ___April___, 19 _85_, before me personally came and appeared
___Tilden P. Holladay, Sr.___, known, and known to me, to be the individual described in
and who executed the foregoing instrument, and who duly acknowledged to me that he/she executed same for the purpose therein contained.

IN WITNESS WHEREOF, I hereunto set my hand and official seal.

Phyllis Moorhouse
             Notary Public

My commission expires: ___September 6, 1987___

Sample of Form 52.1 (*Continued*)

Declaration of Gift

From

Tilden P. Holladay, Sr.
Lazy B Ranch
Box 14
Star Route
Gunlock, Utah 84733

to

Tilden P. Holladay, III
318 Trinity Lane
Ogden, Utah 84401

Dated _____ April 3, _____ 19 __ 85 __

One of the first steps in preparing to write your will should be an evaluation of your estate. Only then can you have a good idea of what should be included in your will, how much your estate is worth, and whether you should establish a giving program, plus a simple trust or two to provide for maximum tax savings.

You can also use such an evaluation as a starting point for building balance into your estate—balance so that it isn't heavily laden with property that could suddenly place hardship on your family at a time when they're least prepared to face payment schedules for land, business expenses, and bank loan obligations.

Such a situation could force an immediate, or at least inopportune, sale of property that might otherwise have continued to provide income or that could have been sold at a better price had time been available. Such a condition can be alleviated by:

1. Providing life insurance, payable to the beneficiaries of your will, that will be adequate to liquidate financial obligations related to any inherited property. It may be wise to present ownership of such insurance policies to your beneficiaries as a gift (as previously explained on page 237) to prevent the policies' proceeds from being counted as part of the value of your taxable estate.
2. Leaving instructions in your will with respect to which assets should be sold first in the event that adequate cash is not available. (A judgment against your estate, related to an accident in which you lost your life, could unexpectedly deplete your estate of much of its value, for example.)

Provisions of the **Economic Recovery Tax Act of 1981** that permit fourteen-year payment of estate taxes due on a qualifying closely held business and that permit "special-use" valuation of qualifying farmland or other land used in connection with a closely held family business (as noted previously on page 236) should also be taken into account.

In evaluating your estate, remember that assets that you transfer to others prior to your death (but which may remain in your possession) or that you transfer to others prior to your death through establishment of a trust—as provided for in the following section, Creating Your Own Trust—should **NOT** be included in the inventory of your estate.

Use Form 53.1 (page F365) to make an estimate of the potential value of your estate. Kept with other papers to be examined at the time of your death, it will also ease the burden of your executor in fulfilling his or her responsibilities.

If you are married and live in a community-property state, remember that almost everything you own is probably one-half owned by your spouse (depending, usually, upon whether acquired before or after marriage and whether the property was inherited or was a gift). Much of what your spouse owns is probably community property too.

In that case, the best way to evaluate your estate is to include the estimated value of everything you believe to be jointly owned under that heading on Form 53.1 and then divide by half to obtain a figure to insert after **ESTIMATED VALUE OF ESTATE AT DEATH, My Share of Jointly Owned,** on the last page of the form.

If you're not married, or are married and do not live in a community-property state, you may still share ownership of a fair amount of property (possibly your house if you are married), and you might also share ownership of a boat or expensive yard or garden tools with a friend or neighbor.

In those cases, list the estimated value of your interest under **Jointly Owned,** followed by a single number (as an aid to your executor) showing the proportion of your interest: $5,000–2, indicating that the value of *your* interest is $5,000 and that the proportion of your interest is one-half.

When you get to **BUSINESS INTERESTS,** item three, listing the extent of your interest in the shorthand of the form may become a bit less well-defined. The main thing is that **you** know what the value of those interests is to your estate.

If you're not married or don't live in a community-property state, listing the estimated value of your interest in a sole proprietorship, partnership, or close corporation is fairly straightforward. Just show your interest as you would with any other property. If you own one-third of a business valued at $2 million, just show $666,666–3 under the heading **Jointly Owned,** again, as an aid to your executor.

If you own the same proportion of the same business but are married and live in a community-property state, you could most easily show your interest as $333,333 under **Owned by Me** since half of your $666,666 investment would, in the event of divorce or your death, be judged the property of your spouse.

If a mortgage exists or payments are due, or if you owe money to banks of others, show those amounts under **Amount Owing** within the appropriate classification.

COMPLETING THE EVALUATION FORM

Before beginning the evaluation, fill in your name, address, and date at the top of the form so that if it later ends up floating around your attorney's or executor's office outside its file, anyone finding it will know where it belongs.

REAL ESTATE

Property listed under REAL ESTATE might be your home (possibly jointly owned), a ranch, farm, or other undeveloped property. Show street address or general location and number of acres. The precise location will be shown on copies of deeds, which you should keep with your will, insurance policies, and other papers. Real estate that you consider part of a business should be listed under BUSINESS INTERESTS.

REAL ESTATE

Property	Owned by Me	Jointly Owned	Amount Owing
Residence, 2417 White Water Arroyo, Douglas, Arizona		$35,000	$7,500

SECURITIES

Securities would include stocks and bonds purchased for long-term investment and speculation, mutual fund shares, credit and savings and loan association shares, U.S. Savings Bonds, etc. If a stock was purchased and is still owned on margin, show the percentage on margin as a value in dollars under **Amount Owing**.

SECURITIES

Property	Owned by Me	Jointly Owned	Amount Owing
1,000 shares IBM common	$52,500		$26,250

BUSINESS INTERESTS

For each sole proprietorship, partnership, or corporation in which you have an active interest (rather than ownership of stock as an investment), list the estimated value of your interest. List your share of each business's accounts payable and other debts under **Amount Owing**. Although your estate would not be liable for a share of the liabilities of a corporation in which you own stock, those debts would reduce the value of that stock to your estate and, as such, should probably still be indicated under **Amount Owing**.

If you are unmarried, or are married and live in a non-community property state, you might show your interest as:

BUSINESS INTERESTS

Property	Owned by Me	Jointly Owned	Amount Owing
Killer Force Exterminators, Incorporated	$2,000,000-3		$50,000

If you are married and live in a community-property state, you might show the same interest as:

Property	Owned by Me	Jointly Owned	Amount Owing
Killer Force Exterminators, Incorporated	$1,000,000-6		$25,000

VEHICLES

List year, make, and model of each vehicle under **Property**; list your interest under **Owned by Me** or **Jointly Owned**, etc.

VEHICLES

Property	Owned by Me	Jointly Owned	Amount Owing
1976 Ford Pick-up	$2,900		
1980 Mazda RX-7	$9,100		$2,500

TOOLS AND EQUIPMENT

Follow procedure described above for VEHICLES.

TOOLS AND EQUIPMENT

Property	Owned by Me	Jointly Owned	Amount Owing
24" Mud Mulker gas engine multi-purpose garden tool		$400-2	

PETS, LIVESTOCK, AND CATTLE

Follow procedure described above for VEHICLES.

PETS, LIVESTOCK, AND CATTLE

Property	Owned by Me	Jointly Owned	Amount Owing
4-year-old bay gelding "Lindy"		$1,750-2	

FURNITURE

List the estimated value of each item of furniture, including carpets, draperies, and antiques, that would accrue to your estate. Show under **Amount Owing** any amount that may be due on any of the above.

APPLIANCES

List the estimated value of major appliances, such as refrigerator, freezer, stove, microwave oven, washer, dryer, sewing machine, etc., that would accrue to your estate. Show under **Amount Owing** any amount that may be due on any of these.

MISCELLANEOUS PERSONAL PROPERTY

Under this heading list all jewelry, furs, objects of art, collections of books, records or tapes, coins, stamps, cameras, guns, hunting and fishing equipment, television, radios, stereo equipment, camping equipment, musical instruments, etc.

LIFE INSURANCE

List the name of the insurer and the policy number (for your executor). Make a list of the amount of benefit payable to your estate.

EMPLOYMENT BENEFITS

List any employer group insurance, retirement, or pension plans that would accrue to your estate. If possible, list the insurer and policy number. Show the estimated value to the estate.

GOVERNMENT BENEFITS

List any social security, veterans, military, or civil service benefits that would accrue to your estate. Again include the estimated value.

ROYALTIES AND PATENTS

Follow procedure described above for GOVERN-MENT BENEFITS.

CASH

Show under **Owned by Me** or **Jointly Owned** all money on deposit in personal or joint checking and savings accounts, on deposit at credit unions and savings associations, in safe-deposit boxes of other vaults, all cash on hand, etc.

MISCELLANEOUS RECEIVABLES

The receivables would include any mortgages, deeds of trust, or promissory notes held by you; any rents due from income property owned by you; and payments due for professional or personal services or property sold by you that are not fully paid for by the purchaser.

MISCELLANEOUS

List any property not shown above.

MISCELLANEOUS PAYABLES

List any debts not shown above under the **Amount Owing** portion of any other classification.

ESTIMATED VALUE OF ESTATE AT DEATH

After adding up the totals under each of the following headings, separately list them as follows:

ESTIMATED VALUE OF ESTATE AT DEATH

Total Owned by Me:	$500,000
My Share of Jointly Owned:	100,000
Life Insurance Benefits Due My Estate at Death:	200,000
	$800,000
Minus Amount Owed:	200,000
Total Estimated Value of Estate at Death:	$600,000

TYPES OF OWNERSHIP: *The type of ownership under which you hold certain assets can often work to your advantage in planning your estate. Some types of ownership you may not be able to do much about; other types of ownership can simplify the transfer of property when you die by keeping it out of your will and out of probate.*

Joint tenancy allows property (in which joint tenants have an undivided interest) to pass legally to the survivor(s) upon the death of a joint tenant. Since state laws with respect to joint tenancy vary somewhat, to make absolutely certain that a joint tenancy will be treated as such upon the death of any joint tenant, be sure that the document of ownership states, "_____ _____ and _____ as joint tenants, survivor take all."

The majority of joint tenants are husband and wife as joint tenant owners of their house, but any two or more persons may be joint tenant owners of almost any kind of property. The proportion of ownership of each would be shown in the **agreement of joint tenancy** *or in the title or deed to the property.*

Property owned in joint tenancy does not pass through your will. Except for ownership shared with your spouse, the percentage of property that you own as a joint tenant will be counted as part of your estate for federal estate tax purposes even though it doesn't pass through your will.

Ownership shared with others as **tenants in common** *does not provide for right of survivorship. If you and a friend share ownership of a weekend cabin or a boat as tenants in common on a fifty–fifty basis, each having contributed one-half toward the purchase price, and one of you dies, that portion of the property owned by the decedent passes to his or her heirs, NOT to the surviving tenant in common.*

Any number of persons may share ownership as tenants in common, the percentage of ownership of each tenant in common being shown in the **agreement of tenancy in common** *or in the title or deed to the property.*

In the eight states having **community-property laws*** *(Arizona, California, Idaho, Louisiana, Nevada, New Mexico, Texas, and Washington), one-half of almost all property owned by either spouse is deemed*

---

*In many states a surviving husband or wife has claim to any real estate that you may own at the time of your death, a right that you cannot "will away" to another person. States having such laws as of January 1, 1982, were:

Alabama	Kentucky	Oregon
Alaska	Louisiana	Pennsylvania
Arkansas	Maryland	Rhode Island
Delaware	Michigan	South Carolina
Florida	Minnesota	Tennessee
Georgia	New Hampshire	Utah
Hawaii	New Jersey	Vermont
Illinois	North Carolina	West Virginia
Kansas	Ohio	Wisconsin

The restriction also applies to residents of New York who were married prior to September 1, 1930, and to residents of Puerto Rico and the District of Columbia.

community property. Property owned by either spouse prior to marriage, property acquired by either spouse as a gift, and property inherited by either spouse is generally excluded. But other property, such as real estate, securities, home furnishings, vehicles, etc., purchased by either spouse with money earned by either spouse after marriage is deemed community property (one-half owned by each spouse), regardless of who paid for it and regardless of which spouse's name may be on the title.

Either spouse may give or sell his or her portion of community property to the other by executing the required legal documents.

Sole ownership is, in many respects, the simplest form of ownership. If you own it, you can sell it or transfer ownership as a gift; you can use it as collateral for a loan; you can transfer it through an *inter vivos* or *testamentary trust;* or you can leave it to (almost) anyone through your will.

If you believe that your bequest might be controversial, though, it might be a good idea to make the transfer through an *inter vivos* trust, with the right to retain possession and use of the property until your death.

During 1982 the will of a man who died that year in New York included a bequest of $50,000 to the Palestine Liberation Organization (PLO), a group having a reputation for international terrorism. The bequest was subject to legal controversy, opponents having filed suit to have that provision of the will set aside as contrary to the public good.

If you'd like to leave a few million for the care of stray cats, though, it's perfectly okay. That provision in scores of wills has been through the courts many times and sustained nary a scratch.

Earlier chapters have introduced some of the language of wills and estates and will making, have shown how taxes can affect your estate—and have shown how planning can affect your estate taxes. In this chapter we'll take apart one of this section's wills to provide the paragraph-by-paragraph knowledge you'll need to complete and use the wills provided by this book.

Although many portions of a will do not exist to comply specifically with a particular legal requirement, they are part of tradition and have been made a part of this book's wills because judges and attorneys, estate tax officials, insurance companies, trust companies, and others have become used to working with them. Every paragraph of every one of the following wills does, however, serve a specific purpose—none have been included without reason.

LETTER PERFECT: *In making your will it's important to know that although all fifty states accept the wills in this book having blanks that you fill in, many states will not recognize as valid a will that bears the mark of even the least change or correction. If you make a mistake completing any page, obtain another photocopy and begin again.*

There's no requirement that any of the wills included in this book be completed using a typewriter. Sufficient space has been provided to fill in all blanks by hand. If you do complete a will by hand, use ink or a nonerasable ballpoint pen and print or write very clearly.

Your name will appear twice at the beginning of your will—once under the heading **Last Will and Testament** and once immediately following the initial "I," which begins the first paragraph.

The following two blanks should contain only the name of the city or town, county, and state of your legal residence—the jurisdiction where you want your will probated. It's been argued that your street address should be included also, but to include a street address could entail the need to write a new will in the event you move. This way no change will be required if you continue to live in the same town.

The initial paragraph further states your declaration that you are of sound and disposing mind, that you are aware that you are making your **Last Will and Testament,** and that you are revoking all previous wills and codicils.

Attorneys advise that the phrase "revoking all previous wills and codicils" be included even though you may never have previously made a will. This is so that any attempted forgery would at least have to be

dated later than the will you are now executing, which makes the job of the forger considerably more difficult.

Last Will and Testament
of
John Williamson

I, _____John Williamson_____, of _____

Chicago	Cook	Illinois
City/Town	*County*	*State*

being of sound and disposing mind, do hereby make, publish and declare the following to be my **Last Will and Testament**, revoking all previous wills and codicils made by me.

The next paragraph identifies the maker's spouse and identifies living children by name and birth date (since this sample is the will of a married man having minor children). Some attorneys make it a practice to include the addresses of children, but our consultants suggest that childrens' addresses, updated along with those of your executor, beneficiaries, family members, and attorney be recorded separately (see Form 51.1 on page F359) and kept with your will and other important papers.

Unused space for the listing of children should either be X'd out or be eliminated by using a typist's "white-out" solution prior to making a photocopy of any of the wills described in this section.*

I declare that I am married to Lucinda Grant Williamson XXXXXXXXXXX and that all references to "my wife" in this will are references to her. I have ____two____ children whose names and birth dates are:

Robert	Weston	Williamson	Feb. 6, 1965
First Name	*Middle*	*Last*	*Date of Birth*
Rayette	Martina	Williamson	Nov. 4, 1970
First Name	*Middle*	*Last*	*Date of Birth*
XXXXXXXXXXXXXXXXXXXXXXXXXXXXXXXXXXXXXXXXXXXXXX			
First Name	*Middle*	*Last*	*Date of Birth*
XXXXXXXXXXXXXXXXXXXXXXXXXXXXXXXXXXXXXXXXXXXXXX			
First Name	*Middle*	*Last*	*Date of Birth*
XXXXXXXXXXXXXXXXXXXXXXXXXXXXXXXXXXXXXXXXXXXXXX			
First Name	*Middle*	*Last*	*Date of Birth*

Use the next brief statement to declare that you have "no" deceased children or to state the number of deceased children.

I have ____one____ deceased children.

One of the characteristics of a well-written will is its ability to provide for future contingencies and for

---

*Note: All insertion rules (or the continuation of a rule on a following line) left blank *should be X'ed out to protect against the possibility of tampering.*

the unexpected. The following paragraph provides for the birth or adoption of additional children and for the inclusion of them within the context of "my children" as referred to in the will. Your will should be replaced with a new one, however, as soon as possible after the birth or adoption of any child.

All references to "my children" in this will include all of the above-named children and also any child hereafter born to or adopted by me.

First Proviso

The following statement, sometimes headed WILLS NOT CONTRACTUAL, has been included in our wills for married couples specifically to state that their wills are not contractual, thus retaining for both husband and wife the unquestioned right to revise or revoke their wills at any time.

FIRST

My wife and I are executing wills at approximately the same time in which each is the primary beneficiary of the other. These wills are not being made because of any contractual agreement between us, and either will may at any time be revoked by either maker at the sole discretion thereof.

Second Proviso

The next provision, sometimes called APPOINT-MENT OF EXECUTOR, lists the primary and alternate executors named by the maker. Some attorneys include the addresses of both individuals in this paragraph, but we feel that this information is best recorded separately so that it can be easily updated without need to revise the will.

SECOND

I appoint my wife _____ Lucinda Grant Williamson _____ as independent executrix of my will. If she is unable or unwilling to act, or to continue to act, as executrix of my will, I then appoint _____ Henry Combstock Sherman _____ as executor/executrix of my will.

My executor or executrix, whether original, substitute or successor, shall hereinafter be referred to as "my executor."

It's essential that you give careful consideration to the naming of an executor of your will. The usual first choice for married couples is the maker's husband or wife, especially those with children. The surviving cohabitant is often a sound choice for cohabitants.

Single men and women of less than middle age often choose a trusted friend of about the same age. This is practical because age has not yet become a major factor in a person's year-to-year survival chances. Older men and women often name a younger person, frequently one of their own children, because a younger person is more likely to survive an older individual. There is no reason why your executor may not also be someone who receives a devise or bequest under the terms of your will. This is a common occurrence when a family member is named as executor of a will.

Your executor will need to have wide discretionary powers regarding the management of your estate if your will is to provide for unforeseeable circumstances. He or she should be someone of integrity, judgment, and maturity who is familiar with your family and financial situation, who is at least acquainted with your principal beneficiaries, and who has no personality conflict with your family or business associates.

The following provision very generally states the powers of the executor relative to the trustee of the trust established later in this will. The responsibilities of an executor of a will that does not establish a trust are usually much greater than those of a will that does establish a trust.

My executor shall have the same powers, rights, obligations and immunities as conferred by this will on the Trustee over the trust estate.

Nearly every jurisdiction requires that the executor of a will be bonded for the faithful performance of his or her duties. Since you wouldn't appoint an executor you didn't trust anyway, the following paragraph has been included to spare your estate the expense of paying for such a bond.

No bond or other security of any kind shall be required of any executor appointed under this will.

If your will is complex or your estate is large, in which case you probably won't be using one of the wills provided by this book, you may want to consider naming coexecutors, your spouse and a bank, or your spouse and a law firm, for example.

Third Proviso

The next paragraph, or one similar to it, is found in nearly every will since the law requires that funeral expenses, taxes, and debts be paid. The provision differs from those in some wills in that it specifies payment of "all of my debts subject to statute of limitations" rather than "all of my debts." This stipulation eliminates the need for payment of alleged old debts, sometimes difficult to refute, which seem to descend upon an estate when death notices are published.

THIRD

I direct that my executor pay all of my funeral expenses, all state and federal estate, inheritance and succession taxes, administration costs and all of my debts subject to statute of limitations, except mortgage notes secured by real estate, as soon as practical.

Although it may be "practical" to pay off the mortgage on your house very soon after your death, it may not be wise to do so if your spouse should desire to keep on living in the house. The above provision gives your executor some leeway in handling his or her financial obligation.

Fourth Proviso

Our sample will being one of a husband, the next paragraph gives that portion of the estate remaining after payment of funeral expenses, taxes, debts, and other expenses to the testator's wife **IF** she survives him for a stipulated time. (You are familiar with the phrases "give, devise and bequeath" and "rest, residue and remainder" from Chapter 51.) The stipulation that the testator's wife survive him for a specified time is included to take into account the possibility that they may be involved in an accident that is fatal to both of them.

If a husband and wife were to be fatally injured in the same accident and it could be proven that the wife survived the husband by even a few minutes, it's possible that his will would be probated (with the resultant taxes, legal expenses, and other costs), leaving everything to her. Then **her** will would be probated, leading to needless payment of additional taxes, court costs, legal fees, etc.

In keeping with the second part of the following provision, the wife is bypassed if she does not survive her husband, thus leaving a larger proportion of his estate to their children.

One hundred and eighty days (six months) is a commonly stipulated period of time, since distribution of property, except for a living allowance to the surviving spouse, is rarely, if ever, made in less than that amount of time anyway.

FOURTH

I give, devise and bequeath all of the rest, residue and remainder of my estate, of whatever kind and character, and wherever located, to my wife _____Lucinda Grant Williamson_____, provided that she survives me by _____one hundred and eighty days_____.

The next paragraph is really a disinheritance clause naming the testator's children. Otherwise, a large proportion of the estate would, by law in some states, have to go to their minor children creating a number of trusteeship and/or property guardianship problems for the surviving spouse. The use of "hereinabove" limits disinheritance to a situation in which the testator's wife survives to care for them.

I make no provision hereinabove for my children _____Robert W. Williamson and Rayette M. Williamson_____, knowing that, as their mother, my wife will continue to be mindful of their needs and requirements.

Fifth Proviso

The following paragraph devises and bequeaths the rest, residue and remainder of the estate to the named trustee to be held in trust and administered as the will (in a later provision) directs.

FIFTH

If my wife does not survive me by _____one hundred and eighty days_____, then I give, devise and bequeath all of the rest, residue and remainder of my estate, of whatever kind and character, and wherever located, to _____Mary Jane Hiplatch_____ as Trustee, in trust, to be held, managed, administered and distributed as herein directed.

Sixth Proviso

The next paragraph, the SIXTH provision, names alternate trustees to serve in the event that the first-named trustee is unable or unwilling to act.

Selecting a primary and substitute trustees is even more difficult than naming an executor since a trustee must have all of the qualifications of an executor and must also be in a position to serve for an extended period of time. If the children of deceased parents are five or six years old at the time of their parents' death, a trustee could expect to administer the estate until the children come of age fifteen or sixteen years in the future.

Trustees' addresses should be updated regularly and kept with your will and other important papers.

SIXTH

If _____Mary Jane Hiplatch_____ is unable or unwilling to act, or to continue to act as Trustee, I then appoint _____Margretta Koehler_____ as Trustee with all of the same powers, rights, obligations and immunities. If the aforesaid _____Mary Jane Hiplatch_____ and _____XXXXXXX Margretta Koehler_____ are each unwilling or unable to act, or continue to act, as Trustee, I then appoint _____Timothy Detweiler_____ as Trustee with all of the same powers, rights, obligations and immunities.

Seventh Proviso

The next provision exempts the trustee from any requirement that he or she provide a bond.

SEVENTH

No bond for the faithful performance of duties shall be required of any Trustee appointed in this will.

Eighth Proviso

Some states base a trustee's compensation on a percentage of the amount of the trust; in other states the probate judge determines the amount of the trustee's fee based upon the amount of time and effort required to manage the trust. Often a family member or friend will waive the right to receive compensation for serving as trustee, particularly if he or she has received a bequest or devise under the will.

EIGHTH

The Trustee shall receive a reasonable fee for the services rendered by him or her.

Ninth Proviso

The following NINTH provision protects the trustee from liability except for gross negligence or willful breach of trust. Considering the responsibility involved and the long-term commitment required, the exemption from liability is not all that much for the trustee to do to reduce some of the risk of accepting an appointment as trustee.

NINTH

No Trustee of the trust created under this will shall at any time be held liable for any action or default of himself or herself, or of his or her agent, or of any other person in connection with the administration of the trust unless caused by his or her own gross negligence or by commission of a willful act of breach of trust.

Tenth Proviso

The next paragraph defines the authority of the trustee with regard to disbursement of principal and of income to meet expenses; it also specifies the state under whose laws the trust is to be administered.

TENTH

The Trustee shall have the sole authority to determine what shall be defined as income and what shall be defined as principal of the trust estate extablished under this will, and to determine what costs, taxes and other expenses shall be paid out of income and which shall be paid out of the principal in accordance with applicable statutes of the state of _____ Illinois _____.

Eleventh Proviso

The ELEVENTH provision sets forth the age at which children are to receive the trust (principal plus accrued income), most commonly stated as "not under the age of twenty-two" or " has attained his (or her) twenty-second birthday" (i.e., having completed his or her twenty-first year). This provision also permits the exercise of wide discretionary powers by the trustee with respect to invasion of the principal, distribution of funds, etc.

ELEVENTH

I direct that the entire trust shall be managed and administered as one trust until no living child of mine is under the age of XXXXXX _____ twenty-two _____. Until that time, the Trustee shall apply the principal and net income of the trust estate as follows:

So long as any of my children are under the age of XXXXXXXX _____ twenty-two _____, the net income of the trust shall be applied to the benefit of, or paid to, any or all of my children in such amounts and at such times as the Trustee shall at his or her discretion decide are necessary for their support, maintenance, welfare and education.

In the event that net income of the trust shall be insufficient to provide any of my said children with the funds necessary for adequate support, maintenance, welfare or education, the Trustee may invade the principal of the trust estate for this purpose. Payments of income or principal to any child of mine pursuant to this paragraph need not be taken into account by the Trustee in any later division of the trust estate into shares for distribution to my children or children of a deceased child of mine. No child of mine who has completed his or her _____ twenty-first _____ year shall receive any of the aforesaid payments from the trust estate.

The Trustee, in exercising his or her discretionary authority regarding the payment of principal or income of the trust estate to any of my children, or to the children of any of my deceased children, may take into consideration any other income or resources available to such beneficiary from sources outside the trust estate which may be known to the Trustee. The decision of the Trustee with regard to the necessity for making payments out of income or principal to any beneficiary shall be conclusive on all persons having any right or interest whatever in the trust.

The Trustee may apply more for or pay more to some bene-ficiaries than others and may entirely omit distribution to any of the beneficiaries during the continuance of the trust estate.

In the event that any of my children shall predecease me or die prior to the termination of the trust estate, interest of such child or children in the trust shall cease, except that if such deceased child or children shall be survived by any child or children of theirs, then the Trustee may apply that same interest for the child or children of a deceased child of mine to such extent as the Trustee at his or her sole descretion may deem necessary for support, maintenance, welfare or education. Payments of income or principal to any child or children of a deceased child of mine pursuant to this paragraph need not be taken into account by the Trustee in any subsequent division of the trust estate into shares for distribution to my children or to the child or children of any deceased child of mine.

The Trustee shall add to the principal of the trust estate any net interest or income not paid out in accordance with the powers, authority and discretion hereinabove conferred on the Trustee.

At such time when no child of mine who is living is under the age of _____ twenty-two _____, the trust shall terminate, and the Trustee shall as soon as practical distribute the residue and remainder of the trust estate in equal shares to my children then living. However, if any deceased child of mine has any child or children then surviving, then an equal share of the trust estate shall be distributed to said surviving issue of each deceased child of mine *per stirpes*.

Twelfth Proviso

The TWELFTH provision of the will gets as close as it's probably practical to do to setting forth specific authority and guidelines for the trustee's management and administration of the trust. The trustee is given what at first may appear to be a surprisingly wide latitude, taking into account a wide range of possible future circumstances that, at the will's writing, are impossible to predict accurately.

The trustee's authority, as described below, is almost exactly the same as stipulated for executors of the balance of the following chapter's wills.

TWELFTH

The Trustee, in addition to all other powers granted by this will and by law, shall have the following additional powers with respect to the trust estate, to be exercised from time to time at his or her discretion without further license or order of any court, subject to any limitations set forth elsewhere in this will:

Business Interests

To sell or otherwise liquidate, or to continue to operate at his or her discretion, any corporation, partnership or other business interest received by the trust estate.

Property of Trust Estate

To retain any and all property and securities of the trust estate for as long as he or she may deem advisable.

Management of Trust Estate

To invest, lease, rent, mortgage, insure, repair, improve or sell any and all real and personal property belonging to the trust estate as he or she may deem advisable.

Mortgages, Pledges and Deeds of Trust

To enforce any and all mortgages, pledges and deeds of trust held by the trust estate and to purchase at any sale thereunder any such real or personal property subject to any mortgage, pledge or deed of trust.

Litigation

To initiate or defend, at his or her discretion, any litigation affecting the trust estate.

Attorneys, Advisors and Agents

To employ and to pay from the trust estate reasonable compensation to such attorneys, accountants, brokers, and investment, tax and other advisors as he or she shall deem advisable.

Adjustment of Claims

To submit to arbitration, to compromise or to release or otherwise adjust, with or without compensation, any and all claims affecting the trust estate.

Distribution of Trust Estate

In distributing the trust estate, to make said distribution wholly or partly in kind by transferring or allotting such real or personal property or undivided interest therein.

Thirteenth Proviso

For the parents of a minor child or children, the THIRTEENTH provision of the will is one of the most important since it names those who would serve as guardians of the children in the event of both parents' deaths.

The nominating of guardians in parents' wills discloses, at a very crucial time, the names of exactly the people whom the parents would most want to care for their children—people with whom that eventuality has been discussed and, as much as possible, been prepared for.

Almost any lawyer or judge familiar with probate matters can recite scores of instances where parents' failure to name guardians has resulted in bitter court battles between children's grandparents or other family factions fighting for custody of the surviving children. Even when these contests are settled, emotional skirmishes often continue over religious training, education, and other matters, all to the emotional detriment of the children.

Occasionally, grandparents may serve as excellent guardians, but often, because of their advanced age, guardianship of young children is a burden they're not prepared to take on. The advanced age of grandparents is also a circumstance that could, within just a few years, subject the children to the trauma of yet another loss of those upon whom they have come to depend as a fixed star in their lives.

Brothers and sisters of the deceased parents often serve as ideal guardians, and reciprocal guardianship arrangements are often provisions of married brothers' and sisters' wills. There's no reason that friends can't serve as guardians, or, for that matter, that a formerly married or single person can't serve. Judges are showing increased willingness to approve parents' choice of a single individual as guardian by confirming such nominations through court appointment.

As with executors and trustees referred to earlier, guardians are exempted, in the following sample provision, from the need to obtain bond for the faithful performance of their responsibilities.

The matter of financial compensation to guardians for the cost of caring for your children should be discussed with the potential guardians before you and your spouse make out your wills.

In the absence of proof that other adequate financial measures have been taken for the support of children, the court will most likely provide an allowance from the property of the estate. But one of the best solutions may simply be to purchase sufficient life insurance on yourself, naming the possible guardians of your children as beneficiaries, then transferring *ownership* of the policy to the guardian(s) as a gift, as described earlier on page 237. Taking such a step will exclude the value of the proceeds of the policy from your taxable estate.

Another option would be to establish a trust fund for the benefit of your children, making the proceeds of the life insurance policy payable to the trust (also as a gift from you to the trust) to be administered by the trustee for the benefit of the children.

THIRTEENTH

If my wife does not survive me, I then appoint _____Robert and Jane Johnson_____ as guardians of the person of each of my minor children, and I hereby request that they seek appointment as guardians of their estates. If both of them qualify and thereafter one of them ceases to act, one may act alone.

If one of them ceases to qualify, or if both cease to act after qualifying, I then appoint _____Saul and Leah Weingarten_____ as new guardians of the person of each of my minor children, and I hereby request that they seek appiontment as guardians of their estates. If both qualify and thereafter either ceases to act, one may act alone.

No bond or other security of any kind shall be required of any of the above parties for the faithful exercise of their responsibilities as guardian of the person or of the estate of any of my minor children.

Fourteenth Proviso

The following provision is frequently included by attorneys as an "insurance clause" in the event that the will or some provision of it is contested by anyone claiming to be an heir of the deceased.

FOURTEENTH

If any person, whether related to me by blood or in any other way, shall attempt, either directly or indirectly, to set aside the probate of my will or oppose any of the provisions hereof, and such person shall establish a right to any portion of my estate, then I give and bequeath the sum of one dollar ($1.00), only that, and no further interest whatever in my estate to such person.

Fifteenth Proviso

The FIFTEENTH paragraph of the will is another "insurance" provision, dealing with two eventualities:

1. That you may become a (married) resident of a community-property state and die before you have an opportunity to make a new will.
2. That although you may continue to maintain legal residence in a non-community property state, you may acquire property (such as a vacation home, real estate investment, or other assets) in a community-property state.

This provision also serves to make this will practical for use by current, married residents of those states that have community-property statutes.

FIFTEENTH

In the event that any of my property, or all of it, at the time of my death is community property under the laws of any jurisdiction, then my will shall be construed as referring only to my community-property interest therein.

Sixteenth Proviso

The SIXTEENTH paragraph is another frequently used "insurance" clause designed to keep as much of the will as possible from being "thrown out of court" in the event that one provision or another is declared invalid due to changes in your legal status, such as marriage or divorce, or the death or birth or adoption of a child whom you did not yet have time to take into account by making a new will.

SIXTEENTH

If any portion of my will shall be held illegal, invalid or otherwise inoperative, it is my intention that all of the other provisions hereof shall continue to be fully effective and operative insofar as is possible and reasonable.

Witnesses

A retired lawyer friend of mine told me to tell you, "The first thing you do after you've made out your will is don't sign it!" What he meant to say, of course, is that in order for your will to be valid it must be signed in the **collective** presence of all the required witnesses to whom you have declared your knowledge that you are signing your **Last Will and Testament.**

You cannot, in other words, merely ask, "Will you please witness my signing of this document?" You must say, "Please witness my signing of my **Last Will and Testament.**" The witnesses must know that **you** know that you are signing your will. And they all have to watch you sign it in the presence of each other. So remember, "The first thing you do after you've made out your will is don't sign it!"

IN WITNESS WHEREOF, I have hereunto set my hand and seal this _____16th_____ day of _____April_____, 19 __85__.

Robert W. Williamson

Signed, sealed, published and declared to be his **Last Will and Testament** by the within-named testator in the presence of all of us, who, in his presence and at his request, and in the presence of each other, have hereunto subscribed our names as witnesses:

Victor Vojnodich

2218 Calumet Park	Chicago	Illinois	60643
Street	City	State	Zip

Josef Holzbauer

7754 Pilsen	Chicago	Illinois	60608
Street	City	State	Zip

Jane Brown

995 Niles	Chicago	Illinois	60648
Street	City	State	Zip

Selecting your witnesses is another one of those decisions that requires a lot of thought. To begin with, good judgment and the law of many states dictate that you *exclude* from selection ALL PERSONS WHO RECEIVE ANY DEVISE OR BEQUEST UNDER THE WILL. That eliminates a lot of people who might otherwise be your most likely choices.

Your witnesses should be:

1. Younger than you are so they'll be likely to outlive you.
2. People who don't move around a lot so they can be easily located for court appearance to attest to the authenticity of your signature.
3. People whose signatures are easy to verify by comparison with other readily available signatures. This is in the event a witness can't be located or has died.

The table **Requirements for Wills in the United States** (see Chapter 51, pages 227–228) shows which states require two witnesses and which require three. Every lawyer we talked with about witnesses to wills suggested that although only two witnesses may be required in your state, you go ahead and use three anyway, particularly since your will just might have to be probated in a three-witness state if you move from a two-witness state and die before making a new will.

The inclusion of witnesses' social security numbers and/or addresses has been suggested as an added means of identification—that your witness is a particular John Jones or Mary Smith and not some one else of the same name.

You should, of course, keep your file of addresses of your executors, trustees, guardians, and witnesses up to date and filed along with other papers, such as trust agreements, life insurance, etc., that are kept with your will.

Form 54.1, an address record form, can be copied from time to time to record and file the latest addresses of people named in your will. It can be found on page F371.

SELF-PROVING AFFIDAVIT

In most states proper execution of a **Self-Proving Affidavit** will eliminate the need for court appearance by witnesses at the time a will is probated. This can be especially important to individuals whose **Last Will and Testament** might not be probated for many years. The affidavit can also save considerable time and expense in cases where a witness may have died and others may have moved away or become unreachable.

If you consult an attorney in connection with the preparation of your will, be sure to ask him or her to also prepare and supervise the execution of a **Self-Proving Affidavit**. If you prepare your own will, be sure to show a photocopy of the following **Self-Proving Affidavit** to the clerk of the appropriate probate court and ask him or her to tell you whether the form is valid in your state.

Follow the sample affidavit on the following page when completing your own form (Form 54.2 on page F377). Make several photocopies of your completed, signed form. Keep the original, signed affidavit with the original copy of your will; keep the photocopies of the affidavit with the photocopies of your will.

Sample of Form 54.2/F377

Self-Proving Affidavit

STATE OF   Colorado   )

) ss:

COUNTY OF   Rio Bravo   )

On this _____ 21st _____ day of _____ December _____, 19 __84__, before me personally came and appeared

_____ Matthew Prescot Clay _____,
Testator/Testatrix

known, and known to me, to be the _____ testator _____, and

_____ Amy Lee Bradshaw _____,
Name of Witness

_____ Sewell D. Henry _____ and
Name of Witness

_____ Bradford L. Bacon _____,
Name of Witness

known, and known to me, to be the _____ testator _____ and witnesses, respectively, whose names are subscribed to the foregoing and annexed **Last Will and Testament**, and all of said persons first being duly sworn by me, said _____ testator _____, _____ Matthew Prescot Clay _____,
Testator/Testatrix

declared to me in the presence of said witnesses that said instrument is __his__ **Last Will and Testament** and that __he__ freely executed same in the presence of the witnesses for the purposes therein expressed and that;

     Said witnesses, each of whom on his/her oath declared to me in the presence of said _____ testator _____ that said _____ testator _____ declared to them in the presence of each other that said instrument is __his__ **Last Will and Testament**, and that __he__ freely executed same and requested each of them to attest to said **Last Will and Testament** as a witness, and;

     Upon their sworn oath each of said witnesses declared that he or she did sign said **Last Will and Testament** as a witness in the presence of said _____ testator _____ and in the presence of said other witnesses and that;

     He or she is legally qualified to witness said **Last Will and Testament**, by reason of having attained legal age and/or compliance with other applicable requirements.

Testator/Testatrix   *Matthew Prescot Clay*

Witness   *Sewell D. Henry*

Witness   *Bradford L. Bacon*

Witness   *Amy Lee Bradshaw*

SUBSCRIBED AND SWORN TO before me by the said _____ Matthew Prescot Clay _____, _____ testator _____, and subscribed and sworn to before me by the said witnesses _____ Amy Lee Bradshaw _____, _____ Sewell D. Henry _____ and _____ Bradford L. Bacon _____ this _____ 21st _____ day of _____ December _____, 19 __84__.

IN WITNESS WHEREOF, I hereunto set my hand and official seal.

                       Olivia Watson
                          Notary Public

My commission expires: _____ June 4, 1986 _____

55 Nine Wills

The nine complete wills listed below, one of which should meet the needs of readers having relatively modest and uncomplicated estates, can be found in the Forms Section, as indicated:

1. Will of husband leaving entire estate to wife, if surviving, otherwise to adult children; appointment of wife as primary executrix (Form 55.1, page F379).
2. Will of wife leaving entire estate to husband, if surviving, otherwise to adult children; appointment of husband as primary executor (Form 55.2, page F383).
3. Will of husband leaving entire estate to wife, if surviving, otherwise in trust for minor children; wife appointed primary executrix (Form 55.3, page F387).
4. Will of wife leaving entire estate to husband, if surviving, otherwise in trust for minor children; husband appointed primary executor (Form 55.4, page F391).
5. Will of husband having no children leaving entire estate to wife, if surviving, otherwise certain bequests and devises; appointment of wife as primary executrix (Form 55.5, page F395).
6. Will of wife having no children leaving entire estate to husband, if surviving, otherwise certain bequests and devises; appointment of husband as primary executor (Form 55.6, page F399).
7. Will of unmarried man having no children leaving entire estate to female cohabitant, if surviving, otherwise certain bequests and devises; appointment of cohabitant as primary executrix (Form 55.7, page F403).
8. Will of unmarried woman having no children leaving entire estate to male cohabitant, if surviving, otherwise certain bequests and devises; appointment of cohabitant as primary executor (Form 55.8, page F407).
9. Will of unmarried man or woman having no children, making certain bequests and devises; appointment of executor or executrix (Form 55.9, page F411).

Not one of these wills is presented as ideal, nor should any of them be viewed as fully adequate to precisely meet your needs and those of your beneficiaries. Only a well-qualified and sensitive attorney can help you prepare such a will.

But if you DON'T have a will now and have for years been putting off making an appointment with an attorney to draw a will for you, your family and others you care about can be provided for much better than they are now if you will take the time to complete one of the above wills and properly execute it before witnesses as soon as you can—today or tonight if possible.

If you are married or living with someone and neither of you have wills, we suggest that each partner complete one of this chapter's wills as soon as possible.

Once your will has been completed, but NOT signed, make copies for your executor, your spouse (or cohabitant), a good friend, and, possibly, your attorney. This will help assure that at least one copy of your will shall be almost immediately available upon your death so that steps can be taken quickly to carry out your instructions.

If your will names a trustee or nominates a guardian of minor children, they too should have unsigned copies of your will. All copies thus circulated should remain unsigned and be marked "COPY" on each page. Finally, you may want to have an unsigned copy of your will handy to review from time to time to make sure that it still meets your current situation and needs.

SAFEKEEPING

Complete agreement is lacking among attorneys about the best place to keep a will. A safe-deposit box may be safe, but it's also likely to be inaccessible for some time after you die, banks being required to seal the box upon notification of your death and to open it only in the presence of court and tax officials, or by court order.

Some married couples meet this challenge by keeping his will in her safe-deposit box and her will in his. This isn't much help if both die in the same accident, but it's better than having one spouse's will unavailable until the required officials can gather at your bank for the opening.

Some banks in some states offer joint safe-deposit boxes and will admit either "boxholder" to the box, even if one has died. There are other places to keep wills—a safe at work if you own a business, or a safe in a friend's office, or even a fireproof file box at home; all are worth considering. Your lawyer's office safe is an obvious possibility, but that hardly seems a fair favor to ask if you've written your own will without the services of an attorney.

AFTER COMPLETING YOUR WILL

Each page of every will in this book is numbered. However, after you have signed your will in the presence of the required number of witnesses, you can help protect your will against tampering by signing your full name, just as you signed in before witnesses, along the left margin of every page. This will discourage the addition or removal of pages.

That done, put the pages of your will together and join them by placing four or five staples along the top, left to right, about half an inch from the edge. This will keep pages from getting lost and will also discourage tampering.

You could even dress up your will a bit with one of those light blue, legal-size covers that lawyers often use to protect legal documents (makes things look like you're getting your money's worth). You could probably even find one with a title panel that says, "Last Will and Testament" in nice, Old English type. But many attorneys advise against using such a cover, feeling that the only thing it does is conceal the original staple holes for someone who has decided to substitute a page in your will.

If you do use such a cover, or if a lawyer who draws a will for you gives it to you with such a cover, sign the cover just like you signed your will. Hardly sure-fire protection, but it helps.

BANK TRAP: *Some banks in some states will strike quick as a rattlesnake to "seal" a joint checking or savings account the minute they learn about the death of either person, often inflicting considerable hardship on the surviving spouse or cohabitant.*

If you now have a joint checking or savings account, we suggest that you learn the policy of your bank. If they assure you that you'll have no problem in the event of the death of your cohabitant or spouse, ask the bank to write you a letter anyway, signed by an officer of the bank. If they won't give you such a letter, consider moving your account to a bank that will, or open separate checking and savings accounts.

---

56 Two Wills Using Tax-Free Interspousal Transfer and Life Income Trust Provisions of the Economic Recovery Tax Act of 1981

We have designed two wills that provide substantial tax savings on the estates of husbands and wives dying during 1984 and whose estates exceed $325,000 —the equivalent tax exemption for that year.

The estate tax exemption, rising in graduated steps from $225,000 in 1982 to $600,000 by 1987 and thereafter (table on page 000), denotes the value of an estate that is free from federal estate tax liability. However, a provision of the **Economic Recovery Tax Act of 1981** exempts all *inter vivos* and *testamentary* transfers of assets between spouses from estate and gift taxes.

By combining the advantages of tax-free interspousal transfers with the equivalent tax exemption in a **Last Will and Testament**, an estate that considerably exceeds the equivalent tax exemption can escape federal tax liability. To accomplish this, you must do the following in your will:

1. Leave the decedent's entire estate (less the amount of the equivalent tax exemption) to the surviving spouse.
2. Establish a testamentary trust (equal to the amount of the equivalent tax exemption) to provide life income to the surviving spouse.
3. Transfer remaining trust assets to the trust beneficiary upon the death of the surviving spouse.

Here's how such an arrangement could work with respect to an estate of $650,000 for a decedent who dies during 1984:

1. There would be no federal estate tax liability on the $325,000 (or any larger amount) transferred through the decedent's will to his or her spouse.
2. There would be no federal estate tax liability on the $325,000 used to establish a trust for the decedent's children (or anyone else) since that amount would be covered by the decedent's equivalent tax exemption.
3. There would be no federal estate tax liability for the $325,000 that the decedent's spouse could leave to the couple's children (or anyone else) since that amount would be covered by his or her 1984 equivalent tax exemption.

Okay, but why go through all that? Why not just leave your entire ($650,000) estate to your spouse? Because if you do that and he or she dies during 1984, for example, there would be a $96,300 federal tax on your spouse's estate (see **Equivalent Tax Exemption Table** on page 255).

So why not leave all of your estate except $325,000 to your spouse and simply give $325,000 outright to your children? Probably not practical unless they're over 18 or 21 years of age—and maybe not even then.

Also, if you create a trust for your children, its income can provide additional tax-free financial support for your spouse—something that money given to your children probably couldn't do.

By now it's fairly obvious that the one hitch with this supposedly neat plan is that you don't know when you're going to die, so you don't know how much to put into the trust. Ideally, the amount should be approximately equal to the equivalent tax exemption for the year of your death—if you want trust assets to pass tax free to beneficiaries upon the death of your spouse.

What you do, within reason, of course, is put in "too much." Given that the 1981 Act allows the trustee to transfer funds tax free to your surviving spouse from the trust's income and **principal assets**, fairly large amounts of principal (as well as income) could be transferred to your spouse each year in order to reduce the value of the trust to an amount more or less equal to the equivalent tax exemption during the year of your death, that is, an amount equal to **your** equivalent tax exemption.

Remember, too, that the amount of your spouse's equivalent tax exemption will be climbing each year as well (see table above). So, assuming that you were to die during 1984 leaving your spouse $325,000 and through your will placed $600,000 in a testamentary trust, the trustee could each year transfer to your spouse an amount equal to the **increase** in his or her equivalent estate tax exemption.

In 1985 the trustee could transfer $75,000; in 1986, $100,000; and in 1987, another $100,000—all while keeping the value of your spouse's estate within the equivalent tax exemption and thus transferable to the beneficiaries of his or her Last Will and Testament free of federal estate tax liability.

At that point (1987), the assets of the trust would be reduced to about $325,000—the amount of the equivalent tax exemption during the year of your death (1984)—and could then pass to the trust beneficiary or beneficiaries tax free.

By 1987, of course, a decedent leaving an estate valued at as much as $600,000 would have no need to create a trust such as we've described above for tax-saving purposes, though there may be other reasons.

Form 56.1, the will of a husband, begins on page F415. The will of a wife, Form 56.2, follows on page F421.

EQUIVALENT TAX EXEMPTION TABLE

Year	Federal Estate Tax Credit	Exemption Equivalent
1982	$ 62,800	$225,000
1983	79,300	275,000
1984	96,300	325,000
1985	121,800	400,000
1986	155,800	500,000
1987 and after	192,800	600,000

57 Custom Fitting Your Will

The range of optional provisions that can be included in your will is possibly greater than the exercise of freedom that can be enjoyed in writing any other legal document. There are more limitations upon the content of articles of incorporation, marriage and cohabitation agreements, credit contracts, and even many bills of sale than there are upon what may be given, devised, and bequeathed by a will.

You may not be able to keep your house red, white, and vacant for a hundred years after you die, but you can leave a million dollars or so for the perpetual (?) care of your cats, and *their* cats, and their cats' cats—at least until the money runs out. And you can leave all your money, at least if you're unmarried and childless, to the United States Treasury without your will being successfully contested on grounds that you are completely insane.

Interestingly, you can't just decide to leave all your money to charity, even the most Godly of charities, unless you make the arrangements to do it well before you die. "Trying to buy his way into Heaven!" the judge is most likely to say, throwing that portion of your estate into the familiar "rest, residue and remainder."

Actually, that precedent, which has found its way into the statutes of many states, isn't as crazy as it sounds, since cases are still turning up in court where spouses and children have been left, or would have been left, penniless where unethical ministers have persuaded gravely ill people to give the church —*their* church—all, in exchange for promises of life everlasting in the Heaven of their choice.

Probate courts routinely reject the provision of **any** will that disinherits spouse and children in favor of a charitable organization. The court will instead almost always award the spouse the required dower or curtesy, distribute the required amount to any children (usually one-half or one-third of the estate), and then allow the remainder, if any, to go to the named charity. If you're single, all bets are pretty much off; you can leave your entire estate as a charitable contribution, but better make the arrangements as early as you can or you might be setting your will up to be contested successfully by your heirs.

The following pages illustrate specific will provisions that, when combined with those of any of the previous chapters' wills, can be used to produce a Last Will and Testament of considerably more scope and flexibility. Each of these ready-to-use will provisions can be found starting on page F427.

Some of the provisions may be used to amplify certain sections of the previous chapters' wills; others are additional provisions for the making of charitable bequests, bequeathing shares of a closely held corpo-

ration, the devising of a home or other real property, the cancellation of debts owed you, etc.

They're worth reading, whether you plan to incorporate any of them into a will taken from this book or whether you plan to see a lawyer first thing in the morning about drafting a will for you. They point out options and ways of distributing property that should be considered whenever you make a will.

To add any of these clauses to any of the previous chapters' wills, simply photocopy the complete will, plus any of the form pages that include provisions you want to add. Using a razor blade and straightedge, slice the pages of the original will apart wherever you want to insert a new clause. (*Note:* If the photocopier you have access to has the capability to make copies on both sides of a page, do **not** use that option when copying the original will. Inserting a new clause on one side of the page will necessarily foul up the provisions on the other side.) Then, using rubber cement according to directions on the container, and using the overlap white space above and below each new provision, assemble your new will. Next, fill in the blanks, number the pages, photocopy, and execute the final result. Really, it's a lot easier to do than read about.

NOTE: There's no legal requirement that the paragraphs of a will be numbered or titled. Therefore, when inserting any of the following optional will provisions in your "custom-fitted" will, you may eliminate any numbers or titles you deem necessary.

OPTIONAL WILL PROVISIONS

Religious Belief

Many men and women wanting to include some expression of religious belief in their wills prefer the following paragraph (Form 57.1, page F427) in lieu of the one at the beginning of the wills in the previous chapters:

Last Will and Testament
of
Timothy Patrick Brody

In the name of God, Amen, I, Timothy Patrick Brody,
of Carlyle Boone Indiana,
City/Town — *County* — *State*
being of sound and disposing mind, and aware of the uncertainties of this life, do hereby make, publish and declare the following to be my **Last Will and Testament,** revoking all previous wills and codicils made by me, so help me, God.

Funeral Instructions

Although a will isn't exactly the best place for funeral instructions, since the will may not be immediately accessable if it's in your safe-deposit box or in the possession of an executor or attorney who happens to be out of town, we include such a paragraph here (Form 57.2, page F427). Better to make your wishes known to your spouse, minister, and friends, and then put everything in a letter just to make sure.

To fill out, insert the name of the appropriate church; insert "buried," "cremated," etc.; and insert the place where the remains are to be buried or what other disposition is to be made of the remains.

I direct that my funeral be carried out according to the ritual of <u>the Catholic Church</u>. I further direct that my remains be <u>embalmed</u> and <u>buried in St. Peter and Paul cemetery in Spring- field, Illinois, in the Brody family plot</u>.

Bequests of Cash

The following (Form 57.3, page F427) may be used to make a cash bequest of any amount to anyone whose name is inserted in the space provided. A contingent beneficiary is provided for in the second example (Form 57.4, page F427). A cash bequest from a savings account is provided for in the third example (Form 57.5, page F427); it should be noted that this bequest will fail if the account is closed. If you want to make several cash bequests, just make several copies of the appropriate paragraphs.

I hereby give and bequeath the sum of <u>$400.00</u> to <u>my niece, Annie Brody</u>. If he/she predeceases me, then this gift shall lapse and the aforesaid sum shall be added to the residual of my estate.

I hereby give and bequeath the sum of <u>$1000.00</u> to <u>my friend, Kevin O'Hanrohan</u>. If he/she predeceases me, then this gift shall lapse, and I direct that the aforesaid sum shall be given to <u>Thomas Dugan</u>, if he/she survives me. If he/she predeceases me, this gift shall lapse and the aforesaid sum shall be added to the residual of my estate.

I hereby give and bequeath the sum of <u>$500.00</u> to <u>Solomon J. Feingold</u> to be paid out of my savings account, number <u>B-456-722-97</u>, at the <u>XXXX</u> <u>Fidelity Savings Bank</u> located in <u>XXXXX</u> <u>Springfield, Illinois</u>. If he/she predeceases me, this gift shall lapse and the aforesaid sum shall be added to the residual of my estate.

Bequests of Personal Property

The first proviso (Form 57.7, page F428) gives all personal property to a husband or wife, if surviving, otherwise to others. Complete the last blank by filling in the name of the beneficiary.

I hereby give and bequeath all of my household furniture and furnishings, books, works of art, silver, jewelry, autos, boats and other vehicles, clothing and all other personal property not otherwise distributed to my spouse <u>George</u>, provided that he/she survives me by <u>thirty (30) days</u>. If he/she shall predecease me or fail to survive me by <u>thirty (30) days</u>, then I give all of my aforementioned personal property to <u>my sister, Ernestene</u>.

Optional Addition to Above Paragraph

Use the following *optional* provision (Form 57.8, page F428) in combination with the above paragraph to give all personal property to a specific individual while using a separate letter requesting him or her to distribute such property according to the wishes expressed in the letter. This provision eliminates the need to make many bequests listing many items—something which could complicate your will. It also provides a simple means of revising the list as many times as desired without making a new will or drafting a codicil.

Make sure that your letter, as does the following paragraph, makes clear that your expression of wishes is a **request**. Otherwise, the letter may have to be probated and could be declared invalid in some states because it does not meet the requirements for proper attestation, etc.

It is my intention to leave in my safe-deposit box at <u>First American Security Bank</u>, of <u>Springfield, Illinois</u>, a letter for the information of <u>my attorney, Thomas J. Blackwell</u> listing items of personal property and indicating those items which I ask be given by him or her to specific persons who are named in the letter. It is my request, but not my direction, that the list be used as a guide in distributing the personal property given and bequeathed to him or her.

The following bequest (Form 57.9, page F428), generally for use by unmarried persons, is similar to the above provision, but gives all personal effects directly to the individual who is requested to make distribution.

I hereby give and bequeath all of my household furnishings and furniture, books, works of art, silver, jewelry, autos, boats and other vehicles, clothing and all other personal property not otherwise distributed by my will to <u>my brother, Robert</u>. If he/she predeceases me, then this gift shall lapse, and I direct that the aforesaid personal property be given to <u>my sister, Jessica</u>, if he/she survives me. If he/she predeceases me, this gift shall lapse and the aforesaid personal property shall be added to the residual of my estate. It is my intention to leave in my safe-deposit box at <u>First Federal Security Trust Farmers Bank</u>, of <u>Chipmunk Hollow, Virginia</u>, a letter for the information of <u>William Smythe</u> or <u>Augusta Smythe</u> listing items of personal property and indicating those items which I ask be given by him or her to specific persons who are also named in the letter. It is my request, but not my direction, that the list be used as a guide in distributing the personal property given and bequeathed to him or her.

Devise of Real Property

The following devise of a home is most often used by persons not having a surviving spouse. It may be used to devise a home to a cohabitant, relative, or anyone named in the space provided.

In devising a home, or any real property for that matter, consider whether you want the beneficiary to receive title to the property free and clear (Form 57.10, page F428) or whether you want him or her to receive only your interest (Form 57.11, page F429). If you want the beneficiary to receive only your interest, it will be necessary to declare that fact in your will because the laws of many states stipulate that a person to whom property is devised is entitled to receive it free and clear and the court may order that any encumbrance be paid from the assets of the estate.

If you want to devise real property "free and clear," it's a good idea to state that fact in your will and to make sure that funds are available for that purpose.

City property can usually be described by street address. Rural property can be described by county and state, number of acres, distance from the nearest town, road on which located, etc. Both types of property can best be described as defined on the deed to the property. Fill in last blank, "through the purchase of life insurance payable to my estate" or "in a (checking) (savings) account number (number) at the (name of bank), located at (city/town, state)."

I hereby give and devise my home, located at ___XXXXXXXXX___ 1621 Wavecrest Road, Malibu, California XXXXXXXXXXXXXXXXXXXXXXXXXXXXXXXXXXXXXXXX, to ___XXX___ ___Debra Lou Ducrot___. If he/she predeceases me, this gift shall lapse, and I then give and devise my aforesaid home to ___Tara Jeane Gruenwald___. If at the time of my death I no longer own the aforesaid property, then this gift shall lapse. It is my intention that the beneficiary of the above devise shall receive title to the aforesaid home free and clear, and I direct my executor to discharge any encumbrance thereon, sufficient funds having been provided for this purpose ___in a___ savings account #4532-654-836 at the Mountain States Bank, located at Big Bear Lake, California .

I hereby give and devise my interest in my home, located at 23 Hidden Cove Road, Lighthouse Point XXXXXXXXXXXXXXXXXXXXXXXXXXXXXXXXXXXXXXXXX, to ___Donald T. Dement___ ___XXXXXXXXXXXXXX___. If he/she predeceases me, this gift shall lapse, and I then give and devise my interest in the aforesaid home to ___Jody B. Jackson___ XXXXXXXXXXXXXXXXXXXXXXXXXXXX. If at the time of my death I no longer own the aforesaid property, this gift shall lapse.

Charitable Gifts

Since charitable gifts are deductible from the value of your estate for federal tax purposes, you may want to consider charitable gifts, if not on their own merits, as a way of reducing the amount of federal tax your estate may have to pay. An accountant or qualified attorney can advise you on these matters.

In making any charitable gift it's important to determine the precise legal name of any organization you plan to make a gift to since many groups are known by a name that differs from their legal name. A phone call to the organization's office is usually all that's required.

The following will provisions (Forms 57.12 and 57.13, page F429) serve slightly different purposes. In this first provision, Form 57.12, fill in the sum to be given, the name and address of the organization, and the appropriate indication of the organization's purpose: "charitable," "religious," "educational," etc.

I hereby give and bequeath the sum of ___$2,500.00___ to ___Cedars of Lebanon Hospital___, of ___Miami, Florida___, to be used for its ___medical research___ purposes.

In this second provision, fill in the sum to be given, the name and address of the charitable, educational, or religious organization, and the purpose for which gift is to be used ("cardiovascular research," "scholarships in the school of agriculture," "the education of orphans," etc.).

I hereby give and bequeath the sum of ___$7,500.00___ to ___St. Edward's University___, of ___Spokane, Washington___, to be used specifically for ___library endowment___ XXXXXXXXXXXXXXXXXXXXXXXXXXXXXXXXXXXXXXXXXXXXXXX.

Bequest of Shares of Close Corporation

Instead of bequeathing shares of a closely held corporation along with the "rest, residue and remainder" of an estate, it may be more practical to bequeath the shares to a specific individual (Form 57.14, page F429). Any such bequest should be discussed ahead of time with business associates to prevent later conflict if there is an existing option agreement with other shareholders.

I hereby give and bequeath all of my stock in ___General___ ___Motors Corporation___ to ___my daughter,___ ___Lynn Abbot___. If he/she predeceases me, this gift shall lapse, and I then give and bequeath all of my stock in the aforesaid corporation to ___my nephew, Harold Wylie___. If I own no shares in the aforesaid corporation at the time of my death, this gift shall lapse.

Gift of Pet

The following provision (Form 57.15, page F429) may be used to bequeath a pet or other animal such as a horse to the named beneficiary. Provision is made for an alternate beneficiary.

I hereby give and bequeath my ___palimino horse, "Rex"___ XXXXXXXXXXXXXXXXXXXXXXXXXXXXXXXXXXXXXXXXXXXXX, together with any documents of pedigree and all equipment which I own and maintain for its care and protection, to ___my niece,___ ___Judy Henderson___. In the event that he/she predeceases me, or is unwilling or unable to accept my aforesaid ___horse___ under this bequest, this gift shall lapse, and I then give and bequeath my aforesaid _____ horse _____, together with any documents of pedigree and all equipment, to _my friend, Jimmy_ _Smith_. If the aforesaid _horse_ _XXXXXXXXXXXXXXXXXX_ is not owned by me at the time of my death, this gift shall lapse.

Delivery of Bequests

The two provisions that follow (Forms 57.16 and 57.17, pages F429–F430) will help clarify, probably to the great relief of your executor, the matter of delivery costs related to various bequests made in your will.

I direct that the expense of moving or shipping any property distributed under my will to a location desired by any beneficiary shall be borne by the beneficiary.

I direct that my executor pay, out of the residue of my estate, any expenses reasonably incurred in the packing, shipping and insurance of any property distributed under my will to any beneficiary of any bequest herein.

Advancements

A frequent source of bad feeling between family members of the deceased is the belief that because of previous gifts to a certain person, provisions of the will leave—in the judgment of some heirs—"too much" to him or her and are "unfair." Use of one or both of the following provisions (Forms 57.18 and 57.19, page F430) will at least clarify your wishes.

From time to time after the execution of my will I may make certain gifts to some of the beneficiaries herein. It is my intention to leave a record of all such gifts in my safe-deposit box at _Miners_ _and Ranchers Bank and Trust, Butte, Montana_, and all gifts so recorded after the execution of my will shall be considered as advancements and shall be deducted from gifts and bequests herein given to those beneficiaries. Any amount so deducted shall be based upon the value of said gift as of the date of the gift.

No devise or bequest provided for herein shall be reduced or extinguished due to any gifts made by me during my lifetime to _my daughter, Barbara Carol_, either before or after the execution of this will.

Cancellation of Debt

The following clause (Form 57.20, page F430) makes possible the cancellation of a debt owed you at the time of your death.

I direct that the balance due, as of the date of my death, on a promissory note in the amount of _$4,700.00_, payable to me and executed by _my son, John_, on _June 23, 1979_, shall be cancelled by my executor and be delivered to _him_, or if he/she has predeceased me, to the executor of his/her estate. If the aforesaid debt has been discharged, this gift shall lapse and resort shall not be had to any asset of my estate for its fulfillment.

Abatement of Bequests and Devises

The abatement provision (Form 57.21, page F430) provides some measure of protection against unforeseen circumstances that could affect devises or bequests that have been made to certain beneficiaries. This provision protects the specified bequest or devise against reduction due to any reduction in the assets of the decedent's estate. Such a reduction of assets would normally result in an apportioned reduction in the value of all bequests and devises.

I direct that in the event my estate shall not have sufficient funds to pay for all of the bequests and devises herein, the bequests and devises which I have made to

my son Hans and my daughter Hilde

XXXXXXXXXXXXXXXXXXXXXXXXXXXXX

shall not abate until all other bequests and devises have been fully abated.

Appointment of Guardian

The following provisions (Forms 57.22 and 57.23, page F431) can be used for the appointment of an individual, rather than a couple as in the previous chapters' wills, as guardian of the person and guardian of the property of a minor child or children.

I hereby appoint _Mary H. Banks_ as guardian of the person of each of my minor children. If he/she is unwilling to act, or to continue to act after qualification, I then appoint _Ruth Banks_ as guardian of the person of each of my minor children.

I hereby appoint _Harry T. Goldman, Esq._ as guardian of the property of each of my minor children. If he/she/it is unwilling to act, or to continue to act after qualification, I then appoint _Samuel J. Brubaker, Esq._ as guardian of the property of each of minor children.

Our addition of "it" to the usual he/she has been made in the second alternative, not out of any belief that you may wish to nominate the *Creature from the Black Lagoon* as guardian of your children's property, but because you may want to nominate a bank or law firm, instead of a person, to fulfill that responsibility.

Contest of Will

This provision (Form 57.24, page F431) is an often used "insurance" clause designed to discourage contest of the will by beneficiaries. Its validity has repeatedly been upheld in court.

If any beneficiary or remainderman under any provision of my will directly or indirectly contests, or in any other manner attacks, this will or any provision thereof, any portion or share whatever of my estate or in any trust established by my will given, devised or bequeathed to said beneficiary or remainderman under my will is revoked and shall be distributed in the same manner as if that contesting beneficiary or remainderman had predeceased me without issue.

CREATING YOUR OWN TRUST

58 A Measure of Trust

The creation and the use of trusts deserve more than passing consideration, even within the context of the previous section's modest estates and simple wills.

- You don't even have to wait until you have a will to create and make use of a trust.
- You don't have to die to make use of a trust.
- You can use a simple trust for the benefit of your spouse, cohabitant, parents, children, or grandchildren.
- You can use a simple trust for tax-saving charitable giving.
- You can even use a simple trust to leave your car, your grandfather's gold watch, your stamp collection, or your stereo equipment to good friends—all outside your will and outside of probate.

A trust is easy to create and doesn't have to be executed with the formality of a will, although it's a good idea to have your signature witnessed and notarized to establish positively the trust's authenticity and the date of its creation. Also, the cost of creating and administering a simple trust is often less than would be the cost of distributing the same property via probate.

As was the case with wills, there are some new terms to be learned before we more fully consider this section's trusts.

A *trust* is created by the transferring of assets belonging to one or more persons (the *trustor* or *trustors*) to another person or persons (the *trustee* or *trustees*) to administer or manage for the benefit of still another person or persons (the *beneficiary* or *beneficiaries*).

A *trustor* (also sometimes called a *grantor, settlor,* or *donor*) is one who creates a trust.

An *inter vivos trust* is created by the trustor during his or her lifetime (not to be confused with a *living will* [page 492], which has to do with the giving of one's vital organs—after death of course!—for medical transplant).

A *revocable trust*, as its name suggests, is a trust that the trustor may revoke at any time.

A *reversionary trust* is a trust in which the assets revert to the trustor upon termination of the trust. The ten-year so-called *Clifford trust* and the *two-year charitable trust* are two of the most popular types of reversionary trusts.

An *irrevocable trust* is a trust that cannot be revoked.

A *life tenancy* is the legal right to receipt of the income of the trust (interest, stock dividends, rents, etc.) during the life of the life-tenancy beneficiary, upon whose death the assets of the trust may be transferred to another beneficiary.

The *corpus* of a trust is the principal body of the trust, more commonly called the *assets* or simply the *principal* of the trust.

A *testamentary trust* is a trust created by the will of the trustor that goes into effect after his or her death.

TRUSTS NOW BETTER THAN EVER

Provisions of the Economic Recovery Tax Act of 1981—

- Increasing from $3,000 to $10,000 the amount that you can give to any individual during each year free of gift tax liability
- Completely eliminating gift and estate taxes on transfers made to your spouse
- Permitting gifts and bequests to your spouse free of gift or estate tax liability (see page 231 of this book's previous section)

greatly expand the flexibility, potential tax savings, and other benefits of simple trusts.

Under provisions of the 1981 Act, for example, you can transfer all of your estate, no matter how large, to your spouse completely free of estate tax liability—your spouse receiving 100 percent of the value of your estate.

But let's look at how a simple trust could provide substantial tax savings on even a relatively modest estate if you and your spouse want your estate plans to provide for your children. We know that you could leave all of your estate to your spouse tax free, but let's see what the federal estate tax liability on your *spouse's* estate would be if your spouse were to die shortly after your death.

If, for example, your spouse were to retain all of a $650,000 estate that you willed to him or her, and then your spouse were to die, the estate would normally be required to pay a federal estate tax of $155,800 plus 37 percent of $150,000 ($55,500), a total of $211,300. To eliminate that considerable tax liability you could, say, leave $325,000 to your spouse through your will and (also through your will) establish a $325,000 trust for your children with the income (and assets if necessary) to go to your spouse tax free for his or her lifetime, with the remaining assets of the trust to be given to your children upon the death of your spouse.

Based upon provisions of the Economic Recovery Tax Act of 1981 (more fully explained beginning on page 231 of Section IX) and upon the **bold face** portions of the Equivalent Tax Exemption and Unified

Rate Schedule tables, you will note the following tax advantages:

1. There would be no federal estate tax liability on the $325,000 (or any larger amount) transferred through your will to your spouse.
2. There would be no federal estate tax liability on the $325,000 used to establish the trust for your children, since that amount would be covered by your 1984 equivalent tax exemption.
3. There would be no federal estate tax liability for the $325,000 that your spouse could leave to your children, since that amount would be covered by his or her 1984 federal estate tax exemption.

Thus, on an estate of $650,000, it is possible for a simple trust to save more than $211,300 in federal estate taxes for a decedent who dies during 1984.

EQUIVALENT TAX EXEMPTION TABLE

Year	Federal Estate Tax Credit	Exemption Equivalent
1982	$ 62,800	$225,000
1983	79,300	275,000
1984	96,300	325,000
1985	121,800	400,000
1986	155,800	500,000
1987 and after	192,800	600,000

UNIFIED RATE SCHEDULE

Column A: Taxable Amount Over	Column B: Taxable Amount Not Over	Column C: Tax on Amount in Column A	Column D: Rate of Tax on Excess Over Amount in Column A
$0	$10,000	$0	18%
10,000	20,000	1,800	20
20,000	40,000	3,800	22
40,000	60,000	8,200	24
60,000	80,000	13,000	26
80,000	100,000	18,200	28
100,000	150,000	23,800	30
150,000	250,000	38,800	32
250,000	500,000	70,800	34
500,000	750,000	155,800	37
750,000	1,000,000	248,300	39
1,000,000	1,250,000	345,800	41
1,250,000	1,500,000	448,300	43
1,500,000	2,000,000	555,800	45
2,000,000	2,500,000	780,800	49
2,500,000	3,000,000	1,025,800	53
3,000,000	3,500,000	1,290,800	57

Even on an estate of $375,000, not unusually large taking into account the value of many homes and the combined face value (amount paid at death) of many personal and employee-paid life insurance policies, a trust such as that described above could still effect an estate tax saving of $23,000.

The trust outlined above, by the way, is an example of a *testamentary trust*, a trust created after your death through your will. A similar trust could be created before your death through a separate **Declaration of Trust**. Such a trust created during your lifetime is called a *revocable inter vivos trust*.

REVOCABLE TRUSTS

Revocable trusts do not provide direct federal tax benefits, but neither do they incur additional tax liabilities. The chief value of revocable trusts is their ability to achieve other goals:

1. To allow property to pass directly to beneficiaries (heirs) outside your will, that is, outside of probate, and thus be more quickly available to beneficiaries than might otherwise be possible.
2. To allow you to maintain a great degree of privacy in post mortem giving, since neither the trust agreement nor property of the trust become part of the public record—as does your last will and testament when filed with the probate court.

3. To enable you in many instances to establish and administer such a trust under the laws of a state other than the state of your legal residence, possibly to take advantage of state tax benefits, to remove property of the trust from contest or easy attack by heirs, or perhaps to gain a special measure of privacy.
4. To allow you to test the management ability of the trustee (who may also be a potential executor of your will) before you die, giving you an opportunity to appoint a different trustee if necessary.
5. To facilitate the smooth transfer of management of the financial affairs of an aging or infirm trustor into the hands of a trustee without the need for court involvement or the appointment of a guardian. (This is a means often selected by those without a living spouse or nearby children as a way of assuring continuity of financial management and whatever personal care may be required.)

Tax Considerations

- Since neither the assets nor the income of a revocable trust are immediately available to the beneficiary, you DO NOT incur a gift tax liability for assets used to establish the trust, nor for income of the trust that is not transferred to the beneficiary.
- You DO pay personal income tax or capital gains tax on any income earned by the trust.

- You DO incur a gift tax liability for the value of any trust assets or income transferred to the beneficiary that exceeds the $10,000 annual exclusion provided for by the Economic Recovery Tax Act of 1981 (ERTA).
- The beneficiary DOES NOT incur a tax liability for the value of assets or income received from a revocable trust.
- Upon your death the value of the principal and any accumulated income of the trust IS counted as part of the value of your estate for federal estate tax purposes.

IRREVOCABLE TRUSTS

An irrevocable trust allows you to achieve goals one, two, and three described under revocable trusts. In addition:

1. It allows you to reduce the value of your estate for federal estate tax purposes by an amount equal to the value of assets used to establish the trust.
2. It allows you to transfer income (earned by the assets of the trust) from your high tax bracket to someone in a lower tax bracket, thus effecting a potential tax saving.
3. If set up as a charitable trust, it allows you to take a tax deduction now, but relinquish the property later. You could, at age 60, for example, place your $100,000 house irrevocably in trust for a charitable, religious, or educational organization, take an immediate federal income tax deduction of $60,000 (see the table on page 266), and continue to live in the house until your death. You could also do the same with an apartment you own, retaining a life interest in income derived from the apartment.
4. It allows you to transfer appreciation and growth (the increased value of securities or real estate, for example) from your estate and high tax bracket to a beneficiary in a lower income tax bracket.

BUT, to avoid having to pay taxes on income earned by an irrevocable trust, two stipulations must be met:

1. The trust and its income MAY NOT be used to meet any of the basic parental obligations (such as food, clothing, and medical care) of a minor child or anyone you are legally required to support—generally a female spouse or disabled male spouse (equalization would have come with the passage of the Equal Rights Amendment) and, in some states, parents.
2. The assets and income of the trust MAY NOT be used to discharge legal obligations—may not, for example, be used to pay off a judgment resulting from a lawsuit.

Tax Considerations

- Generally, you DO incur a gift tax liability for the value of assets used to establish the trust that exceed the $10,000 annual gift tax exclusion provided for by ERTA.

- You DO NOT pay income tax or capital gains tax on the value of any income earned by the trust.
- The beneficiary DOES incur a personal income tax and/or capital gains tax on the value of income earned by the trust.
- Upon your death the value of the assets of the trust ARE NOT counted as part of the value of your estate for federal estate tax purposes.

REVERSIONARY TRUSTS

There is yet another type of trust, called a reversionary trust, which provides many of the tax advantages of an irrevocable trust but which has a life of a predetermined number of years. Upon termination of the trust, the principal of the trust reverts to the trustor, hence its name.

One of the most popular types of reversionary trusts is the so-called Clifford trust, an "irrevocable" trust with a life of ten years or until the death of the beneficiary, "whichever shall first occur."

Clifford Trust

Apart from its nominal ten-year life, the requirements and limitations of a Clifford trust are similar to those of the irrevocable trust, but the limited life of the trust makes it more practical for some purposes than a straight irrevocable trust.

The ten-year Clifford trust is very often used to help pay for the education and other support of ADULT children of the trustor (whom the trustor is no longer legally required to support), as well as, of course, for the benefit of anyone else whom the trustor is not legally required to support.

You pay no gift tax on the value of any amount of property used to establish the trust since the assets of the trust revert to you after ten years and one day. You pay no income or capital gains taxes on income earned by the trust. The beneficiary DOES incur an income and/or capital gains liability for income earned by the trust.

Assuming you are in the 50 percent income tax bracket and you want to establish a trust for your child's college education, you would have to earn $6,000 for every $3,000 you wanted to set aside for the college costs. However, about 90 percent of the first $3,000 income earned by a Clifford trust would remain free of income tax liability if the child had no other income.

The bad news is that once you put assets into a Clifford trust you can't get them back for ten years and one day. Also, every time you add to the trust you automatically add ten years to the life of the trust, dating from the date of each additional contribution.

You can partially get around the ten-year extension associated with each addition to the trust's assets, though, simply by creating a new Clifford trust each time you wish to add assets.

One disadvantage of the Clifford trust is that the child or the trustee must have the right to spend the income of the trust for the child's present interest, which is to say that the child or trustee must have the right to spend trust income immediately. The answer to this potential disadvantage is to choose your trustee very carefully.

The trust may also be used in some states (states that do not require adult children to support their aged or infirm parents) to provide funds for the support of parents in a lower income tax bracket, the income from the trust being paid to them for ten years after which time the assets of the trust revert to the trustor.

Two-Year Reversionary Charitable Trust

A second and less well-known type of reversionary trust is the **two-year reversionary charitable trust**. This trust is essentially the same as the *Clifford trust*, except that its use is restricted to charitable purposes —and, of course, for two years only.

Mutual fund shares are the most often used assets of such trusts since they can be placed in trust and still receive expert (?) management while out of your control and without the expense of bank or other professional trust management.

You pay no tax on income earned by the trust. You have no gift tax liability for any amount of assets used to establish the trust. The charitable organization pays no tax on income earned by the trust. You may take an income tax deduction for the amount of income earned by the trust.

CHARITABLE REMAINDER TRUST

An **irrevocable charitable remainder trust** allows you to take an immediate income tax deduction for a portion of the value of assets (usually securities or income-producing real estate) placed in an **irrevocable** trust naming a religious, educational, or charitable organization as beneficiary.

Although you receive an immediate tax deduction for part of the value of the trust, you continue to receive income from the trust. The charitable remainder trust can be designed to pay income to you for your lifetime, then continue to provide income to your surviving spouse for his or her lifetime, and then, upon the death of your spouse, to transfer trust assets to the charitable organization.

The amount of your immediate tax deduction is based, for the most part, upon your expected longevity in accordance with the following table. The table shows the proportion of the value of a charitable remainder trust's "gift of future interest" that you may deduct from your annual income for any age indicated below.

At age 55, for example, you could deduct 54 percent of the value of a charitable gift of future interest made that year: a $54,000 tax deduction for trust assets worth $100,000 on the day the trust was created, which is the day that assets are **transferred** to the trust rather than the date on which the **Declaration of Trust** is signed.

TAX DEDUCTION FOR CHARITABLE REMAINDER TRUSTS BASED ON AGE OF DONOR

Age	Percent	Age	Percent
50	48%	63	64%
51	49	64	65
52	50	65	66
53	51	66	67
54	52	67	69
55	54	68	70
56	55	69	71
57	56	70	72
58	57	71	73
59	59	72	74
60	60	73	76
61	61	74	77
62	62	75	78

TOTTEN TRUST

One of the simplest kinds of trusts, and also one of the most popular and useful trusts, is called the **Totten trust**. To establish a Totten trust, simply open a checking or savings account in your name and the name of the beneficiary like this:

> Heyward Hoxworth Whipple
> itf [in trust for]
> Hoxworth Bull Channing

That's it.

Upon Whipple's death the assets of the trust go directly to his grandson, Hoxworth, without having to pass through Whipple's will. During Whipple's life he has complete control of the trust and can add to it or subtract from it in whatever manner he desires.

A Totten trust can be established with no particular formality, but it's a good idea to discuss your plan with a senior officer of any bank in which you deposit such funds and to obtain a letter from the bank confirming that it will, indeed, make the funds immediately available to the beneficiary upon receipt of proof of your death.

The Totten trust provides no special tax advantage since the value of trust assets will be counted as part of your estate for federal estate tax purposes. Income earned by the trust will be taxed to you just the same as like income from any other source.

You can convert the revocable Totten trust to an irrevocable trust at any time merely by delivering the passbook to the beneficiary—at which time you will incur a federal gift tax liability for the value of trust assets that exceed the $10,000 annual gift tax exclusion provided for by the Economic Recovery Tax Act of 1981 (as more fully explained in the previous section beginning on page 231).

REVOCABLE *INTER VIVOS* BYPASS TRUST

Passage of ERTA in 1981, allowing unlimited transfers of assets between spouses free of estate and gift taxes, is rapidly making the **revocable** *inter vivos* **bypass trust** one of the most popular trusts.

With the revocable *inter vivos* bypass trust:

- Your estate need not incur federal estate tax liability for trust assets that do not exceed the equivalent tax exemption ($325,000 for 1984, increasing to $600,000 by 1987).
- Income from the trust and/or from the trust principal may be paid to the trustor's surviving spouse during his or her lifetime tax free, with trust principal to be transferred to the trustor's children, tax free, after the death of the trustor's spouse as part of the **trustor's** estate tax exemption.
- Trust assets are kept outside your will; thus, the trust is more rapidly able to benefit trust beneficiaries at the time of your death since it is not involved in time-consuming probate.
- Your trust is more private since it is not part of your will and does not become part of the probate court public record.
- Your trust can begin providing income for your spouse and/or children before you die.

The trustee of an *inter vivos* bypass trust can be authorized to make payments from trust income and/or assets beginning, for example, on the date on which you are unable to be gainfully employed due to disability, or beginning on the date on which you are certified incompetent, or beginning on the date after which you have been missing and your whereabouts unknown for a specified period of time, such as thirty days, six months, or a year—long before you would be declared legally dead, which would be a requirement for payment of life insurance or for probate of your will containing a testamentary trust.

Why not merely place assets in a simple **Totten trust** instead of a *revocable inter vivos bypass trust*? Well, assets of a Totten trust would pass to your spouse, or to any other beneficiary, *only* upon your death. And assets of a Totten trust specifying your spouse as beneficiary could be counted as part of your spouse's taxable estate upon his or her death.

Why not give assets to your spouse outright instead of establishing a revocable *inter vivos* bypass trust? The *inter vivos* bypass trust *assures* that trust assets will be transferred to your children (or other trust beneficiary) upon your spouse's death, rather than according to your spouse's Last Will and Testament. It also protects trust assets from attack by heirs or claimants to the estate of your spouse.

Through its trustee, the *inter vivos* bypass trust can assure sound management of the trust at a time when your spouse may be distressed and open to undue influence by greedy, self-seeking individuals. The trustee can also provide a continuity of trust management for the benefit of your children in the event of the death of your spouse.

THE "CROWN LOAN"

Passage of ERTA quickly spawned more new kinds of trusts than there are tadpoles in a summer pond—most of them probably just as short-lived, as they are challenged by the IRS and disallowed in federal tax courts.

One trust that the IRS is "out to get" is the so-called **Crown loan**. It works like this: assuming that you are in the 50 percent tax bracket (about $41,000 per year for a single person, $86,000 for a married couple), you:

- Borrow $100,000 at, say, 15 percent annual interest (which would actually cost you only 7½ percent since you are in the 50 percent tax bracket).
- Make a $100,000 interest-free loan to a trust established for the benefit of your teenage child, investing the money in high-yield notes that could earn $10,000 per year after taxes.

Here's how a trust funded by a Crown loan could contribute to your child's education:

In three years the trust would have earned:	$30,000
In three years the real cost to you of interest on the loan would be:	$22,500
In three years the amount of "profit" generated for your child's college education would be:	$7,500

A six-year Crown loan trust could provide $15,000 income for your child's college education, more if your income is taxed at greater than the 50 percent rate.

The $100,000 used to fund the trust could be easier to borrow than you think, since the high-yield notes used to fund the trust could remain in custody of the bank as collateral for the loan.

Your Crown loan to the trust must be made to a trust established for the benefit of a *child*, and the loan instrument must be a *demand* note payable at any time *without* interest.

A major advantage of establishing a Crown loan trust arrangement is that, unlike the ten-year Clifford trust, you can reclaim your money at *any* time. You also avoid payment of gift tax on the $90,000 excess beyond the annual $10,000 gift tax exclusion since money used to fund the trust is an *interest-free loan* and not a gift.

Trusts funded by Crown loans (named for the brothers who first established them) have withstood IRS challenge and have been upheld in federal tax court and federal district appeals court litigation.

Although Crown loan trusts are, for the most part, comprised of "boiler-plate" text, trusts funded by Crown loans must meet exacting standards and should only be established with the counsel of a highly qualified financial or estate planning advisor. And don't forget, the IRS is "out to get" the Crown loan.

There are, of course, gifted financial planners who can read a new tax law and almost instantly create a useful and apparently "untouchable" trust the way a gifted composer might hear random auto horns at a traffic jam and create a new symphony. So over the next few years you can expect to be reading about new trusts, some of which will eventually take their place beside the Clifford trust and two-year charitable trust as strong and widely-accepted courtroom survivors of IRS challenge and attack.

UPDATE: *Under the Tax Reform Act of 1984 (Code Sec. 7872), Crown loans now have imputed to them a statutory rate of interest that is taxable to the lender parent. This taxable interest, however, applies only to Crown loans between related parties in excess of $10,000.*

TRUSTEES

You can name almost anyone you want, provided the individual agrees, to serve as trustee of any trust that you establish. In most cases it will probably be most practical to name yourself, your spouse, or cohabitant as primary trustee, nominating a relative or the executor of your estate as successor trustee in the event of the death of the primary trustee.

Lawyers, accountants, stockbrokers, relatives of either the trustor or beneficiary, and, with decreasing frequency, banks are also named as trustee of various kinds of trusts. A stockbroker in whom you have great confidence might, for example, be named trustee of a trust consisting mainly of securities.

Professional trustees will ususally not accept management of a trust having less than $50,000 in assets. Many banks will only serve as trustee of trusts having assets of $250,000 or more. Trust management fees are often based upon a percentage of the value of the trust, usually 0.5 to 1 percent.

You can probably manage trust assets as well as anyone. Even if you don't know everything you'd like to know about managing the trust's assets, there's no law that says you can't make use of expert, outside services while acting as trustee. You can get around the "What happens to the trust if something happens to me?" problem by naming a successor trustee to manage the trust in the event that you die or become incapable of serving as trustee—a provision of all of this section's trust agreements.

Since one of the most frequent uses of trusts is to provide for the trustor's children or grandchildren, it's a good idea to select someone whose values won't come into strong conflict with the beneficiaries' lifestyles.

There are cases on record (some beneficiaries having been forced to take trustees to court) where conservative, business-oriented trustees have told beneficiaries, "Look, you're going to have to stop playing with that rock group," or "You're going to have to stop wasting your life working with stained glass and get into some kind of decent job, or I'm going to have to cut you off." Highly religious trustees have also attempted to use their power as trustee to impose church participation upon beneficiaries.

Discretionary powers accorded to trustees with respect to management and distribution of the trust must be broad if unforeseen circumstances are to be met. Therefore, it's important that any trustee you appoint be able not only to manage efficiently the assets of the trust, but also be able to tolerate, if not accept, the life-styles of beneficiaries of another generation that may differ from those that the trustee might consider ideal.

If you establish a *testamentary trust* (as previously described on pages 263–264) to provide income for your spouse from the date of your death, with assets of the trust to go to your children upon the death of your spouse, a mature and responsible relative, business associate, or good friend could probably handle the responsibilities of trustee if the assets of the trust are not large.

If you establish a ten-year *Clifford trust* (page 265) for the benefit of your children, either parent can act as trustee. If you and your spouse do not frequently travel together, you could name your spouse as successor trustee in the event of your death or incapacity. You can also nominate yet another person to serve as trustee in the event that both you and your spouse should become unable to serve in that capacity.

If you establish a trust naming a child as beneficiary, the trustee must obtain a social security number for the child so that a federal income tax return may be filed and taxes paid. A bank account will also probably have to be opened in the child's name. Gifts of real estate will have to be transferred to the *trust*—not the child. Securities, however, *can* be issued in the name of a child—one instance where a bank account may not have to be established.

If you establish a *two-year charitable trust* (page 266), with income from the trust to go to a charitable organization during the two-year life of the trust and with trust assets to revert to you at the end of that time, you can legally name yourself as trustee, but many financial planners suggest naming a third party (such as the pastor or the beneficiary church, or president of the beneficiary university) as trustee "just because it looks better to the IRS."

If you establish an *irrevocable charitable remainder trust* (page 266), placing securities or real estate such as an apartment in trust for a charitable organization, stipulating that you be paid income from the trust until your death, at which time trust assets become property of the charity, you should name a third party as trustee, possibly an officer or official of the charitable organization.

In the above case, by the way, you would receive an immediate income tax deduction for a portion of the value of trust assets—an amount based, in part, upon your life expectancy (see the table on page 266) and perhaps best negotiated with the IRS by an astute financial planner, possibly the financial consultant of the charity.

NOTE: You can also establish a *charitable remainder trust* that will pay income to you for life, then to your spouse for the remainder of his or her life, and *then* transfer assets of the trust to the charitable organization.

If you establish a *Totten trust* (page 266), you will most probably want to name yourself as trustee. Most probably you will not want to name a successor trustee, since the primary purpose of such a trust is merely to assure that trust assets and income pass promptly and directly to the beneficiary at the time of your death. If you are setting up a trust for any other purpose, one of the above-listed trusts would probably serve better.

If you establish an *inter vivos bypass trust* (page 267), neither you nor your spouse should be trustee. The executor named in your will—unless your executor is your spouse or a beneficiary of the trust— would probably be a good bet as trustee of an *inter vivos* bypass trust since your executor would presumably be familiar with your estate, your will, and other provisions made for your family.

Remember that no one can be required to act as trustee. You should review the trustee's responsibilities as specified in the trust agreements included in this section and should discuss any trustee arrangement ahead of time with the potential trustee and secure his or her agreement in writing.

TRANSFER OF PROPERTY TO TRUSTEE

In creating any of the previously described trusts, it is essential to execute legal transfer of all "title to and interest in" the assets of the trust (real estate, securities, cash, etc.) from your name to the name of the trustee as soon as possible, BECAUSE THE TRUST DOES NOT LEGALLY EXIST UNTIL TRANSFER OF TITLE HAS BEEN COMPLETED.

Your attorney or other financial or estate planning expert should be consulted for any but the most simple transfers of ownership. You should also contact your insurance agent to assure continued coverage of any property that could be lost, stolen, or subject to damage by fire, flood, etc.

If you establish a small revocable trust naming yourself as trustee, with your spouse, attorney, or friend as successor trustee, you or your lawyer can probably handle transfer of title with little difficulty. If you establish a large irrevocable trust naming a third party as trustee, with a bank, brokerage house, law firm, charitable institution, or other organization as successor trustee, your attorney should probably handle the transfer for you.

Although it's almost always legal to name yourself as trustee of an irrevocable trust, tax advisors generally suggest that you name a third person as trustee of an irrevocable trust to help prevent conflict with the IRS.

Remember, too, that bank trust departments and others specializing in the management of trusts are in business to make money, and there can be substantial fees involved for trust administration.

DECLARATION OF GIFT

There may be a time, in connection with your estate and trust planning, when you will want to make a fairly substantial gift under provisions of the **Economic Recovery Tax Act of 1981**. If you do make substantial gifts, consider making use of the **Declaration of Gift**, Form 58.1, on page F433. The completely filled-in and notarized form can:

- Place on the record a gift of your property that the Internal Revenue Service or probate court might otherwise argue should be counted as part of your estate.
- Eliminate claims by acquisitive heirs that the gift recipient's possession of your stamp or coin collection, or boat or fur coat, was the result of theft or borrowing rather than receipt of the item as a gift from you.
- Eliminate claims that property given to an individual shortly before your death was not *legally* transferred to the recipient and thus is part of the "rest and remainder" of your estate for distribution to heirs.
- Help the recipient avoid difficulties with the IRS should he or she be questioned, in connection with a tax audit, for example, about ownership of certain assets that appear to be inconsistent with the recipient's reported income.
- Prove legal ownership, should the time come when the recipient may need to sell or transfer your gift to someone else.

One way of avoiding these kinds of problems— for the recipient, for your estate, and perhaps for yourself—is to make a formal record of the transfer by using the **Declaration of Gift**.

The declaration records the date of the gift, the name of the giver and of the recipient, the value of the item, and a brief description of the item. The accompanying Certificate of Notary eliminates any question that the declaration may be forged or perhaps may have been completed before or after the actual date on which you made the gift.

Our legal consultants point out that the declaration is an ideal means of recording the gift of cash, jewelry, a stamp collection, silverware, valuable antiques or works of art, etc. In the case of most gifts, except cash and securities, it's a good idea to obtain a written appraisal of the gift's value from a qualified appraiser—or two or three appraisers if the gift is costly and its value is likely to be disputed.

The obtaining of a written appraisal is *especially* important when making a charitable contribution of a work of art, an antique, or a collection of one kind or another since it's almost as hard for the IRS to accept the value of those kinds of charitable deductions as it is for some people not to step on a crack in the sidewalk.

Note the value of the gift in the appropriate place on the declaration and attach a copy of the appraisal. Give the original declaration to the recipient; place one copy with your important papers; and give one copy to your attorney, the executor of your estate, and/or your tax consultant.

CAUTION: The Declaration of Gift should not be counted on to serve as a legal instrument for the transfer of title or ownership of property, such as real estate, securities, an auto or boat, etc., for which other means of transfer are traditional and legally required.

A completed sample declaration describing the gift of personal property is provided on page 271.

Since the **Declaration of Gift** can also be utilized in relation to estate planning and the preparation of a will, a declaration (Form 52.1) and completed sample are also provided in the previous section. That section's completed sample form (on pages 238–239) describes the gift of real estate and may also be of interest.

Sample of Form 58.1/F433

Declaration of Gift

TO ALL TO WHOM THESE PRESENTS SHALL COME OR MAY CONCERN, KNOW THAT on this ___4th___

day of ___November___, 19 __84__, I, ___Lucinda Melloweather___,

of ___1895 Patton Place___   ___Biloxi___   ___Mississippi___   ___39530___

       Street   City   State   Zip

being of sound and disposing mind and memory do hereby irrevocably give, bestow and deliver up to _____

___Lodura Jean Funsch___,

of ___45 Waverly Circle___   ___Biloxi___   ___Mississippi___   ___39530___

       Street   City   State   Zip

all of my right, title and interest in the following described property valued at ___twenty-five hundred dollars___

_____, ($ ___2,500.00___):

___Collection of 191 dolls from 32 countries, including 47 dolls more than___

___one hundred years old.___

IN WITNESS WHEREOF, I hereunto set my hand and seal on the date above mentioned.

Lucinda Melloweather

* *

CERTIFICATE OF NOTARY

STATE OF   Mississippi   )
) ss:
COUNTY OF   Morgan   )

On this ___4th___ day of ___November___, 19 __84__, before me personally came and appeared ___Lucinda Melloweather___, known, and known to me, to be the individual described in and who executed the foregoing instrument, and who duly acknowledged to me that he/she executed same for the purpose therein contained.

IN WITNESS WHEREOF, I hereunto set my hand and official seal.

Eleanor Watson
                   Notary Public

My commission expires: ___July 16, 1986___

The Anatomy of a Simple Trust

On the next few pages we'll guide you through a sample trust, paragraph by paragraph, to provide you with a step-by-step guide for completing any of the following chapter's trusts.

Opening Declaration

Declaration of Revocable Trust

This **Declaration of Revocable Trust** is made this _____ 15th _____

day of _____ April _____, 19 _84_, between _____

_____ Sidney J. Goldfarb _____ ,

of _____ 1643 East Cherokee Drive _____

_____ Vero Beach, Florida 32960 _____ ,

hereinafter called the Trustor, and _____ ,

_____ Leah F. Cohen _____ ,

of _____ 117 Cullen Blvd. _____

_____ Vero Beach, Florida 32960 _____ ,

hereinafter called the Trustee.

Fill in the date, the name and address of the trustor, and the name and address of the trustee. Other trusts included in the following chapter provide for the naming of two trustors (usually husband and wife and often used in community-property states) and for the trustors serving as initial trustees, with the provision for a successor trustee to administer the trust after the death of the surviving trustee.

First Proviso

FIRST

The Trustor hereby assigns, conveys and gives to the Trustee, in trust, the following property:

Five thousand shares of IBM common stock

or

One thousand shares of Rampant Lion Mutual Fund

or

Sixteen-family brick, three-story apartment building located at 7856 West Sunset Drive, Vero Beach, Florida, more

particularly described in the Deed of Trust attached hereto.

or

1981 Chevrolet Pickup Truck, Serial #CKU189F180124

or

The Southwest Quarter (SW/4) of the Northeast Quarter (NE/4) of Section Twenty-Six (26), Block D-15, Jefferson County, Tennessee, containing forty (40) acres, more or less [more particularly described in the Deed of Trust attached hereto].

Or, list whatever property you are placing in trust.

TRANSFER OF OWNERSHIP TO TRUSTEE:
Your attorney can assist in making the transfer of title of trust assets from yourself to the trustee. In the case of simple trusts, a well-qualified real estate agent, the county clerk, or a recorder of deeds can assist with the transfer of title to real estate; a stockbroker can assist with the transfer of title to securities; and the state department of motor vehicle registration or county tax assessor's office can assist with the transfer of title to a motor vehicle.

Second Proviso

SECOND

The Trustee shall receive and hold said property, together with any additions thereto, in trust for the use and benefit of _XXXXXX_

_____ David Goldfarb _____

_____ Vero Beach, Florida _____ .

The above blank could have also been filled in:

and benefit of _____ my wife Sadie (359-65-6753), and my _____

_____ two children, Aaron (532-64-8730) and Rhoda _____

_____ (532-64-8731), of Vero Beach, Florida _____ .

Fill in the names of beneficiaries, plus the city and state of their residence. Use of the beneficiaries' social security numbers can help assure positive identification. Your area social security office can issue account numbers for infants and children. Such numbers are often issued for minors who are named beneficiaries of income-producing trusts so that federal income tax returns may be filed by the trustee.

Third Proviso

The third proviso is used to direct the distribution of the income and/or principal assets of the trust.

THIRD

Upon my death, the Trustee shall commence _____ monthly XXXXXXXXXXXXXXX payment of the income of the trust, plus such additional assets from the principal assets of the trust, as the Trustee shall deem proper for the support and benefit of XXXXXXXXXXXXX my wife, Sadie _____. Upon the death of XXXXXXXXXXXX my wife _____, the Trustee shall divide the remainder of the trust assets into equal shares among my children _____ Aaron and Rhoda _____, and to the issue of any deceased child of mine *per stirpes*.

As explained in Chapter 61, Creating a Custom-made Trust, a number of ready-to-use optional distribution provisions have been provided as substitutes for the above paragraph. After filling in a photocopy of the appropriate clause, cut it out to affix in place on the proper page of your trust, prior to making a photo-copy for use.

Fourth Proviso

FOURTH

I reserve the absolute right, during my life, by an instrument in writing signed by me, to revoke, annul and cancel this agreement and the trust created hereby; and to alter, modify or amend this trust in any and all aspects; and to withdraw at any time, and from time to time, any and all of the aforesaid property; and to add thereto at any time, and from time to time, such additional property as I may determine.

This clause reserves the trustor's right of revocation and amendment.

Fifth Proviso

FIFTH

This agreement and the trust created hereby shall be administered, managed, governed and regulated in all respects according to applicable statutes of the State of _____ Florida _____.

Fill in name of the appropriate state.

Sixth through Twelfth Provisions

The following provisions, SIXTH through TWELFTH, contain no blanks to be filled in and are quite similar to like provisions contained in the wills examined in Section IX of this volume.

SIXTH

The Trustee, in addition to all other powers granted by this agreement and by law, shall have the following additional powers with respect to the trust, to be exercised from time to time at the Trustee's discretion:

Management of the Trust

To invest and reinvest, lease, rent, mortgage, insure, repair, improve or sell any of the real and personal property of the trust as he or she may deem advisable.

Business Interests

To sell or otherwise liquidate, or to continue to operate at his or her discretion, any corporation, partnership or other business interest which may be received by the trust.

Mortgages, Pledges and Deeds of Trust

To enforce any and all mortgages, pledges and deeds of trust held by the trust and to purchase at any sale thereunder any such real estate or personal property subject to any mortgage, pledge or deed of trust.

Litigation

To initiate or defend, at his or her discretion, any litigation affecting the trust.

Attorneys, Advisors and Agents

To employ and to pay from the trust reasonable compensation to such attorneys, accountants, brokers, and investment, tax and other advisors as he or she shall deem advisable.

Adjustment of Claims

To submit to arbitration, to compromise or to release or otherwise adjust, with or without compensation, any and all claims affecting the trust estate.

SEVENTH

No bond for the faithful performance of duties shall be required of any Trustee appointed under this agreement.

EIGHTH

The Trustee shall receive reasonable compensation for the services performed by him or her, but such compensation shall not exceed the amount customarily received by corporate fiduciaries in the area for like services.

NINTH

No Trustee of the trust created by this agreement shall at any time be held liable for any action or default of himself or herself, or of his or her agent, or of any other person in connection with the administration and management of this trust unless caused by his or her own gross negligence or by commission of a willful act of breach of trust.

TENTH

The Trustee, by joining in the execution of this agreement, hereby signifies his or her acceptance of this trust.

ELEVENTH

The Trustee shall have sole authority to determine what shall be defined as income and what shall be defined as principal of the trust established by this agreement, and to determine which costs, taxes and other expenses shall be paid out of income and which shall be paid out of principal.

TWELFTH

In the event that any of the property of this trust is community property under the laws of any jurisdiction, then this trust shall be construed as referring only to my community-property interest therein.

Thirteenth Provision and Concluding Statements

THIRTEENTH

In the event that any portion of this trust agreement or the trust created hereby shall be held illegal, invalid or otherwise inoperative, it is my intention that all of the other provisions hereof shall continue to be fully effective and operative insofar as is possible and reasonable.

IN WITNESS WHEREOF, the parties hereto have executed this agreement the day and year first above written.

Sidney G. Goldfarb
Trustor

Leah F. Cohen
Trustee

I, the undersigned _____ wife _____ of the above-described Trustor, do hereby waive and relinquish any and all claim to whatever community-property rights I may have in the hereinabove-described _____ securities _____ and do give and grant my assent to the trust and to the incorporation therein of said _____ securities _____ .

Sadie Goldfarb
Legal Spouse of Trustor

Antonio Rizzo
Witness

Robert Olson
Witness

* *

CERTIFICATE OF NOTARY

STATE OF Florida)
) ss:
COUNTY OF Indian River)

On this _____ 15th _____ day of _____ April _____ , 19 _84_ , before me personally came and appeared _____ Sidney Goldfarb _____ and _____ Leah F. Cohen _____ and XXXXXXXXXXXXXXXXXXXXXX XXXXXXXXXXXXX , known, and known to me, to be the individuals described in and who executed the foregoing instrument, and who duly acknowledged to me that they executed same for the purpose therein contained.

IN WITNESS WHEREOF, I hereunto set my hand and official seal.

Evelyn Davis
Notary Public

My commission expires: _____ September 4, 1987 _____

60 Twelve Trusts (and Two Revocations)

Twelve simple trusts have been provided (Forms 60.1 through 60.12, pages F435 to F482) for which you need only fill in the blanks and:

1. Describe the assets (securities, cash, real estate, etc., that are to be placed in trust) under the trust paragraph titled **FIRST**.
2. Name the beneficiary or beneficiaries of the trust and direct distribution of trust income and/or assets under trust paragraph titled **THIRD** or **FOURTH**, depending upon the trust used.

A number of provisions that you might want to use as **THIRD** or **FOURTH** distribution paragraphs are described in the following chapter, Creating a Custom-made Trust, beginning on page 285. Some of these provisions may serve with little more than filling in the blanks (ready-to-use trust provisions may be found starting on page F487).

There's no reason not to write your own distribution clause, perhaps by combining features from several of the options presented. Just type and insert your own paragraph in the space provided beneath **THIRD** or **FOURTH** on any trust you'll be using.

In reviewing the following list of twelve trusts you may find that you'll want to create more than one trust: an *inter vivos* bypass trust for your spouse and children to take advantage of tax-free interspousal transfers under provisions of **ERTA**; perhaps a ten-year reversionary Clifford trust to provide for children or parents; and possibly a **two-year reversionary charitable trust** or **charitable remainder trust** for charitable gifts that can earn an immediate federal income tax deduction.

The "two-trustor" trusts will most often be used by husbands and wives sharing incomes, property, and financial goals, but, except for the *inter vivos* bypass trust, most of the trusts having two trustors may also be used by nonmarried cohabitants, business partners, and others having jointly owned property to be placed in an agreed-upon trust.

All of the trusts are complete, ready to use by merely filling in the blanks, and are simple to execute. Before turning to these, let us briefly describe each, noting when to use the particular form and pointing out its most evident advantages and disadvantages.

1. Revocable Trust: One trustor, appointment of one trustee (Form 60.1, page F435). Generally suitable for an individual to place a single or limited number of items of personal property in trust for a child, close friend, or cohabitant. Provides privacy and immediate transfer of trust principal to beneficiary upon death of the trustor. Provides no federal tax advantages; value of trust assets will be counted as part of trustor's taxable estate. A slightly more formal way of accomplishing many of the goals of the *Totten trust*, described on page 266.

2. Revocable Trust: Two trustors, appointment of one trustee (Form 60.2, page F439). Same uses, advantages, and disadvantages of the above trust, except generally suitable for use by spouses having jointly owned property and shared purposes in creating the trust.

3. Revocable Trust: One trustor, trustor as initial trustee, provision for appointment of successor trustee (Form 60.3, page F443). Many of the characteristics of the first trust described above, except that the trustor serves as initial trustee. A practical move if the trust is to contain assets such as rental property or securities that require management or administration that the trustor wants to control. Often used by aged individuals or those in poor health to facilitate smooth transfer of trust management in the event of the trustor's illness or death.

4. Revocable Trust: Two trustors, trustors as initial trustees, provision for appointment of successor trustee (Form 60.4, page F447). Similar to the above trust. Provides for management of the trust by cotrustees—who are usually spouses holding jointly owned property that they wish to continue to administer as trustees.

5. Revocable Trust: One trustor, appointment of one trustee, provision for successor trustee, payment of trust income to primary beneficiary commencing upon death of trustor, payment of trust income and/or principal to secondary beneficiary upon death of primary beneficiary (Form 60.5, page F451). A good "lovers' trust." Like the *inter vivos* bypass trust for spouses, provides financial support for the primary beneficiary (cohabitant, for example) commencing with the death of the trustor and continuing throughout the beneficiary's life. Upon the death of the primary beneficiary, trust assets are transferred to the benefit of the secondary beneficiaries—who may be the children of either the trustor or the primary beneficiary (or who may be relatives or friends of either the trustor or primary beneficiary).

Assures privacy and immediate commencement of income to primary beneficiary upon the trustor's death. As with other revocable trusts, provides no federal tax advantages and trust assets will be counted as part of the trustor's taxable estate. (By using the annual $10,000 gift tax exclusion for several years prior to death, it is possible to transfer considerable assets to the trust beneficiary without a trust and without going through probate.)

Note: This lovers' trust provides for children of either the trustor or primary beneficiary as secondary beneficiaries.

6. Revocable *Inter Vivos* Bypass Trust: One trustor, appointment of one trustee (Form 60.6, page F455). Provides tax-free income from the trust income and/or principal to the spouse of the trustor, commencing with the death, disability, or disappearance of the trustor. (A similar *testamentary trust* could not begin to provide for the trustor's spouse until his or her death had been proven.) Upon the death of the trustor's spouse, trust assets are transferred to children of the trustor tax free—provided that the value of trust assets is included within the trustor's equivalent tax exemption (see pages 263–264 for a more complete description).

7. Irrevocable Trust: One trustor, appointment of one trustee (Form 60.7, page F459). Why an irrevocable trust? Unlike a revocable trust, allows you to transfer assets in a way that will remove them from your taxable estate. By making use of the $10,000 annual gift tax exclusion per beneficiary under ERTA, such transfers are tax free (page 263). Also a good way to transfer trust income from your high tax bracket to an individual, such as a child or grandchild, in a lower tax bracket—sometimes completely avoiding payment of federal income tax on income of the trust.

    As with a revocable trust, the trust agreement remains confidential and trust assets can be handed over to the beneficiary by the trustee immediately upon your death, or before if certain conditions are met (see page 265).

8. Irrevocable Trust: Two trustors, appointment of one trustee, trust income to surviving trustor for life, then to secondary beneficiary or beneficiaries (Form 60.8, page F463). Same advantages and disadvantages as the irrevocable trust above, except provides for two trustors who may be unmarried cohabitants or others jointly owning property that they wish to place in irrevocable trust.

9. Ten-Year Reversionary Trust (Clifford Trust): One trustor, appointment of one trustee (Form 60.9, page F467). Allows placing of assets in trust for ten years for the benefit of beneficiaries in a lower income tax bracket, such as children or parents. Neither gift tax liability for any amount of assets used to establish the trust nor federal income tax on income earned by the trust. Income tax liability for beneficiary on income earned by the trust but at a lower rate commensurate with his or her own lower tax rate. Must meet certain IRS requirements (see page 265).

10. Two-Year Reversionary Charitable Trust: One trustor, appointment of one trustee (Form 60.10, page F471). Permits you to place assets in trust for two years for the benefit of a charitable, religious, or educational organization, to take an income tax deduction for the amount of income earned by the trust, and then to have assets revert to you at the end of the trust's two-year life. Assuming trust principal comprised of high-yield bonds (earning, say, about 15 percent), possible for a $10,000 trust to provide both a considerable charitable contribution and a considerable income tax deduction for the trustor.

11. Irrevocable Charitable Remainder Trust: One trustor, appointment of one trustee (Form 60.11, page F475). For use if you want to give your house to a charitable, religious, or educational organization, obtain an immediate income tax deduction, and continue to live in the house until you die—at which time possession transferred by the trustee to the beneficiary. Provision also made for the trustor's spouse to continue to occupy the house until his or her death, with possession being transferred upon the death of the surviving spouse. Can also be used to place other income-producing assets, such as rental property or securities, in trust with income reserved to the trustor and the trustor's surviving spouse for life.

12. Irrevocable Charitable Remainder Trust: Spouses as trustors, appointment of one trustee (Form 60.12, page F479). Similar to the charitable remainder trust above, except provides for spouses as joint trustors and can be used with jointly owned assets.

And now a final word—well, "semifinal" words:

Trusts written for one trustor contain the following provision to comply with the laws of community-property states (listed on pages 227–228). If you are not married or do not live in a community-property state, you can cross out and initial the clause as shown below.

Note: Since the agreement is signed by both the trustor and the trustee, this clause (*and any other clause* which is *deleted* from the agreement) must be initialed by both the trustor and the trustee.

I, the undersigned _____ of the above-described Trustor, do hereby waive and relinquish any and all claim to whatever community-property rights I may have in the hereinabove-described _____ _____ and do give and grant my assent to the trust and to the incorporation therein of said _____.

_____
Legal Spouse of Trustor

Note: If you are married it's not a bad idea to ask your spouse to sign the above clause even though you do not now live in a community-property state. Incorporation of the signed clause in the trust will help avoid problems if you later move to a community-property state or if the IRS or heirs of your spouse contest certain provisions of the trust, claiming that it did not have his/her assent.

Remember:

- Not all states require that trusts be notarized, but having the trust notarized can help protect it against such things as attack by heirs who object to its existence and questions regarding its authenticity.
- The authorities, responsibilities, and limitations of trustees of this section's trusts are generally similar, with any changes being made primarily to accommodate individual trust goals.
- Carefully read every trust that you plan to use; compare one trust with another. Even if a particular trust seems to suit your needs perfectly, review the following chapter's optional trust provisions—one of them might give you a better idea of how you want to go about accomplishing the purpose of any trust you create.
- Be sure that the trustor(s) and trustee *initial each page* of any trust you create to prevent the substitution of pages.
- Make sure that insertion rules left blank (or the continuation, or second half, of a rule on the following line) have been x'ed out to protect against someone—*someone else*—from slipping something in.

THE "LOVERS' TRUST": *The "lovers' trust" (Form 60.5) offers so many options that we have included a completed sample copy (see following page) of the trust indicating several possible beneficiary and distribution clauses. Before using this trust, review the beneficiary and distribution provisions of the inter vivos bypass trust (Form 60.4) and the optional beneficiary and distribution clauses described in the following chapter, Creating a Custom-made Trust.*

To facilitate use of the *inter vivos* **bypass trust** (Form 60.6), we have included on page 282, im-

mediately following the sample of Form 60.5 ("lovers' trust"), a completed sample trust indicating some of the options that are available. After reading this trust, compare its distribution provisions with those of the preceding "lovers' trust" (paragraphs headed **SECOND, THIRD,** and **FOURTH**), since they can, with slight modification, be substituted for those of the *inter vivos* bypass trust.

Now our final word: In spite of all we've said about tax-free interspousal transfers, about the $10,000 annual gift tax exclusion, about revocable and irrevocable trusts, about *testamentary* and *inter vivos* and charitable remainder trusts, and about equivalent tax exemptions and the Economic Recovery Tax Act of 1981—in spite of all that—**FIRST** base your planning on whom you would really like to have what.

Sure, it's fun to plot and plan how we'll do the IRS out of a few thousand here and hang onto a few more thousand there, but what really counts is taking care of the people you love and care for. Do that—then use this book's wills and trusts and tax-saving guides to make the most of whatever you have to give.

REVOCATION OF TRUST

While there's no hard-and-fast rule (nor even a soft-and-slow one), it's generally a good idea to use a notarized document to undo whatever you've used a notarized document to do. So if you want to revoke any trust that you've had notarized, have the **Revocation of Trust** notarized also.

Use the appropriate form to rescind any trust that you wish to cancel. Fill in the date of revocation, the date of the declaration of trust, and the name of the trust beneficiary; list the principal assets of the trust exactly as shown on the **Declaration of Trust.** Revocation forms (Forms 60.13 and 60.14, pages F483–F486) are provided for trusts having one trustor and two trustors.

Sample of Form 60.5/F451

Declaration of Revocable Trust

This **Declaration of Revocable Trust** is made this ____19th____ day of _____March_____, 19 _84_ , between

_____Robert T. Goodwin_____, of

_____1612 Wickford Road, Columbia, Missouri 65201_____ ,

hereinafter called the Trustor, and _____Samuel H. Gotlieb_____, of

_____4365 West Jackson, Columbia, Missouri 65201_____ ,

hereinafter called the Trustee.

FIRST

The Trustor hereby assigns, conveys and gives to the Trustee, in trust, the following property:

> Twelve-family brick, two-story apartment building located at 6901 Athens Avenue, Columbia, Missouri 65201, more particularly described in the Deed of Trust attached hereto, and
>
> Six hundred (600) shares of Exxon common stock.

SECOND

The Trustee shall receive and hold said property, together with any additions thereto, in trust for the use and benefit of:

Alice Griffin, 683 Timber Lane, Clayton, Missouri 63105, whose social security number

is 500-30-6933

xxxxxxxxxxxxxxxxxxxxxxxxxxxxxxxxxxxxxxxxxxxxxxxxxxxxxxxxxxxxx .

THIRD

Upon my death the Trustee shall commence monthly payment of income of the trust, plus such additional assets from the

principal of the trust, as the Trustee shall deem proper for the support of ____the aforesaid Alice Griffin____

xxxxxxxxxxxxxxxxxxxxxxxxxxxxxxxxxxxxxxxxxxxxxxxxxxxxxxxxxxxxxxxxxxxxxxxxxxxxxxxxxxxx

xxxxxxxxxxxxxxxxxxxxxxxxxxxxxxxxxxxxxxxxxxxxxxxxxxxxxxxxxxxxxxxxxxxxxxxxxxxxxxxxxxxx

xxxxxxxxxxxxxxxxxxxxxxxxxxxxxxxxxxxxxxxxxxxxxxxxxxxxxxxxxxxxxxxxx .

RTG SG

Sample of Form 60.5 (*Continued*)

FOURTH

Upon the death of _____ the aforesaid Alice Griffin _____, the Trustee shall divide the remainder of the trust equally into as many parts as there are children of _____ hers _____ then living, and who are deceased, having left issue. The Trustee shall continue to hold, administer and distribute the trust as follows:

1. The Trustee shall each month pay to the guardian of the person of each minor child of _____ hers _____ xxxxxxxxx _____ then living, the income from his/her share of the trust; and the Trustee shall each month pay to the guardian of the person, or to the surviving parent, of the minor issue of each deceased child of _____ hers _____, the income from the share of any deceased child of _____ hers _____ *per stirpes.*

2. The Trustee shall pay to each child of _____ hers _____, and the issue of any deceased child of _____ hers _____, who has attained his/her twenty-first birthday, his/her share of the trust, the payment of said share to the youngest of them thereby terminating the trust.

FIFTH

I reserve the absolute right, during my life, by an instrument in writing signed by me, to revoke, annul and cancel this agreement and the trust created hereby; and to alter, modify or amend this trust in any and all aspects; and to withdraw at any time, and from time to time, any and all of the aforesaid property; and to add thereto at any time, and from time to time, such additional property as I may determine.

SIXTH

This agreement and the trust created hereby shall be administered, managed, governed and regulated in all respects according to applicable statutes of the State of _____ Missouri _____.

SEVENTH

The Trustee shall have with respect to all property held or received by the trust, whether principal or income, until the complete distribution thereof, the following powers to be exercised from time to time, at the discretion of the Trustee, without limitation or further license:

Management of the Trust

To invest, reinvest, lease, rent, mortgage, insure, repair, improve or sell any and all of the real and personal property of the trust as the Trustee may deem advisable.

Business Interests

To sell or otherwise liquidate, or to continue to operate at his or her discretion, any corporation, partnership or other business interest which may be received by the trust.

Mortgages, Pledges and Deeds of Trust

To enforce any and all mortgages, pledges and deeds of trust held by the trust and to purchase at any sale thereunder any such real estate or personal property subject to any mortgage, pledge or deed of trust.

Litigation

To initiate or defend, at his or her discretion, any litigation affecting the trust.

Attorneys, Advisors and Agents

To employ and to pay from the trust reasonable compensation to such attorneys, accountants, brokers, and investment, tax and other advisors as he or she shall deem advisable.

Adjustment of Claims

To submit to arbitration, to compromise or to release or otherwise adjust, with or without compensation, any and all claims affecting the trust estate.

RTG Sh

2

Sample of Form 60.5 (*Continued*)

EIGHTH

No bond for the faithful performance of duties shall be required of any Trustee appointed under this agreement.

NINTH

The Trustee shall receive reasonable compensation for the services performed by him or her, but such compensation shall not exceed the amount customarily received by corporate fiduciaries in the area for like services.

TENTH

No Trustee of the trust created by this agreement shall at any time be held liable for any action or default of himself or herself, or of his or her agent, or of any other person in connection with the administration and management of this trust unless caused by his or her own gross negligence or by commission of a willful act of breach of trust.

ELEVENTH

The Trustee, by joining in the execution of this agreement, hereby signifies his or her acceptance of this trust.

TWELFTH

The Trustee shall have sole authority to determine what shall be defined as income and what shall be defined as principal of the trust established by this agreement, and to determine which costs, taxes and other expenses shall be paid out of income and which shall be paid out of principal.

THIRTEENTH

In the event that any portion of this trust agreement or the trust created hereby shall be held illegal, invalid or otherwise inoperative, it is my intention that all of the other provisions hereof shall continue to be fully effective and operative insofar as is possible and reasonable.

IN WITNESS WHEREOF, the parties hereto have executed this agreement the day and year first above written.

_____
Trustor

_____
Trustee

I, the undersigned _____ of the above-described Trustor, do hereby waive and relinquish any and all claim to whatever community-property rights I may have in the hereinabove-described _____ _____ and do give and grant my assent to the trust and to the incorporation therein of said _____ .

_____
Legal Spouse of Trustor

_____
Witness

_____
Witness

3

Sample of Form 60.5 (*Continued*)

CERTIFICATE OF NOTARY

STATE OF   Missouri   )
)   ss:

COUNTY OF   Boone   )

On this _____19th_____ day of _____March_____, 19 __84__, before me personally came and appeared _____Robert T. Goodwin_____ and _____Samuel H. Gotlieb_____ and _____xxxxxxxxxxxxxxxx_____, known, and known to me, to be the individuals described in and who executed the foregoing instrument, and who duly acknowledged to me that they executed same for the purpose therein contained.

IN WITNESS WHEREOF, I hereunto set my hand and official seal.

Barbara Richards
Notary Public

My commission expires: _____January 6, 1986_____

Declaration of Trust

Dated _____ March 19, _____ 19 __84__

4

Sample of Form 60.6/F455

Declaration of Revocable Trust

This **Declaration of Revocable Trust** is made this _____ 22nd _____ day of _____ November _____, 19 _84_, between

_____ Louis Paulk _____, of

_____ 35 Fairfield Lane, Manchester, N.H. 03101 _____,

hereinafter called the Trustor, and _____ Evelyn Grainger, Esq. _____, of

_____ Suite 277, Lawyers' Title Building, Manchester, N.H. 03101 _____,

hereinafter called the Trustee.

FIRST

The Trustor hereby assigns, conveys and gives to the Trustee, in trust, the following property:

Nine-story office building located at 465 North Central, Manchester, New Hampshire 03101, more particularly described in the Deed of Trust attached hereto.

SECOND

The Trustee shall have and hold the aforesaid property under such terms and conditions, and with such powers, rights and limitations, as are hereinunder set forth:

1. Until (my death) (my incapacity as determined by a licensed physician), the Trustee shall pay the net income of the trust to (my spouse Lucy) (me).

2. Upon (my death) (my incapacity as determined by a licensed physician), the Trustee shall each (month) (quarter) (6 months) pay the net income of the trust, along with such of the principal assets of the trust as may be necessary and reasonable for his/her support, to my spouse _____ Lucy _____.

3. Upon the death of my surviving spouse _____ Lucy _____, the Trustee shall pay the remainder of the trust, in equal shares to those children of _____ ours _____ who are then living, or in the event of the death of any of them, to the issue of any deceased child of (ours) (mine) (his) (hers) _per stirpes_.

THIRD

I reserve the absolute right, during my life, to revoke, annul and cancel this trust; and to alter, modify or amend this trust in any and all respects; and to withdraw at any time, and from time to time, any and all of the aforesaid principal of the trust; and to add thereto at any time, and from time to time, such additional principal as I may determine.

FOURTH

Anything hereinafter to the contrary notwithstanding, none of the powers enumerated herein, nor accorded generally to Trustees by law, shall permit nor be construed to:

A. Allow the Trustee to borrow all or any part of the *corpus* of the trust, nor the income therefrom, directly or indirectly, whether with or without adequate security or adequate interest.

B. Allow the exercise in a nonfiduciary capacity by any person not having written approval of the Trustee, any of the following powers of administration:

1. Any power to control investment of the *corpus* of the trust, either by directing investments or reinvestments or by vetoing any proposed investments or reinvestments, to the extent that the *corpus* of the trust consists of stocks or other securities of corporations in which the holdings of the trust and the Trustor are significant from the viewpoint of voting control; or

2. Any power to vote or direct the voting of stock or other securities of any corporations in which the holdings of the trust and the Trustor are significant from the viewpoint of voting control; or

3. Any power to reacquire the *corpus* of the trust by substituting other property of equal value.

C. Allow the Trustor, the Trustee or any other person to purchase, exchange or otherwise deal with or dispose of the *corpus* of the trust, or the income therefrom, for less than adequate consideration in money or money's worth.

1

Sample of Form 60.6 (*Continued*)

FIFTH

This agreement and the trust created hereby shall be administered, managed, governed and regulated in all respects according to applicable statutes of the State of _____New Hampshire_____.

SIXTH

The Trustee shall have with respect to all property held or received by the trust, whether principal or income, until the complete distribution thereof, the following powers to be exercised from time to time, at the discretion of the Trustee, without limitation or further license:

Management of the Trust

To invest, reinvest, lease, rent, mortgage, insure, repair, improve or sell any and all of the real and personal property of the trust as the Trustee may deem advisable.

Business Interests

To sell or otherwise liquidate, or to continue to operate at his or her discretion, any corporation, partnership or other business interest which may be received by the trust.

Mortgages, Pledges and Deeds of Trust

To enforce any and all mortgages, pledges and deeds of trust held by the trust and to purchase at any sale thereunder any such real estate or personal property subject to any mortgage, pledge or deed of trust.

Litigation

To initiate or defend, at his or her discretion, any litigation affecting the trust.

Attorneys, Advisors and Agents

To employ and to pay from the trust reasonable compensation to such attorneys, accountants, brokers, and investment, tax and other advisors as he or she shall deem advisable.

Adjustment of Claims

To submit to arbitration, to compromise or to release or otherwise adjust, with or without compensation, any and all claims affecting the trust estate.

SEVENTH

No bond for the faithful performance of duties shall be required of any Trustee appointed under this agreement.

EIGHTH

The Trustee shall receive reasonable compensation for the services performed by him or her, but such compensation shall not exceed the amount customarily received by corporate fiduciaries in the area for like services.

NINTH

No Trustee of the trust created by this agreement shall at any time be held liable for any action or default of himself or herself, or of his or her agent, or of any other person in connection with the administration and management of this trust unless caused by his or her own gross negligence or by commission of a willful act of breach of trust.

TENTH

The Trustee, by joining in the execution of this agreement, hereby signifies his or her acceptance of this trust.

ELEVENTH

The Trustee shall have sole authority to determine what shall be defined as income and what shall be defined as principal of the trust established by this agreement, and to determine which costs, taxes and other expenses shall be paid out of income and which shall be paid out of principal.

2

Sample of Form 60.6 (*Continued*)

TWELFTH

In the event that any portion of this trust agreement or the trust created hereby shall be held illegal, invalid or otherwise inoperative, it is our intention that all of the other provisions hereof shall continue to be fully effective and operative insofar as is possible and reasonable.

IN WITNESS WHEREOF, the parties hereto have executed this agreement the day and year first above written.

_____
Trustor

_____
Trustee

I, the undersigned _____ spouse _____ of the above-described Trustor, do hereby waive and relinquish any and all claim to whatever community-property rights I may have in the hereinabove-described ____ office ____ building ____ and do give and grant my assent to the trust and to the incorporation therein of said _____ office building _____ .

_____
Legal Spouse of Trustor

_____
Witness

_____
Witness

* *

CERTIFICATE OF NOTARY

STATE OF   New Hampshire   )
) ss:
COUNTY OF   Hillsborough   )

On this ____ 22nd ____ day of ____ November ____, 19 __84__, before me personally came and appeared ____ Louis Paulk ____ and ____ Lucy Paulk ____ and ____ Evelyn Grainger ____, known, and known to me, to be the individuals described in and who executed the foregoing instrument, and who duly acknowledged to me that they executed same for the purpose therein contained.

IN WITNESS WHEREOF, I hereunto set my hand and official seal.

_____
Notary Public

My commission expires: ____ June 4, 1987 ____

3

61 Creating a Custom-made Trust

This chapter illustrates several types of trust distribution clauses that can be used individually or in combination with others to provide a wide range of options for the use of both income and principal. Each of these ready-to-use trust distribution clauses can be found in the back of the book (starting on page F487).

Here's an example:

First Step

The Trustee, on a _____ quarterly _____ basis, shall pay the net income of the trust to _____ my wife, Melinda Sue _____.

Second Step

Upon the death of _____ her _____, the Trustee shall assign, convey, transfer and pay the principal of the trust to _____ my daughter, Patience Harding Hoxworth _____. If he/she shall not then be living, the trust shall be divided equally among the children of him/her, and the issue of any child of his/hers *per stirpes*.

Here's another combination:

First Step

The Trustee, on a _____ quarterly _____ basis, shall pay the net income of the trust, plus such additional assets of the principal of the trust as the Trustee shall deem proper, to XXXXXXX _____ my son, Gerald _____ for his/her welfare and support.

Second Step

Upon the aforementioned beneficiary attaining his/her XXXXX _____ twenty-fifth _____ birthday, the principal of the trust shall be assigned, conveyed, transferred and paid to* _____ (him) _____ (Tempel Beth Shalom, Miami, Florida) _____ (my brother, Sam) _____, and this trust shall terminate.

The following pages also illustrate clauses that provide for the prompt, probate-free distribution of real and personal property, such as a library, coin collection, automobile, boat, securities, real estate, or stock in a close corporation, upon the death of the testator. Distribution clauses for a ten-year Clifford trust and for a two-year reversionary charitable trust are also shown.

To use the following clauses, do the following:

1. Photocopy the appropriate page or pages of the Optional Trust Provisions (Forms 61.1 to 61.5, pages F487–F495).

*Any of the following, for example.

2. Fill in the appropriate blanks of the clause or clauses you have selected.
3. Cut out and affix the clause or clauses in the space provided after **THIRD** or **FOURTH** on the trust you have chosen to use.

Rubber cement works fine, and if you make copies of the completed pages on a relatively new machine, the lines around the edges of the inserted paragraphs will not even show when you reproduce them to make your "printed" trust.

Many of the distribution clauses presented in this chapter will work perfectly well for many trusts. You can also pick and choose from among their various provisions to write your own.

First-Step Clauses (Form 61.1)

The Trustee, on a _____ monthly _____ basis, shall pay the net income of the trust to _____ my wife, Mary Jane _____.

Fill in the payment schedule—"monthly," "quarterly," "annual," etc., plus the name of the beneficiary.

The Trustee, on a _____ monthly _____ basis, shall pay the net income of the trust, plus such additional assets of the principal of the trust as the Trustee shall deem proper, to XXXXXXX _____ my daughter, Nancy _____ for his/her welfare and support.

Fill in payment schedule, name of beneficiary.

Until the _____ 15th _____ day of _____ March _____, 19 95 _____, the Trustee, on a _____ monthly _____ basis, shall pay the income of the trust to _____ my daughter, Janet _____ for _____ her education and support _____.

Fill in date, payment schedule, name of beneficiary, and purpose for which funds are to be used (e.g., "for tuition and the other direct and indirect expenses of attending law school").

Second-Step Clauses (Form 61.2)

Upon the above date, the Trustee shall assign, convey, transfer and give the remainder of the trust to _____ my brother, Robert _____, to be his/hers absolutely.

Fill in the name of the beneficiary, who may be the same or different from the original beneficiary.

Upon the death of _____ my son, William _____
XXXXXXXXXXXXXXXXXXXXX, the Trustee shall assign, convey, transfer and give the remainder of the trust to XXXXXXXXXXXXXX
_____ my nephew, Frederick _____.

Fill in the name of the original beneficiary, followed by the name of the secondary beneficiary; the latter may be a person or charitable organization.

Upon the death of _____ my husband, Thomas _____
XXXXXXXXXXXXXXXXXX, the Trustee shall divide the remainder of the trust among my children and the issue of any deceased child of mine *per stirpes*.

Fill in the name of the original beneficiary.

Upon the death of _____ my wife, Harriet _____
XXXXXXXXXXXXXXXXX, or my youngest child attaining his/her _____ twenty-first _____ birthday, whichever shall last occur, the remainder of the trust shall be equally divided among my children and the issue of any deceased child of mine *per stirpes*, thereby terminating this trust.

Fill in the name of the original beneficiary and designate birthday.

"Stand-Alone" Clauses (Form 61.3)

Upon my death, the Trustee shall assign, convey, transfer and pay the principal of the trust to _____ St. Luke's Hospital, St. Louis, Missouri _____.

Fill in the name of the beneficiary. This clause is excellent for charitable contributions. If the property is transferred through a revocable trust, the value of the property may be deducted from the value of your estate for federal tax purposes.

Upon my death, the Trustee shall assign, convey, transfer and pay the principal of the trust to _____ my husband, Issac _____ XXXXXXXXXXXXXXXXXX. If he/she shall not then be living, the Trustee shall assign, convey, transfer and pay said principal to _____ my sister, Lucy _____, or, if he/she shall not then be living, said principal shall be equally divided between his/her children and the issue of any deceased child of his/hers *per stirpes*.

Fill in names of primary and secondary beneficiaries.

The Trustee, on a _____ quarterly _____ basis, shall pay the net income of the trust to the Trustor. Upon the death of the Trustor, the Trustee shall assign, convey, transfer and pay the remainder of the trust to _____ my sister, Barbara _____, or, if he/she shall not then be living, the

remainder of the trust shall be equally divided among his/her children and the issue of any deceased child of his/hers *per stirpes*.

Fill in payment schedule and name of beneficiary.

The Trustee, on a _____ quarterly _____ basis, shall pay the net income of the trust to the Trustor. Upon the death of the Trustor, the remainder shall be equally divided among my children and the children of any deceased child of mine *per stirpes*.

Fill in the payment schedule.

Upon my death, the Trustee shall commence _____ monthly _____ XXXXXXXXXXXXX payment of the net income of the trust to _____ my niece, Teresa _____ until such time as he/she shall attain his/her _____ twenty-first _____ birthday, at which time the Trustee shall assign, convey, transfer and pay the remainder of the trust to him/her, or if he/she shall not then be living to _____ Tempel Beth Israel, Atlanta, Georgia _____.

Fill in payment schedule, name beneficiary, specify birthday, and name second beneficiary.

Optional Clause for Use with Two-Year Charitable Trust (Form 61.4)

Until termination of this trust as herein provided, the Trustee, after deducting proper expenses, shall pay the net income of the trust to _____ St. Mary's College, Lincoln, Nebraska _____, for its religious, educational or charitable purposes.

Upon termination of this trust, the principal of the trust, as it is then constituted, shall revert, be assigned, conveyed and transferred with all right and title thereto, to the Trustor to be his/hers absolutely.

If the Trustor shall not then be living, said principal shall be transferred and paid over to his/her executors to be distributed as part of his/her estate.

Fill in the name of the religious, educational, or charitable organization. Remember, in order to obtain its potential tax benefits, the term of a charitable revisionary trust must be for at least two years **and a day**.

A TRUST DOES NOT BEGIN TO EXIST LEGALLY UNTIL TITLE TO THE PRINCIPAL HAS BEEN TRANSFERRED TO THE TRUSTEE—so a two-year charitable trust must be dated no earlier than that date.

Optional Clause for Use with Ten-Year Clifford Trust (Form 61.5)

Until termination of this trust as herein provided, the Trustee, after deducting proper expenses, shall pay to or apply the net income of the trust for the benefit and use of _____ my mother, Louise _____.

Upon termination of this trust, the principal of the trust, as it is then constituted, shall revert, be assigned, conveyed and transferred with all right and title thereto, to the Trustor to be his/hers absolutely.

If the Trustor shall not then be living, said principal shall be transferred and paid over to his/her executors or administrators to be distributed as part of his/her estate.

Fill in the name of the beneficiary. Remember, in order to obtain its potential tax benefits, the term of the Clifford trust must be ten years and a day, or until the death of the beneficiary, whichever shall first occur.

A TRUST DOES NOT BEGIN TO EXIST LEGALLY UNTIL TITLE TO THE PRINCIPAL HAS BEEN TRANSFERRED TO THE TRUSTEE—so a Clifford trust must be dated as of that date.

XI

SELLING YOUR OWN HOUSE

62 You Can Do It Better

Selling your house is sort of like painting a room: it's not so much doing the job, it's getting ready and cleaning up afterward that's the real work. In selling your house, getting ready includes:

- Making needed repairs and cosmetic improvements.
- Obtaining a termite inspection report.
- Clearing clutter from closets, basement, attic, garage, etc.
- Obtaining an appraisal of your home's fair market value for use as a sales tool.
- Making several photocopied sets of your last twelve month's utility and heating bills for use as a sales tool.
- Developing a fact sheet describing your home for use as a sales tool.
- Putting together a fact sheet showing the actual sales prices of similar homes recently sold in your neighborhood for use as a sales tool.
- Becoming an expert on various ways of helping the buyer finance his or her purchase of your home.

All of these items, along with advertising and showing your home, negotiating with buyers, and closing the sale, are covered on the following pages. If there's any consolation in all this, perhaps it's that if you were paying a real estate agent to sell your home for you (about $5,000 on an $85,000 house), you'd still have to do most of these things anyway.

While saving the real estate agent's customary 6 percent commission may make the work a bit more worthwhile, real estate analysts report that the greatest benefits of selling your own home are:

- Owner-sold homes generally sell more quickly than agent-sold homes.
- Owner-sold homes generally net the seller more money than do agent-sold homes.

It's easy to see why. Deducting the 6 percent commission from the price of an $85,000 home reduces its cost by $5,100 to $79,900—which can do a lot more toward selling a house than the most persuasive real estate agent's sales pitch.

Eliminating the real estate agent's commission also makes your house easier to buy since it allows you to substantially reduce the down payment requirement. On an $85,000 home financed with a conventional mortgage, the usual $17,000 down payment could be reduced by $5,000 to $12,000, putting your home within reach of many more prospective buyers.

Taken another way, a $5,000 commission deducted from the price of a house is $5,000 that doesn't have to be included in a mortgage. Five thousand dollars financed over a typical 30-year

mortgage at the 14 percent interest rate common during mid-1984 would cost the buyer $21,330.

It is also true that owner-sold homes are usually sold by smarter, more energetic owners than most agent-sold homes and that nobody knows as much about a home—or cares as much about making the sale—as does the owner.

More than 12 percent of all homes sold during 1981 were owner-sold homes, an impressive figure, especially when you take into account that part of the total sales figure is composed of newly constructed homes marketed by builders and developers.

With preparation out of the way, the worst of the job will probably be behind you. There will be hours of staying close to the phone and seemingly countless times of guiding prospects through your house, answering questions while they peer into your bedroom closet and inspect your bathroom. However, you do not need to be a super salesperson to sell your house. In fact, residential sales experts say that a low-key, "let-the-house-sell-itself" approach works best.

You'll need to be able to justify your home's price, but a written, independent, expert, impartial fair-market appraisal plus your knowledge of the house, the neighborhood, and current sales prices of similar recently sold homes can give you the persuasive facts you'll need.

One of the most effective things you can do to help sell your house is to be in a position to help the buyer secure financing—and a number of options are presented in Chapter 68.

There's always the possibility that because of job changes or other circumstances you'll be placing your house on the market during less than ideal times—during a recession, or at a time when mortgage money is hard to come by, or when interest rates, even for a relatively short mortgage period, make the loan cost a good deal more than the house. But there are ways of making the best of even these situations.

The following chapters deal with separate subjects separately, but that doesn't mean you can't be getting your utility bills together at the same time you're fixing up the yard and studying your home loan agreement to see if there's a provision allowing a qualified buyer to take over your mortgage—a strong sales plus since your original mortgage interest rate is likely to be much lower than anything currently available.

Season and geographical location will obviously affect which jobs you may have to start first. It takes three to four weeks for fertilizer to green up your lawn, but no time at all for paint touch-up to improve your home's salability—provided you don't try to paint it during a snowstorm.

There's nothing particularly complicated about the legal forms used in selling your house yourself. We'll provide most of those that you'll need—and some that you probably won't, just in case some prospective buyer starts throwing around real estate terms in an effort to shake you up. Forms for offer to purchase real estate, counteroffer, and earnest money receipt, plus other forms, are presented in the suc-ceeding chapters.

We can't promise that selling your own home will be a picnic; there's too much work involved for it ever to be that. We've sold homes both ways, though, with real estate agents and without, and after comparing experiences we'll choose "us" over "them" every time.

63 Helping Your House Sell Itself

Getting your home ready to show can be divided into four general areas: exterior of the house, interior of the house, fairly major repairs, and equipment/appliances.

MAJOR REPAIRS

Using our Exterior Checklist (Form 63.1, page F497), note every item that should be repaired: roof, guttering, downspouts, sidewalks, storm windows, screens, steps, fences, garage door, window frames, shutters, etc. In accordance with our checklist instructions—Using the Checklists, page 294—note whether each job is of the do-it-yourself variety or should be contracted out. (Refer to Section IV of this book for suggestions on dealing with roofers, electricians, carpenters, and other home improvement contractors likely to be involved with major repair work on your house.)

Inside the house check for such things as cracked walls or ceilings, doors or windows that stick, carpeting that needs to be replaced, and floors that need to be refinished (see our Interior Checklist, Form 63.2).

In general, try to take care of major repairs before you begin cosmetic improvements, such as painting and carpet and drapery cleaning, since the comings and goings of workers could undo a lot of your cleanup efforts.

CLUTTER CLEANOUT

While repairs are being taken care of, and while you're waiting (and waiting) for repair people to come, begin getting rid of things you've been putting in the garage and stuffing into closets, under the bed, and into the attic and basement for years.

There's nothing that will make your house look more cluttered than a lot of clutter. Closets should look like they're really adequate for a family to live in the house. Storage cabinets should be neat and organized; the basement, garage, and attic should be free of old magazines, outboard motors, used tires, etc.

There are a number of ways to get rid of clutter:

- Sell it, possibly through a garage sale or classified newspaper ads.
- Store it, possibly at a nearby self-storage unit or with friends.
- Give it away to a church or the Salvation Army for an income tax deduction.

Clutter cleanout time may also be an opportunity to do some preliminary packing since you'll be digging into most of your home's nooks and crannies anyway. Books can be packed into carryable cartons; certain furniture items, such as unneeded chairs, small tables, lamps, and even a few pictures, might be removed to give rooms a more spacious look.

Repair and clutter cleanout time is also a good time to remove any appliances and fixtures, such as window air conditioners and chandeliers, that prospective buyers might assume go with the house—or that you don't want to be bargained out of when negotiating your home sale.

EXTERIOR COSMETICS

With major repairs organized, you can begin exterior painting, minor fix-up jobs, and landscaping that you can do yourself. Consider fertilizing your lawn to green up the grass. Think about adding a few shrubs, a small tree or two, or some flowers or plants for the garden.

Consider starting exterior touch-up work on the front of the house just in case the weather changes or something comes up that prevents your finishing the job before you have to start showing the house. Be especially sure your front door is attractive and that all hardware is in good condition.

When showing your house during the spring or fall (the best selling seasons), leave windows uncovered by screens or storm windows. They'll be easier to keep sparkling clean that way and will make the house look better from the outside (as well as make the view look better from the inside).

Drive by your house slowly and try to view it as a prospective buyer would. Walk up the driveway or front sidewalk and judge how the house would look to someone thinking about living there. Remember to keep the garage door closed for appearance's sake during the time that prospective buyers might be viewing it.

Be sure the backyard is kept picked up and free of semiabandoned toys, bicycles, etc. If the yard contains swing sets or other play equipment, considering taking them down to make the yard less crowded. Paint and fix up the doghouse if you have one in the yard. Replace beat-up trash containers. Remove unneeded garden equipment, water hoses, etc. Neaten up the stack of firewood if you have a fireplace.

INTERIOR TOUCH-UP

As with the exterior of your house, try to view the interior as someone would who is thinking about living there. Although the last thing you'll want to do is look for extra work, ask yourself if the walls of some of the rooms should be painted? (Use light, neutral shades if you do paint.) Should carpets be shampooed and in some areas be replaced? Should some of the curtains and draperies be cleaned or replaced with ready-made and inexpensive new ones? What about traverse rods? Are they well-anchored and do they work smoothly? (You're sure to be opening and closing draperies in the presence of prospective buyers.)

Be sure to take a good look at the interior of all of your closets and cabinets. Clean them thoroughly for sure, replacing shelf paper with new, plain (preferably white) paper. Paint them if necessary. Replace small light bulbs in closets with larger ones to make them seem bright and clean looking.

Thoroughly clean broom closets, linen closets, utility areas, around washer and dryer, under the kitchen sink, and around the furnace, the hot water heater, and the central air conditioner. Make sure operating instructions are in plain sight; most buyers will want to look at these items and see how they work.

Keep the garage neat and organized looking; ditto on the children's rooms—if possible.

APPLIANCES AND EQUIPMENT

Appliance and equipment makeready is different from most other home preparation work because the condition of equipment and appliances frequently isn't apparent until a prospective buyer turns something on, or asks you to turn something on, only to be greeted by a wheezing air conditioner, rattling hot water pipes, a growling dishwasher—or nothing. If an appliance is to remain in the house, make sure it works.

Since many equipment and appliance deficiencies don't show, they need to be checked carefully and scheduled for repair early enough so that house calls by repair people won't have to be needlessly duplicated and so that parts that have to be ordered will arrive in time to complete repairs before you need to start showing your house.

USING THE CHECKLISTS

We have provided three forms for use in surveying the condition of your house and for scheduling cosmetic improvements, cleanup, and repairs:

- Exterior Checklist (Form 63.1, page F497)
- Interior Checklist (Form 63.2, page F509)

- Appliance/Equipment Checklist (Form 63.3, page F525)

If possible, have more than one person, each using his or her own photocopy of the appropriate list, check each category to make sure something isn't overlooked or taken for granted. Some people in the family will know more about some things in the house than other people do. By making use of everyone's knowledge, you'll end up with a better survey. When the surveys are completed, hold a family meeting to decide who will be responsible for what.

It was necessary to produce checklists that could be used to survey a wide range of homes—from big, old haunted-house-type homes to newer, much smaller houses. We recognize that few houses have a fireplace in every room, or a basement entry on every side of the house, or window air conditioners and central air conditioning, so just cross out items that don't apply to your house. Conversely, space has been provided in our checklists for the insertion of any items we may have missed—a hot tub on the patio, a greenhouse in the backyard, maybe even a fireplace in one of the bathrooms. Furthermore, by making additional photocopies of some of the forms' pages (see pages F520–F522 and F528–F529), the checklists can accommodate houses with any number of bedrooms or bathrooms.

To complete our ready-to-use checklists, do the following:

1. Under **OK**, place a check mark to the right of every item that needs no work.
2. Under **To Be Done By Us,** fill in the initials of the family member who is responsible for doing each particular job.
3. Under **Our Priority,** number each do-it-yourself item, starting with 1, from the most important on down for every item listed to establish some kind of "first things first" priority. There's no need, nor is it probably even desirable, to hew too closely to your priority list, but it does serve as a useful guide for allocating money, time, and effort.
4. Under **To Be Done By Contractor,** fill in the initials of the family member who is to contact repair people and to:
   - Obtain estimates
   - Arrange for access
   - Be at home while work is being done
   - Make sure work is completed by target date
   - Inspect work after completion
   - Approve payment
5. Under **Contractor Priority,** number each contractor job in order of importance.

Expect the whole job—survey and makeready—to take at least a month and possibly two if the season for tackling certain jobs is wrong or if repair people have long waiting lists. Start as early as you can, but no later than eight weeks prior to the date on which you feel you'll need to be able to start showing your home.

64 What's So Special About Your House?

When prospects visit your home, you'll tell them about your house. However, after looking at maybe ten or fifteen houses, they will have a hard time remembering whether yours was the one with the gazebo in the backyard or the one with the alligator in the basement —they will, that is, unless you give them a concise fact sheet to take home.

Your several-page fact sheet containing information about construction, the number and dimensions of the rooms, appliances that go with the house, site data, facts about the neighborhood, etc., will be a ready reference, but it will also be something they'll keep "tripping" over at home—a constant reminder of your house and all that it has to offer.

Completing our ready-to-use **Fact Sheet** (Form 64.1, page F533) will take a bit of time, but gathering the information will also put at your fingertips the data you're going to need anyway—the data to answer the scores of questions you'll be asked by prospective buyers with different ideas about what they want in a house they're going to own and live in.

At first glance, maybe even at second glance, the fact sheet will probably appear to include more than anyone would ever want to know about a house. But imagine what your thinking would be if you were actually considering *buying* that house. All of a sudden you couldn't have too much information.

Our fact sheet should, of course, be given to prospects, but it can also be taken or mailed to the housing officers of nearby military bases, local colleges and universities, and major corporations. Friends, neighbors, and co-workers should also get copies of the fact sheet.

It's not a bad idea when handing out fact sheets to friends, neighbors, and co-workers to mention that you'll be happy to pay a "bird-dog" fee to anyone who sends you a prospect who actually buys the house. Be sure to mention the amount ($200 to $500 isn't unusual).

The fact sheet (fact sheets, really, because it's several pages in length) is organized into several basic areas, occasionally repeating information that falls into more than one category. The first page contains owners' names and phone numbers, plus some general information about the house. The second page (House and Lot Plan) can be either an outline diagram of the house and lot (similar to the one on page 298) or a photocopy of the plat plan of your house and property taken from your file of house papers. If you can't find a plat plan among your house purchase documents, your mortgage company should be able to supply a copy.

Other fact sheet categories include:

- Construction
- Room Dimensions
- Carpet–Flooring
- Garage–Carport
- Basement
- Heating–Plumbing–Electrical
- Appliances–Built-ins
- Site Data
- Off-Site Improvements
- Taxes, Utilities, and Insurance
- Neighborhood Data
- Community Data
- Major Employers
- General Description

Financial data, such as appraised fair market value, cost per square foot, and mortgage loan information, will be included on a separate sheet that you will also give to buyers but won't be stapled together with the balance of the fact sheet pages (see page F541). This information, including how to determine your home's selling price, will be covered in the next chapter.

COMPLETING YOUR FACT SHEET

Study the sample fact sheet beginning on page 297 before starting to complete your own. Use as few abbreviations as possible. Do use the symbol N/A to indicate "not applicable" if your house does not include a room or appliance listed on the fact sheet— less negative than having to say "no" or "none."

Use your original house plans and specifications, mortgage and other house purchase papers, tax receipts, and utility bills, plus your own information, to complete this form.

You'll probably need at least a hundred copies of the fact sheet, plus an extra twenty-five or so copies of the photo description sheet (see below) and general information sections. These can be produced very inexpensively by a "quick-copy" printer or duplicating service.

HOUSE AND LOT PLAN

If you draw a house and lot plan, don't bother trying to show as much detail as an interior plan. Just show the shape and approximate size of the lot plus an outline of the house and garage, driveway, sidewalks, etc.

Make the drawing as close to scale as possible, but type **NOT TO EXACT SCALE** somewhere on the plan. No use having someone hassle you later because the driveway is 20 feet instead of 22 feet wide. Follow the sample House and Lot Plan provided on page 298.

SEPARATE PHOTO DESCRIPTION SHEET

If possible, take a photograph of your home. Back away far enough to show some of the front lawn if possible, but also try to eliminate from view as many overhead wires and adjacent buildings and as much background clutter as you possibly can. If you can manage to take photos on a slightly hazy day, you can eliminate a lot of harsh, distracting shadows. Also, be sure to take advantage of the best light for photographing your house—either in the morning *or* the afternoon.

If you're not sure of yourself and have a friend who's a pretty good photographer, ask him or her to take the photos for you. You'll probably want a front view from a slight angle, but nothing spectacular.

Have a couple of 5 × 7 prints made of the best picture. Tell whoever makes the prints that they're for reproduction—that way you'll get a photo with slightly more contrast that the printer can more easily work with.

Write a brief, general description of your house (include address, number of rooms, number of bedrooms and baths, amount of square feet in the house, size of the lot, etc., plus any special features) to use as a caption under the photo. Head the sheet with the photo and caption, FOR SALE BY OWNER (see our Sample Photo Description Sheet on page 318). Include it with your fact sheet, but also plan to put it on bulletin boards at supermarkets, laundromats, churches, colleges, universities, etc.—with permission.

Sample of Form 64.1/F533

Fact Sheet

Date _____ April 15, 1984 _____

Owner(s) _____ David and Jodie Newberry _____

Address _____ 2405 Colonial Court, Hinkley, New Bedford 10567 _____

Home Phone __205-432-6891__ **Business Phone** __205-564-6784__ **Business Phone** __205-564-9901__

General Information

Architectural Type _____ Stone and Cedar Shingle Contemporary _____

Selling Price _____ $85,000 _____

Square Feet (House) __1,350__		**No. of Rooms** __Seven__
Square Feet (Lot) __4,890__		**No. of Bedrooms** __Three__
Lot Dimensions __60′ x 81′6″__		**No. of Bathrooms** __Two__
Garage Dimensions __20′ x 22′__		**Basement** __N/A__

This is a well maintained home constructed of generally superior materials. It is sited on a level, well-drained lot on a quiet, block-long residential cul-de-sac. The double garage has been converted to additional living space by replacing the garage doors with aluminum casement, double-pane insulating glass. This space is attractively paneled in weathered cedar, is carpeted, and is adequately heated and cooled. The area is used by the present owners as an art studio and home office. The house contains ample storage space, has a modern kitchen, and has many built-in appliances. The house lacks a garage.

Note: N/A = not applicable.

Sample of Form 64.1 (*Continued*)

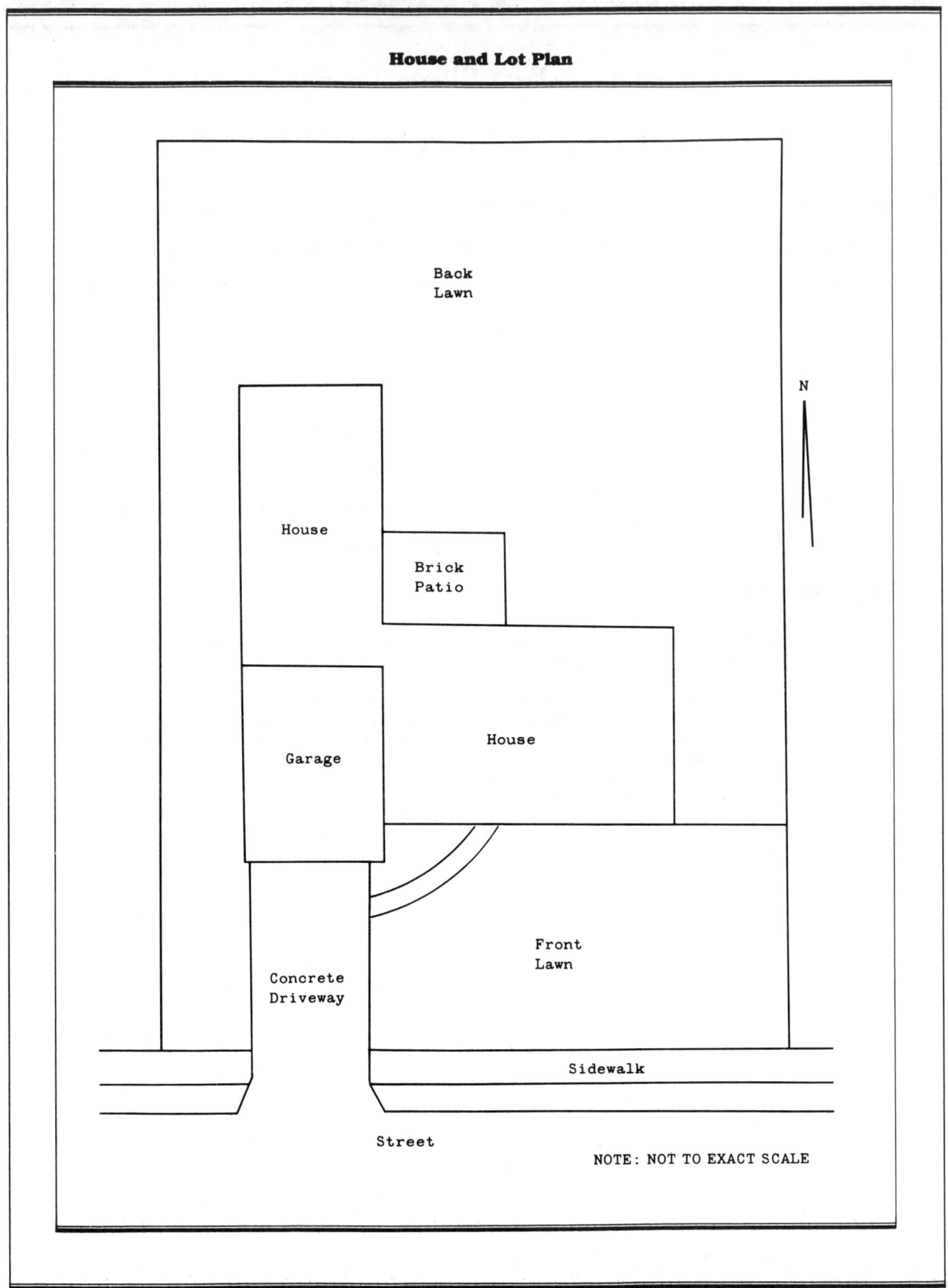

House and Lot Plan

Back Lawn

N

House

Brick Patio

House

Garage

Concrete Driveway

Front Lawn

Sidewalk

Street

NOTE: NOT TO EXACT SCALE

Sample of Form 64.1 (*Continued*)

Construction

Date of Construction ___ 1971 ___	Interior Walls ___ One-half-inch Gypsum Drywall ___
Footings ___ Concrete ___	Interior Doors ___ Interior Slab ___
Foundation Walls ___ N/A ___	Floors (1st Floor) ___ Oak ___
Exterior Walls ___ Stone & Cedar Shingle ___	Floors (2nd Floor) ___ N/A ___
Roof Material ___ Composition Shingle ___	Floors (3rd Floor) ___ N/A ___
Roof Type ___ Gabled ___	Floors (Bathroom #1) ___ Vinyl Tile ___
Framing ___ 2″ x 4″; 16″ Center ___	Floors (Bathroom #2) ___ Vinyl Tile ___
Windows ___ Aluminum Casement ___	Floors (Bathroom #3) ___ N/A ___
Guttering Downspouts ___ Galvanized Steel ___	Fireplace #1 ___ N/A ___
Exterior Doors ___ Solid Oak ___	Fireplace #2 ___ N/A ___
Screens ___ Aluminum ___	
Partitions ___ 2″ x 4″; 16″ Center ___	

Room Dimensions

Entry–Foyer ___ 6′ x 8′ ___	Bedroom #1 ___ 14′ x 14′ ___
Living Room ___ 16′ x 14′ ___	Bedroom #2 ___ 14′ x 12′ ___
Dining Room ___ 14′ x 14′ ___	Bedroom #3 ___ 10′ x 13′ ___
Den–Library ___ N/A ___	Bedroom #4 ___ N/A ___
Kitchen ___ 11′ x 13′ ___	Bedroom #5 ___ N/A ___
Pantry–Laundry Room ___ 6′ x 7′ ___	Family Room ___ N/A ___
Basement ___ N/A ___	Attic ___ N/A ___
Bathroom #1 ___ 6′ x 8′ ___	Garage ___ 22′ x 20′* ___
Bathroom #2 ___ 6′ x 6′ ___	
Bathroom #3 ___ N/A ___	

*Converted to additional living space.

Note: N/A = not applicable.

Sample of Form 64.1 (*Continued*)

Carpet–Flooring

Entry-Foyer	Vinyl Tile (Black-White)	Bedroom #1	Nylon (Off White)
Living Room	Nylon (Light Blue)	Bedroom #2	Nylon (Light Green)
Dining Room	Nylon (Light Blue)	Bedroom #3	Nylon (Yellow)
Den-Library	N/A	Bedroom #4	N/A
Kitchen	Vinyl Tile (Yellow)	Bedroom #5	N/A
Pantry-Laundry Room	Vinyl Tile (Yellow)	Family Room	N/A
Basement	N/A	Attic	N/A
Bathroom #1	Ceramic Tile (Yellow)	Garage	Concrete*
Bathroom #2	Ceramic Tile (Light Blue)		
Bathroom #3	N/A		

Garage–Carport

Attached or Detached?	Attached	Garage or Carport?	Garage
Type of Construction	Stone & Cedar Shingle	Insulation	3½" Rock Wool Batts
Type of Floor	Concrete	Drain	Plugged
Automatic Doors?	Replaced by Aluminum Casement Patio	Heated?	Yes
Roof Type	Gabled	Dimensions	22' x 20'
Roof Material	Composition Shingle	Cooled?	Yes

Basement

Outside Entrance	N/A	Finished Ceiling	N/A
Type of Floor	N/A	Finished Floor	N/A
Floor Drain	N/A		
Square Feet	N/A		
Finished Walls	N/A		

*Converted to living space.

Note: N/A = not applicable.

Sample of Form 64.1 (*Continued*)

Heating–Plumbing–Electrical

Type of Heating ___ Gas ___

Type of Cooling ___ G.E. FF 2241 Central Air ___

Type of Hot Water ___ Gas ___

Hot Water Capacity ___ 30 Gallons ___

Electricity ___ 14-Gallon Copper Romex ___

Plumbing ___ Copper ___

Insulation (Exterior Walls) ___ 3½" Rock Wool Batts ___

Insulation (Floor) ___ N/A ___

Insulation (Ceiling) ___ 6" Rock Wool Batts ___

Insulation (Roof) ___ 6" Rock Wool Batts ___

Appliances–Built-ins

Clothes Washer ___ G.E. WW-8856 ___

Clothes Dryer ___ G.E. WD-7754 ___

Freezer ___ N/A ___

Refrigerator ___ N/A ___

Stove ___ Magic Chef ASD-55-783 ___

Oven ___ Magic Chef ASF-57-9432 ___

Dishwasher ___ G.E. GG SD 250 ___

Trash Compactor ___ N/A ___

Disposer ___ G.E. GGFC 100 ___

Exhaust Fan Hood ___ Rangeaire GTR-813 ___

Site Data

Subdivision ___ GREEN SPRINGS ___

Block No. ___ 32 ___

Square Feet (Lot) ___ 4,890 ___

Lot Shape ___ Rectangle ___

Frontage ___ 60' ___

Elevation ___ Slightly Above Street Level ___

Square Feet (Front Yard) ___ 1,320 ___

Square Feet (Backyard) ___ 780 ___

Lawn Type ___ Merion Blue ___

Fencing Type and Height ___ N/A ___

Driveway Type ___ Concrete ___

Zoned ___ R-1 ___

Lot No. ___ 16 ___

Front Yard Setback ___ 22' ___

Right Side Setback ___ 8' ___

Left Side Setback ___ 7' ___

Rear Setback ___ 13' ___

Served by:

Gas ___ Yes ___   Water ___ Yes ___

Sewer ___ Yes ___   Electricity ___ Yes ___

Telephone ___ Yes ___ Trash P/U ___ Yes ___

Note: N/A = not applicable.

Sample of Form 64.1 (*Continued*)

Off-Site Improvements

Street Surface __Asphalt Paving__   Streetlights? __Yes__

Sidewalk __Concrete__   Trees (Where?) __Both Sides of Street__

Curb–Gutter __Concrete__   _____ _____

Storm Sewers? __Yes__   _____ _____

Alley? __No__   _____ _____

Street Access __Dead End__   _____ _____

Taxes, Utilities, and Insurance

Property Tax (per Year) __$600.00__   Average Electric Bill (Monthly) __$85.00__

School Tax (per Year) __N/A__   Average Fuel Bill (Monthly) __N/A__

Average Trash Pickup Bill (Monthly) __$11.50__   Average Gas Bill (Monthly) __$35.00__

Fire Insurance (per Year) __$224.00__   Average Water Bill (Monthly) __$9.50__

_____ _____   _____ _____

_____ _____   _____ _____

_____ _____   _____ _____

Note: N/A = not applicable.

Sample of Form 64.1 (*Continued*)

Neighborhood Data

Elementary School __Nathan Hale__ (Bus Pickup)

High School __Belle Boyd__ (6 miles)

Junior High School __Seth B. Putnam__ (Bus Pickup)

Nursery School __Humpty Dumpty__ (Bus Pickup)

Junior College __N/A__

College/University __Western State Teachers__ (9 miles)

Downtown __Bus Lines, 20 minutes__ (7 miles)

Shopping Center __Buymor Mall__ (4 miles)

Bus Lines __To Downtown, west; Sommerton & Boston, east__

Hospital __Theodor Aschenbrandt Medical Center__ (6 miles)

Post Office __Hinkley (10567)__ (4 miles)

Fire Station __Hinkley Township__ (4 miles)

Police Station __Hinkley Township__ (4 miles)

Park __Millard Fillmore: swimming & tennis__ (7 miles)

Church __Several within 5 miles__

Trash Pickup __Thursday and Monday mornings__

_____   _____

_____   _____

_____   _____

Note: N/A = not applicable.

Sample of Form 64.1 (*Continued*)

Community Data

City/Town _____ Hinkley _____

County _____ Putnam _____   State _____ New Bedford _____

Mean Summer Temperature ____ 67° ____   Mean Winter Temperature ____ 29° ____

Population 19 70 ____ 315,000 ____   Population 19 79 ____ 385,000 (Est.) ____

Major Employers

Great American Mutual Life	3,200
Internal Revenue Service Regional Office	10,000
Sol-R-Tech, Inc.	3,500
Olde Stone Mill Bakeries, Inc.	2,500

General Description

Hinkley is a well-established community in the eastern portion of the state of New Bedford. Its population has been relatively stable since 1975, when citizens voted to discourage industry and limit the number of commercial and residential building permits. The absence of industrial pollution and the quality of life made possible by the absence of growth have enhanced property values compared to other, nearby, more industrialized communities. Tourism provides significant employment. The area became known as "the handmaiden of democracy" after the army of British General Sir Cecil Drake, who, unable to locate any of New Bedford's townships or villages on his military maps, became lost, retreated to Boston, and shortly thereafter was defeated at the Battle of Lexington on April 19, 1775.

Sample of Form 64.1 (*Continued*)

FINANCIAL DATA

Appraised Fair Market Value __$94,500__   Selling Price __$85,000__   Cost per Square Foot __$62.96__

Mortgage(s) __$44,980__   Mortgage Payments __$463.09__

Property Tax (per Year) __$600.00__   Insurance (per Year) __$544.00__

Average Electric Bill (Monthly) __$85.00__   Average Gas Bill (Monthly) __$35.00__

Average Fuel Bill (Monthly) __$76.00__   Average Water Bill (Monthly) __$9.50__

Average Trash Pickup Bill (Monthly) __$11.50__   School Tax (per Year) __N/A__

Note: N/A = not applicable.

Pricing Your House

There's no shortage of ways to price your house. You can look at newspaper ads to see what apparently similar houses are supposedly selling for, you can ask real estate brokers to tell you what they think you should be able to get, you can ask recent buyers of homes in your neighborhood how much they paid, and you can check the records at your county courthouse to learn the actual selling price for similar houses in your area.

Newspaper ads can tell you asking prices, but they can't tell you selling prices. Real estate brokers, in business to make money selling houses, might "high ball" you, suggesting an unrealistically high price for your home, hoping to persuade you to let them sell it for you (then advising a lower price after your home has been on the market awhile); or they might "low ball" you, suggesting a low price, hoping to make a quick commission on the fast sale of your underpriced home. People who've recently bought or sold in your neighborhood are likely to invent a price that makes them look like a better bargainer than they really are.

Some of these methods might give you an accurate idea of what you could get for your house—and then again, they might not. None of them, no matter how accurate, can give you something absolutely essential that you're going to need: *credibility*.

SELLING PRICE SURVEY

If you cruise your neighborhood and nearby similar neighborhoods, you can probably find a half-dozen houses with **For Sale** signs placarded **SOLD**. Write down the address and name on the mailbox if there is one. If the house is vacant, ask a neighbor for the name of the previous owner and the approximate date of sale.

If the house is occupied, explain to the owner that you are planning to sell your house and are attempting to set a fair price, then ask him if he would mind telling you the selling price. Additionally, find out the date of sale and the current owner's name. With that information the county clerk can tell you what the house *really* sold for.

Depending upon how willing your informant is to talk, see if you can also find out:

1. The number of square feet in the house
2. Number of bedrooms
3. Number of bathrooms
4. Whether one- or two-car garage
5. Dimensions of the lot
6. Amount of frontage

When you've got as much information as you're going to be able to get on, say, half a dozen recently sold houses, make several photocopies of the **Selling Price Comparison Survey** (Form 65.1, page F543) and, using the completed sample on page 309 as a guide, fill in the following information:

- Address
- Buyer–Seller Name
- No. of Bedrooms
- No. of Bathrooms
- Garage Capacity
- Extras
- Date of Sale

The actual amount the house sold for, the price per square foot (PPSF), and the county clerk's file number will be added later.

Give the county clerk a typed copy of the survey form and tell him or her that you'd like to know the price for which each of the houses was sold AND the county clerk's office file number for the transaction. Offer to look up the information yourself or to come back later to pick up the form if that would be more convenient for the clerk.

With the price and total number of square feet in each house in hand, you can easily figure the **selling price per square foot:**

$$\$50,000 \div 1,350 \text{ sq. ft.} = \$37.00 \text{ per sq. ft.}$$

To get a better idea of what your house might sell for, determine the selling price per square foot (PPSF) for every one of your survey houses, add those together, and divide the total by the number of houses to learn the average selling price per square foot:

House No. 1:	$38.00 (PPSF)
House No. 2:	39.00
House No. 3:	32.00
House No. 4:	40.00
House No. 5:	39.00
House No. 6:	39.00
	$227.00

Avg. PPSF = $227.00 ÷ 6 = $37.83

Now, to figure your estimated selling price:

No. sq. ft. Your House	×	Avg. Price per sq. ft.	=	Est. Price Your House
1,350	×	$37.83	=	$51,070

More than being fairly reliable, your survey will provide a figure that is **believable**, a credible price that prospective buyers will have to admit to themselves is reasonable.

There's an interesting thing about home prices: expensive improvements, such as the added living space in our sample home, or such other improvements as a swimming pool don't add much to the value of a house. Some buyers would rather have a garage than an extra room, and many buyers will consider a swimming pool a nuisance, an extra expense, and a hazard that could be a costly liability. Regardless of improvements, you're pretty much locked into the price per square foot of other houses in your neighborhood.

When you're ready to start showing your home, type up a neat copy of your **Selling Price Comparison Survey**, including the county clerk's file number on each transaction, and give a photocopy of the survey to each prospect when the time comes to start talking price. Point out that you have included the county clerk's file number so the buyer can easily confirm your figures.

APPRAISAL OF FAIR MARKET VALUE

Now that you've made your house ready to show, have completed your **Fact Sheet**, and have made several copies of your **Selling Price Comparison Survey**, you're ready to obtain an *appraisal of fair market value*, possibly your most effective selling tool yet.

There are many kinds of appraisals: for replacement cost, for income potential, and for insurance and estate valuation, to name a few. But what you want is an appraisal for *fair market value*, which is generally defined as the price that a willing and informed buyer would pay to a willing and informed seller. In other words, a fair price—fair market value.

Since fair market value not only helps you establish a credible price for your house, but is also a cornerstone of "fair lending value," you'll need a qualified, independent appraiser whose appraisal will be accepted by local mortgage lenders.

The best way to find an appraiser whose appraisal is acceptable to mortgage lenders is to contact a mortgage lender, a savings and loan association, or a mortgage bank close to where you live. The lender who holds your present mortgage might be a good place to start.

Explain that you plan to try selling your house yourself and that you would like to obtain an appraisal that would be acceptable to them. (If it's acceptable to them, it will almost surely be acceptable to other lenders also.) The lender may arrange an appraisal for you by contacting someone whose work is known to them or may give you the names of a few appraisers to contact directly.

Your county courthouse should also have a list of county-approved appraisers. You can also check your phone book under **Real Estate Appraisers** or **Appraisers—Real Estate**, depending upon the whim of whoever organizes your local yellow pages. Just make sure any appraiser you use is acceptable to mortgage lenders.

VA AND FHA APPRAISALS

You may not want to sell your home under a VA-guaranteed or FHA-insured mortgage because of

lenders' practice of charging sellers "points" to compensate themselves for the lower interest rate limits imposed by the VA (Veterans Administration) and FHA (Federal Housing Administration).

One "point" equals 1 percent of the amount of the mortgage, $300, for example, being one "point" on a $30,000 mortgage. A lender making an FHA-insured or VA-guaranteed mortgage on your home might charge you, the seller, five or six points ($1,500 to $1,800) on such a loan. The VA and FHA response to this procedure is that their programs are set up to help people *buy* homes, not *sell* homes. (Have a nice day!)

Even though you may not plan to sell your home under a VA or FHA mortgage, it's a good idea to obtain now a VA Certificate of Reasonable Value/HUD Conditional Commitment [for mortgage insurance], an example of which is supplied on page 313, to avoid delay later on if you find that you *have* to sell your home VA or FHA to get it off your hands.

If you're still on good terms with your mortgage loan officer, go back to him or her and explain that, in addition to an appraisal for conventional mortgage purposes, you'd like to obtain a VA Certificate of Reasonable Value/HUD Conditional Commitment. Such a certificate will state a fair market value for your home (nice to have in addition to the independent appraisal) and will facilitate a quick sale under an FHA or VA mortgage.

When contacted by the mortgage lender, the VA will name someone from its list of approved appraisers; this is the person the lender must use. On the basis of this appraisal, you will receive a VA Certificate of Reasonable Value/HUD Conditional Commitment.

In case you're wondering why your mortgage lender would be willing to go to all this trouble—which really isn't such a bother because lenders do these kinds of things all the time anyway—it's because they do hope to handle the loan. The cost of a VA appraisal, by the way, is fixed at an $85 maximum.

Starting on page 310 we have provided the following blank VA/FHA/HUD forms so that you can familiarize yourself with whatever information is required or supplied by each form:

- Page 310 INSTRUCTIONS FOR PREPARATION OF VA REQUEST FOR DETERMINATION OF REASONABLE VALUE/HUD APPLICATION FOR PROPERTY APPRAISAL AND COMMITMENT
- Page 311 VA REQUEST FOR DETERMINATION OF REASONABLE VALUE (Real Estate)/HUD APPLICATION FOR PROPERTY APPRAISAL AND COMMITMENT
- Page 312 RESIDENTIAL APPRAISAL REPORT
- Page 313 VA CERTIFICATE OF REASONABLE VALUE/HUD CONDITIONAL COMMITMENT
- Page 314 ENDORSEMENT TO CERTIFICATE OF REASONABLE VALUE [for use in the event of modification in the value of previously appraised property]

WORKING WITH YOUR APPRAISER

Before any appraiser sets foot on your property, make sure that your house is in perfect shape to show; otherwise, your appraisal report may contain such buyer turn-off comments as:

- "Missing shingles on roof; estimated cost to repair: $250."
- "Worn vinyl tile flooring in kitchen; estimated cost to replace: $300."
- "Some guttering on rear of house damaged and loose; estimated cost to repair: $125."
- "Hallway carpeting worn; estimated cost to replace: $350."

These are relatively small items and could easily be deducted from the expected selling price—they will certainly be deducted from your home's estimated fair market value by your appraiser—but they're also a sure turn off to any buyer who wants a home that's "ready to go" or who may wonder what else is wrong with the house that the appraiser didn't see.

If the appraiser does spot a deficiency that you somehow missed in making your home ready to show, ask him or her to give you a few days to get it fixed and then come back so the deficiency won't have to be listed in the appraisal report.

There's a funny thing about appraisers. They'll go over your house like a temperance-minded maiden aunt looking for hidden whiskey bottles and when the job seems done will ask, "By the way, what do you think your house is worth?" Then (surprise!) they'll hand in an appraisal listing precisely the figure you mentioned.

So when the appraiser asks what you think your house is worth, mention your comparison survey (though not necessarily showing it) and declare the most optimistic value you can honestly report. After all, who knows your house better than you?

There is yet another turn of the prayer wheel that you can make. There are few more certain ways to endear yourself to someone, almost anyone, than by doing their work for them, and now you're in a position to do just that. Your fact sheet, remember? Sit your appraiser down and give him or her a nice, pristine copy of all those facts and dimensions and interesting things about your house to read while sipping—depending upon the season—a nice cup of hot coffee or something that tastes even better than good, old-fashioned lemonade. Your kindness may be returned by the tacking on of a thousand or two to the value of that highly attractive, extremely well-maintained house you live in.

There are a number of additional financing approaches you can use, some of which considerably reduce the amount of down payment required. These will be covered in the chapter on helping your buyer obtain financing (Chapter 68).

A good appraisal won't be free; at this writing the appraisal fee for an average three-bedroom, two-bath home is between $125 and $175. The cost of a separate VA appraisal, if not done by your original appraiser, is pegged by the VA at an $85 maximum. Since you must have an acceptable appraisal before anyone will finance the purchase of your home, you might as well obtain it early enough to help sell your house.

If you've followed this chapter's suggestions, you'll have the following ammunition to justify your selling price:

- Selling Price Comparison Survey
- Independent Appraisal of Fair Market Value
- VA Certificate of Reasonable Value/HUD Conditional Commitment.

That's a strong, objective, and credible lineup that's hard to argue with.

TERMITE INSPECTION

There's one more document, though not directly related to the pricing of your home, that you'll need and, in some jurisdictions, be required to have. That's a termite inspection report certifying that your house is free of termite infestation and damage.

You'll find plenty of people offering to provide free termite inspection under **Pest Control** in your yellow pages, but ask your mortgage lender for advise so the report you obtain will be acceptable to the lender, FHA, and VA.

Add a photocopy of your termite inspection report to the fact sheet, appraisals, and other information that you have ready to give to prospects.

Sample of Form 65.1/F543

Selling Price Comparison Survey

House No.	Address	No. of Bedrooms	No. of Bathrooms	Garage Capacity	Extras	Sold for	PPSF
1	8814 Burning Tree Road	3	2	2	—	$55,500	$38
	Hinkley				**Square Feet**	1,450	
	M/M Peter Dubinsky	# R-81-465567			**Date of Sale**	July 6, 1984	
2	6430 Hermitge Drive	3	2	2	S.P.	$53,750	$39
	Hinkley				**Square Feet**	1,380	
	M/M A. K. Buckerman	# R-81-465411			**Date of Sale**	June 2, 1984	
3	5161 Azalea	3	2	1	—	$44,000	$32
	Hinkley				**Square Feet**	1,370	
	M/M R. X. Wojclechowski	# R-81-465224			**Date of Sale**	May 31, 1984	
4	5506 Eastshire Drive	3	2	2	—	$56,250	$40
	Hinkley				**Square Feet**	1,390	
	Lillan Rhoulac	# R-81-165578			**Date of Sale**	July 7, 1984	
5	2807 East DeSoto	3	2	2	—	$52,500	$39
	Hinkley				**Square Feet**	1,350	
	M/M Peter Bambach	# R-81-464653			**Date of Sale**	Aug. 3, 1984	
6	124 Strong Point	3	2	2	—	$54,750	$39
	Hinkley				**Square Feet**	1,420	
	M/M L. L. McCall	# R-81-465496			**Date of Sale**	June 28, 1984	

VA/FHA/HUD Forms

Form Approved
OMB No. 2900-0045

INSTRUCTIONS FOR PREPARATION OF VA REQUEST FOR DETERMINATION OF REASONABLE VALUE/HUD APPLICATION FOR PROPERTY APPRAISAL AND COMMITMENT

This form is a combined VA Request for Determination of Reasonable Value and HUD Application For Property Appraisal and Commitment. *All entries must be typed.*

Remove this instruction page and complete page 1 following the instructions below, using the reverse of this instruction page as a worksheet. After completion of page 1, detach page 8 for your records and forward the packet, together with any necessary exhibits, to either the VA office having jurisdiction or the assigned HUD fee appraiser (as applicable).

Since certain selected data from page 1 is transcribed onto the Appraisal Report and the VA Certificate of Reasonable Value/HUD Conditional Commitment, we request that this form be carefully prepared. Incomplete submissions impede timely processing at loss to both the Government and the requester.

This report is authorized by law (38 U.S.C. 1804(a) and 1810(b)(5) or 12 U.S.C. 1709, as applicable). Failure to provide the information requested can result in rejection of the property as security for a loan.

VA-REQUIRED EXHIBITS TO BE SENT WITH APPLICATION

SALES CONTRACTS: In cases involving proposed construction or existing construction not previously occupied, a copy of the executed or proposed sales contract must be submitted or if a previously approved form of contract is to be used the approved contract code number may be shown in Item No. 37.

PROPOSED CONSTRUCTION: 1. Exhibits as specified in VA Pamphlet 26A-3, Revised, Required Exhibits to Accompany Request for Determination of Reasonable Value—Proposed Construction Cases. 2. In Committee Appraisal cases a separate request form must be submitted for each type or model. The lots and blocks involved for each type and model are to be listed in Item 2, Property Address.

EXISTING CONSTRUCTION: 1. ALTERATIONS, IMPROVEMENTS OR REPAIRS—Complete drawings and specifications indicating the work to be done and its relation to the house, in the quantity required by the local VA office. 2. NOT PREVIOUSLY OCCUPIED AND CONSTRUCTION COMPLETED WITHIN 12 CALENDAR MONTHS—Contact local VA office for eligibility criteria and required exhibits.

HUD-REQUIRED EXHIBITS TO BE SENT WITH APPLICATION

HOUSES PROPOSED OR UNDER CONSTRUCTION

1. Complete working drawings, in duplicate, including plot plan, foundation or basement plans, plans of all floors, elevations, grade levels, sectional wall details, and heating layout. (Not required if application is accompanied by VA CRV).

2. If advance approval of additions to or deletions from the basic house is desired, submit Schedule of Alternates, FHA Form 2439. (If application is accompanied by VA CRV, circle additions or deletions on first page of master CRV).

3. Specifications on HUD Form 92005, Description of Materials, in duplicate (Not required if application is accompanied by VA CRV).

4. If an individual water or sewer system is proposed, submit exhibits for each individual property in duplicate. (Not required if application is accompanied by VA CRV).

5. If 5 or more repeat cases are involved, FHA Form 1322 may be submitted. *(First check with local field office. Acceptance of FHA Form 1322 is optional with office. If office is accepting form, obtain copy of HUD Handbook 4115.3).*

Unless application is accompanied by VA CRV, when applications involving repeats of a basic house are simultaneously submitted, submit exhibits for each basic house, with copies of a master plot plan showing location and development of all individual plots, and designating the basic house or variation thereof to be built on each. Unless each plot is clearly shown with an adequate scale on a master plan, individual plot plans are required in triplicate.

EXISTING HOUSES
(Not Required if Application is Accompanied by VA CRV)

1. WITH MAJOR ADDITIONS OR ALTERATIONS PROPOSED:
(a) Complete drawings and specifications, in duplicate, indicating the work to be done and its relation to the house.
(b) Describe minor improvements and illustrate by a sketch.
2. NOT OCCUPIED FOR A FULL YEAR SINCE COMPLETION with Individual Sewerage or Water Systems, or both:
(a) Detail drawings with specifications of Sewerage System, showing cross-section of components with dimensions. If tank is prefab, indicate make, model number and commercial standard label for metal tanks.
(b) Plot Plan showing layout of system indicating distance between its components, dwelling and property lines.
(c) Current Percolation Test Data.
(d) Soil Characteristics depth of at least 6 ft. for disposal field or bed-to-depth of seepage pit when pit is used.
(e) Water Table Data.—Depth at which water is met. Reading should be taken to a point beyond lateral trench or seepage pit depth.
(f) Builder's certification that sewerage system as installed complies with exhibits.
(g) If property has a well show whether well is dug or drilled, give Specifications. Show on Plot Plan, location of well and distance from disposal area, from adjoining properties disposal areas or pits.

SALES CONTRACTS

In cases involving known borrowers accompanied by a Certificate of Reasonable Value issued by VA, lenders must submit a copy of the sales contract and HUD Form 92900, Application for Mortgagor Approval, with the application.

FORM ENTRIES

SECTION OF ACT: Insert section of the National Housing Act requested (HUD CASES ONLY).

NAME, ADDRESS, AND ZIP CODE: Make sure to enter the ZIP Code in all blocks which require an address entry.

LEGAL DESCRIPTION: Insert legal description. If necessary attach 4 copies of a separate sheet showing the legal description.

TITLE LIMITATIONS: Enter known title exceptions. If none are known enter "None." Include easements, special assessments, mandatory homeowners association membership, etc. Exceptions noted on this application will be considered in reasonable value. Attach separate sheet (4 copies) if necessary.

LOT DIMENSIONS: Show frontage X depth. If irregular, indicate dimensions of all perimeter lot lines (FOR HUD CASES, enter total square feet. For irregular lots, estimate square footage to nearest 1000 sq. ft.).

REMOVABLE EQUIPMENT: Personal property, such as furniture, drapes and rugs will not be valued and may not be included in the loan. However, wall to wall carpeting may be included in value and also included in the loan.

BUILDING STATUS—SUBSTAN. REHAB.: Substantial rehabilitation should be indicated if the structure is substandard (dilapidated condition or lack of essential plumbing) and is to be rehabilitated with the proceeds of the loan being applied for. (APPLICABLE TO HUD CASES ONLY.)

NUMBER OF UNITS: Insert number of living units.

CONSTRUCTION COMPLETED: Insert both month and year when property has been completed less than two years. If over two years old, insert year completed only.

COMMENTS ON SPECIAL ASSESSMENTS AND/OR HOMEOWNER ASSOCIATION CHARGES: Indicate special assessments which are now a lien or will become a lien. In the case of a planned unit development, condominium, or a mandatory membership homeowner association, indicate the current monthly or other periodic assessment.

MINERAL RIGHTS: If reserved, explain either in space shown as title exceptions or by separate page.

LEASEHOLD CASES: (Usually Hawaii or Maryland.) If property involves a leasehold, insert the ground rent per year and show whether the lease is for 99 years or renewable, whether it has previously been HUD or VA approved, and its expiration date. In VA cases, submit two copies of the lease agreement.

SALE PRICE: Enter proposed sale price except when application involves an individual owner-occupant building for himself/herself. In such cases, enter estimated cost (house plus lot). If refinancing, enter amount of outstanding indebtedness.

CERTIFICATIONS FOR HUD SUBMISSIONS: Each application must be signed by an authorized official of the mortgagee under the Mortgagee's Certificate. In the case of an existing house, either the mortgagee, builder or seller may sign the Builder/Seller's Agreement. If proposed construction, the Builder/Seller's Agreement must be executed by the Builder or Seller.

NOTE: If title is not "fee simple," submit copies in duplicate of all pertinent legal data providing a full explanation of the title involved.

VA FORM 26-1805, AUG 1980   HUD FORM 92800-1

VA/FHA/HUD Forms (*Continued*)

Form Approved
OMB No. 2900-0045

VA REQUEST FOR DETERMINATION OF REASONABLE VALUE (Real Estate) HUD APPLICATION FOR PROPERTY APPRAISAL AND COMMITMENT	HUD Section of Act	1. CASE NUMBER

2. PROPERTY ADDRESS (Include ZIP Code and county)	3. LEGAL DESCRIPTION	4. TITLE LIMITATIONS AND RESTRICTIVE COVENANTS

1. ☐ CONDOMINIUM   2. ☐ PLANNED UNIT DEVELOPMENT

5. NAME AND ADDRESS OF FIRM OR PERSON MAKING REQUEST/APPLICATION (Include ZIP Code)

6. LOT DIMENSIONS:
1. ☐ IRREGULAR: SQ/FT   2. ☐ ACRES:

7. UTILITIES (✓)	ELEC.	GAS	WATER	SAN. SEWER
1. PUBLIC				
2. COMMUNITY				
3. INDIVIDUAL				

8. EQUIP.
1. ☐ RANGE/OVEN	*4.* ☐ CLOTHES WASHER	*7.* ☐ VENT FAN
2. ☐ REFRIG.	*5.* ☐ DRYER	*8.* ☐ W/W CARPET
3. ☐ DISH-WASHER	*6.* ☐ GARBAGE DISP.	*9.* ☐

9. BUILDING STATUS	10. BUILDING TYPE	11. FACTORY FABRICATED?	12. NUMBER OF UNITS	13A. STREET ACCESS	13B. STREET MAINT.
1. ☐ PROPOSED *3.* ☐ UNDER CONSTR. *2.* ☐ SUBSTANTIAL REHABILITATION *4.* ☐ EXISTING	*1.* ☐ DETACHED *3.* ☐ ROW *2.* ☐ SEMI-DETACHED *4.* ☐ APT. UNIT	*1.* ☐ YES *2.* ☐ NO		*1.* ☐ PRIVATE *2.* ☐ PUBLIC	*1.* ☐ PRIVATE *2.* ☐ PUBLIC

14A. CONSTRUCTION WARRANTY INCLUDED?	14B. NAME OF WARRANTY PROGRAM	14C. EXPIRATION DATE (Month, day, year)	15. CONSTR. COMPLETED (Mo., yr.)
1. ☐ YES *2.* ☐ NO (If "Yes," complete Items 14B and C also.)			

16. NAME OF OWNER	17. PROPERTY:	18. RENT (If applic.)
	☐ OCCUPIED BY OWNER ☐ NEVER OCCUPIED ☐ VACANT ☐ OCCUPIED BY TENANT (Complete Item 18 also)	$ /MONTH

19. NAME OF OCCUPANT	20. TELEPHONE NO.	21. NAME OF BROKER	22. TELEPHONE NO.	23. DATE AND TIME AVAILABLE FOR INSPECTION ☐ AM ☐ PM

24. KEYS AT (Address)	25. ORIGINATOR'S IDENT. NO.	26. SPONSOR'S IDENT. NO.	27. INSTITUTION'S CASE NO.

28. PURCHASER'S NAME AND ADDRESS (Complete mailing address. Include ZIP code.)

EQUAL OPPORTUNITY IN HOUSING

NOTE — Federal laws and regulations prohibit discrimination because of race, color, religion, sex, or national origin in the sale or rental of residential property. Numerous State statutes and local ordinances also prohibit such discrimination. In addition, section 805 of the Civil Rights Act of 1968 prohibits discriminatory practices in connection with the financing of housing.

If HUD/VA finds there is noncompliance with any antidiscrimination laws or regulations, it may discontinue business with the violator.

29. NEW OR PROPOSED CONSTRUCTION — Complete Items 29A through 29G for new or proposed construction cases only.

A. COMPLIANCE INSPECTIONS WILL BE OR WERE MADE BY: ☐ FHA ☐ VA ☐ NONE MADE	B. PLANS (check one) ☐ FIRST SUBMISSION ☐ REPEAT CASE (If checked complete Item 29C.)	C. PLANS SUBMITTED PREVIOUSLY UNDER CASE NO.:

D. NAME AND ADDRESS OF BUILDER	E. TELEPHONE NO.	F. NAME AND ADDRESS OF WARRANTOR	G. TELEPHONE NO.

30. COMMENTS ON SPECIAL ASSESSMENTS OR HOMEOWNERS ASSOCIATION CHARGES	31. ANNUAL REAL ESTATE TAXES $	33. LEASEHOLD CASES (Complete if applicable)
	32. MINERAL RIGHTS RESERVED? ☐ YES (Explain) ☐ NO	LEASE IS: ☐ 99 YEARS ☐ RENEWABLE ☐ HUD/VA APPROVED EXPIRES (Date) ANNUAL GROUND RENT $

34. SALE PRICE OF PROPERTY $	35. REFINANCING – AMOUNT OF PROPOSED LOAN $	36. PROPOSED SALE CONTRACT ATTACHED ☐ YES ☐ NO	37. CONTRACT NUMBER PREVIOUSLY APPROVED BY VA THAT WILL BE USED

CERTIFICATIONS FOR SUBMISSIONS TO HUD

In submitting this application for a conditional commitment for mortgage insurance, it is agreed and understood by the parties involved in the transaction, that if, at the time of application for a Firm Commitment, the identity of the seller has changed, the application for a Firm Commitment will be rejected and the application for a Conditional Commitment will be reprocessed upon request by the mortgagee.

It is further agreed and understood that in submitting the request for a Firm Commitment for mortgage insurance, the seller, the purchaser and the broker involved in the transaction shall each certify that the terms of the contract for purchase are true to his or her knowledge and belief, and that any other agreement entered into by any of these parties in connection with this transaction is attached to the sales agreement.

BUILDER/SELLER'S AGREEMENT: All Houses: The undersigned agrees to deliver to the purchaser HUD's statement of appraised value. **Proposed Construction:** The undersigned agrees, upon sale or conveyance of title within one year from date of initial occupancy, to deliver to the purchaser Form HUD-92544, warranting that the house is constructed in substantial conformity with the plans and specifications on which HUD based its value and to furnish HUD a conformed copy with the purchaser's receipt thereon that the original warranty was delivered to him/her. **All Houses:** In consideration of the issuance of the commitment requested by this application, I (we) hereby agree that any deposit or down payment made in connection with the purchase of the property described above, when received by the undersigned, or an agent of the undersigned, shall upon receipt be deposited in escrow or in trust or in a special account which is not subject to the claims of my creditors and where it will be maintained until it has been disbursed for the benefit of the purchaser or otherwise disposed of in accordance with the terms of the contract of sale.

Signature of: ☐ Mortgagee ☐ Builder ☐ Seller ☐ Other X   Date   19

MORTGAGEE'S CERTIFICATE: The undersigned mortgagee certifies that to the best of his/her knowledge, all statements made in this application and the supporting documents are true, correct and complete.

Signature and Title of Mortgage Officer: X   Date   19

CERTIFICATIONS FOR SUBMISSIONS TO VA

1. On receipt of "Certificate of Reasonable Value" or advice from the Veterans Administration that a "Certificate of Reasonable Value" will not be issued, we agree to forward to the appraiser the approved fee which we are holding for this purpose.
2. CERTIFICATION REQUIRED ON CONSTRUCTION UNDER FHA SUPERVISION (Strike out inappropriate phrases in parentheses)

I hereby certify that plans and specifications and related exhibits, including acceptable FHA Change Orders, if any, supplied to VA in this case, are identical to those (submitted to) (to be submitted to) (approved by) FHA, and that FHA inspections (have been) (will be) made pursuant to FHA approval for mortgage insurance on the basis of proposed construction under Sec.

38. SIGNATURE OF PERSON AUTHORIZING THIS REQUEST	39. TITLE	40. DATE

41. DATE OF ASSIGNMENT	42. NAME OF APPRAISER

WARNING   Section 1010 of Title 18, U.S.C. provides: "Whoever for the purpose of . . . influencing such Administration . . . makes, passes, utters or publishes any statement knowing the same to be false . . . shall be fined not more than $5,000 or imprisoned not more than two years or both."

VA FORM 26-1805, AUG 1980
HUD FORM 92800-1

SUPERSEDES VA FORM 26-1805, AUG 1977, AND
HUD 92800, JUL 1979, WHICH WILL NOT BE USED.

REQUESTER'S COPY 8

VA/FHA/HUD Forms (*Continued*)

Form Approved
OMB No. 2900-0045

RESIDENTIAL APPRAISAL REPORT

	HUD Section of Act	1. CASE NUMBER

2. PROPERTY ADDRESS *(Include ZIP Code and county)*

3. LEGAL DESCRIPTION

4. TITLE LIMITATIONS AND RESTRICTIVE COVENANTS

1. ☐ CONDOMINIUM 2. ☐ PLANNED UNIT DEVELOPMENT

5. NAME AND ADDRESS OF FIRM OR PERSON MAKING REQUEST/APPLICATION *(Include ZIP Code)*

HUD USE ONLY

CONTRACT SALES PRICE

SPEC. ASSESSMENTS

DATE

HUD USE ONLY →

CENSUS TRACT

LOCATION CODE

CLOSING COSTS

6. LOT DIMENSIONS:

1. ☐ IRREGULAR: SQ/FT   2. ☐ ACRES:

7. UTILITIES (√) ELEC. GAS WATER SAN. SEWER

1. PUBLIC

2. COMMUNITY

3. INDIVIDUAL

8. EQUIP.
1. ☐ RANGE/OVEN 4. ☐ CLOTHES WASHER 7. ☐ VENT FAN
2. ☐ REFRIG. 5. ☐ DRYER 8. ☐ W/W CARPET
3. ☐ DISHWASHER 6. ☐ GARBAGE DISP. 9. ☐

9. BUILDING STATUS
1. ☐ PROPOSED
2. ☐ SUBSTANTIAL REHABILITATION
3. ☐ UNDER CONSTRUCTION
4. ☐ EXISTING
5. ☐ ALTERATIONS, IMPROVEMENTS, OR REPAIRS

10. BUILDING TYPE
1. ☐ DETACHED 3. ☐ ROW
2. ☐ SEMI-DETACHED 4. ☐ APT. UNIT

11. FACTORY FABRICATED?
1. ☐ YES 2. ☐ NO

12A. NO. OF BUILDINGS

12B. NO. OF LIVING UNITS

13A. STREET ACCESS
1. ☐ PRIVATE
2. ☐ PUBLIC

13B. STREET MAINT.
1. ☐ PRIVATE
2. ☐ PUBLIC

14. STRUCTURE
1. ☐ FRAME 2. ☐ MASONRY 3. ☐ CONCRETE

15. DESCRIPTION *(Complete only one Item)*
7. ☐ SPLIT FOYER 8. ☐ BI-LEVEL 9. ☐ SPLIT LEVEL OTHER *(Enter No. of Stories)*

16. UNDERGROUND WIRE?
1. ☐ YES 2. ☐ NO

17. CONSTR. WARRANTY INCLUDED?
1. ☐ YES 2. ☐ NO

18. NEIGHBORHOOD DATA

A. CHECK ONE:
1. ☐ URBAN
2. ☐ SUBURBAN
3. ☐ RURAL

B. PRESENT LAND USE
D. BUILT-UP ____ %
E. OWNED ____ %
F. RENTED ____ %
G. VACANT ____ %

C. ANTICIPATED LAND USE

H. TYPICAL RENT $ ____ /MO.

I. TYP. BLDG. AGE ____ YEAR(S)

J. PRICE RANGE

ITEM	DESCRIPTION	COND. *(Observed)*
19. FOUNDATION		
ROOF		
EXT. WALLS		
INT. WALLS		
FLOORS		
HTG. SYSTEM		
PLUMBING		
INSULATION		
ELEC. *(Amps)*		

20. OFFSITE IMPROVEMENTS
1. ☐ CURB
2. ☐ SIDEWALK
3. ☐ GUTTER
4. ☐ STORM SEWER

21. STREET SURFACE

22A. FEDERAL FLOOD HAZARD MAP ISSUED?
1. ☐ YES 2. ☐ NO

22B. PROPERTY IN SPECIAL FLOOD HAZARD AREA?
1. ☐ YES 2. ☐ NO

23. EVIDENCE OF:
1. ☐ DRY ROT 3. ☐ SETTLEMENT
2. ☐ TERMITES 4. ☐ DAMPNESS 5. ☐ NO EVIDENCE

24. UNIT RATING *(Check (√))*

	GOOD	AVG.	POOR
A. GENERAL CONDITION			
B. ROOM SIZES AND LAYOUT			
C. ADEQUACY OF CLOSETS/STORAGE			
D. KITCHEN CABINETS/WORKSPACE			

25. ESTIMATED REMAINING LIFE
YEARS: 1. ☐ ECONOMIC 2. ☐ PHYSICAL

1. ☐ ____ % BSMT.
2. ☐ SLAB
3. ☐ CRAWL SP.
1. ☐ CENT. AIR COND. ☐ FIREPLACE
2. ☐ WALL AIR COND. 2. ☐ REC. ROOM
NO. OF UNITS: 3. ☐

ITEM	SUBJECT PROPERTY	COMPARABLE NO. 1	COMPARABLE NO. 2	COMPARABLE NO. 3
ADDRESS				
PROXIMITY TO SUBJ.				
DATA SOURCE				
TYPE OF FINANCING AND SALE PRICE		$	$	$

26. MARKET DATA ANALYSIS

ITEM	DESCRIPTION ►	DESCRIPTION	(+) (−) ADJ.	DESCRIPTION	(+) (−) ADJ.	DESCRIPTION	(+) (−) ADJ.
ROOM COUNT / TOTAL LIVING AREA *(Square feet)*	ROOMS BDRMS BATH TOTAL S.F.	ROOMS BDRMS BATH TOT.S.F.	$	ROOMS BDRMS BATH TOT.S.F.	$	ROOMS BDRMS BATH TOT. S. F.	$
DATE OF SALE							
LOCATION							
SITE/VIEW							
DESIGN AND APPEAL							
CONSTR. QUALITY							
AGE/CONDITION ►							
BSMT./BSMT FIN. RMS.							
FUNCTIONAL UTILITY							
AIR CONDITIONING							
ENERGY EFFIC. ITEMS							
STORAGE							
PARKING FACILITIES ►							
COMMON ELEMENTS AND MONTHLY ASSESSMENT							
OTHER *(e.g. Fireplace, kitchen equipment, remodeling, etc.)*							
TOTAL NET ADJUSTMENT		ENTER (+) OR (−) $		ENTER (+) OR (−) $		ENTER (+) OR (−) $	
INDICATED VALUE		$		$		$	

RECONCILIATION

27A. INDICATED VALUE BY MARKET DATA APPROACH ► $

27B. INDICATED VALUE BY INCOME APPROACH *(If applicable)* ECON. MRKT. RENT TIMES GROSS RENT MULTIPL. $ ____ /MO. X ► $

27C. IND. VAL. BY COST APPROACH *(If appl.)* *(Attach calculations.)* ► $

28. ESTIMATED LAND VALUE $

29. LEASE DATA *(Complete if applic.)*
A. ANNUAL GROUND RENT $ ____ CAP. AT ____ % = $
B. VAL. OF LEASED FEE $
C. VAL. OF LEASEHOLD EST. $

30. DOES PROP. CONFORM TO APPLICABLE MINIMUM PROPERTY REQUIREMENTS?
1. ☐ YES 2. ☐ NO *(If "No," explain in Item 32.)*

31. APPRAISAL IS MADE:
1. ☐ AS IS 2. ☐ SUBJECT TO COMPLETION PER PLANS/SPECS. 3. ☐ SUBJECT TO REPAIRS, ALTERATIONS, ETC.

32. ADDITIONAL COMMENTS *(Include repairs necessary to make property conform to applicable MPR's, and estimated cost of each. Attach separate sheet if necessary.)*

33. FINAL RECONCILIATION/ESTIMATED VALUE

NOTE: No determination of reasonable value may be made unless a completed appraisal report is received (38 U.S.C. 1810 (VA ONLY)).
I CERTIFY that (a) I have carefully viewed the property described in this report, INSIDE AND OUTSIDE, so far as it has been completed; that (b) it is the same property that is identified by description in my appraisal assignment; that (c) I HAVE NOT RECEIVED, HAVE NO AGREEMENT TO RECEIVE, NOR WILL I ACCEPT FROM ANY PARTY ANY GRATUITY OR PAYMENT OTHER THAN MY APPRAISAL FEE FOR MAKING THIS APPRAISAL (HUD/VA ONLY); that (d) I have no interest, present or prospective, in the applicant, seller, property, or mortgage; that (e) in arriving at the estimated value I have not been influenced in any manner whatsoever by the race, color, religion, national origin, or sex of any person residing in the property or in the neighborhood wherein it is located. I understand that, if I am a fee appraiser, violation of this certification can result in my removal from the fee appraiser's roster.

34A. SIGNATURE OF APPRAISER *(Enter I.D. No. for HUD cases only)*

34B. DATE

OFFICE USE ONLY *(Reviewer's I.D. No. − HUD cases only)*

VA FORM 26-1803, NOV 1982
HUD 92800-3 FmHA 1922-8

NOTE: ON HUD APPRAISALS, SEND THIS COPY TO MANAGEMENT INFORMATION SYSTEMS DIVISION, SINGLE FAMILY INSURED BRANCH.

APPRAISER'S COPY 6

VA/FHA/HUD Forms (*Continued*)

Form Approved
OMB No. 2900-0045

☐ VA CERTIFICATE OF REASONABLE VALUE ☐ HUD CONDITIONAL COMMITMENT	HUD Section of Act	1. CASE NUMBER

2. PROPERTY ADDRESS *(Include ZIP Code and county)*	3. LEGAL DESCRIPTION	4. TITLE LIMITATIONS AND RESTRICTIVE COVENANTS

1. ☐ CONDOMINIUM 2. ☐ PLANNED UNIT DEVELOPMENT

5. NAME AND ADDRESS OF FIRM OR PERSON MAKING REQUEST/APPLICATION *(Include ZIP Code)*

6. LOT DIMENSIONS:

1. ☐ IRREGULAR: SQ/FT 2. ☐ ACRES:

7. UTILITIES (✓)	ELEC.	GAS	WATER	SAN. SEWER
1. PUBLIC				
2. COMMUNITY				
3. INDIVIDUAL				

8. E Q U I P.	*1.* ☐	RANGE/ OVEN	*4.* ☐	CLOTHES WASHER	*7.* ☐	VENT FAN
	2. ☐	REFRIG.	*5.* ☐	DRYER	*8.* ☐	W/W CARPET
	3. ☐	DISH- WASHER	*6.* ☐	GARBAGE DISP.	*9.* ☐	

9. BUILDING STATUS	10. BUILDING TYPE	11. FACTORY FABRICATED?	12. NUMBER OF UNITS	13A. STREET ACCESS	13B. STREET MAINT.
1. ☐ PROPOSED *3.* ☐ UNDER CONSTR. *2.* ☐ SUBSTANTIAL *4.* ☐ EXISTING REHABILITATION	*1.* ☐ DETACHED *3.* ☐ ROW *2.* ☐ SEMI-DETACHED *4.* ☐ APT. UNIT	*1.* ☐ YES *2.* ☐ NO		*1.* ☐ PRIVATE *2.* ☐ PUBLIC	*1.* ☐ PRIVATE *2.* ☐ PUBLIC

14. ESTIMATED REASONABLE VALUE OF PROPERTY	15. REMAINING ECONOMIC LIFE OF PROPERTY IS ESTIMATED TO BE NOT LESS THAN:	16. EXPIRATION DATE
$	YEARS	

17. HUD COMMITMENT TERMS

A. MAXIMUM MORTGAGE AMOUNT	$
B. NO. OF MONTHS	

18. ☐ This Certificate of Reasonable Value is valid only if VA Form 26-1843p showing VA General Conditions and the applicable Specific Conditions is attached.

C. NOTICE OF REJECTION	
D. "AS IS" VALUE	$

19. ADMINISTRATOR OF VETERANS AFFAIRS, BY *(Signature of authorized agent)*, OR HUD AUTHORIZED AGENT	20. DATE ISSUED	21. VA OR HUD OFFICE

E. MONTHLY EXPENSE ESTIMATE

FIRE INSURANCE	$
TAXES	$

22. PURCHASER'S NAME AND ADDRESS *(Complete mailing address. Include ZIP Code.)*

CONDO. COMMUNITY EXPENSE	$
MAINTENANCE AND REPAIRS	$
HEAT AND UTILITIES	$
F. ESTIMATED CLOSING COST	$

G. ☐ EXISTING ☐ PROPOSED	*(See General Condition 3 on attachment.)*
H. IMPROVED LIVING AREA	SQ/FT

I. ☐ This Conditional Commitment is valid only if HUD Form 92800-5a showing HUD General Conditions and the applicable Specific Conditions is attached.

VA FORM 26-1843, AUG 1980   HUD FORM 92800-5

REQUESTER'S COPY 8

VA/FHA/HUD Forms (*Continued*)

ENDORSEMENT TO CERTIFICATE OF REASONABLE VALUE	1. CASE NUMBER

This endorsement takes preference over and specifically amends an outstanding Certificate or Master Certificate of Reasonable Value (VA Form 26-1843 or 26-1843a) having the same identifying number and referring to the same property or properties.

Any condition stated on the outstanding Certificate of Reasonable Value, not specifically referred to and modified herein, remains in full force and effect until expiration of the validity period.

2. NAME AND ADDRESS OF FIRM OR PERSON MAKING REQUEST

3. OUTSTANDING MCRV NUMBER

4. TYPE OF CASE

☐ INDIVIDUAL   ☐ MASTER

5. PROPERTY ADDRESS (*Number and street or rural route, City or P.O., County, State and ZIP Code*)

6. REVISED EXPIRATION OF VALIDITY PERIOD

7. TOTAL REVISED REASONABLE VALUE

$

8. LEGAL DESCRIPTION (*To be stated ONLY if changed from outstanding CRV; continue on reverse, if necessary.*)

9. NAME AND ADDRESS OF COMPLIANCE INSPECTOR

10. REVISED CONDITION (*Continue on reverse, if necessary*)

11. ADMINISTRATOR OF VETERANS' AFFAIRS, BY (*Signature of Authorized Agent*)

12. DATE

13. ADDRESS OF REGIONAL OFFICE

14. NAME AND ADDRESS OF VETERAN

66 Advertising Your Home

Good news! National survey after national survey keeps turning up the fact that most home buyers prefer to deal with homeowners rather than real estate sales people. A recent investigation by *The New York Times*, for example, revealed that FOR SALE BY OWNER ads produce four times more response from the same space than do ads by brokers.

The reasons aren't exactly clear; it's a toss-up whether buyers may feel they'll be able to get a better price (often true due to absence of the need to pay a broker's commission) or whether buyers just sort of resent the feeling of being manipulated by a broker.

Whatever the reason, your most valuable advertising asset is the term FOR SALE BY OWNER in your newspaper ads, on your photo handout, on your fact sheet, and on the sign in your front yard. If there's any magic phrase in home selling, that's it.

FRONT YARD SIGN

If you live in an average suburb near a fairly large city, you can expect that a good front yard FOR SALE sign will bring in about 40 percent of your prospects. No small amount, considering that most prospects will need to have driven by your home to have seen it. But then, some of your best prospects, people who are really looking for a house, and looking for a house in your neighborhood *and* looking for a house in your neighborhood's price range, will be out weekends scouting your area for a house.

Traditionally, FOR SALE signs are placed to best be seen by someone directly in front of your house. A different arrangement (depending upon your lot, its landscaping, and the landscaping of adjacent houses) might be to have **two** signs, each one facing the traffic from a different direction.

It should be noted that some communities have (though not always enforce) prohibitions against front yard FOR SALE signs. However, if you see similar signs displayed in your vicinity you can be fairly certain that you'll be safe in following the practice.

Whether you use one sign facing the street directly, or two signs facing oncoming traffic from both directions, your signs should measure about 21 inches by 24 inches if close to the street and 24 inches by 36 inches if far from the street. Lettering must be large enough to be easily read by someone sitting in a car.

One effective design is simply a white background with large red block letters 4 to 6 inches high saying **BY OWNER** or **FOR SALE BY OWNER**, followed by slightly smaller block letters below saying **By Appointment**, plus your home telephone number. If it's impossible for anyone to be in the house during the day to accept messages, you might also include a work number. But prospects have been found to confuse

two phone numbers, copying them incorrectly and thus being unable to reach you without returning to write them down again.

Either of the following signs would be good:

```
+----------------------------+
|                            |
|   FOR SALE BY OWNER        |
|                            |
|   By Appointment           |
|                            |
|   000-0000                 |
|                            |
+----------------------------+
```

```
+----------------------------+
|                            |
|   BY OWNER                 |
|                            |
|   Shown by Appointment     |
|                            |
|   000-0000                 |
|                            |
+----------------------------+
```

Don't skimp on your sign. Have it made by a good sign painter. Remember, it can bring in 40 percent of your prospects.

If you live in a cul-de-sac or a street having very little traffic that intersects with a fairly busy street, you might use an additional sign or signs near the busier street saying:

```
+----------------------------+
|                            |
|   BY OWNER                 |
|                            |
|   Three-Bedroom            |
|                            |
|   Colonial                 |
|                            |
|   1 Block North            |
|                            |
+----------------------------+
```

Obviously, if you put up *two* additional signs, each facing traffic coming from a different direction on the nearby busy street, you will need signs that indicate different directions, for instance, **1 Block North** and **1 Block South**.

If possible, talk to homeowners close to where you'd like to place additional signs to see if you can get permission to place them on their property, perhaps high enough on a tree to be easily seen from passing cars. Don't be surprised if some of your extra signs disappear; tearing down FOR SALE BY OWNER signs seems to be a favorite pastime of some real estate salespeople.

Even brokers who discount traditional commission rates come in for their share of hostility from the closed society of real estate "six-percenters." Gina Williams, a Northridge, California, broker whose firm charges less than 6 percent, has had her company's signs smashed and her employees harassed by other brokers. Mrs. Williams has received threatening phone calls, has had her office broken into and vandalized, and has had the word "Death" painted on her house—all since her company began discounting the traditional 6 percent commission.

The 6 percent commission has come under increasing attack as a form of illegal price-fixing. In 1977 several Maryland real estate brokers were convicted of price-fixing, a decision that was upheld on appeal by the defendants who claimed that their activities were local in nature and thus not subject to antitrust laws.

In January 1980, the U.S. Supreme Court held that a group of Louisiana real estate brokers could be tried in a civil suit charging them with conspiracy to maintain (in violation of antitrust laws) a fixed, 6 percent sales commission throughout their marketing area.

The 6 percent commission has been so strictly enforced within the real estate industry through coercion (such as refusal to share multiple listings) that some states now require that sales contracts advise homeowners that commission rates are negotiable and not set by law at 6 percent—or any other rate.

NEWSPAPER ADVERTISING

Well-written newspaper ads, frequently run in the right papers during the six to twelve weeks that it takes to sell the average home for an average price, will produce about 50 percent of your prospects.

One of the right newspapers would be the paper in your town that carries the most classified real estate ads. Another of the right papers would probably be the suburban paper that serves your area. In a big city, newcomers will be sure to read ads in the major paper, but people who know the area they want to move to, or who already live near you and don't want to move far from their present location, will check ads in the suburban paper serving the community they're interested in.

Many metropolitan newspapers charge by the line for classified ads, usually with a two-line minimum. Many suburban papers, on the other hand, charge by the word. Since advertising rates are based upon circulation, a good suburban paper can be inexpensive and still pull in some of your best prospects—people who are looking for a home in your specific area.

Advertise at least three times a week in any daily paper you use. You'll have more competition weekends, but you'll have more prospects too. If your budget is anything but the barest minimum, phone your paper to check for special seven-day, ten-day, or other discount rates. Some papers will run your ad Monday, Tuesday, and Wednesday at no additional cost if you advertise Thursday, Friday, Saturday, and Sunday. Others have ten-day package deals that can be renewed as often as you like.

As long as high interest rates continue to inflate the expense of buying a house, many prospective buyers' primary concern will be the amount of the down payment requirement and the amount of monthly payments. If you're willing to carry some of the financing yourself (see Chapter 68, Helping Your Buyer Finance Your House) in a way that can reduce the down payment or monthly payments below the going market, that fact should probably be the "lead" for your ad. There's nothing that gets prospects' attention like a low down payment.

Partial seller financing, by the way, is becoming more the rule than the exception. During 1983 more than 50 percent of all preowned homes were sold with some form of partial seller financing.

The following general guidelines will simplify writing a good ad (examples of which follow):

1. Headline your ad **BY OWNER**.
2. State any special financing advantage, such as low down payment requirement.
3. Describe any unique characteristic of your house that will be of special advantage to some prospects.
4. State the neighborhood or direction from town, unless your paper segregates ads by geographical area.
5. State the number of bedrooms and bathrooms.
6. State the number of square feet.
7. Mention the type of architecture.
8. State the price.
9. Close by saying **Call 000-0000 for appointment.**

BY OWNER
$4,000 moves you in! 3-bedroom, 2-bath colonial 20 minutes from university, large lot. 1,950 sq. ft. Seller will take 12 percent, 5 year second mortgage for partial down payment. $72,000. Call 000-0000 for appointment.

BY OWNER 7½% VA
Save $$$ on 3-bedroom, 2-bath contemporary on corner lot. 1,350 sq. ft. Quiet cul-de-sac ideal for children, one block from Anderson elementary. $86,000. $11,000 equity, assume VA. Call 000-0000 for appointment.

BY OWNER
Kingswood, 3-bedroom, 2-bath French provincial with lots of trees, fireplace. Over 1,500 sq. ft. $78,000. Seller can help arrange low down payment financing. Call 000-0000 for appointment.

BY OWNER
Two blocks from medical center. 3-bedroom, 2-bath Tudor with fireplace. Large, finished basement, superb kitchen. 1,800 sq. ft. Large, secluded lot. $77,500.
Call 000-0000 for appointment.

Be sure that you study your neighborhood before advertising so you'll have some idea of the kind of prospect you should appeal to. Are homeowners in your neighborhood mostly middle-management people with teenage children or are they younger couples with preschoolers, or perhaps older couples whose children are grown? Appeal to prospects who are like your neighbors.

Ads placed by active real estate brokers in your area can be a good source of copy ideas for your own ads. But don't make your ad uninviting by using too many abbreviations, a common fault of some real estate advertisers. And if your copy doesn't produce the response you want, be ready to change it.

Employee newspapers at large corporations and the newspapers of area universities, hospitals, and military bases often run classified ads for very little cost and, sometimes, at no cost at all.

ADDITIONAL ADVERTISING

The final 10 percent of your prospects will come from wide distribution of your fact sheet, your photo description sheet, and the placement of 3 × 5 cards.

Fact Sheet

The multi-page Fact Sheet (Form 64.1, page F533) provides fairly detailed data on your home's construction; floor plan; room dimensions; flooring and carpet; heating, plumbing, and electrical services; built-in appliances; tax and insurance costs; and neighborhood and community data, plus the names, address, and work and home phone numbers of the owners (see the completed sample Fact Sheet on pages 297–305).

The fact sheet should be given to anyone you feel is *seriously* interested in helping you sell your house, as well as to all seriously interested prospects.

Photo Description Sheet

Your photo description sheet (see the following page for a sample) will contain an attractive 4½″ × 7″ photo of your house, a general description of the house, your asking price, and the owners' names, address, and home and work telephone numbers.

Inexpensively produced by "quick copy" type offset printers, the photo description sheet can be given to friends, co-workers, neighbors, church members, and corporate, institutional, and military-base housing managers. It can also be given wide distribution on bulletin boards at some businesses, shopping centers, supermarkets, laundromats, educational institutions, and churches. Give one to every prospect to whom you show your house.

Three-by-Five Cards

Put up 3 × 5 cards, patterned after your classified ads, but including more information, on supermarket, shopping center, laundromat, and other bulletin boards that do not accept larger notices.

You can divide an 8½″ by 11″ piece of paper into five 3 × 5 "cards"; simply type your ad five times on the paper and then run off as many as you'll need on a good photocopy machine. Cut out the "cards" and you'll have a maximum amount of advertising with a minimum amount of typing.

When Your House Is Sold

Keep a record of where you've put cards and photo description sheets on bulletin boards and with whom and at which corporations and institutions you've left fact sheets so that you can let them know when your house is no longer on the market and so that you can remove cards and photo description sheets from bulletin boards when they're no longer needed.

Sample Photo Description Sheet

FOR SALE BY OWNER

$50,000   Shown By Appointment

Well-constructed stone and cedar shingle contemporary home. Three bedrooms, two baths. Children's bedrooms at opposite end of this L-shaped design provide quiet and privacy. The two-car garage has been converted into additional living space by replacing garage doors with aluminum casement, double-pane insulating glass. This space is attractively paneled in weathered cedar, is carpeted, well-insulated and is centrally heated and cooled. Sixty-foot frontage on quiet, block-long cul-de-sac.

David & Jodie Newberry, 2405 Colonial Ct., Hinkley, N.B. 10567

Home: 205-432-6891 Business: 205-564-6784 Business: 205-564-9901

Before showing your home to anyone else, "show" it to yourself. Make a tour through your house and decide which feature is best, second best, etc. Make a list. Prospects will be impressed by what they see first, so plan a tour that begins with your home's most attractive room or with the feature your prospect has stated he or she is especially interested in. And to end your tour in a positive way, show your home's second best feature last.

Organize your tour so that it will have a natural flow through your house and property, avoiding retracing too many steps and making sure potential buyers see your home from its most attractive perspectives.

Before showing the first potential buyer through your house, ask yourself every embarrassing question you can about it, just as a prospect might: "Don't you find the bedroom closet awfully small?" "The basement seems damp. Is it?" "How long have you had that crack in the foundation?"

You can respond to most questions with a positive answer: "Well, we've found there's plenty of room in the attic for storing off-season clothes so the bedroom closet works fine for the clothes we're wearing." "The basement seems a little damp after a heavy rain, but we've never had water in it." "The crack was there when we bought the house and hasn't changed a bit."

If you have a basement that's a bit damp, get a dehumidifier to keep it dry while you're showing the house. They're cheap enough so that you could leave it behind when you move. Also, check for moist or dripping pipes, which, if found, should be wrapped with insulating material to prevent condensation.

If a foundation crack is merely a cosmetic problem (in some parts of the country almost all houses have a crack or two in the foundation), try planting a shrub in front of it or asking your appraiser to make a note about the benign nature of the crack in his or her appraisal report (then refer your prospect to the report).

When your tour is organized, make a run-through or two guiding a friend or your spouse as though you were showing the house to a stranger. Learn where to stand when opening closet and cabinet doors, when to lead (down basement stairs), and where to allow prospects to precede you (into an attractive room). Rehearse your tour and rehearse answering questions in a positive way.

Prospects' very first impression will be gained from the front of your house. Keep the yard extremely neat, trimmed, and picked up.

Make it easy for your prospects to park, and leave an unobstructed view of your home by parking your car down the street, not in front of your house nor in the driveway or garage. Also, there's always the chance, no matter what kind of car you own, that a potential buyer might infer something unfavorable about you based upon the type of car you have.

It may seem a bit ridiculous, but also put other things out of sight that might unfavorably affect the attitude of a perhaps narrow-minded prospect—liquor bottles, nude paintings, controversial magazines, etc. Your object is to *sell* the house. Why do anything to endanger that goal?

As a precaution, place small valuables, jewelry, etc., in a safe place out of sight while showing your home. There are people who inspect houses looking for just such stealables. Check window latches and lock locks after each day of showing your home too.

Finally, before prospects arrive, put fresh soap in bathroom and kitchen soap dishes and hang fresh towels on towel racks. You can whisk them away before any family member has a chance to use them. If you haven't already done so, put new shower curtains in any bathrooms that need them.

WHEN THE PHONE RINGS

Rule number one: While your house is on the market, kids don't answer the phone. PERIOD.

What you might do, if you need to use the phone for other purposes such as business calls or if the kids will *die* if they're cut off from the phone, is just have another phone installed for the time it takes to sell your house. In most parts of the country the cost isn't terribly high, and then you can use *that* number in your ads, on your sign, and on your fact sheet. And, of course, whenever that phone rings you can be fairly sure it's a prospect and answer accordingly.

When a caller says, "I'm calling about your ad," just respond by saying, "I'm glad you called. What can I tell you about the house?"

One purpose of talking with people on the phone will be to separate prospects from nonprospects, and an honest question-and-answer session can do just that. But even though your ad will list the price, the number of bedrooms and baths, and the number of square feet in your house, there will still be people who will phone and ask you the price, the number of bedrooms, and the number of square feet—and then tell you that your house is too expensive (or too small or too large) and hang up.

As a minimum during each call, try to obtain answers to the questions that appear at the top of our **Telephone Log** (Form 67.1, page F545; completed sample appearing on page 322). These will tell you what points to stress when showing and talking about your home and will tell you something about your prospect ahead of time. Remember to make at least a dozen or so photocopies of the log *before* you've started to advertise your home—you'll want to be ready when that first call comes in.

Don't ask where the prospect works—but you might ask if there's an office number where he or she can be reached if you should have to cancel an appointment. When prospects start asking about the amount of your mortgage and what your payments and taxes and utilities cost each month, then you can ask them how much they plan to pay as a down payment, where they plan to place the mortgage, etc.

Real estate salespeople will probably phone asking you to take down your sign while they show a prospect through your house—saying that they will get your asking price, plus their 6 percent commission. When this happened to us, we explained that that would mean we'd be trying to sell our house for two prices: the advertised price, plus a higher price inflated sufficiently to include their commission—and *that* we couldn't do.

You'll possibly also receive calls from real estate people who will play the part of prospects, make appointments to see your home, and then fail to show up—apparently in an effort to discourage your efforts.

Others may play the role of prospects and let you take them through your house so that they can "check out the competition." We expect that *they* would be highly incensed if you were to let them show you what they had for sale so that you could also "check out the competition."

Some callers will want to know if your advertised price is just your "asking" price. Tell them that it's your selling price and that they really need to see the home to appreciate its value. If, after that, anyone wants to make an offer, tell them to put it in writing with an accompanying check and that you will then give their offer your consideration.

About 40 percent of your callers will want to see your home Sunday afternoon, so if other times are convenient to some prospects, try to schedule those appointments then and keep Sunday afternoon available for those who can't inspect your home any other time.

WHEN YOUR PROSPECTS ARRIVE

Nearly 30 percent of the people who make appointments won't show up. Some of those will have driven to your address, looked at the house, and decided not to come in. Nine out of ten people who do tour your house won't like it, and about half of those who say they'll be back will never be seen again. Half of the people who buy a preowned home inspect it at least twice; others inspect it four or five times as they narrow down their choice. Be patient; you only have to make one sale.

Rule number one of showing your house is *no young children and no pets around*. Make advance arrangements to send your kids on short notice to stay with neighbors when prospects are expected. Have a

couple backups ready so you'll always be able to greet tour visitors without the distraction of children.

And since your prospects might not like pets, or may even be allergic to them, find a place for Bruno and Snowflake to stay when potential buyers are scheduled to arrive. Also, turn off the TV and don't use noisy appliances like disposers (garbage disposal units) and dishwashers while potential buyers are in the house.

If the weather's cool enough to justify it, have a fire going in the fireplace. There's no harm in having the house filled with the homelike aroma of baking fresh bread or cookies—but then you can eat only so much bread and cookies.

To repeat, start your tour with your home's best selling point, and as you go through rooms, open cabinets and closets, turn on lights, and lead the way into the basement, attic, garage, and yard. Mention advantages that can't be seen, such as a disposer, copper plumbing, or heavy-duty wiring, but mostly let your house sell itself. No amount of hard sell or psychological pressure will make anyone buy a house they're not comfortable with.

Remember that most people won't like your house and some will feel they have to make disparaging remarks about everything from the condition of your carpets ("This rug will certainly have to be replaced!") to your taste in wallpaper ("We could never live with *that!*"), but just let those kinds of remarks pass. They hardly ever come from a sincere prospect, although there are some who will use this ploy in an attempt to put you on the defensive and set you up for a "low ball" offer later.

After a brief tour, lead your prospects back to a comfortable room and ask if they have further questions. If they appear ready to leave, give them a copy of your fact sheet and invite them to telephone or come back to look at the house again any time.

HANDLING DROP-INS

In spite of your sign, there will be people who will come to your door and say they happened to be in the neighborhood and wondered if they might see your house. Don't turn anyone away; they might be good prospects.

While your house is on the market, try to keep one room, maybe your living room or a family room, always picked up and ready to show. That way you can invite drop-ins into that room, hand them a fact sheet—also perhaps offering them a cup of coffee—and ask them to wait a few minutes while you straighten up.

If your house looks like a cyclone hit it when drop-ins come to the door—unmade beds, laundry being sorted on the floor, etc.—tell them you're in the middle of something and ask if they'd mind returning in fifteen minutes. No serious prospect is likely to feel that your request is unreasonable, and most will be happy to come back. Whatever you do, *never show your house when it isn't ready*. It will never live down a messy impression in prospects' minds, and it will be almost impossible to make the sale.

OPEN HOUSE

After your house has been on the market a week or two, hold a weekend open house. Have two or three easy-to-read signs professionally painted that you can put up at either end of your block and at the entrance to your suburb. All you'll need to say is:

OPEN HOUSE

0000 Your Street

If any real estate brokers are holding open houses in your suburb that weekend, you can place your signs near, but not too near, theirs. Be sure to ask permission of any homeowners in front of whose homes you'd like to place your signs.

You'll also need to run special newspaper ads that can be similar to your regular ad, but which will of course say OPEN HOUSE and will give your complete address:

BY OWNER

OPEN HOUSE, 0000 Avalanche Canyon Rd., Oceanview. Spacious, 1,600 sq. ft., 3-bedroom, 2-bath two-story contemporary on 2 acre wooded lot near university. Fireplace. Pool. $95,000. 10:00 A.M. to 8:00 P.M. Phone 000-0000 for directions.

Be sure to have plenty of fact sheets on hand, give flyers in advance to friends, neighbors, co-workers, and church members, and get permission to put up as many flyers as possible on area bulletin boards. Use Form 67.2 on page F547; follow our completed sample flyer on page 323 for design and format.

Your local "quick copy" type offset printer can run off a hundred open-house announcements quickly and inexpensively. Just don't forget to take along plenty of thumb tacks when putting up your flyers.

Sample of Form 67.1/F545

TELEPHONE LOG, Page No. _3_

1. What special features are you looking for?
2. Number of children and ages.
3. What part of town do you live in now?
4. When is the most convenient time?
5. Your phone number in case we have to call you back?

Caller _Mrs. Lydia Torres_

Date _June 15_ Phone #1 _944-2911_ Phone #2 _476-4620_

Interested in: _House close to work, works at medical center, wants elem. school nearby, large fenced yard._

Appointment for: _2 PM Sat. June 18_

Remarks: _She likes the house and seems able to handle the financing — says she has to talk to her brother, may bring him by —_

Caller _M/M Horace Gakenbeck_

Date _June 15_ Phone #1 _478-9381_ Phone #2 _478-2219_

Interested in: _House on south side of town in a "nice" neighborhood — they have boy seven and girl nine._

Appointment for: _Sunday, June 19_

Remarks: _He liked garage with room for workbench. She liked kitchen but wants larger where she can "keep an eye on the kids." They didn't seem concerned about price. He's an engineer of some kind._

Sample of Form 67.2/F547

OPEN HOUSE

By Owner

June 18, 1984

0000 Avalanche Canyon Road   10:00 A.M. to 8:00 P.M.

Striking 3-bedroom, 3-bath stucco contemporary with fireplace and swimming pool in two-acre wooded, hillside lot near university. 1,800 square
feet. Recent 15' by 15' addition with 16' ceiling and skylight with
adjoining bath would make excellent master bedroom or home office.
Eight-foot privacy fence surrounds pool.

DIRECTIONS: Follow interstate 5 north to Laguna Beach, turn left and
drive west to Avalon, follow Shattuck Road up hill to Avalanche Canyon
Road. Turn left up Avalanche Canyon, go two blocks.

PRICE: $95,000   Conventional or assume $65,000 VA

68 Helping Your Buyer Finance Your Home

Your house won't have to be on the market very long for you to learn that prospective buyers want to know two things almost before they want to know anything else about your house:

- The amount of the down payment
- The amount of the monthly payments

The difference between selling your house and not selling your house will depend, more than anything else, on your ability to arrange financing that will put your home within the range of a sufficient number of buyers.

As you begin taking steps to sell your house, which also means taking steps to *finance* your house, you should know that:

- More than 50 percent of all homes sold during 1983 involved some sort of *seller financing*—a second mortgage, wraparound mortgage, sales contract, etc. (more fully described on the following pages).
- The median selling price of a house during 1983 was close to $80,000. (With a 20 percent down, 30-year, 14 percent, fixed-rate conventional mortgage, the buyer would need to make a $16,000 down payment plus 360 monthly payments of $758.33 for a total mortgage of $272,998.80. To qualify for such a mortgage with most lenders the buyer would need an annual income of $40,000 to $45,000.)

But remember that by eliminating the real estate agent's traditional 6 percent commission ($4,800 on an $80,000 house), you have made it possible to reduce the required down payment from $16,000 to $11,200 ($16,000 − $4,800) and you have lowered the potential selling price of the house from $80,000 to $75,200 ($80,000 − $4,800).

Two factors—affordable down payment and affordable monthly payments—can do more to sell your house than the most persuasive real estate salesperson. And as we noted earlier, you have favorably affected both of these factors by your decision to eliminate the real estate agent's commission by selling your house yourself.

Since many buyers, especially first-time buyers, may know little about home financing, your knowledge and ability to help arrange financing can make the difference between selling your home and not selling your home.

If, from time to time on the following pages, we seem to be telling you more than you ever wanted to know about home financing as a *seller*, it's because we assume that since you are now selling a home you may soon be in the market for another home as a

buyer. We hope what we tell you now as a seller may also be of use to you in the future as a buyer.

In the remainder of this chapter we'll describe a number of home financing methods. Some will be more suitable to your situation than others, but you should know about all of them, since many home sales are arranged through a combination of financing plans:

- Mortgage Assumption
- Conventional Fixed-Rate Mortgage
- Conventional Mortgage with Private Mortgage Insurance
- Variable Interest Rate Mortgage
- Graduated-Payment Mortgage
- FHA-Insured Mortgage
- VA-Guaranteed Mortgage
- Rollover Mortgage
- Zero Percent Mortgage
- Balloon Note Mortgage
- Second Mortgage
- Contract of Sale

Helpful mortgage lenders (not limited, by the way, to those who are local) and your attorney can provide some of the expertise as long as you are familiar with a few of the basics.

Many buyers are completely unaware of down payment and income requirements, so you'll also need to be familiar with these areas to know whether a prospect is "qualified" (in mortgage lender's terms) to purchase your home. (More on buyer qualification beginning on page 343.)

At this writing, though, home financing remains in disarray from the effects of inflation, recession, and high interest rates. However, the bedrock of home financing—conventional mortgages and VA-guaranteed and FHA-insured mortgages—still finance most home sales.

During 1983 the majority of home sales were financed with conventional mortgages, often with the buyer's assumption of the seller's existing mortgage, through a second mortgage or with the seller's acceptance of the buyer's note for part of the down payment. During the same period, about 7 percent of home sales were financed with FHA loans and about 10 percent with VA loans.

The differences between financially stable times and financially unstable times manifest themselves in higher prices, higher rates of interest, and more stringent qualifying income requirements—all of which give birth to buyers' and sellers' creative (for creative read "desperate") financing efforts.

One of the results of unstable economic times, climbing interest rates gave rise to numerous lawsuits that resulted in a June 1982 U.S. Supreme Court decision that significantly affects the shape of nearly all home financing. It's important to be aware of the Court's decision before attempting to help prospective buyers arrange financing for the purchase of your home.

MORTGAGE ASSUMPTION

During the first half of 1982 nearly 70 percent of all "used" homes were sold through the buyer's assumption of the seller's existing mortgage. In assuming the seller's mortgage, the buyer continues to pay an amount equal to the seller's current mortgage payments to the holder of the existing mortgage at the rate of interest stipulated in the seller's existing mortgage—after paying the seller, as a down payment, an amount equal to the seller's equity in the property. If the value of the house had increased since it was purchased, the owner might be able to get more than the amount of his or her equity in the house, thus making a profit.

With rapidly rising interest rates, mortgage lenders were understandably unhappy with mortgage assumptions because they lost money that they could have made if the seller's existing mortgage had been refinanced by the buyer at current (higher) rates of interest.

For many years conventional mortgages, but not FHA-insured nor VA-guaranteed mortgages, have contained a "due-on-sale" clause requiring the owner to pay the mortgage in full whenever the house was sold. Until about 1969, when interest rates began to climb, the due-on-sale clause was seldom enforced because there would be no benefit to the lender.

But as interest rates started to rise, lenders began to attempt to enforce due-on-sale mortgage provisions. Several states outlawed enforcement of due-on-sale provisions and, eventually, the resulting lawsuits ended up before the Supreme Court.

In June 1982 the Supreme Court handed down a decision allowing federally chartered savings and loan associations (S&Ls) to enforce due-on-sale clauses when property is sold.

As a result of that decision, homeowners having conventional mortgages with federally chartered S&Ls can no longer count on mortgage assumption as an attractive, low-interest way of facilitating the sale of their homes. In some states during the first half of 1982, nearly 60 percent of all homes sold involved assumption of the seller's existing mortgage—so the effect of the Supreme Court decision was, to quote some real estate brokers, "catastrophic."

But there's some good news and some bad news. Not all conventional mortgages, especially those written before 1969, contain a due-on-sale clause. Also, federal regulation prohibits the inclusion of a due-on-sale clause in a VA-guaranteed or FHA-insured mortgage. So there's a fair chance that your mortgage may not contain a due-on-sale provision.

Second, the Court's decision directly affects only *federally chartered* S&Ls. It does not affect state-chartered S&Ls, nor does it affect mortgages that homeowners may have signed with other types of lenders, such as mutual savings banks and commercial banks.

The bad news is that a number of state-chartered S&Ls moved to place themselves under the Supreme Court ruling by becoming federally chartered institutions. Also, a number of states have statutes on the books giving state-chartered S&Ls parity with federally chartered S&Ls, so many state-chartered S&Ls can now enforce the due-on-sale provision of any mortgages they hold.

What mortgage lenders are doing at this writing is splitting the difference between the rate of interest on the seller's existing mortgage and the going rate of interest at the time the property is sold. In the case of an existing mortgage having an annual interest rate of, say, 8 percent, the original lender would write the buyer's new mortgage at 11 percent if the going rate of interest on the date of sale was 14 percent.

So, while assumption of the seller's existing mortgage may still be a tool for assisting the buyer's financing efforts, it is a tool that has been blunted somewhat by the 1982 Supreme Court decision. (More on avoiding the due-on-sale clause on page 334.)

CONVENTIONAL MORTGAGES

Since the majority of home sales are financed by conventional mortgages, let's look at those first. During 1983 the average conventional home mortgage down payment was 20 percent of the **appraised value** (not selling price) of a house. The average *fixed-rate* conventional home mortgage rate of interest hovered close to 14 percent and the average payment period was 30 years.

Qualifying Conventional Mortgage Home Buyers

There are several formulas that mortgage lenders use to "qualify" prospective buyers of homes to be financed with conventional mortgages:

1. Under the MGB Rule:
   - The buyer's monthly payment should not exceed one-fourth of his or her **gross monthly income**. A gross monthly income of $2,000 would "qualify" a buyer for monthly payments of $500.
   - The total amount of the buyer's mortgage should not exceed 100 times the amount of his/her monthly mortgage payments. Thus, qualification for $500 monthly payments would also, under the MGB rule, qualify the buyer for a $50,000 mortgage.
2. Under the 54/60 Rule: To qualify under terms of the 54/60 rule, a buyer wishing to obtain a conventional mortgage of $64,000 with monthly payments of $758, approximately the amount needed to pay off a $64,000 mortgage over 30 years at 14 percent,

would need a gross annual income of $40,932 (54 × $758) to $45,480 (60 × $758)—a gross monthly income of $3,411 to $3,790.

3. **Under the Net Income Rule:** The sum of monthly principal, interest, taxes, and insurance (PITI) payments, *plus* maintenance and utilities, should not exceed 35 percent of the buyer's **net monthly income** (income after federal income tax, state income tax, and social security deductions). According to this formula, a buyer would need a net monthly income of $2,166 (based upon $758 ÷ 0.35) *plus* 1/12 the annual estimated cost of utilities and maintenance to qualify for a mortgage having monthly payments of $758.

Regardless of the type of mortgage you work out between the buyer, the lender, and yourself, mortgage lenders pretty much make their first pass at your prospect by "qualifying" the buyer, using whichever of the above rules they've been working with over the years, even if it doesn't precisely fit the situation.

Since bankers will probably be using one of the above qualification yardsticks, it would be a good idea for you to use one too—*before* taking your prospect to the bank.

If your prospect seems seriously interested and appears to be qualified, ask, "How would you like to handle the financing" or "How much of a down payment had you planned to make?" or "What monthly payments had you been thinking about?" And, depending on the situation, you can simply ask the buyer the amount of his or her annual income.

It would also probably be a good idea to obtain a credit report on your prospect through your attorney, your employer, or a friend who owns a business. True, your bank *could* obtain a credit report, but they might not give it to you—meaning that you wouldn't have the report to take to other prospective lenders or to use in making your own evaluation of the prospect if you find it necessary to facilitate the sale through partial self-financing. Anyway, the idea is to take *qualified* prospects to the bank, not question marks.

So, to purchase an $80,000 house under a conventional mortgage a buyer could expect to make a $16,000 down payment and finance $64,000 over 30 years at 14 percent for 360 monthly payments of $758. Actual cost of the house would be $16,000 plus 360 times $758, a total of $288,880. Of that total, $208,880 ($288,880 − $80,000) would be interest that the buyer could deduct from personal income over the 30-year life of the mortgage. To qualify:

- Under the MGB rule, the buyer's *gross* monthly income would need to be $3,032 (4 × $758).
- Under the 54/60 rule, the buyer's *gross* annual income would have to be from $40,932 (54 × $758) to $45,480 (60 × $758).
- Under the 35 percent of net monthly income rule, the buyer's *net* (after taxes) monthly income would have to be at least $2,166 ($758 ÷ 0.35) *plus* 1/12 the estimated monthly cost of maintenance and utilities.

Note that lenders also consider the buyer's income stability, other financial obligations, and credit rating.

A MATTER OF INTEREST: *It doesn't take a long, hard look at home financing to see where the problem is: interest rates. At 14 percent annual interest, commonly charged for fixed rate conventional mortgages during 1984, monthly payments on a $60,000 mortgage financed over 30 years would be $710.93. But look what happens when interest rates are raised or lowered:*

Annual Interest	Years	Monthly Payments	Income to Qualify*	Total Cost
17	30	$855.41	$46,192	$307,947
15	30	758.67	40,968	273,121
14	30	710.93	38,390	255,935
11	30	571.40	30,855	205,704
9	30	482.78	26,070	173,800
7	30	399.19	21,556	143,708

Obviously, many more buyers can qualify for a mortgage having monthly payments of $399.19 than can qualify for a mortgage having payments of $855.41.

PRIVATE MORTGAGE INSURANCE

If your buyer has a good credit rating and a stable income but has only one-fourth of the usual 20 percent conventional mortgage down payment, $4,000 instead of the $16,000 cited in the example of our $80,000 house, there's still hope. In this case, hope is spelled MGIC, **Mortgage Guaranty Insurance Corporation** (MGIC Plaza, Milwaukee, WI 53201, 414-347-6480).

MGIC can insure up to 95 percent of the *appraised fair market value* of a home. What that means is that if both your house *and* your prospective buyer qualify, a lender can grant a conventional mortgage with no more than a 5 percent down payment.

During the first half of 1984, the first year's cost of this coverage to protect the lender was 0.75 percent of the loan amount ($450 on a $60,000 mortgage) and 0.25 percent of the mortgage balance each year thereafter.

On a 10 percent down payment mortgage, MGIC's rate is 0.50 percent of the loan amount for the first year, then 0.25 percent for each year thereafter. (You might want to remember MGIC when you buy a future home, too.)

Since the down payment will be less under a mortgage granted with private mortgage insurance (PMI), the amount of the buyer's mortgage, and the amount of monthly payments, will be more (more principal and more interest) than if the buyer had made a $16,000 instead of $4,000 down payment.

On an $80,000 house purchased with PMI on a 30-year conventional mortgage, the amount of the mortgage would be $76,000 ($80,000 − $4,000) and the monthly payments at 14 percent annual interest would be almost exactly $900 instead of the $758 that would be the case for a 30-year, 14 percent, $64,000 mortgage.

*54 × Monthly Payment.

Under the 54/60 rule, the buyer's gross annual income would have to be $48,600/$54,000 for such a 5 percent down, $76,000 mortgage on an $80,000 house, instead of $40,932/$45,480 for a 20 percent down, $64,000 mortgage on the same house.

Over the 30-year life of such a mortgage, the cost of additional interest would be considerable.

"CONVENTIONAL" MORTGAGE VARIATIONS

Several types of so-called "conventional" mortgage variations have come into use in recent years, mainly to help ensure lenders' profit during uncertain economic times.

Variable Interest Rate Mortgage

Simply stated, the variable interest rate mortgage (also called adjustable interest rate mortgage) is written at an interest rate that may move up or down, usually tied to the Federal Home Loan Bank Board *national mortgage rate index*—the national mortgage interest rate for existing homes.

Variable interest rate mortgages build a "can't lose" profit margin into home mortgage loans for the benefit of lenders. They can be a dangerous gamble for homeowners because under the terms of some variable interest rate loans, monthly payments could go up just when borrowers could least afford the increase, since monthly payments rise in response to higher interest on the unpaid balance of a loan.

As variable interest rate mortgages gain in popularity with lenders, almost driving out fixed-rate conventional mortgages in some parts of the United States, variations of the variable interest rate mortgage are coming into wide use.

The good news about variable interest rate mortgages is that they usually start at an interest rate that is a few percentage points lower than the prevailing interest being charged for fixed-rate mortgages—often 8 percent, for example, at a time when fixed-rate mortgages are being written at 14 percent—since the lender doesn't stand to lose quite so much in the event of future interest rate increases (something very much on the mind of lenders writing mortgages at a fixed rate of interest).

Here's what could happen with monthly payments for a $60,000, 30-year mortgage having an initial rate of 8 percent, increasing as follows:

Year	Interest Rate	Monthly Payment
1	8%	$440.26
2	9	482.78
3	10	526.55
4	11	571.40
5	12	617.17
6	13	663.72
10	15	758.67
15	16	806.86
20	17	855.41
25	18	904.26

Total amount of the home buyer's monthly payment would more than double during the first 25 years, and total interest paid would be considerably more than for a 14 percent, fixed-rate mortgage.

Rate-capped Variable Interest Rate Mortgage. The rate-capped mortgage limits the total amount of interest rate change (up and/or down) during the life of the mortgage—say, 5 percent either way—and often limits the rate at which adjustments may be made, say, once every four or five years.

Each time the interest rate changes, the amount of the borrower's monthly payment is raised or lowered to adjust for the change.

Payment-capped Variable Interest Rate Mortgage. Although the interest rate may vary for a payment-capped mortgage, the borrower's monthly payment remains fixed. If the interest rate goes up, the amount of the unpaid balance is recalculated to reflect the increase by adding to the total number of payments required to retire the mortgage. Thus a 30-year mortgage may become a 31- or 32-year mortgage if written as a payment-capped variable interest rate mortgage.

As with rate-capped mortgages, which limit possible total interest rate increases, many payment-capped mortgages limit the maximum number of payments which can be added.

Many buyers prefer a payment-capped mortgage because it allows them to budget for a known monthly payment, even if they can't be precisely sure how long the mortgage payment period may be.

But a payment-capped mortgage that you might obtain for your buyer from one lender may not necessarily be "better" than a rate-capped mortgage available from another. It all depends on the maximum total possible cost to the buyer—a factor of initial interest rates and the limitations on any increase.

Uncapped Variable Interest Rate Mortgage. There are mortgage lenders who attempt to "sell" variable interest rate mortgages without any "cap" at all on either the *rate* or the *amount* of interest increase, merely telling borrowers that the interest rate charged "will be revised to reflect the cost of funds" or that it will be "tied to the national mortgage rate index." Signing such a mortgage could be a disaster.

Graduated-Payment Mortgage

The *interest rate* on a graduated-payment mortgage remains fixed. Monthly payments start lower than they would for a given mortgage amount under a traditional "straight-line" mortgage, then increase every year, or every few years, during the early years of the mortgage.

Mortgage lenders you talk to about financing the purchase of your house will be quite happy to set up such a plan for you to show to prospects. Originally, graduated-payment mortgages were promoted by residential developers anxious to sell large numbers of new houses they were "stuck with" due to inflation and rapidly rising interest rates.

Lower initial monthly payments allow greater numbers of buyers to "qualify" than would be possible with the higher initial payments that would be required if payments were to be equal throughout the life of the mortgage.

Graduated-payment mortgages (GPMs) were designed for younger, first-time buyers who expected their income to rise during the first few years following the purchase of a house. For this reason, mortgage lenders are more willing to provide GPMs to young borrowers than to those nearing retirement age or whose incomes cannot realistically be expected to rise during the years following the purchase of a house.

Here's how monthly payments would increase on a $70,000, 30-year, 14 percent GPM:

Year	Monthly Payment	Outstanding Balance
1	$645.77	$72,188
2	694.20	74,082
3	746.26	75,593
4	802.23	76,613
5	862.40	77,015
6	927.08	76,649
10	927.08	74,552
15	927.08	69,613
20	927.08	59,707
25	927.08	39,839
30	927.08	0

Note that during the first few years, while monthly payments are rising, the total amount owed also increases. This is because early payments do not cover the cost of interest—which the lender simply adds to the amount due.

Total interest paid during the life of the above GPM would be $323,127, compared to $228,591 for a traditional "straight-line" 30-year, 14 percent mortgage —which would have 360 equal monthly payments of $829.42.

Variable Rate
Graduated-Payment Mortgage

We wouldn't wish a variable interest graduated-payment mortgage on anyone, though quite a few lenders are trying to "market" them. This sort of loan reminds us of the kind of restaurant where the service is bad, but the food is terrible.

Even with payment increases limited to once every five years with a maximum rate of interest limited to, say, 18 percent, payments on such an 11 percent (starting rate), $70,000, 30-year mortgage lender's dream could increase from $666.63 per month during the first year to $1,054.96 per month by the thirtieth year. Total cost of interest for this kind of loan could be close to $400,000, considerably more than the $228,591 that would be charged during the term of a conventional "straight line" 30-year mortgage at a 14 percent annual rate of interest.

FHA-INSURED MORTGAGE

For the buyer of your home, the advantages of an FHA-insured mortgage are lower down payment and a lower rate of interest than for a conventional loan. After a HUD [FHA] CONDITIONAL COMMITMENT (the dual purpose form on page 313 that also serves as a VA CERTIFICATE OF REASONABLE VALUE) has been issued for your house, the FHA (Federal Housing Administration) will insure almost all of the mortgage for a qualified buyer.

On houses valued at *more* than $50,000 the FHA will insure 97 percent of the first $25,000 of a mortgage, plus 95 percent of any amount above that, up to a maximum mortgage of $67,500 (or up to a maximum of $90,000 in some "high cost" areas).

On a $67,500 house, for example, the FHA would insure:

97 percent of the first $25,000:	$24,250
95 percent of the remaining $42,500:	40,375
Total FHA mortgage insurance:	$64,625

With $64,625 of the mortgage on a $67,500 house insured, an FHA-approved lender could grant a mortgage to buy the house with only a $2,875 down payment ($67,500 − $64,625 = $2,875).

On houses valued at $50,000 or less, the FHA will insure 97 percent of the entire mortgage amount, which requires that the buyer make only a 3 percent down payment—about $1,500 on a $50,000 house.

The interest rate on an FHA-insured home loan is often less than the borrower would pay for a conventional mortgage. At one point during 1982 when conventional, fixed-rate mortgages were being written at 18 percent interest in many parts of this country, FHA-insured mortgages cost home buyers only 11½ percent, plus ½ percent for insurance.

To you, the disadvantage of selling your home under an FHA mortgage is the fact that the lender will charge you "points," one "point" being equivalent to 1 percent of the mortgage amount, just for financing the sale of your home under a "low-profit" FHA-insured loan. (The fact that the lender is *insured* against loss under an FHA loan doesn't seem to be taken into account by mortgage lenders.)

On a $48,000 FHA-insured mortgage, one point would be $480. At this writing, many lenders are charging sellers five or six points for granting FHA-insured mortgages on their homes.

Also at this writing, a time when conventional fixed-rate mortgages are being written at 14 percent, FHA-insured mortgages are being written at 12½ percent with a charge to the seller of about five points.

If your buyer wants to arrange an FHA-insured loan because of inability to make the customary 20 percent down payment, or the 5 percent down payment (with larger monthly payments) under private mortgage insurance, you might be wise to lower your price a bit (provided that action will eliminate the buyer's having to secure an FHA-insured loan) since "points" that you would be charged by the lender could cost you several thousand dollars.

A POINT ABOUT POINTS: *Although the law says mortgage lenders can't charge points to the buyer on*

FHA or VA loans, a lender can waive charging any points at all. Occasionally, a lender will waive points on a new mortgage if the borrower obtains the mortgage from the same lender who made the current loan on the property—your mortgage lender.

Discuss with your lawyer the possibility of negotiating such an arrangement before you start to sell your house so that you'll know where to steer a buyer who needs an FHA or VA loan.

VA-GUARANTEED LOAN

Working through a VA-approved mortgage lender, the Veterans Administration will guarantee the first $27,500 of a home loan on *qualified* housing for a veteran or for a qualified spouse of certain deceased veterans. The $27,500 guarantee has the effect of allowing a veteran to buy housing costing up to $110,000 without making a down payment—there being a $110,000 cap on the maximum cost of any house purchased under the no-down-payment program.

If there were no cap, the $27,500 VA guarantee would permit a no-down-payment purchase of housing costing up to $137,500—$27,500 being 20 percent of $137,500.

NOTE: At this writing the VA was expected to announce, during August of 1984, an increase of its guarantee to $30,000 and an increase in the maximum cost of a house purchased under its no-down-payment plan from $110,000 to $135,000.

You can, of course, use a VA loan guarantee in the purchase of *qualified* housing costing any amount; you'll just have to make up the difference between $110,000 and the higher cost of the house in cash as part of the down payment.

Both buyer *and* house must qualify (see page 343); therefore, obtain an early VA appraisal so you'll know before marketing your house whether you can suggest the option of a VA loan to a potential buyer who is a veteran.

Until 1984, VA guaranteed loans were truly "no down payment" loans. Technically, they still are; however, a so-called "funding fee" of ½ percent of the amount financed must now be paid by the borrower directly to the United States Treasury Department when the loan is granted. Veterans who have a service-connected disability for which they are entitled to receive compensation are exempt from payment of the "funding fee."

Interest rates on VA-guaranteed loans were 14 percent during mid-1984, with a "healthy" charge to the seller (by the mortgage lender) for "points."

Mortgage payments on VA-guaranteed loans may run as long as 40 years, depending upon the appraiser's estimate of the "economic life" of the house—how long it may reasonably be expected to last.

Borrower income requirements are pretty much the same for VA loans as for FHA and conventional loans, but mortgage lenders say that VA requirements seem to be a bit less stringent, especially for disabled veterans.

ROLLOVER MORTGAGE

The interest rate on a rollover mortgage is renegotiated every few years, 5 years being the commonly specified time frame. Rollover mortgages also allow for renegotiation of the borrower's right to pay off the mortgage early without penalty, to change the length of the payment period, and to allow assumption of the loan by a new borrower.

A rollover mortgage is usually written for 25 or 30 years, just the same as other mortgages; therefore, there's no need to "renew" the mortgage, and terms remain unchanged unless borrower and lender strike a mutually satisfactory bargain within rate limitations stipulated by law.

As with the previously described variable interest rate mortgage, interest rate adjustments are tied to the Federal Home Loan Bank Board's *national mortgage rate index* or to the mortgage lender's rates at the time of the rollover.

Rollover mortgages aren't necessarily better or worse than other mortgages with built-in variables. "Better" or "worse" would depend upon the specifics of available mortgages.

BY THE BOOK: *Probably the next best thing to having a desk-top computer programmed to figure infinite permutations of variable interest rates and monthly payment schedules over various mortgage lengths is a small booklet usually titled* Comprehensive Mortgage Payment Tables. *You can probably get a copy free for the asking from someone you know at a savings and loan association, credit union, commercial bank, or title insurance company.*

Although the books are not giveaway items to the general public, they're usually in plentiful supply around mortgage lenders and other lending institutions because they are giveaway promotional items with large, national title insurance companies and mortgage companies.

Most mortgage payment table booklets also contain sections of truth-in-lending statutes, points discount tables, amortization schedules, and loan progress tables, but it's the monthly payment tables you'll be most interested in.

Using the monthly payment tables, you'll be able to determine for a prospective buyer the amount of monthly payments on a mortgage having any fixed rate of interest from 7 percent to 18 percent per year, for any number of years from 1 year to 40 years, and for any loan amount from $25 to $100,000. It's simply a matter of consulting the proper column on the proper page.

You'll learn, for example, that monthly payments on a $25.00 loan to be repaid over 30 years at 14 percent interest would be 30¢ a month for a total interest cost of $83.00 (we knew you needed to know that). Or that monthly payments on a $5,000 auto loan at 16 percent interest paid off over five years would amount to $121.60.

You can use the book's tables to determine the monthly payments and cost of interest on any type of loan or repayment schedule.

Statutory interest rate caps that apply to other variable interest rate mortgages also apply to rollover mortgages. At this writing, interest rates are limited to a maximum of five points increase during the life of the mortgage at a rate of no more than ½ percent per year.

One thing that the rollover mortgage does provide is a date certain (as lawyers like to say) when the loan may be renegotiated. Perhaps for this reason, rollover mortgages are generally a bit more liberal than others with respect to a lessened penalty for early payoff and with regard to allowing assumption of the mortgage by a new borrower.

In the absence of fixed-rate mortgage availability, a rollover mortgage could be a better deal for the buyer of your home than any other type of variable interest rate mortgage.

ZERO PERCENT MORTGAGE

Once you're in the real estate market checking out ways of selling your house, you're sure to hear about the zero percent mortgage. The zero percent mortgage is used mostly by developers to sell large numbers of new homes, but it may work for you if you have enough equity in your house.

Here's how it works:

- The buyer makes a 33 to 50 percent down payment.
- The seller then takes a 5- to 7-year mortgage at zero percent interest for the unpaid amount.

On an $80,000 house the buyer could expect to make a $27,000 down payment and pay off the $53,000 balance over 5 years in 60 equal installments of $883.33. Not bad, considering that payments on the customary 30-year, $64,000 mortgage ($80,000 minus the usual 20 percent down payment) would be $758—at a cost of more than $194,480 in interest, more than twice the price of the house!

The large developer's motivation to offer zero percent mortgages is obvious: to unload a large number of new houses he or she is stuck with. But what motivation is there for the usual mortgage lender? Very little.

But if you have enough equity in your home, the tremendous saving in interest that you can offer to a potential buyer just might tilt a sale your way and make the zero percent mortgage a practical way of financing the purchase of your house.

Surprisingly, a section of the Internal Revenue Code states that a simple interest of 10 percent may be imputed where there is an interest charge of less than 9 percent on a home mortgage—the IRS's philosophy perhaps being that the price of the house has been jacked up to compensate for the loss of interest income.

Consult an *experienced real estate attorney* if the zero percent mortgage looks like a possible way of selling your house—and see page 343, which describes ways to obtain ready cash for a portion of the balance due on any mortgage you hold.

BALLOON-NOTE MORTGAGE

The balloon-note mortgage is simple—deadly, but simple. A balloon-note mortgage is set up like a conventional mortgage with monthly payments equal to or somewhat below the amount of monthly payments on a conventional 30-year mortgage. Interest, too, is usually the same as that charged for first mortgages at the time the note is written.

The danger of a balloon note, which is usually written for 3 or 5 years, is that the unpaid balance must be paid in full by the borrower at the end of the rather short mortgage term.

Mortgage lenders love balloon notes because they function much as a completely uncapped variable interest rate mortgage. Many mortgage lenders refuse to guarantee to renew a balloon-note mortgage when it comes due, but even if the lender does guarantee to renew, it's take it or leave it at the lender's going rate or find a way to pay off the note in full.

You would probably never want to accept a balloon-note second mortgage from a buyer unless you had absolute assurance that he/she would be receiving funds, perhaps from a will or trust, to pay off the note when it became due.

SECOND MORTGAGE

If a buyer wants your house and can qualify for a mortgage having the necessary monthly payments, but doesn't have the required down payment, a second mortgage can make it possible for the buyer to purchase your house.

Using the example of a conventional mortgage for which a 20 percent down payment would be required, let's see how a second mortgage might be used if the buyer is able to make only a 5 percent down payment:

Amount of first mortgage on $80,000 house:	$64,000
Buyer's down payment:	4,000
	$68,000

The mortgage lender is willing to grant a $64,000 mortgage; the buyer can make only a $4,000 down payment. So a second mortgage is used to fill the gap between the $68,000 shown above and the $80,000 price of the house.

One option would be for the buyer (possibly with your assistance) to arrange a 5- to 7-year second mortgage from another lender who specializes in second mortgages. Since the interest rate on a second mortgage would probably run 16 to 18 percent when first mortgages are being written at 14 percent, the buyer may feel that he/she can't afford to undertake that obligation.

The second and most commonly used option would be for you to take a second mortgage from the buyer at a rate of interest that is 5 percent or so *less* than the going rate for first mortgages.

Why would you do that? You would do it if it were the only means of selling your house, since the second mortgage is a way of letting the buyer make monthly payments on the down payment *after* he/she has purchased your house.

During the first 5 years of ownership (assuming you've taken a 5-year second mortgage), the buyer will have some stiff monthly payments to make: $758.33 to the mortgage lender on the first mortgage ($64,000/14 percent /30 years), plus $249.11 to you ($12,000/9 percent/5 years) for the second mortgage—a total monthly payment of $1,007.44 for the first 5 years.

If the buyer defaults, you'll have the dubious protection of standing in line after the holder of the first mortgage and will receive any residual after the house is sold—possibly at public auction.

Considering that, at this writing, you could earn 11 percent on 5-year U.S. Treasury notes without taking any credit risk at all, the second mortgage doesn't stack up as a particularly good investment—unless it helps you sell your house when nothing else can.

Of course, you don't have to take a second mortgage for any fixed amount, or at any particular rate of interest. It's just possible that a second mortgage for a minimal amount, and at a rate of interest that will make it worthwhile, may still be a valuable selling tool —particularly if it enables you to sell at your original price rather than at a lowered amount.

You'd be better off if you can help your buyer meet down payment requirements by obtaining private mortgage insurance or an FHA-insured or VA-guaranteed loan. If you do take a second mortgage, be sure you have the advice of an *experienced real estate lawyer.*

CONTRACT OF SALE

During recent years many homeowners have eliminated the need for a mortgage lender by offering the buyer a contract of sale instead of a mortgage. Under a contract of sale the buyer makes a down payment, usually about 10 percent of the selling price, moves in, and then makes monthly payments, which include interest, directly to the seller.

The terms of a contract of sale call for the house to remain the property of the seller until the entire selling price, plus stipulated interest, has been paid. As a practical matter, the buyer and seller understand that the buyer will probably "pay off" the contract of sale within a few years—as soon as the buyer has paid the seller a sufficient amount to equal the customary down payment or as soon as interest rates lower

sufficiently for the buyer to qualify for a conventional mortgage loan.

The amount of the down payment, the interest rate, and the length of the contract of sale are all open to negotiation between the buyer and seller—no one else is involved.

NOTE: The maximum interest rate that may be charged will be affected by your own state's statutes, commonly called *usury laws.* Since no buyer would pay a higher rate of interest on a contract of sale than would be charged by a mortgage lender, this limitation will not normally come into play on a contract of sale.

During the life of the contract, the seller uses the buyer's monthly payments to make his or her own monthly payments to the mortgage lender.

The advantage of a contract of sale to the seller is that it allows him or her to "move" the house much more quickly than would probably be possible if a mortgage lender were involved. The contract of sale also gives the seller more time to look for and purchase another house without tax liability for any profit from the sale of the home, since it isn't "sold" until the deed is transferred.

The lower interest usually charged by sellers under a contract of sale (because of a preexisting, but nonassumable, low interest rate mortgage) often allows them to obtain a better price for the house, since the mortgage lender's higher interest rates do not have to be included in the buyer's monthly payments.

If you decide to sell your house under a contract of sale, have the agreement drawn by an experienced *real estate lawyer.* Also be sure that the down payment is adequate to cover the likely cost of any damage that the buyer might do to your house during occupancy if the contract isn't fulfilled. You should make a careful check to learn the buyer's credit history and ability to pay.

HYPOTHECATE YOUR MORTGAGE: *Chances are that if you sell your house while home mortgage rates remain above 12 percent, you will be providing at least partial seller financing—and in most cases seller financing is spelled SECOND MORTGAGE. The problem with a second mortgage is that while it may help you sell your present home, it won't do much to help you buy the next one.*

Under normal conditions you could let a second mortgage run its course, accepting your buyer's monthly payments until the mortgage is paid in full— usually within 2 to 5 years. But today you'll need all the immediate cash you can get your hands on in order to meet down payment requirements on the next house you plan to buy.

There are two ways you can get immediate cash from a second mortgage:

1. *You can "sell" the mortgage at a discount to a financial institution, usually with the help of your bank or the holder of your home buyer's first mortgage (also sometimes called Deed of Trust).*

Discounts vary, but you might receive only $10,000 to $15,000 for a 5-year, $20,000 second mortgage.

2. *You can "hypothecate" your second mortgage, which is simply financial jargon for using your second mortgage as collateral (security) for a loan from a bank, mortgage broker, credit union, or other lender.*

You won't receive the full face value of your buyer's second mortgage for such a loan; in fact, you'll probably only be able to borrow about half of the value of a second mortgage used as security—a $10,000 loan against a $20,000 second mortgage.

The big advantage of using a second mortgage as security for a loan, instead of discounting it, is that eventually you will receive the full value of the mortgage instead of merely the amount you'd receive if you sold it at a discount.

There is yet another step you can consider when buying your next house: get the seller to take your second mortgage, which you might then arrange to sign in the same amount and for the same monthly payments and rate of interest as the second mortgage that you are holding from the buyer of your home. That way your buyer's payments would merely "pass through" your own bank account on their way to the seller of your newly purchased home.

ESTIMATED PURCHASE DATA

When you've received your independent "conventional" mortgage appraisal and your FHA and VA certificates, sit down on your own or with a mortgage lender or your attorney and complete our **Estimated Purchase Data** form (Form 68.1, page F549). With conventional, VA, and FHA down payments, interest rates, qualifying income, and other requirements differing, the completed form (see our sample on page 333) will put everything at your fingertips.

Refer to the adjacent table (Monthly Payments per $1,000 Amortized Mortgage) to estimate monthly payments required to purchase your house. Be sure to add estimated taxes and insurance (you can do this on the basis of current costs for these items).

Use Form 68.2, **Loan Comparison Data**, to record terms offered by various lenders. Include the name and address of each lender plus the name of the person contacted.

MONTHLY PAYMENTS PER $1,000 AMORTIZED MORTGAGE

Percent Interest	Years						
	10	15	20	25	30	35	40
9	12.67	10.15	9.00	8.40	8.05	7.84	7.72
9½	12.94	10.45	9.33	8.71	8.41	8.22	8.11
10	13.22	10.75	9.66	9.09	8.78	8.60	8.50
10½	13.50	11.06	9.99	9.45	9.15	8.99	8.89
11	13.78	11.37	10.33	9.81	9.53	9.37	9.29
11½	14.06	11.69	10.67	10.17	9.91	9.77	9.69
12	14.35	12.01	11.02	10.54	10.29	10.16	10.09
12½	14.64	12.33	11.37	10.91	10.68	10.56	10.49
13	14.94	12.66	11.72	11.28	11.07	10.96	10.90
13½	15.23	12.99	12.08	11.66	11.46	11.36	11.31
14	15.53	13.32	12.44	12.04	11.85[a]	11.76	11.72
14½	15.83	13.66	12.80	12.43	12.25	12.17	12.13
15	16.14	14.00	13.17	12.81	12.65	12.57	12.54
15½	16.45	14.34	13.54	13.20	13.05	12.98	12.95
16	16.76	14.69	13.92	13.59	13.45	13.39	13.36
16½	17.07	15.04	14.29	13.99	13.86	13.80	13.77
17	17.38	15.40	14.67	14.48	14.26	14.21	14.19
17½	17.70	15.75	15.05	14.78	14.67	14.62	14.60
18	18.02	16.11	15.44	15.18	15.08	15.03	15.02

[a]To figure monthly payments for principal and interest on a $64,000 mortgage over 30 years at an annual interest of 14 percent, for example, multiply the appropriate monthly payment (set in bold face for our example) by the mortgage amount in thousands of dollars ($11.85 × 64 = $758.40). The annual cost of local taxes and insurance must be divided by 12 and added to the $758.40 to determine the total monthly payment for principal, interest, taxes, and insurance (PITI).

Sample of Form 68.1/F549

Estimated Purchase Data

	Conventional		FHA		VA	
Appraised Value	$75,000	(1)	$75,000	(2)	$75,000	(3)
Down Payment Required	$15,000*		$3,000		0	
Annual Interest Rate	14%		14%		14%	
Amount of Mortgage	$60,000		$72,000		$75,000	
Approximate Monthly Payment **30 Years**	$710.93	(4)	$853.12	(4)	$888.66	(4)
Approximate Qualifying Income	$42,656	(5)	$49,987	(5)	$53,320	(5)
Interest Paid Over **30 Years**	$195,935		$235,123		$244,918	

KEY:
(1) Appraised Fair Market Value
(2) FHA Conditional Commitment for Insurance
(3) VA Certificate of Reasonable Value
(4) Add 1/12 of estimated annual local taxes and insurance
   to determine approximate total monthly payment
(5) 60 × approximate monthly payment

*Could be as low as $3,750 (5% of selling price) with private mortgage insurance (PMI)—see page 326.

69 Avoiding the Due-on-Sale Clause

If your existing home mortgage contains an enforceable due-on-sale clause (which requires that you pay off your mortgage in full when your house is sold), you can save your buyer thousands of dollars by using the information in this chapter and our ready-to-use **Lease Agreement with Option to Purchase** to legally avoid the due-on-sale clause.

On a $64,000, 30-year mortgage, the commonly charged interest rate (at this writing) is 14 percent. That works out to $11.85 per thousand per month for a monthly payment of $758.40 ($11.85 × 64). Over 30 years at 14 percent the buyer would pay the mortgage lender $273,024 (360 months × $758.40).

The same $64,000 mortgage at, say, 9 percent, common not many years ago, would be $8.05 per thousand for a monthly payment of $515.20 ($8.05 × 64). Over 30 years at 9 percent the buyer would pay the lender $185,472 (360 months × $515.20), a saving of $87,552 ($273,024 − $185,472) when compared to the 14 percent rate.

Taking into account that the mortgage lender may be willing to let the buyer assume your mortgage at a rate halfway between your original rate of interest, say, for this example, 9 percent, and the lender's current 14 percent rate, savings gained by avoiding the due-on-sale clause could still be substantial. On an $64,000, 30-year mortgage at 11½ percent, monthly payments would be $634.24 ($9.91 × 64) and the total amount paid the lender over 30 years would be $228,326. That's still a saving of $44,698 ($273,024 − $228,326) over the 14 percent rate.

It's easy enough to figure out how much the **Lease Agreement with Option to Purchase** could save your buyer. Just ask your mortgage lender what interest rate would be charged in allowing a buyer to assume your existing mortgage, then use the table on page 332 to compare your present interest rate with the rate charged by the mortgage lender if your buyer assumes your existing mortgage.

Just a few years ago the due-on-sale clause was rarely a problem for anyone. The interest rate may have gone up at most a percentage point or two between an owner's buying and selling a home, but that was all. But as interest rates began to rise and as the rate of increase began to speed up, mortgage lenders began trying to enforce the due-on-sale clause—something the courts of nearly twenty states said they couldn't do.

Then on June 28, 1982, the U.S. Supreme Court handed down a decision that upheld the right of federally chartered savings and loan associations to enforce the due-on-sale clause, thus allowing them to charge going interest rates for mortgages on newly sold, previously financed homes.

The Court's decision affected only *federally* chartered S&Ls. State-chartered S&Ls, commercial banks, mutual savings and loan associations—and VA-guaranteed home loans—were not included in the ruling. Soon, however, many state legislatures, under heavy lobbying pressure from banking interests, passed statutes that allowed state-chartered mortgage lenders in their states to also enforce the due-on-sale clause, leaving only VA-guaranteed loans unaffected by the Supreme Court's decision.

Since your home mortgage probably contains a due-on-sale clause (sometimes called an "accelerated payment" clause), you might want to consider legally avoiding the effect it could have on your chances of selling your home.

There are two ways of legally avoiding the due-on-sale clause. One, the land sales contract, holds dangers for both buyer and seller and presents some complicated income tax problems. Since the land sales contract is not recommended by this volume's legal consultants, we don't offer it here.

The second commonly used method of avoiding the due-on-sale clause is the **Lease Agreement with Option to Purchase** (Form 69.1, page F553). The "Agreement," as we'll call it from now on ("hereinafter" as lawyers like to say), provides protection for both buyer and seller and meets Internal Revenue Code requirements that allow the lessee/buyer to take the same income tax deductions that would normally be taken by the owner of the property (see paragraph 33 of the Agreement).

"Down payment" requirements can be much more flexible since the initial amount paid by the lessee/buyer is completely negotiable between the lessee/buyer and the lessor/seller. In the language of the Agreement (see paragraph 2 of the Agreement), the down payment is termed a "nonrefundable consideration" for making the Agreement, but it's function is substantially the same as a traditional down payment.

Generally, the lessee/buyer must exercise his or her option to purchase the property from the lessor/seller by a specified date, usually within 20 or 30 years of the date of purchase, but that decision is also completely within the control of the buyer and seller.

The Agreement is a fairly long document, longer than a lease and longer than a mortgage note since it contains the major elements of both. But it's written in "bite-size" portions and contains only a few kernels of "legalese"—terms that have been around for so long and that have met so many court tests for interpretation that no one wants to take the risk of changing them.

Given that state laws vary, the following completed sample Agreement (page 336) and its fill-in-the-blanks companion (Form 69.1) are presented as model forms that you can consider and then discuss with a well-qualified real estate attorney. You can save time and money if you'll make a few photocopies of the Agreement to use as work sheets so that when you visit the attorney's office you'll have a copy with all the blanks filled in spelling out exactly what you and your buyer want to do.

Note that, under the Agreement, title to the property remains in your name and you continue to pay the mortgage lender each month with money paid to you by the lessee/buyer, and since existing insurance remains in force (see paragraph 27) the mortgage lender never learns that you have leased your house with an option to sell.

The Agreement may initially seem complicated, but it is a commonly used procedure dating from far before there was any need to avoid the due-on-sale clause, it is well-established in real estate law, and it is not a "gimmick" of so-called "creative" home financing.

USING THE AGREEMENT

The box at the beginning of the Agreement provides space for two lessors and two lessees. This is to accommodate situations where nonmarried individuals (including unmarried cohabitants) may be lessor(s) or lessee(s). In the sample Agreement beginning on page 336, married lessees Hans Lumburg and Freda Lumburg could have been listed separately, filling both lessee spaces, but this would have been unnecessary and was done as it was for simplicity. Note, however, that on page 342 both were required to sign separately, as would also be the case with married lessors.

Paragraph 4 provides space for the lessor to list the name and address of an agent to receive payment from the lessee. If the lessor chooses not to remain in the same area after leasing the property, a local agent—a property management agency, bank, attorney, or real estate agent—can be named.

Paragraph 12 of the Agreement includes provision for an increase in the annual percentage rate of the lessee's promissory note to the lessor every five years during the term of the Agreement, beginning five years after signing. This paragraph was presented to take into account those cases where the lessor may have signed a first mortgage/deed of trust having a similar provision. You would probably not want to include an interest rate escalation clause in any Agreement you sign as lessor if your own mortgage/deed of trust did not contain such a provision.

Paragraph 19 contains the lessor's agreement to sign, before a notary public, a memorandum of the lessee's option to purchase the property. Such a memorandum, recorded with the county clerk, can provide added protection to the lessee since it would give constructive notice to any potential lender or buyer that a purchase option had been sold and thus would cloud the owner's right (and ability) to sell or additionally encumber the property.

Any memorandum of option to purchase should contain the following:

- The option purchaser's name and address.
- The street address and legal description of the property.
- The term covered by the option.
- The statement, "Owner agrees not to further encumber said property during the term of said option."

And it should be drawn by an *experienced real estate attorney.*

Paragraph 25, requiring the lessee to reasonably maintain the property and permanantly attached items, does not specifically list carpets, draperies, electrical fixtures, etc., which are often sold with a house and which the lessor would probably find not practical to remove. These items, plus any others (such as refrigerator, washer, dryer, freezer, and lawn care equipment), could be listed under paragraph 47. Perhaps the simplest way to deal with many of these items would be to sell them separately, either to the lessee or to someone else, prior to leasing the property.

Any lease agreement with option to purchase is negotiated from a wide range of variables: purchase price, term of the agreement, interest rate on the lessee's promissory note to the lessor, the amount of the down payment/nonrefundable consideration for granting the option to purchase, the amount of monthly payments, and so on.

Note: None of the items used in the completed sample Agreement should be taken as indications of what should, or should not, be included in any Agreement that you may use. Those terms should be arrived at by *negotiation* between the lessor and lessee, with the counsel of their own separate and well-qualified real estate attorneys.

Sample of Form 69.1/F553

Lease Agreement with Option to Purchase

Lessor _____ Monroe Earwood _____

Name

7934 Forsythe Boulevard _____ Clayton _____ Missouri _____ 63105

Street Address _____ City _____ State _____ Zip

Lessor _____ xxxxxxxxxxxxxxxxxxxxxxxxxxxxxxxxxxxxxxxxxxxxxxxxxxxxxxxxxxx

Name

xxxxxxxxxxxxxxxxxxxxxxxxxxxxxxxxxxxxxxxxxxxxxxxxxxxxxxxxxxx

Street Address _____ City _____ State _____ Zip

Premises _____ 2620 Freiling _____ St. Louis _____ Missouri _____ 63104

Street Address _____ City _____ State _____ Zip

the legal description of which is _____ Lot 28, Block 14, South Oldendorf Addition

_____

_____

_____

_____

_____

_____

Lessee _____ Hans Lumburg and Freda Lumburg _____

Name

3619 Hofstetter _____ St. Louis _____ Missouri _____ 63147

Street Address _____ City _____ State _____ Zip

Lessee _____ xxxxxxxxxxxxxxxxxxxxxxxxxxxxxxxxxxxxxxxxxxxxxxxxxxxxxxxxx

Name

xxxxxxxxxxxxxxxxxxxxxxxxxxxxxxxxxxxxxxxxxxxxxxxxxxxxxxxxx

Street Address _ Street Address _____ City _____ State _____ Zip

1. The Lessor hereby leases with an option to purchase the above-described premises to _____ Hans Lumburg _____ and _____ Freda Lumburg _____, hereinafter called Lessee, for a term of _____ thirty (30) years _____, beginning _____ May 1, 1984 _____ and ending _____ April 30, 2014 _____.

2. The Lessee agrees to pay the sum of _____ five thousand dollars ($5,000) _____ to the Lessor on or before _____ May 1, 1984 _____, as nonrefundable consideration for granting this lease with option to purchase.

3. The principal balance of the Lessor's existing first mortgage/deed of trust to:

First American Fidelity Savings Bank

Name

720 Olive _____ St. Louis _____ Missouri _____ 63166

Street Address _____ City _____ State _____ Zip

is _____ one hundred and two thousand, six hundred dollars ($102,600) _____, at an interest rate of _____ eleven (11) percent _____, payable at the rate of _____ five hundred and eighty-eight dollars and sixty cents (588.60) _____ per month, which the Lessor shall pay each month to the above-named banking institution.

Sample of Form 69.1 (*Continued*)

4. The balance of the purchase price for the leased premises shall be the attached promissory note of the Lessee to the Lessor, said note secured by this Agreement, dated _____May 1, 1984_____, having a principal balance of _____eighty-nine thousand, six hundred dollars and two cents ($89,600.02)_____, an interest rate of _____thirteen (13) percent_____, payable at the rate of _____nine hundred and eighty-four dollars and fifty-two cents ($984.52)_____ per month, such payments to be made to:

_____Monroe Earwood_____
Name

7934 Forsythe Boulevard   St. Louis   Missouri   63105
Street Address   *City*   *State*   *Zip*

5. Lessee agrees to pay a late charge of _____ten (10) percent_____ of the monthly payment to Lessor if such payment is not made by the Lessee by the __10th__ of each month.

6. Failure of Lessee to make the specified payment within _____thirty (30) days_____ after the date on which due, including any late charge, shall be cause to terminate this Agreement and Lessor shall have the right to retain all payments made by Lessee.

7. Upon tender of any payment in cash, Lessor agrees to issue a receipt stating Lessee's name, a description of the premises, the amount paid and the period for which paid.

8. The Lessor hereby grants to the Lessee an option to purchase the leased property any time Lessee may decide to exercise such option prior to _____April 30, 2014_____, provided that the Lessee shall have met all obligations set forth in this Agreement. At the time of the Lessee's exercise of his/her option to purchase the leased property, the Lessor agrees to convey said property to the Lessee free and clear of any encumbrances, except property taxes and assessments which are to be paid by the Lessee, and except for the herein-described promissory note and first mortgage/deed of trust to _____ First American Fidelity Savings Bank _____.

9. Lessor agrees not to encumber additionally the leased premises, apart from the herein-described encumbrance, which may remain.

10. Lessor hereby agrees to protect and defend the Lessee and the leased property against loss or foreclosure by reason of any encumbrance created by the Lessor and now existing against the leased property.

11. The Lessor agrees that failure of the Lessor to pay promptly in full the amount due _____First American Fidelity Savings Bank_____ each month, as set forth in paragraph three (3) above, or any further encumbrance of the leased property by the Lessor shall be cause for the Lessee to suspend payment to the Lessor, and for Lessee to continue to occupy the leased premises without further payment to the Lessor until such time as the Lessor shall make current the first mortgage/deed of trust to _____First American Fidelity Savings Bank_____ and/or remove any new encumbrance. Lessee shall also have full recourse in a court of law against Lessor for any breach of this Agreement.

12. The Lessor and Lessee agree that the annual rate of interest on the Lessee's promissory note to Lessor may be adjusted on the __first__ day of __May__ of __1992__, __1997__, __2002__, __2007__ and __2012__ to the rate of interest charged by _____First American Fidelity Savings Bank_____ or its successor for home loans made on those dates.

13. At such time as the Lessor shall receive from the Lessee written notice of Lessee's intent to exercise his/her option to purchase the leased property under terms of this Agreement, the Lessor shall, within thirty (30) days of receipt of such notice, deliver to the Lessee a preliminary title search and/or abstract of title. Any defects in title indicated by such title search or abstract shall be remedied by the Lessor within thirty (30) days after notice of such defects shall be given to Lessor. Lessor shall deliver to Lessee on the date of closing of escrow a grant/warranty deed free of all encumbrances except as provided for in paragraph eight (8) above.

Sample of Form 69.1 (*Continued*)

14. At such time as the Lessee shall determine to exercise his/her option to purchase the leased property prior to the expiration of this Agreement, the Lessee shall:

A. Give the Lessor written notice thereof.

B. Make arrangements to assume, pay or take title to the leased property subject to the herein-described encumbrance to _____ First American Fidelity Savings Bank _____ by ____ April 30, ____ 2014 ____, by:

    1) Paying in full to the Lessor the promissory note described in paragraph four (4) above, or

    2) Securing said promissory note by a second mortgage/deed of trust recorded against the property, or

    3) Securing financing elsewhere to pay off the existing first mortgage/deed of trust (together with any prepayment penalty or other charges) and paying the balance of the purchase price owed to the Lessor under Lessee's promissory note to the Lessor, and by

    4) Paying normal escrow, title transfer and title insurance costs for acquisition of property in the county of _____ St. Louis _____, municipality of _____ St. Louis _____.

15. The Lessee acknowledges being advised by the Lessor that the existing first mortgage/deed of trust payable to _____ First American Fidelity Savings Bank _____ contains a provision for accelerated payment of indebtedness, commonly termed a "due-on-sale clause," effective upon transfer of the leased premises. The Lessee agrees, that upon acquisition of said property, he/she shall pay to _____ First American Fidelity Savings Bank _____ any such charges, along with any prepayment penalties and other charges incident to Lessee's acquisition of the property.

16. In the event that proceeds of any new loan not be sufficient to pay in full the remaining balance due the Lessor under this Agreement, the Lessor agrees to accept from the Lessee a promissory note which shall be in the same form as the Lessee's promissory note now attached to and made a part of this Agreement, to be secured by a standard form second mortgage/deed of trust payable to the Lessor under the same terms as contained in the Lessee's original promissory note to the Lessor, described in paragraph four (4) above, with the unpaid balance due no later than _____ April 30, 2014 _____.

17. Purchase of the leased property by Lessee shall be completed by conveyance of the property and payment by the Lessee of all purchase obligations within _____ sixty (60) _____ days from delivery of notice to exercise the purchase option to the Lessor. In the event that such notice is not delivered to the Lessor prior to _____ April 30, 2014 _____, the option to purchase granted under this Agreement shall be null and void, the _____ five thousand dollars _____ _____ ($5,000.00) _____ consideration for granting the herein-described option to purchase being non-refundable as set forth in paragraph two (2) above.

18. All obligations of the Lessee under terms of this Agreement shall terminate upon exercise by the Lessee of the option to purchase and completion of transfer of title of said property to the Lessee or his/her assigns.

19. The Lessor agrees, at any time, to sign before a notary public a memorandum of the Lessee's option to purchase the leased property, which the Lessee may have recorded in the official records of _____ St. Louis County _____, provided that such memorandum shall make no reference to this Agreement.

20. The Lessor covenants that the leased premises are clean, safe, sound and healthful, and that there exists no violation of any applicable housing code, and the Lessee accepts said premises as being in clean, safe, sound and healthful condition and Lessee agrees to accept the property in its current condition with no other warranties or representations by the Lessor.

21. The Lessee agrees to surrender said premises to the Lessor at the end of the term of this Agreement in substantially the same or better condition, except for normal wear and tear and acts of God, unless the Lessee shall have exercised his/her option to purchase said property prior to termination of this agreement.

22. The Lessee agrees to comply with all applicable sanitary laws, ordinances and rules and orders of the Board of Health or other authorities affecting cleanliness, occupancy and preservation of the premises during the term of this Agreement.

23. The Lessee agrees to use the leased premises exclusively as a private residence for no more than _____ five _____ persons unless permission is obtained in writing from the Lessor.

24. The Lessee agrees to keep the premises in good order and repair and Lessee shall pay the cost of all necessary and prudent repairs and maintenance. Any mechanic's lien against the property as a result of work unpaid for by the Lessee shall be cause for immediate termination of this Agreement.

25. The Lessee shall cause to be made, at the Lessee's expense, all necessary and prudent repairs to heating and air conditioning apparatus, plumbing, electric and gas fixtures and other permanently attached items listed in paragraph forty-seven (47).

26. The Lessee shall not keep or have in or about the leased house, outbuildings or grounds any article or thing of a dangerous, inflammable or explosive nature, which might be pronounced "hazardous" or "extra hazardous" by any responsible insurance company. The Lessee agrees not to use the premises in any manner which would increase risks covered by existing insurance on the premises, or which would increase the rate for insurance on said premises. The Lessee agrees to comply, at the Lessee's expense, with all requirements of the insurers applicable to the leased premises in order to maintain fire and public liability insurance covering the house, outbuildings and grounds.

Sample of Form 69.1 (*Continued*)

27. The Lessor agrees to obtain and to maintain in force fire, public liability and extended coverage, plus whatever additional insurance shall be requested in writing by the Lessee, sufficient to protect against loss due to damage by fire of not less than ___ one hundred and fifty-seven thousand dollars ($157,000) ___, Lessor to obtain and maintain in force public liability insurance in a minimum amount of ___ one hundred thousand dollars ($100,000) ___ for each injured person, to a maximum amount of ___ one million dollars ($1,000,000) ___ for any single incident. Said insurance shall be subject to inspection of and approval by both Lessor and Lessee and shall provide coverage for the contingent liability of both Lessor and Lessee against any claims or losses, and shall be paid for by the Lessee within thirty (30) days of receipt of a statement therefor from the insurer or insurer's agent. Failure of Lessee to pay for said insurance within thirty (30) days of receipt of a statement therefor, shall be cause for immediate termination of this Agreement.

28. The Lessee agrees to indemnify the Lessor and hold him/her harmless from any and all damage claims, liability or other obligations incident to or arising from any injuries or losses related to Lessee's occupancy or use of the leased premises.

29. The Lessee shall give prompt notice to the Lessor or his/her agent of any dangerous, defective, unsafe or emergency condition in or on the leased premises, said notice being by any suitable means.

30. Lessor covenants that the Lessee and Lessee's family shall have, hold and enjoy the leased premises for the term of this Agreement, subject to the terms and conditions set forth herein.

31. The Lessee covenants that he/she will not commit nor permit a nuisance in or upon the premises, nor shall Lessee maliciously or by reason of gross negligence substantially damage the house, outbuildings or grounds.

32. The Lessee agrees not to sublet or sublease the leased premises without the express, written consent of the Lessor, who will not unreasonably withhold such consent. Unauthorized sublease or sublet of the premises by the Lessee shall be cause for immediate termination of this Agreement.

33. It is the express intent of the Lessor and Lessee that the Lessee shall, within the term of this Agreement, exercise his/her option to purchase the leased property. Therefore, for income tax purposes this Agreement shall be treated by the Lessor and Lessee as though the Lessee had purchased the leased property from the Lessor on ___ May 1, 1984 ___ xxxxx ___. Pursuant to the Internal Revenue Code, the Lessee shall be entitled to the benefits of ownership of said property, including:

  A. Interest paid on the mortgage/deed of trust to ___ First American Fidelity Savings Bank ___.

  B. Interest paid on the promissory note to the Lessor.

  C. Deduction for operating expenses.

  D. Depreciation of the property and improvements thereto.

The Lessor shall treat all payments of rent made under this Agreement as though a deferred payment installment sale of the property had taken place on ___ May 1, 1984 ___.

34. The Lessee agrees to pay all utilities, including electricity, gas, water and garbage removal and all other expenses of operating the property.

35. Property taxes on the leased premises for the year ending ___ December 31, 1984 ___, and insurance acceptable to the Lessor and Lessee as provided for in paragraph twenty-seven (27) above, along with rent and other current expenses of operating the property enumerated in paragraph thirty-three (33) above, shall be prorated as of the commencement of this Agreement.

36. In the event that proceedings of eminent domain result in condemnation of the leased premises which result in the remaining portion of the property being usable for use as a private residence, such proceedings shall not be cause for termination of this Agreement. All compensation awarded to the Lessee as a result of eminent domain proceedings shall be paid to the Lessor to reduce the balance of the Lessee's promissory note to the Lessor, as secured by this **Lease Agreement with Option to Purchase.**

37. In the event that proceedings of eminent domain result in condemnation of the leased premises which results in the property being unusable for use as a private residence, provisions of paragraph two (2) and paragraph eight (8) above shall apply with regard to Lessee's exercise of the option to purchase.

Sample of Form 69.1 (*Continued*)

38. Lessor and Lessee agree that all notices given under terms of this Agreement, except for notice of **emergency** condition as provided for in paragraph twenty-nine (29) above, shall be by United States certified mail, **return receipt** requested. For purposes of notice under terms of this Agreement, Lessor's address shall be:

Monroe Earwood			
Name			
7934 Forsythe Boulevard	Clayton	Missouri	63105
Street Address	*City*	*State*	*Zip*

and Lessee's address shall be:

Hans or Freda Lumburg			
Name			
2620 Freiling	St. Louis	Missouri	63104
Street Address	*City*	*State*	*Zip*

39. Lessor and Lessee agree that time limits and dates set forth in this Agreement may not be waived or altered **without** the written consent of both parties.

40. If the Lessee breaches this Agreement the Lessor may reenter the premises immediately and shall have the **right to** terminate this Agreement after giving the Lessee _____ thirty (30) _____ days written notice of said termination, **the** reason therefor, and by giving the Lessee an opportunity to correct any breach specified in said notice within ___ thirty ___ (30) _____ days of Lessee's receipt of such notice. The act of reentry by the Lessor shall not constitute termination of this Agreement.

41. After reentry, the Lessor shall have the right to appoint a receiver to take possession of and operate the property, collecting rents therefor. Proceedings by the Lessor for appointment of a receiver, or the appointment of a receiver, **shall not** constitute termination of this Agreement.

42. The Lessee agrees to vacate the leased premises upon any breach of the terms of this Agreement and receipt of **notice** of termination of this Agreement therefor, and to relinquish all rights to any right to recover money spent for improvements, appreciation in market value, rents, or payment made in consideration of this Agreement, or any buildup of equity in **the** premises.

43. The Lessor and Lessee agree that this **Lease Agreement with Option to Purchase** shall have been accepted by both parties when:

A. Both parties have signed both copies of this Agreement, the signatures of each party having been duly **witnessed** and notarized and

B. Lessor has received from Lessee the sum of _____ five thousand dollars ($5,000) _____ xxxxxxxxxxxxx _____, nonrefundable consideration for granting this **Lease Agreement with Option to Purchase** and

C. Lessee has paid to Lessor the sum of ___ nine hundred and eighty-four dollars and fifty-two cents _____ ($984.52) _____ for the period from ___ May 1, 1984 ___ to ___ May 30, 1984 ___ and

D. The Lessee has paid to the Lessor the following sums for:

1)	Fire and liability insurance	$ $311.16
2)	Garbage collection	$ 44.75
3)	Heating oil in tank	$ 55.00
4)	Property taxes	$ 234.35
5)	xxxxxxxxxxxxxxxxxxxxxxxxxxxxxxxxxxxxxxxxxx	$ xxxxxxxx
	For a total of:	$ 645.26

44. This Agreement and its conditions, covenants and terms apply to and are binding upon the assigns, heirs, **executors** and administrators of the Lessor and Lessee.

Sample of Form 69.1 (*Continued*)

45. This **Lease Agreement with Option to Purchase** constitutes the entire agreement between the parties hereto and no changes shall be made herein except by writing, signed by each party and dated. The failure to enforce any right or remedy hereunder shall not be deemed a waiver by either party of such right or remedy, in the absence of a writing as provided for herein.

46. The Lessor and Lessee agree that this **Lease Agreement with Option to Purchase**, when properly executed, is a binding legal obligation.

47. Lessee acknowledges receipt in good order of the following items and agrees to maintain same in good order and repair, normal wear and tear excepted:

Wall-to-wall carpeting in living room, dining room, first-floor hall, second-floor hall, and in all bedrooms.
Draperies in living room, dining room, and all bedrooms.
Model XA-9, America First brand "Tangle-Matic" washer.
Model 445-A-2 Sup-R-Kold brand freezer.

(The above space is provided for such additional terms and conditions as may be agreed to by the parties and must be crossed out to the extent that it is not filled in. DO NOT SIGN IF THERE ARE ANY BLANK SPACES. CROSS OUT OR FILL IN ALL BLANK SPACES BEFORE SIGNING.)

Sample of Form 69.1 (*Continued*)

IN WITNESS WHEREOF, the parties hereto have executed this Agreement.

XXXXXXXXXXXXXXXXXXXXXXXXXXXXXXXXXXXXXXXXXX
Lessor

XXXXXXXXXXXXXXXXXXXXXXXXXXXXXXXXXXXXXX
Witness as to Lessor

XXXXXXXXXXXXXXXXXXXXXXXXXXXXXXXXXXXXXX
Witness as to Lessor

David Cole
Witness as to Lessor

Andrew Cooper
Witness as to Lessor

Monroe Earwood
Lessor

Michael Flynn
Witness as to Lessee

Molly Flynn
Witness as to Lessee

Hans Lumberg
Lessee

Michael Flynn
Witness as to Lessee

Molly Flynn
Witness as to Lessee

Freda Lumberg
Lessee

Dated this _____1st_____ day of _____May_____, 19 __84__.

* *

CERTIFICATE OF NOTARY

STATE OF   Missouri   )
) ss:
COUNTY OF   St. Louis   )

On this ____1st____ day of _____May_____, 19 __84__, before me personally came and appeared ___XXXXXXXXX___ ___XXXXXXXXXXX___, ___Monroe Earwood___, ___Hans Lumburg___ and ___XXXXXXXXXXX___ ___Freda Lumburg___, known, and known to me, to be the individuals described in and who executed the foregoing instrument, and who duly acknowledged to me that they executed same for the purpose therein contained.

IN WITNESS WHEREOF, I hereunto set my hand and official seal.

Jean Palmer
Notary Public

My commission expires: _____April 12, 1987_____

70 Negotiating the Sale

Most people you negotiate with will be honestly interested in buying your house for a fair price. Many will haggle just a bit, probably because they feel they're not the bargainers they'd like to be or because they expect that *you* expect them to haggle.

A decision you'll need to make when people start talking price is whether they're sincere, are just passing the time, or might be trying to steal your house. There are real estate sharks out there, and some of them will rise to your bait. For them, **For Sale by Owner** is like a trail of fresh blood on the water, and they'll come circling around testing for a quick kill. Masters of the depreciatory remark, you can often identify them by their new Cadillacs and old clothes.

There's also the hearty, good ol' boy real estate shark who usually drives a pickup. This species is often looking for a quick fix-up, paint-up house that can be bought cheap and sold high. Your home will probably turn out not to be his type, but since he's taken the trouble to drive by, he'll probably give it a try: "Hi there, I seen your ad in the paper. . . ."

You'll meet many prospective buyers who can afford your house and who won't seriously argue about price. Their only problem will be to gradually narrow down the available houses until they decide which to live in. There's not a lot you can do to sell your house to these kinds of prospects, but there is quite a bit you can do to help them—by learning their needs and then showing them how your house can meet those needs.

It's an old axiom among real estate salespeople that the three most important factors in selling a house are location, location, and location. That may no longer be true, but it's a good device to help you remember to tell your prospect about the advantages of your home's location—on its street, in its neighborhood, and in the community—plus all of the other advantages—schools, public transportation, shopping centers, etc.—that are closely related to location.

Beyond helping such prospects meet their needs, there's not a lot of selling you can do. If, after you've shown your home and explained its advantages and the advantages of location, your prospects still don't feel it's right for them—it probably isn't.

There will also be sincere prospects who will love your house and believe the price is fair, but who feel they just can't quite afford the price you're asking. They'll offer what they believe they can afford, often several thousand dollars less than you're asking, because that's the amount that they decided ahead of time they could afford to pay.

If a prospect says he or she loves your house but can't afford to buy at your price, find out *what* they feel they can't afford. The down payment? The monthly payments? Such a prospect might have an inflated idea of what the down payment has to be, may never have heard of private mortgage insurance and graduated-payment mortgages, and might not believe that it's possible to obtain an FHA or VA loan.

If down payment remains a problem after trying private mortgage insurance, and you have confidence in the buyer's future ability to pay, you might:

1. Accept the buyer's note for part of the down payment.
2. Suggest that the buyer make a loan for part of the down payment at his or her bank and that you cosign the note. You would, of course, receive the proceeds of the loan. There would be a risk that you would have to consider, but it's an option.
3. If the buyer falls slightly short of qualifying for the mortgage amount, say $3,000 short of qualification on a $35,000 mortgage, you might offer to place $3,000 on deposit with the mortgage lender (possibly in a blocked, interest-bearing savings account) to remain on deposit until such time as the lender is satisfied that the buyer is a safe credit risk and is willing to release your money. Your funds would be at risk while on deposit should the buyer default, but it's a way of possibly selling a house that is beginning to seem unsalable.

Once a potential buyer mentions concern about being able to afford the purchase, then the way is open for you to show interest in wanting to help solve the problem. You don't have to begin by asking personal questions. You can, for example, ask:

- Are you familiar with private mortgage insurance?
- Are you familiar with graduated-payment mortgages?
- Are you a veteran (or widow of a veteran)?
- Did you know that an FHA-insured mortgage may be available?

These kinds of questions, without seeming to invade privacy, often naturally lead to a disclosure of how much of a down payment a prospect can afford to make, the amount of monthly payments that can be handled, etc. You can use the tables in Chapter 68 to show your prospect several ways in which he or she can afford to buy your house.

NEGOTIATING PRICE

One thing you've got going for you when selling your house yourself is the fact that you don't have to pay a real estate broker's commission of $4,500 on a $75,000 house.

Another thing you've got going for you when you negotiate selling price is your file of appraisals—conventional, VA, and FHA—which you can give photocopies of to any prospective buyer. With three appraisals of the fair market value of your house in hand, it's not exactly easy for a fair-minded buyer to try to get you to lower your price. There will be people who'll try to do it, but they're hardly fair-minded, and you can, at least during the early stages of your effort, forget about them.

In discussing price you can:

1. Point out that by selling for *only* $72,670, for example, you are splitting the real estate broker's commission with them.
2. Point out that by selling for *only* $70,500 you are saving them the entire $4,500 broker's commission —an additional amount they would presumably have to pay for a similar house across the street if sold through a broker.
3. If the market is strong in your area, you can just go ahead and ask a price equal to the appraised value of your home plus the 6 percent broker's commission that the buyer would have to pay anyway.

There are other areas of give and take in negotiating the sale of your house. If pressed to lower your price, you could say, "OK, but if we do that we'll have to keep the (freezer/washer and dryer/refrigerator/or some other equipment or appliance listed on your fact sheet) as otherwise 'going with the house.'"

On the other hand, if you're close to getting your price, you can offer to "throw in" some appliance or equipment that you had not planned to leave behind, or you could offer to do certain redecorating without charge, such as painting or new carpet installation, before you move out.

WRITTEN OFFERS

"Would you take $67,250?" It may be a sincere offer, it may be a feeler for an even lower offer, or it may just be a face-saving way of getting out the door. Fortunately, there's a way to deal with verbal offers.

"We really hadn't thought about selling for that amount, but if you'll put your offer in writing, we'll give it serious consideration." Your request for a written offer will help separate talkers from serious potential buyers:

"Watsa madder, isn't my word good enough for you?"

"Sure, ol' buddy, but my attorney has advised me to consider only written offers."

"Do you do everything your lawyer tells you?"

"Well, I'm paying for legal advice so I follow it."

A written offer may be in the form of a letter similar to the sample letter at the top of the following column, hand delivered or mailed by the buyer.

Be sure that any letter offer to purchase includes the date, address of your house, price, and buyer's signature.

A printed offer to purchase real estate may be called many things: an **offer** to purchase real estate or property, a **contract** to purchase real estate or property, or an **agreement** to purchase real estate or

July 8, 1984

Mr. and Mrs. Ormond W. Howell
830 York Street
Emeryville, Indiana 47005

Dear Mr. and Mrs. Howell:
    This letter will confirm my offer of $69,500 for your house located at 830 York Street, Emeryville, Indiana. This offer is contingent upon my obtaining financing in the amount of $40,000 for this purchase. This offer is valid for 30 days.
    If this offer is acceptable to you, please sign in the space provided below and return one copy of this letter to me. Upon receipt of your acceptance I will mail you an earnest money check in the amount of four thousand dollars ($4,000.00).

Sincerely,

Agatha Pipes
Agatha Pipes

10 West Brokenrock Ave.
Green Grove, Illinois 61400

Acceptance

I hereby accept your offer.

Ormond W. Howell
Mr. or Mrs. Ormond W. Howell

Date signed: *July 15, 1984*

property. It may even be called a **binder**. The form and format in different parts of the country is often a matter of local custom.

The term "contract" is believed to scare off some prospects, so "contract" is seldom used. Although the form and phrase of an **Offer to Purchase Real Estate** can be just as binding as any document labeled "contract," "offer" is not widely used in the belief that some buyers may not be aware that a legally executed "offer" is binding. The term most commonly used is **Agreement to Purchase Real Estate** (or **Property**).

Being somewhat more formal than offers by letter, printed agreements usually include:

1. Name of seller
2. Name of buyer
3. Address and legal description of property
4. Price
5. Contingent terms
6. Signature of buyer
7. Acceptance signature of seller
8. Signature of witness

Since the use of an ordinary letter constituting an offer to purchase real estate has time and again been held valid in the courts of every state, there is no reason to believe that the agreement provided on page F561 would not also be valid. However, your attorney may have a preference for another format that more closely adheres to local custom. In any event, show Form 70.1 to your lawyer before using it.

There are many forms for an offer to purchase, some of them feasts of legalistic jargon seasoned with myriad demands and exclusions and embellished with Latin italics and Old English type. If anything, their length and verbosity tends to put off prospective buyers who, although realizing they may expect to sign *something*, are still more than a bit uncomfortable about signing *anything*. Try to avoid these kinds of forms.

Much of what needs to be included in an agreement to purchase can be filled in ahead of time: the seller's name, location, legal description of the property, and name of the person (probably your attorney) or escrow agent in whose name the earnest money check is to be made out.

The only item about which you might have a slight problem is the legal description of your property, but that can be copied from your deed of trust or mortgage. If you can't find these documents, you or your attorney can copy the information from county records or obtain it from your mortgage lender.

Terms and conditions desired by the buyer, and the exact amount of earnest money to be paid, may be added when the offer is signed. Sufficient copies of the partially completed **Agreement to Purchase Real Estate** (photocopies of your partially completed master form) should be kept handy for signature when an offer is made.

The primary condition imposed by anyone making an offer is that purchase shall be contingent upon the buyer's ability to obtain financing, a traditional and not unreasonable demand. Some buyers will specify that financing must be available from a particular lender or that a specific type of financing, such as an FHA or VA mortgage, be obtainable.

There are a few possibly confusing terms you should know about. Many buyers will stipulate, in a contract of sale, that the property being purchased shall be "free of all liens and encumbrances," meaning free of all mortgages, unpaid taxes, judgments, etc. Confusion occasionally arises because in some parts of the country the rights of utility companies, etc., to cross property, often called rights of *easement*, are instead termed *liens* or *encumbrances*. So it's possible for your property to be free of all liens and encumbrances while there still may remain upon it (by some definitions) a number of "liens" and "encumbrances." Not to worry, it's a detail for your attorney to work out.

Prior to showing your house, contact savings and loan associations, savings and commercial banks, insurance companies, and other mortgage lenders in your area to learn just how much time a lender usually requires for the period between credit application and approval when granting a home mortgage. Do not allow your buyer, in his or her offer to purchase, to hold you to a time very much beyond that period because from the time you accept an offer until the buyer obtains or is rejected for financing, **your house is off the market**.

Some buyers want to specify in an offer that the house shall contain certain items, such as heating and plumbing fixtures, appliances, etc., or that possession shall be had on a specific date. There's usually no particular objection to adding these provisions, but since the offer is a preliminary document, most lawyers feel these provisions are better left for inclusion in the **Contract for Sale of Real Estate**, usually signed by the buyer and seller *after* the purchaser's loan has been approved.

If either the buyer or seller is married, **both husband and wife** must sign all offers, counteroffers, and acceptances. The signing of these agreements should be viewed by witnesses, so be sure to have a neighbor or two available.

Buyer(s) and seller(s) should each sign three copies of all offers, counteroffers, and acceptances: one copy for seller(s), one for buyer(s), and one to be delivered to the escrow agent (who may be the sellers' attorney) along with the buyers' earnest money check. (The earnest money check should be made out to the escrow agent, with whom arrangements have previously been made.)

When the buyer(s) and seller(s) have signed the agreement and earnest money has been accepted, the buyer(s) should receive a signed copy of the receipt on page F565 (Form 70.3). You'll need an unsigned copy for your records.

Earnest money payments for residential purchases that are to be financed by conventional mortgages are often 5 to 10 percent of the purchase price, $2,500/$5,000 on a $50,000 house. For a purchase that you and the buyer agree must be financed through a VA or FHA loan, the amount may be less, but in no case less than $500 or $1,000 unless some special circumstance exists.

On the first working day after accepting an offer advise your attorney so that he or she may send the buyer an acknowledgment of receipt of earnest money and offer to contact the buyer's attorney, etc. You should also write the buyer a brief note telling him or her that you believe they'll be happy in the house, offering to answer questions, to be of assistance, etc.

COUNTEROFFERS

If you've received an offer that you told the prospect you wanted to think about, and you now want to make a **counteroffer**, use Form 70.2 on page F563, it being only fair that having requested a written offer you respond in kind. In many cases a counteroffer meets the prospect "halfway" between his or her offer and your initial price. Mail a copy of your counteroffer to your attorney when you mail a copy to your prospect.

ACCEPTANCE

Once you formally accept an offer by signing the acceptance provision or by accepting an earnest money payment, your house is off the market. Your house need **not** be taken off the market if you receive a written offer that you have told a prospect you will merely *consider*; as long as you don't accept earnest money, your house is still fair game.

If your prospect signs an agreement to purchase but tells you that he or she doesn't "have the money with me," say that you'll be glad to accept the offer formally, cancel your advertising, and take down your sign just as soon as earnest money has been received.

Sample of Form 70.1/F561

Agreement to Purchase Real Estate

I/We, _____Gerald and Ruth DeForge_____, do hereby agree to purchase from ___Joseph___
___Shusko___ the following described real estate located at:

6255 Lucerne	Millpond	Pennsylvania	18105
Street Address	City/Town	State	Zip

more particularly described as:

Lot. No. Sixty-Two (62), in Block "G," Executive Hills Estates,

Phase Four (4), a subdivision of the town of Millpond, Tracy

County, Pennsylvania, according to the map or plat in Book 187,

Page 145, of the Plat records of Tracy County, Pennsylvania.

for the sum of _____sixty-two thousand dollars_____
($ __62,000.00__) under the following terms and conditions:

This offer shall be contingent upon our obtaining a mortgage in the

amount of $50,000.00, secured by the aforesaid property, payable

over a period of 30 years.

I/We hereby agree to pay to ___Samuel Cohen, escrow agent___ the sum of ___four thousand___
___dollars___ ($ __4,000.00__) as earnest money to be
applied toward the purchase of the above-described property. My/Our deposit shall be fully refunded in the event said
purchase cannot be effected under the terms of this Agreement.

Gerald DeForge
Ruth DeForge

Date signed: ___July 6, 1984___

William Jamison
Witness

Sample of Form 70.1 (*Continued*)

ACCEPTANCE

I/We hereby accept the above offer and agree to all conditions and terms therein stated.

Joseph Shesko

Date of acceptance: _____ July 6, 1984 _____

William Jamison
Witness

71 Closing

Closing the sale of your home is best handled by your attorney. He or she will draw the sales contract and deal with the buyer's attorney and the escrow company if one is used.

Shortly before you begin to advertise and show your house, your attorney will conduct a title search to make sure that you have clear title to your property—except for your mortgage, which will be paid off with the proceeds of the buyer's loan. This precaution can help avoid last-minute hang-ups that could delay or even endanger your sale.

If, as is the custom in many parts of the country, sellers' attorneys in your area act as escrow agent, your lawyer will also:

1. Receive the buyer's earnest money payment.
2. Prepare the new deed for you to sign.
3. Obtain title insurance required to protect the **lender**.
4. See that the buyer signs the new mortgage papers.
5. Pay out money for tax stamps, title insurance, and "points" to the lender.
6. Receive money from the mortgage lender.
7. Collect any outstanding down payment from the buyer.
8. Give you a check for the amount of equity in your house, minus closing costs charged to you.

CONTRACT OF SALE

Before drawing a contract of sale, you and your lawyer should discuss provisions that you want to include in the contract, just as the buyer will discuss with his/her attorney those provisions that he/she wants to be in the contract. When everybody is ready, a meeting can be held to negotiate the contract.

Many provisions are fixed by law or local custom, but you should at least discuss the following items with your attorney ahead of time.

Buyer Move-in Date. Since no one can tell exactly when the sale of your home will legally "close," try to include in the sales contract a provision allowing you to live in the house rent free for ten days after closing. This will give you time to pack last-minute items, contact your mover, call utility companies, etc.

The buyer may agree to let you stay on for ten days but may ask that you pay rent for that period of time—a suggestion that will probably be made by the buyer's attorney. On the other hand, the buyer, once financing has been approved, may ask to move in prior to closing, in which case you may ask for payment of rent.

Payment of Points. In some areas of the country the apportionment of points to buyer and seller in a *conventional* mortgage is a matter of law. In other areas the payment of points, at least some points, is subject to negotiation. Since the 50/50 splitting of points between buyer and seller could save you a few thousand dollars, discuss this with your lawyer.

In some areas and with certain mortgage lenders your lawyer may be able to negotiate with the lender to waive all charges for points if the new borrower's loan is made with the *same* lender that made your mortgage loan.

Appliances and Equipment. Although it will probably not be a matter of contention, the buyer may require that all appliances, fixtures, and equipment listed on your fact sheet as "going with the house" be listed in the contract of sale. Supply your attorney with a list of these items early enough for him or her to send a copy to the buyer's lawyer well ahead of the date set for signing the contract.

Apportionment of Taxes, Insurance, Etc. In many parts of the country residential taxes and insurance are billed and paid annually in advance; thus, if you move out on, say, July 1, you should receive a check from the buyer for one-half of the cost of these items. The same would apply to the cost of any heating oil remaining in your fuel tank.

THE CLOSING MEETING

The closing meeting, or settlement as it is sometimes called, may be held in the office of your attorney, at the office of an escrow or title company, or at the office of the mortgage lender. At that meeting, which your attorney will attend with you, you as the seller can expect to pay for:

- Title search—seller's responsibility in some states
- Title insurance to protect **lender**
- Points charged to seller by lender
- City and county tax stamps
- Any outstanding taxes on your property
- Escrow agent's fee—often split 50/50 with buyer if used
- Final mortgage payment
- Prepayment fee on your mortgage—if a provision of your mortgage
- Plat of survey—if required by lender

The buyer can expect to pay for:

- Remainder of the down payment
- Mortgage processing fee

- Credit report
- Fee for appraisal required by lender—or may accept your appraisal
- Fee for termite inspection if required by lender— or may accept your inspector's inspection report
- State tax stamps
- Title search—buyer's responsibility in some states
- Title insurance to protect **buyer**
- Prorated taxes and insurance
- Heating oil remaining in tank
- Escrow agent's fee—often split 50/50 with seller
- Deed and mortgage recording fees

The expense of closing and settlement costs during 1983 averaged $676 per home sold, but may be much higher than that in some parts of the country.

SETTLEMENT STATEMENT

The laws of most jurisdictions require that at closing, or very shortly thereafter, buyer and seller receive a statement from the escrow agent that lists every settlement expense charged to each. In some areas separate statements are provided to buyer and seller; in others, a combined accounting, listing items and amounts charged to each, is used.

An example of the combined buyer/seller statement of settlement used in compliance with the federal **Real Estate Settlement Procedures Act** (to protect buyers) is provided on pages 351 and 352.

FREE PUBLICATIONS: *There are a number of extremely useful free government booklets that can help you sell your house—and help your purchaser buy it. Order them now by phoning your nearest Housing and Urban Development (HUD) or Veterans Administration office.*

- *Questions & Answers on HUD (FHA) Property Appraisals* HUD-38-H(6)
- *Own—With a Graduated Payment Mortgage* HUD-H-319(2)
- *Lending & Selling with a Graduated Payment Mortgage* HUD-H-318(2)
- *Wise Home Buying* HUD-267-H(8)
- *Settlement Costs* HUD-398-F(2)
- *Buying a Home? Don't Forget Closing Costs* HUD-342-F(7)
- *Home Mortgage Insurance* HUD-43-F(8)
- *Home Buyer's Estimator of Monthly Housing Costs* (*a nifty slide rule for figuring mortgage payments, taxes, insurance, utilities, etc.; fun to use*) HUD-419-(b)-HM
- *Minimum Property Requirements* (*for VA-guaranteed home loans*) VA 26-1
- *A Guide to Veterans Planning to Buy or Build with a GI Loan* VA 26-6
- *Guaranteed and Direct Home Loans for Veterans* VA 26-4
- *Selling Your GI Home?* VA 26-68-1

Plus one Internal Revenue Service Booklet. It won't help you sell your house, but it may save you money on taxes.

- *Tax Information on Selling or Purchasing Your Home* IRS PUB 523

Settlement Statement

Form Approved
OMB NO. 63-R-1501

A.	B. TYPE OF LOAN
U. S. DEPARTMENT OF HOUSING AND URBAN DEVELOPMENT SETTLEMENT STATEMENT	1. ☐ FHA 2. ☐ FmHA 3. ☐ CONV. UNINS. 4. ☐ VA 5. ☐ CONV. INS. 6. File Number: 7. Loan Number: 8. Mortgage Insurance Case Number:

C. NOTE: *This form is furnished to give you a statement of actual settlement costs. Amounts paid to and by the settlement agent are shown. Items marked "(p.o.c.)" were paid outside the closing; they are shown here for informational purposes and are not included in the totals.*

D. NAME OF BORROWER:	E. NAME OF SELLER:	F. NAME OF LENDER:

G. PROPERTY LOCATION:	H. SETTLEMENT AGENT:	I. SETTLEMENT DATE:
	PLACE OF SETTLEMENT:	

J. SUMMARY OF BORROWER'S TRANSACTION		K. SUMMARY OF SELLER'S TRANSACTION	
100. GROSS AMOUNT DUE FROM BORROWER:		**400. GROSS AMOUNT DUE TO SELLER:**	
101. Contract sales price		401. Contract sales price	
102. Personal property		402. Personal property	
103. Settlement charges to borrower *(line 1400)*		403.	
104.		404.	
105.		405.	
Adjustments for items paid by seller in advance		*Adjustments for items paid by seller in advance*	
106. City/town taxes to		406. City/town taxes to	
107. County taxes to		407. County taxes to	
108. Assessments to		408. Assessments to	
109.		409.	
110.		410.	
111.		411.	
112.		412.	
120. GROSS AMOUNT DUE FROM BORROWER		**420. GROSS AMOUNT DUE TO SELLER**	
200. AMOUNTS PAID BY OR IN BEHALF OF BORROWER:		**500. REDUCTIONS IN AMOUNT DUE TO SELLER:**	
201. Deposit or earnest money		501. Excess deposit *(see instructions)*	
202. Principal amount of new loan(s)		502. Settlement charges to seller *(line 1400)*	
203. Existing loan(s) taken subject to		503. Existing loan(s) taken subject to	
204.		504. Payoff of first mortgage loan	
205.		505. Payoff of second mortgage loan	
206.		506.	
207.		507.	
208.		508.	
209.		509.	
Adjustments for items unpaid by seller		*Adjustments for items unpaid by seller*	
210. City/town taxes to		510. City/town taxes to	
211. County taxes to		511. County taxes to	
212. Assessments to		512. Assessments to	
213.		513.	
214.		514.	
215.		515.	
216.		516.	
217.		517.	
218.		518.	
219.		519.	
220. TOTAL PAID BY/FOR BORROWER		**520. TOTAL REDUCTION AMOUNT DUE SELLER**	
300. CASH AT SETTLEMENT FROM/TO BORROWER		**600. CASH AT SETTLEMENT TO/FROM SELLER**	
301. Gross amount due from borrower *(line 120)*		601. Gross amount due to seller *(line 420)*	
302. Less amounts paid by/for borrower *(line 220)*	( )	602. Less reductions in amount due seller *(line 520)*	( )
303. CASH (☐ FROM) (☐ TO) BORROWER		**603. CASH (☐ TO) (☐ FROM) SELLER**	

Settlement Statement (*Continued*)

L. SETTLEMENT CHARGES		PAID FROM BORROWER'S FUNDS AT SETTLEMENT	PAID FROM SELLER'S FUNDS AT SETTLEMENT
700. TOTAL SALES/BROKER'S COMMISSION based on price $ @ % =			
Division of Commission (line 700) as follows:			
701. $ to			
702. $ to			
703. Commission paid at Settlement			
704.			
800. ITEMS PAYABLE IN CONNECTION WITH LOAN			
801. Loan Origination Fee %			
802. Loan Discount %			
803. Appraisal Fee to			
804. Credit Report to			
805. Lender's Inspection Fee			
806. Mortgage Insurance Application Fee to			
807. Assumption Fee			
808.			
809.			
810.			
811.			
900. ITEMS REQUIRED BY LENDER TO BE PAID IN ADVANCE			
901. Interest from to @ $ /day			
902. Mortgage Insurance Premium for months to			
903. Hazard Insurance Premium for years to			
904. years to			
905.			
1000. RESERVES DEPOSITED WITH LENDER			
1001. Hazard insurance months @ $ per month			░░░
1002. Mortgage insurance months @ $ per month			░░░
1003. City property taxes months @ $ per month			░░░
1004. County property taxes months @ $ per month			░░░
1005. Annual assessments months @ $ per month			░░░
1006. months @ $ per month			░░░
1007. months @ $ per month			░░░
1008. months @ $ per month			░░░
1100. TITLE CHARGES			
1101. Settlement or closing fee to			
1102. Abstract or title search to			
1103. Title examination to			
1104. Title insurance binder to			
1105. Document preparation to			
1106. Notary fees to			
1107. Attorney's fees to			
(includes above items numbers;		░░░	░░░
1108. Title insurance to			
(includes above items numbers;		░░░	░░░
1109. Lender's coverage $		░░░	░░░
1110. Owner's coverage $		░░░	░░░
1111.			
1112.			
1113.			
1200. GOVERNMENT RECORDING AND TRANSFER CHARGES			
1201. Recording fees: Deed $; Mortgage $; Releases $			
1202. City/county tax/stamps: Deed $; Mortgage $			
1203. State tax/stamps: Deed $; Mortgage $			
1204.			
1205.			
1300. ADDITIONAL SETTLEMENT CHARGES			
1301. Survey to			
1302. Pest inspection to			
1303.			
1304.			
1305.			
1400. TOTAL SETTLEMENT CHARGES (enter on lines 103, Section J and 502, Section K)			

USING THE FREEDOM OF INFORMATION AND PRIVACY ACTS

72 Your Right to Know

There's some bad news in the next few paragraphs about your right of access to information held by the federal government.

The bad news is that nothing meaningful could be written about citizens' right of access to information held by the federal government without reference to what are widely regarded as efforts of the Reagan Administration to scuttle the **Freedom of Information Act (FOIA)**.

The Freedom of Information Act was passed by Congress in 1966 and went into effect the following year. It has been amended twice, in 1974 and again in 1976. The amendments resulted in a smooth working piece of legislation under which FOIA requests were relatively simple, easy to file, and usually resulted in only modest charges for record searches and document copying.

During their administrations Presidents Nixon and Carter both issued executive orders clarifying the public's right of access and limiting federal officials' authority to arbitrarily classify a wide range of information.

Executive Order 12065, issued by President Carter on June 28, 1978, required that officials be able to cite **identifiable** damage to United States security interests in each instance of information classification. The order also stipulated that specific portions of a document be individually classified, rather than the *entire* document—which might contain much nonclassifiable information of value to the public—being classified.

A thirty-year tide of increasing openness of government was sharply reversed by President Reagan with the issuance of Executive Order 12356 in 1982. The Reagan executive order:

- Vastly expanded the number of federal officials empowered to classify information as top secret, secret, and confidential.
- Removed the requirement that officials be able to cite any identifiable damage at all to U.S. interests that would result from the disclosure of an item of classified information.
- Authorized officials to reclassify information that had been previously declassified and to classify information that had previously never been classified. (Thus the order permits officials to classify information **after** it has been requested under FOIA.)
- Cancelled the long-standing "balancing test" under which officials were required to weigh possible public benefit of the publication of information against any possible need that it remain classified.

Criteria for the classification of information was so broadly defined by the Reagan order that it was described by one Congressional committee as being written to justify classification "of even interstate highway maps." Prior to issuing the executive order, the Reagan administration refused to send witnesses to testify before the House Subcommittee of Government Information and Individual Rights, which was deeply concerned about the consequences of the order.

In a different and almost simultaneous attack on citizens' right to know, administration officials have greatly escalated charges for information searches and document copying.

During 1983 a journalist writing a book about U.S.-Israeli relations submitted an FOIA request for certain information to the Defense Intelligence Agency. His request was not denied; he was advised that his request was estimated to require some 13,000 hours of research, which at $16 per hour would cost the journalist more than $200,000. And he was told that he'd have to pay the entire amount up front, before the agency would even begin to process his request—with no guarantee that the agency would provide any information at all.

In another case, a San Francisco writer submitting a request to the CIA was told that he, too, would have to make an advance payment, this time "only" $61,000, before the agency would begin to search for the requested material—also with no guarantee that any information would actually be provided.

While these amounts are unusual (most FOIA requests require so little research time and document-copying expense that costs for processing the requester's check would exceed the expense of research), the administration has embarked on a program of increasing costs to "price the FOIA out of the market."

Provisions of the Freedom of Information Act specifically provided for waivers of search and document-coping costs for journalists, historians and other academicians, and even for private individuals who could substantiate a need for data but who were too poor to pay. Under the Reagan administration it appears that indirect charges have been added to the direct charges of processing an FOIA request and few waivers of charges are being granted compared to previous administrations.

That's the bad news. However, there may be some good news forthcoming. Soon after issuance of the Reagan executive order, members of both houses of Congress submitted legislation designed to protect the original intent of the FOIA from Presidential abuse and to insure the pubic's continued access to all but properly classified information. Interestingly, legislative leadership in protecting the public's right to know has come from the Republican-dominated Senate.

On March 23, 1983, Senator Durenberger (soon to cosponsor a bill to protect the intent of the Freedom of Information Act) stated that "the recent Presidential directive on safeguarding national security information has aroused proper concern. It carries the risk of severe abuses and could undermine public acceptance of the whole system for protecting national secrets."

Three Senate bills (S. 744, S. 1034, and S. 1335) designed to protect and restore the original intent of FOIA had gained wide bipartisan support among legislators of both houses. They also received strongly favorable testimony from academicians, historians, business and consumer groups, and press associations during committee hearings. Interestingly, two of the three bills were introduced by Republican senators, members of President Reagan's own political party.

The most comprehensive of the three, Senate bill 744, was passed by the Senate on February 27, 1984, and went before the U.S. House of Representatives Government Operations Committee. Although the bill ran into problems in subcommittee and remained bottled up there as the 1984 Congress adjourned, it appears possible at this writing (early 1985) that similar legislation will be reintroduced in 1985—legislation with the intent to restore the FOIA to its original function and purpose.

73 Federally Held Information Only

The **Freedom of Information Act** (Title 5, United States Code, Sec. 552) established for the first time the public's right to all records of the federal agencies not specifically exempt.

The Freedom of Information Act (FOIA) does not require the disclosure of information by any state, county, municipal, or any other governmental unit nor by any nonfederal corporation, institution, partnership, or individual.

(The **Privacy Act**, described separately in Chapter 75, also applies only to federal agencies and contains nothing that would make it illegal, for example, for a nonfederal hospital to display your medical records on its front door, nor would any federal law be broken if your physician were to mail your medical records to a local newspaper that then published them on its front page. The Privacy Act protects you solely from disclosure of personal data by federal agencies—and no one else.)

Although it's true that since 1977 the FOIA has been a smoothly working piece of legislation, its early years were marked by incidents of obstruction by a few government agencies, most notably the Internal Revenue Service and the Federal Bureau of Investigation, to subvert the purpose of the FOIA by charging exorbitant fees, by declaring that records were "lost" or "unavailable," and by engaging in long delays —apparently perpetual if they thought they could get away with it. (Today the FBI is years behind in compliance with individuals' FOIA and Privacy Act requests for data from their personal files.)

It was only through the efforts of concerned members of Congress and citizens' groups such as the Center for National Security Studies and the American Civil Liberties Union that the Freedom of Information Act survived as a practical, workable piece of legislation.

It was essentially because of certain federal agencies' obstruction of the intent of the FOIA that the 1974 amendments, which comprise about 85 percent of the act as it stands today, were passed by Congress.

In requiring federal agencies to disclose all records in their possession not specifically exempt, the FOIA defines "disclose" as meaning to **publish**, to **make available for inspection**, or to **release pursuant to request**, and it is this last definition upon which much FOIA disclosure turns.

But even with the 1974 amendment and a one-paragraph 1977 amendment on the books, some government agencies still attempt to withhold information if it's likely to prove embarrassing—for example:

Only after suit had been filed—*Capitol Hill News Service v. Department of Justice*, Civ. No. 75-2184, Order of March 26, 1976—did the Department of Justice comply with a previously refused FOIA request for information related to a plan to place approximately 15,000 American citizens in detention camps in the event of national emergency.

Only after suit had been filed—*Schaeffer v. Kissinger*, 505 F.2d 398 (D.C. Cir. 75-0675)—did the Department of State comply with a previously refused FOIA request for hundreds of International Red Cross reports on oppressive and unhealthful conditions in South Vietnamese prisoner of war camps.

Only after suit had been filed—*Brandon v. Internal Revenue Service*, 569 F.2d 683 (D.C. Cir. 1977)—did the IRS comply with a previously refused FOIA request for data disclosing improper IRS investigation of politically dissident groups.

Only after suit had been filed—*St. Louis Post-Dispatch v. Federal Bureau of Investigation* (D.C. Cir. 75-1025)—did the FBI comply with a previously refused FOIA request for surveillance and investigative reports compiled over a ten-year period on the Washington bureau of the newspaper and its chief, Richard Dudman.

Only after suit had been filed—*Union of Concerned Scientists v. Nuclear Regulatory Commission*, 76-370, D.C. Order, March 21, 1979—did the NRC comply with a previously refused FOIA request for certain technical reports on (the shortcomings of) nuclear reactor safety.

Generally though, except for the FBI, which is earning itself legions of nonfriends by its foot-dragging response to individuals' requests for information from their personal files, most government agencies are quick to provide information requested under FOIA.

GENERAL USES OF FOIA

The Freedom of Information Act is being used with relative ease today:

- By individuals and consumer organizations to help determine the safety of drugs, foods and food additives, cosmetic preparations, tires, automobiles, appliances, and other manufactured goods such as home insulation, cleaning preparations, insecticides, paint, etc.

- By individuals and consumer organizations to help determine the nutritional value and safety of food products, particularly baby foods, soft drinks sold in plastic containers, etc.
- By businesses and trade organizations to determine the basis for allegations of violations of federal regulations and to determine the basis for federal agency rule making.
- By businesses as an element of their intelligence effort directed toward competitors and adversaries, such as consumer groups, communities, and individuals with whom they may be engaged in federal litigation or other federal adversary proceedings.
- By scholars, reporters, authors, and others engaged in recording and reporting the history of the United States, the rights of citizens, and the operations of government.
- By attorneys and others to determine possible federal agency prejudice in the application and enforcement of laws and government regulations, to obtain discovery, to prove injury, to establish grounds for litigation, or to file FOIA or Privacy Act appeals or initial requests on behalf of clients.

CORPORATE USE OF FOIA

As a matter of interest, by far the greatest percentage of FOIA requests (estimated by some to be as high as 85 percent) appears to be generated by major corporations. Federal agencies most frequently targeted by corporations are the Federal Trade Commission (FTC), the Food and Drug Administration (FDA), and the Environmental Protection Agency (EPA).

A review of corporate FOIA requests indicates a strong interest in direct competitors, in possibly competing products or services, and in the problems of competitors. Corporations also appear to be extremely interested in anyone who makes an FOIA request for information about *them*.

But the game is getting harder to play because corporations are increasingly desirous of wanting to lay their cards on the table face down. Growing numbers of FOIA requesters are using law firms and other information-gathering services to "front" their requests for them, thus concealing the fact of their interest in a particular company, organization, or product.

So great has become corporate interest in who makes which FOIA request about what, that easily the most popular feature in Washington, D.C.'s *Legal Times of Washington* is its weekly listing of the names of law firms that during the previous seven days have

requested information under the Freedom of Information Act.

One D.C. area information-gathering firm, foi services, inc. (of which more later) earns a solid portion of its revenue through publication of its *FOI Log,* a weekly digest of FOIA requests filed with selected government agencies.

The *FOI Log* lists the name and address of each requester, contains a brief description of the information requested, and gives the date received and the receiving agency's control number. Some corporations and law firms subscribe to foi services' telephone-alert service to be assured of prompt notification of any FOIA request for information related to their firm or the firm of any client.

PERSONAL USES OF FOIA

You may want to submit FOIA requests to the FBI, CIA, military services, former civil service employers, and other federal agencies to obtain information about yourself contained in files that they maintain.

We mention the possibility of your taking this action, not out of idle curiosity, but because a significant number of those who have obtained information from personal files have found them to contain inaccurate, biased, untruthful, and potentially damaging data—damaging, for example, if one were to apply or be considered for employment requiring a security clearance.

Although there is no provision under FOIA for correction of any personal file on you maintained by a federal agency, such a provision *does* exist under the Privacy Act, Sec. 552a (b) (3) (see page 368).

Obtaining your personal file from a federal agency is facilitated by provisions of both the Freedom of Information Act and the Privacy Act. Forms and other information needed for filing an FOIA/Privacy Act request for your personal records are provided in Chapters 77 and 78.

As a private individual, you can, of course, initiate an FOIA or Privacy Act request with any government agency for any "records." These records could be provided to any corporation, consumer organization, attorney, or anyone else acting on your behalf and with your authorization.

Filing an FOIA or Privacy Act request, until the 1983 Reagan administration executive order, has been simple and almost always inexpensive, with search and document-copying fees often waived for academic, news media, or other requests that were determined to be primarily in the public interest.

A list of selected government agency addresses and phone numbers beginning on page 392 should provide much of what you need to file an FOIA request with many government agencies.

74 The Freedom of Information Act

There are several ways we could present the **Freedom of Information Act (FOIA)**. We could march through this section of the book, referring to various portions of the Act as might appear necessary (that seemed to work pretty well with other statutes in earlier sections of the book). Or we might include the entire FOIA somewhere toward the end of this section without comment—just daring you to figure it out.

But the entire Act is so short, probably less than 3,500 words, and is so intricately bound, one section with the other and with the function of yet another law, the Privacy Act, that probably the best way to make FOIA understood in any useful manner will be for us to go through the entire Act, adding what we hope will be useful comments along the way.

You don't have to know very much about the Freedom of Information Act or Privacy Act if all you want to do is submit a request to the FBI or CIA for information from your personal file, but if you want to use FOIA in any long-term way for business purposes, for academic research, for reporting or writing, or in a legal practice, then you need to know more than the bare mechanics of filing a request.

We won't comment on *every* part of the FOIA but will concentrate on those that are key portions of the Act, that have been most used in refusing FOIA requests, and that have proven most useful in prevailing in the face of opposition to disclosure.

We have also, in Chapter 78, quoted from President Carter's Executive Order 12065, **National Security Information** (page 383). Two other related documents, the Attorney General's letter to heads of all federal agencies regarding FOIA litigation (page 365) and the Deputy Attorney General's memorandum regarding FOIA and Privacy Act appeals (page 367), are included in this chapter.

The Privacy Act is closely related to, and in some areas overlaps, the Freedom of Information Act; it is the subject of the following chapter.

We don't expect that you'll have any serious problems using FOIA, but a good knowledge of the Act can help you frame a request that zeros in on the exact information you want, avoiding the delays and needless expense of too broad a search by a government agency and by making use of precedents already set by previous litigation, presidential directives, and agency policy directives.

A good working knowledge of the Act can also save you the time and expense of filing and possibly appealing an FOIA request to which an agency's right of refusal has already been established.

Any use of *italics*, **bold face**, or UPPER CASE type for emphasis is ours.

FREEDOM OF INFORMATION ACT
Title 5, USC, Sec. 552

5 USC, Sec. 552 Public information; agency rules, opinions, orders, records, and proceedings.

Comment: RECORDS. Within the context of FOIA, "records" have been defined as all those documents that are in the possession of or subject to the substantial control and/or use of a federal agency. Documents prepared under government contract and uncirculated notes prepared by a federal employee for personal use are NOT "records."

(a) Each [federal] agency shall make available to the public information as follows:

(1) Each agency shall separately state and currently publish in the *Federal Register* for the guidance of the public—

(A) descriptions of its central and field organization and the established places at which, the employees (and in the case of a uniformed service, the members) from whom, and the methods whereby, the public may obtain information, make submittals or requests, or obtain decisions;

(B) statements of the general course and method by which its functions are channeled and determined; including the nature and requirements of all formal and informal procedures available;

(C) rules of procedure, descriptions of forms available or the places at which forms may be obtained, and instructions as to the scope and contents of all papers, reports, or examinations;

(D) substantive rules of general applicability adopted as authorized by law, and statements of general policy or interpretations of general applicability formulated and adopted by the agency; and

(E) each amendment, revision, or repeal of the foregoing.

Except to the extent that a person has actual and timely notice of the terms thereof, a person may not in any manner be required to resort to, or be adversely be affected by, a matter required to be published in the *Federal Register* and not so published. For the purpose of this paragraph, matter reasonably available to the class of persons affected thereby is deemed published in the *Federal Register* when incorporated by reference therein with the approval of the Director of the *Federal Register*.

(2) Each agency, in accordance with published rules, shall make available for public inspection and copying—

    (A) final opinions, including concurring and dissenting opinions, as well as orders, made in the ajudication of cases;

    (B) those statements of policy and interpretations which have been adopted by the agency and are not published in the *Federal Register*; and

    (C) administrative staff manuals and instructions to staff that affect each member of the public;

Comment: AGENCY. A federal "agency" under FOIA is deemed to be any military or executive department, including the Executive Office of the President, any government corporation or federally controlled corporation, or any independent regulatory agency. AMTRAK, for example, is a "federal agency," but the Corporation for Public Broadcasting, though federally funded, is neither controlled nor chartered by the government and thus is not a "federal agency" within the context of FOIA.

unless the materials are promptly published and copies offered for sale. To the extent required to prevent a clearly unwarranted invasion of **personal** privacy, an agency may delete identifying details when it makes available or publishes an opinion, statement of policy, interpretation, or staff manual or instruction. However, in each case the justification for the deletion shall be explained fully in writing. Each agency shall also maintain and make available for public inspection and copying current indexes providing identifying information for the public as to any matter issued, adopted, or promulgated after July 4, 1967, and required by this paragraph to be made available or published. Each agency shall promptly publish, quarterly or more frequently, and distribute (by sale or otherwise) copies of each index or supplements thereto unless it determines by other published in the *Federal Register* that the publication would be unnecessary and impractical, in which case the agency shall nonetheless **provide copies of such index on request at a cost not to exceed the direct cost of duplication.** A final order, opinion, statement of policy, interpretation, or staff manual or instruction that affects a member of the public may be relied on, used, or cited as precedent by an agency against a party other than agency only if—

    (i) it has been indexed and either made available or published as provided by this paragraph; or

    (ii) the party has actual and timely notice of the terms thereof.

Comment: *FEDERAL REGISTER*. The *Federal Register* is usually available in the main library of major city public libraries, in law libraries located in county courthouses and federal district courts, in law school libraries, and in the libraries of large colleges and universities.

Perhaps the most useful compilation of the above material can be found in *Protecting Your Right to Privacy: Digest of Systems of Records,** which contains a listing of the systems of records maintained by each federal agency as published in the *Federal Register.* It's a good place to start and is particularly useful to business managers and consumer organizations who need to know which government agency maintains what kind of records.

(3) Except with respect to the records made available under paragraphs (1) and (2) of this subsection, each agency, upon any request for records which (A) *reasonably describes* such records and (B) is made in accordance with published rules stating the time, place, fees (if any), and procedures to be followed, shall make the records promptly available to any person.

Comment: REASONABLY DESCRIBE. Within the context of FOIA, a reasonable description is one that would "enable a professional employee of the agency who was familiar with the subject area of the request to locate the record with a reasonable amount of effort." [House of Representatives report No. 93-876]

(4) (A) In order to carry out the provisions of this section, each agency shall promulgate regulations, pursuant to notice and receipt of public comment, specifying a uniform schedule of fees applicable to all constituent units of such agency. Such fees shall be limited to *reasonable standard charges for documents search and duplication and provide for recovery of only the direct costs of such search and duplication.* Documents shall be furnished without charge or at a reduced charge where the agency determines that waiver or reduction of the fee is in the public interest because furnishing the information can be considered as primarily benefiting the general public.

Comment: FEES. Any fees charged must be limited to reasonable, direct costs for searches and copying (Senate Report 93-1200) and must be published by each federal agency. Charges may not be made for time spent by an agency reviewing material to determine or excise exempt portions. Payment of fees and advance estimates of fee charges should be made.

Fees may be waived or reduced when disclosure of information is deemed to be primarily in the public interest; however, it's up to the requester to convince an agency that such is the case.

Generally, federal agencies have been quite liberal in recognizing disclosure of information in response to FOIA requests by academic researchers as being in the public interest. Fees are also often waived or reduced for consumer groups and occasionally for reporters and others writing for publication.

*From Superintendent of Documents, Government Printing Office, Washington, D.C. 20402, or from GPO bookstores in major cities. Price: $5.00. Enclose a postal money order to save time waiting for your check to clear. Still, expect mail orders to take forever and a day. (See page 375 for GPO bookstore address and phone number listing.)

In practice, many agencies waive all fees that are computed to be less than $25 to $30, since bookkeeping costs exceed the amount collected. Also, the fact that fees are paid to the U.S. Treasury and not to the agency responding to the request means that an agency loses nothing by its generosity.

(B) On complaint, the district court of the United States in the district in which the complainant resides, or has his [or her] principal place of business, or in which the agency's records are situated, or in the District of Columbia, has jurisdiction to enjoin the agency from withholding agency records and to order production of any agency records improperly withheld from the complainant. In such a case the court shall determine the matter *de novo* [as from the beginning], and may examine the contents of such agency records *in camera* [within the judge's chambers] to determine whether such records or any part thereof shall be withheld under any of the exemptions set forth in subsection (b) of this section, and *the burden is on the agency to sustain its actions.*

Comment: VENUE. A complaint (lawsuit) to obtain information improperly withheld by a government agency may be filed in the district court where the requester resides or has his or her principal place of business, in the **division** of the federal district where the requester resides or has his or her principal place of business, or in the District of Columbia or the appropriate **division** of the federal court district in which the records are located.

Since most federal court districts are made up of several divisions, you can probably file more easily in the division in which you reside than by traveling to a district court.

(C) Notwithstanding any other provision of law, the defendant shall serve an answer [to the complaint] or otherwise plead to any complaint made under this subsection within *thirty days* after service upon the defendant of the pleading in which such complaint is made, unless the court otherwise directs for good cause *shown* [by the defendant].

(D) Except as to cases the court considers of greater importance, proceedings before the district court, as authorized by this subsection, and appeals therefrom, [shall] *take precedence* on the docket over all cases and shall be assigned for hearing and trial or for argument *at the earliest practicable date and expedited in every way.*

(E) The court may assess against the United States reasonable attorney fees and other litigation costs reasonably incurred in any case under this section *in which the complainant has substantially prevailed.*

Comment: ATTORNEY FEES. Voluntary release of records **after** a suit has been filed, but **before** judgment has been handed down, does NOT preclude award of attorney fees in cases where the plaintiff has *substantially* prevailed. It is the intent of Congress to remove the barrier of attorney fee costs that often

has "enabled the government to escape compliance with the law." [*Cuneo v. Rumsfeld*, 553 F.2d 1360, 1363-64 (D.C. Cir. 1977)]

(F) Whenever the court orders the production of any agency records improperly withheld from the complainant and assesses against the United States reasonable attorney fees and other litigation costs, and the court additionally issues a written finding that the circumstances surrounding the withholding raise questions whether agency personnel acted arbitrarily or capriciously with respect to the withholding, the Civil Service Commission shall promptly initiate a proceeding to determine whether disciplinary action is warranted against the officer or employee who was primarily responsible for the withholding. The Commission, after investigation and consideration of the evidence submitted, shall submit its findings and recommendations to the administrative authority of the agency concerned and shall send copies of the findings and recommendations to the officer or employee or his representative. The administrative authority shall take the corrective action that the Commission recommends.

(G) In the event of noncompliance with the order of the court, the district court may punish for contempt the responsible employee, and in the case of a uniformed service, the responsible member.

(5) Each agency having more than one member shall maintain and make available for public inspection a record of the final votes of each member in every agency proceeding.

(6) (A) Each agency, upon any request for records made under paragraph (1), (2), or (3) of this subsection, shall—

(i) determine *within ten days* (excepting Saturdays, Sundays, and legal public holidays) after the receipt of any such request whether to comply with such request and *shall immediately notify* the person making such request of such determination and the reasons therefore, and the right of such person to appeal to the head of the agency any adverse determination; and

(ii) make a determination with respect to any appeal within *twenty days* (excepting Saturdays, Sundays, and legal public holidays) after the receipt of such appeal. If on appeal the denial of the request for records is in the whole or in part upheld, the agency shall notify the person making such request of the provisions for judicial review of that determination under paragraph (4) of this subsection.

Comment: TIME LIMITS. Most agencies respond to, but do not necessarily furnish, requested information within ten days of receipt of an FOIA request. Often an agency's first response to a request will be to provide an estimate of search and duplication costs, to ask for authorization to spend a specific amount, and to ask for an advance, partial payment of estimated fees. A large number of FOIA requests in response to a major legislative, trade, or political development or judicial decision can sometimes create a temporary bottleneck.

The filing of an administrative appeal pursuant to (ii) above (for failure to provide information within a reasonable time or show cause why such was not provided) usually acts as a pretty good squeaky wheel for prompting agencies to disclose information previously withheld. Senior officers who consider appeals seem more motivated than their juniors by practical policy considerations and a desire to avoid attention-getting and potentially costly lawsuits. Federal agencies' desire to avoid litigation being a fairly strong one, an administrative appeal filed by an attorney makes for a very squeaky wheel indeed. (See our administrative appeal form—Form 78.2, page F583).

(B) In unusual circumstances as specified in this subparagraph, the time limits prescribed in either clause (i) or clause (ii) or subparagraph (A) may be extended by *written notice to the person making such request setting forth the reasons for such extension and the date on which a determination is expected to be dispatched. No such notice shall specify a date that would result in an extension for more than ten working days.* As used in this subparagraph, "unusual circumstances" means, but only to the extent reasonably necessary to the proper processing of the particular request—

(i) the need to search for and collect the requested records from field facilities or other establishments that are separate from the office processing the request;

(ii) the need to search for, collect, and appropriately examine a voluminous amount of separate and distinct records which are demanded in a single request; or

(iii) the need for consultation, which shall be conducted with all practicable speed, with another agency having a substantial interest in the determination of the request or among two or more components of the agency having substantial subject-matter interest therein.

Comment: The FBI and CIA routinely fail to meet time limits set for initial requests and appeals and can often be moved to provide personal file information only by the filing of a lawsuit in federal court. Otherwise, plan to be subjected to several years of delays—reportedly designed to reduce the amount of personal file disclosure while those agencies lobby for amendments to FOIA and the Privacy Act that would make them virtually exempt from their provisions.

(C) Any person making a request to any agency for records under paragraph (1), (2), or (3) of this subsection shall be deemed to have exhausted his [or her] administrative remedies with respect to such request *if the agency fails to comply with the applicable time limit provisions of this paragraph.* If the Government can *show* exceptional circumstances exist and that the agency is exercising due diligence in responding to the request, the court may retain jurisdiction and allow the agency additional time to complete its review of the records. Upon any determination by an agency to comply with a request for records, the records shall be made promptly available to such person making such request. Any notification of denial of any requests for records under this subsection shall set forth the names and titles of positions of each person responsible for the denial of such request.

(b) This section does not apply to matters that are—

(1) (A) specifically authorized under criteria established by an Executive order to be kept secret in the interest of national defense or foreign policy *and* (B) are in fact *properly* classified pursuant to such Executive order;

(2) related solely to the internal personnel rules and practices of an agency:

(3) specifically exempted from disclosure by statute (other than section 552b of this title), provided that such statute (A) requires that matters be withheld from the public in such a manner as to leave no discretion on the issue, or (B) establishes particular criteria for withholding or refers to particular types of matters to be withheld;

(4) trade secrets and commercial or financial information obtained from a person and [which is] privileged or confidential;

(5) inter-agency or intra-agency memorandums or letters which would not be available by law to a party other than an agency in litigation with the agency;

(6) personnel and medical files and similar files the disclosure of which would constitute a clearly unwarranted invasion of personal privacy;

(7) investigatory records compiled for law enforcement purposes, but ONLY to the extent that the production of such records would (A) interfere with enforcement proceedings, (B) deprive a person of a right to a fair trial or an impartial adjudication, (C) constitute an unwarranted invasion of personal privacy, (D) disclose the identity of a confidential source and, in the case of a record compiled by a criminal law enforcement authority *in the course of a criminal investigation*, or by an agency conducting a lawful national security intelligence investigation, confidential information furnished only by the confidential source, (E) disclose investigative techniques and procedures, or (F) endanger the life or physical safety of law enforcement personnel;

Comment: EXEMPTIONS. Though now much more narrowly defined by 1974 amendments, the original law gave federal agencies an almost impenetrable barrier (classification of documents) through which no information could be obtained that an agency chose not to release. In a 1973 case (*EPA* v. *Mink*) the Supreme Court held that under FOIA there was "no means to question any executive [agency] decision to stamp any document 'secret,' however cynical, myopic, or even corrupt that decision might have been." The Court also held that in FOIA litigation, courts could not examine documents *in camera* to determine if certain nonclassified portions could be released.

The 1974 amendments gave federal courts the authority to determine *de novo* if information was justifiably classified and whether certain segregable portions of classified documents must be released.

On June 28, 1978, President Carter broadened the public's access to information under FOIA with the issuance of Executive Order 12065, **National Security Information**, which restricted the unwarranted use of document classification to limit disclosure.

E.O. 12065 established categories of classified information, established minimum standards for classification and the duration of classification, and stated that a document may not be classified "to conceal violations of law, inefficiency or administrative error, or to prevent embarrassment to a person, organization or agency, or to restrain competition [Sec. 1-601] or . . . to limit dissemination of information that is not classifiable under the provisions of this order to prevent or delay public release of such information." [Sec. 1-605]

The order also ended the practice of classifying a document only *after* an FOIA request had been received by stating:

"No document originated on or after the effective date of this Order may be classified after an agency has received a request for the document under the Freedom of Information Act or the Mandatory Review provisions of this Order (Section 3-5), unless such classification is consistent with this Order and is authorized by the agency head or deputy agency head. Documents originated before the effective date of this Order and subject to such request may not be classified unless such classification is consistent with this Order and is authorized by the senior official designated to oversee the agency information security program, or by an official with Top Secret classification authority. Classification authority under this provision shall be exercised personally, on a document-by-document basis." [Sec. 1-606]

"Classification may not be restored to documents already declassified and released to the public under this Order or prior Orders." [Sec. 1-607]

(8) contained in or related to examination, operating, or condition reports prepared by, on behalf of, or for the use of an agency responsible for the regulation or supervision of financial institutions; or

(9) geological and geophysical information and data, including maps, [particularly] concerning [oil] wells.

Any reasonably segregable portion of a record shall be provided to any person requesting such record after deletion of the portions which are exempt under this subsection.

(c) This section does not authorize withholding of information or limit the availability of records to the public, except as specifically stated in this section. This section is not authority to withhold information from Congress [or any member of Congress].

Comment: An interesting loophole if you really have a valid case and can convince a member of Congress to request data for you.

(d) On or before March 1 of each calendar year, each agency shall submit a report covering the preceding calendar year to the Speaker of the House of Representatives and President of the Senate for referral to the appropriate committee of the Congress. The report shall include—

(1) the number of determinations made by such agency not to comply with requests for records made to such agency under subsection (a) and the reasons for each such determination;

(2) the number of appeals made by persons under subsection (a)(6), the result of such appeals, and the reason for the action upon each appeal that results in a denial of information;

(3) the names and titles or positions of each person responsible for the denial of records requested under this section, and the number of instances of participation for each;

(4) the results of each proceeding conducted pursuant to subsection (a)(4)(F), including a report of the disciplinary action taken against the officer or employee who was responsible for improperly withholding records or an explanation of why disciplinary action was not taken;

(5) a copy of every rule made by such agency regarding this section;

(6) a copy of the fee schedule and the total amount of fees collected by the agency for making records available under this section; and

(7) such other information as indicates efforts to administer fully this section.

The Attorney General shall submit an annual report on or before March 1 of each calendar year which shall include for the prior calendar year a listing of the number of cases arising under this section, the exemption involved in each case, the disposition of such case, and the cost, fees, and penalties assessed under subsection (a)(4)(E), (F), and (G). Such report shall also include a description of the efforts undertaken by the Department of Justice to encourage agency compliance with this section.

Comment: **FOIA LITIGATION.** On May 5, 1977, Attorney General Griffin Bell sent a letter to the heads of all federal agencies in which he called their attention to the existence of some 600 FOIA lawsuits then pending before federal courts and pointed out that henceforth the Department of Justice would not undertake to defend agencies in FOIA lawsuits unless it was in the public interest to do so, even if there were some arguable legal basis for the withholding of information. The attorney general's letter (pages 365–366), dated a full year prior to E.O. 12065, has done much to encourage agency compliance with FOIA by making administrators aware that justifiable FOIA lawsuits to obtain disclosure of information will not be defended by the Justice Department—the department that would ordinarily defend such suits. (It is unfortunate that similar documents are not available from the current administration.)

(e) For purposes of this section, the term "agency" as defined in section 551(1) of this title includes any executive department, military department, Government corporation, Government controlled corporation, or other establishment in the executive branch of the Government (including the Executive Office of the President), or any independent regulatory agency.

Although the heads of federal agencies, and agency employees assigned to offices that receive and process FOIA requests, will be familiar with the letter starting on the following page, the important thing is that you be familiar with it so that you'll be aware of just how effective an expression of intent to file an FOIA lawsuit—or the actual filing of a lawsuit—can sometimes be. Some agencies have a reputation of frequently denying administrative appeals but then disclosing requested information soon after an FOIA suit has been filed.

The memorandum of Deputy Attorney General Peter Flaherty on page 367 may also be of interest.

ATTORNEYS NOTE: *A 396-page handbook,* Litigation Under the Federal Freedom of Information Act and Privacy Act, *published by the Center for National Security Studies contains almost everything you need to know to become an instant FOIA/Privacy Act litigator.*

It's a cornucopia of analysis of every section of the FOIA and the Privacy Act, plus cites, trial strategy, judicial comment, excerpts from related statutes and sample FOIA requests, administrative appeals, pleadings, motions, and orders as well as useful names and addresses and a complete up-to-date FOIA case list (up to date of publication).

I can almost see it advertised on TV now—

(Conservatively dressed, distinguished-looking talent seated on edge of large, leather-top desk in book-lined, well-appointed office. Holds up product to show cover, flips through pages to display thickness of book—)

"Lawyers! Now offered for the first time on TV—the big, new, 223-page, 1984 edition of Litigation Under the Federal Freedom of Information Act and Privacy Act, *invaluable information and expert advice you* can't *afford to be without!*

"FOIA information acquisition can be a rewarding addition to your corporate practice—make BIG money in FOIA appeals and litigation! Join the ranks of Covington and Burling, Arnold and Porter, all in the privacy of your own office!

"Here's how to order: Send $30.00 in check or money order to Center for National Security Studies, 122 Maryland Avenue, N.E., Washington, D.C. 20002. Just ask for FOIA handbook, *and we'll rush this big, 223-page, money-making volume to you.*

"NOW is the time to get in on this fascinating, fast-growing, financially rewarding form of legal practice. Order today."

(Cut to advertiser name and address, and flashing price: $30.00—$30.00—$30.00.)

Attorney General Bell's Letter

OFFICE OF THE ATTORNEY GENERAL
WASHINGTON, D.C.   20530

May 5, 1977

LETTER TO HEADS OF ALL FEDERAL DEPARTMENTS AND AGENCIES

Re: Freedom of Information Act

I am writing in a matter of great mutual concern to seek your cooperation.

Freedom of Information Act litigation has increased in recent years to the point where there are now over 600 cases pending in federal courts. The actual cases represent only the "tip of the iceberg" and reflect a much larger volume of administrative disputes over access to documents. I am convinced that we should jointly seek to reduce these disputes through concerted action to impress upon all levels of government the requirements, and the spirit, of the Freedom of Information Act. The government should not withhold documents unless it is important to the public interest to do so, even if there is some arguable legal basis for withholding. In order to implement this view, the Justice Department will defend Freedom of Information Act suits only when disclosure is demonstrably harmful, even if the documents technically fall within the exemptions of the Act. Let me assure you that we will certainly counsel and consult with your personnel in making the decision whether to defend. To perform our job adequately, however, we need full access to documents that you desire to withhold, as well as the earliest possible response to our information requests. In the past, we have often filed answers in court without having an adequate exchange with the agencies over the reasons and necessity for the withholding. I hope that this will not occur in the future.

In addition to setting these guidelines, I have requested Barbara Allen Babcock, Assistant Attorney General for the Civil Division, to conduct a review of all pending Freedom of Information Act litigation being handled by the Division. One result of that review may be to determine that litigation against your agency should no longer be continued and that information previously withheld should be released. In that event, I request that you ensure that your personnel work cooperatively with the Civil Division to bring the litigation to an end.

Please refer to 28 CFR 50.9 and accompanying March 9, 1976 memorandum from the Deputy Attorney General. These documents remain in effect, but the following new and additional elements are hereby prescribed:

Attorney General Bell's Letter (*Continued*)

In determining whether a suit against an agency under the Act challenging its denial of access to requested records merits defense, consideration shall be given to four criteria:

(a) Whether the agency's denial seems to have a substantial legal basis,

(b) Whether defense of the agency's denial involves an acceptable risk of adverse impact on other agencies,

(c) Whether there is a sufficient prospect of actual harm to legitimate public or private interests if access to the requested records were to be granted to justify the defense of the suit, and

(d) Whether there is sufficient information about the controversy to support a reasonable judgment that the agency's denial merits defense under the three preceding criteria.

The criteria set forth above shall be considered both by the Freedom of Information Committee and by the litigating divisions. The Committee shall, so far as practical, employ such criteria in its consultations with agencies prior to litigation and in its review of compliance thereafter. The litigating divisions shall promptly and independently consider these factors as to each suit filed.

Together I hope that we can enhance the spirit, appearance and reality of open government.

Yours sincerely,

Griffin B. Bell

Griffin B. Bell
Attorney General

Deputy Attorney General Flaherty's Memo

384   UNITED STATES GOVERNMENT

Memorandum

TO   :   Quin Shea
Director   DATE: June 2, 1977
Office of Information and Privacy Appeals

FROM   :   Peter F. Flaherty   *Pete Flaherty*
Deputy Attorney General

SUBJECT: FOIA Appeals

        The protections of 5 U.S.C. 552(b)(7)(A) -- intended
to preclude interference with law enforcement activities
-- should not be used to conceal unlawful activities,
regardless of the intent with which those activities were
conducted. Similarly, just as this Department will not
obtain information directly by means of unlawful activities,
we will not shield with 5 U.S.C. 552(b)(7)(D) information
which was initially obtained through the use of such means
by other persons or law enforcement organizations. Neither
the use nor methodology of unlawful investigative techniques
or procedures is to be protected by reliance on 5 U.S.C.
552(b)(7)(E).

75 The Privacy Act

The **Privacy Act of 1974** (Title 5, USC, Sec. 552a) is relevant to FOIA information requests because it overlaps the Freedom of Information Act in some areas and augments it in others. The *primary* intent of Congress regarding the Act is expressed in the following sections:

5 USC, Sec. 552a (a)   The Congress finds that—

(1) the privacy of an individual is directly affected by the collection, maintenance, use and dissemination of personal information by Federal agencies;

(2) the increasing use of computers and sophisticated information technology, while essential to the efficient operations of the Government, has greatly magnified the harm to individual privacy that can occur from any collection, maintenance, use, or dissemination of personal information;

(3) the opportunities for an individual to secure employment, insurance, and credit, and his [or her] right to due process, and other legal protections are endangered by the misuse of certain information systems;

(4) the right to privacy is a personal and fundamental right protected by the Constitution of the United States; and

(5) in order to protect the privacy of individuals identified in information systems maintained by Federal agencies, it is necessary and proper for the Congress to regulate the collection, maintenance, use, and dissemination of [personal] information by such agencies.

(b) The purpose of this Act is to provide certain safeguards for an individual against an invasion of personal privacy by requiring Federal agencies, except as otherwise provided by law, to—

(1) permit an individual to determine what records pertaining to him [or her] are collected, maintained, used, or disseminated by such agencies;

(2) permit an individual to prevent records pertaining to him [or her] obtained by such agencies for a particular purpose from being used or made available for another purpose without his [or her] consent;

(3) permit an individual to gain access to information pertaining to him [or her] in Federal agency records, to have a copy made of all or any portion thereof and to correct or amend such records;

(4) collect, maintain, use or disseminate any record of identifiable personal information in a manner that assures that such action is for a necessary and lawful purpose, that the information is current and accurate for its intended use, and that adequate safeguards are provided to prevent misuse of such information;

(5) permit exemptions from the requirements with respect to records provided in this Act only in those cases where there is an important public policy need for such exemption as has been determined by specific statutory authority; and

(6) be subject to civil suit for any damages which occur as a result of willful or intentional action which violates any individual's rights under this Act.

It is the Privacy Act, then, that specifically authorizes an individual to obtain information from federal agency files maintained on him or her and that specifically protects individuals from unwarranted disclosure of personal information by a federal agency.

Although the Privacy Act specifically mentions access to personal records and the FOIA does not, the FOIA is, nevertheless, considered the "stronger" of the two acts with respect to an individual's gaining access to information contained in his or her personal file. Regarding exemptions to disclosure of personal information to an individual, the Privacy Act states:

5 USC, Sec. 552a (j)   General Exemptions—The head of any agency may promulgate rules, in accordance with the requirements (including general notice) of sections 553 (b) (1), (2), and (3), (c), and (e) of this title, to exempt any system of records within the agency from any part of this section except subsections (b), (c)(1) and (2), (e)(4)(A) through (F), (e)(6), (7), (9), (10), and (11), and (i) if the system of records is—

(1) maintained by the Central Intelligence Agency; or

(2) maintained by an agency or component thereof which performs as its principal function any activity pertaining to the enforcement of criminal laws, including police efforts to prevent, control, or reduce crime or to apprehend criminals, and the activities of prosecutors, courts, correctional, probation, pardon, or parole authorities, and which consists of (A) information compiled for the purpose of identifying individual criminal offenders and alleged offenders and consisting only of identifying data and notations of arrests, the nature and disposition of criminal charges, sentencing, confinement, release, and parole and probation status; (B) information compiled for the purpose of a criminal investigation, including reports of informants and investigators, and associated with an identifiable individual; or (C) reports identifiable to an individual compiled at any stage of the process of enforcement of the criminal laws from arrest or indictment through release from supervision.

At the time rules are adopted under this subsection, the agency shall include in the statement required under section 553(c) of this title, the reasons why the system of records is to be exempted from a provision of this section.

(k) **Specific Exemptions**—The head of any agency may promulgate rules in accordance with the requirements (including general notice) of sections 553(b)(1), (2), and (3), (c), and (e) of this title, to exempt any system of records within the agency from subsections (c)(3), (d), (e)(1), (e)(4), (G), (H), and (I) and (f) of this section if the system of records is—

(1) subject to the provisions of section 552(b) (1) of this title;

(2) investigatory material compiled for law enforcement purposes, other than material within the scope of subsection (j)(2) of this section: *Provided, however,* that if any individual is denied any right, privilege, or benefit that he would otherwise be entitled by Federal law, or for which he would otherwise be eligible, as a result of the maintenance of such material, such material shall be provided to such individual, except to the extent that the disclosure of such material would reveal the identity of a source who furnished information to the Government under an express promise that the identity of the source would be held in confidence, or, prior to the effective date of this section, under an implied promise that the identity of the source would be held in confidence;

(3) maintained in connection with providing protective services to the President of the United States or other individuals pursuant to section 3056 of title 18;

(4) required by statute to be maintained and used solely as statistical records;

(5) investigatory material compiled solely for the purpose of determining suitability, eligibility, or qualifications for Federal civilian employment, military service, Federal contracts, or access to classified information, but only to the extent that the disclosure of such material would reveal the identity of a source who furnished information to the Government under an express promise that the identity of the source would be held in confidence, or, prior to the effective date of this section, under an implied promise that the identity of the source would be held in confidence;

(6) testing or examination material used solely to determine individual qualifications for appointment or promotion in the Federal service, the disclosure of which would compromise the objectivity or fairness of the testing or examination process; or

(7) evaluation material used to determine potential for promotion in the armed services but only to the extent that the disclosure of such material would reveal the identity of a source who furnished information to the Government under an express promise that the identity of the source would be held in confidence, or, prior to the effective date of this section, under an implied promise that the identity of the source would be held in confidence.

At the time rules are adopted under this subsection, the agency shall include in the statement required under section 553(c) of this title, the reasons why the

system of records is to be exempted from a provision of this section.

Comment: Taking into account the two sections of the Privacy Act above, the Act seems to—and does—a pretty good job of protecting individuals' records from unwarranted disclosure by a federal agency.

Where the Privacy Act fails, or appears to fail, is through its almost blanket exemptions practically eliminating an individual's right to learn from the FBI or CIA what information is contained in files maintained on him or her.

The key to disclosure (just the kind of thing lawyers love to find) is provided in a tiny subsection of the Privacy Act.

Sec. 552a (q) Effect of Other Laws—No agency shall rely on any exemption contained in section 552 of this title to withhold from an individual any record which is otherwise accessible to such individual under provisions of this section.

Comment: Though it may seem to be talking in circles (and in a way is talking in circles), what Sec. 552a (q), above, is saying is that the Privacy Act (5 USC, Sec. 552a) can't take away access information which is granted under the Freedom of Information Act (552).

There has been a lot of political infighting between the Justice Department and Capitol Hill on this one (at one time the Justice Department presented the FBI as entirely exempt from the FOIA and subject exclusively to the Privacy Act, with its comfortably cozy cloak of exemptions), but it has now been clearly established that you *do* have the right of access to your FBI and CIA files, including information obtained as the result of and in connection with background investigations conducted for the purpose of determining suitability for employment, granting of security clearances, etc.

For an individual not to have access to information compiled in connection with an investigation to determine suitability for employment or granting of a security clearance could be quite serious. As a business owner desirous of obtaining government contracts or as a job applicant for a position with a company having government contracts, he or she might repeatedly be turned down and never know why.

Amendment of Records: If you do discover inaccuracies in a personal file on you maintained by any government agency, they can be corrected under provisions of the Privacy Act, Sec. 552a (d) (B) (i), below. There are also other provisions worth looking at:

(d) **Access to Records**—Each agency that maintains a system of records shall—

(1) upon request by an individual to gain access to his record or to any information pertaining to him which is contained in the system, permit him and upon his request, a person of his own choosing to accompany him, to review the record and have a copy made of all or any portion thereof in a form comprehensible to him, except that the agency may require the individual to

furnish a written statement authorizing discussion of that individual's record in the accompanying person's presence;

Comment: "in a form comprehensible to him" has been interpreted to require translation of information in the event that the individual does not understand the language in which the record is written.

    (2) permit the individual to request amendment of a record pertaining to him and—

        (A) not later than 10 days (excluding Saturdays, Sundays, and legal public holidays) after the date of receipt of such request, acknowledge in writing such request; and;

        (B) promptly, either—

            (i) make any correction of any portion thereof which the individual believes is not accurate, relevant, timely, or complete; or

            (ii) inform the individual of its refusal to amend the record in accordance with his request the reason for the refusal, the procedures established by the agency for the individual to request a review of that refusal by the head of the agency or an officer designated by the head of the agency and the name and business address of that official;

    (3) permit the individual who disagrees with the refusal of the agency to amend his record to request a review of such refusal, and not later than 30 days (excluding Saturdays, Sundays, and legal public holidays) from the date on which the individual requests such review, complete such review and make a final determination unless for good cause shown, the head of the agency extends such 30-day period; and if, after his review, the reviewing official also refuses to amend the record in accordance with the request, permit the individual to file with the agency a concise statement setting forth the reasons for his disagreement with the refusal of the agency, and notify the individual of the provisions for judicial review of the reviewing official's determination under subsection (g)(1)(A) of this section;

    (4) in any disclosure, containing information about which the individual has filed a statement of disagreement, occurring after the filing of the statement under paragraph (3) of this subsection, clearly note any portion of the record which is disputed and provide copies of the statement and, if the agency deems it appropriate, copies of a concise statement of the reasons of the agency for not making the amendments requested, to persons or other agencies to whom the disputed record has been disclosed; and

    (5) nothing in this section shall allow an individual access to any information compiled in reasonable anticipation of a civil action or proceeding.

Comment: Measures to amend a record could include the obtaining of signed statements by persons familiar with you, or with a particular situation cited in the file, who can refuse incorrect comments or other data contained in the file. Examination and comparison of *several* files—FBI, military, and civil service, for example—may reasonably demonstrate that the file you wish to amend is very probably not accurate.

    A former neighbor's statement that you were "a drunkard, argumentative, and often threw loud parties" would be highly suspect in the face of military, civil service, or other employment records affirming you to be "hard-working, well-mannered, and highly thought of." In any event, the inclusion of favorable information from other files, particularly other **government** files, would help to counter any derogatory information that an agency refused to amend.

    There are a few other aspects of the **Privacy Act** that you should be aware of. The Act does not set any time limit within which an agency must provide access. The Office of Management and Budget, the Congressionally appointed watchdog of federal agencies' implementation and compliance with the Privacy Act, suggests in its nonenforceable guidelines that agencies *should* acknowledge information requests within ten business days and *should* provide access within thirty business days. But there's nothing to force any agency to comply with these guidelines.

    There is also no provision in the Privacy Act for the appeal of an agency's decision not to comply with an individual's request for access to information from his or her file maintained by any government agency.

    The good news is that provision for administrative appeal of an agency's refusal to make records available *does* exist under FOIA, and imposition of a time limit for response to an information request is *also provided for under FOIA*—FOIA, Sec. 552 (a)(6)(A)(i) and (ii) (see page 361).

NOTE: *Citations of sections, subsections, paragraphs, and subparagraphs, etc., can sometimes sneak up on you. Sec. 552(a), for example, is the first section of FOIA. Sec. 552a, on the other hand, is almost the entire Privacy Act.*

    As we will report in greater detail in the chapters on filing FOIA and Privacy Act requests, a request for personal file information to a federal agency **may be submitted as a combined FOIA/Privacy Act request,** thus providing requesters with the advantages of each.

    The Privacy Act does have its strong points. It is the Privacy Act, for example, that requires that all federal agencies each year publish in the *Federal Register* a description of each of its systems of records containing personally identifiable information.

    (e) **AGENCY REQUIREMENTS**—Each agency that maintains a system of records shall—

        (4) subject to the provisions of paragraph (11) of this subsection, publish in the *Federal Register* at least annually a notice of the existence

and character of the system of records, which notice shall include—

(A) the name and location of the system;

(B) the categories of individuals on whom records are maintained in the system;

(C) the categories of records maintained in the system;

(D) each routine use of the records maintained in the system, including the categories of users and the purpose of such use;

(E) the policies and practices of the agency regarding storage, retrievability, access controls, retention, and disposal of the records;

(F) the title and business address of the agency official who is responsible for the system of records;

(G) the agency procedures whereby an individual can be notified at his request if the system of records contains a record pertaining to him;

(H) the agency procedures whereby an individual can be notified at his request how he can gain access to any record pertaining to him contained in the system of records, and how he can contest its content; and

(I) the categories of sources of records in the system;

(5) maintain all records which are used by the agency in making any determination about any individual with such accuracy, relevance, timeliness, and completeness as is reasonably necessary to assure fairness to the individual in the determination;

Comment: SYSTEMS OF RECORDS. A complete description of any agency's system of records may be obtained by completing and filing the FOIA request provided on page F571.

Incidentally, even if a record exists but is not maintained in a system of records in which the record may be retrieved by means of an **individual identifier** (name, social security, or other number), it is **not** covered by the Privacy Act.

The Privacy Protection Study Commission, created pursuant to Sec. 5(a)(1) of the Privacy Act, found that certain agencies changed from an individual identifier retrieval system to some other retrieval system in order to circumvent the Privacy Act.*

Here's how an agency might circumvent the Privacy Act. It might, for example, place all sensitive information about an individual on file in a system of records under, say, fingerprint classification or date of birth. Since many people have the same fingerprint classification or date of birth (day, month, and year), such data would *not* be contained in a system of records from which it could be retrieved by use of an *individual* identifier.

By combining several "nonindividual" identifiers, say, sex, date of birth, and initial of last name, the files of all **men** born on **July 4, 1948,** whose last names begin with **J** could be called up on an agency's computer. It would take little time to locate the file of interest.

Sensitive information would thus be easily available to agency personnel but safely beyond reach of the Privacy Act. There are probably much "better" ways for a federal agency to circumvent the law; the above is just one that quickly comes to mind.

Civil Remedies: The following subsection of the Privacy Act is important to be aware of because it clearly states the intent of Congress that personal information contained in any system of records maintained by a federal agency be not unreasonably withheld and provides civil remedies for gaining access to unreasonably withheld information.

Since there remains an area of controversy regarding whether information exempt under the Privacy Act may be withheld when a request is submitted concurrently under FOIA/Privacy Act provisions, you may want to file a lawsuit under provisions of the Privacy Act to gain access to information that is withheld under exemptions of that Act.

While the Department of Justice has determined that all Privacy Act requests *should* be processed under whichever statute (FOIA or Privacy Act) provides the greater access, you can't count on that always being the case. In a 1979 lawsuit—*Terkel* v. *Kelly*, 599 F.2d 214, 216 (7th Cir.)—the court held that "the Freedom of Information Act can not compel disclosure of information which the Privacy Act clearly contemplates to be exempt."

So it's important to be aware of the full extent of Privacy Act civil remedies in the event you are unreasonably refused access to personal information.

Sec. 552a (g) (1) Civil Remedies [emphasis added]

Whenever any agency—

(A) makes a determination under subsection (d)(3) of this section not to amend an individual's record in accordance with his request, or fails to make such review in conformity with that subsection;

(B) REFUSES TO COMPLY WITH AN INDIVIDUAL REQUEST UNDER SUBSECTION (d)(1) OF THIS SECTION;

(C) fails to maintain any record concerning any individual with such accuracy, relevance, timeliness, and completeness as is necessary to assure fairness in any determination relating to the qualifications, character, rights, or opportunities of, or benefits to the individual that may be made on the basis of such record, and consequently a determination is made which is adverse to the individual; or

(D) fails to comply with any other provision of this section, or any rule promulgated thereunder, in such a way as to have an adverse effect on an individual,

the individual may bring a civil action against the

---

*Privacy in an Information Society: Report of the Privacy Protection Study Commission (at 503–504). Available for $5.00 from U.S. Government Printing Office, Washington, D.C. 20402 or from GPO bookstores in major cities.

agency, and the district courts of the United States shall have jurisdiction in the matters under the provisions of this subsection.

(2) (A) In any suit brought under the provisions of subsection (g)(1)(A) of this section, the court may order the agency to amend the individual's record in accordance with his request or in such other way as the court may direct. In such a case the court shall determine the matter *de novo*.

(B) THE COURT MAY ASSESS AGAINST [THE DEFENDANT AGENCY OF] THE UNITED STATES REASONABLE ATTORNEY FEES and other litigation costs reasonably incurred in any case under this paragraph in which the complainant HAS SUBSTANTIALLY PREVAILED.

Comment: ATTORNEY FEES. The above is almost the same, word for word, as the related portion of the Freedom of Information Act [Sec. 552 (a)(4)(E) (*see* page 361)]. On numerous occasions courts have held that the plaintiff has substantially prevailed if substantial portions of records previously withheld were disclosed following judgment for the plaintiff, *even though some* requested records were withheld.

In other cases—*Nationwide Building Maintenance* v. *Sampson*, 559 F.2d 704 (D.C. Cir. 1977) and *Founding Church of Scientology* v. *Miller*, 490 F. Supp. 144 (D.D.C. 1980)—courts have held that judgment is not necessarily a prerequisite to the award of attorney fees.

In *Cox* v. *Department of Justice*, 601 F.2d 1 (D.C. Cir. 1979), the court held that "in order to obtain an award of attorney fees in an FOIA action, a plaintiff must show at minimum, that the prosecution of the action could reasonably have been regarded as necessary and that the action had substantial causative effect on the disclosure of the information."

Awards of attorney fees have been substantial.

So, if you are refused access and if an administrative appeal (under FOIA) is denied, or if administrative appeal is not provided for (as under the Privacy Act) **and** you file suit to obtain access **and** if the court (perhaps after examining the requested records *in camera*) subsequently finds in your favor, you have a damned good chance of receiving an award of attorney fees.

(3) (A) In any suit brought under the provisions of subsection (g)(1)(B) of this section, the court may enjoin the agency from withholding the records and order the production to the complainant of any agency records improperly withheld from him. In such case the court shall determine the matter *de novo*, and may examine the contents of any agency records *in camera* to determine whether the records or any portion thereof may be withheld under any of the exemptions set forth in subsection (k) of this section, AND THE BURDEN IS ON THE AGENCY TO SUSTAIN ITS ACTION. [Same as under FOIA]

(B) THE COURT MAY ASSESS AGAINST THE [DEFENDANT AGENCY OF] THE UNITED STATES REASONABLE ATTORNEY FEES and other litigation costs reasonably incurred in any case under this paragraph in which the complainant has SUBSTANTIALLY PREVAILED.

Other portions of the Privacy Act provide for award by the court for damages sustained by an individual as a result of failure of an agency to disclose personal records in a timely manner—such as, for example, to cause an individual to be refused employment, a security clearance, or a benefit to which he or she would otherwise be entitled. The minimum award established by the Act is $1,000 plus attorney fees and other reasonable costs of litigation.

76 Systems of Records

There's the story of the world-class political prisoner, far too important to just execute or to shoot "while trying to escape," who was being held under guard by the new rulers of his country after a relatively bloodless coup.

Becoming bored with his confinement, he asked if he might be given a few books to read from his multithousand-volume home library. "Certainly," he was told, "if you'll just write down the exact title and full, precise name of the author, publisher, and publication date." Being like many of us, he was unable to meet the requirement for delivery of even a single volume and spent the remainder of his days in prison with nothing to read.

Using the Privacy Act is a lot like that because it stipulates that if you want to learn what information may be contained in any federal agency's record on you, that you "accurately describe the system of records" in which you believe the information may be contained. Section 552a (f) (1) states that each agency "shall establish procedures whereby an individual can be notified in response to his request if any system of records **named by the individual** contains a record pertaining to him." [emphasis added]

So to make practical use of the Privacy Act, at least within the letter of the law selectively applied by some agencies, you must be familiar with the systems of records of any agency you want to query.

But there are several ways out of that minor trap:

1. You can become acquainted with the agency's systems of records by reading them in the *Federal Register* or in *Protecting Your Right to Privacy—A Digest of Systems of Records**; or
2. By asking the agency to send them to you—an ordinary letter request or phone call will probably suffice (see our agency directory on page 392).
3. You can submit your request for personal record information as a combined Privacy Act/FOIA request. That way you can benefit from the "reasonable description" provision—Sec. 552 (a) (3) (A) (see page 360)—of the Freedom of Information Act. (The personal record request forms of Chapter 77 have been prepared as combined Privacy Act/FOIA requests.)

Although the Privacy Act requires that each federal agency annually publish in the *Federal Register* "a notice of the existence of and character of the system(s) of records" maintained, the systems of records described in compliance with that requirement of the Privacy Act are Privacy Act records, that is, people records. They are not records describing agency operations, projects, responsibilities, activities, etc., that could serve as a source of economic, technical, consumer, or educational information.

It would be nice if this chapter could provide a request form that you could submit to a federal agency asking that you be sent a digest of its systems of records other than those pertaining to individuals, but no such digest exists in any of the scores of federal agencies we contacted.

Such a compilation would, in any event, be monumental. The Air Force, for example, maintains more than 450 separate systems of records just on people. The Department of Health and Human Services (formerly Department of Health, Education and Welfare) maintains more than 600 systems of records on people and the tiny Panama Canal Company maintains 130 separate systems of records on people.

To publish a digest of each agency's other, far more numerous, systems of records might be impossible and surely would be impractical.

FOIA SYSTEMS OF RECORDS

There is no single, sure, quick, and easy way of finding out what information is contained in any federal agency's systems of records nor of learning what systems of records it maintains, but that's not quite as bad as it seems because under FOIA all you're required to do is "reasonably describe" the information you're requesting.

You could, of course, submit an FOIA request to an agency "for all information on. . . ," but even then you'd need to have some idea of what to ask for, and requesting information in that way can lead to unnecessary delay and needless expense for records search and copying.

You can usually find out what systems of records an agency maintains in a particular subject area simply by calling and asking—and you may not even need to make a long-distance call if you live in a city with a regional office of the agency you're interested in.

If you can't get a lead on the appropriate systems of records by calling the public information office of an agency's nearest facility, use the directory of selected government agency headquarters' FOIA addresses and telephone numbers beginning on page 392. Most FOIA people can quickly tell you over the phone how to request the records you need. If FOIA telephone people aren't able to guide you, ask that your call be transferred to the appropriate project or office responsible for your area of interest.

---

*Available from Superintendent of Documents, U.S. Government Printing Office, Washington, D.C. 20402, or from GPO bookstores in major cities. Price: $5.00 Stock No. 022-000-00210-5. (See our list of Government Printing Office bookstore addresses and telephone numbers on page 375. Since publication prices may change, a phone call can assure quicker fulfillment of your order.)

Before initiating an FOIA request, there are a couple of other sources you can check that may help you zero in on the information you need.

UNITED STATES GOVERNMENT MANUAL

The *United States Government Manual,** available in even fairly small public libraries, contains, at minimum, a several-page description of the functions and responsibilities of every federal agency. In its description of the Federal Trade Commission (FTC), for example, the manual lists:

- Washington headquarters address
- Telephone number
- Names and titles of 27 top officials
- Descriptions of—
    basic purpose of FTC
    enforcement responsibilities
    legal case work activities
    compliance activities
    cooperative procedures (with other agencies, industry, etc.)
    consumer protection activities, including:
    fair credit
    labeling
    competition
    economic fact-finding activities
- Sources of information—
    contracts and procurement
    employment
    publications (and how to receive a free list of all FTC publications)
    how to receive information on—
    consumer protection
    restraint of trade
    complaints
- Address and phone number of Office of Public Information

The manual also contains fairly extensive information on the legislative and judicial branches of government, plus descriptions of all independent government organizations and corporations, and a guide to government boards, committees, commissions, and quasi-official agencies.

The full text of the Freedom of Information Act, Privacy Act, and Government in the Sunshine Act (regarding the requirement for open meetings within government agencies) are also included in the manual.

CODE OF FEDERAL REGULATIONS

The *Code of Federal Regulations* (CFR)† ia a yearly compilation of all federal regulations published daily in the *Federal Register*, combined with previous regulations that are still in effect. The back of the CFR contains a section titled, "Finding the Code" (commonly referred to as the "code finder"), which is divided into fifty subject areas describing which federal agencies are responsible for what.

The CFR is available in most medium-sized public libraries, many college and university libraries, law school libraries, many county law libraries, and, of course, federal district court law libraries.

PRIVACY ACT SYSTEMS OF RECORDS

If you merely want to submit a Privacy Act request to the FBI or CIA, use the **FBI Privacy Act/FOIA Request** (Form 77.1, page F567) or the **CIA Privacy Act/FOIA Request** (Form 77.2, page F569) as directed in the following chapter.

If you want to submit a Privacy Act request to any other federal agency, you really need to refer to a copy of the *Federal Register* or *Protecting Your Right to Privacy* (to become familiar with an agency's systems of records) if you expect to elicit an adequate response to your request—especially if you feel that an agency may be reluctant to disclose certain information that you believe may be contained in its records on you.

Theoretically, pursuant to a combined Privacy Act/FOIA request, an agency *should* make a search of its records (for which you will be charged under FOIA) for any information that you "reasonably describe" (FOIA, Sec. 552 (a) (3), page 360).

If your request for information contained in personal records is well prepared and requests personal data from accurately described and properly titled systems of records, it's more likely to elicit a satisfactory response because it "comes across" as though you know what you're after and are determined to get it. People responding to your request will want to avoid the hassle of handling a well-prepared and aggressively pursued appeal or lawsuit.

True, under the Privacy Act (Sec. 552a (j), page 368) some federal agencies, most notably the Central Intelligence Agency, plus any agency "which performs

---

*Published by Office of the Federal Register, National Archives and Records Services of the General Services Administration. Price: $6.50. Stock No. 022-003-00982-5. Available from Superintendent of Documents, U.S. Government Printing Office, Washington, D.C. 20402, or from GPO bookstores in major cities (see page 375 for GPO bookstore address and phone number listing).

†The CFR is available on a subscription basis (different portions of the CFR are published quarterly), for $55.00, from Superintendent of Documents, U.S. Government Printing Office, Washington, D.C. 20402. Single copies of the four-volume set may be obtained from GPO bookstores in major cities (see page 375).

as its principal function any activity pertaining to the enforcement of criminal laws [FBI, etc.]" may exempt itself entirely from provisions of the Act.

But, in practice, almost any request for personal data submitted by an individual that is filed as a *combined* Privacy Act/FOIA request is processed pursuant to the provisions of the law that will provide the *greatest* disclosure. Also remember that, in essence, FOIA personal data exemptions are elective. That is, an agency is not *required* to withhold from you personal information contained in its records but, under certain conditions, *may* withhold such information.

In that the Privacy Act doesn't permit federal agencies to charge for time spent searching records, but the Freedom of Information Act *does*, an accurate description of the systems of records to be searched under a combined Privacy Act/FOIA request can save you money.

Additional sources of information are described in Chapter 79, titled (aptly enough) Additional Sources of Information. This chapter lists governmental and nongovernmental sources such as New York City's *FIND/svp* and Washington, D.C.'s *Washington Researchers, Inc.,* and *foi services, inc.*

CORRESPONDING WITH THE GOVERN-MENT: *When corresponding with the government, or with anyone else (as when writing complaint letters, etc.), you'll do better by putting your letters on a printed letterhead than on plain paper.*

The difference between using a printed letterhead and using plain paper is just about as great as the difference between typing your correspondence and writing it in pencil on lined paper from a schoolchild's Big Chief notebook.

Your letterhead doesn't have to be expensive; in fact, you'll probably be surprised to find how little it will cost. For government correspondence and complaint-writing purposes your letterhead should be:

- *On fairly good, plain white, 8½" by 11" paper*
- *Printed in a stodgy, lawyer/accountant-style typeface centered at the top of the page*
- *In black ink*

You should order extra sheets of matching blank paper for use as additional pages for long letters. Envelopes should be printed in the same typeface and should be No. 10 size, 9½" by 4¼".

As effective as they may be, the following chapters' Privacy Act and FOIA request forms will probably require some follow-up correspondence as well as requests for amendment of records, formal appeals, etc., and I can promise you that correspondence typed on a printed letterhead will be infinitely more effective than if submitted on plain paper.

It's not the way things should be, but when it comes to getting a response from government or most businesses, there are two kinds of people: those who write on printed letterheads (who may be important and hence able to cause real trouble) and those ("unimportant" housewives, retirees, etc.) who usually don't have clout.

LIST OF GOVERNMENT PRINTING OFFICE BOOKSTORES

Phone the nearest Government Printing Office bookstore to obtain current publication prices. Some bookstores now accept credit card orders.

Atlanta	275 Peachtree Street, N.E. *404-221-6946*
Birmingham	2121 Eighth Avenue, N. *205-229-1056*
Boston	J. F. Kennedy Federal Building *617-223-6071*
Chicago	219 South Dearborn Street *321-353-5133*
Cleveland	1240 East Ninth Street *216-522-4922*
Columbus	Federal Building, High and Spring Streets *614-469-6956*
Dallas	1100 Commerce Street *214-749-1541*
Denver	1961 Stout Street *303-837-3964*
Detroit	477 Michigan Avenue *313-226-7816*
Houston	9319 Gulf Freeway *713-226-5433*
Jacksonville	400 West Bay Street *904-791-3801*
Kansas City	601 East 12th Street *816-374-2160*
Los Angeles	300 North Los Angeles Street *213-688-5841*
Milwaukee	519 East Wisconsin Avenue *414-224-1304*
New York	26 Federal Plaza *212-264-3825*
Philadelphia	600 Arch Street *215-579-0677*
Pueblo	Public Documents Distribution Center, Pueblo Industrial Park *303-544-5277*
San Francisco	450 Golden Gate Avenue *415-556-6657*
Washington	710 North Capitol *202-275-2091*

77 Filing a Privacy Act Request

You can use the forms on pages F567 and F569 for submitting Privacy Act requests to the FBI and CIA. On each form fill in the date, personal identifying data, amount you are willing to authorize for records search and copying costs, and a telephone number at which you can be reached.

The systems of records to be searched are already described in the printed portion of each form and should be adequate unless you are a previous employee of either agency, a spy, or a fugitive from justice. Follow our completed sample forms on pages 379 and 381 when filling out your own requests.

Since any Privacy Act request for personal data must be notarized, be prepared to appear before a notary bearing sufficient identification to enable him or her to identify you. By itself, a driver's license probably won't be enough and should be supplemented by a birth certificate, passport, military papers, voter registration, etc. Social security cards and employee I.D. cards usually aren't acceptable.

The CIA is getting better about responding to Privacy Act requests, but the FBI will probably take as much time as it thinks it can get away with, and you'll probably have to file an appeal under FOIA (there is no appeal mechanism under the Privacy Act) in order to get them to provide information from your records. It's entirely possible that even after filing an appeal you may have to initiate a lawsuit to get the FBI to move.

OTHER PRIVACY ACT REQUESTS

Use Form 77.3 on page F571 to file a Privacy Act request with any federal agency other than the FBI or CIA. As with FBI and CIA requests, this form is designed as a combined Privacy Act/FOIA request.

Date the request and fill in the address portion of the form using the agency name and address provided in the directory of selected government agencies beginning on page 392. On the basis of descriptions of systems of records contained in the *Federal Register* or *Protecting Your Right to Privacy*, list the specific systems of records that you want searched. Since your request is a combined Privacy Act/FOIA request, you may, instead of describing particular systems of records to be searched, simply ask for "all information contained in any record on me," but results will be better—as well as quicker and cheaper—if you list the systems of records to be searched.

Complete the personal identification portion of the form by listing any information beyond name, address, birth date, social security number, etc., that would be meaningful to the agency: dates and places of employment, occupational classification number, military serial number, discharge date, etc.

Fill in the dollar amount you're willing to authorize for records search and copying costs and have your request notarized. Just to be safe, **do not** sign your request until you are in the presence of the notary who will certify your identity.

There's no requirement that you submit more than an original copy of your request, but you might as well enclose a duplicate since you'll need to make at least six additional copies anyway to attach to any appeal or records amendment request and for use in connection with any lawsuit you may file.

APPEAL OF DENIAL OF ACCESS TO PERSONAL RECORD

Unlike the Freedom of Information Act [Sec. 552 (a) (6)(A)(ii) (page 361)], the Privacy Act contains no provision for appeal of an agency's denial of a request to disclose personal information to you. However, many agencies have their own regulations providing an appeal mechanism. If your request for personal information is denied in whole or in part, use the Sample Format for Privacy Act Records Release Appeal (Form 77.4, page F573) as a guide in framing your own appeal.

Note that, although your request for personal information is primarily a Privacy Act request, the appeal for release of information is based, in part, upon provisions of the Freedom of Information Act that courts have determined may also apply.

The appeal reminds agency officials of FOIA requirements that all segregable nonclassified portions of withheld records be disclosed and asks for a complete enumeration of all documents being withheld with a record-by-record reference to exemptions being claimed by the agency for the withholding of each record.

If necessary, a lawsuit to effect release of information may be initiated in federal court under provisions of FOIA as described in the following chapter.

AMENDMENT OF PERSONAL RECORDS

The Privacy Act does provide, in Sec. 552a (d) (2) (see page 370), for amendment of any personal record that you believe to be inaccurate. A straightforward letter requesting amendment of your record may be all that's needed if you have a convincing argument. In the conduct of background investigations to determine suitability for employment or the granting of security clearances, prejudicial, inaccurate, and unsubstantiated information obtained from neighbors, co-workers, one's former teachers, and others often finds its way into personal records maintained by the FBI, Department of Defense, and various federal employers.

Sometimes, too, inadequately described circumstances or situations that involve an individual may also become part of his or her personal records. An accident in which you were not at fault, for example, may not be fully or accurately described in a record about you. And, of course, there is always the potential for error; derogatory information in your file may actually relate to someone else.

If you find such information in your records, you can, perhaps with the assistance of a good attorney, obtain statements, records, and other data that will convince a fair-minded agency that certain material should no longer be included in your file.

Once you've submitted a request, the agency has ten business days from receipt of the request [Sec. 552a (d) (2) (A) (B) (ii) (see page 370)] in which to acknowledge your request and either:

- Make the requested amendment, or
- Inform you of its refusal to make the amendment, inform you of the reason for the refusal, and advise you of the procedure whereby you may appeal for a review of the refusal to the agency head or a designated appeal officer.

There are too many variables in framing a personal records amendment request for a prepared form to serve any practical purpose. In any event, an individually typed request would be far more effective psychologically than a printed form. You can, however, use the Sample Format for Privacy Act Records Amendment Request (Form 77.5, page F575) to guide you in writing your own request.

Be sure to attach a copy of your initial records request to your amendment request. Also make several photocopies of your *amendment* request so that you will have them later on for use in connection with a records amendment appeal or lawsuit.

AMENDMENT APPEAL

We've been told by so-called "authoritative sources" that since a citizen's next step beyond formal appeal of an agency's refusal to amend records would be to initiate a lawsuit in federal court, an appeal filed on your behalf by an attorney may be somewhat more effective than a *pro se* appeal filed by you because of the implication (indicated by an attorney-filed appeal) that you are prepared to go to court if necessary.

At worst, an appeal is likely to result in the voluntary inclusion in your record by the agency [pursuant to Sec. 552a (d) (4) (page 370)] of your state-

ment, along with any evidence you may have submitted that reasonably refutes any information that you believe to be inaccurate or prejudicial. That information would be sent not only to future recipients of your record, but also to recent past recipients of your record [see Sec. 552a (d) (3) and (4)].

If you do not engage an attorney to file a records amendment appeal for you, use the Sample Format for Privacy Act Records Amendment Appeal (Form 77.6, page F577) as a guide for writing your own appeal.

LEGAL ACTION TO EFFECT RECORDS AMENDMENT

If you are confident that you have evidence that will convince a judge that retention in your record of certain information would be prejudicial and harmful or that retention of the information would violate the Privacy Act requirement [Sec. 552a (g) (1) (C) (page 371)] that a record shall be maintained with "accuracy, relevance, timeliness and completeness" necessary to *assure* fairness, then you may want to consider legal action.

There is, of course, room for argument about the meaning of any or all of those four words. Is a record "complete," for example, if it fails to include valid and verified information that would reasonably tend to refute derogatory statements in your record? Is the fact that some of your activities or lifestyle may be different from those of most people **really** *relevant* to your suitability for federal employment, promotion, or the receipt of a security clearance or government contract? And is something that happened twenty years ago any longer *timely* with respect to the person you are today?

These are questions a judge will have to answer if you file suit in federal court. But you can bet that the judge's opinion will probably be more reasoned than the "police-think" attitudes of some agency officials who'd like to see your former neighbor's unfounded, unsubstantiated statements remain in your file forever.

But maybe we're being a bit unfair. We do know a few FBI and other federal agency investigators who if given scurrilous statements in connection with a background investigation will just forget them and proceed as though the interview never happened.

But if that kind of information is *in* your record, then you've got to live with it unless you get it out— and if a lawsuit is the only way to get it out, then maybe that's the thing to do, especially if there's a chance that a job promotion, future employment, or government benefits may be affected by it.

FILING SUIT

Anyone can file a lawsuit. Using our model complaint form (Model Format for Privacy Act Lawsuit to Effect Amendment of Records, Form 77.7, page F579) plus the knowledge you've probably gained from reading previous sections of this book, you could possibly prepare your own Privacy Act lawsuit in about thirty minutes. The cost would be nominal, $60 to file, and it would be a good complaint—maybe not a *great* complaint, but a good complaint.

It *would* force the agency to do *something* because federal law requires an answer (response) from the defendant within thirty days. If you're in luck, the federal agency might cave in when served with your complaint, and you'd get what you're after: an agreement to amend your record and/or remove the incorrect/prejudicial/harmful material.

But there are more games to be played in court than were ever in the occupational therapy room of a good-sized mental hospital. To begin with, your suit might be a paper tiger because you may not have the time, legal knowledge, or evidence to back it up against opposition. Then, too, especially if someone discovers that you're not a lawyer, the agency may send in *its* paper tiger, a motion to dismiss or a motion for summary judgment. Then you would need to file a cross-motion for summary judgment in your favor.

Remember, to file a complaint (and we're talking here about a complaint to *effect* an amendment of your records, not a complaint to *effect* release of your records), you must first have exhausted all other avenues: request for amendment, appeal of refusal to amend, etc.

In the long run, if it comes to a long run, you'll be much better off using an attorney (who's licensed to practice before a federal court) to handle your suit. But if you have the temperament and the time and are willing to operate on the "cave-in" principle, you might just file your complaint *pro se* and then use an attorney to prosecute your case if the initial complaint fails to produce satisfactory results.

Both the FOIA and the Privacy Act stipulate that you can file a complaint in

- The federal district in which you reside
- The federal district in which you have your principal place of business
- The federal district in which the records are located
- The District of Columbia

There are attorneys who, quite justifiably, will decline to take a case if they feel a potential client has filed a complaint in such a way as to prejudice seriously his or her own interests. If you can afford the expense you'd be wise to have an attorney handle your suit from the very beginning.

Don't foget that under provisions of both the FOIA and the Privacy Act you can be awarded reasonable attorney fees and other costs of litigation if you "substantially prevail" before the court [Privacy Act, Sec. 552a (g)(2)(B) (page 372); and FOIA, Sec. 552 (a)(4)(E) (page 361)].

FINDING AN ATTORNEY

Finding an attorney outside Washington, D.C., who's experienced in FOIA and Privacy Act litigation won't be easy. If you phone your local bar association or lawyer referral service to ask for the names of "a few FOIA/Privacy Act attorneys," the response is likely to be "Huh?" and you'll probably have to remind the person at the other end of the line that FOIA and Privacy Act cases are *federal* cases and that you will need an attorney licensed to practice before a federal court.

Better than a call to the local bar or lawyer referral service would be a call to the nearest office of the American Civil Liberties Union. They'll at least know what an FOIA/Privacy Act case is and should be able to put you in touch with an attorney or two who's experienced before the local federal court and who's temperamentally suited to handling an FOIA/Privacy Act case.

If you can't find a local attorney who can handle your case, write or phone:

Center for National Security Studies
122 Maryland Avenue, N.E.
Washington, DC 20002
202-544-5380

The center can supply you with the names of several Washington area attorneys experienced in handling FOIA and Privacy Act litigation.

If you do find yourself working with a local attorney who's a great lawyer but inexperienced in FOIA/Privacy Act litigation, make him or her a present of the current edition of *Litigation Under the Federal Freedom of Information and Privacy Act* (as mentioned on page 364).

Sample of Form 77.1/F567

March 6, 1984

Director
Federal Bureau of Investigation
J. Edgar Hoover Building
10th Street and Pennsylvania Avenue, N.W.
Washington, D.C. 20535

Attn: FOIA/Privacy Act Branch

This is a request under provisions of Title 5 USC, Sec. 552, the Freedom of Information Act, and Title 5 USC, Sec. 552a, the Privacy Act.

Please furnish me with copies of all records on me retrievable by the use of an individual identifier and by the use of any combination of identifiers (e.g., name + date of birth + social security number, etc.) that are contained in the following systems of records:

National Crime Information Center (NCIC)
Central Records System
Electronic Surveillance (Elsur) Indices

In order to identify myself and to facilitate your search of records systems, I provide the following information:

McCrea	Michael		James
Last Name	*First*		*Middle*
841 Lydia Lane	Chef Menteur	Louisiana	71241
Street	*City*	*State*	*Zip*
April 6, 1947	Wentworth-by-Sea, N.H.	Male	798-65-4364
Date of Birth	*Place of Birth*	*Sex*	*Social Security Number*
Served in U.S. Navy, 1968 to 1971.			

In the event that any part or all of my records are withheld, I request a complete list of all records being withheld and the specific exemption being claimed for the withholding of each.

In the event that search and copying fees are estimated to exceed $ __25.00__ , I request an opportunity to review such records, or to have a duly authorized representative review such records, in order to select those to be copied.

If you have any questions regarding this request, please telephone me at __318-574-4439__ weekdays between __9.00 A.M.__ and __4:30 P.M.__ or write to me at the above address.

As provided for by Sec. 552(a)(6)(i) of the Freedom of Information Act, I shall expect to receive a reply within ten (10) business days.

Sincerely,

Michael J. McCrea

Sample of Form 77.1 (*Continued*)

CERTIFICATE OF NOTARY

STATE OF   Louisiana   )
)   ss:

COUNTY OF   Coushatta   )

On this ____6th____ day of ____March____, 19 _84_, before me personally came and appeared _____ ____Michael J. McCrea____, known, and known to me, to be the individual described in and who executed the foregoing instrument, and who duly acknowledged to me that he/she executed same for the purpose therein contained.

IN WITNESS WHEREOF, I hereunto set my hand and official seal.

_____*Helen Kautzky*_____
Notary Public

My commission expires: ____February 6, 1985____

Sample of Form 77.2/F569

January 2, 1984

Privacy Act/FOIA Coordinator
Central Intelligence Agency
Washington, D.C. 20505

This is a request under provisions of Title 5 USC, Sec. 552, the Freedom of Information Act, and Title 5 USC, Sec. 552a, the Privacy Act.

Please furnish me with copies of all records on me retrievable by the use of an individual identifier and by the use of any combination of identifiers (e.g., name + date of birth + social security number, etc.) that are contained in the following systems of records:

Directorate of Operations Records System
Security Analysis Records
Security Records

In order to identify myself and to facilitate your search of records systems, I provide the following information:

Sharp	Antoinette		Regenia
Last Name	*First*		*Middle*
Apt. G-2, 2843 West Lennox Stockyards	Oklahoma		73108
Street	*City*	*State*	*Zip*
October 14, 1951	Wampsville, New York	Female	643-76-2540
Date of Birth	*Place of Birth*	*Sex*	*Social Security Number*

In the event that any part or all of my records are withheld, I request a complete list of all records being withheld and the specific exemption being claimed for the withholding of each.

In the event that search and copying fees are estimated to exceed $ __25.00__, I request an opportunity to review such records, or to have a duly authorized representative review such records, in order to select those to be copied.

If you have any questions regarding this request, please telephone me at __405-496-3496__ weekdays between __10:30 A.M.__ and __5:00 P.M.__ or write to me at the above address.

As provided for by Sec. 552(a)(6)(i) of the Freedom of Information Act, I shall expect to receive a reply within ten (10) business days.

Sincerely,

Antoinette R. Sharp

Sample of Form 77.2 (*Continued*)

CERTIFICATE OF NOTARY

STATE OF   Oklahoma   )
)   ss:

COUNTY OF   Van Brunt   )

On this _____ 2nd _____ day of _____ January _____ , 19 __84__ , before me personally came and appeared _____ Antoinette R. Sharp ___ , known, and known to me, to be the individual described in and who executed the foregoing instrument, and who duly acknowledged to me that he/she executed same for the purpose therein contained.

IN WITNESS WHEREOF, I hereunto set my hand and official seal.

_____
Notary Public

My commission expires: _____ July 5, 1985 _____

78 Filing an FOIA Request

"There was once a girl who had a little curl right in the middle of her forehead, and when she was good she was very, very good, and when she was bad she was horrid." Using the Freedom of Information Act is sometimes like that.

Filing an FOIA request can be a quick, cheap, and easy means of obtaining information that's available in no other way. Then again, it sometimes seems that government officials are downright sadistic in the extent of their efforts to withhold information. Why else, for example, does the FBI drag its feet in providing individuals with information from their own records?

The two faces of the Freedom of Information Act are *disclosure* and *exemptions* from disclosure, and too often what happens to your FOIA request depends upon whether you seem to be well informed about your rights, appear to be in a position to prosecute aggressively your request, are thought likely to have political influence, or are believed likely or unlikely to embarrass an agency by your use of requested information.

Disclosure

Sec. 552 (a) (3)   [emphasis added]

Except with respect to records made available under paragraphs (1) and (2) of this subsection, each agency, upon any request for records which (A) reasonably describes such records and (B) is made in accordance with published rules stating the time, place, fees (if any), and procedures to be followed, shall make the records **promptly** available to **any** person.

Exemptions from Disclosure

Sec. 552 (b)   [emphasis added]

This section does not apply to matters that are—

(1) (A) specifically authorized under criteria established by an Executive order to be kept secret in the interest of national defense or foreign policy and (B) are in fact properly classified pursuant to such Executive order;

(2) related **solely** to the internal personnel rules and practices of an agency;

3) specifically exempted from disclosure by statute (other than section 552b of this title), provided that such statute (A) **requires** that the matter be withheld from the public in such a manner as to leave **no discretion** on the issue, OR (B) establishes particular criteria for withholding OR refers to particular types of matters to be withheld;

(4) trade secrets and commercial or financial information obtained from a **person** AND privileged or confidential;

(5) inter-agency or intra-agency memorandums or letters which would not be available to a party other than an agency in litigation with the agency;

(6) personnel and medical files and similar files the disclosure of which would constitute a clearly **unwarranted** invasion of **personal** privacy;

(7) investigatory records compiled for law enforcement purposes, but only to the extent that the production of such records would (A) interfere with enforcement proceedings, (B) deprive a person of a right to a fair trial or an impartial adjudication, (C) constitute an unwarranted invasion of personal privacy, (D) disclose the identity of a confidential source and, in the case of a record compiled by a criminal law enforcement authority in the course of a criminal investigation, or by an agency conducting a lawful national security intelligence investigation, confidential information furnished only by the confidential source, (E) disclose [secret] investigative techniques and procedures, or (F) endanger the life or physical safety of law enforcement personnel;

(8) contained in or related to examination, operating, or condition reports prepared by, on behalf of, or for the use of an agency responsible for the regulation or supervision of financial institutions; or

(9) geological and geophysical information and data, including maps, concerning wells.

Your success in obtaining requested information often turns on how the above exemptions are, or are not, applied.

EXEMPTION "GAMES" FEDERAL AGENCIES PLAY

Example A

STATED REASON FOR DENIAL: Disclosure of records denied because records claimed exempt under Sec. 552(b) (1) (A) as secret pursuant to Executive Order [12065] in the interest of national defense or foreign policy.

BACKGROUND: Executive Order 12065, **National Security Information**, June 28, 1978, states, in part:

SECTION 1—Original Classification

1-1   Classification Designation

1-101. Except as provided in the Atomic Energy Act of 1954, as amended, this Order provides the only basis for classifying information. Information may be classified in one of three designations listed below. If there is reasonable doubt which designation is appropriate, or whether the information should be classified at all, the less restrictive designation should be used, or the information should not be classified.

1-102. "Top Secret" shall be applied only to information, the unauthorized disclosure of which reasonably could be expected to cause exceptionally grave damage to national security.

1-103. "Secret" shall be applied only to information, the unauthorized disclosure of which reasonably could be expected to cause serious damage to national security.

1-104. "Confidential" shall be applied to information, the unauthorized disclosure of which reasonably could be expected to cause identifiable damage to national security.

1-3 Classification Requirements

1-301. Information may not be considered for classification unless it concerns:

(a) military plans, weapons, or operations;
(b) foreign government information;
(c) intelligence activities, sources or methods;
(d) foreign relations or foreign activities of the United States;
(e) scientific, technological, or economic matters relating to the national security;
(f) United States Government programs for safeguarding nuclear materials or facilities; or
(g) other categories of information which are related to national security and which require protection against unauthorized disclosure as determined by the President pursuant to Section 1-201, or by an agency head.

1-302. Even though information is determined to concern one or more of the criteria in Section 1-301, it may not be classified unless an original classification authority also determined that its unauthorized disclosure reasonably could be expected to cause at least identifiable damage to the national security.

1-4 Duration of Classification

1-401. Except as permitted in Section 1-402, at the time of the original classification each original classification authority shall set a date or event for automatic declassification no more than six years later.

1-402. Only officials with Top Secret classification authority and agency heads listed in Section 1-2 may classify information for more than six years from the date of the original classification. This authority shall be used sparingly. In such cases, a declassification date or event, or a date for a review, shall be set. This date or event shall be as early as national security permits and shall be no more than twenty years after original classification, except that for foreign government information the date or event may be up to thirty years after original classification.

1-6 Prohibitions

1-601. Classification may not be used to conceal violations of law, or administrative error, to prevent embarrassment to a person, organization or agency, or to restrain competition.

1-606. No document originated on or after the effective date of this Order may be classified after an agency has received a request for the document under the Freedom of Information Act or the Manditory Review provisions of this Order (Section 3-5), unless such classification is consistent with this Order and is authorized by the agency head or deputy head. Documents originated before the effective date of this Order and subject to such request may not be classified unless such classification is consistent with this Order and is authorized by the senior official designated to oversee the agency information security program, or by an official with Top Secret classification authority. Classification authority under this provision shall be exercised personally, on a document-by-document basis.

1-607. Classification may not be restored to documents already declassified to the public under this Order or prior Orders.

3-3 Declassification Policy

3-301. Declassification of classified information shall be given emphasis comparable to that accorded classification. Information classified pursuant to this and prior Orders shall be declassified as early as national security considerations permit. Decisions concerning declassification shall be based on the loss of information sensitivity with the passage of time or on the occurrence of a declassification event.

3-302. When information is reviewed for declassification pursuant to this Order or the Freedom of Information Act, it shall be declassified unless the declassification authority established pursuant to Section 3-1 determines that the information continues to meet the classification requirements prescribed in Section 1-3 despite the passage of time.

APPEAL/LITIGATION RESPONSE:

- Remind agency of 1-101 above.
- Ask for all reasonably segregable portions of withheld records pursuant to Sec. 552 (b) (1) (page 362).
- Ask for a complete list of all withheld records, plus a record-by-record list of exemption(s) claimed for the withholding of each.
- Request date of original classification and date of reclassification to determine whether currently classified and whether classified in response to your request in violation of 1-607 above.
- In litigation, ask for *in camera* review of records.

Example B

STATED REASON FOR DENIAL: Records claimed "lost" or "unavailable."

APPEAL/LITIGATION RESPONSE:

- Ask agency in what system(s) of records the requested information would be contained if it were not "lost" or "unavailable." Then resubmit your request naming those systems of records.
- Request sworn affidavit stating that records are lost and/or why "unavailable."
- File suit in federal court demanding access just as though records were not claimed lost or unavailable.

COMMENT: "Lost" records are surprisingly often "found" soon after an agency's receipt of a request for a sworn affidavit, or soon after a lawsuit has been filed.

Example C

STATED REASON FOR DENIAL: Records are "destroyed."

APPEAL/LITIGATION RESPONSE: Ask for circumstances of the destroying as a preliminary to "determining the possibility of improper agency records destruction procedures."

Example D

STATED REASON FOR DENIAL: Agency refuses to confirm or deny existence of requested records.

APPEAL/LITIGATION RESPONSE: File lawsuit that presumes existence of records. See *Phillippi v. CIA,* 546 F.2d 1099 (D.C. Cir. 1976) and *Kantner v. IRS,* 433 F. Supp. 812 (N.D. Ill. 1977).

Example E

STATED REASON FOR DENIAL: Records claimed exempt under Sec. 552(b) (2) as related solely to the internal personnel rules of the agency.

APPEAL/LITIGATION RESPONSE: Establish that the requested information is a matter in which there is reasonable, substantial public interest. See *Vaughn v. Rosen II,* 523 F.2d 1136 (D.C. Cir. 1975) and *Department of the Air Force v. Rose,* 425 U.S. 352 (1976).

Example F

STATED REASON FOR DENIAL: Records claimed exempt under Sec. 552(b) (3) as specifically exempt by statute.

APPEAL/LITIGATION RESPONSE: Determine whether claimed statute **requires** or merely **authorizes** discretionary withholding. If withholding is merely authorized, file suit based upon complaint form provided on page F585.

Example G

STATED REASON FOR DENIAL: Records are claimed exempt under Sec. 552(b) (4) as trade secrets.

BACKGROUND: Under FOIA a "trade secret" is defined as a commercially valuable, unpatented device, plan, process, or formula used in the preparing, compounding, processing, making, or treating of articles or materials that are trade commodities, the disclosure of which would be likely to result in competitive harm, not merely embarrassment or the release of information, such as deficient labeling, that could result in litigation (see **Reverse FOIA,** page 388).

APPEAL/LITIGATION RESPONSE: Establish that requested information does not fall within the above exemption. Usually, what a corporation is trying to conceal is likely to be poor performance, frequent and costly repairs, hazards and injuries to owners, operators, and users of its products, deficient labeling, etc.

Example H

STATED REASON FOR DENIAL: Records claimed exempt under provisions of Sec. 552 (b) (5) that requested records are interagency or intraagency memoranda or letters that would not be available by law to a party other than an agency in litigation with the agency.

APPEAL/LITIGATION RESPONSE: Determine whether requested records are **predecisional,** which are usually exempt, or are **postdecisional,** which, pursuant to Sec. 552 (a) (2) (A) and (B), page 360, are not exempt. See *Bristol-Myers v. FTC,* 587, F.2d 18, 25-28 (D.C. Cir. 1978).

COMMENT: Other exemptions often claimed with success under Sec. 552 (b) (5) are that the information falls within the attorney–client privilege or that the information is attorney work product—both established (if true) as valid FOIA exemptions.

Example I

STATED REASON FOR DENIAL: Records claimed exempt pursuant to Sec. 552(b) (6) as personal records, the disclosure of which would constitute a clearly unwarranted invasion of personal privacy.

COMMENT: Validity of the claimed exemption may depend upon the nature of the personal information requested, the Supreme Court having found, in *Department of the Air Force v. Rose,* 425 U.S. 352 (1976), that:

> Congressional concern for the protection of the kind of confidential personal data usually included in a personal file is abundantly clear. But Congress also made clear that non-confidential matter was not to be insulated from disclosure merely because it was stored by the Agency in "personal" files. Rather, Congress sought to construct an exemption that would require a balancing of the individual's right of privacy against the preservation of the basic purpose of the Freedom of Information Act, "to open agency action to the light of public scrutiny." The device adopted to achieve that balance was limited to the exemption, where privacy was threatened for "clearly unwarranted" invasions of personal privacy.

And (at 371 of the above decision) the Court stated:

> [W]e find nothing in the wording of exemption six or its legislative history to support the agency claim that Congress created a blanket exemption for personal files. . . .

A federal agency's response may turn on the purpose for which requested information is to be used. The Sec. 552 (b) (6) exemption was used by the Internal Revenue Service to withhold the names and addresses of home wine makers from Wine Hobby USA, Inc., which sought the information for presumably commercial purposes. See *Wine Hobby USA, Inc., v. IRS,* 502 F.2d 133 (D.C. Cir. 1974).

Information regarding health, medical history, legitimacy of children, divorce, custody litigation, reputation, use of alcohol, etc., are generally regarded under FOIA as personal information, the disclosure of which would be a "clearly unwarranted invasion of personal privacy." But **unwarranted** is the key.

APPEAL/LITIGATION RESPONSE: Establish public benefit derived from use of requested personal information to, **in balance**, outweigh any invasion of personal privacy, thus not being an "unwarranted" invasion. Establish that requested information would be held confidential. Establish that disclosure of the requested information could not reasonably be expected to harm the individual(s) concerned.

Example J

STATED BASIS FOR DENIAL: Records claimed exempt pursuant to Sec. 552(b) (7) that requested records are investigatory records compiled for **law enforcement purposes**, and that disclosure would deprive a person of the right to a fair trial or impartial adjudication, constitute an unwarranted invasion of personal privacy, disclose the identity of a confidential source, disclose [secret] investigation techniques, or endanger the life or safety of law enforcement personnel.

APPEAL/LITIGATION RESPONSE: Require the agency to demonstrate that the requested records were compiled for investigatory **AND** law enforcement purposes. Investigatory records, such as background records on an individual considered for federal employment or the granting of a security clearance, may be **investigatory**, may even be compiled by an agency primarily responsible for law enforcement, BUT they were **not** compiled for **law enforcement** purposes. The CIA, of course, may not withhold records on the basis of the Sec. 552(b) (7) exemption because it has no law enforcement authority.

Require the agency to show, in litigation, that disclosure to you would interfere with present, ongoing law enforcement proceedings—this possibly proven to the judge *in camera*. Require that other claims be proven in litigation.

Regarding CIA background investigations, *see Weissman v. CIA*, F.2d 692 (D.C. Cir. 1977) and *Marks v. CIA*, 590 F.2d 997 (D.C. Cir. 1978).

Regarding "interference with law enforcement proceedings," see *NRLB v. Robbins Tire and Rubber Co., Inc.*, 437 U.S. 214 (1978), in which the Supreme Court found that "Congress did not intend to prevent the federal government from determining that, with respect to particular kinds of enforcement proceedings, disclosure of particular kinds of records while a case is pending would generally 'interfere with enforcement proceedings.'"

Nothing contained in the various DENIAL/RESPONSE examples above should be taken as complete, final, or authoritative. To do that would require several volumes the size of this entire book. We have included these examples here merely as an indication that you do not have to accept an agency's allegation that the exemptions cited in denying your request for information are necessarily valid.

A really good lawyer can frame a well-researched appeal or lawsuit that can very often achieve disclosure of information that an agency led you to believe would *never* be disclosed.

SEARCH AND COPYING FEES

Under FOIA [Sec. 552 (a) (4) (A) (page 360)] an agency may require payment of "reasonable standard charges for documents search and duplication," BUT an agency may also "furnish documents without charge or at a reduction in the fee where the agency determines that waiver or reduction of the fee is in the public interest."

Agencies are required to publish fee schedules, which will be mailed to you upon written or telephone request. Each agency's search and copying fees are also printed in the *Federal Register*.

The amount of time spent searching for records depends upon how accurately you describe the information you want and upon how narrowly you define your request. Documents search time charges and copying costs vary between agencies. Here are a few examples:

Department of Defense

Clerical Search Time:	$8.00 per hour
Professional Search Time:	$16.00 per hour
Copying Cost:	10¢ per page

Department of Commerce

Clerical Search Time:	$10.00 per hour
Professional Search Time:	$10.00 per hour
Copying Cost:	7¢ per page

Federal Trade Commission

Clerical Search Time:	$10.00 per hour
Professional Search Time:	$10.00 per hour
Copying Cost:	10¢ per page

Environmental Protection Agency

Clerical Search Time:	$2.50 per half hour
Professional Search Time:	$2.50 per half hour
Copying Cost:	20¢ per page

Department of State

Clerical Search Time:	$6.00 per hour
Professional Search Time:	$12.00 per hour
Copying Cost:	10¢ per page

Although agencies may charge for time spent searching for documents, they may *not* charge for time spent reviewing found documents to select segregable portions, etc.

Some agencies are good about supplying itemized statements of fee charges; others will provide only a total figure for the amount charged. If charges seem excessive, ask for an itemized statement.

WAIVER OR REDUCTION OF FEES

Federal agencies are unhappy with the current FOIA search and duplication arrangement because money you pay goes to the U.S. Treasury and not to the agencies themselves to defray search and copying costs. Although unfair and probably due for change before too long, the situation can work to your advantage because if an agency *does* grant you a waiver or reduction of fees, who cares? It's not costing the agency anything.

That's probably an exaggeration, but some federal agencies are surprisingly liberal when it comes to granting fee waiver and reduction requests. Who for? Well, for:

- **Scholars**, especially those writing on university and other educational institution letterheads.
- **Medical researchers**, ditto regarding letterhead.
- **Graduate students**, especially if the subject of research or dissertation might be useful to the agency.
- **High school students**, if requests are made in a "mature way." (Whatever that is!)
- **Nonprofit organizations**—charitable, religious, or educational groups and consumer groups, sometimes depending upon whether the group is seen as friend or foe.
- **Publications**—newspapers, magazines, etc., that are generally seen as benefiting the public even if profit making and relatively narrow in scope.
- **Electronic media**—radio and television stations, networks, and news services; seen the same as publications.
- **Authors**, usually seen the same as publications. Fee waiver and reduction requests meet with better success if written on publisher's letterhead.
- **Attorneys** (surprise!), especially if the attorney establishes that he or she is representing a "worthy" client and is so doing without fee.

FEE WAIVER AND REDUCTION HINTS

Write a letter to accompany your FOIA request clearly describing public benefit of uses to which the information will be put: to increase public knowledge of the subject, to make available new information, to relate historical and contemporary information in new ways, to make important economic/historical/sociological/medical/educational information more widely available, etc.

Describe where and how the end product resulting from use of the information will be made public—through libraries, used for lectures, published in a book or magazine, used for teaching, in news reporting, etc.

Tell why a fee waiver should be granted: search and copying expense would restrict breadth and depth of the research, thus reducing value/benefit to public; money spent for search and copying costs would take funds from other religious/scientific/educational/charitable causes; or simply that you are a student or other low-income person engaged in *much* research and can't afford to pay.

Whatever you do, offer, in your accompanying letter, to provide the agency with several copies of the completed work product in which the information was used. That's only fair anyway.

FILING AN FOIA REQUEST

Filing an FOIA request is easy. If you use our form letter (Form 78.1, page F581), about the only thing you'll need to do is add the agency's name and address, your name and address, and a reasonable description of the information you want (see our completed sample on page 391).

And there's the rub, "reasonably" describing the information you want. As with many other things—really good medical care, good financial and tax advice, and good legal counsel—the system provides its best to those who can afford the best.

If you operate a large business, your in-house counsel or local law firm will have resources, possibly a Washington-based law firm, with specialized knowledge of FOIA (a new and growing legal specialty), who know where and how to obtain whatever information you need—often even before you know you need it.

But what if you're not a large national corporation, but just an average business owner trying to turn a fair profit? And what if you're not a Washington superlawyer, but just a competent attorney in Denver, or Dallas, or Des Moines, who wants to do the best by your corporate and individual clients? What then?

When you're just beginning to work with the Freedom of Information Act, one of the most frustrating things about it is that it's as though someone opened the door to vast storerooms of information and forgot to turn on the lights.

If you're acquainted with the FOIA at all, you know that General Motors is using it, that Allied Chemical is using it, that ITT and IBM are using it, that E. F. Hutton is using it, and that million-dollar Washington law firms who won't let a corporate client in the door who isn't on the Fortune 500 are daily going to the FOIA well as though it were a fountain of wealth and power—and you don't even know where to begin.

Unfortunately, there's no way you can wander through the FOIA supermarket to view all the available information casually. But you can watch the ads and you can look through the mail-order catalog, from time to time ordering information that you think you might be able to use.

The "ads" of course aren't ads, but the news stories you'll find in the *Wall Street Journal*, good daily newspapers, weekly news magazines, trade magazines, and, occasionally, news stories on radio and TV. Once you begin to think FOIA, you'll automatically pick up on sources of potential FOIA information.

And, of course, the FOIA "mail-order catalog" isn't a mail-order catalog, but is a vast array of government publications that can tell you, in fairly great detail, which federal agency does what and whom you can contact to learn more about it.

The following chapter is devoted to providing you with the names and addresses of federal agencies and their FOIA officers and to detailed descriptions of government publications and other sources that can help you zero in on useful information.

One thing to remember is that under the "reasonable description" provisions of the FOIA, all you really need to have is a pretty good idea of what information you want. You don't even have to know precisely where it is because there's nothing to stop you from firing off FOIA requests to several likely federal agencies.

If, for example, you wanted information on a chemical product, you might file almost the same FOIA requests with the Consumer Product Safety Commission, the Federal Trade Commission, and possibly the Department of Agriculture (if a pesticide), the Food and Drug Administration (if a food product, food preservative, cosmetic, or medication), or the Environmental Protection Agency (if manufacture or use of the product could in any way affect the environment).

Not only is there no harm done by using a shotgun approach, but there very possibly won't be much expense either, since you could ask each agency to notify you in the event that search and copying costs are estimated to exceed $25. Most agencies don't charge for search and copying costs of $25 or less, anyway, because administrative expenses would exceed the amount that would be collected.

If there's any secret in filing successful FOIA requests, it's in developing the knack of phrasing a request so that you'll get the information you're after while at the same time limiting agency search efforts to the narrowest practical area. Limiting the search area saves time and money.

If, for example, you were one of the thousands of owners of recently manufactured General Motors cars having problems with the THM 200 automatic transmission and, after repeated and fruitless attempts to obtain a partial refund of repair and replacement costs from GM, were considering litigation, you might submit the following FOIA request to the Federal Trade Commission:

> Regarding the Federal Trade Commission's investigation into General Motors Corporation's automatic transmissions, please provide me with the following:
>
> 1. The nature of the complaints.
> 2. The number of complaints.
> 3. All documents relating to the differences between the turbohydromatic model 200 and the turbohydromatic model 350 transmissions.
> 4. Final determination or outcome of this proceeding, if available.

This request could provide data useful in pressing GM for reimbursement of repair/replacement costs and/or for instituting litigation against GM.

REVERSE FOIA

Corporations and their law firms take great care to monitor FOIA requests to federal agencies so they may immediately become aware of any FOIA request for information about the corporation or its products and thus may quickly file suit in federal court seeking an injunction that will prevent a federal agency from releasing the requested information.

Many corporations file these "reverse FOIA" lawsuits almost as a matter of course every time they learn that anyone has filed an FOIA request for any information at all about their company. Usually they will claim that the requested information is a "trade secret," or that the information was provided to the government under an express or implied promise of confidentiality, or simply that the requested records are "confidential." In the early days of the FOIA, corporations sought to prevent disclosure of information by claiming the information to be personal information, "the disclosure of which would constitute a clearly unwarranted invasion of personal privacy." It didn't take the courts very long to establish that, within the meaning of the FOIA, a corporation is not a "person."

Often what corporations filing reverse FOIA lawsuits are really concerned about is public disclosure of product defects, widespread consumer problems with service and repair, hazards associated with use of the product, and inadequate labeling of product limitations or hazards of use.

In 1975, for example, an upstate New York resident, Adele Larson, alleging that she had been injured and that her home had been damaged by a "spontaneous fire" while using a cleaning fluid, filed an FOIA request with the Consumer Product Safety Commission asking for information regarding "any labeling deficiencies or history of problems" related to the product, manufactured by the Pierce and Stevens Chemical Corporation.

Upon being informed of the request by the Consumer Product Safety Commission, the company filed suit in a Buffalo district court, charging that the information should be withheld. The Buffalo court found for the company, but the commission appealed. The appeals court ruled in favor of the commission and ordered that the information be released.

In reverse FOIA action the first round will often go to the corporation seeking to prevent disclosure because the corporation is in a position to file a reverse FOIA lawsuit before a sufficient time has elapsed for the information requester to file an administrative appeal.

The requester of information may then be placed in the position of having to file his or her own FOIA suit. And when the corporation's reverse FOIA lawsuit is filed in one federal district court and the requester's suit is filed in a different federal district court, the result can be a legal rat's nest—which is just what the corporation wants.

You can also be sure that any corporation filing a reverse FOIA lawsuit to prevent you from receiving information about the company will file the suit in the court of jurisdiction that will be the most inconvenient for you.

If the government favors withholding the information, it may move to transfer the corporation's suit to a jurisdiction that is not convenient for the requester, say, Delaware, the state of incorporation for many major corporations. As requester, you would not even be officially advised of this change of location, since you are not a party to the *Corporation v. Federal Agency* lawsuit.

If the government is prodisclosure, or merely wants to be fair about the matter, it can, as defendant in the corporation's suit **and** defendant in your suit, move that both cases be heard by a court **reasonably** convenient for *you*. Another tactic possible with a fair-minded federal agency might be for you to join with the agency as codefendant in the litigation.

But things might not get that complicated in surmounting the difficulties presented by a reverse FOIA lawsuit. You could move for dismissal of the corporation's suit by establishing to the court's satisfaction that the requested information is **not** exempt, no matter what the corporation may claim, and that the federal agency **must** disclose the information. See *Sears Roebuck & Co., Inc. v. General Services Administration*, 384 F. Supp. 996 (D.D.C. 1974).

ADMINISTRATIVE APPEAL

You have, under most federal agencies' FOIA regulations, thirty days during which to file an administrative appeal after receiving partial or complete denial of an FOIA request. Pursuant to Sec. 552(a)(6)(A)(ii), page 361, your appeal must be answered within twenty days. An agency may use an additional ten days under "unusual" circumstances, such as the need to contact field offices or other agencies, review a large number of records, etc.

The Act requires that any agency denying your request advise you of your right to administrative appeal and supply you with the name, title, and address of the head of the agency or a designated appeal officer.

Normally, you will be required to have exhausted "administrative remedies" (appeal) before the court will entertain an FOIA lawsuit. Exceptions would be where you initiated litigation in response to a reverse FOIA lawsuit or where a federal agency failed to respond to an administrative appeal within the stipulated time limit (twenty to thirty days).

Some agencies, notably the FBI, will delay as long as possible in answering an FOIA/Privacy Act appeal regarding an individual's request for his or her own personal records, and a lawsuit is often a citizen's only recourse. Many agencies, however, have established a pretty good track record of releasing substantially more information on appeal than in response to initial requests. Whether this is because initial reviewers at some agencies have little discretionary authority or because appeal officers have been encouraged to avoid litigation, no one knows.

Any appeal (as does the one provided on page F583) should do the following:

- Remind agencies of the requirement to release all reasonably segregable portions of requested records after deletion of exempt information.
- Ask for a complete list of all withheld records, plus a record-by-record enumeration of exemptions claimed for the withholding of each.
- State that denial of the appeal may (or will) result in litigation.

Your expression of intent to institute legal action can be quite effective in encouraging the release of requested information, taking into account the letter of the attorney general (page 365) to the heads of all federal agencies stating that the Department of Justice's decision whether to defend an agency in FOIA litigation will, in large measure, be based upon:

1. Whether the agency's denial seems to have a substantial legal basis.
2. Whether defense of the agency's denial involves an acceptable risk of adverse impact upon other agencies (for example, possibly establish a dangerous legal precedent).
3. Whether there is sufficient prospect of actual harm to legitimate public or private interests if access to the requested records were to be granted to justify the defense of the suit.
4. Whether there is sufficient information about the controversy to support a reasonable judgment that the agency's denial merits defense under the three preceding criteria.

There is nothing complicated about filing an FOIA appeal, and typing an individual appeal based upon our Sample Format for FOIA Records Release Appeal (Form 78.2, page F583) requires only the addition of a few names and dates to meet all statutory requirements for an FOIA administrative appeal.

It may be possible, however, to improve the effectiveness of the appeal by adding a paragraph or two (possibly between the form's second and third paragraphs) explaining your need for the material, describing any public benefit to be gained from its release, and politely, but firmly, refuting the agency's claim that requested records are exempt.

There is some indication that an appeal written by an attorney may be more effective than an appeal written by the initial FOIA requester, if for no other reason than an attorney-written appeal lends credence to the statement that denial of the appeal will result in litigation.

FILING AN FOIA LAWSUIT

You would file an FOIA lawsuit to effect release of information—either to release personal records requested under a combination FOIA/Privacy Act request or to bring about disclosure of other information that a federal agency refused to provide, claiming any one or more of the nine exemptions of Sec. 552(b) (see pages 362 and 363).

You may initiate FOIA litigation in the following districts:

- The federal district in which you reside
- The federal district in which you have your principal place of business
- The federal district in which the requested records are located
- The District of Columbia

You have, by custom if not be statute, up to one year from the date of denial of your administrative appeal in which to file an FOIA lawsuit. But if you miss any claimed deadline, you could always file another request, file another appeal, etc.

The defendant agency has thirty days after being served with your complaint in which to respond. You may file for summary judgment twenty days after the defendant has been served.

It's interesting to note that under FOIA the defendant agency withholding records is guilty until proven innocent; that is, the burden of proof is upon the agency to establish to the satisfaction of the court that the records are justifiably withheld.

Since you would ordinarily be at great disadvantage in attempting to argue for disclosure of records you were not allowed to see, courts have often been quite willing, in response to such a motion by the plaintiff, to order the agency to produce the requested records for *in camera* inspection by the judge in order to determine the validity of any exemptions claimed by the agency. Courts have permitted counsel for the plaintiff (FOIA information requester) to participate in the *in camera* inspection, thus providing the plaintiff with a basis upon which to argue for disclosure. See *Vaughn* v. *Rosen (I)*, 484 F.2d 820 (D.C. Cir. 1973); cert. denied, 415 U.S. 977 (1974). This is a milestone case, and you shouldn't move (no pun intended) without it.

It would be interesting to see in a *pro se* FOIA suit involving *in camera* inspection of documents whether the plaintiff, in the role of his/her counsel, would be permitted to view documents from which he/she was barred as FOIA information requester.

You may also petition the court to order the defendant to provide a detailed justification for the withholding of each record, plus an itemization and indexing of all withheld records. See *St. Louis Post-Dispatch* v. *FBI*, 447 F. Supp. 31 (D.C. 1977).

In litigation initiated by the *St. Louis Post-Dispatch* against the Federal Bureau of Investigation to effect disclosure of FBI records related to a ten-year surveillance of the newspaper's Washington bureau and its chief, Richard Dudman, the court ordered, in response to a motion by the plaintiff publication:

> . . . that the defendants deliver, within 30 days of the date of the Complaint in this action, to this Court and to counsel for the plaintiffs, a detailed justification for its allegations that the requested documents are exempt from disclosure under the Freedom of Information Act, 5 USC, Sec. 552, including an itemization and index which correlates specific statements in such justification with actual portions of the requested

documents. [*St. Louis Post-Dispatch* v. *FBI*, 447 F. Supp. 31 (D.C. 1977)]

It's entirely possible, in fact, maybe even probable, that the government's response to your FOIA lawsuit will be a move to dismiss or for summary judgment. But it's also entirely possible that once faced with the actual fact of your lawsuit, the agency will consider the expense, inconvenience, and staff time necessary to prepare a defense, plus possible reluctance of the Department of Justice to defend such a suit, and will decide to provide the requested information.

In a way, filing an FOIA lawsuit *pro se* could be compared to making the opening move in a game of chess. The opening move of a master may be the same as the opening move of a novice, and FOIA litigation is a game that sometimes goes to the individual with the initiative to make the opening move.

Obviously, a good lawyer licensed to practice before a federal court (not all lawyers are) is the ideal person to file and argue an FOIA lawsuit, but, if you must, you can file your own FOIA complaint *pro se*. And, who knows, that may be all you'll need to do. Contact the clerk of the court in which you plan to file to learn the amount of filing fees and the number of required copies. The filing fee, as with most types of federal lawsuits, will be $60. Our Model Format for FOIA Lawsuit to Effect Release of Records (Form 78.3, page F585) may be used as a model in putting together your FOIA lawsuit.

AWARD OF ATTORNEY FEES

The Freedom of Information Act, Sec. 552 (a) (4) (E) (see page 361) provides that the court may assess against the defendant agency reasonable attorney fees and other costs that you incur in connection with any FOIA lawsuit in which you "substantially prevail."

You may be awarded attorney fees and other costs even though the federal agency voluntarily discloses the requested records prior to being ordered to do so by the court. One court, in a generally accepted decision, found that:

> In order to obtain an award of attorney fees in an FOIA action, a plaintiff must show, at minimum, that the prosecution of the action could reasonably have been regarded as necessary and that the action had substantial causative effect on the delivery of the information. [*Vermont Low Income Advocacy Council* v. *Usery*, 546 F.2d 506 [at 513] (2d Cir. 1976)]

In other words, if you file an FOIA request and an agency refuses to provide the information, and if you appeal and the agency still refuses to provide the information, and if you then file suit and the agency *finally* decides to provide the requested information, you have a fairly good chance of receiving an award of attorney's fees.

Sample of Form 78.1/F581

Dated: February 17, 1984

Office of the Secretary
FOIA Office
Federal Trade Commission
6th Street & Pennsylvania Avenue, N.W.
Washington, DC 20580

This is a request under provisions of Title 5 USC, Sec. 552(a), the Freedom of Information Act.

Regarding the Federal Trade Commission's investigation into General Motors Corporation's automatic transmissions (file #792 3042), please provide me with the following:

1. The nature of the complaints.

2. The number of complaints.

3. All documents relating to the difference between the turbohydromatic model 200 and the turbohydromatic 350 transmissions.

4. Final determination or outcome of this proceeding, if available.

This is your authorization to furnish the above information without further notification if search and copying costs are estimated not to exceed $ __35.00__.

Please forward the requested information to:

Sol D. Goldsmith
Apt. H-4
1100 Montclair Avenue
Oak Park, ILL 60301

In the event that any part or all of the requested information is withheld, I request a complete list of all records withheld and the specific exemption(s) being claimed for the withholding of each.

If you have any questions regarding this request, please telephone me at __312-426-9981__ weekdays between __10:00 A.M.__ and __4:30 P.M.__ or write to me at the above address.

As provided for by Sec. 552(a) (6) (i) of the Act, I shall expect to receive a reply within ten (10) business days of your receipt of this request.

Sincerely,

Sol D. Goldsmith

cc: Marvin C. Kaplan, Kaplan, O'Hara and Wyskoski
310 South Michigan Avenue, Chicago, ILL 60604

79 Additional Sources of Information

There are, obviously, countless sources of business/ economic/technical/historical/medical information. The sources provided in this chapter are primarily FOIA sources of information, that is, information sources that will help you frame an FOIA request.

Sources included on the following pages can help you learn which federal agencies may have the information you need and just where, in a particular agency, that information may be. Often, of course, various aspects of information you want may be contained in different federal agencies, requiring several FOIA requests to pull together the data you want.

Included in this chapter are:

- A directory of the names, addresses, telephone numbers, and FOIA officers of more than 100 federal agencies.
- A guide to using the *Congressional Directory.*
- A guide to using the *Guide to Records Retention Requirements.*
- A listing of telephone numbers of more than 80 federal information centers.
- A listing of 1365 federal depository libraries— libraries which have all of the above publications plus many others.
- A description of *INFORMATION U.S.A.*, a guide to more than 10,000 government offices and 3,000 data experts.
- An introduction to foi services, inc., the first company in the United States to specialize exclusively in Freedom of Information Act services.

DIRECTORY OF SELECTED FEDERAL AGENCIES

The following list contains the name, address, phone number, and proper FOIA/Privacy Act addressee of more than 100 federal agencies. As mentioned elsewhere, you may be able to obtain the desired information without the formality, delay, and cost of an FOIA request simply by contacting the appropriate project or activity manager by letter or telephone. An agency's public affairs office is a good place to start your search if you don't know how to locate the information you need.

ACTION — Director, Administrative Services
ACTION
806 Connecticut Avenue, N.W.
Washington, DC 20525
202-254-8105

Department of Agriculture — Department of Agriculture
Records and Communications
Management Branch
Administrative Services Division
Room 3116, Auditors Building
14th Street and Independence
Avenue, S.W.
Washington, DC 20250
202-447-6763

Arms Control and Disarmament Agency — FOIA Officer
Arms Control and Disarmament
Agency
Department of State
Room 1239
2201 C Street, N.W.
Washington, DC 20520
202-632-0760

Central Intelligence Agency — FOIA/Privacy Act Coordinator
Central Intelligence Agency
Washington, DC 20505
703-351-1100

Civil Aeronautics Board — Office of the Secretary
Civil Aeronautics Board
1825 Connecticut Avenue, N.W.
Washington, DC 20428
202-673-5238

Department of Commerce, Bureau of the Census — Associate Director for
Administration
Bureau of the Census
Federal Building 3
Washington, DC 20233
202-763-5238

Department of Commerce, National Oceanic and Atmospheric Administration — Assistant Administrator for
Administration, NOAA
6010 Executive Boulevard
Rockville, MD 20852
301-443-8192

Department of Commerce, National Technical Information Service — Assistant Director, Administration
National Technical Information
Service
Sills Building
Springfield, VA 22161
703-321-9040

Department of Commerce, Office of the Secretary — Assistant Secretary for
Administration
Department of Commerce
Washington, DC 20230
202-377-4217

Commission on Civil Rights — Office of General Counsel
U.S. Commission on Civil Rights
1121 Vermont Avenue, N.W.
Room 600
Washington, DC 20425
202-254-6606

Commission on Fine Arts	Secretary Commission on Fine Arts 708 Jackson Place, N.W. Washington, DC 20006 *202-343-5324*
Community Services Administration	FOIA Records Officer Office of Administration Community Services Administration 1200 19th Street, N.W. Room 436 Washington, DC 20506 *202-254-5794*
Consumer Product Safety Commission	Office of the Secretary Consumer Product Safety Commission 1750 K Street, N.W. Washington, DC 20207 *202-634-7700*
Council on Wage and Price Stability	Office of General Counsel Council on Wage and Price Stability Room 222 600 17th Street, N.W. Washington, DC 20235 *202-456-6210*
Department of Defense, U.S. Air Force	FOIA/Privacy Act Manager HQ USAF, DADF Washington, DC 20330 *202-697-3467*
Department of Defense, Department of the Army	Chief, Records Management Division Office of the Adjutant General Attn: DAAG-AMR-5 Room GA 076 Forrestal Building Washington, DC 20314 *202-693-1847*
Department of Defense, U.S. Marine Corps	Director of Information Code PA, HQ MC Washington, DC 20380 *202-694-4309*
Department of Defense, Department of the Navy	Chief of Naval Operations OP-09-BIF Room 5E593 The Pentagon Washington, DC 20350 *202-697-1459*
Department of Defense, Defense Communications Agency	FOIA/Privacy Act Officer Defense Communications Agency Code 104 Washington, DC 20350 *202-692-2007*
Department of Defense, Defense Intelligence Agency	FOIA/Privacy Act Officer Defense Intelligence Agency Washington, DC 20301 *202-692-5766*
Department of Defense, Defense Mapping Agency	Director Defense Mapping Agency Naval Observatory Building 56 Washington, DC 20305 *202-254-4431*

Department of Defense, Defense Nuclear Agency	Director Defense Nuclear Agency Attn: Public Affairs Office Washington, DC 20305 *202-325-7095*
Department of Defense, Office of the Secretary of Defense	Office of the Assistant Secretary of Defense, Public Affairs Director FOI and Security Review Room 2C757 The Pentagon Washington, DC 20301 *202-697-1160*
Department of Education	Assistant Secretary for Public Affairs 400 Maryland Avenue, S.W. Washington, DC 20202 *202-245-6677*
Department of Education, National Institute of Education	Chief, Office of Government and Public Affairs National Institute of Education 1200 19th Street, N.W. Washington, DC 20036 *202-254-6140*
Energy Research and Development Administration	FOIA/Privacy Act Officer Energy Research and Development Administration Washington, DC 20545 *202-252-5000*
Environmental Protection Agency	FOI Officer Environmental Protection Agency 401 M Street, S.W. Washington, DC 20460 *202-755-2764*
Equal Employment Opportunity Commission	General Counsel Equal Employment Opportunity Commission 2401 E Street, N.W. Washington, DC 20506 *202-634-6460*
Export-Import Bank of the United States	FOI Officer Export-Import Bank 811 Vermont Avenue, N.W. Washington, DC 20571 *202-566-8990*
Farm Credit Administration	FOI Officer Office of Administration Public Affairs Division Farm Credit Administration 490 L'Enfant Plaza, S.W. Washington, DC 20578 *202-755-2170*
Federal Communications Commission	Executive Director Federal Communications Commission 1919 M Street, N.W. Washington, DC 20554 *202-632-6390*
Federal Deposit Insurance Corporation	Executive Secretary Records Unit, FDIC 550 17th Street, N.W. Washington, DC 20429 *202-389-4446*

Federal Election
Commission

General Counsel
Federal Election Commission
1325 K Street, N.W.
Washington, DC 20463
202-382-5162

Federal Energy
Administration

FOI Officer
Federal Energy Administration
12th Street and Pennsylvania
Avenue, N.W.
Washington, DC 20461
202-566-6061

Federal Energy
Regulatory
Commission

FOI Officer
Office of Public Information
Federal Energy Regulatory
Commission
825 North Capitol Street
Washington, DC 20426
202-275-4006

Federal Home Loan
Bank Board

FOI Officer
Federal Home Loan Bank Board
Information Systems Division
Information Disclosure Section
320 First Street, N.W.
Washington, DC 20552
202-337-6138

Federal Maritime
Commission

Secretary
Federal Maritime Commission
1100 L Street, N.W.
Washington, DC 20573
202-523-5725

Federal Mediation
and Conciliation
Service

General Counsel
Federal Mediation and
Conciliation Service
2100 K Street, N.W.
Washington, DC 20427
202-653-5290

Federal Power
Commission

FOI/Privacy Act Officer
Federal Power Commission
825 North Capitol Street
Washington, DC 20426
202-275-4006

Federal Reserve
System

Secretary, Board of Governors
Federal Reserve System
20th Street and Constitution
Avenue, N.W.
Washington, DC 20551
202-452-3000

Federal Trade
Commission

Office of the Secretary
FOIA Office
Federal Trade Commission
6th Street and Pennsylvania
Avenue, N.W.
Washington, DC 20580
202-523-3582

General Services
Administration

Director of Information
General Services Administration
18th and F Streets, N.W.
Washington, DC 20405
202-566-1231

Department of
Health and
Human Services

Assistant Commissioner for
Public Affairs
200 Independence Avenue, S.W.
Washington, DC
202-655-4000

Department of
Health and
Human Services,
Center for
Disease Control

FOI Coordinator
Management Analysis Office
Center for Disease Control
Atlanta, GA 30333
404-329-3311

Department of
Health and
Human Services,
Food and Drug
Administration

Assistant Commissioner for
Public Affairs
Food and Drug Administration
FDA FOI Coordinator
5600 Fischers Lane
Rockville, MD 20852
301-443-4177

Department of
Health and
Human Services,
Health Care
Financing
Administration

Director, Office of Public Affairs
Health Care Financing
Administration
330 C Street, N.W.
Washington, DC 20201
202-245-0381

Department of
Health and
Human Services,
Office of Human
Development

Chief, Public Information Division
FOIA Officer
Office of Human Development
400 6th Street, S.W.
Room 3544
Washington, DC 20201
202-245-6343

Department of
Health and
Human Services,
Social Security
Administration

Chief, Office of Public Information
FOI Officer
Social Security Administration
6401 Security Boulevard
Baltimore, MD 21235
301-594-1995

Department of
Housing and
Urban
Development

FOI Officer
Central Information Center
Department of Housing and
Urban Development
415 7th Street, N.W.
Washington, DC 20410
202-755-6420

Department of the
Interior, Bureau
of Indian Affairs

Director, Office of
Administration
FOI Officer
Interior Building
1951 Constitution Avenue
Washington, DC 20240
202-343-7445

Department of the
Interior, Bureau
of Land
Management

Office of Public Affairs
FOI Officer
Bureau of Land Management
Interior Building
1951 Constitution Avenue
Washington, DC 20240
202-343-5717

Department of the
Interior, Bureau
of Mines

Chief, Office of Mineral
Information
Bureau of Mines
2401 E Street, N.W.
Washington, DC 20241
202-634-1001

Department of the
Interior, Fish and
Wildlife Service

FOI Officer
Fish and Wildlife Service
1717 H Street, N.W.
Potomac Building
Washington, DC 20240
202-343-8914

Department of the
Interior, National
Park Service

FOI Officer
Office of Communications
National Park Service
Interior Building
1951 Constitution Avenue
Washington, DC 20240
202-343-7394

Department of the
Interior, Ocean
Mining
Administration

FOI Officer
Department of the Interior
Ocean Mining Administration
C Street between 18th and 19th
Streets, N.W.
Washington, DC 20240
202-535-1100

Department of the
Interior, U.S.
Geological
Survey

Director, Geological Survey
FOI Officer
USGS National Center
Reston, VA 22092
703-860-7411

Department of the
Interior, Water
Research and
Technology
Office

FOI Officer
Water Research and Technology
Office
C Street between 18th and 19th
Streets, N.W.
Washington, DC 20240
202-343-5881

Inter-American
Foundation

General Counsel
Inter-American Foundation
1515 Wilson Boulevard
Arlington, VA 22209
703-841-3800

International Trade
Commission

Secretary
International Trade Commission
701 E Street, N.W.
Washington, DC 20436
202-523-0161

Interstate
Commerce
Commission

FOIA Officer
Interstate Commerce
Commission
12th Street and Constitution
Avenue, N.W.
Washington, DC 20423
202-275-7076

Department of
Justice, Antitrust
Division

Assistant Attorney General
Antitrust Division
Department of Justice
10th Street and Constitution
Avenue, N.W.
Washington, DC 20530
202-633-2000

Department of
Justice, Bureau of
Prisons

Director, Bureau of Prisons
320 1st Street, N.W.
Washington, DC 20534
202-724-3198

Department of
Justice, Drug
Enforcement
Administration

FOI/Privacy Act Officer
Drug Enforcement Administration
Department of Justice
1405 Eye Street, N.W.
Washington, DC 20537
202-382-5551

Department of
Justice, Federal
Bureau of
Investigation

Director, Federal Bureau of
Investigation
Attn: FOIA/Privacy Act Branch
J. Edgar Hoover Building

10th Street and Pennsylvania
Avenue, N.W.
Washington, DC 20535
202-324-5520

Department of
Justice,
Immigration and
Naturalization
Service

FOI/Privacy Act Officer
Immigration and Naturalization
Service
425 Eye Street, N.W.
Washington, DC 20537
202-655-4000

Department of
Justice, Law
Enforcement
Assistance
Administration

FOI/Privacy Act Officer
Law Enforcement Assistance
Administration
Department of Justice
633 Indiana Avenue, N.W.
Washington, DC 20531
202-376-3604

Department of
Justice, Office of
Assistant
Attorney General,
Criminal Division

Assistant Attorney General,
Criminal Division
Department of Justice
10th Street and Constitution
Avenue, N.W.
Washington, DC 20530
202-633-2000

Department of
Justice, Tax
Division

Assistant Attorney General Tax
Division
Attn: FOI/Privacy Act Officer
10th Street and Constitution
Avenue, N.W.
Washington, DC 20530
202-633-2000

Department of
Labor

Assistant Secretary for
Administration and
Management
Department of Labor
200 Constitution Avenue, N.W.
Washington, DC 20210
202-523-9086

National
Aeronautics and
Space
Administration

Information Center
National Aeronautics and Space
Administration
Washington, DC 20546
202-755-8341

National Labor
Relations Board

FOIA Officer
National Labor Relations Board
1717 Pennsylvania Avenue, N.W.
Washington, DC 20570
202-254-5945

National Science
Foundation

FOI Officer
National Science Foundation
1800 G Street, N.W.
Washington, DC 20550
202-632-5722

National Security
Agency

Director, National Security Affairs
National Security Agency
Central Security Service
Fort Meade, MD 20755
202-688-6542

National
Transportation
Safety Board

Director, Bureau of Administration
National Transportation Safety
Board
800 Independence Avenue, S.W.
Washington, DC 20594
202-472-6111

Nuclear Regulatory Commission
Director, Office of Administration
U.S. Nuclear Regulatory Commission
Washington, DC 20555
202-492-8133

Occupational Safety and Health Review Commission
Director of Information
FOI Officer
OSAHRC
1825 K Street, N.W.
Washington, DC 20006
202-634-7943

Office of Management and Budget
Assistant to the Director for Information
Office of Management and Budget
Old Executive Office Building
17th Street and Pennsylvania Avenue, N.W.
Washington, DC 20530
202-395-4790

Office of Telecommunications Policy
Executive Officer
Attn: FOI Officer
Office of Telecommunications Policy
1800 G Street, N.W.
Washington, DC 20504
202-395-5800

Overseas Private Investment Corporation
Director of Public Affairs
Attn: FOI Officer
Overseas Private Investment Corporation
Washington, DC 20527
202-632-1854

Panama Canal Company
Panama Canal Company
Office of the Secretary
425 13th Street, N.W.
Washington, DC 20004
202-724-0104

Securities and Exchange Commission
FOIA Officer
Securities and Exchange Commission
1100 L Street, N.W.
Washington, DC 20249
202-535-5798

Selective Service System
Director
Selective Service System
Attn: FOI Officer
1724 F Street, N.W.
Washington, DC 20435
202-724-0427

Small Business Administration
Director
Office of Public Information
FOI Officer
Small Business Administration
1441 L Street, N.W.
Washington, DC 20416
202-724-0419

Department of State
Assistant General Counsel
FOI Staff
Bureau of Public Affairs
Department of State
Washington, DC 20520
202-395-2432

Department of State, Agency for International Development
Chief, Public Inquiry Staff
OPA/PI
Agency for International Development
Department of State
320 21st Street, N.W.
Washington, DC 20523
202-632-1850

Tennessee Valley Authority
FOIA Officer
Tennessee Valley Authority
Knoxville, TN 37902
615-632-2101

Department of Transportation, Federal Aviation Administration
Office of Public Affairs
Attn: FOI Officer
Federal Aviation Administration
800 Independence Avenue, S.W.
Washington, DC 20591
202-426-3485

Department of Transportation, Federal Highway Administration
FOI Officer
Office of Management Systems
Federal Highway Administration
400 7th Street, S.W.
Washington, DC 20590
202-426-2718

Department of Transportation, Federal Railroad Administration
Chief Counsel
Attn: FOI Officer
Federal Railroad Administration
Department of Transportation
Washington, DC 20591
202-426-8836

Department of Transportation, National Highway Traffic Safety Administration
FOI Coordinator
Executive Secretariat
Room 5217
DOT Headquarters Building
Washington, DC 20590
202-426-1834

Department of Transportation, Office of the Secretary
Director, Public and Consumer Affairs
Office of the Secretary
Department of Transportation
400 7th Street, S.W.
Washington, DC 20590
202-426-4488

Department of Transportation, Urban Transportation Administration
Director, Public Affairs
Urban Transportation Administration
400 7th Street, S.W.
Washington, DC 20590
202-426-4043

Treasury Department, Bureau of Alcohol, Tobacco and Firearms
Assistant to the Director (Disclosure)
Bureau of Alcohol, Tobacco and Firearms
1200 Pennsylvania Avenue, N.W.
Washington, DC 20226
202-566-7118

Treasury Department, Bureau of Engraving and Printing
Superintendent of Management Services
Attn: FOI Officer
Bureau of Engraving and Printing
14th and C Streets, S.W.
Washington, DC 20228
202-447-1380

Treasury Department, Bureau of the Mint	Chief, Administrative Services Division FOI Officer Bureau of the Mint 501 13th Street, N.W. Washington, DC 20220 202-566-5011
Treasury Department, Comptroller of the Currency	Director, Communications (FOI) Comptroller of the Currency 490 L'Enfant Plaza East, S.W. Washington, DC 20219 202-447-1693
Treasury Department, Internal Revenue Service	Commissioner of Internal Revenue Attn: FOI Officer 1111 Constitution Avenue, N.W. Washington, DC 20224 202-566-4021
Treasury Department, Office of the Secretary	FOIA Officer, OS Treasury Department 15th Street and Pennsylvania Avenue, N.W. Washington, DC 20220 202-566-2327
Treasury Department, U.S. Customs Service	FOI Officer U.S. Customs Service 1301 Constitution Avenue, N.W. Washington, DC 20229 202-964-8195
U.S. Civil Service Commission	Director, Bureau of Management Services U.S. Civil Service Commission FOI Officer 1900 E Street, N.W. Washington, DC 20415 202-655-4000
U.S. Postal Service	Records Officer U.S. Postal Service 475 L'Enfant Plaza West, S.W. Washington, DC 20260 202-245-4142
Veterans Administration	Assistant General Counsel FOI Officer Veterans Administration VA Central Office 810 Vermont Avenue, N.W. Washington, DC 20420 202-389-3632
Water Resources Council	Administrative Officer (FOI) U.S. Water Resources Council 2120 L Street, N.W. Washington, DC 20037 202-254-6448

CONGRESSIONAL DIRECTORY

As most everyone knows, the *Congressional Directory** contains the names and official biographies of

*The *Congressional Directory* is available from the Superintendent of Documents, U.S. Government Printing Office, Washington, D.C. 20402, or from GPO bookstores in major cities (see page 375). Paperbound price: $6.50. Also available in many public libraries and all federal depository libraries (see pages 401–423).

members of both houses of Congress. For FOIA purposes though, the *Directory's* greatest value is probably its listing of the committees and subcommittees of the House and Senate and its detailed organizational descriptions and listings of senior staff members of federal agencies.

Since the FOIA applies only to executive agencies (the legislative and judicial branches of government are totally exempt from the FOIA), Congressional committee staff members have little cause to be anything but helpful in pointing out likely targets on the FOIA horizon.

We cannot overemphasize how helpful Congressional committee and subcommittee staff members can be. People on committees can put you in touch with federal employees and others who are experts on **anything** you need to know. Often, a committee staff member can give you the name of a back-room federal employee who can tell you more about a subject than you'd even think to ask, or a staff member can sometimes guide you to a high-level federal official or agency head who will be glad to arrange for you to have the data you need—possibly without you ever having to file an FOIA request.

But before you phone a committee office (most committees operate under frequent states of crisis and often don't have time or staff to promptly answer mail), use the *Directory* to get some idea of whom to ask for. And **always,** first thing off, ask if you've called at an inconvenient time and offer to call back or accept a collect return call at the individual's convenience. Our saying this may seem superfluous, but you'd be surprised how few people show these courtesies.

Being given a few names to contact can save immeasurable time and can help you begin to build your own network of Washington contacts. Even if you had been able to learn the names elsewhere, it doesn't hurt your cause, when phoning someone at an executive agency, to be able to truthfully say, "Melton Powell over at the House Interstate and Foreign Commerce Committee suggested I give you a call. . . ."

The fact that you were referred by a known committee staff member (and aren't using a Congressman's name) says things that can make the difference between dealing with someone having a closed mind and dealing with someone having a receptive mind.

House and Senate committees are described in two ways in the *Congressional Directory.* Committee members, the committee mailing address, phone number, and meeting days are listed under one heading; committee staff members' names and assignments are listed under a separate heading. If, after looking at staff titles, you aren't sure whom to call, the chief clerk is usually your best bet. He/she can transfer your call once you've explained what you need.

The *Congressional Directory* can also help when you believe you know which agency has the information you want and you'd like to be able to narrow the scope of your request to save time and records search expense.

The *Directory* lists each executive agency's complete organization, plus the names and titles of all senior officials. For the Department of Agriculture, for example, the *Directory* lists the following components:

Office of the Secretary
Office of Communication
Office of the General Counsel
Office of Investigation
Office of Intergovernmental Affairs
Department Administration
    Office of Administrative Law Judges
    Office of Audit
    Office of Automated Data Systems
    Office of Equal Opportunity
    Office of Management and Finance
    Office of Operations
    Office of Personnel
International Affairs and Commodity Programs
    Agricultural Stabilization and Conservation Service
    Commodity Credit Corporation
    Federal Crop Insurance Corporation
    Foreign Agricultural Service
    Foreign Market Development
    International Trade Policy
    Foreign Commodity Analysis
    Agricultural Attaches
    Management
    Office of the General Sales Manager
    Commercial Export Programs
    Operational and Technical Support Staff
Marketing and Consumer Services
    Agricultural Marketing Service
    Animal and Plant Health Inspection Service
    Meat and Poultry Inspection
    Administrative Management
    Federal Grain Inspection Service
    Food and Nutrition Service
    Packers and Stockyards Administration
Rural Development
    Farmers Home Administration
        Program Divisions
        Management Divisions
    Rural Electrification Administration
        Office of the Administrator
        Administration
        Electric Program
        Telephone Program
    Rural Development Service
    Rural Telephone Bank
Agricultural Economics
    Staff Economist Group
    Economic Management Support Center
    Economic Research Service
    Farmer Cooperative Service
    Statistical Reporting Service
Conservation, Research and Education
    Agricultural Research Service
    Cooperative State Research Service
    Extension Service
    Forest Service
    National Agricultural Library
    Soil Conservation Service

The *Directory* further details all federal agency components, as in the following example, also taken from the Department of Agriculture:

Economic Research Service

Administrator's Office: 500 12th St., S.W. Phone 447-8104

Administrator—Quenton M. West

Deputy Administrator, Food and Fiber Economics—Kenneth R. Farrell

Assistant Deputy Administrator, Food and Fiber Economics—Gary C. Taylor

Deputy Administrator, Resource and Development Economics—Lyle P. Schertz

Assistant Deputy Administrator, Resource and Development Economics—Byron Berntson

Outlook and Situation Officer—Rex. F. Daly

Deputy Outlook and Situation Officer—James R. Donald

Assistant Administrator—Allan S. Johnson

Director, National Economic Analysis Division—John E. Lee, Jr.

Director, Commodity Economics Division—John G. Stovall

Director, Foreign Demand and Competition Division—Joseph W. Willett

Director, Natural Resource Economics Division—Melvin L. Cotner

Director, Economic Development Division—Kenneth L. Deavers

Director, Foreign Development Division—William A. Faught

Director, Data Services Center—Gaylor E. Worden

Director, Division of Information—Benjamin R. Blankenship

In addition to information on House and Senate committees and federal executive agencies, the *Congressional Directory* lists all House and Senate members' names, committee assignments, mailing addresses, and phone numbers; federal international organizations; foreign diplomatic representatives and consular offices in the United States; plus international organizations in the United States.

GUIDE TO RECORDS RETENTION REQUIREMENTS

Hardly the world's most exciting title, the compact *Guide to Records Retention Requirements** can be useful in locating possible sources of business, technical, and economic information. It lists many records systems maintained by many federal agencies.

*Available from Superintendent of Documents, U.S. Government Printing Office, Washington, D.C. 20402, or from GPO bookstores in major cities. Price: $3.50. (See page 375 for GPO bookstore list. Since publication prices may change, a phone call can assure quicker fulfillment of your order.)

By way of introduction to the *Guide*, we include below the titles of records systems maintained by a representative federal agency. In the *Guide*, titles are followed by additional information. For "persons" also read "companies."

Environmental Protection Agency

1.1 Persons awarded EPA grants, and contractors for all sub-agreements in excess of $10,000. [Amended]

1.2 Persons obtaining an experimental permit for use of a pesticide chemical for which a temporary tolerance is established.

1.3 Owners or operators of vessels and owners or operators of onshore and offshore facilities using dispersing agents for the removal of spills of oil and other hazardous substances from U.S. waters.

1.4 State agencies participating in relocation assistance programs.

1.5 Owners or operators of any building, structure, facility or installation emitting air pollutants.

1.6 Owners and operators of stationary sources emitting air pollutants for which a national standard is in effect.

1.7 Manufacturers of products subject to noise emission standards and labeling requirements of the Noise Control Act of 1972.

1.8 Persons holding permits to discharge wastes pursuant to the national pollution discharge elimination program. [Amended]

1.9 Contractors of nonpersonal service contracts. [Amended]

1.10 Persons holding permits to allow dumping of material into ocean waters.

1.11 Owners and operators of onshore or offshore facilities engaged in oil activities.

1.12 Owners and operators of thermal processing facilities and land disposal sites.

1.13 Recipients receiving Federal Assistance under the Federal Water Pollution Control Act Amendments of 1972.

1.14 Producers of pesticides and devices, and producers of pesticides pursuant to an experimental use permit.

1.15 State agencies using or applying pesticides pursuant to a quarantine–public health exemption.

1.16 (Reserved)

1.17 (Reserved)

1.18 Refiners, distributors and retailers of gasoline.

1.19 Owners and operators of public water systems.

1.20 Persons who manufacture, process or distribute in commerce any chemical substance or mixture subject to the Toxic Substances Control Act.

1.21 Owners or operators of any stationary sources emitting hazardous pollutants for which a national standard is in effect.

1.22 Manufacturers of new motor vehicles or new motor vehicle engines subject to air pollution control regulations.

1.23 Manufacturers of new motor vehicles or new motor vehicle engines who have been notified that such vehicles or engines are not in conformity with applicable emission standards and regulations.

1.24 Manufacturers of portable air compressors, medium- and heavy-duty trucks, and truck-mounted solid waste compactors subject to the noise emission standards and controls for construction, transportation and general products equipment. [Amended]

1.25 Manufacturers of new gasoline-fueled and diesel light-duty vehicles and new gasoline-fueled and diesel light-duty trucks subject to selective enforcement auditing procedures required by air pollution control regulations.

1.26 Manufacturers of new motor vehicles or new motor vehicle engines subject to defect reporting requirements.

1.27 Manufacturers of new motor vehicles subject to fuel economy regulations.

1.28 Contractors and sub-contractors under negotiated contracts pursuant to 41 USC, Sec. 245(c).

1.29 Contractors with contracts containing Small Business Subcontracting Program clause, and sub-contractors with contracts containing provisions which conform substantially to the language of that clause.

1.30 Contractors with contracts containing Labor Surplus Area Subcontracting Program clause, and sub-contractors with contracts containing provisions which conform substantially to the language of that clause.

1.31 Contractors with fixed-price supply contracts containing the standard inspection clause.

1.32 Contractors with fixed-price contracts in excess of $10,000 for (a) supplies, or (b) experimental, developmental or research work where a profit is contemplated, when such contracts contain the standard long form Termination for Convenience of the Government clause.

1.33 Contractors with fixed-price construction contracts estimated to exceed $10,000, when such contracts contain the standard Termination for Convenience of the Government clause.

1.34 Contractors and sub-contractors required to submit cost and pricing data in conjunction with certain firm fixed-price or fixed-price with escalation negotiated contracts in excess of $100,000 or in conjunction with certain contract modifications in excess of $100,000 or with fixed-price research and development contracts.

1.35 Contractors and sub-contractors having certain cost-reimbursement type, time, material, labor-hour, incentive, research and development, or price redeterminable contracts in excess of $100,000.

1.36 Contractors with fixed-price or cost reimbursement type research and development contracts containing the standard inspection clause.

1.37 Contractor, educational or non-profit institution having fixed-price or cost-reimbursement type research and development contracts without profit or fee.

1.38 Contractors and sub-contractors assigning depreciation of tangible capital assets for contracts in excess of $100,000.

1.39 Contractors operating a system of records on individuals to accomplish an agency function in accordance with the Privacy Act of 1974.

1.40 Contractors with fixed-price or cost type research and development contracts containing the data requirements clause.

1.41 Contractors with fixed-price supply and research and development and cost type contracts which include the Contract Work Hours and Safety Standards Act—Overtime Compensation.

1.42 Contractors with fixed-price construction contracts.

1.43 Contractors with fixed-price supply contracts. [Amended]

1.44 Owners and operators of any facility used for storage or disposal of PCB's or PCB items or facilities using or storing at one time 45 kilograms of PCB's contained in PCB items. [Added]

1.45 Manufacturers or processors of chloroflourocarbons for aerosol propellant uses. [Added]

1.46 State agencies having primary enforcement responsibilities over public water. [Added]

1.47 Manufacturers of hearing protective devices subject to regulatory provisions for noise labeling requirements. [Added]

Persons needing further information about listed record retention requirements should contact the following:

Harold R. Masters
Chief, Administrative Management Branch
Management and Organization (PM-213)
U.S. Environmental Protection Agency
401 M Street, S.W.
Washington, DC 20460
202-755-0840

FEDERAL INFORMATION CENTERS

The more than eighty federal information centers (FIC)—at least one in every state, *except* Delaware, West Virginia, and Wyoming—can steer you to sources of information in any federal agency. Information center people aren't located at every listed city; toll-free tie lines connect some numbers with people located in larger cities. That's actually an advantage because, as a result, these FIC people will handle many more calls than they would answering requests from only one city, and the more experience fielding information requests they have, the more useful they probably will be.

ALABAMA	
Birmingham	322-8591
Mobile	438-1421
ARIZONA	
Phoenix	261-3313
Tucson	622-1511
ARKANSAS	
Little Rock	378-6177
CALIFORNIA	
Los Angeles	688-3800
Sacramento	440-3344
San Diego	293-6030
San Francisco	556-6600
San Jose	275-7422
Santa Ana	836-2386
COLORADO	
Colorado Springs	471-9491
Denver	837-3602
Pueblo	544-9523
CONNECTICUT	
Hartford	527-2617
New Haven	624-4720
DISTRICT OF COLUMBIA	
District of Columbia	755-8660
DELAWARE	None
FLORIDA	
Fort Lauderdale	522-8531
Jacksonville	354-4756
Miami	350-4155
Orlando	422-1800
St. Petersburg	893-3495
Tampa	229-7911
West Palm Beach	833-7566
GEORGIA	
Atlanta	221-6891
HAWAII	
Honolulu	546-8620
ILLINOIS	
Chicago	353-4242
INDIANA	
Gary	883-4110
Indianapolis	269-7373
IOWA	
Des Moines	284-4448
KANSAS	
Topeka	295-2866
Wichita	263-6931
KENTUCKY	
Louisville	582-6261
LOUISIANA	
New Orleans	589-6696
MARYLAND	
Baltimore	962-4980
MASSACHUSETTS	
Boston	223-7121
MICHIGAN	
Detroit	226-7016
Grand Rapids	451-2628
MINNESOTA	
Minneapolis	725-2073
MISSOURI	
Kansas City	374-2466
St. Joseph	233-8206
St. Louis	425-4106
NEBRASKA	
Omaha	221-3353
NEW JERSEY	
Newark	645-3600

Patterson/Passaic	523-0717
Trenton	396-4400
NEW MEXICO	
Alburquerque	766-3091
Santa Fe	983-7743
NEW YORK	
Albany	463-4421
Buffalo	846-4010
New York	264-4464
Rochester	546-5075
Syracuse	476-8545
NORTH CAROLINA	
Charlotte	376-3600
OHIO	
Akron	375-5638
Cincinatti	684-2801
Cleveland	522-4040
Columbus	221-1014
Dayton	223-7377
Toledo	241-3223
OKLAHOMA	
Oklahoma City	231-4868
Tulsa	584-4193
OREGON	
Portland	221-2222
PENNSYLVANIA	
Allentown/Bethlehem	821-7785
Philadelphia	597-7042
Pittsburgh	644-3456
Scranton	346-7081
RHODE ISLAND	
Providence	331-5565
TENNESSEE	
Chattanooga	265-8231
Memphis	521-3285
Nashville	242-5065
TEXAS	
Austin	472-5494
Dallas	749-2131
Fort Worth	334-3624
Houston	226-5711
San Antonio	224-4471
UTAH	
Ogden	399-1347
Salt Lake City	524-5353
VIRGINIA	
Newport News	244-0480
Norfolk	441-6723
Richmond	643-4928
Roanoke	982-8591
WASHINGTON	
Seattle	442-0570
Tacoma	383-5230
WEST VIRGINIA	*None*

WISCONSIN	
Milwaukee	271-2273
WYOMING	*None*

DEPOSITORY LIBRARIES

Depository libraries are generally public and educational institution libraries designated by the federal government to receive significant government publications and public documents. Such government publications held by any depository library must, by law, be available free of cost to the general public.

ALABAMA

Alexander City	Alexander City State Junior College Thomas D. Russell Library
Auburn	Auburn University Ralph Brown Draughon Library
Birmingham	Birmingham Public Library
	Birmingham Southern College Library
	Jefferson State Junior College James B. Allen Library
	Miles College C. A. Kirkendoll Learning Resource Center Library
	Samford University Library
Enterprise	Enterprise State Junior College Learning Resources Center
Fayette	Brewer State Junior College Learning Resources Center Library
Florence	University of North Alabama Collier Library
Gadsden	Gadsden Public Library
Huntsville	University of Alabama in Huntsville Library
Jacksonville	Jacksonville State University Library
Mobile	Mobile Public Library
	Spring Hill College Thomas Byrne Memorial Library
	University of South Alabama Library
Montgomery	Alabama State Department of Archives and History Library
	Alabama Supreme Court and State Law Library
	Auburn University at Montgomery Library REGIONAL DEPOSITORY
	Maxwell Air Force Base Air University Library
Normal	Alabama Agricultural and Mechanical University J. F. Drake Memorial Learning Resources Center

Troy	Troy State University Library	Little Rock	Arkansas State Library REGIONAL DEPOSITORY
Tuskegee Institute	Tuskegee Institute Hollis Burke Frissell Library		Arkansas Supreme Court Library
University	University of Alabama Library REGIONAL DEPOSITORY		Little Rock Public Library
			University of Arkansas at Little Rock Library
	University of Alabama School of Law Library		University of Arkansas at Little Rock Law Library

ALASKA

Anchorage	Anchorage Municipal Libraries Z. J. Loussac Public Library
	Supreme Court of Alaska Library
	University of Alaska at Anchorage Library
	U.S. Department of Interior Alaska Resources Library
Fairbanks	University of Alaska Elmer E. Rasmuson Library
Juneau	Alaska State Library
	University of Alaska-Juneau Library
Ketchikan	Ketchikan Community College Library

Magnolia	Southern Arkansas University Magale Library
Monticello	University of Arkansas at Monticello Library
Pine Bluff	University of Arkansas at Pine Bluff Watson Memorial Library
Russellville	Arkansas Tech University Tomlinson Library
Searcy	Harding University Beaumont Memorial Library
State University	Arkansas State University Dean B. Ellis Library
Walnut Ridge	Southern Baptist College Felix Goodson Library

ARIZONA

Coolidge	Central Arizona College Instructional Materials Center
Flagstaff	Northern Arizona University Library
Phoenix	Department of Library, Archives and Public Records REGIONAL DEPOSITORY
	Grand Canyon College Fleming Library
	Phoenix Public Library
Prescott	Yavapai College Library
Tempe	Arizona State University College of Law Library
	Arizona State University Library
Thatcher	Eastern Arizona College Library
Tucson	Tucson Public Library
	University of Arizona Library REGIONAL DEPOSITORY
Yuma	Yuma City-County Library

ARKANSAS

Arkadelphia	Ouachita Baptist University Riley Library
Batesville	Arkansas College Library
Clarksville	College of the Ozarks Dobson Memorial Library
Conway	Hendrix College Olin C. Bailey Library
Fayetteville	University of Arkansas Library
	University of Arkansas School of Law Library

CALIFORNIA

Anaheim	Anaheim Public Library
Arcadia	Arcadia Public Library
Arcata	Humboldt State University Library
Bakersfield	California State College Bakersfield Library
	Kern County, Beale Memorial Library
Berkeley	University of California General Library
	University of California Law Library
Carson	California State University Dominguez Hills Educational Resources Center
	Carson Regional Library
Chico	California State University at Chico Library
Claremont	Claremont Colleges' Libraries Honnold Library
Coalinga	West Hills Community College Library
Compton	Compton Library
Culver City	Culver City Library
Davis	University of California Shields Library
	University of California at Davis Law Library
Downey	Downey City Library
Fresno	California State University, Fresno Henry Madden Library

Fresno	Fresno County Free Library	Norwalk	Norwalk Public Library
Fullerton	California State University at Fullerton Library	Oakland	Mills College Library
			Oakland Public Library
Garden Grove	Garden Grove Regional Library	Ontario	Ontario City Library
Gardena	Gardena Public Library	Palm Springs	Palm Springs Public Library
Hayward	California State University at Hayward Library	Pasadena	California Institute of Technology Millikan Memorial Library
Huntington Park	Huntington Park Library		Pasadena Public Library
Inglewood	Inglewood Public Library	Pleasant Hill	Contra Costa County Library
Irvine	University of California at Irvine General Library	Redding	Shasta County Library
La Jolla	University of California, San Diego Central University Library	Redlands	University of Redlands Armacost Library
Lakewood	Angelo Iacoboni Public Library	Redwood City	Redwood City Public Library
Lancaster	Lancaster Regional Library	Reseda	West Valley Regional Branch Library
La Verne	University of La Verne College of Law Library	Richmond	Richmond Public Library
Long Beach	California State University at Long Beach Library	Riverside	Riverside Public Library
			University of California at Riverside Library
	Long Beach Public Library	Sacramento	California State Library REGIONAL DEPOSITORY
Los Angeles	California State University at Los Angeles John F. Kennedy Memorial Library		California State University at Sacramento Library
	Los Angeles County Law Library		Sacramento County Law Library
	Los Angeles Public Library		Sacramento Public Library
	Loyola Marymount University Charles Von der Ahe Library		University of the Pacific McGeorge School of Law Library
	Loyola Law School Law Library	San Bernardino	San Bernardino County Library
		San Diego	San Diego County Law Library
	Occidental College Library		San Diego County Library
	Pepperdine University Library		San Diego Public Library
	Southwestern University School of Law Library		San Diego State University Library
	University of California at Los Angeles Research Library		University of San Diego Kratter Law Library
	University of California at Los Angeles Law Library	San Francisco	Golden Gate University School of Law Library
	University of Southern California Library		Hastings College of Law Library
			Mechanics' Institute Library
	University of Southern California Law Library		San Francisco Public Library
	U.S. Court of Appeals 9th Circuit Library		San Francisco State University J. Paul Leonard Library
	Whittier College School of Law Library		Supreme Court of California Library
Menlo Park	Department of Interior U.S. Geological Survey Library		U.S. Court of Appeals Ninth Circuit Library
			University of San Francisco Richard A. Gleeson Library
Montebello	Montebello Library	San Jose	San Jose State University Library
Monterey	U.S. Naval Postgraduate School Dudley Knox Library	San Leandro	San Leandro Community Library Center
Monterey Park	Bruggemeyer Memorial Library	San Luis Obispo	California Polytechnic State University Library
Northridge	California State University at Northridge Delmar T. Oviatt Library	San Rafael	Marin County Free Library
		Santa Ana	Orange County Law Library
			Santa Ana Public Library

Santa Barbara	University of California at Santa Barbara Library
Santa Clara	University of Santa Clara Orradre Library
Santa Cruz	University of California at Santa Cruz McHenry Library
Santa Rosa	Sonoma County Library
Stanford	Stanford University Libraries
	Stanford University Robert Crown Law Library
Stockton	Public Library of Stockton and San Joaquin County
Thousand Oaks	California Lutheran College Library
Torrance	Torrance Civic Center Library
Turlock	California State College Stanislaus Library
Vallejo	Solano County, John F. Kennedy Library
Valencia	Valencia Regional Library
Ventura	Ventura County Library Services Agency
Visalia	Tulare County Free Library
Walnut	Mount San Antonio College Library
West Covina	West Covina Regional Library
Whittier	Whittier College Wardman Library

CANAL ZONE

Balboa Heights	Panama Canal Commission Library Services Branch

COLORADO

Alamosa	Adams State College Learning Resources Center
Boulder	University of Colorado at Boulder Government Publications Library REGIONAL DEPOSITORY
Colorado Springs	Colorado College Charles Leaming Tutt Library
	University of Colorado at Colorado Springs Library
Denver	Auraria Library
	Colorado State Library
	Colorado Supreme Court Library
	Denver Public Library REGIONAL DEPOSITORY
	Department of the Interior Water and Power Resources Service Library
	Regis College Dayton Memorial Library
	U.S. Court of Appeals Tenth Circuit Library

Denver	University of Denver Penrose Library
	University of Denver School of Law Library
Fort Collins	Colorado State University Libraries
Golden	Colorado School of Mines Arthur Lakes Library
Grand Junction	Mesa County Public Library
Greeley	University of Northern Colorado Library
Gunnison	Western State College Leslie J. Savage Library
La Junta	Otero Junior College Wheeler Library
Lakewood	Jefferson County Public Library Lakewood Library
Pueblo	Pueblo Library District
	University of Southern Colorado Library
USAF Academy	U.S. Air Force Academy Library

CONNECTICUT

Bridgeport	Bridgeport Public Library
	University of Bridgeport School of Law Library
Danbury	Western Connecticut State College Ruth A. Haas Library
Danielson	Quinebaug Valley Community College Library
Enfield	Enfield Central Library
Hartford	Connecticut State Library REGIONAL DEPOSITORY
	Hartford Public Library
	Trinity College Library
Middletown	Wesleyan University Olin Library
Mystic	Mystic Seaport Museum, Incorporated G. W. Blunt White Library
New Britain	Central Connecticut State College Elihu Burritt Library
New Haven	Southern Connecticut State College Hilton C. Buley Library
	Yale Law Library
	Yale University Library
New London	Connecticut College Library
	U.S. Coast Guard Academy Library
Stamford	The Ferguson Library Stamford's Public Library
Storrs	University of Connecticut Library
Waterbury	Post College Traurig Library
	Silas Bronson Public Library

West Hartford	University of Connecticut School of Law Library	Washington	Federal Election Commission Library
West Haven	University of New Haven Peterson Library		Federal Labor Relations Authority Law Library

DELAWARE

Dover — Delaware State College William C. Jason Library

State Law Library in Kent County

Georgetown — Delaware Technical and Community College Library

Sussex County Law Library

Newark — University of Delaware Library

Wilmington — Delaware Law School Library

New Castle County Law Library

DISTRICT OF COLUMBIA

Washington — Administrative Conference of the United States Library

Advisory Commission on Intergovernmental Relations Library

Catholic University of America Robert J. White Law Library

Civil Aeronautics Board Library

Department of the Army Library Office of the Adjutant General

Department of Commerce Library

Department of Energy Library

Department of Health and Human Services

Department of Housing and Urban Development Library

Department of the Interior Library Natural Resources Library

Department of Justice Main Library

Department of Labor Library

Department of the Navy Library

Department of State Law Library

Department of State Library

Department of Transportation, National Highway Traffic Safety Administration Library Technical Reference Branch

Department of the Treasury Library

District of Columbia Court of Appeals Library

District of Columbia Public Library Documents Department

Executive Office of the President, Office of Administration Library and Information Service Division

Federal Deposit Insurance Corporation Library

Washington (cont.):

Federal Election Commission Library

Federal Labor Relations Authority Law Library

Federal Mine Safety and Health Review Commission Library

Federal Reserve System Board of Governors Research Library

Federal Reserve System Law Library

General Accounting Office Library

General Services Administration Library

Georgetown University Law Center Fred O. Dennis Law Library

Georgetown University Library

George Washington University National Law Center Jacob Burns Law Library

Library of Congress Congressional Research Service Library Service Division

Library of Congress Serial and Government Publications Documents Unit

Merit Systems Protection Board Library

National Defense University Library

U.S. Court of Appeals Judges' Library

U.S. Office of Personnel Management Library

U.S. Postal Service Library

U.S. Senate Library

U.S. Supreme Court Library

University of the District of Columbia Library

Veterans' Administration Library Central Office Library

FLORIDA

Boca Raton — Florida Atlantic University S. E. Wimberly Library

Clearwater — Clearwater Public Library

Coral Gables — University of Miami Library

Daytona Beach — Volusia County Library Center

De Land — Stetson University duPont-Ball Library

Fort Lauderdale — Broward County Library East Regional Branch

Nova University Law Library

Fort Pierce — Indian River Community College Library

Gainesville	University of Florida College of Law Library	Atlanta	Atlanta Public Library
	University of Florida Libraries REGIONAL DEPOSITORY		Atlanta University Center Robert W. Woodruff Library
Jacksonville	Haydon Burns Library		Emory University School of Law Library
	Jacksonville University Swisher Library		Emory University Robert W. Woodruff Library
	University of North Florida Thomas G. Carpenter Library		Georgia Institute of Technology Price Gilbert Memorial Library
Lakeland	Lakeland Public Library		Georgia State Library
Leesburg	Lake-Sumter Community College Library		George State University William Russell Pullen Library
Melbourne	Florida Institute of Technology Library		U.S. Court of Appeals 5th Circuit Court Library
Miami	Florida International University Library	Augusta	Augusta College Reese Library
	Miami Public Library	Brunswick	Brunswick-Glynn County Regional Library
North Miami	Florida International University North Miami Campus Library	Carrollton	West Georgia College Irvine Sullivan Ingram Library
Opa Locka	Biscayne College Library	Columbus	Columbus College Simon Schwob Memorial Library
Orlando	University of Central Florida Library	Dahlonega	North Georgia College Stewart Library
Palatka	Saint Johns River Community College Library	Dalton	Dalton Junior College Library
Pensacola	University of West Florida John C. Pace Library	Decatur	DeKalb Community College South Campus Learning Resources Center
Port Charlotte	Charlotte County Library System		
Saint Petersburg	Saint Petersburg Public Library	Macon	Mercer University Stetson Memorial Library
	Stetson University College of Law Charles A. Dana Library		Mercer University Walter F. George School of Law Library
Sarasota	Selby Public Library		
Tallahassee	Florida Agricultural and Mechanical University Coleman Learning Resources Center	Marietta	Kennesaw College Memorial Library
	Florida State University College of Law Library	Milledgeville	Georgia College at Milledgeville Ina Dillard Russell Library
	Florida State University Robert M. Strozier Library	Mount Berry Savannah	Berry College Memorial Library Chatham-Effingham-Liberty Regional Library
	Florida Supreme Court Library		
	State Library of Florida	Statesboro	Georgia Southern College Library
Tampa	Tampa-Hillsborough County Public Library	Valdosta	Valdosta State College Library
	University of South Florida Library		
	University of Tampa Merl Kelce Library		**GUAM**
Winter Park	Rollins College Mills Memorial Library	Agana	Nieves M. Flores Memorial Library
		Mangilao	University of Guam Robert F. Kennedy Memorial Library
	GEORGIA		
Albany	Albany-Dougherty Public Library		**HAWAII**
Americus	Georgia Southwestern College James Earl Carter Library	Hilo	University of Hawaii at Hilo Library
Athens	University of Georgia Libraries REGIONAL DEPOSITORY	Honolulu	Hawaii Medical Library, Incorporated
	University of Georgia School of Law Library		Hawaii State Library
			Municipal Reference and Records Center
			Supreme Court Law Library

Honolulu	University of Hawaii Library REGIONAL DEPOSITORY	Chicago	Loyola University School of Law Library
	University of Hawaii School of Law Library		Northeastern Illinois University Library
Laie	Brigham Young University Joseph F. Smith Library		Northwestern University School of Law Library
Lihue	Kauai Regional Library		University of Chicago Law Library
Pearl City	Leeward Community College Library		University of Chicago Library
Wailuku	Maui Public Library		University of Illinois at Chicago Circle Library

IDAHO

			William J. Campbell Library of the U.S. Courts
Boise	Boise Public Library and Information Center	Decatur	Decatur Public Library
	Boise State University Library	De Kalb	Northern Illinois University Founders' Memorial Library
	Idaho State Law Library	Des Plaines	Oakton Community College Learning Resource Center
	Idaho State Library	Edwardsville	Southern Illinois University Lovejoy Memorial Library
Caldwell	College of Idaho Terteling Library	Elsah	Principia College Marshall Brooks Library
Moscow	University of Idaho College of Law Library	Evanston	Northwestern University Library
	University of Idaho Library REGIONAL DEPOSITORY	Freeport	Freeport Public Library
Pocatello	Idaho State University Library	Galesburg	Galesburg Public Library
Rexburg	Ricks College David O. McKay Library	Glen Ellyn	Northern Illinois University College of Law Library
Twin Falls	College of Southern Idaho Library	Jacksonville	MacMurray College Henry Pfeiffer Library

ILLINOIS

		Kankakee	Olivet Nazarene College Benner Library and Learning Resource Center
Bloomington	Illinois Wesleyan University Libraries	Lake Forest	Lake Forest College Donnelley Library
Carbondale	Southern Illinois University at Carbondale Morris Library	Lebanon	McKendree College Holman Library
	Southern Illinois University School of Law Library	Lisle	Illinois Benedictine College Theodore F. Lownik Library
Carlinville	Blackburn College Lumpkin Library	Macomb	Western Illinois University Libraries
Carterville	Shawnee Library System	Moline	Black Hawk College Learning Resources Center
Champaign	University of Illinois Law Library	Monmouth	Monmouth College Hewes Library
Charleston	Eastern Illinois University Booth Library	Mount Carmel	Wabash Valley College Bauer Media Center
Chicago	Chicago Public Library	Mount Prospect	Mount Prospect Public Library
	Chicago State University Paul and Emily Douglas Library	Normal	Illinois State University Milner Library
	DePaul University Law Library	Oak Park	Oak Park Public Library
	Field Museum of Natural History Library	Oglesby	Illinois Valley Community College Jacobs Memorial Library
	Illinois Institute of Technology Chicago-Kent College of Law Library	Palos Hills	Moraine Valley Community College Library
	Illinois Institute of Technology Kemper Library	Park Forest South	Governors' State University Library
	John Crerar Library	Peoria	Bradley University Cullom-Davis Library
	John Marshall Law School Library		Peoria Public Library
	Loyola University of Chicago E. M. Cudahy Memorial Library		

River Forest	Rosary College Rebecca Crown Library
Rockford	Rockford Public Library
Romeoville	Lewis University Library
Springfield	Illinois State Library REGIONAL DEPOSITORY
Streamwood	Poplar Creek Public Library District
Urbana	University of Illinois Library
Wheaton	Wheaton College Library
Woodstock	Woodstock Public Library

INDIANA

Anderson	Anderson College Charles E. Wilson Library
Bloomington	Indiana University Law Library
	Indiana University Library
Crawfordsville	Wabash College Lilly Library
Evansville	Evansville and Vanderburgh County Public Library
	Indiana State University at Evansville Evansville Campus Library
Fort Wayne	Indiana University–Purdue University at Fort Wayne Helmke Library
	Allen County Public Library
Franklin	Franklin College Library
Gary	Gary Public Library
	Indiana University Northwest Campus Library
Greencastle	De Pauw University Roy O. West Library
Hammond	Hammond Public Library
Hanover	Hanover College Duggan Library
Huntington	Huntington College Loew Alumni Library
Indianapolis	Butler University Irwin Library
	Indianapolis–Marion County Public Library
	Indiana State Library REGIONAL DEPOSITORY
	Indiana Supreme Court Law Library
	Indiana University School of Law Library
	Indiana University–Purdue University Library
Kokomo	Indiana University at Kokomo Learning Resource Center
Lafayette	Purdue University Libraries and Audio-Visual Center
Muncie	Ball State University Library
	Muncie Public Library

New Albany	Indiana University Southeastern Campus Library
Notre Dame	University of Notre Dame Memorial Library
Rensselaer	Saint Joseph's College Library
Richmond	Earlham College Lilly Library
	Morrison-Reeves Library
South Bend	Indiana University at South Bend Library
Terre Haute	Indiana State University Cunningham Memorial Library
Valparaiso	Valparaiso University Moellering Memorial Library
	Valparaiso University Law Library

IOWA

Ames	Iowa State University Library
Cedar Falls	University of Northern Iowa Library
Council Bluffs	Free Public Library
	Iowa Western Community College Herbert Hoover Library
Davenport	Davenport Public Library
Des Moines	Drake University Cowles Library
	Drake University Law Library
	Public Library of Des Moines
	State Library of Iowa
Dubuque	Carnegie-Stout Public Library
	Loras College Wahlert Memorial Library
Fayette	Upper Iowa University Henderson-Wilder Library
Grinnell	Grinnell College Library
Iowa City	University of Iowa College of Law Library
	University of Iowa Libraries REGIONAL DEPOSITORY
Lamoni	Graceland College Frederick Madison Smith Library
Mason City	North Iowa Area Community College Library
Mount Vernon	Cornell College Russell D. Cole Library
Orange City	Northwestern College Ramaker Library
Sioux City	Sioux City Public Library

KANSAS

Atchison	Benedictine College Library
Baldwin City	Baker University Collins Library
Colby	Colby Community College H. F. Davis Memorial Library
Emporia	Emporia State University William Allen White Library

Hays	Fort Hays State University Forsyth Library
Hutchinson	Hutchinson Public Library
Fort Scott	Fort Scott Community College Learning Resources Center Library
Lawrence	University of Kansas Law Library
	University of Kansas REGIONAL DEPOSITORY Watson Library
Manhattan	Kansas State University Farrell Library
Pittsburg	Pittsburg State University Leonard H. Axe Library
Salina	Kansas Wesleyan University Memorial Library
Shawnee Mission	Johnson County Library
Topeka	Kansas State Historical Society Library
	Kansas State Library
	Kansas Supreme Court Law Library
	Washburn University of Topeka Law Library
Wichita	Wichita State University Ablah Library

KENTUCKY

Ashland	Boyd County Public Library
Barbourville	Union College Abigail E. Weeks Memorial Library
Bowling Green	Western Kentucky University Helm-Cravens Graduate Center and Library
Fort Mitchell	Thomas More College Library
Danville	Centre College Grace Doherty Library
Frankfort	Kentucky Department of Libraries and Archives
	Kentucky State Law Library
	Kentucky State University Blazer Library
Highland Heights	Northern Kentucky University W. Frank Steely Library
Hopkinsville	Hopkinsville Community College Library
Lexington	University of Kentucky Law Library
	University of Kentucky Libraries REGIONAL DEPOSITORY
Louisville	Louisville Free Public Library
	University of Louisville Ekstrom Library–Belnap Campus Government Publications Department
	University of Louisville Law Library

Morehead	Morehead State University Camden-Carroll Library
Murray	Murray State University Waterfield Library
Owensboro	Kentucky Wesleyan College Library Learning Center
Richmond	Eastern Kentucky University John Grant Crabbe Library

LOUISIANA

Baton Rouge	Louisiana State Library
	Louisiana State University Middleton Library REGIONAL DEPOSITORY
	Louisiana State University Paul M. Hebert Law Center Library
	Southern University Law School Library
	Southern University Library
Eunice	Louisiana State University at Eunice LeDoux Library
Hammond	Southeastern Louisiana University Sims Memorial Library
Lafayette	University of Southwestern Louisiana Library
Lake Charles	McNeese State University Lether E. Frazar Memorial Library
Monroe	Northeast Louisiana University Sandel Library
Natchitoches	Northwestern State University Watson Memorial Library
New Orleans	Law Library of Louisiana
	Loyola University Library
	Loyola University Law Library
	New Orleans Public Library Business and Science Division
	Our Lady of Holy Cross College Library
	Southern University in New Orleans Library
	Tulane University Howard-Tilton Memorial Library
	Tulane University Law Library
	U.S. Court of Appeals Fifth Circuit Library
	University of New Orleans Earl K. Long Library
Pineville	Louisiana College Richard W. Norton Memorial Library
Ruston	Louisiana Technical University Prescott Memorial Library REGIONAL DEPOSITORY
Shreveport	Louisiana State University at Shreveport Library
	Shreve Memorial Library

Thibodaux	Nicholls State University Ellender Memorial Library

MAINE

Augusta	Maine Law and Legislative Reference Library
	Maine State Library
Bangor	Bangor Public Library
Brunswick	Bowdoin College Library
Castine	Maine Maritime Academy Nutting Memorial Library
Lewiston	Bates College George and Helen Ladd Library
Orono	University of Maine REGIONAL DEPOSITORY Raymond H. Fogler Library Tri-State Regional Documents Depository
Portland	Portland Public Library
	University of Maine School of Law Library
Presque Isle	University of Maine at Presque Isle Library/Learning Resources Center
Springvale	Nasson College Library
Waterville	Colby College Miller Library

MARYLAND

Annapolis	Maryland State Law Library
	U.S. Naval Academy Nimitz Library Acquisitions Branch
Baltimore	Enoch Pratt Free Library
	Johns Hopkins University Milton S. Eisenhower Library
	Morgan State College Soper Library
	University of Baltimore University Library
	University of Baltimore Law Library
	University of Maryland School of Law Marshall Law Library
Bel Air	Harford Community College Library
Beltsville	Department of Agriculture National Agricultural Library
Bethesda	Department of Health and Human Services National Library of Medicine
Catonsville	University of Maryland, Baltimore County University Library
Chestertown	Washington College Clifton M. Miller Library
College Park	University of Maryland REGIONAL DEPOSITORY McKeldin Library

Cumberland	Allegany Community College Library
Frostburg	Frostburg State College Library
Patuxent River	U.S. Naval Air Station Library
Rockville	Montgomery County Department of Public Libraries
Salisbury	Salisbury State College Blackwell Library
Towson	Goucher College Julia Rogers Library
	Towson State University Cook Library
Westminster	Western Maryland College Hoover Library

MASSACHUSETTS

Amherst	Amherst College Library
	University of Massachusetts Goodell Library
Belmont	Belmont Memorial Library
Boston	Boston Athenaeum Library
	Boston Public Library REGIONAL DEPOSITORY
	Boston University School of Law Pappas Law Library
	Northeastern University Robert G. Dodge Library
	State Library of Massachusetts
	Suffolk University Law Library
	Supreme Judicial Court Social Law Library
	U.S. Court of Appeals First Circuit Library
Brookline	Public Library of Brookline
Cambridge	Harvard College Library
	Harvard Law School Library
	Massachusetts Institute of Technology Libraries
Chestnut Hill	Boston College Bapst Library
Chicopee	College of Our Lady of the Elms Alumnae Library
Lowell	University of Lowell Alumni-Lydon Library
Lynn	Lynn Public Library
Marlborough	Marlborough Public Library
Medford	Tufts University Library
Milton	Curry College Levin Library
New Bedford	New Bedford Free Public Library
Newton Centre	Boston College Law School Library
North Dartmouth	Southeastern Massachusetts University Library
North Easton	Stonehill College Cushing-Martin Library
Springfield	Springfield City Library

Springfield	Western New England College Law Library
Waltham	Brandeis University Library
Wellesley	Wellesley College Library
Wenham	Gordon College Winn Library
Williamstown	Williams College Library
Worcester	American Antiquarian Society Library
	University of Massachusetts Medical Center Lamar Soutter Library
	Worcester Public Library

MICHIGAN

Albion	Albion College Stockwell Memorial Library
Allendale	Grand Valley State College Zumberge Library
Alma	Alma College Library
Ann Arbor	University of Michigan Harlan Hatcher Library
	University of Michigan Law Library
Benton Harbor	Benton Harbor Public Library
Bloomfield Hills	Cranbrook Institute of Science Library
Dearborn	Henry Ford Centennial Library
	Henry Ford Community College Library
Detroit	Detroit College of Law Library
	Detroit Public Library REGIONAL DEPOSITORY
	Marygrove College Library
	Mercy College of Detroit Library
	University of Detroit Library
	University of Detroit School of Law Library
	Wayne State University G. Flint Purdy Library
	Wayne State University Arthur Neef Law Library
Dowagiac	Southwestern Michigan College Matthews Library
East Lansing	Michigan State University Library
Farmington Hills	Oakland Community College Martin L. King Learning Resources Center
Flint	Flint Public Library
	University of Michigan–Flint Library
Grand Rapids	Calvin College and Seminary Library
	Grand Rapids Public Library
Houghton	Michigan Technological University Library
Jackson	Jackson District Library

Kalamazoo	Kalamazoo Public Library
	Western Michigan University Dwight B. Waldo Library
Lansing	Michigan State Library REGIONAL DEPOSITORY
	Thomas M. Cooley Law School Library
Livonia	Schoolcraft College Library
Madison Heights	Madison Heights Public Library
Marquette	Northern Michigan University Olson Library
Monroe	Monroe County Library System
Mount Clemens	Macomb County Library
Mount Pleasant	Central Michigan University Library
Muskegon	Hackley Public Library
Olivet	Olivet College Library
Petoskey	North Central Michigan College Library
Port Huron	Saint Clair County Library
Rochester	Oakland University Kresge Library
Saginaw	Hoyt Public Library
Sault Ste. Marie	Lake Superior State College Kenneth Shouldice Library
Traverse City	Northwestern Michigan College Mark Osterlin Library
University Center	Delta College Learning Resources Center
Warren	Warren Public Library Arthur J. Miller Branch
Wayne	Wayne Oakland Federated Library System
Ypsilanti	Eastern Michigan University Library

MICRONESIA

Ponape, E. Caroline Islands	Community College of Micronesia Library

MINNESOTA

Bemidji	Bemidji State University A. C. Clark Library
Collegeville	Saint John's University Alcuin Library
Duluth	Duluth Public Library
Mankato	Mankato State University Memorial Library
Minneapolis	Anoka County Library
	Hennepin County Libraries
	Minneapolis Public Library
	University of Minnesota Law School Library
	University of Minnesota REGIONAL DEPOSITORY Wilson Library
Moorhead	Moorhead State University Library

Morris	University of Minnesota, Morris Rodney Briggs Library	Fulton	Westminster College Reeves Library
Northfield	Carleton College Library	Jefferson City	Lincoln University Inman E. Page Library
	Saint Olaf College Rolvaag Memorial Library		Missouri State Library
Saint Cloud	Saint Cloud State University Learning Resources Center		Missouri Supreme Court Library
Saint Paul	Hamline University School of Law Library	Joplin	Missouri Southern State College Library
	Minnesota Historical Society Library	Kansas City	Kansas City Public Library
			Rockhurst College Greenlease Library
	Minnesota State Law Library		University of Missouri at Kansas City
	Saint Paul Public Library		General Library
	University of Minnesota Saint Paul Campus Library		University of Missouri at Kansas City
	William Mitchell College of Law Library		Leon E. Bloch Law Library
Saint Peter	Gustavus Adolphus College Library	Kirksville	Northeast Missouri State University Pickler Memorial Library
Stillwater	Stillwater Public Library	Liberty	William Jewell College Charles F. Curry Library
Willmar	Crow River Regional Library		
Winona	Winona State University Maxwell Library	Maryville	Northwest Missouri State University Wells Library

MISSISSIPPI

		Rolla	University of Missouri-Rolla Curtis Laws Wilson Library
Cleveland	Delta State University W. B. Roberts Library	Saint Charles	Lindenwood Colleges Margaret Leggat Butler Library
Columbus	Mississippi University for Women John Clayton Fant Memorial Library	Saint Joseph	Saint Joseph Public Library
Hattiesburg	University of Southern Mississippi Joseph A. Cook Memorial Library	Saint Louis	Maryville College Library
			Saint Louis County Library
Jackson	Jackson State University Henry Thomas Sampson Library		Saint Louis Public Library
	Millsaps College Millsaps-Wilson Library		Saint Louis University Law Library
	Mississippi College School of Law Library		Saint Louis University Pius XII Memorial Library
	Mississippi Library Commission		U.S. Court of Appeals Eighth Circuit Library
	Mississippi State Library		University of Missouri at Saint Louis
Lorman	Alcorn State University Library		Thomas Jefferson Library
Mississippi State	Mississippi State University Mitchell Memorial Library		Washington University John M. Olin Library
University	University of Mississippi Law Library		Washington University Law Library
	University of Mississippi Library REGIONAL DEPOSITORY	Springfield	Drury College Walker Library
			Southwest Missouri State University Library

MISSOURI

		Warrensburg	Central Missouri State University Ward Edwards Library
Cape Girardeau	Southeast Missouri State University Kent Library		

MONTANA

Columbia	University of Missouri, Columbia Library	Billings	Eastern Montana College Library
	University of Missouri, Columbia Law Library	Bozeman	Montana State University Renne Library
Fayette	Central Methodist College George M. Smiley Library	Butte	Montana College of Mineral Science and Technology Library

Havre	Northern Montana College Library
Helena	Carroll College Library
	Montana Historical Society Library
	Montana State Library
	State Law Library of Montana
Missoula	University of Montana Maurene and Mike Mansfield Library REGIONAL DEPOSITORY

NEBRASKA

Blair	Dana College Dana-LIFE Library
Crete	Doane College Perkins Library
Fremont	Midland Lutheran College Luther Library
Kearney	Kearney State College Calvin T. Ryan Library
Lincoln	Nebraska Library Commission REGIONAL DEPOSITORY, in cooperation with University of Nebraska at Lincoln
	Nebraska State Library
	University of Nebraska-Lincoln College of Law Library
	University of Nebraska-Lincoln Don L. Love Memorial Library REGIONAL DEPOSITORY
Omaha	Creighton University Alumni Memorial Library
	Creighton University Law Library
	Omaha Public Library W. Dale Clark Library
	University of Nebraska at Omaha University Library
Scottsbluff	Scottsbluff Public Library
Wayne	Wayne State College U.S. Conn Library

NEVADA

Carson City	Nevada State Library
	Nevada Supreme Court Library
Las Vegas	Clark County Library District
	University of Nevada at Las Vegas James Dickinson Library
Reno	National Judicial College Law Library
	Nevada Historical Society Library
	University of Nevada Library REGIONAL DEPOSITORY
	Washoe County Library

NEW HAMPSHIRE

Concord	Franklin Pierce Law Center Library
	New Hampshire State Library
Durham	University of New Hampshire Library
Hanover	Dartmouth College Library
Henniker	New England College Danforth Library
Manchester	Manchester City Library
	New Hampshire College H. A. B. Shapiro Memorial Library
	Saint Anselm's College Geisel Library
Nashua	Nashua Public Library

NEW JERSEY

Bayonne	Bayonne Free Public Library
Bloomfield	Bloomfield Public Library
Bridgeton	Cumberland County Library
Camden	Rutgers University, Camden Camden Library
	Rutgers University, Camden School of Law Library
Convent Station	College of Saint Elizabeth Mahoney Library
East Brunswick	East Brunswick Public Library
East Orange	East Orange Public Library
Elizabeth	Free Public Library of Elizabeth
Glassboro	Glassboro State College Savitz Learning Resource Center
Hackensack	Johnson Free Public Library
Irvington	Free Public Library of Irvington
Jersey City	Jersey City Public Library
	Jersey City State College Forrest A. Irwin Library
Lawrenceville	Rider College Franklin F. Moore Library
Madison	Drew University Rose Memorial Library
Mahwah	Ramapo College Library
Mount Holly	Burlington County Library
New Brunswick	New Brunswick Free Public Library
	Rutgers University Alexander Library
Newark	Newark Public Library REGIONAL DEPOSITORY
	Rutgers, The State University John Cotton Dana Library
	Rutgers, The State University Law School Justice Henry E. Ackerson Law Library
	Seton Hall University School of Law Library
Passaic	Passaic Public Library
Pemberton	Burlington County College Library
Phillipsburg	Phillipsburg Free Public Library
Plainfield	Plainfield Public Library
Pomona	Stockton State College Library

Princeton	Princeton University Library
Randolph Township	County College of Morris Sherman H. Masten Learning Resource Center
Rutherford	Fairleigh Dickinson University Messler Library
Shrewsbury	Monmouth County Library Eastern Branch
South Orange	Seton Hall University McLaughlin Library
Teaneck	Fairleigh Dickinson University Teaneck/Hackensack Campus Library
Toms River	Ocean County College Learning Resources Center
Trenton	New Jersey State Library
	Trenton Free Public Library
Union	Kean College of New Jersey Nancy Thompson Library
Upper Montclair	Montclair State College Harry A. Sprague Library
Wayne	Wayne Public Library
West Long Beach	Monmouth College Guggenheim Memorial Library
Woodbridge	Free Public Library of Woodbridge

NEW MEXICO

Albuquerque	University of New Mexico REGIONAL DEPOSITORY General Library
	University of New Mexico Medical Center Library
	University of New Mexico School of Law Library
Hobbs	New Mexico Junior College Pannell Library
Las Cruces	New Mexico State University Library
Las Vegas	New Mexico Highlands University Donnelly Library
Portales	Eastern New Mexico University Golden Library
Santa Fe	New Mexico State Library REGIONAL DEPOSITORY
	New Mexico Supreme Court Law Library
Silver City	Western New Mexico University Miller Library

NEW YORK

Albany	Albany Law School Library
	New York State Library REGIONAL DEPOSITORY
	State University of New York at Albany University Library
Auburn	Seymour Library
Bayside	Queensborough Community College Library

Binghamton	State University of New York at Binghamton Glenn G. Bartle Library
Brockport	State University of New York at Brockport Drake Memorial Library
Bronx	Fordham University Library
	Herbert H. Lehman College Library
	New York Public Library Mott Haven Branch
	State University of New York Maritime College Stephen B. Luce Library
Brooklyn	Brooklyn College Library
	Brooklyn Law School Library
	Brooklyn Public Library
	Polytechnic Institute of New York Spicer Library
	Pratt Institute Library
	State University of New York Downstate Medical Center Library
Buffalo	Buffalo and Erie County Public Library
	State University of New York at Buffalo Charles B. Sears Law Library
	State University of New York at Buffalo Lockwood Memorial Library
Canton	Saint Lawrence University Owen D. Young Library
Cheektowaga	Cheektowaga Public Library Reinstein Memorial Branch
Corning	Corning Community College Arthur A. Houghton Jr. Library
Cortland	State University of New York, College at Cortland Memorial Library
Delhi	State University Agricultural and Technical College Library
Douglaston	Cathedral College Library
East Islip	East Islip Public Library
Elmira	Elmira College Gannett Tripp Learning Center
Farmingdale	State University of New York at Farmingdale Library
Flushing	Queens College Paul Klapper Library
Garden City	Adelphi University Swirbul Library
Geneseo	State University of New York at Geneseo Milne Library
Greenvale	Long Island University B. Davis Schwartz Memorial Library

Hamilton	Colgate University Everett Needham Case Library Reference Department	Plattsburgh	State University College at Plattsburgh Benjamin F. Feinberg Library
Hempstead	Hofstra University Library	Potsdam	Clarkson College of Technology Harriet Call Burnap Memorial Library
	Hofstra University School of Law Library		State University College at Potsdam
Ithaca	Cornell University Library		Frederick W. Crumb Memorial Library
	Cornell Law Library		
	New York State College of Agriculture and Human Economics	Poughkeepsie	Vassar College Library
	Albert R. Mann Library	Purchase	State University of New York, College at Purchase Library
Jamaica	Queens Borough Public Library	Rochester	Rochester Public Library
	Saint John's University Library		University of Rochester Rush Rhees Library
	Saint John's University School of Law Library	Saint Bonaventure	Saint Bonaventure University Friedsam Memorial Library
Kings Point	U.S. Merchant Marine Academy Library	Saratoga Springs	Skidmore College Library
Long Island City	Fiorello H. LaGuardia Community College Library	Schenectady	Union College Schaffer Library
Mount Vernon	Mount Vernon Public Library	Southampton	Southampton College Library
New Paltz	State University College at New Paltz	Staten Island	Wagner College Horrmann Library
	Sojourner Truth Library	Stony Brook	State University of New York at Stony Brook
New York City	Cardoza Law School Library		Main Library
	City University of New York City College Library	Syracuse	Onondaga County Public Library
	College of Insurance Library		Syracuse University Library
	Columbia University Libraries		Syracuse University William C. Ruger Law Library
	Columbia University School of Law Library	Troy	Troy Public Library
	Cooper Union for the Advancement of Science and Arts Library	Uniondale	Nassau Library System
		Utica	Utica Public Library
	Medical Library Center of New York		SUNY College of Technology Library
	New York Law Institute Library	West Point	U.S. Military Academy Cadet Library
	New York Law School Library	White Plains	Pace University Law School Library
	New York Public Library Astor Branch	Yonkers	Sarah Lawrence College Library
	New York Public Library Lenox Branch		Yonkers Public Library Getty Square Branch
	New York University Elmer Holmes Bobst Library	Yorktown Heights	Mercy College Library
	New York University Law Library		
	U.S. Court of Appeals Second Circuit Library		**NORTH CAROLINA**
	Yeshiva University Pollack Library	Asheville	University of North Carolina D. Hiden Ramsey Library
Newburgh	Newburgh Free Library	Boiling Springs	Gardner-Webb College Dover Memorial Library
Niagara Falls	Niagara Falls Public Library	Boone	Appalachian State University Library
Oakdale	Dowling College Library		
Oneonta	State University College at Oneonta	Buies Creek	Campbell University Carrie Rich Memorial Library
	James M. Milne Library	Chapel Hill	University of North Carolina at Chapel Hill
Oswego	State University College at Oswego Penfield Library		Wilson Library REGIONAL DEPOSITORY

Chapel Hill	University of North Carolina Law Library	Winston-Salem	Forsyth County Public Library
Charlotte	Public Library of Charlotte and Mecklenburg County		Wake Forest University Z. Smith Reynolds Library

Chapel Hill	University of North Carolina Law Library
Charlotte	Public Library of Charlotte and Mecklenburg County
	Queens College Everett Library
	University of North Carolina at Charlotte Atkins Library
Cullowhee	Western Carolina University Hunter Library
Davidson	Davidson College Library
Durham	Duke University School of Law Library
	Duke University William R. Perkins Library
	North Carolina Central University Law Library
	North Carolina Central University James E. Shepard Memorial Library
Elon College	Elon College Iris Holt McEwen Library
Fayetteville	Fayetteville State University Charles W. Chestnutt Library
Greensboro	North Carolina Agricultural and Technical State University F. D. Bluford Library
	University of North Carolina at Greensboro Walter Clinton Jackson Library
Greenville	East Carolina University J. Y. Joyner Library
Laurinburg	Saint Andrews Presbyterian College DeTamble Library
Lexington	Davidson County Public Library
Mount Olive	Mount Olive College Moye Library
Murfreesboro	Chowan College Whitaker Library
Pembroke	Pembroke State University Mary H. Livermore Library
Raleigh	Department of Cultural Resources Divison of State Library
	North Carolina State University D. H. Hill Library
	North Carolina Supreme Court Library
	Wake County Public Library
Rocky Mount	North Carolina Wesleyan College Library
Salisbury	Catawba College Library
Wilmington	University of North Carolina at Wilmington William M. Randall Library
Wilson	Atlantic Christian College Clarence L. Hardy Library

Winston-Salem	Forsyth County Public Library
	Wake Forest University Z. Smith Reynolds Library

NORTH DAKOTA

Bismarck	North Dakota State Library
	North Dakota Supreme Court Law Library
	State Historical Society of North Dakota Research and Reference Library
	Veterans' Memorial Public Library
Dickinson	Dickinson State College Stoxen Library
Fargo	Fargo Public Library
	North Dakota State University Library
	REGIONAL DEPOSITORY, in cooperation with University of North Dakota Chester Fritz Library
Grand Forks	University of North Dakota Chester Fritz Library
Minot	Minot State College Memorial Library
Valley City	Valley City State College Library

OHIO

Ada	Ohio Northern University J. P. Taggart Law Library
Akron	Akron-Summit County Public Library
	University of Akron Bierce Library
	University of Akron School of Law Library C. Blake McDowell Law Center
Alliance	Mount Union College Library
Ashland	Ashland College Library
Athens	Ohio University Library
Batavia	University of Cincinnati at Batavia Clermont General and Technical College Library
Bluffton	Bluffton College Musselman Library
Bowling Green	Bowling Green State University Library
Canton	Malone College Everett L. Cattell Library
Chardon	Geauga County Public Library
Cincinnati	Public Library of Cincinnati and Hamilton County
	University of Cincinnati Central Library
	University of Cincinnati College of Law Marx Law Library

Cleveland	Case Western Reserve University Freiberger Library	Steubenville	Public Library of Steubenville and Jefferson County
	Case Western Reserve University Franklin Thomas Backus School of Law Library	Tiffin	Heidelberg College Beeghly Library
	Cleveland Heights–University Heights Public Library	Toledo	Toledo-Lucas County Public Library
	Cleveland Public Library		University of Toledo College of Law Library
	Cleveland State University Cleveland-Marshall College of Law Joseph W. Bartunek III Law Library	Westerville	University of Toledo Library Otterbein College Courtright Memorial Library
	Cleveland State University Library	Wooster	College of Wooster Andrews Library
	John Carroll University Grasselli Library	Youngstown	Public Library of Youngstown and Mahoning County
	Municipal Reference Library		Youngstown State University William F. Maag Library
Columbus	Capital University Law School Library		
	Capital University Library	**OKLAHOMA**	
	Ohio State University Libraries	Ada	East Central Oklahoma State University Linscheid Library
	Ohio Supreme Court Law Library		
	Public Library of Columbus and Franklin County	Alva	Northwestern Oklahoma State University Library
	State Library of Ohio REGIONAL DEPOSITORY	Bartlesville	U.S. Department of Energy Bartlesville Energy Research Center Library
Dayton	Dayton and Montgomery County Public Library	Bethany	Bethany Nazarene College R. T. Williams Library
	University of Dayton Roesch Library	Durant	Southeastern Oklahoma State University Library
	Wright State University Library	Edmond	Central State University Library
Delaware	Ohio Wesleyan University L. A. Beeghly Library	Enid	Public Library of Enid and Garfield County
Elyria	Elyria Public Library	Langston	Langston University G. Lamar Harrison Library
Findlay	Findlay College Shafer Library		
Gambier	Kenyon College Library	Muskogee	Muskogee Public Library
Granville	Denison University Libraries William Howard Doane Library	Norman	University of Oklahoma Libraries Bizzell Memorial Library
Hiram	Hiram College Teachout-Price Memorial Library		University of Oklahoma Law Library
Kent	Kent State University Libraries	Oklahoma City	Metropolitan Library System
Marietta	Marietta College Dawes Memorial Library		Oklahoma City University Library
Marion	Marion Public Library		Oklahoma Department of Libraries REGIONAL DEPOSITORY
Middletown	Miami University at Middletown Gardner-Harvey Library	Shawnee	Oklahoma Baptist University Library
New Concord	Muskingum College Library	Stillwater	Oklahoma State University Library REGIONAL DEPOSITORY
Oberlin	Oberlin College Library		
Oxford	Miami University at Oxford King Library	Tahlequah	Northeastern Oklahoma State University John Vaughan Library
Portsmouth	Portsmouth Public Library		
Rio Grande	Rio Grande College and Community College Jeanette Albiez Davis Library	Tulsa	Tulsa City-County Library System
			University of Tulsa College of Law Library
Springfield	Warder Public Library		University of Tulsa McFarlin Library
Steubenville	College of Steubenville Starvaggi Memorial Library		

Weatherford	Southwestern Oklahoma State University Al Harris Library	Coraopolis	Robert Morris College Library
		Doylestown	Bucks County Free Library Center County Branch
	OREGON	East Stroudsburg	East Stroudsburg State College Kemp Library
Ashland	Southern Oregon State College Library	Erie	Erie County Library System
Corvallis	Oregon State University Library	Greenville	Thiel College Langenheim Memorial Library
Eugene	University of Oregon Law Library	Harrisburg	State Library of Pennsylvania REGIONAL DEPOSITORY
	University of Oregon Library	Haverford	Haverford College Magill Library
Forest Grove	Pacific University Harvey W. Scott Library		
Klamath Falls	Oregon Institute of Technology Learning and Resources Center	Hazleton	Hazleton Area Public Library
		Indiana	Indiana University of Pennsylvania Rhodes R. Stabley Library
La Grande	Eastern Oregon College Walter M. Pierce Library	Johnstown	Cambria County Library System Glosser Memorial Library
McMinnville	Linfield College Northup Library	Lancaster	Franklin and Marshall College Fackenthal Library
Monmouth	Western Oregon State College Library	Lewisburg	Bucknell University Ellen Clarke Bertrand Library
Portland	Lewis and Clark College Aubrey R. Watzek Library	Mansfield	Mansfield State College Library
	Library Association of Portland	Meadville	Allegheny College Lawrence Lee Pelletier Library
	Northwestern School of Law Paul L. Boley Law Library	Millersville	Millersville State College Helen A. Ganser Library
	Portland State University Library REGIONAL DEPOSITORY	Monessen	Monessen Public Library
	Reed College Library	New Castle	New Castle Public Library
	U.S. Department of Energy Bonneville Power Administration Library	Newton	Bucks County Community College Library
Salem	Oregon State Library	Norristown	Montgomery County–Norristown Public Library
	Oregon Supreme Court Library	Philadelphia	Drexel University Library
	Willamette University College of Law Library		Free Library of Philadelphia
	Willamette University Main Library		Saint Joseph's University Drexel Library
	PENNSYLVANIA		Temple University Paley Library
Allentown	Muhlenberg College Haas Library		Temple University Law Library
Altoona	Altoona Area Public Library		Thomas Jefferson University Scott Memorial Library
Bethel Park	Bethel Park Public Library		U.S. Court of Appeals Third Circuit Library
Bethlehem	Lehigh University Libraries Linderman Library #30		University of Pennsylvania Biddle Law Library
Blue Bell	Montgomery County Community College Learning Resources Center		University of Pennsylvania Library
		Pittsburgh	Allegheny County Law Library
Bradford	University of Pittsburgh at Bradford Bradford Campus Library		Carnegie Library of Pittsburgh
			Carnegie Library of Pittsburgh Allegheny Regional Branch
Carlisle	Dickinson College Boyd Lee Spahr Library		Duquesne University Law Library
	Dickinson School of Law Sheeley-Lee Law Library		La Roche College John J. Wright Library
Cheyney	Cheyney State College Leslie Pinckney Hill Library		U.S. Department of Interior Bureau of Mines Library
Collegeville	Ursinus College Myrin Library		University of Pittsburgh Hillman Library

Pittsburgh	University of Pittsburgh Law Library
Pottsville	Pottsville Free Public Library
Reading	Reading Public Library
Scranton	Scranton Public Library
Shippensburg	Shippensburg State College Ezra Lehman Memorial Library
Slippery Rock	Slippery Rock State College Bailey Library
Swarthmore	Swarthmore College Library
University Park	Pennsylvania State University Libraries
Villanova	Villanova University Law School Pulling Law Library
Warren	Warren Library Association Warren Public Library
Washington	Washington and Jefferson College U. Grant Miller Library
Waynesburg	Waynesburg College Library
West Chester	West Chester State College Francis Harvey Green Library
Wilkes-Barre	King's College D. Leonard Corgan Library
Williamsport	Lycoming College Library
York	York College of Pennsylvania Schmidt Library
Youngwood	Westmoreland County Community College Learning Resources Center

PUERTO RICO

Mayaguez	University of Puerto Rico Mayaguez Campus Library
Ponce	Catholic University of Puerto Rico Encarnacion Valdes Library
	Catholic University of Puerto Rico School of Law Library
Rio Piedras	University of Puerto Rico General Library

RHODE ISLAND

Kingston	University of Rhode Island Library
Newport	U.S. Naval War College Library
Providence	Brown University John D. Rockefeller Jr. Library
	Providence College Phillips Memorial Library
	Providence Public Library
	Rhode Island College James P. Adams Library
	Rhode Island State Law Library
	Rhode Island State Library
Warwick	Warwick Public Library
Westerly	Westerly Public Library
Woonsocket	Woonsocket Harris Public Library

SOUTH CAROLINA

Charleston	Baptist College at Charleston L. Mendel Rivers Library
	The Citadel Daniel Library
	College of Charleston Robert Scott Small Library
Clemson	Clemson University Library
Columbia	Benedict College Payton Learning Resources Center
	South Carolina State Library
	University of South Carolina Thomas Cooper Library
Conway	University of South Carolina Coastal Carolina College Kimbel Library
Due West	Erskine College McCain Library
Florence	Florence County Library
	Francis Marion College James A. Rogers Library
Greenville	Furman University Library
	Greenville County Library
Greenwood	Lander College Larry A. Jackson Library
Orangeburg	South Carolina State College Miller F. Whittaker Library
Rock Hill	Winthrop College Dacus Library
Spartanburg	Spartanburg County Public Library

SOUTH DAKOTA

Aberdeen	Northern State College Library
Brookings	South Dakota State University H. M. Briggs Library
Pierre	South Dakota State Library
	South Dakota Supreme Court Library
Rapid City	Rapid City Public Library
	South Dakota School of Mines and Technology Devereaux Library
Sioux Falls	Augustana College Mikkelsen Library and Learning Resource Center
	Sioux Falls Public Library
Spearfish	Black Hills State College Library Learning Center
Vermillion	University of South Dakota I. D. Weeks Library
Yankton	Yankton College James Lloyd Library

TENNESSEE

Bristol	King College E. W. King Library

Chattanooga	Chattanooga-Hamilton County Bicentennial Library
	U.S. Tennessee Valley Authority Technical Library
Clarksville	Austin Peay State University Felix G. Woodward Library
Cleveland	Cleveland State Community College Library
Columbia	Columbia State Community College John W. Finney Memorial Library
Cookeville	Tennessee Technological University Jere Whitson Memorial Library
Jackson	Lambuth College Luther L. Gobbel Library
Jefferson City	Carson-Newman College Library
Johnson City	East Tennessee State University Sherrod Library
Knoxville	Public Libraries Knoxville-Knox County Lawson McGhee Library
	University of Tennessee at Knoxville James D. Hoskins Library
	University of Tennessee Law Library
Martin	University of Tennessee at Martin Paul Meek Library
Memphis	Memphis-Shelby County Public Library and Information Center
	Memphis State University Cecil C. Humphreys School of Law Library
	Memphis State University John W. Brister Library
Murfreesboro	Middle Tennessee State University Andrew L. Todd Library
Nashville	Fisk University Library
	Public Library of Nashville and Davidson County
	Tennessee State Law Library
	Tennessee State Library and Archives
	Tennessee State University Brown-Daniel Library
	Vanderbilt University Law Library
	Vanderbilt University Library
Sewanee	University of the South Jesse Ball duPont Library

TEXAS

Abilene	Abilene Christian University Margaret and Herman Brown Library
	Hardin-Simmons University Rupert and Pauline Richardson Library

Arlington	Arlington Public Library
	University of Texas at Arlington Library
Austin	Texas State Law Library
	Texas State Library REGIONAL DEPOSITORY
	University of Texas at Austin Perry-Castañeda Library
	University of Texas at Austin Lyndon B. Johnson School of Public Affairs Library
	University of Texas at Austin Tarlton Law Library
Baytown	Lee College Library
Beaumont	Lamar University Mary and John Gray Library
Brownwood	Howard Payne University Walker Memorial Library
Canyon	West Texas State University Cornette Library
College Station	Texas Agricultural and Mechanical University Library
Commerce	East Texas State University Library
Corpus Christi	Corpus Christi State University Library
Corsicana	Navarro College Gaston T. Gooch Library
Dallas	Bishop College Zale Library
	Dallas Baptist College Vance Memorial Library
	Dallas Public Library
	Southern Methodist University Fondren Library
	University of Texas Health Science Center—Dallas Library
Denton	North Texas State University Library
Edinburg	Pan American University Library
El Paso	El Paso Public Library
	University of Texas at El Paso Documents and Maps Library
Fort Worth	Fort Worth Public Library
	Texas Christian University Mary Couts Burnett Library
Galveston	Rosenberg Library
Houston	Houston Public Library
	North Harris County College Learning Resource Center
	Rice University, Fondren Library
	South Texas College of Law Library
	University of Houston at Clear Lake City Library
	University of Houston Library

Houston	University of Houston School of Law Library	Ogden	Weber State College Stewart Library
Huntsville	Sam Houston State University Library	Provo	Brigham Young University Harold B. Lee Library
Irving	Irving Public Library System		Brigham Young University J. Reuben Clark Law Library
Kingsville	Texas Arts and Industries University Jernigan Library	Salt Lake City	University of Utah Eccles Health Sciences Library
Laredo	Laredo Junior College Harold R. Yeary Library		University of Utah Law Library
Longview	Nicholson Memorial Public Library		University of Utah Marriott Library
Lubbock	Texas Tech University Library REGIONAL DEPOSITORY		Utah State Library
	Texas Tech University School of Law Library		Utah State Supreme Court Law Library

UTAH

Cedar City	Southern Utah State College Library
Ephraim	Snow College Lucy A. Phillips Library
Logan	Utah State University REGIONAL DEPOSITORY Merrill Library and Learning Resources Center

VERMONT

Burlington	University of Vermont Bailey Library
Castleton	Castleton State College Calvin Coolidge Library
Johnson	Johnson State College John Dewey Library
Lyndonville	Lyndon State College Samuel Reed Hall Library
Middlebury	Middlebury College Egbert Starr Library
Montpelier	Vermont Department of Libraries
Northfield	Norwich University Library
South Royalton	Vermont Law School Library

VIRGIN ISLANDS

Saint Croix	Florence Williams Public Library
Saint Thomas	College of the Virgin Islands Ralph M. Paiewonsky Library
	Enid M. Baa Library and Archives

VIRGINIA

Alexandria	Department of the Navy Library Office of the Judge Advocate General
Arlington	George Mason University School of Law Library
Blacksburg	Virginia Polytechnic Institute and State University Carol M. Newman Library
Bridgewater	Bridgewater College Alexander Mack Memorial Library
Charlottesville	University of Virginia REGIONAL DEPOSITORY Alderman Library
	University of Virginia Arthur J. Morris Law Library
Chesapeake	Chesapeake Public Library
Danville	Danville Community College Learning Resources Center
Emory	Emory and Henry College Kelly Library

Texas (continued)

Marshall	Wiley College Thomas Winston Cole Sr. Library
Nacogdoches	Stephen F. Austin State University Steen Library
Plainview	Wayland Baptist University Van Howeling Memorial Library
Richardson	University of Texas at Dallas Library
San Angelo	Angelo State University Porter Henderson Library
San Antonio	Saint Mary's University Academic Library
	San Antonio College Library
	San Antonio Public Library
	Trinity University Library
	University of Texas at San Antonio Library
San Marcos	Southwest Texas State University Library
Seguin	Texas Lutheran College Blumberg Memorial Library
Sherman	Austin College Arthur Hopkins Library
Texarkana	Texarkana Community College Palmer Memorial Library
Victoria	Victoria College/University of Houston Victoria Campus Library
Waco	Baylor University Moody Memorial Library
Wichita Falls	Midwestern University Moffett Library

Fairfax	George Mason University Fenwick Library		Cheney	Eastern Washington University JFK Library
Fredericksburg	Mary Washington College E. Lee Trinkle Library		Ellensburg	Central Washington University Library
Hampden-Sydney	Hampden-Sydney College Eggleston Library		Everett	Everett Public Library
Hampton	Hampton Institute Huntington Memorial Library		Olympia	Evergreen State College Daniel J. Evans Library
Harrisonburg	James Madison University Madison Memorial Library			Washington State Law Library
Hollins College	Hollins College Fishburn Library			Washington State Library REGIONAL DEPOSITORY
Lexington	Virginia Military Institute Preston Library		Port Angeles	North Olympic Library System Port Angeles Branch
	Washington and Lee University University Library		Pullman	Washington State University Library
	Washington and Lee University Wilbur C. Hall Law Library		Seattle	Seattle Public Library
Martinsville	Patrick Henry Community College Library			University of Washington Libraries
Norfolk	Norfolk Public Library			University of Washington Marian Gould Gallagher Law Library
	Old Dominion University Library			U.S. Court of Appeals 9th Circuit Library
	U.S. Armed Forces Staff College Library		Spokane	Gonzaga University School of Law Library
Petersburg	Virginia State University Johnston Memorial Library			Spokane Public Library
Quantico	Federal Bureau of Investigation Academy Library		Tacoma	Tacoma Public Library
	U.S. Marine Corps Schools James Carson Breckinridge Library			University of Puget Sound Collins Memorial Library
				University of Puget Sound School of Law Library
Reston	Department of the Interior Geological Survey National Center Library		Vancouver	Fort Vancouver Regional Library
			Walla Walla	Whitman College Penrose Memorial Library

West Virginia

Richmond	U.S. Court of Appeals Fourth Circuit Library		Athens	Concord College Library
	University of Richmond Boatwright Memorial Library		Bluefield	Bluefield State College Hardway Library
	University of Richmond Law School Library		Charleston	Kanawha County Public Library
	Virginia Commonwealth University James Branch Cabell Library			West Virginia Library Commission
				West Virginia Supreme Court Law Library
	Virginia State Law Library		Elkins	Davis and Elkins College Library
	Virginia State Library		Fairmont	Fairmont State College Library
Roanoke	Roanoke Public Library		Glenville	Glenville State College Robert F. Kidd Library
Salem	Roanoke College Library		Huntington	Marshall University James E. Morrow Library
Williamsburg	College of William and Mary Marshall-Wythe Law Library		Institute	West Virginia College of Graduate Studies Library
	College of William and Mary Swem Library			West Virginia State College Drain-Jordan Library
Wise	Clinch Valley College John Cook Wyllie Library		Morgantown	West Virginia University Library REGIONAL DEPOSITORY
			Salem	Salem College Library
			Shepherdstown	Shepherd College Ruth Scarborough Library

Washington

Bellingham	Western Washington University Mabel Zoe Wilson Library		Weirton	Mary H. Weir Public Library

WISCONSIN

Appleton	Lawrence University Seeley G. Mudd Library
Beloit	Beloit College Col. Robert H. Morse Library
Eau Claire	University of Wisconsin–Eau Claire William D. McIntyre Library
Fond Du Lac	Fond Du Lac Public Library
Green Bay	University of Wisconsin–Green Bay Library Learning Center
La Crosse	La Crosse Public Library
	University of Wisconsin–La Crosse Murphy Library
Madison	Madison Public Library
	State Historical Society Library REGIONAL DEPOSITORY, in cooperation with University of Wisconsin–Madison
	University of Wisconsin–Madison Memorial Library
	University of Wisconsin–Madison Law Library
	Wisconsin State Law Library
Milwaukee	Alverno College Library/Media Center
	Medical College of Wisconsin, Inc. Todd Wehr Library
	Milwaukee County Law Library
	Milwaukee Public Library REGIONAL DEPOSITORY
	Mount Mary College Library
	University of Wisconsin–Milwaukee Library
Oshkosh	University of Wisconsin–Oshkosh Forrest R. Polk Library
Platteville	University of Wisconsin–Platteville Karrmann Library
Racine	Racine Public Library
Ripon	Ripon College Library
River Falls	University of Wisconsin–River Falls Chalmer Davee Library
Stevens Point	University of Wisconsin–Stevens Point Learning Resources Center
Superior	Superior Public Library
	University of Wisconsin–Superior Jim Dan Hill Library
Waukesha	Waukesha Public Library
Wausau	Marathon County Public Library
Whitewater	University of Wisconsin–Whitewater Harold Anderson Library

WYOMING

Casper	Natrona County Public Library
Cheyenne	Wyoming State Law Library
	Wyoming State Library REGIONAL DEPOSITORY
Gillette	George Amos Memorial Library
Laramie	University of Wyoming Coe Library
	University of Wyoming Law Library
Powell	Northwest Community College Library
Riverton	Central Wyoming College Library
Rock Springs	Western Wyoming College Library
Sheridan	Sheridan College Library

INFORMATION U.S.A.

Published in 1983 by Viking Press, this comprehensive, 990-page directory of federal agencies by Matthew Lesko provides the names, addresses, and telephone numbers of more than 10,000 government offices and 3,000 data experts.

The book's detailed descriptions of the many separate functions of each government agency (under **Major Sources of Information**), plus the names and telephone numbers of each agency's experts in every area of its activities, enables you to talk directly with people who can help you zero in on systems of records containing information you need. It may even enable you to obtain desired data without the time and expense of filing an FOIA request.

For example, under **Federal Trade Commission** (in the book's listing of Agencies, Boards, Commissions, Committees, and Government Corporations) the directory describes in detail and provides addresses and contact telephone numbers for:

- Administrative Law Judges
- Advertising Substantiation
- Advisory Opinions
- Antitrust Compliance
- Children's Advertising
- Cigarette Advertising and Labeling
- Competition and Antitrust
- Compliance with Consumer Protection Orders
- Consumer Bibliography
- Consumer Dispute Resolution
- Consumer Leasing
- Credit Billing
- Credit Discrimination Complaints
- Creditors' Remedies
- Design Defects
- Energy and Product Information
- Equal Credit Opportunity
- Evaluation [of Consumer Protection]
- Fair Credit Reporting
- Finance Statistics (Contains a listing of more than 32 FTC economic and statistical reports and studies.)
- Food and Nutrition Advertising
- Franchising and Business Opportunities

- Freedom of Information Act Requests
- FTC Meetings (Phone number for recorded message detailing FTC meetings.)
- FTC News (Phone number for recorded message of latest FTC activities, findings, decisions, etc.)
- Funeral Industry
- Housing Problems
- Industry Analysis (Economic studies of individual industries and their trade practices, etc.)
- Insurance
- Land Sale Abuses
- Library
- Mobile Homes
- New Consumer Problems
- Occupational Deregulation
- Over-the-Counter Drug Advertising
- Point-of-Sale Practices
- Product Registration Numbers
- Publications (A listing of more than 40 FTC consumer publications—many free.)
- Public Funding of FTC [Hearings] Participants
- Public Records
- Regional Office [Consumer Protection] Programs
- Requests for Closed Meetings
- Standards and Certification
- Trade Regulation Rules and Industry Guides (A listing of more than 50 industry guides and guidelines.)
- Truth-in-Lending
- Warranties
- How Can the Federal Trade Commission Help You? (Contact telephone number and address for assistance in locating FTC information and resources.)

The above FTC listing, though impressive, is by no means atypical. The **Sources of Information** heading under Department of Agriculture lists 241 such sources; under Department of Defense, 232 "sources of information" are listed—all with detailed descriptions, addresses, and contact telephone numbers.

The book is priced at $19.95 and is available at many bookstores.

FOI SERVICES, INC.

Foi services, inc., is a private corporation that specializes exclusively in Freedom of Information Act services. It is the first and largest service of its type in the United States. Many law firms, corporations, management consultants, academic researchers, and other professionals use foi services, inc., to meet their FOIA needs.

Although the company does not ordinarily work with private individuals, it may do so on occasion after telephone arrangements have been made.

The company provides several services:

- It submits FOIA requests for clients on the basis of a letter or phone call. Its broad experience in filing FOIA requests and its knowledge of how to phrase

a request can often save clients the expense of its fee in reduced records search fees charged by federal agencies.
- By submitting requests in its own name, rather than the name of a client, foi services, inc., prevents the subject of your request from learning that you are the requester, although the filing of a request will still tip them off that *someone* is interested in their corporation, its products, or its particular government problems.
- Foi services publishes weekly logs that list the names of FOIA requesters and the subjects of their requests. As of January 1984, FOIA logs were published listing all FOIA requests filed with the U.S. Food and Drug Administration (FDA) and the Environmental Protection Agency (EPA). The company's FOI logs are provided on an annual subscription basis; individual sample copies are provided free to prospective clients. A sample from the foi services' weekly log of FOIA requests received by the FDA may be found on the following page.

You don't have to study our *FOI Log* excerpt for very long to appreciate the extent of FOIA uses by business, nor do you have to consider for very long whether you would want to be informed of any FOIA requests regarding your own firm.

A regular reading of the various FOI logs can suggest information that you might want to acquire. If someone wants to know about a company or product affecting your industry, then maybe you'd better find out about it too. Also, the weekly log isn't a bad place to learn "FOIA-speak"—the language of FOIA request writing.

At this writing, *FOI Log* yearly subscription rates range from $230 to $360, depending upon the agency whose requests you're interested in learning about. Foi services' telephone alert service will inform you the same day that an FOIA request about any specified company or product is received by any of the federal agency FOIA offices that it monitors. The telephone alert service is $280 per year in addition to the basic *FOI Log* subscription rate.

- In cooperation with **CompuServe Information Service**, foi services operates the **FOI:Newsline**, a computer database containing many federal documents and other data that may be accessed via a client's computer terminal and a **modem** device for computer communication over telephone lines.

Charges for filing FOIA requests are $20 for subscribers and $25 for nonsubscribers.

To obtain more complete information about services provided by the company, write on your company or professional letterhead to:

John E. Carey, Manager
foi services, inc.
12315 Wilkins Avenue
Rockville, MD 20852
301-881-0410

foi services FDA Freedom of Information Log

Issue Date: 8 July 1983

This publication lists the Freedom of Information Act requests received by the U.S. Food and Drug Administration.

Official Title: "FOI Services — FDA Freedom of Information Log." Published weekly by FOI Services, Inc., 12315 Wilkins Avenue, Rockville, Maryland 20852. Phone 301/881-0410. All Rights Reserved. Subscription Rates: $340 per year, $180 for additional copies mailed in the same envelope. ISSN 0161-7044

CONTROL #	RECVD DUE	ACTION OFFICES	REQUESTER/FIRM	SUBJECT
F83019193	0627 0712	HFR8100	KANE, M MEADOW FRESH FARMS INC	INFO RE MEADOW FRESH FARMS INC SALT LAKE CITY UT
F83019194	0627 0712	HFO420	YOUNG, P BELL PHARMACAL CORP	EIR 483 &/OR QAP FOR FRESH LABS INC WARREN, MI; NEWTRON PHARMACEUTICALS INC BOHEMIA NY
F83019195	0627 0712	HFO420	GRISSO, T CARGILL	EIR FOR LAUHOFF BUSHNELL Il 1970-1983; CENTRAL SOYA GIBSON CITY IL; A E STALEY DECATUR IL 1982-1983; ETC
F83019196	0627 0712	HFN804	SANCHEZ, J MEDICAL SCIENCES INT'L	ESTABLISHMENTS & PRODUCT BOOKLET
F83019197	0627 0712	HFV236	MASON, M MASON, M	NDA PERTAINING TO STDS RE MASOTEN (DYLOX)
F83019215	0627 0712	HFN5	FOI SERVICES INC 30230 FOI SERVICES INC	LIST OF APRVD NDA'S FOR ANITMICROBIAL PRODS, CHEMICAL CLASS & INDICATIONS FOR WHICH THEY ARE APRVD
F83019216	0627 0712	HFN5	BESTA, G BERLEX LABORATORIES	CURRENT LIST OF THOSE DRUGS WHICH HAVE BEEN DESIGNATED AS ORPHAN DRUGS
F83019217	0627 0712	HFN5	MCILHENNY, H PFIZER PHARM	ALL DISC REVIEWERS' COMMENTS & APRVD LBLG FOR ZANTAC (RANITIDINE HYDRO-CHLORIDE
F83019218	0627 0712	HFN5	FRANCO, D FRANCO, D	INFO RE FERTILITY DRUG KLOMED
F83019219	0627 0712	HFN5	KUTTNER, B KUTTNER, TONER & DIBENEDETT	ANY/ALL INFO FDA MAY HAVE ACCUMULATED RE POSSIBLE RELATIONSHIP BTWN BIRTH CONTROL PILLS & PITUITARY TUMORS; ETC
F83019220	0627 0712	HFN5	RUBILLO, T LAWRIMORE, RUBILLO & LUMPKI	ANY ADV DRUG RCTN RPTS RE AMINOPHYLLINE (THEOPHYLLINE) & THEO-DUR
F83019221	0627 0712	HFN5	HUGHES, J CALBIOCHEM-BEHRING	LIST OF ALL HOLDERS OF DMF FOR COMPOUND L-5-HYDROXYTRYPTOPHAN
F83019222	0627 0712	HFN804	D'ARCO, J MILES PHARMACEUTICAL	TRANS OF ALLERGY PNL MTG 6/23/83

XIII

PERSONAL, FAMILY, AND FINANCIAL FORMS

80 Direct Mail Forms

In the Forms section of this volume you will find four forms that you can use either to reduce or increase the amount of direct mail advertising material you receive. With the more than 30 billion pieces of junk mail being fed into the postal system each year (more than 150 pieces for every man, woman, and child in the United States), you may feel you've had enough.

One California man, Vincent Napoli, of Cupertino, considered junk mail so obnoxious that he turned it as a weapon of spite against a neighbor with whom he was engaged in a dispute over location of a front-yard tree. The neighbor received more than 7,000 pieces of junk mail during the year following Napoli's attempt to bury him under unwanted paper—until the neighbor learned the identity of the "culprit" and filed a criminal complaint. Napoli soon found himself in jail facing a one-year term and $5,000 fine.

The Direct Mail Marketing Association (DMMA), which has nearly 2,000 members (and to which two of this chapter's forms are addressed), advertises that it wants to clean up the storm of unwanted junk mail, but a DMMA spokesperson admitted during 1979 that no more than 200 of the association's members have agreed to voluntarily remove consumers' names from mailing lists upon request.

As things now stand, you can't expect much help from the federal government in stemming the tide of junk mail. Unsolicited advertising material generates about one-third of the Post Office Department's yearly income, and, of course, many Congressmen send junk mail too. But the Privacy Protection Study Commission, created under provisions of the Privacy Act of 1974, has suggested that direct mailers should advise customers if they regularly rent or sell mailing lists and should give customers the option of having their names removed from such lists.

If you want to receive **less** direct mail advertising material, complete and mail a photocopy of Form 80.1 (page F587) to the Direct Mail Marketing Association and mail photocopies of Form Letter 80.2 (page F589) to any companies that you believe may sell or rent mailing lists containing your name.

Finally, make several photocopies of Form 80.3 (page F591) so that when you order anything by mail you can attach one of the small notices requesting that your name not be added to the seller's mailing lists.

If you'd like to receive **more** direct mail advertising material, complete and mail a photocopy of Form 80.4 (page F593).

81 Medical Forms

We have provided four medical forms that may prove useful, one of which we hope you will use. That one is, of course, the Uniform Donor Card (Form 81.1, page F595).

UNIFORM DONOR CARD

The Uniform Donor Card conforms to the federal Uniform Anatomical Gift Act and is regarded by law as the donor's last will and testament. Carrying the card in your wallet or purse, as against signing and filing a form with your other important papers, is important because for organs to be transplanted with any chance of survival they must be removed almost at once. For example, kidneys must be removed almost immediately after death and donated corneas must be removed within six hours after death—hardly time for notification of next of kin or discovery of a form tucked away with your insurance papers and other documents.

In all, about twenty-five kinds of organs and tissues can be used for medical transplants. Hearts, kidneys, and corneas are the ones we hear most about, but blood vessels, pituitary and parathyroid glands, and, increasingly, livers and lungs are also being transplanted.

During 1982, more than 5,000 kidney transplants were performed and at any moment in time there were about 15,000 people who could accept transplants if organs were available. With increased success in reducing organ rejection by a recipient's immune system, it's believed that many, if not all, of these people could be helped if the frequency of use of the Uniform Donor Card were to be increased by 20 percent.

SPECIAL MEDICAL POWER OF ATTORNEY

If you have children, complete and use a photocopy of the Special Medical Power of Attorney (Form 81.2, page F597) every time you leave your child or children in the care of a friend or neighbor who may need to authorize emergency surgery or other medical care. Each power of attorney can be made to remain valid for as long as you like; therefore, you'll need to provide only one form for each person who cares for your children.

LIST OF EMERGENCY NAMES AND NUMBERS

Give a photocopy of the list on page F599 (Form 81.3) to anyone in whose care you leave your children, and place a copy near your telephone when leaving chil-dren at home in the care of a babysitter, relative, or friend. Send it with your children whenever they travel or visit with friends for several days.

AUTHORIZATION TO INSPECT MEDICAL RECORDS

The chances are great that whenever you make an insurance claim for illness or injury that you will be asked (perhaps required) to give permission for an insurance company representative to inspect your medical records at a hospital or the office of your physician.

Release forms usually presented by insurance companies include provisions that, in effect, give the company access to all your medical records, at any time and for all time in the future. Here's an excerpt from a typical insurance company medical information release:

> I hereby authorize any licensed physician, medical practitioner, hospital, clinic or other medical or medically related facility, insurance company, the Medical Information Bureau or other organization, institution, or person that has any knowledge of me, or my dependents, or has attended, or who will hereafter attend me, to give the _____ Insurance Company any such information.

Considering such companies' demonstrated failure to properly hold such information confidential, and considering hospitals' and physicians' demonstrated failure to safeguard such information from improper disclosure, you may want to reject the form given to you by an insurance company representative and instead use a photocopy of the Authorization to Inspect Hospital Medical Records (Form 17.1, page F137) or the Authorization to Inspect Physician's Medical Records (Form 17.2, page F139). Both of these forms are related to Section III of this volume, Accidents and Injuries.

The use of either form won't cure a physician's office assistant or hospital records custodian of sloppy procedures, nor will it guarantee that he or she won't hand over your records to a friendly insurance company representative, but it might help. At the very least, it should put everyone on notice that you are assertive in protecting your privacy and are the sort of person who just might take aggressive legal action if your privacy is violated.

Given the nature of the two medical records release forms, it would be extremely difficult for your insurance company, or anyone else's insurance company, to use improperly disclosed information against you in litigation, because to reveal possession of such information during a trial would be to leave the improper discloser of such information wide open to a substantial lawsuit. Our legal consultants point out, too, that your attorney could object to the introduction of any such information on the basis that it was improperly disclosed.

If your insurance company doesn't like either form, tell the company to see your lawyer. The forms do meet legal requirements for compliance with reasonable requests for access to medical records.

82 Rental Agreements

This chapter concerns itself with agreements that you can use for renting a friend's pickup (to carry building materials for a home-improvement project, for example) or for renting out your own car or pickup; for renting a friend's boat, motor, and trailer for a few days (or for renting out yours); and for renting, or renting out, almost any kind of personal property, such as scuba tanks, a post hole digger, a paint sprayer, or anything else.

You may read the provisions of the agreements and swear to "never a renter or rentee be." (I suppose that, strictly speaking, a "rentee" is one who or that which is rented.) But even so, just remember that most of the scary clauses merely put into print the practical effect of various laws (bailment, for example—see page 456) that are on the books anyway.

Before you rent out your car or boat, read your insurance policies and talk with your insurance agent because **your coverage may be null and void** while either is rented out. Remember, too, that if you merely **lend** personal property, such as a car, truck, or boat, you are normally only required (should a liability suit involving an accident get to court) to exercise **ordinary** care in the maintenance of such property. But if you *rent* out such property, you will probably be required to show that you have exercised **extraordinary** care in its maintenance to be absolved of legal liability in the event of an accident related to a defect or fault of the car, truck, or boat.

In *some* states, with respect to renting out a car or truck or boat, extraordinary care has been shown to be ordinary, good maintenance, plus a state safety inspection immediately prior to turning the vehicle over to the renter.

Make photocopies of Forms 82.1, 82.2, and 82.3 (pages F601–F606) for actual use, returning originals to the pocket at the back of the book.

83 Real Estate Forms

In addition to the wide range of leases, rental agreements, and rental applications provided in Section II of this volume (Landlord–Tenant, beginning on page 27), we have provided you with six ready-to-use real estate forms that will be useful whether you happen to own a house, cabin, or cottage that you occasionally rent out or whether you own several rental properties for regular income purposes. These forms are much less complex than the Section II forms, but just as useful. They are as follows:

- Rent Receipt (Form 83.1, page F607)

- Notice of Rent Due (Form 83.2, page F609)
- Notice of Overdue Rent (Form 83.3, page F611)
- Notice to Quit Premises (Form 83.4, page F613)
- Furnishings Inspection and Inventory (Form 83.5, page F615)
- Property Management Agreement (Form 83.6, page F619)

As with other forms in this book, make photocopies for actual use and return the originals to the pocket at the back of the book.

84 Employment Application

Employment Application—Form 84.1 on page F621 —meets federal fair employment practices requirements as well as the needs of many employers. It's typical of most applications that you, as a prospective employee, will be asked to complete, and it will serve as a good work sheet for pulling together dates, places, and names you should be able to provide. If you complete a photocopy of this application before visiting employment agencies or personnel offices, you will be able to quickly fill in any form you're given.

Age

It's not legal for a prospective employer to ask you your date of birth, but it is legal to ask if you are between 18 and 65 years of age because of certain employment and insurance limitations that apply to workers under 18 and over 65.

Health

Prospective employers may ask if you have any health problems or physical limitations that might affect your ability to perform the job for which you are applying. You may not be presented with a list of illnesses and disabilities and then be asked to check those that you have or may have had in the past.

Police Record

You may be asked if you have been convicted of any crime. You may not be asked if you have been arrested for any crime.

Psychological Tests

The U.S. Supreme Court (*Griggs* v. *Duke Power Company*) has determined that you may be asked to take certain psychological tests as a condition to employment if it can be reasonably shown that such tests are job-related.

Lie Detectors

There is no federal prohibition of the use of polygraphs (lie detectors) for preemployment screening, and only a handful of states prohibit their use. On the basis of the intrusiveness and unreliability of the polygraph, the Privacy Protection Study Commission has recommended "that Federal law be enacted or amended to forbid an employer from using a polygraph or other truth-verification equipment to gather information from an applicant or employee."

For the present, at least, preemployment screening is the single greatest area of polygraph use, with about 300,000 preemployment polygraph examinations being administered each year.

Race and Religion

An employer may not ask your race or religion unless either is clearly job-related, as in the case of a black or oriental model or job applicant for certain positions with a religious institution.

Sex

An employer may not ask your sex unless it is clearly job-related, as in the case of a male model or actor or salesperson of women's clothing. Generally, credit applications can legally require the disclosure of much more personal information than can employment applications—which says something, although I'll leave it to you to decide exactly what, about our hierarchy of values.

After Employment

You may be asked all sorts of questions after employment that would not be permitted prior to employment: about your health (because of company-sponsored health insurance), about dependents (because of federal income tax deductions), and even about race (because of an employer's need to complete federal forms designed to obtain data regarding compliance with affirmative action and equal employment opportunity programs).

There is no federal law that requires an employer to allow you to inspect your personnel file, although many employers do give employees this right.

85 Bills of Sale

We have provided two ready-to-use forms each for the sale of a boat and the sale of personal property:

- **Bill of Sale of Boat**—Individual Buyer and Seller (Form 85.1, page F625)
- **Bill of Sale of Boat**—Joint Buyers and Sellers (Form 85.2, page F627)

and

- **Bill of Sale of Personal Property**—Individual Buyer and Seller (Form 85.3, page F629)
- **Bill of Sale of Personal Property**—Joint Buyers and Sellers (Form 85.4, page F631)

If joint sellers are selling to an individual, use the joint buyer/seller form and cross out the provision for the joint buyer. For an individual owner selling to joint buyers, also use the joint form and cross out the provision for a joint seller.

BILL OF SALE OF BOAT

Many states have boat title, registration, and licensing requirements that stipulate that any bill of sale for a boat be notarized. Some states don't require notarization, but you can use either boat bill of sale in any state by having it notarized.

It's a good idea to have the bill of sale notarized anyway in case the new owner ever wants to register and title the boat in a state that does require a notarized bill of sale.

BILL OF SALE OF PERSONAL PROPERTY

Obviously, you won't be required by law to have a bill of sale notarized for the purchaser of a used chain saw or a sewing machine, but you should consider it for the sale of an outboard motor, firearm, stereo equipment, or other type of item that is often stolen so that the buyer can prove ownership in the event he or she ever wants to sell or insure the item or prove ownership if it is stolen.

In some states you may be **required** to have a bill of sale notarized for the transfer of a boat, trailer, motor home, or firearm.

If you sell anything used in a business, or for which you have taken a tax deduction, be sure to make an extra photocopy of the bill of sale for your business and tax records.

The forms for selling your own car are simple enough —a bill of sale, a couple of receipts, and a federal odometer mileage statement warranting that you haven't turned the mileage indicator back or driven the car without recording mileage at all.

But selling your own car usually isn't the kind of thing you do for fun. You sell it yourself because you believe you can come out better financially that way than by trading with a dealer in the kind of bargain where he gives you *wholesale* price for your car and you pay him *retail* price for his.

There are many people who would rather buy a used car from an individual than from a dealer. They'll consider buying on price because they believe that individuals sell for less than do dealers (often true) and because they believe they can drive a better bargain with an individual owner than with a dealer—also often true.

Prospects are interested in buying from individuals because they feel they can learn something about the car's use and maintenance background that they can't learn from a dealer. They have nearly all seen auto transport trailers on the highway hauling used cars to or from an auction, or have seen one used car towing another, dealer plates hanging crookedly on the back of each, the lead car driven into the afternoon sun by a bottom-of-the-rung salesman for some brightly lighted used-car lot somewhere along "automobile strip" in the nearest big city up ahead. Nobody feels comfortable about buying a car like that.

So, in selling your own car you have a lot going for you. When prospects see a cleaned-up used car on a lot, swept out, vacuumed, and polished, with the engine steam cleaned and the 100,000-mile interior liberally sprayed with aersol "new-car smell," it's somehow not believable. But when you show a clean car and step out of the house in fresh clothes into a neat, well-kept front yard, that makes most used-car buyers feel safe.

Most people who buy used cars from individuals are looking for a better than average car—better running, better looking, and one that has had better care. They also often hope to save a bit of money. You shouldn't have any trouble selling for *several* hundred dollars *less* than they'd have to pay a dealer—while at the same time receiving $300 or $500 or $700 *more* than a dealer would pay you.

Getting your car ready to sell yourself will probably require about two weekends' effort, plus possibly a few dollars for mechanical or body work—work that would have to be done anyway if you kept the car. Getting top dollar for your car will depend more upon these things than upon anything else. With a clean car you don't have to know much about selling cars; your car will sell itself. (There are, of course, cars that don't

deserve fixing up before sale, but we'll assume that yours is in better shape than that.)

To aid you in this process we'll provide a shopping list describing in some detail most of the items you'll need for making your car look new. The secret word to making your car look attractive is **original**—like it was when it came from the factory.

MECHANICAL CONDITION

Obviously, the car must start easily, idle quietly, accelerate and run smoothly, shift smoothly, steer well, and stop when you apply the brakes. These things it **MUST** do.

Engine

If your car's engine doesn't operate smoothly, it should be tuned. If you're not ready to tackle this job yourself, ask around among your friends and neighbors and check with a used-car lot to learn who does their tune-up work. Watch for tune-up specials in the newspaper, but make sure the price includes parts and labor. Not long ago, for example, Gem Chevrolet in Willimatic, Connecticut, ran a V-8 tune-up "special" for $48.48, "plus tax, parts and labor."

Make sure any suspicious noises are eliminated. These will turn off a prospect all out of proportion to their actual menace. Squeaky belts might merely be loose. They can be easily tightened, or you can ask the tune-up mechanic to do it (probably for no charge). A few squirts of *belt dressing* will do the job if tightening them doesn't completely cure the problem.

Change the oil and oil filter. **Everybody** checks the oil to see if it's clean, even though **everybody** knows you'll have just changed it and its cleanliness doesn't mean a thing. Also top off the levels of transmission fluid, brake fluid, battery water, radiator water, windshield washer, etc.

Have the car greased to stop squeaks. Many shops that advertise tune-up specials also advertise "lube job" and oil change specials in the same ad and will quote you a "special special" if you have both done at the same time.

If a mechanic confirms that your car's engine is really hopeless, consider a "short block"—a rebuilt engine block with reconditioned or new crankshaft, rods, camshaft bearings, main and connecting rod bearings, pistons, pins, rings, timing chain, and other major and minor parts. In 1984, J. C. Whitney's price for a Chevrolet, 8-cylinder, 305 cc. "short block" was $549.00. There will also, of course, be a charge for installation. If this seems like a lot, it is, but remember your car would require this investment if you kept it to use. Before giving your money to Sears, though, get estimates from several local engine rebuilders and check with used-car dealers to find out who does their engine rebuilding.

Transmission

If a trustworthy mechanic confirms that your transmission needs work, ask a few used-car dealers who does their work. In many towns and cities there are individual mechanics, often semiretired and highly qualified, who do transmission and other overhaul work for car dealers. These mechanics almost always work in their home garage or basement and almost never advertise. You'll never find out about them unless you ask used-car dealers. If used-car dealers can't steer you to someone, check classified ads for *nonfranchised*, local transmission repair shops.

Brakes

If your brakes pull left or right, or grab or squeal, or just plain don't work, they may only need adjusting. If the brake pedal is too low or slowly sinks when you maintain pressure on it, you may need brake fluid or possibly a rebuilt master cylinder.

If inspection confirms that you need to have your car's brakes relined, watch for specials and check with used-car dealers. Remember that if a mechanic shows you your car's brake shoes and tells you that your lining is "half gone" on a 50,000-mile car, he's also telling you that you have half of it left—and that's a lot of remaining use.

Clutch

If you have a manual transmission, your clutch must not slip or grab. If it does, it may need adjustment or possible rebuilding. Back to used-car dealers again.

Shock Absorbers

Step on your front bumper and push down hard and fast. If the bumper comes back up and "bounces" a few times you could need new shock absorbers. Watch for specials in the newspaper.

Accessories

You must make sure that **everything** works perfectly: headlights, taillights, stop lights, backup lights, windshield wipers, windshield washers, turn indicators, horn, windows, interior lights, instrument lights, glove compartment light, trunk light, glove compartment latch and lock, heater, defroster, air conditioner, radio, stereo, interior door locks, clock, cruise control, dimmer switch, etc. Everything must work.

The money-saving word to remember when it comes to most replacement parts is **rebuilt**. Almost everything that's available in rebuilt condition is nearly as good as, and sometimes even better than, new. And it's a lot cheaper!

EXTERIOR APPEARANCE

Exterior appearance makes your car's first impression. In reacting to your car's exterior appearance, prospective buyers will be affected by the condition of the body—paint, chrome, windows, tires, etc.—and what

I call exterior details—bumpers, license plate frames, license plates, wheels, hubcaps, etc. More on all of these items later.

Engine Compartment

The engine compartment is a logical place to begin improving your car's sales appearance, if for no other reason than the fact that it's a messy job. In some locations you can have an engine compartment steam cleaned. This is quick and obviously easy. One disadvantage in steam cleaning an engine compartment is that the high-pressure steam is likely to blast off a lot of paint and may leave things looking worse than before.

One excellent way to do the job is to use a can or two of *Gunk Engine Brite* (see our shopping list— Form 86.1, page F633). First locate a coin-op car wash that provides hot, high-pressure, soapy water controlled by a coin box timer similar to that on a laundromat washing machine. Plan to clean your car's engine during an off hour when there will be few other customers.

Remove the car's air cleaner and cover the carburetor and distributor with plastic bags tied to keep out the cleaner and high-pressure hot water. Let the cleaner soak on the engine for fifteen minutes or so and then go over any greasy parts with a brush and additional cleaner.

While the engine is soaking, squirt a bit of cleaner on any areas on the underside of the car that are covered with thick, old dust and dirt-laden grease. Next, turn the hot, soapy water into the car's wheel wells to wash out any caked mud and grease. Thoroughly wash off the bottom of the car; then turn the hot water on the engine to rinse off the *Gunk Engine Brite*. Inspect. Add more Gunk if necessary, soaking a few minutes and rinsing with high-pressure hot water again. Brush and rinse the battery and battery terminals.

Wipe off the engine in a sort of gross way with old towels, remove the plastic bags, replace the air cleaner, and drive home.

Now that the engine is clean and mostly dry, inspect the fan belt, alternator belt, and air conditioner compressor drive belt to see if they're worn or shabby looking. Check hoses and wiring for the same thing, and make a note to buy any needed replacements.

You'll *finish* the engine compartment in a few days, after it's thoroughly dry and you're ready to install any replacement parts.

Trim Replacement

Replace any missing exterior trim, chrome strips, hubcaps, etc. Replace rusty dealer name or "I'd Rather Be Fishin'" license plate frames with plain chrome ones. Wheels should be covered with original-type full wheel covers—usually obtainable at large junkyards.

Replace all broken light lenses and burnt-out bulbs. Light lenses and light frames can also be found at junkyards. Scrape off all bumper stickers and window stickers. Leave the inspection sticker until you have the car inspected a day or two before you plan to advertise it.

Replace both wiper blades unless they're near perfect. No use having streaky wipers if your prospect has to test drive the car on a rainy day or decides to test the washers.

Tires

Tires should not look worn out or nearly worn out. Check filling stations, tire companies, and junkyards for good used tires. Don't use recaps—they look sleazy, and if you'd try that, what else might you try to get away with?

Check newspaper ads (usually on the sports pages) for tire sales, and visit a few dealers to ask if they have any "blems" (slightly blemished, but perfectly safe tires) for sale. New tires are a definite sales plus even if they're not radials—but they **must** be whitewalls. Save the best of your old tires for use as a spare.

Mag Wheels

OFF! Unless you're selling a sports car, mag wheels should be replaced with factory-type wheels from a junkyard, large filling station, or tire company. New-car dealers will charge you at least twice as much as a tire company for new wheels. Mag wheels will scare off a family car buyer who'll believe you may have been "hot rodding" the car or that you are a "hot-rod-type" driver. Wash, dry, and spray any replacement wheels glossy black before mounting tires.

Trailer Hitch

OFF! Many prospects will fear you've strained the transmission and engine by towing a heavy trailer.

Body

Any dents should probably be fixed and painted. Any rusted-through areas **must** be fixed and painted. Check with car dealers for the names of body shops. If it's impossible because of time or money to have a dent repaired, get several written estimates to show prospective buyers. Explain that your car's price is as low as it is because you haven't had time to get the dents taken care of. Offer to have them repaired by adding the average cost of the estimates to the price of the car (they'll never take you up on it).

Paint

If polishing compound and auto polish won't bring your car's paint to life, you'll probably need to have it painted. Have it done in the same color to eliminate complications. You can increase the quality of a $100 paint job to that approaching a $200 paint job by removing everything that you can from the car— headlight trim, grille, taillight and side light trim, antennas, windshield wiper arms and blades, etc.— before you deliver the car to be painted. What you can't remove, mask yourself. You'll do it more carefully than the piecework-paid painter's assistant who would otherwise do the job.

Check with used-car dealers to get the names of small, local paint shops. There's one franchise operation we know of which does a pretty good job on its cheapest paint job; that's *Maaco*. Quality can vary with the franchise operator. Make sure they wipe down the car thoroughly **after** sanding and just **before** painting to help eliminate dust particles.

Windows

Scrape off all stickers except for the inspection sticker. Replace any cracked or gravel-chipped windows. Check junkyards for replacements.

Trunk

Take everything out of the trunk and vacuum it thoroughly. If you don't have a vacuum cleaner that you can use for this, check filling stations and coin-op car washes. You can also rent industrial vacuum cleaners at rental companies.

Next, paint the entire interior of the trunk using flat, grey/white, brown/white, or black/white "spackle" paint made especially for this purpose (see page F633). While the paint is drying, remove rust from all the tire tools and paint glossy black. Paint the spare wheel if you haven't done that.

If your car's trunk carpet is shoddy looking, use the old carpet as a pattern for a new carpet. If your trunk has no carpet, use wrapping paper to make one. Most auto upholstery shops carry several types of trunk carpet to meet the needs of auto dealers who realize the importance of installing fresh carpet.

You can "tack" the carpet in place with a light coat of spray adhesive to keep it from sliding around. As with everything else you do to make your car ready to sell, the carpet and trunk paint should look "original."

Vinyl Top

You may be able to get by with a thorough cleaning using a commercial vinyl top cleaner followed by a vinyl top restorer. If that doesn't do the job, buy a can of spray vinyl top paint in a matching color from an auto paint supply house or an upholstery shop. If you spray the top, you'll have to plan on masking and draping the entire car. Use inexpensive, plastic painter's drop cloths held in place with masking tape. Do the job out of the wind and follow directions carefully.

If your car's vinyl top is too far gone to paint, ask used-car dealers to suggest someone who can replace it for you.

Engine Compartment (Round Two)

We could give you a long list of details to take care of, but we won't. Just inspect the engine compartment and clean and paint anything that needs cleaning or painting. The metalwork just aft of the grille, which acts to stabilize both the grille and the radiator (and upon which the hood latch is also often mounted), will probably be rusty in several places. Since this is one of the first things a prospect sees when raising the hood, it should look "original."

Don't try to touch up rusty spots. Using green Scotch-Brite kitchen scouring pads and fine emery cloth, remove rust spots and blend your sanding into the surrounding paint. Go over the entire area with a green Scotch-Brite scouring pad so that new paint will adhere.

Next, check around the battery and everyplace else you can see for rust. Check between the grille and radiator and the back of the radiator for missing paint. If the air cleaner is rusty and pitted, you'll have to take it off and remove old paint with paint remover, neutralize the paint remover, sand pitted areas, and repaint.

Before you paint anything in the engine compartment, you'll need to mask and drape with rags everything that doesn't require painting. There will probably be one or two decals on the metal surface you've sanded that bridge the grille and radiator. Carefully mask these, using a razor blade to precisely trim the tape to match the edges of the decals.

To paint these areas (unless they were not originally black), use *Krylon Semi-Flat Black* (stock No. 1613) from a spray can (see our shopping list—Form 86.1, page F633). Any painted parts of the engine itself can also be painted with *Krylon* spray paint made in thirteen different colors and shades to match those of most auto manufacturers.

After paint has had time to dry, wipe down everything (except the surfaces you've just painted) with *Armorall Protectant* (see our shopping list). *Armorall* is manufactured for vinyl care, but it will make your engine's wiring, hoses, accessories, etc., look fresh and new, it won't collect dust, and it won't harm anything it touches.

Before you close the hood, lightly coat the (cleaned) battery terminals with *Vaseline* and lubricate the hood mechanism and hood latch. Remove masking tape.

Exterior Details

Now that the interior of your car's trunk and engine compartment are immaculate, missing trim and wheel covers replaced, any needed bodywork done (or estimates obtained), window and bumper stickers removed, license plate frames added or replaced, cracked or broken light lenses replaced, burned-out bulbs replaced, wiper blades replaced, worn tires replaced, and the car polished and waxed—it's ready for the detail work.

Oil all door hinges and lubricate all door latches and the trunk's hinges and latch. Wipe down all rubber weather stripping lightly with *Armorall*. This will restore their original color and new look. Wipe down any rubber or plastic bumper trim or inserts with *Armorall*. This will restore their new color and remove any excess auto polish and chrome cleaner.

We suggest that you **not** paint the sides of your car's tires with tire dressing. This makes them look *too* new—too much like you've gone to a lot of effort to "dress up" the car—when you actually want them to look as though they have had tender loving care since the first day you owned them.

Another problem with tire dressing, apart from being a lot of trouble to apply, is that you will need to keep your car looking immaculate *every* day until you sell it, and successive coats of tire dressing will soon become too thick.

Do this instead: after your tires are scrubbed and dry, wipe them down with *Armorall*, taking care to keep it away from the white portion of the sidewalls. *Armorall* will make your tires look fresh and new without calling attention to itself and can be reapplied as often as necessary.

Paint wheel weights to match wheels. Clean and polish the license plate. Spray any parts of the car's underside that show with *Krylon* semiflat black.

Spray the wheel wells, which you previously washed out when you cleaned the car's engine, with *Krylon* semiflat black or with spray-on black undercoating. Without your buyer quite realizing it, black, clean-looking wheel wells will add a lot to the cared-for appearance of your car.

Remove filling station and garage oil-change stickers from the left front door edge.

INTERIOR APPEARANCE

First, remove the car's rear seat to clean out coins, peanuts, gum wrappers, ball-point pens, supermarket checkout receipts, and the lost report card. Vacuum the area beneath the rear seat, and thoroughly sweep out and vacuum the remainder of the car's interior, using a long, thin nozzle attachment to reach into remote areas under the front seats. Replace the rear seat. If the rear seat belts have been squished down behind the seat, be sure to leave these out for use by the new owner.

Place a round, soft brush accessory on the vacuum cleaner hose and gently vacuum the car's headliner, both sides of the sun visors, the instrument panel, and the underside of the panel. Empty out, vacuum, and **leave empty** the glove compartment (the car, in every respect, should look "ready to go" to the new buyer). Vacuum the rear deck beneath the back window and vacuum the seats, door arm rests, and (pulling each out to its full length) all seat belts. Next, wipe everything down with a clean, soft, slightly damp cloth.

General Interior Inspection

Check to make sure that everything works so that you can pick up replacement parts next time you use the car. Check interior lights, instrument panel lights, glove compartment light, glove compartment latch and lock, seat-belt and brake warning lights, heater, defroster, air conditioner, radio, horn, cartridge or cassette player, seat-belt retractors, seat-belt buckles, seat adjustment, interior door locks, turn indicators, cruise control, window adjustments, tilt wheel, windshield wipers and washers, etc.

Remove, thoroughly scrub out, dry, and replace all ashtrays. Don't use them again while showing your car. Carry a small "bean bag" ashtray if you have to, but don't use the car's ashtrays.

Steering Wheel

There's nothing like a "yucky" steering wheel to turn off a prospective buyer. Use a strong cleaner like *409* to get the wheel pristine so that it will look and feel clean when a prospect test drives your car. If your steering wheel has one of those "leather" wraparound covers, remove it. The car should be o-r-i-g-i-n-a-l.

For detail cleaning use *Q-Tips* and an old, soft toothbrush. The auto polishing compound you bought for your car's paint is excellent for cleaning steering wheel chrome. Toothpaste is an excellent polish for plastic parts and for "fragile chrome," such as chrome-plated plastic. (Toothpaste is also great for polishing plastic watch crystals like new. Just thought you might like to know.)

Instrument Panel

You've already vacuumed the panel's nooks and crannies. Now wipe everything with a clean, soft, slightly damp cloth. Use *Q-Tips* to clean mininooks and crannies. Use black paste shoe polish to make air conditioner outlet louvers and other black plastic parts look new. (Later on, you'll make a small-area test application of *Armorall* to the plastic padded portion, but not now.)

Seats

Your car's seats must look perfect. Shabby seats are about as bad a minus as worn-looking tires. If your car's vinyl, leather, or fabric seats are just dirty, clean them with upholstery cleaner. (*K-Mart* sells a combination fabric/vinyl/leather upholstery cleaner that will save you from having to buy several types.)

If a car's seats have reached the point of needing replacement, it's almost always just the driver's seat or a burn or tear in one of the other seats. The automobile trade word for what such seats need is "inserting."

Auto upholstery shops do inserting all the time for used-car dealers who know how much a worn-out looking driver's seat detracts from the sales potential of a car by making it seem as though the car has had hard use. In doing inserting, an upholstery shop will remove and replace only the fabric or vinyl portion of the seat that must be replaced. This is done with factory original material, and the work will almost always be invisible—and always a lot cheaper than complete reupholstering. As a matter of fact, inserting will probably cost less than a set of seat covers.

There are kits available (you've seen them advertised on TV) for supposedly making invisible repairs in torn or punctured vinyl. But there's a better way. In nearly every city worth its "automobile row" there is sure to be at least one "detailer." What a "detailer" is, is someone who goes around to used-car lots and does all of the things we've been telling you to do to get your car ready to sell. Well, almost everything. Like maids who "don't do windows," most detailers will tell you they "don't do engines."

So, if your car's vinyl seats need tear or puncture repair, call on a couple of used-car lots and ask who does their "detailing." When you've got a few names, make a couple of calls, describe what you need to have done, and set up an appointment—which will probably be at a large used-car lot. Don't ask for estimates over the phone.

Detailers usually work out of vans and carry every kind of cleaner, paint, polish, and wax; they are equipped with paint sprayers, vacuum cleaners, sewing machines, and most types of auto carpet, vinyl top material, and many kinds of vinyl and auto upholstery fabric. A good detailer with a well-established route will earn about $400 a day.

Seat Belts

Clean. Nothing will lose prospects faster than having your seat belts leave marks on their clothing. Clean them with upholstry cleaner and tie them to keep them extended until completely dry. Clean and polish buckles.

Carpet

Almost never will more than a small area of an auto's carpet need replacement—and that area will usually be on the front left side just aft of the "kick-pad" where the driver's heel has left its mark. Since wear in this area is common, many auto upholstery shops carry and can sew into place a slightly oversize "kick-pad" that will completely cover this wear.

If you've been using rubber protective mats since you purchased the car, it's carpet can probably be made new looking with little more than vacuuming and shampooing plus perhaps a bit of spot cleaning with a grease solvent.

Many sports cars have flat floor areas between the drive shaft tunnel, and matching new carpet can very easily be installed after being cut to fit the original carpet's pattern. Binding usually will not need to be sewn around the edges, and the cost will be slight because the small area requires very little carpet.

Finally, invest a few dollars in a set of new, factorylike rubber floor mats.

Doors

Wipe down all doors with a clean, soft, damp cloth. Clean any dirty areas with *409*. Clean and polish door handles and window cranks (or electric buttons). Clean door lock pulls and replace worn chrome with new door lock pulls. (We'll be back with *Armorall* later.)

Interior Painted Surfaces

Auto supply stores and, nationally, Sears carry small cans of spray paint to match most cars. You can use these to touch up interior surfaces; the only catch is that these spray paints don't come in shades that match your car's interior, nor do they come in the flat or semiflat finishes used in auto interiors. No matter.

At the store pick out a handful of colors that you think are very close to the right color. Hand the clerk a

$10 bill and tell him you'd like to take them outside to match your car's paint. You can almost always find a perfect or near-perfect match that way.

Here's how to spray "flat" with glossy paint. First give the area a very light coat and wait until it's just started to dry. Painters call this the "tack" coat. Next, hold the can far enough away from the surface so that the paint droplets are almost dry when they reach the surface. Apply several very light coats, waiting for each coat to dry before applying the next; it helps if the surface is warm or almost hot. You can use a hair dryer to accomplish this—but NOT while there are paint fumes in the air!

Whenever using a spray can, don't just hold the spray button down and wave the can around pointing the spray toward whatever you're trying to paint. Make each pass of the spray overlap the previous spray slightly. Stop spraying as the spray passes beyond the area you're painting, and start again only after your hand has begun moving back the other way. Alternate horizontal strokes with vertical strokes. If you were born with God-given spray can talent equal to a great surgeon's operating room technique, you can probably carry this off.

On the other hand . . . auto paint supply houses **do** custom mix flat and semiflat interior paints by factory formula to match your car's interior paint perfectly. But you'll need a paint sprayer and will have to mask and drape almost all of your car's interior to use them.

One area where you almost have to use this type of paint is on the uncarpeted metal rear deck of a station wagon. With many station wagons it's easier, almost cheaper—and a lot nicer looking—to obtain and fit auto carpeting that matches the station wagon's floor carpeting. Make a paper pattern and secure the carpet in place with spray adhesive. Don't forget to replace the carpet in the wagon's rear storage "well" if you add or replace rear-deck carpet.

Molded Interior Plastic

Door moldings, window frames, seat frames, under dash kick panels, rear decks, and instrument panels are almost always plastic in cars manufactured since the early 1970s. For restoring original color and appearance nothing works like *Armorall*!

You can also impart a new look to vinyl seats with *Armorall*, but it can make them "squeaky" and, for our taste, a bit too shiny. You can prevent much of the shiny look by rubbing seats with a soft, dry cloth immediately after applying the *Armorall* to remove most of it. Any remaining squeakiness will vanish in a day or two—possibly after your clothes have absorbed the surplus *Armorall*.

If your padded dash is faded, try a little *Armorall* in an inconspicuous area to see what happens. If it restores the original color and doesn't make the area too shiny, treat the entire padded portion of your instrument panel. If it's a bit too shiny, go over it thoroughly with a soft dry cloth to remove the excess *Armorall*.

Disaster Areas

Molded plastic trim and even vinyl seats can be made new looking by using spray *Mar-Hyde*. *Mar-Hyde* isn't always easy to find, but upholstery shops, used-car dealers, and auto paint supply houses in larger cities can usually steer you to a source. *Mar-Hyde* is available in spray cans in sixteen colors, and distributors can mix *Mar-Hyde* to match your car's interior **and** provide it to you in pressure cans for spray application. *Mar-Hyde* sounds too good to be true, but it does cover, does go on evenly, and does not crack, peel, or fade.

PRICING YOUR CAR

Don't make the mistake of checking dealers' ads in the newspaper and thinking you can ask that amount for your car. Well, you can **ask** it, but you probably won't get it. To begin with, a large dealer usually offers a 90-day warranty with maybe a longer 50–50 warranty. (You pay 50 percent and the dealer pays 50 percent of any needed parts and labor during the 50–50 warranty period.) A large dealer is also probably in a position to arrange quick financing and take a buyer's old car off his or her hands. You're probably not in a position to do any of these things. Beyond that, the price you see advertised is probably the dealer's **asking** price with room for a bit of negotiating.

By all means check ads, but check individuals' small classified ads too. Visit a new-car dealer and ask to look at the National Automobile Dealers Association (NADA) "blue book"(actually it's orange) to check the current price for your car. There will be several prices, depending upon condition.

Also visit a few used-car dealers to see what they're asking for cars like yours. Don't drive the car you're planning to sell. Few used-car salespeople were born yesterday.

Using these sources—ads, the "blue book," and visits to used-car dealers—you should have a pretty good idea of how to start figuring out a selling price for your car. Try halfway between the price asked by large dealers and the price asked by individuals advertising cars similar to yours.

You can't ignore competition since competition will affect the price you can get for your car. In fact, if there are many cars like yours advertised in your price range, you might be better off to wait a week or two until some of your competition is off the market before you advertise.

Never advertise a price in even thousands or ending in even hundreds. Check how car dealers do it—probably ending in 95. Never end a price in 99; it looks like you're trying to squeeze out the last cent. Go the car dealers one better: end your price in 75.

ADVERTISING AND SHOWING YOUR CAR

There are many ways you can advertise your car: by telling friends and co-workers; by putting up 3″ × 5″

cards on bulletin boards at work and school, in laundromats, in apartment-complex laundry rooms, etc.; by placing FOR SALE signs on your car; and by placing ads in newspapers.

You can also very effectively "advertise" your car by parking it in highly visible locations at shopping centers, movie parking lots, vacant filling stations (of which there are currently 80,000 in the U.S.), and other locations you can scout in your neighborhood or town. Big cities, small towns, and rural areas each offer unique opportunities.

We'll get back to displaying your car later, but first you'll want to place newspaper ads so they'll be working for you while you're displaying your car.

Usually the best place to advertise your car will be the newspaper in your town that carries the most classified ads. If your area has neighborhood or "shopper" newspapers, these are also likely places. Increasing numbers of "shopper" papers offer free classified advertising to individuals. For autos, Friday, Saturday, and Sunday are usually the best days.

Before writing an ad, read those appearing in the paper you're planning to advertise in and see what attracts you. Here are a few dealer ads:

```
'75 Dodge Dart, 4-door, 6-
cylinder, automatic transmis-
sion, factory air, power steer-
ing and brakes, white walls.
Very nice.            $2,695
```

```
'78 VW Scirroco, 4-speed, fac-
tory air, AM–FM, extra clean.
                     $4,595
```

```
'74 Mercury Comet, 2-door,
standard transmission, factory
air, new tires. Nice Car. $2,195
```

```
'65 Mustang, six-cylinder, three
speed, factory air, AM–FM.
Very clean.          $1,695
```

What's good about these ads? All state the price; none use abbreviations. All say that the car is very clean, very nice, excellent, etc.; none mention things you'd expect any car to have, such as radio, heater, etc. They don't end in even hundreds.

Could they be improved upon? Maybe, but perhaps not as much as you might think. Here's the Mercury Comet ad again, with a few underlined changes:

```
'74 Mercury Comet, 2-door, six-
cylinder,  economical  three-
speed, factory air, AM–FM.
Very clean.          $2,195
```

The original ad didn't mention the engine, which would make me suspect that it's probably eight-cylinder. If it were an eight and happened to be the small eight, one might say economical small eight. But saying economical three-speed is too much. The buyer knows whether he believes a three-speed is economical, and besides, a three-speed isn't *that* economical. A four-speed or a three-speed with overdrive would be economical.

Here are some ads placed by individuals:

```
MGB GT, 1973, good condition.
Very reasonable.     $2,300
            000-0000
```

What's the matter with this car that it's just in "good" condition? The seller has said nothing to make the car seem attractive. Either the price is reasonable or it isn't, but you don't have to tell the reader. $2,275 would be a better price.

```
'65 VW, new paint, clutch and
seat covers. $650.00 000-0000
```

The new paint job makes me wonder how much body work might be hidden. The new clutch and seat covers make the car seem to have had hard use. I *know* a '65 car has earned its right to have a new clutch and seat covers, but the seller would be better off saying something like "runs perfect" or "economical transportation" and not mentioning the clutch and seat covers.

```
Camaro, 1967, spoiler, mag
wheels.     $1,495 negotiable.
            000-0000
```

What size engine? Automatic or manual transmission? Factory air? What does the seller mean by "negotiable"? That he'll get $1,495 out of you if he can, but that if he can't, he'll take what he can get? Better to state a price that truly reflects the car's value.

Ford Galaxy 500. Fully loaded.
After 7 pm weekdays and all day
weekends.   000-0000

Why did the seller bother to tell us the make and model? We don't have to tell you what's wrong with this ad.

When writing ads don't mention items that raise more questions than they answer. **New transmission** makes the reader wonder **why** the car needed a new transmission. Pulling a heavy trailer? (Bad for the engine too.) "Tore up"? (Maybe "hot rodding" the car.) If a car has **two new tires**, what about the other two?

Mention items that will make the car *seem* desirable: **runs good, economical transportation, wife's car** (hell, maybe even **husband's car**), **can't be told from new** (if a very recent model), **very clean, very nice, excellent,** etc. And especially today, **uses economical regular gas.** If it's a wreck, **mechanic's special.** You can say something nice about almost *any* car.

Always state the price, but never add **firm** or **negotiable,** or state that it's an **asking price.** But I must admit that I've always liked the rather quaint way brokers' ads price yachts—"try $350,000."

Three-by-Five Cards

You can easily make many 3″ × 5″ "cards" by drawing lines on a piece of ordinary 8½″ × 11″ paper to represent four 3″ × 5″ cards. Then type whatever you want to say four times, once within each 3″ × 5″ space, so that you'll have a "master" from which you can photocopy four cards to place wherever you want to.

On a card you'll be able to say more than you might want to pay to say in a newspaper ad, but don't be tempted to single space your typing to squeeze in too many words. Single spaced ads aren't inviting to read.

Here's a sample card:

1979 Pontiac Grand Prix

    Small V-8, automatic transmission, power
steering, power brakes, factory air,
AM/FM/stereo cassette, tilt wheel, bucket
seats and more. Excellent radials. $4,195.

56,000 miles Immaculate Geoff: 686-7492

Window Sticker

Another effective way to help sell your car is to type up a factory-style "window sticker," listing the vehicle's engine type and size, plus all the accessories. Also list the price, mileage, condition, and your name and telephone number.

Leave room on the right side of the sticker to paste in the page for your car's make, year, and model from the National Automobile Dealers Association *Official Used Car Guide.* The *Guide* is published monthly and lists, among other things, the average trade-in price, average loan value, and average retail price for almost all cars, plus the average loan value and average retail price of most auto accessories and options, such as automatic transmission, air conditioning, power windows, stereo, sun roof, etc.

You can probably obtain a photocopy of the appropriate page of the *Guide* from a new car or used car dealer. If you've been looking at a new car to replace your present auto as soon as it's sold, or if you've recently bought a car, the salesman you dealt with will probably be willing to give you a copy of last month's *Guide.* Month-to-month prices often remain the same.

After you've typed your "master" sticker and pasted on the appropriate *Guide* page, make several dozen photocopies; one to place in your car's rear left-hand window and the remainder to use as "handouts" to people who stop by to look at your car (see our Sample Window Sticker on page 447).

On each *photocopy,* underline the average loan value and average retail price in red. Place a bright red dot opposite the price of each option and accessory included in your car.

FOR SALE Signs

Make three **FOR SALE** signs for your car. Use letters at least four inches high for **FOR SALE.** Under **FOR SALE** list your phone number in numbers at least two and a half inches high. You can obtain large stencils and heavy white illustration board from many office supply and art supply stores.

Place one sign more or less permanently inside your car on the far right side of the rear window. When displaying your car, place one sign on the outside of the right front window and another on the outside of the windshield on the right side. That way you can easily remove the "outside" signs whenever anyone test drives your car. Place those same signs in the same locations *inside* your car when you park it for any length of time.

Displaying Your Car

At some locations, such as large shopping-center parking lots, you can park your car in a highly visible place and leave it all day while you're at work. At night you can park your car as close to a movie entrance as possible—and under a strong light if there's one nearby.

For best results on weekends, stay with your car if you can to answer questions, offer to accompany prospective buyers on test drives, and give each prospect a "handout" copy of your window sticker.

If possible, stay with your car, but not IN it. Prospects who see you sitting in the car will often hesitate to approach you, thinking that you may be waiting for someone or might not want to be bothered.

When we've displayed cars in the past, we've waited in another, nearby auto and only approached prospects who seemed to be seriously looking at our car. If you wait in a nearby auto, you can also have an ice chest with something to drink, plus a sandwich or two—hardly appropriate items to keep in any car that's likely to be inspected from engine compartment to trunk.

Keep paper towels, window cleaner, and a whisk broom handy for quick cleanups after test drives.

Magic Words

If there's a magic phrase you can add to any sales pitch or advertisement, it's "Priced below loan value." That means that any buyer with good credit can finance the purchase of your car with no down payment at all.

As we mentioned above, you can determine a car's average loan value by checking the National Automobile Dealers Association (NADA) *Official Used Car Guide* for the year, make, and model of your car. The average loan value is usually about two-thirds of its average retail value.

Since "average retail value" tends to be a bit elevated (after all, dealers will be showing the book to prospective used car buyers to prove what a good deal they're offering) and because your price will be somewhat less than "average retail," you may find that the price you were planning to ask for is quite close to "loan value." Shaving your price just a bit to "loan" can make for a quick sale that could save you a lot of time and advertising expense.

JUST THE FACTS

People who look at your car and people who phone will have a lot of questions, many of which could be answered by reading your ad or window sticker. Legitimate questions you can expect are:

How many miles? The average owner drives a car 10,000 to 12,000 miles a year. If your four-year-old car has 40,000 to 50,000 miles on it, you have nothing to be defensive about. If the car has a lot of miles on it, say 80,000 during four years, then be sure to mention if they were mostly highway miles. *Now* is the time to mention a new transmission or overhauled engine.

What kind of mechanical condition is it in? Answer questions about mechanical condition by saying that it "runs very good" or "is very dependable" or "runs like new." Be careful about getting too specific because the prospect's next question might be, "Are you a mechanic?" and if you say you're not, then the buyer is likely to ask how come you know so much about the engine or clutch or transmission or whatever.

What kind of shape is the body in? Answer this by stating that it has no dents, no rust, has never been wrecked, etc., if true. If the body does have a dent, for example, get several estimates and say where the dent is and that you have estimates "averaging $85" but that you haven't had time to get it fixed. Be sure to mention that the reason the car is priced "so low" is because you haven't had time to get the dent fixed—and that you'll be happy to have it fixed for the additional cost of the average estimated expense if he or she buys the car (and no, you won't take off the estimated cost of the repair; you've already done that).

Are you the original owner? If you are, say so; if you're not, simply say "no"—period!

What kind of gas mileage does it get? This is a tough one. To avoid getting into an argument ("That sounds like awful good mileage to me. Are you sure you get that much?"), it's probably best to explain that the car is used in the city and on the highway and that your wife or husband sometimes drives it and that you haven't kept specific records.

Remind the caller that it's an economical six or an economical small eight and that it has an economical manual transmission, overdrive, etc. You can say more over the phone than you can convincingly say in an ad. Also, now you are responding to a *question*. If the car is a recent enough model to have a published EPA mileage rating, tell the caller what it is.

SHOWING YOUR CAR

Let your car sell itself. Don't try to be a used-car salesperson. Answer all questions truthfully. Whatever you do, don't talk too much. Remember that if your prospect starts finding fault with the car, that's because he or she *wants* it!

By all means, readily allow a prospect to drive your car—if only for a few minutes "because I have some other prospects coming to look at it." If you're selling a small sports car or a late-model subcompact, do the initial demonstration drive yourself, performance being a major concern of many first-time small-car buyers.

And, by all means, readily agree to let a prospect have his or her mechanic inspect the car—although only "after Monday because there are quite a few people coming to look at the car." Many prospects will be merely testing you when they ask this question, but when a prospect's mechanic does inspect your car, make arrangements to drive it there yourself and wait.

Be sure to park your car so that it's easy for your prospect to drive. Don't park it so that he or she must back it out of your driveway into the street, for example.

If you regularly park in your driveway, remove all traces of oil and grease from its surface. One drop of oil looks like a tablespoon and one tablespoon looks like a quart.

Wipe off your car daily while it's for sale. Keep it swept out, and make sure the windshield is clean. Also keep the car's gas tank full while showing the car. There's just something about a full gas tank. Like, did you *ever* notice how much better your car runs just after you've waxed it? Same thing.

OFFERS

You're standing there at the curb with the prospect. He drove the car with you, shook his head in slight disappointment when accelerating, but said nothing, and now, after bending down and sighting along the car's frame and asking, "Ever wrecked?" he turns to you and asks, "How much did you say you hoped to get for this car?"

"The price," you say, "is $4,675."

"Would you take $4,400?"

"Gee, I hadn't thought about that," you reply, reaching into the brown manilla envelope of the car's papers you've been carrying. "Why don't you fill out and sign this written offer for that amount, and I'll sure be glad to think about it. Here's a pen."

If you had said that you'd take $4,400, maybe he would ask you if you'd take $4,200. By inviting him to make a written offer, you have, in a way, asked him to put up or shut up. Most prospects who've been playing games will back away, but the nice thing about handing such a person a written offer to sign is that if they're sincere, you've given them a chance to show it. And who knows, if the car doesn't sell in two or three weeks, maybe you'll be glad to get $4,400.

The signed **Offer to Purchase Motor Vehicle** (Form 86.2, page F635) isn't binding upon you; it's the **prospect's** written offer to buy. In some jurisdictions the offer might not even be binding upon the prospect, but it looks very formal, legal, and binding and is an assertive, yet nonargumentative, way of calling the prospect's bluff—if that's what it is.

THE RULES OF THE GAME: *The game of buying and selling is pretty much a game with two sets of rules, and the "two-rule" formula especially applies to buying and selling cars.*

What we've outlined so far are guidelines from the rule book of selling. Here (forewarned is forearmed, remember) are a few excerpts from the rule book of buying, the rule book your prospect will probably be following:

1. *Wear old clothes; this will maybe make the seller think your low offer is really all you can afford to pay. Leave your gold Rolex at home, and don't arrive in a new car.*

2. *Don't get emotionally involved with the car; don't let your interest show. Like a hooker with a variable price, the seller is likely to add a few dollars if your enthusiasm is all that evident.*

3. *Ask the owner why he or she is selling the car. The sooner the car must be sold (getting married, getting divorced, being transferred overseas), the lower the price the seller may be willing to accept.*

4. *Give the impression that you have several other cars to look at—that if the seller doesn't accept your offer you very probably won't be back.*

5. *Don't let your offer be affected by what the seller may tell you about other potential buyers' interest in the car: "One guy just left here to get approval from his bank."*

6. *Take along a friend (with the day's classified section in hand with lots of ads circled in red) to act as devil's advocate. Your friend can often be the one to save face and help make a deal you want after the seller has turned down your "best offer"— an offer that you really might be willing to raise just a bit to get the car.*

7. *Even if the ad says, "Make Offer," never make an offer. Ask the seller to tell you the minimum amount he or she will accept. That way you have a low figure at which to begin your bargaining.*

8. *If your bargaining reaches a stalemate, take another look at the car, maybe giving your friend a signal to say, "Aw, Joe, that price ain't too bad" or some such.*

9. *Take cash so that if you do strike a bargain, you won't lose the deal to some other cash buyer who arrives while you've gone after the money.*

   Let the seller SEE that you have cash (as much cash as possible) in hand. An effective ploy of insurance claims adjusters is to lay a giant roll of twenties and hundreds on the table in front of a personal injury claimant when attempting to settle a multithousand dollar lawsuit. You'd be surprised how many times it works!

10. *Don't get carried away. Make what you feel is a fair offer and stick to it. If the seller doesn't accept, give him or her a card with your name and phone number. You may receive a call later.*

And remember: nothing personal, it's just the rules of the game.

GETTING PAID

When a buyer makes an acceptable offer for your car, bind the deal with a nonrefundable deposit. (Use our **Receipt for Nonrefundable Deposit**, Form 86.3, page F637.) Make the deposit substantial, at least $200, and tell the buyer that you will take the car off the market as soon as you have the deposit and that in the process you will miss many prospective buyers—so the deposit *must* be nonrefundable.

Don't be too eager to accept a deposit though. After making an offer that he or she really wasn't too sure of, the prospect might be embarrassed into giving you a deposit when, in fact, they're really not too comfortable about doing it. That being the case, the prospect will run down to the bank first thing Monday morning and stop payment on the check.

It's better to give the prospect every graceful way out of making a deposit so that both of you are sure the offer is sincere. Of course, when you've accepted a deposit, you must take your car off the market and tell callers that you have a deposit on the car and that you believe it's sold.

You might let a buyer take the car on the basis of a full payment check, and, then again, you might not. If the buyer is known to you, or if the buyer can show plenty of identification—driver's license, credit cards, etc.—it might be OK to let him or her drive the car home. On the other hand, if the buyer can't show satisfactory identification, or if things just don't feel right, offer to meet him or her at the bank Monday morning. Since your buyer may need to finance the car, it's possible you'll need to make a trip to the bank anyway. In any event, keep the car's title and registration until you have cash or a bank cashier's check in hand.

In addition to a **Bill of Sale** (Forms 86.4 and 86.5, pages F639 and F641) and a federal **Odometer Mileage Statement** (Form 86.6, page F643), you'll have to sign over your car's title and, in some states, make arrangements to turn in your car's license plates. Before advertising your car, visit the county courthouse or state department of motor vehicles to pick up any state forms you'll need.

FORMS

Fix-up Materials Shopping List

We've included our shopping list (Form 86.1, page F633) in the Forms section since it's meant to be removed, photocopied, and taken on a shopping trip.

Written Offer to Purchase

Use the written **Offer to Purchase Motor Vehicle** (Form 86.2) for dealing with less than satisfactory offers for your car. Don't be discouraged if you receive quite a few offers for substantially less than you're asking; some people just **have** to make a "low-ball" offer; if you're firm, they will go ahead and pay your price. Inviting the "low-ball" bargainer to make a written offer will save you the hassle of haggling about price.

Receipt for Nonrefundable Deposit

The receipt (Form 86.3) makes very clear the fact that the prospect is making (and that you are accepting) a **nonrefundable** deposit. It won't prevent anyone from stopping payment on a check, but it will discourage someone from making an offer unless he or she fully intends to buy your car.

Bill of Sale

Two bills of sale have been provided:

- **Bill of Sale of Motor Vehicle**—Individual Buyer and Seller (Form 86.4)
- **Bill of Sale of Motor Vehicle**—Joint Buyers and Sellers (Form 86.5)

If joint sellers are selling to an individual, use the joint buyer/seller form and cross out the provision for the joint buyer. For an individual owner selling to joint buyers, also use the joint form and cross out the provision for a joint seller.

Both bills of sale acknowledge receipt of payment, so you won't need a separate form for this purpose. A partial payment may be recorded on the **Receipt for Nonrefundable Deposit**.

Odometer Mileage Statement

Federal regulations require that you state the odometer mileage upon transfer of ownership of your motor vehicle. Use our **Odometer Mileage Statement** (Form 86.6, page F643) for this purpose. **Note:** an inaccurate or untruthful statement may make you liable for damages to your transferee, for attorney fees, and for civil and criminal penalties, pursuant to sections 409, 412, and 413 of the Motor Vehicle Information and Cost Savings Act of 1972 (Public Law 92-513, as amended by Public Law 94-364).

Sample Window Sticker

1981 CHEVROLET MONTE CARLO

301 V-8

Automatic Transmission

Power Steering

Power Brakes

Factory Air

AM/FM/Stereo Cassette

Tilt Wheel

Tinted Glass

Rear Window Defroster

Bucket Seats

Console

Electric Clock

Inside Hood Release

Full-Size Spare Tire

Affix Appropriate
Page from NADA
*Official Used
Car Guide* Here.

Almost new steel radials.   36,000 miles.   Immaculate. $6,195

Phone Geoff: 686-7492

⑧⑦ Financial Forms

This chapter concerns ten financial and credit forms:

- Credit Application
- Personal Financial Statement
- Joint Financial Statement
- Promissory Note
- Installment Note
- Series Promissory Note
- Security Agreement
- Chattel Mortgage
- Request for Reason for Adverse Credit Action
- Request for Disclosure of Credit Information

CREDIT APPLICATION

The **Credit Application** (Form 87.1) on page F645 meets all federal requirements and is appropriate for use in evaluating applicants for a wide range of credit purposes. It's also a good work sheet for individuals who expect to be applying for credit. The names, dates, and references that you will need to fill out our form will also be needed for completion of any credit application given out by a store, credit card company, bank, or other lender. Our form works equally well for individual and joint credit applicants.

PERSONAL FINANCIAL STATEMENT

You will probably be asked by a bank, credit union, or other lender to complete a **Personal Financial Statement** (in addition to a credit application) for any major personal loan, business loan, home purchase, or other significant amount of credit. As with many other forms in this book, make a photocopy of Form 87.2 (page F649) to serve as a work sheet and return the original to the pocket at the back of the book.

JOINT FINANCIAL STATEMENT

Our **Joint Financial Statement** (Form 87.3, page F653) is designed primarily for use by spouses and cohabitants who may share certain bank accounts and charge accounts and who may also have separate assets and liabilities. Business partners, on the other hand, should each complete separate copies of the individual **Personal Financial Statement**.

PROMISSORY NOTE

The individual **Promissory Note** (Form 87.4), of which several copies are printed on page F657, is useful for formalizing almost any kind of personal loan

or debt. Be sure that any rate of interest charged is within legal limits set by your state. Some states may declare an entire debt null and void—as being an "illegal," and hence unenforceable, contract—if any included interest rate exceeds the legal limit.

Show the amount of the note in the upper left-hand corner of the document in the space provided after the dollar sign. This amount, in figures, should be the same as the amount specified in the body of the note following "the sum of."

If you lend money to Smith and if repayment of the loan in the event of default by Smith is guaranteed by Jones, then Jones is the "endorser" and should sign in the space provided.

INSTALLMENT NOTE

Our **Installment Note** (Form 87.5, page F659) is similar to the individual promissory note, except that it provides for repayment of a loan in regular, monthly installments rather than in full on a specific date. Be sure that the rate of interest is within the legal limits set by your state.

SERIES PROMISSORY NOTE

Unlike the installment note, the **Series Promissory Note** (Form 87.6) can provide for irregularly spaced payments. This series note, of which several copies are found on page F661, is designed for use in conjunction with similar notes, each becoming due at a specified time.

SECURITY AGREEMENT

Security agreements are often used by retailers as a means of financing the sale of major appliances; banks and other lenders often use such agreements in financing borrowers' purchase of autos. They are also used by banks and other lenders to obtain a security interest in a borrower's property when granting personal loans.

You might want to use a photocopy of our short-form **Security Agreement** (Form 87.7, page F663) to provide protection for yourself if you sell an auto, boat, or other property to a buyer who must pay in installments.

Thoroughly describe the item sold (or offered as security for a loan) under "Collateral," listing any serial numbers, model numbers, motor numbers, or similar identifying data, along with color, size, type, make, year of manufacture, etc.

Under "Obligation," stipulate the amount to be paid and the schedule for repayment. Be sure that any interest rate charged is within the legal limits set by your state.

CHATTEL MORTGAGE

Like the security agreement, our **Chattel Mortgage** (Form 87.8, page F665) is often used by retailers and lenders for the financing of appliances, furniture, and autos, as well as being used to obtain security when making loans.

A chattel mortgage is very similar to a security agreement, except that in many jurisdictions chattel mortgages used by retailers and lenders clearly state that title to the mortgaged chattels does not pass to the borrower/purchaser until the mortgage is paid in full. (A chattel, by the way, is simply any kind of movable personal property.)

You may not need to fill in all the blanks under "terms" in every case, since excise tax is not charged on the sale of many items and not all states and cities impose a sales tax. Once more, be sure that any interest rate charged (as the finance charge) is within the legal limits of your state.

In many states a notarized copy of a chattel mortgage may also be used to record mortgaged property at county courthouses.

REQUEST FOR REASON FOR ADVERSE CREDIT ACTION

You may want to mail **Request for Reason for Adverse Credit Action** (Form 87.9, page F669) to any store, credit card company, lender, or other credit source that has refused to grant credit. Although the credit grantor (or in this case, credit nongrantor) is required by federal law to reply, your request may be accorded greater and more prompt attention if it is individually typed, rather than photocopied from this book and filled out.

Our printed form, a typed letterhead, or a printed letterhead (which you should have anyway for complaint letters, etc.) should have your name and address centered at the top of the page:

Your Complete Name
Street Address
City, State, Zip

The form must be notarized as proof that you are the actual requestor and should be mailed within thirty days of any credit refusal.

REQUEST FOR DISCLOSURE OF CREDIT INFORMATION

You don't have to wait until you're denied credit in order to mail the **Request for Disclosure of Credit Information** (Form 87.10, page F671) to local credit bureaus. Since nobody's perfect, errors can creep into anyone's credit file, and it's probably a good idea to learn as much as you can about your credit bureau file by requesting a disclosure of information every year or so.

Helpful as they are, federal fair credit reporting laws only require that consumer credit bureaus disclose to you the "nature and substance" of credit information in your file. A far better way of checking up is to have a friend who is a business owner or manager order a copy of the bureau's report on you. Employers, particularly small employers, are often happy to do this for employees upon request.

88 Attorney Forms

"In my name, place and stead" to act "as fully as I might or could do if I were personally present"—that's what a power of attorney that you grant allows another person to do.

While not exactly an awesome power, it's certainly enough to get you into trouble if such a person commits the equivalent of a physician taking out the wrong person's gall bladder. Such little mistakes as buying the wrong supertanker and selling the wrong shopping center have happened. Of course, you could argue negligence, but you may have to pay for the supertanker or give up your shopping center first and then try to straighten things out in court later.

But, assuming that someone to whom you grant a power of attorney is of good judgment and is knowledgeable in the area in which you want him or her to function, a **Power of Attorney** can allow action to be taken when you can't (or don't want) to be there.

POWER OF ATTORNEY

An open **Power of Attorney** (Form 88.1, page F673) can allow your attorney or accountant to negotiate and settle up with the IRS if you don't want to be around to be asked questions; it can allow another person to sell your house or car for you; it can allow another person to buy property you're not able to view personally; and it can permit someone else to temporarily operate your business, deposit checks, and pay your bills.

Of course, you aren't limited to granting a power of attorney to a lawyer; it can be granted to anyone of sound mind and legal age. Real estate agents, insurance agents, accountants, stock brokers, and bankers are often granted powers of attorney. A person to whom you have granted a power of attorney is called your "attorney-in-fact."

The sample power of attorney provisions on page F675 (Form 88.2) should give you some idea of the kinds of powers that are often granted to an attorney-in-fact.

AFFIDAVIT OF ATTORNEY

An affidavit of attorney will often be required of an attorney-in-fact acting in behalf of the grantor. The affidavit is a sworn statement by the attorney-in-fact that he or she is, indeed, attorney-in-fact for the grantor and that the grantor is alive and of sound mind and has not revoked the power of attorney.

The exercise of specific powers related to an action taken by an attorney-in-fact should be described in the space provided following, "THAT I make this affidavit for the purpose of."

Anyone acting under authority granted by a power of attorney should have several photocopies of this volume's **Affidavit of Attorney** (Form 88.3, page F677) on hand whenever exercising such powers in the event he or she is asked to provide an affidavit.

AUTO DEALER'S POWER OF ATTORNEY

This very limited power of attorney allows a third party to sell an auto belonging to the grantor. Such powers of attorney are often employed by used-car dealers who routinely sell cars left with them on consignment.

You could use our auto dealer's **Power of Attorney** forms (Form 88.4, page F679) to grant another person authority to sell your car for you, but the form provided on page F673 would probably be more acceptable to a skeptical buyer.

REVOCATION OF POWER OF ATTORNEY

Whenever you **revoke** a power of attorney be sure to mail one copy, registered or certified mail, return receipt requested, to the individual whose power of attorney you are revoking. You may want to hand him or her a copy, too, before mail might be delivered, but receipt for delivery of the **Revocation of Power of Attorney** (Form 88.5, page F681) is your protection in the event he or she later acts without authority.

While you're at it, also mail copies of the revocation to anyone whom you expect the former attorney-in-fact might have dealings with pertaining to the now revoked power of attorney.

RETAINER

The **Retainer** of attorney (Form 88.6, page F683) may or may not involve the concurrent granting of a power of attorney. The most common use of the retainer is to set down the understanding between an attorney and client. It describes what the attorney is to do and how he or she is to be paid.

CONTINGENT FEE RETAINER

A Contingent Fee Retainer (Form 88.7, page F685) is often the basis for an agreement between an attorney and a client who desires to file suit for personal injury. Such cases are often chancy, and the personal-injury victims are frequently individuals who could not ordinarily afford an attorney. Thus the contingent fee retainer works to the advantage of both. Payment of the attorney for legal services is contingent upon a judgment or settlement in favor of the client.

A contingent fee retainer permits even a penniless client to obtain good legal counsel while often permitting the attorney a return on his or her investment of time and effort on litigation.

Although a contingent fee arrangement is negotiable, attorney payment usually amounts to about 33 percent of any sum received by the client if the case goes to trial, less if settlement is accepted prior to trial, and more if the case is won on appeal.

RETAINER OF ATTORNEY BY EXECUTOR

There's not much chance you'll be named as executor in someone's will without your at least being asked if you're willing, but sometimes it happens. Our Retainer of Attorney by Executor (Form 88.8, page F687) is at least something you can photocopy, complete, and send off in the mail if you find that you must suddenly, or with little notice, act as executor of the estate of someone who unexpectedly died in another state or town.

AFFIDAVIT

Form 88.9 (page F689) serves as framework on which to hang almost any type of sworn affidavit that may be required. A sworn affidavit, by the way, is merely a signed statement that has been sworn to and notarized.

⑧⑨ Living Will

At this writing, "right-to-die" laws were in effect in twenty-one states and the District of Columbia: Alabama, Arkansas, California, Delaware, Florida, Georgia, Idaho, Illinois, Kansas, Mississippi, Nevada, New Mexico, North Carolina, Oregon, Texas, Vermont, Virginia, Washington, West Virginia, Wisconsin, and Wyoming. In these states having "right-to-die" laws, usually termed the state's *Natural Death Act*, a **Living Will** is considered a valid legal document if properly executed *after* you have been diagnosed as having a terminal illness or diagnosed as "being in a terminal condition"—as from a head injury sustained in an auto accident, for example.

But even in "right-to-die" states, and of course in states lacking such laws, a Living Will is only *informative*, merely advising your physician and family of your wishes.

If the execution of a Living Will *prior* to diagnosis of a terminal condition isn't legally binding, then why sign one? Well, the reason is simple. Execution of a Living Will *prior* to terminal illness or injury is one way of placing your wishes on record so that if you later reaffirm your desire by executing a Living Will again *after* diagnosis of a terminal condition, there can be little question of the willful and voluntary nature of your action.

Although a Living Will executed prior to diagnosis is **not** legally binding, a caring physician will often carry out your wishes even though not legally required to honor such a request.

Once you have signed a Living Will in the presence of *qualified* witnesses and are still in the office of the certifying notary public, make half a dozen or so photocopies. The notary can then certify these as true copies of the original. Give one to your physician, one to your spouse or a close friend, one to your attorney, and one to anyone else who may be contacted in the event of accident or sudden illness.

The forms for **Living Will** (Forms 89.1 and 89.2) on pages F691 and F693 are exactly the same, except that Form 89.2 contains a pregnancy clause for use by women. The **Living Will** on page F695 (Form 89.3), for use *after* diagnosis of a terminal condition, is valid in any state having a Natural Death Act.

Read each form carefully before use, making sure that none of your witnesses fall within the exclusions stated in the form.

XIV

GLOSSARY

The following glossary contains nearly 1,000 legal terms, many more than appear in the preceding text, but which you may encounter when presented with various contracts, insurance forms, employment agreements, sales agreements, credit applications, purchase or sale offers, etc.

*   *   *

A

Abandon To give up rights, property, or a family relationship by desertion without intention to return or reclaim.

Abate To reduce or diminish, as in the abatement of noise.

Abet To stir up, encourage, or incite.

Abscond To leave a jurisdiction and hide to avoid legal process.

Abstract of Title A condensed, chronological history of the titles to a piece of real estate.

Acceleration Clause States that the balance of a debt shall be considered due upon the occurrence of an event, for instance the default of a single installment.

Acceptance The creating of a binding contract by receiving something with the intention of keeping it. Also, creating a binding contract by agreeing to the terms of an offer.

Acre 4,840 square yards or 43,560 square feet.

Action A judicial proceeding to assert one's rights. A lawsuit.

Actionable That which may be grounds for an action or lawsuit.

Act of God A natural phenomenon, such as lightning, earthquakes, or tornadoes, that is the cause of an accident or casualty.

Actual Cash Value The market value. The reasonable market price of goods or property under normal circumstances.

Addendum Something added; a supplement.

Ademption The withdrawal of a devise or bequest by a testator's act that clearly indicates intent.

Adhesion Contract A standard form, submitted by one party to another on a take-it-or-leave-it basis, often presented in situations where the buyer's position is significantly weaker than the seller's.

Adjudication Settlement by judicial decision.

Adjunct Additional, but not essential part of.

Adjuster An insurance company employee who investigates and settles property damage and personal injury claims.

Administrator A person appointed by a probate court to manage the settlement of the estate of a deceased person when there is no qualified executor—as in cases where there is no valid will.

Administrator *De Bonis Non* (D.B.N.) An administrator who is appointed by the court to distribute or manage any part of an estate not completely administered by a former executor or administrator.

Advancement A financial or real estate settlement made to an individual by another against an amount that the recipient would be receiving under the will of the person who makes the advancement.

Adversary Proceeding A court action where disputing parties present their conflicting and opposing views for litigation.

Adverse Possession Continuous, open, hostile, and notorious possession and occupation of real estate for a statutory length of time by a trespasser attempting to claim or establish title.

Advocate One who assists in defense of or pleads the cause of another.

Affiant A person who swears to and signs an affidavit.

Affidavit A written and signed statement sworn to under oath.

Aforesaid Previously mentioned.

Agency An arrangement whereby a person or corporation acts on behalf of another person or corporation with his/her/its permission.

Agent One who represents, does business for, or acts on behalf of another with the other's permission.

Aggravated Assault Severe, intentional violence against another.

Aggrieved One upon whom injury is inflicted or who is unjustly treated.

Agreement of Sale A binding agreement between buyer and seller.

Alienable That which can be transferred or conveyed to another.

Alienation The transfer of title of land or other property from one person to another.

Alimony Regular payments that one spouse is ordered by the court to pay to the other after legal separation or divorce.

Allegation An unproven statement, assertion, or charge.

Allege To assert that something is a true fact that has not yet been proved to be true or false.

Amenable Answerable; accountable; liable.

Amend To revise, change, or alter.

Amenities Pleasant, extra features pertaining to premises or real estate in addition to the normal, expected necessities.

Amicable Action A judicial proceeding that is conducted with mutual, agreeable understanding between the parties.

Amicus Brief A brief submitted by a friend of the court.

Amicus Curiae A friend of the court. A qualified person who gives opinion or information that might otherwise escape the attention of the court.

Amortization Reduction of a debt, such as a mortgage, by regular payments on the principal along with each periodic interest payment.

Annuity An arrangement whereby a specific sum is paid to a person in periodic payments of one or more per year.

Annulment A voiding; a cancellation.

Answer A defendant's legal, written response to the plaintiff's complaint in a civil lawsuit.

Antenuptial Agreement A prewedding contract made between a man and woman declaring the agreed rights and obligations of each during their marriage and any subsequent divorce or separation.

Appeal The application to a higher court for review of judicial decision when the applicant believes he or she was unjustly defeated in a lawsuit.

Appearance Notice to the court of the representation of a litigant by his lawyer or by himself (*pro se*).

Appellant A person who appeals a judicial decision.

Appellate Court An appeals court. Also termed court of appeals.

Apportionment The distribution of assets and liabilities according to the interests of the parties involved.

Appraisal The value of property as estimated by a disinterested expert.

Appropriate To take possession or set apart for a specific purpose; often used to imply that possession was taken without permission.

Arbitration The settling of a dispute between parties by a designated third party or parties who, after considering the arguments of both sides, determine an equitable settlement.

Arrears The amount that a debt is overdue or unpaid.

Arrogation The legal adoption of a fully competent adult.

Artificial Person A "person," such as a corporation, created by law, as distinguished from a natural person.

Assault An intentional and unlawful verbal or physical threat causing fear of violence and expectation that the threat will be carried out.

Assessment The setting of value on property for taxation purposes.

Asset Anything of value that could be used, directly or indirectly, to pay a debt.

Assign To convey or transfer, as to assign property, rights, or interests to another.

Assignment The transfer of property by the assignor to the assignee.

Assumpsit An express or implied, written or oral promise; a simple contract. In common law, also a form of action for recovery of a debt on a simple contract or promise.

Attachment The lawful taking or seizure of property to bring it under the custody of a civil court.

Attest To certify the signatures on a document by signing the document as a witness.

Attorney-at-Law A lawyer. A person who is licensed to practice law, try cases in court, and give legal advice.

Attorney-in-Fact A person, not necessarily a lawyer, who has a written and signed power of attorney to transact business and act on behalf of another person.

Attractive Nuisance A condition on someone's property that is both attractive to and dangerous to others, especially children, such as a deep hole or an insufficiently fenced swimming pool. The owner of an attractive nuisance may be liable for death or injury.

Auction The public sale of property to the highest bidder.

Audit An official examination and verification of an account or accounts.

Award Damages Declare an amount to be paid by one party to an action to another party.

B

Bail Money deposited with the court to secure release of a suspect from police custody. Bail may be forfeited if the suspect fails to appear for trial and sentencing.

Bailiff A court officer who guards the deliberations of a jury and keeps order in the courtroom.

Bailment A written or unwritten agreement that provides for the possession of the owner's (bailor's) property by another (the bailee) for a specific purpose.

Balloon Payment A final payment that is more than twice the amount of earlier, regular payments.

Bankrupt The condition of an insolvent debtor in

which his or her property is turned over, under jurisdiction of a federal bankruptcy court, to a trustee to be distributed for the benefit of creditors.

Bar The place in a courtroom from which attorneys address the court and jury, at which prisoners are arraigned or sentenced, and where litigants stand to plead their cases. Also refers to the legal profession or to lawyers as a group.

Battery Physical violence or unlawful touching done by one person to another without consent. Assault and battery refers to the threat of violence and the actual carrying out of violence against another.

Bench The seat occupied by the judge in a courtroom. Also refers to judges as a group.

Bench Trial A trial before a judge only.

Bench Warrant A warrant issued by a judge for the apprehension of a person for contempt of court or for failure to appear after being ordered to do so.

Beneficiary A person to whom the benefits of an insurance policy, a trust, or the proceeds of an estate are payable.

Bequeath To leave personal property to someone by will; to make a bequest.

Bigamy The criminal offense of marrying one person while married to another.

Bilateral Contract A contract between two parties with binding agreements made by both parties, making each party both a promisor and a promisee.

Bill A written statement or declaration. Also an itemized statement of an amount due and payable.

Bill of Exchange An instrument written by a person ordering a certain sum to be paid to another by a third party.

Bill of Sale A document attesting to the conveyance of ownership of property, other than real estate, from the seller to the buyer.

Binder A preliminary agreement. In insurance, a binder serves to provide immediate coverage until such time as a written policy is issued.

Binding Arbitration Arbitration with the settlement binding upon all parties to the controversy.

Blackmail The crime of extorting money or valuables by intimidation or threats of exposure.

Blanket Mortgage A mortgage that covers more than one piece of real estate.

Blanket Policy A flexible insurance policy with broad coverage.

Bodily Heirs Direct decendants. Most often used to refer to children of a deceased and their children.

Boiler Plate Portions of a contract that do not deal with the individual particulars of the contract; contract clauses in common use.

Bond A sum of money posted as surety or bail.

Bondsman A person who provides surety or bond for another in exchange for payment of a fee.

Breach An intentional or unintentional infraction of the law, a failure to fulfill an obligation, or the breaking of one's written or oral contract or promise.

Breach of Contract Failure to perform one or more conditions of a contract without a legal excuse.

Breach of the Peace Disorderly conduct or riotous behavior that disturbs the public peace.

Breach of Warranty A nonfraudulent violation of a manufacturer's, distributor's, or seller's promise as to quality, condition, or content of goods.

Bribery The crime of attempting to influence a public official by giving or offering something of value.

Brief A concise statement of a plaintiff's or defendant's case, usually prepared by an attorney.

Broker A middle person who transacts business for the benefit of others for a commission, as does a real estate broker, stockbroker, etc.

Burden of Proof The obligation to prove a disputed fact in a legal action. In a civil suit the burden of proof lies with the plaintiff.

Burglary Unlawful entry into a building or premises with intent to commit a crime. In some states it must be during the nighttime.

C

Capital Assets All assets of a business except those held for sale to customers in the ordinary course of business.

Causa Mortis Because of death. A gift *causa mortis* is one made in contemplation of death, but one that becomes void if the donor survives the contemplated cause of death.

Causa Proxima The proximate or most closely related legal cause.

Cause of Action The legal basis upon which a plaintiff's lawsuit is founded; the reason for going to court.

Cede To yield; to give up; to assign.

Chain of Title All of the transfers of ownership of a piece of real estate from the first record to the present time.

Chancery A court of equity; equitable jurisprudence.

Chattel Personal, tangible, movable property.

Chattel Mortgage A mortgage on personal, movable property, such as furniture, an auto, or cattle.

Chose in Action A thing that is recoverable in a lawsuit.

Chose in Possession   A thing actually possessed or possessable.

Circuit Court   A lower court that sometimes sits at two or more places within a judicial district between which the judge travels.

Citation   An official notice ordering a person to appear in court at a certain time; a summons. Also a reference to a court decision and other legal precedents.

Civil Action   A noncriminal judicial proceeding.

Civil Injury   An infringement of a civil right as distinguished from a criminal injury.

Civil Law   The body of law that is concerned with the individual and his or her rights of person and property.

Civil Liberty   The right of liberty for all that is restricted only by such laws as are necessary for the common good; civil freedoms.

Civil Rights   The rights of citizens guaranteed by the Bill of Rights, the Constitution, acts of Congress, and especially the Thirteenth and Fourteenth Amendments to the Constitution.

Claimant   A person who demands or asserts a claim.

Class Action   A lawsuit brought on behalf of a group of persons having a common complaint.

Clear Title   A title to property that has been determined to be free from all liens and encumbrances.

Closing   The meeting at which the buyer and seller of a piece of real estate transfer ownership with the exchange of money and the deed to the property.

Cloud on a Title   A possible claim to real estate that would diminish the rights of the owners.

Codicil   A supplement that makes a change or changes in an existing will.

Coercion   To force by pressure or threat.

Cohabitation   The act of living together by a man and woman not necessarily holding themselves out to be husband and wife.

Collateral   Property used as security for a loan. Also refers to that which is supporting, corroborating, or secondary. Collateral evidence.

Collusion   A secret, deceitful conspiracy between two or more persons made for improper or unlawful purposes.

Comaker   A person who by his or her signature guarantees the payment of a debt should the original borrower default. A cosigner.

Common Carrier   A person or company in the business of transporting people or goods for anyone who choses to hire such service.

Common Law   Those principles of law that originated in the customs and usage of old (olde?) English law.

Common-Law Marriage   The relationship between a man and woman living together and holding themselves out to be husband and wife, which is recognized in some states as marriage even though no marriage ceremony has been performed.

Community Property   A principle recognized in some states whereby property acquired by a husband or wife during their marriage to each other becomes the property of both. Inheritances and gifts are often exempt.

Comparative Negligence   A legal principle followed in some states that takes into account the degree of negligence on the part of the plaintiff as well as that of the defendant in a civil action.

Compensatory Damages   A financial award to the plaintiff in a lawsuit as compensation for injury to his person, property, or reputation.

Complainant   One who institutes legal proceedings against another.

Complaint   The legal document containing the plaintiff's cause of action or reasons for initiating a lawsuit against the defendant.

Compromise   An out-of-court settlement of a dispute.

Condemnation   A legal declaration taking privately owned real estate for public use without the owner's consent but with the payment of compensation. This may be done pursuant to a governmental body's right of eminent domain. Also the declaring of a premises to be unsafe for habitation.

Conditional Sale   An agreement whereby partial payment is made for goods or property with transfer of title to take place only upon payment of any remaining amount due.

Conjugal   Pertaining to the relationship of a husband and wife.

Consent Judgment   A court-approved settlement agreed to by the plaintiff and defendant.

Consideration   The price or inducement of a contract; necessary for a contract to be binding.

Consignment   The delivery of goods by the owner (consignor) to the receiver (consignee) who is either to sell the goods and pay the owner the amount of the sale less any commission or to return the goods to the owner.

Consortium   A husband or wife's right to the affection, help, and companionship of the other without interference by a third party.

Constructive   Assumed or inferred by legal interpretation.

Constructive Eviction Eviction by breach of covenant or agreement; forced eviction by a landlord's violation of a tenant's rights.

Constructive Notice Inferred notice—as when a notice is delivered to a person's attorney, it is legally inferred that the notice has been delivered to the person.

Contempt The disobedience of and disregard of the rules, orders, process authority, and dignity of a judicial or legislative body, punishable by fine or imprisonment or both.

Contiguous Touching or adjoining.

Contingent Fee An attorney's fee that, by mutual agreement, shall be paid only if a lawsuit is successful, usually an agreed-upon percentage of client's award.

Continuance Postponement of a judicial proceeding.

Contract A legally enforceable, explicit, written agreement between two or more parties and made for a consideration.

Contract, Implied A contract not explicitly written but presumed or implied by law as deduced from the circumstances or conduct of the parties.

Contract, Quasi An implied contract arising from the relationship of the parties, without express agreement.

Contract, Time-of-the-Essence A contract containing time limitations after which neither party can demand an extension of performance.

Contributory Negligence The legal principle followed in some states whereby if both parties in an accident are negligent to any degree, neither may collect damages in a civil action. Certain other states follow the principle of comparative negligence.

Conversion Unauthorized appropriation or use of another's personal property.

Convey To transfer ownership of property.

Conveyance The document by which title to property is transferred from one party to another. Also, the act of transferring ownership of property.

Corespondent A person charged with having committed adultery with the defendant spouse in a divorce suit.

Corporation An association of one or more shareholders having its own legal entity separate from the individual shareholders.

Corporation, Alien A corporation that is incorporated outside the United States or its territories.

Corporation, Close A corporation incorporated by a small group of individuals, such as a family, in which the majority of stock is ordinarily held by the officers and directors.

Corporation, Domestic Incorporated under the laws of the state in which it conducts business.

Corporation, Foreign Incorporated under the laws of a state other than the state or states in which it conducts business.

Corporation, Subchapter S A corporation that chooses, as permitted by the Internal Revenue Service, to be taxed as a partnership. Stockholders' individual incomes are taxed rather than that of the corporation.

Corporeal Hereditaments Tangible, real, or personal property that may be inherited.

Cosigner A person who, by his or her signature, guarantees the payment of a debt should the original signer default; a comaker.

Counterclaim A claim made by the defendant against the plaintiff in the same suit as that brought by the plaintiff.

Court Costs Certain expenses, such as filing fees, process server's fees, witnesses' fees, and deposition fees, for which the winner of a lawsuit is entitled to be reimbursed by the loser.

Covenant An agreement or special provision of a deed or lease fixing certain uses and nonuses of the property or promising certain things to be done or not to be done by the landlord or tenant. To covenant is to promise by means of a covenant.

Covenant, Real A covenant in a deed that is binding upon future owners of the land.

Covenant, Restrictive An agreement written into a deed or lease that prohibits certain uses or disposal of land.

Creditor One to whom a debt is owed.

Creditor's Bill A filing by a creditor for an accounting of the settlement of the estate of a deceased debtor.

Cross Claim A claim litigated by coplaintiffs or by codefendants against each other rather than against the other side in a lawsuit. A contractor and subcontractor may enter cross claims against each other in a lawsuit filed by a homeowner.

Cruelty The deliberate causing of physical or mental pain and suffering of one person by another. A common cause of action in divorce suits.

Curtesy Possession for life by a husband to a part of his deceased wife's estate.

Custody The legal right to the physical care and keeping of a person or property.

D

Damages Monetary compensation awarded by the court to the injured party as the result of a lawsuit.

Damages, Actual Compensation awarded in the amount of actual loss sustained.

Damages, Compensatory Compensation awarded for pain, loss, or injury sustained by the plaintiff. General damages.

Damages, Exemplary Compensation awarded in excess of the plaintiff's actual loss, intended partly to serve as punishment for willfully malicious, vicious behavior on the part of the defendant. Punitive damages.

Damages, General Compensation awarded for pain, injury, or loss sustained by the plaintiff. Compensatory damages.

Damages, Liquidated The amount stipulated in a contract that must be paid as compensation by the defaulting party to the other in the event of default or breach of contract.

Damages, Nominal A nominal compensation awarded, when the plaintiff's injury or loss is minimal, to establish the responsibility of the defendant.

Damages, Punitive Compensation awarded in excess of the plaintiff's actual loss, intended partly to serve as punishment for willfully malicious, vicious behavior on the part of the defendant. Exemplary damages.

Damages, Special Compensation awarded for specific financial losses, such as loss of earnings, that flow from another injury sustained by the plaintiff.

d.b.a. Doing business as. Used to denote an unincorporated business affiliation of an individual, as in Lana Pipes d.b.a. Georgetown Booksellers.

Debt Anything specific, usually money, owed by a debtor to a creditor; a financial obligation.

Debtor Anyone owing to another.

Decedent A person who has died; the deceased.

Decision A judgment or determination of the court in deciding litigation.

Declaration A plaintiff's written statement declaring his or her grounds for a lawsuit. Also means any formal written or oral statement or announcement.

Decree A judicial decision or judgment; an order with the authority of law.

Deed The legal instrument or document used to transfer the ownership of real estate.

Deed, Bargain-and-Sale A deed in which marketable title to real estate is implied but in which title is not warranted by the seller.

Deed, Bargain-and-Sale, with Covenant Against Grantor's Act Similar to a bargain-and-sale deed but one in which the seller declares that he or she has done nothing to encumber the title except that which may be recorded on the deed.

Deed, Grant A deed that warrants that the property is free from encumbrances.

Deed, Warranty A deed in which the seller agrees to defend the title against any liens or claims, thereby warranting the title.

Deed, Quitclaim A deed relinquishing and denouncing all claims to a property by the seller but does not guarantee against claims by others.

Defamation Oral or written publication of anything injurious to the reputation of another.

Default Failure to meet a legal obligation, as in failure to pay a debt when due. Also failure to take steps required in a legal action.

Defeasible Capable of being revoked, changed, or voided.

Defect, Apparent A readily detectable, not hidden, defect. A patent defect.

Defect, Latent A hidden, not readily discoverable, defect.

Defect, Patent A readily detectable, not hidden, defect. An apparent defect.

Defendant One against whom a court action is brought; the person defending himself or herself against the plaintiff in a civil suit. In criminal law, the suspect charged with a crime.

Defense Action taken by the defendant in response to allegations made against him or her in litigation. Also refers to the defendant and his or her attorney.

Deferred Payment Payment made in installments or in a specified sum on a stipulated date.

Deficiency Judgment A judgment for the amount still owing after applying the proceeds of a foreclosure sale to the amount owed.

Defraud To take from another by deceit, misrepresentation, or trickery; to commit fraud.

Delinquent Account An overdue bill.

Demand Note A loan payable upon demand by the lender.

Demise To convey; the conveyance of real property by will or by lease.

Demised Premises Leased premises.

Demurrer A defendant's formal objection to the legal basis for a lawsuit while admitting that the facts of the plaintiff's complaint are true.

De Novo As from the beginning.

Deponent One who gives evidence or makes a deposition under oath.

Deposition A written, signed record of an oral statement, given under oath, that may be submitted as evidence in a court.

Depreciation A loss of value due to deterioration or the passage of time.

Descent The passing of a person's estate to an heir by inheritance through a will or by the laws of intestate succession.

Desertion Willful abandonment of property or of another person to whom one is legally bound, such as a spouse or child.

Designee A person appointed for a particular purpose; a person who has been designated.

Detainer The keeping of a person from real or personal property to which he or she has a legal right.

Devisable Legally capable of being conveyed from one person to another by a will.

Devise To give real property by will. Also refers to property thus conveyed. A devise is devised by a divisor to a divisee.

Dilatory Delaying, as in dilatory tactics employed by an attorney or insurance company.

Direct Examination The first questioning of a witness by the person who calls him or her to the witness stand. In a civil suit, direct examination of the plaintiff is normally conducted by the plaintiff's attorney; direct examination of the defendant is conducted by the defendant's attorney. Cross-examination, which usually follows direct examination, is conducted by the opposing attorney.

Disability Incapacity to act due to failure to meet legal requirements. Also lack of capacity resulting from injury or disease.

Disaffirm To refuse to be bound by an agreement; to renege.

Discharge To satisfy an obligation; to set free; to acquit.

Disclaimer The denial of rights, interests, or responsibilities.

Discovery The procedure whereby a party may gain pretrial information from the opposition's depositions, interrogatories, facts, documents, etc.

Discrimination To make a favorable or unfavorable distinction of any person or persons over another person or persons.

Dismiss To refuse further judicial hearing on a legal action; to excuse.

Dismiss with Prejudice To refuse further judicial hearing of a case and to refuse reinstatement of the case at a later date.

Disposition The outcome, as in the final disposition of a lawsuit.

Dispossess To put out of possession or occupancy by court order as petitioned by a landlord.

Dispute A controversy; a disagreement.

Distraint The legal taking over and holding of personal property of a debtor until the debt is paid or until the property is sold for payment of the debt.

Distress The illegal taking over and holding of one's personal property by an injured party in an attempt to obtain payment of a claim.

Divorce The legal dissolution of a marriage.

Docket The list of cases on a court's calendar.

Doctrine A principle; a theory.

Document A paper on which formal, legal information is printed or written.

Domicile One's permanent residence; where a person lives and expects to return to when he or she goes home.

Double Indemnity An agreed obligation of an insurer to pay the beneficiary double the face amount of a policy if the insured dies as the result of an accident.

Double Jeopardy To try a suspect twice for the same offense. Prohibited by the Fifth Amendment of the Constitution.

Dower The share of a deceased husband's property that is given by law to his widow for life.

Duress Force, coercion, threats, or pressure brought against an individual to cause him or her to do something that he or she would not otherwise do.

E

Earnest Money A deposit on a purchase, made by the buyer, that binds both parties to the terms of a sales agreement.

Easement The legal right to use of a limited portion of another's land for a specific purpose, usually for the user's access to his or her own land.

Emancipation The releasing of a minor from parental custody and control and giving him or her legal status as an adult.

Embezzlement The fraudulent appropriation or conversion to one's own use of money, goods, or property of another.

Eminent Domain The right of a governmental unit to take private property for public use without the owner's consent but upon payment of just compensation.

Emolument The salary, fees, or pay that a person receives from gainful employment.

Encroachment An intrusion or trespass onto one's property or rights.

Encumbrance A claim or lien against real or personal property.

Endorse To sign one's name on a legal document, as to endorse a check upon cashing or to endorse (cosign) the note of another to guarantee payment in the event of the original signer's default. Also to signify one's approval, as to endorse for membership or election.

Enjoin To prohibit or enforce an action by order of a court.

Entrust To deliver something into the care of another with the mutual understanding that it will be used or held as agreed.

Equity The amount of interest that one has in property. Also refers to a supplemental system of law that grants relief in cases where the payment of money does not provide adequate compensation. Fairness.

Escheat The transfer of property to the state for lack of an owner, as when property is abandoned or when no heir to an estate can be found.

Escrow The delivery of a document, money, or property to a third party to be held in trust by the third party until certain conditions of an agreement between other parties have been met.

Estate All property in which one has an interest and that must be administered and distributed according to a will or the laws of intestacy after one's death.

Estate, Freehold Includes estates of inheritance and estates for life.

Estate by the Entirety The ownership of tangible or intangible property by a husband and wife together. Also called tenancy by the entirety.

Estate for Life Giving one the right of possession of or benefits of an estate during his or her lifetime or the lifetime of another specified person.

Estate of Inheritance The owner having full, legal ownership with clear title and right to possession. Also an estate in fee or in fee simple absolute.

Estoppel A restraint to prevent a person from producing evidence to contradict or deny his or her own previous assertion.

et al. And others.

Eviction The dispossession, usually of a tenant, from property by legal process.

Evidence Any matter that can be used as proof in a court of law.

Exception An objection or nonacceptance by a litigant to a court's action or ruling.

Execute To fulfill all legal formalities and requirements; to make a document such as a contract or will valid.

Execution Sale The legally authorized sale of property on which a mortgage has been foreclosed.

Executor A man named in a will to execute the will and administer an estate.

Executory Contract A contract to be executed in the future at such time when all formalities and requirements have been fulfilled.

Executrix A woman named in a will to execute the will and administer an estate.

Exemption An immunity or exception from an obligation to which others are subject.

Express Unmistakable; explicit.

Express Contract One in which all provisions are explicitly stated and agreed upon, as distinguished from an implied contract.

Extrinsic Evidence Evidence found outside and separate from the body of a contract, document, or agreement.

F

Face of an Instrument The express language of a document and the exact meaning therein.

Face Value The value of a document as determined by its explicit wording and without resorting to outside interpretations or further information.

Facsimile An exact copy or reproduction.

Factor An agent; a commission merchant; a person who sells goods for another. He or she also holds accounts receivable as security for loans or acts as collection agent for those accounts.

Fair Comment Usually a plea by a defendant that untrue statements that resulted in a suit for libel were believed to be true at the time they were made and were neither made with malice nor with any intent to damage the plaintiff.

Fair Market Value A reasonable price that encourages a reasonable buyer to buy and a reasonable seller to sell.

False Arrest The unlawful, unjustified seizure and detention of a person by an officer of the law.

False Pretenses Willful misrepresentation with intent to defraud.

Family Car Doctrine The legal principle, followed in some states, that maintains that the owner of a family car is legally responsible when any member of the family is driving the car with the owner's knowledge and consent.

Feasance A doing; an act.

Fee Simple Describes an estate, the inheritance of which confers unconditional ownership and possession of real property that can be sold or left to heirs without restriction. Also expressed as "in fee" or "fee simple and absolute." Real property so conveyed is usually conveyed "to Jones in fee simple."

Fee Tail Describes an estate with inheritance limited to a specified holder and certain classified bodily heirs, such as male or female only.

Felonious With intent to commit a felony; pertaining to a felony.

Felony A serious crime punishable by a severe sentence.

Fiduciary A person having a position founded upon trust and confidence; a trustee.

File To introduce a legal document into the public record.

Final Disposition The final judgment of the court settling a dispute.

Finding A verdict; a legal decision.

Fine Money paid to the court as penalty for an offense.

Fixed Asset An item of value basic to the operation of a business, such as a printing press would be to a printer.

Fixture An item of personal property attached to a piece of real property that may be deemed to be a part of the real property if its removal would damage the real property.

Forbearance Refraining from or delaying a possible legal action to enforce rights.

Forced Sale A sale made in execution of a court judgment.

Force Majeur A superior or immovable force.

Foreclose To legally terminate a mortgage and take possession of the mortgaged property by court order after default by a borrower.

Foreman The member of a jury who presides during its deliberations and who reports its verdict to the court.

Forensic Medicine Those aspects of medicine as they apply to the law.

Forgery The act of making or altering a document with intent to deceive or defraud.

Fraud An act of deceit, misrepresentation, or trickery used to mislead, deceive, or cheat. To defraud is to commit fraud.

Full Faith and Credit A requirement of the Constitution that the results of a judicial proceeding in one state be respected by the other states.

G

Garnishment A legal proceeding whereby a debtor's salary is withheld from him or her by the debtor's employer and paid to a judgment creditor instead of to the debtor.

Gift The voluntary transfer of any property from the giver to the recipient without any contract, obligation, compensation, or exchange of money or property.

Gift Over To make a gift to the ultimate recipient but with temporary ownership by an intermediate third party.

Good Cause A substantial or sufficient legal justification.

Good Samaritan Doctrine A legal doctrine followed in many states that holds that a person who attempts to render aid to another person in apparent, imminent danger may not be held liable for any harm to that person other than that which results from his or her negligence.

Good Title A title of ownership to real or personal property that is free from valid liens, claims, and encumbrances, making it a valid and marketable title.

Grand Jury A jury of inquiry that hears accusations against a suspect in a criminal case and determines if he or she is to be indicted.

Grant To formally transfer real property by sale, gift, or lease. Land is granted by the grantor to the grantee.

Gratuitous Given without compensation or obligation.

Gratuitous Guest A person riding in a vehicle with the permission and knowledge of the driver but without payment.

Gross Negligence Willful, wanton disregard for the safety of others.

Gross Profits Profits before deductions for costs of operation, taxes, etc.

Ground Rent Rent payable for the use of leased land.

Guarantee To promise to be responsible for a debt or legal obligation of another in the event of default. To promise that one will do a specific thing. A warranty to assure the continued quality of a thing. To furnish security for an arrangement.

Guardian A person appointed by the court to protect the person or interests of a minor or legally incompetent person.

H

Harass To annoy and disturb repeatedly and persistently.

Hearing A preliminary examination or proceeding; an equity trial.

Hearsay Generally inadmissible evidence that comes from information based upon what one witness was told by another rather than by the witness's personal knowledge and observation.

Heir (or Heiress) A person who inherits property.

Heir, Legal One who inherits property pursuant to the laws of intestacy; an heir at law.

Heir at Law   One who inherits property pursuant to the laws of intestacy. A legal heir.

Heir by Devise   One who inherits property by will.

Heirloom   An item of personal property passed from one generation to the next within a family.

Hereditament   Any real or personal property that can be inherited.

Hereditary   Having title or possession pass to another by inheritance.

Holdover Tenant   A tenant who retains possession of property beyond expiration of his or her lease.

Holographic Will   A will written entirely in the hand of the maker.

Homestead   A residence and related property exempt from execution for general debts in bankruptcy.

Hung Jury   A jury unable to reach agreement after hearing evidence in a trial.

Hypothecate   To pledge property as security but without transfer of title or possession to the lender.

I

Illusory   Having a deceptive, false appearance.

Immunity   Freedom from a certain law, penalty, or obligation.

Implied   Presumed; suggested; may be deduced from behavior or circumstances. Implied rather than expressed.

Impute   To charge one with negligence or knowledge of something over which he or she has indirect responsibility; to attribute, in a negative sense.

Inalienable   That which cannot be transferred.

In Camera   Within the judge's chambers.

Inchoate   Recently begun; incomplete.

Incident to   Dependent upon and a part of another thing.

Incite   To urge to act; to provoke into action.

Incompetent   One physically or mentally unfit to handle his or her own affairs.

Incorporeal Hereditament   Something intangible and inheritable that is derived from property, such as rents.

Incriminate   To state or imply a person's association with a wrongful act; to blame or inculpate.

Inculpable   Blameless; free of guilt.

Inculpate   To incriminate; to implicate in guilt.

Inculpatory   Tending to establish guilt or blame.

Indefeasible   That which cannot be voided or altered in any way.

Indemnify   To secure against loss or damage; to insure.

Indemnity   Security against loss or liability; insurance.

Indenture   A properly executed legal document between two parties.

Indictment   The written charge of a grand jury accusing a suspect of a serious crime.

Indigent   A needy person without money, property, or resources.

Inducement   An explanatory introduction to the main allegations in a legal action. Anything that persuades one to act.

Infant   A person under legal age; a minor.

In Fee   Describes an estate, the inheritance of which confers unconditional ownership and possession of real property that can be sold or left to heirs without restriction. Also expressed as "in fee simple and absolute."

Infra   Below; in a following part of a document that one is reading, as compared to *supra*—above or preceding.

Infraction   A breach; a violation; a failure to fulfill an obligation, as in breach of contract or breach of warranty.

Infringement   A trespass; a violation of a right or a disregard of an obligation; going beyond a certain limit.

Inherently Dangerous   Intrinsically dangerous in itself with no additional circumstances necessary for possible hazardous effects.

Inheritance   Real or personal property that is passed to heirs after the owner's death.

Inheritance Tax   A tax levied upon the value of inherited property. A death tax.

Injunction   A written court order that prohibits the taking of an action or that requires that an action be taken.

Injury   Damage or wrong done to a person, or his or her rights, property, or reputation. In a court proceeding, the injury is alleged to have been caused by a wrongful act of the defendant.

In Medias Res   Right into the middle of the thing.

In Re   In the matter of. A legal proceeding where there is a nonadversary matter requiring the court's attention.

Intangible   That which has no physical property or has no value in itself but represents value.

Inter Alia   Among other things.

Interdiction   A forbidding; a prohibition.

Interest A degree of ownership in property. Also refers to the price of borrowed money, such as interest on a mortgage.

Interlocutory Preliminary; provisional.

Interrogatories A formally presented set of oral or written questions that must be answered under oath.

Inter Se Among themselves.

Inter Vivos Between the living, as in an *inter vivos* gift.

Intestacy, Laws of Laws that provide for the legal distribution of a deceased person's estate to his or her legal heirs if he or she did not leave a valid will. Also called the laws of descent and distribution.

Intestate A person, or a legal status of a person, who dies without having executed a valid will.

Intestate Succession The disposition of property among legal heirs of a deceased according to the laws of intestacy if there is no valid will.

Intrust To deliver something into the care of another with the mutual understanding that it will be used or held as agreed. To entrust.

Inure To pass to; to result.

Invitee One who goes onto the property of another either by implied or express invitation.

Irreconcilable Differences Feelings, beliefs, and differences incapable of compromise, adjustment, or harmony.

Irrefutable Incapable of being disproved; factual.

Irreparable Incapable of being returned to a former good condition or state of repair.

Irrevocable Incapable of being retracted or changed.

Issue of Fact A point to be determined by the jury.

Issue of Law A point to be resolved by the court.

J

Jeopardy Danger or peril.

Joinder A uniting of causes of action or of parties in an action, as, for example, codefendants or coplaintiffs.

Joint Shared; united; common to more than one party.

Joint Lives A designation used wherein an estate in the names of two or more parties would terminate upon the death of either party.

Joint Will A single will executed by more than one person that is the will of each of them.

Judgment The final determination of a court.

Judgment, Summary A judgment rendered in response to the plaintiff's or defendant's motion, where evidence shows there is no issue as to material fact and that the plaintiff or defendant is entitled to a judgment in his or her favor as a matter of law.

Judgment Creditor A creditor in whose favor a judgment has been made but who has not yet been paid by the judgment debtor.

Judgment Debtor A debtor against whom the court has rendered a judgment but who has not yet made payment to the judgment creditor.

Judicial Action An action taken in or by a court of law.

Judicial Proceedings Activities within the realm of the court.

Judiciary Refers to the system of courts of law and to the judges of the courts.

Jurant One who takes an oath.

Juridicial Days Days when a court is in session.

Jurisdiction The extent of the authority of a court or other government entity such as a law enforcement agency.

Jurisdiction, Appellate Authority to review previous decisions of a lower court.

Jurisdiction, Original Authority to decide a question properly presented to the court.

Jurisprudence The science and philosophy of law and the systems of law.

Jurist A person having expert knowledge in the field of law.

Juror A member of a jury.

Jury A body of citizens brought together in a court of law to hear and decide a case on the evidence presented before it.

Just Honorable; fair; equitable; sound.

Justice The fair administration of law.

Justice of the Peace An official of a lower court with authority to perform marriages, administer oaths, act on minor offenses, and refer major offenses to a higher court.

K

Kangaroo Court Slang expression for a court whose procedures are as irregular as the leaps and bounds of a kangaroo. Usually refers to an illegal court using illegal procedures.

Kiting Issuing a negotiable instrument, such as a check, without funds to honor the instrument but with the expectation that a deposit will be made in time for the instrument to be honored—for the check to clear.

Kleptomania A persistent, neurotic impulse to steal.

L

Laches Unreasonable delay in asserting a legal right or claim.

Landlord The owner of real property who rents or leases it to another.

Lapse The termination of a right or privilege through neglect or a failure to continue to meet requirements.

Larceny Stealing; the unlawful taking away of personal property belonging to another.

Last Resort, Court of A court from which no appeal may be made.

Lawsuit An action taken by a plaintiff to recover a right or claim in a court of law.

Lawyer Attorney; a person who is licensed by examination to practice law, try cases in court, and give legal advice.

Leading Case The case setting a precedent upon which a principle of law is established.

Lease A written contract in which a landlord (lessor) and a tenant (lessee) agree to the conditions whereby the tenant has a right to the possession and use of a specific property for a specific consideration.

Leasehold Possession by lease.

Legacy A bequest; an inheritance; a gift of personal property made by will.

Legal Established by, concerned with, or authorized by law.

Legal Age Usually 18 or 21; the age at which a minor person assumes the legal responsibilities of an adult. In states that confer partial legal responsibilities at age 18, the attainment of 21 years of age is referred to as "full legal age."

Legal Aid Society A group of attorneys in a local area who will provide free or low-cost legal advice and representation to those in need.

Legal Consideration An amount of money (legal tender) that changes hands to bind a contract.

Legal Separation A court order that stipulates the individual legal rights of a separated husband and wife.

Legatee The inheritor of a gift of personal property left by a legator in a will.

Legatee, Residuary The person named in a will to receive the balance (residue) of an estate after all debts and specific bequests have been satisfied.

Legitime The share of a deceased parent's estate that by law passes to his or her children.

Lessee One who leases or rents real property.

Lessor The owner of real property who rents or leases it to another.

Letters Testamentary A probate court document certifying the appointment of the person named in a decedent's will to act as executor of his or her will.

Letters of Administration Probate court document certifying the appointment of an administrator of the estate of a decedent who died without leaving a valid will or without naming an executor.

Levy The court-ordered seizure of property by an officer such as a sheriff or marshal. Also, to impose or assess a tax.

Liable Legally responsible and answerable for damages or injury to another.

Libel A malicious statement expressed in writing, print, film, or recording that defames one's character or exposes him or her to ridicule. Libel is actionable even without proof of actual damage.

License Legal permission to engage in an activity that would be illegal without the authority of the license.

Lien A legal claim that one party has against the property of another as security for a debt.

Lineal Descendant A person directly descended from another, as one is a lineal descendant of his or her parents.

Liquid Assets Cash or property that can readily be converted to cash.

Liquidate To convert assets to cash. To settle a business affair or pay off a debt or obligation.

Liquidated Damages A sum of money, expressly agreed upon by the parties to a contract, to be paid by one to the other in the event of a default or breach of the agreement.

Litigant A party to a lawsuit, either the plaintiff or defendant.

Litigation A lawsuit.

Litigious Person One who is prone to become involved in numerous lawsuits, especially as a plaintiff.

Long-Arm Statute A statute that permits a court to acquire jurisdiction over a defendant who is outside the court's ordinary jurisdiction.

Long-Term Capital Gains or Losses Those gains or losses from the buying, selling, or exchange of capital assets that one has held for more than six months if acquired after June 22, 1984, and more than 12 months if acquired before June 23, 1984.

M

Magistrate Judge of a lower court of limited jurisdiction.

Maim To cripple or severely injure one's limb, as to be maimed by the attack (battery) of another or in an accident.

Majority A person who has attained legal age. A person who has attained his or her majority is no longer a minor.

Maker One who makes or signs a promissory note payable to another.

Malfeasance The intentional commission of an illegal act; unlawful conduct.

Malice The intention of committing an unlawful act that will result in the injury of another; the intent to injure another through an unlawful act.

Malicious Mischief The intentional damaging of the property of another.

Malpractice Professional misconduct through negligence, malice, or unreasonable incompetence.

Manslaughter Unpremeditated, unlawful killing of another without malice. The killing of another through gross negligence or incompetence, as in the taking of a life when driving an auto while intoxicated.

Marketable Title A title that any reasonably informed buyer can assume to be sufficiently free and clear of encumbrances for the transaction of business.

Marriage Settlement A financial settlement made by one spouse, before or after marriage, for the benefit of the other.

Master in Chancery A court-appointed officer (often an attorney in private practice) empowered to hear testimony and report to the judge. Increasingly used in cases of uncontested or "no-fault" divorce.

Material Evidence Evidence that is relevant to the matter at hand.

Mayhem The violent, willful injuring of another, especially if such action deprives the victim of the use of a part of his or her body necessary for self-defense.

Merchantable Reasonably fit for the general use for which the item is manufactured and sold.

Meretricious Unlawful sexual relations.

Metes and Bounds Used in a surveyor's description of real property. Bounds are the lines that join the metes, or corner points.

Mineral Rights An interest in or right to the removal of minerals from real property.

Minor A person, usually under 18 or 21 years of age, who has not reached majority and who does not have the legal rights and responsibilities of an adult.

Minor Offense A less serious offense; a lesser infraction of the law.

Misappropriate To appropriate dishonestly; to take wrongful possession for one's own use; to embezzle.

Misdemeanor A criminal offense less grave than a felony. Usually punishable by a fine and/or a jail sentence of less than one year.

Misfeasance The improper, negligent, or injurious performance of an otherwise lawful act.

Misrepresentation The making of a false, misleading statement. The inadequate representation of his or her constituency by an elected representative.

Mistrial A trial from which there was no verdict due to a major error in the conduct of the trial or in which the jury was unable to render a verdict.

Mitigate To diminish, reduce, moderate, or make less severe.

Modify To change or alter.

Mortgage A contract pledging real property as security for a debt, the lender being the mortgagee and the borrower being the mortgagor.

Motion An application to the court for a rule or an order.

Multiple Wills Duplicates of the same will, each executed as an original. All duplicates must be presented to the court in order for the will to be probated.

Mutuality of Contract Obligations in common to which all parties of a contract are bound.

Mutual or Reciprocal Wills Separate wills, executed under an agreement made by separate individuals, that contain reciprocal provisions for the disposition of their individual properties, usually for the benefit of each other.

N

Natural Person A human being, as distinguished from an artificial person created by law such as a corporation.

Necessaries Essentials, such as food, clothing, shelter, medical care, education, etc., needed for the maintenance of a dependent person—and that are compatible with his or her usual standard of living.

Negligence Failure to exercise the degree of care and caution that would be exercised by a reasonable person.

Negligence, Comparative A legal principle, adhered to in some states, that takes into account the degree of negligence on the part of the plaintiff as well as that of the defendant, with any damages awarded on the basis of the court's determination of which party was the most negligent.

Negligence, Contributory A legal principle, adhered to in some states, providing that in cases of negligence by both parties in, say, an accident, neither may be awarded damages—a measure intended to prevent plaintiffs from profiting from their own negligence.

Negligence, Gross A willful, wanton disregard for the safety of others. A defendant charged with gross negligence usually faces criminal charges and may also be ordered by the court to pay punitive civil damages.

Negotiable Instrument A document such as a check, draft, promissory note, bill of exchange, etc., that when properly executed and delivered is transferable from one person to another as a means of exchange or of credit.

Net Applies to that portion of profit that remains after expenses and other direct and indirect costs have been deducted from the gross profit.

Nominal A stated minimal, rather than actual, value; a token amount.

Noncupative Will A will made orally in the presence of two or more persons, written down then or later by one of them and witnessed by at least two of those present. Valid in some states if made during the last illness of the decedent or if made by a person in military service in anticipation of combat. Generally, an oral will.

Nonfeasance Failure to perform an act that is one's legal duty to perform.

Nonsuit A judgment against a plaintiff for failure to prosecute his or her case or to provide evidence.

Notary Public A person authorized by law to perform certain public functions such as witnessing signatures, administering oaths, and taking affidavits.

Notice A formal written declaration of intent, usually required pursuant to an agreement, to be given by one party to the other at a specified time, such as notice given a landlord in advance of vacating leased premises. Also may be delivery of a formal, written instrument of the court—such as an order or writ.

Notice to Produce A legal, written notice requiring a party in a court action to produce specified evidence, usually a document.

Novation The writing of a new contract that supersedes a previous contract between the same parties and that is related to the same matters.

Nuisance A condition that is annoying, harmful, or damaging to others.

Nullify To render invalid; to void.

O

Oath A solemn avowal made as to the truth of a matter, the intentional breaking of which is cause for prosecution for perjury.

Obstruction of Justice Interference with witnesses, destruction of evidence, false statements to police, or any other act intended to deter the activities of the court from proceeding in a straightforward manner.

Offense Any violation of any law; any violation of another's rights.

Offer A formal proposal that, if accepted, is a legally binding preliminary step toward a contract, sale, or purchase.

Offset Set-off; a counterclaim not directly related to a plaintiff's claim, whereby the defendant attempts to reduce or cancel a claim against him or her.

Ombudsman A person designated to investigate grievances and take or recommend corrective measures.

Option An agreement giving one of the parties the right to buy or sell property at a specific price within a specific time.

Oral Spoken; verbal.

Order of the Court A direction or order from a judge that a specific act be performed or not be performed.

Ordinance A statute or regulation, especially as established and enforced by a municipal government.

Overrule To void a lower court's judgment by the judgment of a higher court; to invalidate by higher authority.

P

Paramount Title Superior to all other titles making the same claim. A paramount title is usually dated earlier than other titles.

Parol Oral; spoken; verbal, as in parol evidence.

Partition The dividing up of a property and its rights between its owners.

Partnership, General A relationship between two or more parties, usually defined by a written agreement, whereby each furnishes specific material or nonmaterial assets (such as labor) for the joint conduct of a business and each shares profits and losses therefrom in specific proportions.

Partnership, Limited A contract between two or more persons whereby the active partner or partners operate a business and are solely responsible for its debts and commitments and who share its profits with others, limited partners, who have invested only money (rather than time and effort) in the venture.

Party An individual; a litigant or person directly involved in a legal action.

Party Wall A single wall shared in common by two buildings or a wall on the boundary between two parcels of land.

Patent A document granted by the federal government giving an inventor exclusive rights to manufacture, sell, and otherwise exploit an invention for a specific period of time.

Peculate To embezzle or steal goods or money entrusted to one by another.

Pecuniary Relating to money; monetary.

Pendente Lite Pending the outcome of a lawsuit or other legal action, as in support *pendente lite* paid by one spouse to the other pending the granting of a decree of divorce.

Per Capita According to the number of individuals.

Peremptory Challenge The challenge an attorney may make to a prospective juror disqualifying him or her for no stated reason; an arbitrary disqualification.

Performance of a Contract The fulfillment of the conditions and obligations of a contract.

Perjury To lie willfully under oath; to swear falsely to a document.

Perpetrator An individual who has committed or carried out an act, usually one who has committed an offense—as an alleged perpetrator, an expression much loved by police.

Perpetuity Forever; without definite end.

Persecute To harass and annoy willfully and constantly.

Persona A natural or artificial person.

Personal Property Any property, excluding real estate.

Per Stirpes In the laws of descent, refers to the division of an estate whereby a class of heirs, such as siblings, receives and divides the part of an estate that would have gone to a deceased ancestor of theirs.

Petit Petty; on a lesser scale; of minor significance, as distinguished from grand.

Petition A formal request for action—usually court action.

Plaintiff A complainant; one who initiates a lawsuit against the defendant.

Plat A map of an area that shows streets, lots, and the locations of boundary markers, including measurements as surveyed.

Plea An answer to charges made in a legal action.

Pleading The formal, written document stating the position of a party to a lawsuit.

Pledge The bailment or delivery of personal property to a creditor as security for payment of a loan.

Polygamy Having more than one spouse at the same time.

Possession The actual holding of goods or occupancy of real estate with or without ownership but with the right to occupy or hold the property.

Possession, Constructive Possession that is imputed to a person by law, even though he or she doesn't have actual possession.

Possessory Action A lawsuit that seeks to regain possession of real property, as when a landlord brings action against tenant who refused to vacate property.

Posthumous Occurring or continuing after one's death.

Power of Attorney A written document that gives a person the legal authority to act on behalf of another to the degree specified in the document.

Practicable Capable of being put into practice; capable of being done.

Praecipe A legal writ ordering an individual to do a particular thing. If the person refuses to do so, that individual should appear in court and state why he or she refuses to do so.

Prayer for Relief A request to the court by a plaintiff for relief that he or she believes is due.

Precedent A judicial decision that serves as a guide in subsequent similar litigation. Also that which is said or done to justify further acts.

Preempt To assert a right to perform an act or possess property before someone else beats you to it.

Preferred Stock A class of corporate stock that is entitled to priority over common stock in the distribution of corporate dividends (profits). Preferred stock is often nonvoting stock.

Premeditation The giving of prior consideration to an act before carrying it out; forethought.

Premises A specific parcel of land or specific portion of a building. Also refers to the preliminary statements explaining or describing a document.

Preponderance of Evidence The greater quantity and/or quality of evidence needed to prove a case.

Prescription Acquisition of an easement or right to real property by virtue of long, uninterrupted, non-hostile use for a statutory period.

Presumptive Assumed.

Pretermitted Heir An inheritor omitted from a will inadvertently, such as a child born after a will is executed having no provision for future children.

Pretrial Procedure A system used by many courts to encourage and assist settlement before and instead of trial.

Prima Facie At first sight; on its face and not requiring further support to establish credibility.

Principal A person who gives an agent authority (sometimes through use of a power of attorney) to act for him or her.

Principle The basis for a fundamental law or belief.

Priority The right of a specific creditor or class of creditors to be paid first from the assets of a bankrupt.

Privilege A right, immunity, exemption, or benefit that applies to one or to a class of people.

Privileged Communication   Knowledge given as a professional confidence to an attorney, physician, clergyman, or rabbi that he or she is bound not to divulge to another.

Privity   The relationship between two or more persons who have a common legal interest.

Privity of Estate   A mutual or successive relationship to, or interest in, a parcel of real estate.

Privy to   Shares personal or confidential information, as in, "He is privy to all of that information."

Probate   To prove officially after the death of a testate that his or her will is authentic, valid, and properly executed so that its provisions may be carried out.

Probative Facts   Evidence that proves the truth of a matter and that determines the facts of a case.

Probative Value   The relative weight and value of evidence to be introduced in litigation.

Probity   Honesty; integrity.

Pro Bono Publico   For the public good or welfare, such as legal work done by an attorney without fee, *pro bono publico.*

Proceedings   The formal, legal steps taken to initiate, conduct, and conclude a court action.

Proceeds   The amount of money gained; the financial yield or profits from a particular venture. Also the amount of a money judgment handed down by a court.

Process   The course of legal action. Also a summons or writ.

Process Server   An official of the court who delivers a writ or summons demanding one's appearance in court.

Pro Forma   As a matter of form.

Prolixity   The tendency to make verbose, overly wordy, long statements.

Promissory Note   A written instrument in which the maker promises to pay the bearer of the note a specific sum, with interest, at a specific time, or on demand, in payment of a debt.

Promulgate   To put a new law, doctrine, or decree into effect by public, official announcement.

Proof   Evidence that determines the facts of a case.

Property   Any thing that can be owned. Real property refers to land and its buildings. Property other than real property (real estate) is referred to as personal property, personalty, or chattels.

Proponent   One who offers a will for probate. Also one who is in favor of something, as a proponent of the death penalty.

Pro Rata   According to the rate; proportionately.

Pro Se   For one's self. Refers to a person representing himself or herself without an attorney.

Prosecute   To initiate and carry out legal proceedings to a resolution.

Proviso   A condition, restriction, or qualification included in a document.

Proximate Cause   The direct cause of an injury or accident.

Public Policy   A principle that states that a person may not act contrary to the common, public good.

Punitive Damages   An award to the plaintiff by the court as punishment to the defendant. Also called exemplary damages.

Purview   Scope; purpose; range.

Putative Father   The alleged father of an illegitimate child.

Q

Quiet Enjoyment   Refers to a tenant's right, either implied or by express covenant in a lease, not to be wrongfully disturbed by the acts or omissions of the landlord or by anyone claiming paramount title.

Quitclaim Deed   A deed relinquishing or renouncing all claims to a property by the seller but not guaranteeing against claims by others.

Quit the Premises   To leave permanently with one's belongings.

R

Real Property   Real estate; land and the buildings and fixtures permanently attached to it.

Rebate   A deduction; an abatement; a return of part of a payment.

Rebut   To contradict, answer, or refute.

Receiver   A court-appointed officer who holds possession of a defendant's property during civil litigation and who then may be ordered to dispose of the property under direction of the court, as in a foreclosure or bankruptcy. Such property is said to be in receivership.

Reciprocity   The recognition in one state of the laws, judgments, rights, and licenses granted by another state in exchange for similiar recognition of such laws, judgments, rights, and licenses by the other state.

Reckless   Carelessly heedless of danger; acting with willful lack of caution.

Recover Damages   To obtain a legal judgment in one's favor and be awarded a sum of money to be paid by the defendant; to be compensated for a loss.

Redress   To set right; to compensate for; to make amends; to give relief.

Referee   A court-appointed officer having the power to take testimony, hear arguments, and arbitrate disputes.

Release   A document relinquishing a claim or freeing one from an obligation or responsibility.

Remainderman   One who is entitled to an estate by gift or bequest but only after the termination of someone else's interest in that estate.

Remand   To order returned; to send back.

Remedy   The desired result of an action.

Removal of Cause   A change of venue from one state court to another or from a state court to a federal court.

Replication   The answer of a plaintiff to the plea of a defendant.

Repudiate   To reject or to refuse to acknowledge.

Res   A thing, as opposed to a person.

Rescind   To cancel or annul; to make no longer legally binding and to return the parties to a contract to a position of never having made the contract.

Res Ipsa Loquitur   The thing speaks for itself.

Resolution   A determination by the court; the successful arbitration of a dispute.

Respondent   A defendant; one who answers in a legal proceeding.

Restitution   The return of a person's property or the receipt of funds equal in value to that of lost property.

Retainer   An initial, advance payment to an attorney to secure professional services and, occasionally as a matter of legal tactics, to secure an attorney's refusal to represent one's adversary in a case.

Retract   To withdraw, disavow, or take back.

Return   A report from an officer of the court regarding the carrying out of an order, as in an officer's return to the court regarding the serving of a subpoena.

Reversal   The changing of a lower court's decision by a higher court.

Revert   To return to.

Revoke   To annul by recalling; to rescind.

Rider   An addition to an insurance policy or contract.

Right of Action   The basis for bringing a lawsuit against another; a claim that is the grounds for suing another.

Right of Way   The right of one vehicle's driver to proceed across the path of another. Also the right to pass over another person's land at a particular place.

Rights   The moral and legal privileges to which one is entitled.

Riparian Rights   The special rights of an owner whose land borders on rivers, streams, and other waterways.

Risk   A specific type of loss or damage covered by an insurance policy.

Robbery   The crime of taking personal property from another by force or fear of force.

Run with the Land   A covenant is said to run with the land when it passes from one owner to the next with the title, such as a restriction upon a particular use of the land or type of building to be constructed thereon.

S

Sale   The transfer of ownership of property in exchange for a sum of money.

Sale, Absolute   Occurs when title to property is passed upon fulfillment of a sales contract between the buyer and seller.

Sale, Conditional   Occurs when possession is passed to the buyer but title is withheld until full payment has been made.

Sale, Executed   A completed sale.

Sale, Execution   A sheriff's sale; a court-authorized sale of a debtor's property to satisfy the claims of creditors against the owner.

Sale, Executory   An incomplete sale; a sale that will be complete when all conditions of the sales contract have been met.

Sale, Public   A sale in which the public may bid after public notice of the sale has been made.

Sale, Sheriff's   An execution sale.

Sale, Tax   A legally authorized sale of a person's property to pay delinquent taxes.

Satisfaction   Payment of or in some other manner discharging an obligation or debt.

Satisfaction of Judgment   Documents filed with the court by a plaintiff and a defendant stating that a judgment has been satisfied.

Satisfaction Piece   A document stating that a mortgage has been paid in full.

Scienter   Knowingly—refers to one's knowledge that his or her act is illegal.

Seal   To authenticate or confirm. A stamp or other device used to certify or authenticate a document.

Search Warrant   A judicial order authorizing the search that describes the exact premises to be searched and the item or evidence that is being sought.

Section   One square mile of land; 640 acres.

Secure To guarantee payment of a debt or obligation.

Security Property pledged to guarantee payment of a loan. If the loan is not paid, ownership of the property is transferred from the debtor to the creditor.

Security Deposit Money left on deposit with a landlord by a tenant to insure that the tenant will abide by a lease agreement. A landlord may use all or part of a security deposit to pay for any damages that may be caused by a tenant. Such a deposit may also be used to pay liquidated damages in the event that a tenant requests premature termination of a lease.

Seize To take into possession.

Seizin (or Seisin) The legal ownership and possession of real property.

Self-defense The right to act to repel or prevent an attack upon one's person, family, or property.

Separation A decree or agreement that allows husband and wife to live separately and apart, but without being divorced.

Sequester To set apart.

Sequestration Proceedings to attach a person's property that is to be sold to pay a debt or to pay alimony.

Service of Process The personal delivery of a legal notice, such as a summons, subpoena, or citation, to effect legal notification of the named person.

Service of Process, Substitute Service of process by publication in a newspaper or by delivery to an agent of the person being served.

Servient Estate A property upon which the owner of another property has an easement.

Set Aside To declare a proceedings or verdict to be void.

Settlement A resolution and compromise reached by adversaries that eliminates the need for a trial or judicial decision.

Settlor One who places property in the possession of a trustee for the benefit of a third party, the beneficiary, thereby creating an express trust.

Severalty Refers to the holding of property alone and without another person having any right of ownership.

Show Cause Order A court order that requires a litigating party to appear and show why certain things should or should not be done.

Simultaneous Death The deaths of two or more persons in circumstances, such as an auto accident, that make it necessary for the court to declare that they died at the same time, there being no evidence by which to determine that one died before the other or others.

Slander A malicious, oral defamation of another's character.

Small Claims Court A court of limited jurisdiction in which one may bring a minor civil suit without representation by an attorney.

Solvency The ability to pay one's debts as they become due.

Sound Mind The healthy, normal mental capacity necessary for a person to legally execute a binding contract or document such as a will.

Special Endorsement An endorsement transferring a negotiable instrument to a specific, named person.

Specific Performance A court order requiring a defendant to perform a specific act rather than pay damages. For example, an order requiring a roofer to properly redo the work rather than pay the plaintiff a full or partial refund.

Spendthrift Trust A trust created to provide for the possibly financially irresponsible beneficiary that prevents him or her from squandering money or having claims made against it.

Spouse A married partner; a husband or wife.

ss Scilicet; that is to say; it is permitted to know; namely.

Statute A law enacted by a legislative body.

Statute of Frauds A requirement that certain types of contracts must be written in order to be valid and enforceable.

Statute of Limitations A law limiting the time between the occurrence of a grievance and the date legal action is initiated.

Statutory Period A period of time determined by statute.

Stay A temporary, court-ordered delay in legal proceedings until the occurrence of a specific event or until a specified date.

Stipulation A condition to an agreement or court order.

Stock A certificate held by a stockholder as evidence of ownership of a stated number of shares of a corporation.

Stockholder One who owns stock in a corporation.

Sublet The renting by a tenant, to a third party, of all or part of the premises that the tenant is leasing from a landlord.

Subornation The crime of inducing another person to commit perjury.

Subpoena A court order requiring a witness to appear in court at a specific time to give testimony.

Subpoena *Duces Tecum* A subpoena requiring a witness to bring specific evidence, usually documents, to court.

Subrogation The substitution of one creditor for another.

Subscribe To consent to or to affirm the contents of a document by signing one's name to the document.

Substantial Performance The carrying out of the essential terms of a contract although there may be some minor omissions in the strict performance of the contract.

Sue To begin a court action to recover a right or to obtain damages; to begin legal proceedings against another.

Suit A lawsuit; a legal action taken by a plaintiff to recover a right or claim against a defendant.

Summation An attorney's closing statement to a jury.

Summons A written notice ordering a person (or party) to appear in court.

Supra Above; a preceding part of the document that one is reading, as compared to *infra*—below or following.

Surety A guarantee; a person who agrees to guarantee a debt.

Surrogate A county officer with jurisdiction to administer matters relating to the settlement of estates of deceased persons. Also means substitute.

Survive To live longer than another.

Survivorship Right A right to property by outliving another who had an interest in the property.

T

Tangible Material; capable of being touched, as distinguished from intangibles, such as easements and rights.

Tenancy A right to possess property either by lease or by title.

Tenancy, Holdover The possessing of real property beyond the expiration of a lease, not necessarily illegal.

Tenancy, Joint The joint ownership of real property by two or more persons with the right of survivorship.

Tenancy, Periodic The possessing of real property by lease for a specific period of time but with the expectation by both the landlord and tenant that the period will be extended. If it is not to be extended, either the landlord or tenant must terminate the tenancy with a written "notice to quit."

Tenancy at Will The possessing of real property with a lease of indefinite term. Either landlord or tenant may terminate the tenancy by written notice to quit.

Tenancy by the Entirety The holding of real property by a husband and wife jointly, with the right of survivorship so that on the death of either the other becomes sole owner. Neither can sell his or her interest without the consent of the other.

Tenancy for Life The possessing of real property for the duration of one's life.

Tenancy for Years The possessing of real property for a specified, limited time, usually for years, but may be for weeks or months.

Tenancy in Common The ownership of real property by two or more people, each with an undivided interest in it and all with equal right to possession of it. The undivided interests may or may not be equal. Upon the death of a tenant in common, his or her interest does not pass to the survivors but becomes part of his or her estate.

Tenant One who holds title, lease, or right to possession of real property.

Tender An offer or proposal of willingness.

Tenement A building occupied by tenants. A holding or interest in real property.

Tenement, Dominant An estate that has easement rights or interest in another estate.

Tenement, Servient An estate in which another estate has easement rights or interest.

Term A predetermined period of time.

Testamentary A disposition of property made by will.

Testate To die leaving a valid will (see Intestate).

Testator One who executes a valid will.

Testify To give evidence, based upon personal knowledge, under oath in a court of law.

Testimonial A declaration of the worth of property or of a person's good character.

Testimony A declaration of evidence, based upon personal knowledge, given under oath.

Title Legal ownership of property; a document proving ownership.

Title, Adverse A title claimed to have been acquired by adverse possession.

Title, Clear Title to a property that has been reasonably determined, without reference to public record, to be free and clear of liens or encumbrances.

Title, Clear, of Record A clear title as determined by evidence of public record.

Title, Cloud on a A possible claim to real estate that would diminish the rights of the owners.

Title, Color of Having the appearance of a title but not being a valid title.

Title, Legal A valid title.

Title, Marketable or Good A title without encumbrances or cloud; usually a clear title.

Title, Quiet A court proceeding to establish, from among several claims, the rightful title to property.

Title Search A review of public records to assure that the title to a parcel of real estate is free of encumbrances (such as mortgages, judgments, tax, or other liens), restrictions, or easements.

Tort A wrongful civil act, as distinguished from a criminal act, that violates the rights of another, except in matters of contracts.

Tort-Feasor One who commits a tort.

Tortious Injurious; wrongful; incurring liability.

To Wit Namely; as follows; viz.

Transfer To convey or pass ownership from one person to another; to sell.

Transfer Clause An agreement between landlord and tenant, which may be written into a lease, that releases the tenant from the obligation of a lease if transferred to another area by his or her employer. When applied to a tenant in military service, called a military clause.

Traverse A general or special denial of an allegation made by a litigant in a court proceeding.

Trespass An illegal intrusion into real property, or a disturbance of real property, that is in the legal possession of another.

Trial A judicial, public hearing examining evidence, and the application of law to such evidence, for a determination to be made by a judge or by a jury concerning specific claims and charges.

Trust An arrangement made by a trustor or settlor for the administration and distribution of property by another party, the trustee, for the benefit of a third party, the beneficiary.

Trust, Irrevocable A trust established in which the trustor relinquishes his or her right to revoke the arrangement.

Trust, Testamentary A trust that is created by the will of the testator/trustor.

Trust, Totten A bank account opened and used by the trustor, which becomes the property of a named beneficiary upon the death of the trustor. A Totten trust need not be probated but is figured as part of the decedent's estate for tax purposes.

Trustee One who administers a trust.

Trustor One who establishes a trust.

U

Unconscionable Not guided by conscience; unreasonable.

Underlet The renting out, by a tenant, of a portion of premises leased by the tenant while continuing to occupy the remainder of the leased premises, as in renting one bedroom of a leased apartment to a third party.

Underwriter An insurer; one who assumes the liability for specific insured losses.

Undivided Interest The right or interest in real property whereby each tenant in common, tenant by the entirety, or joint tenant has equal right to use of the entire property.

Undue Influence That amount of threat or persuasion that overpowers the will of another and causes him or her to act in favor of the person exerting the influence rather than to act under his or her own free will and best judgment.

Unilateral Contract A contract having binding promises made by one party only, generally invalid as lacking mutuality of consideration.

Unlawful Assembly A meeting of three or more persons who have the intent to riot or commit a crime by use of open force.

Unlawful Detainer Illegal retention of real estate, as when a tenant refuses to give up an apartment at the termination of a lease or when served notice to quit the premises for nonpayment of rent.

Usury The crime of charging a rate of interest on a loan that is greater than the amount permitted by law.

V

V. (or v.) Versus; against, as in *Smith v. Brown*. Also vs.

Vacate To set aside or annul a judgment. Also, in real estate law, to quit a premises.

Valid Properly executed; legally binding. Based upon incontestable truth or fact.

Validate To declare or mark as valid.

Valuable Consideration Anything of value given in exchange for performance or the promise of performance by another.

Venue A location; the place where a trial is to be held; a place within which jurisdiction is established.

Verdict The finding or decision of a judge or jury.

Verification A sworn statement affirming the truth or authenticity of a document.

Vicarious Liability Liability that occurs when a person is held legally responsible for the actions of another, as when an employer is held responsible for certain acts of employees.

Vinculo Matrimoni A complete dissolution of a marriage, as opposed to a divorce "from bed and board," which in some jurisdictions is the equivalent of a legal separation.

Viz.   Namely; to wit.

Void   Of no legal force; null; invalid.

Voluntary Assignment   A debtor's conveyance of property in trust for the benefit of creditors.

Voluntary Nonsuit   Occurs when a plaintiff abandons a case and accepts the consequences of a judgment and court costs.

Voucher   A signed or stamped document that serves as evidence of a transaction.

vs.   Versus; against, as in *Brown* vs. *Smith*.

W

Waiver   A voluntary relinquishment or renunciation of a claim, right, or privilege.

Ward   A person under the legal care and protection of a guardian.

Warrant   A judicial writ authorizing the execution of a judgment or the making of a search, seizure, or arrest.

Warranty   A statement of assurance by the seller or manufacturer that goods are as represented to the buyer; also an assurance that goods or property will be repaired or made serviceable if found defective within a stipulated period of time.

Waste   Damage, injury, or deterioration beyond normal wear and tear inflicted upon real property by anyone who is in legal possession of such property.

Will   A legal instrument by which a person declares how his or her property is to be distributed after death.

Willful   Deliberate; intentional.

Witness   One who saw or heard an occurrence and who is called into court to testify. Also refers to one who is present when a document is executed and who swears to its authenticity.

Writ   A written court order commanding that something be done or not be done.

Y

Yield   To surrender; to give up.

Z

Zoning   The setting apart of specified areas of a town, village, or municipality for specified activities or types of construction.

XV

INDEX

Abatement, in will, 226
Accidents, and injuries, reports of, 39–57
  Auto Accident Report, 42–46, F53–F75
    Minor Accident Report, 46, F77–F81
  Boating/Marine Accident Report, 47–48, F83–F93
    Float Plan, 47, F95–F96
  miscellaneous reports, 49–50
    Animal Accident Report, 49, F111–F114
    Attorney's Accident Work Sheet, 45, 50, F119–F135
    Building Accident Report, 49, F97–F102
    Defective Product Accident Report, 49, F107–F110
    Public Transportation Accident Report, 50, F115–F118
Adhesion contract, 27
Administrator, 226
Administratrix, 226
Affidavit, 451, F689–F690
  Affidavit of Attorney, 450, F677–F678
  Affidavit of completion, 64, 73
    Contractor's Affidavit of Completion, 73, F189–F190
  Self-proving Affidavit, 249–250, F377
    completed sample, 251
Affirmative defense, 154
Agreement, out-of-court settlement for small claims court, 153, F239
  completed sample, 156
Agreement Between Contractor and Subcontractor, 70, F165–F166
Agreement Between Husband and Wife, see Marriage
Agreement Between Owner and Contractor, 65–68, F149–F152
Agreement Between Owner and Contractor—Short Form, 65, 68, F155–F156
Agreement for Submission of an Existing Dispute to Arbitration
  form for one arbitrator, 87, F191–F192
  form for three arbitrators, 87, F199–F200
Agreement in Contemplation of Marriage, see Marriage
Agreement of joint tenancy, 242
Agreement of tenancy in common, 242
Agreement to Live Together, see Living together, agreement for
Agreement to Purchase Real Estate, 345–346, F561–F562
  completed sample, 347–348
Alimony, see Marriage, Agreement in Contemplation of
  Marriage, possible dissolution of the marriage
American Arbitration Association (AAA), 81–85
  commercial arbitration rules of, 82–83
Animal Accident Report, 49, F111–F114
Answer, of defendant, 21
Apartments, rental of, see Lease agreements, apartment
Appeal, 23
  from small claims court, 169
  under provisions of the Privacy Act, 370
Appeals courts, 23
Appellate courts, 9
Appliance/Equipment Checklist, 294, F525–F532
Application for Subpoena, 148, F235–F236
  completed sample, 149–150
Appraisal, of house, see House(s), selling your own
Arbitration, 81–90
  Agreement for Submission of an Existing Dispute to
      Arbitration, 87
    form for one arbitrator, 87, F191–F192
    form for three arbitrators, 87, F199–F200
  avoidance of, 81–85
  Demand for Arbitration, 87–88
    form for one arbitrator, 87–88, F193–F194
    form for three arbitrators, 87–88, F201–F202
  Guidelines for Arbitration, 88
    form for one arbitrator, 88, F195–F198
    form for three arbitrators, 88, F203–F206
  model arbitration agreement for insertion in a contract, 89
    Agreement Using One Arbitrator, 89, F207
    Agreement Using Three Arbitrators, 89, F209
  Petition for the Appointment of Arbitrator, 89–90, F211–F212
Assault, 18–19
  and battery, 18
Assets, of trust, 263
Assumption of risk, 17

Attorney
  advice by, in writing your own marriage contract, 175, 177, 190–191, 194, 197–198
  duties of, in estate probate and administration, 229–230
  fees of, 12–13
    award of, per FOIA, 361, 378
    award of, per Privacy Act, 372, 378
  finding, 13–14
  responsibilities of, as escrow agent, 349
  retainer of, see Retainer, of attorney
  when to consult, 5, 21, 154, 216, 237, 269, 272, 330, 331, 335, 344, 349, 377, 378
  where to find, for FOIA and Privacy Act litigation, 378
  working with, 14
  see also Attorney forms
Attorney forms, 50, 53, 450–451
  Affidavit, 451, F689–F690
  Affidavit of Attorney, 450, F677–F678
  Attorney's Accident Work Sheet, 45, 50, F119–F135
  Auto Dealer's Powers of Attorney, 450, F679
  Contingent Fee Retainer, 451, F685
  Power of Attorney, 53, 450, F145, F673–F674
    miscellaneous provisions for insertion in, 450, F675
  Release of All Rights and Claims, 54–55, F147–F148
    completed sample, 56–57
  Retainer, 450, F683
  Retainer and Power of Attorney, 53, F143–F144
  Retainer of Attorney by Executor, 451, F687
  Revocation of Power of Attorney, 450, F681–F682
Attorney's Accident Work Sheet, 45, 50, F119–F135
Authority to Represent the Owner, 69, F159, F161
Authorization to Inspect Hospital Medical Records, 51, 430–431, F137–F138
Authorization to Inspect Physician's Medical Records, 51, 430–431, F139–F140
Auto, bill of sale of, see Car, selling your own
Auto accident, what to do first after, 42
Auto Accident Report, 42–46, F53–F75
  Minor Accident Report, 46, F77–F81
Auto Dealer's Powers of Attorney, 450, F679
Auto rental contract, 19
Auto/Truck Rental Agreement, 432, F601–F602

Bailee, 17
Bailment, 17–18
Battery, 18
Beneficiary, 263
Bequeath, 225
Bid and Proposal, 71, F177–F178
Bids, obtaining, from contractor, 62
Bill of Rights, 4–5
Bill(s) of sale, 19, 435, 446
  Bill of Sale of Boat, 435
    form for individual buyer and seller, 435, F625–F626
    form for joint buyers and sellers, 435, F627–F628
  Bill of Sale of Motor Vehicle, see Car, selling your own
  Bill of Sale of Personal Property, 435
    form for individual buyer and seller, 435, F629–F630
    form for joint buyers and sellers, 435, F631–F632
  of car, see Car, selling your own
Boat, bills of sale of, see Bill(s) of sale
Boating/Marine Accident Report, 47–48, F83–F93
  Float Plan, 47, F95–F96
Boat Rental Agreement, 432, F603–F604
Building Accident Report, 49, F97–F102

Car, selling your own, 436–447
  advertising and showing, 441–444, 447
    average loan value of car, 444
    displaying car, 443–444
    FOR SALE signs, 443
    three-by-five cards, use of, 443
    window sticker, 443, 447
  Bill of Sale of Motor Vehicle, 446
    form for individual buyer and seller, 446, F639–F640
    form for joint buyers and sellers, 446, F641–F642

Car, selling your own (*cont.*)
  exterior appearance, 437–439
    Fix-up Materials Shopping List, 446, **F633**
  facts in, 444
  interior appearance, 439–441
    Fix-up Materials Shopping List, 446, **F633**
  mechanical condition, 436–437
  Odometer Mileage Statement, 446, **F643**
  Offer to Purchase Motor Vehicle, 445, 446, **F635**
  pricing, 441
  Receipt for Nonrefundable Deposit, 445, 446, **F637**
Charitable remainder trust, *see* Trust(s), charitable remainder
Chattel Mortgage, 449, **F665–F668**
CIA Privacy Act/FOIA Request, 374, 376, **F569–F570**
  completed sample, 381–382
Civil law, 8
Clayton Act of 1914, 126
Clifford trust, *see* Trust(s), Clifford
Close corporation, bequest of shares of, 258, **F429**
Code of Federal Regulations (CFR), 374
Codicil, 224–225
Cohabitants, unmarried, *see* Living together, agreement for
Common-law marriage, 216
Community property, 242–243
  division of, in Agreement in Contemplation of Marriage, 175,
    183
  in trust, 274, 276
  in will, 225, 226, 227–228, 248–249
Comparative negligence, 17
Comparison Shopping Checklist, 97, 98, **F213–F214**
Complaint(s)
  consumer, *see* Consumer complaints
  in court, 21
Congressional Directory, 397–398
Constitution, U.S., 4–6
Consumer complaints, 101–111
  art of complaining, 105
  communication of, 102–103
    by letter, 103, 104
      sample follow-up letter, 104, 109
      sample initial complaint letter, 104, 107–108
      sample letter to third-party organization, 104, 110–111
    by personal visit, 103
    by telephone, 102–103
      Telephone Log, 134, **F229–F230**
  organization of, 101–102
  for small claims court, *see* Small claims court(s), making and
    filing complaint to
  techniques and tactics to use, 103–105
  when complaining fails, 105–106; *see also* Small claims
    court(s)
Consumer Complaint Report, FTC, 126, **F223–F224**
Consumer organizations, 130–134
  San Francisco Consumer Action (SFCA), 131
  state-sponsored consumer protection agencies, 131–134
    list of, by state, 131–133
Consumer Product Complaint Form, 130, **F227**
Consumer Product Safety Commission, U.S., 49, 130, 388; *see
  also* Consumer Product Complaint Form
Consumer Questionnaire, ICC, 128, **F225–F226**
Consumer rights, 93–134
  how to avoid consumer hassles, 94–95
  shopping, protecting your consumer rights while, 98–100
    Comparison Shopping Checklist, 97, 98, **F213–F214**
    Warranty Comparison Checklist, 97, 98–100, **F215**
  warranty rights, 96–97
    exercising, 97
    full warranty, 96
    implied warranty, 96–97
      of fitness for a particular purpose, 97; *see also*
        Revocation of Acceptance
      of merchantability, 97; *see also* Revocation of Acceptance
      protection against consequential damages, 97
      see also Uniform Commercial Code (UCC)
    limited warranty, 96
  see also Consumer complaints; Consumer organizations;

Consumer Product Safety Commission, U.S.;
  Federal Trade Commission (FTC); Interstate
  Commerce Commission (ICC); Revocation of
  Acceptance; Small claims court(s); Uniform
  Commercial Code (UCC); U.S. Office of Consumer
  Affairs (OCA)
Consumers, justice for, *see* Small claims court(s)
Contesting a will, 226
Contingent Fee Retainer, 451, **F685**
Contract(s), 19–20
  conditions for, 19
Contractor
  finding, 61, 62
  liens, *see* Homeowner, and contractor, liens
  negotiating contract with, by homeowner, 62–63
  obtaining bids from, 62
    Bid and Proposal, 71, **F177–F178**
  owner as, 71, 74–77
    dealing with subcontractors, 74–75
    Job Estimate Work Sheet, 71, **F167–F175**
    savings, 75–76
      on contractor profit, 75
      on interest, 75–76
      on labor, 75
      on materials, 75
      sweat equity, 76
    sources of information, 76–77
    working with architect, 76
  and subcontractor, 70
    Agreement Between Contractor and Subcontractor, 70,
      F165–F166
    Job Estimate Work Sheet, 71, **F167–F175**
  see also Homeowner; House(s)
Contractor's Affidavit of Completion, 73, **F189–F190**
Contributory negligence, 16, 17
Conversion, 17, 18
Corporation, close, bequest of shares of, 258, **F429**
Corpus, of trust, 263
Counterclaim, 154, 169
Counteroffer, 345, **F563**
Court(s)
  declaring marriage agreement "contrary to public policy,"
    189–190
  enforcement of Agreement in Contemplation of Marriage by,
    177, 195
  going to, 21–23
    cost of, 23
  staying out of, 15–20
  see also entries for particular kinds of courts
Court(s) of claims, 9
Court system, 9–11
Credit
  Credit Application, 448, **F645–F647**
  Request for Disclosure of Credit Information, 449, **F671**
  Request for Reason for Adverse Credit Action, 449, **F669**
Criminal law, 8
Cross-claim, 154, 169
Cross-examination, 22
Crown loan, *see* Trust(s), Crown loan
Curtesy, 226

Declaration of Gift, 237–239, 269–271
  for gift of personal property, 269–270, **F433–F434**
    completed sample, 271
  for gift of real estate, 237, **F363–F364**
    completed sample, 238–239
  see also Trust(s); Will(s)
Declaration and Notice of Motion to Vacate Judgment, 158,
    F241–F242
  completed sample, 160–161
Deed of Trust, 331
Default judgment, against defendant, in small claims court, 158
Defective Product Accident Report, 49, **F107–F110**
Defendant, 8
Defendant's answer, 21

Demand for Arbitration, 87–88
    form for one arbitrator, 87–88, **F193–F194**
    form for three arbitrators, 87–88, **F201–F202**
Departing Tenant Cleanup Letter, 35, **F49**
Deposition(s), 22
    Notice to Take Deposition, 154–155
Depository libraries, federal, 401–423
Devise, 225
Direct examination, 22
Direct mail forms, 429
    for less mail
        form letter to companies, requesting removal of name from
            mailing list, 429, **F589**
        form letter to Direct Mail Marketing Association (DMMA),
            429, **F587**
        Notices Not to Add Name to Mailing List, 429, **F591**
    for more mail, form letter to DMMA, 429, **F593–F594**
Direct Mail Marketing Association (DMMA), see Direct mail
    forms
Discovery, 22
Disinherit, 226
Dispute, with contractor, 64
Document to Be Kept with the Last Will and Testament, 249,
    F371–F375
Donor, 263; see also Uniform Donor Card
Dowager, 226
Dower, 226

Earnest Money Receipt, 345–346, **F565**
Easement, right of, 345
Economic Recovery Tax Act of 1981 (ERTA), 231–232, 233, 235,
    236–237, 240, 254–255, 263–264, 265, 269
    tax-free interspousal transfer and life income trust provisions
        of, two wills using, 254–255
        will of husband, 254–255, **F415–F420**
        will of wife, 254–255, **F421–F426**
    and trusts, 263–264, 265, 269
Emergency Names and Numbers, list of, 430, **F599**
Employment Application, 434, **F621–F624**
Encumbrance, 345
Enforcement, by court, of Agreement in Contemplation of
    Marriage, 177, 195
Environmental Protection Agency (EPA), 358, 388
Equal Credit Opportunity Act of 1975, 126
Equivalent Tax Exemption Table, 231, 232, 255, 264
ERTA, see Economic Recovery Tax Act of 1981 (ERTA)
Estate, 225
    evaluating, 240–243
        Informal Estate Evaluation, 240–242, **F365–F370**
    guardian of the, 225
Estate planning specialist, when to consult, 237, 269, 272
Estate probate, 225, 229, 230
Estate taxes, federal, minimizing, 231–239
    through gifts from estate, 231–235, 237–239
        Declaration of Gift, 237–239, 269–271
            for gift of personal property, 269–270, **F433–F434**
                completed sample, 271
            for gift of real estate, 237, **F363–F364**
                completed sample, 238–239
        deduction of excess amount of gift from lifetime equivalent
            estate tax exemption, 232–233
        financial planner, finding, 235–236
        gifts, 233–235
            charitable gifts, 234–235
            to children, 233
            for educational and medical expenses, 235
            of life insurance, 234
            of real estate, 234
            of securities, 233
            larger gifts, 234
            qualifications for, 233
            unmarried cohabitants, deprived of benefits of marital
              estate tax exclusion, 235
    see also Wills, estate evaluation
Estimated Purchase Data, 332, **F549**
    completed sample, 333

Evidence
    in Agreement in Contemplation of Marriage, 195
    collecting, in making consumer complaint, 98, 103–104
    in small claims court, 98, 147, 157–158
Examination, direct and cross-, 22
Executor, 225
    alternate, 229
    appointment of, provision for, in will, 245
    duties of, in estate probate and administration, 229–230
    Retainer of Attorney by Executor, 451, **F687**
    see also Will(s)
Executive Order 12065, National Security Information, 355, 363,
    383–384
Executive Order 12356, 355–356
Executrix, see Executor
Exhibit A, 198, 217–218, **F325**
    completed sample, 214
Exhibit B, 198, 217–218, **F327**
    completed sample, 215
Extension of Lease, 31, **F21**
Exterior Checklist, 294, **F497–F508**
Extraordinary care, 17

Fact Sheet, 295–296, 317, 321, **F533–F541**
    completed sample, 297–305
Fair Credit Billing Act of 1975, 126
Fair Credit Reporting Act of 1970, 126
Fair market value, of house, 307
Fair Packaging and Labeling Act of 1966, 126
FBI Privacy Act/FOIA Request, 374, 376, **F567–F568**
    completed sample, 379–380
Federal agencies, directory of, 392–397
Federal bankruptcy courts, 10
Federal courts, 10
Federal estate taxes, see Estate taxes, federal, minimizing
Federal Hazardous Substances Act, 130
Federal Housing Administration (FHA)
    appraisal of house by, 307, 308, 310 314
        VA/FHA/HUD forms, 310–314
    mortgage insured by, 324, 325, 328–329
Federal information centers (FIC), 400–401
Federally-held information, see Freedom of Information Act
    (FOIA); Privacy Act
Federal Register, 360, 370–371, 373, 374, 376, 386
Federal Rules of Civil Procedure, 144
Federal Trade Commission (FTC), 95, 98, 99, 125–127, 358, 388
    Consumer Complaint Report, 126, **F223–F224**
    Federal Trade Commission consumer notice and form, 126,
        F219–F222
    law administered by, 126
    reports and booklets of, 127
FHA forms, see VA/FHA/HUD forms
FIND/svp, 375
Financial forms, 448–449
    Chattel Mortgage, 449, **F665–F668**
    Credit Application, 448, **F645–F647**
    Installment Note, 448, **F659**
    Joint Financial Statement, 448, **F653–F655**
    Personal Financial Statement, 448, **F649–F652**
    Promissory Note, 448, **F657**
    Request for Disclosure of Credit Information, 449, **F671**
    Request for Reason for Adverse Credit Action, 449, **F669**
    Security Agreement, 448–449, **F663–F664**
    Series Promissory Note, 448, **F661**
Financial planner, finding, 235–236
Financial statement, 448
    Joint Financial Statement, 448, **F653–F655**
    Personal Financial Statement, 448, **F649–F652**
Financing
    for home improvement, 63–64
    of house, see House, selling your own, helping buyer finance
Fitness for a particular purpose, implied warranty of, 97, 113,
    114, 123–124
Fix-up Materials Shopping List, 446, **F633**
Flammable Fabrics Act, 130
Float Plan, 47, **F95–F96**

FOIA, *see* Freedom of Information Act (FOIA)
foi services, inc., 358, 424–425
  FOI Log excerpt, 425
Food and Drug Administration (FDA), 130, 358, 388
Freedom of Information Act (FOIA), 355–425
  administrative appeal, after denial of FOIA request, 389
    Sample Format for FOIA Records Release Appeal, 389,
      F583–F584
  application of, to federally held information only, 357–358
  Executive Order 12065, National Security Information, 355,
    363, 383–384
  Executive Order 12356, 355–356
  filing FOIA lawsuit to effect release of information, 389–390
    award of attorney fees, 390
    Model Format for FOIA Lawsuit to Effect Release of
      Records, 390, **F585–F586**
    where to initiate litigation, 378, 389–390
  filing FOIA request to effect release of information, 383–389,
    391
    exemptions that federal agencies use, 383–386
    Freedom of Information Act Request, 387–388, **F581**
      completed sample, 391
    reverse FOIA, 388–389
    see also Privacy Act, filing Privacy Act request to effect
      release of information
  finding attorney for litigation involving, 378
  letter from Attorney General Griffin Bell, 363, 365–366, 389
  *Litigation Under the Federal Freedom of Information Act and
    Privacy Act*, 364, 378
  memorandum from Deputy Attorney General Peter Flaherty,
    364, 367
  search and copying fees, 386–387, 388
    waiver or reduction of, 386–387
  sources of information to help frame FOIA request, 392–425
    Congressional Directory, 397–398
    depository libraries, federal, list of, 401–423
    federal agencies, directory of, 392–397
    federal information centers (FIC), 400–401
    foi services, inc., 424–425
      FOI Log excerpt, 425
    Guide to Records Retention Requirements, 398–400
    Information U.S.A., 423–424
  systems of records, 373–374
  Title 5, USC, Sec. 552, 359–364, 383
  uses of, 357–358
    corporate, 358
    general, 357–358
    personal, 358
  see also Privacy Act
Full warranty, 96
Furnishings Inspection and Inventory, 433, **F615–F617**
Fur Products Labeling Act of 1951, 126

Garnishee Summons, 164, **F295–F296**
Garnishment, 164
General Waiver of Liens, 72, **F179–F184**
Gifts, *see* Estate taxes, federal, minimizing
Gift taxes and gift tax credits, *see* Estate taxes, federal,
    minimizing
Government Printing Office (GPO) bookstores, U.S., list of, 375
Grantor, 263
Great care, 16, 17
Guardian(s)
  of children, in will, 248
  of the person, 225
  of the property/estate, 225
Guidelines for Arbitration, 88
  form for one arbitrator, 88, **F195–F198**
  form for three arbitrators, 88, **F203–F206**
Guide to Records Retention Requirements, 398–400

Heir, 226
Heiress, 226
Holdover tenant, 29
Holographic wills, 226

Home improvement, 61–64
Homeowner
  and contractor, 61–77
    agreements and forms between, 64, 65–68, 69, 71, 72–73
      Agreement Between Owner and Contractor, 65–68,
        F149–F152
        Alternate Articles, 65, 67, 68, **F153**
        Authority to Represent the Owner, 69, **F159**
      Agreement Between Owner and Contractor—Short
        Form, 65, 68, **F155–F156**
        Alternate Articles, 68, **F157**
        Authority to Represent the Owner, 69, **F161**
      Bid and Proposal, 71, **F177–F178**
      Contractor's Affidavit of Completion, 73, **F189–F190**
      General Waiver of Liens, 72, **F179–F184**
      Receipt for Conditional Payment, 72, **F187**
      Revocation of Authority to Represent the Owner, 69,
        F163
      Waiver of Lien, 64, 72, **F185–F186**
    liens, 63, 64, 72, 73
      mechanic's lien, 64, 72
      surety bond, 63, 64
      see also agreements and forms between *subentry* (*above*)
    performance bond, 62
  as contractor, *see* Contractor, owner as
  dispute with contractor, 64
  financing home improvements, 63–64
    payment schedule, 65, 72
  finding contractor, 61, 62
  negotiating contract with contractor, 62–63
  see also Contractor; House(s)
House(s)
  building your own, *see* Contractor, owner as
  rental of, *see* Lease agreement(s), house; Real estate forms
  selling your own, 291–352
    advertising, 315–318
      Fact Sheet, 295–296, 317, 321, **F533–F541**
        completed sample, 297–305
      front yard sign, 315–316
      after house sold, 317
      newspaper ads, 316–317, 321
      OPEN HOUSE Flyer, 321, **F547**
        completed sample, 323
      photo description sheet, 296, 317
        sample, 318
      three-by-five cards, 317
    closing, 349–352
      attorney responsibilities, as escrow agent, 349
      closing meeting, 349–350
        buyer, expected payments of, 349–350
        seller, expected payments of, 349
      contract of sale, 349
        appliances and equipment, 349
        move-in date, of buyer, 349
        points, payment of, 349
        taxes and insurance, apportionment of, 349
      settlement statement, 350–352
    due-on-sale clause
      avoidance of, 334–335
        Lease Agreement with Option to Purchase, 334–335,
          F553–F559
          completed sample, 336–342
      enforcement of, 325
    Fact Sheet, 295–296, 317, 321, **F533–F541**
      completed sample, 297–305
      financial data, 295, 305, **F541**
      house and lot plan in, 295–296, 298
      photo description sheet with, use of, 296, 317, 318
    government publications, free, list of, 350
    helping buyer finance, 324–333, 334–342, 343
      contract of sale, 331
      Estimated Purchase Data, 332, **F549**
        completed sample, 333
        monthly payments per $1,000 amortized mortgage,
          table of, 332
      Loan Comparison Data, 332, **F551**

House(s) (*cont.*)
  selling your own (*cont.*)
    helping buyer finance (*cont.*)
      mortgage(s)
        balloon-note, 330
        buyer qualifications for, 325–326, 343
        buyer's assumption of seller's, 325
          due-on-sale clause
            avoidance of, 334–335; *see also* Lease Agreement with Option to Purchase *subentry*
            enforcement of, 325
            federally chartered savings and loan associations (S&Ls), June 28, 1982, U.S. Supreme Court decision concerning, 325, 334
            Lease Agreement with Option to Purchase, 334–335, **F553–F559**
              completed sample, 336–342
        conventional, 325–328
          fixed-rate, 325–327
          formulas that "qualify" prospective buyers, 325–326
            54/60 rule, 325–326
            MGB rule, 325
            net income rule, 326
          graduated-payment, 327–328
            variable rate, 328
          interest rates, effect on qualifying income, 326
          private mortgage insurance, Mortgage Guaranty Insurance Corporation (MGIC), 326–327
          variable interest rate, 327
            payment-capped, 327
            rate-capped, 327
            uncapped, 327
        FHA-insured, 324, 325, 328–329; *see also* pricing house, appraisal of fair market value, VA and FHA appraisals *subentry*
        payment table booklets, 329–330
        rollover, 329–330
        second, 330–331, 332
        VA-guaranteed, 324, 325, 329; *see also* pricing house, appraisal of fair market value, VA and FHA appraisals *subentry*
        zero percent, 330
    improvements to make before sale of house, 293–294
      appliances and equipment, 294
        Appliance/Equipment Checklist, 294, **F525–F532**
      clean out clutter, 293
      exterior appearance, 293
        Exterior Checklist, 293, 294, **F497–F508**
      interior appearance, 294
        Interior Checklist, 293, 294, **F509–F523**
      major repairs, 293
    negotiating sale of house, 343–348
      Counteroffer, 345, **F563**
      discussing price, 343–344
      Earnest Money Receipt, 345–346, **F565**
      written offers, 344–346
        acceptance of, 344–346
        Agreement to Purchase Real Estate, 344–346, **F561–F562**
          completed sample, 347–348
        sample letter, 344
    pricing house, 306–314
      appraisal of fair market value, 307
        independent appraiser, how to find, 307
        VA and FHA appraisals, 307, 308
          VA/FHA/HUD forms, 310–314
            Endorsement to Certificate of Reasonable Value, 314
            Instructions for Preparation of VA Request for Determination of Reasonable Value/HUD Application for Property Appraisal and Commitment, 310
            Residential Appraisal Report, 312
            VA Certificate of Reasonable Value/HUD Conditional Commitment, 313
            VA Request for Determination of Reasonable

            Value (Real Estate)/HUD Application for Property Appraisal and Commitment, 311
        working with appraiser, 308
      Selling Price Comparison Survey, 306–307, **F543**
        completed sample, 309
    showing house, 319–323
      arrival of prospects, 320
      drop-ins, how to handle, 320–321
      open house, holding, 321, 323
      OPEN HOUSE Flyer, 321, **F547**
        completed sample, 323
      organizing tour, 319
      phone calls from prospects, 319–320, 322
        Telephone Log, 319–320, **F545**
          completed sample, 322
    termite inspection, 308
    see also Contractor; Homeowner
HUD forms, *see* VA/FHA/HUD forms
Husband, and wife, agreement between, *see* Marriage

Implied warranty, 96–97
Imputed negligence, 17
Informal Estate Evaluation, 240–242, **F365–F370**
Information U.S.A., 423–424
Injuries, accidents and, *see* Accidents, and injuries, reports of
Installment Note, 448, **F659**
Insurance adjuster, talking with, 39–40
Interest, legal rate of, on promissory note, 19–20
Interior Checklist, 294, **F509–F523**
Internal Revenue Service Code, 232, 233
Interrogatories, 162–164, 167–168
  Petition for Order to Answer (Written) Interrogatories, 144, 163, **F247–F248**
    completed sample, 167–168
  Plaintiff's Interrogatories in Aid of Judgment, 163, **F251–F294**
  Summons to Answer Interrogatories, 163, **F249–F250**
Interstate Commerce Commission (ICC), 127–129
  Consumer Questionnaire, 128, **F225–F226**
  reports and booklets of, 128
Inter vivos trust, *see* Trust(s), *inter vivos*
Intestate, dying, 223
Irrevocable trust, *see* Trust(s), irrevocable
Issue, in probate, 226

Job Estimate Work Sheet, 71, **F167–F175**
Joint bank accounts, after death of spouse, 253
Joint Financial Statement, 448, **F653–F655**
Joint tenancy, 242
Joint wills, 226
Judge or jury option, 21–22
Judicial mechanisms for small claims litigation, state-by-state, table of, 170–171
Jurisdiction, 9
  of small claims court, 169
Jury or judge option, 21–22
Justice of the Peace (JP) courts, 170–171

Landlords, and tenants, 27–35; *see also* Lease agreement(s)
Last Will and Testament, *see* Will(s)
Law
  amendments to the Constitution, 5–6
  American, basis of, 4–7
  Bill of Rights, 4–5
  civil, 8
  criminal, 8
  FTC-administered, 126
  religious, 7
  "unwritten," 6–7
Lawyer, *see* Attorney
Lease agreement(s), 27–29, 30–31, 32–33
  apartment
    furnished, 30, **F5–F8**
      List of Furnishings, 30, 34, **F43**
      subleases of, for use by tenant, 32–33, **F37–F38**
      Permission to Sublet, 33, **F39–F40**
      Permission to Underlet, 33, **F41–F42**

Lease agreements (*cont.*)
  apartment (*cont.*)
    Rental Application, 34, **F45–F46**
    unfurnished, 30, **F1–F4**
      subleases of
        for use by landlord, 32, **F33–F34**
        for use by tenant, 32, **F35–F36**
  Departing Tenant Cleanup Letter, 35, **F49**
  Extension of Lease, 31, **F21**
  house
    furnished, 30, **F13–F16**
      country/seashore, seasonal, 30, **F17–F19**
      List of Furnishings, 30, 34, **F43**
      sublease of, for use by tenant, 32–33, **F37–F38**
    with option to purchase, 334–335, **F553–F559**
      completed sample, 336–342
    Permission to Sublet, 33, **F39–F40**
    Permission to Underlet, 33, **F41–F42**
    unfurnished, 30, **F9–F12**
      subleases of
        for use by landlord, 32, **F33–F34**
        for use by tenant, 32, **F35–F36**
  monthly tenancy, 32
    furnished premises, 32, **F31–F32**
    unfurnished apartment, 32, **F29–F30**
  Notice of Intent to Vacate, 35, **F47**
  parking space, 31, **F23–F24**
  short term, 32–33
  storage space, 31, **F25–F27**
  Transfer Clause, 29, 35, **F51**
  see also Real estate forms
Legacy, 225
"Legalese," 20
Legatee, 225
Letters, making complaints by, *see* Consumer complaints
Liens, 63, 64, 72, 73, 345; *see also* General Waiver of Liens;
    Waiver of Lien
Life income trust provisions of ERTA, and tax-free interspousal
    transfer provisions of ERTA, two wills using, 254–255
  will of husband, 254–255, **F415–F420**
  will of wife, 254–255, **F421–F426**
Life tenancy, 263
Lifetime equivalent estate tax exemption, deduction from, 232–
    233
Limited warranty, 96
List of Furnishings, 30, 32, 34, **F43**
List of Important People and Papers, 229, **F359–F362**
*Litigation Under the Federal Freedom of Information Act and
    Privacy Act*, 364, 378
Living together, agreement for, 176–177, 216–218, **F329–F355**
  children, 216
  common-law marriage, 216
  completion of, 217–218
  disclosure in, 218
  Exhibits A and B in, 217–218, **F325, F327**
  need for, 216–217
  provisions of, 217
    future marriage not a condition precedent, 217
    means of dissolution, 217
    names of the parties, 217
    paternity, 217
Living Will, 452, **F691–F692**
  with pregnancy clause, 452, **F693–F694**
  for use after diagnosis of a terminal condition, 452, **F695–F696**
Loan Comparison Data, 332, **F551**
Local courts, 9
"Lovers' trust," *see* Trust(s), "lovers'"

Magnuson-Moss Warranty/Federal Trade Improvement Act of
    1975, 95, 126, 137–138
Market value, fair, of house, 307
Marriage
  Agreement Between Husband and Wife, 176, 219, **F357–F358**
  Agreement in Contemplation of Marriage, 175–177, 178–215,
    F297–F324
    advice by attorney in, 175, 177, 190–191, 194, 197–198

children, Article III provisions, 187–189
  care and support of children, 188
  education of children, 189
  mutual agreement not to have children, 188
  names of children, 189
  religious instruction of children, 189
  rights of children, 189
community-property states, 175, 183, 225, 227–228, 242–243
completed sample, 198–199, 200–213
completion of, 199
conditions of the agreement, Article I provisions, 179–181
  acceptance of obligations, 179
  children by previous marriage, 181
  declaration of principle, 179
  incapacitation of either party, 181
  marriage as a condition precedent, 179
  names of the parties, 180
  neither party presently married, 179
  openness between parties, 179–180
  present employment of the parties, 180–181
  previous children, 181
  purpose, 179
  sexual exclusivity, 180
  sexual nonexclusivity, 180
  use of living space, 181
  voluntary, 179
  waiver of rights, 179
enforcement by court, 177, 195
Exhibits A and B, 198, **F325, F327**
  completed samples, 214, 215
general provisions, of Article VI, 194–198
  advice by counsel, 194
  affidavit of counsel, 197–198
  attestation of notary, 197
  counterparts, 195
  enforcement by court, 195
  entire agreement, 195
  evidence, 195
  execution of agreement, 196
  execution of documents, 195
  fair and equitable, 195
  governing law, 195–196
  headings, 194
  independent counsel, 194
  partial invalidity, 194–195
  parties bound, 195
  resident agent, 196
possible dissolution of the marriage, Article IV provisions,
    189–192
  advice of counsel, 190, 191
  child custody, 192
  child support in the event of dissolution of the marriage,
    192
  compliance with applicable law, 191–192
  payments in lieu of alimony (and support), 191
  removal of children from jurisdiction of the court, 192
  support *pendente lite*, 192
  waiver of alimony, 190–191
  waiver of alimony and support, 190
    provision for child support, 190
property and financial provisions, of Article II, 181–187
  bank accounts
    household, 184
    joint, 183
    separate, 184
  credit transactions by the parties, 184–185
  disclosure, 182
  existing financial obligations, 184
  financial support, 186
    revision of shared financial support, 186
  gainful employment and education, 186–187
  home care and maintenance, 187
  household expenses, 185
    revision of shared household expenses, 185–186
  partition of community property, 183
  present property of the parties, 182

Marriage (cont.)
  Agreement in Contemplation of Marriage (cont.)
    property and financial provisions, of Article II (cont.)
      property held as tenants by the entirety, 182–183
      right to make voluntary transfers not waived, 183
      separate property, 182
      taxes, 185
      waiver by future husband, 182
      waiver by future wife, 182
    protection from court with, 175
    testementary provisions, of Article V, 192–194
      agreement between the parties, 193
      life insurance, 194
  common-law, 216
Martindale Hubbell Law Directory, 13
Mechanic's lien, 64
Medical forms, 430–431
  Authorization to Inspect Hospital Medical Records, 51, 430–431, F137–F138
  Authorization to Inspect Physician's Medical Records, 51, 430–431, F139–F140
  (List of) Emergency Names and Numbers, 430, F599
  Special Medical Power of Attorney, 430, F597–F598
  Uniform Donor Cards, 430, F595–F596
Merchantability, implied warranty of, 97, 112, 114, 121–122
Minor Accident Report, 46, F77–F81
Mortgage Guaranty Insurance Corporation (MGIC), 326–327
Mortgages, see House(s), selling your own
Motor vehicle, bill of sale of, see Car, selling your own

Natural Death Act, 452
Negligence, 15–17
No fault insurance, 46
Notes, and interest, 19–20
Notice of Intent to Vacate, 35, F47
Notice of Overdue Rent, 433, F611
Notice of Rent Due, 433, F609
Notice of Revocation of Acceptance, see Revocation of Acceptance
Notices Not to Add Name to Mailing List, 429, F591
Notice to Quit Premises, 433, F613
Notice to Take Deposition, 154–155
Nuisance, 18
Nuncupative wills, 226

Odometer Mileage Statement, 446, F643
Offer to Purchase Motor Vehicle, 445, 446, F635
Office of Consumer Affairs (OCA), U.S., 130
OPEN HOUSE flyer, 321, F547
  completed sample, 323
"Open" Rental Agreement, 432, F605–F606
Operation Identification, 34
Oral wills, 226
Ordinary care, 17
Orphans courts, 9
Out-of-court settlement, 52, 53; see also Release of All Rights and Claims; Settlement, outside of small claims court

Parking Space Lease, 31, F23–F24
Per capita, in wills, 225
Peremptory challenges, 22
Performance bond, 62
Permission to Sublet, 33, F39–F40
Permission to Underlet, 33, F41–F42
Personal Financial Statement, 448, F649–F652
Personal property, 225
  bill of sale of, see Bill(s) of sale
Per stirpes, 225
Petition for Order to Answer (Written) Interrogatories, 144, 163, F247–F248
  completed sample, 167–168
Petition for the Appointment of Arbitrator, 89–90, F211–F212
Petition for Writ of Execution, 162, F243–F244
  completed sample, 165–166
Plaintiff, 8
Plaintiff's Interrogatories in Aid of Execution, 163

Plaintiff's Interrogatories in Aid of Judgment, 163, F251–F294
Poison Prevention Packaging Act, 130
Police, answering questions of, at scene of accident, 45, 52
Police blotter and/or accident report, request for a copy of, 52, F141
Power of Attorney, 53, 450, F145, F673–F674
  Auto Dealer's Powers of Attorney, 450, F679
  miscellaneous clauses for, 450, F675
  Retainer and Power of Attorney, 53, F143–F144
  Revocation of Power of Attorney, 450, F681–F682
  Special Medical Power of Attorney, 430, F597–F598
Precedent(s), 6–7, 22
Pretrial hearing, for small claims court, 140
Pretrial maneuvers, for small claims court, see Small claims court(s), pretrial maneuvers
Pretrial motions, 22
Principal, of trust, 263
Privacy Act, 355–425
  amendment appeal, 377
    Sample Format for Privacy Act Records Amendment Appeal, 377, F577–F578
  amendment of personal records, 376–377
    Sample Format for Privacy Act Records Amendment Request, 377, F575–F576
  appeal of denial of access to personal records, 376
    Sample Format for Privacy Act Records Release Appeal, 376, F573–F574
  filing Privacy Act request to effect release of information, 374–375, 376–382
    CIA Privacy Act/FOIA Request, 374, 376, F569–F570
      completed sample, 381–382
    FBI Privacy Act/FOIA Request, 374, 376, F567–F568
      completed sample, 379–380
    Privacy Act/FOIA Request, 376, F571–F572
  finding attorney for litigation involving, 378
  legal action to effect records amendment, 377–378
    Model Format for Privacy Act Lawsuit to Effect Amendment of Records, 377–378, F579
    where to file complaint, 378
  Litigation Under the Federal Freedom of Information Act and Privacy Act, 364, 378
  sources of information to help frame Privacy Act request, see Freedom of Information Act (FOIA), sources of information to help frame FOIA request
  systems of records, 373, 374–375
  Title 5, USC, Sec. 552a, 368–372
  see also Freedom of Information Act (FOIA)
Private nuisance, 18
Probate, estate, 225, 229, 230
Probate courts, 9, 225
Promissory Note, 448, F657
  Series Promissory Note, 448, F661
Property
  community, see Community property
  guardian of the, 225
  personal, 225
    bill of sale of, see Bill(s) of sale
  real, 225
  transfer of, to trustee, 269
Property Management Agreement, 433, F619–F620
Protecting Your Right to Privacy: Digest of Systems of Records, 360, 373, 374, 376
Public nuisance, 18
Public Transportation Accident Report, 50, F115–F118

Real estate appraisers, 307–308
Real estate forms, 433
  Furnishings Inspection and Inventory, 433, F615–F617
  Notice of Overdue Rent, 433, F611
  Notice of Rent Due, 433, F609
  Notice to Quit Premises, 433, F613
  Property Management Agreement, 433, F619–F620
  Rent Receipt, 433, F607
  see also House(s), selling your own; Lease agreement(s)
Real Estate Settlement Procedures Act, 350
Real property, 225

Receipt for Conditional Payment, 72, **F187**
Receipt for Nonrefundable Deposit, 445, 446, **F637**
Records, systems of, federal, 359, 370–371, 373–375
Refrigerator Safety Act, 130
Release of All Rights and Claims, 54–55, **F147–F148**
  completed sample, 56–57
Rental agreements, 432
  Auto/Truck Rental Agreement, 432, **F601–F602**
  Boat Rental Agreement, 432, **F603–F604**
  "Open" Rental Agreement, 432, **F605–F606**
  see also Lease agreement(s); Real estate forms
Rental Application, 34, **F45–F46**
Rent Receipt, 433, **F607**
Request for Copy of Police Blotter and/or Accident Report, 52,
  F141
Request for Disclosure of Credit Information, 449, **F671**
Request for Reason for Adverse Credit Action, 449, **F669**
"Rest, residue and remainder," 225
Retainer, of attorney, 450, **F683**
  Contingent Fee Retainer, 451, **F685**
  Retainer of Attorney by Executor, 451, **F687**
  Retainer and Power of Attorney, 53, **F143–F144**
Reverse FOIA, 388–389
Reversionary trust, *see* Trust(s), reversionary
Revocable trust, *see* Trust(s), revocable
Revocation of Acceptance, 105–106, 117–124
  Notice of Revocation of Acceptance, 117–119, **F217–F218**
    completed samples
      failing to meet the implied warranty of fitness for a
        particular purpose, 123–124
      failing to meet the implied warranty of merchantability,
        121–122
    table of state UCC citations, for use with, 119–120
Revocation of Authority to Represent the Owner, 69, **F163**
Revocation of Power of Attorney, 450, **F681–F682**
Revocation of Trust, 277
  for trusts having one trustor, 277, **F483–F484**
  for trusts having two trustors, 277, **F485–F486**
Rights and claims, release of all, 54–57, **F147–F148**
Rules of Civil Practice and Procedure, 144
Rules of the Court, for small claims court, 144–146

Sale, bills of, *see* Bill(s) of sale
San Francisco Consumer Action (SFCA), 131
Securities, gifts of, in will, 233
Security Agreement, 448–449, **F663–F664**
Self-Proving Affidavit, 249–250, **F377**
  completed sample, 251
Selling Price Comparison Survey, 306–307, **F543**
  completed sample, 309
Series Promissory Note, 448, **F661**
Service, of summons, 21, 139
Settlement, outside of small claims court, 139, 140, 153, 156
  Agreement, 153, **F239**
    completed sample, 156
Settlor, 263
Small claims court(s), 137–138
  appeal in, 169
  collecting award in, 162–168
    garnishment, 164
      Garnishee Summons, 164, **F295–F296**
      Petition for Garnishment, 164
    interrogatories, 162–164
      asking court to order defendant to submit to, 162–163
      Petition for Order to Answer (Written) Interrogatories,
        144, 163, **F247–F248**
        completed sample, 167–168
      Plaintiff's Interrogatories in Aid of Judgment, 163, **F251–
        F294**
      Summons to Answer Interrogatories, 163, **F249–F250**
    Petition for Writ of Execution, 162, **F243–F244**
      completed sample, 165–166
    Writ of Execution, 162, **F245–F246**
  evidence for case in, 98, 103–104, 147, 157–158
  judicial mechanisms for handling small claims litigation, by
    state, 169

table of, 170–171
  jurisdiction of, 169
  making and filing complaint to, 139–143
    Summons and Complaint, 139–140, **F231–F233**
      certificate, for mail service of, 139, 140
      completed sample, 141–143
      Statement of Complaint, 139
    Trial Notice, 139, 140
  pretrial hearing for, 140
  pretrial maneuvers, 153–155
    by defendant/defendant's attorney, 153–154
      affirmative defense, 154
      counterclaim, 154, 169
      cross-claim, 154, 169
      letter requesting delay of trial, 153–154
      Notice to Take Deposition, 154–155
      written interrogatories, 154
  requirements of suit to be brought before, 138
  rules of, 144–146
  settlement, out-of-court, 153, 156
    Agreement, 153, **F239**
      completed sample, 156
  statute of limitations of, 169
  transfer of case from, 169
  trial, 157–161
    default judgment, against defendant, 158
      Declaration and Notice of Motion to Vacate Judgment,
        158, **F241–F242**
        completed sample, 160–161
    dress, 158
    evidence, 157–158
    judgment, 158, 159
      typical small claims judgment form, 159
    procedure of, 157
    witnesses, 158
  venue of, 169
  waiting time for, 169
  what must be determined before taking case to, 138
  witnesses for, 147–148, 158
    subpoena(s) of, 23, 147–148, 158
      Application for Subpoena, 148, **F235–F236**
        completed sample, 149–150
      Subpoena Duces Tecum, 23, 148, 158, **F237–F238**
        completed sample, 151–152
      Subpoena for Witness, 148
Small claims litigation, judicial mechanisms for, by state, table
  of, 170–171
Sole ownership, 243
Special Medical Power of Attorney, 430, **F597–F598**
Standard & Poor's Register of Corporations, 102
Standard wills, 226
State-sponsored consumer protection agencies, 131–134
State courts, 9–10
State courts of appeals, 9
State Supreme Court, 9
Statute of limitations, 21
  for small claims court, 169
Storage Space Lease, 31, **F25–F27**
Street/Sidewalk Accident Report, 49, **F103–F106**
Subcontractor, *see* Contractor, owner as; Contractor, and
  subcontractor
Subleases, *see* Lease agreement(s)
Subpoena(s), 23, 147–152, 158
  Application for Subpoena, 148, **F235–F236**
    completed sample, 149–150
  Subpoena Duces Tecum, 23, 148, 158, **F237–F238**
    completed sample, 151–152
  Subpoena for Witness, 148
Summons, 21, 139
  Garnishee Summons, 164, **F295–F296**
Summons to Answer Interrogatories, 163, **F249–F250**
Summons and Complaint, for small claims court, 139–140,
  F231–F233
  completed sample, 141–143
Supreme Court, U.S., *see* U.S. Supreme Court
Surety bond, 63, 64

Surrogate courts, 9, 225
Sweat equity, 76
Sworn affidavit, 451; *see also* Affidavit

Tax(es)
    and charitable remainder trust, 266
    estate, federal, *see* Estate taxes, federal, minimizing
    gift, *see* Estate taxes, federal, minimizing
    and irrevocable trusts, 265
    and revocable trusts, 264–265
    see also Economic Recovery Tax Act of 1981 (ERTA)
Tax-free interspousal transfer and life income trust provisions of
        ERTA, two wills using, 254–255
    will of husband, 254–255, **F415–F420**
    will of wife, 254–255, **F421–F426**
Tax Reform Act of 1976, 231, 234
Tax Reform Act of 1984, 268
Telephone
    making complaint by, 102–103
        Telephone Log, 134, **F229–F230**
    in selling house, 319–320, 322
        Telephone Log, 319–320, **F545**
            completed sample, 322
Tenants
    in common, 242
    forms for departing, 35
    landlords and, 27–35
    see also Lease agreement(s)
Testamentary trust, *see* Trust(s), testamentary
Testator, 225
Testatrix, 225
Textile Fiber Products Identification Act of 1958, 126
Torts, 15–19
Totten trust, *see* Trust(s), Totten
Transfer Clause, of lease, 29, 35, **F51**
Trial, 22–23
Trial memorandum, 22
Trial Notice, for small claims court, 139, 140
Trust(s), 225, 263–287
    assets of, 263
    charitable remainder, *see* Trust(s), irrevocable charitable
        remainder
    Clifford, 263, 265–266, 268; *see also* Trust(s), reversionary
    concluding statements of, 274
    Crown loan, 267–268
    Declaration of Gift, 237–239, 269–271
        for gift of personal property, 269–270, **F433–F434**
            completed sample, 271
        for gift of real estate, 237, **F363–F364**
            completed sample, 238–239
    distribution clause(s), 285–287
        first-step, 285, **F487**
        optional
            for ten-year Clifford trust, 286–287, **F495**
            for two-year charitable trust, 286, **F493**
        second step, 285–286, **F489**
        "stand-alone," 286, **F491**
    evaluation and definition of, 225, 263–270
    inter vivos, 225, 243, 263
    inter vivos bypass, revocable, 267, 269
        one trustor, one trustee, 276, 277, **F455–F458**
            completed sample, 282–284
    irrevocable, 263, 265, 269
        one trustor, one trustee, 276, **F459–F462**
        two trustors, one trustee, trust income to surviving trustor
            for life, then to secondary beneficiary(ies), 276,
            F463–F466
    irrevocable charitable remainder, 265, 266, 268–269
        one trustor, one trustee, 276, **F475–F478**
        spouses as trustors, one trustee, 276, **F479–F482**
    life tenancy, 263
    "lovers'," 277, **F451–F454**
        completed sample, 278–281
    opening declaration, 272
    principal of, 263
    providing tax savings, 263–267

    provisions of, 272–274
        community property, 274, 276
        name of state, 273
        names of beneficiaries, 272–273
        partial invalidity, 274
        property placed in trust, 272
        trustee in
            acceptance of trust by, 273
            authority of, with regard to disbursement of principal and
                income to meet expenses, 273
            compensation of, 273
            distribution of income and assets by, 273
            exemption of, from providing bond, 273
            guidelines for administration and management of trust by,
                273
            liability of, 273
        trustor's right of revocation and amendment, 273
    reversionary, 263, 265–266, 268
        ten-year (Clifford), one trustor, one trustee, 276, **F467–F470**
        two-year charitable, one trustor, one trustee, 276, **F471–
            F474**
    revocable, 263, 264–265, 269
        one trustor, one trustee, 275, **F435–F438**
        one trustor, one trustee, provision for successor trustee,
            payment of trust income to primary beneficiary upon
            death of trustor, payment of trust income and/or
            principal to secondary beneficiary upon death of
            primary beneficiary, 275–276, **F451–F454**
            completed sample, 278–281
        one trustor, trustor as initial trustee, provision for
            successor trustee, 275, **F443–F446**
        two trustors, one trustee, 275, **F439–F442**
        two trustors, trustors as initial trustees, provision for
            successor trustee, 275, **F447–F450**
        see also Trust(s), *inter vivos* bypass, revocable
    Revocation of Trust, 277
        for trusts having one trustor, 277, **F483–F484**
        for trusts having two trustors, 277, **F485–F486**
    terminology of, 263
    testamentary, 225, 243, 263, 264, 268
    Totten, 266, 269
    transfer of assets of trust to trustee, 269, 272
    trustee(s) of, *see* Trust(s), provisions of, trustee in; Trustee(s)
    see also Economic Recovery Tax Act of 1981 (ERTA)
Trustee(s), 263, 268–269
    transfer of property to, 269, 272
    in will, 225; *see also* Will(s), provisions of, trustee(s) in
    see also Trust(s), provisions of, trustee in
Trustor, 225, 263
Truth in Lending Act of 1969, 126
Two-year charitable trust, *see* Trust(s), reversionary, two-year
        charitable

Unified Rate Schedule, 232, 264
Uniform Commercial Code (UCC), 93, 95, 96–97, 105, 112–116,
        117, 119–120, 138
    listing of statutory citations of, by state, table of, 119–120
    pertinent court decisions involving, 115–116
    sections of, 112–115
        buyer's incidental and consequential damages, 113–114, 115
        contractual modification or limitation of remedy, 114, 115
        exclusion or modification of warranties, 113, 114
        implied warranty of fitness for a particular purpose, 113,
            114
        implied warranty of merchantability, 112, 114
Uniform Donor Cards, 430, **F595–F596**
Uniform Gifts to Minors Act, 233
United States Government Manual, 374
Unmarried cohabitants, *see* Living together, agreement for
U.S. Consumer Product Safety Commission, *see* Consumer
        Product Safety Commission, U.S.
U.S. Court of Appeals, 22
U.S. Court of Claims, 10
U.S. Court of Customs and Patent Appeals, 10
U.S. Courts of Appeals, 10
U.S. Customs Court, 10

U.S. District Courts, 10
U.S. Office of Consumer Affairs (OCA), 130
U.S. Supreme Court, 10–11, 22, 325, 334, 362
Usury laws, 331

VA/FHA/HUD forms, 310–314
Venue, 169, 361
Veterans Administration (VA)
  appraisal of house by, 307, 308, 310–314
    VA/FHA/HUD forms, 310–314
  guaranteed house loan of, 329

Waiver of Lien, 64, 72, **F185–F186**
Warranties, 96–97
Warranty Comparison Checklist, 97, 98–100, **F215**
  guidelines for filling out, 98–100
Washington Researcher's, Inc., 375
Wife, husband and, agreement between, *see* Marriage
Will(s), 223–259
  after completion of, 252–253
  assets that remain outside, 224
  attorney, duties of, in estate probate and administration, 229–230
  bank trap concerning, 253
  cost of probating, 229
  Declaration of Gift, 237–239, 269–271
    for gift of personal property, 269–270, **F433–F434**
      completed sample, 271
    for gift of real estate, 237, **F363–F364**
      completed sample, 238–239
  disinherit children in, 226
  disinherit spouse in, 226
  Document to Be Kept with the Last Will and Testament, 249, **F371–F375**
  dying without, 223
  estate evaluation, 240–243
    Informal Estate Evaluation, 240–242, **F365–F370**
  executor, duties of, in estate probate and administration, 229, 230
  functions of, 228
  holographic, 226
  of husband
    leaving estate to wife
      otherwise in trust for minor children, wife as executrix, 224, 252, **F387–F390**
      otherwise to adult children, wife as executrix, 223, 252, **F379–F382**
    with no children, leaving estate to wife, otherwise certain bequests and devises, wife as executrix, 224, 252, **F395–F398**
    using tax-free interspousal transfer and life income trust provisions of ERTA, 254–255, **F415–F420**
  joint, 226
  List of Important People and Papers, 229, **F359–F362**
  Living Will, 452, **F691–F692**
    with pregnancy clause, 452, **F693–F694**
    for use after diagnosis of a terminal condition, 452, **F695–F696**
  minimizing federal estate taxes under terms of, *see* Economic Recovery Tax Act of 1981 (ERTA); Estate taxes, federal, minimizing
  nuncupative, 226
  oral, 226
  provisions of, 244–249, 256–259
    age at which children are to receive trust, 247
    appointment of executor, 245
    bequests and devises, to wife/husband, stipulation of survival for specified time, 245–246
    community property, 248–249
    disinheritance of children, 246
    guardians of children, 248

"insurance" clause in event that will or provision is contested by someone claiming to be an heir, 248
    optional will provisions, 256–259, **F427–F431**
      abatement of bequests and devises, 259, **F430**
      advancements, 259, **F430**
      appointment of guardian, 259, **F431**
      bequests
        of cash, 257, **F427**
        delivery of, 259, **F429–F430**
        of personal property (and optional addition to), 257, **F428**
        of shares of close corporation, 258, **F429**
      cancellation of debt, 259, **F430**
      charitable gifts, 258, **F429**
      contest of will, 259, **F431**
      devise of real property, 258, **F428–F429**
      funeral instructions, 257, **F427**
      gift of pet, 258–259, **F429**
      religious belief, 256, **F427**
    partial invalidity, 249
    payment of debts, 245
    trustee(s) in
      alternate, naming of, 246
      authority of, with regard to disbursement of principal and income to meet expenses, 247
      bequests and devises to, 246
      exemption of, from providing bond, 246
      fee of, 246
      guidelines for administration and management of trust by, 247–248
      liability of, 246–247
    wills not contractual, 245
  requirements for, in United States, table of, 227–228
  safekeeping of, 252
  Self-Proving Affidavit, 249–250, **F377**
    completed sample, 251
  standard, 226
  state of legal residence, 226, 244
  terminology of, 224–226
  of unmarried man
    with no children, leaving estate to female cohabitant, otherwise certain bequests and devises, cohabitant as executrix, 224, 252, **F403–F406**
    or woman, with no children, making certain bequests and devises, appointment of executor or executrix, 224, 252, **F411–F414**
  of unmarried woman, with no children, leaving estate to male cohabitant, otherwise certain bequests and devises, cohabitant as executor, 224, 252, **F407–F410**
  what happens with, after you die, 228–229
  of wife
    leaving estate to husband
      otherwise in trust for minor children, husband as executor, 224, 252, **F391–F394**
      otherwise to adult children, husband as executor, 223, 252, **F383–F386**
    with no children, leaving estate to husband, otherwise certain bequests and devises, husband as executor, 224, 252, **F399–F402**
    using tax-free interspousal transfer and life income trust provisions of ERTA, 254–255, **F421–F426**
  witnesses to, 249; *see also* Self-Proving Affidavit
Witnesses, 23
  auto accident, 43
  to lease, 29
  for small claims court, *see* Small claims court(s), witnesses for
  subpoena(s) of, *see* Small claims court(s), witnesses for
  to will, 249; *see also* Self-Proving Affidavit
Wool Products Labeling Act of 1939, 126
Writ of Execution, 162, 163, **F245–F246**
  Petition for Writ of Execution, 162, **F243–F244**
    completed sample, 165–166

XVI

LEGAL FOOTNOTES

SECTION I

Search and Seizure When police officer threatened to impound van if defendant did not drive it to police station, officer seized van just as effectively as if he had had the van towed. *Wilder v. Superior Court of Tulane County*, 154 Cal. Rptr. 494, 92 C.A.3d 90. [*chap. 2, p. 5, col. 2, par. 2**]

Abortion A minor has a basic constitutional right to an abortion. The state's power to limit this right should extend only to protect the minor from the special consequences of her minority: immaturity and lack of informed understanding. *Baird v. Bellotti*, 443 U.S. 662. [*chap 2, p. 7, col. 2, par. 2*]

Tort An action in tort will lie for intentional interference by a third person with a contractual relationship either by unlawful means or by means otherwise lawful when there is a lack of sufficient justification. *Richardson v. La Rancherita La Jolla, Inc.*, 159 Cal. Rptr. 285, 98 C.A.3d 73. [*chap. 6, p. 15, col. 2, par. 2*]

Animal Accident Recovery denied in action by a schoolgirl against the owner of a horse which reached over a high fence and bit the girl's ear. *Leipske v. Guenther*, 7 Wis.2d 86, 95 N.W.2d 774. [*chap. 6, p. 16, col. 2, par. 9*]

Boating Accident Guest in motorboat may assume host knows what he is doing when he asks guest to pour gasoline into carburetor. *Warnken v. Moody*, 22 F.2d 960. [*chap. 6, p. 16, col. 2, par. 9*]

Conversion Defendant on moving into a building found plaintiff's barrels of wine left in building cellar for storage. Assuming they were abandoned, he sold them for junk. Defendant was held liable for conversion. *Poggi v. Scott*, 167 Cal. 372, 139 P. 815. [*chap. 6. p. 17, col. 2, par. 1*]

Conversion If a garage delays for a month the return of the plaintiff's parked car, it is conversion. *Thomas v. Westbrook*, 206 Ark. 841, 177 S.W.2d 931. [*chap. 6, p. 17, col. 2, par. 1*]

Bailment When pickup truck and camper unit was delivered to the automotive shop for repairs, bailment of the pickup truck and camper unit was created. *Kern v. Harris*, 567 P.2d 1069, 30 Or. App. 723. [*chap. 6, p. 17, col. 2, par. 7*]

Negligence Supermarket was not guilty of negligence which proximately caused the death of a four year old boy who wandered away from his mother in supermarket's parking lot. Child ran off to ride amusement machine and was struck by an automobile traveling in a properly marked lane in parking lot. *Cole v. Delchamps, Inc.*, 152 So.2d 911. [*chap. 6, p. 18, col. 1, par. 8*]

Negligence Defendant may be held liable for negligence if he turns his automobile over to one who is intoxicated. *Mueller v. Winston Bros. Co.*, 165 Wash. 130, 4 P.2d 854. [*chap. 6, p. 18, col. 1, par. 8*]

Nuisance Operation of a pig farm in a semi-residential area was a nuisance which interfered with neighboring residents' use and enjoyment of their property. *Jewett v. Deerhorn Enterprises, Inc.*, 575 P.2d 164, 281 Or. 469. [*chap. 6, p. 18, col. 1, par. 9*]

Nuisance A dog which makes evenings and nights hideous with his howls is a nuisance. *Hubbard v. Preston*, 90 Mich. 221, 51 N.W. 209. [*chap. 6, p. 18, col. 1, par. 9*]

Assault Where defendant leaned over a woman's bed and made indecent proposals in such a way as to put the woman in fear, an assault was committed. *Newell v. Whitcher*, 53 Vt. 589. [*chap. 6, p. 18, col. 2, par. 6*]

Common Law Marriage A woman living with a man for several years may recover under an express or implied theory of contract. *Marvin v. Marvin*, 18 Cal.3d 660. [*chap. 6, p. 19, col. 1, par. 3*]

Pretrial Procedure Where plaintiff was permitted to amend her personal injury complaint to increase the ad damnum clause from $300,000 to $900,000, defendants were entitled to another physical examination and further discovery. *Streit v. Parker*, 404 N.Y.S.2d 308, 94 Misc.2d 295. [*chap. 7, p. 22, col. 1, par. 3*]

SECTION II

Alterations Short of waste, tenant may make nonstructural alterations consistent with use of premises contemplated by his possession of them. *Rumiche Corp. v. Eisenreich*, 386 N.Y.S.2d 208. [*chap. 8, p. 28, col. 1, par. 5*]

Unconscionable Clauses Clause of lease agreement which obligated tenants to pay landlord additional rent of $100 for attorney's fees if landlord was required to bring proceeding due to tenant's default was unconscionable in equity. *Weedman v. Tomaselli*, 386 N.Y.S.2d 276. [*chap. 8, p. 28, col. 2, par. 6*]

SECTION V

Public Policy Arbitration, the object of which is to achieve a final disposition of differences between parties in an easier, more expeditious and less expensive manner, is favored by public policy in resolution of private disputes, as well as those in the field of collective bargaining. *Maye v. Bluestein*, 351 N.E.2d 717. [*chap. 28, p. 81, col. 1, par. 2*]

Remedies The remedies available in arbitration are not confined to traditional forms at law, and, thus, if a claim is substantially related to matters encompassed by the substantive agreement, it is immaterial, in applying the statute of limitations whether the claim lies in "contract" or "tort." *Steinver v. Wenning*, 386 N.Y.S.2d 429. [*chap. 28, p. 83, col. 1, par. 5*]

Power of Arbitrators Arbitrators generally are not bound by principles of substantive law; furthermore, arbitrators generally are free to fashion remedy appropriate to wrong, if they find one, but authentic remedy is compensatory and measured by harm caused and how it may be corrected. These broad principles are tolerable so long as arbitrators are not thereby empowered to ride roughshod over strong policies in law which control coercive private conduct and which confine to state and its courts infliction of punitive sanctions on wrongdoers. *Garrity v. Lyle Stuart, Inc.*, 353 N.E.2d 793. [*chap. 28, p. 84, col. 1. par. 6*]

---

*Paragraph number refers to complete paragraphs only. All lists and extracts count as paragraphs.

Modification of Award Though modification of arbitrator's award would be in jeopardy under principle that questions of law determined by arbitrator are not open to resolution by judicial intervention, order of Appellate Division making such modification would be affirmed where appeal of parties aggrieved by such modification had been dismissed under nine-month rule. *Maye v. Bluestein*, 351 N.E.2d 717. [*chap. 28, p. 84, col. 2, par. 5*]

Power of Arbitrators That arbitrator's award of punitive damages, in violation of public policy, was quite modest was immaterial. *Garrity v. Lyle Stuart, Inc.*, 353 N.E.2d 793. [*chap. 28, p. 85, col. 1, par. 1*]

SECTION VII

Collecting Your Award In attempting to execute on a judgement, first it must be established that the party requesting issuance of a writ fieri facias is a judgement creditor based on a valid and final judgement. *Board of Trustees of East Baton Rouge Mortg. Finance Authority v. All Taxpayers*, 361 So.2d 292. [*chap. 45, p. 162, col. 1, par. 6*]

Writ of Execution Execution becomes a lien on personal property from the time the writ is delivered to the sheriff and is superior to liens created by writs delivered to sheriff at a later time. *Krauth v. First Continental Dev-Con, Inc.*, 351 So.2d 1106. [*chap. 45, p. 162, col. 1, par. 7*]

Verbal vs. Written A party is generally free to choose between interrogatories and oral depositions and the order in which to use them. Such freedom, however, is subject to judicial intervention if the process is abused. *Barouh Eaton Allen Corp. v. International Business Machines Corp.* 429 N.Y.S.2d 33, 76 A.D.2d 873. [*chap. 45, p. 163, col. 1, par. 4*]

Petition for Order Party required to answer interrogatories is entitled to rely on date set forth in order for compliance and he may reasonably expect a case will not be called for trial until sometime after that date. *Fanfarillo v. East End Motor Co.*, 411 A.2d 1167, 172 N.J. Super 309. [*chap. 45, p. 163, col. 2, par. 1*]

Interrogatories Discovery rules governing interrogatories and production of documents must be liberally construed in order to ensure that a litigant's right to discover is broad and flexible. *United Nuclear Corp. v. Gen. Atomic Co.*, 629 P.2d 231, 96 N.M. 155, appeal dismissed, cert. denied 101 S. Ct. 1966, 451 U.S. 901, 68 L. Ed.2d 289, rehearing denied 101 S. Ct. 3070, 452 U.S. 932, 69 L. Ed.2d 433. [*chap. 45, p. 163, col. 2, par. 8*]

Interrogatories Only limitation to discovery is relevancy to subject matter involved in action; test in determining relevance of interrogatories is whether testimony sought reasonably may be expected to lead to discovery of admissible evidence. *Lurus v. Bristol Laboratories Inc.*, 574 P.2d 391, 89 Wash.2d 632. [*chap. 45, p. 163, col. 2, par. 8*]

Contempt Any contempt for failing to answer interrogatories filed by opposing party is "indirect contempt." *Opinion of the Clerk*, 386 So.2d 737. [*chap. 45, p. 164, col. 1, par. 2*]

Appeal Right to Appeal is truly statutory and an appeal taken without statutory authority must be dismissed for want of jurisdiction. *Hallman v. City of Northport*, 386 So.2d 756. [*chap. 46, p. 169, col. 2, par. 5*]

Appeal Any right of appeal in either a civil or criminal case must find its source in an act of the Legislature. *State v. Bailey*, 422 A.2d 1021, 289 Md. 143. [*chap. 46, p. 169, col. 2, par. 5*]

SECTION VIII

Acceptance of Obligation Spouses have mutual obligations to care for and support the other, including obligation to provide medical care. *Hawkins v. Superior Ct. of San Bernardino County*, 152 Cal. Rptr. 491, 89 C.A.3d 413. [*chap. 47, p. 175, col. 1, par. 6*]

Agreement in Contemplation of Marriage Relief predicated upon a promise of marriage has been barred since 1935 by the Heart Balm Act, NJSA 2A:23 1 et seq. *Kozlowski v. Kozlowski*, 403 A.2d 902, 80 N.J. 378. [*chap. 47, p. 176, col. 2, par. 5*]

Cohabitation Cohabitation within commonwealth in absence of formal soleminization of marriage does not create relationship of husband and wife. *Davis v. Misiano*, 366 N.E.2d 750, 373 Mass. 261. [*chap. 47, p. 176, col. 2, par. 6*]

Dissolution Authority to grant dissolution of marriage is entirely statutory in origin and nature; court's authority is limited thereby. *In remarriage of Cohn*, 50 Ill. Dec. 621, 419 N.E.2d 729, 94 Ill. App.3d 732. [*chap. 47, p. 177, col. 1, par. 4*]

Employment of Parties A husband may not quit his job to avoid his familial obligations. *Levine v. Levine*, 373 So.2d 1380. [*chap. 48, p. 180, col. 2, par. 1*]

Separate Property In absence of statute, state courts are without power to transfer property of either spouse to the other or to change the parties' rights or estates in that property, not withstanding a wife's nonmonetary contributions to the marriage. *Wimmer v. Wimmer*, 414 A.2d 1254, 287 Md. 663. [*chap. 48, p. 182, col. 1, par. 5*]

Separate Property Spouse does have present vested right to half of community property. *Harper v. New Mexico Dept. of Human Services, Income Support Division*, 623 P.2d 985, 95 N.M. 471. [*chap. 48, p. 182, col. 1, par. 5*]

Tenants by Entirety Upon the death of a tenant by the entirety, survivor becomes sole owner either by right of survivorship or as an incident of the original grant or devise. *Matter of Houghton's Estate*, 383 A.2d 713, 75 N.J. 462. [*chap. 48, p. 182, col. 2, par. 6*]

Bank Accounts Where joint checking account and certificates of deposit were in name of "Mr. or Mrs. Pepper," there was a rebuttable presumption that spouses intended to hold funds as joint tenants with survivorship rather than as tenants in common. *Vaughn v. Perkins*, 576 S.W.2d 257. [*chap. 48, p. 184, col. 1, par. 3*]

Child Custody Divorce court has duty to decide between contesting parents when issue of child custody is raised. *Cradie v. Cradie*, 544 S.W.2d 605. [*chap. 48, p. 187, col. 2, par. 9*]

Child Support As long as the parties are married and the wife has not abandoned the husband without just cause, it is the duty of the husband to support her and his minor children according to their station in life. *Evans v. Evans*, 564 S.W.2d 505, 263 Ariz. 291. [*chap. 48, p. 188, col. 1, par. 8*]

Child Support Provision in final judgment of dissolution requiring parental support of each child until the child attains age of 21 years was modified to 18 years. *Mohammad v. Mohammad*, 371 So.2d 1070. [*chap. 48, p. 188, col. 1, par. 8*]

Alimony Allowance of alimony installments not in gross is subject to modification as circumstances may warrant. *Phillips v. Phillips*, 344 So.2d 786. [*chap. 48, p. 190, col. 1, par. 2*]

Alimony Party in whose favor the judgement was rendered may make arrangements with the party liable for payment of alimony or child support in a way other than direct payments or may waive rights under the judgement. *Seifert v. Seifert*, 374 So.2d 157. [*chap. 48, p. 190, col. 1, par. 2*]

Alimony Alimony paid pendente lite is not recoverable by person paying same even if award is eventually found to be erroneous. *Atkins v. Atkins*, 388 So.2d 34. [*chap. 48, p. 190, col. 1, par. 2*]

Support Cause of marital separation must be considered in cases involving suit for separate maintenance brought by one spouse against another; separation without justification is a defense to such actions. *Edge v. Commissioner of Welfare*, 388 A.2d 1193, 34 Conn. Sup. 284. [*chap. 48, p. 191, col. 1, par. 4*]

Removal of Child from Jurisdiction Removal of child of divorced parents from jurisdiction may be judicially permitted where it is made clear that the best interests of the child will be served. *Hart v. Hart*, 539 S.W.2d 679. [*chap. 48, p. 192, col. 2, par. 6*]

Capacity of Either Party A marriage contract will not be declared void because one party did not have mental capacity to enter into it unless there existed at time of marriage such a want of understanding as to render party incapable of assenting thereto. *Edwards v. Edwards*, 287 N.W.2d 420, 205 Neb. 255. [*chap. 48, p. 195, col. 1, par. 4*]

SECTION IX

Capacity Evidence, in proceeding in which probate of a purported will was denied, did not support determination that testatrix lacked testamentary capacity or that she was under the constraint of undue influence. *Matter of Cottone*, 374 N.Y.S.2d 45. [*chap. 51, p. 225, col. 1, par. 1*]

Future Estates Future estates of residuary legatees identified by name in will were vested immediately at testator's death and the estates were descendible, devisable, and alienable in same manner as estates in possessions. *Matter of Newton's Estate*, 54 A.D.2d 452. [*chap. 51, p. 226, col. 1, par. 1*]

Residuary Clauses When a will contains a residuary clause it manifests an intention on the part of the testator to make a testamentary disposition of his estate and to avoid

intestacy as to any part thereof. *Will of Van Inwegen*, 386 N.Y.S.2d 517. [*chap. 51, p. 226, col. 1, par. 1*]

Who May Contest Evidence in probate proceeding established that contestant was not the son of decedent and, hence, was not a distributee entitled to contest the propounded writing. *Will of Esther T.*, 382 N.Y.S.2d 916. [*chap. 51, p. 226, col. 1, par. 8*]

Who May Contest Contestant was a party to preliminary hearing to determine his status as decedent's surviving child, and, as such, he had a right to be present at the hearing. *Will of Esther T.*, 382 N.Y.S.2d 916. [*chap. 51, p. 226, col. 1, par. 8*]

Holographic Wills A determination that decedent was domiciled in Germany at time of her death was essential to establishment of holographic will executed by decedent in Germany. *Estate of Hahnel*, 389 N.Y.S.2d 970. [*chap. 51, p. 226, col. 2, par. 2*]

Joint Wills Mere execution of joint will may not, in and of itself, suffice to establish binding contract to dispose of property in particular way. *Matter of Warych's Estate*, 389 N.Y.S.2d 49. [*chap. 51, p. 226, col. 2, par. 4*]

Repudiation of Legacy In order to repudiate or renounce a legacy, an affirmative act is required. *Matter of Bertram's Estate*, 389 N.Y.S.2d 999. [*chap. 51, p. 228, col. 1, par. 1*]

Undue Influence Generally, any rule that a bequest to attorney draftsman gives rise to inference or presumption of undue influence does not apply where attorney is named executor only. *Matter of Weinstock's Estate*, 351 N.E.2d 647. [*chap. 51, p. 229, col. 2, par. 2*]

SECTION X

Constructive Trust Even without an express promise, courts of equity have imposed a constructive trust on property transferred in reliance on a confidential relationship. In such a situation a promise may be implied or inferred from the transaction itself. *Sharp v. Kosmalski*, 351 N.E.2d 721. [*chap. 58, p. 263, col. 1, par. 5*]

Relationship Needed A marital or other family relationship is not essential for existence of a confidential relation warranting imposition of a constructive trust. *Sharp v. Kosmalski*, 351 N.E.2d 721. [*chap. 58, p. 263, col. 1, par. 5*]

Invading Principal Petition of life income beneficiary of testamentary trust to invade principal to aid in defraying nursing home costs could not be granted in absence of consent by immediate contingent remainderman. *Matter of Harold's Estate*, 386 N.Y.S.2d 972. [*chap. 58, p. 268, col. 2, par. 1*]

Removal of Trustees It is possible that removal proceedings should be considered if there was a continual refusal by trustee to render proper accounting of trust which by its terms had terminated. *Kelly v. Sassower*, 382 N.Y.S.2d 88. [*chap. 58, p. 269, col. 1, par. 3*]

Corporate Stock Rule that retention by corporate trustee of shares of its own stock is subject to testatrix's authorization that they be retained also covers instances where corporation is subsequently merged or consolidated with another corporation. *In re Heidenreich's Will*, 378 N.Y.S.2d 982.   [*chap. 58, p. 269, col. 1, par. 4*]

Elements of Valid Trust   Essential elements of a valid trust are a designated beneficiary, a designated trustee who is not the beneficiary, an identifiable fund, and actual delivery of the fund to the trustee. *Matter of Bertram's Estate*, 389 N.Y.S.2d 999.   [*chap. 58, p. 269, col. 1, par. 4*]

XVII

FORMS

Lease Agreement—Unfurnished Apartment

Landlord _____

_____
                       Address   *Phone*

Managing Agent _____

_____
                       Address   *Phone*

Premises _____
                       Address   *Apt. No.*

Tenant _____

Tenant _____

1. The LANDLORD hereby leases to _____ (and) _____, hereinafter termed TENANT, the premises described above for a term of _____ beginning _____ _____ and ending _____, at a monthly rate of $ _____, making a total rental amount payable under this lease of $ _____.

2. The tenant agrees to pay the rent herein provided subject to the terms and conditions set forth herein.

3. Rent shall be payable in equal monthly installments to be paid in advance on the _____ day of each month.

4. Rent shall be payable in the following manner:

(Specify above if payments are to be made by mail, and if so, to what address. If payments are to be made to the landlord or the landlord's agent in person, state the place where, and the person to whom, payments are to be made.)

5. Upon receiving any payment of rent in cash, the landlord agrees to issue a receipt stating the tenant's name, a description of the premises, the amount of rent paid, the date paid and the period for which rent is paid.

6. The landlord covenants that the leased premises are, to the best of his or her knowledge, clean, safe, sound and healthful and that there exists no violation of any applicable housing code, law or regulation of which he or she is aware.

7. The tenant agrees to comply with all sanitary laws, ordinances and rules and all orders of the Board of Health or other authorities affecting the cleanliness, occupancy and preservation of the premises during the term of this lease.

8. The tenant shall use the leased premises exclusively as a private residence for no more than _____ persons, and the tenant will not make alterations therein without the written consent of the landlord.

9. The tenant shall keep fixtures in said apartment in good order and repair, and the tenant shall cause to be made, at the tenant's expense, all required repairs to heating and air-conditioning apparatus, refrigerator, range, electric and gas fixtures and plumbing work whenever such damage shall have resulted from misuse, waste or neglect, it being understood that the landlord is to have same in good order and repair when giving possession.

10. The tenant shall not keep or have in the leased premises any article or thing of a dangerous, inflammable or explosive nature that might be pronounced "hazardous" or "extra hazardous" by any responsible insurance company.

11. The tenant shall give prompt notice to the landlord of any dangerous, defective, unsafe or emergency condition in the leased premises, said notice being given by any suitable means. The landlord shall repair and correct said conditions promptly upon receiving notice thereof from the tenant.

12. The landlord covenants that all essential services are now provided and shall be provided at all times during the term of this lease and any extension, renewal or continuation thereof, except where any interruption of essential services shall be for maintenance or for cause beyond control of the landlord such as strike, storm, civil insurrection, fire or acts of God. "Essential services" hereunder are defined as heat, hot and cold running water, a properly functioning toilet, light in public areas and suitable building security.

13. The _____ shall pay for gas and electricity except to the extent otherwise set forth herein.

14. The landlord covenants that consumption of electricity for the public halls and other common areas and use and consumption of gas for heat or hot water in public areas are recorded on separate meters, and that said electricity and gas are and will at all times be billed to and paid by the landlord.

15. The tenant covenants that during the last 30 days of this lease, or any renewal thereof, the landlord or his agents, with reasonable notice, and at reasonable hours, have the privilege of showing the premises to prospective buyers or tenants.

16. The tenant shall, at reasonable times, give access to the landlord or his agents for any reasonable and lawful purpose. Except in situations of compelling emergency, or to show the premises for rental or sale, the landlord agrees to give the tenant 24 hours' notice, stating the time and date when access will be sought, and the reason therefore.

17. The landlord covenants that the tenant and the tenant's family shall have, hold and enjoy the leased premises for the term of this lease, subject to the provisions and conditions set forth herein.

18. The tenant covenants that he shall not commit nor permit a nuisance in or upon the premises, that he shall not maliciously or by reason of gross negligence damage the premises and that he shall not engage in conduct so as to interfere substantially with the comfort and safety of occupants of adjacent apartments or buildings.

19. The tenant agrees to place a security deposit with the landlord in the amount of $ _____, to be used by the landlord for the cost of replacing and/or repairing damage, if any, to the premises caused by the intentional or negligent acts of the tenant.

20. The landlord agrees, within ten days of receiving said security deposit, to deposit same in an interest-bearing account in a banking organization, in which said deposit shall earn interest at a rate which shall be the prevailing rate earned by other such deposits made with banking organizations in such circumstances.

21. The landlord agrees, within ten days of making such deposit, to notify the tenant, in writing, of the name and address of the banking organization in which the deposit of security money has been made.

22. The landlord shall be entitled to receive, as administrative expenses, an amount equal to one percent per annum upon the security payment so deposited, which shall be in lieu of all other administrative and custodial expenses. The balance of the interest paid by the banking organization shall be the money of the tenant and shall be paid to the tenant on each anniversary of this lease or any extension or renewal thereof.

23. The landlord agrees to return said security deposit to the tenant within ten days of the tenant's vacating the leased premises subject to the terms and conditions set forth herein.

24. In the event of any breach by the tenant of any of the tenant's covenants or agreements herein, the landlord may give the tenant five days' notice to cure said breach, setting forth in writing which covenants or agreements have been breached. If any breach is not cured within said five-day period, or reasonable steps to effectuate said cure are not commenced and diligently pursued within said five-day period and thereafter until said breach has been cured, the landlord may terminate this lease upon five days' additional notice to the tenant, with said notice being in lieu of a Notice to Quit, which tenant hereby waives. The tenant shall then become liable for the cost of landlord's normal redecorating and cleaning expenses related to preparation of the premises for rental to a succeeding tenant.

Said termination shall be ineffective if the tenant cures said breach or commences and diligently pursues reasonable steps to effectuate such cure at any time prior to the expiration of said five-day termination. Upon terminating this lease as provided herein, the landlord or his agent may commence proceedings against the tenant for his removal as provided for by law.

25. In the event of any breach by the landlord of any of the landlord's covenants or agreements herein, the tenant may give the landlord ten days' notice to cure said breach, setting forth in writing the manner in which said covenants and agreements have been breached. If said breach is not cured within said ten-day period, or reasonable steps to effectuate said cure are not commenced and diligently pursued within said ten-day period and thereafter until said breach has been cured, rent hereunder shall be fully abated from the time at which said ten days' notice expired until such time as the landlord has fully cured the breach set forth in the notice provided for in this paragraph.

26. In no case shall any abatement of rent hereunder be effected where the condition set forth in the notice provided for herein was created by the intentional or negligent act of the tenant, but the landlord shall have the burden of proving that rent abatement may not be effected for the foregoing reason.

27. The landlord agrees to deliver possession of the leased premises at the beginning of the term provided for herein. In the event of the landlord's failure to deliver possession at the beginning of said term, the tenant shall have the right to rescind this lease and to recover any consideration paid under terms of this agreement.

28. The tenant agrees that this lease shall be subject to and subordinate to any mortgage or mortgages now on said premises or which any owner of said premises may hereafter at any time elect to place on said premises.

29. Unless otherwise provided for elsewhere in this lease, any notice required or authorized herein shall be given in writing, one copy of said notice mailed via U.S. certified mail, return receipt requested, and one copy of said notice mailed via U.S. first-class mail.

Notice to the tenant shall be mailed to him at the leased premises. Notice to the landlord shall be mailed to him, or to the managing agent, at their respective addresses as set forth herein, or at such new address as to which the tenant has been duly notified.

30. This lease constitutes the entire agreement between the parties hereto. No changes shall be made herein except by writing, signed by each party and dated. The failure to enforce any right or remedy hereunder, and the payment and acceptance of rent hereunder, shall not be deemed a waiver by either party of such right or remedy in the absence of a writing as provided for herein.

31. In the event legal action is required to enforce any provision of this agreement, the prevailing party shall be entitled to recover reasonable attorney's fees and costs.

32. The landlord and tenant agree that this apartment lease, when filled out and signed, is a binding legal obligation.

(DO NOT SIGN IF THERE ARE ANY BLANK SPACES. CROSS OUT OR FILL IN ALL BLANK SPACES BEFORE SIGNING.)

(The above space is provided for such additional terms and conditions as may be agreed to by the parties and must be crossed out to the extent that it is not filled in.)

IN WITNESS WHEREOF, the parties hereto have executed this agreement.

_____

Landlord

By _____

_____
Witness as to landlord

_____
Witness as to landlord

_____

Tenant

_____
Witness as to tenant

_____
Witness as to tenant

_____

Tenant

_____
Witness as to tenant

_____
Witness as to tenant

Dated this _____ day of _____, 19____.

Lease of Unfurnished Apartment

Landlord

Tenant

Premises

From _____

To _____

Monthly rent

Lease Agreement—Furnished Apartment

Landlord _____

_____
                               Address   *Phone*

Managing Agent _____

_____
                               Address   *Phone*

Premises _____
                               Address   *Apt. No.*

Tenant _____

Tenant _____

1. The LANDLORD hereby leases to _____ (and) _____,
hereinafter termed TENANT, the furnished premises described above for a term of _____ beginning
_____ and ending _____, at a monthly rate of $ _____, making a total
rental amount payable under this lease of $ _____.

2. The described premises are leased furnished, to include all furnishings enumerated on the **List of Furnishings**, which is a part of this lease, signed by both parties and dated, and incorporated herein by reference for all purposes.

3. The tenant agrees to pay the rent herein provided subject to the terms and conditions set forth herein.

4. Rent shall be payable in equal monthly installments on the _____ day of each month.

5. Rent shall be payable in the following manner:

(Landlord specify if payments are to be made by mail, and if so, to what address. If payments are to be made to the landlord or to the landlord's agent in person, state the place where, and the person to whom, payments are to be made.)

6. Upon receiving any payment of rent in cash, the landlord agrees to issue a receipt stating the tenant's name, a description of the premises, the amount of rent paid, the date paid and the period for which rent is paid.

7. The landlord covenants that the leased premises are, to the best of his or her knowledge, clean, safe, sound and healthful and that there exists no violation of any applicable housing code, law or regulation of which he or she is aware.

8. The tenant agrees to comply with all sanitary laws, ordinances and rules and all orders of the Board of Health or other authorities affecting the cleanliness, occupancy and preservation of the premises and furnishings during the term of this lease.

9. The tenant shall use the leased premises exclusively for a private residence, unless otherwise specified herein, and the tenant will not make alterations to the premises or furnishings therein without the written consent of the landlord.

10. The tenant agrees to take good care of the furniture, carpets, draperies, appliances and other household goods, and of the personal effects of the landlord, and further agrees that he or she will deliver up same to the landlord in good condition at the end of this lease, normal wear and tear excepted.

11. The tenant will repair or replace, at the tenant's expense, all loss of or damage to any of the listed furniture, carpets, draperies, appliances and other household goods, and personal effects of the landlord, whenever such damage or loss shall have resulted from the tenant's misuse, waste or neglect of said furnishings and personal effects of the landlord.

12. The tenant shall keep fixtures in said apartment in good order and repair, and the tenant shall cause to be made, at the tenant's expense, all required repairs to heating and air-conditioning apparatus, refrigerator, range, electric and gas fixtures and plumbing work whenever such damage shall have resulted from the tenant's misuse, waste or neglect, it being understood that the landlord is to have same in good order and repair when giving possession.

13. The tenant will not keep or have in the leased premises any article or thing of a dangerous, flammable or explosive nature that might be pronounced "hazardous" or "extra hazardous" by any responsible insurance company.

14. The tenant shall give prompt notice to the landlord of any dangerous, defective, unsafe or emergency condition in the leased premises, said notice being given by any suitable means. The landlord shall repair and correct said conditions promptly upon receiving notice thereof from the tenant.

15. The landlord covenants that all essential services are now provided and shall be provided at all times during the term of this lease and any extension, renewal or continuation thereof, except where any interruption of essential services shall be for maintenance or for cause beyond control of the landlord, such as strike, storm, civil insurrection, fire or acts of God. "Essential services" hereunder are defined as heat, hot and cold running water, electricity, a properly functioning toilet, light in public areas and suitable building security.

16. The _____ shall pay for gas and electricity except to the extent otherwise set forth herein.

17. The landlord covenants that consumption of electricity for the public halls and other common areas and use and consumption of gas for heat or hot water in public areas are recorded on separate meters, and that said electricity and gas are and will at all times be billed to and paid by the landlord.

18. The tenant covenants that during the last 30 days of this lease, or any renewal thereof, the landlord or his agents, with reasonable notice, and at reasonable hours, have the privilege of showing the premises to prospective buyers or tenants.

19. The tenant shall, at reasonable times, give access to the landlord or his agents for any reasonable and lawful purpose. Except in situations of compelling emergency, or to show the premises for rental or sale, the landlord agrees to give the tenant 24 hours' notice, stating the time and date when access will be sought, and the reason therefore.

20. The landlord covenants that the tenant and the tenant's family shall have, hold and enjoy the leased premises for the term of this lease, subject to the provisions and conditions set forth herein.

21. The tenant covenants that he shall not commit nor permit a nuisance in or upon the premises, that he shall not maliciously or by reason of gross negligence damage the premises and that he shall not engage in conduct so as to interfere substantially with the comfort and safety of occupants of adjacent apartments or buildings.

22. The tenant agrees to place a security deposit with the landlord in the amount of $ _____ , to be used by the landlord at the termination of this lease for the cost of replacing and/or repairing damage, if any, to the premises or furnishings resulting from the intentional or negligent acts of the tenant.

23. The landlord agrees, within ten days of receiving said security payment, to deposit same in an interest-bearing account in a banking organization, in which said deposit shall earn interest at a rate which shall be the prevailing rate earned by other such deposits made with banking organizations in such circumstances.

24. The landlord agrees, within ten days of making such a deposit, to notify the tenant of the name and address of the banking organization in which the deposit of security money has been made.

25. The landlord shall be entitled to receive, as administrative expenses, an amount equal to one percent per annum upon the security payment so deposited, which shall be in lieu of all other administrative and custodial expenses. The balance of the interest paid by the banking organization shall be the money of the tenant and shall be paid to the tenant on each anniversary of this lease or any extension or renewal thereof.

26. The landlord agrees to return said security deposit to the tenant within ten days of the tenant's vacating the leased premises subject to the terms and conditions set forth herein.

27. In the event of any breach by the tenant of any of the tenant's covenants or agreements herein, the landlord may give the tenant five days' notice to cure said breach, setting forth in writing which covenants or agreements have been breached. If any breach is not cured within said five-day period, or reasonable steps to effectuate said cure are not commenced and diligently pursued within said five-day period and thereafter until said breach has been cured, the landlord may terminate this lease upon five days' additional notice to the tenant, with said notice being in lieu of a Notice to Quit, which tenant hereby waives.

Said termination shall be ineffective if the tenant cures said breach or commences and diligently pursues reasonable steps to effectuate such cure at any time prior to the expiration of said five-day termination. Upon terminating this lease as provided herein, the landlord or his agent may commence proceedings against the tenant for his removal as provided for by law.

28. In the event of any breach by the landlord of any of the landlord's covenants or agreements herein, the tenant may give the landlord ten days' notice to cure said breach, setting forth in writing the manner in which said covenants and agreements have been breached. If said breach is not cured within said ten-day period, or reasonable steps to effectuate said cure are not commenced and diligently pursued within said ten-day period and thereafter until said breach has been cured, rent hereunder shall be fully abated from the time at which said ten days' notice expired until such time as the landlord has fully cured the breach set forth in the notice provided for in this paragraph.

29. In no case shall any abatement of rent hereunder be effected where the condition set forth in the notice provided for herein was created by the intentional or negligent act of the tenant, but the landlord shall have the burden of proving that rent abatement may not be effected for the foregoing reason.

30. The landlord agrees to deliver possession of the leased premises at the beginning of the term provided for herein. In the event of the landlord's failure to deliver possession at the beginning of said term, the tenant shall have the right to rescind this lease and to recover any consideration paid under terms of this agreement.

31. The tenant agrees that this lease shall be subject to and subordinate to any mortgage or mortgages now on said premises or which any owner of said premises may hereafter at any time elect to place on said premises.

32. Unless otherwise provided for elsewhere in this lease, any notice required or authorized herein shall be given in writing, one copy of said notice mailed via U.S. certified mail, return receipt requested, and one copy of said notice mailed via U.S. first-class mail.

Notice to the tenant shall be mailed to him at the leased premises. Notice to the landlord shall be mailed to him, or to the managing agent, at their respective addresses as set forth herein, or at such new address as to which the tenant has been duly notified.

33. This lease constitutes the entire agreement between the parties hereto. No changes shall be made herein except by writing, signed by each party and dated. The failure to enforce any right or remedy hereunder, and the payment and acceptance of rent hereunder, shall not be deemed a waiver by either party of such right or remedy in the absence of a writing as provided for herein.

34. In the event legal action is required to enforce any provision of this agreement, the prevailing party shall be entitled to recover reasonable attorney's fees and costs.

35. The landlord and tenant agree that this apartment lease, when filled out and signed, is a binding legal obligation.

(DO NOT SIGN IF THERE ARE ANY BLANK SPACES. CROSS OUT OR FILL IN ALL BLANK SPACES BEFORE SIGNING.)

(The above space is provided for such additional terms and conditions as may be agreed to by the parties and must be crossed out to the extent that it is not filled in.)

IN WITNESS WHEREOF, the parties hereto have executed this agreement.

Landlord

By _____

_____
Witness as to landlord
_____
Witness as to landlord

_____
Tenant

_____
Witness as to tenant
_____
Witness as to tenant

_____
Tenant

_____
Witness as to tenant
_____
Witness as to tenant

Dated this _____ day of _____, 19___.

Lease of Furnished Apartment

Landlord

Tenant

Premises

From _____
To _____
Monthly rent

Lease Agreement—Unfurnished House

Landlord _____

_____
  Address   *Phone*

Managing Agent _____

_____
  Address   *Phone*

Premises _____

_____

Tenant _____

Tenant _____

1. The LANDLORD hereby leases to _____ (and) _____, hereinafter termed TENANT, the premises described above for a term of _____ beginning _____ _____ and ending _____, at a monthly rate of $_____, making a total rental payable under this lease of $ _____.

2. The tenant agrees to pay the rent herein provided subject to the terms and conditions set forth herein.

3. Rent shall be payable in equal monthly installments to be paid in advance on the _____ day of each month.

4. Rent shall be paid in the following manner:

(Landlord specify if the payments are to be made by mail, and if so, to what address. If payments are to be made to the landlord or his agent in person, state the place where, and the person to whom, payments are to be made.)

5. Upon any payment of the rent in cash, the landlord agrees to issue a receipt stating the tenant's name, a description of the premises, the amount of rent paid and the period for which rent is paid.

6. The tenant shall pay for all electricity, water, fuel oil and gas used during the term of this lease and any extension or renewal thereof.

7. The landlord covenants that the leased premises are, to the best of his or her knowledge, clean, safe, sound and healthful and that there exists no violation of any applicable housing code, law or regulation of which he or she is aware.

8. The tenant agrees to comply with all sanitary laws, ordinances and rules and all orders of the Board of Health or other authorities affecting the cleanliness, occupancy and preservation of the premises during the term of this lease.

9. The tenant shall use the leased premises exclusively as a private residence for no more than _____ persons unless otherwise specified herein, and the tenant shall not make any alterations to the house, outbuildings or grounds without the written consent of the landlord.

10. The tenant shall keep the premises, including exterior, lawn and grounds, in good order and repair and shall advise the landlord or the landlord's agent of any needed maintenance or repairs reasonably expected to cost $ _____ or more.

11. The tenant shall cause to be made, at the tenant's expense, all required repairs to heating and air-conditioning apparatus, electric and gas fixtures and plumbing work whenever such damage shall have resulted from misuse, waste or neglect of the tenant, it being understood that the landlord is to have same in good order and repair when giving possession.

12. The tenant shall not keep or have in or on the leased house, outbuildings or grounds any article or thing of a dangerous, flammable or explosive nature that might be pronounced "hazardous" or "extra hazardous" by any responsible insurance company.

13. The tenant shall give prompt notice to the landlord or his agent of any dangerous, defective, unsafe or emergency condition in or on the leased premises, said notice being by any suitable means. The landlord or his agent shall repair and correct said conditions promptly upon receiving notice thereof from the tenant.

14. The landlord covenants that the tenant and the tenant's family shall have, hold and enjoy the leased premises for the term of this lease, subject to the conditions set forth herein.

15. The tenant covenants that he shall not commit nor permit a nuisance in or upon the premises, that he shall not maliciously or by reason of gross negligence damage the house, outbuildings or grounds, and that he shall not engage, nor permit any member of his family to engage, in conduct so as to interfere substantially with the comfort and safety of residents of adjacent buildings.

16. The tenant agrees to place a security deposit with the landlord in the amount of $ _____ , to be used by the landlord for the cost of replacing or repairing damage, if any, to the house, outbuildings or grounds caused by the intentional or negligent acts of the tenant, or any other damages or charges resulting from the tenant's breach of this lease for which the landlord may be liable.

17. The landlord agrees, within ten days of receiving said security deposit, to deposit same in an interest-bearing account in a banking organization, in which said deposit shall earn interest at a rate which shall be the prevailing rate earned by other such deposits made with banking organizations in such circumstances.

18. The landlord agrees, within ten days of making such a deposit, to notify the tenant in writing of the name and address of the banking organization in which the deposit of security money has been made.

19. The landlord shall be entitled to receive, as administrative expenses, an amount equal to one percent per annum upon the security payment so deposited, which shall be in lieu of all other administrative and custodial expenses. The balance of the interest paid by the banking organization shall be the money of the tenant and shall be paid to the tenant on each anniversary of this lease or any extension or renewal thereof.

20. The landlord agrees to return said security deposit to the tenant upon the tenant's vacating the leased premises subject to the terms and conditions set forth herein.

21. The tenant shall, at reasonable times, give access to the landlord or his agents for any reasonable and lawful purpose. Except in situations of compelling emergency, the landlord or his agents shall give the tenant at least 24 hours' notice of intention to seek access, the date and time at which access will be sought, and the reason therefore.

22. In the event of default by the tenant, the tenant shall remain liable for all rent due, or to become due, during the term of this lease. The landlord or his agents shall have the obligation to relet the premises in the landlord's name for the balance of the term, or longer, and will apply the proceeds of such reletting toward the reduction of the tenant's obligations enumerated herein.

23. The tenant shall permit the landlord or his agents to show the premises at reasonable hours, to persons desiring to rent or purchase same, 30 days prior to the expiration of this lease, and will permit the notice "To Let" or "For Sale" to be placed on said premises and remain thereon without hindrance or molestation after said date.

24. In the event of any breach by the tenant of any of the tenant's covenants or agreements herein, the landlord or his agents may give the tenant five days' notice to cure said breach, setting forth in writing which covenants or agreements have been breached. If any breach is not cured within said five-day period, or reasonable steps to effectuate said cure are not commenced and diligently pursued within said five-day period and thereafter until said breach has been cured, the landlord or his agents may terminate this lease upon five days' additional notice to the tenant, with said notice being in lieu of a Notice to Quit, which tenant hereby waives. The tenant shall then become liable for the cost of landlord's normal redecorating and cleaning expenses related to preparation of the premises for rental to a succeeding tenant.

Said termination shall be ineffective if the tenant cures said breach or commences and diligently pursues reasonable steps to effectuate such cure at any time prior to the expiration of said five-day termination. Upon terminating this lease as provided herein, the landlord or his agent may commence proceedings against the tenant for his removal as provided for by law.

25. In the event of any breach by the landlord of any of the landlord's covenants or agreements herein, the tenant may give the landlord ten days' notice to cure said breach, setting forth in writing the manner in which said covenants and agreements have been breached. If said breach is not cured within said ten-day period, or reasonble steps to effectuate said cure are not commenced and diligently pursued within said ten-day period and thereafter until said breach has been cured, rent hereunder shall be fully abated from the time at which said ten days' notice expired until such time as the landlord has fully cured the breach set forth in the notice provided for in this paragraph.

26. In no case shall any abatement of rent hereunder be effected where the condition set forth in the notice provided for herein was created by the intentional or negligent act of the tenant, but the landlord shall have the burden of proving that rent abatement may not be effected for the foregoing reason.

27. The landlord agrees to deliver possession of the leased premises at the beginning of the term provided for herein. In the event of the landlord's failure to deliver possession at the beginning of said term, the tenant shall have the right to rescind this lease and to recover any consideration paid under terms of this agreement.

28. The tenant agrees that this lease shall be subject to and subordinate to any mortgage or mortgages now on said premises or which any owner of said premises may hereafter at any time elect to place on said premises.

29. Unless otherwise provided for elsewhere in this lease, any notice required or authorized herein shall be given in writing, one copy of said notice mailed via U.S. certified mail, return receipt requested, and one copy of said notice mailed via U.S. first-class mail.

Notice to the tenant shall be mailed to him at the leased premises. Notice to the landlord or his agent shall be mailed to the addresses set forth herein, or at such new address as to which the tenant has been duly informed.

30. The tenant shall, in case of fire, give immediate notice to the proper authorities and to the landlord or his agent who will cause the damage to be promptly repaired, but if the premises be so damaged that the landlord or his agent shall decide to terminate this lease, then upon ten days' personal or written notice to the tenant this lease shall terminate and the accrued rent shall be paid up to the time of the fire.

31. The tenant shall not assign this lease, nor underlet or underlease the premises, or any part thereof.

32. This lease constitutes the entire agreement between the parties hereto. No changes shall be made herein except by writing, signed by each party and dated. The failure to enforce any right or remedy hereunder, and the payment and acceptance of rent hereunder, shall not be deemed a waiver by either party of such right or remedy in the absence of a writing as provided for herein.

33. In the event legal action is required to enforce any provision of this agreement, the prevailing party shall be entitled to recover reasonable attorney's fees and costs.

34. The landlord and tenant agree that this lease, when filled out and signed, is a binding legal obligation.

(DO NOT SIGN IF THERE ARE ANY BLANK SPACES. CROSS OUT OR FILL IN ALL BLANK SPACES BEFORE SIGNING.)

(The above space is provided for such additional terms and conditions as may be agreed to by the parties and must be crossed out to the extent that it is not filled in.)

IN WITNESS WHEREOF, the parties hereto have executed this agreement.

Landlord

By _____

_____
Witness as to landlord

_____
Witness as to landlord

_____
Tenant

_____
Witness as to tenant

_____
Witness as to tenant

_____
Tenant

_____
Witness as to tenant

_____
Witness as to tenant

Dated this _____ day of _____, 19____.

Lease of Unfurnished House

Landlord

Tenant

Premises

From _____

To _____

Monthly rent _____

Lease Agreement—Furnished House

Landlord _____

_____

                                Address   *Phone*

Managing Agent _____

_____

                                Address   *Phone*

Premises _____

_____

Tenant _____

Tenant _____

1. The LANDLORD hereby leases to _____ (and) _____,
hereinafter termed TENANT, the furnished premises described above for a term of _____ beginning _____
_____ and ending _____, at a monthly rate of $ _____, making a total
rental payable under this lease of $ _____.

2. The described premises are leased furnished, to include all furnishings enumerated on the **List of Furnishings**, which is
a part of this lease, signed by both parties and dated.

3. The tenant agrees to pay the rent herein provided subject to the terms and conditions set forth herein.

4. Rent shall be payable in equal monthly installments on the _____ day of each month.

5. Rent shall be payable in the following manner:

(Landlord specify if payments are to be made by mail, and if so, to what address. If payments are to be made to the landlord
or his or her agent in person, state the place where, and the person to whom, payments are to be made.)

6. The tenant shall pay for all electricity, water, fuel oil and gas during the term of this lease and any extension or renewal
thereof.

7. The landlord covenants that the leased premises are, to the best of his or her knowledge, clean, safe, sound and
healthful and that there exists no violation of any applicable housing code, law or regulation of which he or she is aware.

8. The tenant agrees to comply with all sanitary laws, ordinances and rules and all orders of the Board of Health or other
authorities affecting the cleanliness, occupancy and preservation of the premises during the term of this lease.

9. The tenant shall use the leased premises exclusively for a private residence for occupancy by no more than _____
_____ persons, unless otherwise specified herein, and the tenant shall not make any alterations to the house,
outbuildings or grounds without written consent of the landlord.

10. The tenant shall keep the premises in good order and repair and shall advise the landlord or the landlord's agent of
any needed repairs or maintenance reasonably expected to cost $ _____ or more.

11. The tenant agrees to take good care of the furniture, carpets, draperies, appliances and other household goods, and the personal effects of the landlord, and further agrees that he will deliver up same to the landlord in good condition at the end of the term of this lease, normal wear and tear excepted.

12. The tenant shall repair or replace, at the tenant's expense, all loss or damage to any of the listed furniture, carpets, draperies, appliances and other household goods, and personal effects of the landlord, whenever such damage or loss shall have resulted from the tenant's misuse, waste or neglect of said furnishings and personal effects of the landlord.

13. The tenant shall cause to be made, at the tenant's expense, all required repairs to heating and air-conditioning apparatus, electric and gas fixtures and plumbing work whenever such damage shall have resulted from misuse, waste or neglect of the tenant, it being understood that the landlord is to have same in good order and repair when giving possession.

14. The tenant shall not keep or have in or on the leased house, outbuildings or grounds any article or thing of a dangerous, flammable or explosive nature that might be pronounced "hazardous" or "extra hazardous" by any responsible insurance company.

15. The tenant shall give prompt notice to the landlord or his agent of any dangerous, defective, unsafe or emergency condition in or on the leased premises, said notice being by any suitable means. The landlord or his agent shall repair and correct said conditions promptly upon receiving notice thereof from the tenant.

16. The landlord covenants that the tenant and the tenant's family shall have, hold and enjoy the leased premises for the term of this lease, subject to the conditions set forth herein.

17. The tenant covenants that he shall not commit nor permit a nuisance in or upon the premises, that he shall not maliciously or by reason of gross negligence damage the house, outbuildings or grounds, and that he shall not engage, nor permit any member of his family to engage, in conduct so as to interfere substantially with the comfort and safety of residents of adjacent buildings.

18. The tenant agrees to place a security deposit with the landlord in the amount of $ _____, to be used by the landlord at the termination of this lease for the cost of replacing or repairing damage, if any, to the house, outbuildings, grounds, furnishings or personal effects of the landlord resulting from the intentional or negligent acts of the tenant.

19. The landlord agrees, within ten days of receiving said security deposit, to deposit same in an interest-bearing account in a banking organization, in which said deposit shall earn interest at a rate which shall be the prevailing rate earned by other such deposits made with banking organizations in such circumstances.

20. The landlord agrees, within ten days of making such a deposit, to notify the tenant of the name and address of the banking organization in which the deposit of security money has been made.

21. The landlord shall be entitled to receive, as administrative expenses, an amount equal to one percent per annum upon the security payment so deposited, which shall be in lieu of all other administrative and custodial expenses. The balance of the interest paid by the banking organization shall be the money of the tenant and shall be paid to the tenant on each anniversary of this lease or any extension or renewal thereof.

22. The landlord agrees to return said security deposit to the tenant within ten days of the tenant's vacating the leased premises subject to the terms and conditions set forth herein.

23. The tenant shall, at reasonable times, give access to the landlord or his agents for any reasonable and lawful purpose. Except in situations of compelling emergency, the landlord or his agents shall give the tenant at least 24 hours' notice of intention to seek access, the date and time at which access will be sought, and the reason therefore.

24. In the event of default by the tenant, the tenant shall remain liable for all rent due or to become due during the term of this lease. The landlord or his agents shall have the obligation to relet the premises in the landlord's name for the balance of the term, or longer, and will apply proceeds of such reletting toward the reduction of the tenant's obligations enumerated herein.

25. The tenant shall permit the landlord or his agents to show the premises at reasonable hours, to persons desiring to rent or purchase same, 30 days prior to the expiration of this lease, and will permit the notice "To Let" or "For Sale" to be placed on said premises and remain thereon without hindrance or molestation after said date.

26. In the event of any breach by the tenant of any of the tenant's covenants or agreements herein, the landlord or his agents may give the tenant five days' notice to cure said breach, setting forth in writing which covenants or agreements have been breached. If any breach is not cured within said five-day period, or reasonable steps to effectuate said cure are not commenced and diligently pursued within said five-day period and thereafter until said breach has been cured, the landlord or his agents may terminate this lease upon five days' additional notice to the tenant, with said notice being in lieu of a Notice to Quit, which tenant hereby waives.

Said termination shall be ineffective if the tenant cures said breach or commences and diligently pursues reasonable steps to effectuate such cure at any time prior to the expiration of said five-day termination. Upon terminating this lease as provided herein, the landlord or his agent may commence proceedings against the tenant for his removal as provided for by law.

27. In the event of any breach by the landlord of any of the landlord's covenants or agreements herein, the tenant may give the landlord ten days' notice to cure said breach, setting forth in writing the manner in which said covenants and agreements have been breached. If said breach is not cured within said ten-day period, or reasonable steps to effectuate said cure are not commenced and diligently pursued within said ten-day period and thereafter until said breach has been cured, rent hereunder shall be fully abated from the time at which said ten days' notice expired until such time as the landlord has fully cured the breach set forth in the notice provided for in this paragraph.

28. In no case shall any abatement of rent hereunder be effected where the condition set forth in the notice provided for herein was created by the intentional or negligent act of the tenant, but the landlord shall have the burden of proving that rent abatement may not be effected for the foregoing reason.

29. The landlord agrees to deliver possession of the leased premises at the beginning of the term provided for herein. In the event of the landlord's failure to deliver possession at the beginning of said term, the tenant shall have the right to rescind this lease and recover any consideration paid under terms of this agreement.

30. The tenant agrees that this lease shall be subject to and subordinate to any mortgage or mortgages now on said premises or which any owner of said premises may hereafter at any time elect to place on said premises.

31. Unless otherwise provided for elsewhere in this lease, any notice required or authorized herein shall be given in writing, one copy of said notice mailed via U.S. certified mail, return receipt requested, and one copy of said notice mailed via U.S. first-class mail.

Notice to the tenant shall be mailed to him at the leased premises. Notice to the landlord shall be mailed to him, or to the managing agent, at their respective addresses as set forth herein, or at such new address as to which the tenant has been duly notified.

32. This lease constitutes the entire agreement between the parties hereto. No changes shall be made herein except by writing, signed by each party and dated. The failure to enforce any right or remedy hereunder, and the payment and acceptance of rent hereunder, shall not be deemed a waiver by either party of such right or remedy in the absence of a writing as provided for herein.

33. In the event legal action is required to enforce any provision of this agreement, the prevailing party shall be entitled to recover reasonable attorney's fees and costs.

34. The landlord and tenant agree that this apartment lease, when filled out and signed, is a binding legal obligation.

(DO NOT SIGN IF THERE ARE ANY BLANK SPACES. CROSS OUT OR FILL IN ALL BLANK SPACES BEFORE SIGNING.)

(The above space is provided for such additional terms and conditions as may be agreed to by the parties and must be crossed out to the extent that it is not filled in.)

IN WITNESS WHEREOF, the parties hereto have executed this agreement.

Landlord

By _____

Witness as to landlord

Witness as to landlord

Tenant

_____

_____

Witness as to tenant

Witness as to tenant

Tenant

_____

_____

Witness as to tenant

Witness as to tenant

Dated this _____ day of _____, 19____.

Lease of Furnished House

Landlord

Tenant

Premises

From _____

To _____

Monthly rent

Seasonal Lease Agreement—Furnished Country/Seashore House

Landlord _____

_____
Address   *Phone*

Managing Agent _____

_____
Address   *Phone*

Premises _____

_____

Tenant _____

_____
Address   *Phone*

Tenant _____

_____
Address   *Phone*

1. The LANDLORD hereby leases to _____ (and) _____, hereinafter termed TENANT, the premises described above for a term of _____ beginning _____ _____ and ending _____, at a monthly rate of $ _____, making a total rental amount payable under this lease of $ _____.

2. The tenant agrees to pay the rent in the following manner:

(Landlord specify if payments are to be made by mail, and if so, to what address. If payments are to be made to the landlord or his agent in person, state the place where, and the person to whom, payments should be made.)

3. The tenant, in addition to rent, agrees to pay all charges for water, gas, fuel oil and electricity used during the term of the lease, such charges to be paid monthly in addition to rent.

4. Upon receipt of any payment for rent or utilities in cash, the landlord agrees to issue a receipt stating the tenant's name, a description of the premises, the amount paid, the date paid and the period for which rent or utilities is paid.

5. The tenant agrees to place a security deposit of $ _____, to be used by the landlord at the termination of this lease for the cost of replacing or repairing damage, if any, to the premises or furnishings caused by the intentional or negligent acts of the tenant.

6. The landlord agrees to return said security deposit to the tenant upon the tenant's vacating the premises subject to the terms and conditions herein.

7. The tenant agrees to take good care of the premises and of the furnishings therein, and at the end of the term of this lease to deliver up to the landlord the premises and furnishings in good order, normal wear and tear excepted.

8. The landlord covenants that the leased premises are, to the best of his or her knowledge, clean, safe, sound and healthful and that there exists no violation of any applicable housing code, law or regulation of which he or she is aware, and that no such violation will be permitted to exist during the term of this lease or any extension thereof.

9. The tenant shall promptly comply with all laws, orders, ordinances and regulations pertaining to his or her use of the premises, and the tenant shall not keep therein any article or thing of a dangerous, flammable or explosive nature that might be pronounced "hazardous" or "extra hazardous" by any responsible insurance company.

10. The tenant shall, in case of fire, give immediate notice to the proper authorities and to the landlord who will cause the damage to be promptly repaired; but if the premises be so damaged that the landlord shall decide to terminate this lease, then upon ten days' personal or written notice to the tenant this lease shall terminate and the accrued rent shall be paid up to the time of the fire.

11. The tenant shall do no cooking in any room used for sleeping purposes, but shall have the right to use jointly with any other tenants a room set aside by the landlord for that purpose.

12. The tenant shall, at reasonable times, give access to the landlord or his agents for any reasonable and lawful purpose. Except in situations of compelling emergency, the landlord shall give the tenant at least 24 hours' notice of intention to seek access, the date and time at which access will be sought, and the reason therefore.

13. In the event of default by the tenant, the tenant shall remain liable for all rent due or to become due during the term of this lease. The landlord shall have the obligation to relet the premises in the landlord's name for the balance of the term, or longer, and will apply proceeds of such reletting toward the reduction of the tenant's obligations enumerated herein.

14. The tenant shall permit the landlord or his agents to show the premises at reasonable hours, to persons desiring to rent or purchase same, 30 days prior to the expiration of this lease, and will permit the notice "To Let" or "For Sale" to be placed on said premises and remain thereon without hindrance or molestation after said date.

15. The tenant shall not assign this lease, nor underlet or underlease the premises, or any part thereof, nor make any alterations to the premises, nor permit same to be used at any time during the term of this lease for any other purpose than a private residence.

16. This lease, and any attached **List of Furnishings** signed by both parties and dated, and incorporated herein by reference for all purposes, constitutes the entire agreement between the parties hereto. No changes shall be made herein except by writing, signed by each party and dated.

17. In the event legal action is required to enforce any provision of this agreement, the prevailing party shall be entitled to recover reasonable attorney's fees and costs.

18. This lease, when filled out and signed, is a binding legal obligation.

(DO NOT SIGN IF THERE ARE ANY BLANK SPACES. CROSS OUT OR FILL IN ALL BLANK SPACES BEFORE SIGNING.)

(The above space is provided for such additional terms and conditions as may be agreed to by the parties and must be crossed out to the extent that it is not filled in.)

IN WITNESS WHEREOF, the parties hereto have executed this agreement.

Landlord _____

By _____

_____
Witness as to landlord

_____
Witness as to landlord

Tenant _____

_____
Witness as to tenant

_____
Witness as to tenant

Tenant _____

_____
Witness as to tenant

_____
Witness as to tenant

Dated this _____ day of _____, 19____.

Seasonal Lease

Landlord

Tenant

Premises

From _____

To _____

Monthly rent _____

Extension of Lease

Landlord _____

_____
                          Address   *Phone*

Managing Agent _____

_____
                          Address   *Phone*

Premises _____

Tenant _____

Tenant _____

Date of Lease _____

Beginning _____ Ending _____

1. The above-described lease, due to expire on _____, is hereby renewed for a term of _____ beginning _____ and ending _____.

2. All terms, provisions and covenants of the above-described lease shall remain in full force for the duration of the extended term, except as noted.

3. In connection with this renewal, the rent, payable monthly, shall be $ _____ per month, making a total rental of $ _____ payable under this agreement.

(The above space is provided for such additional terms and conditions as may be agreed to by the parties and must be crossed out to the extent that it is not filled in.)

IN WITNESS WHEREOF, the parties hereto have executed this agreement.

_____
Landlord

By _____

_____
Tenant

_____
Tenant

Dated this _____ day of _____, 19_____.

Parking Space Lease

Landlord _____

_____
                           Address   *Phone*

Managing Agent _____

_____
                           Address   *Phone*

Premises _____

Tenant _____
                           Address   *Phone*

1. The LANDLORD hereby leases to the TENANT parking space located at _____ and designated as space No. _____, for a term of _____ beginning _____ and ending _____, at a monthly rent of $_____.

2. The tenant agrees to pay the stipulated rent in advance on the _____ day of each month to the landlord or his agent by mail or in person to the landlord or his agent at their respective addresses as noted above.

3. Upon receiving any payment of parking space rent in cash, the landlord agrees to issue a receipt stating the name of the tenant, the amount of rent paid, the designation of the parking space and the period for which said rent is paid.

4. The tenant affirms his/her understanding that the landlord does not furnish attendants for the parking of automobiles, and if any employee of the landlord shall, at the request of the tenant, handle, move, park or drive any vehicle placed in the parking area, then, and in every case, such employee shall be deemed the agent of the tenant, and the tenant, not the landlord, shall be liable for any loss, damage, injury or expense that may be suffered or sustained in connection therewith or arising from the acts of the tenant or any employee who may be acting as agent of the tenant.

5. The landlord is not responsible for items left in any vehicle parked in the designated space.

(The above space is provided for such additional terms and conditions as may be agreed to by the parties and must be crossed out to the extent that it is not filled in.)

IN WITNESS WHEREOF, the parties hereto have executed this agreement.

_____

Landlord

By _____

_____
Witness as to landlord

_____
Witness as to landlord

_____

Tenant

_____
Witness as to tenant

_____
Witness as to tenant

_____

Tenant

_____
Witness as to tenant

_____
Witness as to tenant

Dated this _____ day of _____, 19____.

Storage Space Lease

Lessor _____

_____
Address   Phone

Lessor's Agent _____

_____
Address   Phone

Premises _____

_____

_____

Tenant _____

_____
Address   Phone

1. The LESSOR hereby leases to _____, hereinafter termed the TENANT, the premises described above for a term of _____ beginning _____ and ending _____ _____, at a monthly rate of $_____, making a total rental payable under this lease of $_____.

2. The tenant agrees to pay the rent herein provided subject to the terms and conditions set forth herein.

3. Rent shall be payable in equal monthly installments to be paid in advance on the _____ day of each month.

4. Rent shall be paid in the following manner:

(Lessor specify if payments are to be made by mail, and if so, to what address. If payments are to be made to the lessor or his agent in person, state the place where and the person to whom payments are to be made.)

5. Upon receiving any payment of the rent in cash, the lessor agrees to issue a receipt stating the tenant's name, a description of the premises, the amount of rent paid, the date paid and the period for which rent is paid.

6. The lessor covenants that the leased premises are clean and dry and that there exists no violation of any applicable building code, law or regulation.

7. The tenant agrees to use the premises exclusively for the storage of a vehicle, boat or trailer or for the storage of personal property, merchandise, supplies or other material owned by the tenant and for no other use.

8. The tenant understands and agrees that the use of electricity for food freezers, refrigerators and other appliances is not allowed.

9. The tenant agrees to keep the immediate premises in good order and to advise the lessor or his agent of any needed maintenance or repairs.

10. The tenant shall not store any items outside the storage area nor dispose of any trash outside the storage area other than in containers provided by the lessor.

11. The tenant shall not keep or have in or on the leased premises any article or thing which might be pronounced "hazardous" or "extra hazardous" by any responsible insurance company.

12. The tenant agrees not to commit a nuisance in or upon said premises so as to substantially interfere with the comfort or safety of occupants of adjacent buildings.

13. The lessor is not responsible for any loss or damage due to fire, theft, water, wind, hurricane or any cause whatsoever to the property of the tenant, nor is the lessor required to carry any insurance to cover same.

14. The tenant, at his own expense, shall obtain his own insurance, if any, to the property stored in said premises.

15. The tenant shall not sublease said premises without the written consent of the lessor.

16. The tenant may not make any alterations to the premises without the written consent of the lessor.

17. The tenant agrees to make a security deposit in the amount of $_____ to be used by the lessor at the termination of this lease for the cost of repairs, if any, to the premises caused by the intentional or negligent acts of the tenant.

18. The lessor agrees to return said security deposit to the tenant upon the tenant's vacating the premises in a clean condition subject to the terms and conditions set forth herein.

19. The lessor shall have the right to enter said premises at any time to inspect same, to make repairs or to enforce this lease.

20. The tenant, at his own expense, may provide a suitable means of locking said premises, giving a key or combination to any locking device to the lessor so that he or his agent may effect entry for any of the purposes enumerated above.

21. The tenant agrees to notify the lessor in writing 15 days in advance of vacating the premises.

22. The tenant agrees that this lease shall be subject and subordinate to any mortgage or mortgages now on said premises, or which the owner of said premises may hereafter at any time elect to place upon said premises.

23. The lessor and tenant agree that this lease, when filled out and signed, is a binding legal obligation.

24. This lease constitutes the entire agreement between the parties hereto.

(The above space is provided for such additional terms and conditions as may be agreed to by the parties and must be crossed out to the extent that it is not filled in.)

IN WITNESS WHEREOF, the parties hereto have executed this agreement.

_____
Landlord

By _____

_____
Witness as to landlord

_____
Witness as to landlord

_____
Tenant

_____
Witness as to tenant

_____
Witness as to tenant

_____
Tenant

_____
Witness as to tenant

_____
Witness as to tenant

Dated this _____ day of _____, 19____.

Lease Agreement—Monthly Tenancy of Unfurnished Apartment

Landlord _____

_____
                    Address   *Phone*

Managing Agent _____

_____
                    Address   *Phone*

Premises _____
                    Address   *Apt. No.*

Tenant _____

Tenant _____

1. The LANDLORD hereby leases to _____ (and) _____,
hereinafter termed TENANT, the above-described premises on a month-to-month basis at a monthly rental of $_____,
payable in advance on the _____ day of each month, the first payment being due _____,
all rents payable at _____.

2. The landlord covenants that the tenant shall have quiet enjoyment of said premises during the term of this agreement.

3. The tenant agrees to pay rent in the amount and manner described herein.

4. The tenant further agrees:

    A. To leave the premises in like good condition as found.
    B. To use said premises exclusively as a residence.
    C. Not to assign nor sublet said premises without written permission of the landlord.
    D. Not to create a nuisance which shall disturb other tenants or occupants of adjoining buildings.
    E. To give the landlord, in writing, 30 days' notice of intention to quit the premises.

5. The tenant agrees to take good care of any carpets, draperies, appliances or other household goods and further agrees to deliver up same to the landlord in good condition at the end of the term of this lease, normal wear and tear excepted.

6. The tenant shall cause to be made, at the tenant's expense, all required repairs to any carpets, draperies, appliances, heating and air-conditioning apparatus, electric and gas fixtures and plumbing work whenever such damage shall have resulted from misuse, waste or neglect of the tenant, it being understood that the landlord is to have same in good order and repair when giving possession.

7. The tenant agrees to place a security deposit in the amount of $ _____ to be used by the landlord for making any repairs necessitated by the intentional or negligent acts of the tenant.

8. The landlord agrees to refund promptly said security deposit upon the tenant's vacating the premises subject to the terms of this agreement.

9. The landlord may reenter for default of _____ days in the payment of any installment of rent, or for the breach by the tenant of any of the covenants or conditions herein.

10. In the event legal action is required to enforce any provision of this agreement, the prevailing party shall be entitled to recover reasonable attorney's fees and costs.

(The above space is provided for such additional terms and conditions as may be agreed to by the parties and must be crossed out to the extent that it is not filled in.)

FORM 10.1/F30

IN WITNESS WHEREOF, the parties hereto have executed this agreement.

_____
Landlord
By _____

_____
Witness as to landlord

_____
Witness as to landlord

_____
Tenant

_____
Witness as to tenant

_____
Witness as to tenant

_____
Tenant

_____
Witness as to tenant

_____
Witness as to tenant

Dated this _____ day of _____, 19____.

Monthly Tenancy Agreement

Landlord

Tenant

Premises

From _____
Until _____
Monthly rent _____

Lease Agreement—Monthly Tenancy of Furnished Premises

Landlord _____

_____

$\qquad$ *Address* $\qquad$ *Phone*

Managing Agent _____

_____

$\qquad$ *Address* $\qquad$ *Phone*

Premises _____

$\qquad$ *Address*

Tenant _____

Tenant _____

1. The LANDLORD hereby leases to _____ (and) _____, hereinafter termed TENANT, the above-described furnished premises on a month-to-month basis at a monthly rental of $ _____, payable in advance on the _____ day of each month, the first payment being due _____ _____, all rents payable at _____.

2. The landlord covenants that the tenant shall have quiet enjoyment of said premises during the term of this agreement.

3. The tenant agrees that furnishings in the above-described premises are received in good order and condition and covenants to deliver up same, in like condition, normal wear and tear excepted, to the landlord at the end of this agreement.

4. The tenant agrees to pay rent in the amount and manner described herein.

5. The tenant further agrees:

   A. To leave the premises in like good condition as found.
   B. To use said premises exclusively as a residence.
   C. Not to assign nor sublet said premises without written permission of the landlord.
   D. Not to create a nuisance which shall disturb other tenants or occupants of adjoining buildings.
   E. To give the landlord, in writing, 30 days' notice of intention to quit the premises.

6. The tenant agrees to place a security deposit in the amount of $ _____ to be used by the landlord for making any repairs necessitated by the intentional or negligent acts of the tenant.

7. The landlord agrees to refund promptly said security deposit upon the tenant's vacating the premises subject to the terms of this agreement.

8. The landlord may reenter for default of _____ days in the payment of any installment of rent, or for the breach by the tenant of any of the covenants or conditions herein.

9. In the event legal action is required to enforce any provision of this agreement, the prevailing party shall be entitled to recover reasonable attorney's fees and costs.

(The above space is provided for such additional terms and conditions as may be agreed to by the parties and must be crossed out to the extent that it is not filled in.)

IN WITNESS WHEREOF, the parties hereto have executed this agreement.

_____

Landlord

By _____

_____
Witness as to landlord

_____
Witness as to landlord

_____

Tenant

_____
Witness as to tenant

_____
Witness as to tenant

_____

Tenant

_____
Witness as to tenant

_____
Witness as to tenant

Dated this _____ day of _____, 19____.

Monthly Tenancy Agreement

Landlord

Tenant

Premises

From

Until

Monthly rent

Lease Agreement—Sublease of Unfurnished Apartment or House

Landlord _____

_____
         Address   *Phone*

Managing Agent _____

_____
         Address   *Phone*

Premises _____
         Address

Subtenant _____

Subtenant _____

1. The LANDLORD hereby subleases to _____ (and) _____, hereinafter termed SUBTENANT, the unfurnished premises described above for a term of _____ beginning _____ and ending _____, at a monthly rate of $ _____, making a total rental of $_____ payable under this sublease.

2. The above-described premises are the same premises referred to in a lease between the landlord and _____ _____, dated _____.

3. The subtenant affirms that he has read, understands and will fully comply with all terms and conditions of said lease, an exact copy of which is attached.

4. In the event legal action is required to enforce any provision of this agreement, the prevailing party shall be entitled to recover reasonable attorney's fees and costs.

5. The terms, provisions and conditions of said lease are incorporated herein for all purposes and shall be binding upon the landlord and tenant.

(The above space is provided for such additional terms and conditions as may be agreed to by the parties and must be crossed out to the extent that it is not filled in.)

IN WITNESS WHEREOF, the parties hereto have executed this agreement.

_____

Landlord

By _____

_____
Witness as to landlord

_____
Witness as to landlord

_____
Subtenant

_____
Witness as to subtenant

_____
Witness as to subtenant

_____
Subtenant

_____
Witness as to subtenant

_____
Witness as to subtenant

Dated this _____ day of _____, 19____.

Sublease

Landlord

Subtenant

Premises

From

To

Monthly rent

Lease Agreement—Sublease of Unfurnished Apartment or House

Tenant _____

_____
      Address   *Phone*

Tenant's Agent _____

_____
      Address   *Phone*

Premises _____

_____

Subtenant _____

_____
      Address   *Phone*

Subtenant _____

_____
      Address   *Phone*

1. The TENANT hereby subleases to _____ (and) _____, hereinafter termed SUBTENANT, the premises described above for a term of _____ beginning _____ _____ and ending _____ _____, at a monthly rate of $ _____, making a total rental of $_____ payable under the terms of this sublease.

2. The above-described premises are the same premises referred to in a lease between the landlord and _____ _____, dated _____.

3. The subtenant affirms that he/she has read, understands and will fully comply with said lease, an exact copy of which is attached.

4. The terms, provisions and conditions of said lease are incorporated by reference herein for all purposes and shall be binding upon the tenant as landlord and upon the subtenant as tenant.

5. The subtenant shall deposit with the tenant the sum of $_____ as security deposit to be used by the tenant at the termination of this agreement for the cost of repairing damage, if any, to the premises caused by the intentional or negligent acts of the subtenant.

6. The tenant agrees to pay the subtenant interest on said security deposit at a rate equal to that earned by the security deposit of the tenant under terms of the tenant's lease with the landlord.

7. The tenant agrees to refund to the subtenant said security deposit paid under this agreement upon subtenant's vacating the subleased premises subject to the terms and conditions set forth herein.

8. The subtenant, in addition to rent, agrees to pay all charges for gas, electricity, fuel oil and water used during the term of this sublease, such charges to be paid monthly to the tenant or to the tenant's agent.

9. In the event legal action is required to enforce any provision of this agreement, the prevailing party shall be entitled to recover reasonable attorney's fees and costs.

(The above space is provided for such additional terms and conditions as may be agreed to by the parties and must be crossed out to the extent that it is not filled in.)

IN WITNESS WHEREOF, the parties hereto have executed this agreement.

_____
Tenant

_____
Witness as to tenant
_____
Witness as to tenant

_____
Subtenant

_____
Witness as to subtenant
_____
Witness as to subtenant

_____
Subtenant

_____
Witness as to subtenant
_____
Witness as to subtenant

Dated this _____ day of _____, 19____.

Sublease

Tenant

Subtenant

Premises

From _____
To _____
Monthly rent _____

Lease Agreement—Sublease of Furnished Apartment or House

Tenant _____

_____
Address   Phone

Tenant's Agent _____

_____
Address   Phone

Premises _____

_____

Subtenant _____

_____
Address   Phone

Subtenant _____

_____
Address   Phone

1. The TENANT hereby leases to _____ (and) _____, hereinafter termed SUBTENANT, the furnished premises described above for a term of _____ beginning _____ and ending _____, at a monthly rate of $ _____, making a total rental of $ _____ payable under terms of this sublease.

2. These premises are the same premises referred to in the lease between _____ (landlord) and _____ (tenant), signed by them and dated _____.

3. The subtenant affirms that he or she has read, understands and will fully comply with said lease, an exact copy of which is attached hereto.

4. The terms, provisions and conditions of said lease are incorporated by reference herein for all purposes and shall be binding upon the tenant as landlord and upon the subtenant as tenant.

5. The described premises are subleased furnished, to include all furnishings enumerated on the **List of Furnishings**, which is a part of this lease, signed by both parties and dated and incorporated herein by reference for all purposes.

6. The subtenant agrees to take good care of the furniture, carpets, draperies, appliances and other household goods, and of the personal effects of the tenant, and further agrees to deliver up same to the tenant in good condition at the end of the term of this sublease, normal wear and tear excepted.

7. The subtenant will repair or replace, at the subtenant's expense, all loss of, or damage to, any of the listed furniture, carpets, draperies, appliances and other household goods, and personal effects of the tenant, whenever such damage or loss shall have resulted from the subtenant's misuse, waste or neglect of said furnishings or personal effects of the tenant.

8. The subtenant agrees to make a security deposit with the tenant in the amount of $_____, to be used by the tenant at the termination of this sublease for the cost of replacing or repairing damage, if any, to the furnishings, premises or personal effects of the tenant resulting from the intentional or negligent acts of the subtenant.

9. The tenant agrees to pay the subtenant interest on said security deposit at a rate equal to that earned by the security deposit of the tenant under terms of the tenant's lease with the landlord.

10. The tenant agrees to refund to the subtenant said security deposit paid under this agreement upon subtenant's vacating the subleased premises subject to the terms and conditions set forth herein.

11. The subtenant, in addition to rent, agrees to pay all charges for gas, electricity, fuel oil and water used during the term of this sublease, such charges to be paid monthly to the tenant or to the tenant's agent.

12. In the event legal action is required to enforce any provision of this agreement, the prevailing party shall be entitled to recover reasonable attorney's fees and costs.

(The above space is provided for such additional terms and conditions as may be agreed to by the parties and must be crossed out to the extent that it is not filled in.)

IN WITNESS WHEREOF, the parties hereto have executed this agreement.

_____
Tenant

_____
Witness as to tenant

_____
Witness as to tenant

_____
Subtenant

_____
Witness as to subtenant

_____
Witness as to subtenant

_____
Subtenant

_____
Witness as to subtenant

_____
Witness as to subtenant

Dated this _____ day of _____, 19____.

Sublease

Tenant

Subtenant

Premises

From _____
To _____
Monthly rent _____

Permission to Sublet

Landlord _____

Premises _____

Tenant _____

Date of Lease _____

1. Permission is hereby granted to the above-named tenant to sublease the premises described above for a term of _____ beginning _____ and ending _____.

2. Any and all subtenants shall be required to conform to all obligations and covenants of the tenant as set forth in the above-described lease, all provisions of said lease remaining in full force and effect for the entire term of the sublease.

3. Any and all adult subtenants shall be required to complete the landlord's standard rental application and must meet the usual character, employment and credit requirements for tenancy.

4. In the event legal action is required to enforce any provision of this agreement, the prevailing party shall be entitled to recover reasonable attorney's fees and costs.

5. This permission to sublease in no way releases the above-named tenant from any obligation, responsibility or duty of a tenant as set forth in the above-described lease.

(The above space is provided for such additional terms and conditions as the parties may agree to and must be crossed out to the extent that it is not filled in.)

FORM 10.6/F40

IN WITNESS WHEREOF, the parties hereto have executed this agreement.

_____
Landlord

By _____

_____
Witness as to landlord

_____
Witness as to landlord

_____
Tenant

_____
Witness as to tenant

_____
Witness as to tenant

_____
Tenant

_____
Witness as to tenant

_____
Witness as to tenant

Dated this _____ day of _____, 19____.

Permission to Underlet

Landlord _____

Premises _____

Tenant _____

Date of Lease _____

1. Permission is hereby granted by the LANDLORD to the above-named TENANT to underlet a portion of the above-described premises for a term of _____ beginning _____ and ending _____ .

2. Any person who underlets hereunder shall be required to conform to all obligations and covenants of the tenant as set forth in the above-described lease.

3. Any and all adult persons who underlet shall be required to complete the landlord's standard rental application and must meet the usual character, employment and credit requirements for residency.

4. Any person underletting hereunder shall do so for the sole purpose of a residence.

5. In the event legal action is required to enforce any provision of this agreement, the prevailing party shall be entitled to recover reasonable attorney's fees and costs.

6. The landlord reserves the right to cancel this authorization any time that a person underletting said premises shall fail to fully and wholly comply with the convenants and obligations of a tenant under terms of the lease described above.

(The above space is provided for such additional terms and conditions as may be agreed to by the parties and must be crossed out to the extent that it is not filled in.)

FORM 10.7/F42

IN WITNESS WHEREOF, the parties hereto have executed this agreement.

_____

Landlord

By _____

_____

Witness as to landlord

_____

Witness as to landlord

_____

Tenant

_____

Witness as to tenant

_____

Witness as to tenant

_____

Tenant

_____

Witness as to tenant

_____

Witness as to tenant

Dated this _____ day of _____, 19____.

List of Furnishings

1. The following listed furnishings and items of personal property belonging to _____ are located at the premises described in the attached agreement between _____ and _____ _____, dated _____.

2. _____ hereby acknowledges receipt of the above-listed furnishings and other items in good order and repair.

3. At the end of the term of the attached agreement between _____ and _____ _____, dated the _____ day of _____, 19_____, _____ agrees to deliver up to _____ the herein-listed furnishings and items of personal property in good order and repair, normal wear and tear excepted.

4. Under terms of the attached agreement described above, _____ shall deposit with _____ _____ the sum of $_____ as security deposit to be used by _____ for the cost of replacing or repairing damage, if any, to the listed furnishings and items of personal property caused by the intentional or negligent acts of _____.

5. In the event of early termination of this agreement by _____, he or she shall then become liable for the cost of normal redecorating required for rental of the premises to a subsequent tenant.

(Signed) _____

(Signed) _____

(Signed) _____

Rental Application

Date _____

Application is hereby made to rent premises known as

_____
_____
Apartment No.   *Building Name*

_____
Street & Number   *City*   *State*   *Zip*

for a term of _____ beginning the _____ day
of _____, 19 _____, and ending the _____ day of _____
_____, 19 _____, for which monthly rental shall be $_____
payable in advance, and for which a security deposit of $_____ shall be due prior to
occupancy of the above-described premises.

A deposit of $_____ is made herewith on account of the first month's rent, with
the understanding that if this application is accepted and the applicant fails to execute a lease before the
beginning date specified above, or to pay the balance due as first month's rent, said payment will be forfeited
as liquidated damages.

It is also understood that if this application is not accepted, or if the premises are not ready for occupancy
by the applicant on the date specified above, said deposit shall be refunded to the applicant forthwith, upon
applicant's request.

APPLICANT

Name _____

Present Address _____ How Long? _____

Previous Address _____ How Long? _____

Married? _____ Spouse's Name _____ No. to Live in Apt. _____

Children? _____ How Many? _____ Ages? _____

Pets? _____ What Kind? _____ How Many? _____

YOUR EMPLOYMENT

Employer _____

Employer Address _____

Supervisor _____ Bus. Phone _____

How Long on Present Job? _____ Annual Income _____

SPOUSE'S EMPLOYMENT

Employer _____

Employer Address _____

Supervisor _____ Bus. Phone _____

How Long on Present Job? _____ Annual Income _____

REFERENCES

Bank _____ Phone _____

Personal Reference _____ Phone _____

Credit Reference _____ Phone _____

Credit Reference _____ Phone _____

_____
Applicant's Signature

The information provided herein may be used by the landlord or his agent to determine whether to accept this application. Upon written request within 60 days, the landlord or his agent will disclose to applicant in writing the nature and scope of any investigation landlord has requested, and will, if this application is refused, state in writing the reason for said refusal.

Accepted _____ Refused _____ By _____

Notice of Intent to Vacate

Date: _____

Premises: _____

    In accordance with terms of a rental agreement between the undersigned tenant and the landlord of the above-described premises, dated _____, notice is hereby given of intention to vacate said premises on _____.

_____
Tenant

_____
Tenant

Forwarding Address: _____

_____

Dear Tenant:

When you moved in, you found clean, livable quarters. Now that you are moving out, we expect that you will want to leave a clean apartment.

Under the terms of your rental agreement you are required to leave your apartment in the same clean condition as when you moved in. Specifically, you should:

-- Remove all food, debris and other refuse.

-- Clean and defrost refrigerator.

-- Clean stove top, oven, and other appliances.

-- Clean all closets, kitchen cabinets, and medicine cabinet.

-- Clean all floors.

-- Report all damage.

After you have vacated the apartment, it will be inspected for compliance with your rental agreement and the expense of cleaning or repairing damage, if any, will be charged against your security deposit.

Most departing tenants do leave clean apartments. Some, however, neglect this responsibility and need a reminder.

It has been a pleasure to have you with us, and we hope that our facilities and services have been such that you can recommend us to friends who may be seeking similar accommodations.

Sincerely,

P.S. Don't forget to turn in your keys. Thanks!

Transfer Clause

The landlord agrees that upon presentation of proof of transfer, the tenant shall be relieved of the requirement of this lease with respect to term, and may vacate under provisions of this lease pertaining to quitting the premises at the expiration of the original term.

Auto Accident Report

EMERGENCY MEDICAL SERVICE

_____ _____
Fire Department Phone   *Rescue Squad Phone*

_____ _____
City/County Hospital Phone   *Other*

CLAIMANT DATA

_____
Claimant Name   *Phone*

_____
Street   *City*   *State*   *Zip*

Insurer _____ Policy No. _____ Phone _____

_____
Street   *City*   *State*   *Zip*

ACCIDENT DATA

Date of Accident _____ Time of Accident _____

Location _____

_____

_____

WITNESSES

_____
Name   *(Occupation)*

_____
Address   *Phone*

_____
Name   *(Occupation)*

_____
Address   *Phone*

FORM 14.1/F54

WITNESSES

_____
Name   (Occupation)

_____
Address   Phone

_____
Name   (Occupation)

_____
Address   Phone

_____
Name   (Occupation)

_____
Address   Phone

_____
Name   (Occupation)

_____
Address   Phone

_____
Name   (Occupation)

_____
Address   Phone

_____
Name   (Occupation)

_____
Address   Phone

_____
Name   (Occupation)

_____
Address   Phone

_____
Name   (Occupation)

_____
Address   Phone

_____
Name   (Occupation)

_____
Address   Phone

_____
Name   (Occupation)

_____
Address   Phone

INJURIES

Other Vehicle

DVR: Driver	**RFP:** Right Front Passenger	**CRP:** Center Rear Passenger
CFP: Center Front Passenger	**LRP:** Left Rear Passenger	**RRP:** Right Rear Passenger

DVR	CFP	RFP	LRP	CRP	RRP	
——	——	——	——	——	——	Dead at scene.
——	——	——	——	——	——	Visible signs of injury, such as bleeding wound or distorted arm, leg, etc. Had to be carried from scene.
——	——	——	——	——	——	Visible bruises, abrasions, swelling, limping, etc.
——	——	——	——	——	——	No visible injury but complaint of pain or momentary unconsciousness.
——	——	——	——	——	——	No apparent injury.
——	——	——	——	——	——	Not ejected from vehicle.
——	——	——	——	——	——	Partially ejected from vehicle.
——	——	——	——	——	——	Ejected from vehicle.

Pedestrian/Other

P#1	P#2	P#3	P#4	O#1	O#2	
——	——	——	——	——	——	Dead at scene.
——	——	——	——	——	——	Visible signs of injury, such as bleeding wound or distorted arm, leg, etc. Had to be carried from scene.
——	——	——	——	——	——	Visible bruises, abrasions, swelling, limping, etc.
——	——	——	——	——	——	No visible injury but complaint of pain or momentary unconsciousness.

SAFETY EQUIPMENT (APPARENTLY) USED

Other Vehicle

| DVR: Driver | RFP: Right Front Passenger | CRP: Center Rear Passenger |
| CFP: Center Front Passenger | LRP: Left Rear Passenger | RRP: Right Rear Passenger |

DVR	CFP	RFP	LRP	CRP	RRP	
___	___	___	___	___	___	No restraint used
___	___	___	___	___	___	Seat belt
___	___	___	___	___	___	Harness
___	___	___	___	___	___	Seat belt and harness
___	___	___	___	___	___	Child restraint
___	___	___	___	___	___	Air bag
___	___	___	___	___	___	Helmet (cyclist)

Your Vehicle

DVR	CFP	RFP	LRP	CRP	RRP	
___	___	___	___	___	___	No restraint used
___	___	___	___	___	___	Seat belt
___	___	___	___	___	___	Harness
___	___	___	___	___	___	Seat belt and harness
___	___	___	___	___	___	Child restraint
___	___	___	___	___	___	Air bag
___	___	___	___	___	___	Helmet (cyclist)

SAFETY EQUIPMENT (APPARENTLY) USED

Additional Vehicle #1

DVR: Driver
CFP: Center Front Passenger

RFP: Right Front Passenger
LRP: Left Rear Passenger

CRP: Center Rear Passenger
RRP: Right Rear Passenger

DVR	CFP	RFP	LRP	CRP	RRP	
___	___	___	___	___	___	No restraint used
___	___	___	___	___	___	Seat belt
___	___	___	___	___	___	Harness
___	___	___	___	___	___	Seat belt and harness
___	___	___	___	___	___	Child restraint
___	___	___	___	___	___	Air bag
___	___	___	___	___	___	Helmet (cyclist)

Additional Vehicle #2

DVR	CFP	RFP	LRP	CRP	RRP	
___	___	___	___	___	___	No restraint used
___	___	___	___	___	___	Seat belt
___	___	___	___	___	___	Harness
___	___	___	___	___	___	Seat belt and harness
___	___	___	___	___	___	Child restraint
___	___	___	___	___	___	Air bag
___	___	___	___	___	___	Helmet (cyclist)

OTHER VEHICLE

Vehicle

License Plate No.   State   Expiration Date   Type of Vehicle

Make   Body Style   Color(s)   Year

Apparent Condition (see **Vehicle Condition** below for additional details)

(Windshield Clean?)   (Tires Smooth?)   (Seat Belts Accessible?)

Driver

Last Name   First   Middle   Phone

Street   City   State   Zip

Driver's License No.   State   Expiration Date

Vehicle Condition

____ Worn or slick tires   ____ Chains in use   ____ Puncture or blowout

____ Defective lights   ____ Motor trouble   ____ Steering defective

____ Expired inspection sticker   ____ Brakes defective (skid marks)   ____ No noted defects

Other _____

Driver Apparent Condition (*Your Best Estimate*)

____ Not wearing corrective glasses   ____ Hearing apparently defective   ____ Apparently been drinking, not visibly affected

____ Wearing corrective glasses   ____ Possibly ill   ____ Apparently been drinking, visibly affected

____ Wearing sunglasses   ____ Possibly fell asleep

____ Not wearing sunglasses   ____ Apparently not drinking   ____ Obviously drunk

Other _____

INJURIES

Additional Vehicles

DVR: Driver   RFP: Right Front Passenger   CRP: Center Rear Passenger
CFP: Center Front Passenger   LRP: Left Rear Passenger   RRP: Right Rear Passenger

---

Additional Vehicle #1

DVR	CFP	RFP	LRP	CRP	RRP	
—	—	—	—	—	—	Dead at scene.
—	—	—	—	—	—	Visible signs of injury, such as bleeding wound or distorted arm, leg, etc. Had to be carried from scene.
—	—	—	—	—	—	Visible bruises, abrasions, swelling, limping, etc.
—	—	—	—	—	—	No visible injury but complaint of pain or momentary unconsciousness.
—	—	—	—	—	—	No apparent injury.
—	—	—	—	—	—	Not ejected from vehicle.
—	—	—	—	—	—	Partially ejected from vehicle.
	—	—	—	—	Ejected from vehicle.

Additional Vehicle #2

DVR	CFP	RFP	LRP	CRP	RRP	
—	—	—	—	—	—	Dead at scene.
—	—	—	—	—	—	Visible signs of injury, such as bleeding wound or distorted arm, leg, etc. Had to be carried from scene.
—	—	—	—	—	—	Visible bruises, abrasions, swelling, limping, etc.
—	—	—	—	—	—	No visible injury but complaint of pain or momentary unconsciousness.
—	—	—	—	—	—	No apparent injury.
—	—	—	—	—	—	Not ejected from vehicle.
—	—	—	—	—	—	Partially ejected from vehicle.
—	—	—	—	—	—	Ejected from vehicle.

FORM 14.1/F60

ADDITIONAL VEHICLE #1

Vehicle

License Plate No.	State	Expiration Date	Type of Vehicle

Make	Body Style	Color(s)	Year

Apparent Condition (see **Vehicle Condition** below for additional details)

(Windshield Clean?)	(Tires Smooth?)	(Seat Belts Accessible?)

Driver

Last Name	First	Middle	Phone

Street	City	State	Zip

Driver's License No.	State	Expiration Date

Vehicle Condition

____ Worn or slick tires	____ Chains in use	____ Puncture or blowout
____ Defective lights	____ Motor trouble	____ Steering defective
____ Expired inspection sticker	____ Brakes defective (skid marks)	____ No noted defects

Other _____

Driver Apparent Condition (*Your Best Estimate*)

____ Not wearing corrective glasses	____ Hearing apparently defective	____ Apparently been drinking, not visibly affected
____ Wearing corrective glasses	____ Possibly ill	____ Apparently been drinking, visibly affected
____ Wearing sunglasses	____ Possibly fell asleep	
____ Not wearing sunglasses	____ Apparently not drinking	____ Obviously drunk

Other _____

ADDITIONAL VEHICLE #2

Vehicle

License Plate No.   State   Expiration Date   Type of Vehicle

Make   Body Style   Color(s)   Year

Apparent Condition (see **Vehicle Condition** below for additional details)

(Windshield Clean?)   (Tires Smooth?)   (Seat Belts Accessible?)

Driver

Last Name   First   Middle   Phone

Street   City   State   Zip

Driver's License No.   State   Expiration Date

Vehicle Condition

____ Worn or slick tires   ____ Chains in use   ____ Puncture or blowout

____ Defective lights   ____ Motor trouble   ____ Steering defective

____ Expired inspection   ____ Brakes defective   ____ No noted defects
　　　 sticker   　　　 (skid marks)

Other _____

Driver Apparent Condition (*Your Best Estimate*)

____ Not wearing corrective   ____ Hearing apparently   ____ Apparently been
　　　 glasses   　　　 defective   　　　 drinking, not visibly
　　　　　　　　　　　　　　　　　　　　　　　　　　　　　　　 affected

____ Wearing corrective   ____ Possibly ill
　　　 glasses   ____ Possibly fell asleep   ____ Apparently been
　　　　　　　　　　　　　　　　　　　　　　　　　　　　　 drinking, visibly
____ Wearing sunglasses   　　　　　　　　　　　　 affected
　　　　　　　　　　　　　　　　 ____ Apparently not
____ Not wearing sunglasses   　　　 drinking   ____ Obviously drunk

Other _____

INJURIES

Your Vehicle

DVR: Driver	**RFP:** Right Front Passenger	**CRP:** Center Rear Passenger
CFP: Center Front Passenger	**LRP:** Left Rear Passenger	**RRP:** Right Rear Passenger

DVR	CFP	RFP	LRP	CRP	RRP	
——	——	——	——	——	——	Dead at scene.
——	——	——	——	——	——	Visible signs of injury, such as bleeding wound or distorted arm, leg, etc. Had to be carried from scene.
——	——	——	——	——	——	Visible bruises, abrasions, swelling, limping, etc.
——	——	——	——	——	——	No visible injury but complaint of pain or momentary unconsciousness.
——	——	——	——	——	——	No apparent injury.
——	——	——	——	——	——	Not ejected from vehicle.
——	——	——	——	——	——	Partially ejected from vehicle.
——	——	——	——	——	——	Ejected from vehicle.

FORM 14.1/F63

INJURED PERSONS

DVR: Driver   RFP: Right Front Passenger   CRP: Center Rear Passenger
CFP: Center Front Passenger   LRP: Left Rear Passenger   RRP: Right Rear Passenger

_____   _____
Name   (Occupation)

_____   _____
Address   Phone

Other Vehicle ____ Addl. Vehicle #1 ____ Addl. Vehicle #2 ____ My Vehicle ____ Ped./Other ____

_____   _____
Name   (Occupation)

_____   _____
Address   Phone

Other Vehicle ____ Addl. Vehicle #1 ____ Addl. Vehicle #2 ____ My Vehicle ____ Ped./Other ____

_____   _____
Name   (Occupation)

_____   _____
Address   Phone

Other Vehicle ____ Addl. Vehicle #1 ____ Addl. Vehicle #2 ____ My Vehicle ____ Ped./Other ____

_____   _____
Name   (Occupation)

_____   _____
Address   Phone

Other Vehicle ____ Addl. Vehicle #1 ____ Addl. Vehicle #2 ____ My Vehicle ____ Ped./Other ____

_____   _____
Name   (Occupation)

_____   _____
Address   Phone

Other Vehicle ____ Addl. Vehicle #1 ____ Addl. Vehicle #2 ____ My Vehicle ____ Ped./Other ____

_____   _____
Name   (Occupation)

_____   _____
Address   Phone

Other Vehicle ____ Addl. Vehicle #1 ____ Addl. Vehicle #2 ____ My Vehicle ____ Ped./Other ____

_____   _____
Name   (Occupation)

_____   _____
Address   Phone

Other Vehicle ____ Addl. Vehicle #1 ____ Addl. Vehicle #2 ____ My Vehicle ____ Ped./Other ____

_____   _____
Name   (Occupation)

_____   _____
Address   Phone

Other Vehicle ____ Addl. Vehicle #1 ____ Addl. Vehicle #2 ____ My Vehicle ____ Ped./Other ____

ACCIDENT DIAGRAM

Fill in the dotted lines on one of the above diagrams to indicate the appropriate roadways and intersections. Mark your vehicle **Y**, the other vehicle **O**, and additional vehicles **#1**, **#2**, etc. Show positions of injured pedestrians and others with a circle enclosing the appropriate number. Indicate north with an arrow and an **N**. You might also indicate the placement of signs, signals, railroad crossings, etc. If you're particularly enterprising, use *both* diagrams to indicate the passage of time.

TRAFFIC CONTROL

____ No traffic control

____ Officer or watchman

____ Traffic signal

____ Stop sign

____ Slow or warning sign

____ Yield sign

____ Traffic lanes marked

____ No-passing lanes

____ Railroad crossing with markings and signs

____ Railroad crossing with signals

____ Railroad crossing with gate and signals

____ One-way road or street

Traffic device working? ____

Other _____

_____

_____

TRAFFIC SIGN/SIGNAL

____ None

____ Electric signal

____ Sign

____ Two-way stop, my street

____ Two-way stop, other street

____ Yield, my street

____ Yield, other street

____ Flashing yellow, my street

____ Signal not operating

____ Signal obscured from my view

____ Sign obscured from my view

____ Signal green, my street

____ Signal red, my street

____ Signal yellow, my street

____ Flashing red, my street

____ Sign in bad condition

Other _____

_____

_____

ROADWAY

Condition

___ Dry	___ Icy	___ Cement
___ Wet	___ Muddy	___ Asphalt
___ Snowy	___ Oily	___ Blacktop
___ Slushy	___ Flooded	___ Dirt
		___ Gravel

Other _____

_____

Grade and Curvature

___ Level, straight	___ Upgrade, curve	___ Hill crest, straight
___ Level, curve	___ Dip, straight	___ Hill crest, curve
___ Upgrade, straight	___ Dip, curve	

Other _____

_____

Defects

___ No defect	___ Under repair	___ Slick surface
___ Holes, ruts, bumps	___ Loose material	___ Obstructed
___ Soft or low shoulder	___ Restricted width	___ No traffic lane lines

Other defects _____

_____

VEHICLE MOTION/DIRECTION

Other Vehicle

____ Going straight ahead	____ Stopping	____ Parked
____ Making right turn	____ Starting in traffic lane	____ Backing up
____ Making left turn		____ Passing, in right lane
____ Making U-turn	____ Starting from parked position	____ Passing, in left lane
____ Slowing	____ Stopped in traffic lane	____ Changing lanes

Other _____

_____

Your Vehicle

____ Going straight ahead	____ Stopping	____ Parked
____ Making right turn	____ Starting in traffic lane	____ Backing up
____ Making left turn		____ Passing, in right lane
____ Making U-turn	____ Starting from parked position	____ Passing, in left lane
____ Slowing	____ Stopped in traffic lane	____ Changing lanes

Other _____

_____

Additional Vehicles (*mark with #1, #2, etc.*)

____ Going straight ahead	____ Stopping	____ Parked
____ Making right turn	____ Starting in traffic lane	____ Backing up
____ Making left turn		____ Passing, in right lane
____ Making U-turn	____ Starting from parked position	____ Passing, in left lane
____ Slowing	____ Stopped in traffic lane	____ Changing lanes

Other _____

TYPE OF COLLISION

Collision with Vehicle (*mark with 0, #1, #2, etc.*)

_____ Head-on

_____ Rear end

_____ Angle,
      same direction

_____ Angle,
      opposite direction

_____ Perpendicular

_____ Backed into

_____ Sideswipe,
      same direction

_____ Sideswipe,
      opposite direction

Other type _____

Collision with Fixed Object

_____ Fixed object in road

_____ Bank or ledge

_____ Utility pole

_____ Guard rail or post

_____ Fence or fence post

_____ Parked vehicle

_____ Ran off road, right

_____ Ran off road, left

_____ Sign or traffic signal

_____ Bridge, underpass,
      culvert

_____ Impact cushioning
      device

Other fixed object _____

SKIDDING (*Your Estimate*)

Other Vehicle

_____ Before application of brakes

_____ After application of brakes

_____ Before and after application of brakes

_____ No skidding

Your Vehicle

_____ Before application of brakes

_____ After application of brakes

_____ Before and after application of brakes

_____ No skidding

Additional Vehicle #1

_____ Before application of brakes

_____ After application of brakes

_____ Before and after application of brakes

_____ No skidding

Additional Vehicle #2

_____ Before application of brakes

_____ After application of brakes

_____ Before and after application of brakes

_____ No skidding

VEHICLE DAMAGE

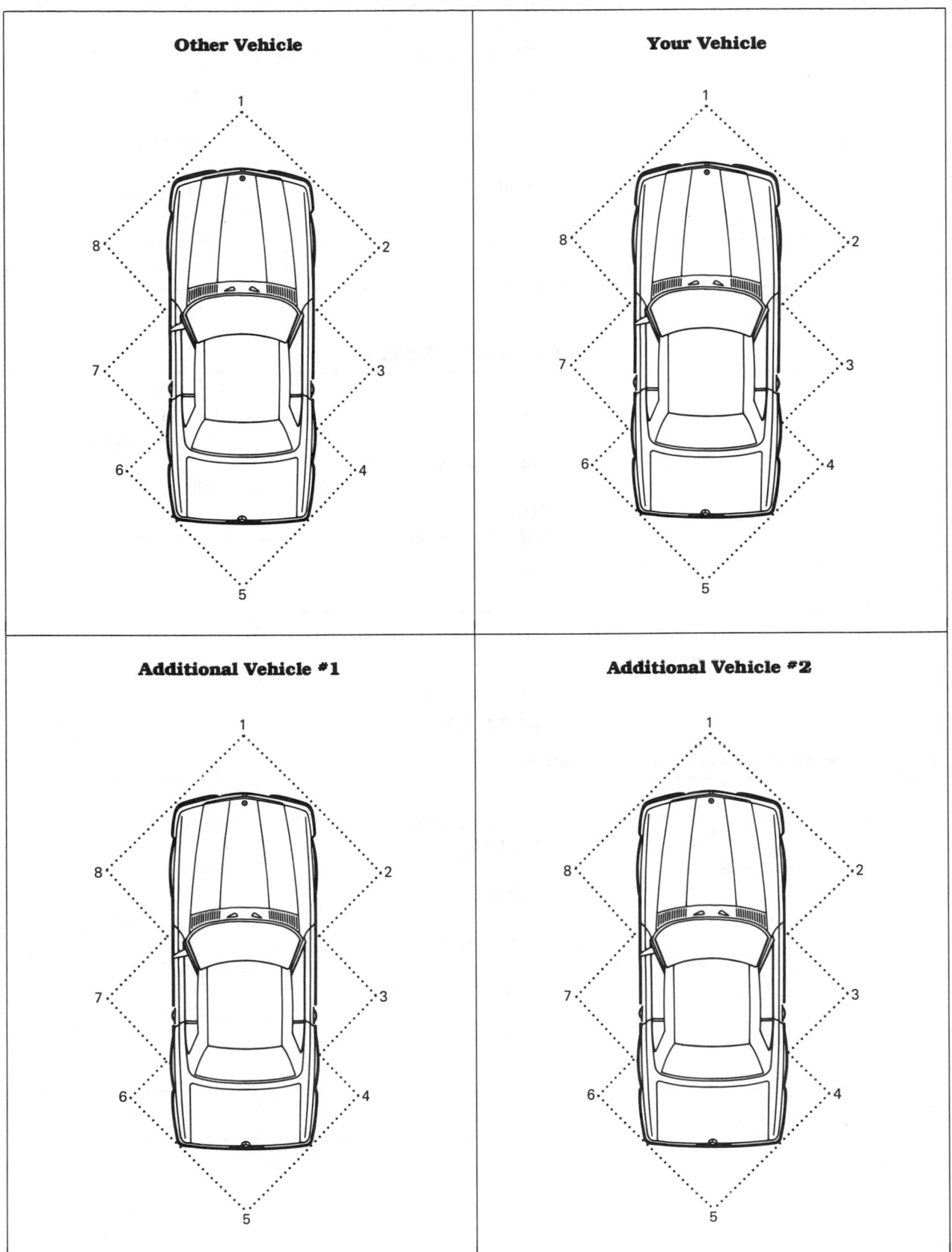

Circle numbers indicating areas of impact resulting in vehicle damage.

WEATHER CONDITIONS

___ Clear   ___ Rain   ___ Smoke, dust

___ Cloudy   ___ Snow   ___ Strong winds

___ Fog   ___ Sleet   ___ Storm winds

___ Mist   ___ Hail   ___ Hurricane, tornado

Other _____

LIGHT CONDITIONS

___ Dawn   ___ Hazy   ___ Dark, street or highway unlighted

___ Dusk   ___ Partly cloudy   ___ Twilight

___ Sunny   ___ Dark, street or highway lighted

___ Overcast   ___ Eclipse of sun or moon (*just checking*)

Other _____

VISION OBSCURED

Other Vehicle Driver Vision (*Your Estimate*)

___ Not obscured   ___ Obstructed by load on vehicle   ___ Hill crest

___ Rain on windshield   ___ Building   ___ Parked vehicle

___ Snow on windshield   ___ Embankment   ___ Moving vehicle

___ Windshield otherwise obscured   ___ Signboard, signpost   ___ Sunlight glare

___ Trees, hedges, crops   ___ Banked or drifted snow   ___ Headlight glare

Other _____

VISION OBSCURED

Your Vision

____ Not obscured	____ Obstructed by load on vehicle	____ Hill crest
____ Rain on windshield		____ Parked vehicle
____ Snow on windshield	____ Building	____ Moving vehicle
	____ Embankment	
____ Windshield otherwise obscured	____ Signboard, signpost	____ Sunlight glare
		____ Headlight glare
____ Trees, hedges, crops	____ Banked or drifted snow	

Other _____

Additional Vehicle #1 Driver Vision (*Your Estimate*)

____ Not obscured	____ Obstructed by load on vehicle	____ Hill crest
____ Rain on windshield		____ Parked vehicle
____ Snow on windshield	____ Building	____ Moving vehicle
	____ Embankment	
____ Windshield otherwise obscured	____ Signboard, signpost	____ Sunlight glare
		____ Headlight glare
____ Trees, hedges, crops	____ Banked or drifted snow	

Other _____

Additional Vehicle #2 Driver Vision (*Your Estimate*)

____ Not obscured	____ Obstructed by load on vehicle	____ Hill crest
____ Rain on windshield		____ Parked vehicle
____ Snow on windshield	____ Building	____ Moving vehicle
	____ Embankment	
____ Windshield otherwise obscured	____ Signboard, signpost	____ Sunlight glare
		____ Headlight glare
____ Trees, hedges, crops	____ Banked or drifted snow	

Other _____

DRIVERS' ACTIONS (*Your Best Estimate*)

You	Other	A#1	A#2	
——	——	——	——	None
——	——	——	——	Exceeded speed limit
——	——	——	——	Exceeded safe speed
——	——	——	——	Overtook vehicle on hill
——	——	——	——	Overtook vehicle on curve
——	——	——	——	Overtook vehicle at intersection
——	——	——	——	Cut in on vehicle
——	——	——	——	Did not have right-of-way
——	——	——	——	Followed too close
——	——	——	——	Failed to signal or made improper signal
——	——	——	——	Made improper wide right turn
——	——	——	——	Made improper wide left turn
——	——	——	——	Made improper turn from wrong lane
——	——	——	——	Disregarded stop–go light
——	——	——	——	Disregarded stop or yield sign
——	——	——	——	Drove through safety zone
——	——	——	——	Failed to set out flares or flags
——	——	——	——	Avoided pedestrian
——	——	——	——	Avoided other vehicle
——	——	——	——	Hit and run
——	——	——	——	Drove inattentively
——	——	——	——	Backed up improperly
——	——	——	——	Was crowded off roadway
——	——	——	——	Other _____
——	——	——	——	Other _____

PEDESTRIANS' ACTIONS (*Your Best Estimate*)

P#1	P#2	P#3	P#4	
___	___	___	___	Crossed at intersection, with signal
___	___	___	___	Crossed at intersection, against signal
___	___	___	___	Crossed at intersection, no signal
___	___	___	___	Crossed, not at intersection
___	___	___	___	Emerged from between parked vehicles
___	___	___	___	Played in roadway
___	___	___	___	Walked in roadway, sidewalk available
___	___	___	___	Walked in roadway, sidewalk not available
___	___	___	___	Got on or off bus
___	___	___	___	Got in or out of stopped/parked car
___	___	___	___	Stood in roadway
	___	___	___	Worked in roadway
___	___	___	___	Not in roadway
___	___	___	___	Walked on sidewalk
___	___	___	___	Played on sidewalk
___	___	___	___	Ran/jogged on sidewalk
___	___	___	___	Ran/jogged in roadway
___	___	___	___	Rode bicycle on sidewalk
___	___	___	___	Rode bicycle in roadway
___	___	___	___	Roller skated on sidewalk
___	___	___	___	Roller skated in roadway
___	___	___	___	Other _____
___	___	___	___	Other _____
___	___	___	___	Other _____
___	___	___	___	Other _____

YOUR VEHICLE

Vehicle

License Plate No.	State	Expiration Date	Type of Vehicle
Make	Body Style	Color(s)	Year

Apparent Condition (see **Vehicle Condition** below for additional details)

(Windshield Clean?)	(Tires Smooth?)	(Seat Belts Accessible?)

Driver (*if other than claimant*)

Last Name	First	Middle	Phone
Street	City	State	Zip
Driver's License No.		State	Expiration Date

Vehicle Condition

____ Worn or slick tires	____ Chains in use	____ Puncture or blowout
____ Defective lights	____ Motor trouble	____ Steering defective
____ Expired inspection sticker	____ Brakes defective (skid marks)	____ No noted defects

Other _____

Driver Condition

____ Not wearing corrective glasses	____ Not wearing sunglasses	____ Not drinking
____ Wearing corrective glasses	____ Hearing defective	____ Some drinking, did not feel affected
____ Wearing sunglasses	____ Felt ill	____ Some drinking, may have been affected
	____ Felt drowsy	____ I may have been drunk
	____ Fell asleep	

Other _____

MANNER OF ACCIDENT (*Narrative Description*)

_____

_____

_____

_____

_____

_____

_____

_____

_____

_____

_____

_____

_____

_____

_____

_____

_____

PERSON FILLING OUT REPORT

_____

Last Name   *First*   *Middle*

Street   *City*   *State*   *Zip*

Home Phone _____ Business Phone _____

(Signed) _____

_____
(*Print Name Here*)

Date of Report _____

Minor Accident Report

CLAIMANT DATA

_____
Claimant Name   Phone

_____
Street   City   State   Zip

Insurer _____ Policy No. _____ Phone _____

_____
Street   City   State   Zip

ACCIDENT DATA

Date of Accident _____ Time of Accident _____

Location _____

_____

_____

OTHER VEHICLE

License Plate No. _____ State _____ Expires _____

Make _____ Type _____

Color(s) _____ Year _____

Damage _____

_____ Est. Cost of Repair _____

OTHER VEHICLE

Driver

Last Name		First		Middle
Street	City	State		Zip
Driver's License No.		State		Expires

Owner

Last Name		First		Middle
Street	City	State		Zip
Driver's License No.		State		Expires

Driver's Insurance Company

Name of Insurance Company

Street	City	State	Zip

Policy No. _____ Policy Period _____
From   To

Owner's Insurance Company (*Not Agent*)

Name of Insurance Company

Street	City	State	Zip

Policy No. _____ Policy Period _____
From   To

YOUR VEHICLE

Vehicle

License Plate No. _____ State _____ Expires _____

Make _____ Type _____

Color (s) _____ Year _____

Damage _____

_____ Est. Cost of Repair _____

You or Driver

Last Name	First	Middle

Street	City	State	Zip

Driver's License No.	State	Expires

WITNESSES

Last Name	First	Middle

Street	City	State	Zip

Home Phone _____ Business Phone _____

Last Name	First	Middle

Street	City	State	Zip

Home Phone _____ Business Phone _____

Last Name	First	Middle

Street	City	State	Zip

Home Phone _____ Business Phone _____

Last Name	First	Middle

Street	City	State	Zip

Home Phone _____ Business Phone _____

VEHICLE DAMAGE

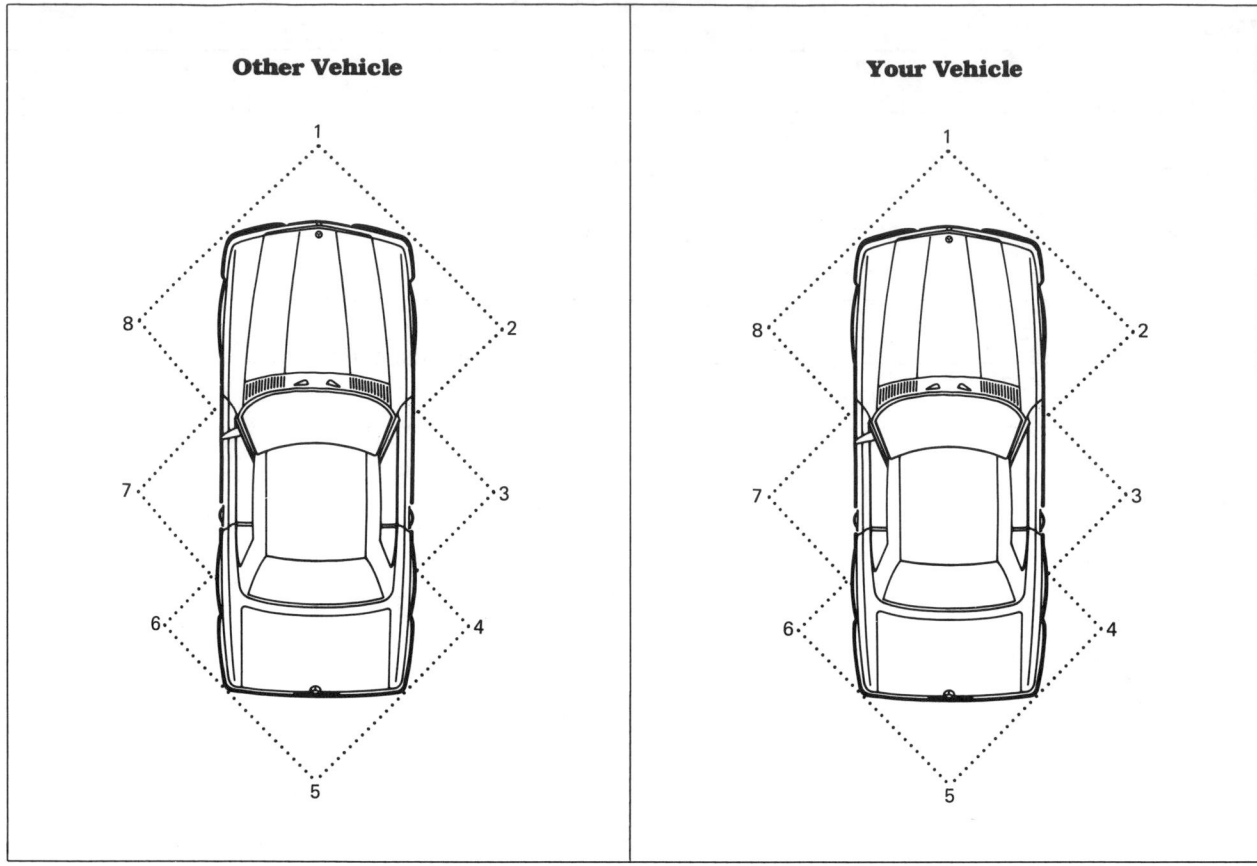

Circle numbers indicating areas of impact resulting in vehicle damage.

SKIDDING (*Your Estimate*)

Other Vehicle

____ Before application of brakes

____ After application of brakes

____ Before and after application of brakes

____ No skidding

Your Vehicle

____ Before application of brakes

____ After application of brakes

____ Before and after application of brakes

____ No skidding

MANNER OF ACCIDENT (*Narrative Description*)

_____

_____

_____

_____

_____

_____

_____

_____

_____

_____

_____

_____

_____

_____

(Signed) _____

_____
(*Print Name Here*)

Date Signed _____

Boating/Marine Accident Report

CLAIMANT DATA

_____
Claimant Name   _Phone_

_____
Street   _City_   _State_   _Zip_

Insurer _____ Policy No. _____ Phone _____

_____
Street   _City_   _State_   _Zip_

ACCIDENT DATA

Date of Accident _____ Time of Accident _____

Location _____

_____

TYPE OF ACCIDENT

____ Fire   ____ Grounding   ____ Capsized

____ Explosion   ____ Broke up   ____ Sinking

Person(s) Overboard _____ Drowning(s) _____

Collision with _____

Loss of Sail/Rigging/Mast _____ Loss of Power _____

Other _____

_____

Overdue—Last Heard from _____

_____

Missing—Last Heard from _____

_____

FORM 15.1/F84

VESSEL/BOAT #1

Vessel Description

Name _____

Registry _____ Home Port _____

State Where Licensed _____ License No. _____

Documented? _____ Registration No. _____ Year Built _____

Type of Vessel _____ Type of Construction _____

Manufacturer/Builder _____

Length _____ Beam _____ Draft _____ Displacement_____

Hull Color _____ Deck Color _____ Trim Color _____

Sails (Number/Color) _____

_____

No. of Masts _____ Height of Tallest Mast _____

No. of Engines _____ Type _____

Capacity (Persons) _____ Capacity (Weight) _____

Owner/Captain

Last Name	First	Middle	Occupation
Street	City	State	Zip

Home Phone _____ Business Phone _____

Licensed? _____ Type of License? _____

Training/Qualifications _____

_____

VESSEL/BOAT #1

Voyage/Activity

Departed from _____

Date of Departure _____ Time of Departure _____

Destination _____

Routing _____

Due to Arrive (Date/Time) _____

Purpose of Voyage/Activity _____

_____

Crew/Passengers

No. of Adults _____ No. of Children _____

Name _____ Age _____ Sex _____

Address _____

Name _____ Age _____ Sex _____

Address _____

Name _____ Age _____ Sex _____

Address _____

Name _____ Age _____ Sex _____

Address _____

Name _____ Age _____ Sex _____

Address _____

Name _____ Age _____ Sex _____

Address _____

Name _____ Age _____ Sex _____

Address _____

VESSEL/BOAT #1

Navigation/Communications Equipment (*Please Specify Type*)

VHF-FM _____ AM _____ SSB _____ CB _____ Other _____

Short Wave (Ham) _____ EPIRB _____ Other _____

Radar _____ Depth Finder _____ DF _____ Loran _____

Sextant _____ Other _____ Other _____

Safety/Survival Gear

No. of Life Jackets _____ Color _____ Type _____

No. of Life Rings _____ Color _____ Type _____

Inflatable Raft _____ Color _____

Skiff _____ Color _____ Outboard _____

Smoke Flares _____ Night Flares _____ Mirror _____

Aerial Flares _____ Dye Marker _____ Strobe _____

Radar Reflector _____ Flashlight _____ Other _____

Auxiliary Electrical Power _____ Type _____

Emergency Food (Days) _____ Emergency Water (Days) _____

Stores/Rations

Please note for information provided below: _____ At departure _____ At time of accident

Gallons of Fuel Aboard _____ Type _____

Gallons of Water _____ No. of Days of Food _____

Other _____

_____

VESSEL/BOAT #2

Vessel Description

Name _____

Registry _____ Home Port _____

State Where Licensed _____ License No. _____

Documented? _____ Registration No. _____ Year Built _____

Type of Vessel _____ Type of Construction _____

Manufacturer/Builder _____

Length _____ Beam _____ Draft _____ Displacement_____

Hull Color _____ Deck Color _____ Trim Color _____

Sails (Number/Color) _____

_____

No. of Masts _____ Height of Tallest Mast _____

No. of Engines _____ Type _____

Capacity (Persons) _____ Capacity (Weight) _____

Owner/Captain

Last Name	First	Middle	Occupation
Street	City	State	Zip

Home Phone _____ Business Phone _____

Licensed? _____ Type of License? _____

Training/Qualifications _____

_____

VESSEL/BOAT #2

Voyage/Activity

Departed from _____

Date of Departure _____ Time of Departure _____

Destination _____

Routing _____

Due to Arrive (Date/Time) _____

Purpose of Voyage/Activity _____

_____

Crew/Passengers

No. of Adults _____ No. of Children _____

Name _____ Age _____ Sex _____

Address _____

Name _____ Age _____ Sex _____

Address _____

Name _____ Age _____ Sex _____

Address _____

Name _____ Age _____ Sex _____

Address _____

Name _____ Age _____ Sex _____

Address _____

Name _____ Age _____ Sex _____

Address _____

Name _____ Age _____ Sex _____

Address _____

VESSEL/BOAT #2

Navigation/Communications Equipment (*Please Specify Type*)

VHF-FM _____ AM _____ SSB _____ CB _____ Other _____

Short Wave (Ham) _____ EPIRB _____ Other _____

Radar _____ Depth Finder _____ DF _____ Loran _____

Sextant _____ Other _____ Other _____

Safety/Survival Gear

No. of Life Jackets _____ Color _____ Type _____

No. of Life Rings _____ Color _____ Type _____

Inflatable Raft _____ Color _____

Skiff _____ Color _____ Outboard _____

Smoke Flares _____ Night Flares _____ Mirror _____

Aerial Flares _____ Dye Marker _____ Strobe _____

Radar Reflector _____ Flashlight _____ Other _____

Auxiliary Electrical Power _____ Type _____

Emergency Food (Days) _____ Emergency Water (Days) _____

Stores/Rations

Please note for information provided below: ____ At departure ____ At time of accident

Gallons of Fuel Aboard _____ Type _____

Gallons of Water _____ No. of Days of Food _____

Other _____

_____

MANNER OF ACCIDENT

DIAGRAM OF ACCIDENT

Use the above box to diagram accident; clearly indicate boats #1 and #2 (and any other vessels/landmarks).

INJURED PERSONS

Last Name _____ First _____ Middle _____ Phone _____

Street _____ City _____ State _____ Zip _____

Injury _____

Hospitalized? _____ How Taken? _____

Name of Hospital _____

Last Name _____ First _____ Middle _____ Phone _____

Street _____ City _____ State _____ Zip _____

Injury _____

Hospitalized? _____ How Taken? _____

Name of Hospital _____

Last Name _____ First _____ Middle _____ Phone _____

Street _____ City _____ State _____ Zip _____

Injury _____

Hospitalized? _____ How Taken? _____

Name of Hospital _____

Last Name _____ First _____ Mtddle _____ Phone _____

Street _____ City _____ State _____ Zip _____

Injury _____

Hospitalized? _____ How Taken? _____

Name of Hospital _____

Last Name _____ First _____ Middle _____ Phone _____

Street _____ City _____ State _____ Zip _____

Injury _____

Hospitalized? _____ How Taken? _____

Name of Hospital _____

FORM 15.1 / F92

WITNESSES

Last Name   _First_   _Middle_

Street   _City_   _State_   _Zip_

Home Phone _____ Business Phone _____

Summary of Statement _____

_____

_____

Last Name   _First_   _Middle_

Street   _City_   _State_   _Zip_

Home Phone _____ Business Phone _____

Summary of Statement _____

_____

_____

Last Name   _First_   _Middle_

Street   _City_   _State_   _Zip_

Home Phone _____ Business Phone _____

Summary of Statement _____

_____

_____

Last Name   _First_   _Middle_

Street   _City_   _State_   _Zip_

Home Phone _____ Business Phone _____

Summary of Statement _____

_____

_____

WEATHER (*Narrative Description*)

In Accident Area _____   In Departure Area _____   Forecast _____   Actual _____

Weather Conditions (Seas, winds, visibility, etc.) _____

_____

_____

_____

_____

_____

_____

_____

_____

_____

PERSON FILLING OUT REPORT

_____
Last Name   *First*   *Middle*

_____
Street   *City*   *State*   *Zip*

Home Phone _____ Business Phone _____

Date of Report _____

Signed _____

Float Plan

Complete the relevant portions of this form and leave copies with a family member or friend and/or the marina or boat dock from which you will depart so that, in the event you fail to return or reach your destination on time, a search can be instituted.

Search and Rescue Data

Name of Vessel _____ Owner/Operator _____

Address _____

Home Phone _____ Work Phone _____

Based at _____ Departed from _____

Time of Departure _____ Destination _____

Routing _____

Estimated Time of Arrival _____

Purpose of Trip _____

Miscellaneous Information _____

Crew

No. of Adults _____ No. of Children _____

Vessel

Home Port _____

Length _____

Type _____

Numbers _____

Hull Color _____ Deck Color _____ Trim Color _____

Hull Material _____

Prominent Features _____

_____

Number and Color of Sails _____

_____

Electronics (Please Specify Type)

Radio: AM _____   VHF-FM _____   SSB _____   CB _____   EPIRB _____

Short Wave (Ham): Frequencies _____

Radar _____   Depth Finder _____   DF _____   Loran A _____   Loran C _____

Survival Equipment

Life Jackets (#) _____   Color _____

Life Rings (#) _____   Color _____

Smoke Flares (#) _____   Night Flares (#) _____

Mirror _____   Dye Marker _____   Strobe _____

Aerial Flares _____   Flashlights (#) _____

Inflatable Raft (#) _____   Color _____   Color _____

Skiff _____   Color _____

Lifeboat (#) _____   Color _____   Color _____

Radar Reflector _____   Spotlight _____

Auxillary Electrical Power _____   Type _____

Food (Days) _____   Water (Days) _____

Remarks

_____

_____

_____

_____

_____

_____

_____

_____

_____

Building Accident Report

CLAIMANT DATA

_____
Claimant Name   Phone

_____
Street   City   State   Zip

Insurer _____ Policy No. _____ Phone _____

_____
Street   City   State   Zip

Date of Accident _____ Time of Accident _____

BUILDING

_____
Name of Building

_____
Street   City   State   Zip

Building Type _____ No. of Floors _____ _____

Type of Construction _____ Date of Construction _____

No. of Apartments _____ No. of Stores/Offices _____

OWNER/MANAGEMENT

_____
Name of Owner   Phone

_____
Street   City   State   Zip

_____
Name of Agent   Phone

_____
Street   City   State   Zip

_____
Name of Superintendent   Phone

_____
Street   City   State   Zip   Apt. No.

_____
Name of Manager   Phone

_____
Street   City   State   Zip   Apt. No.

ACCIDENT LOCATION

Elevator

Which Elevator? _____

Operated by _____ _____
             Passenger   *Building Employee*

How Used at Time of Accident? _____

Current Inspection Certificate? _____ Date _____

Maintenance Company _____
                                                        Phone

_____ _____ _____ _____
Street   *City*   *State*   *Zip*

Manufacturer _____

_____ _____ _____ _____
Street   *City*   *State*   *Zip*

Manufacturer Model No. _____ Date of Manufacture _____

Stairway

Which Stairway? _____ Which Step? _____

Type of Construction _____ Condition _____

Type of Covering _____ Condition _____

Object on Stairway? _____

Handhold or Railing? _____ Adequate Lighting? _____

Hallway

Which Hallway? _____ Adequate Lighting? _____

Type of Construction _____ Condition _____

Type of Covering _____ Condition _____

ACCIDENT LOCATION

Fallen/Dropped Object

Fell from _____

Landed _____

Type of Object _____ Size _____ Weight _____

Apartment

No. of Apartment _____ Floor _____

Name of Tenant _____
Last _____ _First_ _____ _Middle_

Which Room? _____ Phone _____

Store

Address of Store _____

Name of Business _____
Phone

Manager _____
Phone

Business Owner _____
Phone

Where in Store? _____

Building Common Area

____ Lobby   ____ Roof   ____ Restroom

____ Parking lot   ____ Office   ____ Laundry room

____ Loading dock   ____ Pool   ____ Basement

____ Recreation room ____ Driveway   ____ Work area

Other area _____

MANNER OF ACCIDENT (*Narrative Description*)

_____
_____
_____
_____
_____
_____
_____
_____

INJURED PERSONS

Last Name	First	Middle	Phone

Street	City	State	Zip

Injury _____

Hospitalized? _____ How Taken? _____

Name of Hospital _____

Last Name	First	Middle	Phone

Street	City	State	Zip

Injury _____

Hospitalized? _____ How Taken? _____

Name of Hospital _____

Last Name	First	Middle	Phone

Street	City	State	Zip

Injury _____

Hospitalized? _____ How Taken? _____

Name of Hospital _____

WITNESSES

Last Name	First	Middle

Street	City	State	Zip

Home Phone _____ Business Phone _____

Summary of Statement _____

_____

_____

Last Name	First	Middle

Street	City	State	Zip

Home Phone _____ Business Phone _____

Summary of Statement _____

_____

_____

Last Name	First	Middle

Street	City	State	Zip

Home Phone _____ Business Phone _____

Summary of Statement _____

_____

_____

Last Name	First	Middle

Street	City	State	Zip

Home Phone _____ Business Phone _____

Summary of Statement _____

_____

_____

FORM 16.1/F102

Last Name   _First_   _Middle_

Street   _City_   _State_   _Zip_

Home Phone _____ Business Phone _____

Date of Report _____

Signed _____

Street/Sidewalk Accident Report

CLAIMANT DATA

_____   _____
                Claimant Name   *Phone*

_____
    Street   *City*   *State*   *Zip*

Insurer _____ Policy No. _____ Phone _____

_____
    Street   *City*   *State*   *Zip*

Date of Accident _____   Time of Accident _____

LOCATION

_____
  Street   *City*   *State*   *Zip*

Sidewalk ____   Street ____   Alleyway ____   Driveway ____   Steps/Ramp ____

Distance from Curb _____ Distance from Building _____

Distance from Corner _____ Streets _____

Type of Street (Surface/Condition) _____

Type of Sidewalk (Surface/Condition) _____

Type of Alleyway (Surface/Condition) _____

Type of Driveway (Surface/Condition) _____

Type of Steps/Ramp (Surface/Condition) _____

Other Location Details _____

_____

_____

ADJACENT BUILDING

Building Type _____ Type of Construction _____

Primary Use of Building _____

_____
Name of Owner   Phone

_____
Street   City   State   Zip

_____
Name of Management/Manager   Phone

_____
Street   City   State   Zip

CONDITION OF STREET/SIDEWALK

___ Dry   ___ Potholes   ___ Cement

___ Wet   ___ Cracked Surface   ___ Asphalt

___ Icy   ___ Uneven surface   ___ Blacktop

___ Snowy   ___ Loose bricks   ___ Gravel

___ Slushy   ___ Protruding tree roots ___ Earth

___ Muddy   ___ Well maintained   ___ Brick

___ Flooded   ___ Poorly maintained   ___ Cobblestones

Other/Description of Defects _____

_____

WEATHER/LIGHT CONDITIONS

___ Dry   ___ Fog   ___ Dusk

___ Rain   ___ Sunny   ___ Dark, lighted

___ Snow   ___ Partly cloudy   ___ Dark, unlighted

___ Sleet   ___ Overcast   ___ Strong winds

___ Mist   ___ Dawn   ___ Storm winds

Temperature _____ Last Rain (Date/Time) _____ Wind Velocity _____

MANNER OF ACCIDENT (*Narrative Statement*)

_____

_____

_____

_____

_____

_____

_____

_____

INJURED PERSONS

Last Name	First	Middle	Phone
Street	City	State	Zip

Injury _____

Hospitalized? _____ How Taken? _____

Name of Hospital _____

Last Name	First	Middle	Phone
Street	City	State	Zip

Injury _____

Hospitalized? _____ How Taken? _____

Name of Hospital _____

Last Name	First	Middle	Phone
Street	City	State	Zip

Injury _____

Hospitalized? _____ How Taken? _____

Name of Hospital _____

WITNESSES

Last Name   First   Middle

Street   City   State   Zip

Home Phone _____ Business Phone _____

Summary of Statement _____

_____

_____

Last Name   First   Middle

Street   City   State   Zip

Home Phone _____ Business Phone _____

Summary of Statement _____

_____

_____

Last Name   First   Middle

Street   City   State   Zip

Home Phone _____ Business Phone _____

Summary of Statement _____

_____

_____

PERSON FILLING OUT REPORT

Last Name   First   Middle

Street   City   State   Zip

Home Phone _____ Business Phone _____

Date of Report _____

Signed _____

Defective Product Accident Report

CLAIMANT DATA

_____

Claimant Name   *Phone*

_____

Street   *City*   *State*   *Zip*

Insurer _____ Policy No. _____ Phone _____

_____

Street   *City*   *State*   *Zip*

Date of Accident _____ Time of Accident _____

PRODUCT

Type of Product _____

Trade Name of Product _____

Model No. _____ Serial No. _____

Name of Manufacturer _____

Phone

_____

Street   *City*   *State*   *Zip*

STORE/SELLER

Name of Store/Seller _____

Phone

_____

Street   *City*   *State*   *Zip*

Name of Salesperson _____

Date of Purchase _____ Manner of Purchase _____

Price _____ How Paid _____ Date Paid _____

WARRANTY

Full? _____ Limited? _____ Combination (Full/Limited)? _____

Warrantor _____

_____
                                     Phone

_____
  Street   *City*   *State*   *Zip*

Warranty Period _____

Store Warranty/Money Back? _____

LOCATION OF ACCIDENT

Home ____   Store ____   At Work ____   Outside ____   Office ____

Other _____

_____
  Name (Store, company, homeowner, place, etc.)   *Phone*

_____
  Street   *City*   *State*   *Zip*

WEATHER/LIGHT CONDITIONS (*leave blank if weather is not a factor*)

____ Dry   ____ Fog   ____ Dusk

____ Rain   ____ Sunny   ____ Dark, lighted

____ Snow   ____ Partly cloudy   ____ Dark, unlighted

____ Sleet   ____ Overcast   ____ Strong winds

____ Mist   ____ Dawn   ____ Storm winds

Temperature _____ Last Rain (Date/Time) _____ Wind Velocity _____

MANNER OF ACCIDENT (*Narrative Statement*)

_____

_____

_____

_____

_____

_____

_____

_____

INJURED PERSONS

Last Name	*First*	*Middle*	*Phone*
Street	*City*	*State*	*Zip*

Injury _____

Hospitalized? _____ How Taken? _____

Name of Hospital _____

Last Name	*First*	*Middle*	*Phone*
Street	*City*	*State*	*Zip*

Injury _____

Hospitalized? _____ How Taken? _____

Name of Hospital _____

Last Name	*First*	*Middle*	*Phone*
Street	*City*	*State*	*Zip*

Injury _____

Hospitalized? _____ How Taken? _____

Name of Hospital _____

WITNESSES

Last Name   First   Middle

Street   City   State   Zip

Home Phone ———————— Business Phone ————————

Summary of Statement ————————

Last Name   First   Middle

Street   City   State   Zip

Home Phone ———————— Business Phone ————————

Summary of Statement ————————

Last Name   First   Middle

Street   City   State   Zip

Home Phone ———————— Business Phone ————————

Summary of Statement ————————

PERSON FILLING OUT REPORT

Last Name   First   Middle

Street   City   State   Zip

Home Phone ———————— Business Phone ————————

Date of Report ————————

Signed ————————

Animal Accident Report

CLAIMANT DATA

_____
Claimant Name   Phone

_____
Street   City   State   Zip

Insurer _____ Policy No. _____ Phone _____

_____
Street   City   State   Zip

ACCIDENT DATA

Date of Accident _____ Time of Accident _____

Location _____

_____

_____

ANIMAL

____ Dog   ____ Snake   ____ Spider

____ Cat   ____ Lizard   ____ Fish/shark

____ Horse   ____ Bee   ____ Mongoose

____ Bird   ____ Wasp   ____ Rat

Other _____

Breed _____ Color _____ Weight _____ Size _____

Sex _____ Altered _____ Age _____

Licensed by _____ License No. _____

How Restrained _____

Previous Trouble or Complaint _____

_____

FORM 16.4/F112

VETERINARIAN

Last Name	First	Middle

Street	City	State	Zip

Office Hours _____ Phone _____

VETERINARIAN'S EXAMINATION

Animal's Apparent Condition _____

_____

_____

_____

_____

Previous Treatment _____

_____

_____

Date of Last Rabies Shots _____ Given by _____

Any Special Training? _____

OWNER

Last Name	First	Middle

Street	City	State	Zip

Home Phone _____ Business Phone _____

Owner's Qualifications _____

MANNER OF ACCIDENT (*Narrative Statement*)

_____
_____
_____
_____
_____
_____
_____
_____

INJURED PERSONS

Last Name	First	Middle	Phone
Street	City	State	Zip

Injury _____

Hospitalized? _____ How Taken? _____

Name of Hospital _____

Last Name	First	Middle	Phone
Street	City	State	Zip

Injury _____

Hospitalized? _____ How Taken? _____

Name of Hospital _____

Last Name	First	Middle	Phone
Street	City	State	Zip

Injury _____

Hospitalized? _____ How Taken? _____

Name of Hospital _____

WITNESSES

_____
Last Name   First   Middle

_____
Street   City   State   Zip

Home Phone _____ Business Phone _____

Summary of Statement _____

_____

_____

_____

_____
Last Name   First   Middle

_____
Street   City   State   Zip

Home Phone _____ Business Phone _____

Summary of Statement _____

_____

_____

_____

_____
Last Name   First   Middle

_____
Street   City   State   Zip

Home Phone _____ Business Phone _____

Summary of Statement _____

_____

_____

PERSON FILLING OUT REPORT

_____
Last Name   First   Middle

_____
Street   City   State   Zip

Home Phone _____ Business Phone _____

Date of Report _____

Signed _____

Public Transportation Accident Report

CLAIMANT DATA

_____
Claimant Name   Phone

_____
Street   City   State   Zip

Insurer _____ Policy No. _____ Phone _____

_____
Street   City   State   Zip

Date of Accident _____ Time of Accident _____

TYPE OF TRANSPORTATION

Bus ____   Taxi ____   Subway ____   Airline ____   Train ____

Other _____

Name of Operating Company _____
                                                    Phone

_____
Street   City   State   Zip

DRIVER/OPERATOR

_____
Last Name   First   Middle

License No. _____ Badge No. _____

LOCATION

Line or Route No. _____

Nearest Address _____
                Street   City   State   Zip

Platform _____ Waiting Room _____ Station _____ Street _____

On Vehicle _____ Other _____

WEATHER/LIGHT CONDITIONS

____ Dry   ____ Fog   ____ Dusk

____ Rain   ____ Sunny   ____ Dark, lighted

____ Snow   ____ Partly cloudy   ____ Dark, unlighted

____ Sleet   ____ Overcast   ____ Strong winds

____ Mist   ____ Dawn   ____ Storm winds

Temperature _____ Last Rain (Date/Time) _____ Wind Velocity _____

MANNER OF ACCIDENT (*Narrative Description*)

_____

_____

_____

_____

_____

INJURED PERSONS

Last Name	First	Middle	Phone
Street	City	State	Zip

Injury _____

Hospitalized? _____ How Taken? _____

Name of Hospital _____

Last Name	First	Middle	Phone
Street	City	State	Zip

Injury _____

Hospitalized? _____ How Taken? _____

Name of Hospital _____

INJURED PERSONS

Last Name   _First_   _Middle_   _Phone_

Street   _City_   _State_   _Zip_

Injury _____

Hospitalized? _____ How Taken? _____

Name of Hospital _____

Last Name   _First_   _Middle_   _Phone_

Street   _City_   _State_   _Zip_

Injury _____

Hospitalized? _____ How Taken? _____

Name of Hospital _____

Last Name   _First_   _Middle_   _Phone_

Street   _City_   _State_   _Zip_

Injury _____

Hospitalized? _____ How Taken? _____

Name of Hospital _____

Last Name   _First_   _Middle_   _Phone_

Street   _City_   _State_   _Zip_

Injury _____

Hospitalized? _____ How Taken? _____

Name of Hospital _____

Last Name   _First_   _Middle_   _Phone_

Street   _City_   _State_   _Zip_

Injury _____

Hospitalized? _____ How Taken? _____

Name of Hospital _____

WITNESSES

Last Name   _First_   _Middle_

Street   _City_   _State_   _Zip_

Home Phone _____ Business Phone _____

Summary of Statement _____

_____

_____

Last Name   _First_   _Middle_

Street   _City_   _State_   _Zip_

Home Phone _____ Business Phone _____

Summary of Statement _____

_____

_____

Last Name   _First_   _Middle_

Street   _City_   _State_   _Zip_

Home Phone _____ Business Phone _____

Summary of Statement _____

_____

_____

PERSON FILLING OUT REPORT

Last Name   _First_   _Middle_

Street   _City_   _State_   _Zip_

Home Phone _____ Business Phone _____

Date of Report _____

Signed _____

Attorney's Accident Work Sheet

File No. _____

Date _____

Attorney Name _____

CASE

Date Received _____

Referred by _____

Previous Client? _____

How Long Known? _____

This Case (*Include Description of Injury*) _____

_____

_____

_____

_____

_____

Previous Case _____

_____

_____

_____

_____

_____

PLAINTIFF-CLAIMANT

Last Name   _First_   _Middle_

Street   _City_   _State_   _Zip_

Home Phone _____ Date of Birth _____ Sex _____

Employment

Employer

Street   _City_   _State_   _Zip_

Phone _____ Ext. _____ Supervisor _____

Type of Business _____

Occupation _____

How Long Employed There? _____

Earnings _____

Spouse/Parent/Guardian

Last Name   _First_   _Middle_

Street   _City_   _State_   _Zip_

Home Phone _____ Business Phone _____

Employer _____

Street   _City_   _State_   _Zip_

Relationship to Plaintiff-Claimant _____

PLAINTIFF-CLAIMANT

Previous Injuries or Hospitalizations (*Before Accident*)

Injury or Illness _____

From _____ To _____

Where Were You Living Then? _____

Name of Physician _____

Name of Hospital _____

Injury or Illness _____

From _____ To _____

Where Were You Living Then? _____

Name of Physician _____

Name of Hospital _____

Injury or Illness _____

From _____ To _____

Where Were You Living Then? _____

Name of Physician _____

Name of Hospital _____

Injury or Illness _____

From _____ To _____

Where Were You Living Then? _____

Name of Physician _____

Name of Hospital _____

PLAINTIFF-CLAIMANT

Subsequent Injuries or Hospitalizations (*Since Accident*)

Injury or Illness _____

From _____ To _____

Where Were You Living Then? _____

Name of Physician _____

Name of Hospital _____

Injury or Illness _____

From _____ To _____

Where Were You Living Then? _____

Name of Physician _____

Name of Hospital _____

Present Disability, If Any (*Narrative Description*)

_____

_____

_____

_____

Previous Disability, If Any (*Narrative Description*)

_____

_____

_____

_____

OTHER LAWSUITS

Have you ever been involved in any other lawsuits related to this case, or to any *other* case, before or after the above-described claim?

Nature of Suit _____

Date _____

Location _____

Name of Opposing Party _____

Name of Opposing Attorney _____

Damages or Award For or Against You _____

Nature of Suit _____

Date _____

Location _____

Name of Opposing Party _____

Name of Opposing Attorney _____

Damages or Award For or Against You _____

Nature of Suit _____

Date _____

Location _____

Name of Opposing Party _____

Name of Opposing Attorney _____

Damages or Award For or Against You _____

DEFENDANT

Last Name	First	Middle

Street	City	State	Zip

Home Phone _____ Date of Birth _____ Sex _____

Employment

_____

Employer

Street	City	State	Zip

Phone _____ Ext. _____ Supervisor _____

Type of Business _____

Occupation _____

How Long Employed There? _____ Earnings _____

Type of Injury _____ Time Lost _____

Spouse/Parent/Guardian

Last Name	First	Middle

Street	City	State	Zip

Phone _____ Relationship _____

DEFENDANT

_____
Last Name   First   Middle

_____
Street   City   State   Zip

Home Phone _____ Date of Birth _____ Sex _____

Employment

_____
Employer

_____
Street   City   State   Zip

Phone _____ Ext. _____ Supervisor _____

Type of Business _____

Occupation _____

How Long Employed There? _____ Earnings _____

Type of Injury _____ Time Lost _____

Spouse/Parent/Guardian

_____
Last Name   First   Middle

_____
Street   City   State   Zip

Phone _____ Relationship _____

PLAINTIFF-CLAIMANT INSURER

_____
Name of Insurance Company

_____
Street   *City*   *State*   *Zip*

Adjuster _____ Phone _____

Days in Office _____ Claim or File No. _____

DEFENDANT INSURER

_____
Name of Insurance Company

_____
Street   *City*   *State*   *Zip*

Adjuster _____ Phone _____

Days in Office _____ Claim or File No. _____

DEFENDANT ATTORNEY(S)

_____
Firm

_____
Street   *City*   *State*   *Zip*

Attorney _____ Phone _____

_____
Firm

_____
Street   *City*   *State*   *Zip*

Attorney _____ Phone _____

_____
Firm

_____
Street   *City*   *State*   *Zip*

Attorney _____ Phone _____

HOSPITAL CARE

Patient _____
         Last Name   *First*   *Middle*

_____
Name of Hospital

_____
  Street   *City*   *State*   *Zip*

Phone _____ Ext. _____

How Taken? _____

Admitted _____ Discharged _____

Examination, Tests, X-rays, etc. _____

_____

_____

_____

_____

Treatment _____

_____

_____

_____

_____

Staff Physician _____
                Last Name   *First*   *Middle*

Staff Physician _____
                Last Name   *First*   *Middle*

Patient's Own M.D. _____
                Last Name   *First*   *Middle*

Amount of Hospital Bill $ _____ Paid by _____ Date _____

HOSPITAL CARE

Patient _____
          Last Name   *First*   *Middle*

_____
                          Name of Hospital

_____
   Street   *City*   *State*   *Zip*

Phone _____ Ext. _____

How Taken? _____

Admitted _____ Discharged _____

Examination, Tests, X-rays, etc. _____

_____

_____

_____

_____

Treatment _____

_____

_____

_____

_____

Staff Physician _____
                 Last Name   *First*   *Middle*

Staff Physician _____
                 Last Name   *First*   *Middle*

Patient's Own M.D. _____
                    Last Name   *First*   *Middle*

Amount of Hospital Bill $ _____ Paid by _____ Date _____

OUT-PATIENT CARE

Patient _____
            Last Name   *First*   *Middle*

Physician _____
             Last Name   *First*   *Middle*

_____
   Street   *City*   *State*   *Zip*

Phone _____

Date(s) Seen _____

_____

Examination, Tests, X-rays, etc. _____

_____

_____

_____

_____

Treatment _____

_____

_____

_____

_____

_____

Confined to: ____ Bed ____ Wheelchair ____ Home Other (Describe) _____

Prognosis _____

_____

_____

_____

Amount of Bill $ _____ Paid by _____ Date _____

Other Expenses (Nursing Care, Household Help, Sickroom Equipment) _____

_____

_____

OUT-PATIENT CARE

Patient _____
  Last Name   First   Middle

Physician _____
  Last Name   First   Middle

_____
  Street   City   State   Zip

Phone _____

Date(s) Seen _____

_____

Examination, Tests, X-rays, etc. _____

_____

_____

_____

_____

Treatment _____

_____

_____

_____

_____

Confined to: ____ Bed   ____ Wheelchair   ____ Home   Other (Describe) _____

Prognosis _____

_____

_____

_____

Amount of Bill $ _____ Paid by _____ Date _____

Other Expenses (Nursing Care, Household Help, Sickroom Equipment) _____

_____

_____

WITNESSES

Last Name   _First_   _Middle_

Street   _City_   _State_   _Zip_

Phone _____ Date of Birth _____

Employer

Street   _City_   _State_   _Zip_

Phone _____ Supervisor _____

Occupation _____ Earnings _____

Summary of Statement _____

Last Name   _First_   _Middle_

Street   _City_   _State_   _Zip_

Phone _____ Date of Birth _____

Employer

Street   _City_   _State_   _Zip_

Phone _____ Supervisor _____

Occupation _____ Earnings _____

Summary of Statement _____

Last Name   _First_   _Middle_

Street   _City_   _State_   _Zip_

Phone _____ Date of Birth _____

Employer

Street   _City_   _State_   _Zip_

Phone _____ Supervisor _____

Occupation _____ Earnings _____

Summary of Statement _____

WITNESSES

Last Name _____ First _____ Middle _____

Street _____ City _____ State _____ Zip _____

Phone _____ Date of Birth _____

Employer _____

Street _____ City _____ State _____ Zip _____

Phone _____ Supervisor _____

Occupation _____ Earnings _____

Summary of Statement _____

Last Name _____ First _____ Middle _____

Street _____ City _____ State _____ Zip _____

Phone _____ Date of Birth _____

Employer _____

Street _____ City _____ State _____ Zip _____

Phone _____ Supervisor _____

Occupation _____ Earnings _____

Summary of Statement _____

Last Name _____ First _____ Middle _____

Street _____ City _____ State _____ Zip _____

Phone _____ Date of Birth _____

Employer _____

Street _____ City _____ State _____ Zip _____

Phone _____ Supervisor _____

Occupation _____ Earnings _____

Summary of Statement _____

MANNER OF ACCIDENT (*Narrative Description*)

Note: Be sure to include date, location, time, type of injury, and whether work-related both in narrative *and* in separate spaces provided below.

_____

_____

_____

_____

_____

_____

_____

_____

_____

_____

_____

_____

_____

_____

_____

_____

_____

_____

_____

Date _____ Time _____

_____
Street   *City*   *State*   *Zip*

Type of Injury _____

Work-related? _____

WORK-RELATED ACCIDENT (*Narrative Description*)

If the accident was in *any* way related to plaintiff/claimant's work, describe it in detail. Describe precisely what plaintiff was doing when the accident took place; name the person who told him or her to carry out that activity; and/or describe *how* the activity is related to the performance of the plaintiff's duties and/or how the plaintiff was acting on behalf of his or her employer when the accident took place.

_____

_____

_____

_____

_____

_____

_____

_____

_____

_____

_____

_____

_____

_____

_____

_____

_____

POLICE OFFICER(S)

_____
Last Name   First   Middle

Precinct Address _____
                 Street   City   State   Zip

Shield No. _____ Phone _____

File or Report No. _____

_____
Last Name   First   Middle

Precinct Address _____
                 Street   City   State   Zip

Shield No. _____ Phone _____

File or Report No. _____

_____
Last Name   First   Middle

Precinct Address _____
                 Street   City   State   Zip

Shield No. _____ Phone _____

File or Report No. _____

_____
Last Name   First   Middle

Precinct Address _____
                 Street   City   State   Zip

Shield No. _____ Phone _____

File or Report No. _____

DISPOSITION

File or Report No. _____

Arrest? _____

Summons? _____

Trial Set for _____

At _____

Authorization to Inspect
Hospital Medical Records

_____
Date

TO: CUSTODIAN OF RECORDS:

_____

_____

_____

I HEREBY AUTHORIZE YOU to permit _____, of

_____,

and his, her or their representative(s), to inspect any and all medical records, x-rays, etc., that you may have on file ONLY relative to the examination, treatment and/or confinement in your hospital directly related to injuries sustained by _____
_____ on or about _____.
Name of Person   *Date*
_____ was treated at your hospital on or about _____.
Name of Person   *Date*

Inspection of said records is authorized only upon your making permanent notation in my file of the NAME of the individual making such inspection and the DATE of such inspection.

NOTICE

This is NOT an authorization to permit the inspection of **any** medical records of _____
Name of Person

other than those referred to above and is LIMITED to the inspection of medical records relative ONLY to said examination, treatment and/or confinement.

(Signed) _____

_____
Print Name of Signer

_____
Street Address

_____
City   *State*   *Zip*
Telephone: _____

Witness _____

CERTIFICATE OF NOTARY

STATE OF   )

)   ss:

COUNTY OF   )

On this _____ day of _____, 19 _____, before me personally came and appeared _____, known, and known to me, to be the individual described in and who executed the foregoing instrument, and who duly acknowledged to me that he or she executed same for the purpose therein contained.

IN WITNESS WHEREOF, I hereunto set my hand and official seal.

_____

Notary Public

My commission expires: _____

Authorization to Inspect
Physician's Medical Records

_____
Date

TO: _____, M.D. _____

_____

_____

I HEREBY AUTHORIZE YOU to permit _____, of

_____,

and his, her or their representative(s), to inspect any and all medical records, x-rays, etc., that you may have on file ONLY relative to examination and/or treatment by you in connection with injuries sustained by _____
_____ on or about _____.
    Name of Person   *Date*

_____ was treated by you for said injuries on or about _____.
    Name of Person   *Date*

    Inspection of said records is authorized only upon your making a permanent notation in my file of the NAME of the individual making such inspection and the DATE of such inspection.

NOTICE

    This is NOT an authorization to permit the inspection of **any** medical records of _____
                                                                 Name of Person

other than those referred to above and is LIMITED to the inspection of medical records relative ONLY to said examination and treatment.

(Signed) _____

_____
Print Name of Signer

_____
Street Address

_____
City   *State*   *Zip*

Telephone: _____

Witness _____

CERTIFICATE OF NOTARY

STATE OF   )

)   ss:

COUNTY OF   )

On this _____ day of _____, 19 _____, before me personally came and appeared _____, known, and known to me, to be the individual described in and who executed the foregoing instrument, and who duly acknowledged to me that he or she executed same for the purpose therein contained.

IN WITNESS WHEREOF, I hereunto set my hand and official seal.

_____

Notary Public

My commission expires: _____

Request for a Copy of Police Blotter and/or Accident Report

_____
Date

To: _____

_____

_____

Kindly furnish _____
Name

_____
Address

with a copy of the police blotter and/or any accident report relative to the accident in which _____

_____, of
Name

_____,
Address

was injured at _____ (AM) (PM) on the _____ day of _____, 19 _____,

at _____.
Location

Signed _____

Witness _____

* *

CERTIFICATE OF NOTARY

STATE OF ⠀⠀⠀⠀⠀⠀⠀⠀⠀)
⠀⠀⠀⠀⠀⠀⠀⠀⠀⠀⠀⠀⠀⠀⠀) ss:
COUNTY OF ⠀⠀⠀⠀⠀⠀⠀)

⠀⠀⠀On this _____ day of _____, 19 _____, before me personally came and appeared _____, known, and known to me, to be the individual who executed the foregoing instrument and who duly acknowledged to me that he or she executed same for the purpose therein contained.

⠀⠀⠀IN WITNESS WHEREOF, I hereunto set my hand and official seal.

_____
Notary Public

My commission expires: _____

Retainer and Power of Attorney

I, THE UNDERSIGNED, residing at _____

_____ ,

do hereby retain _____

_____

to prosecute and adjust for me claims arising from _____

_____ ,

sustained by _____

on the _____ day of _____, 19 _____, through the negligence or other unlawful acts of

_____

_____ or against anyone else responsible for same.

I represent that said claim is a true one and has not been settled. I hereby agree that I will not settle nor in any way compromise said claim without the written consent of my attorney(s), nor take any action to jeopardize aforesaid claim in any way.

In consideration of the services to be rendered by said attorney(s) in the prosecution of said claim, I promise to pay to said attorney(s) a sum of money equal to _____ percent of any sum I may receive as a result of a settlement prior to trial; _____ percent of any sum I may receive as a result of any judgment or verdict arising from any trial; and _____ percent of any sum I may receive as a result of any appeal undertaken by said attorney(s). I further agree that my attorney(s) shall have a lien thereon. I further agree to reimburse said attorney(s) for all costs and disbursements incurred in connection herewith.

POWER OF ATTORNEY

I hereby further appoint said attorney(s) to be my lawful attorney(s) in this matter, granting said attorney(s) exclusive right to take any and all steps to legally prosecute and enforce my claim, and to act as I might and could do if personally present, and;

I do hereby confirm and ratify all whatsoever said attorney(s) or his, her or their substitute(s) shall do or cause to be done in the prosecution of my claim by virtue of this **Power of Attorney**.

This **Retainer and Power of Attorney** may not be changed orally.

IN WITNESS WHEREOF, I set my hand this _____ day of _____, 19 _____.

Signed _____

Witness _____

CERTIFICATE OF NOTARY

STATE OF _____)
)   ss:
COUNTY OF _____)

On this _____ day of _____, 19 _____, before me personally came and appeared _____, known, and known to me, to be the individual described in and who executed the foregoing instrument, and who duly acknowledged to me that he or she executed same for the purpose therein contained.

IN WITNESS WHEREOF, I hereunto set my hand and official seal.

_____
Notary Public

My commission expires: _____

Power of Attorney

I, THE UNDERSIGNED, residing at _____

_____ ,

do hereby appoint _____

_____

to be my lawful attorney(s) in the matter of _____

_____

_____

_____ ,

granting said attorney(s) exclusive right to take any and all steps necessary to legally prosecute and enforce my claim, and to act as I might and could do if personally present, and;

To constitute and appoint in his, her or their place and stead, as his, her or their substitute(s), one or more attorneys for me, with full power of revocation, and;

I do hereby confirm and ratify all whatsoever said attorney(s) or his, her or their substitute(s) shall do or cause to be done in the prosecution of my claim by virtue of this **Power of Attorney**, and;

I represent that my claim is a true one and has not been settled. I hereby agree that I will not settle nor in any way compromise said claim without the written consent of my attorney(s), nor take any action to jeopardize said claim in any way.

This **Power of Attorney** may not be changed orally.

IN WITNESS WHEREOF, I set my hand this _____ day of _____, 19 _____.

Signed _____

Witness _____

* *

CERTIFICATE OF NOTARY

STATE OF   )
)   ss:
COUNTY OF   )

On this _____ day of _____, 19 _____, before me personally came and appeared _____, known, and known to me, to be the individual described in and who executed the foregoing instrument, and who duly acknowledged to me that he or she executed same for the purpose therein contained.

IN WITNESS WHEREOF, I hereunto set my hand and official seal.

_____
Notary Public

My commission expires: _____

Release of All Rights and Claims

I, _____ , age _____ , residing at _____

_____ ,

in exchange for _____ ($ _____), which I have received from

_____ ,

do hereby forever _____ and discharge _____

_____ ,

and their heirs, executors, administrators, successors and assigns, from every right and claim which I may now have, or may hereafter have, on account of any injuries, disabilities and/or illnesses suffered by me as follows:

_____

_____

_____

I hereby acknowledge that by signing this _____ I am forever settling in full for any injuries, disabilities and/or illnesses which I have previously had, which I now have and which I may have in the future, either on account of the specific occurrence mentioned above, or because of any other occurrence in the past, or because of both, even though I do not know that I already have had, have now or may in the future have such injuries, disabilities and/or illnesses, and even though they are not mentioned specifically in this release; and I do this regardless of what any person or persons may have told me about my injuries, disabilities and/or illnesses, or about anything else.

I KNOW THAT DOCTORS, LAWYERS AND OTHERS MAKE MISTAKES AND I REALIZE THAT WHAT OTHER PEOPLE MAY HAVE TOLD ME COULD BE WRONG. I REALIZE I AM TAKING THE RISK THAT THEY MIGHT BE WRONG ABOUT MY CASE, AND IF THEY ARE WRONG, IT IS MY LOSS AND I CANNOT BACK OUT OF THIS _____ AND SETTLEMENT.

I am signing this _____ in exchange for the money which I am being paid, and I have not been promised anything else.

I realize that payment of the above-mentioned money is not an admission by anyone that anyone is liable to me for anything.

CLAIMANT: Please answer the following questions in your own handwriting:

1. Have you read this paper from beginning to end? _____

2. What is this paper you are signing? _____

3. Do you realize that signing this paper forever settles and ends every right and/or claim which you may now have for any damages as well as for past or future medical treatment, care, cure, maintenance and/or wages?

_____

4. Are you satisfied with this settlement? _____

THEREFORE, I am signing my name upon the words, THIS IS A RELEASE, which is printed below to show that I understand and mean everything which is said in this paper.

Signature: _____   THIS IS A RELEASE

Dated this _____ day of _____ , 19 _____ .

CERTIFICATE OF WITNESSES

WE, THE UNDERSIGNED, do hereby certify that the **Release of All Rights and Claims** set forth on the reverse side of this paper was executed in our presence by _____ and that said claimant acknowledged that he or she fully understood the contents and that it was a release of everything and that he or she executed the same as his or her free act and deed in exchange for _____ ($ _____), as therein set forth, and for that only.

WITNESS our hands and seals this _____ day of _____ , 19 _____ .

_____
Signature

_____
Address

_____
Signature

_____
Address

_____
Signature

_____
Address

* *

CERTIFICATE OF NOTARY

STATE OF   )
) ss:
COUNTY OF   )

On this _____ day of _____ , 19 _____ , before me personally came and appeared said claimant, _____ , known, and known to me, to be the individual described in and who executed the foregoing document, and who duly acknowledged to me that he or she executed same for the purpose therein contained.

IN WITNESS WHEREOF, I hereunto set my hand and official seal.

_____
Notary Public

My commission expires: _____

Agreement Between Owner and Contractor

THIS AGREEMENT is hereby entered into this _____ day of _____, 19 _____, between

_____ , of

_____
| Street Address | City | State | Zip | Phone |

hereafter called Owner, and _____ , of

_____
| Street Address | City | State | Zip | Phone |

hereafter called the Contractor.

The said parties, for the considerations hereinafter mentioned, hereby agree to the following:

Description of the Work

1. The Contractor shall provide all materials and labor required to perform all of the work for:

as shown on the drawing(s), and set forth in the specifications and/or description(s) prepared by _____,
which drawing(s) and specifications and/or description(s) are identified by the signatures of the parties to this agreement,
and which form a part of this agreement and are incorporated by reference herein for all purposes.

Payment

2. Under the terms of this agreement, the Owner agrees to pay the Contractor, for materials to be furnished and work to
be done, the sum of _____
_____ ($_____), subject to any additions or deductions as hereinafter provided for in
this agreement, and to make the following payments:

and that the final payment shall be made subject to the hereinafter stated conditions of this agreement.

It is agreed that no payment made under this agreement shall be considered conclusive evidence of full performance of
this contract, either wholly or in part by the Contractor, and that acceptance of payment shall not be considered by the
Contractor to be acceptance by the Owner of any defective materials or workmanship.

Liens

3. Final payment shall not be due until such time as the Contractor has provided the Owner with a release of any liens
arising from this agreement; or receipts for payment in full for all materials and labor for which a lien could be filed; or a
bond satisfactory to the Owner indemnifying the Owner against any lien.

Timely Completion of the Work

4. The Contractor agrees that the various portions of the work shall be completed on or before the following dates:

and the entire work shall be completed on or before the _____ day of _____, 19 _____.

In the event the work is not completed by the aforementioned date, the Owner shall be entitled to receive as damages from the Contractor, the sum of _____ ($_____) per _____, it being agreed that the aforementioned sum is reasonable, taking into account the difficulty in determining the exact amount of damages the Owner would sustain in the event of said delay, and that the agreed sum shall be considered as liquidated damages.

If the Contractor is delayed in the completion of the work by any changes ordered in the work, by acts of God, fire, flood or any other unavoidable casualties; or by labor strikes, late delivery of materials; or by neglect of the Owner, his agents or representatives; or by any subcontractor employed by the Contractor; the time for completion of the work shall be extended for the same period as the delay occasioned by any of the aforementioned causes.

Surveys and Easements

5. The Owner shall provide and pay for all surveys. All easements for access across the property of another, and for permanent changes, and for the construction or erection of structures shall also be obtained and paid for by the Owner.

Licenses, Permits and Building Codes

6. The Contractor shall obtain and pay for all permits and licenses required for the prosecution and timely completion of the work. The Contractor shall comply with all appropriate regulations relating to the conduct of the work and shall advise the Owner of any specifications or drawings which are at variance therewith.

Materials and Equipment

7. The Contractor shall provide and pay for all materials, tools and equipment required for the prosecution and timely completion of the work. Unless otherwise specified in writing, all materials shall be new and of good quality.

Samples

8. Whenever the Owner may require, the Contractor will furnish for approval all samples as directed, and the work shall be in accordance with approved samples.

Labor and Supervision

9. In the prosecution of the work the Contractor shall at all times keep a competent foreman and a sufficient number of workers skilled in their trades to suitably perform the work.

The foreman shall represent the Contractor and, in the absence of the Contractor, all instructions given by the Owner to the foreman shall be binding upon the Contractor as though given to the Contractor. Upon request of the foreman, instructions shall be in writing.

Alterations and Changes

10. All changes and deviations in the work ordered by the Owner must be in writing, the contract sum being increased or decreased accordingly by the Contractor. Any claims for increases in the cost of the work must be presented by the Contractor to the Owner in writing, and written approval of the Owner shall be obtained by the Contractor before proceeding with the ordered change or revision.

In the event that additional work, not shown on the drawings and/or not described in the specifications, is required to comply with laws, regulations or building codes, such additional work shall be considered as done under the terms of this agreement.

Correction of Deficiencies

11. The Contractor agrees to reexecute any work which does not conform to the drawings and specifications, warrants the work performed, and further agrees that he shall remedy any defects resulting from faulty materials or workmanship which shall become evident during a period of one year after completion of the work. This provision shall apply with equal force to all work performed by subcontractors as to work that is performed by direct employees of the Contractor.

Protection of the Work

12. It shall be the responsibility of the Contractor to reasonably protect the work, the property of the Owner, and adjacent property and the public, and the Contractor shall be responsible for any damage, injury or death resulting from his negligence or from any intentional act of the Contractor or the Contractor's employees, agents or subcontractors.

Cleaning Up

13. The Contractor shall keep the premises free from the accumulation of waste and, upon completion of the work, shall remove all waste, equipment and other materials and leave the premises in broom-clean condition.

Contractor's Liability Insurance

14. The Contractor shall obtain insurance to protect himself against claims for property damage arising out of his or any subcontractor's performance of this contract; and to protect himself against claims under provisions of Workman's Compensation and any similar employee benefit acts, and from claims for bodily injury, including death, due to performance of this contract by the Contractor or any subcontractor employed for the performance of this contract.

Owner's Liability Insurance

15. It shall be the responsibility of the Owner, at the Owner's option, to obtain insurance to protect himself from the contingent liability of claims for property damage and bodily injury, including death, that may arise from the performance of this contract.

Fire Insurance with Extended Coverage

16. The Owner shall obtain fire insurance with extended coverage at 100 percent of the value of the entire structure, including materials and labor related to the work described in this agreement. Certificates of insurance shall be filed with the Contractor if he so requests. The aforesaid fire insurance need not include tools, equipment, scaffolding or forms owned or rented by the Contractor, any subcontractor or their respective employees.

Owner's Right to Terminate the Agreement

17. In the event the Contractor shall fail to meet the provisions of this agreement, the Owner shall, after seven (7) days' written notice to the Contractor and his surety, have the right to take possession of the premises in order to complete the work as specified in the agreement. The Owner may deduct the cost thereof from any payment then and thereafter due to the Contractor or may, at his option, terminate the agreement, take possession of any materials and complete the work as he deems appropriate. If the unpaid balance of the contracted sum exceeds the Owner's expenses of completing the work, such excess shall be paid to the Contractor. If such expense shall exceed the unpaid balance, the Contractor shall pay the difference to the Owner.

Contractor's Right to Terminate the Agreement

18. In the event the Owner shall fail to pay the Contractor within seven (7) days after the date upon which payment shall become due, the Contractor shall have the right, after seven (7) days' written notice to the Owner, to stop work and may, at his option, terminate the agreement and recover from the Owner payment for all work executed, plus any loss sustained, plus a reasonable profit, plus damages.

In the event the work is stopped by any court or other public authority for a period of thirty (30) days through no fault of the Contractor, the Contractor shall have the right to stop work and may, at his option, terminate the agreement and recover from the Owner payment for all work executed, plus any loss sustained, plus a reasonable profit, plus damages.

Assignment of Rights

19. Neither the Owner nor Contractor shall have the right to assign any rights or interest occurring under this agreement without the written consent of the other, nor shall the Contractor assign any sums due, or to become due, to him under the provisions of this agreement.

Access and Inspection

20. The Owner, Owner's representative and public authorities shall at all times have access to the work.

An appropriately licensed representative of the Owner, whose authority shall be set forth in writing by the Owner, shall have the authority to direct the removal of any materials and the taking down of any portions of the work failing to meet drawings, specifications, laws, regulations or building codes; the reexecution of said work deemed as being done under the provisions of Article 11 of this agreement.

Any other removal of materials or taking down of any portions of the work as directed by the Owner's representative shall be in writing and at the sole expense of the Owner.

Attorney Fees

21. Attorney fees and court costs shall be paid by the defendant in the event that judgment must be obtained, and is, to enforce this agreement or any breach thereof.

IN WITNESS WHEREOF, the parties hereto set their hands and seals the day and year written above.

_____   _____
Witness as to Owner   *Owner*

_____   _____
Witness as to Contractor   *Contractor*

𝕬𝖌𝖗𝖊𝖊𝖒𝖊𝖓𝖙 𝕭𝖊𝖙𝖜𝖊𝖊𝖓 𝕺𝖜𝖓𝖊𝖗 𝖆𝖓𝖉 𝕮𝖔𝖓𝖙𝖗𝖆𝖈𝖙𝖔𝖗

Owner

Contractor

Dated _____ 19 _____

Amount $ _____

Alternate Articles

Access and Inspection

20. The Owner, Owner's representative and public authorities shall at all times have access to the work.

An appropriately licensed representative of the Owner, whose authority shall be set forth in writing by the Owner, shall have the authority to direct the removal of any materials and the taking down of any portions of the work failing to meet drawings, specifications, laws, regulations or building codes; the reexecution of said work deemed as being done under the provisions of Article 11 of this agreement. If the Contractor deems himself aggrieved thereby, the matter shall be submitted to arbitration as provided for in Article 21 of this agreement.

Arbitration

21. All disputes arising under this agreement shall be submitted to arbitration at the option of the Owner or Contractor. The demand for arbitration must be filed by the aggrieved party, and each party shall name one arbitrator. An umpire shall be chosen by the arbitrators within ten (10) days after the date of written demand for arbitration. In the event the arbitrators shall fail to select an umpire, one shall be named by the appropriate court of jurisdiction.

The arbitrators shall attempt to resolve the dispute in a timely manner and the decision of any two shall be binding upon Owner and Contractor. A decision of the arbitrators in an attempt to resolve any dispute arising out of this agreement shall be a condition precedent to any right to legal action by Owner or Contractor.

Attorney Fees

22. Attorney fees and court costs shall be paid by the defendant in the event that judgment must be, and is, obtained to enforce a decision or award of the arbitrator or arbitrators in any dispute related to this agreement.

IN WITNESS WHEREOF, the parties hereto set their hands and seals the day and year written above.

_____
Witness as to Owner

_____
Owner

_____
Witness as to Contractor

_____
Contractor

Agreement Between Owner and Contractor—Short Form

THIS AGREEMENT is hereby entered into this _____ day of _____, 19 _____, between

_____ , of

_____ ,

Street Address	City	State	Zip	Phone

hereafter called Owner, and _____ , of

_____ ,

Street Address	City	State	Zip	Phone

hereafter called Contractor.

The said parties, for the considerations hereinafter mentioned, hereby agree to the following:

1. The Contractor agrees to provide all of the material and labor required to perform the following work for:

as shown by the drawing(s) and described in the specifications prepared by _____
and provided by the Owner, which are identified by the signatures of the parties to this agreement and which form a part of this agreement.

2. The Owner hereby agrees to pay the Contractor, for the aforesaid materials and labor, the sum of _____
_____ _____ ($ _____),
in the following manner:

3. The Contractor agrees that the various portions of the above-described work shall be completed on or before the following dates:

and the entire above-described work shall be completed no later than the _____ day of _____,
19 _____ .

4. The Contractor agrees to provide and pay for all materials, tools and equipment required for the prosecution and timely completion of the work. Unless otherwise specified, all materials shall be new and of good quality.

5. In the prosecution of the work the Contractor shall employ a sufficient number of workers skilled in their trades to suitably perform the work.

6. All changes and deviations in the work ordered by the Owner must be in writing, the contract sum being increased or decreased accordingly by the Contractor. Any claims for increases in the cost of the work must be presented by the Contractor to the Owner in writing, and written approval of the Owner shall be obtained by the Contractor before proceeding with the ordered change or revision.

7. The Owner, Owner's representative and public authorities shall at all times have access to the work.

8. The Contractor agrees to reexecute any work which does not conform to the drawings and specifications, warrants the work performed, and agrees to remedy any defects resulting from faulty materials or workmanship which shall become evident during a period of one year after completion of the work.

9. The Owner agrees to maintain full insurance on the above-described work during the progress of the work, in his own name and that of the Contractor.

10. In the event the Contractor is delayed in the prosecution of the work by acts of God, fire, flood or any other unavoidable casualties; or by labor strikes, late delivery of materials; or by neglect of the Owner; the time for completion of the work shall be extended for the same period as the delay occasioned by any of the aforementioned causes.

11. In the event the work is delayed due to neglect of the Contractor, the Contractor agrees to pay the Owner the sum of _____ ($ _____) per _____ as liquidated damages until such time as the work is completed.

12. The Contractor agrees to obtain insurance to protect himself against claims for property damage, bodily injury or death due to his performance of this agreement.

13. Neither the Owner nor Contractor shall have the right to assign any rights or interest occurring under this agreement without the written consent of the other, nor shall the Contractor assign any sums due, or to become due, to him under the provisions of this agreement.

Attorney Fees

14. Attorney fees and court costs shall be paid by the defendant in the event that judgment must be, and is, obtained to enforce this agreement or any breach thereof.

IN WITNESS WHEREOF, the parties hereto set their hands and seals the day and year written above.

_____
Witness as to Owner

_____
Witness as to Contractor

_____
Owner

_____
Contractor

Agreement Between Owner and Contractor

Owner

Contractor

Dated _____ 19 ___

Amount $ _____

Alternate Articles

14. All disputes arising under this agreement shall be submitted to arbitration, one arbitrator appointed by the Owner and one appointed by the Contractor, those two having the power to name an umpire, whose decision shall be binding upon the parties.

Attorney Fees

15. Attorney fees and court costs shall be paid by the defendant in the event that judgment must be, and is, obtained to enforce a decision or award of the arbitrator or arbitrators in any dispute related to this agreement.

IN WITNESS WHEREOF, the parties hereto set their hands and seals the day and year written above.

_____
Witness as to Owner

_____
Witness as to Contractor

_____
Owner

_____
Contractor

Authority to Represent the Owner

I, _____ , Owner of property located at _____

_____ ,

do hereby appoint _____ , of

_____ ,

Street Address   *City*   *State*   *Zip*

who is duly licensed as _____ by _____ ,

as my representative under the provisions of Article 20 of the agreement dated _____

between the undersigned Owner and _____ , of

Name of Contractor

_____ .

Street Address   *City*   *State*   *Zip*

    Aforesaid representative is hereby empowered to take all steps legally to act in my place and stead, and I do hereby ratify whatsoever said representative shall do or cause to be done by virtue of the authority hereby granted.

    Right to revoke said authority is reserved by the undersigned and shall become effective upon presentation of written notice of revocation to said representative and said contractor.

Dated _____

_____

Owner

Witness _____

Authority to Represent the Owner

I, _____, Owner of property located at _____

_____,

do hereby appoint _____, of

_____,

Street Address   City   State   Zip

who is duly licensed as _____ by _____,

as my representative under the provisions of Paragraph 7 of the agreement dated _____

between the undersigned Owner and _____, of

Name of Contractor

_____.

Street Address   City   State   Zip

    Aforesaid representative is hereby empowered to take all steps legally to act in my place and stead, and I do hereby ratify whatsoever said representative shall do or cause to be done by virtue of the authority hereby granted.

    Right to revoke said authority is reserved by the undersigned and shall become effective upon presentation of written notice of revocation to said representative and said contractor.

Dated _____

_____

Owner

Witness _____

Revocation of Authority to Represent the Owner

I hereby revoke, effective immediately, the authority granted to _____

by the **Authority to Represent the Owner** dated _____ and signed by me on that date.

Dated _____

_____
Owner

Witness _____

Revocation of Authority to Represent the Owner

I hereby revoke, effective immediately, the authority granted to _____

by the **Authority to Represent the Owner** dated _____ and signed by me on that date.

Dated _____

_____
Owner

Witness _____

Revocation of Authority to Represent the Owner

I hereby revoke, effective immediately, the authority granted to _____

by the **Authority to Represent the Owner** dated _____ and signed by me on that date.

Dated _____

_____
Owner

Witness _____

Agreement Between Contractor and Subcontractor

THIS AGREEMENT is hereby entered into this _____ day of _____, 19 _____, between

_____ , of

| Street Address | City | State | Zip | Phone |

hereafter called Contractor, and _____, of

| Street Address | City | State | Zip | Phone |

hereafter called Subcontractor.

The said parties, for the considerations hereinafter mentioned, hereby agree to the following:

1. The Subcontractor agrees to provide all materials and labor to perform the following portions of work specified in an agreement between the Contractor and _____, described therein as Owner, in accordance with the terms, drawings, plans and specifications provided by the Owner, which are identified by the signatures of the parties hereto, and which form a part of the agreement, to wit:

2. The Contractor agrees to pay the Subcontractor, for the aforesaid materials and labor, the sum of _____ _____ ($_____), in the following manner:

3. The Subcontractor agrees that the various portions of the above-described work shall be completed on or before the following dates:

and that the entire above-described work shall be completed no later than the _____ day of _____, 19 _____.

4. The Subcontractor agrees to provide and pay for all materials, tools and equipment required for the prosecution and timely completion of the work. Unless otherwise specified, all materials shall be new and of good quality.

5. In the prosecution of the work the Subcontractor shall employ a sufficient number of workers skilled in their trades to suitably perform the work.

1

6. All changes in the work must be ordered by the Contractor in writing, the contract sum being increased or decreased accordingly by the Subcontractor. Any claims for increases in the cost of the work presented by the Subcontractor to the Contractor shall be in writing, and written approval of the Contractor shall be obtained by the Subcontractor before proceeding with the ordered change.

7. The Subcontractor agrees to reexecute any work which does not conform to the drawings and specifications, and further agrees to remedy any defects resulting from faulty materials or workmanship which shall become evident during a period of one year after completion of the work.

8. The Contractor agrees to pay the Subcontractor a just share of any fire insurance sums which may be received by the Contractor under provisions of the aforesaid agreement between the Owner and Contractor.

9. In the event the Subcontractor is delayed in the prosecution of the work by acts of God, fire, flood or any other unavoidable casualties; or by labor strikes, late delivery of materials; or by neglect of the Owner or Contractor; the time for completion of the work shall be extended for the same period as the delay occasioned by any of the aforementioned causes.

10. In the event the work is delayed due to neglect of the Subcontractor, the Subcontractor agrees to pay the Contractor the sum of _____ ($_____) per _____ as liquidated damages until such time as the work is completed.

11. The Subcontractor agrees to obtain insurance to protect himself against claims for property damage, bodily injury or death arising from his performance of this contract.

12. The Subcontractor agrees to assume toward the Contractor such responsibilities and obligations in so far as the same may be applicable to the materials and labor herein described, as the Contractor assumes toward the Owner.

13. The Contractor agrees to be bound to the Subcontractor by all responsibilities and obligations that the Owner assumes toward the Contractor, and by all aforementioned plans, drawings and specifications as they may be applicable to the materials and labor herein described.

14. The Contractor agrees that in the event of arbitration of any dispute relating to the materials and/or labor described in this agreement, the Subcontractor shall have the opportunity to be present and to give evidence relative thereto; and that the Contractor shall name as arbitrator whomsoever may be named by the Subcontractor, if the sole cause of the dispute shall be the materials and/or labor provided by the Subcontractor under provisions of this agreement; or, if the cause of the dispute shall be the joint responsibility of the Contractor and Subcontractor, or of said Subcontractor and any other Subcontractor, to name as arbitrator such person upon whom both shall agree.

15. Attorney fees and court costs shall be paid by the defendant in the event that judgment must be, and is, obtained to enforce this agreement or any breach thereof.

IN WITNESS WHEREOF, the parties hereto set their hands and seals the day and year written above.

_____
Witness as to Contractor

_____
Witness as to Subcontractor

_____
Contractor

_____
Subcontractor

Agreement Between Contractor and Subcontractor

Contractor

Subcontractor

Dated _____ 19 ____

Amount $ _____

Job Estimate Work Sheet

Owner: _____

_____

Architect: _____

_____

_____

Type of Job: _____

_____

Lottery No. _____ Block _____ Tract _____

Description _____ No. Square Feet _____

Date of Estimate _____

Estimated by _____

ARCHITECTURAL

Plans and Specifications _____ $_____

Engineering _____ $_____

LEGAL

Building Permit _____ $_____

Street Deposit _____ $_____

Construction Water _____ $_____

Water Tap _____ $_____

Miscellaneous _____ $_____

FORM 25.1/F168

INSURANCE

Liability _____ $_____

Compensation _____ $_____

Fire _____ $_____

Surety _____ $_____

PRELIMINARY

Survey _____ $_____

Wrecking _____ $_____

EXCAVATING

Excavate _____ Yards @ _____ $_____

Grading and Filling _____ $_____

Hauling _____ $_____

MASONRY

Face Brick _____ M @ _____ $_____

Common Brick _____ M @ _____ $_____

Hollow Tile _____ M @ _____ $_____

Concrete Block _____ M @ _____ $_____

Stonework _____ $_____

Chimneys and Fireplaces _____ $_____

Mantles _____ $_____

Other _____ $_____

Other _____ $_____

CONCRETE

Walls _____ Cubic Feet @ _____ $_____

Floors _____ Square Feet @ _____ $_____

Walks _____ Square Feet @ _____ $_____

CONCRETE (*Continued*)

Driveways _____ Square Feet @ _____ $_____

Curbs _____ Linear Feet @ _____ $_____

Steps _____ Linear Feet @ _____ $_____

Light Weight _____ Square Feet @ _____ $_____

Concrete Block _____ $_____

Reinforcing Steel _____ $_____

Pans _____ $_____

Other _____ $_____

Other _____ $_____

Other _____ $_____

LUMBER

Rough _____ M @ _____ $_____

Finish _____ M @ _____ $_____

Other _____ $_____

CARPENTRY

Rough _____ $_____

Finish _____ $_____

Other _____ $_____

LATH AND PLASTERING

Exterior _____ Yards @ _____ $_____

Interior _____ Yards @ _____ $_____

Staff Work _____ $_____

Dry Wall _____ $_____

Other _____ $_____

Other _____ $_____

FORM 25.1 / F170

CEILING

Acoustic _____ $_____

Other _____ $_____

Other _____ $_____

MILLWORK

Frames _____ $_____

Sash _____ $_____

Doors _____ $_____

Screens _____ $_____

Stair Work _____ $_____

Cabinets _____ $_____

Interior Finish _____ $_____

Other _____ $_____

Other _____ $_____

ROOF

Trusses _____ $_____

Tile _____ $_____

Composition _____ $_____

Tarring _____ $_____

Other _____ $_____

FLOORS

Hardwood _____ Yards @ _____ $_____

Parquet _____ Yards @ _____ $_____

Asphalt/Vinyl _____ Yards @ _____ $_____

Composition _____ Yards @ _____ $_____

Carpet _____ Yards @ _____ $_____

Other _____ Yards @ _____ $_____

GLAZING

Plate Glass _____ $ _____

Mirrors _____ $ _____

Miscellaneous Glass _____ $ _____

Weather Stripping _____ $ _____

Other _____ $ _____

Other _____ $ _____

TILE

Glazed Tile _____ $ _____

Unglazed Tile _____ $ _____

Tile Setting _____ $ _____

METALWORK

Structural Steel _____ $ _____

Ornamental Iron _____ $ _____

Sheet Metal _____ $ _____

Steel Sash _____ $

Other _____ $ _____

PLUMBING

Pipe _____ $ _____

Fixtures _____ $ _____

Plumbing Work _____ $ _____

Other _____ $ _____

SANITATION

Sewer _____ $ _____

Septic Tank _____ $ _____

Other _____ $ _____

FORM 25.1/F172

HEATING

Furnace _____ $_____

Solar Unit _____ $_____

Other _____ $_____

Other _____ $_____

AIR CONDITIONING

Central Unit _____ $_____

Ducting _____ $_____

Individual Units _____ $_____

Other _____ $_____

INSULATION

Insulating Material _____ $_____

Insulation Work _____ $_____

Storm Windows _____ $_____

Other _____ $_____

HARDWARE

Rough _____ $_____

Finish _____ $_____

Other _____ $_____

Other _____ $_____

ELECTRICAL

Wiring _____ $_____

Fixtures _____ $_____

Electrical Work _____ $_____

Other _____ $_____

Other _____ $_____

APPLIANCES

Stove _____ $ _____

Microwave Oven _____ $ _____

Convector Oven _____ $ _____

Exhaust Hoods _____ $ _____

Refrigerator _____ $ _____

Freezer _____ $ _____

Dishwasher _____ $ _____

Garbage Disposer _____ $ _____

Trash Compactor _____ $ _____

Washer _____ $ _____

Dryer _____ $ _____

Other _____ $ _____

FIRE PREVENTION

Smoke Detectors _____ $ _____

Sprinkler System _____ $ _____

Fire Escapes _____ $ _____

Extinguishers _____ $ _____

Other _____ $ _____

Other _____ $ _____

PAINTING AND DECORATING

Paint _____ $ _____

Interior Stain _____ $ _____

Exterior Stain _____ $ _____

Waterproofing _____ $ _____

Wallpaper _____ $ _____

Wallpapering _____ $ _____

PAINTING AND DECORATING (*Continued*)

Draperies/Curtains _____ $_____

Other _____ $_____

Other _____ $_____

Other _____ $_____

LANDSCAPING

Sod _____ $_____

Sprigging _____ $_____

Trees, Shrubbery _____ $_____

Sprinkler System _____ $_____

Fence _____ $_____

Other _____ $_____

DETACHED GARAGE

Materials _____ $_____

Labor _____ $_____

Driveway _____ $_____

Other _____ $_____

SWIMMING POOL

Construction _____ $_____

Filter _____ $_____

Gas/Electric Heater _____ $_____

Solar Heater _____ $_____

Cover _____ $_____

Other _____ $_____

MISCELLANEOUS

Sauna _____ $_____

Exterior Heated Soaking Tub _____ $_____

Interior Heated Soaking Tub _____ $_____

Soundproofing _____ $_____

Awnings _____ $_____

Shades/Blinds _____ $_____

Shutters _____ $_____

Burglar Alarm System _____ $_____

Exterior Lighting _____ $_____

Other _____ $_____

Other _____ $_____

CLEANUP

Removing Exterior Debris _____ $_____

Interior Cleanup (Broom Clean) _____ $_____

Clean Windows _____ $_____

EXTRAS

1. _____ $_____

2. _____ $_____

3. _____ $_____

4. _____ $_____

5. _____ $_____

6. _____ $_____

Total Cost $_____

Profit $_____

Bid $_____

Bid and Proposal

TO: _____

_____

_____

FROM: _____

_____

_____

We propose to provide all materials and supply all labor required for:

The above-described work shall be completed in a substantial and workmanlike manner according to standard practices and in conformance with all applicable building codes and regulations on or before the _____ day of _____, 19 _____, for the sum of _____ _____ ($_____).

All materials will be of good quality and will be new unless otherwise specified in writing and accepted by the Owner.

All workers will be skilled in their trades and be under the supervision of the Contractor or his representative.

Changes in or departures from the above-described work shall be executed only upon written orders and the cost of the work will be adjusted accordingly by the Contractor.

Payment shall be made:

This bid and proposal shall remain in effect for thirty (30) days.

_____

_____

Dated this _____ day of _____, 19 _____.

ACCEPTED

You are hereby authorized to proceed with the work in accordance with the aforementioned description and conditions for which _____ agree(s) to pay the sum of _____ _____ ($ _____).

Accepted this _____ day of _____ , 19 _____ .

_____
Owner

General Waiver of Liens

WHEREAS, we, the undersigned subscribers, have provided materials and labor for:

located at _____,
we hereby agree to waive and release any and all right which we now have, or may hereafter have, to any lien upon the aforementioned property, building(s), equipment or furnishings.

We individually warrant that we have the right to execute and subscribe to this waiver of lien and that we have not assigned our right to lien, nor our right to payment, and that all suppliers and all workers employed by us have been paid in full and have no right of claim against the aforementioned property, building(s), equipment or furnishings.

IN WITNESS WHEREOF, we have set our hands and seals on the date written opposite our respective signatures.

NAME		DATE	WITNESS
_____	Excavating	_____	_____
_____	Stone	_____	_____
_____	Stonework	_____	_____
_____	Lime and Cement	_____	_____
_____	Ready-mixed Concrete	_____	_____
_____	Concrete Block	_____	_____
_____	Sand and Gravel	_____	_____
_____	Reinforcing Steel	_____	_____
_____	Cement Work	_____	_____
_____	Face Brick	_____	_____
_____	Common Brick	_____	_____
_____	Glazed Tile	_____	_____
_____	Hollow Tile	_____	_____
_____	Tile Setting	_____	_____
_____	Brick Layer	_____	_____
_____	Lumber	_____	_____
_____	Doors	_____	_____

NAME		DATE	WITNESS
_____	Garage Doors	_____	_____
_____	Carpet	_____	_____
_____	Carpet Layer	_____	_____
_____	Structural Steel	_____	_____
_____	Sheet Metal	_____	_____
_____	Steel Sash	_____	_____
_____	Ornamental Iron	_____	_____
_____	Metalwork	_____	_____
_____	Ironwork	_____	_____
_____	Pipe	_____	_____
_____	Plumber	_____	_____
_____	Plumber	_____	_____
_____	Plumbing Fixtures	_____	_____
_____	Plumbing Fixtures	_____	_____
_____	Oil/Gas Furnace	_____	_____
_____	Electric Heat	_____	_____
_____	Solar Heating Unit	_____	_____
_____	Gas/Electric Water Heater	_____	_____
_____	Solar Water Heater	_____	_____
_____	Central Air Conditioner	_____	_____
_____	Duct Work	_____	_____
_____	Insulation Material	_____	_____
_____	Insulating	_____	_____
_____	Sash	_____	_____
_____	Frames	_____	_____
_____	Windows	_____	_____
_____	Plate Glass	_____	_____

NAME		DATE	WITNESS
————————————	Mirrors	———————	————————————
————————————	Cabinets	———————	————————————
————————————	Carpenter	———————	————————————
————————————	Carpenter	———————	————————————
————————————	Stair Work	———————	————————————
————————————	Weather Stripping	———————	————————————
————————————	Dry Wall	———————	————————————
————————————	Plaster Material	———————	————————————
————————————	Plastering	———————	————————————
————————————	Composition Roofing	———————	————————————
————————————	Roofing Tile	———————	————————————
————————————	Tarring	———————	————————————
————————————	Roofer	———————	————————————
————————————	Hardwood Flooring	———————	————————————
————————————	Parquet Flooring	———————	————————————
————————————	Asphalt/Vinyl	———————	————————————
————————————	Linoleum	———————	————————————
————————————	Composition	———————	————————————
————————————	Terrazo	———————	————————————
————————————	Electrical Wiring	———————	————————————
————————————	Electrical Fixtures	———————	————————————
————————————	Electrician	———————	————————————
————————————	Electrician	———————	————————————
————————————	Rough Hardware	———————	————————————
————————————	Finish Hardware	———————	————————————
————————————	Stove	———————	————————————
————————————	Oven	———————	————————————

NAME		DATE	WITNESS
_____	Exhaust Hood	_____	_____
_____	Dishwasher	_____	_____
_____	Trash Compactor	_____	_____
_____	Garbage Disposer	_____	_____
_____	Refrigerator	_____	_____
_____	Freezer	_____	_____
_____	Clothes Washer	_____	_____
_____	Clothes Dryer	_____	_____
_____	Sprinkler System	_____	_____
_____	Smoke Detectors	_____	_____
_____	Intercom System	_____	_____
_____	Burglar Alarm System	_____	_____
_____	Interior Paint	_____	_____
_____	Exterior Paint	_____	_____
_____	Interior Stain	_____	_____
_____	Exterior Stain	_____	_____
_____	Painter, Interior	_____	_____
_____	Painter, Exterior	_____	_____
_____	Wallpaper	_____	_____
_____	Paperhanger	_____	_____
_____	Window Shades/ Blinds	_____	_____
_____	Awnings	_____	_____
_____	Shutters	_____	_____
_____	Sod	_____	_____
_____	Sprigging	_____	_____
_____	Trees and Shrubbery	_____	_____
_____	Landscape Work	_____	_____

NAME		DATE	WITNESS
_____	Fence	_____	_____
_____	Swimming Pool Heater	_____	_____
_____	Swimming Pool Filter	_____	_____
_____	Swimming Pool Contractor	_____	_____
_____	Scaffolding	_____	_____
_____	Equipment Rental	_____	_____
_____	Equipment Rental	_____	_____
_____	_____	_____	_____
_____	_____	_____	_____
_____	_____	_____	_____
_____	_____	_____	_____

* *

CERTIFICATE TO OBTAIN PAYMENT

_____ , 19 _____

(I) (We) hereby certify unto _____ that the signatures on the annexed **General Waiver of Liens** comprise a true, full and complete list of all individuals and corporations who have contracted for and/or provided any and all materials and fixtures of every description for, in or about the construction, improvement or repair of the premises or building(s) described in the aforementioned **General Waiver of Liens** and who are, or have been, subcontractors upon aforesaid premises, building(s) or any part thereof, or for providing any and all fixtures, furnishings, repairs or improvements to aforesaid premises or building(s) under any contract or agreement with the undersigned.

(I) (We) warrant that (I) (we) have the right to execute this waiver and that (I) (we) have not assigned (my) (our) right to lien nor (my) (our) right to payment.

_____

By _____

Title _____

_____

By _____

Title _____

5

CERTIFICATE OF NOTARY

STATE OF   )

)   ss:

COUNTY OF   )

On this _____ day of _____, 19 _____, before me personally came and appeared _____ (and) _____, known, and known to me, to be the individual(s) described in and who executed the foregoing instrument, and who duly acknowledged to me that he, she, or they executed same for the purpose therein contained.

IN WITNESS WHEREOF, I hereunto set my hand and official seal.

_____
Notary Public

My commission expires: _____

General Waiver of Liens

TO

IN RE

Dated _____ 19 ____

Waiver of Lien

In consideration of value received, having furnished:

for property located at _____

and owned by _____,

(I) (we) do hereby waive and release any and all right which (I) (we) now or hereafter may have to a lien upon the aforementioned property.

    (I) (We) warrant that (I) (we) have the right to execute this waiver and that (I) (we) have not assigned (my) (our) right to lien nor (my) (our) right to payment, and that all suppliers and all workers employed by (me) (us) have been paid in full and have no right to claim against the property or materials.

_____

By _____

Title _____

_____

By _____

Title _____

* *

CERTIFICATE OF NOTARY

STATE OF   )

)   ss:

COUNTY OF   )

    On this _____ day of _____, 19 _____, before me personally came and appeared _____ (and) _____, known, and known to me, to be the individual(s) described in and who executed the foregoing instrument, and who duly acknowledged to me that he, she, or they executed same for the purpose therein contained.

    IN WITNESS WHEREOF, I hereunto set my hand and official seal.

_____

Notary Public

My commission expires: _____

Waiver of Lien

Owner

Contractor

2

Dated ———————————— 19 ——

Receipt for Conditional Payment

(I) (We) acknowledge that payment of _____
_____ ($ _____), received from the Owner this _____
day of _____ , 19 _____ , is not an acceptance by the Owner of the following claimed defects and/or departures from specifications, drawings or plans:

(I) (We) hereby agree to correct the above no later than the _____ day of _____ , 19 _____ .

_____

By _____

Title _____

_____

By _____

Title _____

Contractor's Affidavit of Completion

STATE OF _____)
)   ss:
COUNTY OF _____)

On this _____ day of _____, 19 _____, before me personally came and appeared _____
_____, who, first being duly sworn, says that:

1. On the _____ day of _____, 19 _____, the Contractor, _____,
entered into an agreement with _____, Owner of property located at _____
_____.

2. The work described in aforesaid agreement has been fully performed. All suppliers and workers dealing with the Contractor in connection with said agreement have been fully paid and their releases hereto attached, with the following exceptions:
(Show name, materials or services supplied, and amount due.)

3. In consideration of the balance due to the above-listed creditors, the Contractor hereby agrees to pay promptly in full and obtain the release of any liens or claims, and hold the Owner harmless from any loss or damage which may result from the Contractor's failure to do so.

4. The Contractor has in no way pledged or assigned the aforesaid agreement, nor any amount due or hereafter to become due.

5. The undersigned is either the owner or a principal officer of the Contractor, and has personally supervised the performance of this contract.

_____

By _____

Title _____

1

CERTIFICATE OF NOTARY

STATE OF ⎫

⎬ ss:

COUNTY OF ⎭

On this _____ day of _____, 19 _____, before me personally came and appeared _____, known, and known to me, to be the individual described in and who executed the foregoing instrument, and who duly acknowledged to me that he or she executed same for the purpose therein contained.

IN WITNESS WHEREOF, I hereunto set my hand and official seal.

_____
Notary Public

My commission expires: _____

....

OWNER'S RECEIPT

Received from _____, Owner, this _____ day of _____, 19 _____, the sum of _____ ($_____), as final payment in full of all amounts due and to become due in connection with (my) (our) performance of aforesaid agreement.

_____

By _____

Title _____

Contractor's Affidavit of Completion

Owner

Contractor

Dated _____ 19 __

2

Agreement for Submission of an Existing Dispute to Arbitration—One Arbitrator

We, the undersigned, hereby agree to submit to arbitration the following dispute:

_____

_____

_____

_____

_____

Selection of an Arbitrator

The parties to the dispute shall select and equally pay an Arbitrator. In the event the parties are unable to agree upon an Arbitrator within ten (10) days of signing this agreement, an Arbitrator shall be named by the appropriate court of jurisdiction.

Costs

The costs of arbitration shall be borne equally by the parties to the dispute, provided that fees paid to expert witnesses, and the costs of travel, laboratory tests, etc., shall be borne by the party incurring them.

Procedure

The Arbitrator shall hear and attempt to resolve the dispute in a timely manner, and the written dicision of the Arbitrator shall be binding equally upon all parties to the dispute. Unless otherwise agreed to by the parties, the arbitration shall be conducted in the county and state of the appropriate court of jurisdiction, in accordance with the guidelines accepted by the parties and in conformance with accepted rules governing the admission of evidence in courts of law.

Award

Judgment upon award rendered by the Arbitrator may be entered in the appropriate court of jurisdiction.

IN WITNESS WHEREOF, we, the parties hereto, hereby set our hands and seals this date.

(Signed) _____

(Signed) _____

Dated _____

FORM 29.1/F192

Agreement for Arbitration

BETWEEN

and

Dated _____ 19 ___

𝔇𝔢𝔪𝔞𝔫𝔡 𝔣𝔬𝔯 𝔄𝔯𝔟𝔦𝔱𝔯𝔞𝔱𝔦𝔬𝔫—𝔒𝔫𝔢 𝔄𝔯𝔟𝔦𝔱𝔯𝔞𝔱𝔬𝔯

TO:

YOU WILL PLEASE TAKE NOTICE that the undersigned hereby demands arbitration of the dispute(s) herein raised pursuant to the terms of the agreement dated _____ , two (2) copies of which are attached hereto. Arbitration is demanded upon the issue(s) enumerated in the following statement of complaint.

Statement of Complaint

_____

_____

_____

_____

_____

Nature of Claim or Relief Sought

_____

_____

_____

_____

_____

Dated this _____ day of _____ , 19 _____ .

(Signed) _____

Title _____

_____
Name of Claimant

_____
Street Address

_____
   City   *State*   *Zip*

CERTIFICATE OF SERVICE

I hereby certify that a copy of the foregoing was mailed this _____ day of _____ , 19 _____ , postage prepaid, via United States registered mail, return receipt requested, to:

_____

_____

_____

(Signed) _____

Demand for Arbitration

TO

Dated _____ 19 ___

Guidelines for Arbitration—One Arbitrator

AGREEMENT OF PARTIES

The undersigned hereby agree that the dispute they are submitting to arbitration shall be arbitrated according to the following guidelines as a part of their arbitration agreement dated _____.

INITIATION OF ARBITRATION

The complaining party shall give notice of his or her intent to seek arbitration by forwarding a **Demand for Arbitration** via United States certified mail, return receipt requested, to the defending party, which shall include a **statement of complaint** and a description of the **claim or relief sought.**

NAMING OF ARBITRATOR

Within ten (10) days of the date of the defending party's receipt of the **Demand for Arbitration**, the parties of this agreement shall select and agree to equally and mutually pay an Arbitrator. In the event the parties are unable to agree upon a mutually satisfactory Arbitrator within the specified time, they agree to accept an Arbitrator named by the appropriate court of jurisdiction.

ORDER OF PROCEEDINGS

1. The arbitration hearings shall be held at a time and place designated by the Arbitrator within the framework of these guidelines.
2. The hearings shall be held in the presence of the complaining and defending parties and their counsel, if any.
3. At the opening of the hearings the Arbitrator may ask for statements to clarify the issues involved.
4. The complaining party shall then present his or her claim, exhibits and witnesses, who shall be subject to question and/or other examination.
5. The defending party shall then present his or her defense, exhibits and witnesses, who shall be subject to question and/or other examination.
6. Upon determining that both parties, and/or their counsel, have presented all statements, briefs, exhibits and witnesses, the Arbitrator shall declare the hearings closed and shall then consider the evidence and render his or her decision in a timely manner.

LOCALE

The hearings shall be held in the county and state of the appropriate court of jurisdiction.

DATE AND TIME

The Arbitrator shall set the date and time of each hearing.

EVIDENCE AND EXHIBITS

Exhibits submitted by either party may be received in evidence by the Arbitrator, who shall determine the relevance and materiality of the exhibits presented.

OATHS

Either party may require that oaths be administered to all persons giving testimony, provided that the requesting party shall bear the expense of the taking and recording of oaths.

INSPECTION

Whenever the Arbitrator may so decide, he or she shall set a date and time and shall advise both parties of his or her intent to inspect any locale, building or other physical evidence relevant and material to the hearings. In the event that either party cannot be present, the Arbitrator shall make a verbal or written report to both parties and invite their comment.

CUSTODY OF EVIDENCE AND EXHIBITS

The Arbitrator shall direct the safekeeping of all evidence and exhibits.

ADJOURNMENTS

The Arbitrator may adjourn the hearings upon the request of either party, or upon his or her own initiative.

RECORD OF HEARINGS

A stenographic record of the hearings may be made and shall be paid for by the party requesting the record.

Tape recordings of the hearings shall also be permitted, and the cost of the recordings shall be paid for by the party requesting or making them.

COMMUNICATION WITH THE ARBITRATOR

There shall be no communication by either party with the Arbitrator other than at the hearings, except to advise the Arbitrator of a party's inability to attend a scheduled hearing or to request an adjournment of the hearings.

REOPENING OF HEARINGS

The hearings may be reopened by the Arbitrator upon his or her own initiative, or upon the motion of either party, any time before the award is made.

TIME OF AWARD

The award must be made no later than thirty (30) days after the closing of the hearings.

FORM OF AWARD

The award must be in writing and signed by the Arbitrator and shall be executed in the manner prescribed by law.

SCOPE OF THE AWARD

The Arbitrator may award real and/or punitive damages, the specific performance of a contract, the assessment of arbitration fees and expenses, or may grant any other award which could lawfully be handed down by the appropriate court of jurisdiction.

DELIVERY OF THE AWARD

Delivery of the award by the Arbitrator shall be deemed to have been accomplished within ten (10) days after forwarding the award via United States registered mail, return receipt requested, to the last known address of each party, by service of the award, or by filing the award in any manner prescribed by law.

APPLICATION TO COURT

Both parties to the arbitration agree that judgment upon the arbitration award may be entered in the appropriate court of jurisdiction.

INTERPRETATION AND APPLICATION OF ARBITRATION GUIDELINES

The Arbitrator shall interpret and apply the above guidelines.

WE, THE UNDERSIGNED, having read and understood the above arbitration guidelines, hereby agree to make them a part of our arbitration agreement, and further agree to abide by said guidelines.

(Signed) _____

(Signed) _____

Dated _____

FORM 29.3 / F198

Guidelines for Arbitration

Agreed to Between

and

Dated _____ 19 ____

Agreement for Submission of an Existing Dispute to Arbitration—Three Arbitrators

We, the undersigned, hereby agree to submit to arbitration the following dispute:

_____

_____

_____

_____

_____

Selection of Arbitrators

We further agree that each party to the aforementioned dispute shall name one Arbitrator and shall pay that Arbitrator. An Umpire shall be chosen by the Arbitrators within ten (10) days of the signing of this agreement. In the event the Arbitrators shall be unable to agree upon an Umpire, one shall be named by the appropriate court of jurisdiction. The cost of the Umpire shall be borne equally by the parties to the dispute.

Costs

The costs of arbitration, apart from the costs of Arbitrators, shall be borne equally by the parties to the dispute, provided that fees paid to expert witnesses, and the costs of travel, laboratory tests, etc., shall be borne by the party incurring them.

Procedure

The Arbitrators shall hear and attempt to resolve the dispute in a timely manner, and the written decision of any two shall be binding equally upon all parties to the dispute. Unless otherwise agreed to by the parties, the arbitration shall be conducted in the county and state of the appropriate court of jurisdiction, in accordance with the guidelines accepted by the parties and in conformance with accepted rules governing the admission of evidence in courts of law.

Award

Judgment upon award rendered by the Arbitrators may be entered in the appropriate court of jurisdiction.

IN WITNESS WHEREOF, we, the parties hereto, hereby set our hands and seals this date.

(Signed) _____

(Signed) _____

Dated _____

Agreement for Arbitration

BETWEEN

and

Dated ——————————— 19 ——

Demand for Arbitration—Three Arbitrators

TO:

    YOU WILL PLEASE TAKE NOTICE that the undersigned hereby demands arbitration of the dispute(s) herein raised pursuant to the terms of the agreement dated _____, two (2) copies of which are attached hereto. Arbitration is demanded upon the issue(s) enumerated in the following statement of complaint.

Statement of Complaint

_____

_____

_____

_____

_____

Nature of Claim or Relief Sought

_____

_____

_____

_____

_____

    PLEASE TAKE FURTHER NOTICE that under provisions of the above-referenced agreement I have named as my selection for Arbitrator:

First Name	Middle	Last

Street Address

City	State	Zip	Phone

    Please instruct the Arbitrator of your choice to contact the above-named individual in a timely manner so that an Umpire may be selected by our two Arbitrators within ten (10) days of your receipt of this **Demand for Arbitration**.

FORM 29.5/F202

Dated this _____ day of _____, 19 _____.

(Signed) _____

Title _____

_____
Name of Claimant

_____
Street Address

_____
City   *State*   *Zip*

* *

CERTIFICATE OF SERVICE

I hereby certify that a copy of the foregoing was mailed this _____ day of _____, 19 _____, postage prepaid, via United States registered mail, return receipt requested, to:

_____

_____

_____

(Signed) _____

Demand for Arbitration

TO

Dated _____ 19 ___

Guidelines for Arbitration—Three Arbitrators

AGREEMENT OF PARTIES

The undersigned hereby agree that the dispute they are submitting to arbitration shall be arbitrated according to the following guidelines as a part of their arbitration agreement dated _____.

INITIATION OF ARBITRATION

The complaining party shall give notice of his or her intent to seek arbitration **by** forwarding a **Demand for Arbitration** via United States certified mail, return receipt requested, to the defending party, which shall include a **statement of complaint** and a description of the **claim or relief sought.**

NAMING OF ARBITRATORS

The name and address of the Arbitrator chosen by the complaining party shall **be** included in the **Demand for Arbitration**. Within ten (10) days of receipt of the **Demand for Arbitration**, the defending party shall select and inform the complaining party via United States certified mail, return receipt requested, of the name and address of the Arbitrator chosen by the defending party so that the Arbitrators chosen by each party may select an Umpire (third Arbitrator) within ten (10) days of receipt by the complaining party of the name and address of the Arbitrator chosen by the defending party.

ORDER OF PROCEEDINGS

1. The arbitration hearings shall be held at a time and place designated by the Umpire within the framework of these guidelines.

2. The hearings shall be held in the presence of the complaining and defending parties and their counsel, if any.

3. At the opening of the hearings the Umpire and/or the Arbitrators chosen **by** either party may ask for statements to clarify the issues involved.

4. The complaining party shall then present his or her claim, exhibits and witnesses, who shall be subject to question and/or other examination.

5. The defending party shall then present his or her defense, exhibits and witnesses, who shall be subject to question and/or other examination.

6. Upon determining that both parties, and/or their counsel, have presented all statements, briefs, exhibits and witnesses, the Arbitrators shall declare the hearings closed and shall then consider the evidence and render their decision in a timely manner.

LOCALE

The hearings shall be held in the county and state of the appropriate court of jurisdiction.

DATE AND TIME

The Umpire shall set the date and time of each hearing.

EVIDENCE AND EXHIBITS

Exhibits submitted by either party may be received in evidence by the Arbitrators, a majority of whom shall determine the relevance and materiality of the exhibits presented.

OATHS

Either party may require that oaths be administered to all persons giving testimony, provided that the requesting party shall bear the expense of the taking and recording of oaths.

INSPECTION

Whenever the Arbitrators may so decide, they shall set a date and time and shall advise both parties of their intent to inspect any locale, building or other physical evidence relevant and material to the hearings. In the event that either party cannot be present, the Umpire shall make a verbal or written report to both parties and invite their comment.

CUSTODY OF EVIDENCE AND EXHIBITS

The Umpire shall direct the safekeeping of all evidence and exhibits.

ADJOURNMENTS

The Umpire may adjourn the hearings upon the request of either party, or upon his own initiative.

DECISION OF ARBITRATORS

Any decision of the Arbitrators must be by at least a majority.

RECORD OF HEARINGS

A stenographic record of the hearings may be made and shall be paid for by the party requesting the record.

Tape recordings of the hearings shall also be permitted, and the cost of the recordings shall be paid for by the party requesting or making them.

COMMUNICATION WITH THE UMPIRE AND ARBITRATORS

There shall be no communication by either party with the Umpire or Arbitrators other than at hearings, except to advise the Umpire or an Arbitrator of a party's inability to attend a scheduled hearing or to request an adjournment of the hearings.

REOPENING OF HEARINGS

The hearings may be reopened by the Arbitrators upon their own initiative, or upon the motion of either party, any time before the award is made.

AWARD BY ARBITRATORS

Any and all awards by the Arbitrators must be by at least a majority.

TIME OF AWARD

The award must be made no later than thirty (30) days after the closing of the hearings.

FORM OF AWARD

The award must be in writing and signed by a majority of the Arbitrators and shall be executed in the manner prescribed by law.

SCOPE OF AWARD

The Arbitrators may award real and/or punitive damages, the specific performance of a contract, the assessment of arbitration fees and expenses, or may grant any other award which could lawfully be handed down by an appropriate court of jurisdiction.

DELIVERY OF THE AWARD

Delivery of the award by the Arbitrators shall be deemed to have been accomplished within ten (10) days after forwarding the award via United States registered mail, return receipt requested, to the last known address of each party, by service of the award, or by filing the award in any manner prescribed by law.

APPLICATION TO COURT

Both parties to the arbitration agree that judgment upon the arbitration award may be entered in the appropriate court of jurisdiction.

INTERPRETATION AND APPLICATION OF ARBITRATION GUIDELINES

The Umpire shall interpret and apply the above guidelines.

WE, THE UNDERSIGNED, having read and understood the above arbitration guidelines, hereby agree to make them a part of our arbitration agreement, and further agree to abide by said guidelines.

(Signed) _____

(Signed) _____

Date _____

FORM 29.6 / F206

Guidelines for Arbitration

Agreed to Between

and

Dated _____ 19 ___

Agreement Using One Arbitrator

ARBITRATION

Any dispute or claim arising out of this agreement, or any breach thereof, shall be submitted to arbitration at the option of any party thereto. The **Demand for Arbitration** shall be filed in writing and forwarded by United States registered mail, return receipt requested, by the complaining party.

Selection of Arbitrator

The parties to the dispute shall select and equally pay an Arbitrator. In the event the parties are unable to agree upon an Arbitrator within ten (10) days of the defending party's receipt of the **Demand for Arbitration**, an Arbitrator shall be named by the appropriate court of jurisdiction.

Costs

The costs of arbitration, apart from the cost of the Arbitrator, shall be borne equally by the parties to the dispute, provided that fees paid to expert witnesses and costs of travel, laboratory tests, etc., shall be borne by the party incurring them.

Procedure

The Arbitrator shall hear and attempt to resolve the dispute in a timely manner, and the written decision of the Arbitrator shall be binding equally upon all parties to the dispute. Unless otherwise agreed to by the parties, the arbitration shall be conducted in the county and state of the appropriate court of jurisdiction, in accordance with the guidelines accepted by the parties and in conformance with accepted rules governing the admission of evidence in courts of law.

Award

Judgment upon award rendered by the Arbitrator may be entered in the appropriate court of jurisdiction.

Agreement Using Three Arbitrators

ARBITRATION

Any dispute or claim arising out of this agreement, or any breach thereof, shall be submitted to arbitration at the option of any party thereto. The **Demand for Arbitration** shall be filed in writing and forwarded by United States registered mail, return receipt requested, by the complaining party.

Selection of Arbitrators

Each party shall name one Arbitrator and shall pay this Arbitrator. An Umpire shall be chosen by the Arbitrators within ten (10) days after delivery of the written **Demand for Arbitration**. In the event the Arbitrators shall be unable to agree upon an Umpire, one shall be named by the appropriate court of jurisdiction. The cost of the Umpire shall be borne equally by the parties to the dispute.

Costs

The costs of arbitration, apart from the costs of Arbitrators, shall be borne equally by the parties to the dispute, provided that fees paid to expert witnesses and costs of travel, laboratory tests, etc., shall be borne by the party incurring them.

Procedure

The Arbitrators shall hear and attempt to resolve the dispute in a timely manner, and the written decision of any two shall be binding equally upon all parties to the dispute. Unless otherwise agreed to by the parties, the arbitration shall be conducted in the county and state of the appropriate court of jurisdiction, in accordance with the guidelines accepted by the parties and in conformance with accepted rules governing the admission of evidence in courts of law.

Award

Judgment upon award rendered by the Arbitrators may be entered in the appropriate court of jurisdiction.

IN THE MATTER FOR
ARBITRATION BETWEEN

)
)
)
)
)
)
)
and   )
)
)
)
)
)
)
)
)

𝔓etition for the 𝔄ppointment of 𝔄rbitrator

In accordance with the **Agreement for Arbitration** between them dated _____,
a copy of which is attached hereto, the parties ask the honorable Court to enter an order appointing an Arbitrator, a citizen of this state, who shall be vested by the Court with the power and authority, and charged with the duty, to hear their dispute, to determine the issues between them and to enter an award disposing of the issues thereto.
  The fee of the Arbitrator shall be paid equally by the parties to the dispute.

We ask for this:

_____   _____

Petition for Appointment of Arbitrator

TO

Dated ——————————— 19 ———

Comparison Shopping Checklist

Date _____

Retailer/Seller's Name _____

Street Address _____ City _____ State _____ Zip _____

Salesperson's Name _____ Title _____ Department _____

Owner or Manager's Name _____

Product or Service _____

Brand _____ Model No. _____ Name _____ Quality Level _____

Tested in Store? _____ Serial No. _____

Delivery Promised _____
Date   Time

Delivered _____
Date   Time

Installation Promised _____
Date   Time

Installed _____
Date   Time

Tested OK upon Delivery or Installation? _____

Use the following space to note specific product features such as capacity, power requirements, size, etc.:

_____

_____

_____

_____

_____

FORM 33.1 / F214

Attach or note the following and keep on file together with the **Warranty Comparison Checklist** for the product purchased:

Payment Receipt _____   Manufacturer Ads _____

Invoice _____   Seller Ads _____

Finance Agreement _____   Brochures _____

Manufacturer Warranty _____   Owner's Manual _____

Seller Warranty _____   Salesperson's Card _____

Sales Agreement _____   Care Instructions _____

Canceled Check _____   Credit Card/Charge Slip _____

Warranty Comparison Checklist

1. _____
   Name of Manufacturer

2. _____
   Product or Service

3. _____
   Model No. or Service Quality Level

4. _____
   Name and Address of Seller

5. _____
   Salesperson   *Department*   *Phone*

6. _____
   Is Warranty Text Readily Available in Store?

7. _____
   Is Warranty Text in Mail-Order Catalog or Offered by Seller?

8. _____
   Who Is the Warrantor?

9. _____
   Full or Limited Warranty?

10. _____
    Duration of Full Warranty (Portion)?

11. _____
    Duration of Limited Warranty (Portion)?

12. _____
    Any Additional Guarantees?

13. _____
    What Parts/Components Are Covered?

14. _____
    What Parts/Components Are Excluded?

15. _____
    Any Special Conditions or Limitations?

16. _____
    To Whom Is the Warranty Extended?

17. _____
    When Does Warranty Date Commence?

18. _____
    What Are Your Obligations Under the Warranty?

19. _____
    Is Return of Registration Card a Precondition to Receiving Warranty Service?

20. _____
    Who Do You Notify to Obtain Warranty Service?

21. _____
    Who Authorizes Exchange or Refund?

22. _____
    Any Charge for Warranty Service?

23. _____
    Any Limitation upon Your Warranty Rights?

24. _____
    Is There a Requirement That You Utilize an Industry-related "Consumer Action Panel" Prior to Taking Legal Action?

_____

_____

_____

Notice of Revocation of Acceptance

Notice of Revocation of Acceptance

IN THE MATTER OF

TO

Dated ———————— 19 ——

Federal Trade Commission

Cleveland Regional Office

Suite 500
The Mall Building
118 St. Clair Avenue
Cleveland, Ohio 44114
Area Code (216) 522-4207

GENERAL MOTORS CORPORATION INVESTIGATION

Because of the national publicity concerning this office's inquiry into certain problems consumers have with General Motors cars, we have received many phone calls and letters. This has made it impossible to handle all questions individually.

If you would like to submit to us your experience with a General Motors car, we would greatly appreciate it. A form and envelope has been enclosed for your convenience. If you attach documents to the complaint form, do not attach originals: photocopies only, please.

You should be aware, however, that we cannot assist you individually with regard to your car. There are just too many complaints, and Congress did not intend the Federal Trade Commission to resolve individual disputes between consumers and businesses. Our role is to achieve broad remedies for identified legal violations that will affect the public in general. Thus, we need information that you can supply through the form we have enclosed.

If you have a dispute with General Motors, there are steps that you can take to resolve it yourself. First, car companies sometimes pay for repairs after the warranty period ends. This payment may depend on how persistent you are and on how well you have kept records on your problem. The car dealership is usually not authorized to make such decisions to pay. Therefore, you may wish to talk to the car company's representative, sometimes called a "service representative" or "zone representative," about your problem. The telephone number is usually in your owner's manual or in the telephone book under the company name.

If this step does not work, you may wish to consider legal action. You could consider small claims court, where you can sue without a lawyer. Or, you can consult a lawyer. You may also wish to write for a book put out by the Attorney General of Maine, which explains some of the rights of car owners. Write to: Richard S. Cohen, Attorney General, State House, Consumer Protection Division, Augusta, Maine 04333.

You should always save your papers and records. Write down the names of the people or companies with whom you communicate in trying to resolve your problem. You may need this later to prove what happened.

GENERAL MOTORS CORPORATION

File No. 792 3042

1. PERSONAL IDENTIFICATION.

Your Name: _____

Address: _____

_____ ZIP Code: _____

Home Phone: (Area Code _____) _____ Business Phone: _____

2. AUTOMOBILE IDENTIFICATION

Make of Car: _____ Model of Car: _____

Year of Car: _____ Car Purchased: NEW [] USED []

Dealer's Name
and Address: _____

_____

_____ ZIP Code: _____

TRANSMISSION:
Engine Size: _____ No. Cylinders: _____ Automatic [] Manual []

Transmission Name
and/or Series (if known): _____

<u>GENERAL MOTORS CORPORATION</u>

File No. 792 3042

3.   PROBLEM IDENTIFICATION

Part of the car with a problem: _____

Mileage at which the   Age of the Car at which
Problem First Occurred: _____   Problem First Occurred: _____

Was the car under warranty at the time the problem first occurred? YES [] NO []

Please describe (a) the problem in detail, (b) who you have contacted to fix the
problem, (c) whether or not the problem has been adequately repaired:

_____

_____

_____

_____

_____

_____

_____

_____

_____

_____

_____

_____

_____

_____

(If you need additional space or wish to make other comments, please use the back of this
form. If you wish to attach documents, attach photocopies only; save your originals.)

FORM 37.1/F222

GENERAL MOTORS CORPORATION

File No. 792 3042

4. ADDITIONAL INFORMATION

What was the cost to you for repairs? _____

Did the dealer or GM cover any of the cost?   YES []   GM []
                                           NO []   DEALER []

    If YES, do you know how much? _____

Please provide the names and titles of people that you dealt with from GM and
the dealer:

_____

_____

_____

_____

_____

_____

PRIVACY ACT DISCLOSURE STATEMENT

The Federal Trade Commission Act is the authority for collecting the above
information. The principal purpose for which this information is intended
is to assist in determining whether companies are violating the Federal
Trade Commission Act. The routine uses which may be made of the information
are: to determine whether any law enforcement or other actions by the Federal
Trade Commission may be warranted; to refer matters to other federal, state,
or local government agencies where the matter comes within their jurisdictions;
to respond to correspondence. Providing the information requested is voluntary.
There is no effect on the individual for not providing all or any part of the
requested information.

Consumer Complaint Report

Date _____

TO: Federal Trade Commission
          Office of the Secretary
          Correspondence Branch
          Room 701
          6th Street and Pennsylvania Avenue, N.W.
          Washington, DC 20580

FROM:

Brief description of the product or service: _____

_____

_____

_____

_____

Model number or code number on the article or package, if a product: _____

Manufacturer, if a product: _____

_____

_____

Seller of the product or service: _____

_____

_____

When was the product or service purchased? _____

BE SURE TO INCLUDE YOUR COMPLETE NAME AND ADDRESS FOLLOWING "FROM" ABOVE. KEEP A COPY OF THIS FORM FOR YOUR RECORDS.

FORM 37.2/F224

Please describe the problem you encountered with the product or service: _____

_____

_____

_____

_____

_____

_____

Your telephone number: _____

Consumer Questionnaire

TO: Interstate Commerce Commission
12th Street and Constitution Avenue, N.W.
Washington, DC 20423

    Attn: Household Goods Branch
          Bureau of Operations

I, _____ , recently made an interstate move from _____
City or Town and State

_____ to _____ . My household goods were picked up by
City or Town and State

_____ . The number of the bill of lading issued on my shipment
Name of Mover or Mover's Agent

was _____ and the mover's number was ICC-MC No. _____ .

	Yes	No
1. Did you receive Form BOp 103, Summary of Information for Shippers of Household Goods, before signing an order for service?	___	___
2. Was your shipment picked up within the agreed dates on the bill of lading?	___	___
3. Was the tare (preloading) weight entered on your copy of the bill of lading before your shipment was loaded?	___	___
4. Did you go to the scale and view the weighing of your shipment?	___	___
5. Were you given copies of two weight tickets obtained on your shipment?	___	___
6. a. Did you request that your shipment be reweighed?	___	___
b. Was it done?	___	___
7. If so, was the weight of your shipment on reweigh lower than the original weight?	___	___
8. Was your shipment delivered by the same carrier that picked it up?	___	___
9. Was your shipment delivered within the agreed dates on the bill of lading?	___	___
10. If your shipment was delivered late, were you notified by the carrier of the reason for the delay and location and condition of your shipment?	___	___
11. Did you furnish the carrier with a destination address and/or phone number or point of contact?	___	___
12. Did you request assistance from an ICC field office?	___	___
13. Was the total of your transportation charges within 10% above or below the estimate of those charges made by your mover?	___	___
14. a. Were any of your goods lost or damaged?	___	___
b. If so, have you filed or do you plan to file a claim for loss or damage with your mover?	___	___
c. If you have filed, has your mover acknowledged receipt of your claim in writing?	___	___
15. Was your move satisfactory?	___	___
16. Was your move paid for by		
a. the Department of Defense?	___	___
b. your employer?	___	___
c. yourself?	___	___

Additional Comments: _____

_____

_____

_____

_____

Date _____

Name _____

Address _____

_____

NOTE: If your moving experience has given you an idea as to how service can be improved, please write and tell us about it.

U.S. CONSUMER PRODUCT SAFETY COMMISSION
Consumer Product Complaint Form

To: Consumer Product Safety Commission
5401 Westbard Avenue
Bethesda, MD 20207

1. NAME OF ARTICLE OR A BRIEF DESCRIPTION: _____

_____

_____

2. STOCK OR CODE NUMBERS ON ARTICLE OR PACKAGE: _____

_____

3. COUNTRY OF ORIGIN (IF IMPORTED): _____

_____

4. MANUFACTURER OR IMPORTER (IF KNOWN): _____

_____

5. WHERE AND WHEN WAS THE ARTICLE PURCHASED? _____

_____

6. WHAT IS HAZARDOUS ABOUT THIS PRODUCT? _____

_____

_____

_____

7. YOUR NAME, ADDRESS, AND PHONE NUMBER: _____

_____

_____

_____

8. DATE: _____

Telephone Log

Nature of Problem _____

Name of Seller _____

First Call

Date _____ Time _____

Number Called _____ Department _____ Ext. _____

Name of Person You Spoke with _____ Title _____

What He/She Told You: _____

_____

What You Then Said/Did: _____

_____

Name of Person to Whom You Were Referred _____ Title _____

Phone Number _____ Department _____ Title _____

Address _____

_____

Second Call

Date _____ Time _____

Number Called _____ Department _____ Ext. _____

Name of Person You Spoke with _____ Title _____

What He/She Told You: _____

_____

What You Then Said/Did: _____

_____

Name of Person to Whom You Were Referred _____ Title _____

Phone Number _____ Department _____ Title _____

Address _____

_____

FORM 38.2/F230

Third Call

Date _____ Time _____

Number Called _____ Department _____ Ext. _____

Name of Person You Spoke with _____ Title _____

What He/She Told You: _____

_____

What You Then Said/Did: _____

_____

Name of Person to Whom You Were Referred _____ Title _____

Phone Number _____ Department _____ Title _____

Address _____

_____

Comments: _____

_____

_____

Status Date of Last Contact with Seller: _____

_____

_____

Summons and Complaint

STATE OF NEW BEDFORD

COUNTY OF PUTNAM   TO:

YOU ARE HEREBY SUMMONED to appear and state your defense to the annexed complaint of:

Plaintiff, in a civil action, Small Claims Division, of Putnam County District Court, to be held at the Putnam County Courthouse, 101 Courthouse Square, Sommerton, N.B.

TAKE NOTICE that unless you appear before the court on _____ at _____, a judgment by default may be entered against you for the money damages demanded in the statement of claim. If this occurs, your wages or bank account may be attached or withheld, or any personal property owned by you may be taken and sold to pay the judgment.

Hon. _____

Presiding Judge, Putnam County District Court at Sommerton

_____

Attorney or Plaintiff

_____

Address

_____

City / Township   Zip

_____

Clerk or Deputy Clerk

(Bring this **Summons and Complaint** with you at all times.)

FORM 40.1/F232

PUTNAM COUNTY DISTRICT COURT, DIVISION OF SMALL CLAIMS
101 Courthouse Square, Sommerton, N.B. 10560

Plaintiff _____   vs.   Defendant _____

Address _____   Address _____

Township _____ Zip   Township _____ Zip

....

No. _____

STATEMENT OF CLAIM

Judgment will be claimed in the sum of $ _____ together with interest and costs of suit.

STATE OF NEW BEDFORD)
) ss:
COUNTY OF PUTNAM   )

_____, Plaintiff, being duly sworn on oath, says the foregoing is a just and true statement of the amount owed by the Defendant to said Plaintiff.

_____
Plaintiff

_____
Attorney for Plaintiff (if any)

_____
Address

_____
Township   Zip

Subscribed and sworn to before me this _____ of _____, 19 _____.

_____
Deputy Clerk/Notary Public

My appointment/commission expires: _____.

INSTRUCTIONS TO DEFENDANT(S)

You may come with or without a lawyer. The Statement of Claim indicates whether the Plaintiff has a lawyer. If the Plaintiff does have a lawyer and you wish either to dispute the claim or to attempt to arrange a compromise settlement, it would be in your best interest to have your own lawyer.

If you wish to have legal advice and feel that you cannot afford to pay an attorney, you may contact the Putnam County Legal Aid Society, 751-1775, or the New Bedford University Law Students in Court Project, 387-7000, to ask for help. Act promptly.

If it is impossible for you to appear on the date set for trial, notify the Clerk of the Division of Small Claims in person or by phone, 569-4189. The Clerk will assist you in requesting a new date. In arranging this new date you may wish to consider that the court holds sessions on weekdays at 10:00 A.M., Thursday evenings at 6:30 P.M., and Saturday mornings at 9:00 A.M. If you do not appear on the new date, judgment may be entered against you.

If you have witnesses, photographs, receipts, writings or other evidence bearing upon this claim, you should bring them with you at the time of the hearing.

If you wish to have witnesses summoned, contact the Clerk at once for assistance.

If you admit the claim but desire additional time to pay, you must come to the hearing in person and state your circumstances to the court.

A CORPORATION MAY APPEAR ONLY THROUGH AN ATTORNEY.

(Bring this **Summons and Complaint** with you at all times.)

I served the within **Summons and Complaint** _____ on _____ said defendant by giving (him) (her) a copy thereof.

_____
Sheriff/Deputy

The said defendant not being found, I served the **Summons and Complaint** by _____ leaving a copy thereof at the place of abode with a competent person residing therein, of the age of sixteen years or more.

_____
Sheriff/Deputy

I served the within **Summons and Complaint** _____ on _____ (she) being the _____ , (he) of _____ said _____ , by giving (him) (her) a copy thereof.

_____
Sheriff/Deputy

the _____ , being said _____ of _____ and (he) (she) not being found, I served the **Summons and Complaint** by _____ leaving a copy thereof at the abode or place of business with a competent person of the age of sixteen years or more.

_____
Sheriff/Deputy

No. _____

Summons and Complaint

vs.

Amount of Claim $ _____

Dated _____ 19 ____

Returnable _____ 19 ____

STATE OF NEW BEDFORD

𝕬pplication for 𝕾ubpoena

———————————————————————, 19 ————

TO: Hon. JUDGE of the
———————————————— County District Court
Division of Small Claims

vs.

No. ————————————————————

    I HEREBY REQUEST that you issue a subpoena for each of the following witnesses, represented to reside within the jurisdiction of said court where the suit above described is pending.

Name	County	Address	D.O.S.*

Such subpoena(s) to be made returnable no later than the ———————— day of ———————————, 19 ————.

(Signed) ————————————————————————

† ————————————————————————

*Date of subpoena to be filled in by clerk of the court.

†Show Plaintiff, Defendant, or Attorney for Plaintiff or Defendant.

No. _____

Application
for
Subpoena

vs.

_____ Court

_____ County, New Bedford

Filed _____ day of _____, 19 ___

(Bring this **Subpoena** with you at all times.)

STATE OF NEW BEDFORD

𝕾ubpoena 𝕯uces 𝕿ecum

No. _____

_____ vs. _____

TO ANY SHERIFF, CONSTABLE OR OTHER PERSON WHO IS NOT A PARTY AND WHO IS NOT LESS THAN EIGHTEEN YEARS OF AGE, A CITIZEN OF THE STATE OF NEW BEDFORD, GREETING:

YOU ARE HEREBY COMMANDED TO SUMMON _____

_____

to be and personally appear at _____ o'clock, ____M., on the _____ day of _____, 19 ____;
before the HONORABLE JUDGE of the District Court, Division of Small Claims, _____ County, New Bedford, held within said county at the courthouse thereof, _____
_____, New Bedford, then and there to testify and say the truth on behalf of the _____
in the above-styled and -numbered case, now pending before said Court, and there to remain from day to day, and from term to term, until discharged by said Court.

Said named witness is further commanded to produce at said time and place above, as now set forth, the following books, papers, documents and/or other tangible things, to wit:

HEREIN FAIL NOT, and make due return thereof, showing how you have executed same.

Issued and given under my hand and seal of said Court at office, this _____ day of _____, 19 ____.

Clerk _____

_____ County, New Bedford

By _____
Deputy

RETURN

Came to hand the _____ day of _____, 19 ____, at _____ o'clock ____M., and executed the
_____ day of _____, 19 ____, at _____ o'clock ____M., by delivering to the within-named
witness at _____ in _____ County, New Bedford, in person, a true copy of this Subpoena.

(Signed) _____

* _____

*Show Sheriff, Constable, Marshal or Citizen.

ACCEPTANCE OF SERVICE

The undersigned witness named in the Subpoena acknowledges receipt of a copy thereof and hereby accepts and waives service of such Subpoena.

(Signed) _____

_____
Date

RETURN ORIGINAL TO CLERK OF THE COURT
(Bring this **Subpoena** with you at all times.)

No. _____

Subpoena
Duces Tecum

vs.

Issued _____ 19 ____

_____ *Clerk*

_____ *Court*

_____ *County, New Bedford*

By _____ *Deputy Clerk*

Agreement

IN ACCORDANCE with the terms set forth herein,

_____, Plaintiff, and _____

_____, Defendant, in the action of _____vs. _____

_____, Docket No. _____, in _____

_____, agree that the above action between them is

hereby settled without trial for the sum of $ _____ to be paid by the Defendant to the Plaintiff _____

_____.

    It is further agreed that prior to the date for trial the Plaintiff shall advise the court of this Agreement and discontinue the above action.

    The Plaintiff shall have the right, in the event of default of payment of the above sum, to collect same from the Defendant, in addition to court costs, interest and reasonable attorney's fees.

_____
                                     Plaintiff

_____
                                     Defendant

Dated _____, 19 _____.

STATE OF NEW BEDFORD

No. _____

_____)
Plaintiff   )   PUTNAM COUNTY DISTRICT COURT
)
)   DIVISION OF SMALL CLAIMS
)
        vs.   )
)   101 Courthouse Square
)
_____)   Sommerton, N.B. 10560
Defendant

𝕯eclaration and 𝕹otice of 𝕸otion
to 𝖁acate 𝕵udgment

    WHEREAS I, the undersigned Defendant in the above-styled action; that on _____
judgment was entered against me; I was not present at the trial and did not notify the court before trial that I could not be
present because:

_____

_____

_____

    I believe I can prove to the Court that the facts support my defense, to wit: _____

_____

_____

_____

_____

    WHEREFORE, I request that said judgment against me be vacated and the case be tried on its merits.
I declare under penalty of perjury that the aforesaid statements are true and correct.

                     (Signed) _____
                                                       Defendant

Executed this _____ day of _____, 19 _____.

NOTICE OF MOTION

To: _____

    _____

    _____

PLEASE TAKE NOTICE that on the _____ day of _____, 19 _____, _____
_____ will move the Court for an order vacating the judgment heretofore entered in
this case and for trial forthwith.

_____
Signature of Moving Party

Dated this _____ day of _____, 19 _____.

* *

COURT ORDER

The above motion is hereby _____, and trial is set for the _____ day
of _____, 19 _____.

_____
Judge
PUTNAM COUNTY DISTRICT COURT

Dated this _____ day of _____, 19 _____.

No. _____

Declaration and Notice of Motion

vs.

19 _____

Dated

STATE OF NEW BEDFORD

No. _____

In the PUTNAM COUNTY DISTRICT COURT, DIVISION OF SMALL CLAIMS:

_____)
Plaintiff)
)
)
)
vs.)
)
)
)
_____)
Defendant

𝔓etition for 𝔚rit of 𝔈xecution

TO THE HONORABLE _____, Judge:

YOUR PETITIONER, _____, Plaintiff in the above-styled and -numbered case, respectfully shows Your Honor that on the _____ day of _____, 19 _____, judgment was awarded by the _____ in favor of Your Petitioner against said Defendant in the sum of _____ _____ ($ _____), which amount was due and payable in full on the _____ day of _____, 19 _____; that said judgment has not been satisfied; and that Your Petitioner is entitled to recover said sum.

WHEREFORE Your Petitioner asks for a **Writ of Execution** against the estate, real and personal, of the Defendant, and that sufficient real and personal property of said Defendant be seized and sold to satisfy the claim of Your Petitioner and be applied to the satisfaction thereof.

And Your Petitioner will ever pray, etc.

_____
Plaintiff

* *

CERTIFICATE OF NOTARY

STATE OF NEW BEDFORD)
) ss:
COUNTY OF PUTNAM)

BEFORE ME, the undersigned, on this day personally appeared _____, who, first being duly sworn, made oath that (he) (she) is cognizant of the facts stated in the foregoing petition and that they are true.

GIVEN UNDER MY HAND, this _____ day of _____, 19 _____.

_____
Notary Public

ORDER OF THE COURT

WHEREAS, on this _____ day of _____, 19 _____, came _____
_____, petitioning the Court for a **Writ of Execution** for the reasons set out in said petition, the same having been duly considered, the Court is of the opinion that the reasons stated are good and sufficient to order said **Writ**. It is therefore, considered, adjudged and ordered that the petitioned **Writ** be granted forthwith.

_____
Judge
PUTNAM COUNTY DISTRICT COURT
Division of Small Claims
Sommerton, N.B.

No. _____

Petition for Writ of Execution

vs.

19 _____

Dated _____

STATE OF NEW BEDFORD

Writ of Execution

To Any Sheriff or Constable Within the State of New Bedford, GREETING:

WHEREAS, on the _____ day of _____, 19 _____, in _____

_____,

in case No. _____, _____, Plaintiff vs. _____,

Defendant, _____ recovered a judgment against _____

for the sum of $ _____, with interest thereon from the _____ day of _____,

19 _____, at the rate of _____% per annum, and all costs of suit.

THEREFORE, you are commanded that out of the property of said _____,

subject to execution by law, you cause to be made the sum of $ _____ with interest thereon from the _____

day of _____, 19 _____, at the rate of _____% per annum, together with the sum of $ _____,

cost of suit, and also of executing this Writ and you will forthwith execute this Writ according to law and the mandates thereof.

HEREIN FAIL NOT and have you the said monies, together with this Writ before the said Court at the Courthouse

thereof in _____, New Bedford, showing how you have executed same within

_____ days from the date hereof.

ISSUED AND GIVEN UNDER MY HAND AND SEAL OF SAID COURT at _____,

New Bedford, this _____ day of _____, 19 _____.

(Signed) _____

Clerk _____ Court,

_____, New Bedford

(The Rules of Civil Procedure do not require an execution to show upon its face the number of previous executions that may have been issued on a judgment.)

* *

SHERIFF'S/CONSTABLE'S RETURN

CAME TO HAND the _____ day of _____, 19 _____, and executed at _____

_____ in _____ County, New Bedford, on the _____ day of _____,

19 _____, by levying and seizing upon the following described property of the Defendant, and situated in _____

_____ County, New Bedford, viz:

And afterward, on the _____ day of _____, 19 _____, advertised the same for sale at

the Courthouse door of _____ County, on the _____ day of _____,

19 _____, said advertisement published once a week for three consecutive weeks preceding such sale, starting _____

days previous to such sale, stating in the advertisement the authority by virtue of which such sale was to be made, the time and place of sale and a brief description of the property to be sold; and also delivered or mailed one copy of each advertisement to the within-named Defendant(s); and also delivered or mailed a copy of said notice of sale to _____

_____, the Defendant's attorney of record (if any), in said cause.

AND ON SAID _____ day of _____, 19 _____, between the hours of 10 o'clock A.M. and 4 o'clock P.M., at the Courthouse door of said _____ County, in pursuance to said advertisement, sold said property at public sale for the highest secured bid for same. And after first satisfying the Sheriff's/Constable's costs accruing under this Writ, amounting to the sum of $ _____, and the further sum of $ _____, original Court costs, the remainder being the sum of $ _____, was paid to _____ _____, whose receipt for the same is herewith presented, and this Writ hereby returned on this _____ day of _____, 19 _____.

By _____
Deputy

Sheriff's/Constable's Fees

Executing or Attempting to Execute Writ—Making Return	$ _____
Executing Deeds	$ _____
Executing Bills of Sale	$ _____
Advertising Sale	$ _____
Commissions	$ _____
_____	$ _____
_____	$ _____
TOTAL	$ _____
Original Court Costs	$ _____
TOTAL COSTS	$ _____

No. _____

Writ of Execution

vs.

Issued _____ 19 _____

Filed _____ 19 _____

STATE OF NEW BEDFORD

No. _____

In the PUTNAM COUNTY DISTRICT COURT, DIVISION OF SMALL CLAIMS:

_____)
Plaintiff)
)
)
)
)
vs.)
)
)
)
_____)
Defendant)

𝔓etition for 𝔒rder to 𝔄nswer 𝔚ritten 𝔍nterrogatories

TO THE HONORABLE _____, Judge:

YOUR PETITIONER, _____, Plaintiff in the above-number and -styled case, respectfully shows Your Honor that on the _____ day of _____, 19 ____, judgment was awarded by the _____ in favor of Your Petitioner against said Defendant in the sum of _____ _____ ($ _____), which amount was due and payable in full on the _____ day of _____, 19 ____; that said judgment has not been satisfied; and that Your Petitioner is entitled to recover same.

WHEREFORE Your Petitioner asks that an **Order to Answer Written Interrogatories** be issued by the Court to the Defendant requiring said Defendant to answer questions contained in said Interrogatory in aid of aforesaid judgment against the Defendant.

And Your Petitioner will ever pray, etc.

_____
Plaintiff

* *

CERTIFICATE OF NOTARY

STATE OF NEW BEDFORD)
) ss:
COUNTY OF PUTNAM)

BEFORE ME, the undersigned, on this day personally appeared _____, who, first being duly sworn, made oath that (he) (she) is cognizant of the facts stated in the foregoing petition and that they are true.

GIVEN UNDER MY HAND, this _____ day of _____, 19 ____.

_____
Notary Public

ORDER OF THE COURT

WHEREAS, on this _____ day of _____, 19 ____, came _____
_____, to petition the Court for an Order to answer **Plaintiff's Interrogatories in Aid of Judgment**, for the reasons set out in said petition, the same having been duly considered, the Court is of the opinion that the reasons so stated are good and sufficient to issue said Order.

It is, therefore, considered, adjudged and ordered that the petitioned Order be granted forthwith.

_____
Judge
PUTNAM COUNTY DISTRICT COURT
Division of Small Claims
Sommeton, N.B.

No. _____

Petition for Order to Answer Written Interrogatories

vs.

_____ 19 ____

Dated _____

STATE OF NEW BEDFORD

Summons to Answer Interrogatories

To the Sheriff of _____ County, Greeting:

    WHEREAS, a judgment was rendered in _____ Court on the _____ day of _____, 19 _____, in favor of _____, Plaintiff, against _____, Defendant, for the sum of $ _____ with interest thereon from the _____ day of _____, 19 _____, to accrue at the rate of _____% per annum until paid, and $ _____ costs.

    NOW THEREFORE, upon application of said execution creditor, I command you to summon the said _____ _____, Defendant, to appear before _____, a Commissioner in Chancery of said Court on the _____ day of _____, 19 _____, at _____ o'clock _____M., to answer such interrogatories as may be legally propounded to him or her by the Plaintiff, by counsel for said execution creditor or by said Commissioner, in order to ascertain the estate of the said Defendant, upon which the aforesaid execution is a lien, or any real estate to which said Defendant is entitled.

    Given under my hand, this _____ day of _____, 19 _____.

By _____

(Title) _____

FORM 45.4/F250

No. _____

Summons to Answer Interrogatories

vs.

Returnable _____ 19 ____

Before Commissioner _____

No. _____

_____)
Plaintiff)   PUTNAM COUNTY DISTRICT COURT
)
)   DIVISION OF SMALL CLAIMS
vs.)
)
)   101 Courthouse Square
)
_____)   Sommerton, N.B. 10560
Defendant

Plaintiff's Interrogatories in Aid of Judgment

I, _____ , Judgment Debtor in the above-titled action, first being duly sworn, make the following answers in compliance with a **Summons to Answer Interrogatories**, of the Putnam County District Court, dated the _____ day of _____, 19 _____.

_____
Defendant–Judgment Debtor

FORM 45.5/F252

No. _____

_____)
Plaintiff   )   PUTNAM COUNTY DISTRICT COURT
)
)   DIVISION OF SMALL CLAIMS
          vs.   )
)   101 Courthouse Square
)
_____)   Sommerton, N.B. 10560
Defendant   )

𝕻laintiff's 𝕴nterrogatories in 𝕬id of 𝕵udgment

TO:

Under Rules 171 and 659a, New Bedford Rules of Civil Procedure, you are required to:

(1) answer in complete detail and in writing each or the succeeding interrogatories or questions numbered 1 through 100;

(2) sign your answers to the questions;

(3) swear to the truth of your answers before a notary public or other judicial officer;

(4) deliver a complete, signed, and notarized copy of your answers to the undersigned within 15 days; and

(5) file a true copy of your answers with the clerk of the Court shown above, together with proof of service thereof.

If you fail to comply with the requirements above, the Court may order you held in contempt, fined and confined in jail until you obey all orders of the Court, and pay all additional costs and attorney's fees.

DATED and served as shown below.

By _____

* *

CERTIFICATE OF SERVICE

I certify that a true and correct copy of the foregoing **Plaintiff's Interrogatories in Aid of Judgment** was mailed to the above-named Defendant–Judgment Debtor by certified mail, return receipt requested, this _____ day of _____, 19 _____.

By _____

1. WHAT IS YOUR FULL LEGAL NAME? _____

2. HAVE YOU EVER BEEN KNOWN BY ANY OTHER NAME? If so, state name:

_____

3. DATE OF BIRTH: _____

4. WHAT IS YOUR HOME ADDRESS? _____

_____

5. WHAT TYPE OF PREMISES DO YOU OCCUPY? (Apartment, house, duplex, condominium, motor home, trailer, etc.)

_____

6. WITH WHOM DO YOU LIVE?

Name	*Relationship*
Name	*Relationship*
Name	*Relationship*
Name	*Relationship*
Name	*Relationship*
Name	*Relationship*

7. WHAT IS THE AMOUNT OF THE MONTHLY RENT OR MORTGAGE PAYMENT? $ _____

8. IF PREMISES RENTED OR LEASED, STATE NAME AND ADDRESS OF OWNER OR RENTAL AGENT:

_____
Name of Rental Agent or Owner

_____
Complete Address

9. HOW MUCH SECURITY DEPOSIT DO YOU HAVE WITH THE LANDLORD? $ _____

10. HOW LONG HAVE YOU LIVED THERE? _____

11. ARE YOU NOW OR HAVE YOU EVER BEEN MARRIED? If so, state:

_____
Name of Spouse   *Marriage Date*

Date Widowed or Divorced _____

_____
Present Address of Spouse

FORM 45.5 / F254

Name of Spouse _____ _Marriage Date_

Date Widowed or Divorced _____

Present Address of Spouse _____

12. DO YOU HAVE ANY CHILDREN? If so, state:

Name _____ _Date of Birth_

Present Address _____

Employed _____ Occupation _____

Name _____ _Date of Birth_

Present Address _____

Employed _____ Occupation _____

Name _____ _Date of Birth_

Present Address _____

Employed _____ Occupation _____

Name _____ _Date of Birth_

Present Address _____

Employed _____ Occupation _____

13. WHAT IS YOUR OCCUPATION? _____

14. WHO IS YOUR EMPLOYER? _____

15. COMPLETE ADDRESS OF EMPLOYER: _____

_____

16. WHAT SALARY DO YOU RECEIVE? $ _____ per _____

17. WHAT OTHER INCOME DO YOU RECEIVE FROM THAT EMPLOYMENT? $ _____

18. HOW ARE YOU PAID? (Check, cash, etc.) _____

19. DO YOU HAVE OTHER EMPLOYMENT? _____

20. NAME OF ADDITIONAL EMPLOYER: _____

21. COMPLETE ADDRESS OF ADDITIONAL EMPLOYER: _____

_____

22. WHAT INCOME DO YOU DERIVE FROM THAT ADDITIONAL EMPLOYMENT? $ _____ per _____

23. HAVE YOU BEEN SELF-EMPLOYED OR CONDUCTED A BUSINESS DURING THE PAST TWO YEARS? If so, state:

_____

Trade or Assumed Name

_____

Complete Address

_____

Nature of Business

Income Derived from That Business: $_____ per _____

_____

Trade or Assumed Name

_____

Complete Address

_____

Nature of Business

Income Derived from That Business: $_____ per _____

24. GIVE THE FULL NAME AND ADDRESS OF EACH PERSON WHO ENGAGED IN ANY PARTNERSHIP OR BUSINESS ENTERPRISE WITH YOU:

_____

Name

_____

Address

_____

Name

_____

Address

_____

Name

_____

Address

25. WHAT IS THE PRESENT LOCATION OF ALL FUNDS RECEIVED FROM EMPLOYMENT AND/OR BUSINESS ENTERPRISE IN WHICH YOU ARE OR HAVE BEEN ENGAGED?

_____

_____

_____

_____

26. IF FUNDS RECEIVED FROM YOUR EMPLOYMENT OR BUSINESS ENTERPRISE ARE IN A SAVINGS OR CHECKING ACCOUNT, THEN, FOR EACH ACCOUNT, STATE:

Name of Institution

Complete Address

Account No.   _Present Balance_   _Signatures Authorized_

Name of Institution

Complete Address

Account No.   _Present Balance_   _Signatures Authorized_

Name of Institution

Complete Address

Account No.   _Present Balance_   _Signatures Authorized_

Name of Institution

Complete Address

Account No.   _Present Balance_   _Signatures Authorized_

27. HAVE YOU FURNISHED A FINANCIAL STATEMENT TO ANY PERSON OR INSTITUTION DURING THE PAST TWO YEARS? If so, state with respect to each:

Name   _Date_

Address

Name   _Date_

Address

Name   _Date_

Address

Name   _Date_

Address

Name   _Date_

Address

28. DO YOU HAVE AN OWNERSHIP OR INTEREST OR A LEASEHOLD INTEREST IN ANY REAL ESTATE? If so, then state with respect to each parcel:

	1st Tract	**2nd Tract**
Street Address		
Full Legal Description		
Description of Each Structure or Improvement		

29. DOES ANYONE ELSE HAVE AN OWNERSHIP INTEREST IN THE PROPERTY? If so, state with respect to each:

	1st Tract	**2nd Tract**
Name		
Address		
Name		
Address		
Name		
Address		

30. HOW IS OWNERSHIP OF THE PROPERTY STATED IN DOCUMENTS OF TITLE?

1st Tract: _____

_____

2nd Tract: _____

_____

31. IS ANY REAL ESTATE OWNED BY YOU ENCUMBERED BY ANY TYPE OF LIEN? If so, then state with respect to each:

	1st Tract	**2nd Tract**
Description of Property Encumbered	_____	_____
	_____	_____
	_____	_____
	_____	_____
Nature and Type of Encumberance	_____	_____
	_____	_____
Date of Encumberance	_____	_____
Name and Address of Holder of Encumberance Name	_____	_____
Address	_____	_____
	_____	_____
Consideration Received for Encumberance	$ _____	$ _____
Date and Place of Recordation of Encumberance	_____	_____
	Date	*Date*
	_____	_____
	Volume *Page*	*Volume* *Page*
	_____	_____
	Records	*Records*
	_____	_____
	County	*County*
	_____	_____
	State	*State*

32. DO YOU OWN ANY MOTOR VEHICLES, MOTOR HOMES, TRAILERS, MOTORCYCLES, ETC.? If so, state:

	1st Vehicle	**2nd Vehicle**	**3rd Vehicle**	**4th Vehicle**
Type of Vehicle	_____	_____	_____	_____
Year	_____	_____	_____	_____
Make	_____	_____	_____	_____
Model	_____	_____	_____	_____
Serial No.	_____	_____	_____	_____
Motor No.	_____	_____	_____	_____
Registration No.	_____	_____	_____	_____
State	_____	_____	_____	_____
Estimated value	_____	_____	_____	_____
Location	_____	_____	_____	_____

33. DO YOU OWN ANY BOATS OR BOATING EQUIPMENT? If so, then state, with respect to each:

Item: _____

_____	_____	_____	_____
Year	Make	Model	Serial No.

_____ $ _____ _____
Registration No.   Estimated Value   Location

Item: _____

_____	_____	_____	_____
Year	Make	Model	Serial No.

_____ $ _____ _____
Registration No.   Estimated Value   Location

Item: _____

_____	_____	_____	_____
Year	Make	Model	Serial No.

_____ $ _____ _____
Registration No.   Estimated Value   Location

34. DO YOU OWN ANY AIRCRAFT? If so, state:

Make and Model _____

Year _____ Registration No. _____ Serial No. _____

Location _____

Avionics Equipment _____

Make and Model _____

Year _____ Registration No. _____ Serial No. _____

Location _____

Avionics Equipment _____

35. DO YOU OWN A COLLECTION OF ANY KIND, SUCH AS COIN, STAMP, ETC.? If so, state with respect to each:

Description _____

Estimated Market Value $ _____

Location _____

Description _____

Estimated Market Value $ _____

Location _____

Description _____

Estimated Market Value $ _____

Location _____

36. DO YOU OWN ANY TOOLS OR EQUIPMENT OF ANY SORT? If so, state with respect to each:

Description _____

Estimated Market Value $ _____

Location _____

Description _____

Estimated Market Value $ _____

Location _____

Description _____

Estimated Market Value $ _____

Location _____

37. DO YOU OWN ANY SPORTING GOODS OR FIREARMS? If so, state with respect to each:

Description _____

Estimated Market Value $ _____   Registration or Serial No. _____

Location _____

Description _____

Estimated Market Value $ _____   Registration or Serial No. _____

Location _____

Description _____

Estimated Market Value $ _____   Registration or Serial No. _____

Location _____

38. DO YOU OWN ANY ANTIQUES? If so, state:

Description _____

Estimated Market Value $ _____   Maker or Designer _____

Location _____

Description _____

Estimated Market Value $ _____   Maker or Designer _____

Location _____

Description _____

Estimated Market Value $ _____   Maker or Designer _____

Location _____

Description _____

Estimated Market Value $ _____   Maker or Designer _____

Location _____

39. DO YOU OWN ANY PAINTINGS, CARPETS, SCULPTURE, RARE OR VALUABLE BOOKS, OR DOCUMENTS OF ANY KIND? If so, state with respect to each:

Description _____

Estimated Market Value $ _____   Artist or Author _____

Location _____

Description _____

Estimated Market Value $ _____   Artist or Author _____

Location _____

Description _____

Estimated Market Value $ _____   Artist or Author _____

Location _____

Description _____

Estimated Market Value $ _____   Artist or Author _____

Location _____

40. DO YOU OWN ANY JEWELRY, GEMS, GOLD, SILVER, OR PRECIOUS METALS OF ANY KIND? If so, state with respect to each:

Description _____

Estimated Market Value $ _____

Location _____

Description _____

Estimated Market Value $ _____

Location _____

Description _____

Estimated Market Value $ _____

Location _____

Description _____

Estimated Market Value $ _____

Location _____

41. IS ANY OF THE PERSONAL PROPERTY DESCRIBED ABOVE AS OWNED BY YOU ENCUMBERED BY ANY SECURITY AGREEMENT OR ANY OTHER TYPE OF LIEN? If so, state with respect to each:

	Item 1	Item 2
Description of Each Property Encumbered		
Nature and Type of Encumberance		
Date of Encumberance		
Name and Address of Holder of Encumberance Name		
Address		
Date and Place of Recordation of Encumberance	Date	Date
	Volume _____ Page	Volume _____ Page
	Records	Records
	County	County
	State	State
Consideration Received by You for Encumberance	$	$

42. HAS ANY OF THE PERSONAL PROPERTY DESCRIBED ABOVE AS OWNED BY YOU BEEN PAWNED OR PLEDGED TO SECURE A DEBT? If so, state with respect to each:

	Item 1	**Item 2**
Description of Property Pledged		
Amount of Debt So Secured	$ _____	$ _____
How Was Debt Incurred?		
Date on Which Debt Was Incurred		
Date on Which Possession Was Transferred to Pledgee		
Name and Address of Pledgee	*Name* _____ *Address* _____	*Name* _____ *Address* _____

43. ARE YOU NOW AN OWNER OR PART OWNER OF ANY BUSINESS, FIRM, OR CORPORATION? If so, state:

_____
Full Name of the Business

_____
Address of the Principal Place of Business or General Office

Address of each place where business is conducted:

_____

_____

_____

_____

_____
Type of Business Conducted

_____
Form of Business Organization

_____
Percentage of Total Your Interest Represents

_____
Date You Acquired Your Interest

Your Office or Responsibilities

Exact Present Value of Your Interest

Full name and address of each officer and director or partner:

Name	*Address*
Name	*Address*
Name	*Address*
Name	*Address*
Name	*Address*
Name	*Address*

44. FOR ANY BANK OR OTHER INSTITUTION AT WHICH THE BUSINESS MAINTAINS AN ACCOUNT, STATE:

Name and Address of Institution

Complete Address

Name of Account

Type of Account _____   No. of Account _____

Name and Address of Institution

Complete Address

Name of Account

Type of Account _____   No. of Account _____

45. DO YOU OWN ANY STOCKS, BONDS, OR OTHER SECURITIES OF ANY CLASS IN ANY GOVERNMENT, GOVERNMENT AGENCY, COMPANY, FIRM, OR CORPORATION? If so, state:

Name of Organization in Which Interest Is Owned

Complete Address

Description of the Security

Serial or Certificate Number(s)

Date on Which Acquired _____

Method of Acquisition _____

Name of Person or Firm from Which the Security Was Acquired

Complete Address

Name of Person or Firm with Whom Any Joint or Community Interest Is Shared

Complete Address

Location of the Security

Name and address of any person or firm to whom the securities are pledged or mortgaged or subject to an option to repurchase:

Name

Address

Name of Organization in Which Interest Is Owned

Complete Address

Description of Security

Serial or Certificate Number(s)

Date on Which Acquired _____

Method of Acquisition _____

Name of Person or Firm from Which the Security Was Acquired

Complete Address

Name of Person or Firm with Whom Any Joint or Community Interest Is Shared

Complete Address

Location of the Security

Name and address of any person or firm to whom the securities are pledged or mortgaged or subject to an option to repurchase:

Name

Address

46. DO YOU MAINTAIN ANY BUSINESS BANK ACCOUNTS? If so, state:

Name of Account   *Account No.*

Name of Bank

Complete Address of Bank

Authorized Signatures

Present Balance $ _____

Name of Account   *Account No.*

Name of Bank

Complete Address of Bank

Authorized Signatures

Present Balance $ _____

Name of Account   *Account No.*

Name of Bank

Complete Address of Bank

Authorized Signatures

Present Balance $ _____

47. DO YOU MAINTAIN ANY PERSONAL CHECKING OR SAVINGS ACCOUNTS? If so, state:

Name of Account   *Account No.*

Name of Bank

Complete Address of Bank

Authorized Signatures

Present Balance $ _____

Name of Account   *Account No.*

Name of Bank

Complete Address of Bank

Authorized Signatures

Present Balance $ _____

Name of Account   Account No.

Name of Bank

Complete Address of Bank

Authorized Signatures

Present Balance $ _____

48. DO YOU HAVE ANY JOINT SAVINGS OR CHECKING ACCOUNTS? If so, state:

Name of Account   Account No.

Name of Bank

Complete Address of Bank

Authorized Signatures

Present Balance $ _____

Name of Account   Account No.

Name of Bank

Complete Address of Bank

Authorized Signatures

Present Balance $ _____

Name of Account   Account No.

Name of Bank

Complete Address of Bank

Authorized signatures

Present Balance $ _____

49. DURING THE PAST YEAR HAS ANY MONEY BELONGING TO YOU OR EARNED BY YOU BEEN DE-POSITED IN ANY BANK ACCOUNT NOT LISTED ABOVE? If so, state:

Name of Account   Account No.

Name of Bank

Complete Address of Bank

Authorized Signatures

Present Balance $ _____

Name of Account _____ Account No. _____

Name of Bank _____

Complete Address of Bank _____

Authorized Signatures _____

Present Balance $ _____

50. DO YOU HAVE ANY ACCOUNTS IN ANY BANK OR OTHER INSTITUTION THAT YOU ARE HOLDING IN TRUST FOR ANYONE? If so, state:

Name of Account _____ Account No. _____

Name of Bank _____

Complete Address of Bank _____

Authorized Signatures _____

Date on Which Account Opened _____

Source of Deposits to Account _____

51. CONCERNING EACH PERSON HAVING AN INTEREST IN THE ACCOUNT, STATE:

Name _____ Relationship to You ____

Address _____

Name _____ Relationship to You ____

Address _____

Name _____ Relationship to You ____

Address _____

52. DO YOU HAVE ACCESS TO ANY SAFE-DEPOSIT BOX OR OTHER DEPOSITORY FOR VALUABLES, CASH, SECURITIES, ETC.? If so, state:

Name of Bank or Institution Where Located _____

Complete Address _____

FORM 45.5/F270

Complete description of all items in depository as of five days ago:

_____

_____

_____

_____

_____

With respect to each person having access to the depository, state:

_____
Name

_____
Complete Address

_____
Name

_____
Complete Address

_____
Name

_____
Complete Address

53. WHEN DID YOU LAST ENTER THE DEPOSITORY? _____
                                                                  Date

54. HAVE ANY OF THE CONTENTS OF THE DEPOSITORY BEEN REMOVED DURING THE PAST YEAR? If so, state:

_____
Description of Item Removed

_____
Reason for Removal

_____
Date of Removal

_____
Name of Person Removing

_____
Complete Address of Person Removing

_____
Description of Item Removed

_____
Reason for Removal

_____
Date of Removal

_____
Name of Person Removing

_____
Complete Address of Person Removing

Description of Item Removed

Reason for Removal

Date of Removal

Name of Person Removing

Complete Address of Person Removing

55. DO YOU OWN ANY INTEREST IN ANY KIND OF PATENT OR COPYRIGHT? If so, state:

Description

Registry No. _____

Approximate Yearly Income $ _____

Description

Registry No. _____

Approximate Yearly Income $ _____

Description

Registry No. _____

Approximate Yearly Income $ _____

56. DOES ANY PERSON OR FIRM SHARE ANY PATENT OR COPYRIGHT WITH YOU? If so, state:

Name

Complete Address

Percentage of Interest Owned by You _____

Approximate Yearly Income Received by You $ _____

Name

Complete Address

Percentage of Interest Owned by You _____

Approximate Yearly Income Received by You $ _____

57. DURING THE PAST TWO YEARS HAVE YOU PAID, OR HAD PAID FOR YOU, THE PREMIUMS ON ANY LIFE INSURANCE? If so, state:

Policy No. 1

Name of Beneficiary

Complete Address

Name of Issuing Company

Complete Address of Issuing Company

Policy No. _____ Present Cash Value $ _____

Date Policy Issued _____

Face Value of Policy upon Death of Insured $ _____

Name of Premium Payer

Complete Address of Premium Payer

Date of Last Payment _____ Amount of Last Payment $ _____

Location of Contract of Insurance

Policy No. 2

Name of Beneficiary

Complete Address

Name of Issuing Company

Complete Address of Issuing Company

Policy No. _____ Present Cash Value $ _____

Date Policy Issued _____

Face Value of Policy upon Death of Insured $ _____

Name of Premium Payer

Complete Address of Premium Payer

Date of Last Payment _____ Amount of Last Payment $ _____

Location of Contract of Insurance

58. DO YOU NOW HAVE ANY CLAIMS AGAINST OTHERS BY REASON OF LOANS, NOTES, CLAIMS FOR DAMAGES, ETC.? If so, state:

_____ $ _____
Description of Claim   *Amount Claimed*

_____
Name of Person Indebted to You

_____
Complete Address

_____ $ _____
Description of Claim   *Amount Claimed*

_____
Name of Person Indebted to You

_____
Complete Address

_____ $ _____
Description of Claim   *Amount Claimed*

_____
Name of Person Indebted to You

_____
Complete Address

59. HAS ANY SUIT OR ACTION BEEN BROUGHT TO REDUCE ANY ABOVE-DESCRIBED CLAIM TO JUDGMENT? If so, state:

Number of Case _____

Style of Case _____

vs.

_____

Date of Filing _____

_____
Court in Which the Case Is Pending

_____
Status of Case

Amount of Any Offer of Settlement $ _____

_____
Name of Person Offering Settlement

_____
Complete Address

Details of settlement offer, if any:

_____

_____

_____

_____

FORM 45.5 / F274

60. IS ANY PROPERTY NOW BEING HELD FOR YOU IN THE NAME OF ANY PERSON OR FIRM OTHER THAN YOURSELF? If so, state:

_____
Description of Item

_____
Name of Holder

_____
Complete Address

Date of Transfer _____   Estimated Value $_____

_____
Description of Item

_____
Name of Holder

_____
Complete Address

Date of Transfer _____   Estimated Value $_____

_____
Description of Item

_____
Name of Holder

_____
Complete Address

Date of Transfer _____   Estimated Value $_____

61. HAVE YOU SOLD, TRANSFERRED, OR ASSIGNED IN BULK ALL OR A SUBSTANTIAL PART OF YOUR STOCK IN TRADE OR TRADE FIXTURES DURING THE PAST SIX MONTHS? If so, state:

_____
Type and Nature of Business Sold

_____
Name of Transferee   *Date of Transfer*

_____
Complete Address

_____
Location of Any Notice or Recording of Sale or Transfer

_____
Name of Any Newspaper Publishing Any Notice of Sale or Transfer

_____
Complete Address

Description of each item disposed of:

_____ $ _____
Item   *Sold for*

_____ $ _____
Item   *Sold for*

_____ $ _____
Item   *Sold for*

_____ $ _____
Item   *Sold for*

_____ $ _____
Item   *Sold for*

62. HAVE YOU ENTERED INTO ANY TRANSACTION WITH YOUR SPOUSE OR ANY OTHER RELATIVE INVOLVING A TRANSFER, CONVEYANCE, ASSIGNMENT, OR OTHER DISPOSITION OF ANY OF YOUR REAL OR PERSONAL PROPERTY IN THE PAST TWO YEARS? If so, for each transaction state:

Description

Date of Transaction _____ Consideration Received $ _____

Description

Date of Transaction _____ Consideration Received $ _____

Description

Date of Transaction _____ Consideration Received $ _____

Description

Date of Transaction _____ Consideration Received $ _____

63. HAVE YOU TRANSFERRED ANY OF YOUR REAL OR PERSONAL PROPERTY TO ANY OTHER PERSON OR FIRM DURING THE PAST TWO YEARS IN CONSIDERATION OF FUTURE SUPPORT? If so, state:

Description of Item

Date of Transfer _____ Estimated Value $ _____

Name of Transferee

Complete Address

Description of Item

Date of Transfer _____ Estimated Value $ _____

Name of Transferee

Complete Address

Description of Item

Date of Transfer _____ Estimated Value $ _____

Name of Transferee

Complete Address

64. ARE YOU A PARTY TO ANY CONTRACT OR OTHER AGREEMENT WHEREBY YOU CREATED, DURING THE PAST TWO YEARS, AN OPTION FOR ANY OTHER PERSON OR FIRM TO PURCHASE ANY OF YOUR REAL OR PERSONAL PROPERTY? If so, state:

_____
Description of Property Covered by the Agreement

_____
Location Where Agreement Was Made

Date of Agreement _____   Consideration Received $ _____

_____
Description of Terms of the Agreement

_____
Name of Person or Firm Furnishing Consideration

_____
Complete Address

_____
Name of Any Other Person or Firm That Is a Party to the Agreement

_____
Complete Address

_____
Name of Any Other Person or Firm That Is a Party to the Agreement

_____
Complete Address

65. HAVE YOU CREATED OR CONTRIBUTED TO ANY TRUST FOR THE BENEFIT OF OTHERS DURING THE PAST TWO YEARS? If so, state:

_____ $ _____
Description of Item Contributed   *Est. Value*

_____ $ _____
Description of Item Contributed   *Est. Value*

_____ $ _____
Description of Item Contributed   *Est. Value*

Amount of Money Contributed $ _____

Date of Creation of Trust _____

For each beneficiary, state:

_____
Name   *Relationship to You*

_____
Complete Address

_____
Name   *Relationship to You*

_____
Complete Address

_____
Name   *Relationship to You*

_____
Complete Address

_____
Total Amount of Consideration Received by You for All Contributions and Transfers

66. DO YOU HOLD ANY PROPERTY AS TRUSTEE OF ANY TRUST? If so, state:

Description of Property

Name of Trustor or Settlor

Complete Address

Name of Beneficiary   _Relationship to You_

Complete Address

Name of Beneficiary   _Relationship to You_

Complete Address

Name of Beneficiary   _Relationship to You_

Complete Address

Name of Beneficiary   _Relationship to You_

Complete Address

Date of Creation of Trust _____   Duration or Life of Trust _____

Description of Any General Powers of Appointment That You Have

Terms and Conditions of Trust

67. ARE YOU AN HEIR-AT-LAW OR BENEFICIARY OF THE ESTATE OF ANY PERSON NOW DECEASED? If so, state:

Name of Decedent

Name of Any Person Possessing Will Not Yet Offered for Probate

Complete Address

Name of Court in Which Estate Is Pending

Complete Address of Court

Date of Any Renunciation of Bequest or Legacy _____

Amount of Any Advancements Received $ _____

Name of Any Person Whose Interest Was Enhanced by Renunciation

Complete Address

68. HAVE YOU CONVEYED OR DISPOSED OF ANY PROPERTY, EITHER BY SALE, GIFT, OR OTHERWISE, DURING THE PAST TWO YEARS? If so, state:

_____

Description of Item Disposed of

Date of Disposition _____   Consideration Received $ _____

_____

Manner of Disposition

_____

Name of Person Receiving

_____

Complete Address

_____

Description of Item Disposed of

Date of Disposition _____   Consideration Received $ _____

_____

Manner of Disposition

_____

Name of Person Receiving

_____

Complete Address

_____

Description of Item Disposed of

Date of Disposition _____   Consideration Received $ _____

_____

Manner of Disposition

_____

Name of Person Receiving

_____

Complete Address

69. HAVE YOU MADE ANY CONVEYANCES, TRANSFERS, GIFTS, OR OTHER DISPOSITIONS OF PROPERTY WITHIN THE PAST TWO YEARS WITH ANY RESERVATION OF RIGHTS, BENEFITS, OR OPTIONS RUNNING TO YOU FOR THE REACQUISITION OF THE PROPERTY AT SOME FUTURE DATE? If so, state:

_____

Description of Property Conveyed

_____

Nature of Reservation, Benefit, or Option Reserved

Date of Conveyance _____

_____

Name of Transferee

_____

Complete Address

Description of Property Conveyed

Nature of Reservation, Benefit, or Option Reserved

Date of Conveyance _____

Name of Transferee

Complete Address

70. HAVE YOU ASSIGNED ANYTHING OR "CHOSE IN ACTION" (CLAIMS OR DEBT) DURING THE PAST TWO YEARS? If so, state:

Description of Item Assigned

Date of Assignment _____   Consideration Received $ _____

Name of Assignee

Complete Address

Description of Item Assigned

Date of Assignment _____   Consideration Received $ _____

Name of Assignee

Complete Address

71. HAVE YOU SUFFERED ANY CASUALTY LOSS FROM FIRE, WIND, THEFT, OR OTHERWISE DURING THE PAST TWO YEARS? If so, state:

Description of Item Lost or Damaged

Cause of Loss

Date of Loss _____   Amount of Loss $ _____

Name of Insurance Carrier Covering Loss

Policy No. _____   Policy Limits $ _____

Date of Filing Claim _____

Date of Payment of Claim _____

Amount of Claim Payment $ _____

Description of Item Lost or Damaged

Cause of Loss

Date of Loss _____   Amount of Loss $ _____

Name of Insurance Carrier Covering Loss

Policy No. _____   Policy Limits $ _____

Date of Filing Claim _____

Date of Payment of Claim _____

Amount of Claim Payment $ _____

72. IS YOUR SPOUSE EMPLOYED? If so, state:

Name of Employer

Complete Address

Nature of the Business

Nature of Spouse's Occupation

How Long Employed There _____   Annual Income $ _____

73. DOES YOUR SPOUSE OWN AN AUTOMOBILE, TRAILER, BOAT, AIRCRAFT, OR ANY OTHER VEHICLE?
    If so, state:

	1st Vehicle	2nd Vehicle	3rd Vehicle	4th Vehicle
Type of Vehicle				
Make				
Year				
Model				
Serial No.				
Motor No.				
Registration No.				
State				
Estimated Value				
Location				

74. ARE ANY OF THE ABOVE-LISTED VEHICLES COVERED BY A CHATTEL MORTGAGE, CONDITIONAL SALE, OR SECURITY AGREEMENT? If so, state:

_____ $ _____
Description of Vehicle   *Amount Owed*

_____ $ _____
Description of Vehicle   *Amount Owed*

_____ $ _____
Description of Vehicle   *Amount Owed*

_____ $ _____
Description of Vehicle   *Amount Owed*

75. DOES YOUR SPOUSE OWN OR HAVE AN INTEREST IN ANY REAL ESTATE? If so, state:

	1st Tract	**2nd Tract**
Street Address	_____	_____
	_____	_____
Full Legal Description	_____	_____
	_____	_____
	_____	_____
Description of Each Structure or Improvement	_____	_____
	_____	_____
	_____	_____
Is the Tract Encumbered?	_____	_____
Amount of Encumberance	$ _____	$ _____

76. DOES YOUR SPOUSE HAVE AN OWNERSHIP INTEREST IN ANY BUSINESS? If so, state:

_____
Full Name of the Business

_____
Address of the Principal Place of Business

_____
Type of Business Conducted

_____
Percentage of Total Your Spouse's Interest Represents

_____
Spouse's Responsibilities

_____
Exact Present Value of Spouse's Interest

77. DOES YOUR SPOUSE OWN ANY STOCKS, BONDS, OR OTHER SECURITIES OF ANY CLASS IN ANY GOVERNMENT, GOVERNMENT AGENCY, COMPANY, FIRM, OR CORPORATION? If so, state:

_____
Name of Organization in Which Interest Is Owned

_____
Complete Address

_____
Description of the Security

Date When Acquired _____

Is the security pledged, mortgaged, or subject to an option to repurchase? _____

Estimated Value $ _____

_____
Name of Organization in Which Interest Is Owned

_____
Complete Address

_____
Description of the Security

Date When Acquired _____

Is the security pledged, mortgaged, or subject to an option to repurchase? _____

Estimated Value $ _____

78. DOES YOUR SPOUSE OWN ANY JEWELRY? If so, state:

_____ *Description*	$ _____ *Estimated Value*
_____ *Description*	$ _____ *Estimated Value*
_____ *Description*	$ _____ *Estimated Value*
_____ *Description*	$ _____ *Estimated Value*
_____ *Description*	$ _____ *Estimated Value*

79. DOES YOUR SPOUSE HAVE ANY CHECKING OR SAVINGS ACCOUNTS? If so, state:

_____
Name of Account   *Account No.*

_____
Name of Bank

_____
Complete Address of Bank

_____
Authorized Signatures

Present Balance $ _____

Name of Account   _Account No._

Name of Bank

Complete Address of Bank

Authorized Signatures

Present Balance $ _____

80. DO YOU OWE ANY DEBTS? If so, state:

Name and Address of Creditor	Amount Owed	Date Debt Incurred	How Incurred	Security Given

FORM 45.5/F284

Name and Address of Creditor	Amount Owed	Date Debt Incurred	How Incurred	Security Given
_____	_____	_____	_____	_____
_____				
_____				
_____	_____	_____	_____	_____
_____				
_____				
_____	_____	_____	_____	_____
_____				
_____				
_____	_____	_____	_____	_____
_____				
_____				
_____	_____	_____	_____	_____
_____				
_____				
_____	_____	_____	_____	_____
_____				
_____				

81. HAVE YOU MADE ANY PAYMENTS TO CREDITORS DURING THE PAST SIX MONTHS? If so, state:

Name and Address of Each Creditor	Amount of Each Payment	Date of Each Payment
_____	$_____	_____
_____		
_____		
_____	$_____	_____
_____		
_____		
_____	$_____	_____
_____		
_____		
_____	$_____	_____
_____		
_____		
_____	$_____	_____
_____		
_____		
_____	$_____	_____
_____		
_____		
_____	$_____	_____
_____		
_____		

Name and Address of Each Creditor	Amount of Each Payment	Date of Each Payment
_____	$ _____	_____
_____		
_____		
_____	$ _____	_____
_____		
_____		
_____	$ _____	_____
_____		
_____		
_____	$ _____	_____
_____		
_____		

82. DO YOU HAVE ANY ACCOUNTS RECEIVABLE? If so, state:

Name and Address of Each Person or Firm Owing You	Amount Owed
_____	$ _____
_____	
_____	
_____	$ _____
_____	
_____	
_____	$ _____
_____	
_____	
_____	$ _____
_____	
_____	

Name and Address of Each Person or Firm Owing You   **Amount Owed**

_____ $_____

_____

_____ $_____

_____

_____ $_____

_____

_____ $_____

_____

_____ $_____

_____

_____ $_____

_____

_____ $_____

_____

_____ $_____

_____

_____

_____

83. HAVE ANY OF YOUR ACCOUNTS RECEIVABLE BEEN ASSIGNED OR OTHERWISE DISPOSED OF OTHER THAN BY COLLECTION DURING THE PAST YEAR? If so, state:

_____
Name of Account

_____
Name of Assignee

_____
Complete Address

Date of Assignment _____   Amount of Reserve Due You $ _____

_____
Name of Account

_____
Name of Assignee

_____
Complete Address

Date of Assignment _____   Amount of Reserve Due You $ _____

_____
Name of Account

_____
Name of Assignee

_____
Complete Address

Date of Assignment _____   Amount of Reserve Due You $ _____

84. TO WHAT EXTENT WERE FUTURE ACCOUNTS RECEIVABLE COVERED?

_____

85. WHAT WAS THE AMOUNT OF CONSIDERATION RECEIVED? $ _____

86. HAVE YOU SOLD OR ASSIGNED ANY ACCOUNTS RECEIVABLE AND HAVE ANY RESERVE FUNDS BEEN ESTABLISHED FOR YOUR BENEFIT OUT OF SUCH ACCOUNTS RECEIVABLE? If so, state:

_____
Name of Account

_____
Name of Person or Firm Holding Fund

_____
Complete Address

Amount of Fund $ _____

_____
Name of Account

_____
Name of Person or Firm Holding Fund

_____
Complete Address

Amount of Fund $ _____

Name of Account

Name of Person or Firm Holding Fund

Complete Address

Amount of Fund $ _____

87. HAVE YOU TAKEN AN INVENTORY OF YOUR PERSONAL OR BUSINESS PROPERTY DURING THE PAST TWO YEARS? If so, state:

Name of Person Supervising or Taking Inventory

Complete Address

Name of Person Having a Copy of the Inventory

Complete Address

Total Value of Property as Stated in Inventory $ _____

Means of Valuation of Inventory

88. WHAT WERE THE MAJOR ITEMS OF PROPERTY INCLUDED IN THE INVENTORY?

Description of Item $ _____ _Estimated Value_

Description of Item $ _____ _Estimated Value_

Description of Item $ _____ _Estimated Value_

Description of Item $ _____ _Estimated Value_

Description of Item $ _____ _Estimated Value_

Description of Item $ _____ _Estimated Value_

Description of Item $ _____ _Estimated Value_

Description of Item $ _____ _Estimated Value_

Description of Item $ _____ _Estimated Value_

Description of Item $ _____ _Estimated Value_

89. DO YOU HAVE ANY INTEREST IN ANY PENSION PLAN, RETIREMENT FUND, OR PROFIT-SHARING PLAN? If so, state:

Name of Administrator of Plan

Complete Address

Nature of Plan _____

Value of Your Interest in Plan $ _____

Description of terms under which you may receive money or property pursuant to the plan:

_____

_____

_____

90. HAVE YOU KEPT ANY BOOKS OR WRITTEN MEMORANDA OF YOUR INCOME AND BUSINESS AFFAIRS DURING THE PAST TWO YEARS? If so, state:

_____
Form in Which Books Were Kept

Date Books Were First Kept _____

Do the books accurately reflect income stated in federal income tax return each year? _____

_____
Name of Person Who Prepared Books—First Year

_____
Complete Address

_____
Name of Person Who Prepared Books—Second Year

_____
Complete Address

_____
Name of Person Who Has Custody of Books

_____
Complete Address

91. HAVE YOU DESTROYED OR DISPOSED OF ANY BOOKS OF ACCOUNT, ANY MEMORANDA, OR OTHER RECORDS RELATING TO YOUR BUSINESS OR INCOME DURING THE PAST TWO YEARS? If so, state:

_____
Description of Books or Memoranda Destroyed

_____
Reason for Destroying

Date Books or Memoranda Were Destroyed _____

_____
Name of Person Destroying

_____
Complete Address

92. HAVE YOU EMPLOYED, OR HAD EMPLOYED IN YOUR BEHALF, THE SERVICES OF ANY ACCOUNTANT DURING THE PAST TWO YEARS? If so, state:

_____
Name of Accountant or Firm

_____
Complete Address

_____
Services Performed

Period of Employment _____

Name of Accountant or Firm

Complete Address

Services Performed

Period of Employment _____

Name of Accountant or Firm

Complete Address

Services Performed

Period of Employment _____

93. HAVE YOU PREVIOUSLY BEEN EXAMINED AS A JUDGMENT DEBTOR? If so, state:

No. of Case _____ Date of Examination _____

vs.

Style of Case

Court

Location/Address

Status of Case

No. of Case _____ Date of Examination _____

vs.

Style of Case

Court

Location/Address

Status of Case

94. ARE THERE ANY JUDGMENTS AGAINST YOU? If so, state:

No. of Case _____ Date of Judgment _____

vs.

Style of Case

Court

Location/Address

Amount of Judgment $ _____

Amount of Judgment That Has Been Paid $ _____

FORM 45.5/F292

No. of Case _____   Date of Judgment _____

_____ vs. _____
Style of Case

_____
Court

_____
Location/Address

Amount of Judgment $ _____

Amount of Judgment That Has Been Paid $ _____

95. DO YOU HAVE ANY SOURCE OF INCOME OTHER THAN PREVIOUSLY STATED HEREIN? If so, state:

_____
Source

_____
Complete Address of Source

_____
How Paid

Amount Paid During Past Year $ _____

_____
Source

_____
Complete Address of Source

_____
How Paid

Amount Paid During Past Year $ _____

96. WITH WHAT IRS OFFICE DID YOU FILE YOUR FEDERAL INCOME TAX FOR THE PAST TWO YEARS?

_____
Address of IRS Office Where Filed for Year Ending 12/31/

_____
Address of IRS Office Where Filed for Year Ending 12/31/

97. IN WHAT STATE DID YOU FILE YOUR STATE INCOME TAX FOR THE PAST TWO YEARS?

_____
Address of State Office Where Filed for Year Ending 12/31/

_____
Address of State Office Where Filed for Year Ending 12/31/

98. ARE YOU ENTITLED TO A REFUND OF FEDERAL INCOME TAX PAID?

Estimated Amount $ _____

99. ARE YOU ENTITLED TO A REFUND OF STATE INCOME TAX PAID?

Estimated Amount $ _____

100. DO YOU CLAIM THAT ANY OF THE REAL OR PERSONAL PROPERTY OWNED BY YOU IS EXEMPT FROM CLAIMS OF YOUR CREDITORS? If so, state:

_____ $ _____
Description of Item   *Estimated Value*

_____
Basis for Claimed Exemption

_____ $ _____
Description of Item   *Estimated Value*

_____
Basis for Claimed Exemption

_____ $ _____
Description of Item   *Estimated Value*

_____
Basis for Claimed Exemption

_____ $ _____
Description of Item   *Estimated Value*

_____
Basis for Claimed Exemption

_____ $ _____
Description of Item   *Estimated Value*

_____
Basis for Claimed Exemption

_____ $ _____
Description of Item   *Estimated Value*

_____
Basis for Claimed Exemption

_____ $ _____
Description of Item   *Estimated Value*

_____
Basis for Claimed Exemption

SIGNED this _____ day of _____, 19 _____.

_____
Defendant–Judgment Debtor

FORM 45.5/F294

CERTIFICATE OF NOTARY

STATE OF   )

)   ss:

COUNTY OF   )

    BEFORE ME, the undersigned, on this day personally appeared _____,
who, being first duly sworn, stated that each and all of the foregoing Answers to Interrogatories are true and correct.

    SUBSCRIBED AND SWORN to this _____ day of _____, 19 _____.

                                _____

                                 Notary Public

                                 _____ County, _____

STATE OF NEW BEDFORD

Garnishee Summons

To the Sheriff of the County of _____, Greeting:

WHEREAS, on the _____ day of _____, 19 _____, an execution was duly issued and delivered to _____, upon a judgment rendered in the _____ _____ on the _____ day of _____, 19 _____, in favor of _____ _____, Plaintiff, against _____, Defendant, for the sum of $ _____, with legal interest thereon from the _____ day of _____, 1984, until payment, and $ _____ costs; and it being suggested by the Plaintiff that by reason of the lien such execution there is a liability upon the Garnishee.

THEREFORE WE COMMAND YOU, in the name of the State of New Bedford, to summon _____ _____, Garnishee, to appear before the Court at _____ o'clock _____M., on the _____ day of _____, 19 _____, to answer such suggestion, having then and there this writ; and the Garnishee named above shall withhold from the Defendant any sums of money to which the Defendant is or may be entitled from the Garnishee for the period between the date of service of this summons on the Garnishee and the date of the Garnishee's appearance in Court as specified above, except such sums of money as may be exempt from garnishment pursuant to State of New Bedford Code 34-29, which reads as follows:

34-29. Maximum portion of disposable earnings subject to garnishment . . . (a) Except as provided in subsection (b) and (bl), the maximum part of the aggregate of disposable earnings of an individual for any work week which is subjected to garnishment may not exceed the lesser of the following amounts:

(1) Twenty-five (25) per centum of his disposable earnings for that week, or

(2) The amount by which his disposable earnings for that week exceed thirty (30) times the federal minimum hourly wage prescribed by 206 (a) (1) of Title 29 of the United States Code in effect at the time earnings are payable. In case of earnings for any pay period other than a week, the State Commissioner of Labor and Industry shall by regulation prescribe a multiple of the federal minimum hourly wage equivalent in effect to that set forth in this section.

(b) The restrictions of subsection (a) do not apply in case of:

(1) Any order for the support of any person issued by a court of competent jurisdiction or in accordance with an administrative procedure established by State law, which affords substantial due process, and which is subject to judicial review.

(2) Any order of any court of bankruptcy under Chapter XIII of the Bankruptcy Act.

(3) Any debt due for any state or federal tax.

(bl) The maximum part of the aggregate disposable earnings of an individual for any work week which is subject to garnishment to enforce any order for the support of any person shall not exceed:

(1) Sixty (60) per centum of such individual's disposable earnings for that week; or

(2) If such individual is supporting a spouse or dependent child other than the spouse or child with respect to whose support such order was issued, fifty (50) per centum of such individual's disposable earnings for that week. The fifty (50) per centum specified in clause (bl) (2) shall be fifty-five (55) per centum and the sixty (60) per centum specified in clause (bl) (1) shall be sixty-five (65) per centum in and to the extent that such earnings are subject to garnishment to enforce an order for support for a period which is more than twelve (12) weeks prior to the beginning of such work week.

(c) No court of the State and no State agency or officer may make, execute or enforce any order or process in violation of this section.

The exemptions allowed herein shall be granted to any person so entitled without any further proceedings.

(d) For the purposes of this section:

(1) The term "earnings" means compensation paid or payable for personal services, whether denominated as wages, salary, commissions, bonus or otherwise, and includes periodic payments pursuant to a pension or retirement program.

(2) The term "disposable earnings" means that part of the earnings of any individual remaining after the deduction from those earnings of any amounts required by law to be withheld, and

(3) The term "garnishment" means any legal or equitable procedure through which the earnings of any individual are required to be withheld for payment of any debt.

(e) Every assignment, sale, transfer, pledge or mortgage of the wages or salary of an individual which is exempted by this section, to the extent of the exemption provided by this section, shall be void and unenforceable by any process of law.

(f) No employer may discharge any employee by reason of the fact that his earnings have been subjected to garnishment for any one indebtedness.

GIVEN UNDER MY HAND, this _____ day of _____, 19 _____.

_____
Clerk

By _____
Deputy Clerk

No. —————

Garnishee Summons

vs.

Returnable ————— 19 —————

ANSWER MUST BE FILED BY
GARNISHEE BY RETURN DATE

Agreement in Contemplation of Marriage

THIS AGREEMENT in contemplation of marriage is made this _____ day of _____,
19 _____, by and between

_____, of

Street Address	*Apt. No.*	*City*	*State*	*Zip*

hereinafter referred to as _____, and

_____, of

Street Address	*Apt. No.*	*City*	*State*	*Zip*

hereinafter referred to as _____.

WHEREAS _____ and _____ are contemplat-
ing marriage, and each party wishes to settle between themselves questions of separate and jointly owned property; separate
and joint financial responsibilities; children, if any, and their care, financial support and education; location of domicile; the
sharing of household space, expenses and housekeeping responsibilities; the gainful employment and education of each party;
the names of each; the possible incapacitation of each; possible dissolution of the marriage; maintenance and support; alimony;
and the death of either party; and

WHEREAS, for and in consideration of the sum of twenty dollars ($20.00), and other good and valuable consideration,
the receipt whereof is hereby acknowledged, and in further consideration of the parties entering into this agreement and making
the mutual convenants herein contained to be performed by the parties, the parties hereto mutually agree and covenant as
follows:

ARTICLE I: CONDITIONS OF THE AGREEMENT

Neither Party Presently Married   (1)

_____ hereby states that he is not presently married and has never been married, is
_____ (_____) years of age and is competent to enter into a valid marriage, and
_____ hereby states that she is not presently married and has never been married, is
_____ (_____) years of age and is competent to enter into a valid marriage.

ARTICLE I: CONDITIONS OF THE AGREEMENT

Neither Party Presently Married   (2)

_____ hereby states that he is not presently married and that if previously married
has received a final decree of divorce and is competent to enter into a valid marriage, and _____
hereby states that she is not presently married and that if previously married has received a final decree of divorce and is
competent to enter into a valid marriage.

Purpose   (1)

The purpose of the parties for entering into a state of matrimony under the laws of the State of _____
is to receive public recognition of the relationship between them as defined by this agreement and to receive mutually the
benefits thus obtained.

Purpose   (2)

The purpose of the parties for entering into a state of matrimony within the embrace of their religious faith and under the laws of the State of _____ is an expression of their religious belief and their love and commitment to each other.

Voluntary

Each party acknowledges that this agreement is being entered into voluntarily and that it is not the result of duress, coercion or undue influence.

Marriage as a Condition Precedent

This agreement shall become effective immediately upon the marriage of the parties to each other, but shall have no force or effect until that time.

Declaration of Principle   (1)

The parties value and accept the principle of independence and of the equal distribution of responsibility and authority between them and that each is a fully equal and independent partner in their relationship with each other.

Declaration of Principle   (2)

The parties value and accept the principle of independence and of equal distribution of responsibility and authority between them and that each is a fully equal partner in their relationship with each other.

Waiver of Rights   (1)

Both parties hereby waive, relinquish and renounce whatever rights, duties, obligations and privileges which either might have which may be derived from or related to a state of matrimony between them, other than those which are included in and made a part of this agreement.

Acceptance of Obligations   (2)

Both parties voluntarily and fully accept all legal, moral and religious duties, rights, obligations and privileges derived from or related to a state of matrimony between them.

Openness Between Parties   (1)

Both parties anticipate and expect the sharing of each other's emotional and sexual lives to the extent as may benefit both, without infringing upon the privacy, independence or solitude of the other.

Openness Between Parties   (2)

Both parties anticipate the sharing of their religious faith and experience and each other's emotional and sexual lives to the extent as may benefit both, without infringing upon the privacy, independence or solitude of the other.

Sexual Nonexclusivity   (1)

Each party recognizes the right of the other to be open to, and to maintain, additional emotional and sexual relationships beyond the one existing between them, neither party expecting nor demanding sexual exclusivity.

Sexual Exclusivity   (2)

Each party anticipates and pledges complete sexual fidelity during the marriage, each party promising to forsake all other such relationships out of love, commitment and deep personal belief.

Names of the Parties   (1)

The parties agree that neither shall change his or her name as a result of the marriage. We shall continue to be known, respectively, as _____ and _____.

Names of the Parties   (2)

The parties agree that, following their marriage, they shall adopt the surname of _____, being known, respectively, as _____ and _____.

Present Employment of the Parties   (1)

(a) The parties acknowledge their understanding that _____ is presently gainfully employed as _____ with an approximate annual income of $_____ and presently intends to continue such employment, and that;

(b) _____ is presently gainfully employed as _____ with an approximate annual income of $_____ and presently intends to continue such employment.

Present Employment of the Parties (2)

(a) The parties acknowledge their understanding that _____ is presently gainfully employed as _____ with an approximate annual income of $_____ and presently intends to continue such employment indefinitely, and that;

(b) _____ is not employed and _____ plan to become employed during the next _____ in order to _____ _____.

Present Employment of the Parties (3)

(a) The parties acknowledge their understanding that _____ is presently gainfully employed as _____ with an approximate annual income of $_____ and presently intends to continue such employment, and that;

(b) _____ is presently gainfully employed as _____ with an approximate annual income of $_____, but that he/she presently intends to terminate such employment _____ in order to _____.

Present Employment of the Parties (4)

The parties acknowledge their understanding that neither is presently gainfully employed and that _____ shall diligently seek gainful employment so that _____ may _____ _____.

Present Employment of the Parties (5)

The parties acknowledge that neither party is presently gainfully employed and that neither presently plans to become gainfully employed.

Children by Previous Marriage (1)

The parties acknowledge their understanding that _____ has previously been married and has a child or children born of or adopted during such marriage for whom he/she is obligated to provide $_____ per _____ in financial support and who shall, for approximately _____ _____ of each year, live with the parties.

Children by Previous Marriage (2)

The parties acknowledge their understanding that _____ has previously been married and has a child or children born of or adopted during such marriage for whom he/she has a right to receive child support in the amount of $ _____ per _____ and who shall, for approximately _____ _____ of each year, live with the parties.

Children by Previous Marriage (3)

The parties acknowledge their understanding that _____ has previously been married and has a child or children born of or adopted during such marriage for whom he/she receives no child support and who shall, for approximately _____ of each year, live with the parties.

Previous Children

The parties acknowledge their understanding that _____ has a child or children adopted during or born of a previous relationship for whom he/she _____ child support and who shall, for approximately _____ of each year, live with the parties.

Incapacitation of Either Party

The parties agree that in the event of incapacitation of either party during the marriage the other party shall assume complete responsibility for the care and financial support of such party to the extent of his or her income, assets and time.

Use of Living Space

(a) The parties agree to live together at a residence of their mutual choice, recognizing, however, that it may be necessary or desirable from time to time for one to live away from the other for a period of up to several months as determined by the educational, employment or other needs of either party. Each party hereby waives whatever right he or she may have to determine solely the domicile of the parties, and the parties further agree that;

(b) The parties shall have equal right to use of all living space in their home and that all decisions regarding its use shall be by mutual consent only, except that the right of each party to the quiet enjoyment and security of shared living space shall take precedence over all other uses.

ARTICLE II: PROPERTY AND FINANCIAL PROVISIONS
Disclosure (1)

Each party has made a full and complete disclosure of his or her assets, liabilities and net worth to the other.

ARTICLE II: PROPERTY AND FINANCIAL PROVISIONS
Disclosure (2)

Each party has made a full and complete disclosure of his or her assets, liabilities and net worth to the other by means of documents which are attached hereto and made a part of this agreement as exhibits; the disclosure of _____ _____ being **Exhibit A**, and the disclosure of _____ being **Exhibit B.**

Present Property of the Parties

Each of the parties has acquired all of his or her separate property independently of, and without the assistance of, the other and desires to keep separate all of his or her real and/or personal property, whether now owned or hereafter acquired, free from any claim by virtue of a marriage between them.

Separate Property

(a) For all purposes of this agreement, as used herein, the term "separate property" shall mean, with respect to a party hereto, all of such party's right, title and interest, legal or beneficial, in and to any and all property and interests in property, whether real, personal or mixed, wherever situated, and regardless of whether now owned or hereafter acquired, and;

(b) Each party shall, during his or her remaining lifetime, retain the sole ownership of all of his or her separate property, and shall have the exclusive right to dispose of any and all of such property during his or her remaining lifetime, by *inter vivos* or testamentary transfer, or by any and all other dispositions, and/or to encumber, pledge or hypothecate same, without any interference on the part of the other in such manner as shall be determined at the sole discretion of such owner thereof, as if their marriage had not taken place.

Waiver by Future Husband

Except as specifically provided herein, _____ hereby waives, relinquishes and releases all right, title and interest in and to any and all separate property of _____, accruing to, or vesting in him, or in which he may otherwise be entitled as husband of _____, or her widower, heir-at-law, next of kin or distributee, upon or by virtue of a termination of the marriage of the parties by death, divorce, dissolution, annulment, or otherwise, including, but not limited to such rights as curtesy, statutory or other allowances to a spouse of a decedent, distributions by way of intestacy, rights of election to take against the will of _____, or against any other alimony, support and/or other property settlement.

Waiver by Future Wife

Except as specifically provided herein, _____ hereby waives, relinquishes and releases all right, title and interest in and to any and all separate property of _____, accruing to, or vesting in her, or in which she may otherwise be entitled as wife of _____, or his widow, heir-at-law, next of kin or distributee, upon or by virtue of a termination of the marriage of the parties by death, divorce, dissolution, annulment, or otherwise, including, but not limited to such rights as dower, statutory or other allowances of a spouse of a decedent, distributions by way of intestacy, rights of election to take against the will of _____, or against any other alimony, support and/or other property settlement.

Property Held as Tenants by the Entirety

(a) Any other provisions of this agreement to the contrary notwithstanding, _____ and _____ may, during the marriage, acquire property or interests therein, in both names, with or without rights of survivorship. In such event, the signatures of both parties shall be required to sell, transfer, convey, pledge, encumber or hypothecate such jointly held property; and, upon the death of either party, any and all such property jointly held by both parties with rights of survivorship shall pass outright to the survivor in accordance with applicable law. Entry into such arrangements shall not in any way be deemed a waiver of or abandonment of this agreement or any part hereof.

(b) Upon termination of the marriage of the parties by divorce, dissolution, annulment or any other means while both are living, each party shall become a tenant in common with the other party and thereby entitled to an undivided one-half interest in said property. Should either party have contributed more than one-half toward the purchase, maintenance or improvement of such property, said party shall be entitled to a special equity in such property according to his or her respective contribution.

Partition of Community Property

The parties hereby agree that, if at any time after their marriage, either shall have or acquire any property which shall be derived from or related to separately owned property, or which is income from such property, or which is derived from or related to the labor of either party, then, upon request of either party, the parties will promptly execute such documents and instruments as may be required by applicable law to partition such community property into the separate property of the parties.

Right to Make Voluntary Transfers Not Waived

Any other provisions of this agreement to the contrary notwithstanding, each party shall have the right to voluntarily transfer or convey to the other any property or interest therein which may be lawfully transferred or conveyed, during his or her lifetime, or by will or otherwise upon death; and neither party intends by this agreement to limit nor restrict in any way the right and power of the other to receive any such voluntary transfer or conveyance. All such ostensible voluntary transfers or conveyances shall be deemed to be voluntary gifts from the transferor to the transferee and shall not in any way be deemed a waiver or abandonment of this agreement or any part hereof.

Joint Bank Accounts (1)

Any other provisions of this agreement to the contrary notwithstanding, the parties may, from time to time during the marriage, establish joint bank checking and/or savings accounts as tenants by the entirety requiring the signatures of both parties for the withdrawal of funds from such accounts. Upon the death of either party, any and all sums in any such bank accounts jointly held by both parties shall pass outright to the survivor in accordance with applicable law.

Joint Bank Accounts (2)

Any other provisions of this agreement to the contrary notwithstanding, the parties may, from time to time during the marriage, establish joint bank savings and/or checking accounts requiring the signature of either party for the withdrawal of funds from such accounts. Upon the death of either party, any and all sums in any such bank accounts jointly held by the parties shall pass outright to the survivor in accordance with applicable law.

Separate Bank Accounts

The parties agree that each may, from time to time during the marriage, establish various bank savings and/or checking accounts which shall be "separate property" under terms of this agreement and that all funds deposited therein, and all income derived therefrom, shall be "separate property" of the party in whose name such funds are held. The parties further agree to instruct any bank holding funds as provided for in this paragraph, that such funds shall be the separate property of the party in whose name such funds are being held.

Household Bank Accounts (1)

(a) The parties agree that they may, from time to time during the marriage, establish various jointly held bank checking accounts for convenience in the payment of household expenses and which require the signature of either party for the withdrawal of funds, and that;

(b) Funds shall be equally deposited therein by both parties in accord with their agreement to equally share payment of household expenses, and that;

(c) Upon the death or either party, any and all such sums in any such jointly held accounts shall pass outright to the surviving party in accordance with applicable law.

Household Bank Accounts (2)

(a) The parties agree that they may, from time to time during the marriage, establish various jointly held bank checking accounts for convenience in the payment of household expenses and which require the signature of either party for the withdrawal of funds, and that;

(b) Funds deposited therein shall be deposited _____ percent by _____ and _____ percent by _____, and that;

(c) Upon the death of either party, any and all sums in any such bank accounts jointly held by the parties shall pass outright to the surviving party in accordance with applicable law.

Household Bank Accounts (3)

(a) The parties agree that they may, from time to time during the marriage, establish various jointly held bank checking accounts for convenience in the payment of household expenses and which require the signature of either party for the withdrawal of funds, and that;

(b) Any and all funds deposited therein by either party shall be deemed the equal and undivided property of both, and that;

(c) Upon the death of either party, any and all sums in any such bank accounts jointly held by the parties shall pass outright to the surviving party in accordance with applicable law.

Existing Financial Obligations

(a) Each of the parties acknowledges that he or she is presently indebted to various persons and/or business entities as described by each in the hereinabove-mentioned disclosures to each other. With regard to these financial obligations, the parties hereby agree that they shall each individually be responsible for the payment of all antenuptial debts existing at the time of marriage, _____ paying for all antenuptial debts incurred by himself on his behalf, and _____ paying for all antenuptial debts incurred by herself on her behalf.

(b) Each party agrees to indemnify the other for all damage and cost incurred by reason of any suit against said party for debts which the other party has agreed in subparagraph (a) hereof to be responsible.

(c) In consideration of payment of any antenuptial debt of one party by the other, the party whose debt is thus paid agrees that the party satisfying such debt shall be entitled to a special equity in the property of the other, equal in value to the amount of any such debt so paid.

Credit Transactions by the Parties

The parties hereby agree that when either party enters into a transaction where credit is extended to such party, and such party becomes a debtor on the basis of credit extended solely by virtue of his or her assets, liabilities, income and credit history, then such party shall be fully and individually liable for the timely payment of any such obligation and shall hold the other party harmless from any such obligation and indemnify him or her in the event that he or she shall ever be required to satisfy same.

Taxes

Any other provisions of this agreement to the contrary notwithstanding, the parties recognize that the Internal Revenue Code and regulations thereunder, and other codes and regulations of the several states and of foreign nations, do, in certain instances, provide substantial savings in taxes paid by married couples filing joint returns. If such be the case, the parties hereby agree that the filing of any such joint returns, and/or the combining of their separate incomes and deductions, shall not in any way be deemed a waiver of, or abandonment of, this agreement or any part hereof, and that each party shall be fully responsible for the payment of his or her portion of any federal, state or other taxes attributable to his or her income or personal or real property.

Household Expenses (1)

(a) The parties agree to equally share responsibility for payment of household expenses, which for all purposes of this agreement, as used herein, shall mean mortgage or rent payments on the residence of the parties, all maintenance and improvement of same, utilities, food, shared entertainment and travel and medical expenses. The parties also agree that the mutually agreed-upon purchase and maintenance of household furniture, draperies, carpets, appliances, etc., shall also be "household expenses" for all purposes of this agreement and shall be shared equally by the parties, and the parties further agree that;

(b) Distribution of any such jointly owned property between the parties in the event the marriage is dissolved *vinculo matrimoni* by divorce, annulment, or any other means during the lifetime of both parties shall be carried out as provided for under **Possible Dissolution of the Marriage** as set forth herein, and that;

(c) The parties may determine, from time to time, to equally share the cost of insurance on their residence and its contents and the costs of medical and hospitalization insurance on both parties.

Household Expenses (2)

(a) _____ agrees to provide for payment of all household expenses during the marriage and to establish and adequately fund a joint bank checking account from which either party may withdraw funds for convenience in the payment of household expenses. For all purposes of this agreement, "household expenses" shall mean mortgage or rent payments on the residence of the parties, all maintenance and improvement of same, utilities, food, shared entertainment and travel and medical expenses. The mutually agreed-upon purchase and maintenance of household furniture, draperies, carpets, appliances, etc., shall also be "household expenses" for all purposes of this agreement, and;

(b) Distribution of any such jointly owned property between the parties in the event the marriage is dissolved *vinculo matrimoni* by divorce, annulment, or any other means during the lifetime of both parties shall be carried out as provided for under **Possible Dissolution of the Marriage** as set forth herein, and;

(c) _____ also agrees to provide for payment of insurance on their residence and its contents and for medical and hospitalization insurance on both parties.

Household Expenses (3)

(a) The parties agree to share responsibility for the payment of household expenses as follows:

(i) _____ shall provide for the payment of _____ percent of all reasonable household expenses, and

(ii) _____ shall provide for the payment of _____ percent of all reasonable household expenses, and

the parties agree to establish and fund a joint bank checking account for convenience in the payment of household expenses. For all purposes of this agreement, "household expenses" shall mean mortgage or rent payments on the residence of the parties, all maintenance and improvement of same, utilities, food, shared entertainment and travel and medical expenses. The parties also agree that the mutually agreed-upon purchase and maintenance of household furniture, draperies, carpets, appliances, etc., shall also be "household expenses" for all purposes of this agreement and shall be shared in the same proportion as provided for under (i) and (ii) hereinabove, and the parties further agree that;

(b) Distribution of any such jointly owned property between the parties in the event the marriage is dissolved *vinculo matrimoni* by divorce, annulment or any other means during the lifetime of both parties shall be carried out as provided for under **Possible Dissolution of the Marriage**, as set forth herein, and that;

(c) The parties may determine, from time to time, to share the cost of insurance on their residence and its contents and the costs of medical and hospitalization insurance on both parties. Any such insurance shall be paid for by the parties in the same proportion as "household expenses," as provided for under subparagraph (a), (i) and (ii), hereinabove.

Revision of Shared Household Expenses

The parties agree to revise the proportion of household expenses shared by each, and of household, medical and hospitalization insurance paid by each, whenever there is a substantial revision in the ratio between the incomes of the parties, so that the proportion of such shared household and insurance expenses remains closely related to the ratio between the individual incomes of the parties.

Financial Support   (1)

The parties agree to each be fully responsible for the payment of all expenses related to his or her own personal financial support and maintenance during the marriage.

Financial Support   (2)

(a) The parties agree to each be fully responsible for the payment of all expenses related to his or her own personal financial support and maintenance during the marriage, and;

(b) _____ agrees to be responsible for payment of _____ percent of the expense of the personal financial support of _____ during said marriage.

Financial Support   (3)

(a) The parties agree to each be fully responsible for the payment of all expenses related to his or her own personal financial support and maintenance during the marriage, and;

(b) _____ agrees to be responsible for payment of _____ percent of the expense of the personal financial support of _____ during said marriage, and further;

(c) Agrees to be responsible for the payment of _____ percent of the expense of the personal financial support of _____ during said marriage.

Financial Support   (4)

(a) The parties agree to each be fully responsible for the payment of all expenses related to his or her own personal financial support and maintenance during the marriage, and further agree that;

(b) Each party shall be responsible for the financial support and maintenance of _____ as follows:

(i) _____ shall be responsible for payment of _____ percent of such financial support and maintenance, and

(ii) _____ shall be responsible for payment of _____ percent of such financial support and maintenance.

Financial Support   (5)

(a) _____ agrees to be fully responsible for the payment of all expenses related to _____ own financial support and maintenance and agrees to be responsible for payment of _____ percent of all expenses for the personal financial support and maintenance of _____, and;

(b) _____ agrees to be fully responsible for the payment of _____ percent of all expenses related to _____ own personal financial support and maintenance.

Revision of Shared Financial Support

The parties agree to revise the proportion of financial support hereinabove-apportioned between the parties whenever there is a substantial change in the ratio of incomes between the parties, so that the proportion of shared financial support remains closely related to the ratio between the individual incomes of the parties.

Gainful Employment and Education   (1)

The parties agree that each shall have full autonomy regarding the choice of occupation, employment, career and education during the marriage, while in no way waiving nor renouncing the binding nature of their agreement providing for payment of household expenses and financial support as set forth herein.

Gainful Employment and Education   (2)

The parties agree that each shall have full autonomy regarding the choice of occupation, employment, career and education during the marriage, while recognizing the binding agreement of _____ to provide for payment of household expenses, financial support and maintenance as set forth herein.

Gainful Employment and Education   (3)

(a) The parties agree that each shall alternately be responsible for the payment of all reasonable household expenses and for the financial support and maintenance of both parties during such times when the other party is enrolled in school, namely:

_____ shall be responsible for payment of the household expenses, financial support and maintenance of both parties during such times as _____ shall be enrolled substantially full time in school diligently pursuing the educational goal of _____; and _____ shall be responsible for payment of the household expenses, financial support and maintenance of both parties during such times as _____ shall be enrolled substantially full time in school diligently pursuing the educational goal of _____. The enrollment of either party in school and the responsibility of the other for payment of household expenses, financial support and maintenance shall be determined solely by mutual consent.

(b) If after one party has provided for payment of the household expenses, financial support and maintenance of both parties for a period of approximately _____ so that the other may be enrolled in school pursuant to subparagraph (a) hereof, and then the party having been enrolled in school fails to provide for payment of the household expenses, financial support and maintenance of both parties for a subsequent equal period of time, the party failing to fulfill such obligation shall be indebted to the other party for a sum equal to one-half the amount reasonably expended for the household expenses, financial support and maintenance of both parties during the previous _____ _____.

Home Care and Maintenance   (1)

The parties agree to share equally, in terms of time, effort and expense, the responsibility for all housekeeping and the care and maintenance of their living space and any real property jointly owned or used.

Home Care and Maintenance (2)

In consideration of the obligation herein accepted by _____ to provide for payment of household expenses and for the financial support of _____ during the marriage, _____ hereby agrees to accept responsibility for the housekeeping, care and maintenance of shared living space, with such assistance as _____ may voluntarily provide.

Home Care and Maintenance (3)

The parties agree to share the responsibility for the housekeeping, care and maintenance of shared living space and any real property jointly owned or used as follows:

(a) _____ accepts responsibility for _____ percent of the necessary time and effort and _____ percent of the reasonable expense for the care and maintenance of shared living space and any real property jointly owned or used, and;

(b) _____ accepts responsibility for _____ percent of the necessary time and effort and _____ percent of the reasonable expense for the care and maintenance of shared living space and any real property jointly owned or used.

Home Care and Maintenance (4)

(a) It is agreed by the parties that _____ shall be responsible for the necessary time and effort for the care and maintenance of shared living space and any real property jointly owned or used during the marriage, for which he/she shall be paid the weekly sum of $_____ by _____ in addition to any other sums provided by _____ for household expenses, maintenance and the personal financial support of _____ as herein provided, and;

(b) _____ accepts responsibility for _____ percent of the reasonable expense for the care and maintenance of shared living space and any real property jointly owned or used, and that;

(c) _____ accepts responsibility for _____ percent of the reasonable expense for the care and maintenance of shared living space and any real property jointly owned or used.

ARTICLE III: CHILDREN

Mutual Agreement Not to Have Children

(a) Each party agrees that no children shall be born of the marriage, nor shall any children be adopted by either party during the marriage, unless both parties mutually agree in writing, and;

(b) It is further agreed that if a child is born during the marriage without the written agreement of both parties, then the wife waives all right to child support and the husband waives all right to visitation, and;

(c) _____ agrees to inform _____ immediately upon obtaining knowledge that she is pregnant, and further agrees that the withholding of such information from _____ _____ shall be deemed a waiver by her of child-support payments in the event of divorce, annulment or dissolution of the marriage by any other means during the lifetime of both parties, and;

(d) _____ realizes that the Courts look upon with disfavor as being contrary to public policy, agreements containing the provisions in subparagraphs (a), (b) and (c), hereof, but she strongly urges that those provisions be enforced to the letter. This provision shall be null and void where for medical reasons the wife must deliver a child.

ARTICLE III: CHILDREN

Care and Support of Children   (1)

The parties agree to share fully and equally all responsibilities related to the care and financial support of any and all children whom they may mutually agree to have or to adopt during the marriage.

ARTICLE III: CHILDREN

Care and Support of Children   (2)

In consideration of the agreement by _____ to provide for payment of all household expenses and for the financial support and maintenance of _____ and any and all children whom the parties may mutually agree to have or to adopt during the marriage, _____ agrees to accept primary responsibility for the care of any such children.

ARTICLE III: CHILDREN

Care and Support of Children   (3)

(a) The parties agree to share fully and equally during the marriage all responsibilities related to the financial support and care of the children of _____, of whom he/she is parent by previous marriage or by adoption, and;

(b) Further agree to share fully and equally all responsibilities related to the financial support and care of any and all children whom they may mutually agree to have or to adopt during the marriage.

ARTICLE III: CHILDREN

Care and Support of Children   (4)

(a) The parties agree to share fully and equally during the marriage all responsibilities related to the financial support and care of the children of _____, of whom she is parent by previous marriage or by adoption, and the children of _____, of whom he is parent by previous marriage or by adoption, and;

(b) Further agree to share fully and equally all responsibilities related to the financial support and care of any and all children whom they may mutually agree to have or to adopt during the marriage.

ARTICLE III: CHILDREN

Care and Support of Children   (5)

The parties agree to share fully and equally during the marriage all responsibilities related to the financial support and care of the children of _____, of whom he/she is parent by previous marriage or by adoption.

ARTICLE III: CHILDREN

Care and Support of Children   (6)

The parties agree to share fully and equally during the marriage all responsibilities related to the financial support and care of the children of _____, of whom he is parent by previous marriage or by adoption, and for the financial support and care of the children of _____, of whom she is parent by previous marriage or by adoption.

ARTICLE III: CHILDREN

Care and Support of Children   (7)

The parties agree to share fully and equally during the marriage all responsibilities related to the financial support and care of the children of _____, of whom he/she is parent.

Education of Children

It is mutually agreed by the parties that any child or children of them, or of either of them, shall have the benefit of a public school education up to and through high school level and that the parties shall mutually determine no later than during each child's junior year in high school whether it is desirable that such child have additional education and the manner of paying therefore.

Religious Instruction   (1)

It is mutually agreed by the parties that any child or children of them shall receive instruction in the _____ _____ faith and be encouraged by the parties to continue in that faith.

Religious Instruction   (2)

It is mutually agreed by the parties that any child or children of them shall receive no religious instruction from either parent, nor from any religious organization recommended by either parent, it being agreed by the parties that any child or children of theirs may seek his or her own religious instruction without influence or hindrance of either parent and that it shall be up to each child to pursue his or her own religious interest.

Religious Instruction   (3)

(a) It is mutually agreed by the parties that any child or children of them shall receive no religious instruction from either parent, nor from any religious organization recommended by either parent, it being agreed by the parties that any child or children of theirs may seek his or her own religious instruction without influence or hindrance of either parent and that it shall be up to each child to pursue his or her own religious interest, it being further agreed between the parties, however, that:

(b) Any child of _____, of whom he or she is parent by previous marriage or adoption, may be instructed in the _____ faith, this being deemed in the best interests of the child by _____.

Religious Instruction   (4)

(a) It is mutually agreed by the parties that any child or children of them shall receive no religious instruction from either parent, nor from any religious organization recommended by either parent, it being agreed by the parties that any child or children of theirs may seek his or her own religious instruction without influence or hindrance of either parent and that it shall be up to each child to pursue his or her own religious interest, it being further agreed between the parties, however, that;

(b) Any child of _____, of whom he is parent by previous marriage or by adoption, may be instructed in the _____ faith, this being deemed in the best interests of such child by _____, and, that;

(c) Any child of _____, of whom she is parent by previous marriage or by adoption, may be instructed in the _____ faith, this being deemed in the best interests of such child by _____.

Names of Children

It is agreed by the parties that any child whom the parties mutually agree to have or to adopt during the marriage shall bear the surname of _____.

Rights of Children

The parties recognize that they might, during the course of their marriage, mutually determine to have or to adopt a child or children and hereby agree that the provisions of this agreement are not intended to govern nor affect the rights of any such children in or to the separate property of either party hereto, and the parties further agree that all such rights in and to such separate property and/or financial support shall be governed by applicable law.

ARTICLE IV: POSSIBLE DISSOLUTION OF THE MARRIAGE

Waiver of Alimony and Support   (1)

(a) In accordance with the parties' full and complete acceptance of the principle of independence and equal responsibility and authority between them, and in further accordance with the parties' waiver and relinquishment of whatever rights, duties, obligations and privileges which either might or could have derived from or related to a state of matrimony between them, other than those which may be included in and made a part of this agreement, each party hereby waives, relinquishes and renounces whatever right he or she may have to alimony, maintenance or support in the event the marriage is dissolved *vinculo matrimoni* by divorce, annulment or any other means during the lifetime of both parties.

(b) The parties recognize that the Courts look upon with disfavor as being contrary to public policy, marriage agreements anticipating dissolution of the marriage or the waiver of alimony and/or support by either party. The above notwithstanding, the parties strongly urge the Court to enforce this agreement to the letter.

Advice of Counsel

In connection with provisions of the above paragraph, **Waiver of Alimony and Support**, and particularly regarding the waiver, relinquishment and renouncing of whatever right either party may have to alimony, maintenance or support in the event the marriage is dissolved by divorce, annulment or any other means during the lifetime of both parties, each party hereby acknowledges receipt of specific advice pertaining thereto by separate, independent counsel of each party's own choice, each paying for his or her own counsel's advice and aid. Each party acknowledges that as a part of such advice his or her counsel has thoroughly discussed current _____ statutes concerning the dissolution of marriage and of alimony in connection therewith, as well as pertinent judicial decisions.

ARTICLE IV: POSSIBLE DISSOLUTION OF THE MARRIAGE

Waiver of Alimony, Provision for Child Support   (2)

(a) In accordance with the parties' full and complete acceptance of the principle of independence and equal responsibility and authority between them, and in further accordance with the parties' waiver and relinquishment of whatever rights, duties, obligations and privileges which either might or could have derived from or related to a state of matrimony between them, other than those which may be included in and made a part of this agreement, each party hereby waives, relinquishes and renounces whatever right he or she may have to alimony, maintenance and support in the event the marriage is dissolved *vinculo matrimoni* by divorce, annulment or any other means during the lifetime of both parties except that;

(b) The party having primary custody of any child or children whom the parties may mutually have agreed to have or to adopt during the marriage shall receive from the other party a monthly sum equal to _____ percent of the reasonable cost of the maintenance and support of any such child or children until reaching eighteen (18) years of age.

(c) The parties recognize that the Courts look with disfavor as being contrary to public policy, marriage agreements anticipating dissolution of the marriage or the waiver of alimony and/or support by either party. The above notwithstanding, the parties strongly urge the Court to enforce this agreement to the letter.

Advice of Counsel

In connection with provisions of the above paragraph, **Waiver of Alimony, Provision for Child Support**, and particularly regarding the waiver, relinquishment and renouncing of whatever right either party may have to alimony, maintenance or support in the event the marriage is dissolved by divorce, annulment or any other means during the lifetime of both parties, each party hereby acknowledges receipt of specific advice pertaining thereto by separate, independent counsel of each party's own choice, each paying for his or her own counsel's advice and aid. Each party acknowledges that as a part of such advice, his or her counsel has thoroughly discussed current _____ statutes concerning the dissolution of marriage, and of alimony in connection therewith, as well as pertinent judicial decisions.

ARTICLE IV: POSSIBLE DISSOLUTION OF THE MARRIAGE

Waiver of Alimony   (3)

(a) Each party hereby waives, relinquishes and renounces in perpetuity his or her right to receive any type of alimony, whether it be temporary, permanent, continuous, lump sum, rehabilitative, periodic or otherwise, from the other party, regardless of whether or not either party has experienced a substantial change in his or her financial circumstances.

(b) The parties recognize that the Courts look upon with disfavor as being contrary to public policy, marriage agreements anticipating dissolution of the marriage or the waiver of alimony and/or support by either party. The above notwithstanding, the parties strongly urge the Court to enforce this agreement to the letter.

Advice of Counsel

In connection with provisions of the above paragraph, **Waiver of Alimony**, and particularly regarding the waiver, relinquishment and renouncing of whatever right either party may have to alimony, maintenance or support in the event the marriage is dissolved by divorce, annulment or any other means during the lifetime of both parties, each party hereby acknowledges receipt of specific advice pertaining thereto by separate, independent counsel of each party's own choice, each paying for his or her own counsel's advice and aid. Each party acknowledges that as a part of such advice, his or her own counsel has thoroughly discussed _____ statutes concerning the dissolution of marriage, and of alimony in connection therewith, as well as pertinent judicial decisions.

ARTICLE IV: POSSIBLE DISSOLUTION OF THE MARRIAGE
Payments in Lieu of Alimony (4)

While the parties contemplate a long and lasting marriage terminated only by the death of one of the parties, they also recognize the possibility that their marriage may be terminated by way of divorce or dissolution during the lifetime of both. In the event of such termination of the marriage *vinculo matrimoni* during the lifetime of both parties by way of divorce, annulment or any other means, regardless of which party hereto shall initiate such action, the parties hereby specifically agree:

(a) _____ shall not receive any alimony, support or separate property which might otherwise be available to him or her in accordance with applicable law.

(b) _____ shall accept from _____, in limitation of alimony and support, and in lieu of and instead of any obligation of _____ for the costs and attorney's fees of _____, payments as set forth below for a period equal to the number of months of marriage between the parties, or ten (10) years, whichever is less, and subject to the provisions of paragraph (d) hereof:

(i) For the first _____ months from and after issuance of the final decree of dissolution (termination date) of the marriage, _____ shall receive the sum of _____ _____ ($_____) per month;

(ii) Thereafter, the sum of _____ ($_____) per month for _____ consecutive months.

(iii) The aforesaid sums shall be payable by _____, by depositing a check therefore in the mails of the United States Postal Service, first class, postage prepaid, on or before the first day of each month to such address as _____ may from time to time designate in writing to _____ _____. The first such monthly payment shall be made for the first calendar month following the termination date of the marriage.

(iv) It is further agreed that the maximum monthly payments made by _____ hereunder shall at no time exceed _____ percent of the net worth of _____.

(c) It is hereby agreed by the parties that all payments made pursuant to provisions of the immediately preceding subparagraph (b) shall, for federal income tax purposes, be deemed and considered by both parties as payments of alimony or as payments in lieu thereof, and;

(d) All such obligations of and payments by _____ shall terminate conclusively and forever upon the first occurrence of the death of or the remarriage of _____, or his/her continuously residing with an adult of the opposite sex other than a blood relative; and no obligation of any kind as set forth in this paragraph, **Payments in Lieu of Alimony,** shall survive such first occurrence of said events, and;

(e) It is further agreed that such obligations of _____ shall be legal and binding obligations of and upon the estate and property in which _____ had a legal or beneficial interest prior to death, and;

(f) _____ hereby specifically recognizes and agrees that he/she shall have no right to receive additional payments of alimony or support in any manner at any time and upon the occurrence of any event from and after the aforesaid termination of marriage, and that he/she shall have no right to receive any separate property of _____ _____ at any time, or upon the occurrence of any event, and _____ further recognizes and ratifies his/her waiver, relinquishment and release of all such rights, and;

(g) The parties recognize that the Courts look upon with disfavor as being contrary to public policy, marriage agreements anticipating dissolution of the marriage or the waiver of alimony and/or support by either party. The above notwithstanding, the parties strongly urge the Court to enforce this agreement to the letter.

Advice of Counsel

In connection with provisions of the above paragraph, **Payments in Lieu of Alimony,** and particularly regarding the waiver, relinquishment and renouncing of whatever right either party may have to alimony, maintenance or support in the event the marriage is dissolved *vinculo matrimoni* by divorce, annulment or any other means during the lifetime of the parties, each party hereby acknowledges receipt of specific advice pertaining thereto by separate, independent counsel of each party's own choice, each paying for his or her own counsel's advice and aid. Each party acknowledges that as a part of such advice, his or her own counsel has thoroughly discussed _____ statutes concerning the dissolution of marriage, and of alimony in connection therewith, as well as pertinent judicial decisions.

Compliance with Applicable Law

Each party further acknowledges that he or she has sought meticulously to comply with applicable law concerning marital agreements regarding alimony, dower and curtesy rights and property rights, and that, among other things, each:

(a) Has fully and fairly advised the other, and been advised by the other, of their respective financial situations, and;

(b) Has a fair understanding of the financial status of the other and specifically understands that the other party is possessed of certain assets, as set forth in the annexed **Exhibits A** and **B**, which are made a part of this agreement, and;

(c) Considers the proposed payments in limitation of alimony or support as more than he or she would presently regard as fair under the current and probable future circumstances of each party and, in sum;

(d) Considers and believes after full and fair examination of the other's finances and after the advice of independent counsel that each has made a full disclosure to the other, each has a reasonable approximation of the financial situation of the other, and each considers the payments in limitation of and in lieu of all further obligation under provisions of said paragraph, **Payments in Lieu of Alimony**, to be more than fair.

Support *Pendente Lite*

The parties realize that in the event of dissolution of the marriage *vinculo matrimoni* by divorce, annulment or any other means during the lifetime of both parties, this agreement does not govern nor provide for support payments for the period beginning with the initiation of legal proceedings by either party for termination of the marriage and ending with the issuance of the final decree of termination in accordance with applicable law. To the extent enforceable and valid under _____ law, the parties agree that support *pendente lite* shall not exceed _____ _____ ($ _____) per week and that each party shall bear his or her own costs and attorney's fees related thereto.

Child Support in the Event of Dissolution of the Marriage

(a) The parties shall attempt to arrive at a sum which they mutually agree shall constitute reasonable monthly payments for support of any child or children whom the parties, by mutual consent, may agree to have or to adopt during the marriage, in the event of legal separation of the parties or dissolution of the marriage *vinculo matrimoni* by divorce, annulment or any other means during the lifetime of both parties. In the event that they are unable to agree upon such a sum, the Court shall decide the issue, and;

(b) The parties each agree that neither party shall attempt to include an amount which would have been used for alimony in the sum designated for child-support payments. This provision also applies to temporary child support.

Child Custody   (1)

The parties shall attempt, in the event of dissolution of the marriage, to arrive at an agreement for the custody of any child or children whom the parties may mutually agree to have or to adopt during the marriage. Such agreement shall take into consideration the best interests of any such child or children and the ability of each parent to provide for the financial support and care of any such children. In the event the parties are unable to agree upon child custody, the Court shall decide the issue.

Child Custody (2)

(a) It is agreed between the parties that _____ shall have primary custody of any child or children whom the parties mutually agree to have or to adopt during the marriage, subject to the following conditions:

(b) _____ shall have liberal visitation rights with any such child or children and shall give _____ reasonable advance notice of each visit, so that plans may be made by _____ so that the children will not be disturbed to their detriment, unless the parties have agreed to a fixed schedule which may be adhered to without notice to _____ by _____, and;

(c) _____ shall have custody of any such child or children for a _____ period during the summer and _____ of every other Christmas vacation and up to one week every other Thanksgiving. _____ shall have liberal visitation rights during all periods of custody of any such child or children by _____.

Removal of Children from Jurisdiction of the Court

It is mutually agreed by the parties that, in the event of dissolution of the marriage, neither party shall attempt to remove from the jurisdiction of the Court, without the written permission of the other party, any child or children whom the parties mutually agreed to have or to adopt during the marriage.

ARTICLE V: TESTEMENTARY PROVISIONS

Agreement Between the Parties (1)

(a) In the event that the marriage shall be terminated by the death of _____, and if at the time of such death the parties are living together as husband and wife, then, upon such death, _____ shall receive from the estate of _____, or from trust funds in which _____ may have a beneficial interest, together with all other funds and/or property which _____ may receive upon, and by virtue of the death of _____ (from, without limitation, joint bank accounts with or without rights of survivorship, other jointly held assets, life insurance and other property held in trust for the benefit of _____), a sum which shall be equal to the lesser of _____ ($_____) or _____ percent of the gross estate of _____, for Federal Estate Tax purposes, and;

(b) Any additional sum which may be needed to achieve said amount of $_____ or said _____ percent, as the case may be, shall be distributed to _____ by the executors of the estate of _____ and/or trustees of said estate, as the case may be, in cash or other forms of property capable of being converted to cash without material reduction in value, and such distribution shall be made as soon as practicable after the death of _____, but no later than six (6) months after the date of such death, and;

(c) The provisions required under subparagraphs (a) and (b) hereof shall be set forth in the **Last Will and Testament** of _____, or if an *inter vivos* trust agreement contains substantially all of the dispositive provisions concerning the assets of _____ at his or her death, then upon the request of _____, at any time during their marriage, _____ shall deliver to _____ a copy of the portion of such then current will and/or trust containing such provisions. The said obligation to set forth said provision in the said will and/or trust shall be an additional obligation of _____, but failure to perform such additional obligation shall have no effect upon the existence or validity of the obligation of _____ to make provision and payment as set forth in subparagraphs (a) and (b) hereof, and;

(d) In the event that at the time of the death of _____, the parties shall have not been married, or shall not then be living together as husband and wife, or the said marriage shall have been dissolved prior thereto, the obligations set forth hereinabove shall be null and void and of no force or effect whatever.

ARTICLE V: TESTEMENTARY PROVISIONS
Agreement Between the Parties   (2)

(a) In the event the marriage shall be terminated by the death of _____, and if at the time of such death the parties shall be living together as husband and wife, then _____ accepts as full discharge, settlement and satisfaction of any and all other statutory and/or other right, title and interest which she, as widow, heir-at-law, next of kin or distributee, upon termination of the marriage by death might or could acquire by virtue of the death of _____, the provisions of any **Last Will and Testament** of _____ _____, and hereby waives, relinquishes and renounces any right which she may have to share in the estate of _____ by way of intestacy, dower or right of election to take against the estate of _____, and;

(b) The consideration of the agreement of _____ as provided in subparagraph (a) hereof, _____ hereby agrees to take out and maintain in force during the marriage, life insurance which will pay an amount not less than _____ ($_____) to _____ in the event of the death of _____ by illness or accident, or, alternatively, to make an *inter vivos* gift to, or to establish an irrevocable trust for the benefit of, _____ in said amount and;

(c) In the event the marriage shall be terminated by the death of _____, and if at the time of such death the parties shall be living together as husband and wife, then _____ accepts as full discharge, settlement and satisfaction of any and all other statutory and other right, title and interest which he, as widower, heir-at-law, next of kin or distributee, upon termination of the marriage by death might or could acquire by virtue of the death of _____, the provisions of any **Last Will and Testament** of _____ _____, and hereby waives, relinquishes and renounces any right which he may have to share in the estate of _____ by way of intestacy, curtesy or right of election to take against the estate of _____, and;

(d) In consideration of the agreement of _____ as provided in subparagraph (c) hereof, _____ hereby agrees to take out and maintain in force during the marriage, life insurance which will pay an amount not less than _____ ($_____) to _____ in the event of the death of _____ by illness or accident, or, alternatively, to make an *inter vivos* gift to, or to establish an irrevocable trust for the benefit of, _____ in said amount.

Life Insurance

(a) _____ hereby agrees to take out and maintain in force during the marriage, life insurance which will pay an amount not less than _____ ($_____) to _____ in the event of the death of _____ by illness or accident, or, alternatively, to make an *inter vivos* gift to, or to establish an irrevocable trust for the benefit of, _____ in said amount and;

(b) _____ hereby agrees to take out and maintain in force during the marriage, life insurance which will pay an amount not less than _____ ($_____) to _____ in the event of the death of _____ by illness or accident, or, alternatively, to make an *inter vivos* gift to, or to establish an irrevocable trust fund for the benefit of, _____ in said amount.

ARTICLE VI: GENERAL PROVISIONS

Independent Counsel (1)

(a) The parties hereto jointly and severally acknowledge that each has consulted with separate and independent legal counsel with respect to the legal and other effects of this agreement, the rights and privileges waived and granted hereby, and all other matters pertaining thereto, and;

(b) Both parties further jointly and severally acknowledge their complete understanding of such legal and other effects of this agreement, and;

(c) Each of the parties hereby warrants and represents that the legal counsel of each party executing this agreement was and is the sole and exclusive legal counsel consulted by such party with regard to the matters contained herein, and;

(d) Each acknowledges his or her understanding that he or she is relinquishing and waiving certain rights which might or could have great value in consideration of the provisions of this agreement, and each does so willingly and free of all duress or coercion.

ARTICLE VI: GENERAL PROVISIONS

Advice by Counsel (2)

(a) The parties hereto acknowledge that they have jointly obtained the advice and counsel of an attorney with respect to the legal and other effects of this agreement, the rights and privileges waived and granted hereby, and all other matters pertaining hereto, and;

(b) The parties acknowledge that as a part of such counsel's advice, said counsel has thoroughly discussed _____ _____ statutes concerning the dissolution of marriage, alimony, support, dower and curtesy rights and property rights, as well as pertinent judicial decisions, and;

(c) Each party acknowledges his/her understanding that he/she is accepting certain rights, duties and obligations hereby, and is also waiving certain rights which might or could have great value in consideration for the provisions of this agreement, and each does so willingly and free from all duress or coercion.

Headings

The headings of the several paragraphs hereof are inserted solely for the convenience of reference and shall have no further meaning, force or effect.

Partial Invalidity

If any provision of this agreement is held to be invalid or unenforceable, all other provisions hereof shall nevertheless remain in full force and effect.

Fair and Equitable

Each party acknowledges that this agreement is fair and equitable.

Parties Bound

This agreement shall inure to the benefit of and be legally binding upon the parties hereto, and the heirs, executors, administrators, successors and assigns of each of them, but shall take effect only in the event the parties become legally married to each other.

Enforcement by Court

The parties hereto strongly urge the Court to enforce this agreement to the letter, even though some provisions contained herein may be void as against public policy and even though a substantial change may have occurred in the financial circumstances of either or both parties.

Entire Agreement

This agreement contains the entire understanding and agreement between the parties, and no amendment or future understanding shall be binding upon either party unless reduced to writing and executed by both parties.

Evidence

Neither party shall object to this agreement being entered in evidence in any action for permanent separation, divorce, dissolution of the marriage, or other similar action in any Court of law.

Execution of Documents

Each party shall, at any time and from time to time, upon the request of the other party, execute, acknowledge and deliver any and all documents which may be necessary or advisable to carry out the intentions and provisions of this agreement, including, but not limited to, such instruments as may be required by the laws of any jurisdiction now in effect or hereafter enacted which may affect the property or other rights of the parties *inter se*, or between the parties hereto and third parties; and further, specifically including all portions of this agreement, or amendments thereto, in recordable form, which may, at the option of either party, be filed of record with any Court in any county wherein is located any separate property of either party hereto.

Counterparts

This agreement may be executed in one or more counterparts, each of which shall be considered as an original.

Governing Law (1)

This agreement shall be construed and governed in accordance with the laws of the State of _____.

Governing Law (2)

(a) This agreement shall be executed and delivered in the State of _____, and the provisions hereof shall be construed and enforced in accordance with the laws of said State, regardless of any change of domicile by either or both parties, and;

(b) Any and all actions brought in any Court of law relating directly or indirectly to the marriage or any terms of this agreement, shall be brought in the appropriate Court of the State of _____, and;

(c) Such Court shall have exclusive jurisdiction and venue thereof, and;

(d) Both parties hereby specifically agree to submit to the personal jurisdiction of such Court, regardless of their respective domiciles or residences, at any time any such action is brought.

Resident Agent

Each party hereby makes, constitutes and appoints the following as his or her resident agent for service of process and other notices as herein provided, waives his or her right to service by publication, and agrees that any and all such service may be made on:

(i) The party personally,

(ii) Said designated agent, or

(iii) By certified or registered mail.

PARTY	REGISTERED AGENT
_____	_____
_____	_____
_____	_____
_____	_____
_____	_____
_____	_____
_____	_____

Execution of Agreement

IN WITNESS WHEREOF, the parties hereto set their hands and seals this _____ day of _____,
19 _____.

_____
Witness

_____

_____

_____ (Seal)

_____
Witness

_____

_____

_____
Witness

_____

_____

_____ (Seal)

_____
Witness

_____

_____

* *

Attestation of Notary

STATE OF   )
)   ss:

COUNTY OF   )

On this _____ day of _____, 19 _____, before me personally came and appeared _____, who, first being duly sworn, stated that he has read the foregoing **Agreement in Contemplation of Marriage** and that he signed same for the purpose therein contained.

IN WITNESS WHEREOF, I hereunto set my hand and official seal.

_____
                                      Notary Public

My commission expires: _____

STATE OF   )
)   ss:

COUNTY OF   )

On this _____ day of _____, 19 _____, before me personally came and appeared _____, who, first being duly sworn, stated that she has read the foregoing **Agreement in Contemplation of Marriage** and that she signed same for the purpose therein contained.

IN WITNESS WHEREOF, I hereunto set my hand and official seal.

_____
                                      Notary Public

My commission expires: _____

* *

AFFIDAVIT OF COUNSEL   (1)

The undersigned hereby certifies that he/she is and has been legal counsel to _____
in connection with the preparation, review and execution of the foregoing **Agreement in Contemplation of Marriage**; and

The undersigned further certifies that he/she has consulted with and rendered independent legal advice to said client concerning provisions of the aforesaid **Agreement in Contemplation of Marriage,** the financial, legal and other effects thereof, and has thoroughly discussed _____ statutes concerning the dissolution of marriage, and of alimony in connection therewith, as well as judicial decisions related thereto.

IN WITNESS WHEREOF, I hereunto set my hand and seal this _____ day of _____,
19 _____.

_____ (Seal)

_____
Witness

_____

_____

_____
Witness

_____

Attestation of Notary

STATE OF   )
)   ss:
COUNTY OF   )

On this _____ day of _____, 19 _____, before me personally came and appeared
_____, who, first being duly sworn, stated that he/she executed the foregoing **Affidavit of Counsel** for the purpose therein contained.

IN WITNESS WHEREOF, I hereunto set my hand and official seal.

_____
                                    Notary Public

My commission expires: _____

* *

AFFIDAVIT OF COUNSEL (2)

The undersigned hereby certifies that he/she is and has been legal counsel to _____
and _____ in connection with the preparation, review and execution of the foregoing
Agreement in Contemplation of Marriage; and

The undersigned further certifies that he/she has consulted with and rendered legal advice to said clients concerning provisions of the aforesaid **Agreement in Contemplation of Marriage**, the financial, legal and other effects thereof, and has thoroughly discussed _____ statutes concerning the dissolution of marriage, and of alimony in connection therewith, as well as judicial decisions related thereto.

IN WITNESS WHEREOF, I hereunto set my hand and seal this _____ day of _____,
19 _____.

_____ (Seal)

_____

Witness

_____

_____

Witness

_____

_____

Attestation of Notary

STATE OF   )
) ss:
COUNTY OF   )

On this _____ day of _____, 19 _____, before me personally came and appeared
_____, who, first being duly sworn, stated that he/she executed the foregoing **Affidavit of Counsel** for the purpose therein contained.

IN WITNESS WHEREOF, I hereunto set my hand and official seal.

_____
Notary Public

My commission expires: _____

Agreement in Contemplation of Marriage

Between

and

Dated _____ 19 _____

Exhibit A

It is mutually agreed by _____ and _____ that all of the following listed real and personal property was acquired by _____ independent of and without the assistance of _____ , and shall hereafter be the separate property of _____ .

Acknowledged:

_____ (Seal)

_____ (Seal)

Exhibit B

It is mutually agreed by _____ and _____ that all of the following listed real and personal property was acquired by _____ independent of and without the assistance of _____ , and shall hereafter be the separate property of _____ .

Acknowledged:

_____ (Seal)

_____ (Seal)

Agreement to Live Together

THIS AGREEMENT is made this _____ day of _____, 19 _____, by and between

_____, of

| Street Address | Apt. No. | City | State | Zip |

hereinafter referred to as _____, and

_____, of

| Street Address | Apt. No. | City | State | Zip |

hereinafter referred to as _____.

WHEREAS _____ and _____ agree to live together, each party wishes to settle between themselves the nature of their relationship; property; financial responsibility; children, if any, and their care, support and education; location of domicile; the sharing of household space, expenses and housekeeping responsibilities; the gainful employment and education of each party; the names of each; possible incapacitation of each; possible dissolution of the herein-described relationship; the financial support and maintenance of either party thereafter; and the death of either party; and

WHEREAS, for and in consideration of the sum of twenty dollars ($20.00), and other good and valuable consideration, the receipt whereof is hereby acknowledged, and in further consideration of the parties entering into the herein-described relationship and making the mutual covenants herein contained to be performed by the parties, the parties hereto mutually agree and covenant as follows:

ARTICLE I: CONDITIONS OF THE AGREEMENT

Purpose (1)

The purpose of the parties for living together is to share more of themselves and their time, energy and affection than would be possible if they were living apart.

ARTICLE I: CONDITIONS OF THE AGREEMENT

Purpose (2)

The purpose of the parties for living together is to share more of themselves and their time, energy and affection and their financial resources and property than would be possible if they were living apart.

Voluntary

Each party acknowledges that this agreement is being entered into voluntarily and that it is not the result of duress, coercion or undue influence.

Future Marriage Not a Condition Precedent

The parties mutually and severally acknowledge that neither has made nor expects any commitment, promise or offer of marriage now or at any time hereafter, in consideration of, nor in any way related to nor derived from, any of the promises, covenants or effects of this agreement.

Declaration of Principle (1)

The parties value and accept the principle of independence and of the equal distribution of responsibility and authority between them and that each is a fully equal and independent partner in their relationship with each other.

Declaration of Principle (2)

The parties value and accept the principle of independence and of the equal distribution of responsibility and authority between them and that each is a fully equal partner in their relationship with each other.

Openness Between the Parties (1)

Both parties anticipate and expect the sharing of each other's lives to the extent as may benefit both, without infringing upon the privacy, independence or solitude of the other.

Openness Between the Parties (2)

Both parties anticipate and expect the sharing of each other's lives to the extent as may benefit both, without infringing upon the privacy or solitude of the other.

Names of the Parties (1)

The parties agree not to hold themselves out to be husband and wife and further agree that each shall continue to use his or her own name, being known, respectively, as _____ and _____ _____ .

Names of the Parties (2)

The parties agree that they shall use the surname of _____ and shall be known during the herein-described relationship as _____ and _____ _____ .

Present Employment of the Parties (1)

(a) The parties acknowledge their understanding that _____ is presently gainfully employed as _____ with an approximate annual income of $ _____ _____ and presently intends to continue such employment, and that;

(b) _____ is presently gainfully employed as _____ _____ with an approximate annual income of $ _____ and presently intends to continue such employment.

Present Employment of the Parties (2)

(a) The parties acknowledge their understanding that _____ is presently gainfully employed as _____ with an approximate annual income of $ _____ _____ and presently intends to continue such employment, and that;

(b) _____ is not employed and _____ plan to become employed during the next _____ in order to _____ _____ .

Present Employment of the Parties (3)

(a) The parties acknowledge their understanding that _____ is presently gainfully employed as _____ with an approximate annual income of $ _____ _____ and presently intends to continue such employment, and that;

(b) _____ is presently gainfully employed as _____ _____ with an approximate annual income of $ _____ , but that he/she presently intends to terminate such employment _____ in order to _____ _____ .

Present Employment of the Parties (4)

The parties acknowledge their understanding that neither is presently gainfully employed and that _____ _____ shall diligently seek employment in order that _____ may _____ .

Children by Previous Marriage (1)

The parties acknowledge their understanding that _____ has previously been married and has a child or children born of or adopted during such marriage for whom he/she is obligated to provide $ _____ per _____ in financial support and who shall, for approximately _____ of each year, live with the parties.

Children by Previous Marriage (2)

The parties acknowledge their understanding that _____ has previously been married and has a child or children born of or adopted during such marriage for whom he/she has the right to receive child support in the amount of $ _____ per _____ and who shall, for approximately _____ of each year, live with the parties.

Children by Previous Marriage   (3)

The parties acknowledge their understanding that _____ has previously been married and has a child or children born of or adopted during such marriage for whom he/she receives no child support and who shall, for approximately _____ of each year, live with the parties.

Previous Children

The parties acknowledge their understanding that _____ has a child or children adopted during or born of a previous relationship for whom he/she _____ child support and who shall, for approximately _____ of each year, live with the parties.

Incapacitation of Either Party

The parties agree that in the event of the incapacitation of either party during the herein-described relationship the other party shall assume complete responsibility for the care and financial support of the other party to the extent of his or her income, assets and time.

Commitment

Both parties anticipate and offer commitment, loyalty and support during the herein-described relationship, freely given in time of need.

Use of Living Space

(a) The parties agree to live together at a residence of their mutual choice, recognizing, however, that it may be necessary or desirable from time to time for one to live away from the other for a period of up to several months as determined by the educational, employment or other needs of either party. Each party hereby waives whatever right he or she may have to determine solely the domicile of the parties, and the parties further agree that;

(b) The parties shall have equal right to use of all living space in their home and that all decisions regarding its use shall be by mutual consent only, except that the right of each party to the quiet enjoyment and security of shared living space shall take precedence over all other uses.

ARTICLE II: PROPERTY AND FINANCIAL PROVISIONS

Disclosure   (1)

Each party has made a full and complete disclosure of his or her assets, liabilities and net worth to the other.

ARTICLE II: PROPERTY AND FINANCIAL PROVISIONS

Disclosure (2)

Each party has made a full and complete disclosure of his or her assets, liabilities and net worth to the other by means of documents which are attached hereto and made a part of this agreement as exhibits: the disclosure of _____ _____ being **Exhibit A,** and the disclosure of _____ being **Exhibit B.**

Present Property of the Parties

Each of the parties has acquired all of his or her separate property independently of, and without the assistance of, the other and desires to keep separate all of his or her real and/or personal property, whether now owned or hereafter acquired, free from any claim by virtue of the herein-described relationship between the parties.

Separate Property

(a) For all purposes of this agreement, as used herein, the term "separate property" shall mean, with respect to a party hereto, all of such party's right, title and interest, legal and beneficial, in and to any and all property and interests in property, whether real, personal or mixed, wherever situated, and regardless of whether now owned or hereafter acquired, and;

(b) Each party shall, during his or her remaining lifetime, retain the sole ownership of all of his or her separate property, and shall have exclusive right to dispose of any and all of such property during his or her remaining lifetime, by *inter vivos* or testamentary transfer, or by any and all other dispositions, and/or to encumber, pledge or hypothecate same, without any interference on the part of the other in such manner as shall be determined at the sole discretion of such owner thereof, as if the herein-described relationship did not exist and had not taken place.

Jointly Held Property

(a) Any other provisions of this agreement to the contrary notwithstanding, _____ and _____ may, during the herein-described relationship, acquire property or interests therein in joint tenancy, in both names. In such event the signatures of both parties shall be required to sell, transfer, convey, pledge, encumber or hypothecate such jointly held property, and;

(b) Any and all such property jointly held by both parties shall pass outright to the survivor in accordance with applicable law, and;

(c) Entry into such arrangements shall not in any way be deemed a waiver or abandonment of this agreement or any part hereof.

Right to Make Voluntary Transfers Not Waived

Any other provisions of this agreement to the contrary notwithstanding, each party shall have the right to voluntarily transfer or convey to the other any property or interest therein which may be lawfully transferred or conveyed, during his or her remaining lifetime, or by will or otherwise upon death; and neither party intends by this agreement to limit nor restrict in any way the right and power of the other to receive any such voluntary transfer or conveyance. All such ostensible voluntary transfers or conveyances shall be deemed to be voluntary gifts from the transferor to the transferee and shall not in any way be deemed a waiver or abandonment of this agreement or any part thereof.

Joint Bank Accounts   (1)

Any other provisions of this agreement to the contrary notwithstanding, the parties may, from time to time during the herein-described relationship, establish joint bank checking and/or savings accounts requiring the signatures of both parties for the withdrawal of funds from such accounts. Upon the death of either party, any and all sums in any such bank accounts jointly held by the parties shall pass outright to the survivor in accordance with applicable law.

Joint Bank Accounts   (2)

Any other provisions of this agreement to the contrary notwithstanding, the parties may, from time to time during the herein-described relationship, establish joint bank checking and/or savings accounts requiring the signature of either party for the withdrawal of funds from such accounts. Upon the death of either party, any and all sums in any such bank accounts jointly held by the parties shall pass outright to the survivor in accordance with applicable law.

Separate Bank Accounts

The parties agree that each may, from time to time during the herein-described relationship, establish various bank checking and/or savings accounts which shall be "separate property" under terms of this agreement and that all funds deposited therein, and all income derived therefrom, shall be "separate property" of the party in whose name such funds are held. The parties further agree to instruct any bank holding such funds as provided for in this paragraph that such funds shall be the separate property of the party in whose name such funds are being held.

Household Bank Accounts   (1)

(a) The parties agree that they may, from time to time during the herein-described relationship, establish various jointly held bank checking accounts for convenience in the payment of household expenses and which require the signature of either party for the withdrawal of funds, and that;

(b) Funds shall be equally deposited therein by both parties in accord with their agreement to equally share the payment of household expenses, and that;

(c) Upon the death of either party, any and all sums in any such jointly held bank accounts shall pass outright to the survivor in accordance with applicable law.

Household Bank Accounts   (2)

(a) The parties agree that they may, from time to time during the herein-described relationship, establish various jointly held bank checking accounts for convenience in the payment of household expenses and which require the signature of either party for the withdrawal of funds, and that;

(b) Funds deposited therein shall be deposited _____ percent by _____ _____ and _____ percent by _____, and that;

(c) Upon the death of either party, any and all sums in any such bank accounts jointly held by the parties shall pass outright to the survivor in accordance with applicable law.

Household Bank Accounts   (3)

(a) The parties agree that they may, from time to time during the herein-described relationship, establish various jointly held bank checking accounts for convenience in the payment of household expenses and which require the signature of either party for the withdrawal of funds, and that;

(b) Any and all funds deposited therein by either party shall be deemed the equal and undivided property of both, and that;

(c) Upon the death or either party, any and all sums in any such bank accounts jointly held by the parties shall pass outright to the survivor in accordance with applicable law.

Existing Financial Obligations

(a) Each of the parties acknowledges that he or she is presently indebted to various persons and/or business entities as described by each in the hereinabove-mentioned disclosures to each other. With regard to these financial obligations, the parties hereby agree that they shall each individually be responsible for the payment of all debts existing on the date of this agreement, _____ paying for all such debts incurred by himself on his behalf, and _____ paying for all such debts incurred by herself on her behalf, and;

(b) Each party agrees to indemnify the other for all damage and cost incurred by reason of any suit against said party for debts which the other party has agreed in subparagraph (a) hereof to be responsible for, and;

(c) In consideration of payment of any such debts of one party by the other, the party whose debt is thus paid agrees that the party satisfying such debt shall be entitled to a special equity in the property of the other, equal in value to the amount of any such debt so paid.

Credit Transactions by the Parties

The parties agree that when either party enters into a transaction where credit is extended to such party, and such party becomes a debtor on the basis of credit extended solely by virtue of his or her assets, liabilities, income and credit history, then such party shall be fully and individually liable for the timely payment of any such obligation and shall hold the other party harmless from any such obligation and indemnify him or her in the event that he or she shall ever be required to satisfy same.

Taxes

The parties agree that each shall be responsible for payment of his or her portion of any taxes attributable to his or her income or personal or real property and that each party shall pay his or her portion of any taxes upon any real or personal property which is jointly owned by the parties.

Household Expenses (1)

(a) The parties agree to equally share responsibility for payment of household expenses, which for all purposes of this agreement, as used herein, shall mean mortgage or rent payments on the residence of the parties, all maintenance and improvement of same, utilities, food, shared entertainment and travel and medical expenses. The parties also agree that the mutually agreed-upon purchase and maintenance of household furniture, draperies, carpets, appliances, etc., shall also be "household expenses" for all purposes of this agreement and shall be shared equally by the parties, and the parties further agree that;

(b) Distribution of such jointly owned property between the parties in the event of dissolution of the herein-described relationship shall be carried out as provided for under **Possible Dissolution of the Relationship** as set forth herein, and that;

(c) The parties may determine, from time to time, to equally share the cost of insurance on their residence and its contents and the costs of medical and hospitalization insurance on both parties.

Household Expenses (2)

(a) _____ agrees to provide for payment of all household expenses and to establish and adequately fund a joint bank checking account from which either party may withdraw funds for convenience in the payment of household expenses. For all purposes of this agreement, as used herein, "household expenses" shall mean mortgage or rent payments on the residence of the parties, all maintenance and improvement of same, utilities, food, shared entertainment and travel and medical expenses. The mutually agreed-upon purchase and maintenance of household furniture, draperies, carpets, appliances, etc., shall also be "household expenses" for all purposes of this agreement, and;

(b) Distribution of any such jointly owned property between the parties in the event of dissolution of the herein-described relationship shall be carried out as provided for under **Possible Dissolution of the Relationship** as set forth herein, and;

(c) _____ also agrees to provide for payment of insurance on their residence and its contents and for medical and hospitalization insurance on both parties.

Household Expenses   (3)

(a) The parties agree to share responsibility for the payment of household expenses as follows:

(i) _____ shall provide for the payment of _____

percent of all reasonable household expenses, and

(ii) _____ shall provide for the payment of _____

percent of all reasonable household expenses, and
the parties agree to establish and fund a joint bank checking account for convenience in the payment of household expenses. For all purposes of this agreement, "household expenses" shall mean mortgage or rent payments on the residence of the parties, all maintenance and improvement of same, utilities, food, shared entertainment and travel and medical expenses. The parties also agree that the mutually agreed-upon purchase and maintenance of household furniture, draperies, carpets, appliances, etc., shall also be "household expenses" for all purposes of this agreement and shall be shared in the same proportion as provided for under (i) and (ii) hereinabove, and the parties further agree that;

(b) Distribution of any such jointly owned property between the parties in the event of dissolution of the herein-described relationship between the parties shall be carried out as provided for under **Possible Dissolution of the Relationship** as set forth herein, and that;

(c) The parties may determine, from time to time, to share the cost of insurance on their residence and its contents and the costs of medical and hospitalization insurance on both parties. Any such insurance shall be paid for by the parties in the same proportion as "household expenses," as provided for under subparagraph (a), (i) and (ii), hereinabove.

Revision of Shared Household Expenses

The parties agree to revise the proportion of household expenses shared by each, and of household, medical and hospitalization insurance paid by each, whenever there is a substantial revision in the ratio between the incomes of the parties, so that the proportion of such shared household and insurance expenses remains closely related to the ratio between the individual incomes of the parties.

Financial Support   (1)

The parties agree to each be fully responsible for the payment of all expenses related to his or her own personal financial support and maintenance during the herein-described relationship.

Financial Support   (2)

(a) _____ hereby accepts responsibility for payment of all expenses related
to _____ own personal financial support and maintenance during the herein-described relationship, and further;

(b) Agrees to be responsible for payment of _____ percent of the personal financial support and maintenance of _____ during said relationship.

Financial Support   (3)

(a) _____ hereby accepts responsibility for payment of all expenses related
to _____ own personal financial support and maintenance during the herein-described relationship, and;

(b) Agrees to be responsible for payment of _____ percent of the personal financial support and maintenance of _____ during said relationship, and further;

(c) Agrees to be responsible for payment of _____ percent of the personal financial support and maintenance of _____ during said relationship.

Financial Support   (4)

(a) The parties agree to each be fully responsible for the payment of all expenses related to his or her own personal financial support and maintenance during the herein-described relationship, and further agree that;

(b) Each party shall be responsible for payment of the financial support and maintenance of _____ _____ as follows:

(i) _____ shall be responsible for payment of _____ percent of such financial support and maintenance, and

(ii) _____ shall be responsible for payment of _____ percent of such financial support and maintenance.

Revision of Shared Financial Support

The parties agree to revise the proportion of financial support hereinabove-apportioned between the parties whenever there is a substantial revision in the ratio between the incomes of the parties, so that the proportion of such shared financial support remains closely related to the ratio between the individual incomes of the parties.

Gainful Employment and Education   (1)

The parties agree that each shall have full autonomy regarding the choice of occupation, employment, career and education during the herein-described relationship, while in no way waiving nor renouncing the binding nature of their agreement providing for payment of household expenses, financial support and maintenance as set forth herein.

Gainful Employment and Education   (2)

The parties agree that each shall have full autonomy regarding the choice of occupation, employment, career and education during the herein-described relationship, while recognizing the binding agreement of _____ _____ to provide for payment of household expenses, financial support and maintenance as set forth herein.

Gainful Employment and Education   (3)

(a) The parties agree that each shall alternately be responsible for the payment of all reasonable household expenses and for the financial support and maintenance of both parties during such times when the other party is enrolled in school, namely:

_____ shall be responsible for payment of the household expenses, financial support and maintenance of both parties during such times as _____ shall be enrolled substantially full time in school diligently pursuing the educational goal of _____ ; and _____ shall be responsible for payment of the household expenses, financial support and maintenance of both parties during such times as _____ shall be enrolled substantially full time in school diligently pursuing the educational goal of _____ . The enrollment of either party in school and the responsibility of the other for payment of household expenses, financial support and maintenance shall be determined solely by mutual consent.

(b) If after one party has provided for the payment of the household expenses, financial support and maintenance of both parties for a period of approximately _____ so that the other may be enrolled in school pursuant to subparagraph (a) hereof, and then the party having been enrolled in school fails to provide for payment of the household expenses, financial support and maintenance of both parties for a subsequent equal period of time, the party failing to fulfill such obligation shall be indebted to the other party for a sum equal to one-half the amount reasonably expended for the household expenses, financial support and maintenance of both parties during the previous

_____ .

Home Care and Maintenance   (1)

The parties agree to share equally, in terms of time, effort and expense, the responsibility for housekeeping and the care and maintenance of their living space and any real property jointly owned or used.

Home Care and Maintenance   (2)

In consideration of the obligation herein accepted by _____ to provide payment of household expenses and for the financial support of _____ during the herein-described relationship, _____ hereby agrees to accept responsibility for the housekeeping, care and maintenance of shared living space and any real property jointly owned or used.

Home Care and Maintenance   (3)

The parties agree to share the responsibility for the housekeeping, care and maintenance of shared living space and any real property jointly owned or used as follows:

(a) _____ accepts responsibility for _____ percent of the necessary time and effort and _____ percent of the reasonable expense for the care and maintenance of shared living space and any real property jointly owned or used, and;

(b) _____ accepts responsibility for _____ percent of the necessary time and effort and _____ percent of the reasonable expense for the care and maintenance of shared living space and any real property jointly owned or used.

Home Care and Maintenance   (4)

(a) It is agreed by the parties that _____ shall be responsible for the necessary time and effort for the care and maintenance of shared living space and any real property jointly owned or used during the herein-described relationship, for which he/she shall be paid the weekly sum of $_____ by _____ in addition to any other sums provided by _____ for household expenses, maintenance and the personal financial support of _____ as herein provided, and;

(b) _____ accepts responsibility for _____ percent of the reasonable expense for the care and maintenance of shared living space and any real property jointly owned or used, and that;

(c) _____ accepts responsibility for _____ percent of the reasonable expense for the care and maintenance of shared living space and any real property jointly owned or used.

ARTICLE III: CHILDREN
Mutual Agreement Not to Have Children

(a) Each party agrees that no children shall be born of the herein-described relationship, nor shall any children be adopted by either party during said relationship, unless both parties mutually agree in writing, and;

(b) It is further agreed that if a child is born during said relationship without the written agreement of both parties, then _____ waives all right to child support and _____ _____ waives all right to visitation, and;

(c) _____ agrees to inform _____ immediately upon obtaining knowledge that she is pregnant, and further agrees that the withholding of such information from _____ shall be deemed a waiver by her of child-support payments, and;

(d) _____ realizes that the Courts may look upon with disfavor as being contrary to public policy, agreements containing the provisions in subparagraphs (b) and (c) hereof, but she strongly urges that those provisions be enforced to the letter. This provision shall be null and void where for medical reasons _____ _____ must deliver a child.

ARTICLE III: CHILDREN
Care and Support of Children   (1)

The parties agree to share fully and equally all responsibilities related to the care and financial support of any and all children whom they may mutually agree to have or to adopt during the herein-described relationship.

ARTICLE III: CHILDREN
Care and Support of Children   (2)

In consideration of the agreement by _____ to provide for payment of all household expenses and for the financial support and maintenance of _____ and any and all children whom the parties may mutually agree to have or to adopt during the herein-described relationship, _____ agrees to accept primary responsibility for the care of any such children.

ARTICLE III: CHILDREN
Care and Support of Children   (3)

(a) The parties agree to share fully and equally during the herein-described relationship all responsibilities related to the financial support and care of the children of _____, of whom he/she is parent by previous marriage or by adoption, and;

(b) The parties further agree to share fully and equally all responsibilities for the financial support and care of any and all children whom they may mutually agree to have or to adopt during said relationship.

ARTICLE III: CHILDREN
Care and Support of Children   (4)

(a) The parties agree to share fully and equally during the herein-described relationship all responsibilities related to the financial support and care of the children of _____, of whom she is parent by previous marriage or by adoption, and the children of _____, of whom he is parent by previous marriage or by adoption, and;

(b) Further agree to share fully and equally all responsibilities related to the financial support and care of any and all children whom they may mutually agree to have or to adopt during the herein-described relationship.

ARTICLE III: CHILDREN

Care and Support of Children   (5)

The parties agree to share fully and equally during the herein-described relationship all responsibilities related to the financial support and care of the children of _____, of whom he/she is parent by previous marriage or by adoption.

ARTICLE III: CHILDREN

Care and Support of Children   (6)

The parties agree to share fully and equally during the herein-described relationship all responsibilities related to the financial care and support of the children of _____, of whom she is parent by previous marriage or by adoption, and for the financial support and care of the children of _____, of whom he is parent by previous marriage or by adoption.

ARTICLE III: CHILDREN

Care and Support of Children   (7)

The parties agree to share fully and equally during the herein-described relationship all responsibilities related to the financial support and care of the children of _____, of whom he/she is parent.

Education of Children

It is mutually agreed by the parties that any child or children of them, or of either of them, shall have the benefit of a public school education up to and through high school level and that the parties shall mutually determine no later than during each child's junior year in high school whether it is desirable that such child have additional education and the manner of paying therefore.

Religious Instruction   (1)

It is mutually agreed by the parties that any child or children of them shall receive instruction in the _____ _____ faith and be encouraged by the parties to continue in that faith.

Religious Instruction   (2)

It is mutually agreed by the parties that any child or children of them shall receive no religious instruction from either parent, nor from any religious organization recommended by either parent, it being agreed by the parties that any child or children of theirs may seek his or her own religious instruction without influence or hindrance of either parent and that it shall be up to each child to pursue his or her own religious interest.

Religious Instruction   (3)

(a) It is mutually agreed by the parties that any child or children of them shall receive no religious instruction from either parent, nor from any religious organization recommended by either parent, it being agreed by the parties that any child or children of theirs may seek his or her own religious instruction without influence or hindrance of either parent and that it shall be up to each child to pursue his or her own religious interest, it being further agreed by the parties, however, that;

(b) Any child of whom _____ is parent by previous marriage or by adoption may be instructed in the _____ faith, this being deemed in the best interests of the child by _____ .

Religious Instruction   (4)

(a) It is mutually agreed by the parties that any child or children of them shall receive no religious instruction from either parent, nor from any religious organization recommended by either parent, it being agreed by the parties that any child or children of theirs may seek his or her own religious instruction without influence or hindrance of either parent and that it shall be up to each child to pursue his or her own religious interest, it being further agreed between the parties, however, that;

(b) Any child of whom _____ is parent by previous marriage or by adoption may be instructed in the _____ faith, this being deemed in the best interests of such child by _____ , and, that;

(c) Any child of whom _____ is parent by previous marriage or by adoption may be instructed in the _____ faith, this being deemed in the best interests of such child by _____ .

Paternity

In the event of the birth of a child to _____ during the herein-described relationship or during the nine months immediately following the termination of said relationship, _____ agrees to execute, within ten days of the birth of any such child, an affidavit acknowledging paternity of such child, unless advised by _____ that he is not the father of said child or it has been medically determined that he is not the father of said child.

Names of Children

It is agreed by the parties that any child whom the parties mutually agree to have or to adopt during the herein-described relationship shall bear the surname of _____ .

Rights of Children

The parties recognize that they might, during the course of the herein-described relationship, mutually determine to have or to adopt a child or children and agree that the provisions of this agreement are not intended to govern nor affect the rights of any such children in or to the separate property of either party hereto, and the parties further agree that all such rights in and to such separate property and/or financial support shall be governed by applicable law.

ARTICLE IV: POSSIBLE DISSOLUTION OF THE RELATIONSHIP
Means of Dissolution

(a) The parties mutually agree that the herein-described relationship may be dissolved by either party at any time by the initiating party's moving his or her personal property from the parties' shared living space to a separate living space, and;

(b) The parties further agree that any such action will not be taken capriciously, nor in the heat of argument, but only after diligent, considerate and thoughtful efforts to achieve reconciliation, taking into account the feelings of the parties and the possible effects upon any child or children of the parties.

ARTICLE IV: POSSIBLE DISSOLUTION OF THE RELATIONSHIP
Waiver of Support   (1)

(a) In accordance with the parties' full and complete acceptance of the principle of independence and equal responsibility and authority between them, and in further accordance with the parties' waiver and relinquishment of whatever rights, duties, obligations and privileges which either might or could have related to the herein-described relationship between them, other than those which may be included in and made a part of this agreement, each party hereby waives, relinquishes and renounces whatever right he or she may have to rehabilitative financial support, maintenance or any other kind of support and/or maintenance in the event said relationship is dissolved by either party.

(b) The parties recognize that the Courts may look upon with disfavor as being contrary to public policy, agreements waiving any and all types of financial support and/or maintenance for either party in the event of the dissolution of relationships such as that described herein. The above notwithstanding, the parties strongly urge the Court to enforce this agreement to the letter.

Advice of Counsel

In connection with provisions of the above paragraph, **Waiver of Support**, and particularly regarding the waiver, relinquishment and renouncing of whatever right either party might have to rehabilitative financial support, maintenance or any other kind of support or maintenance in the event the relationship is dissolved by either party, each party hereby acknowledges receipt of specific advice pertaining thereto by separate, independent counsel of each party's own choice, each paying for his or her own counsel's advice and aid. Each party acknowledges that as a part of such advice his or her counsel has thoroughly discussed current _____ statutes regarding such relationships and such agreements, as well as judicial decisions related thereto.

ARTICLE IV: POSSIBLE DISSOLUTION OF THE RELATIONSHIP
Waiver of Support   (2)

(a) Each party hereby waives, relinquishes and renounces in perpetuity his or her right to receive any type of financial rehabilitative support or maintenance, or any other kind of support or maintenance, whether it be temporary, permanent, continuous, lump sum, periodic or otherwise, from the other party, regardless of whether or not either party has experienced a substantial change in his or her financial circumstances.

(b) The parties recognize that the Courts may look upon with disfavor as being contrary to public policy, agreements waiving any and all types of financial support and/or maintenance for either party in the event of the dissolution of relationships such as that described herein. The above notwithstanding, the parties strongly urge the Court to enforce this agreement to the letter.

Advice of Counsel

In connection with provisions of the above paragraph, **Waiver of Support**, and particularly regarding the waiver, relinquishment and renouncing of whatever right either party might have to rehabilitative financial support, maintenance or any other kind of support or maintenance in the event the relationship is dissolved by either party, each party hereby acknowledges receipt of specific advice pertaining thereto by separate, independent counsel of each party's own choice, each paying for his or her own counsel's advice and aid. Each party acknowledges that as a part of such advice his or her counsel has thoroughly discussed current _____ statutes regarding such relationships and such agreements, as well as judicial decisions related thereto.

ARTICLE IV: POSSIBLE DISSOLUTION OF THE RELATIONSHIP
Waiver of Support for Either Party, Provision for Child Support   (3)

(a) In accordance with the parties' full and complete acceptance of the principle of independence and equal responsibility and authority between them, and in further accordance with the parties' waiver and relinquishment of whatever rights, duties, obligations and privileges which either might or could have derived from or related to the herein-described relationship, other than those which may be included in and made a part of this agreement, each party hereby waives, relinquishes and renounces whatever right he or she might have to rehabilitative financial support, maintenance or any other kind of support or maintenance in the event said relationship is dissolved by either party except that;

(b) The party having primary custody of any child or children whom the parties may mutually have agreed to have or to adopt during the said relationship shall receive from the other party a monthly sum equal to _____ _____ of the reasonable cost of the financial support and maintenance of any such child or children until such time as said child or children shall reach eighteen (18) years of age.

(c) The parties recognize that the Courts look upon with disfavor as being contrary to public policy, agreements waiving any and all types of financial support and/or maintenance for either party in the event of the dissolution of relationships such as that described herein. The above notwithstanding, the parties strongly urge the Court to enforce this agreement to the letter.

Advice of Counsel

In connection with provisions of the above paragraph, **Waiver of Support for Either Party, Provision for Child Support**, and particularly regarding the waiver, relinquishment and renouncing of whatever right either party might have to rehabilitative financial support, maintenance or any other kind of support or maintenance in the event the relationship is dissolved by either party, each party hereby acknowledges receipt of specific advice pertaining thereto by separate, independent counsel of each party's own choice, each paying for his or her own counsel's advice and aid. Each party acknowledges that as a part of such advice his or her counsel has thoroughly discussed current _____ _____ statutes regarding such relationships and such agreements, as well as judicial decisions related thereto.

ARTICLE IV: POSSIBLE DISSOLUTION OF THE RELATIONSHIP
Payments in Lieu of Support (4)

While the parties contemplate that the herein-described relationship will be a long and lasting one, they also recognize that it may be dissolved by either party. In the event of such dissolution during the lifetime of both parties, regardless of which party may initiate such dissolution, the parties hereby specifically agree:

(a) _____ shall not receive any rehabilitative support, maintenance or any other support or maintenance which might otherwise be available to him/her in accordance with applicable law.

(b) _____ shall accept from _____,
in limitation of any such support or maintenance, and in lieu of any obligation of _____
for costs or attorney's fees of _____ in connection with said dissolution, payments as set forth below for a period equal to the number of months which the parties lived together under the terms of this agreement, or ten (10) years, whichever is less, subject to the provisions of subparagraph (c) hereof:

(i) For the first _____ months from and after the date of dissolution of the relationship (date on which the initiating party moved out of shared living space), _____ shall receive the sum of _____
($_____) per month;

(ii) Thereafter, the sum of _____
($_____) per month;

(iii) The aforesaid sums shall be payable by _____, by depositing a check therefore in the mails of the United States Postal Service, first class, postage prepaid, on or before the first day of each month to such address as _____ may from time to time designate in writing. The first such monthly payment shall be made for the first calendar month following the termination of the relationship as set forth in subparagraph (i) above.

(iv) It is further agreed that the maximum monthly payments made by _____ hereunder shall at no time exceed _____ percent of the net worth of _____.

(c) All such obligations and payments by _____ shall terminate conclusively and forever upon the first occurrence of the death of or the marriage of _____, or his/her continuously residing with an adult of the opposite sex other than a blood relative; and no obligation of any kind as set forth in this paragraph, **Payments in Lieu of Support**, shall survive such first occurrence of said events, and;

(d) It is further agreed that such obligations of _____ shall be legal and binding obligations of and upon the estate and property in which _____ had a legal or beneficial interest prior to death, and;

(e) _____ hereby specifically recognizes and agrees that he/she shall have no right to receive additional payments of support or maintenance in any manner at any time and upon the occurrence of any event from and after the aforesaid dissolution of the parties' herein-described relationship, and that he/she shall have no right to receive any separate property of _____ at any time, or upon the occurrence of any event, and _____ further recognizes and ratifies his/her waiver, relinquishment and release of all such rights.

Advice of Counsel

In connection with provisions of the above paragraph, **Payments in Lieu of Support**, and particularly regarding the waiver, relinquishment and renouncing of whatever right either party may have to rehabilitative financial support, maintenance or any other kind of support or maintenance in the event the relationship is dissolved by either party, each party hereby acknowledges receipt of specific advice pertaining thereto by separate, independent counsel of each party's own choice, each paying for his or her own counsel's advice and aid. Each party acknowledges that as a part of such advice his or her counsel has thoroughly discussed current _____ statutes regarding such relationships and such agreements, as well as judicial decisions related thereto.

Child Support in the Event of Dissolution of the Relationship

(a) The parties shall attempt to arrive at a sum which they mutually agree shall constitute reasonable monthly payments for support of any child or children whom the parties, by mutual consent, may agree to have or to adopt during the herein-described relationship, in the event of the dissolution of the relationship of the parties during the lifetime of both. In the event that they are unable to agree upon such a sum, the Court shall decide the issue, and;

(b) The parties each agree that neither party shall attempt to include an amount which would have been used for financial support and maintenance of the other party in any sum designated for child-support payments.

Child Custody   (1)

The parties shall attempt, in the event of the dissolution of the herein-described relationship, to arrive at an agreement for the custody of any child or children whom the parties may mutually agree to have or to adopt during said relationship. Such agreement shall take into consideration the best interests of any such child or children and the ability of each parent to provide for the financial support and care of any such children. In the event the parties are unable to agree upon child custody, the Court shall decide the issue.

Child Custody   (2)

(a) It is agreed between the parties that _____ shall have primary custody of any child or children whom the parties mutually agree to have or to adopt during the herein-described relationship, subject to the following conditions:

(b) _____ shall have liberal visitation rights with any such child or children and shall give _____ reasonable advance notice of each visit, so that plans may be made by _____ so that the children will not be disturbed to their detriment, unless the parties have agreed to a fixed schedule which may be adhered to without notice to _____ by _____, and;

(c) _____ shall have custody of any such child or children for a _____ _____ period during the summer and _____ of every other Christmas vacation and up to one week every other Thanksgiving. _____ shall have liberal visitation rights during all periods of custody of any such child or children by _____.

Removal of Children from Jurisdiction of the Court

It is mutually agreed by the parties that, in the event of the dissolution of the herein-described relationship, neither party shall attempt to remove from the jurisdiction of the Court, without the written permission of the other party, any child or children whom the parties mutually agree to have or to adopt during said relationship.

ARTICLE V: TESTEMENTARY PROVISIONS
Agreement Between the Parties (1)

(a) In the event that the herein-described relationship shall be terminated by the death of _____ , and if at the time of such death the parties are living together under the terms of this agreement, then, upon such death, _____ shall receive from the estate of _____ , or from trust funds in which _____ may have a beneficial interest, together with all other funds and/or property which _____ may receive upon, and by virtue of the death of _____ (from, without limitation, joint bank accounts with or without rights of survivorship, other jointly held assets, life insurance and other property held in trust for the benefit of _____ _____), a sum which shall be equal to the lesser of _____ _____ ($_____) or _____ percent of the gross estate of _____ , for Federal Estate Tax purposes, and;

(b) Any additional sum which may be needed to achieve said amount of $_____ or said _____ percent, as the case may be, shall be distributed to _____ by the executors of the estate of _____ and/or trustees of said estate, as the case may be, in cash or other forms of property capable of being converted to cash without material reduction in value, and such distribution shall be made as soon as practicable after the death of _____ , but no later than six (6) months after the date of such death, and;

(c) The provisions required under subparagraphs (a) and (b) hereof shall be set forth in the **Last Will and Testament** of _____ , or if an *inter vivos* trust agreement contains substantially all of the dispositive provisions concerning the assets of _____ at his death, then upon the request of _____ , at any time during the said relationship, _____ _____ shall deliver to _____ a copy of the portion of such then current will and/or trust containing such provisions. The said obligation to set forth said provision in the said will and/or trust shall be an additional obligation of _____ , but failure to perform such additional obligation shall have no effect upon the existence or validity of the obligation of _____ _____ to make provision and payment as set forth in subparagraphs (a) and (b) hereof, and;

(d) In the event that at the time of the death of _____ , the parties shall not be living together under terms of this agreement, the obligations set forth hereinabove shall be null and void and of no force or effect whatever.

ARTICLE V: TESTEMENTARY PROVISIONS
Agreement Between the Parties   (2)

(a) In the event that herein-described relationship between the parties shall be terminated by the death of _____ _____, and if at the time of such death the parties shall be living together under terms of this agreement, then _____ accepts as full discharge, settlement and satisfaction of any and all other right, title or interest which she might or could acquire in the property of _____ _____, by virtue of the death of _____, the provisions of the **Last Will and Testament** of _____, and hereby waives, relinquishes and re-nounces any right which she may have to share in the estate of _____, and;

(b) In consideration of the agreement of _____ as provided in subparagraph (a) hereof, _____ agrees to take out and maintain in force during the herein-described relationship, life insurance which will pay an amount not less than _____ _____ ($_____) to _____ in the event of the death of _____ by illness or accident, or, alternatively, to make an *inter vivos* gift to, or to establish an irrevocable trust for the benefit of, _____ in said amount, and;

(c) In the event the herein-described relationship shall be terminated by the death of _____, and if at the time of such death the parties are living together under the terms of this agreement, then _____ accepts as full discharge, settlement and satisfaction of any and all other right, title or interest which he might or could acquire in the estate of _____, by virtue of the death of _____, the provisions of the **Last Will and Testament** of _____ _____, and hereby waives, relinquishes and renounces any right which he may have to share in the estate of _____, and;

(d) In consideration of the agreement of _____ as provided in subparagraph (c) hereof, _____ agrees to take out and maintain in force during the herein-described relationship, life insurance which will pay an amount not less than _____ _____ ($_____) to _____ in the event of the death of _____ by illness or accident, or, alternatively, to make an *inter vivos* gift to, or to establish an irrevocable trust for the benefit of, _____ in said amount.

Life Insurance

(a) _____ hereby agrees to take out and maintain in force during the herein-described relationship, life insurance which will pay an amount not less than _____ _____ ($_____) to _____ in the event of the death of _____ by illness or accident, or, alternatively, to make an *inter vivos* gift to, or to establish an irrevocable trust for the benefit of, _____ in said amount, and;

(b) _____ hereby agrees to take out and maintain in force during the herein-described relationship, life insurance which will pay an amount not less than _____ _____ ($_____) to _____ in the event of the death of _____ by illness or accident, or, alternatively, to make an *inter vivos* gift to, or to establish an irrevocable trust for the benefit of, _____ in said amount.

ARTICLE VI: GENERAL PROVISIONS
Independent Counsel   (1)

(a) The parties hereto jointly and severally acknowledge that each has consulted with separate and independent legal counsel with respect to the legal and other effects of this agreement, the rights and privileges waived and granted hereby, and all other matters pertaining hereto, and;

(b) Both parties further jointly and severally acknowledge their complete understanding of such legal and other effects of this agreement, and;

(c) Each of the parties hereby warrants and represents that the legal counsel of each party executing this agreement was and is the sole and exclusive legal counsel consulted by such party with regard to the matters contained herein, and;

(d) Each acknowledges his or her understanding that he or she is relinquishing and waiving certain rights which might or could have great value in consideration of the provisions of this agreement, and each does so willingly and free of all duress or coercion.

ARTICLE VI: GENERAL PROVISIONS
Advice by Counsel   (2)

(a) The parties hereto acknowledge that they have jointly obtained the advice and counsel of an attorney with respect to the legal and other effects of this agreement and the herein set forth rights, duties and obligations which each of the parties has agreed to hereby, as well as the rights and privileges hereby waived, and all other matters pertaining to the herein-described relationship, and;

(b) The parties acknowledge that as a part of such counsel's advice, said counsel has thoroughly discussed current _____ statutes regarding such relationships, as well as pertinent judicial decisions, and;

(c) Each party acknowledges his/her understanding that he/she is accepting certain rights, duties and obligations hereby, and is also waiving certain rights which might or could have great value in consideration for the provisions of this agreement, and each does so willingly and free from all duress and coercion.

Headings

The headings of the several paragraphs hereof are inserted solely for the convenience of reference and shall have no further meaning, force or effect.

Partial Invalidity

If any provision of this agreement is held to be invalid or unenforceable, all other provisions hereof shall nevertheless remain in full force and effect.

Fair and Equitable

Each party acknowledges that this agreement is fair and equitable.

Parties Bound

This agreement shall inure to the benefit of and be legally binding upon the parties hereto, and the heirs, executors, administrators, successors and assigns of each of them.

Enforcement by Court

The parties hereto strongly urge the Court to enforce this agreement to the letter, even though some provisions contained herein may be void as against public policy and even though a substantial change may have occurred in the financial circumstances of either or both parties.

Entire Agreement

This agreement contains the entire understanding and agreement between the parties, and no amendment or future understanding shall be binding unless reduced to writing and executed by both parties.

Evidence

Neither party shall object to this agreement being entered in evidence in any action for distribution of property, financial support or maintenance, the sharing of expenses or child care or custody, dissolution of the relationship, or any other action between the parties in any Court of law.

Execution of Documents

Each party shall, at any time and from time to time, upon the request of the other, execute, acknowledge and deliver any and all documents which may be necessary or advisable to carry out the intentions and provisions of this agreement, including, but not limited to, such instruments as may be required by the laws of any jurisdiction now in effect or hereafter enacted which may affect the property or other rights of the parties *inter se*, or between the parties hereto and third parties; and further, specifically including all portions of this agreement, or amendments thereto, in recordable form, which may, at the option of either party, be filed of record with any Court in any county wherein is located any separate property of either party hereto.

Counterparts

This agreement may be executed in one or more counterparts, each of which shall be considered as an original.

Governing Law   (1)

This agreement shall be construed and governed in accordance with the laws of the State of _____.

Governing Law   (2)

(a) This agreement shall be executed and delivered in the State of _____, and the provisions hereof shall be construed and enforced in accordance with the laws of said State, regardless of any change of domicile by either or both parties hereto, and;

(b) Any and all actions brought in any Court of law relating directly or indirectly to the herein-described relationship or to any of the terms of this agreement, shall be brought in the appropriate Court of the State of _____ _____, and;

(c) Such Court shall have exclusive jurisdiction and venue thereof, and;

(d) Both parties hereby specifically agree to submit to the personal jurisdiction of such Court, regardless of their respective domiciles or residences, at any time any such action is brought.

Resident Agent

Each party hereby makes, constitutes and appoints the following as his or her resident agent for service of process and other notices as herein provided, waives his or her right to service by publication, and agrees that any and all such service may be made on:

(i) The party personally,

(ii) Said designated agent, or

(iii) By certified or registered mail.

PARTY	REGISTERED AGENT
_____	_____
_____	_____
_____	_____
_____	_____
_____	_____
_____	_____
_____	_____

Execution of Agreement

IN WITNESS WHEREOF, the parties hereto set their hands and seals this _____ day of _____,
19 _____.

_____
Witness

_____

_____

_____ (Seal)

_____
Witness

_____

_____

_____
Witness

_____

_____

_____ (Seal)

_____
Witness

_____

_____

FORM 49.1/F352

* *

Attestation of Notary

STATE OF   )

)   ss:

COUNTY OF   )

On this _____ day of _____, 19 _____, before me personally came and appeared _____, who, first being duly sworn, stated that he has read the foregoing **Agreement to Live Together** and that he signed same for the purpose therein contained.

IN WITNESS WHEREOF, I hereunto set my hand and official seal.

_____
                                     Notary Public

My commission expires: _____

STATE OF   )

)   ss:

COUNTY OF   )

On this _____ day of _____, 19 _____, before me personally came and appeared _____, who, first being duly sworn, stated that she has read the foregoing **Agreement to Live Together** and that she signed same for the purpose therein contained.

IN WITNESS WHEREOF, I hereunto set my hand and official seal.

_____
                                     Notary Public

My commission expires: _____

* *

AFFIDAVIT OF COUNSEL (1)

The undersigned hereby certifies that he/she is and has been legal counsel to _____
in connection with the preparation, review and execution of the foregoing **Agreement to Live Together**; and

The undersigned further certifies that he/she has consulted and rendered independent legal advice to said client concerning provisions of the aforesaid **Agreement to Live Together**, the financial, legal and other effects thereof, and has thoroughly discussed _____ statutes regarding such relationships and such agreements, as well as judicial decisions related thereto.

IN WITNESS WHEREOF, I hereunto set my hand and seal this _____ day of _____,
19 _____.

_____ (Seal)

Witness

_____

_____

Witness

_____

_____

Attestation of Notary

STATE OF   )
)   ss:
COUNTY OF   )

On this _____ day of _____, 19 _____, before me personally came and appeared
_____, who, first being duly sworn, stated that he/she executed the foregoing
Affidavit of Counsel for the purpose therein contained.

IN WITNESS WHEREOF, I hereunto set my hand and official seal.

_____
Notary Public

My commission expires: _____

* *

AFFIDAVIT OF COUNSEL   (2)

The undersigned hereby certifies that he/she is and has been legal counsel to _____
and _____ in connection with the preparation, review and execution of the
foregoing **Agreement to Live Together**; and

The undersigned further certifies that he/she has consulted with and rendered legal advice to said clients concerning
provisions of the aforesaid **Agreement to Live Together**, the financial, legal and other effects thereof, and has thoroughly
discussed _____ statutes regarding such relationships and such agreements, as
well as judicial decisions related thereto.

IN WITNESS WHEREOF, I hereunto set my hand and seal this _____ day of _____,
19 _____.

_____ (Seal)

_____
Witness

_____

_____

_____
Witness

_____

_____

Attestation of Notary

STATE OF   )
) ss:
COUNTY OF   )

On this _____ day of _____, 19 _____, before me personally came and appeared
_____, who, first being duly sworn, stated that he/she executed the foregoing
Affidavit of Counsel for the purpose therein contained.

IN WITNESS WHEREOF, I hereunto set my hand and official seal.

_____
Notary Public

My commission expires: _____

Agreement to Live Together

Between

and

Dated _____ 19 ____

Agreement Between Husband and Wife

THIS AGREEMENT is made this _____ day of _____, 19 _____, by and between

_____, of

_____,

| Street Address | Apt. No. | City | State | Zip |

hereinafter referred to as _____, and

_____, of

_____,

| Street Address | Apt. No. | City | State | Zip |

hereinafter referred to as _____.

WHEREAS _____ and _____ have been married to each other continuously since the _____ day of _____, 19 _____, and the parties wish to clarify between themselves for the purpose of the continued harmony of their relationship, the questions of separate and jointly owned property; separate and joint financial responsibilities; children, if any, and their care, financial support and education; location of domicile; the sharing of household space, expenses and housekeeping responsibilities; the gainful employment and education of each party; the names of each; the possible incapacitation of each; possible dissolution of the marriage; maintenance and support; alimony; and the death of either party; and

WHEREAS, for and in consideration of the sum of twenty dollars ($20.00), and other good and valuable consideration, the receipt whereof is hereby acknowledged, and in further consideration of the parties entering into this agreement and making the mutual covenants herein contained to be performed by the parties, the parties hereto mutually agree and covenant as follows:

FORM 50.1 / F358

Agreement Between Husband and Wife

Between

and

Dated _____ 19 _____

List of Important People and Papers

Name _____

Home Address _____

_____

Employer Company Name _____

Office Address _____

_____

Name of Person to Contact at Work _____

Home Phone _____ Business Phone _____

Social Security Number _____ VA Claim Number _____

Location Guide

1. Office desk
2. Home desk
3. Office safe
4. Home safe
5. Lawyer's office
6. My safe-deposit box
7. Spouse's safe-deposit box

8. Fireproof box in bedroom closet
9. Stockbroker
10. Home filing cabinet
11. Office filing cabinet
12. _____
13. _____
14. _____

LIST OF IMPORTANT PAPERS

Item	Location	Item	Location
1. My will, original	_____	13. Living will for medical transplants	_____
2. My will, copy	_____	14. Document naming children's guardian	_____
3. List of special bequests	_____	15. Checkbooks	_____
4. Spouse's will, original	_____	16. Savings passbooks	_____
5. Spouse's will, copy	_____	17. Certificates of deposit	_____
6. Life insurance, personal	_____	18. Stock certificates	_____
7. Life insurance, company	_____	19. Shares, close corporation	_____
8. Life insurance, VA	_____	20. Brokerage account records	_____
9. Life insurance, other	_____	21. Record of investments	_____
10. Trust agreements	_____	22. List of bank accounts	_____
11. Burial instructions	_____	23. Bank statements	_____
12. Document authorizing medical care	_____	24. Mutual fund shares	_____

LIST OF IMPORTANT PAPERS

Item	Location	Item	Location
25. Bonds	_____	48. Income tax returns, other	_____
26. IRA/Keogh plan	_____	49. Gift tax returns	_____
27. Company retirement plan	_____	50. Other tax returns and records	_____
28. Stock purchase plan	_____	51. Important receipts	_____
29. Stock option plan	_____	52. Birth certificate	_____
30. Profit-sharing plan	_____	53. Marriage certificate	_____
31. Annuities	_____	54. Divorce certificate	_____
32. Health insurance, personal	_____	55. Passport	_____
33. Health insurance, company	_____	56. Military papers	_____
34. Auto insurance	_____	57. Children's birth certificates	_____
35. Property/casualty insurance	_____	58. Children's adoption papers	_____
36. Homeowner's insurance	_____	59. Citizenship papers	_____
37. Title insurance	_____	60. List of memberships	_____
38. Real estate titles and deeds	_____	61. List of friends	_____
39. Partnership agreements	_____	62. Medical records	_____
40. Employment contracts	_____	63. _____	_____
41. Home mortgage	_____	64. _____	_____
42. Loans I owe	_____	65. _____	_____
43. Loans made to others	_____	66. _____	_____
44. List of valuable possessions	_____	67. _____	_____
45. List of loaned possessions	_____	68. _____	_____
46. Vehicle ownership records	_____	69. _____	_____
47. Income tax returns, federal	_____	70. _____	_____

LIST OF IMPORTANT PEOPLE

Lawyer _____

_____

_____ Phone _____

Accountant _____

_____

_____ Phone _____

Insurance Agent _____

_____

_____ Phone _____

Physician _____

_____

_____ Phone _____

Executor _____

_____

_____ Phone _____

Stockbroker _____

_____

_____ Phone _____

Trustee _____

_____

_____ Phone _____

Banker _____

_____

_____ Phone _____

LIST OF IMPORTANT PEOPLE

Business Associate _____

_____

_____ Phone _____

Former Spouse _____

_____

_____ Phone _____

Children's Mother/Father _____

_____

_____ Phone _____

Child _____

_____

_____ Phone _____

_____   _____

_____

_____ Phone _____

_____   _____

_____

_____ Phone _____

_____   _____

_____

_____ Phone _____

Declaration of Gift

TO ALL TO WHOM THESE PRESENTS SHALL COME OR MAY CONCERN, KNOW THAT on this _____

day of _____, 19 _____, I, _____,

of _____,
                    Street   *City*   *State*   *Zip*

being of sound and disposing mind and memory, do hereby irrevocably give, bestow and deliver up to _____

_____,

of _____,
                    Street   *City*   *State*   *Zip*

all of my right, title and interest in the following described property valued at _____

_____ ($_____):

_____

_____

_____

_____

_____

_____

_____

_____

_____

    IN WITNESS WHEREOF, I hereunto set my hand and seal on the date above mentioned.

_____

* *

CERTIFICATE OF NOTARY

STATE OF   )
) ss:
COUNTY OF   )

    On this _____ day of _____, 19 _____, before me personally came and appeared
_____, known, and known to me, to be the individual described in
and who executed the foregoing instrument, and who duly acknowledged to me that he/she executed same for the purpose
therein contained.

    IN WITNESS WHEREOF, I hereunto set my hand and official seal.

_____
                                       Notary Public

My commission expires: _____

FORM 52.1 / F364

Declaration of Gift

From

to

Dated _____ 19 ___

Informal Estate Valuation

of

_____

_____

_____

REAL ESTATE

Property	Owned by Me	Jointly Owned	Amount Owing

SECURITIES

Property	Owned by Me	Jointly Owned	Amount Owing

FORM 53.1 / F366

BUSINESS INTERESTS

Property	Owned by Me	Jointly Owned	Amount Owing

VEHICLES

Property	Owned by Me	Jointly Owned	Amount Owing

TOOLS AND EQUIPMENT

Property	Owned by Me	Jointly Owned	Amount Owing

PETS, LIVESTOCK, AND CATTLE

Property	Owned by Me	Jointly Owned	Amount Owing

MISCELLANEOUS PERSONAL PROPERTY

Property	Owned by Me	Jointly Owned	Amount Owing

LIFE INSURANCE

Property	Owned by Me	Jointly Owned	Amount Owing

EMPLOYMENT BENEFITS

Property	Owned by Me	Jointly Owned	Amount Owing

GOVERNMENT BENEFITS

Property	Owned by Me	Jointly Owned	Amount Owing

ROYALTIES AND PATENTS

Property	Owned by Me	Jointly Owned	Amount Owing

CASH

Property	Owned by Me	Jointly Owned	Amount Owing

MISCELLANEOUS RECEIVABLES

Property	Owned by Me	Jointly Owned	Amount Owing

MISCELLANEOUS

Property	Owned by Me	Jointly Owned	Amount Owing

MISCELLANEOUS PAYABLES

Property	Owned by Me	Jointly Owned	Amount Owing

ESTIMATED VALUE OF ESTATE AT DEATH

Total Owned by Me:

My Share of Jointly Owned:

Life Insurance Benefits Due My Estate at Death: _____

Minus Amount Owed: _____

Total Estimated Value of Estate at Death:

Document to Be Kept with the
Last Will and Testament
of

_____

Date _____

Primary Executor

Name _____ Phone _____

Street _____

City/State _____

Alternate Executor

Name _____ Phone _____

Street _____

City/State _____

Primary Trustee

Name _____ Phone _____

Street _____

City/State _____

1st Alternate Trustee

Name _____ Phone _____

Street _____

City/State _____

2nd Alternate Trustee

Name _____ Phone _____

Street _____

City/State _____

Primary Guardians

Name _____ Phone _____

Street _____

City/State _____

Alternate Guardians

Name _____ Phone _____

Street _____

City/State _____

1st Witness

Name _____ Phone _____

Street _____

City/State _____

2nd Witness

Name _____ Phone _____

Street _____

City/State _____

3rd Witness

Name _____ Phone _____

Street _____

City/State _____

CHILDREN

Name _____ Phone _____

Street _____

City/State _____

Name _____ Phone _____

Street _____

City/State _____

Name _____ Phone _____

Street _____

City/State _____

Name _____ Phone _____

Street _____

City/State _____

Name _____ Phone _____

Street _____

City/State _____

BENEFICIARIES

Name _____ Phone _____

Street _____

City/State _____

Name _____ Phone _____

Street _____

City/State _____

BENEFICIARIES

Name _____ Phone _____

Street _____

City/State _____

Name _____ Phone _____

Street _____

City/State _____

ATTORNEY

Name _____ Phone _____

Street _____

City/State _____

INSURANCE

Insurer _____ Phone _____

Street _____

City/State _____

Agent _____ Phone _____

Street _____

City/State _____

Policy No. _____ Type/Coverage _____

Insurer _____ Phone _____

Street _____

City/State _____

Agent _____ Phone _____

Street _____

City/State _____

Policy No. _____ Type/Coverage _____

TRUSTS

Trustee _____ Phone _____

Street _____

City/State _____

Type _____

Beneficiary _____

Trustee _____ Phone _____

Street _____

City/State _____

Type _____

Beneficiary _____

BANK ACCOUNTS

Bank _____ Phone _____

Street _____

City/State _____

Account No. _____ Officer _____

Bank _____ Phone _____

Street _____

City/State _____

Account No. _____ Officer _____

Self-Proving Affidavit

STATE OF _____)
) ss:
COUNTY OF _____)

On this _____ day of _____, 19 _____, before me personally came and appeared

_____,
Testator/Testatrix

known, and known to me, to be the _____, and

_____,
Name of Witness

_____ and
Name of Witness

_____,
Name of Witness

known, and known to me, to be the _____ and witnesses, respectively, whose names are subscribed to the foregoing and annexed **Last Will and Testament,** and all of said persons first being duly sworn by me, said _____, _____,
Testator/Testatrix

declared to me in the presence of said witnesses that said instrument is _____ **Last Will and Testament** and that _____ freely executed same in the presence of the witnesses for the purposes therein expressed and that;

    Said witnesses, each of whom on his/her oath declared to me in the presence of said _____ that said _____ declared to them in the presence of each other that said instrument is _____ **Last Will and Testament,** and that _____ freely executed same and requested each of them to attest to said **Last Will and Testament** as a witness, and;

    Upon their sworn oath each of said witnesses declared that he or she did sign said **Last Will and Testament** as a witness in the presence of said _____ and in the presence of said other witnesses and that;

    He or she is legally qualified to witness said **Last Will and Testament,** by reason of having attained legal age and/or compliance with other applicable requirements.

Testator/Testatrix _____

      Witness _____

      Witness _____

      Witness _____

    SUBSCRIBED AND SWORN TO before me by the said _____,
_____, and subscribed and sworn to before me by the said witnesses _____,
_____ and _____
this _____ day of _____, 19 _____.

    IN WITNESS WHEREOF, I hereunto set my hand and official seal.

_____
Notary Public

My commission expires: _____

Last Will and Testament
of

_____

I, _____, of

_____,

| _City/Town_ | _County_ | _State_ |

being of sound and disposing mind, do hereby make, publish and declare the following to be my **Last Will and Testament**, revoking all previous wills and codicils made by me.

I declare that I am married to _____ and that all references to "my wife" in this will are references to her. I have _____ children now living whose names and birth dates are:

First Name	_Middle_	_Last_	_Date of Birth_
First Name	_Middle_	_Last_	_Date of Birth_
First Name	_Middle_	_Last_	_Date of Birth_
First Name	_Middle_	_Last_	_Date of Birth_
First Name	_Middle_	_Last_	_Date of Birth_

I have _____ deceased children.

All references to "my children" in this will include all of the above-named children and also any child hereafter born to or adopted by me.

FIRST

My wife and I are executing wills at approximately the same time in which each is the primary beneficiary of the other. These wills are not being made because of any contractual agreement between us, and either will may at any time be revoked by either maker at the sole discretion thereof.

SECOND

I appoint my wife _____ as independent executrix of my will. If she is unable or unwilling to act, or to continue to act, as executrix of my will, I then appoint _____ as executor/executrix of my will.

No bond or other security of any kind shall be required of any executor/executrix appointed in this will.

My executor or executrix, whether original, substitute or successor, shall hereafter be referred to as my "executor."

THIRD

I direct that my executor pay all of my funeral expenses, all state and federal estate, inheritance and succession taxes, administration costs and all of my debts subject to statute of limitations, except mortgage notes secured by real estate, as soon as practical.

FOURTH

I give, devise and bequeath all of the rest, residue and remainder of my estate, of whatever kind and character, and wherever located, to my wife _____, provided that she survives me by _____

_____.

I make no provision hereinabove for my children _____

_____, knowing that, as their mother, my wife will continue to be mindful of their needs and requirements.

FIFTH

If my wife does not survive me by _____,
then I give, devise and bequeath all of the rest, residue and remainder of my estate, of whatever kind and character, and wherever located, to my children *per stirpes*, and I direct that the share of any child of mine who shall have died leaving no issue shall be divided among my surviving children in equal shares *per stirpes*.

SIXTH

My executor shall have the following additional powers with respect to my estate, to be exercised from time to time at his or her discretion without further license or order of any court:

Business Interests

To sell or otherwise liquidate, or to continue to operate at his or her discretion, any corporation, partnership or other business interest received by my estate.

Property of My Estate

To retain any and all property and securities of my estate in the name of my executor as executor or in his or her own name.

Retention of Assets

To retain all property and securities of my estate for as long as my executor deems advisable.

Management of Estate

To invest, lease, rent, mortgage, insure, repair, improve or sell any and all real and personal property belonging to my estate as my executor deems advisable.

Mortgages, Pledges and Deeds of Trust

To enforce any and all mortgages, pledges and deeds of trust held by my estate and to purchase at any sale thereunder any such real or personal property subject to any mortgage, pledge or deed of trust.

Litigation

To initiate or defend, at his or her discretion, any litigation affecting my estate.

Attorneys, Advisors and Agents

To employ and to pay from my estate reasonable compensation to such attorneys, accountants, brokers, and investment, tax and other advisors as he or she shall deem advisable.

Adjustment of Claims

To submit to arbitration, to compromise or to release or otherwise adjust, with or without compensation, any and all claims affecting my estate.

Distribution of My Estate

In distributing my estate, to make said distribution wholly or partly in kind by transferring or allotting such real or personal property or undivided interest therein.

SEVENTH

If any person, whether or not related to me by blood or in any way, shall attempt, either directly or indirectly, to set aside the probate of my will or oppose any of the provisions hereof, and such person shall establish a right to any portion of my estate, then I give and bequeath the sum of one dollar ($1.00), only that, and no further interest whatever in my estate to such person.

EIGHTH

In the event that any of my property, or all of it, at the time of my death is community property under the laws of any jurisdiction, then my will shall be construed as referring only to my community-property interest therein.

NINTH

If any portion of my will shall be held illegal, invalid or otherwise inoperative, it is my intention that all of the other provisions hereof shall continue to be fully effective and operative insofar as is possible and reasonable.

IN WITNESS WHEREOF, I have hereunto set my hand and seal this _____ day of _____, 19 _____.

_____

Signed, sealed, published and declared to be his **Last Will and Testament** by the within-named testator in the presence of all of us, who, in his presence and at his request, and in the presence of each other, have hereunto subscribed our names as witnesses:

_____

Street   *City*   *State*   *Zip*

_____

Street   *City*   *State*   *Zip*

_____

Street   *City*   *State*   *Zip*

FORM 55.1 / F382

Last Will and Testament of

_____

19 _____

Dated _____

Last Will and Testament
of

_____

I, _____, of

_____,

| *City/Town* | *County* | *State* |

being of sound and disposing mind, do hereby make, publish and declare the following to be my **Last Will and Testament**, revoking all previous wills and codicils made by me.

I declare that I am married to _____ and that all references to "my husband" in this will are references to him. I have _____ children now living whose names and birth dates are:

First Name	*Middle*	*Last*	*Date of Birth*
First Name	*Middle*	*Last*	*Date of Birth*
First Name	*Middle*	*Last*	*Date of Birth*
First Name	*Middle*	*Last*	*Date of Birth*
First Name	*Middle*	*Last*	*Date of Birth*

I have _____ deceased children.

All references to "my children" in this will include all of the above-named children and also any child hereafter born to or adopted by me.

FIRST

My husband and I are executing wills at approximately the same time in which each is the primary beneficiary of the other. These wills are not being made because of any contractual agreement between us, and either will may at any time be revoked by either maker at the sole discretion thereof.

SECOND

I appoint my husband _____ as independent executor of my will. If he is unable or unwilling to act, or to continue to act, as executor of my will, I then appoint _____ as executor/executrix of my will.

No bond or other security of any kind shall be required of any executor/executrix appointed in this will.

My executor or executrix, whether original, substitute or successor, shall hereafter be referred to as my "executor."

THIRD

I direct that my executor pay all of my funeral expenses, all state and federal estate, inheritance and succession taxes, administration costs and all of my debts subject to statute of limitations, except mortgage notes secured by real estate, as soon as practical.

FOURTH

I give, devise and bequeath all of the rest, residue and remainder of my estate, of whatever kind and character, and wherever located, to my husband _____, provided that he survives me by

_____.

I make no provision hereinabove for my children _____

_____, knowing that, as their father, my husband will continue to be mindful of their needs and requirements.

FIFTH

If my husband does not survive me by _____,
then I give, devise and bequeath all of the rest, residue and remainder of my estate, of whatever kind and character, and wherever located, to my children *per stirpes*, and I direct that the share of any child of mine who shall have died leaving no issue shall be divided among my surviving children in equal shares *per stirpes*.

SIXTH

My executor shall have the following additional powers with respect to my estate, to be exercised from time to time at his or her discretion without further license or order of any court:

Business Interests

To sell or otherwise liquidate, or to continue to operate at his or her discretion, any corporation, partnership or other business interest received by my estate.

Property of My Estate

To retain any and all property and securities of my estate in the name of my executor as executor or in his or her own name.

Retention of Assets

To retain all property and securities of my estate for as long as my executor deems advisable.

Management of Estate

To invest, lease, rent, mortgage, insure, repair, improve or sell any and all real and personal property belonging to my estate as my executor deems advisable.

Mortgages, Pledges and Deeds of Trust

To enforce any and all mortgages, pledges and deeds of trust held by my estate and to purchase at any sale thereunder any such real or personal property subject to any mortgage, pledge or deed of trust.

Litigation

To initiate or defend, at his or her discretion, any litigation affecting my estate.

Attorneys, Advisors and Agents

To employ and to pay from my estate reasonable compensation to such attorneys, accountants, brokers, and investment, tax and other advisors as he or she shall deem advisable.

Adjustment of Claims

To submit to arbitration, to compromise or to release or otherwise adjust, with or without compensation, any and all claims affecting my estate.

Distribution of My Estate

In distributing my estate, to make said distribution wholly or partly in kind by transferring or allotting such real or personal property or undivided interest therein.

SEVENTH

If any person, whether or not related to me by blood or in any way, shall attempt, either directly or indirectly, to set aside the probate of my will or oppose any of the provisions hereof, and such person shall establish a right to any portion of my estate, then I give and bequeath the sum of one dollar ($1.00), only that, and no further interest whatever in my estate to such person.

EIGHTH

In the event that any of my property, or all of it, at the time of my death is community property under the laws of any jurisdiction, then my will shall be construed as referring only to my community-property interest therein.

NINTH

If any portion of my will shall be held illegal, invalid or otherwise inoperative, it is my intention that all of the other provisions hereof shall continue to be fully effective and operative insofar as is possible and reasonable.

IN WITNESS WHEREOF, I have hereunto set my hand and seal this _____ day of _____, 19 _____.

_____

Signed, sealed, published and declared to be her **Last Will and Testament** by the within-named testatrix in the presence of all of us, who, in her presence and at her request, and in the presence of each other, have hereunto subscribed our names as witnesses:

_____

| _Street_ | _City_ | _State_ | _Zip_ |

_____

| _Street_ | _City_ | _State_ | _Zip_ |

_____

| _Street_ | _City_ | _State_ | _Zip_ |

Last Will and Testament of

Dated _____ 19 ____

4

Last Will and Testament
of

_____

I, _____ , of

_____ ,

City/Town	County	State

being of sound and disposing mind, do hereby make, publish and declare the following to be my **Last Will and Testament**, revoking all previous wills and codicils made by me.

I declare that I am married to _____ and that all references to "my wife" in this will are references to her. I have _____ children now living whose names and birth dates are:

First Name	Middle	Last	Date of Birth
First Name	Middle	Last	Date of Birth
First Name	Middle	Last	Date of Birth
First Name	Middle	Last	Date of Birth
First Name	Middle	Last	Date of Birth

I have _____ deceased children.

All references to "my children" in this will include all of the above-named children and also any child hereafter born to or adopted by me.

FIRST

My wife and I are executing wills at approximately the same time in which each is the primary beneficiary of the other. These wills are not being made because of any contractual agreement between us, and either will may at any time be revoked by either maker at the sole discretion thereof.

SECOND

I appoint my wife _____ as independent executrix of my will. If she is unable or unwilling to act, or to continue to act, as executrix of my will, I then appoint _____ as executor/executrix of my will.

My executor or executrix, whether original, substitute or successor, shall hereinafter be referred to as "executor."

My executor shall have the same powers, rights, obligations and immunities as conferred by this will on the Trustee over the trust estate.

No bond or other security of any kind shall be required of any executor appointed in this will.

THIRD

I direct that my executor pay all of my funeral expenses, all state and federal estate, inheritance and succession taxes, administration costs and all of my debts subject to statute of limitations, except mortgage notes secured by real estate, as soon as practical.

FOURTH

I give, devise and bequeath all of the rest, residue and remainder of my estate, of whatever kind and character, and wherever located, to my wife _____ _____ , provided that she survives me by _____ _____ .

I make no provision hereinabove for my children _____ _____ _____ , knowing that, as their mother, my wife will continue to be mindful of their needs and requirements.

FIFTH

If my wife does not survive me by _____, then I give, devise and bequeath all of the rest, residue and remainder of my estate, of whatever kind and character, and wherever located, to _____ _____ as Trustee, in trust, to be held, managed, administered and distributed as herein directed.

SIXTH

If _____ is unable or unwilling to act, or to continue to act as Trustee, I then appoint _____ as Trustee with all of the same powers, rights, obligations and immunities. If the aforesaid _____ and _____ are each unwilling or unable to act, or to continue to act, as Trustee, I then appoint _____ as Trustee with all of the same powers, rights, obligations and immunities.

SEVENTH

No bond for the faithful performance of duties shall be required of any Trustee appointed in this will.

EIGHTH

The Trustee shall receive a reasonable fee for the services rendered by him or her.

NINTH

No Trustee of the trust created under this will shall at any time be held liable for any action or default of himself or herself, or of his or her agent, or of any other person in connection with the administration of the trust unless caused by his or her own gross negligence or by commission of a willful act of breach of trust.

TENTH

The Trustee shall have the sole authority to determine what shall be defined as income and what shall be defined as principal of the trust estate established under this will, and to determine what costs, taxes and other expenses shall be paid out of income and which shall be paid out of principal in accordance with applicable statutes of the State of _____ _____.

ELEVENTH

I direct that the entire trust shall be managed and administered as one trust until no living child of mine is under the age of _____. Until that time, the Trustee shall apply the principal and net income of the trust estate as follows:

So long as any of my children are under the age of _____, the net income of the trust shall be applied to the benefit of, or paid to, any or all of my children in such amounts and at such times as the Trustee shall at his or her discretion decide are necessary for their support, maintenance, welfare and education.

In the event that net income of the trust shall be insufficient to provide any of my said children with the funds necessary for adequate support, maintenance, welfare or education, the Trustee may invade the principal of the trust estate for this purpose. Payments of income or principal to any child of mine pursuant to this paragraph need not be taken into account by the Trustee in any later division of the trust estate into shares for distribution to my children or children of a deceased child of mine. No child of mine who has completed his or her _____ year shall receive any of the aforesaid payments from the trust estate.

The Trustee, in exercising his or her discretionary authority regarding the payment of principal or income of the trust estate to any of my children, or to the children of any of my deceased children, may take into consideration any other income or resources available to such beneficiary from sources outside the trust estate which may be known to the Trustee. The decision of the Trustee with regard to the necessity for making payments out of income or principal to any beneficiary shall be conclusive on all persons having any right or interest whatever in the trust.

The Trustee may apply more for or pay more to some beneficiaries than others and may entirely omit distribution to any of the beneficiaries during the continuance of the trust estate.

In the event that any of my children shall predecease me or die prior to the termination of the trust estate, interest of such child or children in the trust shall cease, except that if such deceased child or children shall be survived by any child or children of theirs, then the Trustee may apply that same interest for the child or children of a deceased child of mine to such extent as the Trustee at his or her sole discretion may deem necessary for support, maintenance, welfare or education. Payments of income or principal to any child or children of a deceased child of mine pursuant to this paragraph need not be taken into account by the Trustee in any subsequent division of the trust estate into shares for distribution to my children or to the child or children of any deceased child of mine.

The Trustee shall add to the principal of the trust estate any net interest or income not paid out in accordance with the powers, authority and discretion hereinabove conferred on the Trustee.

At such time when no child of mine who is living is under the age of _____ , the trust shall terminate, and the Trustee shall as soon as practical distribute the remainder and residue of the trust estate in equal shares to my children then living. However, if any deceased child of mine has any child or children then surviving, then an equal share of the trust estate shall be distributed to said surviving issue of each deceased child of mine *per stirpes*.

TWELFTH

The Trustee, in addition to all other powers granted by this will and by law, shall have the following additional powers with respect to the trust estate, to be exercised from time to time at his or her discretion without further license or order of any court, subject to any limitations set forth elsewhere in this will:

Business Interests

To sell or otherwise liquidate, or to continue to operate at his or her discretion, any corporation, partnership or other business interest received by the trust estate.

Property of Trust Estate

To retain any and all property and securities of the trust estate for as long as he or she may deem advisable.

Management of Trust Estate

To invest, lease, rent, mortgage, insure, repair, improve or sell any and all real and personal property belonging to the trust estate as he or she may deem advisable.

Mortgages, Pledges and Deeds of Trust

To enforce any and all mortgages, pledges and deeds of trust held by the trust estate and to purchase at any sale thereunder any such real or personal property subject to any mortgage, pledge or deed of trust.

Litigation

To initiate or defend, at his or her discretion, any litigation affecting the trust estate.

Attorneys, Advisors and Agents

To employ and to pay from the trust estate reasonable compensation to such attorneys, accountants, brokers, and investment, tax and other advisors as he or she shall deem advisable.

Adjustment of Claims

To submit to arbitration, to compromise or to release or otherwise adjust, with or without compensation, any and all claims affecting the trust estate.

Distribution of Trust Estate

In distributing the trust estate, to make said distribution wholly or partly in kind by transferring or allotting such real or personal property or undivided interest therein.

THIRTEENTH

If my wife does not survive me, I then appoint _____ _____ and _____ as guardians of the person of each of my minor children, and I hereby request that they seek appointment as guardians of their estates. If both of them qualify and thereafter either ceases to act, one may act alone.

If one of them fails to qualify, or if both cease to act after qualifying, I then appoint _____ _____ and _____ as new guardians of the person of each of my minor children, and I hereby request that they seek appointment as guardians of their estates. If both qualify and thereafter either ceases to act, one may act alone.

No bond or other security of any kind shall be required of any of the above parties for the faithful exercise of their responsibilities as guardian of the person or of the estate of any of my minor children.

FOURTEENTH

If any person, whether or not related to me by blood or in any other way, shall attempt, either directly or indirectly, to set aside the probate of my will or oppose any of the provisions hereof, and such person shall establish a right to any portion of my estate, then I give and bequeath the sum of one dollar ($1.00), only that, and no further interest whatever in my estate to such person.

FIFTEENTH

In the event that any of my property, or all of it, at the time of my death is community property under the laws of any jurisdiction, then my will shall be construed as referring only to my community-property interest therein.

SIXTEENTH

If any portion of my will shall be held illegal, invalid or otherwise inoperative, it is my intention that all of the other provisions hereof shall continue to be fully effective and operative insofar as is possible and reasonable.

IN WITNESS WHEREOF, I have hereunto set my hand and seal this _____ day of _____, 19 _____.

_____

Signed, sealed, published and declared to be his **Last Will and Testament** by the within-named testator in the presence of all of us, who, in his presence and at his request, and in the presence of each other, have hereunto subscribed our names as witnesses:

_____

| _Street_ | _City_ | _State_ | _Zip_ |

_____

| _Street_ | _City_ | _State_ | _Zip_ |

_____

| _Street_ | _City_ | _State_ | _Zip_ |

𝕷𝖆𝖘𝖙 𝖂𝖎𝖑𝖑 𝖆𝖓𝖉 𝕿𝖊𝖘𝖙𝖆𝖒𝖊𝖓𝖙 𝖔𝖋

Dated _____ 19 _____

Last Will and Testament
of

_____

I, _____, of

_____,

| City/Town | County | State |

being of sound and disposing mind, do hereby make, publish and declare the following to be my **Last Will and Testament,** revoking all previous wills and codicils made by me.

I declare that I am married to _____ and that all references to "my husband" in this will are references to him. I have _____ children now living whose names and birth dates are:

First Name	Middle	Last	Date of Birth
First Name	Middle	Last	Date of Birth
First Name	Middle	Last	Date of Birth
First Name	Middle	Last	Date of Birth
First Name	Middle	Last	Date of Birth

I have _____ deceased children.

All references to "my children" in this will include all of the above-named children and also any child hereafter born to or adopted by me.

FIRST

My husband and I are executing wills at approximately the same time in which each is the primary beneficiary of the other. These wills are not being made because of any contractual agreement between us, and either will may at any time be revoked by either maker at the sole discretion thereof.

SECOND

I appoint my husband _____ as independent executor of my will. If he is unable or unwilling to act, or to continue to act, as executor of my will, I then appoint _____ as executor/executrix of my will.

My executor or executrix, whether original, substitute or successor, shall hereinafter be referred to as "executor."

My executor shall have the same powers, rights, obligations and immunities as conferred by this will on the Trustee over the trust estate.

No bond or other security of any kind shall be required of any executor appointed in this will.

THIRD

I direct that my executor pay all of my funeral expenses, all state and federal estate, inheritance and succession taxes, administration costs and all of my debts subject to statute of limitations, except mortgage notes secured by real estate, as soon as practical.

FOURTH

I give, devise and bequeath all of the rest, residue and remainder of my estate, of whatever kind and character, and wherever located, to my husband _____, provided that he survives me by

_____.

I make no provision hereinabove for my children _____

_____, knowing that, as their father, my husband will continue to be mindful of their needs and requirements.

FIFTH

If my husband does not survive me by _____ , then I give, devise and bequeath all of the rest, residue and remainder of my estate, of whatever kind and character, and wherever located, to _____ _____ as Trustee, in trust, to be held, managed, administered and distributed as herein directed.

SIXTH

If _____ is unable or unwilling to act, or to continue to act, as Trustee, I then appoint _____ as Trustee with all of the same powers, rights, obligations and immunities. If the aforesaid _____ and _____ are each unwilling or unable to act, or to continue to act, as Trustee, I then appoint _____ as Trustee with all of the same powers, rights, obligations and immunities.

SEVENTH

No bond for the faithful performance of duties shall be required of any Trustee appointed in this will.

EIGHTH

The Trustee shall receive a reasonable fee for the services rendered by him or her.

NINTH

No Trustee of the trust created under this will shall at any time be held liable for any action or default of himself or herself, or of his or her agent, or of any other person in connection with the administration of the trust unless caused by his or her own gross negligence or by commission of a willful act of breach of trust.

TENTH

The Trustee shall have the sole authority to determine what shall be defined as income and what shall be defined as principal of the trust estate established under this will, and to determine what costs, taxes and other expenses shall be paid out of income and which shall be paid out of principal in accordance with applicable statutes of the State of _____ _____ .

ELEVENTH

I direct that the entire trust shall be managed and administered as one trust until no living child of mine is under the age of _____ . Until that time, the Trustee shall apply the principal and net income of the trust estate as follows:

So long as any of my children are under the age of _____ , the net income of the trust shall be applied to the benefit of, or paid to, any or all of my children in such amounts and at such times as the Trustee shall at his or her discretion decide are necessary for their support, maintenance, welfare and education.

In the event that net income of the trust shall be insufficient to provide any of my said children with the funds necessary for adequate support, maintenance, welfare or education, the Trustee may invade the principal of the trust estate for this purpose. Payments of income or principal to any child of mine pursuant to this paragraph need not be taken into account by the Trustee in any later division of the trust estate into shares for distribution to my children or children of a deceased child of mine. No child of mine who has completed his or her _____ year shall receive any of the aforesaid payments from the trust estate.

The Trustee, in exercising his or her discretionary authority regarding the payment of principal or income of the trust estate to any of my children, or to the children of any of my deceased children, may take into consideration any other income or resources available to such beneficiary from sources outside the trust estate which may be known to the Trustee. The decision of the Trustee with regard to the necessity for making payments out of income or principal to any beneficiary shall be conclusive on all persons having any right or interest whatever in the trust.

The Trustee may apply more for or pay more to some beneficiaries than others and may entirely omit distribution to any of the beneficiaries during the continuance of the trust estate.

In the event that any of my children shall predecease me or die prior to the termination of the trust estate, interest of such child or children in the trust shall cease, except that if such deceased child or children shall be survived by any child or children of theirs, then the Trustee may apply that same interest for the child or children of a deceased child of mine to such extent as the Trustee at his or her sole discretion may deem necessary for support, maintenance, welfare or education. Payments of income or principal to any child or children of a deceased child of mine pursuant to this paragraph need not be taken into account by the Trustee in any subsequent division of the trust estate into shares for distribution to my children or to the child or children of any deceased child of mine.

The Trustee shall add to the principal of the trust estate any net interest or income not paid out in accordance with the powers, authority and discretion hereinabove conferred on the Trustee.

At such time when no child of mine who is living is under the age of _____, the trust shall terminate, and the Trustee shall as soon as practical distribute the remainder and residue of the trust estate in equal shares to my children then living. However, if any deceased child of mine has any child or children then surviving, then an equal share of the trust estate shall be distributed to said surviving issue of each deceased child of mine *per stirpes.*

TWELFTH

The Trustee, in addition to all other powers granted by this will and by law, shall have the following additional powers with respect to the trust estate, to be exercised from time to time at his or her discretion without further license or order of any court, subject to any limitations set forth elsewhere in this will:

Business Interests

To sell or otherwise liquidate, or to continue to operate at his or her discretion, any corporation, partnership or other business interest received by the trust estate.

Property of Trust Estate

To retain any and all property and securities of the trust estate for as long as he or she may deem advisable.

Management of Trust Estate

To invest, lease, rent, mortgage, insure, repair, improve or sell any and all real and personal property belonging to the trust estate as he or she may deem advisable.

Mortgages, Pledges and Deeds of Trust

To enforce any and all mortgages, pledges and deeds of trust held by the trust estate and to purchase at any sale thereunder any such real or personal property subject to any mortgage, pledge or deed of trust.

Litigation

To initiate or defend, at his or her discretion, any litigation affecting the trust estate.

Attorneys, Advisors and Agents

To employ and to pay from the trust estate reasonable compensation to such attorneys, accountants, brokers, and investment, tax and other advisors as he or she shall deem advisable.

Adjustment of Claims

To submit to arbitration, to compromise or to release or otherwise adjust, with or without compensation, any and all claims affecting the trust estate.

Distribution of Trust Estate

In distributing the trust estate, to make said distribution wholly or partly in kind by transferring or allotting such real or personal property or undivided interest therein.

THIRTEENTH

If my husband does not survive me, I then appoint _____ and _____ as guardians of the person of each of my minor children, and I hereby request that they seek appointment as guardians of their estates. If both of them qualify and thereafter either ceases to act, one may act alone.

If one of them fails to qualify, or if both cease to act after qualifying, I then appoint _____ and _____ as new guardians of the person of each of my minor children, and I hereby request that they seek appointment as guardians of their estates. If both qualify and thereafter either ceases to act, one may act alone.

No bond or other security of any kind shall be required of any of the above parties for the faithful exercise of their responsibilities as guardian of the person or of the estate of any of my minor children.

FOURTEENTH

If any person, whether or not related to me by blood or in any other way, shall attempt, either directly or indirectly, to set aside the probate of my will or oppose any of the provisions hereof, and such person shall establish a right to any portion of my estate, then I give and bequeath the sum of one dollar ($1.00), only that, and no further interest whatever in my estate to such person.

FIFTEENTH

In the event that any of my property, or all of it, at the time of my death is community property under the laws of any jurisdiction, then my will shall be construed as referring only to my community-property interest therein.

SIXTEENTH

If any portion of my will shall be held illegal, invalid or otherwise inoperative, it is my intention that all of the other provisions hereof shall continue to be fully effective and operative insofar as is possible and reasonable.

IN WITNESS WHEREOF, I have hereunto set my hand and seal this _____ day of _____, 19 _____.

_____

Signed, sealed, published and declared to be her **Last Will and Testament** by the within-named testatrix in the presence of all of us, who, in her presence and at her request, and in the presence of each other, have hereunto subscribed our names as witnesses:

_____

| *Street* | *City* | *State* | *Zip* |

_____

_____

| *Street* | *City* | *State* | *Zip* |

_____

_____

| *Street* | *City* | *State* | *Zip* |

Last Will and Testament of

19 _____

Dated _____

4

Last Will and Testament
of

_____

I, _____ , of

_____ ,

| City/Town | County | State |

being of sound and disposing mind, do hereby make, publish and declare the following to be my **Last Will and Testament,** revoking all previous wills and codicils made by me.

I declare that I am married to _____ and that all references to "my wife" in this will are references to her. I have no children now living.

FIRST

My wife and I are executing wills at approximately the same time in which each is the primary beneficiary of the other. These wills are not being made because of any contractual agreement between us, and either will may at any time be revoked by either maker at the sole discretion thereof.

SECOND

I appoint my wife _____ as independent executrix of my will. If she is unable or unwilling to act, or to continue to act, as executrix of my will, I then appoint _____ as executor/executrix of my will.

No bond or other security of any kind shall be required of any executor/executrix appointed in this will.

My executor or executrix, whether original, substitute or successor, shall hereafter be referred to as my "executor."

THIRD

I direct that my executor pay all of my funeral expenses, all state and federal estate, inheritance and succession taxes, administration costs and all of my debts subject to statute of limitations, except mortgage notes secured by real estate, as soon as practical.

FOURTH

I give, devise and bequeath all of the rest, residue and remainder of my estate, of whatever kind and character, and wherever located, to my wife _____ , provided that she survives me by

_____ .

FIFTH

If my wife does not survive me by _____ , then I give, devise and bequeath all of the rest, residue and remainder of my estate, of whatever kind and character, and wherever located, per capita, to:

First Name	Middle	Last

First Name	Middle	Last

First Name	Middle	Last

First Name	Middle	Last

SIXTH

My executor shall have the following additional powers with respect to my estate, to be exercised from time to time at his or her discretion without further license or order of any court:

Business Interests

To sell or otherwise liquidate, or to continue to operate at his or her discretion, any corporation, partnership or other business interest received by my estate.

Property of My Estate

To retain any and all property and securities of my estate in the name of my executor as executor or in his or her own name.

Retention of Assets

To retain all property and securities of my estate for as long as my executor deems advisable.

Management of Estate

To invest, lease, rent, mortgage, insure, repair, improve or sell any and all real and personal property belonging to my estate as my executor deems advisable.

Mortgages, Pledges and Deeds of Trust

To enforce any and all mortgages, pledges and deeds of trust held by my estate and to purchase at any sale thereunder any such real or personal property subject to any mortgage, pledge or deed of trust.

Litigation

To initiate or defend, at his or her discretion, any litigation affecting my estate.

Attorneys, Advisors and Agents

To employ and to pay from my estate reasonable compensation to such attorneys, accountants, brokers, and investment, tax and other advisors as he or she shall deem advisable.

Adjustment of Claims

To submit to arbitration, to compromise or to release or otherwise adjust, with or without compensation, any and all claims affecting my estate.

Distribution of My Estate

In distributing my estate, to make said distribution wholly or partly in kind by transferring or allotting such real or personal property or undivided interest therein.

SEVENTH

If any person, whether or not related to me by blood or in any way, shall attempt, either directly or indirectly, to set aside the probate of my will or oppose any of the provisions hereof, and such person shall establish a right to any portion of my estate, then I give and bequeath the sum of one dollar ($1.00), only that, and no further interest whatever in my estate to such person.

EIGHTH

In the event that any of my property, or all of it, at the time of my death is community property under the laws of any jurisdiction, then my will shall be construed as referring only to my community-property interest therein.

NINTH

If any portion of my will shall be held illegal, invalid or otherwise inoperative, it is my intention that all of the other provisions hereof shall continue to be fully effective and operative insofar as is possible and reasonable.

IN WITNESS WHEREOF, I have hereunto set my hand and seal this _____ day of _____, 19 _____.

_____

Signed, sealed, published and declared to be his **Last Will and Testament** by the within-named testator in the presence of all of us, who, in his presence and at his request, and in the presence of each other, have hereunto subscribed our names as witnesses:

_____

| *Street* | *City* | *State* | *Zip* |

_____

| *Street* | *City* | *State* | *Zip* |

_____

| *Street* | *City* | *State* | *Zip* |

FORM 55.5 / F398

Last Will and Testament of

_____

4

Dated _____ 19 _____

Last Will and Testament
of

_____

I, _____ , of

_____ ,

| *City/Town* | *County* | *State* |

being of sound and disposing mind, do hereby make, publish and declare the following to be my **Last Will and Testament**, revoking all previous wills and codicils made by me.

I declare that I am married to _____ and that all references to "my husband" in this will are references to him. I have no children now living.

FIRST

My husband and I are executing wills at approximately the same time in which each is the primary beneficiary of the other. These wills are not being made because of any contractual agreement between us, and either will may at any time be revoked by either maker at the sole discretion thereof.

SECOND

I appoint my husband _____ as independent executor of my will. If he is unable or unwilling to act, or to continue to act, as executor of my will, I then appoint _____ as executor/executrix of my will.

No bond or other security of any kind shall be required of any executor/executrix appointed in this will.

My executor or executrix, whether original, substitute or successor, shall hereafter be referred to as my "executor."

THIRD

I direct that my executor pay all of my funeral expenses, all state and federal estate, inheritance and succession taxes, administration costs and all of my debts subject to statute of limitations, except mortgage notes secured by real estate, as soon as practical.

FOURTH

I give, devise and bequeath all of the rest, residue and remainder of my estate, of whatever kind and character, and wherever located, to my husband _____ , provided that he survives me by

_____ .

FIFTH

If my husband does not survive me by _____ , then I give, devise and bequeath all of the rest, residue and remainder of my estate, of whatever kind and character, and wherever located, per capita, to:

First Name	*Middle*	*Last*
First Name	*Middle*	*Last*
First Name	*Middle*	*Last*
First Name	*Middle*	*Last*

SIXTH

My executor shall have the following additional powers with respect to my estate, to be exercised from time to time at his or her discretion without further license or order of any court:

Business Interests

To sell or otherwise liquidate, or to continue to operate at his or her discretion, any corporation, partnership or other business interest received by my estate.

Property of My Estate

To retain any and all property and securities of my estate in the name of my executor as executor or in his or her own name.

Retention of Assets

To retain all property and securities of my estate for as long as my executor deems advisable.

Management of Estate

To invest, lease, rent, mortgage, insure, repair, improve or sell any and all real and personal property belonging to my estate as my executor deems advisable.

Mortgages, Pledges and Deeds of Trust

To enforce any and all mortgages, pledges and deeds of trust held by my estate and to purchase at any sale thereunder any such real or personal property subject to any mortgage, pledge or deed of trust.

Litigation

To initiate or defend, at his or her discretion, any litigation affecting my estate.

Attorneys, Advisors and Agents

To employ and to pay from my estate reasonable compensation to such attorneys, accountants, brokers, and investment, tax and other advisors as he or she shall deem advisable.

Adjustment of Claims

To submit to arbitration, to compromise or to release or otherwise adjust, with or without compensation, any and all claims affecting my estate.

Distribution of My Estate

In distributing my estate, to make said distribution wholly or partly in kind by transferring or allotting such real or personal property or undivided interest therein.

SEVENTH

If any person, whether or not related to me by blood or in any way, shall attempt, either directly or indirectly, to set aside the probate of my will or oppose any of the provisions hereof, and such person shall establish a right to any portion of my estate, then I give and bequeath the sum of one dollar ($1.00), only that, and no further interest whatever in my estate to such person.

EIGHTH

In the event that any of my property, or all of it, at the time of my death is community property under the laws of any jurisdiction, then my will shall be construed as referring only to my community-property interest therein.

NINTH

If any portion of my will shall be held illegal, invalid or otherwise inoperative, it is my intention that all of the other provisions hereof shall continue to be fully effective and operative insofar as is possible and reasonable.

IN WITNESS WHEREOF, I have hereunto set my hand and seal this _____ day of _____, 19 _____.

_____

Signed, sealed, published and declared to be her **Last Will and Testament** by the within-named testatrix in the presence of all of us, who, in her presence and at her request, and in the presence of each other, have hereunto subscribed our names as witnesses:

_____

Street   *City*   *State*   *Zip*

_____

Street   *City*   *State*   *Zip*

_____

Street   *City*   *State*   *Zip*

Last Will
and
Testament
of

Dated _____ 19 ____

4

Last Will and Testament
of

_____

I, _____, of

_____,
City/Town   _County_   _State_

being of sound and disposing mind, do hereby make, publish and declare the following to be my **Last Will and Testament,** revoking all previous wills and codicils made by me.

I declare that I am the cohabitant of _____ and that all references to "my cohabitant" in this will are references to her.

I am not now married to any person, and I have no children now living.

FIRST

My cohabitant and I are executing wills at approximately the same time in which each is the primary beneficiary of the other. These wills are not being made because of any contractual agreement between us, and either will may at any time be revoked by either maker at the sole discretion thereof.

SECOND

I appoint my cohabitant _____ as independent executrix of my will. If she is unable or unwilling to act, or to continue to act, as executrix of my will, I then appoint _____ as executor/executrix of my will.

No bond or other security of any kind shall be required of any executor/executrix appointed in this will.

My executor or executrix, whether original, substitute or successor, shall hereafter be referred to as my "executor."

THIRD

I direct that my executor pay all of my funeral expenses, all state and federal estate, inheritance and succession taxes, administration costs and all of my debts subject to statute of limitations, except mortgage notes secured by real estate, as soon as practical.

FOURTH

I give, devise and bequeath all of the rest, residue and remainder of my estate, of whatever kind and character, and wherever located, to my cohabitant _____, provided that she survives me by _____

_____.

FIFTH

If my cohabitant _____ does not survive me by _____, then I give, devise and bequeath all of the rest, residue and remainder of my estate, of whatever kind and character, and wherever located, per capita, to:

First Name	_Middle_	_Last_
First Name	_Middle_	_Last_
First Name	_Middle_	_Last_
First Name	_Middle_	_Last_

SIXTH

My executor shall have the following additional powers with respect to my estate, to be exercised from time to time at his or her discretion without further license or order of any court:

Business Interests

To sell or otherwise liquidate, or to continue to operate at his or her discretion, any corporation, partnership or other business interest received by my estate.

Property of My Estate

To retain any and all property and securities of my estate in the name of my executor as executor or in his or her own name.

Retention of Assets

To retain all property and securities of my estate for as long as my executor deems advisable.

Management of Estate

To invest, lease, rent, mortgage, insure, repair, improve or sell any and all real and personal property belonging to my estate as my executor deems advisable.

Mortgages, Pledges and Deeds of Trust

To enforce any and all mortgages, pledges and deeds of trust held by my estate and to purchase at any sale thereunder any such real or personal property subject to any mortgage, pledge or deed of trust.

Litigation

To initiate or defend, at his or her discretion, any litigation affecting my estate.

Attorneys, Advisors and Agents

To employ and to pay from my estate reasonable compensation to such attorneys, accountants, brokers, and investment, tax and other advisors as he or she shall deem advisable.

Adjustment of Claims

To submit to arbitration, to compromise or to release or otherwise adjust, with or without compensation, any and all claims affecting my estate.

Distribution of My Estate

In distributing my estate, to make said distribution wholly or partly in kind by transferring or allotting such real or personal property or undivided interest therein.

SEVENTH

If any person, whether or not related to me by blood or in any way, shall attempt, either directly or indirectly, to set aside the probate of my will or oppose any of the provisions hereof, and such person shall establish a right to any portion of my estate, then I give and bequeath the sum of one dollar ($1.00), only that, and no further interest whatever in my estate to such person.

EIGHTH

In the event that any of my property, or all of it, at the time of my death is community property under the laws of any jurisdiction, then my will shall be construed as referring only to my community-property interest therein.

NINTH

If any portion of my will shall be held illegal, invalid or otherwise inoperative, it is my intention that all of the other provisions hereof shall continue to be fully effective and operative insofar as is possible and reasonable.

IN WITNESS WHEREOF, I have hereunto set my hand and seal this _____ day of _____, 19 _____.

_____

Signed, sealed, published and declared to be his **Last Will and Testament** by the within-named testator in the presence of all of us, who, in his presence and at his request, and in the presence of each other, have hereunto subscribed our names as witnesses:

_____

| *Street* | *City* | *State* | *Zip* |

_____

| *Street* | *City* | *State* | *Zip* |

_____

| *Street* | *City* | *State* | *Zip* |

Last Will and Testament of

Dated _____ 19 _____

Last Will and Testament
of

_____

I, _____ , of

_____ ,

| City/Town | County | State |

being of sound and disposing mind, do hereby make, publish and declare the following to be my **Last Will and Testament**, revoking all previous wills and codicils made by me.

I declare that I am the cohabitant of _____ and that all references to "my cohabitant" in this will are references to him.

I am not now married to any person, and I have no children now living.

FIRST

My cohabitant and I are executing wills at approximately the same time in which each is the primary beneficiary of the other. These wills are not being made because of any contractual agreement between us, and either will may at any time be revoked by either maker at the sole discretion thereof.

SECOND

I appoint my cohabitant _____ as independent executor of my will. If he is unable or unwilling to act, or to continue to act, as executor of my will, I then appoint _____ as executor/executrix of my will.

No bond or other security of any kind shall be required of any executor/executrix appointed in this will.

My executor or executrix, whether original, substitute or successor, shall hereafter be referred to as my "executor."

THIRD

I direct that my executor pay all of my funeral expenses, all state and federal estate, inheritance and succession taxes, administration costs and all of my debts subject to statute of limitations, except mortgage notes secured by real estate, as soon as practical.

FOURTH

I give, devise and bequeath all of the rest, residue and remainder of my estate, of whatever kind and character, and wherever located, to my cohabitant _____ , provided that he survives me by _____ _____ .

FIFTH

If my cohabitant _____ does not survive me by _____ , then I give, devise and bequeath all of the rest, residue and remainder of my estate, of whatever kind and character, and wherever located, per capita, to:

First Name	Middle	Last
First Name	Middle	Last
First Name	Middle	Last
First Name	Middle	Last

SIXTH

My executor shall have the following additional powers with respect to my estate, to be exercised from time to time at his or her discretion without further license or order of any court:

Business Interests

To sell or otherwise liquidate, or to continue to operate at his or her discretion, any corporation, partnership or other business interest received by my estate.

Property of My Estate

To retain any and all property and securities of my estate in the name of my executor as executor or in his or her own name.

Retention of Assets

To retain all property and securities of my estate for as long as my executor deems advisable.

Management of Estate

To invest, lease, rent, mortgage, insure, repair, improve or sell any and all real and personal property belonging to my estate as my executor deems advisable.

Mortgages, Pledges and Deeds of Trust

To enforce any and all mortgages, pledges and deeds of trust held by my estate and to purchase at any sale thereunder any such real or personal property subject to any mortgage, pledge or deed of trust.

Litigation

To initiate or defend, at his or her discretion, any litigation affecting my estate.

Attorneys, Advisors and Agents

To employ and to pay from my estate reasonable compensation to such attorneys, accountants, brokers, and investment, tax and other advisors as he or she shall deem advisable.

Adjustment of Claims

To submit to arbitration, to compromise or to release or otherwise adjust, with or without compensation, any and all claims affecting my estate.

Distribution of My Estate

In distributing my estate, to make said distribution wholly or partly in kind by transferring or allotting such real or personal property or undivided interest therein.

SEVENTH

If any person, whether or not related to me by blood or in any way, shall attempt, either directly or indirectly, to set aside the probate of my will or oppose any of the provisions hereof, and such person shall establish a right to any portion of my estate, then I give and bequeath the sum of one dollar ($1.00), only that, and no further interest whatever in my estate to such person.

EIGHTH

In the event that any of my property, or all of it, at the time of my death is community property under the laws of any jurisdiction, then my will shall be construed as referring only to my community-property interest therein.

NINTH

If any portion of my will shall be held illegal, invalid or otherwise inoperative, it is my intention that all of the other provisions hereof shall continue to be fully effective and operative insofar as is possible and reasonable.

IN WITNESS WHEREOF, I have hereunto set my hand and seal this _____ day of _____, 19 _____.

_____

Signed, sealed, published and declared to be her **Last Will and Testament** by the within-named testatrix in the presence of all of us, who, in her presence and at her request, and in the presence of each other, have hereunto subscribed our names as witnesses:

_____

| Street | City | State | Zip |

_____

| Street | City | State | Zip |

_____

| Street | City | State | Zip |

Last Will
and
Testament
of

Dated _____ 19 ___

4

Last Will and Testament
of

_____

I, _____, of

_____ ,

| City/Town | County | State |

being of sound and disposing mind, do hereby make, publish and declare the following to be my **Last Will and Testament,** revoking all previous wills and codicils made by me.

I declare that I am not married and have no children now living.

FIRST

I appoint _____ as independent executor/executrix of my will. If he or she is unable or unwilling to act, or to continue to act, I then appoint _____ as executor/executrix of my will.

SECOND

No bond or other security of any kind shall be required of any executor/executrix appointed in this will.

My executor or executrix, whether original, substitute or successor, shall hereafter be referred to as my "executor."

THIRD

I direct that my executor pay all of my funeral expenses, all state and federal estate, inheritance and succession taxes, administration costs and all of my debts subject to statute of limitations, except mortgage notes secured by real estate, as soon as practical.

FOURTH

I give, devise and bequeath all of the rest, residue and remainder of my estate, of whatever kind and character, and wherever located, per capita, to:

First Name	Middle	Last
First Name	Middle	Last
First Name	Middle	Last
First Name	Middle	Last

FIFTH

My executor shall have the following additional powers with respect to my estate, to be exercised from time to time at his or her discretion without further license or order of any court:

Business Interests

To sell or otherwise liquidate, or to continue to operate at his or her discretion, any corporation, partnership or other business interest received by my estate.

Property of My Estate

To retain any and all property and securities of my estate in the name of my executor as executor or in his or her own name.

Retention of Assets

To retain all property and securities of my estate for as long as my executor deems advisable.

Management of Estate

To invest, lease, rent, mortgage, insure, repair, improve or sell any and all real and personal property belonging to my estate as my executor deems advisable.

Mortgages, Pledges and Deeds of Trust

To enforce any and all mortgages, pledges and deeds of trust held by my estate and to purchase at any sale thereunder any such real or personal property subject to any mortgage, pledge or deed of trust.

Litigation

To initiate or defend, at his or her discretion, any litigation affecting my estate.

Attorneys, Advisors and Agents

To employ and to pay from my estate reasonable compensation to such attorneys, accountants, brokers, and investment, tax and other advisors as he or she shall deem advisable.

Adjustment of Claims

To submit to arbitration, to compromise or to release or otherwise adjust, with or without compensation, any and all claims affecting my estate.

Distribution of My Estate

In distributing my estate, to make said distribution wholly or partly in kind by transferring or allotting such real or personal property or undivided interest therein.

SEVENTH

If any person, whether or not related to me by blood or in any way, shall attempt, either directly or indirectly, to set aside the probate of my will or oppose any of the provisions hereof, and such person shall establish a right to any portion of my estate, then I give and bequeath the sum of one dollar ($1.00), only that, and no further interest whatever in my estate to such person.

EIGHTH

In the event that any of my property, or all of it, at the time of my death is community property under the laws of any jurisdiction, then my will shall be construed as referring only to my community-property interest therein.

NINTH

If any portion of my will shall be held illegal, invalid or otherwise inoperative, it is my intention that all of the other provisions hereof shall continue to be fully effective and operative insofar as is possible and reasonable.

IN WITNESS WHEREOF, I have hereunto set my hand and seal this _____ day of _____, 19 _____.

_____

Signed, sealed, published and declared to be his/her **Last Will and Testament** by the within-named testator/testatrix in the presence of all of us, who, in his/her presence and at his/her request, and in the presence of each other, have hereunto subscribed our names as witnesses:

_____

| Street | City | State | Zip |

_____

| Street | City | State | Zip |

_____

| Street | City | State | Zip |

FORM 55.9/F414

𝕷𝖆𝖘𝖙 𝖂𝖎𝖑𝖑
𝖆𝖓𝖉
𝕿𝖊𝖘𝖙𝖆𝖒𝖊𝖓𝖙
𝖔𝖋

Dated _____ 19 ___

4

Last Will and Testament
of

_____

I, _____, of

_____ ,

| City/Town | County | State |

being of sound and disposing mind, do hereby make, publish and declare the following to be my **Last Will and Testament**, revoking all previous wills and codicils made by me.

I declare that I am married to _____ and that all references to "my wife" or "my spouse" made in this will are references to her. I have _____ children whose names and birth dates are:

First Name	Middle	Last	Date of Birth
First Name	Middle	Last	Date of Birth
First Name	Middle	Last	Date of Birth
First Name	Middle	Last	Date of Birth
First Name	Middle	Last	Date of Birth

I have _____ deceased children.

All references to "my children" in this will include all of the above-named children and also any child hereafter born to or adopted by me.

FIRST

My wife and I are executing wills at approximately the same time in which each is the primary beneficiary of the other. These wills are not being made because of any contractual agreement between us, and either will may at any time be revoked by either maker at the sole discretion thereof.

SECOND

I appoint my wife _____ as independent executrix of my will. If she is unable or unwilling to act, or to continue to act, as executrix of my will, I then appoint _____ _____ as executor/executrix of my will.

My executor or executrix, whether original, substitute or successor, shall hereinafter be referred to as "executor."

No bond or other security of any kind shall be required of any executor appointed under this will.

THIRD

I direct that my executor pay all of my funeral expenses, all state and federal estate, inheritance and succession taxes, administration costs and all of my debts subject to statute of limitations, except mortgage notes secured by real estate, as soon as practical.

FOURTH

I give, devise and bequeath the following described personal, real and other property of my estate, wherever located, to my wife _____, provided that she survives me by _____ _____ :

_____

_____

_____

_____

_____

_____

_____

_____

_____

_____

I make no provision hereinabove for my children _____

_____ ,

knowing that, as their mother, my wife will continue to be mindful of their needs and requirements.

FIFTH

If my wife does not survive me by _____, then I give, devise and bequeath all of the above-described property of my estate, wherever located, along with all of the rest, residue and remainder of my estate to _____, as Trustee, in trust, for the benefit of my children, to be held, managed, administered and distributed as herein directed.

SIXTH

If my wife does survive me by _____, I hereby give, devise and bequeath the following described personal, real and other property of my estate, wherever located, to _____ _____, as Trustee, in trust, to be held, managed, administered and distributed as herein directed:

_____

_____

_____

_____

_____

_____

_____

_____

_____

_____

_____

The Trustee shall pay any and all income from said trust established with the immediately above described assets to my surviving wife no less frequently than _____, commencing _____ _____, and continuing during her lifetime.

The Trustee may also at his/her discretion transfer to my spouse such of the principal assets of the trust at any time as may be necessary or advisable for her continued maintenance and welfare during her lifetime.

Upon the death of my spouse the Trustee shall hold, manage, administer and distribute the remaining principal assets of said trust as hereinbelow directed.

SEVENTH

If _____ is unable or unwilling to act, or to continue to act, as Trustee, I then appoint _____ as Trustee with all of the same powers, rights, obligations and immunities. If the aforesaid _____ and _____ are each unwilling or unable to act, or to continue to act, as Trustee, I then appoint _____ as Trustee with all of the same powers, rights, obligations and immunities.

EIGHTH

No bond for the faithful performance of duties shall be required of any Trustee appointed in this will.

NINTH

The Trustee shall receive a reasonable fee for the services rendered by him or her.

TENTH

No Trustee of any trust created under this will shall at any time be held accountable for any action or default of himself or herself, or his or her agent, or of any other person in connection with the administration of such trust unless caused by his or her own gross negligence or by commission of a willful act of breach of trust.

ELEVENTH

The Trustee shall have the sole authority to determine what shall be defined as income and what shall be defined as principal of any trust established under this will, and to determine what costs, taxes and other expenses shall be paid out of income and what shall be paid out of principal in accordance with applicable statutes of the State of _____ _____.

TWELFTH

I direct that any trust established under **FIFTH**, above, or, after the death of my surviving wife, that any trust established under **SIXTH**, above, shall be held, managed, administered and distributed as one trust until no living child of mine is under the age of _____. Until that time, the Trustee shall apply the principal and net income of the trust as follows:

So long as any of my children are under the age of _____, the net income of the trust shall be applied to the benefit of, or paid to, any or all of my children in such amounts and at such times as the Trustee shall at his or her discretion decide are necessary for their support, maintenance, welfare and education.

In the event that net income of the trust shall be insufficient to provide any of my said children with the funds necessary for adequate support, maintenance, welfare or education, the Trustee may invade the principal of the trust for this purpose. Payments of trust income or principal to any child of mine pursuant to this paragraph need not be taken into account by the Trustee in any later division of the trust into shares for distribution to my children or children of a deceased child of mine. No child of mine who has completed his or her _____ year shall receive any of the aforesaid payments from the trust estate.

The Trustee, in exercising his or her discretionary authority regarding the payment of principal or income of the trust estate to any of my children, or to the children of any of my deceased children, may take into consideration any other income or resources available to such beneficiary from sources outside the trust estate which may be known to the Trustee. The decision of the Trustee with regard to the necessity for making payments out of income or principal to any beneficiary shall be conclusive on all persons having any right or interest whatever in the trust.

The Trustee may apply more for or pay more to some beneficiaries than others and may entirely omit distribution to any of the beneficiaries during the continuance of the trust estate.

In the event that any of my children shall predecease me or die prior to the termination of the trust estate, interest of such child or children in the trust shall cease, except that if such deceased child or children shall be survived by any child or children of theirs, then the Trustee may apply that same interest for the child or children of a deceased child of mine to such extent as the Trustee at his or her sole discretion may deem necessary for support, maintenance, welfare or education. Payments of income or principal to any child or children of a deceased child of mine pursuant to this paragraph need not be taken into account by the Trustee in any subsequent division of the trust estate into shares for distribution to my children or to the child or children of any deceased child of mine.

The Trustee shall add to the principal of the trust estate any net interest or income not paid out in accordance with the powers, authority and discretion hereinabove conferred on the Trustee.

At such time when no child of mine who is living is under the age of _____, the trust shall terminate, and the Trustee shall as soon as practical distribute the remainder and residue of the trust estate in equal shares to my children then living. However, if any deceased child of mine has any child or children then surviving, then an equal share of the trust estate shall be distributed to said surviving issue of each deceased child of mine *per stirpes*.

THIRTEENTH

The Trustee, in addition to all other powers granted by this will and by law, shall have the following additional powers with respect to the trust estate, to be exercised from time to time at his or her discretion without further license or order of any court, subject to any limitations set forth elsewhere in this will:

Business Interests

To sell or otherwise liquidate, or to continue to operate at his or her discretion, any corporation, partnership or other business interest received by the trust estate.

Property of Trust Estate

To retain any and all property and securities of the trust estate for as long as he or she may deem advisable.

Management of Trust Estate

To invest, lease, rent, mortgage, insure, repair, improve or sell any and all real and personal property belonging to the trust estate as he or she may deem advisable.

Mortgages, Pledges and Deeds of Trust

To enforce any and all mortgages, pledges and deeds of trust held by the trust estate and to purchase at any sale thereunder any such real or personal property subject to any mortgage, pledge or deed of trust.

Litigation

To initiate or defend, at his or her discretion, any litigation affecting the trust estate.

Attorneys, Advisors and Agents

To employ and to pay from the trust estate reasonable compensation to such attorneys, accountants, brokers, and investment, tax and other advisors as he or she shall deem advisable.

Adjustment of Claims

To submit to arbitration, to compromise or to release or otherwise adjust, with or without compensation, any and all claims affecting the trust estate.

Distribution of Trust Estate

In distributing the trust estate, to make said distribution wholly or partly in kind by transferring or allotting such real or personal property or undivided interest.

FOURTEENTH

If my wife does not survive me, I then appoint _____
_____ and _____
as guardians of the person of each of my minor children, and I hereby request that they seek appointment as guardians of their estates. If both of them qualify and thereafter either ceases to act, one may act alone.

If one of them fails to qualify, or if both cease to act after qualifying, I then appoint _____
_____ and _____
as new guardians of the person of each of my minor children, and I hereby request that they seek appointment as guardians of their estates. If both qualify and thereafter either ceases to act, one may act alone.

No bond or other security of any kind shall be required of any of the above parties for the faithful exercise of their responsibilities as guardian of the person or of the estate of any of my minor children.

FIFTEENTH

If any person, whether or not related to me by blood or in any other way, shall attempt, either directly or indirectly, to set aside the probate of my will or oppose any of the provisions hereof, and such person shall establish a right to any portion of my estate, then I give and bequeath the sum of one dollar ($1.00), only that, and no further interest whatever in my estate to such person.

SIXTEENTH

In the event that any of my property, or all of it, at the time of my death is community property under the laws of any jurisdiction, then my will shall be construed as referring only to my community-property interest therein.

SEVENTEENTH

If any portion of my will shall be held illegal, invalid or otherwise inoperative, it is my intention that all of the other provisions hereof shall continue to be fully effective and operative insofar as is possible and reasonable.

IN WITNESS WHEREOF, I have hereunto set my hand and seal this _____ day of _____, 19 _____.

_____   _____

Signed, sealed, published and declared to be his **Last Will and Testament** by the within-named testator in the presence of all of us, who, in his presence and at his request, and in the presence of each other, have hereunto subscribed our names as witnesses:

_____

| _Street_ | _City_ | _State_ | _Zip_ |

_____

| _Street_ | _City_ | _State_ | _Zip_ |

_____

| _Street_ | _City_ | _State_ | _Zip_ |

Last Will
and
Testament
of

Dated _____ 19 ____

Last Will and Testament
of

_____

I, _____, of

_____,
City/Town   *County*   *State*

being of sound and disposing mind, do hereby make, publish and declare the following to be my **Last Will and Testament,** revoking all previous wills and codicils made by me.

I declare that I am married to _____ and that all references to "my husband" or "my spouse" made in this will are references to him. I have _____ children whose names and birth dates are:

First Name	*Middle*	*Last*	*Date of Birth*
First Name	*Middle*	*Last*	*Date of Birth*
First Name	*Middle*	*Last*	*Date of Birth*
First Name	*Middle*	*Last*	*Date of Birth*
First Name	*Middle*	*Last*	*Date of Birth*

I have _____ deceased children.
All references to "my children" in this will include all of the above-named children and also any child hereafter born to or adopted by me.

FIRST

My husband and I are executing wills at approximately the same time in which each is the primary beneficiary of the other. These wills are not being made because of any contractual agreement between us, and either will may at any time be revoked by either maker at the sole discretion thereof.

SECOND

I appoint my husband _____ as independent executor of my will. If he is unable or unwilling to act, or to continue to act, as executor of my will, I then appoint _____ _____ as executor/executrix of my will.

My executor or executrix, whether original, substitute or successor, shall hereinafter be referred to as "executor."
No bond or other security of any kind shall be required of any executor appointed under this will.

THIRD

I direct that my executor pay all of my funeral expenses, all state and federal estate, inheritance and succession taxes, administration costs and all of my debts subject to statute of limitations, except mortgage notes secured by real estate, as soon as practical.

FOURTH

I give, devise and bequeath the following described personal, real and other property of my estate, wherever located, to my husband _____, provided that he survives me by _____ _____ :

_____

_____

_____

_____

_____

_____

_____

_____

_____

_____

I make no provision hereinabove for my children _____
_____,
knowing that, as their father, my husband will continue to be mindful of their needs and requirements.

FIFTH

If my husband does not survive me by _____, then I give, devise and bequeath all of the above-described property of my estate, wherever located, along with all of the rest, residue and remainder of my estate to _____, as Trustee, in trust, for the benefit of my children, to be held, managed, administered and distributed as herein directed.

SIXTH

If my husband does survive me by _____, I hereby give, devise and bequeath the following described personal, real and other property of my estate, wherever located, to _____
_____, as Trustee, in trust, to be held, managed, administered and distributed as herein directed:

_____

_____

_____

_____

_____

_____

_____

_____

_____

_____

_____

The Trustee shall pay any and all income from said trust established with the immediately above described assets to my surviving husband no less frequently than _____, commencing _____ _____, and continuing during his lifetime.

The Trustee may also at his/her discretion transfer to my spouse such of the principal assets of the trust at any time as may be necessary or advisable for his continued maintenance and welfare during his lifetime.

Upon the death of my spouse the Trustee shall hold, manage, administer and distribute the remaining principal assets of said trust as hereinbelow directed.

SEVENTH

If _____ is unable or unwilling to act, or to continue to act, as Trustee, I then appoint _____ as Trustee with all of the same powers, rights, obligations and immunities. If the aforesaid _____ and _____ are each unwilling or unable to act, or to continue to act, as Trustee, I then appoint _____ as Trustee with all of the same powers, rights, obligations and immunities.

EIGHTH

No bond for the faithful performance of duties shall be required of any Trustee appointed in this will.

NINTH

The Trustee shall receive a reasonable fee for the services rendered by him or her.

TENTH

No Trustee of any trust created under this will shall at any time be held accountable for any action or default of himself or herself, or his or her agent, or of any other person in connection with the administration of such trust unless caused by his or her own gross negligence or by commission of a willful act of breach of trust.

ELEVENTH

The Trustee shall have the sole authority to determine what shall be defined as income and what shall be defined as principal of any trust established under this will, and to determine what costs, taxes and other expenses shall be paid out of income and what shall be paid out of principal in accordance with applicable statutes of the State of _____ _____.

TWELFTH

I direct that any trust established under **FIFTH,** above, or, after the death of my surviving husband, that any trust established under **SIXTH,** above, shall be held, managed, administered and distributed as one trust until no living child of mine is under the age of _____. Until that time, the Trustee shall apply the principal and net income of the trust as follows:

So long as any of my children are under the age of _____, the net income of the trust shall be applied to the benefit of, or paid to, any or all of my children in such amounts and at such times as the Trustee shall at his or her discretion decide are necessary for their support, maintenance, welfare and education.

In the event that net income of the trust shall be insufficient to provide any of my said children with the funds necessary for adequate support, maintenance, welfare or education, the Trustee may invade the principal of the trust for this purpose. Payments of trust income or principal to any child of mine pursuant to this paragraph need not be taken into account by the Trustee in any later division of the trust into shares for distribution to my children or children of a deceased child of mine. No child of mine who has completed his or her _____ year shall receive any of the aforesaid payments from the trust estate.

The Trustee, in exercising his or her discretionary authority regarding the payment of principal or income of the trust estate to any of my children, or to the children of any of my deceased children, may take into consideration any other income or resources available to such beneficiary from sources outside the trust estate which may be known to the Trustee. The decision of the Trustee with regard to the necessity for making payments out of income or principal to any beneficiary shall be conclusive on all persons having any right or interest whatever in the trust.

The Trustee may apply more for or pay more to some beneficiaries than others and may entirely omit distribution to any of the beneficiaries during the continuance of the trust estate.

In the event that any of my children shall predecease me or die prior to the termination of the trust estate, interest of such child or children in the trust shall cease, except that if such deceased child or children shall be survived by any child or children of theirs, then the Trustee may apply that same interest for the child or children of a deceased child of mine to such extent as the Trustee at his or her sole discretion may deem necessary for support, maintenance, welfare or education. Payments of income or principal to any child or children of a deceased child of mine pursuant to this paragraph need not be taken into account by the Trustee in any subsequent division of the trust estate into shares for distribution to my children or to the child or children of any deceased child of mine.

The Trustee shall add to the principal of the trust estate any net interest or income not paid out in accordance with the powers, authority and discretion hereinabove conferred on the Trustee.

At such time when no child of mine who is living is under the age of _____ , the trust shall terminate, and the Trustee shall as soon as practical distribute the remainder and residue of the trust estate in equal shares to my children then living. However, if any deceased child of mine has any child or children then surviving, then an equal share of the trust estate shall be distributed to said surviving issue of each deceased child of mine *per stirpes*.

THIRTEENTH

The Trustee, in addition to all other powers granted by this will and by law, shall have the following additional powers with respect to the trust estate, to be exercised from time to time at his or her discretion without further license or order of any court, subject to any limitations set forth elsewhere in this will:

Business Interests

To sell or otherwise liquidate, or to continue to operate at his or her discretion, any corporation, partnership or other business interest received by the trust estate.

Property of Trust Estate

To retain any and all property and securities of the trust estate for as long as he or she may deem advisable.

Management of Trust Estate

To invest, lease, rent, mortgage, insure, repair, improve or sell any and all real and personal property belonging to the trust estate as he or she may deem advisable.

Mortgages, Pledges and Deeds of Trust

To enforce any and all mortgages, pledges and deeds of trust held by the trust estate and to purchase at any sale thereunder any such real or personal property subject to any mortgage, pledge or deed of trust.

Litigation

To initiate or defend, at his or her discretion, any litigation affecting the trust estate.

Attorneys, Advisors and Agents

To employ and to pay from the trust estate reasonable compensation to such attorneys, accountants, brokers, and investment, tax and other advisors as he or she shall deem advisable.

Adjustment of Claims

To submit to arbitration, to compromise or to release or otherwise adjust, with or without compensation, any and all claims affecting the trust estate.

Distribution of Trust Estate

In distributing the trust estate, to make said distribution wholly or partly in kind by transferring or allotting such real or personal property or undivided interest.

FOURTEENTH

If my husband does not survive me, I then appoint _____
_____ and _____
as guardians of the person of each of my minor children, and I hereby request that they seek appointment as guardians of their estates. If both of them qualify and thereafter either ceases to act, one may act alone.

If one of them fails to qualify, or if both cease to act after qualifying. I then appoint _____
_____ and _____
as new guardians of the person of each of my minor children, and I hereby request that they seek appointment as guardians of their estates. If both qualify and thereafter either ceases to act, one may act alone.

No bond or other security of any kind shall be required of any of the above parties for the faithful exercise of their responsibilities as guardian of the person or of the estate of any of my minor children.

FIFTEENTH

If any person, whether or not related to me by blood or in any other way, shall attempt, either directly or indirectly, to set aside the probate of my will or oppose any of the provisions hereof, and such person shall establish a right to any portion of my estate, then I give and bequeath the sum of one dollar ($1.00), only that, and no further interest whatever in my estate to such person.

SIXTEENTH

In the event that any of my property, or all of it, at the time of my death is community property under the laws of any jurisdiction, then my will shall be construed as referring only to my community-property interest therein.

SEVENTEENTH

If any portion of my will shall be held illegal, invalid or otherwise inoperative, it is my intention that all of the other provisions hereof shall continue to be fully effective and operative insofar as is possible and reasonable.

IN WITNESS WHEREOF, I have hereunto set my hand and seal this _____ day of _____, 19 _____.

_____

Signed, sealed, published and declared to be her **Last Will and Testament** by the within-named testatrix in the presence of all of us, who, in her presence and at her request, and in the presence of each other, have hereunto subscribed our names as witnesses:

_____

| *Street* | *City* | *State* | *Zip* |

_____

| *Street* | *City* | *State* | *Zip* |

_____

| *Street* | *City* | *State* | *Zip* |

Last Will

and

Testament

of

Dated _____ 19 ___

Last Will and Testament Provisions

In the name of God, Amen, I, _____ ,

of _____ ,
      City/Town   *County*   *State*

being of sound and disposing mind, and aware of the uncertainties of this life, do hereby make, publish and declare the following to be my **Last Will and Testament,** revoking all previous wills and codicils made by me, so help me, God.

I direct that my funeral be carried out according to the ritual of _____ .
I further direct that my remains be _____ and _____
_____ .

I hereby give and bequeath the sum of _____ to _____ . If he/she predeceases me, then this gift shall lapse and the aforesaid sum shall be added to the residual of my estate.

I hereby give and bequeath the sum of _____ to _____ . If he/she predeceases me, then this gift shall lapse, and I direct that the aforesaid sum shall be given to _____ _____ , if he/she survives me. If he/she predeceases me, this gift shall lapse and the aforesaid sum shall be added to the residual of my estate.

I hereby give and bequeath the sum of _____ to _____ to be paid out of my savings account, number _____ , at the _____ located in _____ . If he/she predeceases me, this gift shall lapse and the aforesaid sum shall be added to the residual of my estate.

Last Will and Testament Provisions

I hereby give and bequeath all of my household furniture and furnishings, books, works of art, silver, jewelry, autos, boats and other vehicles, clothing and all other personal property not otherwise distributed to my spouse _____ _____, provided that he/she survives me by _____. If he/she shall predecease me or fail to survive me by _____, then I give all of my aforementioned personal property to _____.

It is my intention to leave in my safe-deposit box at _____, of _____, a letter for the information of _____, listing items of personal property and indicating those items which I ask be given by him or her to specific persons who are named in the letter. It is my request, but not my direction, that the list be used as a guide in distributing the personal property given and bequeathed to him or her.

I hereby give and bequeath all of my household furnishings and furniture, books, works of art, silver, jewelry, autos, boats and other vehicles, clothing and all other personal property not otherwise distributed by my will to _____ _____. If he/she predeceases me, then this gift shall lapse, and I direct that the aforesaid personal property be given to _____, if he/she survives me. If he/she predeceases me, this gift shall lapse and the aforesaid personal property shall be added to the residual of my estate.

It is my intention to leave in my safe-deposit box at _____ _____, of _____, a letter for the information of _____ or _____, listing items of personal property and indicating those items which I ask be given by him or her to specific persons who are also named in the letter. It is my request, but not my direction, that the list be used as a guide in distributing the personal property given and bequeathed to him or her.

I hereby give and devise my home, located at _____ _____, to _____. If he/she predeceases me, this gift shall lapse, and I then give and devise my aforesaid home to _____. If at the time of my death I no longer own the aforesaid property, then this gift shall lapse. It is my intention that the beneficiary of the above devise shall receive title to the aforesaid home free and clear, and I direct my executor to discharge any encumbrance thereon, sufficient funds having been provided for this purpose _____ _____.

Last Will and Testament Provisions

I hereby give and devise my interest in my home, located at _____ _____, to _____. If he/she predeceases me, this gift shall lapse, and I then give and devise my interest in the aforesaid home to _____. If at the time of my death I no longer own the aforesaid property, this gift shall lapse.

I hereby give and bequeath the sum of _____ to _____, of _____, to be used for its _____ purposes.

I hereby give and bequeath the sum of _____ to _____, of _____, to be used specifically for _____ _____.

I hereby give and bequeath all of my stock in _____ to _____. If he/she predeceases me, this gift shall lapse, and I then give and bequeath all of my stock in the aforesaid corporation to _____. If I own no shares in the aforesaid corporation at the time of my death, this gift shall lapse.

I hereby give and bequeath my _____, together with any documents of pedigree and all equipment which I own and maintain for its care and protection, to _____. In the event that he/she predeceases me, or is unwilling or unable to accept my aforesaid _____ under this bequest, this gift shall lapse, and I then give and bequeath my aforesaid _____, together with any documents of pedigree and all equipment to _____. If the aforesaid _____ is not owned by me at the time of my death, this gift shall lapse.

I direct that the expense of moving or shipping any property distributed under my will to a location desired by any beneficiary shall be borne by the beneficiary.

Last Will and Testament Provisions

I direct that my executor pay, out of the residue of my estate, any expenses reasonably incurred in the packing, shipping and insurance of any property distributed under my will to any beneficiary of any bequest herein.

From time to time after the execution of my will I may make certain gifts to some of the beneficiaries herein. It is my intention to leave a record of all such gifts in my safe-deposit box at _____ _____, and all gifts so recorded after the execution of my will shall be considered as advancements and shall be deducted from gifts and bequests herein given to those beneficiaries. Any amount so deducted shall be based upon the value of said gift as of the date of the gift.

No devise or bequest provided for herein shall be reduced or extinguished due to any gifts made by me during my lifetime to _____, either before or after the execution of this will.

I direct that the balance due, as of the date of my death, on a promissory note in the amount of _____, payable to me and executed by _____, on _____, shall be cancelled by my executor and be delivered to _____, or if he/she has predeceased me, to the executor of his/her estate. If the aforesaid debt has been discharged, this gift shall lapse and resort shall not be had to any asset of my estate for its fulfillment.

I direct that in the event my estate shall not have sufficient funds to pay for all of the bequests and devises herein, the bequests and devises which I have made to

_____

_____

shall not abate until all other bequests and devises have been fully abated.

Last Will and Testament Provisions

I hereby appoint _____ as guardian of the person of each of my minor children. If he/she is unwilling to act, or to continue to act after qualification, I then appoint _____ as guardian of the person of each of my minor children.

I hereby appoint _____ as guardian of the property of each of my minor children. If he/she/it is unwilling to act, or to continue to act after qualification, I then appoint _____ _____ as guardian of the property of each of my minor children.

If any beneficiary or remainderman under any provision of my will directly or indirectly contests, or in any other manner attacks, this will or any provision thereof, any portion or share whatever of my estate or in any trust established by my will given, devised or bequeathed to said beneficiary or remainderman under my will is revoked and shall be distributed in the same manner as if that contesting beneficiary or remainderman had predeceased me without issue.

Declaration of Gift

TO ALL TO WHOM THESE PRESENTS SHALL COME OR MAY CONCERN, KNOW THAT on this _____

day of _____, 19 _____, I, _____,

of _____,
          Street   *City*   *State*   *Zip*

being of sound and disposing mind and memory do hereby irrevocably give, bestow and deliver up to _____

_____,

of _____,
          Street   *City*   *State*   *Zip*

all of my right, title and interest in the following described property valued at _____

_____, ($ _____):

_____

_____

_____

_____

_____

_____

_____

_____

IN WITNESS WHEREOF, I hereunto set my hand and seal on the date above mentioned.

_____

* *

CERTIFICATE OF NOTARY

STATE OF   )
)   ss:

COUNTY OF   )

On this _____ day of _____, 19 _____, before me personally came and appeared _____, known, and known to me, to be the individual described in and who executed the foregoing instrument, and who duly acknowledged to me that he/she executed same for the purpose therein contained.

IN WITNESS WHEREOF, I hereunto set my hand and official seal.

_____
                                       Notary Public

My commission expires: _____

FORM 58.1 / F434

Declaration
of Gift

From

To

Dated _____ 19 _____

Declaration of Revocable Trust

This **Declaration of Revocable Trust** is made this _____ day of _____ , 19 _____ , between

_____ , of

_____ ,

hereinafter called the Trustor, and _____ , of

_____ ,

hereinafter called the Trustee.

FIRST

The Trustor hereby assigns, conveys and gives to the Trustee, in trust, the following property:

SECOND

The Trustee shall receive and hold said property, together with any additions thereto, in trust for the use and benefit of:

_____

_____

_____ .

THIRD

FOURTH

I reserve the absolute right, during my life, by an instrument in writing signed by me, to revoke, annul and cancel this agreement and the trust created hereby; and to alter, modify or amend this trust in any and all aspects; and to withdraw at any time, and from time to time, any and all of the aforesaid property; and to add thereto at any time, and from time to time, such additional property as I may determine.

FIFTH

This agreement and the trust created hereby shall be administered, managed, governed and regulated in all respects according to applicable statutes of the State of _____ .

SIXTH

The Trustee, in addition to all other powers granted by this agreement and by law, shall have the following additional powers with respect to the trust, to be exercised from time to time at the Trustee's discretion:

Management of the Trust

To invest and reinvest, lease, rent, mortgage, insure, repair, improve or sell any of the real and personal property of the trust as he or she may deem advisable.

Business Interests

To sell or otherwise liquidate, or to continue to operate at his or her discretion, any corporation, partnership or other business interest which may be received by the trust.

Mortgages, Pledges and Deeds of Trust

To enforce any and all mortgages, pledges and deeds of trust held by the trust and to purchase at any sale thereunder any such real estate or personal property subject to any mortgage, pledge or deed of trust.

Litigation

To initiate or defend, at his or her discretion, any litigation affecting the trust.

Attorneys, Advisors and Agents

To employ and to pay from the trust reasonable compensation to such attorneys, accountants, brokers, and investment, tax and other advisors as he or she shall deem advisable.

Adjustment of Claims

To submit to arbitration, to compromise or to release or otherwise adjust, with or without compensation, any and all claims affecting the trust estate.

SEVENTH

No bond for the faithful performance of duties shall be required of any Trustee appointed under this agreement.

EIGHTH

The Trustee shall receive reasonable compensation for the services performed by him or her, but such compensation shall not exceed the amount customarily received by corporate fiduciaries in the area for like services.

NINTH

No Trustee of the trust created by this agreement shall at any time be held liable for any action or default of himself or herself, or of his or her agent, or of any other person in connection with the administration and management of this trust unless caused by his or her own gross negligence or by commission of a willful act of breach of trust.

TENTH

The Trustee, by joining in the execution of this agreement, hereby signifies his or her acceptance of this trust.

ELEVENTH

The Trustee shall have sole authority to determine what shall be defined as income and what shall be defined as principal of the trust established by this agreement, and to determine which costs, taxes and other expenses shall be paid out of income and which shall be paid out of principal.

TWELFTH

In the event that any portion of this trust agreement or the trust created hereby shall be held illegal, invalid or otherwise inoperative, it is my intention that all of the other provisions hereof shall continue to be fully effective and operative insofar as is possible and reasonable.

IN WITNESS WHEREOF, the parties hereto have executed this agreement the day and year first above written.

_____
Trustor

_____
Trustee

....

I, the undersigned _____ of the above-described Trustor, do hereby waive and relinquish any and all claim to whatever community-property rights I may have in the hereinabove-described _____ _____ and do give and grant my assent to the trust and to the incorporation therein of said _____ _____ .

_____
Legal Spouse of Trustor

....

_____
Witness

_____
Witness

* *

CERTIFICATE OF NOTARY

STATE OF   )
) ss:
COUNTY OF   )

On this _____ day of _____ , 19 _____ , before me personally came and appeared _____ and _____ and _____ , known, and known to me, to be the individuals described in and who executed the foregoing instrument, and who duly acknowledged to me that they executed same for the purpose therein contained.

IN WITNESS WHEREOF, I hereunto set my hand and official seal.

_____
Notary Public

My commission expires: _____

3

Declaration of Trust

Dated _____ 19 ____

4

Declaration of Revocable Trust

This **Declaration of Revocable Trust** is made this _____ day of _____, 19 _____, between

_____

and _____, of

_____ ,

hereinafter called the Trustors, and _____, of

_____ ,

hereinafter called the Trustee.

FIRST

The Trustors hereby assign, convey and give to the Trustee, in trust, the following property:

SECOND

The Trustee shall receive and hold said property, together with any additions thereto, in trust for the use and benefit of:

_____

_____

_____ .

THIRD

FOURTH

The Trustors reserve the right, by an instrument in writing signed by both, to revoke, annul and cancel this agreement and the trust created hereby; and to alter, modify or amend this trust in any and all aspects; and to withdraw at any time, and from time to time, any and all of the aforesaid property; and to add thereto at any time, and from time to time, such additional property as they may determine.

Upon the death of either Trustor, the survivor shall have the right to act alone as sole Trustor, with all of the powers and rights enumerated herein.

FIFTH

This agreement and the trust created hereby shall be administered, managed, governed and regulated in all respects according to applicable statutes of the State of _____ .

SIXTH

The Trustee, in addition to all other powers granted by this agreement and by law, shall have the following additional powers with respect to the trust, to be exercised from time to time at the Trustee's discretion:

Management of the Trust

To invest and reinvest, lease, rent, mortgage, insure, repair, improve or sell any of the real and personal property of the trust as he or she may deem advisable.

Business Interests

To sell or otherwise liquidate, or to continue to operate at his or her discretion, any corporation, partnership or other business interest which may be received by the trust.

Mortgages, Pledges and Deeds of Trust

To enforce any and all mortgages, pledges and deeds of trust held by the trust and to purchase at any sale thereunder any such real estate or personal property subject to any mortgage, pledge or deed of trust.

Litigation

To initiate or defend, at his or her discretion, any litigation affecting the trust.

Attorneys, Advisors and Agents

To employ and to pay from the trust reasonable compensation to such attorneys, accountants, brokers, and investment, tax and other advisors as he or she shall deem advisable.

Adjustment of Claims

To submit to arbitration, to compromise or to release or otherwise adjust, with or without compensation, any and all claims affecting the trust estate.

SEVENTH

No bond for the faithful performance of duties shall be required of any Trustee appointed under this agreement.

EIGHTH

The Trustee shall receive reasonable compensation for the services performed by him or her, but such compensation shall not exceed the amount customarily received by corporate fiduciaries in the area for like services.

NINTH

No Trustee of the trust created by this agreement shall at any time be held liable for any action or default of himself or herself, or of his or her agent, or of any other person in connection with the administration and management of this trust unless caused by his or her own gross negligence or by commission of a willful act of breach of trust.

TENTH

The Trustee, by joining in the execution of this agreement, hereby signifies his or her acceptance of this trust.

ELEVENTH

The Trustee shall have sole authority to determine what shall be defined as income and what shall be defined as principal of the trust established by this agreement, and to determine which costs, taxes and other expenses shall be paid out of income and which shall be paid out of principal.

TWELFTH

In the event that any portion of this trust agreement or the trust created hereby shall be held illegal, invalid or otherwise inoperative, it is our intention that all of the other provisions hereof shall continue to be fully effective and operative insofar as is possible and reasonable.

IN WITNESS WHEREOF, the parties hereto have executed this agreement the day and year first above written.

_____
Trustor

_____
Trustor

_____
Trustee

_____
Witness

_____
Witness

* *

CERTIFICATE OF NOTARY

STATE OF   )
) ss:
COUNTY OF   )

On this _____ day of _____, 19 _____, before me personally came and appeared _____ and _____ and _____, known, and known to me, to be the individuals described in and who executed the foregoing instrument, and who duly acknowledged to me that they executed same for the purpose therein contained.

IN WITNESS WHEREOF, I hereunto set my hand and official seal.

_____
Notary Public

My commission expires: _____

FORM 60.2/F442

Declaration
of
Trust

Dated _____ 19 ___

Declaration of Revocable Trust

I, _____ , of

_____ ,

hereby make and declare this **Revocable Trust** this _____ day of _____ , 19 _____ .

FIRST

Whereas I am the sole and undisputed owner of the following property:

I hereby declare that I do now hold said property, as Trustee, with all title, right and interest thereto, in trust for the use

and benefit of _____

_____

_____

_____ .

SECOND

I reserve the absolute right, during my life, to revoke, annul and cancel this trust; and to alter, modify or amend this trust in any and all respects; and to withdraw at any time, and from time to time, any and all of the aforesaid property; and to add thereto at any time, and from time to time, such additional property as I may determine.

THIRD

I reserve the absolute right to deliver, transfer, convey and give to the beneficiary/beneficiaries, at any time, and from time to time, during my lifetime, any and all of the above-described property.

FOURTH

FIFTH

In the event of my death or legal incapacity, I hereby appoint _____ ,
of _____ , as my Successor Trustee. If _____
_____ is unwilling or unable to act, or to continue to act, as Successor Trustee, I then appoint
_____ , of _____
_____ , with all of the same powers, rights, obligations and immunities.

SIXTH

No bond for the faithful performance of duties shall be required of any Successor Trustee appointed under this declaration.

SEVENTH

My Successor Trustee shall receive a reasonable fee for the services performed by him or her.

EIGHTH

No Successor Trustee of the trust created by this declaration shall at any time be held liable for any action or default of himself or herself, or of his or her agent, or of any other person in connection with the exercise of the duties of Trustee unless caused by his or her own gross negligence or by commission of a willful act of breach of trust.

NINTH

In the event that any of the property of this trust is community property under the laws of any jurisdiction, then this trust shall be construed as referring only to my community-property interest therein.

TENTH

In the event that any portion of this declaration and the trust created hereby shall be held illegal, invalid or otherwise inoperative, it is my intention that all of the other provisions hereof shall continue to be fully effective and operative insofar as is possible and reasonable.

ELEVENTH

This declaration and the trust created hereby shall be administered, governed and regulated in all respects according to applicable statutes of the State of _____.

IN WITNESS WHEREOF, I hereby set my hand and seal this _____ day of _____, 19 _____.

_____
Trustor

_____
Witness

_____
Witness

* *

CERTIFICATE OF NOTARY

STATE OF   )
) ss:
COUNTY OF   )

On this _____ day of _____, 19 _____, before me personally came and appeared _____, known, and known to me, to be the individual who executed the foregoing instrument, and who duly acknowledged to me that he/she executed same for the purpose therein contained.

IN WITNESS WHEREOF, I hereunto set my hand and official seal.

_____
Notary Public

My commission expires: _____

Declaration
of
Trust

Dated _____ 19 _____

4

Declaration of Revocable Trust

We, _____ and _____ , of

_____ ,

hereby make and declare this **Revocable Trust** this _____ day of _____ , 19 _____.

FIRST

Whereas we are the sole and undisputed owners of the following property:

We hereby declare that we do now hold said property, as Trustees, with all title, right and interest thereto, in trust for the

use and benefit of _____

_____

_____

_____ .

SECOND

The Trustors reserve the right, by an instrument in writing signed by both, to revoke, annul and cancel this declaration and the trust created hereby; and to alter, modify or amend this trust in any and all respects; and to withdraw at any time, and from time to time, any and all of the aforesaid property; and to add thereto at any time, and from time to time, such additional property as they may determine.

Upon the death of either Trustor, the survivor shall have the right to act alone as sole Trustor, with all of the powers and rights enumerated herein.

THIRD

We reserve the absolute right, by an instrument in writing signed by both, to deliver, transfer, convey and give to the beneficiary/beneficiaries, at any time, and from time to time, any and all of the above-described property.

FOURTH

FIFTH

In the event of the legal incapacity of both of us, and in the event of the death of the survivor of us, we hereby appoint _____, of _____, as our Successor Trustee. If _____ is unwilling or unable to act, or to continue to act, as Successor Trustee, we then appoint _____, of _____, with all of the same powers, rights, obligations and immunities.

SIXTH

No bond for the faithful performance of duties shall be required of any Successor Trustee appointed under this declaration.

SEVENTH

Our Successor Trustee shall receive a reasonable fee for the services performed by him or her.

EIGHTH

No Successor Trustee of the trust created by this declaration shall at any time be held liable for any action or default of himself or herself, or of his or her agent, or of any other person in connection with the exercise of the duties of Trustee unless caused by his or her own gross negligence or by commission of a willful act of breach of trust.

NINTH

In the event that any portion of this declaration and the trust created hereby shall be held illegal, invalid or otherwise inoperative, it is our intention that all of the other provisions hereof shall continue to be fully effective and operative insofar as is possible and reasonable.

TENTH

This declaration and the trust created hereby shall be administered, governed and regulated in all respects according to applicable statutes of the State of _____.

IN WITNESS WHEREOF, we each set our hand and seal this _____ day of _____, 19 _____.

_____
Trustor

_____
Trustor

_____
Witness

_____
Witness

* *

CERTIFICATE OF NOTARY

STATE OF   )
)   ss:
COUNTY OF   )

On this _____ day of _____, 19 _____, before me personally came and appeared _____ and _____,
known, and known to me, to be the individuals who executed the foregoing instrument, and who duly acknowledged to me that they executed same for the purpose therein contained.

IN WITNESS WHEREOF, I hereunto set my hand and official seal.

_____
Notary Public

My commission expires: _____

3

Declaration of Trust

Dated _____ 19 _____

Declaration of Revocable Trust

This **Declaration of Revocable Trust** is made this _____ day of _____, 19 _____, between

_____, of

_____ ,

hereinafter called the Trustor, and _____, of

_____ ,

hereinafter called the Trustee.

FIRST

The Trustor hereby assigns, conveys and gives to the Trustee, in trust, the following property:

SECOND

The Trustee shall receive and hold said property, together with any additions thereto, in trust for the use and benefit of:

_____

_____

_____.

THIRD

Upon my death the Trustee shall commence monthly payment of income of the trust, plus such additional assets from the

principal of the trust, as the Trustee shall deem proper for the support of _____

_____

_____

_____.

FOURTH

Upon the death of _____, the Trustee shall divide the remainder of the trust equally into as many parts as there are children of _____ then living, and who are deceased, having left issue. The Trustee shall continue to hold, administer and distribute the trust as follows:

1. The Trustee shall each month pay to the guardian of the person of each minor child of _____ _____ then living, the income from his/her share of the trust; and the Trustee shall each month pay to the guardian of the person, or to the surviving parent, of the minor issue of each deceased child of _____, the income from the share of any deceased child of _____ *per stirpes*.

2. The Trustee shall pay to each child of _____, and the issue of any deceased child of _____, who has attained his/her twenty-first birthday, his/her share of the trust, the payment of said share to the youngest of them thereby terminating the trust.

FIFTH

I reserve the absolute right, during my life, by an instrument in writing signed by me, to revoke, annul and cancel this agreement and the trust created hereby; and to alter, modify or amend this trust in any and all aspects; and to withdraw at any time, and from time to time, any and all of the aforesaid property; and to add thereto at any time, and from time to time, such additional property as I may determine.

SIXTH

This agreement and the trust created hereby shall be administered, managed, governed and regulated in all respects according to applicable statutes of the State of _____.

SEVENTH

The Trustee shall have with respect to all property held or received by the trust, whether principal or income, until the complete distribution thereof, the following powers to be exercised from time to time, at the discretion of the Trustee, without limitation or further license:

Management of the Trust

To invest, reinvest, lease, rent, mortgage, insure, repair, improve or sell any and all of the real and personal property of the trust as the Trustee may deem advisable.

Business Interests

To sell or otherwise liquidate, or to continue to operate at his or her discretion, any corporation, partnership or other business interest which may be received by the trust.

Mortgages, Pledges and Deeds of Trust

To enforce any and all mortgages, pledges and deeds of trust held by the trust and to purchase at any sale thereunder any such real estate or personal property subject to any mortgage, pledge or deed of trust.

Litigation

To initiate or defend, at his or her discretion, any litigation affecting the trust.

Attorneys, Advisors and Agents

To employ and to pay from the trust reasonable compensation to such attorneys, accountants, brokers, and investment, tax and other advisors as he or she shall deem advisable.

Adjustment of Claims

To submit to arbitration, to compromise or to release or otherwise adjust, with or without compensation, any and all claims affecting the trust estate.

EIGHTH

No bond for the faithful performance of duties shall be required of any Trustee appointed under this agreement.

NINTH

The Trustee shall receive reasonable compensation for the services performed by him or her, but such compensation shall not exceed the amount customarily received by corporate fiduciaries in the area for like services.

TENTH

No Trustee of the trust created by this agreement shall at any time be held liable for any action or default of himself or herself, or of his or her agent, or of any other person in connection with the administration and management of this trust unless caused by his or her own gross negligence or by commission of a willful act of breach of trust.

ELEVENTH

The Trustee, by joining in the execution of this agreement, hereby signifies his or her acceptance of this trust.

TWELFTH

The Trustee shall have sole authority to determine what shall be defined as income and what shall be defined as principal of the trust established by this agreement, and to determine which costs, taxes and other expenses shall be paid out of income and which shall be paid out of principal.

THIRTEENTH

In the event that any portion of this trust agreement or the trust created hereby shall be held illegal, invalid or otherwise inoperative, it is my intention that all of the other provisions hereof shall continue to be fully effective and operative insofar as is possible and reasonable.

IN WITNESS WHEREOF, the parties hereto have executed this agreement the day and year first above written.

_____
Trustor

_____
Trustee

I, the undersigned _____ of the above-described Trustor, do hereby waive and relinquish any and all claim to whatever community-property rights I may have in the hereinabove-described _____ _____ and do give and grant my assent to the trust and to the incorporation therein of said _____ _____ .

_____
Legal Spouse of Trustor

_____
Witness

_____
Witness

3

CERTIFICATE OF NOTARY

STATE OF _____)
) ss:
COUNTY OF _____)

On this _____ day of _____, 19 _____, before me personally came and appeared
_____ and _____
and _____, known, and known to me, to be the individuals described in and who executed the foregoing instrument, and who duly acknowledged to me that they executed same for the purpose therein contained.

IN WITNESS WHEREOF, I hereunto set my hand and official seal.

_____
Notary Public

My commission expires: _____

Declaration of Trust

Dated _____ 19 _____

Declaration of Revocable Trust

This **Declaration of Revocable Trust** is made this _____ day of _____, 19 _____, between

_____, of

_____,

hereinafter called the Trustor, and _____, of

_____,

hereinafter called the Trustee.

FIRST

The Trustor hereby assigns, conveys and gives to the Trustee, in trust, the following property:

SECOND

The Trustee shall have and hold the aforesaid property under such terms and conditions, and with such powers, rights and limitations, as are hereinunder set forth:

1. Until _____, the Trustee shall pay the net income of the trust to _____.

2. Upon _____, the Trustee shall each _____ pay the net income of the trust, along with such of the principal assets of the trust as may be necessary and reasonable for his/her support, to my spouse _____.

3. Upon the death of my surviving spouse _____, the Trustee shall pay the remainder of the trust, in equal shares to those children of _____ who are then living, or in the event of the death of any of them, to the issue of any deceased child of _____ *per stirpes*.

THIRD

I reserve the absolute right, during my life, to revoke, annul and cancel this trust; and to alter, modify or amend this trust in any and all respects; and to withdraw at any time, and from time to time, any and all of the aforesaid principal of the trust; and to add thereto at any time, and from time to time, such additional principal as I may determine.

FOURTH

Anything hereinafter to the contrary notwithstanding, none of the powers enumerated herein, nor accorded generally to Trustees by law, shall permit nor be construed to:

A. Allow the Trustee to borrow all or any part of the *corpus* of the trust, nor the income therefrom, directly or indirectly, whether with or without adequate security or adequate interest.

B. Allow the exercise in a nonfiduciary capacity by any person not having written approval of the Trustee, any of the following powers of administration:

1. Any power to control investment of the *corpus* of the trust, either by directing investments or reinvestments or by vetoing any proposed investments or reinvestments, to the extent that the *corpus* of the trust consists of stocks or other securities of corporations in which the holdings of the trust and the Trustor are significant from the viewpoint of voting control; or

2. Any power to vote or direct the voting of stock or other securities of any corporations in which the holdings of the trust and the Trustor are significant from the viewpoint of voting control; or

3. Any power to reacquire the *corpus* of the trust by substituting other property of equal value.

C. Allow the Trustor, the Trustee or any other person to purchase, exchange or otherwise deal with or dispose of the *corpus* of the trust, or the income therefrom, for less than adequate consideration in money or money's worth.

1

FIFTH

This agreement and the trust created hereby shall be administered, managed, governed and regulated in all respects according to applicable statutes of the State of _____.

SIXTH

The Trustee shall have with respect to all property held or received by the trust, whether principal or income, until the complete distribution thereof, the following powers to be exercised from time to time, at the discretion of the Trustee, without limitation or further license:

Management of the Trust

To invest, reinvest, lease, rent, mortgage, insure, repair, improve or sell any and all of the real and personal property of the trust as the Trustee may deem advisable.

Business Interests

To sell or otherwise liquidate, or to continue to operate at his or her discretion, any corporation, partnership or other business interest which may be received by the trust.

Mortgages, Pledges and Deeds of Trust

To enforce any and all mortgages, pledges and deeds of trust held by the trust and to purchase at any sale thereunder any such real estate or personal property subject to any mortgage, pledge or deed of trust.

Litigation

To initiate or defend, at his or her discretion, any litigation affecting the trust.

Attorneys, Advisors and Agents

To employ and to pay from the trust reasonable compensation to such attorneys, accountants, brokers, and investment, tax and other advisors as he or she shall deem advisable.

Adjustment of Claims

To submit to arbitration, to compromise or to release or otherwise adjust, with or without compensation, any and all claims affecting the trust estate.

SEVENTH

No bond for the faithful performance of duties shall be required of any Trustee appointed under this agreement.

EIGHTH

The Trustee shall receive reasonable compensation for the services performed by him or her, but such compensation shall not exceed the amount customarily received by corporate fiduciaries in the area for like services.

NINTH

No Trustee of the trust created by this agreement shall at any time be held liable for any action or default of himself or herself, or of his or her agent, or of any other person in connection with the administration and management of this trust unless caused by his or her own gross negligence or by commission of a willful act of breach of trust.

TENTH

The Trustee, by joining in the execution of this agreement, hereby signifies his or her acceptance of this trust.

ELEVENTH

The Trustee shall have sole authority to determine what shall be defined as income and what shall be defined as principal of the trust established by this agreement, and to determine which costs, taxes and other expenses shall be paid out of income and which shall be paid out of principal.

TWELFTH

In the event that any portion of this trust agreement or the trust created hereby shall be held illegal, invalid or otherwise inoperative, it is our intention that all of the other provisions hereof shall continue to be fully effective and operative insofar as is possible and reasonable.

IN WITNESS WHEREOF, the parties hereto have executed this agreement the day and year first above written.

_____
Trustor

_____
Trustee

....

I, the undersigned _____ of the above-described Trustor, do hereby waive and relinquish any and all claim to whatever community-property rights I may have in the hereinabove-described _____ _____ and do give and grant my assent to the trust and to the incorporation therein of said _____ _____ .

_____
Legal Spouse of Trustor

....

_____
Witness

_____
Witness

* *

CERTIFICATE OF NOTARY

STATE OF   )
) ss:
COUNTY OF   )

On this _____ day of _____ , 19 _____ , before me personally came and appeared _____ and _____ and _____ , known, and known to me, to be the individuals described in and who executed the foregoing instrument, and who duly acknowledged to me that they executed same for the purpose therein contained.

IN WITNESS WHEREOF, I hereunto set my hand and official seal.

_____
Notary Public

My commission expires: _____

Declaration
of
Trust

Dated ——————————— 19 ———

Declaration of Irrevocable Trust

This **Declaration of Irrevocable Trust** is made this _____ day of _____ , 19 _____ , between

_____ , of

_____ ,

hereinafter called the Trustor, and _____ , of

_____ ,

hereinafter called the Trustee.

FIRST

The Trustor hereby irrevocably assigns, conveys and gives to the Trustee, in trust, the following property:

SECOND

The Trustee shall receive and hold said property, together with any additions thereto, in trust for the use and benefit of:

_____

_____

_____

THIRD

FOURTH

This trust shall be irrevocable and unamendable. I am aware of the consequences of establishing an irrevocable trust and hereby affirm that the trust created by this agreement shall be irrevocable by me or by any other person, it being my intention to make to the beneficiary/beneficiaries named herein an absolute gift of the property described in paragraph ONE, above.

FIFTH

This agreement and the trust created hereby shall be administered, managed, governed and regulated in all respects according to applicable statutes of the State of _____ .

SIXTH

The Trustee, in addition to all other powers granted by this agreement and by law, shall have the following additional powers with respect to the trust, to be exercised from time to time at the Trustee's discretion:

Management of the Trust

To invest and reinvest, lease, rent, mortgage, insure, repair, improve or sell any of the real and personal property of the trust as he or she may deem advisable.

Business Interests

To sell or otherwise liquidate, or to continue to operate at his or her discretion, any corporation, partnership or other business interest which may be received by the trust.

Mortgages, Pledges and Deeds of Trust

To enforce any and all mortgages, pledges and deeds of trust held by the trust and to purchase at any sale thereunder any such real estate or personal property subject to any mortgage, pledge or deed of trust.

Litigation

To initiate or defend, at his or her discretion, any litigation affecting the trust.

Attorneys, Advisors and Agents

To employ and to pay from the trust reasonable compensation to such attorneys, accountants, brokers, and investment, tax and other advisors as he or she shall deem advisable.

Adjustment of Claims

To submit to arbitration, to compromise or to release or otherwise adjust, with or without compensation, any and all claims affecting the trust estate.

SEVENTH

No bond for the faithful performance of duties shall be required of any Trustee appointed under this agreement.

EIGHTH

The Trustee shall receive reasonable compensation for the services performed by him or her, but such compensation shall not exceed the amount customarily received by corporate fiduciaries in the area for like services.

NINTH

No Trustee of the trust created by this agreement shall at any time be held liable for any action or default of himself or herself, or of his or her agent, or of any other person in connection with the administration and management of this trust unless caused by his or her own gross negligence or by commission of a willful act of breach of trust.

TENTH

The Trustee, by joining in the execution of this agreement, hereby signifies his or her acceptance of this trust.

ELEVENTH

The Trustee shall have sole authority to determine what shall be defined as income and what shall be defined as principal of the trust established by this agreement, and to determine which costs, taxes and other expenses shall be paid out of income and which shall be paid out of principal.

TWELFTH

In the event that any portion of this trust agreement or the trust created hereby shall be held illegal, invalid or otherwise inoperative, it is my intention that all of the other provisions hereof shall continue to be fully effective and operative insofar as is possible and reasonable.

IN WITNESS WHEREOF, the parties hereto have executed this agreement the day and year first above written.

_____
Trustor

_____
Trustee

....

I, the undersigned _____ of the above-described Trustor, do hereby waive and relinquish any and all claim to whatever community-property rights I may have in the hereinabove-described _____ _____ and do give and grant my assent to the trust and to the incorporation therein of said _____ _____ .

_____
Legal Spouse of Trustor

....

_____
Witness

_____
Witness

* *

CERTIFICATE OF NOTARY

STATE OF   )
) ss:
COUNTY OF   )

On this _____ day of _____, 19 _____, before me personally came and appeared _____ and _____ and _____ , known, and known to me, to be the individuals described in and who executed the foregoing instrument, and who duly acknowledged to me that they executed same for the purpose therein contained.

IN WITNESS WHEREOF, I hereunto set my hand and official seal.

_____
Notary Public

My commission expires: _____

Declaration of Trust

Dated _____ 19 _____

Declaration of Irrevocable Trust

This **Declaration of Irrevocable Trust** is made this _____ day of _____, 19 _____, between

_____ and _____ , of

_____ ,

hereinafter called the Trustors, and _____ , of

_____ ,

hereinafter called the Trustee.

FIRST

The Trustors hereby irrevocably assign, convey and give to the Trustee, in trust, the following property:

SECOND

The Trustee shall receive and hold said property, together with any additions thereto, in trust for the use and benefit of:

_____

_____

_____

THIRD

FOURTH

This trust shall be irrevocable and unamendable. We are aware of the consequences of establishing an irrevocable trust and hereby affirm that the trust created by this agreement shall be irrevocable by us or by any other person, it being our intention to make to the beneficiary/beneficiaries named herein an absolute gift of the property described in paragraph ONE, above, with income therefrom reserved to us, or the survivor of us, for his or her lifetime.

FIFTH

This agreement and the trust created hereby shall be administered, managed, governed and regulated in all respects according to applicable statutes of the State of _____ .

SIXTH

The Trustee, in addition to all other powers granted by this agreement and by law, shall have the following additional powers with respect to the trust, to be exercised from time to time at the Trustee's discretion:

Management of the Trust

To invest and reinvest, lease, rent, mortgage, insure, repair, improve or sell any of the real and personal property of the trust as he or she may deem advisable.

Business Interests

To sell or otherwise liquidate, or to continue to operate at his or her discretion, any corporation, partnership or other business interest which may be received by the trust.

Mortgages, Pledges and Deeds of Trust

To enforce any and all mortgages, pledges and deeds of trust held by the trust and to purchase at any sale thereunder any such real estate or personal property subject to any mortgage, pledge or deed of trust.

Litigation

To initiate or defend, at his or her discretion, any litigation affecting the trust.

Attorneys, Advisors and Agents

To employ and to pay from the trust reasonable compensation to such attorneys, accountants, brokers, and investment, tax and other advisors as he or she shall deem advisable.

Adjustment of Claims

To submit to arbitration, to compromise or to release or otherwise adjust, with or without compensation, any and all claims affecting the trust estate.

SEVENTH

No bond for the faithful performance of duties shall be required of any Trustee appointed under this agreement.

EIGHTH

The Trustee shall receive reasonable compensation for the services performed by him or her, but such compensation shall not exceed the amount customarily received by corporate fiduciaries in the area for like services.

NINTH

No Trustee of the trust created by this agreement shall at any time be held liable for any action or default of himself or herself, or of his or her agent, or of any other person in connection with the administration and management of this trust unless caused by his or her own gross negligence or by commission of a willful act of breach of trust.

TENTH

The Trustee, by joining in the execution of this agreement, hereby signifies his or her acceptance of this trust.

ELEVENTH

The Trustee shall have sole authority to determine what shall be defined as income and what shall be defined as principal of the trust established by this agreement, and to determine which costs, taxes and other expenses shall be paid out of income and which shall be paid out of principal.

TWELFTH

In the event that any portion of this trust agreement or the trust created hereby shall be held illegal, invalid or otherwise inoperative, it is our intention that all of the other provisions hereof shall continue to be fully effective and operative insofar as is possible and reasonable.

IN WITNESS WHEREOF, the parties hereto have executed this agreement the day and year first above written.

_____
Trustor

_____
Trustor

_____
Trustee

_____
Witness

_____
Witness

* *

CERTIFICATE OF NOTARY

STATE OF   )
) ss:
COUNTY OF   )

On this _____ day of _____, 19 _____, before me personally came and appeared _____ and _____ and _____, known, and known to me, to be the individuals described in and who executed the foregoing instrument, and who duly acknowledged to me that they executed same for the purpose therein contained.

IN WITNESS WHEREOF, I hereunto set my hand and official seal.

_____
Notary Public

My commission expires: _____

Declaration of Trust

Dated _____ 19 ____

Ten-Year Reversionary Trust (Clifford Trust)

This **Declaration of Trust** is made this _____ day of _____, 19 _____, between

_____, of

_____ ,

hereinafter called the Trustor, and _____, of

_____ ,

hereinafter called the Trustee.

FIRST

The Trustor hereby irrevocably assigns, conveys and gives to the Trustee, in trust, for the duration of this trust, the following property:

SECOND

The Trustee, his/her successors and assigns shall have and hold the aforesaid property under such terms and conditions, and with such powers, rights and limitations as are hereunder set forth:

A. The trust created by this agreement shall be irrevocable and unamendable.

B. This trust shall terminate on the _____ day of _____, 19 _____, or upon the death of the beneficiary, whichever shall first occur.

C. Upon termination of the trust, the principal of said trust, as it is then constituted, shall revert to the Trustor and shall be transferred, conveyed and paid over to the Trustor with all right and title thereto, to be his/hers absolutely.

D. In the event that the Trustor shall not then be living, said property shall then be transferred and paid over to the executor/administrator of the Trustor's estate and shall become part of said estate.

THIRD

Until termination of this trust as hereinbefore provided, the Trustee shall collect and receive all interest, dividends, rents and other income of the trust and, after paying administrative and other proper expenses, shall each _____ _____ pay to, or apply the net income of the trust for the use and benefit of, _____ _____, hereinafter called the Beneficiary.

FOURTH

Anything hereinafter to the contrary notwithstanding, none of the powers enumerated herein, nor accorded generally to Trustees by law, shall permit nor be construed to:

A. Allow the Trustor to borrow all or any part of the *corpus* of the trust, nor the income therefrom, directly or indirectly, whether with or without adequate security or adequate interest.

B. Allow the exercise in a nonfiduciary capacity by any person not having written approval of the Trustee, any of the following powers of administration:

1. Any power to control investment of the *corpus* of the trust, either by directing investments or reinvestments or by vetoing any proposed investments or reinvestments, to the extent that the *corpus* of the trust consists of stocks or other securities of corporations in which the holdings of the trust and the Trustor are significant from the viewpoint of voting control; or

2. Any power to vote or direct the voting of stock or other securities of any corporations in which the holdings of the trust and the Trustor are significant from the viewpoint of voting control; or

3. Any power to reacquire the *corpus* of the trust by substituting other property of equal value.

C. Allow the Trustor, the Trustee or any other person to purchase, exchange or otherwise deal with or dispose of the *corpus* of the trust, or the income therefrom, for less than adequate consideration in money or money's worth.

FIFTH

This agreement and the trust created hereby shall be administered, managed, governed and regulated in all respects according to applicable statutes of the State of _____.

SIXTH

The Trustee shall have with respect to all property held or received by the trust, whether principal or income, until the complete distribution thereof, the following powers to be exercised from time to time, at the discretion of the Trustee, without limitation or further license:

Management of the Trust

To invest, reinvest, lease, rent, mortgage, insure, repair, improve or sell any and all of the real and personal property of the trust as the Trustee may deem advisable.

Business Interests

To sell or otherwise liquidate, or to continue to operate at his or her discretion, any corporation, partnership or other business interest which may be received by the trust.

Mortgages, Pledges and Deeds of Trust

To enforce any and all mortgages, pledges and deeds of trust held by the trust and to purchase at any sale thereunder any such real estate or personal property subject to any mortgage, pledge or deed of trust.

Litigation

To initiate or defend, at his or her discretion, any litigation affecting the trust.

Attorneys, Advisors and Agents

To employ and to pay from the trust reasonable compensation to such attorneys, accountants, brokers, and investment, tax and other advisors as he or she shall deem advisable.

Adjustment of Claims

To submit to arbitration, to compromise or to release or otherwise adjust, with or without compensation, any and all claims affecting the trust estate.

SEVENTH

No bond for the faithful performance of duties shall be required of any Trustee appointed under this agreement.

EIGHTH

The Trustee shall receive reasonable compensation for the services performed by him or her, but such compensation shall not exceed the amount customarily received by corporate fiduciaries in the area for like services.

NINTH

No Trustee of the trust created by this agreement shall at any time be held liable for any action or default of himself or herself, or of his or her agent, or of any other person in connection with the administration and management of this trust unless caused by his or her own gross negligence or by commission of a willful act of breach of trust.

TENTH

The Trustee, by joining in the execution of this agreement, hereby signifies his or her acceptance of this trust.

ELEVENTH

The Trustee shall have sole authority to determine what shall be defined as income and what shall be defined as principal of the trust established by this agreement, and to determine which costs, taxes and other expenses shall be paid out of income and which shall be paid out of principal.

TWELFTH

In the event that any portion of this trust agreement or the trust created hereby shall be held illegal, invalid or otherwise inoperative, it is my intention that all of the other provisions hereof shall continue to be fully effective and operative insofar as is possible and reasonable.

IN WITNESS WHEREOF, the parties hereto have executed this agreement the day and year first above written.

_____
Trustor

_____
Trustee

- -

I, the undersigned _____ of the above-described Trustor, do hereby waive and relinquish any and all claim to whatever community-property rights I may have in the hereinabove-described _____
_____ and do give and grant my assent to the trust and to the incorporation therein of said _____
_____ .

_____
Legal Spouse of Trustor

- -

_____
Witness

_____
Witness

CERTIFICATE OF NOTARY

STATE OF   )

)   ss:

COUNTY OF   )

On this _____ day of _____, 19 _____, before me personally came and appeared _____ and _____ and _____, known, and known to me, to be the individuals described in and who executed the foregoing instrument, and who duly acknowledged to me that they executed same for the purpose therein contained.

IN WITNESS WHEREOF, I hereunto set my hand and official seal.

_____
Notary Public

My commission expires: _____

Declaration of Trust

Dated _____ 19 _____

Two-Year Reversionary Charitable Trust

This **Declaration of Trust** is made this _____ day of _____, 19 _____, between

_____, of

_____,

hereinafter called the Trustor, and _____, of

_____,

hereinafter called the Trustee.

FIRST

The Trustor hereby irrevocably assigns, conveys and gives to the Trustee, in trust, for the duration of this trust, the following property:

SECOND

The Trustee, his/her successors and assigns shall have and hold the aforesaid property under such terms and conditions, and with such powers, rights and limitations as are hereunder set forth:

A. The trust created by this agreement shall be irrevocable and unamendable.

B. This trust shall terminate on the _____ day of _____, 19 _____.

C. Upon termination of the trust, the principal of said trust, as it is then constituted, shall revert to the Trustor and shall be transferred, conveyed and paid over to the Trustor with all right and title thereto, to be his/hers absolutely.

D. In the event that the Trustor shall not then be living, said property shall then be transferred and paid over to the executor/administrator of the Trustor's estate and shall become part of said estate.

THIRD

Until termination of this trust as hereinbefore provided, the Trustee shall collect and receive all interest, dividends, rents and other income of the trust and, after paying administrative and other proper expenses, shall each _____ _____ pay to, or apply the net income of the trust for the use and benefit of, _____ _____, hereinafter called the Beneficiary.

FOURTH

Anything hereinafter to the contrary notwithstanding, none of the powers enumerated herein, nor accorded generally to Trustees by law, shall permit nor be construed to:

A. Allow the Trustor to borrow all or any part of the *corpus* of the trust, nor the income therefrom, directly or indirectly, whether with or without adequate security or adequate interest.

B. Allow the exercise in a nonfiduciary capacity by any person not having written approval of the Trustee, any of the following powers of administration:

1. Any power to control investment of the *corpus* of the trust, either by directing investments or reinvestments or by vetoing any proposed investments or reinvestments, to the extent that the *corpus* of the trust consists of stocks or other securities of corporations in which the holdings of the trust and the Trustor are significant from the viewpoint of voting control; or

2. Any power to vote or direct the voting of stock or other securities of any corporations in which the holdings of the trust and the Trustor are significant from the viewpoint of voting control; or

3. Any power to reacquire the *corpus* of the trust by substituting other property of equal value.

C. Allow the Trustor, the Trustee or any other person to purchase, exchange or otherwise deal with or dispose of the *corpus* of the trust, or the income therefrom, for less than adequate consideration in money or money's worth.

FIFTH

This agreement and the trust created hereby shall be administered, managed, governed and regulated in all respects according to applicable statutes of the State of _____.

SIXTH

The Trustee, in addition to all other powers granted by this agreement and by law, shall have the following additional powers with respect to the trust, to be exercised from time to time at the Trustee's discretion:

Management of the Trust

To invest and reinvest, lease, rent, mortgage, insure, repair, improve or sell any of the real and personal property of the trust as the Trustee may deem advisable.

Business Interests

To sell or otherwise liquidate, or to continue to operate at his or her discretion, any corporation, partnership or other business interest which may be received by the trust.

Mortgages, Pledges and Deeds of Trust

To enforce any and all mortgages, pledges and deeds of trust held by the trust and to purchase at any sale thereunder any such real estate or personal property subject to any mortgage, pledge or deed of trust.

Litigation

To initiate or defend, at his or her discretion, any litigation affecting the trust.

Attorneys, Advisors and Agents

To employ and to pay from the trust reasonable compensation to such attorneys, accountants, brokers, and investment, tax and other advisors as he or she shall deem advisable.

Adjustment of Claims

To submit to arbitration, to compromise or to release or otherwise adjust, with or without compensation, any and all claims affecting the trust estate.

SEVENTH

No bond for the faithful performance of duties shall be required of any Trustee appointed under this agreement.

EIGHTH

The Trustee shall receive reasonable compensation for the services performed by him or her, but such compensation shall not exceed the amount customarily received by corporate fiduciaries in the area for like services.

NINTH

No Trustee of the trust created by this agreement shall at any time be held liable for any action or default of himself or herself, or of his or her agent, or of any other person in connection with the administration and management of this trust unless caused by his or her own gross negligence or by commission of a willful act of breach of trust.

TENTH

The Trustee, by joining in the execution of this agreement, hereby signifies his or her acceptance of this trust.

ELEVENTH

The Trustee shall have sole authority to determine what shall be defined as income and what shall be defined as principal of the trust established by this agreement, and to determine which costs, taxes and other expenses shall be paid out of income and which shall be paid out of principal.

TWELFTH

In the event that any portion of this trust agreement or the trust created hereby shall be held illegal, invalid or otherwise inoperative, it is our intention that all of the other provisions hereof shall continue to be fully effective and operative insofar as is possible and reasonable.

IN WITNESS WHEREOF, the parties hereto have executed this agreement the day and year first above written.

_____
Trustor

_____
Trustee

- -

I, the undersigned _____ of the above-described Trustor, do hereby waive and relinquish any and all claim to whatever community-property rights I may have in the hereinabove-described _____ _____ and do give and grant my assent to the trust and to the incorporation therein of said _____ _____ .

_____
Legal Spouse of Trustor

- -

_____
Witness

_____
Witness

* *

CERTIFICATE OF NOTARY

STATE OF   )
)   ss:
COUNTY OF   )

On this _____ day of _____, 19 _____, before me personally came and appeared _____ and _____ and _____, known, and known to me, to be the individuals described in and who executed the foregoing instrument, and who duly acknowledged to me that they executed same for the purpose therein contained.

IN WITNESS WHEREOF, I hereunto set my hand and official seal.

_____
Notary Public

My commission expires: _____

3

Declaration
of
Trust

19 _____

Dated _____

4

Declaration of
Irrevocable Charitable Remainder Trust

This **Declaration of Irrevocable Charitable Remainder Trust** is made this _____ day of _____ , 19 _____ ,

between _____ , of

_____ ,

hereinafter called the Trustor, and _____ , of

_____ ,

hereinafter called the Trustee.

FIRST

The Trustor hereby irrevocably assigns, conveys and gives to the Trustee, in trust, the following property:

SECOND

Until my death, I shall have full and complete right to the _____ of the hereinabove-described property, and following my death, _____ shall have the right to the _____ of the hereinabove-described property.

THIRD

Until my death, the Trustee shall _____ pay the net income of the trust, if any, to me, and upon my death shall _____ pay the net income of the trust, if any, to _____ , until the death of _____ for his/her welfare and support.

FOURTH

Upon my death, or the death of _____ , whichever shall last occur, the Trustee shall transfer possession, use and any income of the hereinabove-described _____ to _____ , of _____ .

FIFTH

This trust shall be irrevocable and unamendable. I am aware of the consequences of establishing an irrevocable trust and hereby affirm that the trust created by this agreement shall be irrevocable by me or by any other person.

SIXTH

This agreement and the trust created hereby shall be administered, managed, governed and regulated in all respects according to applicable statutes of the State of _____.

SEVENTH

No bond for the faithful performance of duties shall be required of any Trustee appointed under this agreement.

EIGHTH

No Trustee of the trust created by this agreement shall at any time be held liable for any action or default of himself or herself, or of his or her agent, or of any other person in connection with the administration and management of this trust unless caused by his or her own gross negligence or by commission of a willful act of breach of trust.

NINTH

The Trustee, by joining in the execution of this agreement, hereby signifies his or her acceptance of this trust.

TENTH

In the event that any portion of this trust agreement or the trust created hereby shall be held illegal, invalid or otherwise inoperative, it is my intention that all of the other provisions hereof shall continue to be fully effective and operative insofar as is possible and reasonable.

IN WITNESS WHEREOF, the parties hereto have executed this agreement the day and year first above written.

_____
Trustor

_____
Trustee

I, the undersigned _____ of the above-described Trustor, do hereby waive and relinquish any and all claim to whatever community-property rights I may have in the hereinabove-described _____ _____ and do give and grant my assent to the trust and to the incorporation therein of said _____ _____.

_____
Legal Spouse of Trustor

_____
Witness

_____
Witness

CERTIFICATE OF NOTARY

STATE OF)
) ss:
COUNTY OF)

On this _____ day of _____, 19 _____, before me personally came and appeared
_____ and _____
and _____, known, and known to me, to be the individuals described in and who
executed the foregoing instrument, and who duly acknowledged to me that they executed same for the purpose therein
contained.

IN WITNESS WHEREOF, I hereunto set my hand and official seal.

_____
Notary Public

My commission expires: _____

FORM 60.11/F478

Declaration
of
Trust

Dated _____ 19 ____

Declaration of
Irrevocable Charitable Remainder Trust

This **Declaration of Irrevocable Charitable Remainder Trust** is made this _____ day of _____ , 19 ____ ,

between _____ and _____ , of

_____ ,

hereinafter called the Trustors, and _____ , of

_____ ,

hereinafter called the Trustee.

FIRST

The Trustors hereby irrevocably assign, convey and give to the Trustee, in trust, the following property:

SECOND

We shall retain full and complete right to the _____
of the hereinabove-described property, and following the death of either of us, the survivor shall have full and complete right to
the _____ of the hereinabove-described property until his or her
death.

THIRD

The Trustee shall _____ pay the net monthly income of the
trust, if any, jointly to us, and, upon the death of either of us, the Trustee shall pay the net income of the trust, if
any, _____ to the survivor of us until his or her death.

FOURTH

Upon the death of the surviving Trustor, the Trustee shall transfer possession, use and any income of the hereinabove-
described _____ to _____ ,
of _____ .

FIFTH

This trust shall be irrevocable and unamendable. We are aware of the consequences of establishing an irrevocable trust and
hereby affirm that the trust created by this agreement shall be irrevocable by us or by any other person.

SIXTH

This agreement and the trust created hereby shall be administered, managed, governed and regulated in all respects
according to applicable statutes of the State of _____ .

SEVENTH

No bond for the faithful performance of duties shall be required of any Trustee appointed under this agreement.

EIGHTH

No Trustee of the trust created by this agreement shall at any time be held liable for any action or default of himself or herself, or of his or her agent, or of any other person in connection with the administration and management of this trust unless caused by his or her own gross negligence or by commission of a willful act of breach of trust.

NINTH

The Trustee, by joining in the execution of this agreement, hereby signifies his or her acceptance of this trust.

TENTH

In the event that any portion of this trust agreement or the trust created hereby shall be held illegal, invalid or otherwise inoperative, it is our intention that all of the other provisions hereof shall continue to be fully effective and operative insofar as is possible and reasonable.

IN WITNESS WHEREOF, the parties hereto have executed this agreement on the day and year first above written.

_____
Trustor

_____
Trustor

_____
Trustee

_____
Witness

_____
Witness

CERTIFICATE OF NOTARY

STATE OF   )

)   ss:

COUNTY OF   )

On this _____ day of _____, 19 _____, before me personally came and appeared
_____ and _____
and _____, known, and known to me, to be the individuals described in and who executed the foregoing instrument, and who duly acknowledged to me that they executed same for the purpose therein contained.

      IN WITNESS WHEREOF, I hereunto set my hand and official seal.

_____
                                   Notary Public

My commission expires: _____

Declaration of Trust

Dated _____ 19 ____

Revocation of Trust

This **Revocation of Trust** is made this _____ day of _____, 19 _____.

WHEREAS, on the _____ day of _____, 19 _____, I created by written declaration a revocable trust for the use and benefit of _____ _____, and having reserved the right to revoke, annul and cancel said trust and the declaration creating it, I do now hereby revoke said trust, with all of the following principal thereof reverting absolutely to me, with all right and title thereto:

I further declare the Trustee(s) of said trust free and discharged from all further responsibility for the administration and management of said trust and the principal thereof.

_____
Trustor

_____
Witness

_____
Witness

* *

CERTIFICATE OF NOTARY

STATE OF)
) ss:
COUNTY OF)

On this _____ day of _____, 19 _____, before me personally came and appeared _____, known, and known to me, to be the individual described in and who executed the foregoing instrument, and who duly acknowledged to me that he/she executed same for the purpose therein contained.

IN WITNESS WHEREOF, I hereunto set my hand and official seal.

_____
Notary Public

My commission expires: _____

**Revocation
of
Trust**

Dated _____ 19 _____

Revocation of Trust

This **Revocation of Trust** is made this _____ day of _____, 19 _____.

WHEREAS, on the _____ day of _____, 19 _____, we created by written declaration a revocable trust for the use and benefit of _____

_____, and having reserved the right to revoke, annul and cancel said trust and the declaration creating it, we do now hereby revoke said trust, with all of the following principal thereof reverting absolutely to us, with all right and title thereto:

We further declare the Trustee(s) of said trust free and discharged from all further responsibility for the administration and management of said trust and the principal thereof.

_____
Trustor

_____
Trustor

_____
Witness

_____
Witness

* *

CERTIFICATE OF NOTARY

STATE OF   )
) ss:
COUNTY OF   )

On this _____ day of _____, 19 _____, before me personally came and appeared _____ and _____, known, and known to me, to be the individuals described in and who executed the foregoing instrument, and who duly acknowledged to me that they executed same for the purpose therein contained.

IN WITNESS WHEREOF, I hereunto set my hand and official seal.

_____
Notary Public

My commission expires: _____

Revocation
of
Trust

Dated _____ 19 _____

Optional Trust Provisions—First-Step Clauses

The Trustee, on a _____ basis, shall pay the net income of the trust to _____
_____.

The Trustee, on a _____ basis, shall pay the net income of the trust, plus such additional assets of the principal of the trust as the Trustee shall deem proper, to _____
_____ for his/her welfare and support.

Until the _____ day of _____, 19 _____, the Trustee, on a _____
_____ basis, shall pay the income of the trust to _____ for _____
_____.

Optional Trust Provisions—Second-Step Clauses

Upon the above date, the Trustee shall assign, convey, transfer and give the remainder of the trust to _____ _____, to be his/hers absolutely.

Upon the death of _____, the Trustee shall assign, convey, transfer and give the remainder of the trust to _____.

Upon the death of _____, the Trustee shall divide the remainder of the trust among my children and the issue of any deceased child of mine *per stirpes.*

Upon the death of _____, or my youngest child attaining his/her _____ _____ birthday, whichever shall last occur, the remainder of the trust shall be equally divided among my children and the issue of any deceased child of mine *per stirpes,* thereby terminating this trust.

Optional Trust Provisions—Second-Step Clauses

Optional Trust Provisions—"Stand-Alone" Clauses

Upon my death, the Trustee shall assign, convey, transfer and pay the principal of the trust to _____ _____.

Upon my death, the Trustee shall assign, convey, transfer and pay the principal of the trust to _____ _____. If he/she shall not then be living, the Trustee shall assign, convey, transfer and pay said principal to _____, or, if he/she shall not then be living, said principal shall be equally divided between his/her children and the issue of any deceased child of his/hers *per stirpes.*

The Trustee, on a _____ basis, shall pay the net income of the trust to the Trustor. Upon the death of the Trustor, the Trustee shall assign, convey, transfer and pay the remainder of the trust to _____ _____, or, if he/she shall not then be living, the remainder of the trust shall be equally divided among his/her children and the issue of any deceased child of his/hers *per stirpes.*

The Trustee, on a _____ basis, shall pay the net income of the trust to the Trustor. Upon the death of the Trustor, the remainder shall be equally divided among my children and the children of any deceased child of mine *per stirpes.*

Upon my death, the Trustee shall commence _____ payment of the net income of the trust to _____ until such time as he/she shall attain his/her _____ birthday, at which time the Trustee shall assign, convey, transfer and pay the remainder of the trust to him/her, or if he/she shall not then be living to _____ _____.

Optional Trust Provision—For Use with Two-Year Charitable Trust

Until termination of this trust as herein provided, the Trustee, after deducting proper expenses, shall pay the net income of the trust to _____, for its religious, educational or charitable purposes.

Upon termination of this trust, the principal of the trust, as it is then constituted, shall revert, be assigned, conveyed and transferred with all right and title thereto, to the Trustor to be his/hers absolutely.

If the Trustor shall not then be living, said principal shall be transferred and paid over to his/her executors to be distributed as part of his/her estate.

Optional Trust Provision—For Use with
Ten-Year Clifford Trust

Until termination of this trust as herein provided, the Trustee, after deducting proper expenses, shall pay to or apply the net income of the trust for the benefit and use of _____

_____.

Upon termination of this trust, the principal of the trust, as it is then constituted, shall revert, be assigned, conveyed and transferred with all right and title thereto, to the Trustor to be his/hers absolutely.

If the Trustor shall not then be living, said principal shall be transferred and paid over to his/her executors or administrators to be distributed as part of his/her estate.

Exterior Checklist

Item	OK	To Be Done By Us	Our Priority	To Be Done By Contractor	Contractor's Priority	Target Completion Date	Finished
FRONT							
Roof	___	_____	_____	_____	_____	_____	_____
Guttering	___	_____	_____	_____	_____	_____	_____
Downspouts	___	_____	_____	_____	_____	_____	_____
Roof Antenna	___	_____	_____	_____	_____	_____	_____
Roof Ventilator	___	_____	_____	_____	_____	_____	_____
	___	_____	_____	_____	_____	_____	_____
Chimney	___	_____	_____	_____	_____	_____	_____
Windows	___	_____	_____	_____	_____	_____	_____
Window Frames	___	_____	_____	_____	_____	_____	_____
Shutters	___	_____	_____	_____	_____	_____	_____
Awnings	___	_____	_____	_____	_____	_____	_____
	___	_____	_____	_____	_____	_____	_____
Screens	___	_____	_____	_____	_____	_____	_____
Storm Windows	___	_____	_____	_____	_____	_____	_____
Front Door	___	_____	_____	_____	_____	_____	_____
Door Hardware	___	_____	_____	_____	_____	_____	_____
Paint	___	_____	_____	_____	_____	_____	_____
Brick/Masonry	___	_____	_____	_____	_____	_____	_____
Foundation	___	_____	_____	_____	_____	_____	_____
Front Porch	___	_____	_____	_____	_____	_____	_____
Entry Walk	___	_____	_____	_____	_____	_____	_____
Doormat	___	_____	_____	_____	_____	_____	_____
Porch Light	___	_____	_____	_____	_____	_____	_____
Porch Furniture	___	_____	_____	_____	_____	_____	_____

Item	OK	To Be Done By Us	Our Priority	To Be Done By Contractor	Contractor's Priority	Target Completion Date	Finished
FRONT (*Continued*)							
Porch Steps	——	——	——	——	——	——	——
_____	——	——	——	——	——	——	——
Mailbox	——	——	——	——	——	——	——
Garage Door	——	——	——	——	——	——	——
Driveway	——	——	——	——	——	——	——
_____	——	——	——	——	——	——	——
Basement Windows	——	——	——	——	——	——	——
Lawn	——	——	——	——	——	——	——
Garden #1	——	——	——	——	——	——	——
Garden #2	——	——	——	——	——	——	——
Shrubs	——	——	——	——	——	——	——
_____	——	——	——	——	——	——	——
Hedge	——	——	——	——	——	——	——
Trees	——	——	——	——	——	——	——
Fence	——	——	——	——	——	——	——
Gate	——	——	——	——	——	——	——
_____	——	——	——	——	——	——	——
Sidewalk	——	——	——	——	——	——	——
Curb	——	——	——	——	——	——	——
Electric/Gas Light	——	——	——	——	——	——	——
House Number	——	——	——	——	——	——	——
Hose Connection	——	——	——	——	——	——	——
_____	——	——	——	——	——	——	——
_____	——	——	——	——	——	——	——
_____	——	——	——	——	——	——	——

Item	OK	To Be Done By Us	Our Priority	To Be Done By Contractor	Contractor's Priority	Target Completion Date	Finished
RIGHT SIDE							
Roof	——	——	——	——	——	——	——
Guttering	——	——	——	——	——	——	——
Downspouts	——	——	——	——	——	——	——
Attic Exhaust Fan	——	——	——	——	——	——	——
_____	——	——	——	——	——	——	——
Chimney	——	——	——	——	——	——	——
Windows	——	——	——	——	——	——	——
Window Frames	——	——	——	——	——	——	——
Shutters	——	——	——	——	——	——	——
Awnings	——	——	——	——	——	——	——
_____	——	——	——	——	——	——	——
Screens	——	——	——	——	——	——	——
Storm Windows	——	——	——	——	——	——	——
Basement Windows	——	——	——	——	——	——	——
Basement Entry	——	——	——	——	——	——	——
Basement Door	——	——	——	——	——	——	——
Door Hardware	——	——	——	——	——	——	——
Exterior Light	——	——	——	——	——	——	——
_____	——	——	——	——	——	——	——
Porch	——	——	——	——	——	——	——
Porch Screens	——	——	——	——	——	——	——
Steps	——	——	——	——	——	——	——
Side Door	——	——	——	——	——	——	——
_____	——	——	——	——	——	——	——

Item	OK	To Be Done By Us	Our Priority	To Be Done By Contractor	Contractor's Priority	Target Completion Date	Finished
RIGHT SIDE (*Continued*)							
Paint	___	___	___	___	___	___	___
Brick/Masonry	___	___	___	___	___	___	___
Metal Trim/Railings	___	___	___	___	___	___	___
Foundation	___	___	___	___	___	___	___
Walkway	___	___	___	___	___	___	___
_____	___	___	___	___	___	___	___
Breezeway	___	___	___	___	___	___	___
Breezeway Light	___	___	___	___	___	___	___
Lawn	___	___	___	___	___	___	___
Garden #1	___	___	___	___	___	___	___
Garden #2	___	___	___	___	___	___	___
Shrubs	___	___	___	___	___	___	___
Hedge	___	___	___	___	___	___	___
_____	___	___	___	___	___	___	___
Trees	___	___	___	___	___	___	___
Fence	___	___	___	___	___	___	___
Gate	___	___	___	___	___	___	___
Swimming Pool	___	___	___	___	___	___	___
Lawn Furniture	___	___	___	___	___	___	___
_____	___	___	___	___	___	___	___
_____	___	___	___	___	___	___	___
_____	___	___	___	___	___	___	___
_____	___	___	___	___	___	___	___
_____	___	___	___	___	___	___	___

Item	OK	To Be Done By Us	Our Priority	To Be Done By Contractor	Contractor's Priority	Target Completion Date	Finished
RIGHT SIDE (*Continued*)							
Side Door to House	___	___	___	___	___	___	___
Door Hardware	___	___	___	___	___	___	___
Exterior Light	___	___	___	___	___	___	___
_____	___	___	___	___	___	___	___
Woodpile	___	___	___	___	___	___	___
Doghouse	___	___	___	___	___	___	___
Trash Containers	___	___	___	___	___	___	___
Children's Swings, etc.	___	___	___	___	___	___	___
_____	___	___	___	___	___	___	___
Barbecue	___	___	___	___	___	___	___
Clothesline	___	___	___	___	___	___	___
_____	___	___	___	___	___	___	___
_____	___	___	___	___	___	___	___
_____	___	___	___	___	___	___	___
_____	___	___	___	___	___	___	___
_____	___	___	___	___	___	___	___
_____	___	___	___	___	___	___	___
_____	___	___	___	___	___	___	___
_____	___	___	___	___	___	___	___
_____	___	___	___	___	___	___	___
_____	___	___	___	___	___	___	___

FORM 63.1 / F502

Item	OK	To Be Done By Us	Our Priority	To Be Done By Contractor	Contractor's Priority	Target Completion Date	Finished
LEFT SIDE							
Roof	——	——	——	——	——	——	——
Guttering	——	——	——	——	——	——	——
Downspouts	——	——	——	——	——	——	——
Attic Exhaust Fan	——	——	——	——	——	——	——
————	——	——	——	——	——	——	——
Chimney	——	——	——	——	——	——	——
Windows	——	——	——	——	——	——	——
Window Frames	——	——	——	——	——	——	——
Shutters	——	——	——	——	——	——	——
Awnings	——	——	——	——	——	——	——
————	——	——	——	——	——	——	——
Screens	——	——	——	——	——	——	——
Storm Windows	——	——	——	——	——	——	——
Basement Windows	——	——	——	——	——	——	——
Basement Entry	——	——	——	——	——	——	——
Basement Door	——	——	——	——	——	——	——
Door Hardware	——	——	——	——	——	——	——
Exterior Light	——	——	——	——	——	——	——
————	——	——	——	——	——	——	——
Porch	——	——	——	——	——	——	——
Porch Screens	——	——	——	——	——	——	——
Steps	——	——	——	——	——	——	——
Side Door	——	——	——	——	——	——	——
————	——	——	——	——	——	——	——

Item	OK	To Be Done By Us	Our Priority	To Be Done By Contractor	Contractor's Priority	Target Completion Date	Finished
LEFT SIDE (*Continued*)							
Paint	___	___	___	___	___	___	___
Brick/Masonry	___	___	___	___	___	___	___
Metal Trim/Railings	___	___	___	___	___	___	___
Foundation	___	___	___	___	___	___	___
Walkway	___	___	___	___	___	___	___
_____	___	___	___	___	___	___	___
Breezeway	___	___	___	___	___	___	___
Breezeway Light	___	___	___	___	___	___	___
Lawn	___	___	___	___	___	___	___
Garden #1	___	___	___	___	___	___	___
Garden #2	___	___	___	___	___	___	___
Shrubs	___	___	___	___	___	___	___
Hedge	___	___	___	___	___	___	___
_____	___	___	___	___	___	___	___
Trees	___	___	___	___	___	___	___
Fence	___	___	___	___	___	___	___
Gate	___	___	___	___	___	___	___
Swimming Pool	___	___	___	___	___	___	___
Lawn Furniture	___	___	___	___	___	___	___
_____	___	___	___	___	___	___	___
_____	___	___	___	___	___	___	___
_____	___	___	___	___	___	___	___
_____	___	___	___	___	___	___	___
_____	___	___	___	___	___	___	___

FORM 63.1 / F504

Item	OK	To Be Done By Us	Our Priority	To Be Done By Contractor	Contractor's Priority	Target Completion Date	Finished
LEFT SIDE (*Continued*)							
Side Door to House	____	_____	_____	_____	_____	_____	_____
Door Hardware	____	_____	_____	_____	_____	_____	_____
Exterior Light	____	_____	_____	_____	_____	_____	_____
_____	____	_____	_____	_____	_____	_____	_____
Woodpile	____	_____	_____	_____	_____	_____	_____
Doghouse	____	_____	_____	_____	_____	_____	_____
Trash Containers	____	_____	_____	_____	_____	_____	_____
Children's Swings, etc.	____	_____	_____	_____	_____	_____	_____
_____	____	_____	_____	_____	_____	_____	_____
Barbecue	____	_____	_____	_____	_____	_____	_____
Clothesline	____	_____	_____	_____	_____	_____	_____
_____	____	_____	_____	_____	_____	_____	_____
_____	____	_____	_____	_____	_____	_____	_____
_____	____	_____	_____	_____	_____	_____	_____
_____	____	_____	_____	_____	_____	_____	_____
_____	____	_____	_____	_____	_____	_____	_____
_____	____	_____	_____	_____	_____	_____	_____
_____	____	_____	_____	_____	_____	_____	_____
_____	____	_____	_____	_____	_____	_____	_____
_____	____	_____	_____	_____	_____	_____	_____
_____	____	_____	_____	_____	_____	_____	_____
_____	____	_____	_____	_____	_____	_____	_____

Item	OK	To Be Done By Us	Our Priority	To Be Done By Contractor	Contractor's Priority	Target Completion Date	Finished
REAR							
Roof	——	——	——	——	——	——	——
Guttering	——	——	——	——	——	——	——
Downspouts	——	——	——	——	——	——	——
Attic Exhaust Fan	——	——	——	——	——	——	——
Roof Ventilator	——	——	——	——	——	——	——
Roof Antenna	——	——	——	——	——	——	——
————	——	——	——	——	——	——	——
Chimney	——	——	——	——	——	——	——
Windows	——	——	——	——	——	——	——
Window Frames	——	——	——	——	——	——	——
Shutters	——	——	——	——	——	——	——
Awnings	——	——	——	——	——	——	——
————	——	——	——	——	——	——	——
Patio	——	——	——	——	——	——	——
Patio Door	——	——	——	——	——	——	——
Exterior Light	——	——	——	——	——	——	——
Screens	——	——	——	——	——	——	——
Storm Windows	——	——	——	——	——	——	——
Basement Windows	——	——	——	——	——	——	——
Basement Entry	——	——	——	——	——	——	——
Basement Door	——	——	——	——	——	——	——
Door Hardware	——	——	——	——	——	——	——
————	——	——	——	——	——	——	——
————	——	——	——	——	——	——	——

Item	OK	To Be Done By Us	Our Priority	To Be Done By Contractor	Contractor's Priority	Target Completion Date	Finished
REAR (*Continued*)							
Exterior Light	___	___	___	___	___	___	___
Porch	___	___	___	___	___	___	___
Porch Steps	___	___	___	___	___	___	___
Porch Screens	___	___	___	___	___	___	___
Porch Door	___	___	___	___	___	___	___
_____	___	___	___	___	___	___	___
Rear Entry	___	___	___	___	___	___	___
Rear Door	___	___	___	___	___	___	___
Door Hardware	___	___	___	___	___	___	___
_____	___	___	___	___	___	___	___
Paint	___	___	___	___	___	___	___
Brick/Masonry	___	___	___	___	___	___	___
Metal Trim/Railings	___	___	___	___	___	___	___
Foundation	___	___	___	___	___	___	___
_____	___	___	___	___	___	___	___
_____	___	___	___	___	___	___	___
Walk	___	___	___	___	___	___	___
Lawn	___	___	___	___	___	___	___
Garden #1	___	___	___	___	___	___	___
Garden #2	___	___	___	___	___	___	___
Shrubs	___	___	___	___	___	___	___
_____	___	___	___	___	___	___	___
_____	___	___	___	___	___	___	___
_____	___	___	___	___	___	___	___

Item	OK	To Be Done By Us	Our Priority	To Be Done By Contractor	Contractor's Priority	Target Completion Date	Finished
REAR (*Continued*)							
Hedge	——	————	———	————	————	————	————
Trees	——	————	———	————	————	————	————
Fence	——	————	———	————	————	————	————
Gate	——	————	———	————	————	————	————
Swimming Pool	——	————	———	————	————	————	————
————	——	————	———	————	————	————	————
Lawn Furniture	——	————	———	————	————	————	————
Trash Containers	——	————	———	————	————	————	————
Woodpile	——	————	———	————	————	————	————
Doghouse	——	————	———	————	————	————	————
Barbecue	——	————	———	————	————	————	————
Clothesline	——	————	———	————	————	————	————
————	——	————	———	————	————	————	————
Children's Swings, etc.	——	————	———	————	————	————	————
————	——	————	———	————	————	————	————
————	——	————	———	————	————	————	————
————	——	————	———	————	————	————	————
————	——	————	———	————	————	————	————
————	——	————	———	————	————	————	————
————	——	————	———	————	————	————	————
————	——	————	———	————	————	————	————
————	——	————	———	————	————	————	————

Item	OK	To Be Done By Us	Our Priority	To Be Done By Contractor	Contractor's Priority	Target Completion Date	Finished
GARAGE							
Roof	——	——	——	——	——	——	——
Windows	——	——	——	——	——	——	——
Paint	——	——	——	——	——	——	——
Exterior Walls	——	——	——	——	——	——	——
Brick/Masonry	——	——	——	——	——	——	——
Door	——	——	——	——	——	——	——
————	——	——	——	——	——	——	——
————	——	——	——	——	——	——	——
————	——	——	——	——	——	——	——
————	——	——	——	——	——	——	——
————	——	——	——	——	——	——	——
————	——	——	——	——	——	——	——
————	——	——	——	——	——	——	——

Interior Checklist

Item	OK	To Be Done By Us	Our Priority	To Be Done By Contractor	Contractor's Priority	Target Completion Date	Finished
ENTRY HALL							
Door #1	___	___	___	___	___	___	___
Door #2	___	___	___	___	___	___	___
Carpet	___	___	___	___	___	___	___
Floor	___	___	___	___	___	___	___
Windows	___	___	___	___	___	___	___
Window Latches	___	___	___	___	___	___	___
Drapes/Curtains	___	___	___	___	___	___	___
Traverse Rods	___	___	___	___	___	___	___
Light Fixtures	___	___	___	___	___	___	___
Closet/Door	___	___	___	___	___	___	___
North Wall	___	___	___	___	___	___	___
South Wall	___	___	___	___	___	___	___
East Wall	___	___	___	___	___	___	___
West Wall	___	___	___	___	___	___	___
Ceiling	___	___	___	___	___	___	___
Ceiling Fixture	___	___	___	___	___	___	___
_____	___	___	___	___	___	___	___
LIVING ROOM							
Door #1	___	___	___	___	___	___	___
Door #2	___	___	___	___	___	___	___
Fireplace	___	___	___	___	___	___	___
Floor	___	___	___	___	___	___	___
Carpet	___	___	___	___	___	___	___
Windows	___	___	___	___	___	___	___

Item	OK	To Be Done By Us	Our Priority	To Be Done By Contractor	Contractor's Priority	Target Completion Date	Finished
LIVING ROOM (*Continued*)							
Window Latches	___	_____	___	_____	_____	_____	_____
Drapes/Curtains	___	_____	___	_____	_____	_____	_____
Traverse Rods	___	_____	___	_____	_____	_____	_____
Closet Door	___	_____	___	_____	_____	_____	_____
Closet Interior	___	_____	___	_____	_____	_____	_____
Ceiling	___	_____	___	_____	_____	_____	_____
_____	___	_____	___	_____	_____	_____	_____
Ceiling Fixture	___	_____	___	_____	_____	_____	_____
_____	___	_____	___	_____	_____	_____	_____
North Wall	___	_____	___	_____	_____	_____	_____
South Wall	___	_____	___	_____	_____	_____	_____
East Wall	___	_____	___	_____	_____	_____	_____
West Wall	___	_____	___	_____	_____	_____	_____
_____	___	_____	___	_____	_____	_____	_____
_____	___	_____	___	_____	_____	_____	_____
_____	___	_____	___	_____	_____	_____	_____
DINING ROOM							
Door #1	___	_____	___	_____	_____	_____	_____
Door #2	___	_____	___	_____	_____	_____	_____
Other Door	___	_____	___	_____	_____	_____	_____
Fireplace	___	_____	___	_____	_____	_____	_____
Floor	___	_____	___	_____	_____	_____	_____
_____	___	_____	___	_____	_____	_____	_____
_____	___	_____	___	_____	_____	_____	_____

Item	OK	To Be Done By Us	Our Priority	To Be Done By Contractor	Contractor's Priority	Target Completion Date	Finished
DINING ROOM (*Continued*)							
Carpet	___	___	___	___	___	___	___
Windows	___	___	___	___	___	___	___
Window Latches	___	___	___	___	___	___	___
Traverse Rods	___	___	___	___	___	___	___
Drapes/Curtains	___	___	___	___	___	___	___
Light Fixtures	___	___	___	___	___	___	___
North Wall	___	___	___	___	___	___	___
South Wall	___	___	___	___	___	___	___
East Wall	___	___	___	___	___	___	___
West Wall	___	___	___	___	___	___	___
_____	___	___	___	___	___	___	___
Ceiling Fixture	___	___	___	___	___	___	___
Ceiling	___	___	___	___	___	___	___
_____	___	___	___	___	___	___	___
_____	___	___	___	___	___	___	___
_____	___	___	___	___	___	___	___
_____	___	___	___	___	___	___	___
DEN/LIBRARY							
Door #1	___	___	___	___	___	___	___
Door #2	___	___	___	___	___	___	___
Bookcases	___	___	___	___	___	___	___
Floor	___	___	___	___	___	___	___
Carpet	___	___	___	___	___	___	___
_____	___	___	___	___	___	___	___

Item	OK	To Be Done By Us	Our Priority	To Be Done By Contractor	Contractor's Priority	Target Completion Date	Finished
DEN/LIBRARY							
(Continued)							
Windows	——	———	———	———	———	———	———
Window Latches	——	———	———	———	———	———	———
Drapes/Curtains	——	———	———	———	———	———	———
Traverse Rods	——	———	———	———	———	———	———
————	——	———	———	———	———	———	———
————	——	———	———	———	———	———	———
North Wall	——	———	———	———	———	———	———
South Wall	——	———	———	———	———	———	———
East Wall	——	———	———	———	———	———	———
West Wall	——	———	———	———	———	———	———
————	——	———	———	———	———	———	———
Light Fixtures	——	———	———	———	———	———	———
Ceiling Fixture	——	———	———	———	———	———	———
Ceiling	——	———	———	———	———	———	———
————	——	———	———	———	———	———	———
————	——	———	———	———	———	———	———
————	——	———	———	———	———	———	———
FAMILY ROOM							
Door #1	——	———	———	———	———	———	———
Door #2	——	———	———	———	———	———	———
Bookcases	——	———	———	———	———	———	———
Floor	——	———	———	———	———	———	———
Carpet	——	———	———	———	———	———	———
————	——	———	———	———	———	———	———

Item	OK	To Be Done By Us	Our Priority	To Be Done By Contractor	Contractor's Priority	Target Completion Date	Finished
FAMILY ROOM (*Continued*)							
Windows							
Window Latches							
Drapes/Curtains							
Traverse Rods							
Fireplace							
Light Fixtures							
Ceiling Fixture							
Ceiling							
North Wall							
South Wall							
East Wall							
West Wall							

FORM 63.2/F514

Item	OK	To Be Done By Us	Our Priority	To Be Done By Contractor	Contractor's Priority	Target Completion Date	Finished
KITCHEN							
Door #1	——	———	———	———	———	———	———
Door #2	——	———	———	———	———	———	———
Door #3	——	———	———	———	———	———	———
Floor	——	———	———	———	———	———	———
Carpet/Area Rug	——	———	———	———	———	———	———
———————	——	———	———	———	———	———	———
Cabinet #1	——	———	———	———	———	———	———
Cabinet #2	——	———	———	———	———	———	———
Cabinet #3	——	———	———	———	———	———	———
Cabinet #4	——	———	———	———	———	———	———
Cabinet #5	——	———	———	———	———	———	———
———————	——	———	———	———	———	———	———
———————	——	———	———	———	———	———	———
Windows	——	———	———	———	———	———	———
Window Latches	——	———	———	———	———	———	———
Drapes/Curtains	——	———	———	———	———	———	———
Traverse Rods	——	———	———	———	———	———	———
———————	——	———	———	———	———	———	———
Counter Top	——	———	———	———	———	———	———
Storage Drawers #1	——	———	———	———	———	———	———
Storage Drawers #2	——	———	———	———	———	———	———
Light Fixtures	——	———	———	———	———	———	———
———————	——	———	———	———	———	———	———
———————	——	———	———	———	———	———	———

Item	OK	To Be Done By Us	Our Priority	To Be Done By Contractor	Contractor's Priority	Target Completion Date	Finished
KITCHEN (*Continued*)							
Ceiling Fixture	——	———	———	———	———	———	———
Ceiling	——	———	———	———	———	———	———
————————	——	———	———	———	———	———	———
North Wall	——	———	———	———	———	———	———
South Wall	——	———	———	———	———	———	———
East Wall	——	———	———	———	———	———	———
West Wall	——	———	———	———	———	———	———
————————	——	———	———	———	———	———	———
————————	——	———	———	———	———	———	———
————————	——	———	———	———	———	———	———
————————	——	———	———	———	———	———	———
PANTRY—LAUNDRY/ UTILITY ROOM							
Door #1	——	———	———	———	———	———	———
Door #2	——	———	———	———	———	———	———
Floor	——	———	———	———	———	———	———
Carpet	——	———	———	———	———	———	———
————————	——	———	———	———	———	———	———
————————	——	———	———	———	———	———	———
Shelves #1	——	———	———	———	———	———	———
Shelves #2	——	———	———	———	———	———	———
Shelves #3	——	———	———	———	———	———	———
Windows	——	———	———	———	———	———	———
Window Latches	——	———	———	———	———	———	———
————————	——	———	———	———	———	———	———

Item	OK	To Be Done By Us	Our Priority	To Be Done By Contractor	Contractor's Priority	Target Completion Date	Finished
PANTRY—LAUNDRY/ UTILITY ROOM (*Continued*)							
Cabinet #1	___	___	___	___	___	___	___
Cabinet #2	___	___	___	___	___	___	___
Cabinet #3	___	___	___	___	___	___	___
Cabinet #4	___	___	___	___	___	___	___
_____	___	___	___	___	___	___	___
_____	___	___	___	___	___	___	___
Storage Drawers #1	___	___	___	___	___	___	___
Storage Drawers #2	___	___	___	___	___	___	___
Storage Drawers #3	___	___	___	___	___	___	___
_____	___	___	___	___	___	___	___
Curtains	___	___	___	___	___	___	___
Light Fixtures	___	___	___	___	___	___	___
Ceiling Fixture	___	___	___	___	___	___	___
Ceiling	___	___	___	___	___	___	___
_____	___	___	___	___	___	___	___
North Wall	___	___	___	___	___	___	___
South Wall	___	___	___	___	___	___	___
East Wall	___	___	___	___	___	___	___
West Wall	___	___	___	___	___	___	___
_____	___	___	___	___	___	___	___
_____	___	___	___	___	___	___	___
_____	___	___	___	___	___	___	___
_____	___	___	___	___	___	___	___
_____	___	___	___	___	___	___	___

Item	OK	To Be Done By Us	Our Priority	To Be Done By Contractor	Contractor's Priority	Target Completion Date	Finished
BASEMENT							
Door to Basement	___	___	___	___	___	___	___
Basement Stairway	___	___	___	___	___	___	___
_____	___	___	___	___	___	___	___
Stairway Carpet	___	___	___	___	___	___	___
_____	___	___	___	___	___	___	___
Floor	___	___	___	___	___	___	___
Floor Drain	___	___	___	___	___	___	___
Area Carpet	___	___	___	___	___	___	___
Windows	___	___	___	___	___	___	___
Window Latches	___	___	___	___	___	___	___
_____	___	___	___	___	___	___	___
Outside Door	___	___	___	___	___	___	___
Permanent Tubs	___	___	___	___	___	___	___
Light Fixtures	___	___	___	___	___	___	___
Overhead/Ceiling	___	___	___	___	___	___	___
_____	___	___	___	___	___	___	___
_____	___	___	___	___	___	___	___
Storage Cabinets	___	___	___	___	___	___	___
Workbench	___	___	___	___	___	___	___
Bar Top	___	___	___	___	___	___	___
Back Bar	___	___	___	___	___	___	___
Storeroom	___	___	___	___	___	___	___
_____	___	___	___	___	___	___	___
_____	___	___	___	___	___	___	___

Item	OK	To Be Done By Us	Our Priority	To Be Done By Contractor	Contractor's Priority	Target Completion Date	Finished
BASEMENT (*Continued*)							
North Wall	——	————	————	————	————	————	————
South Wall	——	————	————	————	————	————	————
East Wall	——	————	————	————	————	————	————
West Wall	——	————	————	————	————	————	————
————————	——	————	————	————	————	————	————
————————	——	————	————	————	————	————	————
————————	——	————	————	————	————	————	————
————————	——	————	————	————	————	————	————
————————	——	————	————	————	————	————	————
————————	——	————	————	————	————	————	————
————————	——	————	————	————	————	————	————
STAIRWAY TO SECOND FLOOR							
Stairway	——	————	————	————	————	————	————
Light Fixture	——	————	————	————	————	————	————
Stairway Carpet	——	————	————	————	————	————	————
Railing	——	————	————	————	————	————	————
————————	——	————	————	————	————	————	————
Window/Latch	——	————	————	————	————	————	————
Curtain/Drape	——	————	————	————	————	————	————
————————	——	————	————	————	————	————	————
SECOND-FLOOR HALLWAY							
Door #1	——	————	————	————	————	————	————
Door #2	——	————	————	————	————	————	————
Door #3	——	————	————	————	————	————	————

Item	OK	To Be Done By Us	Our Priority	To Be Done By Contractor	Contractor's Priority	Target Completion Date	Finished
SECOND-FLOOR HALLWAY (*Continued*)							
Door #4	____	_____	_____	_____	_____	_____	_____
Door #5	____	_____	_____	_____	_____	_____	_____
Door #6	____	_____	_____	_____	_____	_____	_____
_____	____	_____	_____	_____	_____	_____	_____
Floor	____	_____	_____	_____	_____	_____	_____
Carpet	____	_____	_____	_____	_____	_____	_____
Windows	____	_____	_____	_____	_____	_____	_____
Window Latches	____	_____	_____	_____	_____	_____	_____
_____	____	_____	_____	_____	_____	_____	_____
Drapes/Curtains	____	_____	_____	_____	_____	_____	_____
Traverse Rods	____	_____	_____	_____	_____	_____	_____
Closet	____	_____	_____	_____	_____	_____	_____
Light Fixtures	____	_____	_____	_____	_____	_____	_____
Ceiling Fixture	____	_____	_____	_____	_____	_____	_____
Ceiling	____	_____	_____	_____	_____	_____	_____
_____	____	_____	_____	_____	_____	_____	_____
North Wall	____	_____	_____	_____	_____	_____	_____
South Wall	____	_____	_____	_____	_____	_____	_____
East Wall	____	_____	_____	_____	_____	_____	_____
West Wall	____	_____	_____	_____	_____	_____	_____
_____	____	_____	_____	_____	_____	_____	_____
_____	____	_____	_____	_____	_____	_____	_____
_____	____	_____	_____	_____	_____	_____	_____
_____	____	_____	_____	_____	_____	_____	_____

FORM 63.2/F520

Item	OK	To Be Done By Us	Our Priority	To Be Done By Contractor	Contractor's Priority	Target Completion Date	Finished
BEDROOM NO. ___							
Door #1	___	___	___	___	___	___	___
Door #2	___	___	___	___	___	___	___
Floor	___	___	___	___	___	___	___
Carpet	___	___	___	___	___	___	___
Bookcases	___	___	___	___	___	___	___
Windows	___	___	___	___	___	___	___
Window Latches	___	___	___	___	___	___	___
Drapes/Curtains	___	___	___	___	___	___	___
Traverse Rods	___	___	___	___	___	___	___
_____	___	___	___	___	___	___	___
Light Fixtures	___	___	___	___	___	___	___
Ceiling Fixture	___	___	___	___	___	___	___
Ceiling	___	___	___	___	___	___	___
Closet	___	___	___	___	___	___	___
_____	___	___	___	___	___	___	___
North Wall	___	___	___	___	___	___	___
South Wall	___	___	___	___	___	___	___
East Wall	___	___	___	___	___	___	___
West Wall	___	___	___	___	___	___	___
_____	___	___	___	___	___	___	___
_____	___	___	___	___	___	___	___
_____	___	___	___	___	___	___	___
_____	___	___	___	___	___	___	___
_____	___	___	___	___	___	___	___

Item	OK	To Be Done By Us	Our Priority	To Be Done By Contractor	Contractor's Priority	Target Completion Date	Finished
BATHROOM NO. ___							
Door #1	___	___	___	___	___	___	___
Door #2	___	___	___	___	___	___	___
Floor	___	___	___	___	___	___	___
Carpet	___	___	___	___	___	___	___
Basin/Fixtures	___	___	___	___	___	___	___
_____	___	___	___	___	___	___	___
_____	___	___	___	___	___	___	___
_____	___	___	___	___	___	___	___
_____	___	___	___	___	___	___	___
Toilet	___	___	___	___	___	___	___
Tub/Fixtures	___	___	___	___	___	___	___
Shower/Fixtures	___	___	___	___	___	___	___
Enclosure	___	___	___	___	___	___	___
_____	___	___	___	___	___	___	___
_____	___	___	___	___	___	___	___
_____	___	___	___	___	___	___	___
_____	___	___	___	___	___	___	___
Windows	___	___	___	___	___	___	___
Window Latches	___	___	___	___	___	___	___
Medicine Cabinet	___	___	___	___	___	___	___
Mirror	___	___	___	___	___	___	___
_____	___	___	___	___	___	___	___
_____	___	___	___	___	___	___	___
_____	___	___	___	___	___	___	___

Item	OK	To Be Done By Us	Our Priority	To Be Done By Contractor	Contractor's Priority	Target Completion Date	Finished
BATHROOM NO. ____ (Continued)							
Light Fixtures	____	____	____	____	____	____	____
Ceiling Fixture	____	____	____	____	____	____	____
Ceiling	____	____	____	____	____	____	____
_____	____	____	____	____	____	____	____
North Wall	____	____	____	____	____	____	____
South Wall	____	____	____	____	____	____	____
East Wall	____	____	____	____	____	____	____
West Wall	____	____	____	____	____	____	____
_____	____	____	____	____	____	____	____
_____	____	____	____	____	____	____	____
_____	____	____	____	____	____	____	____
Linen Storage #1	____	____	____	____	____	____	____
Linen Storage #2	____	____	____	____	____	____	____
_____	____	____	____	____	____	____	____
_____	____	____	____	____	____	____	____
_____	____	____	____	____	____	____	____
_____	____	____	____	____	____	____	____
_____	____	____	____	____	____	____	____

Item	OK	To Be Done By Us	Our Priority	To Be Done By Contractor	Contractor's Priority	Target Completion Date	Finished
ATTIC							
Attic Door	____	_____	_____	_____	_____	_____	_____
Attic Stairway	____	_____	_____	_____	_____	_____	_____
Stairway Carpet	____	_____	_____	_____	_____	_____	_____
_____	____	_____	_____	_____	_____	_____	_____
Railing	____	_____	_____	_____	_____	_____	_____
Floor	____	_____	_____	_____	_____	_____	_____
Carpet	____	_____	_____	_____	_____	_____	_____
Windows	____	_____	_____	_____	_____	_____	_____
Window Latches	____	_____	_____	_____	_____	_____	_____
_____	____	_____	_____	_____	_____	_____	_____
_____	____	_____	_____	_____	_____	_____	_____
Drapes/Curtains	____	_____	_____	_____	_____	_____	_____
Traverse Rods	____	_____	_____	_____	_____	_____	_____
Light Fixtures	____	_____	_____	_____	_____	_____	_____
Ceiling Fixture	____	_____	_____	_____	_____	_____	_____
Ceiling	____	_____	_____	_____	_____	_____	_____
_____	____	_____	_____	_____	_____	_____	_____
_____	____	_____	_____	_____	_____	_____	_____
North Wall	____	_____	_____	_____	_____	_____	_____
South Wall	____	_____	_____	_____	_____	_____	_____
East Wall	____	_____	_____	_____	_____	_____	_____
West Wall	____	_____	_____	_____	_____	_____	_____
_____	____	_____	_____	_____	_____	_____	_____
_____	____	_____	_____	_____	_____	_____	_____

Appliance/Equipment Checklist

Item	OK	To Be Done By Us	Our Priority	To Be Done By Contractor	Contractor's Priority	Target Completion Date	Finished
FRONT DOORWAY							
Door Lock	____	_____	_____	_____	_____	_____	_____
Doorbell	____	_____	_____	_____	_____	_____	_____
Door (Stick?)	____	_____	_____	_____	_____	_____	_____
Weather Stripping	____	_____	_____	_____	_____	_____	_____
Exterior Light	____	_____	_____	_____	_____	_____	_____
_____	____	_____	_____	_____	_____	_____	_____
_____	____	_____	_____	_____	_____	_____	_____
ENTRY HALL							
Light Switch	____	_____	_____	_____	_____	_____	_____
Wall Outlets	____	_____	_____	_____	_____	_____	_____
Smoke Alarm	____	_____	_____	_____	_____	_____	_____
_____	____	_____	_____	_____	_____	_____	_____
_____	____	_____	_____	_____	_____	_____	_____
_____	____	_____	_____	_____	_____	_____	_____
LIVING ROOM							
Light Switches	____	_____	_____	_____	_____	_____	_____
Wall Outlets	____	_____	_____	_____	_____	_____	_____
Window Air Conditioner	____	_____	_____	_____	_____	_____	_____
Fireplace Blower	____	_____	_____	_____	_____	_____	_____
Intercom	____	_____	_____	_____	_____	_____	_____
Smoke Alarm	____	_____	_____	_____	_____	_____	_____
_____	____	_____	_____	_____	_____	_____	_____
_____	____	_____	_____	_____	_____	_____	_____
_____	____	_____	_____	_____	_____	_____	_____

Item	OK	To Be Done By Us	Our Priority	To Be Done By Contractor	Contractor's Priority	Target Completion Date	Finished
DINING ROOM							
Light Switches	____	_____	_____	_____	_____	_____	_____
Wall Outlets	____	_____	_____	_____	_____	_____	_____
Window Air Conditioner	____	_____	_____	_____	_____	_____	_____
Fireplace Blower	____	_____	_____	_____	_____	_____	_____
Intercom	____	_____	_____	_____	_____	_____	_____
Smoke Alarm	____	_____	_____	_____	_____	_____	_____
_____	____	_____	_____	_____	_____	_____	_____
FAMILY ROOM							
Light Switches	____	_____	_____	_____	_____	_____	_____
Wall Outlets	____	_____	_____	_____	_____	_____	_____
Window Air Conditioner	____	_____	_____	_____	_____	_____	_____
Fireplace Blower	____	_____	_____	_____	_____	_____	_____
Intercom	____	_____	_____	_____	_____	_____	_____
Smoke Alarm	____	_____	_____	_____	_____	_____	_____
_____	____	_____	_____	_____	_____	_____	_____
LIBRARY/DEN							
Light Switches	____	_____	_____	_____	_____	_____	_____
Wall Outlets	____	_____	_____	_____	_____	_____	_____
Window Air Conditioner	____	_____	_____	_____	_____	_____	_____
Fireplace Blower	____	_____	_____	_____	_____	_____	_____
Intercom	____	_____	_____	_____	_____	_____	_____
Smoke Alarm	____	_____	_____	_____	_____	_____	_____
_____	____	_____	_____	_____	_____	_____	_____

Item	OK	To Be Done By Us	Our Priority	To Be Done By Contractor	Contractor's Priority	Target Completion Date	Finished
KITCHEN							
Light Switches	——	———	———	———	———	———	———
Wall Outlets	——	———	———	———	———	———	———
Window Air Conditioner	——	———	———	———	———	———	———
Exhaust Fan	——	———	———	———	———	———	———
Intercom	——	———	———	———	———	———	———
————	——	———	———	———	———	———	———
————	——	———	———	———	———	———	———
Stove	——	———	———	———	———	———	———
Oven	——	———	———	———	———	———	———
Refrigerator	——	———	———	———	———	———	———
Freezer	——	———	———	———	———	———	———
————	——	———	———	———	———	———	———
————	——	———	———	———	———	———	———
Disposer	——	———	———	———	———	———	———
Dishwasher	——	———	———	———	———	———	———
Trash Compactor	——	———	———	———	———	———	———
————	——	———	———	———	———	———	———
————	——	———	———	———	———	———	———
Clothes Washer	——	———	———	———	———	———	———
Dryer	——	———	———	———	———	———	———
Smoke Alarm	——	———	———	———	———	———	———
————	——	———	———	———	———	———	———
————	——	———	———	———	———	———	———
————	——	———	———	———	———	———	———

Item	OK	To Be Done By Us	Our Priority	To Be Done By Contractor	Contractor's Priority	Target Completion Date	Finished
PANTRY—LAUNDRY/ UTILITY ROOM							
Light Switches	——	————	————	————	————	————	————
Wall Outlets	——	————	————	————	————	————	————
Clothes Washer	——	————	————	————	————	————	————
Dryer	——	————	————	————	————	————	————
————————	——	————	————	————	————	————	————
————————	——	————	————	————	————	————	————
BEDROOM NO. ——							
Door (Stick?)	——	————	————	————	————	————	————
Lock	——	————	————	————	————	————	————
Light Switches	——	————	————	————	————	————	————
Wall Outlets	——	————	————	————	————	————	————
Window Air Conditioner	——	————	————	————	————	————	————
Fireplace Blower	——	————	————	————	————	————	————
Intercom	——	————	————	————	————	————	————
Smoke Alarm	——	————	————	————	————	————	————
————————	——	————	————	————	————	————	————
————————	——	————	————	————	————	————	————
————————	——	————	————	————	————	————	————
BATHROOM NO. ——							
Door (Stick?)	——	————	————	————	————	————	————
Lock	——	————	————	————	————	————	————
Toilet	——	————	————	————	————	————	————
Basin Faucets	——	————	————	————	————	————	————
Basin Drain	——	————	————	————	————	————	————

Item	OK	To Be Done By Us	Our Priority	To Be Done By Contractor	Contractor's Priority	Target Completion Date	Finished
BATHROOM NO. ___							
(*Continued*)							
Shower Faucets	___	___	___	___	___	___	___
Shower Head	___	___	___	___	___	___	___
Shower Drain	___	___	___	___	___	___	___
Tub Faucets	___	___	___	___	___	___	___
Tub Drain	___	___	___	___	___	___	___
Shower/Tub Enclosure	___	___	___	___	___	___	___
Exhaust Fan	___	___	___	___	___	___	___
Light Switches	___	___	___	___	___	___	___
Wall Outlets	___	___	___	___	___	___	___
_____	___	___	___	___	___	___	___
_____	___	___	___	___	___	___	___
_____	___	___	___	___	___	___	___
_____	___	___	___	___	___	___	___
ATTIC							
Door (Stick?)	___	___	___	___	___	___	___
Light Switches	___	___	___	___	___	___	___
Wall Outlets	___	___	___	___	___	___	___
Window Air Conditioner	___	___	___	___	___	___	___
Exhaust Fan	___	___	___	___	___	___	___
Smoke Alarm	___	___	___	___	___	___	___
_____	___	___	___	___	___	___	___
_____	___	___	___	___	___	___	___
_____	___	___	___	___	___	___	___
_____	___	___	___	___	___	___	___

Item	OK	To Be Done By Us	Our Priority	To Be Done By Contractor	Contractor's Priority	Target Completion Date	Finished
BASEMENT							
Clothes Washer	___	___	___	___	___	___	___
Dryer	___	___	___	___	___	___	___
Dehumidifier	___	___	___	___	___	___	___
Light Fixtures	___	___	___	___	___	___	___
Wall Outlets	___	___	___	___	___	___	___
Floor Drain	___	___	___	___	___	___	___
Smoke Alarm	___	___	___	___	___	___	___
Freezer	___	___	___	___	___	___	___
_____	___	___	___	___	___	___	___
_____	___	___	___	___	___	___	___
_____	___	___	___	___	___	___	___
_____	___	___	___	___	___	___	___
GARAGE							
Door (Opener)	___	___	___	___	___	___	___
Light Switches	___	___	___	___	___	___	___
Wall Outlets	___	___	___	___	___	___	___
Clothes Washer	___	___	___	___	___	___	___
Dryer	___	___	___	___	___	___	___
Smoke Alarm	___	___	___	___	___	___	___
_____	___	___	___	___	___	___	___
_____	___	___	___	___	___	___	___
_____	___	___	___	___	___	___	___
_____	___	___	___	___	___	___	___

CENTRAL HEAT

Open the vents/radiator valves in every room and turn on the heat. Check main unit for unusual sounds and smells. Check each room to assure that heat is being delivered. Close and open the vents/radiator valves to check their effectiveness and freedom of operation. After the unit has been operating for some time, check for water, gas, and oil leaks. Check oil tank for leaks. Check operation of the thermostat.

	OK	Not OK		OK	Not OK		OK	Not OK
Heating Unit	___	___	Basement	___	___	Bedroom #4	___	___
Entry Hall	___	___	Garage	___	___	Bedroom #5	___	___
Living Room	___	___	Bathroom #1	___	___	Attic	___	___
Dining Room	___	___	Bathroom #2	___	___	Thermostat	___	___
Den/Library	___	___	Bathroom #3	___	___	Oil Tank	___	___
Family Room	___	___	Bedroom #1	___	___	_____	___	___
Kitchen	___	___	Bedroom #2	___	___	_____	___	___
Pantry	___	___	Bedroom #3	___	___	_____	___	___

CENTRAL AIR CONDITIONING

Open the vents in every room and turn on the air conditioning. Check main unit for unusual sounds and smells. Check each room to assure that cool air is being delivered. Close and open the vents to check their effectiveness and freedom of operation. After unit has been operating for some time, check for refrigerant leaks. Check operation of the thermostat.

	OK	Not OK		OK	Not OK		OK	Not OK
Cooling Unit	___	___	Basement	___	___	Bedroom #4	___	___
Entry Hall	___	___	Garage	___	___	Bedroom #5	___	___
Living Room	___	___	Bathroom #1	___	___	Attic	___	___
Dining Room	___	___	Bathroom #2	___	___	Thermostat	___	___
Den/Library	___	___	Bathroom #3	___	___	Refrigerator Leak	___	___
Family Room	___	___	Bedroom #1	___	___	_____	___	___
Kitchen	___	___	Bedroom #2	___	___	_____	___	___
Pantry	___	___	Bedroom #3	___	___	_____	___	___

HOT WATER

Carefully inspect the hot water heater for cleanliness, strange smells, evidence of leaks, worn wiring, and loose connections. Check operation of the thermostat.

	OK	Not OK		OK	Not OK
Cleanliness	____	____	Worn Wiring	____	____
Smells	____	____	Loose Connections	____	____
Leaks	____	____	Thermostat	____	____

SWIMMING POOL

	OK	Not OK		OK	Not OK
Exterior Lights	____	____	Heater	____	____
Underwater Lights	____	____	Drain	____	____
Filter	____	____	Pump	____	____
Vacuum	____	____	Cover	____	____

Fact Sheet

Date _____

Owner(s) _____

Address _____

Home Phone _____ Business Phone _____ Business Phone _____

General Information

Architectural Type _____

Selling Price _____

Square Feet (House) _____ No. of Rooms _____

Square Feet (Lot) _____ No. of Bedrooms _____

Lot Dimensions _____ No. of Bathrooms _____

Garage Dimensions _____ Basement _____

Note: N/A = not applicable.

House and Lot Plan

Construction

Date of Construction _____

Footings _____

Foundation Walls _____

Exterior Walls _____

Roof Material _____

Roof Type _____

Framing _____

Windows _____

Guttering Downspouts _____

Exterior Doors _____

Screens _____

Partitions _____

_____ _____

Interior Walls _____

Interior Doors _____

Floors (1st Floor) _____

Floors (2nd Floor) _____

Floors (3rd Floor) _____

Floors (Bathroom #1) _____

Floors (Bathroom #2) _____

Floors (Bathroom #3) _____

Fireplace #1 _____

Fireplace #2 _____

_____ _____

_____ _____

Room Dimensions

Entry–Foyer _____

Living Room _____

Dining Room _____

Den–Library _____

Kitchen _____

Pantry–Laundry Room _____

Basement _____

Bathroom #1 _____

Bathroom #2 _____

Bathroom #3 _____

_____ _____

Bedroom #1 _____

Bedroom #2 _____

Bedroom #3 _____

Bedroom #4 _____

Bedroom #5 _____

Family Room _____

Attic _____

Garage _____

_____ _____

_____ _____

_____ _____

Note: N/A = not applicable.

Carpet–Flooring

Entry–Foyer _____   Bedroom #1 _____

Living Room _____   Bedroom #2 _____

Dining Room _____   Bedroom #3 _____

Den–Library _____   Bedroom #4 _____

Kitchen _____   Bedroom #5 _____

Pantry–Laundry Room _____   Family Room _____

Basement _____   Attic _____

Bathroom #1 _____   Garage _____

Bathroom #2 _____   _____ _____

Bathroom #3 _____   _____ _____

_____ _____   _____ _____

Garage–Carport

Attached or Detached? _____   Garage or Carport? _____

Type of Construction _____   Insulation _____

Type of Floor _____   Drain _____

Automatic Doors? _____   Heated? _____

Roof Type _____   Dimensions _____

Roof Material _____   _____ _____

Basement

Outside Entrance _____   Finished Ceiling _____

Type of Floor _____   Finished Floor _____

Floor Drain _____   _____ _____

Square Feet _____   _____ _____

Finished Walls _____   _____ _____

Note: N/A = not applicable.

Heating–Plumbing–Electrical

Type of Heating _____   Insulation (Exterior Walls) _____

Type of Cooling _____   Insulation (Floor) _____

Type of Hot Water _____   Insulation (Ceiling) _____

Hot Water Capacity _____   Insulation (Roof) _____

Electricity _____   _____   _____

Plumbing _____   _____   _____

Appliances–Built-ins

Clothes Washer _____   Oven _____

Clothes Dryer _____   Dishwasher _____

Freezer _____   Trash Compactor _____

Refrigerator _____   Disposer _____

Stove _____   Exhaust Fan Hood _____

_____   _____   _____   _____

Site Data

Subdivision _____

Block No. _____   Lot No. _____

Square Feet (Lot) _____   Front Yard Setback _____

Lot Shape _____   Right Side Setback _____

Frontage _____   Left Side Setback _____

Elevation _____   Rear Setback _____

Square Feet (Front Yard) _____   Served by:

Square Feet (Backyard) _____   Gas _____   Water _____

Lawn Type _____   Sewer _____   Electricity _____

Fencing Type and Height _____   Telephone _____   _____   ____

Driveway Type _____   _____   _____

Zoned _____   _____   _____

_____   _____   _____   _____

Note: N/A = not applicable.

Off-Site Improvements

Street Surface _____   Streetlights? _____

Sidewalk _____   Trees (Where?) _____

Curb–Gutter _____   _____   _____

Storm Sewers? _____   _____   _____

Alley? _____   _____   _____

Street Access _____   _____   _____

Taxes, Utilities, and Insurance

Property Tax (per Year) _____   Average Electric Bill (Monthly) _____

School Tax (per Year) _____   Average Fuel Bill (Monthly) _____

Average Trash Pickup Bill (Monthly) _____   Average Gas Bill (Monthly) _____

Fire Insurance (per Year) _____   Average Water Bill (Monthly) _____

_____   _____   _____   _____

_____   _____   _____   _____

_____   _____   _____   _____

Note: N/A = not applicable.

Neighborhood Data

Elementary School _____

High School _____

Junior High School _____

Nursery School _____

Junior College _____

College/University _____

Downtown _____

Shopping Center _____

Bus Lines _____

Hospital _____

Post Office _____

Fire Station _____

Police Station _____

Park _____

Church _____

Trash Pickup _____

_____ _____

_____ _____

_____ _____

Note: N/A = not applicable.

FORM 64.1/F540

Community Data

City/Town _____

County _____ State _____

Mean Summer Temperature _____ Mean Winter Temperature _____

Population 19___ _____ Population 19___ _____

Major Employers

_____

_____

_____

_____

_____

_____

_____

General Description

FINANCIAL DATA

Appraised Fair Market Value _____ Selling Price _____ Cost per Square Foot _____

Mortgage(s) _____ Mortgage Payments _____

Property Tax (per Year) _____ Insurance (per Year) _____

Average Electric Bill (Monthly) _____ Average Gas Bill (Monthly) _____

Average Fuel Bill (Monthly) _____ Average Water Bill (Monthly) _____

Average Trash Pickup Bill (Monthly) _____ School Tax (per Year) _____

_____ _____   _____ _____

_____ _____   _____ _____

_____ _____   _____ _____

Note: N/A = not applicable.

Selling Price Comparison Survey

House No.	Address	No. of Bedrooms	No. of Bathrooms	Garage Capacity	Extras	Sold for	PPSF
_____	_____	_____	_____	_____	____	_____	_____
	_____				Square Feet	_____	
	_____	# _____			Date of Sale	_____	
_____	_____	_____	_____	_____	____	_____	_____
	_____				Square Feet	_____	
	_____	# _____			Date of Sale	_____	
_____	_____	_____	_____	_____	____	_____	_____
	_____				Square Feet	_____	
	_____	# _____			Date of Sale	_____	
_____	_____	_____	_____	_____	____	_____	_____
	_____				Square Feet	_____	
	_____	# _____			Date of Sale	_____	
_____	_____	_____	_____	_____	____	_____	_____
	_____				Square Feet	_____	
	_____	# _____			Date of Sale	_____	
_____	_____	_____	_____	_____	____	_____	_____
	_____				Square Feet	_____	
	_____	# _____			Date of Sale	_____	

TELEPHONE LOG, Page No. ____

1. What special features are you looking for?
2. Number of children and ages.
3. What part of town do you live in now?
4. When is the most convenient time?
5. Your phone number in case we have to call you back?

Caller _____

Date _____ Phone #1 _____ Phone #2 _____

Interested in: _____

_____

_____

Appointment for: _____

Remarks: _____

_____

_____

_____

Caller _____

Date _____ Phone #1 _____ Phone #2 _____

Interested in: _____

_____

_____

Appointment for: _____

Remarks: _____

_____

_____

_____

OPEN HOUSE

By Owner

Estimated Purchase Data

	Conventional	FHA	VA
Appraised Value	_____ (1)	_____ (2)	_____ (3)
Down Payment Required	_____	_____	_____
Annual Interest Rate	_____	_____	_____
Amount of Mortgage	_____	_____	_____
Approximate Monthly Payment	_____ (4)	_____ (4)	_____ (4)
Approximate Qualifying Income	_____ (5)	_____ (5)	_____ (5)
Interest Paid Over	_____	_____	_____

KEY:
(1) Appraised Fair Market Value
(2) FHA Conditional Commitment for Insurance
(3) VA Certificate of Reasonable Value
(4) Add 1/12 of estimated annual local taxes and insurance
  to determine approximate total monthly payment
(5) 60 × approximate monthly payment

Loan Comparison Data (Page No. ___)

Lender	Down	Interest	Years	Points
_____	_____	_____	_____	_____
_____				
_____				
_____				
_____	_____	_____	_____	_____
_____				
_____				
_____				
_____	_____	_____	_____	_____
_____				
_____				
_____				
_____	_____	_____	_____	_____
_____				
_____				
_____				
_____	_____	_____	_____	_____
_____				
_____				

Loan Comparison Data (Page No. ___)

Lender	Down	Interest	Years	Points

Lease Agreement with Option to Purchase

Lessor _____

Name

_____
Street Address   *City*   *State*   *Zip*

Lessor _____

Name

_____
Street Address   *City*   *State*   *Zip*

Premises _____

Street Address   *City*   *State*   *Zip*

the legal description of which is _____

_____

_____

_____

_____

_____

_____ .

Lessee _____

Name

_____
Street Address   *City*   *State*   *Zip*

Lessee _____

Name

_____
Street Address   *City*   *State*   *Zip*

1. The Lessor hereby leases with an option to purchase the above-described premises to _____ and _____, hereinafter called Lessee, for a term of _____, beginning _____ and ending _____.

2. The Lessee agrees to pay the sum of _____ to the Lessor on or before _____, as nonrefundable consideration for granting this lease with option to purchase.

3. The principal balance of the Lessor's existing first mortgage/deed of trust to:

_____

Name

_____
Street Address   *City*   *State*   *Zip*

is _____, at an interest rate of _____, payable at the rate of _____ per month, which the Lessor shall pay each month to the above-named banking institution.

4. The balance of the purchase price for the leased premises shall be the attached promissory note of the Lessee to the Lessor, said note secured by this Agreement, dated _____, having a principal balance of _____ _____, an interest rate of _____ _____, payable at the rate of _____ _____ per month, such payments to be made to:

_____

Name

Street Address	*City*	*State*	*Zip*

5. Lessee agrees to pay a late charge of _____ of the monthly payment to Lessor if such payment is not made by the Lessee by the _____ of each month.

6. Failure of Lessee to make the specified payment within _____ after the date on which due, including any late charge, shall be cause to terminate this Agreement and Lessor shall have the right to retain all payments made by Lessee.

7. Upon tender of any payment in cash, Lessor agrees to issue a receipt stating Lessee's name, a description of the premises, the amount paid and the period for which paid.

8. The Lessor hereby grants to the Lessee an option to purchase the leased property any time Lessee may decide to exercise such option prior to _____, provided that the Lessee shall have met all obligations set forth in this Agreement. At the time of the Lessee's exercise of his/her option to purchase the leased property, the Lessor agrees to convey said property to the Lessee free and clear of any encumbrances, except property taxes and assessments which are to be paid by the Lessee, and except for the herein-described promissory note and first mortgage/deed of trust to _____ _____.

9. Lessor agrees not to encumber additionally the leased premises, apart from the herein-described encumbrance, which may remain.

10. Lessor hereby agrees to protect and defend the Lessee and the leased property against loss or foreclosure by reason of any encumbrance created by the Lessor and now existing against the leased property.

11. The Lessor agrees that failure of the Lessor to pay promptly in full the amount due _____ _____ each month, as set forth in paragraph three (3) above, or any further encumbrance of the leased property by the Lessor shall be cause for the Lessee to suspend payment to the Lessor, and for Lessee to continue to occupy the leased premises without further payment to the Lessor until such time as the Lessor shall make current the first mortgage/deed of trust to _____ and/or remove any new encumbrance. Lessee shall also have full recourse in a court of law against Lessor for any breach of this Agreement.

12. The Lessor and Lessee agree that the annual rate of interest on the Lessee's promissory note to Lessor may be adjusted on the _____ day of _____ of _____, _____, _____, _____ and _____ to the rate of interest charged by _____ or its successor for home loans made on those dates.

13. At such time as the Lessor shall receive from the Lessee written notice of Lessee's intent to exercise his/her option to purchase the leased property under terms of this Agreement, the Lessor shall, within thirty (30) days of receipt of such notice, deliver to the Lessee a preliminary title search and/or abstract of title. Any defects in title indicated by such title search or abstract shall be remedied by the Lessor within thirty (30) days after notice of such defects shall be given to Lessor. Lessor shall deliver to Lessee on the date of closing of escrow a grant/warranty deed free of all encumbrances except as provided for in paragraph eight (8) above.

14. At such time as the Lessee shall determine to exercise his/her option to purchase the leased property prior to the expiration of this Agreement, the Lessee shall:

A. Give the Lessor written notice thereof.

B. Make arrangements to assume, pay or take title to the leased property subject to the herein-described encumbrance to _____ by _____ _____, by:

    1) Paying in full to the Lessor the promissory note described in paragraph four (4) above, or

    2) Securing said promissory note by a second mortgage/deed of trust recorded against the property, or

    3) Securing financing elsewhere to pay off the existing first mortgage/deed of trust (together with any prepayment penalty or other charges) and paying the balance of the purchase price owed to the Lessor under Lessee's promissory note to the Lessor, and by

    4) Paying normal escrow, title transfer and title insurance costs for acquisition of property in the county of _____, municipality of _____.

15. The Lessee acknowledges being advised by the Lessor that the existing first mortgage/deed of trust payable to _____ contains a provision for accelerated payment of indebtedness, commonly termed a "due-on-sale clause," effective upon transfer of the leased premises. The Lessee agrees, that upon acquisition of said property, he/she shall pay to _____ any such charges, along with any prepayment penalties and other charges incident to Lessee's acquisition of the property.

16. In the event that proceeds of any new loan not be sufficient to pay in full the remaining balance due the Lessor under this Agreement, the Lessor agrees to accept from the Lessee a promissory note which shall be in the same form as the Lessee's promissory note now attached to and made a part of this Agreement, to be secured by a standard form second mortgage/deed of trust payable to the Lessor under the same terms as contained in the Lessee's original promissory note to the Lessor, described in paragraph four (4) above, with the unpaid balance due no later than _____.

17. Purchase of the leased property by Lessee shall be completed by conveyance of the property and payment by the Lessee of all purchase obligations within _____ days from delivery of notice to exercise the purchase option to the Lessor. In the event that such notice is not delivered to the Lessor prior to _____, the option to purchase granted under this Agreement shall be null and void, the _____ _____ consideration for granting the herein-described option to purchase being non-refundable as set forth in paragraph two (2) above.

18. All obligations of the Lessee under terms of this Agreement shall terminate upon exercise by the Lessee of the option to purchase and completion of transfer of title of said property to the Lessee or his/her assigns.

19. The Lessor agrees, at any time, to sign before a notary public a memorandum of the Lessee's option to purchase the leased property, which the Lessee may have recorded in the official records of _____, provided that such memorandum shall make no reference to this Agreement.

20. The Lessor covenants that the leased premises are clean, safe, sound and healthful, and that there exists no violation of any applicable housing code, and the Lessee accepts said premises as being in clean, safe, sound and healthful condition and Lessee agrees to accept the property in its current condition with no other warranties or representations by the Lessor.

21. The Lessee agrees to surrender said premises to the Lessor at the end of the term of this Agreement in substantially the same or better condition, except for normal wear and tear and acts of God, unless the Lessee shall have exercised his/her option to purchase said property prior to termination of this agreement.

22. The Lessee agrees to comply with all applicable sanitary laws, ordinances and rules and orders of the Board of Health or other authorities affecting cleanliness, occupancy and preservation of the premises during the term of this Agreement.

23. The Lessee agrees to use the leased premises exclusively as a private residence for no more than _____ persons unless permission is obtained in writing from the Lessor.

24. The Lessee agrees to keep the premises in good order and repair and Lessee shall pay the cost of all necessary and prudent repairs and maintenance. Any mechanic's lien against the property as a result of work unpaid for by the Lessee shall be cause for immediate termination of this Agreement.

25. The Lessee shall cause to be made, at the Lessee's expense, all necessary and prudent repairs to heating and air conditioning apparatus, plumbing, electric and gas fixtures and other permanently attached items listed in paragraph forty-seven (47).

26. The Lessee shall not keep or have in or about the leased house, outbuildings or grounds any article or thing of a dangerous, inflammable or explosive nature, which might be pronounced "hazardous" or "extra hazardous" by any responsible insurance company. The Lessee agrees not to use the premises in any manner which would increase risks covered by existing insurance on the premises, or which would increase the rate for insurance on said premises. The Lessee agrees to comply, at the Lessee's expense, with all requirements of the insurers applicable to the leased premises in order to maintain fire and public liability insurance covering the house, outbuildings and grounds.

27. The Lessor agrees to obtain and to maintain in force fire, public liability and extended coverage, plus whatever additional insurance shall be requested in writing by the Lessee, sufficient to protect against loss due to damage by fire of not less than _____, Lessor to obtain and maintain in force public liability insurance in a minimum amount of _____ _____ for each injured person, to a maximum amount of _____ _____ for any single incident. Said insurance shall be subject to inspection of and approval by both Lessor and Lessee and shall provide coverage for the contingent liability of both Lessor and Lessee against any claims or losses, and shall be paid for by the Lessee within thirty (30) days of receipt of a statement therefor from the insurer or insurer's agent. Failure of Lessee to pay for said insurance within thirty (30) days of receipt of a statement therefor, shall be cause for immediate termination of this Agreement.

28. The Lessee agrees to indemnify the Lessor and hold him/her harmless from any and all damage claims, liability or other obligations incident to or arising from any injuries or losses related to Lessee's occupancy or use of the leased premises.

29. The Lessee shall give prompt notice to the Lessor or his/her agent of any dangerous, defective, unsafe or emergency condition in or on the leased premises, said notice being by any suitable means.

30. Lessor covenants that the Lessee and Lessee's family shall have, hold and enjoy the leased premises for the term of this Agreement, subject to the terms and conditions set forth herein.

31. The Lessee covenants that he/she will not commit nor permit a nuisance in or upon the premises, nor shall Lessee maliciously or by reason of gross negligence substantially damage the house, outbuildings or grounds.

32. The Lessee agrees not to sublet or sublease the leased premises without the express, written consent of the Lessor, who will not unreasonably withhold such consent. Unauthorized sublease or sublet of the premises by the Lessee shall be cause for immediate termination of this Agreement.

33. It is the express intent of the Lessor and Lessee that the Lessee shall, within the term of this Agreement, exercise his/her option to purchase the leased property. Therefore, for income tax purposes this Agreement shall be treated by the Lessor and Lessee as though the Lessee had purchased the leased property from the Lessor on _____ _____. Pursuant to the Internal Revenue Code, the Lessee shall be entitled to the benefits of ownership of said property, including:

    A. Interest paid on the mortgage/deed of trust to _____.

    B. Interest paid on the promissory note to the Lessor.

    C. Deduction for operating expenses.

    D. Depreciation of the property and improvements thereto.

The Lessor shall treat all payments of rent made under this Agreement as though a deferred payment installment sale of the property had taken place on _____.

34. The Lessee agrees to pay all utilities, including electricity, gas, water and garbage removal and all other expenses of operating the property.

35. Property taxes on the leased premises for the year ending _____, and insurance acceptable to the Lessor and Lessee as provided for in paragraph twenty-seven (27) above, along with rent and other current expenses of operating the property enumerated in paragraph thirty-three (33) above, shall be prorated as of the commencement of this Agreement.

36. In the event that proceedings of eminent domain result in condemnation of the leased premises which result in the remaining portion of the property being usable for use as a private residence, such proceedings shall not be cause for termination of this Agreement. All compensation awarded to the Lessee as a result of eminent domain proceedings shall be paid to the Lessor to reduce the balance of the Lessee's promissory note to the Lessor, as secured by this **Lease Agreement with Option to Purchase.**

37. In the event that proceedings of eminent domain result in condemnation of the leased premises which results in the property being unusable for use as a private residence, provisions of paragraph two (2) and paragraph eight (8) above shall apply with regard to Lessee's exercise of the option to purchase.

38. Lessor and Lessee agree that all notices given under terms of this Agreement, except for notice of emergency condition as provided for in paragraph twenty-nine (29) above, shall be by United States certified mail, return receipt requested. For purposes of notice under terms of this Agreement, Lessor's address shall be:

_____

Name

_____

Street Address   *City*   *State*   *Zip*

and Lessee's address shall be:

_____

Name

_____

Street Address   *City*   *State*   *Zip*

39. Lessor and Lessee agree that time limits and dates set forth in this Agreement may not be waived or altered without the written consent of both parties.

40. If the Lessee breaches this Agreement the Lessor may reenter the premises immediately and shall have the right to terminate this Agreement after giving the Lessee _____ days written notice of said termination, the reason therefor, and by giving the Lessee an opportunity to correct any breach specified in said notice within _____ _____ days of Lessee's receipt of such notice. The act of reentry by the Lessor shall not constitute termination of this Agreement.

41. After reentry, the Lessor shall have the right to appoint a receiver to take possession of and operate the property, collecting rents therefor. Proceedings by the Lessor for appointment of a receiver, or the appointment of a receiver, shall not constitute termination of this Agreement.

42. The Lessee agrees to vacate the leased premises upon any breach of the terms of this Agreement and receipt of notice of termination of this Agreement therefor, and to relinquish all rights to any right to recover money spent for improvements, appreciation in market value, rents, or payment made in consideration of this Agreement, or any buildup of equity in the premises.

43. The Lessor and Lessee agree that this **Lease Agreement with Option to Purchase** shall have been accepted by both parties when:

A. Both parties have signed both copies of this Agreement, the signatures of each party having been duly witnessed and notarized and

B. Lessor has received from Lessee the sum of _____ _____ , nonrefundable consideration for granting this **Lease Agreement with Option to Purchase** and

C. Lessee has paid to Lessor the sum of _____ _____ for the period from _____ to _____ and

D. The Lessee has paid to the Lessor the following sums for:

1) _____ $ _____

2) _____ $ _____

3) _____ $ _____

4) _____ $ _____

5) _____ $ _____

For a total of: $ _____

44. This Agreement and its conditions, covenants and terms apply to and are binding upon the assigns, heirs, executors and administrators of the Lessor and Lessee.

FORM 69.1/F558

45. This **Lease Agreement with Option to Purchase** constitutes the entire agreement between the parties hereto and no changes shall be made herein except by writing, signed by each party and dated. The failure to enforce any right or remedy hereunder shall not be deemed a waiver by either party of such right or remedy, in the absence of a writing as provided for herein.

46. The Lessor and Lessee agree that this **Lease Agreement with Option to Purchase**, when properly executed, is a binding legal obligation.

47.

(The above space is provided for such additional terms and conditions as may be agreed to by the parties and must be crossed out to the extent that it is not filled in. DO NOT SIGN IF THERE ARE ANY BLANK SPACES. CROSS OUT OR FILL IN ALL BLANK SPACES BEFORE SIGNING.)

IN WITNESS WHEREOF, the parties hereto have executed this Agreement.

_____
Lessor

_____
Witness as to Lessor

_____
Witness as to Lessor

_____
Lessor

_____
Witness as to Lessor

_____
Witness as to Lessor

_____
Lessee

_____
Witness as to Lessee

_____
Witness as to Lessee

_____
Lessee

_____
Witness as to Lessee

_____
Witness as to Lessee

Dated this _____ day of _____, 19 _____.

* *

CERTIFICATE OF NOTARY

STATE OF   )
)   ss:
COUNTY OF   )

On this _____ day of _____, 19 _____, before me personally came and appeared _____
_____, _____, _____ and _____
_____, known, and known to me, to be the individuals described in and who executed the foregoing
instrument, and who duly acknowledged to me that they executed same for the purpose therein contained.

IN WITNESS WHEREOF, I hereunto set my hand and official seal.

_____
Notary Public

My commission expires: _____

Agreement to Purchase Real Estate

I/We, _____, do hereby agree to purchase from _____

_____ the following described real estate located at:

_____

Street Address   *City/Town*   *State*   *Zip*

more particularly described as:

_____

_____

_____

_____

_____

for the sum of _____

($ _____) under the following terms and conditions:

_____

_____

_____

_____

_____

I/We hereby agree to pay to _____ the sum of _____

_____ ($ _____) as earnest money to be
applied toward the purchase of the above-described property. My/Our deposit shall be fully refunded in the event said
purchase cannot be effected under the terms of this Agreement.

_____

_____

Date signed: _____

_____

Witness

ACCEPTANCE

I/We hereby accept the above offer and agree to all conditions and terms therein stated.

_____

_____

Date of acceptance: _____

_____
Witness

Counteroffer

To: _____

    I/We hereby submit the following counteroffer for the sale of real estate located at:

_____
   Street Address   *City/Town*   *State*   *Zip*
more fully described in a written offer from you dated _____.

    I/We hereby agree to sell the above-described property to you under the terms of said offer for the sum of _____
_____ ($ _____).

    This counteroffer shall terminate _____.

                                       _____

                                       _____

Date of counteroffer: _____

ACCEPTANCE

    I/We hereby accept the above counteroffer, and;

    I/We hereby pay the sum of _____ ($ _____)
as earnest money to be applied toward purchase of the above-described property. My/Our deposit shall be fully refunded in
the event said purchase cannot be effected under the contingent terms of my/our original offer.

                                       _____

                                       _____

Date of acceptance: _____

Earnest Money Receipt

_____
Date

Received from _____, the sum of _____

_____ ($ _____), earnest money upon the purchase of real estate

located at:

_____

Street Address   _City/Town_   _State_   _Zip_

more fully described in an agreement between the parties hereto dated _____.

    The above sum is to be refunded fully in the event purchase of said property is not effected under terms of the afore-mentioned agreement.

_____

_____ Personal Check   _____ Cash

_____ Money Order   _____ _____

_____ Cashier's Check

FBI Privacy Act/FOIA Request

Director
Federal Bureau of Investigation
J. Edgar Hoover Building
10th Street and Pennsylvania Avenue, N.W.
Washington, D.C. 20535

Attn: FOIA/Privacy Act Branch

   This is a request under provisions of Title 5 USC, Sec. 552, the Freedom of Information Act, and Title 5 USC, Sec. 552a, the Privacy Act.

   Please furnish me with copies of all records on me retrievable by the use of an individual identifier and by the use of any combination of identifiers (e.g., name + date of birth + social security number, etc.) that are contained in the following systems of records:

   National Crime Information Center (NCIC)
   Central Records System
   Electronic Surveillance (Elsur) Indices

   In order to identify myself and to facilitate your search of records systems, I provide the following information:

Last Name	First	Middle

Street	City	State	Zip

Date of Birth	Place of Birth	Sex	Social Security Number

   In the event that any part or all of my records are withheld, I request a complete list of all records being withheld and the specific exemption being claimed for the withholding of each.

   In the event that search and copying fees are estimated to exceed $_____, I request an opportunity to review such records, or to have a duly authorized representative review such records, in order to select those to be copied.

   If you have any questions regarding this request, please telephone me at _____ weekdays between _____ and _____ or write to me at the above address.

   As provided for by Sec. 552(a)(6)(i) of the Freedom of Information Act, I shall expect to receive a reply within ten (10) business days.

                                                            Sincerely,

FORM 77.1 / F568

CERTIFICATE OF NOTARY

STATE OF   )

)   ss:

COUNTY OF   )

On this _____ day of _____, 19 _____, before me personally came and appeared _____ _____, known, and known to me, to be the individual described in and who executed the foregoing instrument, and who duly acknowledged to me that he/she executed same for the purpose therein contained.

    IN WITNESS WHEREOF, I hereunto set my hand and official seal.

_____
Notary Public

My commission expires: _____

CIA Privacy Act/FOIA Request

Privacy Act/FOIA Coordinator
Central Intelligence Agency
Washington, D.C. 20505

This is a request under provisions of Title 5 USC, Sec. 552, the Freedom of Information Act, and Title 5 USC, Sec. 552a, the Privacy Act.

Please furnish me with copies of all records on me retrievable by the use of an individual identifier and by the use of any combination of identifiers (e.g., name + date of birth + social security number, etc.) that are contained in the following systems of records:

Directorate of Operations Records System
Security Analysis Records
Security Records

In order to identify myself and to facilitate your search of records systems, I provide the following information:

Last Name	*First*	*Middle*

Street	*City*	*State*	*Zip*

Date of Birth	*Place of Birth*	*Sex*	*Social Security Number*

In the event that any part or all of my records are withheld, I request a complete list of all records being withheld and the specific exemption being claimed for the withholding of each.

In the event that search and copying fees are estimated to exceed $_____, I request an opportunity to review such records, or to have a duly authorized representative review such records, in order to select those to be copied.

If you have any questions regarding this request, please telephone me at _____ weekdays between _____ and _____ or write to me at the above address.

As provided for by Sec. 552(a)(6)(i) of the Freedom of Information Act, I shall expect to receive a reply within ten (10) business days.

Sincerely,

FORM 77.2 / F570

CERTIFICATE OF NOTARY

STATE OF   )

)   ss:

COUNTY OF   )

On this _____ day of _____ , 19 _____ , before me personally came and appeared _____ _____ , known, and known to me, to be the individual described in and who executed the foregoing instrument, and who duly acknowledged to me that he/she executed same for the purpose therein contained.

IN WITNESS WHEREOF, I hereunto set my hand and official seal.

_____

Notary Public

My commission expires: _____

Privacy Act/FOIA Request

Attn:

This is a request under provisions of Title 5 USC, Sec. 552, the Freedom of Information Act, and Title 5 USC, Sec. 552a, the Privacy Act.

Please furnish me with copies of all records on me retrievable by the use of an individual identifier and by the use of any combination of identifiers (e.g., name + date of birth + social security number, etc.) that are contained in the following systems of records:

In order to identify myself and to facilitate your search of records systems, I provide the following information:

Last Name	First	Middle
Street	City	State	Zip
Date of Birth	Place of Birth	Sex	Social Security Number

In the event that any part or all of my records are withheld, I request a complete list of all records being withheld and the specific exemption being claimed for the withholding of each.

In the event that search and copying fees are estimated to exceed $ _____, I request an opportunity to review such records, or to have a duly authorized representative review such records, in order to select those to be copied.

If you have any questions regarding this request, please telephone me at _____ weekdays between _____ and _____ or write to me at the above address.

As provided for by Sec. 552(a)(6)(i) of the Freedom of Information Act, I shall expect to receive a reply within ten (10) business days.

Sincerely,

FORM 77.3/F572

CERTIFICATE OF NOTARY

STATE OF   )

)   ss:

COUNTY OF   )

On this _____ day of _____ , 19 _____ , before me personally came and appeared _____ _____ , known, and known to me, to be the individual described in and who executed the foregoing instrument, and who duly acknowledged to me that he/she executed same for the purpose therein contained.

IN WITNESS WHEREOF, I hereunto set my hand and official seal.

_____
Notary Public

My commission expires: _____

Sample Format for Privacy Act
Records Release Appeal

Your Complete Name
Street Address
City and State
Zip Code

Date

Agency Head
Title
Name of Agency
Address
City, State, Zip

Re: Privacy Act/FOIA
     Records Release Appeal

Dear _____:

In the attached request dated _____, I asked that I be provided with copies of all records on me contained in the specified systems of records.

My request for disclosure of those records was (partially) denied by Mr./Ms. _____. A copy of his/her denial is enclosed.

This letter is my appeal of that denial.

As you recall, the Freedom of Information Act, Sec. 552(a)(b), provides that any reasonably segregable portion of a record shall be provided to any person requesting such record after deletion of the portions that are exempt under that section.

Pursuant to the above provision of FOIA, I hereby request copies of all portions of all records on me that are not specifically exempt under FOIA. I also hereby request a complete list of all records withheld, as well as a record-by-record reference to each exemption claimed for the withholding of each record.

As provided for by Sec. 552(a)(6)(A)(ii), I expect to receive your reply within twenty (20) business days of your receipt of this appeal.

Sincerely,

cc: (If appropriate, name and address of attorney with whom you may have discussed this appeal.)

FORM 77.5/F575

Sample Format for Privacy Act
Records Amendment Request

Your Complete Name
Street Address
City and State
Zip Code

Date

Agency Head or
  Designated Official
Title
Name of Agency
Address
City, State, Zip

Re: Privacy Act
     Request for Amendment of Record(s)

Dear _____:

    In the attached request dated _____, I asked that

I be furnished with _____

_____.

    In reviewing the portion(s) of my record(s) that I have noted in red, I

found them/it to be "inaccurate," "untimely," "outdated," "irrelevant to the

purpose of _____(name agency)_____," "incomplete," "prejudicial and

potentially damaging" as follows:

_____

_____

_____

Therefore, pursuant to Title 5 USC, Sec. 552a(d)(2), I hereby request that my record be amended in the following manner:

_____

_____

_____

In accordance with Sec. 552a(d)(2)(A) of the Act, I expect to receive your acknowledgment of this request within ten (10) business days of its receipt.

Thank you for your cooperation in this matter.

Sincerely,

cc: (If appropriate, name and address of attorney with whom you may have discussed this request.)

Sample Format for Privacy Act
Records Amendment Appeal

Your Complete Name
Street Address
City and State
Zip Code

Date

Agency Head or
   Designated Appeal Officer
Title
Name of Agency
Address
City, State, Zip

Re: Privacy Act
     Records Amendment Appeal

Dear _____:

 In the attached letter to Mr./Ms. _____,

dated _____, I asked that certain "inaccurate,"

"untimely," "outdated," "irrelevant to the purpose of _____(name agency)_____,"

"incomplete," "prejudicial and potentially damaging" information in my record

be amended.

 My amendment request was denied by Mr./Ms. _____,

and I am, pursuant to Sec. 552a(d)(3) of the Act, appealing that denial.

 I trust that upon consideration of the facts, and of the potential for

damage to me, that you will approve this appeal for corrective amendment of

my record.

It will be necessary for me to initiate legal action in the event this appeal for amendment of my record(s) is denied.

Thank you for your cooperation in this matter.

                    Sincerely,

cc: (If appropriate, name and address of attorney with whom you have spoken regarding this appeal.)

Model Format for Privacy Act Lawsuit
to Effect Amendment of Records

UNITED STATES DISTRICT COURT
FOR THE _____ DISTRICT OF _____

YOUR COMPLETE NAME)
)
Street Address)
City, State, Zip)
)
          Plaintiff)
)
           vs.)

)   Civil Action No. _____
NAME OF AGENCY)   (No. to be obtained from clerk of court)
(Having your records))
)
Street Address of Agency)   **Complaint for Declaratory**
City, State, Zip)   **and Injunctive Relief**
)
NAME OF HEAD OF AGENCY)
Title)
)
Street Address of Agency Headquarters)
City, State, Zip)
)
         Defendants)

(Here describe the related records and specific inaccuracies and list specific corrections that you desire to be made.)

Freedom of Information Act Request

Dated:

This is a request under provisions of Title 5 USC, Sec. 552(a), the Freedom of Information Act.

This is your authorization to furnish the above information without further notification if search and copying costs are estimated not to exceed $_____.

Please forward the requested information to:

In the event that any part or all of the requested information is withheld, I request a complete list of all records withheld and the specific exemption(s) being claimed for the withholding of each.

If you have any questions regarding this request, please telephone me at _____ weekdays between _____ and _____ or write to me at the above address.

As provided for by Sec. 552(a) (6) (i) of the Act, I shall expect to receive a reply within ten (10) business days of your receipt of this request.

Sincerely,

cc: (*If appropriate, name and address of any attorney with whom you may have discussed this request.*)

Sample Format for FOIA
Records Release Appeal

Your Complete Name
Street Address
City and State
Zip Code

Date

Agency Head or
  Designated Appeal Officer
Title
Name of Agency
Street Address
City, State, Zip

Re: FOIA Appeal

Dear _____:

In the attached request dated _____, I asked

that I be provided with information specified in my request. My request for

that information was (partially) denied by Mr./Ms. _____.

A copy of his/her denial dated _____ is enclosed.

This letter is my appeal, pursuant to subsection (a)(6) of the Freedom

of Information Act, of that denial.

As you recall, the Freedom of Information Act, Sec. 552(a)(b), provides

that any reasonably segregable portion of a record shall be provided to any

person requesting such record after deletion of the portions that are exempt

under that subsection.

Pursuant to the above provision of FOIA, I hereby request copies of all portions of all requested records that are not specifically exempt under FOIA. I also hereby request a complete list of all records withheld, as well as a record-by-record reference to each exemption claimed for the withholding of each record.

As provided for by Sec. 552(a)(6)(A)(ii) of the Act, I expect to receive your reply within twenty (20) business days of your receipt of this appeal.

It will be necessary for me to initiate legal action in the event this appeal is denied.

Sincerely,

cc: (If appropriate, name and address of attorney with whom you may have discussed this appeal.)

Model Format for FOIA Lawsuit
to Effect Release of Records

UNITED STATES DISTRICT COURT
FOR THE _____ DISTRICT OF _____

YOUR COMPLETE NAME	)
	)
Street Address	)
City, State, Zip	)
	)
Plaintiff	)
	)
vs.	)
	)
	)
NAME OF AGENCY	)
(Having requested information)	)
	)
Street Address	)
City, State Zip	)
	)
	)
NAME OF HEAD OF AGENCY	)
Title	)
	)
Street Address of Agency	)
City, State, Zip	)
	)
Defendants	)

Civil Action No. _____

**Complaint for Declaratory
and Injunctive Relief**

JURISDICTION

1. This is an action under the Freedom of Information Act, Title 5 U.S.C., Sec. 552, to order the defendant to produce certain records for inspection and copying, viz., _____

_____
(here list information or records as specified in your initial request as well as

_____
any records listed by the agency in response to your appeal)

(hereinafter called the requested records).

2. The court has jurisdiction over this action pursuant to Title 5 U.S.C., Sec. 552(a) (4); Title 28 U.S.C., Sec. 1361; and the First and Fifth Amendments.

PARTIES

3. Plaintiff is _____

_____
(here describe who you are and why you want/need the requested information) .

4. Defendant is _____*(here name the agency)*_____, an agency of the Executive Branch which has custody and control of the requested records; Defendant is _____*(here name head of agency plus his/her title)*_____; he/she is sued in his/her official capacity as custodian of the requested records, and as head of the agency wherein the requested records are located.

CAUSE OF ACTION

5. By request dated _____, addressed to _____, a copy of which is attached hereto as Exhibit A, Plaintiff requested access to the requested record(s).

6. By letter dated _____, a copy of which is attached hereto as Exhibit B, the Plaintiff's request was (in part) denied.

7. By letter dated _____, addressed to _____, a copy of which is attached hereto as Exhibit C, Plaintiff appealed the initial denial of his/her request.

8. By letter dated _____, a copy of which is attached hereto as Exhibit D, the Plaintiff's administrative appeal was denied.

9. The plaintiff has exhausted his/her administrative remedies.

10. Plaintiff is entitled, pursuant to Title 5 U.S.C., Sec. 552(a), to inspect and copy the requested records.

WHEREFORE, Plaintiff prays (1) that the Court order defendants to produce the requested records to him/her for inspection and copying, (2) that this Court award Plaintiff his/her costs and disbursements in this action pursuant to Title 5 U.S.C., Sec. 552(a) (4) (e), (3) that this Court grant such other and further relief as the Court shall deem just and proper, and (4) provide for expedition of proceedings on this complaint pursuant to Title 5 U.S.C., Sec. 552(a) (4) (C) (D).

Dated: _____

  City   State

_____

               Date

(Signed) _____

                    Plaintiff or Attorney for Plaintiff

                    _____

                    Street Address

                    _____

                    City   State   Zip

Date:

Direct Mail Marketing Association
6 East 43rd Street
New York, N.Y. 10017

Attn: Mail Preference Service

Please list my name (as shown below) in your NAME REMOVAL FILE so that members may REMOVE my name from their mailing lists at the earliest possible date:

_____

_____

_____

_____

My name is furnished herein for the sole purpose of its removal from mailing lists and its use for any other purpose is not authorized.

Thank you for your attention to this matter.

Very truly yours,

Date:

To:

Dear Sirs:

Please remove my name as shown below from your mailing lists at the earliest possible date:

_____

_____

_____

_____

Thank you for your prompt attention to this matter.

Very truly yours,

Notices Not to Add Name to Mailing List

PLEASE TAKE NOTICE

My name and address as included in the attached order are provided solely for use in fulfillment of said order and use of my name for any other purpose is not authorized.

_____

PLEASE TAKE NOTICE

My name and address as included in the attached order are provided solely for use in fulfillment of said order and use of my name for any other purpose is not authorized.

_____

PLEASE TAKE NOTICE

My name and address as included in the attached order are provided solely for use in fulfillment of said order and use of my name for any other purpose is not authorized.

_____

PLEASE TAKE NOTICE

My name and address as included in the attached order are provided solely for use in fulfillment of said order and use of my name for any other purpose is not authorized.

_____

PLEASE TAKE NOTICE

My name and address as included in the attached order are provided solely for use in fulfillment of said order and use of my name for any other purpose is not authorized.

_____

PLEASE TAKE NOTICE

My name and address as included in the attached order are provided solely for use in fulfillment of said order and use of my name for any other purpose is not authorized.

_____

PLEASE TAKE NOTICE

My name and address as included in the attached order are provided solely for use in fulfillment of said order and use of my name for any other purpose is not authorized.

_____

PLEASE TAKE NOTICE

My name and address as included in the attached order are provided solely for use in fulfillment of said order and use of my name for any other purpose is not authorized.

_____

Date:

Direct Mail Marketing Association
6 East 43rd Street
New York, N.Y. 10017

Attn: Mail Preference Service

I would like to receive more direct mail advertising material on the

subjects that I have checked below:

____	Autos, parts & accessories	____	Insurance
____	Books	____	Magazines
____	Charitable Organizations	____	Plants & Flowers
____	Civic Organizations	____	Photography
____	Clothing	____	Records & Tapes
____	Cooking	____	Sewing & Needlework
____	Foods	____	Sports & Camping
____	Gifts	____	Stamps & Coins
____	Grocery Bargains	____	Stocks & Bonds
____	Health Foods	____	Tools & Equipment
____	Home Furnishings	____	Travel
		____	Office Furniture & Supplies

The requested advertising material should be addressed as follows:

_____

_____

_____

_____

Thank you for your attention to this matter.

Very truly yours,

Uniform Donor Cards

In the hope that I may help others, I hereby make this anatomical gift, if medically acceptable, to take effect upon my death. The words and marks below indicate my desires.

I give: (a) ☐ my body for anatomical study if needed
(b) ☐ any needed organs or parts
(c) ☐ only the following organs or parts

_____

Specify which organ(s) or part(s) for the purposes of transplantation, therapy, medical research or education.

_____
LIMITATIONS OR SPECIAL WISHES, IF ANY

Signed by the Donor and the following two witnesses in the presence of each other:

_____
Signature of Donor   *Donor's Birthplace*

_____
City and State Where Signed   *Date Signed*

_____
Witness   *Witness*

THIS IS A LEGAL DOCUMENT UNDER THE UNIFORM ANATOMICAL GIFT ACT OR SIMILAR LAWS

In the hope that I may help others, I hereby make this anatomical gift, if medically acceptable, to take effect upon my death. The words and marks below indicate my desires.

I give: (a) ☐ my body for anatomical study if needed
(b) ☐ any needed organs or parts
(c) ☐ only the following organs or parts

_____

Specify which organ(s) or part(s) for the purposes of transplantation, therapy, medical research or education.

_____
LIMITATIONS OR SPECIAL WISHES, IF ANY

Signed by the Donor and the following two witnesses in the presence of each other:

_____
Signature of Donor   *Donor's Birthplace*

_____
City and State Where Signed   *Date Signed*

_____
Witness   *Witness*

THIS IS A LEGAL DOCUMENT UNDER THE UNIFORM ANATOMICAL GIFT ACT OR SIMILAR LAWS

In the hope that I may help others, I hereby make this anatomical gift, if medically acceptable, to take effect upon my death. The words and marks below indicate my desires.

I give: (a) ☐ my body for anatomical study if needed
(b) ☐ any needed organs or parts
(c) ☐ only the following organs or parts

_____

Specify which organ(s) or part(s) for the purposes of transplantation, therapy, medical research or education.

_____
LIMITATIONS OR SPECIAL WISHES, IF ANY

Signed by the Donor and the following two witnesses in the presence of each other:

_____
Signature of Donor   *Donor's Birthplace*

_____
City and State Where Signed   *Date Signed*

_____
Witness   *Witness*

THIS IS A LEGAL DOCUMENT UNDER THE UNIFORM ANATOMICAL GIFT ACT OR SIMILAR LAWS

In the hope that I may help others, I hereby make this anatomical gift, if medically acceptable, to take effect upon my death. The words and marks below indicate my desires.

I give: (a) ☐ my body for anatomical study if needed
(b) ☐ any needed organs or parts
(c) ☐ only the following organs or parts

_____

Specify which organ(s) or part(s) for the purposes of transplantation, therapy, medical research or education.

_____
LIMITATIONS OR SPECIAL WISHES, IF ANY

Signed by the Donor and the following two witnesses in the presence of each other:

_____
Signature of Donor   *Donor's Birthplace*

_____
City and State Where Signed   *Date Signed*

_____
Witness   *Witness*

THIS IS A LEGAL DOCUMENT UNDER THE UNIFORM ANATOMICAL GIFT ACT OR SIMILAR LAWS

Uniform Donor Cards (Reverse)

Emergency Medical
Uniform Donor Card

_____
Donor's Name

_____
Social Security Number

_____
Name of Next of Kin

_____
Kin's Street Address

_____
City   *State*   *Zip*

_____
Area Code/Telephone Number

THIS IS A LEGAL DOCUMENT UNDER THE UNIFORM ANATOMICAL GIFT ACT OR SIMILAR LAWS

Emergency Medical
Uniform Donor Card

_____
Donor's Name

_____
Social Security Number

_____
Name of Next of Kin

_____
Kin's Street Address

_____
City   *State*   *Zip*

_____
Area Code/Telephone Number

THIS IS A LEGAL DOCUMENT UNDER THE UNIFORM ANATOMICAL GIFT ACT OR SIMILAR LAWS

Emergency Medical
Uniform Donor Card

_____
Donor's Name

_____
Social Security Number

_____
Name of Next of Kin

_____
Kin's Street Address

_____
City   *State*   *Zip*

_____
Area Code/Telephone Number

THIS IS A LEGAL DOCUMENT UNDER THE UNIFORM ANATOMICAL GIFT ACT OR SIMILAR LAWS

Emergency Medical
Uniform Donor Card

_____
Donor's Name

_____
Social Security Number

_____
Name of Next of Kin

_____
Kin's Street Address

_____
City   *State*   *Zip*

_____
Area Code/Telephone Number

THIS IS A LEGAL DOCUMENT UNDER THE UNIFORM ANATOMICAL GIFT ACT OR SIMILAR LAWS

Special Medical Power of Attorney

I, _____, of

_____,
Street Address   Apt. No.   City   State   Zip

do hereby constitute and appoint _____, of

_____,
Street Address   Apt. No.   City   State   Zip

as my Attorney-in-Fact to act as follows; giving and granting to my said Attorney-in-Fact full power to:

AUTHORIZE AND EXECUTE CONSENT FOR ANY AND ALL MEDICAL AND HOSPITAL CARE AND TREATMENT, INCLUDING MAJOR SURGERY, DEEMED NECESSARY BY A DULY LICENSED PHYSICIAN SELECTED BY MY ATTORNEY-IN-FACT FOR THE HEALTH AND WELL-BEING OF MY FOLLOWING NAMED CHILD(REN):

_____

_____

_____

_____

_____

FURTHER, I hereby authorize my aforesaid Attorney-in-Fact to perform all necessary acts in the execution of the aforesaid authorization with the same validity and right as I could effect if personally present. Any act or thing lawfully done hereunder by my said Attorney-in-Fact shall be binding upon me and my heirs, administrators, executors, successors and assigns.

FURTHER, I hereby agree to hold harmless my said Attorney-in-Fact from any liability, claims, charges or costs related to his/her execution of the aforesaid authorization.

FURTHER, unless sooner revoked by me, this **Special Medical Power of Attorney** shall become NULL and VOID from and after the _____ day of _____, 19 _____.

IN WITNESS WHEREOF, I have hereunto set my hand and seal this _____ day of _____, 19 _____.

(Signed) _____

* *

CERTIFICATE OF NOTARY

STATE OF _____)
) ss:
COUNTY OF _____)

On this _____ day of _____, 19 _____, before me personally came and appeared _____, known, and known to me, to be the individual described in and who executed the foregoing instrument, and who duly acknowledged to me that he/she executed same for the purpose therein contained.

IN WITNESS WHEREOF, I hereunto set my hand and official seal.

_____
Notary Public

My commission expires: _____

Medical Power of Attorney

To

19 ___

Dated ___

Emergency Names and Numbers

Fire .... _____

Police .... _____

Sheriff .... _____

Ambulance .... _____

Dr. _____ (*Physician*) .... Office _____
Home _____

Dr. _____ (*Physician*) .... Office _____
Home _____

Mother's Work No. .... _____

Father's Work No. .... _____

_____ (*Neighbor*) .... _____

_____ (*Neighbor*) .... _____

_____ (*Building Superintendent*) .... _____

CHILDRENS' BLOOD TYPES

_____ ____ _____ ____

_____ ____ _____ ____

_____ ____ _____ ____

WHERE I CAN BE REACHED NOW

_____ _____
Name *Phone*

_____
Address

SPECIAL INSTRUCTIONS

_____

_____

_____

_____

Auto/Truck Rental Agreement

THIS AGREEMENT is made this _____ day of _____, 19 _____, between

_____, of

Street Address	*City*	*State*	*Zip*

hereinafter called "Owner," and _____, of

Street Address	*City*	*State*	*Zip*

hereinafter called "Renter."

Vehicle

The vehicle which the Owner hereby agrees to rent is:

Year	*Make*	*Model*

Serial No.	*License No.*	*State*	*Year*

Mileage at termination of rental period: _____

Mileage at beginning of rental period: _____

Total miles driven: _____

Condition of Vehicle as Determined by Renter
*(Renter to Initial Each Item as **OK** or **Not OK**)*

OK	Not OK		OK	Not OK	
_____	_____	Tires	_____	_____	Wipers
_____	_____	Headlights	_____	_____	Exterior Mirror
_____	_____	Taillights	_____	_____	Rearview Mirror
_____	_____	Stop Lights	_____	_____	Seat Belts
_____	_____	Turn Indicators	_____	_____	Steering
_____	_____	Brakes	_____	_____	Horn
_____	_____	Parking Brake	_____	_____	

The Owner represents that to the best of his/her knowledge and belief that said vehicle is in sound and safe condition and free of any known faults or defects which would affect its safe operation under normal use.

Rental Period

The Owner agrees to rent the above-described vehicle to the Renter for a period of _____ beginning at _____.M. on _____ and ending at _____.M. on _____.

Use of Vehicle

_____

_____

_____

_____

_____

The Renter further agrees (A) that the rented vehicle shall not be used to carry passengers or property for hire; (B) that the rented vehicle shall not be used to carry passengers other than in the interior or cab of the vehicle; (C) that the rented vehicle shall not be used to carry passengers in excess of the capacity thereof; (D) not to use the vehicle to push, propel or tow another vehicle, trailer or any other thing without the written permission of the owner; (E) not to use the vehicle for any race or competition; (F) not to use the vehicle for any illegal purpose; (G) not to operate the vehicle in a negligent manner; (H) not to permit the vehicle to be operated by any other person without the written permission of the owner; and (I) not to carry passengers, property or materials in excess of the rated weight carrying capacity of the vehicle.

Insurance

The Renter hereby agrees that he/she shall fully indemnify the Owner for any and all loss of or damage to the vehicle or equipment during the term of this Agreement whether caused by collision, fire, flood, vandalism, theft or any other cause, except that which shall be determined to be caused by a fault or defect of the vehicle or equipment.

Rental Rate

The Renter hereby agrees to pay the Owner at the rate of $_____ per _____ for the use of said vehicle, plus the sum of _____ per mile for each mile driven during the term of this Agreement. All fuel used shall be paid for by the Renter.

Deposit

The Renter further agrees to make a deposit of $_____ with the Owner, said deposit to be used, in the event of loss of or damage to the vehicle or equipment during the term of this Agreement, to defray fully or partially the cost of necessary repairs or replacement. In the absence of damage or loss, said deposit shall be credited toward payment of the rental fee and any excess shall be returned to the Renter.

Return of Vehicle to Owner

The Renter hereby agrees to return said vehicle to the Owner at _____
_____ no later than _____.

Termination of Agreement

It is mutually agreed that the Renter shall have the right to terminate this Agreement at any time by payment for all miles driven and all fuel used, plus one full day's rental for each 24-hour period or any part thereof, during which the Renter has retained possession of the vehicle during the term of this Agreement.

IN WITNESS WHEREOF, the parties hereto hereby execute this Agreement.

(Signed) _____
Renter

(Signed) _____
Owner

Boat Rental Agreement

THIS AGREEMENT is made this _____ day of _____, 19 _____, between

_____, of

| Street Address | City | State | Zip |

hereinafter called "Owner," and _____, of

| Street Address | City | State | Zip |

hereinafter called "Renter."

Boat

The boat which the Owner agrees to rent is:

Year	Make	Model
Length	Capacity (Persons)	Capacity (Weight)

Motor	Make	Horsepower	Serial No.

| State or Other License No. | Year |

The Owner represents that to the best of his/her knowledge and belief that said boat (and motor, if any) is free from any known faults or deficiencies which would affect safe and reliable operation under normal and prudent usage.

The Owner further represents that all required lifesaving and safety equipment are aboard the boat and in good order and condition at the time of delivery to the Renter.

Rental Period

The Owner agrees to rent the above-described boat (and motor) to the Renter for a period of _____ beginning at _____.M. on _____ and ending at _____.M. on _____.

Use of Boat

_____

_____

_____

_____

_____

The Renter further agrees (A) that the rented boat shall not be used to carry passengers or property for hire; (B) that the rented boat shall not be used to carry passengers or property in excess of the rated capacity of the boat; (C) not to use the boat (or motor) for water skiing; (D) not to use the boat to tow or propel any other boat, barge or thing without the owner's written permission; (E) not to use the boat (or motor) in any race or competition; (F) not to use the boat (or motor) for any illegal purpose; (G) not to operate the boat (or motor) in a negligent manner; (H) not to operate the boat (or motor) outside the area of use designated in this Agreement; (I) not to permit the boat (or motor) to be operated by any other person without written permission of the Owner; and (J) not to remove the motor from the boat for any use whatsoever.

Area of Operation

The Renter agrees to operate the boat (and motor) only within the following area(s):

_____

_____

_____

Insurance

The Renter hereby agrees that he/she shall fully indemnify the Owner for any and all damage to or loss of the boat, motor or equipment during the term of this Agreement whether caused by collision, grounding, fire, theft, sinking, vandalism or any other cause, except that which shall be determined to be caused by a fault or deficiency of the boat, motor or equipment.

Rental Rate

The Renter hereby agrees to pay the Owner at the rate of $ _____ per _____ for the use of said boat (and motor). All fuel used shall be paid for by the Renter.

Deposit

The Renter further agrees to make a deposit of $_____ with the Owner, said deposit to be used, in the event of loss of or damage to the boat, motor or equipment during the term of this Agreement, to defray fully or partially the cost of necessary repairs or replacement. In the absence of damage or loss, said deposit shall be credited toward payment of the rental fee and any excess shall be returned to the Renter.

Return of Boat, Motor and Equipment to Owner

The Renter hereby agrees to return the boat, motor and equipment to the Owner at _____
_____ _____ no later than _____.

Termination of Agreement

It is mutually agreed that the Renter shall have the right to terminate this Agreement at any time by payment for all fuel used, plus one full day's rental for each 24-hour period or any part thereof, during which the Renter has retained possession of the boat (and motor) during the term of this Agreement.

Trailer

This Agreement shall include rental of the Owner's boat trailer for transportation of the rented boat/motor/equipment during the term of this Agreement, and such use shall be subject to the general conditions and limitations of this Agreement.

IN WITNESS WHEREOF, the parties hereto hereby execute this Agreement.

(Signed) _____
Renter

(Signed) _____
Owner

"Open" Rental Agreement

THIS AGREEMENT is made this _____ day of _____, 19 _____, between

_____, of

_____,

Street Address   *City*   *State*   *Zip*

hereinafter called "Owner," and _____, of

_____,

Street Address   *City*   *State*   *Zip*

hereinafter called "Renter."

Property

_____

_____

_____

_____

_____

_____

Year   *Make*   *Model/Type*

_____

Capacity   *Horsepower*   *Serial No.*

The Owner warrants that to the best of his/her knowledge and belief that the aforesaid property is free of any known faults or deficiencies which would affect its safe and dependable operation under normal and prudent usage.

Rental Period

The Owner agrees to rent the above-described property to the Renter for a period of _____ beginning _____ and ending _____.

Use of Property

_____

_____

_____

_____

_____

The Renter further agrees that the rented property (A) shall not be used beyond any rated capacity; (B) shall not be used for any illegal purpose; (C) shall not be used in any manner for which it was not designed, built or designated by the manufacturer; (D) will not be used in a negligent manner; (E) will not be operated by any other person without the written permission of the Owner; and (F) will not be removed from the designated area of use or operation.

Area of Use or Operation

The Renter agrees to operate/use the above-described property only at the following location or within the following described area(s):

_____

_____

_____

Insurance

The Renter hereby agrees that he/she shall fully indemnify the Owner for any and all damage to or loss of the rented property and any accessories or related equipment during the term of this Agreement whether caused by fire, theft, flood, vandalism or any other cause, except that which shall be determined to have been caused by a fault or deficiency of the rented property, accessories or equipment.

Rental Rate

The Renter hereby agrees to pay the Owner at the rate of $_____ per _____ for the use of said property and any accessories/equipment. Any fuel used shall be paid for by the Renter.

Deposit

The Renter further agrees to make a deposit of $_____ with the Owner, said deposit to be used, in the event of loss of or damage to the rented property and any accessories/equipment during the term of this Agreement, to defray fully or partially the cost of necessary repairs or replacement. In the absence of any damage or loss, said deposit shall be credited toward payment of the rental fee and any excess shall be returned to the Renter.

Return of Property to Owner

The Renter hereby agrees to return the rented property and any accessories/equipment to the Owner at _____ _____ no later than _____.

Termination of Agreement

It is mutually agreed that the Renter shall have the right to terminate this Agreement at any time by payment of one full day's rental for each 24-hour period or any part thereof, during which the Renter has retained possession of the property and any accessories/equipment during the term of this Agreement.

IN WITNESS WHEREOF, the parties hereto hereby execute this Agreement.

(Signed) _____
Renter

(Signed) _____
Owner

Rent Receipt

Date: _____

To:

Received from _____ the sum of $_____ , rent

for the period of _____ for _____

_____ .

By _____

_____ *Owner*   _____ *Manager*

_____

_____

Phone: _____

Notice of Rent Due

Date: _____

To:

Your rent is now due in the sum of $ _____ for the period of _____
_____.

If this matter has been overlooked, please remit promptly to:

_____

_____

_____

By _____
　　　____ Owner　　____ Manager

_____

_____

Phone: _____

Notice of Overdue Rent

Date: _____

To:

Rent in the amount of $ _____ was due on _____ for the period of _____ for _____ _____. Please bring your payment to the address shown below or telephone us immediately. Please disregard this notice if you have already sent us your remittance.

By _____
_____ *Owner* _____ *Manager*

_____

_____

Phone: _____

Notice of Overdue Rent

Date: _____

To: _____

Rent in the amount of $ _____ was due on _____ for the period
of _____ for _____

Please bring payment to the address shown below, or call the phone number listed. If
you have already paid this amount, you have already so that your confirmation.

By _____ Signature _____

_____

Phone _____

Notice to Quit Premises

Date: _____

To:

You are required within _____ days after service of this Notice to pay all delinquent rent (in the sum of $_____) on the premises described above, or the undersigned will initiate legal proceedings to recover possession.

The undersigned hereby declares a forfeiture of the lease or rental agreement under which you hold the herein-described premises if you do not remit the full amount of rent due as shown above by _____.

By _____
_____ *Owner*   _____ *Manager*

_____

_____

Phone: _____

Date: _____

Furnishings Inspection and Inventory

Room/Item	Condition In	Condition Out	Room/Item	Condition In	Condition Out
LIVING ROOM			**KITCHEN**		
Carpeting	_____	_____	Floor	_____	_____
Floor	_____	_____	Walls	_____	_____
Walls	_____	_____	Curtains	_____	_____
Drapes	_____	_____	Fixtures	_____	_____
Fixtures	_____	_____	Sink	_____	_____
Windows	_____	_____	Cabinets	_____	_____
_____	_____	_____	Windows	_____	_____
_____	_____	_____	_____	_____	_____
_____	_____	_____	_____	_____	_____
DINING ROOM			**KITCHEN APPLIANCES**		
Carpeting	_____	_____	Refrigerator	_____	_____
Floor	_____	_____	Freezer	_____	_____
Walls	_____	_____	Dishwasher	_____	_____
Drapes	_____	_____	Disposer	_____	_____
Fixtures	_____	_____	Stove	_____	_____
Windows	_____	_____	Oven	_____	_____
_____	_____	_____	_____	_____	_____
_____	_____	_____	_____	_____	_____
_____	_____	_____	_____	_____	_____

Furnishings Inspection and Inventory

Room/Item	Condition In	Condition Out	Room/Item	Condition In	Condition Out
BATHROOM #1			**BEDROOM #1**		
Floor	_____	_____	Carpeting	_____	_____
Walls	_____	_____	Floor	_____	_____
Curtains	_____	_____	Walls	_____	_____
Fixtures	_____	_____	Drapes	_____	_____
Cabinet	_____	_____	Fixtures	_____	_____
Heater	_____	_____	Windows	_____	_____
Ceiling Fan	_____	_____	_____	_____	_____
Mirror	_____	_____	_____	_____	_____
Tub	_____	_____	_____	_____	_____
Enclosure	_____	_____	_____	_____	_____
Toilet	_____	_____	_____	_____	_____
Sink	_____	_____	**BEDROOM #2**		
Windows	_____	_____	Carpeting	_____	_____
_____	_____	_____	Floor	_____	_____
OTHER ROOM			Walls	_____	_____
Carpeting	_____	_____	Drapes	_____	_____
Floor	_____	_____	Fixtures	_____	_____
Walls	_____	_____	Windows	_____	_____
Drapes	_____	_____	_____	_____	_____
Fixtures	_____	_____	_____	_____	_____
Windows	_____	_____			
_____	_____	_____	_____	_____	_____
_____	_____	_____	_____	_____	_____

Furnishings Inspection and Inventory

Room/Item	Condition In	Condition Out	Room/Item	Condition In	Condition Out
BEDROOM #3			**BATHROOM #2**		
Carpeting	_____	_____	Floor	_____	_____
Floor	_____	_____	Walls	_____	_____
Walls	_____	_____	Curtains	_____	_____
Drapes	_____	_____	Fixtures	_____	_____
Fixtures	_____	_____	Cabinet	_____	_____
Windows	_____	_____	Heater	_____	_____
_____	_____	_____	Ceiling Fan	_____	_____
_____	_____	_____	Mirror	_____	_____
_____	_____	_____	Tub	_____	_____
_____	_____	_____	Enclosure	_____	_____
_____	_____	_____	Toilet	_____	_____
APPLIANCES			Sink	_____	_____
Washer	_____	_____	Windows	_____	_____
Dryer	_____	_____	_____	_____	_____
Vacuum	_____	_____	_____	_____	_____
Freezer	_____	_____			
Central Air Conditioning	_____	_____	**GARAGE**		
Heating Unit	_____	_____	Door	_____	_____
Room Air Conditioner	_____	_____	Fixtures	_____	_____
Room Air Conditioner	_____	_____	**YARD/GROUNDS**		
Room Air Conditioner	_____	_____	Fence	_____	_____
_____	_____	_____	Shrubs	_____	_____
_____	_____	_____	Trees	_____	_____
			_____	_____	_____

Property Management Agreement

STATE OF   )
)   ss:

COUNTY OF   )

KNOW YE ALL MEN BY THESE PRESENTS,

That _____, of

_____,

    Street Address   *City*   *State*   *Zip*

hereinafter called "Owner," and _____, of

_____,

    Street Address   *City*   *State*   *Zip*

hereinafter called "Manager," do hereby agree as follows:

The Owner hereby employs the services of the Manager to manage, operate, control, rent and lease the following property:

_____

_____

_____

_____

Responsibilities of Manager

The Owner hereby appoints the Manager as his/her lawful agent and attorney-in-fact with full authority to do any and all lawful things necessary for the fulfillment of this Agreement, including the following:

1. To collect all rents due and as they become due, giving receipts therefore; to render to the Owner a monthly accounting of rents received and expenses paid out; and to remit to the Owner all income, less any sums paid out.
2. To make or cause to be made all decorating, maintenance, alterations and repairs to said property and to hire and supervise all employees and other labor for the accomplishment of same.
3. To advertise the property and display signs thereon; to rent and lease the property; to sign, renew and cancel rental agreements and leases for the property or any part thereof; to sue and recover for rent and for loss of or damage to any part of the property and/or furnishings thereof; and, when expedient, to compromise, settle and release any such legal proceedings or lawsuits.

Liability of Manager

The Owner hereby agrees to hold the Manager harmless from any and all claims, charges, debts, demands and lawsuits, including attorney's fees related to his/her management of the herein-described property, and from any liability for injury on or about the property which may be suffered by any employee, tenant or guest upon the property.

Compensation of Manager

The Owner agrees to compensate the Manager as follows:

_____

_____

_____

_____

_____

Sale of Property

In the event the herein-described property or any part thereof is sold during the initial term of this Agreement, the Owner agrees to pay the Manager a commission of _____ percent of the gross sales price of the property.

Term of Agreement

The term of this Agreement shall commence on the _____ day of _____, 19 _____, and end on the _____ day of _____, 19 _____.

Upon expiration of the above initial term, this Agreement shall automatically be renewed and extended for a like period of time unless terminated in writing by either party 30 days prior to the date for such renewal.

This Agreement may also be terminated by mutual agreement of the parties at any time upon payment to the Manager of all fees, commissions and expenses due the Manager under terms of this Agreement.

Extent of Agreement

This document represents the entire Agreement between the parties hereto.

This Agreement shall be binding upon the heirs, administrators, executors, successors and assigns of the Owner.

Dated this _____ day of _____, 19 _____.

By _____
Owner

By _____
Manager

𝔓𝔯𝔬𝔭𝔢𝔯𝔱𝔶 𝔐𝔞𝔫𝔞𝔤𝔢𝔪𝔢𝔫𝔱 𝔄𝔤𝔯𝔢𝔢𝔪𝔢𝔫𝔱

Dated _____ 19 _____

Employment Application

Date: _____

Position Applied For: _____

PERSONAL INFORMATION

Last Name	*First*	*Middle*	*Home Phone*	*Other Phone*

Present Street Address	*Apt. No.*	*City*	*State*	*Zip*

1. Are you between the ages of 18 and 70? _____

2. Are you a U.S. citizen (or have legal right to work and remain in the U.S.)? _____

3. Have you ever been *convicted* of any crime other than traffic violations? _____

SEEKING

_____ Full Time	_____ Day Shift	_____ Immediate
_____ Part Time	_____ Evening Shift	_____ _____
_____ Temporary	_____ Night Shift	_____ _____

Salary desired: $ _____ per _____

Available beginning: _____

EDUCATION

Grammar School

Name _____

Location _____
        City   *State*

From _____ To _____ Graduate? _____

High School

Name _____

Location _____
        City   *State*

Best Subjects _____ Grade Average _____

From _____ To _____ Graduate? _____

Last Name

First

Middle

Trade/Vocational School

Name _____

Location _____
   City   *State*

Subjects _____ Grade Average _____

From _____ To _____ Graduate? _____

College

Name _____

Location _____
   City   *State*

Major _____ Grade Average _____

From _____ To _____ Graduate? _____

Other Education

Name _____

Location _____
   City   *State*

Subjects _____ Grade Average _____

From _____ To _____ Graduate? _____

Indicate areas of academic interest plus any school activities which you believe would be relevant to the employment you are seeking with us. (*Exclude organizations or activities the name of which would indicate race, creed, color or national origin.*)

_____

_____

_____

_____

MILITARY SERVICE

Indicate any military service or training which you believe would be relevant to the employment you are seeking with us:

_____

_____

_____

_____

PREVIOUS EMPLOYMENT

(List Most Recent Employment First)

Dates of Employment	Name and Address of Employer	Salary
_____ *From*	_____	$ _____
_____ *To*	_____	per
	_____	_____

Duties _____

_____

_____

_____

Supervisor _____ Telephone _____

Reason for Leaving _____

Dates of Employment	Name and Address of Employer	Salary
_____ *From*	_____	$ _____
_____ *To*	_____	per
	_____	_____

Duties _____

_____

_____

_____

Supervisor _____ Telephone _____

Reason for Leaving _____

Dates of Employment	Name and Address of Employer	Salary
_____ *From*	_____	$ _____
_____ *To*	_____	per
	_____	_____

Duties _____

_____

FORM 84.1/F624

_____

_____

Supervisor _____ Telephone _____

Reason for Leaving _____

MAY WE CONTACT YOUR PRESENT EMPLOYER NOW? _____

INTERESTS, SKILLS AND ABILITIES

Indicate any interests, skills and abilities such as hobbies, athletic activities, language fluency, etc., which you believe would be relevant to the employment you are seeking with us. (*Exclude any organizations or activities the name or character of which would indicate race, creed, color or national origin.*)

_____

_____

_____

_____

_____

REFERENCES

List three persons, NOT related to you, who have known you for at least one year:

Last Name	First		Telephone
Street Address	City	State	Zip

Last Name	First		Telephone
Street Address	City	State	Zip

Last Name	First		Telephone
Street Address	City	State	Zip

I authorize the investigation of all statements contained in this application and hereby authorize my previous employers and references to furnish relevant information concerning my character, work habits, job performance and employment record. I understand that misrepresentation or omission of facts relevant to my employment is cause for dismissal.

(Signed) _____

Bill of Sale of Boat

STATE OF _____)
) ss:

COUNTY OF _____)

KNOW YE ALL MEN BY THESE PRESENTS,

That I, _____, of

_____,

    Street Address   *City*   *State*   *Zip*

for and in consideration of payment of the sum of $ _____, the receipt of which is hereby acknowledged, do hereby grant, bargain, sell and convey to:

_____, of

_____,

    Street Address   *City*   *State*   *Zip*

and his/her heirs, executors, administrators, successors and assigns the following boat:

Year	*Make*	*Model*

Length	*Serial No.*	*Registration or Documentation No.*

Engine/Motor No. 1 _____

	Year	*Make*	*Horsepower*	*Type*	*Serial No.*

Engine/Motor No. 2 _____

	Year	*Make*	*Horsepower*	*Type*	*Serial No.*

together with the following equipment:

    I hereby warrant that I am the lawful owner of said boat and equipment and that I have full legal right, power and authority to sell said property. I further warrant said boat and equipment to be free of all encumbrances and that I will warrant and defend said boat and equipment hereby sold against any and all persons whomsoever.

    IN WITNESS WHEREOF, I, the seller, have hereto set my hand and seal this _____ day of _____ _____, 19 _____.

(Signed) _____

                                                Seller

FORM 85.1 / F626

CERTIFICATE OF NOTARY

STATE OF   )

)   ss:

COUNTY OF   )

On this _____ day of _____, 19 _____, before me personally came and appeared _____, known, and known to me, to be the individual described in and who executed the foregoing instrument, and who duly acknowledged to me that he/she executed same for the purpose therein contained.

IN WITNESS WHEREOF, I hereunto set my hand and official seal.

_____
Notary Public

My commission expires: _____

Bill of Sale of Boat

To

from

Dated _____ 19 _____

Bill of Sale of Boat

STATE OF ⎯⎯⎯⎯⎯⎯⎯⎯)
⎯⎯⎯⎯⎯⎯⎯⎯⎯⎯⎯⎯⎯⎯) ss:
COUNTY OF ⎯⎯⎯⎯⎯⎯⎯)

KNOW YE ALL MEN BY THESE PRESENTS,

That I/We, _____, of

Street Address	*City*	*State*	*Zip*

and _____, of

Street Address	*City*	*State*	*Zip*

for and in consideration of payment of the sum of $ _____, the receipt of which is hereby acknowledged, do hereby grant, bargain, sell and convey to:

_____, of

Street Address	*City*	*State*	*Zip*

and _____, of

Street Address	*City*	*State*	*Zip*

and his/her/their heirs, executors, administrators, successors and assigns the following boat:

Year	*Make*	*Model*
Length	*Serial No.*	*Registration or Documentation No.*

Engine/Motor No. 1 _____

Year	*Make*	*Horsepower*	*Type*	*Serial No.*

Engine/Motor No. 2 _____

Year	*Make*	*Horsepower*	*Type*	*Serial No.*

together with the following equipment:

I/We hereby warrant that I/we are the lawful owner(s) of said boat and equipment and that I/we have full legal right, power and authority to sell said property. I/We further warrant said boat and equipment to be free of all encumbrances and that I/we will warrant and defend said boat and equipment hereby sold against any and all persons whomsoever.

IN WITNESS WHEREOF, I/we, the seller(s), have hereto set my/our hand and seal this _____ day of _____, 19 _____.

(Signed) _____
Seller

(Signed) _____
Seller

FORM 85.2 / F628

CERTIFICATE OF NOTARY

STATE OF _____)
) ss:
COUNTY OF _____)

On this _____ day of _____, 19 _____, before me personally came and appeared
_____ and _____, known, and known
to me, to be the individual(s) described in and who executed the foregoing instrument, and who duly acknowledged to me
that he/she/they executed same for the purpose therein contained.

IN WITNESS WHEREOF, I hereunto set my hand and official seal.

_____
Notary Public

My commission expires: _____

𝔅𝔦𝔩𝔩 𝔬𝔣 𝔖𝔞𝔩𝔢
𝔬𝔣 𝔅𝔬𝔞𝔱

To

from

Dated _____ 19 ____

Bill of Sale
of

_____

STATE OF   )
)   ss:
COUNTY OF   )

KNOW YE ALL MEN BY THESE PRESENTS,

That I, _____, of

_____,
    Street Address   _City_   _State_   _Zip_

for and in consideration of payment of the sum of $ _____, the receipt of which is hereby acknowledged, do hereby grant, bargain, sell and convey to:

_____, of

_____,
    Street Address   _City_   _State_   _Zip_

and his/her heirs, executors, administrators, successors and assigns the following property:

I hereby warrant that I am the lawful owner of said property and that I have full legal right, power and authority to sell said property. I further warrant said property to be free of all encumbrances and that I will warrant and defend said property hereby sold against any and all persons whomsoever.

IN WITNESS WHEREOF, I, the seller, have hereto set my hand and seal this _____ day of _____ _____, 19 _____.

(Signed) _____
                                        Seller

CERTIFICATE OF NOTARY

STATE OF   )
)   ss:
COUNTY OF   )

On this _____ day of _____, 19 _____, before me personally came and appeared _____, known, and known to me, to be the individual described in and who executed the foregoing instrument, and who duly acknowledged to me that he/she executed same for the purpose therein contained.

IN WITNESS WHEREOF, I hereunto set my hand and official seal.

_____
Notary Public

My commission expires: _____

𝕭𝖎𝖑𝖑 𝖔𝖋 𝕾𝖆𝖑𝖊

of

To

from

Dated _____ 19 _____

Bill of Sale
of

_____

STATE OF _____)
) ss:
COUNTY OF _____)

KNOW YE ALL MEN BY THESE PRESENTS,

That I/We, _____, of

| _____ | _____ | _____ | _____ |
| Street Address | City | State | Zip |

and _____, of

| _____ | _____ | _____ | _____ |
| Street Address | City | State | Zip |

for and in consideration of payment of the sum of $ _____, the receipt of which is hereby acknowledged, do hereby grant, bargain, sell and convey to:

_____, of

| _____ | _____ | _____ | _____ |
| Street Address | City | State | Zip |

and _____, of

| _____ | _____ | _____ | _____ |
| Street Address | City | State | Zip |

and his/her/their heirs, executors, administrators, successors and assigns the following property:

I/We hereby warrant that I/we are the lawful owner(s) of said property and that I/we have full legal right, power and authority to sell said property. I/We further warrant said property to be free of all encumbrances and that I/we will warrant and defend said property hereby sold against any and all persons whomsoever.

IN WITNESS WHEREOF, I/we, the seller(s), have hereto set my/our hand and seal this _____ day of _____, 19 _____.

(Signed) _____
                                                 Seller

(Signed) _____
                                                 Seller

FORM 85.4/F632

CERTIFICATE OF NOTARY

STATE OF   )

)   ss:

COUNTY OF   )

On this _____ day of _____, 19 _____, before me personally came and appeared _____ and _____, known, and known to me, to be the individual(s) described in and who executed the foregoing instrument, and who duly acknowledged to me that he/she/they executed same for the purpose therein contained.

    IN WITNESS WHEREOF, I hereunto set my hand and official seal.

_____
Notary Public

My commission expires: _____

Bill of Sale

of

To

from

Dated _____

19 ____

Fix-up Materials Shopping List

Polishing Compound   Finer than rubbing compound, more coarse than toothpaste, polishing compound should be your product of next resort if ordinary auto polish fails to make your car's finish sparkle.

Rubbing Compound   Much more coarse than polishing compound, rubbing compound is normally used to smooth newly sprayed auto paint. When a painter applies paint, he/she "lays on" a sufficient amount of paint to compensate for the fact that in "polishing out" with rubbing compound a considerable amount of paint will be removed. Since paint on an older car has already been worn away to some extent, be extremely careful when using rubbing compound or you may remove paint right down to the primer. Rubbing compound is a good chrome cleaner.

Toothpaste   This is a very nice, fine compound for polishing molded plastic to a shine and for gently polishing out any interior paint that should be glossy.

Auto Polish   Almost all auto polishes are good. There are two basic types: those without "cleaner" and those with "cleaner." For "cleaner," read "mild abrasive." Obviously, if you regularly polish a car with a product having an abrasive, you will run out of paint a few years before you run out of car.

Armorall   A whitish, moderately water-soluble solution that beautifully restores vinyl, molded plastic, and "printed" station wagon wood grain. Tends to make vinyl seats a bit shiny and "squeaky." This can sometimes be remedied by rubbing with a soft, dry cloth immediately after application. Six ounces should be plenty.

Krylon Semi-Flat Black Paint   This paint provides a very "factorylike" finish, not too glossy and not too flat. It is available in spray cans from auto parts stores, many hardware stores, and some artists' supply stores. Perfect for restoring a new appearance to almost anything on your car that is painted black.

Krylon Engine Paint   Comes in sixteen colors to match original engine paint on most makes of cars.

Gunk Engine Brite   Available in 20-ounce spray cans to clean auto engines. Easy to use by following directions on the can. You'll probably need two cans though. Plan on cleaning your auto's engine at a coin-op car wash during off hours. It would make a disaster area of your driveway.

Spray Undercoat   Black, rubbery auto undercoat similar to dealer-applied undercoating. Use to renew appearance of a car's wheel wells and various areas of a car's underside. Available in spray cans at most auto supply stores.

Belt Dressing   Quiets squeaky fan belts (try tightening your car's belts first though). Comes in spray cans. *Krylon* makes one brand but only in a 16-ounce can, which should last you until the coming of the next ice age.

Door Ease   Looks like a five-inch *Chap-Stick*. Use on auto door mechanisms to help them operate smoothly.

Spray Adhesive   Rubber cement in a spray can. Used extensively in auto upholstery shops. Use it to stick carpets, trim, etc., back into place. Available from auto upholstery shops and artists' supply stores.

Mar-Hyde   Unbelievable! Mostly because it works. *Mar-Hyde* can restore the color and new appearance of vinyl and molded plastic trim. Available from many auto supply stores in sixteen colors in spray cans. Distributors can mix to match your car's interior and put in spray cans for you. Check with used-car dealers if you have trouble finding it.

Upholstery Cleaner   Most are made for use on fabric and carpets. Some, such as one sold by K-Mart, are advertised as being suitable for vinyl, leather, and fabric.

Paste Shoe Polish   Useful for restoring the appearance of plastic and vinyl, but not, of course, seat cushions.

Dupli-Color Spray Paint   Auto touch-up spray paint sold in auto supply stores and Sears. Car's make and year are printed on the top of the can—which matches color of contents. To touch up small nicks and chips, spray a bit of paint into the top of the can, dip a small, camel's hair brush into that, and then apply. Don't attempt spray touch-up work unless you *really* know what you're doing.

Q-Tips   Useful for cleaning mininooks and crannies.

Offer to Purchase Motor Vehicle

STATE OF _____)

_____) ss:

COUNTY OF _____)

KNOW YE ALL MEN BY THESE PRESENTS,

That I, _____ , of

_____ ,

| Street Address | Apt. No. | City | State | Zip |

do hereby offer to purchase from _____ , of

_____ ,

| Street Address | Apt. No. | City | State | Zip |

the following motor vehicle:

_____

| Year | Make | Model | Serial No. | Engine No. |

for the sum of _____ ($_____).

This offer shall be binding upon me for a period of three days from the date of execution of this instrument.

IN WITNESS WHEREOF, I set my hand and seal this _____ day of _____ , 19 _____ .

(Signed) _____

Receipt for Nonrefundable Deposit

Received of _____ , the sum of _____

($_____) as NONREFUNDABLE DEPOSIT toward the purchase of _____

_____ ,

to be sold to the above-named individual by _____ ,

owner of said vehicle, on or before the _____ day of _____ , 19 _____ , for a total price of _____ ($_____), this NON-REFUNDABLE DEPOSIT being a part thereof.

    I understand and agree that if I fail to pay the remaining $_____ due by the above date, said NONREFUNDABLE DEPOSIT shall be forfeit.

    The seller, _____ , hereby agrees in consideration of payment of said NON-REFUNDABLE DEPOSIT to withdraw said vehicle from the market until the above date and to transfer title to said vehicle to _____ upon receipt of the remaining amount due.

(Signed) _____
                                    Purchaser

(Signed) _____
                                      Seller

Bill of Sale of Motor Vehicle

STATE OF _____)

)   ss:

COUNTY OF _____)

KNOW YE ALL MEN BY THESE PRESENTS,

That I, _____, of

_____,

   Street Address   *City*   *State*   *Zip*

for and in consideration of payment of the sum of $ _____, the receipt of which is hereby acknowledged, do hereby grant, bargain, sell and convey to:

_____, of

_____,

   Street Address   *City*   *State*   *Zip*

and his/her heirs, executors, administrators, successors and assigns the following motor vehicle:

_____

   Year   *Make*   *Model*   *Serial No.*   *Engine No.*

    Said vehicle is sold to the buyer with current (State) (County) (Municipal) inspection sticker and current (State) (County) (Municipal) tax sticker and a total mileage of _____, with no other warranties or representations express or implied.

    I hereby warrant that I am the lawful owner of said vehicle and that I have full legal right, power and authority to sell said vehicle. I further warrant said vehicle to be free from all encumbrances and that I will warrant and defend said vehicle hereby sold against any and all persons whomsoever.

    IN WITNESS WHEREOF, I, the seller, have hereto set my hand and seal this _____ day of _____

_____, 19 _____.

(Signed) _____

                                            Seller

* *

Buyer's Acceptance

I, _____, buyer of said vehicle, hereby accept the above-described vehicle in good order and repair pursuant to the hereinbefore BILL OF SALE this _____ day of _____, 19 _____.

(Signed) _____

                                          Buyer

CERTIFICATE OF NOTARY

STATE OF   )

)   ss:

COUNTY OF   )

On this _____ day of _____, 19 _____, before me personally came and appeared _____, known, and known to me, to be the individual described in and who executed the foregoing instrument, and who duly acknowledged to me that he/she executed same for the purpose therein contained.

IN WITNESS WHEREOF, I hereunto set my hand and official seal.

_____

Notary Public

My commission expires: _____

Bill of Sale of Motor Vehicle

To

from

Dated _____ 19 ___

Bill of Sale of Motor Vehicle

STATE OF _____)
) ss:
COUNTY OF _____)

KNOW YE ALL MEN BY THESE PRESENTS,

That I/we, _____, of

_____,
Street Address   _City_   _State_   _Zip_

and _____, of

_____,
Street Address   _City_   _State_   _Zip_

for and in consideration of payment of the sum of $ _____, the receipt of which is hereby acknowledged, do hereby grant, bargain, sell and convey to:

_____, of

_____,
Street Address   _City_   _State_   _Zip_

and _____, of

_____,
Street Address   _City_   _State_   _Zip_

and his/her/their heirs, executors, administrators, successors and assigns the following motor vehicle:

_____
Year   _Make_   _Model_   _Serial No._   _Engine No._

Said vehicle is sold to the buyer(s) with current (State) (County) (Municipal) inspection sticker and current (State) (County) (Municipal) tax sticker and a total mileage of _____, with no other warranties or representations express or implied.

I/We hereby represent that I/we are the lawful owner(s) of said vehicle and that I/we have full legal right, power and authority to sell said vehicle. I/We further warrant said vehicle to be free from all encumbrances and that I/we will warrant and defend said vehicle hereby sold against any and all persons whomsoever.

IN WITNESS WHEREOF, I/we, the seller(s), have hereto set my/our hand and seal this _____ day of _____, 19 _____.

(Signed) _____
                                 Seller

(Signed) _____
                                 Seller

* *

Buyer's Acceptance

I/We, _____ and _____, buyer(s) of said vehicle, hereby accept the above-described vehicle in good order and repair pursuant to the hereinbefore BILL OF SALE this _____ day of _____, 19 _____.

(Signed) _____
                                 Buyer

(Signed) _____
                                 Buyer

FORM 86.5/F642

CERTIFICATE OF NOTARY

STATE OF   )

)   ss:

COUNTY OF   )

On this _____ day of _____, 19 _____, before me personally came and appeared _____ and _____, known, and known to me, to be the individual(s) described in and who executed the foregoing instrument, and who duly acknowledged to me that he/she/they executed same for the purpose therein contained.

    IN WITNESS WHEREOF, I hereunto set my hand and official seal.

_____
                                          Notary Public

My commission expires: _____

Bill of Sale of Motor Vehicle

To

from

Dated _____ 19 _____

Odometer Mileage Statement

I, _____ , state that the odometer of the vehicle described below now reads
_____ miles/kilometers.

Check one box only.

☐ 1. I hereby certify that to the best of my knowledge the odometer reading as stated above reflects the actual mileage of the vehicle described below.

☐ 2. I hereby certify that to the best of my knowledge the odometer reading as stated above reflects the amount of mileage in excess of the designed mechanical odometer limit of 99,999 miles/kilometers of the vehicle described below.

☐ 3. I hereby certify that to the best of my knowledge the odometer reading as stated above is NOT the actual mileage of the vehicle described below, and should not be relied upon.

Make	*Model*	*Body Type*
Year	*Vehicle Identification No.*	*Last Plate No.*

Check one box only.

☐ 1. I hereby certify that the odometer of said vehicle was not altered, set back, or disconnected while in my possession, and I have no knowledge of anyone else doing so.

☐ 2. I hereby certify that the odometer was altered for repair or replacement purposes while in my possession and that the mileage registered on the repaired or replacement odometer was identical to that before such service.

☐ 3. I hereby certify that the repaired or replacement odometer was incapable of registering the same mileage, that it was reset to zero, and that the mileage on the original odometer or the odometer before repair was _____ miles/kilometers.

Transferor's (Seller's) Address:

_____
Street Address   *City*   *State*   *Zip*

Transferor's Signature _____ Date of Statement _____

Transferee's (Buyer's) Name _____

_____
Street Address   *City*   *State*   *Zip*

Receipt of Copy Acknowledged   (Signed) _____
                                                        Transferee/Buyer

Credit Application

IMPORTANT: *READ THESE DIRECTIONS BEFORE COMPLETING THIS APPLICATION.*

1. If you are applying for individual credit in your own name and relying on your own income or assets and not the income or assets of another person as the basis for repayment of the credit requested, complete Sections A and C, omitting Section B.

2. If this is an application for joint credit with another person, complete all sections, providing information in B about the joint applicant.

3. If you are applying for individual credit, but are relying on income from alimony, child support, or separate maintenance or on the income or assets of another person as the basis for repayment of the credit requested, complete all sections to the extent possible, providing information in B about the person on whose alimony, support, or maintenance payments you are relying.

Section A—Applicant

First Name	Middle	Last

Present Street Address/Apt. No. (How Long?)   City   State   Zip

Home Telephone _____ Work Telephone _____

Previous Street Address/Apt. No. (How Long?)   City   State   Zip

Name of Mortgage Holder or Landlord   Telephone

Street Address   City   State   Zip

Date of Birth _____ Social Security No. _____

Current Annual Gross Income   Monthly Housing Payment

No. of Dependents _____ Ages: _____

Name of Present Employer   Years There   Telephone

Street Address   City   State   Zip

Duties/Title   Supervisor

Name of Previous Employer   Years There   Telephone

Street Address   City   State   Zip

Duties/Title   Supervisor

Name of Bank   Branch/Office

Checking Account No.   Savings Account No.

Current Loan? _____ _____
                      Yes   No

Previous Loan? _____ _____
                       Yes   No

Are you obligated to make regular alimony, child support or maintenance payments? _____ _____
                                                                                                                        Yes   No

NOTE: Alimony, child support, or separate maintenance income need not be revealed if you do not wish to have it considered as a basis for repaying this obligation.

Section B—Coapplicant

First Name   Middle   Last

Present Street Address/Apt. No. (How Long?)   City   State   Zip

Home Telephone _____ Work Telephone _____

Previous Street Address/Apt. No. (How Long?)   City   State   Zip

Name of Mortgage Holder or Landlord   Telephone

Street Address   City   State   Zip

Date of Birth _____ Social Security No. _____

Current Annual Gross Income   Monthly Housing Payment

No. of Dependents _____ Ages: _____

Name of Present Employer   Years There   Telephone

Street Address   City   State   Zip

Duties/Title   Supervisor

Name of Previous Employer	Years There		Telephone

Street Address	City	State	Zip

Duties/Title			Supervisor

Name of Bank	Branch/Office

Checking Account No.	Savings Account No.

Current Loan? _____ _____
               Yes   *No*

Previous Loan? _____ _____
               Yes   *No*

Are you obligated to make regular alimony, child support or maintenance payments? _____ _____
                                                                                            Yes   *No*

Section C—Credit Experience of Applicant and Coapplicant

List current financial obligations including banks, department stores, and credit cards. Indicate debts of applicant alone with an **A**, debts of coapplicant alone with a **C**, and debts which are jointly obligated with a **J**.

Name of Creditor	Account No.

Original Amount _____ Monthly Payment _____ Balance _____

Name of Creditor	Account No.

Original Amount _____ Monthly Payment _____ Balance _____

Name of Creditor	Account No.

Original Amount _____ Monthly Payment _____ Balance _____

* *

    Everything that I have stated in this application is true and correct to the best of my knowledge. I understand that you will retain this application and/or financial statement, if it has been tendered or required, whether or not it is approved. You are authorized to investigate my credit and employment history and to answer questions about your credit experience with me.

(Signed) _____
                          Applicant

_____
                          Date

(Signed) _____
                          Coapplicant

_____
                          Date

Personal Financial Statement

Date _____

First Name		Middle			Last

Street Address	Apt. No.	City	State	Zip

For the purpose of obtaining credit from _____, I submit the following financial statement and hereby warrant same to be a true and complete representation of my assets and liabilities as of the _____ day of _____, 19 _____.

Assets	**Liabilities**

Cash on Hand

_____ $_____

Checking Accounts   **Loans Payable to Banks**

_____ _____   _____ $_____

_____ _____   _____ _____

_____ _____   _____ _____

_____ _____   _____ _____

Savings Accounts   **Loans Payable to Others**

_____ _____   _____ _____

_____ _____   _____ _____

_____ _____   _____ _____

_____ _____   _____ _____

Certificates of Deposit   **Owed on Real Property**

_____ _____   _____ _____

_____ _____   _____ _____

_____ _____   _____ _____

_____ _____   _____ _____

	Assets		Liabilities

Insurance Cash Value

_____ _____

_____ _____

_____ _____

Stocks and Bonds

_____ _____

_____ _____

_____ _____

_____ _____

Real Property

_____ _____

_____ _____

_____ _____

_____ _____

Vehicles

_____ _____

_____ _____

_____ _____

_____ _____

Owed on Vehicles

_____ _____

_____ _____

_____ _____

_____ _____

Owed on Credit Card Accounts

_____ _____

_____ _____

_____ _____

Owed on Charge Accounts

_____ _____

_____ _____

_____ _____

_____ _____

_____ _____

_____ _____

_____ _____

Assets	Liabilities

Debts Owed to You

_____ _____

_____ _____

_____ _____

_____ _____

Household Goods

_____ _____

_____ _____

Personal Property

_____ _____

_____ _____

_____ _____

_____ _____

Other Assets

_____ _____

_____ _____

_____ _____

_____ _____

_____ _____

Total Assets: $_____

Other Liabilities

_____ _____

_____ _____

_____ _____

_____ _____

_____ _____

_____ _____

Total Liabilities: $_____

FORM 87.2 / F652

1. Nature of security given to banks, finance companies and others as collateral to secure loans: _____

_____

2. Do you have any contingent indebtedness as a guarantor or endorser of any notes, loans or indebtedness of others? _____ **Yes** _____ **No**

3. Are any of your debts owing past due? _____ **Yes** _____ **No**

4. Have you filed bankruptcy at any time during the past seven years? _____ **Yes** _____ **No**

5. Are there any judgments against you? _____ **Yes** _____ **No**

6. Are there any lawsuits pending against you? _____ **Yes** _____ **No**

7. Are you a co-owner of any real or personal property not listed above? If so, give details:

_____

_____

_____

_____

   I have reviewed and carefully checked all of the information contained herein and certify all data to be accurate and complete to the best of my knowledge and belief.

(Signed) _____

_____
Date

Joint Financial Statement

Date _____

First Name		Middle		Last

Street Address	Apt. No.	City	State	Zip

and

First Name		Middle		Last

Street Address	Apt. No.	City	State	Zip

For the purpose of obtaining credit from _____ , we submit the following financial statement and hereby warrant same to be a true and complete representation of our assets and liabilities as of the _____ day of _____ , 19 _____ .

Assets		**Liabilities**	
Cash on Hand			
_____ $_____			
Checking Accounts		*Loans Payable to Banks*	
_____ _____		_____ $_____	
_____ _____		_____ _____	
_____ _____		_____ _____	
_____ _____			
Savings Accounts		*Loans Payable to Others*	
_____ _____		_____ _____	
_____ _____		_____ _____	
_____ _____		_____ _____	
_____ _____		_____ _____	

Assets	Liabilities

Certificates of Deposit

_____ _____

_____ _____

_____ _____

_____ _____

Insurance Cash Value

_____ _____

_____ _____

_____ _____

Stocks and Bonds

_____ _____

_____ _____

_____ _____

_____ _____

_____ _____

Real Property

_____ _____

_____ _____

_____ _____

_____ _____

Vehicles

_____ _____

_____ _____

_____ _____

_____ _____

Owed on Real Property

_____ _____

_____ _____

_____ _____

_____ _____

Owed on Vehicles

_____ _____

_____ _____

_____ _____

_____ _____

Owed on Credit Card Accounts

_____ _____

_____ _____

_____ _____

_____ _____

Owed on Charge Accounts

_____ _____

_____ _____

_____ _____

_____ _____

_____ _____

_____ _____

Assets		Liabilities	

Debts Owed to You

_____ _____

_____ _____

_____ _____

_____ _____

Other Liabilities

_____ _____

_____ _____

_____ _____

_____ _____

_____ _____

_____ _____

Household Goods

_____ _____

_____ _____

Total Liabilities: $_____

Personal Property

_____ _____

_____ _____

_____ _____

_____ _____

_____ _____

Other Assets

_____ _____

_____ _____

_____ _____

_____ _____

_____ _____

Total Assets: $_____

FORM 87.3/F656

1. Nature of security given to banks, finance companies and others as collateral to secure loans: _____

   _____

2. Do you have any contingent indebtedness as a guarantor or endorser of any notes, loans or indebtedness of others? _____ **Yes** _____ **No**

3. Are any of your debts owing past due? _____ **Yes** _____ **No**

4. Have either of you filed bankruptcy at any time during the past seven years? _____ **Yes** _____ **No**

5. Are there any judgments against either of you? _____ **Yes** _____ **No**

6. Are there any lawsuits pending against either of you? _____ **Yes** _____ **No**

7. Is either of you a co-owner of any real or personal property not listed above? If so, give details:

   _____

   _____

   _____

   _____

We have reviewed and carefully checked all of the information contained herein and certify all data to be accurate and complete to the best of our knowledge and belief.

(Signed) _____

_____
Date

(Signed) _____

_____
Date

Promissory Note

$_____

Date _____

_____ after the above date I promise to pay to the order of _____
Number of Days

_____ the sum of _____

_____ ($_____), together with interest at _____ percent per annum,
payable at _____.

The maker and endorser of this note further agree to waive demand, notice of nonpayment and protest, and in case suit shall be brought for the collection hereof, or the same has to be collected upon demand of an attorney, to pay reasonable attorney's fees for making such collection. Deferred interest payments to bear interest from maturity at _____ percent per annum, payable semiannually.

(Signed) _____
Maker

(Signed) _____
Endorser

Due _____

Promissory Note

$_____

Date _____

_____ after the above date I promise to pay to the order of _____
Number of Days

_____ the sum of _____

_____ ($_____), together with interest at _____ percent per annum,
payable at _____.

The maker and endorser of this note further agree to waive demand, notice of nonpayment and protest, and in case suit shall be brought for the collection hereof, or the same has to be collected upon demand of an attorney, to pay reasonable attorney's fees for making such collection. Deferred interest payments to bear interest from maturity at _____ percent per annum, payable semiannually.

(Signed) _____
Maker

(Signed) _____
Endorser

Due _____

Installment Note

$_____

Date _____

I promise to pay the sum of _____
_____ ($_____) to the order of _____
_____ at _____
_____ in the following manner:

The sum of $ _____ on the _____ day of _____, 19 _____; and the sum of
$_____ on the _____ of each month thereafter until the entire amount is repaid, together
with interest at the rate of _____ percent per annum, payable with each installment of the principal.

The maker and endorser of this note further agree to waive demand, notice of nonpayment and protest, and
in case suit shall be brought for the collection hereof, or the same has to be collected upon demand of an
attorney, to pay reasonable attorney's fees for making such collection. Deferred interest payments to bear
interest from maturity at _____ percent per annum, payable semiannually.

(Signed) _____
                          Maker

(Signed) _____
                          Endorser

Series Promissory Note

$_____

Date _____

On _____, I promise to pay to the order of _____
_____ the sum of _____
_____ ($_____), together with interest at _____ percent per annum, payable at
_____.

This note is number _____ of a series of _____ notes. I agree that upon default in the payment of this or any of the remaining notes, all of the remaining notes shall immediately become due and payable without notice at the option of the holder thereof. The maker and endorser (if any) hereby waive presentment for payment, protest, notice of protest and notice of nonpayment.

The maker and endorser of this note further agree to waive demand, notice of nonpayment and protest, and in case suit shall be brought for the collection hereof, or the same has to be collected upon demand of an attorney, to pay reasonable attorney's fees for making such collection.

For value received.

(Signed) _____
                                    Maker

(Signed) _____
                                    Endorser

Note No. _____ Due _____

Series Promissory Note

$_____

Date _____

On _____, I promise to pay to the order of _____
_____ the sum of _____
_____ ($_____), together with interest at _____ percent per annum, payable at
_____.

This note is number _____ of a series of _____ notes. I agree that upon default in the payment of this or any of the remaining notes, all of the remaining notes shall immediately become due and payable without notice at the option of the holder thereof. The maker and endorser (if any) hereby waive presentment for payment, protest, notice of protest and notice of nonpayment.

The maker and endorser of this note further agree to waive demand, notice of nonpayment and protest, and in case suit shall be brought for the collection hereof, or the same has to be collected upon demand of an attorney, to pay reasonable attorney's fees for making such collection.

For value received.

(Signed) _____
                                    Maker

(Signed) _____
                                    Endorser

Note No. _____ Due _____

Security Agreement

STATE OF _____)

) ss:

COUNTY OF _____)

KNOW YE ALL MEN BY THESE PRESENTS,

That I, _____ , of

_____ ,

   Street Address   *Apt. No.*   *City*   *State*   *Zip*

hereinafter called "Debtor," hereby grant to _____ , of

_____ ,

   Street Address   *Apt. No.*   *City*   *State*   *Zip*

hereinafter called the "Secured Party," a security interest in the following described property as collateral to secure payment of the obligation described herein.

Collateral

_____

_____

_____

_____

Obligation

_____

_____

_____

_____

Default in the payment of all or any part of the obligation described is a default under this Agreement. Upon such default the Secured Party may declare all of the above-described obligation(s) immediately due and payable and shall have the remedies of a secured party under provisions of the Uniform Commercial Code. In the event legal action is required to enforce any provision of this Agreement, the prevailing party shall be entitled to recover reasonable attorney's fees and costs.

The Debtor hereby agrees to exercise reasonable caution and care in use of the herein-described collateral; to adequately insure or keep insured the described collateral; not to attempt to sell, assign or dispose of said collateral or his/her interest therein; not to encumber nor to permit any encumbrance against same; and not to remove said collateral from the county where the Debtor resides without written permission of the Secured Party.

EXECUTED this _____ day of _____ , 19 _____ .

(Signed) _____

                                 Debtor

(Signed) _____

                               Secured Party

FORM 87.7 / F664

Security Agreement

19 _____

Dated _____

Chattel Mortgage

STATE OF   )

) ss:

COUNTY OF   )

KNOW YE ALL MEN BY THESE PRESENTS,

That I, _____ , of

_____ ,

| *Street Address* | *Apt. No.* | *City* | *State* | *Zip* |

hereinafter called the "Purchaser," hereby purchase from _____ , of

_____ ,

| *Street Address* | *Apt. No.* | *City* | *State* | *Zip* |

hereinafter called the "Seller," the following property:

_____

_____

_____

_____

_____

Under the following terms:

1. Selling Price $_____

2. State Tax $_____

3. City Tax $_____

4. Excise Tax $_____

5. Total Cash Selling Price $_____

6. Less Down Payment $_____

7. Unpaid Amount $_____

8. Finance Charge $_____

9. Balance Payable in Installments $_____

10. **Annual Percentage Rate:** $_____

I promise to pay the Seller the above balance in _____ successive, equal monthly installments beginning on the _____ day of _____, 19 _____, payment to be made at _____ _____, or otherwise as may be designated by the Seller.

Use and Care of Chattel(s)

The Purchaser hereby agrees to use said chattel(s) with reasonable skill, caution and care and to keep same in good order and repair and will not attempt to sell, assign or dispose of said chattel(s) or his/her interest therein; will not encumber nor permit any encumbrance or lien against same; and will not remove same from the county where Purchaser resides without written permission of the Seller.

Insurance

The Purchaser agrees to obtain insurance upon said chattel(s), to include, but not necessarily be limited to, the following coverage:

_____

_____

Purchaser agrees that in the event he/she fails to insure said chattel(s), Seller may obtain insurance coverage for same and that any sums of money so expended by the Seller shall be secured by the herein-described property and shall be payable with interest at the rate of _____ percent per annum by the Purchaser to the Seller.

Late Payment

A charge of _____ percent of any installment not paid within _____ days of due date will be payable by the Purchaser to the Seller, in addition to the amount of the payment due.

Default

In the event of default in the payment of said obligation, the whole amount herein secured shall become due and payable and the Seller (at his/her option, notice of which is hereby expressly waived) may foreclose this mortgage by legal proceedings or otherwise and the Seller is hereby authorized to enter upon the premises where said chattel(s) may be and remove and/or sell same and all equity of the Purchaser therein.

Said Purchaser may buy said chattel(s) at any such sale in the same manner, and to have the same effect, as any person having no interest therein.

Attorney's Fees

In the event of default, reasonable attorney's fees and costs of collection will be charged where permitted by law.

Prepayment Rebate

In the event of prepayment in full the Purchaser shall be entitled to a rebate of the finance charge in accordance with the rule of 78.

Validity of Agreement

Any provision of this mortgage which is contrary to the laws of this state shall be inoperative, but shall not invalidate other provisions of this mortgage.

THIS MORTGAGE CONSTITUTES THE ENTIRE AGREEMENT BETWEEN THE PARTIES.

IN WITNESS WHEREOF, the parties hereto have executed this mortgage this _____ day of _____, 19 ____.

(Signed) _____
Purchaser

(Signed) _____
Guarantor

(Signed) _____
Seller

Chattel Mortgage

From _____

to _____

Deposited in my office this ____ day

of ____, 19 ___ at ____ M., and

duly numbered ____ and entered in

volume ____, page ____, of the Chattel

Mortgage Register of

County.

_____
County Clerk ____ County

state of _____

By _____
Deputy

Date: _____

REQUEST FOR REASON FOR ADVERSE CREDIT ACTION

Dear

On _____, I was notified that my application for credit dated _____
_____ was denied based upon information received by you from a source other than a consumer credit reporting agency.

Pursuant to my right under the Fair Credit Reporting Act, Title 15 USC, Sec. 1681 m(b), I hereby request that the nature of the information received by you be disclosed to me.

Please forward such information to me at the above address.

Thank you for your prompt attention to this matter.

Sincerely,

* *

CERTIFICATE OF NOTARY

STATE OF)
) ss:
COUNTY OF)

On this _____ day of _____, 19 _____, before me personally came and appeared _____, known, and known to me, to be the individual described in and who executed the foregoing instrument, and who duly acknowledged to me that he/she executed same for the purpose therein contained.

IN WITNESS WHEREOF, I hereunto set my hand and official seal.

_____
Notary Public

My commission expires: _____

Date: _____

REQUEST FOR DISCLOSURE OF CREDIT INFORMATION

Dear

Pursuant to my rights under the Fair Credit Reporting Act, Title 15 USC, Sec. 1681(h), I hereby request that you provide to me a clear and accurate disclosure of the nature, substance and sources of all information (other than medical) in your files that pertains to me.

I also hereby request the names and addresses of all recipients of any credit reports, oral or written, on me furnished by you.

Please forward such information to me at the above address.

Thank you for your prompt attention to this matter.

Sincerely,

* *

CERTIFICATE OF NOTARY

STATE OF   )

)   ss:

COUNTY OF   )

On this _____ day of _____, 19 ____, before me personally came and appeared _____, known, and known to me, to be the individual described in and who executed the foregoing instrument, and who duly acknowledged to me that he/she executed same for the purpose therein contained.

IN WITNESS WHEREOF, I hereunto set my hand and official seal.

_____
Notary Public

My commission expires: _____

Power of Attorney

STATE OF   )

)   ss:

COUNTY OF   )

KNOW YE ALL MEN BY THESE PRESENTS,

That I, _____, of

_____,

Street Address   *Apt. No.*   *City*   *State*   *Zip*

do hereby make, constitute and appoint _____, of

_____,

Street Address   *City*   *State*   *Zip*

as my true and lawful Attorney-in-Fact, for me and in my name, place and stead to:

_____

_____

_____

_____

I further give and grant to my said Attorney-in-Fact full power and authority to do and perform every act necessary and proper to be done in the exercise of any of the foregoing powers as fully as I might or could do if personally present, with full power of substitution and revocation, hereby ratifying and confirming all that my said Attorney-in-Fact shall lawfully do, or cause to be done by virtue hereof.

This instrument may not be changed orally.

IN WITNESS WHEREOF, I have hereunto set my hand and seal this _____ day of _____, 19 _____.

(Signed) _____

* *

CERTIFICATE OF NOTARY

STATE OF   )

)   ss:

COUNTY OF   )

On this _____ day of _____, 19 _____, before me personally came and appeared _____, known, and known to me, to be the individual described in and who executed the foregoing instrument, and who duly acknowledged to me that he/she executed same for the purpose therein contained.

IN WITNESS WHEREOF, I hereunto set my hand and official seal.

_____

Notary Public

My commission expires: _____

Power of Attorney

To

Dated _____ 19 ___

Miscellaneous Power of Attorney Clauses

To demand, collect, recover and receive any and all monies, sums, profits, dividends, interests, claims and debts whatsoever now due or to become due to me, and to execute and deliver receipts, releases or other discharges of debt.

To receive, endorse and collect checks payable to my order and to deposit same in _____ _____ at _____ .

To pay, settle, compromise, arbitrate and adjust all monies, sums, claims and debts whatsoever now or in the future owed by me.

To make, execute and deliver any lease, mortgage or deed pertaining to any real property, real estate, lands or mineral and/or other rights.

To take possession of and enter upon any real property, real estate, lands, tenements or hereditaments which may now or in the future belong to me, the possession of which I am now or in the future will be entitled.

To employ, hire, retain and contract for attorneys, consultants, accountants, engineers, architects, contractors, clerks, laborers and others; to remove them and/or appoint others in their place; and to pay such persons fees, wages, salaries, expenses and other remunerations as he/she shall deem proper.

Affidavit of Attorney

STATE OF _____)
)   ss:
COUNTY OF _____)

_____, first being duly sworn, deposes and says:
Name of Attorney-in-Fact

That _____, of

_____,

  Street Address   *Apt. No.*   *City*   *State*   *Zip*

did, by letter of attorney dated the _____ day of _____, 19 _____, make, constitute and appoint me as his/her true and lawful Attorney-in-Fact, and that attached hereto, and hereby made a part hereof, is a true copy of said letter of attorney.

    THAT as Attorney-in-Fact of the aforesaid _____ and under and by virtue of said **Power of Attorney**, this _____ day of _____, 19 _____, I have:

_____

_____

_____

_____

    I represent that the aforesaid _____ is now alive, is of sound mind and has not, at any time, revoked, countermanded nor made null and void the aforesaid **Power of Attorney** and that the aforesaid **Power of Attorney** is in full force and effect.

    THAT I make this Affidavit for the purpose of:

as executed by me in my capacity as Attorney-in-Fact for and in the name, place and stead of _____ _____, with full knowledge that _____ in accepting execution of the aforesaid **Power of Attorney** will rely upon this Affidavit and the attached true copy of said **Power of Attorney**.

    IN WITNESS WHEREOF, I have hereunto set my hand and seal this _____ day of _____, 19 _____.

                                   (Signed) _____
                                                      Attorney-in-Fact

CERTIFICATE OF NOTARY

STATE OF   )

)   ss:

COUNTY OF   )

On this _____ day of _____, 19 _____, before me personally came and appeared _____, known, and known to me, to be the individual described in and who executed the foregoing instrument, and who duly acknowledged to me that he/she executed same for the purpose therein contained.

    IN WITNESS WHEREOF, I hereunto set my hand and official seal.

_____
Notary Public

My commission expires: _____

Affidavit of Attorney

To

from

Dated _____ 19 _____

Auto Dealer's Powers of Attorney

Power of Attorney

KNOW YE ALL MEN BY THESE PRESENTS,

That the undersigned _____ ,
Buyer, Seller, or Legal Owner

of the following described Motor Vehicle:

19 _____ License No. _____ Engine No. _____

Make _____ Type _____

Year Built _____ Model _____

does hereby constitute and appoint _____ ,

of _____ , County of _____ , State _____ ,

my (or our) true and lawful Attorney to sign in the name, place and stead of the undersigned any Certificates of Ownership issued by the Division of Motor Vehicles of the State covering the vehicle described above in whatever manner necessary to transfer any registration of said vehicle as they may deem fit and proper.

IN WITNESS WHEREOF, the undersigned does hereby set his hand and seal this _____ day

of _____ , 19 _____ .

_____   _____
Witness   *Name*

_____   _____
Address   *Address*

SWORN TO AND SUBSCRIBED BEFORE me, the undersigned authority, on this the _____

_____ day of _____ A.D., 19 _____ .

_____
Notary Public

Power of Attorney

KNOW YE ALL MEN BY THESE PRESENTS,

That the undersigned _____ ,
Buyer, Seller, or Legal Owner

of the following described Motor Vehicle:

19 _____ License No. _____ Engine No. _____

Make _____ Type _____

Year Built _____ Model _____

does hereby constitute and appoint _____ ,

of _____ , County of _____ , State _____ ,

my (or our) true and lawful Attorney to sign in the name, place and stead of the undersigned any Certificates of Ownership issued by the Division of Motor Vehicles of the State covering the vehicle described above in whatever manner necessary to transfer any registration of said vehicle as they may deem fit and proper.

IN WITNESS WHEREOF, the undersigned does hereby set his hand and seal this _____ day

of _____ , 19 _____ .

_____   _____
Witness   *Name*

_____   _____
Address   *Address*

SWORN TO AND SUBSCRIBED BEFORE me, the undersigned authority, on this the _____

_____ day of _____ A.D., 19 _____ .

_____
Notary Public

Power of Attorney

KNOW YE ALL MEN BY THESE PRESENTS,

That the undersigned _____ ,
Buyer, Seller, or Legal Owner

of the following described Motor Vehicle:

19 _____ License No. _____ Engine No _____

Make _____ Type _____

Year Built _____ Model _____

does hereby constitute and appoint _____ ,

of _____ , County of _____ , State _____ ,

my (or our) true and lawful Attorney to sign in the name, place and stead of the undersigned any Certificates of Ownership issued by the Division of Motor Vehicles of the State covering the vehicle described above in whatever manner necessary to transfer any registration of said vehicle as they may deem fit and proper.

IN WITNESS WHEREOF, the undersigned does hereby set his hand and seal this _____ day

of _____ , 19 _____ .

_____   _____
Witness   *Name*

_____   _____
Address   *Address*

SWORN TO AND SUBSCRIBED BEFORE me, the undersigned authority, on this the _____

_____ day of _____ A.D., 19 _____ .

_____
Notary Public

Power of Attorney

KNOW YE ALL MEN BY THESE PRESENTS,

That the undersigned _____ ,
Buyer, Seller, or Legal Owner

of the following described Motor Vehicle:

19 _____ License No. _____ Engine No. _____

Make _____ Type _____

Year Built _____ Model _____

does hereby constitute and appoint _____ ,

of _____ , County of _____ , State _____ ,

my (or our) true and lawful Attorney to sign in the name, place and stead of the undersigned any Certificates of Ownership issued by the Division of Motor Vehicles of the State covering the vehicle described above in whatever manner necessary to transfer any registration of said vehicle as they may deem fit and proper.

IN WITNESS WHEREOF, the undersigned does hereby set his hand and seal this _____ day

of _____ , 19 _____ .

_____   _____
Witness   *Name*

_____   _____
Address   *Address*

SWORN TO AND SUBSCRIBED BEFORE me, the undersigned authority, on this the _____

_____ day of _____ A.D., 19 _____ .

_____
Notary Public

Revocation of Power of Attorney

STATE OF _____)
) ss:
COUNTY OF _____)

KNOW YE ALL MEN BY THESE PRESENTS,

That I, _____, of

_____,
Street Address   Apt. No.   City   State   Zip

in and by a letter of attorney dated the _____ day of _____, 19 _____, did make, constitute and appoint

_____, of

_____,
Street Address   City   State   Zip

by said letter of attorney as my Attorney-in-Fact.

    BY THESE PRESENTS, I do hereby revoke, countermand and make null and void the aforesaid letter of attorney, and all right, power and authority thereby given, or intended to be given, to the aforesaid _____
                                                            Name of Attorney-in-Fact
_____.

    IN WITNESS WHEREOF, I have hereunto set my hand and seal this _____ day of _____, 19 _____.

(Signed) _____

* *

CERTIFICATE OF NOTARY

STATE OF _____)
) ss:
COUNTY OF _____)

    On this _____ day of _____, 19 _____, before me personally came and appeared _____, known, and known to me, to be the individual described in and who executed the foregoing instrument, and who duly acknowledged to me that he/she executed same for the purpose therein contained.

    IN WITNESS WHEREOF, I hereunto set my hand and official seal.

_____
                                       Notary Public

My commission expires: _____

Revocation of Power of Attorney

19 _____

Dated

Retainer

STATE OF _____)
) ss:
COUNTY OF _____)

KNOW YE ALL MEN BY THESE PRESENTS,

THIS AGREEMENT is made this _____ day of _____, 19 _____, between

_____, of

_____ ,
  Street Address   *City*   *State*   *Zip*

hereinafter called "Attorney," and _____ , of

_____ ,
  Street Address   *Apt. No.*   *City*   *State*   *Zip*

hereinafter called "Client."

The Client hereby retains and employs the Attorney to:

The Attorney shall charge for his/her services at the rate of _____ for time actually devoted to the service of the Client.

The Client agrees to pay the Attorney each month for services rendered during the preceding month, together with reimbursement for all expenses pertaining thereto.

In consideration for said payment, the Attorney agrees to:

In the event legal action is required to enforce any provision of this Agreement, the prevailing party shall be entitled to recover reasonable attorney's fees and costs.

IN WITNESS WHEREOF, we have hereunto set our hands and seals this _____ day of _____, 19 _____.

(Signed) _____
                                       Client

(Signed) _____
                                      Attorney

Contingent Fee Retainer

STATE OF _____)
) ss:
COUNTY OF _____)

KNOW YE ALL MEN BY THESE PRESENTS,

THIS AGREEMENT is made this _____ day of _____, 19 _____, by and between

_____, of

_____,
  Street Address   *City*   *State*   *Zip*

hereinafter called "Attorney," and _____, of

_____,
  Street Address   *City*   *State*   *Zip*

hereinafter called "Client."

WHEREAS the Client desires to initiate proceedings against _____, of

_____,
  Street Address   *City*   *State*   *Zip*

the Client hereby retains and employs the Attorney to prosecute said action to final judgment or to any other settlement satisfactory to the Client.

The Client agrees to pay the Attorney for his/her services under this Agreement a sum equal to _____ percent of any monies or property obtained or received by the Client as the result of voluntary compromise or other out-of-court settlement; _____ percent if received after judgment; and _____ percent if received by the Client after appeal.

The Client further agrees to reimburse the Attorney for all proper expenses incurred by the Attorney pertaining to such action or settlement.

Except as provided herein, the Attorney shall not be entitled to any other compensation from the Client for legal services related to this Agreement.

It is agreed between the parties hereto that the Attorney shall have a lien for payment of his/her fee on all monies or property obtained, received or recovered by compromise, settlement, judgment or any other means whatsoever.

In the event legal action is required to enforce any provision of this Agreement, the prevailing party shall be entitled to recover reasonable attorney's fees and costs.

IN WITNESS WHEREOF, we set our hands and seals this _____ day of _____, 19 _____.

(Signed) _____ (Seal)
                                 Client

(Signed) _____ (Seal)
                               Attorney

Retainer of Attorney by Executor

KNOW YE ALL MEN BY THESE PRESENTS,

That I, _____, of

_____,
Street Address   *City*   *State*   *Zip*

as Executor/Executrix of the estate of _____,

now deceased and late of _____,
                                              Address

do hereby retain and employ _____, of

_____,
Street Address   *City*   *State*   *Zip*

as Attorney to take any and all proceedings which he/she may deem necessary and proper in the _____

_____,
                  Name Court, County and State

and I do further appoint said Attorney as lawful attorney to represent me in all matters and proceedings pertaining to the estate of the deceased _____ and to execute and perform all acts and things which he/she may deem necessary and proper; particularly to demand, collect, recover and receive all monies, sums, profits, interests, claims and debts owed, whether now due or to become due, to the estate of _____ _____, deceased.

IN WITNESS WHEREOF, I hereunto set my hand and seal this _____ day of _____, 19 ____.

(Signed) _____
                                     Executor/Executrix

Affidabit

STATE OF _____)
)   ss:
COUNTY OF _____)

KNOW YE ALL MEN BY THESE PRESENTS,

That on this _____ day of _____, 19 _____, personally came and appeared before me

_____ , of

_____ ,

| Street Address | Apt. No. | City | State | Zip |

known, and known to me, who, after being first duly sworn, deposes and says:

(Signed) _____

* *

SUBSCRIBED TO AND SWORN TO BEFORE ME THIS _____ day of _____, 19 _____.

(Signed) _____
                                             Notary Public

My commission expires: _____

Affidavit

of

to

Dated _____ 19 _____

Living Will

Directive to Physicians:

I, _____, of

_____,
Street Address   Apt. No.   City   State   Zip

being of sound mind, do hereby willfully and voluntarily make known my desire that my life not be prolonged under any of the following conditions, and do hereby further declare:

1. If I should, at any time, have an incurable condition caused by any disease or illness, or by any accident or injury, and be determined by any two or more physicians to be in a terminal condition whereby the use of "heroic measures" or the application of life-sustaining procedures would only serve to delay the moment of my death, and where my attending physician has determined that my death is imminent whether or not such "heroic measures" or life-sustaining measures are employed, I direct that such measures and procedures be withheld or withdrawn and that I be permitted to die naturally.

2. In the event of my inability to give directions regarding the application of life-sustaining procedures or the use of "heroic measures," it is my intention that this directive shall be honored by my family and physicians as my final expression of my right to refuse medical and surgical treatment, and my acceptance of the consequences of such refusal.

3. I am mentally, emotionally and legally competent to make this directive and I fully understand its import.

4. I reserve the right to revoke this directive at any time.

5. This directive shall remain in force until revoked.

IN WITNESS WHEREOF, I have hereunto set my hand and seal this _____ day of _____, 19 _____.

(Signed) _____

Declaration of Witnesses

The declarant is personally known to me and I believe him/her to be of sound mind and emotionally and legally competent to make the herein-contained **Directive to Physicians**. I am not related to the declarant by blood or marriage, nor would I be entitled to any portion of the declarant's estate upon his/her decease, nor am I an attending physician of the declarant, nor an employee of the attending physician, nor an employee of a health care facility in which the declarant is a patient, nor a patient in a health care facility in which the declarant is a patient, nor am I a person who has any claim against any portion of the estate of the declarant upon his/her decease.

(Signed) _____
                                        Witness

_____
                                        Address

_____

(Signed) _____
                                        Witness

_____
                                        Address

_____

FORM 89.1/F692

CERTIFICATE OF NOTARY

STATE OF   )

)   ss:

COUNTY OF   )

On this _____ day of _____, 19 _____, before me personally came and appeared _____ _____, declarant, and _____, witness, and _____ _____, witness, known, and known to me, to be the individuals described in and whose names are subscribed in the foregoing instrument in their respective capacities, and who duly acknowledged to me that they executed same for the purpose therein contained.

      IN WITNESS WHEREOF, I hereunto set my hand and official seal.

_____

                                          Notary Public

My commission expires: _____

Living Will

of

Dated _____ 19 _____

2

Living Will

Directive to Physicians:

I, _____, of

_____,
| Street Address | Apt. No. | City | State | Zip |

being of sound mind, do hereby willfully and voluntarily make known my desire that my life not be prolonged under any of the following conditions, and do hereby further declare:

1. If I should, at any time, have an incurable condition caused by any disease or illness, or by any accident or injury, and be determined by any two or more physicians to be in a terminal condition whereby the use of "heroic measures" or the application of life-sustaining procedures would only serve to delay the moment of my death, and where my attending physician has determined that my death is imminent whether or not such "heroic measures" or life-sustaining measures are employed, I direct that such measures and procedures be withheld or withdrawn and that I be permitted to die naturally.

2. In the event of my inability to give directions regarding the application of life-sustaining procedures or the use of "heroic measures," it is my intention that this directive shall be honored by my family and physicians as my final expression of my right to refuse medical and surgical treatment, and my acceptance of the consequences of such refusal.

3. **If I have been diagnosed as pregnant and such diagnosis is known to my physicians, this directive shall have no force or effect during the course of my pregnancy.**

4. I am mentally, emotionally and legally competent to make this directive and I fully understand its import.

5. I reserve the right to revoke this directive at any time.

6. This directive shall remain in force until revoked.

IN WITNESS WHEREOF, I have hereunto set my hand and seal this _____ day of _____, 19 _____.

(Signed) _____

Declaration of Witnesses

The declarant is personally known to me and I believe her to be of sound mind and emotionally and legally competent to make the herein-contained **Directive to Physicians**. I am not related to the declarant by blood or marriage, nor would I be entitled to any portion of the declarant's estate upon her decease, nor am I an attending physician of the declarant, nor an employee of the attending physician, nor an employee of a health care facility in which the declarant is a patient, nor a patient in a health care facility in which the declarant is a patient, nor am I a person who has any claim against any portion of the estate of the declarant upon her death.

(Signed) _____
| | Witness |

_____
| | Address |

(Signed) _____
| | Witness |

_____
| | Address |

1

CERTIFICATE OF NOTARY

STATE OF   )
)   ss:

COUNTY OF   )

On this _____ day of _____, 19 _____, before me personally came and appeared _____ _____, declarant, and _____, witness, and _____ _____, witness, known, and known to me, to be the individuals described in and whose names are subscribed in the foregoing instrument in their respective capacities, and who duly acknowledged to me that they executed same for the purpose therein contained.

     IN WITNESS WHEREOF, I hereunto set my hand and official seal.

_____
Notary Public

My commission expires: _____

Living Will

of

Dated _____ 19 ___

Living Will

Directive to Physicians:

I, _____, of

Street Address	*Apt. No.*	*City*	*State*	*Zip*

have been diagnosed and notified by _____, M.D., of

Street Address	*City*	*State*	*Zip*

and by _____, M.D., of

Street Address	*City*	*State*	*Zip*

as having a terminal condition caused by disease, illness, accident or injury; therefore:

1. Being of sound mind, I do hereby willfully and voluntarily make known my desire that my life not be prolonged by the use of "heroic measures" or by the application of life-sustaining procedures which would only serve to delay the moment of my death.

2. I direct that such measures be withheld or withdrawn and that I be permitted to die naturally.

3. In the event of my inability to give directions regarding the application of life-sustaining procedures or the use of "heroic measures," it is my intention that this directive shall be honored by my family and physicians as my final expression of my right to refuse medical or surgical treatment, and my acceptance of the consequences of such refusal.

4. I am mentally, emotionally and legally competent to make this directive and I fully understand its import.

5. I reserve the right to revoke this directive at any time.

6. This directive shall remain in force until revoked.

IN WITNESS WHEREOF, I have hereunto set my hand and seal this _____ day of _____, 19 _____.

(Signed) _____

Declaration of Witnesses

The declarant is personally known to me and I believe him/her to be of sound mind and emotionally and legally competent to make the herein-contained **Directive to Physicians.** I am not related to the declarant by blood or marriage, nor would I be entitled to any portion of the declarant's estate upon his/her decease, nor am I an attending physician of the declarant, nor an employee of the attending physician, nor an employee of a health care facility in which the declarant is a patient, nor a patient in a health care facility in which the declarant is a patient, nor am I a person who has any claim against any portion of the estate of the declarant upon his/her decease.

(Signed) _____
Witness

_____
Address

_____

(Signed) _____
Witness

_____
Address

_____

NOTICE: This Living Will is for use ONLY AFTER DIAGNOSIS OF A TERMINAL CONDITION.

CERTIFICATE OF NOTARY

STATE OF _____)
) ss:
COUNTY OF _____)

On this _____ day of _____, 19 _____, before me personally came and appeared _____ _____, declarant, and _____, witness, and _____ _____, witness, known, and known to me, to be the individuals described in and whose names are subscribed in the foregoing instrument in their respective capacities, and who duly acknowledged to me that they executed same for the purpose therein contained.

    IN WITNESS WHEREOF, I hereunto set my hand and official seal.

_____
                                       Notary Public

My commission expires: _____

Living Will

of

Dated _____ 19 ____